THE
PUBLIC GENERAL ACTS
AND GENERAL SYNOD MEASURES
1982

[IN THREE PARTS]

PART I

(Chapters 1–39)

with
Lists of the Public General Acts
Local Acts and an Index

LONDON
HER MAJESTY'S STATIONERY OFFICE
1983
£115·00 net

ISBN 0 11 840225 0 *

e

CONTENTS

PART I

PART II

PART III

TABLE I

Alphabetical List of
the Public General Acts of 1982

TABLE II

Chronological List of
the Public General Acts of 1982

*Consolidation Act.

*Consolidation Act.

TABLE III

Alphabetical List of
the Local and Personal Acts of 1982

TABLE IV

Chronological List of
the General Synod Measures of 1982

---

*Measures passed by the General Synod of the Church of England which received
the Royal Assent during the year* 1982

THE PUBLIC GENERAL ACTS OF 1982

Civil Aviation (Amendment) Act 1982

1982 CHAPTER 1

An Act to make further provision with respect to the financial limits applying to the British Airports Authority and the British Airways Board; and to make amendments designed to facilitate, or otherwise desirable in connection with, the consolidation of certain enactments relating to civil aviation.

[2nd February 1982]

B E IT ENACTED by the Queen's most Excellent Majesty, by and with the advice and consent of the Lords Spiritual and Temporal, and Commons, in this present Parliament assembled, and by the authority of the same, as follows:—

1.—(1) In subsection (4) of section 5 of the Airports Authority Act 1975 (limit of £125 million on borrowing and commencing capital debt of British Airports Authority) for the words "£125 million" there shall be substituted the words "£200 million but the Secretary of State may by order increase that limit to £300 million ". *Increase of financial limit of British Airports Authority. 1975 c. 78.*

(2) After subsection (4) of that section there shall be inserted—
    " (4A) The power to make an order under subsection (4) above shall be exercisable by statutory instrument and no such order shall be made unless a draft of it has been approved by resolution of the House of Commons."

2. In section 9(1) of the British Airways Board Act 1977 (limit of £1,000 million on borrowing by and government investment in British Airways Board) for the words " £1,000 million " there shall be substituted the words "£1,200 million but the Secretary of State may by order increase that limit to £1,400 million and by a further order to £1,600 million." *Increase of financial limit of British Airways Board. 1977 c. 13.*

Part I   A

Application of
financial limit
of British
Airways
Board to
foreign
currency
borrowings.
1977 c. 13.

3.—(1) For the purposes of section 9(1) of the British Airways Board Act 1977 the sterling equivalent of any amount borrowed by the British Airways Board (whether before or after the passing of this Act) in a currency other than sterling shall, subject to subsections (3) and (4) below, be determined by reference to the London market spot selling rate for sterling at the close of the last working day before that on which that amount was received by the Board or, if there is no such rate, by reference to such rate as may be specified by the Secretary of State.

(2) Where in the case of any loan amounts have been received by the Board on different days and an amount less than the aggregate of those amounts has been repaid, any question under subsection (1) above as to the day on which the outstanding amount was received shall, in the absence of any indication to the contrary, be determined by apportioning the repayment rateably between the amounts received.

(3) Where pursuant to a scheme established by the Treasury the Board has (whether before or after the passing of this Act) contracted to purchase currency other than sterling for the purpose of enabling the Board to repay money borrowed by it in that currency, the sterling equivalent of any amount comprised in the money to which the contract relates shall for the purposes of the said section 9(1) be determined by reference to the rate of exchange specified in the contract.

(4) Subsection (1) above does not apply to money borrowed by overdraft.

Pre-
consolidation
amendments
of Civil
Aviation Acts.

4.—(1) Schedule 1 to this Act shall have effect for making amendments designed to facilitate, or otherwise desirable in connection with, the consolidation of certain enactments relating to civil aviation.

1949 c. 67.
1971 c. 75.

(2) In that Schedule " the Act of 1949 " and " the Act of 1971 " mean respectively the Civil Aviation Act 1949 and the Civil Aviation Act 1971.

(3) The enactments mentioned in Schedule 2 to this Act are hereby repealed to the extent specified in the third column of that Schedule.

(4) Neither Schedule 1 nor Schedule 2 to this Act affects any liability or penalty for, or proceedings in respect of, an offence committed before the passing of this Act.

Short title
and extent.

5.—(1) This Act may be cited as the Civil Aviation (Amendment) Act 1982.

(2) This Act extends to Northern Ireland.

SCHEDULES

SCHEDULE 1

PRE-CONSOLIDATION AMENDMENTS

Power to extend enactments relating to civil aviation outside the United Kingdom

1.—(1) Section 30 of the Civil Aviation Act 1980 (power to extend 1980 c. 60.
Act outside the United Kingdom) shall apply, as it applies to that
Act, to—

(*a*) the Act of 1949 ;

(*b*) the Civil Aviation (Eurocontrol) Act 1962 ;   1962 c. 8.

(*c*) the Tokyo Convention Act 1967 (except section 4) ;   1967 c. 52.

(*d*) sections 16 and 17 of the Civil Aviation Act 1968 ;   1968 c. 61.

(*e*) the Act of 1971 ; and

(*f*) the Civil Aviation Act 1978.   1978 c. 8.

(2) Accordingly, sections 66 and 67 of the Act of 1949, section 9
of the said Act of 1962, sections 16(3) and 17(3) of the said Act of
1968, paragraph (*a*) of section 66(1) of the Act of 1971 and subsections (4) and (5)(*b*) of section 16 of the said Act of 1978 shall
cease to have effect ; and section 8 of the said Act of 1967 shall
apply only in relation to the said section 4.

(3) The preceding provisions of this paragraph shall not affect
the law in force in any country or territory which is outside the
United Kingdom and is not a relevant overseas territory for the purposes of subsection (1) of section 30 of the Civil Aviation Act 1980.

Criminal penalties in Northern Ireland

2.—(1) There shall be no limit to the amount of the fine which
may be imposed in Northern Ireland on conviction on indictment of
an offence against an order under section 25 of the Act of 1949
(power to prohibit or restrict use of civil aerodromes).

(2) The maximum fine which may be imposed in Northern Ireland
on summary conviction of an offence under section 38 of the Act
of 1949 (trespassing on licensed aerodromes) shall be £25 and on
summary conviction of an offence under section 29(2) or 55(1) of
that Act (obstruction and contravention of provision about registration of births and deaths) shall be £50.

(3) Paragraph (*e*) of section 26(2) of the Act of 1971 (regulation of
provision of accommodation on aircraft) shall have effect in Northern
Ireland as if the maximum fine on summary conviction which may
be provided for in pursuance of that paragraph were a fine of the
statutory maximum.

(4) The maximum fine which may be imposed in Northern Ireland on summary conviction of any offence to which this sub-paragraph applies shall be a fine of the statutory maximum.

(5) Sub-paragraph (4) above applies to the following offences, that is to say—

    (*a*) an offence against an order under section 25 of the Act of 1949 ;

    (*b*) an offence under section 6(3) or (4) of the Civil Aviation (Eurocontrol) Act 1962 (furnishing false particulars or certifying a false document) ;

    (*c*) an offence under subsection (5) or (7) of section 21 of the Act of 1971 (restriction of unlicensed carriage for reward) ;

    (*d*) an offence under section 24(7) of the Act of 1971 (furnishing false information) ;

    (*e*) any offence falling within section 35(4)(*b*) of the Act of 1971 (furnishing false information) ; and

    (*f*) an offence under section 36(3) of the Act of 1971 (disclosing confidential information).

(6) In this paragraph " the statutory maximum " means the prescribed sum within the meaning of section 32 of the Magistrates' Courts Act 1980 (that is to say, £1,000 or another sum fixed by order under section 143 of that Act to take account of changes in the value of money) ; and for the purposes of this paragraph the provisions of the said Act of 1980 which relate to that sum shall extend to Northern Ireland.

Incidental, supplementary and transitional provisions

3.—(1) Any power to which this paragraph applies shall include power to make such incidental, supplementary or transitional provision as the authority exercising the power thinks fit.

(2) This paragraph applies to the following powers, that is to say—

    (*a*) the power to make an Order in Council under any enactment to which Part VI of the Act of 1949 applies or under that Part of that Act ;

    (*b*) any power to make regulations conferred by the Civil Aviation (Licensing) Act 1960 ;

    (*c*) the power to make regulations under section 4 of the Civil Aviation (Eurocontrol) Act 1962 (charges for air navigation services, etc.) ;

    (*d*) any power to make an order under section 3(4), 6(5) or 14(10) of the Civil Aviation Act 1968 (power to repeal local enactments) ;

    (*e*) any power to make an Order in Council under section 16 or 17 of the said Act of 1968 (mortgaging of and other rights in aircraft) ;

(f) any power to make an order or to make regulations which is conferred on the Secretary of State by the Act of 1971 (excluding section 15); — Sch. 1

(g) any power conferred by the Civil Aviation Act 1978 to make an order or to make regulations; and — 1978 c. 8.

(h) the power to make an Order in Council under section 30 of the Civil Aviation Act 1980. — 1980 c. 60.

Amendments of the Civil Aviation Act 1949 — 1949 c. 67.

4.—(1) In section 8 of the Act of 1949 (Air Navigation Orders)—

(a) in subsection (4), for the words from " thereof " to " taking " there shall be substituted the words " thereof, provide—

(a) subject to subsection (4A) of this section, for persons to be guilty of offences in such circumstances as may be specified in the Order and to be liable on conviction of those offences to such penalties as may be so specified; and

(b) in the case of a provision having effect by virtue of paragraph (l) of subsection (2) of this section, for the taking "; and

(b) after subsection (4) there shall be inserted the following subsections—

" (4A) The power conferred by virtue of subsection (4)(a) of this section shall not include power—

(a) to provide for offences to be triable only on indictment;

(b) to authorise the imposition, on summary conviction of any offence, of any term of imprisonment or of a fine exceeding the statutory maximum;

(c) to authorise the imposition, on conviction on indictment of an offence, of a term of imprisonment exceeding two years.

(4B) In subsection (4A) above ' the statutory maximum ' means—

(a) in England and Wales and Northern Ireland, the prescribed sum within the meaning of section 32 of the Magistrates' Courts Act 1980 (that is to say, £1,000 or another sum fixed by order under section 143 of that Act to take account of changes in the value of money); and — 1980 c. 43.

(b) in Scotland, the prescribed sum within the meaning of section 289B of the Criminal Procedure (Scotland) Act 1975 (that is to say, £1,000 or — 1975 c. 21.

another sum fixed by order under section 289D of that Act for that purpose) ;

and for the purposes of the application of this definition in Northern Ireland the provisions of the Magistrates' Courts Act 1980 which relate to the sum mentioned in paragraph (*a*) above shall extend to Northern Ireland.".

(2) For the purposes of any Order in Council made at any time before the coming into force of sub-paragraph (1) above, it is hereby declared that at all material times the power conferred by virtue of subsection (4) of the said section 8 has included power to provide—

 (*a*) for offences triable only summarily ; and

 (*b*) for maximum fines and maximum periods of imprisonment of less than the maximums specified in that subsection.

5. In section 9 of the Act of 1949 (control of aviation in time of war or emergency)—

 (*a*) in subsection (1), for the words " this Act " there shall be substituted the words " any enactment relating to civil aviation " ; and

 (*b*) in subsection (3), for the words from " principles " to " shall, with " there shall be substituted the words " principles of the Land Compensation Act shall, with " and at the end of that subsection there shall be added the words—

  " In this subsection ' the Land Compensation Act '—

   (*a*) in relation to England and Wales, means the Land Compensation Act 1961 ;

   (*b*) in relation to Scotland, means the Land Compensation (Scotland) Act 1963 ; and

   (*c*) in relation to Northern Ireland, means the Acquisition of Land (Assessment of Compensation) Act 1919.".

6. In section 10 of the Act of 1949 (investigation of accidents), in subsection (2)(*d*), the words " this Part of this Act or " shall be omitted, and after the word " licence ", in the second and third places where it occurs, there shall be inserted the words " or certificate ".

7. Subsections (6) and (8) of section 19 of the Act of 1949 (power of local authority to appropriate and dispose of land and to borrow for the purposes of section 19) shall cease to have effect.

8. In section 23 of the Act of 1949—

 (*a*) subsection (1) (which confers power on the Secretary of State to acquire land under the Military Lands Acts for civil aviation purposes) shall cease to have effect ; and

 (*b*) in subsection (7) (enforcement of certain rights in land), the words from " This subsection shall " onwards shall be omitted ; and (*c*) subsections (8), (9) and (10) (which provide for the application of certain enactments to land vested in the Secretary of State) shall cease to have effect.

9. In section 28 of the Act of 1949 (power to stop up and divert highway)—

(*a*) in paragraph (*a*) of subsection (7) (Scottish adaptations), for the words " county or town " there shall be substituted the words " regional, islands or district " ;

(*b*) in paragraph (*d*) of subsection (8) (Northern Irish adaptations), for the words " the said subsection " and the words " the said Act " there shall be substituted respectively the words " the said Article 53 " and the words " the said Order ".

10. Subsections (2) and (6) of section 31 of the Act of 1949 (which relate to displacements from land in Northern Ireland) shall cease to have effect.

11. In subsection (5)(*a*) of section 33 of the Act of 1949 (registration of certain rights and instruments in Northern Ireland)—

(*a*) for the words " Local Registration of Title (Ireland) Act 1891 " there shall be substituted the words " Land Registration Act (Northern Ireland) 1970 " ; and

1891 c. 66.
1970 c. 18.
(N.I.).

(*b*) the words " under subsection (2) of section eighty-one of the said Act " shall be omitted.

12. Section 36 of the Act of 1949 (which provides for the compensation of officers in connection with the acquisition of an aerodrome by the Secretary of State) shall cease to have effect.

13. In subsection (1) of section 40 of the Act of 1949 (liability for trespass, etc.), for the words from " Part II and " onwards there shall be substituted the words " any Orders in Council under section 8 of this Act and of any orders under section 9 of this Act are duly complied with and there has been no breach of section 11 of this Act ".

14. In section 55 of the Act of 1949 (registration of births and deaths on aircraft), in subsections (1)(*a*) and (9)(*a*) for the words " Great Britain and Northern Ireland " there shall be substituted the words " the United Kingdom ".

15. After section 62 of the Act of 1949 there shall be inserted the following section—

" Offences by bodies corporate.

62A.—(1) Where an offence under section 24(8), 25(4), 29(2) or 55 of this Act which has been committed by a body corporate is proved to have been committed with the consent or connivance of, or to be attributable to any neglect on the part of, any director, manager, secretary or other similar officer of the body corporate or any person who was purporting to act in any such capacity, he, as well as the body corporate, shall be guilty of that offence and be liable to be proceeded against and punished accordingly.

(2) Where the affairs of a body corporate are managed by its members, the preceding subsection shall apply in relation to the acts and defaults of a member in connection with his functions of management as if he were a director of the body corporate.".

16. In section 63(1) of the Act of 1949 (interpretation)—

(*a*) for the definition of " land " there shall be substituted the following definition—

1978 c. 30. " ' land ' has the same meaning as, by virtue of Schedule 1 and paragraph 4 of Schedule 2 to the Interpretation Act 1978, it has in an Act passed on or after 1st January 1979 ; "

(*b*) in the definition of " local authority " at the end there shall be inserted the words " and, in relation to Northern Ireland,
1972 c. 9 (N.I.) a district council established under the Local Government Act (Northern Ireland) 1972 " ;

(*c*) before the definition of " owner " there shall be inserted the following definitions—

" ' modifications ' includes additions, omissions and amendments, and ' modify ' shall be construed accordingly ;
1971 c. 75. ' operator ', in relation to an aircraft, has the same meaning as in the Civil Aviation Act 1971 ; " and

(*d*) the definition of " purposes of civil aviation " shall be omitted.

17. For subsection (4) of section 65 of the Act of 1949 (modification of references to Lands Tribunal in application of Act to Northern Ireland) there shall be substituted the following subsection—

" (4) In the application of this Act to Northern Ireland any reference to the Lands Tribunal shall be construed as a reference to the Lands Tribunal for Northern Ireland.".

18. In paragraph 9 of Schedule 1 to the Act of 1949 (application of provisions relating to land compensation), for the words from " provisions " onwards there shall be substituted the words " provisions of the Land Compensation Act shall have effect accordingly.

In this paragraph ' the Land Compensation Act '—

(*a*) in relation to England and Wales, means the Land Compensation Act 1961 ;

(*b*) in relation to Scotland, means the Land Compensation (Scotland) Act 1963 ; and

(*c*) in relation to Northern Ireland, means the Acquisition of Land (Assessment of Compensation) Act 1919.".

19. In sub-paragraph (*b*) of paragraph 2 of Schedule 4 to the Act of 1949 (power to apply certain provisions), the words from "including" onwards shall be omitted.

20. In paragraph 2 of Schedule 8 to the Act of 1949 (fixing etc. of security in respect of patent claim involving a detained aircraft), for the words from "fixed" onwards there shall be substituted the words "fixed by the Secretary of State or some person duly authorised on his behalf ; and payment thereof shall be made or secured to the Secretary of State in such manner as the Secretary of State shall approve.".

21. In paragraph 1(2) of Schedule 11 to the Act of 1949 (modifications of section 143 of the Public Health Act 1936 in relation to the Secretary of State's aerodromes), for paragraphs (*a*) and (*b*) there shall be substituted the following paragraphs—

" (*a*) in subsection (1) the proviso shall be omitted ;

(*b*) in subsection (3) for the words from ' shall specify ' to ' executed ' there shall be substituted the words ' may provide for their enforcement and execution by officers designated for that purpose by the Secretary of State ' and paragraphs (i) and (ii) of the proviso shall be omitted ; and

(*c*) in subsection (4) for the words ' Authorised officers of any such authority ' there shall be sustituted the words ' Officers designated as aforesaid '.".

Amendment of the Civil Aviation (Licensing) Act 1960

22. In section 6 of the Civil Aviation (Licensing) Act 1960, for the words from " In this subsection '" in subsection (6) (offences committed by bodies corporate) to the end of that subsection there shall be substituted the following subsection—

" (6A) Where the affairs of a body corporate are managed by its members the preceding subsection shall apply in relation to the acts and defaults of a member in connection with his functions of management as if he were a director of the body corporate.".

Amendments of the Civil Aviation (Eurocontrol) Act 1962

23. In paragraph (*c*) of section 6(2) of the Civil Aviation (Eurocontrol) Act 1962 (duty not to disclose certain information except in specified circumstances), for the words from " this Act " onwards there shall be substituted the words " the said section 4, of proceedings brought by virtue of section 7(3)(*b*) of this Act or of any criminal proceedings whether or not arising out of this Act ; or ".

24. In section 8(1) of the said Act of 1962 (interpretation), for the definition of " navigation services " there shall be substituted the following definitions—

" ' land ' has the same meaning as, by virtue of Schedule 1 and paragraph 4 of Schedule 2 to the Interpretation Act 1978, it has in any Act passed on or after 1st January 1979 ;

'navigation services' means any air navigation services within the meaning of the Civil Aviation Act 1971 ; ".

Amendments of the Tokyo Convention Act 1967

25. In section 5(1)(*b*) of the Tokyo Convention Act 1967 (admissibility in evidence of depositions made outside the United Kingdom), for the words from "which is" to "jurisdiction" there shall be substituted the words " which was part of Her Majesty's dominions at the time the deposition was made or in which Her Majesty had jurisdiction at that time ".

26. In subsection (1) of section 6 of the said Act of 1967 (evidential effect of certain documents and records)—

 (*a*) in paragraph (*a*)(ii), the words " or this Act " shall be omitted ; and

 (*b*) at the end there shall be inserted the words—

  " In this subsection ' record ' has the same meaning as in the Civil Aviation (Eurocontrol) Act 1962.".

27. In section 7(1) of the said Act of 1967 (interpretation), after the definition of " military aircraft " there shall be inserted the following definition—

  " ' modifications ' includes additions, omissions and amendments ; ".

Amendments of the Civil Aviation Act 1968

28. In section 14(5)(*a*) of the Civil Aviation Act 1968 (application of proceeds of sale of aircraft sold for unpaid airport charges), for the words " purchase tax " there shall be substituted the words " value added tax ".

29. In subsection (4) of section 18 of the said Act of 1968 (interpretation), for the words from " ' relevant " onwards there shall be substituted the words " ' enactment ' has the same meaning as in
the Civil Aviation Act 1949 and ' relevant overseas territory ' has the same meaning as in section 30(1) of the Civil Aviation Act 1980."

30. In section 28(3) of the said Act of 1968 (interpretation), at the end there shall be added the words " ; and ' modifications ' includes additions, omissions and amendments.".

Amendments of the Civil Aviation Act 1971

31. In section 4 of the Act of 1971 (Secretary of State's directions in the national interest, etc.), for the words " this Act " in subsection (1)(*b*) and the words " any provision of this Act " in subsections (2A)

and (3) there shall be substituted the words " any enactment or instru-   Sᴄʜ. 1
ment relating to the Authority ".

32. In subsection (9) of section 14 of the Act of 1971 (adaptations
for Scotland and Northern Ireland)—

    (*a*) paragraph (*c*) shall be omitted ; and

    (*b*) for the words from " to subsection (2) " onwards there shall
        be substituted the words " to paragraphs 2 and 3 of
        Schedule 7 to the Roads (Northern Ireland) Order 1980 S.I.
        and to Article 40 of that Order.".   1980 No. 1085
                                                  (N.I. 11).

33. In section 15 of the Act of 1971 (compulsory purchase of
land in Northern Ireland)—

    (*a*) for subsection (2) there shall be substituted the following
        subsection—

        " (2) Schedule 6 to the Local Government Act (Northern 1972 c. 9. (N.I.).
        Ireland) 1972 shall, subject to the modifications specified
        in Schedule 4 to this Act, apply for the purposes of the
        acquisition of land by means of an order under this
        section in the same manner as it applies to the acquisition
        of land by means of a vesting order under that Act." ;

    (*b*) subsection (3) and in subsection (4) the words " Schedule 4 to
        this Act and the said Schedule 5 as incorporated in this
        Act," and the words from " and in Schedule 4 " onwards
        shall be omitted.

34. In subsection (1) of section 16 of the Act of 1971 (land rights
granted to CAA to bind grantor's successors), at the end there shall
be added the following paragraph—

    " Section 63(2) of the Civil Aviation Act 1949 shall apply for 1949 c. 67.
        the purposes of this subsection as it applies for the purposes
        of that Act.".

35. In subsection (2)(*e*) of section 36 of the Act of 1971 (disclosure
of certain information for the purposes of criminal proceedings
arising out of that Act or an Air Navigation Order), for the words
" this Act or an Air Navigation Order " there shall be substituted
the words " any enactment relating to civil aviation ".

36. In section 63 of the Act of 1971 (orders and regulations)—

    (*a*) in subsection (1), the words " (except orders appointing a
        day) " shall be omitted ; and

    (*b*) in subsection (3), the words from " but " onwards shall be
        omitted.

37. In section 64(1) of the Act of 1971 (interpretation)—

    (*a*) for the definition of " land " there shall be substituted the
        following definition—

        " ' land ' has the same meaning as, by virtue of

Schedule 1 and paragraph 4 of Schedule 2 to the Interpretation Act 1978, it has in an Act passed on or after
1st January 1979 ; " and

(b) for the definition of " relevant overseas territory " there
shall be substituted the following definition—
" ' relevant overseas territory ' has the same meaning
1980 c. 60.   as in section 30(1) of the Civil Aviation Act 1980 ; ".

38. In section 65(1) of the Act of 1971, paragraph (a) (construction of references in application of Act to Northern Ireland) shall
be omitted.

39.—(1) Section 66 of the Act of 1971 (which, as amended by
paragraph 1(2) above, provides for the extension of any provision of
that Act to certain aircraft registered otherwise than in the United
Kingdom) shall apply, as it applies to any provision of the Act of
1971, to—

(a) any provision of any enactment to which Part IV of the Act
of 1949 applies ;

(b) any provision of that Part of that Act ;

1968 c. 61.   (c) section 16 of the Civil Aviation Act 1968 ; and

(d) any provision of any Order in Council or regulation made
by virtue of any provision mentioned in paragraphs (a) to
(c) above.

(2) Subsection (2) of section 59 of the Act of 1949 (which contains
provision, in relation to the matters mentioned in sub-paragraph
(1)(a), (b) and (d) above, which is comparable to that made by the said
section 66) shall cease to have effect except for the purposes of any
Order in Council made under that subsection and in force immediately before the coming into operation of this paragraph and for
the purpose of amending or revoking such an Order.

40. It is hereby declared that the survey in relation to which a
power of entry is conferred by virtue of paragraph 9(2) of Schedule
3 to the Act of 1971 is any survey which the Secretary of State or
the Civil Aviation Authority requires to be made for the purpose
of any steps to be taken in consequence of the order in question or,
as the case may be, for the purpose of determining whether the
order should be made.

41. For Schedule 4 to the Act of 1971 (modifications of Schedules
5 and 6 to the Roads Act (Northern Ireland) 1948) there shall be
substituted the following Schedule—

" SCHEDULE 4

MODIFICATIONS OF SCHEDULE 6 TO THE LOCAL
GOVERNMENT ACT (NORTHERN IRELAND) 1972

1. For references to the department concerned there shall be
substituted references to the Secretary of State.

2. For references to a district council there shall be substituted   SCH. 1
references to the Civil Aviation Authority.

3. References to Schedule 6 to the Local Government Act (Nor- 1972 c. 9 (N.I.).
thern Ireland) 1972 shall be construed as references to that
Schedule as modified by this Schedule.

4. For paragraph 1 there shall be substituted the following paragraph—

'1. An application by the Civil Aviation Authority
to the Secretary of State for a vesting order shall be in the
prescribed form.'.

5. For paragraph 6(2) there shall be substituted the following
sub-paragraph—

'(2) To the extent to which compensation is payable in
accordance with the provisions of this Schedule, as from
the date of vesting the rights and claims of all persons
in respect of any land acquired by the vesting order shall
be transferred and attached to the funds of the Civil
Aviation Authority (in this Schedule referred to as "the
compensation fund") and shall be discharged by payments made by the Civil Aviation Authority.'.

6. In paragraph 12(2) for the words 'the clerk of the council'
there shall be substituted the words 'such person as may be
designated for the purposes of this Schedule by the Civil
Aviation Authority'.

7. Paragraph 20(2) shall be omitted.".

42. In paragraph 3 of Schedule 9 to the Act of 1971 (which,
in relation to Northern Ireland, makes provision about staff transferred to the Civil Aviation Authority)—

(*a*) in sub-paragraph (3), for the words "paragraph 7 of Schedule
2 to the Act of 1965" there shall be substituted the words
"paragraph 8 of Schedule 2 to the Industrial Relations S.I.
(Northern Ireland) Order 1976" and for the words from 1976 No. 1043
"paragraph 10" onwards there shall be substituted the (N.I. 16).
words "Schedule 1 to the Act of 1965 shall be construed
as a reference to that Schedule as it has effect by virtue
of sub-paragraph (1) above"; and

(*b*) in sub-paragraph (5), for the words "or 2 to that Act"
there shall be substituted the words "to that Act or to
Schedule 2 to the Industrial Relations (Northern Ireland)
Order 1976".

Amendment of the Air Travel Reserve Fund Act 1975   1975 c. 36.

43. In subsection (2) of section 7 of the Air Travel Reserve Fund
Act 1975 (which applies certain provisions of the Act of 1971)—

(*a*) for the words "sections 63(1) and (4) and 66 of that Act"
there shall be substituted the words "section 63(1) and (4)
of that Act and paragraphs 1 and 3 of Schedule 1 to the
Civil Aviation (Amendment) Act 1982".

(*b*) for the words " that Act " in the third, fourth arid fifth places where they occur there shall be substituted the words " the said Act of 1971 ".

Amendment of the Airports Authority Act 1975

44. It is hereby declared that the survey in relation to which a power of entry is conferred by virtue of paragraph 9(1) of Schedule 3 to the Airports Authority Act 1975 is any survey which the Secretary of State or the British Airports Authority requires to be made for the purpose of any steps to be taken in consequence of the order in question or, as the case may be, for the purpose of determining whether the order should be made.

Amendments of the Civil Aviation Act 1978

45. In section 1(4) of the Civil Aviation Act 1978 (deposit with certain institutions of money in the Aviation Security Fund), for the words from " with any " to " 1963 " there shall be substituted the words " with a recognised bank or licensed institution within the meaning of the Banking Act 1979 ".

46. In section 14(3) of the said Act of 1978 (power to amend local Acts), after the words " local authority " there shall be inserted the words " (within the meaning of the Civil Aviation Act 1949) ".

47. In sub-paragraph (3) of paragraph 2 of Schedule 1 to the said Act of 1978 (power of entry for survey in case of order made or to be made by virtue of that paragraph), after the words " in consequence of the order " there shall be inserted the words " or, as the case may be, for the purpose of determining whether the order should be made ".

Amendment of the Land Registration (Scotland) Act 1979

48.—(1) In subsection (1) of section 28 of the Land Registration (Scotland) Act 1979 (interpretation) at the end of the definition of the word " deed " there shall be inserted the words " and includes any such instrument as is mentioned in subsection (1) of section 33 of the Civil Aviation Act 1949 ; ".

(2) The amendment made by this paragraph shall be deemed for all purposes to have had effect from the coming into operation of the said section 28.

The Civil Aviation Act 1980

49. The enactments and instruments with respect to which provision may be made by Order in Council in pursuance of section 1(1)(*h*) of the Hovercraft Act 1968 (power to apply enactments and instruments in relation to hovercraft etc.) shall include the Civil Aviation Act 1980 and any instrument made under it.

SCHEDULE 2

REPEALS

Chapter	Short title	Extent of repeal
12, 13 & 14 Geo. 6. c. 67.	The Civil Aviation Act 1949.	In section 10(2)(*d*), the words " this Part of this Act or ". In section 19, subsections (6) and (8) and in subsection (9) the words " and the expression ' land ' includes any right in or over land ". In section 23, subsection (1), in subsection (2) the words " also " and " otherwise than under the said Acts " and the words from " any estate " onwards, in subsection (3) the words from " In this subsection " onwards, in subsection (4) the word " adaptations " and the words " and exceptions ", in subsection (7) the words from " This subsection shall " onwards and subsections (8), (9) and (10). Section 24(10). Section 25(7). Section 29(4). In section 31, subsections (2) and (6). In section 33(5)(*a*), the words " under subsection (2) of section eighty-one of the said Act ". Section 36. In section 51(2), the words " exceptions, adaptations and ". Section 55(3). In section 57(1), the words from " may contain " to " Order and ". Section 59(2). In section 63(1), the definition of " purposes of civil aviation ". Sections 66 and 67. In Schedule 4, in sub-paragraph (*b*) of paragraph 2 the words from " (including " onwards and paragraph 10. In Schedule 9, in Part I the words " in section twenty-three, subsections (8), (9), (10) and (11) " and Part II.

Chapter	Short title	Extent of repeal
		In paragraph 1(5) of Schedule 11, the word " exceptions " and the words " and adaptations ".
8 & 9 Eliz. 2. c. 38.	The Civil Aviation (Licensing) Act 1960.	In subsection (3) of section 5, the words from " and " onwards.
10 & 11 Eliz. 2. c. 8.	The Civil Aviation (Euro-control) Act 1962.	In section 4, in subsection (1) the words from " and may " onwards and in subsection (1C), paragraph (*c*) and the word " and " immediately preceding it. Section 9.
1967 c. 52.	The Tokyo Convention Act 1967.	In section 6(1)(*a*)(ii), the words " or this Act ". In section 8(1), the words " exceptions, adaptations and ".
1968 c. 61	The Civil Aviation Act 1968.	In section 1(2), the words " exceptions, adaptations or ". In subsection (4) of section 3, the word " which " in the third place where it occurs and the words from " may contain " onwards. In subsection (5) of section 6, the word " which " in the third place where it occurs and the words from " may contain " onwards. In subsection (10) of section 14, the words from " and any " onwards. In section 16, in subsection (2)(*a*) the words " adaptations or " and subsection (3). Section 17(3). In section 18, in subsection (2), the words from " contain " to " and may " and in subsection (3), the proviso.
1969 c. 48.	The Post Office Act 1969.	Section 88(3).
1971 c. 75.	The Civil Aviation Act 1971.	Section 14(9)(*c*). In section 15, subsection (3) and in subsection (4), the words " Schedule 4 to this Act and the said Schedule 5 as incorporated in this Act " and the words from " and in " onwards. Section 62(1).

Chapter	Short title	Extent of repeal
		In section 63, in subsection (1) the words "(except orders appointing a day)", in subsection (3) the words from "but" onwards and in subsection (4), paragraph (*b*) and the word "and" immediately preceding it.
		Section 65(1)(*a*).
		Section 66(1)(*a*).
1972 c. 70.	The Local Government Act 1972.	Section 131(2)(*h*).
1973 c. 27.	The Bahamas Independence Act 1973.	In Schedule 2, paragraph 8.
1978 c. 8.	The Civil Aviation Act 1978.	Section 5(3)(*a*).
		Section 13(2).
		In section 16, subsection (4), in subsection (5) paragraph (*b*) and the word "and" immediately preceding it and in subsection (6) the words "(4) and".
1978 c. 15.	The Solomon Islands Act 1978.	In the Schedule, paragraph 6.
1978 c. 20.	The Tuvalu Act 1978.	In Schedule 2, paragraph 6.
1979 c. 27.	The Kiribati Act 1979.	In the Schedule, paragraph 7.
1981 c. 52.	The Belize Act 1981.	In Schedule 2, paragraph 6.

Social Security (Contributions) Act 1982

1982 CHAPTER 2

An Act to make provision in connection with certain contributions payable under the Social Security Act 1975.
[2nd February 1982]

BE IT ENACTED by the Queen's most Excellent Majesty, by and with the advice and consent of the Lords Spiritual and Temporal, and Commons, in this present Parliament assembled, and by the authority of the same, as follows:—

Increase in contributions.

1.—(1) In regulation 7 of the Contributions Regulations (lower and upper earnings limits for Class 1 contributions)—

 (*a*) for the words " 6th April 1981 " there are substituted the words " 6th April 1982 " ; and

 (*b*) for " £27 " and " £200 " there are substituted respectively " £29·50 " and " £220 ".

(2) In section 4(6)(*a*) of the principal Act (amount of primary Class 1 contribution) for the words " 7·75 per cent." there are substituted the words " 8·75 per cent.".

(3) In regulation 104 of the Contributions Regulations (reduced rate Class 1 contribution of married women and widows) for the words " 2·75 per cent." there are substituted the words " 3·2 per cent.".

(4) In section 7 of the principal Act (amount of Class 2 contribution)—

 (*a*) in subsection (1) (weekly rate) for " £3·40 " there is substituted " £3·75 " ;

 (*b*) in subsection (5) (small earnings exception) for " £1,475 " there is substituted " £1,600 ".

(5) In regulation 98(*c*) of the Contributions Regulations (amount of Class 2 contribution of share fishermen) for " £5·15 " there is substituted " £5·85 ".

(6) In section 8(1) of the principal Act (amount of Class 3 contribution) for " £3·30 " there is substituted " £3·65 ".

(7) In sections 9(2) and 10(1) of the principal Act (Class 4 contributions recoverable under Tax Acts and regulations)—

   (*a*) for the words " 5·75 per cent." (amount of contribution) there are substituted, in each case, the words " 6 per cent." ;

   (*b*) for " £3,150 " (lower limit) wherever that amount appears there is substituted " £3,450 " ;

   (*c*) for " £10,000 " (upper limit) there is substituted, in each case, " £11,000 ".

2.—(1) In section 1(5) of the principal Act (Treasury supplement to contributions to be a fixed percentage of so much of all contributions paid in the year concerned as remains after deducting the appropriate national health service allocation and the appropriate employment protection allocation) for the words " 14·5 per cent. " there are substituted the words " 13 per cent.". *Alteration of Treasury supplement to contributions.*

(2) In section 1(5A) of the principal Act (power by order to vary percentage rate) for the words " 1981-82 " there are substituted the words " 1982-83 ".

3.—(1) Section 134(4) of the principal Act is amended as follows. *Allocation of contributions.*

(2) In the definition of " the appropriate national health service allocation "—

   (*a*) in paragraph (*a*) (primary Class 1 contributions) for the words " 0·65 per cent." there are substituted the words " 0·75 per cent. ", and

   (*b*) in paragraph (*e*) (Class 4 contributions) for the words " 0·85 per cent." there are substituted the words " 0·95 per cent.".

(3) In the definition of " the appropriate employment protection allocation ", for the words from " in the case of " to " this subsection " there are substituted the words " means—

>   (i) in the case of primary Class 1 contributions, 0·35 per cent. of the amount determined to be that of the earnings in respect of which those contributions were paid ; and

          (ii) in the case of secondary Class 1 contributions, 0·2 per cent. of the amount determined to be that of the earnings in respect of which those contributions were paid ;

and in this subsection ".

<table>
<tr><td>Supplemental.</td><td>

4.—(1) In this Act—</td></tr>
</table>

Supplemental.

S.I. 1979/591.

1975 c. 14.

4.—(1) In this Act—

    " Contributions Regulations " means the Social Security (Contributions) Regulations 1979 ; and

    " principal Act " means the Social Security Act 1975.

(2) This Act does not apply in respect of any tax year before the tax year beginning with 6th April 1982.

(3) The consequential amendments set out in Schedule 1 to this Act shall have effect and the enactments specified in Schedule 2 are hereby repealed to the extent specified in the third column.

(4) Nothing in section 120 of the principal Act (annual review of contributions) shall be taken to require the Secretary of State to carry out a review of earnings with a view to determining whether an order should be made under that section to have effect in relation to the tax year beginning with 6th April 1982.

1974 c. 28.

(5) An Order in Council under paragraph 1(1)(*b*) of Schedule 1 to the Northern Ireland Act 1974 (legislation for Northern Ireland in the interim period) which states that it is made only for purposes corresponding to those of this Act—

    (*a*) shall not be subject to paragraph 1(4) and (5) of that Schedule (affirmative resolution of both Houses of Parliament) ; but

    (*b*) shall be subject to annulment in pursuance of a resolution of either House.

(6) The amendment by this Act of any provision of the Contributions Regulations shall not be taken to prejudice any power to make further regulations varying or revoking that provision.

Short title and extent.

5.—(1) This Act may be cited as the Social Security (Contributions) Act 1982.

(2) Subsections (5) and (6) of section 4 and paragraph 3(3) of Schedule 1 extend to Northern Ireland, but otherwise this Act does not extend to Northern Ireland.

SCHEDULES

SCHEDULE 1

Section 4(3).

CONSEQUENTIAL AMENDMENTS

Social Security Act 1975 (c. 14)

1.—(1) Section 122 of the principal Act (additional power to alter contributions) is amended as follows.

(2) In subsection (3)(*b*), for the words " any percentage " there are substituted the words " one or other, or both, of the percentages ".

(3) In subsection (4), for the words from " the percentage rate " to the end there are substituted the words " one or other, or both, of the percentage rates (primary and secondary Class 1 contributions) specified in paragraphs (*a*) and (*b*) ".

(4) For subsection (5) there is substituted the following subsection—

" (5) An order under subsection (4) above which increases or reduces the percentage rate for a Class 1 contribution shall also amend the definition of " the appropriate employment protection allocation " in section 134(4) of this Act by increasing or, as the case may be, reducing by the same amount the percentage specified there in relation to that contribution.".

Employment Protection (Consolidation) Act 1978 (c. 44)

2.—(1) In section 105 of the Employment Protection (Consolidation) Act 1978 (payment to employers out of redundancy fund in respect of certain employees who are not entitled to redundancy payments), after subsection (4) there are inserted the following subsections—

" (5) Where the Secretary of State has determined a class of employees under subsection (3) above he may also make payments out of the fund to employees of that class and may determine, with the approval of the Treasury, the amounts of the payments which may be so made.

(6) The payments made to an employee by virtue of this section shall not, in respect of any period, exceed the amount appearing to the Secretary of State to be equal to the amount paid into the fund from the appropriate employment protection allocation from all primary Class 1 contributions paid by or on behalf of that employee under Part I of the Act of 1975.".

(2) In section 113 of the Act of 1978 (employment under government of overseas territory) for subsection (2) there is substituted the following subsection—

" (2) The reference in subsection (1) to employer's contributions is a reference—

(*a*) in relation to any period before 6th April 1975, to employer's contributions within the meaning of the National Insurance Act 1965 ;

SCH. 1

    (*b*) in relation to any period after 5th April 1975 and before 6th April 1982, to secondary Class 1 contributions in respect of the person in question payable by persons who were, in relation to him, secondary Class 1 contributors by virtue of section 4(4)(*a*) of the Social Security Act 1975 ; and

    (*c*) in relation to any period after 5th April 1982, to such contributions as are mentioned in paragraph (*b*) together with primary Class 1 contributions in respect of the person in question payable as so mentioned.".

Social Security (Contributions) Regulations 1979 (*S.I.* 1979/591)

3.—(1) Regulations 89, 115, 133 and 134 of the Contributions Regulations (reduction of Class 1 contributions in respect of mariners, serving members of the forces and registered dock workers) are amended as follows.

(2) In regulation 89(1)—

    (*a*) for the words " section 4(6)(*b*) of the Act (secondary contributions) " there are substituted the words " section 4(6) of the Act (Class 1 contributions) " ;

    (*b*) in sub-paragraph (*a*), for the words from " specified " to the end there are substituted the words " of the primary Class 1 contribution specified in section 4(6)(*a*) of the Act and of the reduced primary Class 1 contribution specified in regulation 104 of these regulations shall be reduced by 0·35 and that of the secondary Class 1 contribution specified in section 4(6)(*b*) by 0·15 " ;

    (*c*) in sub-paragraph (*b*), for the words " said percentage rate " there are substituted the words " percentage rate of the secondary Class 1 contribution specified in section 4(6)(*b*) of the Act ".

(3) In regulation 115(1)(*a*), for " 0·7 " and " 0·15 " there are substituted respectively " 1·05 " and " 0·5 ".

(4) In regulation 133—

    (*a*) the word " secondary ", in the first place where it occurs in paragraph (1) and in each place where it occurs in paragraphs (2) and (4), is omitted ; and

    (*b*) in paragraph (1), for the words from " of the secondary " to the end there are substituted the words " of the primary Class 1 contribution specified in section 4(6)(*a*) of the Act shall be reduced by 0·35 and that of the secondary Class 1 contribution specified in section 4(6)(*b*) by 0·15.".

(5) In regulation 134, in paragraphs (*b*) and (*c*)—

    (*a*) the word " secondary ", in each case where first occurring, is omitted ; and

    (*b*) for the words " ' secondary Class 1 contributions, means ' " there are substituted, in each case, the words " ' employment protection allocation means ' ".

SCHEDULE 2

REPEALS

Chapter	Short title	Extent of repeal
1975 c. 14.	The Social Security Act 1975.	In section 134, in subsections (1)(*b*) and (5)(*b*), the word " secondary ".
1981 c. 1.	The Social Security (Contributions) Act 1981.	Section 1. Section 2(1). Section 3(2)(*a*) and (*d*). Section 4(3), (4) and (7). In section 5(2), the words " Subject to section 4(4) ".

Currency Act 1982

1982 CHAPTER 3

An Act to replace section 1(1) of the Decimal Currency Act 1967 so as to sanction references to the new penny as the penny.   [2nd February 1982]

BE IT ENACTED by the Queen's most Excellent Majesty, by and with the advice and consent of the Lords Spiritual and Temporal, and Commons, in this present Parliament assembled, and by the authority of the same, as follows:—

Denominations of money.

1.—(1) The denominations of money in the currency of the United Kingdom shall be the pound sterling and the penny or new penny, being one hundredth part of a pound sterling.

1967 c. 47.

(2) Section 1(1) of the Decimal Currency Act 1967 (which is superseded by subsection (1) above) is hereby repealed.

Short title.

2. This Act may be cited as the Currency Act 1982.

Shipbuilding Act 1982

1982 CHAPTER 4

An Act to raise the limits imposed by section 11 of the Aircraft and Shipbuilding Industries Act 1977 in relation to the finances of British Shipbuilders and its wholly owned subsidiaries; and to provide for extending the period in relation to which schemes under the Shipbuilding (Redundancy Payments) Act 1978 operate.   **[25th February 1982]**

B E IT ENACTED by the Queen's most Excellent Majesty, by and with the advice and consent of the Lords Spiritual and Temporal, and Commons, in this present Parliament assembled, and by the authority of the same, as follows:—

1.—(1) In section 11(7) of the Aircraft and Shipbuilding Industries Act 1977 (which imposes an overall limit, increased from £500 million to £600 million by the British Shipbuilders Borrowing Powers (Increase of Limit) Order 1981, on certain sums borrowed by British Shipbuilders and its wholly owned subsidiaries and on its public dividend capital) for " £500 million " and " £600 million " (which were substituted by section 1 of the Shipbuilding Act 1979) there shall be substituted respectively " £700 million " and " £800 million ".

Limit on borrowing etc. of British Shipbuilders.
1977 c. 3.
S.I. 1981/1726.
1979 c. 59.

(2) Section 1 of the Shipbuilding Act 1979 is hereby repealed and the British Shipbuilders Borrowing Powers (Increase of Limit) Order 1981 is hereby revoked.

2.—(1) In section 2(4) of the Shipbuilding (Redundancy Payments) Act 1978 (which, as amended by section 5 of the Industry Act 1981, gives the Secretary of State power to amend any scheme under the said Act of 1978 by extending the period in relation to which the scheme operates from two years to four years and from four years to six years) for the words from " by

Payments to redundant workers in shipbuilding industry.
1978 c. 11.
1981 c. 6.

substituting " to the end there shall be substituted the following paragraphs—

> " (*a*) by substituting four years for the said period of two years;
>
> (*b*) in a case where he has exercised the power conferred by paragraph (*a*) above, by substituting six years for the said period of four years; and
>
> (*c*) in a case where he has exercised the power conferred by paragraph (*b*) above, by substituting eight years for the said period of six years. "

1981 c. 6.

(2) Section 5 of the Industry Act 1981 is hereby repealed.

Short title and extent.

3.—(1) This Act may be cited as the Shipbuilding Act 1982.

(2) This Act extends to Northern Ireland.

Hops Marketing Act 1982

1982 CHAPTER 5

An Act to revoke the Hops Marketing Scheme 1932, to make provision with respect to the forward contracts and other property, rights and liabilities of the Hops Marketing Board and to provide for the dissolution or winding up of that Board.   [25th February 1982]

B E IT ENACTED by the Queen's most Excellent Majesty, by and with the advice and consent of the Lords Spiritual and Temporal, and Commons, in this present Parliament assembled, and by the authority of the same, as follows:—

1.—(1) Subject to the provisions of this Act—

   (*a*) the Hops Marketing Scheme 1932 (in this Act referred to as " the Scheme ") ; and

   (*b*) the orders under the Agricultural Marketing Act 1958 set out in the Schedule to this Act (by which the Scheme and the amendments to it were approved),

are hereby revoked.

Revocation of Hops Marketing Scheme.

1958 c. 47.

(2) Subsection (1) above shall come into force on such day (in this Act referred to as " the appointed day ") as the Minister of Agriculture, Fisheries and Food may appoint by an order made by statutory instrument.

(3) Paragraph 6 of Schedule 1 to the said Act of 1958 and paragraph 6(2) of Schedule 2 to that Act (which contain savings where a scheme is revoked under that Act) shall have effect on

the revocation of the Scheme by this section as if it had then been revoked under that Act.

2.—(1) The Hops Marketing Board (in this Act referred to as " the Board ") shall cause a poll of the producers registered under the Scheme to be taken on the question whether the property, rights and liabilities of the Board should on the appointed day be transferred to such person or persons respectively as may be specified by the Board in the voting paper for the poll.

(2) If—

(*a*) the result of the poll under subsection (1) above shows that the requisite majority of registered producers is in favour of the proposal that the property, rights and liabilities of the Board should be transferred as mentioned in that subsection ; and

(*b*) at any time before the appointed day a resolution is passed by the Board incorporating the terms of that proposal and confirming the Board's approval of it,

the property, rights and liabilities of the Board shall on that day and by virtue of this Act become the property, rights and liabilities of such person or persons respectively as are specified in the resolution.

(3) In subsection (2)(*a*) above " the requisite majority " means a majority comprising—

(*a*) not less than two-thirds of the total number of registered producers voting on the poll ; and

(*b*) such number of registered producers as are together capable of producing not less than two-thirds of the quantity of hops produced in England which all the registered producers voting on the poll are together capable of producing.

(4) Paragraphs 25(*b*), 25A to 29 and 79 of, and the First Schedule to, the Scheme shall apply in relation to the poll under subsection (1) above as they apply in relation to polls held under the Scheme, except that the reference in paragraph 29(2) to the number of registered producers voting in favour of or against the amendment or revocation of the Scheme shall be construed as a reference to the number of registered producers voting in favour of or against the proposal that the property, rights and liabilities of the Board should be transferred as mentioned in subsection (1) above.

(5) The Board shall cause the poll under subsection (1) above to be taken as soon as practicable after the passing of this Act, and if the result of the poll under that subsection is such

that subsection (2)(*a*) above does not apply, the Board may at any time before the appointed day cause a further poll or polls of registered producers to be taken under this section; and subsections (1) to (4) above shall apply in relation to any such further poll as if it were the poll required to be taken under subsection (1) above.

(6) Nothing in section 47(2) of the Agricultural Marketing 1958 c. 47. Act 1958 (restriction on disclosure of information) shall preclude the disclosure of any information reasonably required by a person in connection with any property, rights or liabilities transferred to him by virtue of this Act.

(7) For the purposes of the Employment Protection (Con- 1978 c. 44. solidation) Act 1978 there shall be deemed to have been no break in the employment of any person who is transferred by virtue of this Act from the employment of the Board to that of another person.

3.—(1) Where a resolution is passed by the Board as men- Forward tioned in section 2(2)(*b*) above, the provisions of this section contracts of shall have effect on and after the appointed day with respect to the Board. contracts to which subsection (2) below applies.

(2) Without prejudice to the effect of subsection (2) of section 2 above, any offer of hops made to and accepted by the Board before the appointed day under a Forward Contract Plan established by them for a crop season after 1980 shall be treated as having been made to and accepted by such person as is specified in that behalf in the resolution mentioned in paragraph (*b*) of that subsection.

(3) The relevant provisions of the Scheme shall, notwithstanding section 1 above, continue to apply so far as necessary for giving effect to any contract to which subsection (2) above applies, references to the Board in those provisions and in the Forward Contract Plan in question being construed, as respects anything falling to be done on or after the appointed day, as references to the person referred to in that subsection.

(4) Where a contract to which subsection (2) above applies relates to a crop season before 1984, the hops which the producer shall be required to consign under the contract in the case of any variety of hops offered by him are—

    (*a*) if the offer specified a maximum sales quantity for that variety, all the hops of that variety produced by him in that season up to that quantity, or up to such revised maximum sales quantity as may be subsequently specified by the producer with the consent of the Board given before the appointed day or with the consent of the person referred to in subsection (2) above given on or after that day ; or

(b) if the offer did not specify a maximum sales quantity for that variety, all the hops of that variety so produced by him up to the quantity specified in the offer as the producer's expected production quantity, or up to such revised expected production quantity as may be subsequently specified as aforesaid ;

but nothing in this subsection shall require a producer to consign a quantity of hops of any variety in excess of the quantity of those hops actually produced by him in the season in question.

(5) In this section—

" Forward Contract Plan " means a Plan within paragraph 3(4)(b) of the Fourth Schedule to the Scheme ; and

" the relevant provisions of the Scheme " means paragraphs 19, 37, 51 to 58, 75, 76, 78 and 79 of, and the Second and Fourth Schedules to, the Scheme.

Winding up and dissolution of the Board.

4.—(1) No general election of members of the Board shall be held under paragraph 7 of the Scheme after the passing of this Act, and the term of office of any member of the Board or of any committee appointed under paragraph 10 of the Scheme shall, instead of expiring at any other time, expire at such time as the Board are dissolved under subsection (7) below or in consequence of being wound up under subsection (8) below.

(2) Where a resolution is passed by the Board as mentioned in section 2(2)(b) above, subsections (3) to (7) below shall have effect on and after the appointed day with respect to the Board, and notwithstanding section 1 above—

(a) paragraph 32 of the Scheme (which relates to accounts, audit and reports) shall continue to have effect on and after that day in relation to the Board so as to require them to comply with the provisions of that paragraph in respect of their financial year which ends (or is by virtue of subsection (3) or (4) below deemed to end) immediately before that day and, in so far as those provisions have not already been complied with in respect thereof, in respect of any preceding financial year ; and

(b) Part II of the Scheme shall accordingly continue to have effect in relation to the Board (subject to subsection (1) above) until such time as the Board are dissolved under subsection (7) below.

(3) Subject to subsection (4) below, if the appointed day is other than 1st April, the Board's financial year then current shall be deemed to have ended with the day before the appointed day.

(4) If the appointed day falls on or after 2nd April but before 2nd July in any year, the Board's financial year which would apart from this section have ended on the preceding 31st March shall instead be deemed to have ended with the day before the appointed day.

(5) The Board shall have all such powers as are necessary for the performance of their duties under paragraph 32 of the Scheme or for otherwise winding up their affairs, including, in particular, power to make arrangements with any person for the use by the Board of the services of a person whose contract of employment has been transferred to that person pursuant to a resolution under section 2(2)(*b*) above, or for the use of any office accommodation which has been so transferred.

(6) Any expenses incurred by the Board on or after the appointed day under the preceding provisions of this section shall be defrayed by the person in whom the fund established under paragraph 30 of the Scheme has vested in accordance with section 2(2) above (or if it has so vested in more than one person, by those persons rateably according to the proportions in which it has so vested in them).

(7) As soon as the Minister of Agriculture, Fisheries and Food is satisfied that the requirements of paragraph 32 of the Scheme have been complied with on the part of the Board in respect of their financial years up to and including the one ending immediately before the appointed day, and on being notified by them that they have wound up their affairs, the Minister shall, after consulting the Board, make an order by statutory instrument dissolving the Board on such day as is specified in the order.

(8) If no resolution is passed by the Board as mentioned in section 2(2)(*b*) above the said Minister shall present a petition for the winding up of the Board in accordance with the Scheme and Schedule 2 to the Agricultural Marketing Act 1958; and 1958 c. 47. if, in the event of the Board being so wound up, any assets of the Board remain after the discharge of their debts and liabilities and the payment of the costs and expenses incurred in the winding up, those assets shall be distributed to the producers who would have been by virtue of paragraph 5 of that Schedule liable to contribute in the winding up, and shall be so distributed in proportion to their respective liabilities in that behalf.

5.—(1) This Act may be cited as the Hops Marketing Act 1982. Short title and interpretation.

(2) In this Act—

"the appointed day" means the day appointed by the Minister under section 1(2) above ;

"the Board" means the Hops Marketing Board ;

"the Scheme" means the Hops Marketing Scheme 1932.

SCHEDULE

ORDERS REVOKED

Number	Title
S.R. & O. 1932 No. 505 ...	The Hops Marketing Scheme (Approval) Order 1932.
S.R. & O. 1934 No. 841 ...	The Hops Marketing Scheme (Amendment) Order 1934.
S.R. & O. 1939 No. 444 ...	The Hops Marketing Scheme (Amendment) Order 1939.
S.R. & O. 1945 No. 1486 ...	The Hops Marketing Scheme (Amendment) Order 1945.
S.I. 1948 No. 642	The Hops Marketing Scheme (Amendment) Order 1948.
S.I. 1949 No. 2456	The Hops Marketing Scheme (Amendment) Order 1949.
S.I. 1950 No. 655	The Hops Marketing Scheme (Amendment) Order 1950.
S.I. 1955 No. 464	The Hops Marketing Scheme (Amendment) Order 1955.
S.I. 1965 No. 406	The Hops Marketing Scheme (Amendment) Order 1965.
S.I. 1972 No. 1427	The Hops Marketing Scheme (Amendment) Order 1972.
S.I. 1974 No. 2030	The Hops Marketing Scheme (Amendment) Order 1974.
S.I. 1977 No. 1280	The Hops Marketing Scheme (Amendment) Order 1977.

Transport (Finance)
Act 1982

1982 CHAPTER 6

An Act to increase certain limits relating to the indebtedness of the British Railways Board and the National Bus Company, to the amount of compensation payable in respect of certain public service obligations of the Board, and to the amount of certain financial assistance given to the Port of London Authority and the Mersey Docks and Harbour Company; and to enable the Treasury to guarantee the discharge of the Board's liabilities to the European Company for the Financing of Railroad Rolling Stock.   [25th February 1982]

B E IT ENACTED by the Queen's most Excellent Majesty, by and with the advice and consent of the Lords Spiritual and Temporal, and Commons, in this present Parliament assembled, and by the authority of the same, as follows:—

British Railways Board

Increased borrowing limit for the Board.

1968 c. 73.

1. In section 42(6) of the Transport Act 1968 (which limits the aggregate amount outstanding in respect of the principal of money borrowed by the British Railways Board and its commencing capital debt to £600 million or such greater sum not exceeding £900 million as the Secretary of State may by order specify) for " £600 million " and " £900 million " there shall be substituted respectively " £1,100 million " and " £1,300 million ".

2. For section 3(4) of the Railways Act 1974 (directions to Increased Board not to involve compensation under certain Community limit relating regulations beyond a limit, now £3,000 million for periods after to 1978) there shall be substituted— compensation.

1974 c. 48.

"(4) The power of giving directions under subsection (1) above shall be so exercised that the aggregate amount of any compensation payable under the relevant transport regulations, for periods after the end of 1978, in respect of all obligations imposed by directions under that subsection shall not exceed £6,000 million or such greater sum not exceeding £10,000 million as may be specified by Order in Council.".

3.—(1) If the British Railways Board becomes a member of the Treasury European Company for the Financing of Railroad Rolling Stock, guarantee. the Treasury may guarantee the discharge of the Board's liabilities to the Company.

(2) Immediately after a guarantee is given under this section the Treasury shall lay a statement of the guarantee before each House of Parliament, and where any sum is issued for fulfilling the guarantee the Treasury shall, as soon as possible after the end of each financial year, beginning with that in which the sum is issued and ending with that in which all liability in respect of the principal of the sum and in respect of interest on it is finally discharged, lay before each House of Parliament a statement relating to that sum.

(3) Any sums required by the Treasury for fulfilling the guarantee shall be charged on and issued out of the Consolidated Fund.

(4) If any sums are issued in fulfilment of the guarantee, the Board shall make to the Treasury, at such times and in such manner as the Treasury may from time to time direct, payments of such amounts as the Treasury may so direct in or towards repayment of the sums so issued, and payments of interest at such rate as the Treasury may so direct on what is outstanding for the time being in respect of sums so issued.

(5) Any sums received by the Treasury under subsection (4) above shall be paid into the Consolidated Fund.

National Bus Company

4.—(1) Section 27 of the Transport Act 1968 (subsection (3)(i) Increased of which limits the aggregate amount outstanding in respect of borrowing the principal of money borrowed by the National Bus Company limit for and its commencing capital debt to £200 million) shall be amended National Bus as follows. Company.

1968 c. 73.

(2) In subsection (3)(i) for " £200 million " there shall be substituted " the limit mentioned in subsection (4) of this section ".

(3) After subsection (3) there shall be added—

" (4) The limit referred to in subsection (3)(i) of this section is £250 million or such greater sum not exceeding £275 million as the Secretary of State may specify by order.

(5) No order shall be made under subsection (4) of this section unless a draft of the order has been laid before and approved by resolution of the House of Commons."

Port of London Authority and
Mersey Docks and Harbour Company

Increased financial assistance.
1981 c. 21.

5. In section 1(3) of the Ports (Financial Assistance) Act 1981 (limit of £160 million on financial assistance to the Port of London Authority and the Mersey Docks and Harbour Company) for " £160 million " there shall be substituted " £360 million ".

General

Repeals.

6. The enactments mentioned in Part I of the Schedule to this Act are hereby repealed to the extent specified in the third column of that Schedule and the instruments mentioned in Part II of that Schedule are hereby revoked.

Short title.

7. This Act may be cited as the Transport (Finance) Act 1982.

SCHEDULE

REPEALS

PART I

ACTS

Chapter	Short title	Extent of repeal
1974 c. 48.	The Railways Act 1974.	Section 2.
1975 c. 55.	The Statutory Corporations (Financial Provisions) Act 1975.	Section 4.
1978 c. 55.	The Transport Act 1978.	Section 14.

PART II

STATUTORY INSTRUMENTS

Number	Title
S.I. 1979 No. 944.	The British Railways Board (Borrowing Powers) Order 1979.
S.I. 1981 No. 441.	The British Railways Board (Increase of Compensation Limit) Order 1981.

New Towns Act 1982

1982 CHAPTER 7

An Act to increase the limit imposed by section 60 of the New Towns Act 1981 on the amounts which may be borrowed by development corporations and the Commission for the New Towns. [25th February 1982]

B E IT ENACTED by the Queen's most Excellent Majesty, by and with the advice and consent of the Lords Spiritual and Temporal, and Commons, in this present Parliament assembled, and by the authority of the same, as follows:—

Increase of limit on borrowing.
1981 c. 64.

1. In section 60 of the New Towns Act 1981 (limit on borrowing by development corporations and Commission for New Towns) for "£3,625 million or such greater sum not exceeding £4,000 million" there shall be substituted "£4,500 million or such greater sum not exceeding £5,000 million".

Citation and extent.

2.—(1) This Act may be cited as the New Towns Act 1982.

(2) This Act does not extend to Northern Ireland.

Consolidated Fund Act 1982

1982 CHAPTER 8

An Act to apply certain sums out of the Consolidated Fund to the service of the years ending on 31st March 1981 and 1982.   [22nd March 1982]

Most Gracious Sovereign,

WE, Your Majesty's most dutiful and loyal subjects, the Commons of the United Kingdom in Parliament assembled, towards making good the supply which we have cheerfully granted to Your Majesty in this Session of Parliament, have resolved to grant unto Your Majesty the sums hereinafter mentioned; and do therefore most humbly beseech Your Majesty that it may be enacted, and be it enacted by the Queen's most Excellent Majesty, by and with the advice and consent of the Lords Spiritual and Temporal, and Commons, in this present Parliament assembled, and by the authority of the same, as follows:—

1. The Treasury may issue out of the Consolidated Fund of the United Kingdom and apply towards making good the supply granted to Her Majesty for the service of the year ending on 31st March 1981 the sum of £14,620,065·17.

Issue out of the Consolidated Fund for the year ending 31st March 1981.

2. The Treasury may issue out of the Consolidated Fund of the United Kingdom and apply towards making good the supply granted to Her Majesty for the service of the year ending on 31st March 1982 the sum of £1,459,337,000.

Issue out of the Consolidated Fund for the year ending 31st March 1982.

3. This Act may be cited as the Consolidated Fund Act 1982.

Short title.

Agricultural Training
Board Act 1982

1982 CHAPTER 9

An Act to consolidate the law relating to the Agricultural
Training Board.   [29th March 1982]

B E IT ENACTED by the Queen's most Excellent Majesty, by and
with the advice and consent of the Lords Spiritual and
Temporal, and Commons, in this present Parliament
assembled, and by the authority of the same, as follows:—

The Agricultural Training Board

1.—(1) The provisions of this Act shall have effect in relation The
to the Agricultural Training Board.

(2) In this Act—

> " agriculture " has the same meaning as in the Agriculture 1947 c. 48.
> Act 1947 or the Agriculture (Scotland) Act 1948 ; 1948 c. 45.

> " the Board " means the Agricultural Training Board which
> was established by the Industrial Training (Agricultural, S.I. 1966/969.
> Horticultural and Forestry Board) Order 1966 ;

> " employee " includes a person engaged under a contract
> for services, and " employer " shall be construed accor-
> dingly ;

> " employment " means employment under a contract of
> service or apprenticeship or a contract for services or
> otherwise than under a contract, and " employed "
> shall be construed accordingly ;

(marginal note) Agricultural Training Board.

1964 c. 16.
1982 c. 10.
" industrial training board " means a board established under section 1 of the Industrial Training Act 1964 or section 1 of the Industrial Training Act 1982 ;

" the industry " means the activities in relation to which the Board exercises functions in accordance with the Industrial Training (Agricultural, Horticultural and Forestry Board) Order 1966 (as for the time being amended) ;

S.I. 1966/969.

" the Ministers " means the Ministers concerned with agriculture in England, Scotland and Wales, acting jointly.

(3) Schedule 1 to this Act shall have effect with respect to the Board.

Establishment
of committees.

2.—(1) The Board may—

(*a*) appoint committees (which need not include members of the Board) ;

(*b*) join with one or more other industrial training boards in appointing joint committees consisting of such persons (whether or not members of an industrial training board) as may be determined by the Board and the other board or boards ;

and delegate to any such committee all or any of the functions conferred on the Board by section 4 or by virtue of section 6 below.

(2) The Board may pay or, as the case may be, join in paying—

(*a*) to the members of such a committee such travelling, subsistence and other allowances (including allowances for loss of remunerative time) as the Ministers may determine with the approval of the Treasury ; and

(*b*) to the chairman of any such committee to which functions mentioned in subsection (1) above are delegated such remuneration as the Ministers may so determine.

(3) The Board may make such arrangements as the Ministers may specify with the approval of the Treasury—

(*a*) for the payment of pensions, superannuation allowances and gratuities to or in respect of the chairmen of such committees as are mentioned in subsection (2)(*b*) above ;

(*b*) for the payment of compensation to a person who ceases to be such a chairman otherwise than on the expiry of his term of office where it appears to the Ministers that there are special circumstances which make it right for him to receive compensation.

(4) Subject to any directions of the Board or, in the case of a committee appointed under subsection (1)(*b*) above, the Board and the other board or boards which appointed it, a committee appointed under this section may regulate its own procedure and fix a quorum for its proceedings.

3.—(1) The Ministers may by order—

    (*a*) amend the Industrial Training (Agricultural, Horticultural and Forestry Board) Order 1966 (as for the time being amended) ; or

    (*b*) revoke that order.

Amendment or revocation of order establishing the Board.

S.I. 1966/969.

(2) Before making an order under subsection (1)(*a*) above the Ministers shall consult the Board and any organisation or association appearing to them to be representative—

    (*a*) of employers engaged in activities to be included in or excluded from the order by virtue of the amendments in question ; and

    (*b*) of employees engaged in those activities.

(3) Before making an order under subsection (1)(*b*) above the Ministers shall consult the Board and any organisation or association of organisations appearing to them to be representative—

    (*a*) of substantial numbers of employers engaging in the activities with which the Board is concerned ; and

    (*b*) of substantial numbers of persons employed in the activities mentioned in paragraph (*a*) above.

(4) An order under subsection (1)(*a*) above may, besides including or without including provisions with respect to any activities of industry or commerce, include provisions with respect to activities relating to agriculture which are not carried on in the course of industry or commerce.

(5) An order under subsection (1)(*b*) above shall provide for the winding up of the Board.

(6) An order under subsection (1) above may provide for any incidental, transitional or consequential matter for which it appears to the Ministers to be necessary or expedient to provide.

(7) The power to make an order under subsection (1) above shall be exercisable by statutory instrument which shall be subject to annulment in pursuance of a resolution of either House of Parliament.

Functions of the Board

4.—(1) The Board—

(a) shall provide or secure the provision of such courses and other facilities (which may include residential accommodation) for the training of persons employed or intending to be employed in the industry as may be required, having regard to any courses or facilities otherwise available to such persons;

(b) may approve such courses and facilities provided by other persons;

(c) shall from time to time consider such employments in the industry as appear to require consideration and publish recommendations with regard to the nature and length of the training for any such employment and the further education to be associated with the training, the persons by and to whom the training ought to be given, the standards to be attained as a result of the training and the methods of ascertaining whether those standards have been attained;

(d) may apply or make arrangements for the application of selection tests and of tests or other methods for ascertaining the attainment of any standards recommended by the Board and may award certificates of the attainment of those standards;

(e) may assist persons in finding facilities for being trained for employment in the industry;

(f) may take part in any arrangements made in pursuance of section 2(1) or (2), 3(4) or 8 of the Employment and Training Act 1973 (which relate to arrangements for persons to select, train for and obtain suitable employments and to obtain suitable employees);

(g) may carry on or assist other persons in carrying on research into any matter relating to training for employment in the industry;

(h) may provide advice about training connected with the industry;

(i) may enter into agreements with persons for the making by them of payments to the Board in respect of the exercise by the Board of any of its functions.

(2) The Board may enter into contracts of service or apprenticeship with persons who intend to be employed in the industry and to attend courses or avail themselves of other facilities provided or approved by the Board.

(3) The Board may, at the request of another industrial training board, provide advice for the other board and courses and other facilities for the training of persons employed or intending to be employed in the industry for which that other board is established.

(4) The Board may—

   (a) pay maintenance and travelling allowances to persons attending courses provided or approved by the Board ;

   (b) make grants or loans to persons providing courses or other facilities approved by the Board ;

   (c) pay fees to persons providing further education in respect of persons who receive it in association with their training in courses provided or approved by the Board ;

   (d) make payments to persons in connection with arrangements under which they or employees of theirs make use of courses or other facilities provided or approved by the Board.

5.—(1) The Board may, with the consent of the Ministers, exercise such functions in connection with training for employment outside Great Britain of persons temporarily in Great Britain as are exercisable by it under section 4(1) and (4) above in connection with the training of persons employed or intending to be employed in the industry.

Training for employment overseas.

(2) The Board may delegate any power exercisable by it by virtue of this section to a committee (which need not include members of the Board) appointed for that purpose or to any committee appointed under section 2 above.

6.—(1) The Ministers may give to the Board such directions as they think fit with respect to the performance by the Board of its functions ; and it shall be the duty of the Board, notwithstanding anything in any other provision of this Act, to comply with the directions.

Directions by the Ministers.

(2) Any such directions may require the Board to exercise on behalf of the Ministers functions exercisable by the Ministers, whether by virtue of an enactment or otherwise, which are connected with the provision of training or advice for persons employed or intending to be employed in agriculture or in agriculture or horticulture business within the meaning of section 64 of the Agriculture Act 1967 (excluding a function of making regulations or any other instrument having the force of law).

1967 c. 22.

7. The Minister of Agriculture, Fisheries and Food and the Secretary of State may, for the purpose of assisting the Board in planning and carrying out activities (including research) connected with the functions conferred on it by section 4(1)(a) above, disclose to the Board any information about—

Disclosure of information to the Board.

   (a) the kind of crops grown on any land and the areas of land on which crops of any kind are grown ; and

> (*b*) the number and description of persons employed on any land and employed in disposing of the produce of any land ; and
>
> (*c*) the kinds of machinery used on any land,

1947 c. 48.
1979 c. 13.

which has been furnished to him in pursuance of section 78 of the Agriculture Act 1947 or section 1 of the Agricultural Statistics Act 1979.

Reports and accounts.

8.—(1) The Board shall keep proper accounts and other records in relation to the accounts and prepare in respect of each of its financial years a statement of account in such form as the Ministers may, with the approval of the Treasury, determine.

(2) The accounts of the Board shall be audited by auditors appointed by the Board and no person shall be qualified to be so appointed unless he is a member of one or more of the following bodies : —

> (*a*) the Institute of Chartered Accountants in England and Wales ;
>
> (*b*) the Institute of Chartered Accountants of Scotland ;
>
> (*c*) the Association of Certified Accountants ;
>
> (*d*) the Institute of Chartered Accountants in Ireland ;

1948 c. 38.

> (*e*) any other body of accountants established in the United Kingdom and for the time being recognised, for the purposes of section 161(1)(*a*) of the Companies Act 1948, by the Secretary of State ;

but a Scottish firm may be so appointed if each of the partners is qualified to be so appointed.

(3) The Board shall for each of its financial years make a report of its activities to the Ministers and that report shall include a statement of the accounts of the Board for that year together with a copy of any report made by the auditors on the accounts.

(4) The Ministers shall lay a copy of every such report before Parliament.

General

Financial assistance and investment.

9.—(1) The Minister of Agriculture, Fisheries and Food may with the approval of the Treasury make grants and loans to the Board out of moneys provided by Parliament.

(2) The Board shall not invest any money otherwise than in such manner as the Ministers may approve.

10.—(1) In relation to accidents happening to employed earners (within the meaning of Chapter IV of Part II of the Social Security Act 1975) who attend courses or avail themselves of other facilities provided or approved by the Board, sections 52 to 54 of that Act have effect subject to the following modifications.

Industrial injuries benefit for accidents in training.

1975 c. 14.

(2) For the purposes of section 52, any act done by the employed earner for the purposes of and in connection with his training shall, if it is not done for the purposes of and in connection with his employer's trade or business, be deemed to be so done.

(3) For the purposes of section 53, a vehicle (within the meaning of that section) which is operated by or on behalf of the Board or some other person by whom it is provided in pursuance of arrangements made with the Board shall, if not operated and provided as mentioned in subsection (1)(*b*)(i) of that section, be deemed to be so operated and provided.

(4) For the purposes of section 54, any premises at which an employed earner is for the time being employed for the purposes of his training shall, if they are not premises at which he is for the time being employed for the purposes of his employer's trade or business, be deemed to be such premises.

Supplemental

11.—(1) The enactments specified in Schedule 2 to this Act are hereby repealed to the extent specified in the third column of that Schedule but none of those repeals shall affect any of those enactments as they have effect in relation to any industrial training board other than the Board.

Consequential provisions, repeals and savings.

(2) The repeals made by this Act in sections 6 and 14 of the Employment and Training Act 1973 and the repeal of paragraph 7 of the Schedule to the Industrial Training Act 1964 shall not affect the validity of any order made under the said Act of 1964 in respect of the Board but this subsection is without prejudice to the powers conferred by section 3 above to amend or revoke such an order.

1973 c. 50.
1964 c. 16.

(3) In section 127(1) of the Employment Protection Act 1975 after paragraph (*b*) there shall be inserted—

1975 c. 71.

" (*bb*) the Agricultural Training Board Act 1982 ".

(4) Where any period of time specified in or under an enactment repealed by this Act is current at the commencement of this Act, this Act shall have effect as if the corresponding provision of this Act had been in force when that period began to run.

Short title,
extent and
commence-
ment.

12.—(1) This Act may be cited as the Agricultural Training Board Act 1982.

(2) This Act does not extend to Northern Ireland.

(3) This Act shall come into force at the expiry of the period of three months beginning with the day on which it is passed.

SCHEDULES

SCHEDULE 1

The Agricultural Training Board

1. The Board shall be a body corporate and shall continue to be known as the Agricultural Training Board.

2. The members of the Board shall be appointed by the Ministers.

3. The Board shall consist of a chairman, who shall be a person appearing to the Ministers to have industrial or commercial experience, and—

   (a) an equal number of persons appointed after consultation with such organisations or associations of organisations representative of employers engaging in the industry and of persons employed in the industry respectively as appear to the Ministers to be appropriate ;

   (b) persons appointed after consultation with the Ministers concerned with education in England, Scotland and Wales ;

and, if the Ministers think fit to appoint as deputy chairman a person appearing to them to have industrial or commercial experience, the deputy chairman so appointed ; and references in the following provisions of this Schedule to a chairman shall include a deputy chairman.

4. The Board shall pay to its chairman such remuneration (if any) as the Ministers may from time to time with the approval of the Treasury determine and may make such arrangements for the payment of pensions, superannuation allowances and gratuities to or in respect of its chairman as the Ministers may specify with the approval of the Treasury.

5. Where a person ceases to be the chairman of the Board otherwise than on the expiry of his term of office and it appears to the Ministers that there are special circumstances which make it right for him to receive compensation, the Board may make him a payment of such amount as the Ministers may determine with the approval of the Treasury.

6. The Ministers, the Minister concerned with education in Scotland, the Ministers concerned with education in England and Wales (acting jointly), the Manpower Services Commission and, if the Ministers think fit in a particular case, such other Ministers in charge of government departments as they may specify may each appoint one person to attend the meetings of the Board ; and any person so appointed shall be entitled to take part in the proceedings of the Board and receive copies of all documents distributed to its members, but shall have no vote.

7. An order under section 3 of this Act may make provision with respect to—

   (a) the tenure of office of the members of the Board ;

(*b*) the quorum and, subject to paragraph 6 above, the proceedings and meetings of the Board ;

(*c*) the execution of instruments by and on behalf of the Board and the proof of documents purporting to be executed, issued or signed by the Board or a member, officer or servant of the Board ;

and any provision made by virtue of sub-paragraph (*b*) above may enable votes to be cast by proxy.

8. Subject to paragraph 6 above and to any provision of the kind mentioned in paragraph 7 above which is contained in the Industrial Training (Agricultural, Horticultural and Forestry Board) Order 1966 (as for the time being amended) either by virtue of that paragraph or of paragraph 7 of the Schedule to the Industrial Training Act 1964, the Board shall have power to regulate its own procedure.

9. The proceedings of the Board shall not be invalidated by any vacancy in the membership of the Board or by any defect in the appointment of any member.

10. The Board may appoint such officers and servants, upon such terms as to remuneration, pension rights and other conditions of service, as the Board may determine with the approval of the Ministers given with the consent of the Treasury.

11. The Board may pay to its members such travelling, subsistence and other allowances (including allowances for loss of remunerative time) as the Ministers may determine with the approval of the Treasury.

SCHEDULE 2

Repeals

Chapter	Short title	Extent of repeal
1964 c. 16.	The Industrial Training Act 1964.	The whole Act except section 16.
1973 c. 50.	The Employment and Training Act 1973.	Section 6(3), (4). In section 14(2), the words from " but " onwards. In Schedule 2, Parts III and IV.
1975 c. 18.	The Social Security (Consequential Provisions) Act 1975.	In Schedule 2, paragraph 11.
1979 c. 13.	The Agricultural Statistics Act 1979.	In Schedule 1, paragraph 3.

Industrial Training Act 1982

1982 CHAPTER 10

An Act to consolidate the law relating to industrial training boards. [29th March 1982]

BE IT ENACTED by the Queen's most Excellent Majesty, by and with the advice and consent of the Lords Spiritual and Temporal, and Commons, in this present Parliament assembled, and by the authority of the same, as follows:—

Establishment and winding up of industrial training boards

1.—(1) For the purpose of making better provision for the training of persons over compulsory school age (in Scotland school age) for employment in any activities of industry or commerce the Secretary of State may, subject to the provisions of this section, make an order specifying those activities and establishing a board to exercise in relation to them the functions conferred on industrial training boards by the following provisions of this Act. *Establishment of industrial training boards.*

(2) In this Act—

" the Commission " means the Manpower Services Commission ;

" employee " includes a person engaged under a contract for services, and " employer " shall be construed accordingly ;

" employment " means employment under a contract of service or apprenticeship or a contract for services or otherwise than under a contract, and " employed " shall be construed accordingly ;

" exemption certificate " has the meaning assigned to it by section 13(1) below ;

1964 c. 16.

" industrial training board " means (subject to section 20(2) below) a board established under this section or section 1 of the Industrial Training Act 1964 ;

" industrial training order " means an order under this section ;

" the industry ", in relation to an industrial training board, means the activities in relation to which it exercises functions ;

" levy order " has the meaning assigned to it by section 11(2) below ; and

" levy proposals " has the meaning assigned to it by section 11(1) below.

(3) The provisions of Schedule 1 to this Act shall have effect with respect to industrial training boards.

(4) The Secretary of State shall not make an industrial training order unless—

(a) the Commission has submitted proposals to him for an order together with a statement of the views of the persons consulted by it in accordance with subsection (5) below, or

(b) he has consulted the Commission and the Commission has given him such a statement (whether or not the Commission has also given him its own views).

(5) Where the Commission proposes to submit to the Secretary of State proposals for the making of an industrial training order or is consulted by the Secretary of State in connection with the making of such an order, the Commission shall consult—

(a) such organisations or associations of organisations appearing to the Commission to be representative of substantial numbers of employers or employees and such bodies established for the purpose of carrying on under national ownership any industry or part of an industry or undertaking as the Commission thinks fit ; and

(b) such other organisations, associations or bodies (if any) as the Secretary of State may direct.

(6) Any consultations required to be carried out under this section may be in such form and in respect of such matters (whether or not related to the making of a specific order) as the Secretary of State or, in a case where the consultations are carried out by it, the Commission thinks fit.

(7) An industrial training order may provide for any incidental or supplementary matter for which it appears to the Secretary of State to be necessary or expedient to provide and an order amending or revoking such an order may provide for any incidental, transitional or consequential matter for which it appears

to the Secretary of State to be necessary or expedient to provide ; and, without prejudice to the generality of the foregoing or to the powers implied in section 3(2) below, the matters for which orders under this section may provide shall include the amendment or revocation of an order under that section.

(8) The power to make an industrial training order shall be exercisable by statutory instrument, which shall be subject to annulment in pursuance of a resolution of either House of Parliament.

2.—(1) An industrial training board may—
    (*a*) appoint committees (which need not include members of the board) ;
    (*b*) join with one or more other industrial training boards in appointing joint committees consisting of such persons (whether or not members of an industrial training board) as may be determined by the boards ;

Establishment of committees.

and delegate to any such committee, to such extent as may be stated in proposals submitted to and approved by the Commission under section 5(5) below, all or any of the functions conferred on the board by section 5 or section 14(5) below.

(2) An industrial training board may pay or, as the case may be, join in paying—
    (*a*) to the members of such a committee such allowances for loss of remunerative time as the Secretary of State may, with the approval of the Treasury, determine and such travelling, subsistence and other allowances as the board or, as the case may be, the boards may determine ; and
    (*b*) to the chairman of any such committee to which functions mentioned in subsection (1) above are delegated such remuneration as the board or, as the case may be the boards may determine.

(3) An industrial training board may make, or as the case may be join in making, such arrangements as the board may determine—
    (*a*) for the payment of pensions, superannuation allowances and gratuities to or in respect of the chairmen of such committees as are mentioned in subsection (2)(*b*) above ;
    (*b*) for the payment of compensation to a person who ceases to be such a chairman otherwise than on the expiry of his term of office where it appears to the board that there are special circumstances which make it right for him to receive compensation.

(4) Subject to any directions of the board or boards which appointed it, a committee appointed under this section may regulate its own procedure and fix a quorum for its proceedings.

Transfer of establishments' activities from industry of one board to that of another.

3.—(1) If an employer in the industry of an industrial training board requests the Commission in writing to secure that the activities carried on at a particular establishment of his shall, instead of being included for the purposes of this Act in that industry, be included for those purposes in the industry of another industrial training board, the Commission shall, after consulting both boards in question about the request, submit it to the Secretary of State together with a statement of the boards' views and may also submit its recommendation as to whether he should give effect to that request.

(2) Where the Commission submits such a request to the Secretary of State, he may if he thinks fit make an order giving effect to the request; and the power to make such an order shall be exercisable by statutory instrument.

Winding up of boards.

4.—(1) An order made under section 1 above revoking an industrial training order (in this section referred to as " a revocation order ") shall provide for the winding up of the industrial training board.

(2) A revocation order may provide—

(*a*) for the imposition of a levy on employers in the industry (whether or not exemption certificates have been issued to them), other than such (if any) as may be exempted by the order, for the purpose of raising the whole or part of any amount by which the assets of the board may be insufficient to meet its liabilities and the expenses of the winding up ; and

(*b*) for the application for specified purposes of any amount by which those assets may exceed those liabilities and expenses.

(3) A revocation order making provision for the imposition of a levy—

(*a*) may provide for payments by way of levy to accrue due from day to day over a period specified in the order ; and

(*b*) may contain provisions as to the evidence by which a person's liability to the levy or his discharge of that liability may be established and as to the time at which any amount payable by any person by way of levy shall (whether or not any period over which that amount accrues due has expired) become due and recoverable by the board.

(4) A person assessed to levy imposed under a revocation order may appeal to an industrial tribunal and a revocation order imposing a levy shall make provision as to the time within which such an appeal may be made.

(5) On an appeal under subsection (4) above—

(a) if the appellant satisfies the tribunal that he ought not to have been assessed to the levy or ought to have been assessed in a smaller amount, the tribunal shall rescind or, as the case may be, reduce the assessment but (subject to paragraph (b) below) in any other case shall confirm it ; and

(b) if it appears to the tribunal that the appellant ought to have been assessed to the levy in a larger amount, the tribunal may increase the assessment accordingly.

(6) Where a revocation order has been made for the winding up of an industrial training board the Secretary of State may out of moneys provided by Parliament—

(a) pay such pension, superannuation allowance or gratuity to or in respect of the former chairman of the board as he may with the approval of the Treasury determine ; and

(b) pay such sums as he may so determine to the trustees of the Industrial Training Boards' Combined Pension Fund for the purpose of meeting the whole or part of any shortfall in the assets of the Fund referable to the pensions, superannuation allowances and gratuities payable in respect of the former officers and servants of the board.

Functions of boards

5.—(1) For the purpose of encouraging adequate training of persons employed or intending to be employed in the industry, an industrial training board— Functions of boards.

(a) may provide or secure the provision of such courses and other facilities (which may include residential accommodation) for the training of those persons as the board considers adequate, having regard to any courses or facilities otherwise available to those persons ;

(b) may approve such courses and facilities provided by other persons ;

(c) may from time to time consider such employments in the industry as appear to require consideration and publish recommendations with regard to the nature and length of the training for any such employment and the further education to be associated with the training, the persons by and to whom the training ought to be given, the standards to be attained as a result of the training and the methods of ascertaining whether those standards have been attained ;

(d) may apply or make arrangements for the application of selection tests and of tests or other methods for ascertaining the attainment of any standards recommended by the board and may award certificates of the attainment of those standards ;

(e) may assist persons in finding facilities for being trained for employment in the industry ;

(f) may carry on or assist other persons in carrying on research into any matter relating to training for employment in the industry ;

(g) may provide advice about training connected with the industry.

(2) An industrial training board may enter into contracts of service or apprenticeship with persons who intend to be employed in the industry and to attend courses or avail themselves of other facilities provided or approved by the board.

(3) An industrial training board may—

(a) at the request of another industrial training board provide advice for the other board and courses and other facilities for the training of persons employed or intending to be employed in the industry for which that other board is established ;

(b) at the request of the Commission provide such other advice, and such other courses and facilities for training, as are mentioned in the request ;

(c) at the request of an employer in the industry provide for him advice about training connected with activities carried on in Northern Ireland or outside the United Kingdom, which, if they were carried on in Great Britain, would be included in the industry ;

(d) enter into agreements with persons for the making by them of payments to the board in respect of the exercise by the board of any of its functions ;

1973 c. 50.

(e) take part in any arrangements made in pursuance of section 2(1) or (2), 3(4) or 8 of the Employment and Training Act 1973 (which relate to arrangements for persons to select, train for and obtain suitable employments and to obtain suitable employees) ;

but any expense incurred by the board in pursuance of paragraph (c) above shall not be defrayed out of sums received by way of levy.

(4) An industrial training board may—

    (*a*) pay maintenance and travelling allowances to persons attending courses provided or approved by the board ;

    (*b*) make grants or loans to persons providing courses or other facilities approved by the board, to persons who make studies for the purpose of providing such courses or facilities and to persons who maintain arrangements to provide such courses or facilities which are not for the time being in use ;

    (*c*) pay fees to persons providing further education in respect of persons who receive it in association with their training in courses provided or approved by the board ;

    (*d*) make payments to persons in connection with arrangements under which they or employees of theirs make use of courses or other facilities provided or approved by the board.

(5) An industrial training board—

    (*a*) shall from time to time submit to the Commission for its approval proposals for the exercise of functions conferred on the board by this section ; and

    (*b*) may from time to time submit to the Commission for its approval proposals for the delegation of all or any of those functions to committees established under section 2 above ;

and the board shall exercise its functions under this section in accordance with proposals submitted to the Commission and approved by it.

(6) An industrial training board shall give to the Commission such information or facilities for obtaining information with regard to the exercise of its functions, in such manner and at such times as the Commission may reasonably require.

6.—(1) An industrial training board may require employers in the industry to furnish such returns and other information of a kind approved by the Secretary of State and to keep such records of a kind approved by him and produce them for examination on behalf of the board as appear to the board to be necessary for carrying out its functions.

    Power to obtain information from employers.

(2) Subject to subsection (3) below, returns and other information furnished in pursuance of subsection (1) above and any information obtained on an examination made in pursuance of that subsection shall not, without the consent of the employer to whose business the returns or information relate, be disclosed otherwise than to the Secretary of State or one of his officers, or to an industrial training board or a committee

appointed by such a board, or an officer of such a board or committee or any person entitled to take part in the proceedings of such a board or to the Commission or an officer of the Commission.

(3) Subsection (2) above shall not apply—

(a) to the disclosure of returns or information in the form of a summary of similar returns or information furnished by or obtained from a number of employers, if the summary is so framed as not to enable particulars relating to any individual business to be ascertained from it ;

(b) to any disclosure of information made for the purposes of any legal proceedings pursuant to this Act or any criminal proceedings, whether pursuant to this Act or not, or for the purposes of any report of any such proceedings.

(4) A certificate purporting to be issued by or on behalf of the Secretary of State and stating that he has approved any kind of information, return or record for the purposes of subsection (1) above shall in any legal proceedings be evidence, and in Scotland sufficient evidence, of the facts stated in the certificate.

(5) If any person fails to comply with any requirement made under subsection (1) above he shall be liable on summary conviction to a fine not exceeding £100 or, on a second or subsequent conviction, £200.

(6) If any person—

(a) knowingly or recklessly furnishes, in pursuance of any requirement made under subsection (1) above, any return or other information which is false in a material particular, or

(b) wilfully makes a false entry in any record required to be produced under that subsection or, with intent to deceive, makes use of any such entry which he knows to be false, or

(c) discloses any information in contravention of subsection (2) above,

he shall be liable on summary conviction to imprisonment for a term not exceeding three months or to a fine not exceeding the prescribed sum or to both, or on conviction on indictment to imprisonment for a term not exceeding two years or to a fine or to both.

(7) In subsection (6) above " the prescribed sum " means—

(a) if the offence was committed in England or Wales, the prescribed sum within the meaning of section 32 of the

Magistrates' Courts Act 1980 (£1,000 or other sum 1980 c. 43. substituted by order under section 143(1) of that Act) ; and

(*b*) if the offence was committed in Scotland, the prescribed sum within the meaning of section 289B of the Crim- 1975 c. 21. inal Procedure (Scotland) Act 1975 (£1,000 or other sum substituted by order under section 289D(1) of that Act).

(8) Where an offence under this section committed by a body corporate is proved to have been committed with the consent or connivance of, or to be attributable to any neglect on the part of, any director, manager, secretary or other similar officer of the body corporate, or any person who was purporting to act in any such capacity, he, as well as the body corporate, shall be guilty of that offence and be liable to be proceeded against and punished accordingly.

7.—(1) The Commission may, with the approval of the Secre- Provisions tary of State, direct an industrial training board to exercise the supplementary power to require the furnishing of information which is conferred to s. 6. on the board by section 6(1) above (in this section referred to as " the information power ") so as to require employers in the industry to furnish to the board, in such form and on such occasions as are specified in the direction, such information as the Commission considers that it needs for the purposes of its functions and as is so specified ; and it shall be the duty of the board to comply with the direction.

(2) An industrial training board shall not exercise the information power except—

(*a*) in pursuance of a direction given by virtue of subsection (1) above ; or

(*b*) with the approval of the Secretary of State and in accordance with the conditions, if any, of the approval ;

and any application by a board for approval in pursuance of paragraph (*b*) above must be made to the Commission and contain such information as the Commission may require with respect to the proposed exercise of the information power.

(3) Where the Commission receives such an application from a board the Commission—

(*a*) may request the board to withdraw or alter the application ; and

(*b*) shall, if it does not so request or the board declines to comply with the request or complies with a request to alter the application, transmit the application to the Secretary of State ;

and it shall be the duty of the Commission on transmitting the application to the Secretary of State to inform him whether in its opinion he should reject the application or approve it with specified conditions or without conditions.

(4) An approval of an application given by the Secretary of State in pursuance of subsection (2)(*b*) above may be given subject to conditions that the board in question may exercise the information power only for the purpose of requiring the furnishing of information in such forms and on such occasions as are specified in the instrument of approval.

Reports and accounts.

8.—(1) An industrial training board shall keep proper accounts and other records in relation to the accounts and prepare in respect of each of its financial years a statement of account in such form as the Commission may, with the approval of the Secretary of State and the Treasury, determine.

(2) The accounts of an industrial training board shall be audited by auditors appointed by the board and no person shall be qualified to be so appointed unless he is a member of one or more of the following bodies: —

(*a*) the Institute of Chartered Accountants in England and Wales ;

(*b*) the Institute of Chartered Accountants of Scotland ;

(*c*) the Association of Certified Accountants ;

(*d*) the Institute of Chartered Accountants in Ireland ;

(*e*) any other body of accountants established in the United Kingdom and for the time being recognised for the purposes of section 161(1)(*a*) of the Companies Act 1948 by the Secretary of State ;

1948 c. 38.

but a Scottish firm may be so appointed if each of the partners is qualified to be so appointed.

(3) An industrial training board shall for each of its financial years make a report of its activities to the Commission and that report shall include a statement of the accounts of the board for that year together with a copy of any report made by the auditors on the accounts.

(4) The Commission shall send a copy of every such report to the Secretary of State and he shall lay a copy of every such report before Parliament.

Publication of information.

9.—(1) Subject to subsection (2) below, the Secretary of State may, after consultation with the Commission, direct an industrial training board to publish in the report made by it under section 8(3) above, or otherwise as he may direct, such information in the possession of the board as he may specify in the direction.

(2) No direction under this section shall require any information which is so framed as to enable particulars relating to any individual employer or establishment of an employer to be ascertained from it to be published without the consent of the employer in question.

10.—(1) An industrial training board may, with the consent Training for of the Commission given with the approval of the Secretary employment of State, exercise such functions in connection with training for overseas. employment outside Great Britain of persons temporarily in Great Britain as are exercisable by it under section 5(1) and (4) above in connection with the training of persons employed or intending to be employed in the industry ; and the board may enter into agreements for the making of payments to the board in respect of the exercise in pursuance of this subsection of functions by the board.

(2) An industrial training board may delegate any power exercisable by it by virtue of this section to a committee (which need not include members of the board) appointed for that purpose or to any committee appointed under section 2 above.

(3) An industrial training board shall keep separate accounts—

(*a*) with respect to its functions under this section ; and

(*b*) with respect to its other functions under this Act ;

and no money raised by a levy imposed under this Act shall be carried to an account kept in pursuance of paragraph (*a*) above, and any expenses and liabilities incurred by the board under this section shall be disregarded for the purposes of section 4(2) above and section 11(1) below.

Levies

11.—(1) An industrial training board may from time to time, Levies. submit to the Commission for the Commission's approval proposals (in this Act referred to as " levy proposals ") for the raising and collection of a levy to be imposed for the purpose of raising money towards meeting the board's expenses and the Commission shall submit any proposals approved by it to the Secretary of State.

(2) The levy shall be imposed in accordance with an order made by the Secretary of State (in this Act referred to as " a levy order ") which shall give effect to levy proposals approved by the Commission under subsection (1) above and shall provide for the levy to be imposed on employers in the industry, except in so far as they are exempted from it by the industrial training

order, the levy order or an exemption certificate ; but nothing in this Act shall be construed as requiring the Secretary of State to make a levy order in a case in which he considers it inexpedient to make one.

(3) Levy proposals must include proposals for exempting from the levy any employer who, in view of the small number of his employees, ought in the opinion of the board to be exempted and the Secretary of State shall not make a levy order in pursuance of levy proposals unless they provide for the exemption of employers who, in view of the small number of their employees, ought in his opinion to be exempted.

(4) Subject to subsection (5) below, levy proposals may include proposals for securing—

(a) that any exemption certificates issued by the board shall not exempt from the whole or a portion of the levy the employers or some of the employers in the industry, or

(b) that no exemption certificates shall be issued by the board ;

and the Secretary of State shall not make a levy order in pursuance of any levy proposals unless he is satisfied that the proposals published by the board under section 13(5) below provide for exemption certificates relating to levy (other than that payable by virtue of this subsection) in such cases as he considers appropriate.

(5) If, as a result of such levy proposals as are mentioned in subsection (4) above—

(a) in a case within paragraph (a) of that subsection, the amount of the levy from which an exemption certificate will not exempt any person will exceed 0·2 per cent. of the relevant emoluments ; or

(b) in a case within paragraph (b) of that subsection, the amount of the levy payable by any person will exceed that percentage of the relevant emoluments,

then the Commission shall not approve the levy proposals unless it is of the opinion that they are necessary to encourage adequate training in the industry and the Secretary of State shall not make a levy order in pursuance of the levy proposals unless he is satisfied that the proposals are necessary for that purpose and one of the conditions mentioned in subsection (6) below is satisfied.

(6) The conditions referred to in subsection (5) above are—

(a) that the relevant organisations consider, after taking reasonable steps to ascertain the views of the persons they represent, that the proposals are necessary to encourage adequate training in the industry ;

(*b*) that the order will be made less than two years after the making of a former levy order giving effect to proposals made by the board in respect of which the Secretary of State was satisfied that the condition in paragraph (*a*) above applied and either—

(i) the proposals to which the former order gave effect were that no exemption certificates should be issued or that the exemption certificates to be issued should not exempt employers from any of the levy, or

(ii) the proposals to which the former order gave effect were that exemption certificates should not exempt employers from a portion of the levy and the percentage of the relevant emoluments from which under the current proposals the exemption certificates will not exempt any person will not exceed the percentage of relevant emoluments from which he was not exempted under the former order ;

(*c*) that neither of the conditions mentioned in paragraphs (*a*) and (*b*) above applies but the proposals are considered by the Secretary of State to be appropriate in the circumstances.

(7) The Secretary of State shall not make a levy order in pursuance of any levy proposals unless the amount which, disregarding any exemption, he estimates would, if the order were made, be payable by virtue of it by any employer in the industry either—

(*a*) does not exceed an amount which the Secretary of State estimates is equal to one per cent. of the relevant emoluments, or

(*b*) does exceed the amount mentioned in paragraph (*a*) above but is considered by him to be appropriate in the circumstances.

(8) In this section—

" the relevant emoluments " in relation to any person means the aggregate of the emoluments and payments intended to be disbursed as emoluments which are paid and payable by him to or in respect of persons employed in the industry in respect of the period specified in the levy proposals as the period which is relevant for the purposes of this section, and

"the relevant organisations" means organisations appearing to the Secretary of State to represent more than half the persons who he considers are likely to be liable to make payments by way of levy in consequence of the proposals and organisations appearing to him to represent persons who he considers are together likely to be liable to make payments by way of levy in consequence of the levy proposals which amount to more than half the aggregate amount of those payments.

Provisions supplementary to s. 11.

12.—(1) Levy proposals must include such information or further information as the Commission directs the board to furnish, and any additional information which the board considers appropriate, for the purpose of assisting the Secretary of State to decide—

(a) in a case where the levy proposals include such proposals as are mentioned in section 11(4) above, whether a levy order made in pursuance of them would fall within section 11(5) above and, if so, whether the condition mentioned in section 11(6)(a) above would be satisfied, and

(b) whether a levy order made in pursuance of the proposals would fall within paragraph (a) or (b) of section 11(7) above ;

and a levy order which falls within section 11(5) above in a case where the condition mentioned in section 11(6)(c) above is satisfied or which falls within section 11(7)(b) above shall state that fact.

(2) Levy proposals may provide for the amendment of a previous levy order and may make different provision in relation to different classes or descriptions of employer and, in particular—

(a) proposals made in pursuance of subsection (3) of section 11 above may be made in respect of different numbers of employees for different employers or classes of employers and may provide for numbers of employees or for employers or classes of employers to be determined by reference to such factors as are specified in the proposals ; and

(b) different proposals may be made in pursuance of subsection (4) of that section as respects different portions of the levy.

(3) A levy order—

(a) may provide for payments by way of levy to accrue due from day to day over a period specified in the order ;

(b) may contain provisions as to the evidence by which a person's liability to the levy or his discharge of that liability may be established and as to the time at which any amount payable by any person by way of the levy shall (whether or not any period over which that amount accrues due has expired) become due and recoverable by the industrial training board.

(4) A person assessed to levy imposed under a levy order may appeal to an industrial tribunal and the levy order shall make provision as to the time within which such an appeal may be made.

(5) On an appeal under subsection (4) above—

   (*a*) if the appellant satisfies the tribunal that he ought not to have been assessed to the levy or ought to have been assessed in a smaller amount, the tribunal shall rescind or, as the case may be, reduce the assessment but (subject to paragraph (*b*) below) in any other case shall confirm it ; and

   (*b*) if it appears to the tribunal that the appellant ought to have been assessed to the levy in a larger amount, the tribunal may increase the assessment accordingly.

(6) The power to make a levy order shall be exercisable by statutory instrument, which shall be subject to annulment in pursuance of a resolution of either House of Parliament unless the instrument contains only an order which includes such a statement as is mentioned in subsection (1) above ; and no levy order which includes such a statement shall be made unless a draft of the order has been approved by a resolution of each House of Parliament.

13.—(1) An industrial training board may from time to time Proposals for and, subject to subsection (2) below, shall always at or before the exemption time when it submits levy proposals under section 11 above certificates. submit to the Commission for its approval proposals for the issue of certificates (in this Act referred to as " exemption certificates ") which while in force are to exempt from relevant levy employers in the industry who—

   (*a*) make arrangements for the training, or the training and further education associated with training, of persons employed or to be employed in the industry ; and

   (*b*) satisfy the board by reference to criteria specified in the proposals that the arrangements are adequate and are to a material extent being implemented ;

and in this subsection " relevant levy " means levy which, apart from any exemption certificate, is payable to the board in question by virtue of this Act by employers in the industry, other than levy which the levy order authorising it provides is to be payable notwithstanding any exemption certificate.

(2) An industrial training board shall not be obliged to submit proposals under subsection (1) above for the issue of exemption certificates to any category of employer at or before the time

C

when it submits levy proposals in respect of a levy on those employers which include—

> (a) proposals that no exemption certificates will be issued by the board to employers in that category ; or
>
> (b) proposals by virtue of which the levy payable by any employer in that category (disregarding any exemptions) will not exceed 0·2 per cent. of the relevant emoluments within the meaning of section 11(8) above ; or
>
> (c) proposals within section 11(4)(a) above by virtue of which any exemption certificates issued to those employers will not exempt them from any of the levy.

(3) The criteria for arrangements made by employers which by virtue of paragraph (b) of subsection (1) above are to be specified in proposals submitted under that subsection must relate to the quality or amount of training, or training and education, provided for by the arrangements, but need not relate solely to the needs of establishments of the employers and the proposals may specify different criteria as respects arrangements made by different categories of employers.

(4) The Secretary of State and the Commission may issue guidance concerning the criteria which by virtue of paragraph (b) of subsection (1) above are to be specified in proposals submitted under that subsection.

(5) If the Commission approves proposals submitted to it by a board under subsection (1) above the Commission shall submit them to the Secretary of State and, where the board is informed by the Commission that the Commission and the Secretary of State approve the proposals, the board shall arrange for them to be published as soon as practicable in a manner approved by the Commission.

(6) Proposals made by a board in pursance of subsection (1) above—

> (a) must include proposals as to the arrangements for the reconsideration of decisions in pursuance of section 14(5) below ; and
>
> (b) may include proposals for altering or cancelling any previous proposals made by the board in pursuance of subsection (1) above ;

but proposals made by virtue of paragraph (b) above shall not affect the operation of any exemption certificates issued in pursuance of previous proposals.

Exemption certificates.

14.—(1) Where an industrial training board is satisfied, on an application made in writing to the board by an employer liable apart from this section to pay to the board any levy from which exemption may be conferred on him by an exemption certificate, that the arrangements made by him for the training, or the training and further education associated with training, of persons employed or to be employed in the industry are such that, in accordance with proposals published by the board in pursuance of section 13 above, an exemption certificate falls to be issued to him in respect of any establishment of his, it shall be the duty of the board to issue such a certificate to him.

(2) A person to whom an exemption certificate is issued (in this section referred to as " the holder ") shall, while the certificate is in force, be exempt from levy payable to the board by virtue of this Act in respect of persons employed at the establishment to which the certificate relates, other than levy which the levy order authorising it provides is to be payable notwithstanding any exemption certificate.

(3) An exemption certificate—

> (a) may require the holder to comply with such conditions relating to the training, or the training and education, of persons employed or to be employed in the industry (including in particular conditions as to the inspection on behalf of the relevant board of the arrangements for the training or the training and education) as are specified in the certificate and are in accordance with the proposals mentioned in subsection (1) above ;
>
> (b) shall specify the date on which the certificate is to come into force ;
>
> (c) shall specify the period (not exceeding three years beginning with that date) at the expiration of which it shall cease to be in force unless it has previously ceased to be in force by virtue of subsection (4) below ;
>
> (d) may provide that the certificate shall be deemed to have been in force for such period before the date on which it comes into force as is specified in the certificate (which shall not begin before the period of one year ending with the date on which the said board received the application in pursuance of which it issues the certificate) ;

and any levy paid to the said board by a person for a period in respect of which by virtue of paragraph (d) above it becomes not payable shall be repayable by the board to that person.

(4) An exemption certificate issued by an industrial training board shall cease to be in force if the board gives notice in writing to the holder stating that in the opinion of the board he has failed to comply with conditions specified in the certificate

C 2

and mentioned in the notice ; but for the purposes of the preceding provisions of this subsection a notice given in pursuance of this subsection shall be disregarded if the board subsequently informs the person to whom it was given that the notice is withdrawn.

(5) If a person who is liable apart from any exemption certificate to pay an industrial training board levy from which exemption may be conferred by an exemption certificate is dissatisfied with the decision of the board—

(a) to refuse to issue to him an exemption certificate relating to such levy in respect of a particular establishment, or

(b) to refuse to include in an exemption certificate issued to him provisions or different provisions authorised by subsection (3)(b) or subsection (3)(d) above, or

(c) to include in an exemption certificate provisions requiring him to comply with conditions, or

(d) to give a notice to him in pursuance of subsection (4) above,

and requests the board in writing to reconsider the decision, it shall be the duty of the board to reconsider it or to secure that it is reconsidered by a committee authorised to deal with such requests by virtue of section 2(1) above ; and if, on reconsidering the decision, the board or committee decides not to alter it, or not to alter it in a manner which the person who made the request considers is satisfactory, that person may refer the decision to a body established in pursuance of subsection (6) below.

(6) It shall be the duty of the Secretary of State to make regulations establishing a body to which decisions are to be referred in pursuance of subsection (5) above ; and regulations made by virtue of this subsection may include provisions as to the powers and procedure of the body and such other provisions (including provisions for defraying the body's expenses out of moneys provided by Parliament or otherwise) as the Secretary of State considers appropriate for the purpose of facilitating the exercise by the body of its functions.

(7) Without prejudice to the generality of subsection (6) above regulations made by virtue of that subsection may—

(a) require a board to draw the attention of a person to his right to refer a decision to the body ;

(b) authorise the body to direct a board whose decision is referred to the body to alter the decision in a manner specified in the direction ; and

(c) require the board to comply with the direction and provide for any case in which it fails to do so.

(8) Regulations under subsection (6) above shall be made by statutory instrument which shall be subject to annulment in pursuance of a resolution of either House of Parliament.

(9) No appeal shall lie to an industrial tribunal in respect of such a decision as is mentioned in subsection (5) above.

General provisions

15.—(1) The Commission may direct an industrial training board to submit proposals to it under section 5(5), 11(1) or 13(1) above within the time specified in the direction and it shall be the duty of the board to comply with such a direction.

Default powers in relation to proposals.

(2) Where proposals submitted to the Commission under section 5(5), 11(1) or 13(1) above appear unsatisfactory to the Commission, it may direct the board to submit fresh proposals within a specified time, stating in the direction in what respect the proposals already submitted appear to the Commission unsatisfactory; and where the fresh proposals also appear unsatisfactory to the Commission it shall report on them to the Secretary of State and, if it appears to the Secretary of State after he has considered the Commission's report that the fresh proposals are unsatisfactory, he may make an order (in this section referred to as " a default order ") declaring the board to be in default.

(3) Where the Commission has given a board a direction under subsection (1) above in pursuance of a direction given to the Commission under section 3(1)(*b*) of the Employment and Training Act 1973, the Commission shall report to the Secretary of State on the proposals submitted in pursuance of the direction and, if it appears to the Secretary of State after he has considered the Commission's report that the proposals are unsatisfactory, he may direct the Commission to direct the board to submit fresh proposals to the Commission within a specified time and such a direction by the Commission shall state in what respect the proposals already submitted appear to the Secretary of State unsatisfactory.

1973 c. 50.

(4) Where fresh proposals are submitted to the Commission in pursuance of a direction under subsection (3) above, the Commission shall report on them to the Secretary of State and, if it appears to the Secretary of State after he has considered the Commission's report that the proposals are unsatisfactory, he may make a default order.

(5) Where a board has failed to comply with a direction of the Commission under subsection (1), (2) or (3) above within the time specified in the direction, the Commission shall report that fact to the Secretary of State and the Secretary of State may make a default order.

(6) On the making of a default order the members of the board shall forthwith vacate their office and the order may contain such provisions as seem to the Secretary of State expedient for authorising any person to act in place of the members of the board during such period, not exceeding six months, as may elapse before new members are appointed.

(7) While a default order is in force with respect to a board paragraph 3 of Schedule 1 to this Act and any provision of the industrial training order made by virtue of paragraph 8(*a*) of that Schedule shall not apply in relation to it, and accordingly (but without prejudice to any provision made under subsection (8) below) paragraph 6 of that Schedule shall not apply.

(8) A default order may contain such incidental or supplementary provisions as appear to the Secretary of State to be necessary or expedient and may be varied or revoked by a subsequent order.

(9) The Secretary of State may out of moneys provided by Parliament defray the expenses of any person acting in the place of the members of a board in pursuance of subsection (6) above and recover from the board any expenses so defrayed.

Enterprise zones.

1980 c. 65.

16.—(1) No employer shall be liable to any levy imposed under this Act in respect of any establishment situated wholly or mainly within an area designated as an enterprise zone under Schedule 32 to the Local Government, Planning and Land Act 1980 ; and for the purposes of any levy order such an establishment shall be treated as if it were not carrying on business.

(2) No levy shall be imposed under this Act by reference to emoluments paid or payable to an employee whose employment is carried on at or from such an establishment as is mentioned in subsection (1) above.

(3) An employer shall not be obliged to comply with a requirement imposed under section 6 above in respect of an establishment or employee if—

(*a*) at the time the requirement is imposed the establishment is situated as mentioned in subsection (1) above or, as the case may be, the employee's employment is carried on at or from such an establishment, or

(*b*) the requirement relates to a period during which the establishment was so situated or, as the case may be, the employee's employment was so carried on.

(4) The Secretary of State may by order made by statutory instrument provide that this section shall not apply in relation to

such employees or such establishments as he may specify in the order or shall apply to them with such modifications as he may so specify ; but no such order shall be made unless the Secretary of State has first consulted the Commission or the Commission has submitted proposals to him for an order under this subsection.

(5) An order made by virtue of subsection (4) above shall be subject to annulment by a resolution of either House of Parliament.

17.—(1) The Commission may with the approval of the Secretary of State make grants and loans to an industrial training board. Financial provisions.

(2) The Commission may give to an industrial training board such directions as the Commission thinks fit for the purpose of securing—

> (a) that the board's expenditure for a purpose specified in the directions does not exceed an amount so specified ; and
>
> (b) that the whole or part of any grant or loan made to the board in pursuance of subsection (1) above is used only for the purposes specified in the directions ;

and it shall be the duty of the board to comply with the directions.

(3) An industrial training board may, with the consent of the Commission or in accordance with the terms of any authority given by the Commission, borrow temporarily from any other person by way of overdraft or otherwise such sums as it may require.

(4) An industrial training board may give security for any money borrowed by it.

(5) An industrial training board shall not invest any money otherwise than in such manner as the Commission may approve.

18.—(1) In relation to accidents happening to employed earners (within the meaning of Chapter IV of Part II of the Socal Security Act 1975) who attend courses or avail themselves of other facilities provided or approved by an industrial training board, sections 52 to 54 of that Act have effect subject to the following modifications. Industrial injuries benefit for accidents in training. 1975 c. 14.

(2) For the purposes of section 52, any act done by the employed earner for the purposes of and in connection with his training shall, if it is not done for the purposes of and in connection with his employer's trade or business, be deemed to be so done.

C 4

(3) For the purposes of section 53, a vehicle (within the meaning of that section) which is operated by or on behalf of an industrial training board or some other person by whom it is provided in pursuance of arrangements made with an industrial training board shall, if not operated and provided as mentioned in subsection (1)(*b*)(i) of that section, be deemed to be so operated and provided.

(4) For the purposes of section 54, any premises at which an employed earner is for the time being employed for the purposes of his training shall, if they are not premises at which he is for the time being employed for the purposes of his employer's trade or business, be deemed to be such premises.

The Industrial Training Boards' Combined Pension Fund.

19. The trustees of the Industrial Training Boards' Combined Pension Fund may, with the consent of three-quarters of the number of the industrial training boards whose officers and servants are eligible to benefit from the Fund, make such amendments of the rules of the Fund as they think fit.

Supplemental

Transitional and consequential provisions, repeals and savings.

1978 c. 30.

20.—(1) Schedule 2 (transitional and saving provisions) and Schedule 3 (consequential amendments) to this Act shall have effect, but without prejudice to the operation of sections 15 to 17 of the Interpretation Act 1978 (which relate to the effect of repeals).

(2) Sections 1 to 18 above and Schedules 1 and 2 to this Act shall not have effect in relation to the Agricultural Training Board ; and accordingly the references in those provisions to industrial training boards (except in sections 2(1)(*b*) and 5(3)(*a*)) do not include that Board.

(3) The enactments specified in Schedule 4 to this Act are hereby repealed to the extent mentioned in the third column of that Schedule.

Short title, extent and commencement.

21.—(1) This Act may be cited as the Industrial Training Act 1982.

(2) Paragraph 4 of Schedule 3 to this Act extends to Northern Ireland, but except as aforesaid this Act shall not extend there.

(3) This Act shall come into force at the expiry of the period of three months beginning with the day on which it is passed.

SCHEDULES

SCHEDULE 1

INDUSTRIAL TRAINING BOARDS

1. An industrial training board shall be a body corporate, by such name as may be specified in the industrial training order.

2. The members of an industrial training board shall be appointed by the Secretary of State.

3. An industrial training board shall consist of a chairman, who shall be a person appearing to the Secretary of State to have industrial or commercial experience, and—

 (*a*) an equal number of persons appointed after consultation with such organisations or associations of organisations representative of employers engaging in the industry and of persons employed in the industry respectively as appear to the Secretary of State to be appropriate ;

 (*b*) persons appointed after consultation with the Ministers concerned with education in England, Scotland and Wales ;

and, if the Secretary of State thinks fit to appoint as deputy chairman a person appearing to him to have industrial or commercial experience, the deputy chairman so appointed ; and references in the following provisions of this Schedule to a chairman shall include a deputy chairman.

4. An industrial training board shall pay to its chairman such remuneration (if any) as the Secretary of State may from time to time with the approval of the Treasury determine and may make such arrangements for the payment of pensions, superannuation allowances and gratuities to or in respect of its chairman as the Secretary of State may specify with the approval of the Treasury.

5. Where a person ceases to be the chairman of an industrial training board otherwise than on the expiry of his term of office and it appears to the Secretary of State that there are special circumstances which make it right for him to receive compensation, the board may make him a payment of such amount as the Secretary of State may determine with the approval of the Treasury.

6. The chairman and the members appointed as mentioned in sub-paragraph (*b*) of paragraph 3 above shall not vote on any matter relating to the imposition of a levy and no such matter shall be decided except in accordance with the votes of the majority of the members who were appointed as mentioned in sub-paragraph (*a*) of that paragraph after consultation with organisations or associations of organisations representative of employers engaging in the industry.

7.—(1) The Secretary of State, the Minister concerned with education in Scotland, the Ministers concerned with education in England and Wales (acting jointly), the Manpower Services Commission and, if the Secretary of State thinks fit in a particular case, such other Ministers in charge of government departments as he may specify may each appoint one person to attend the meetings of an industrial training board ; and any person so appointed shall be entitled to take part in the proceedings of the board and receive copies of all documents distributed to its members, but shall have no vote.

(2) The Commission may appoint one or more persons to attend the meetings of a committee of an industrial training board ; and a person so appointed shall be entitled to take part in the proceedings of the committee and receive copies of all documents distributed to its members but shall have no vote.

8. An industrial training order may make provision with respect to—

(a) the tenure of office of the members of the board ;

(b) the quorum and, subject to paragraphs 6 and 7 above, the proceedings and meetings of the board ;

(c) the execution of instruments by and on behalf of the board and the proof of documents purporting to be executed, issued or signed by the board or a member, officer or servant thereof ;

and any provision made by virtue of sub-paragraph (b) above may enable votes to be cast by proxy.

9. Subject to paragraphs 6 and 7 and to any provision made by virtue of paragraph 8 above, a board shall have the power to regulate its own procedure.

10. The proceedings of an industrial training board shall not be invalidated by any vacancy in the membership of the board or by any defect in the appointment of any member.

11. An industrial training board may appoint such officers and servants, upon such terms as to remuneration, pension rights and other conditions of service, as the board may determine.

12. An industrial training board may pay to its members such allowances for loss of remunerative time as the Secretary of State may determine with the approval of the Treasury and such travelling, subsistence and other allowances as the board may determine.

13. For the purposes of this Schedule any body established for the purpose of carrying on under national ownership any industry or part of an industry or undertaking shall be treated as if it were an organisation representative of employers.

SCHEDULE 2

Section 20(1).

TRANSITIONAL PROVISIONS AND SAVINGS

1. Where any consultations are required by virtue of section 1 of this Act and the Secretary of State is satisfied that adequate consultations took place before 31st July 1981, no further consultations shall be required.

2.—(1) If at the commencement of this Act any provision of the Employment and Training Act 1981 mentioned in column 1 of the following Table is not in force for any purpose of that provision, then the provision of this Act set out in column 2 of the Table opposite that provision shall have effect for that purpose with the modification there specified.

1981 c. 57.

TABLE

Provision of Employ-ment and Training Act 1981	*Modification of this Act*
Section 2(1)	In section 11(1), for " raising money towards meeting its expenses " substitute " encouraging adequate training in the industry ".
Schedule 1, paragraph 1.	In section 2—
	(*a*) In subsection (2)(*a*) for " allowances " in the first place where it occurs to the end substitute " travelling, subsistence and other allowances (including allowances for loss of remunerative time) as the Secretary of State may determine with the approval of the Treasury " ;
	(*b*) in subsection (2)(*b*) for " board " to the end substitute " Secretary of State may so determine " ;
	(*c*) in subsection (3) for " board may determine " substitute " Secretary of State may specify with the approval of the Treasury " ;
	(*d*) in subsection (3)(*b*) for " board " substitute " Secretary of State ".
Schedule 1, paragraph 7.	In paragraph 11 of Schedule 1, at end insert " with the approval of the Secretary of State given with the consent of the Treasury ".
Schedule 1, paragraph 8.	In paragraph 12 of Schedule 1 for " allowances " to the end substitute " travelling, subsistence and other allowances (including allowances for loss of remunerative time) as the Secretary of State may determine with the approval of the Treasury ".

(2) The Secretary of State may by order made by statutory instrument provide that on such day as he may appoint sub-paragraph (1) above shall cease to have effect and the order—

    (*a*) may appoint different days for the purposes of different provisions or for different purposes of the same provision ;

    (*b*) may contain such transitional, incidental and supplementary provisions as the Secretary of State considers appropriate in connection with the order.

3.—(1) Any sum paid to an industrial training board in pursuance of a levy imposed under a levy order made before the relevant day may be used by the board to meet any of its expenses.

(2) In sub-paragraph (1) above " the relevant day " means—

    (*a*) the day appointed under section 11(3) of the Employment and Training Act 1981 for the coming into force of section 2(1) of that Act, or

    (*b*) if at the commencement of this Act no such day has been appointed, such day as the Secretary of State may appoint under paragraph 2(2) above in relation to the said section 2(1).

(3) If at the commencement of this Act section 2(2) of the said Act of 1981 is not in force for any purpose of that provision sub-paragraph (1) above shall not have effect for that purpose until such date as the Secretary of State may by order made by statutory instrument appoint and an order under this sub-paragraph may—

    (*a*) appoint different dates for different purposes of that section ; and

    (*b*) contain such transitional, incidental and supplementary provisions as the Secretary of State considers appropriate in connection with the order.

4. Any transitional, incidental and supplementary provisions made by any order made under section 11(3) of the Employment and Training Act 1981 in connection with the bringing into force of any provision of that Act shall not cease to have effect by virtue of the repeal by this Act of that section but—

    (*a*) in the case of any provisions mentioned in column 1 of the Table in paragraph 2(1) above, shall be construed so as to produce a corresponding effect in connection with the provision of this Act mentioned in column 2 of the Table opposite that provision ; and

    (*b*) in the case of section 2(2) of that Act, shall be construed so as to produce a corresponding effect in paragraph 3(1) above.

5. If at the date of the commencement of this Act an order has been made under section 11(3) of the Employment and Training Act 1981 (whether or not that order has come into force by that date) appointing a day after that date for the coming into force of any provision of that Act for any purpose, paragraphs 2 to 4 above shall have effect from that day—

    (*a*) in the case of an order which is not in force at that date, as if the order had come into force before that date ; and

    (*b*) as if the day appointed were a day before that date.

6. Nothing in this Act shall affect the enactments repealed by this Act in their operation in relation to offences committed before the commencement of this Act.

7. Where any period of time specified in or under an enactment repealed by this Act is current at the commencement of this Act, this Act shall have effect as if the corresponding provision of this Act had been in force when that period began to run.

SCHEDULE 3

Section 20.

Consequential Amendments

1. In section 51(1) of the Docks and Harbours Act 1966 for the words from " a tribunal" onwards there shall be substituted the words " an industrial tribunal ". 1966 c. 28.

2. In paragraphs 10 and 38 of Part I of Schedule 1 to the Tribunals and Inquiries Act 1971 for the words " section 12 of the Industrial Training Act 1964 (c.16)" there shall be substituted the words " section 128 of the Employment Protection (Consolidation) Act 1978 (c.44) ". 1971 c. 62.

3. In sections 4(4) and 11(3) of the Employment and Training Act 1973 for the words " within the meaning of the Industrial Training Act 1964 " there shall be substituted the words " established under section 1 of the Industrial Training Act 1964 or section 1 of the Industrial Training Act 1982." 1973 c. 50.

4. In Part III of Schedule 1 to the House of Commons Disqualification Act 1975 after the words " constituted under the Industrial Training Act 1964 " there shall be inserted the words " or the Industrial Training Act 1982 " and for the words " that Act " there shall be substituted the words " either of those Acts ". 1975 c. 24.

5. In the Sex Discrimination Act 1975— 1975 c. 65.

    (*a*) at the end of section 14(2)(*a*) there shall be inserted the words " or section 1 of the Industrial Training Act 1982." ; and

    (*b*) the definition of " industrial tribunal " in section 82(1) shall cease to have effect.

6. In section 127(1) of the Employment Protection Act 1975 for paragraph (*b*) there shall be substituted— 1975 c. 71.

    " (*b*) the Industrial Training Act 1982."

7. In the Race Relations Act 1976— 1976 c. 74.

    (*a*) at the end of section 13(2)(*a*) there shall be inserted the words " or section 1 of the Industrial Training Act 1982 " ; and

    (*b*) the definition of " industrial tribunal " in section 78(1) shall cease to have effect.

SCHEDULE 4

ENACTMENTS REPEALED

Chapter	Short title	Extent of repeal
1964 c. 16.	The Industrial Training Act 1964.	The whole Act except section 16 (save as that Act applies to the Agricultural Training Board).
1973 c. 50.	The Employment and Training Act 1973.	Section 6(1), (2) and (5). In Schedule 2, Parts I and II.
1975 c. 18.	The Social Security (Consequential Provisions) Act 1975.	In Schedule 2, paragraph 11, save as it applies to the Agricultural Training Board.
1975 c. 65.	The Sex Discrimination Act 1975.	In section 82(1) the definition of " industrial tribunal ".
1976 c. 74.	The Race Relations Act 1976.	In section 78(1) the definition of " industrial tribunal ".
1978 c. 44.	The Employment Protection (Consolidation) Act 1978.	In Schedule 16, paragraph 4.
1981 c. 57.	The Employment and Training Act 1981.	Sections 1 to 8 and 11(3). Schedule 1. In Schedule 2, paragraph 4.

Canada Act 1982

1982 CHAPTER 11

An Act to give effect to a request by the Senate and House of Commons of Canada.   [29th March 1982]

Whereas Canada has requested and consented to the enactment of an Act of the Parliament of the United Kingdom to give effect to the provisions hereinafter set forth and the Senate and the House of Commons of Canada in Parliament assembled have submitted an address to Her Majesty requesting that Her Majesty may graciously be pleased to cause a Bill to be laid before the Parliament of the United Kingdom for that purpose:

Be it therefore enacted by the Queen's Most Excellent Majesty, by and with the advice and consent of the Lords Spiritual and Temporal, and Commons, in this present Parliament assembled, and by the authority of the same, as follows:

Constitution Act, 1982 enacted

1. The Constitution Act, 1982 set out in Schedule B to this Act is hereby enacted for and shall have the force of law in Canada and shall come into force as provided in that Act.

Termination of power to legislate for Canada

2. No Act of the Parliament of the United Kingdom passed after the Constitution Act, 1982 comes into force shall extend to Canada as part of its law.

French version.

3. So far as it is not contained in Schedule B, the French version of this Act is set out in Schedule A to this Act and has the same authority in Canada as the English version thereof.

Short title.

4. This Act may be cited as the Canada Act 1982.

SCHEDULE (ANNEXE) A

Loi donnant suite à une demande du Sénat et de la Chambre des communes du Canada.

Sa Très Excellente Majesté la Reine, considérant :

qu'à la demande et avec le consentement du Canada, le Parlement du Royaume-Uni est invité à adopter une loi visant à donner effet aux dispositions énoncées ci-après et que le Sénat et la Chambre des communes du Canada réunis en Parlement ont présenté une adresse demandant à Sa Très Gracieuse Majesté de bien vouloir faire déposer devant le Parlement du Royaume-Uni un projet de loi à cette fin,

sur l'avis et du consentement des Lords spirituels et temporels et des Communes réunis en Parlement, et par l'autorité de celui-ci, édicte :

1. La Loi constitutionnelle de 1982, énoncée à l'annexe B, est édictée pour le Canada et y a force de loi. Elle entre en vigueur conformément à ses dispositions. <small>Adoption de la Loi constitutionnelle de 1982</small>

2. Les lois adoptées par le Parlement du Royaume-Uni après l'entrée en vigueur de la Loi constitutionnelle de 1982 ne font pas partie du droit du Canada. <small>Cessation du pouvoir de légiférer pour le Canada</small>

3. La partie de la version française de la présente loi qui figure à l'annexe A a force de loi au Canada au même titre que la version anglaise correspondante. <small>Version française</small>

4. Titre abrégé de la présente loi : Loi de 1982 sur le Canada. <small>Titre abrégé</small>

SCHEDULE B

CONSTITUTION ACT, 1982

PART I

CANADIAN CHARTER OF RIGHTS AND FREEDOMS

Whereas Canada is founded upon principles that recognize the supremacy of God and the rule of law:

Guarantee of Rights and Freedoms

Rights and freedoms in Canada

1. The *Canadian Charter of Rights and Freedoms* guarantees the rights and freedoms set out in it subject only to such reasonable limits prescribed by law as can be demonstrably justified in a free and democratic society.

Fundamental Freedoms

Fundamental freedoms

2. Everyone has the following fundamental freedoms:

    (*a*) freedom of conscience and religion ;

    (*b*) freedom of thought, belief, opinion and expression, including freedom of the press and other media of communication ;

    (*c*) freedom of peaceful assembly ; and

    (*d*) freedom of association.

Democratic Rights

Democratic rights of citizens

3. Every citizen of Canada has the right to vote in an election of members of the House of Commons or of a legislative assembly and to be qualified for membership therein.

Maximum duration of legislative bodies

4.—(1) No House of Commons and no legislative assembly shall continue for longer than five years from the date fixed for the return of the writs at a general election of its members.

Continuation in special circumstances

(2) In time of real or apprehended war, invasion or insurrection, a House of Commons may be continued by Parliament and a legislative assembly may be continued by the legislature beyond five years if such continuation is not opposed by the votes of more than one-third of the members of the House of Commons or the legislative assembly, as the case may be.

Annual sitting of legislative bodies

5. There shall be a sitting of Parliament and of each legislature at least once every twelve months.

Mobility Rights

Mobility of citizens

6.—(1) Every citizen of Canada has the right to enter, remain in and leave Canada.

Rights to move and gain livelihood

(2) Every citizen of Canada and every person who has the status of a permanent resident of Canada has the right

    (*a*) to move to and take up residence in any province ; and

    (*b*) to pursue the gaining of a livelihood in any province.

ANNEXE B

LOI CONSTITUTIONNELLE DE 1982

Partie I

Charte Canadienne Des Droits Et Libertés

Attendu que le Canada est fondé sur des principes qui reconnaissent la suprématie de Dieu et la primauté du droit :

Garantie des droits et libertés

1. La *Charte canadienne des droits et libertés* garantit les droits et libertés qui y sont énoncés. Ils ne peuvent être restreints que par une règle de droit, dans des limites qui soient raisonnables et dont la justification puisse se démontrer dans le cadre d'une société libre et démocratique. Droits et libertés au Canada

Libertés fondamentales

2. Chacun a les libertés fondamentales suivantes : Libertés fondamentales

   (*a*) liberté de conscience et de religion ;

   (*b*) liberté de pensée, de croyance, d'opinion et d'expression, y compris la liberté de la presse et des autres moyens de communication ;

   (*c*) liberté de réunion pacifique ;

   (*d*) liberté d'association.

Droits démocratiques

3. Tout citoyen canadien a le droit de vote et est éligible aux élections législatives fédérales ou provinciales. Droits démocratiques des citoyens

4.—(1) Le mandat maximal de la Chambre des communes et des assemblées législatives est de cinq ans à compter de la date fixée pour le retour des brefs relatifs aux élections générales correspondantes. Mandat maximal des assemblées

(2) Le mandat de la Chambre des communes ou celui d'une assemblée législative peut être prolongé respectivement par le Parlement ou par la législature en question au-delà de cinq ans en cas de guerre, d'invasion ou d'insurrection, réelles ou appréhendées, pourvu que cette prolongation ne fasse pas l'objet d'une opposition exprimée par les voix de plus du tiers des députés de la Chambre des communes ou de l'assemblée législative. Prolongations spéciales

5. Le Parlement et les législatures tiennent une séance au moins une fois tous les douze mois. Séance annuelle

Liberté de circulation et d'établissement

6.—(1) Tout citoyen canadien a le droit de demeurer au Canada, d'y entrer ou d'en sortir. Liberté de circulation

(2) Tout citoyen canadien et toute personne ayant le statut de résident permanent au Canada ont le droit : Liberté d'établissement

   (*a*) de se déplacer dans tout le pays et d'établir leur résidence dans toute province ;

   (*b*) de gagner leur vie dans toute province.

Limitation

(3) The rights specified in subsection (2) are subject to

(*a*) any laws or practices of general application in force in a province other than those that discriminate among persons primarily on the basis of province of present or previous residence ; and

(*b*) any laws providing for reasonable residency requirements as a qualification for the receipt of publicly provided social services.

Affirmative action programs

(4) Subsections (2) and (3) do not preclude any law, program or activity that has as its object the amelioration in a province of conditions of individuals in that province who are socially or economically disadvantaged if the rate of employment in that province is below the rate of employment in Canada.

Legal Rights

Life, liberty and security of person

7. Everyone has the right to life, liberty and security of the person and the right not to be deprived thereof except in accordance with the principles of fundamental justice.

Search or seizure

8. Everyone has the right to be secure against unreasonable search or seizure.

Detention or imprisonment

9. Everyone has the right not to be arbitrarily detained or imprisoned.

Arrest or detention

10. Everyone has the right on arrest or detention

(*a*) to be informed promptly of the reasons therefor ;

(*b*) to retain and instruct counsel without delay and to be informed of that right ; and

(*c*) to have the validity of the detention determined by way of *habeas corpus* and to be released if the detention is not lawful.

Proceedings in criminal and penal matters

11. Any person charged with an offence has the right

(*a*) to be informed without unreasonable delay of the specific offence ;

(*b*) to be tried within a reasonable time ;

(*c*) not to be compelled to be a witness in proceedings against that person in respect of the offence ;

(*d*) to be presumed innocent until proven guilty according to law in a fair and public hearing by an independent and impartial tribunal ;

(*e*) not to be denied reasonable bail without just cause ;

(*f*) except in the case of an offence under military law tried before a military tribunal, to the benefit of trial by jury where the maximum punishment for the offence is imprisonment for five years or a more severe punishment ;

(3) Les droits mentionnés au paragraphe (2) sont subordonnés : Restriction

    (*a*) aux lois et usages d'application générale en vigueur dans une province donnée, s'ils n'établissent entre les personnes aucune distinction fondée principalement sur la province de résidence antérieure ou actuelle ;

    (*b*) aux lois prévoyant de justes conditions de résidence en vue de l'obtention des services sociaux publics.

(4) Les paragraphes (2) et (3) n'ont pas pour objet d'interdire les lois, programmes ou activités destinés à améliorer, dans une province, la situation d'individus défavorisés socialement ou économiquement, si le taux d'emploi dans la province est inférieur à la moyenne nationale. Programmes de promotion sociale

Garanties juridiques

7. Chacun a droit à la vie, à la liberté et à la sécurité de sa personne ; il ne peut être porté atteinte à ce droit qu'en conformité avec les principes de justice fondamentale. Vie. liberté et sécurité

8. Chacun a droit à la protection contre les fouilles, les perquisitions ou les saisies abusives. Fouilles, perquisitions ou saisies

9. Chacun a droit à la protection contre la détention ou l'emprisonnement arbitraires. Détention ou emprisonnement

10. Chacun a le droit, en cas d'arrestation ou de détention : Arrestation ou détention

    (*a*) d'être informé dans les plus brefs délais des motifs de son arrestation ou de sa détention ;

    (*b*) d'avoir recours sans délai à l'assistance d'un avocat et d'être informé de ce droit ;

    (*c*) de faire contrôler, par *habeas corpus,* la légalité de sa détention et d'obtenir, le cas échéant, sa libération.

11. Tout inculpé a le droit : Affaires criminelles et pénales

    (*a*) d'être informé sans délai anormal de l'infraction précise qu'on lui reproche ;

    (*b*) d'être jugé dans un délai raisonnable ;

    (*c*) de ne pas être contraint de témoigner contre lui-même dans toute poursuite intentée contre lui pour l'infraction qu'on lui reproche ;

    (*d*) d'être présumé innocent tant qu'il n'est pas déclarè coupable, conformément à la loi, par un tribunal indépendant et impartial à l'issue d'un procès public et équitable ;

    (*e*) de ne pas être privé sans juste cause d'une mise en liberté assortie d'un cautionnement raisonnable ;

    (*f*) sauf s'il s'agit d'une infraction relevant de la justice militaire, de bénéficier d'un procès avec jury lorsque la peine maximale prévue pour l'infraction dont il est accusé est un emprisonnement de cinq ans ou une peine plus grave :

(g) not to be found guilty on account of any act or omission unless, at the time of the act or omission, it constituted an offence under Canadian or international law or was criminal according to the general principles of law recognized by the community of nations ;

(h) if finally acquitted of the offence, not to be tried for it again and, if finally found guilty and punished for the offence, not to be tried or punished for it again ; and

(i) if found guilty of the offence and if the punishment for the offence has been varied between the time of commission and the time of sentencing, to the benefit of the lesser punishment.

Treatment or punishment

12. Everyone has the right not to be subjected to any cruel and unusual treatment or punishment.

Self-crimina-tion

13. A witness who testifies in any proceedings has the right not to have any incriminating evidence so given used to incriminate that witness in any other proceedings, except in a prosecution for perjury or for the giving of contradictory evidence.

Interpreter

14. A party or witness in any proceedings who does not understand or speak the language in which the proceedings are conducted or who is deaf has the right to the assistance of an interpreter.

Equality Rights

Equality before and under law and equal protection and benefit of law

15.—(1) Every individual is equal before and under the law and has the right to the equal protection and equal benefit of the law without discrimination and, in particular, without discrimination based on race, national or ethnic origin, colour, religion, sex, age or mental or physical disability.

Affirmative action programs

(2) Subsection (1) does not preclude any law, program or activity that has as its object the amelioration of conditions of disadvantaged individuals or groups including those that are disadvantaged because of race, national or ethnic origin, colour, religion, sex, age or mental or physical disability.

Official Languages of Canada

Official languages of Canada

16.—(1) English and French are the official languages of Canada and have equality of status and equal rights and privileges as to their use in all institutions of the Parliament and government of Canada.

Official languages of New Brunswick

(2) English and French are the official languages of New Brunswick and have equality of status and equal rights and privileges as to their use in all institutions of the legislature and government of New Brunswick.

Advancement of status and use

(3) Nothing in this Charter limits the authority of Parliament or a legislature to advance the equality of status or use of English and French.

(*g*) de ne pas être déclaré coupable en raison d'une action ou d'une omission qui, au moment où elle est survenue, ne constituait pas une infraction d'après le droit interne du Canada ou le droit international et n'avait pas de caractère criminel d'après les principes généraux de droit reconnus par l'ensemble des nations ;

(*h*) d'une part de ne pas être jugé de nouveau pour une infraction dont il a été définitivement acquitté, d'autre part de ne pas être jugé ni puni de nouveau pour une infraction dont il a été définitivement déclaré coupable et puni ;

(*i*) de bénéficier de la peine la moins sévère, lorsque la peine qui sanctionne l'infraction dont il est déclaré coupable est modifiée entre le moment de la perpétration de l'infraction et celui de la sentence.

12. Chacun a droit à la protection contre tous traitements ou peines cruels et inusités. _{Cruauté}

13. Chacun a droit à ce qu'aucun témoignage incriminant qu'il donne ne soit utilisé pour l'incriminer dans d'autres procédures, sauf lors de poursuites pour parjure ou pour témoignages contradictoires. _{Témoignage incriminant}

14. La partie ou le témoin qui ne peuvent suivre les procédures, soit parce qu'ils ne comprennent pas ou ne parlent pas la langue employée, soit parce qu'ils sont atteints de surdité, ont droit à l'assistance d'un interprète. _{Interprète}

Droits à l'égalité

15.—(1) La loi ne fait acception de personne et s'applique également à tous, et tous ont droit à la même protection et au même bénéfice de la loi, indépendamment de toute discrimination, notamment des discriminations fondées sur la race, l'origine nationale ou ethnique, la couleur, la religion, le sexe, l'âge ou les déficiences mentales ou physiques. _{Égalité devant la loi, égalité de bénéfice et protection égale de la loi}

(2) Le paragraphe (1) n'a pas pour effet d'interdire les lois, programmes ou activités destinés à améliorer la situation d'individus ou de groupes défavorisés, notamment du fait de leur race, de leur origine nationale ou ethnique, de leur couleur, de leur religion, de leur sexe, de leur âge ou de leurs déficiences mentales ou physiques. _{Programmes de promotion sociale}

Langues officielles du Canada

16.—(1) Le français et l'anglais sont les langues officielles du Canada ; ils ont un statut et des droits et privilèges égaux quant à leur usage dans les institutions du Parlement et du gouvernement du Canada. _{Langues officielles du Canada}

(2) Le français et l'anglais sont les langues officielles du Nouveau-Brunswick ; ils ont un statut et des droits et privilèges égaux quant à leur usage dans les institutions de la Législature et du gouvernement du Nouveau-Brunswick. _{Langues officielles du Nouveau-Brunswick}

(3) La présente charte ne limite pas le pouvoir du Parlement et des législatures de favoriser la progression vers l'égalité de statut ou d'usage du français et de l'anglais. _{Progression vers l'égalité}

Proceedings of
Parliament

17.—(1) Everyone has the right to use English or French in any debates and other proceedings of Parliament.

Proceedings of
New Brunswick
legislature

(2) Everyone has the right to use English or French in any debates and other proceedings of the legislature of New Brunswick.

Parliamentary
statutes and
records

18.—(1) The statutes, records and journals of Parliament shall be printed and published in English and French and both language versions are equally authoritative.

New Brunswick
statutes and
records

(2) The statutes, records and journals of the legislature of New Brunswick shall be printed and published in English and French and both language versions are equally authoritative.

Proceedings in
courts
established by
Parliament

19.—(1) Either English or French may be used by any person in, or in any pleading in or process issuing from, any court established by Parliament.

Proceedings in
New Brunswick
courts

(2) Either English or French may be used by any person in, or in any pleading in or process issuing from, any court of New Brunswick.

Cummunica-
tions by public
with federal
institutions

20.—(1) Any member of the public in Canada has the right to communicate with, and to receive available services from, any head or central office of an institution of the Parliament or government of Canada in English or French, and has the same right with respect to any other office of any such institution where

  (*a*) there is a significant demand for communications with and services from that office in such language ; or

  (*b*) due to the nature of the office, it is reasonable that communications with and services from that office be available in both English and French.

Communica-
tions by public
with New
Brunswick
institutions

(2) Any member of the public in New Brunswick has the right to communicate with, and to receive available services from, any office of an institution of the legislature or government of New Brunswick in English or French.

Continuation of
existing
constitutional
provisions

21. Nothing in sections 16 to 20 abrogates or derogates from any right, privilege or obligation with respect to the English and French languages, or either of them, that exists or is continued by virtue of any other provision of the Constitution of Canada.

Rights and
privileges
preserved

22. Nothing in sections 16 to 20 abrogates or derogates from any legal or customary right or privilege acquired or enjoyed either before or after the coming into force of this Charter with respect to any language that is not English or French.

Minority Language Educational Rights

Language of
instruction

23.—(1) Citizens of Canada

  (*a*) whose first language learned and still understood is that of the English or French linguistic minority population of the province in which they reside, or

17.—(1) Chacun a le droit d'employer le français ou l'anglais dans les débats et travaux du Parlement.

<small>Travaux du
Parlement</small>

(2) Chacun a le droit d'employer le français ou l'anglais dans les débats et travaux de la Législature du Nouveau-Brunswick.

<small>Travaux de la
Législature du
Nouveau-
Brunswick</small>

18.—(1) Les lois, les archives, les comptes rendus et les procès-verbaux du Parlement sont imprimés et publiés en français et en anglais, les deux versions des lois ayant également force de loi et celles des autres documents ayant même valeur.

<small>Documents
parlementaires</small>

(2) Les lois, les archives, les comptes rendus et les procès-verbaux de la Législature du Nouveau-Brunswick sont imprimés et publiés en français et en anglais, les deux versions des lois ayant également force de loi et celles des autres documents ayant même valeur.

<small>Documents de
la Législature
du Nouveau-
Brunswick</small>

19.—(1) Chacun a le droit d'employer le français ou l'anglais dans toutes les affaires dont sont saisis les tribunaux établis par le Parlement et dans tous les actes de procédure qui en découlent.

<small>Procédures
devant les
tribunaux
établis par le
Parlement</small>

(2) Chacun a le droit d'employer le français ou l'anglais dans toutes les affaires dont sont saisis les tribunaux du Nouveau-Brunswick et dans tous les actes de procédure qui en découlent.

<small>Procédures
devant les
tribunaux du
Nouveau-
Brunswick</small>

20.—(1) Le public a, au Canada, droit à l'emploi du français ou de l'anglais pour communiquer avec le siège ou l'administration centrale des institutions du Parlement ou du gouvernement du Canada ou pour en recevoir les services ; il a le même droit à l'égard de tout autre bureau de ces institutions là où, selon le cas :

<small>Communica-
tions entre les
administrés et
les institutions
fédérales</small>

   (*a*) l'emploi du français ou de l'anglais fait l'objet d'une demande importante ;

   (*b*) l'emploi du français et de l'anglais se justifie par la vocation du bureau.

(2) Le public a, au Nouveau-Brunswick, droit à l'emploi du français ou de l'anglais pour communiquer avec tout bureau des institutions de la législature ou du gouvernement ou pour en recevoir les services.

<small>Communica-
tions entre les
administrés et
les institutions
du Nouveau-
Brunswick</small>

21. Les articles 16 à 20 n'ont pas pour effet, en ce qui a trait à la langue française ou anglaise ou à ces deux langues, de porter atteinte aux droits, privilèges ou obligations qui existent ou sont maintenus aux termes d'une autre disposition de la Constitution du Canada.

<small>Maintien en
vigueur de
certaines
dispositions</small>

22. Les articles 16 à 20 n'ont pas pour effet de porter atteinte aux droits et privilèges, antérieurs ou postérieurs à l'entrée en vigueur de la présente charte et découlant de la loi ou de la coutume, des langues autres que le français ou l'anglais.

<small>Droits préservés</small>

Droits à l'instruction dans la langue de la minorité

23.—(1) Les citoyens canadiens :

<small>Langue
d'instruction</small>

   (*a*) dont la première langue apprise et encore comprise est celle de la minorité francophone ou anglophone de la province où ils résident,

(*b*) who have received their primary school instruction in Canada in English or French and reside in a province where the language in which they received that instruction is the language of the English or French linguistic minority population of the province,

have the right to have their children receive primary and secondary school instruction in that language in that province.

Continuity of
language
instruction

(2) Citizens of Canada of whom any child has received or is receiving primary or secondary school instruction in English or French in Canada, have the right to have all their children receive primary and secondary school instruction in the same language.

Application
where numbers
warrant

(3) The right of citizens of Canada under subsections (1) and (2) to have their children receive primary and secondary school instruction in the language of the English or French linguistic minority population of a province

(*a*) applies wherever in the province the number of children of citizens who have such a right is sufficient to warrant the provision to them out of public funds of minority language instruction ; and

(*b*) includes, where the number of those children so warrants, the right to have them receive that instruction in minority language educational facilities provided out of public funds.

Enforcement

Enforcement of
guaranteed
rights and
freedoms

24.—(1) Anyone whose rights or freedoms, as guaranteed by this Charter, have been infringed or denied may apply to a court of competent jurisdiction to obtain such remedy as the court considers appropriate and just in the circumstances.

Exclusion of
evidence
bringing
administration
of justice into
disrepute

(2) Where, in proceedings under subsection (1), a court concludes that evidence was obtained in a manner that infringed or denied any rights or freedoms guaranteed by this Charter, the evidence shall be excluded if it is established that, having regard to all the circumstances, the admission of it in the proceedings would bring the administration of justice into disrepute.

General

Aboriginal
rights and
freedoms not
affected by
Charter

25. The guarantee in this Charter of certain rights and freedoms shall not be construed so as to abrogate or derogate from any aboriginal, treaty or other rights or freedoms that pertain to the aboriginal peoples of Canada including

(*a*) any rights or freedoms that have been recognized by the Royal Proclamation of October 7, 1763 ; and

(*b*) any rights or freedoms that may be acquired by the aboriginal peoples of Canada by way of land claims settlement.

Other rights
and freedoms
not affected by
Charter

26. The guarantee in this Charter of certain rights and freedoms shall not be construed as denying the existence of any other rights or freedoms that exist in Canada.

(*b*) qui ont reçu leur instruction, au niveau primaire, en français ou en anglais au Canada et qui résident dans une province où la langue dans laquelle ils ont reçu cette instruction est celle de la minorité francophone ou anglophone de la province,

ont, dans l'un ou l'autre cas, le droit d'y faire instruire leurs enfants, aux niveaux primaire et secondaire, dans cette langue.

(2) Les citoyens canadiens dont un enfant a reçu ou reçoit son instruction, au niveau primaire ou secondaire, en français ou en anglais au Canada ont le droit de faire instruire tous leurs enfants, aux niveaux primaire et secondaire, dans la langue de cette instruction. Continuité d'emploi de la langue d'instruction

(3) Le droit reconnu aux citoyens canadiens par les paragraphes (1) et (2) de faire instruire leurs enfants, aux niveaux primaire et secondaire, dans la langue de la minorité francophone ou anglophone d'une province : Justification par le nombre

(*a*) s'exerce partout dans la province où le nombre des enfants des citoyens qui ont ce droit est suffisant pour justifier à leur endroit la prestation, sur les fonds publics, de l'instruction dans la langue de la minorité ;

(*b*) comprend, lorsque le nombre de ces enfants le justifie, le droit de les faire instruire dans des établissements d'enseignement de la minorité linguistique financés sur les fonds publics.

Recours

24. (1) Toute personne, victime de violation ou de négation des droits ou libertés qui lui sont garantis par la présente charte, peut s'adresser à un tribunal compétent pour obtenir la réparation que le tribunal estime convenable et juste eu égard aux circonstances. Recours en cas d'atteinte aux droits et libertés

(2) Lorsque, dans une instance visée au paragraphe (1), le tribunal a conclu que des éléments de preuve ont été obtenus dans des conditions qui portent atteinte aux droits ou libertés garantis par la présente charte, ces éléments de preuve sont écartés s'il est établi, eu égard aux circonstances, que leur utilisation est susceptible de déconsidérer l'administration de la justice. Irrecevabilité d'éléments de preuve qui risqueraient de déconsidérer l'administration de la justice

Dispositions générales

25. Le fait que la présente charte garantit certains droits et libertés ne porte pas atteinte aux droits ou libertés — ancestraux, issus de traités ou autres—des peuples autochtones du Canada, notamment : Maintien des droits et libertés des autochtones

(*a*) aux droits ou libertés reconnus par la Proclamation royale du 7 octobre 1763 ;

(*b*) aux droits ou libertés acquis par règlement de revendications territoriales.

26. Le fait que la présente charte garantit certains droits et libertés ne constitue pas une négation des autres droits ou libertés qui existent au Canada. Maintien des autres droits et libertés

Multicultural heritage

27. This Charter shall be interpreted in a manner consistent with the preservation and enhancement of the multicultural heritage of Canadians.

Rights guaranteed equally to both sexes

28. Notwithstanding anything in this Charter, the rights and freedoms referred to in it are guaranteed equally to male and female persons.

Rights respecting certain schools preserved

29. Nothing in this Charter abrogates or derogates from any rights or privileges guaranteed by or under the Constitution of Canada in respect of denominational, separate or dissentient schools.

Application to territories and territorial authorities

30. A reference in this Charter to a province or to the legislative assembly or legislature of a province shall be deemed to include a reference to the Yukon Territory and the Northwest Territories, or to the appropriate legislative authority thereof, as the case may be.

Legislative powers not extended

31. Nothing in this Charter extends the legislative powers of any body or authority.

Application of Charter

Application of Charter

32.—(1) This Charter applies

(*a*) to the Parliament and government of Canada in respect of all matters within the authority of Parliament including all matters relating to the Yukon Territory and Northwest Territories ; and

(*b*) to the legislature and government of each province in respect of all matters within the authority of the legislature of each province.

Exception

(2) Notwithstanding subsection (1), section 15 shall not have effect until three years after this section comes into force.

Exception where express declaration

33.—(1) Parliament or the legislature of a province may expressly declare in an Act of Parliament or of the legislature, as the case may be, that the Act or a provision thereof shall operate notwithstanding a provision included in section 2 or sections 7 to 15 of this Charter.

Operation of exception

(2) An Act or a provision of an Act in respect of which a declaration made under this section is in effect shall have such operation as it would have but for the provision of this Charter referred to in the declaration.

Five year limitation

(3) A declaration made under subsection (1) shall cease to have effect five years after it comes into force or on such earlier date as may be specified in the declaration.

Re-enactment

(4) Parliament or the legislature of a province may re-enact a declaration made under subsection (1).

Five year limitation

(5) Subsection (3) applies in respect of a re-enactment made under subsection (4).

Citation

Citation

34. This Part may be cited as the *Canadian Charter of Rights and Freedoms*.

27. Toute interprétation de la présente charte doit concorder avec l'objectif de promouvoir le maintien et la valorisation du patrimoine multiculturel des Canadiens. Maintien du patrimoine culturel

28. Indépendamment des autres dispositions de la présente charte, les droits et libertés qui y sont mentionnés sont garantis également aux personnes des deux sexes. Égalité de garantie des droits pour les deux sexes

29. Les dispositions de la présente charte ne portent pas atteinte aux droits ou privilèges garantis en vertu de la Constitution du Canada concernant les écoles séparées et autres écoles confessionnelles. Maintien des droits relatifs à certaines écoles

30. Dans la présente charte, les dispositions qui visent les provinces, leur législature ou leur assemblée législative visent également le territoire du Yukon, les territoires du Nord-Ouest ou leurs autorités législatives compétentes. Application aux territoires

31. La présente charte n'élargit pas les compétences législatives de quelque organisme ou autorité que ce soit. Non-élargissement des compétences législatives

Application de la charte

32.—(1) La présente charte s'applique : Application de la charte

    (*a*) au Parlement et au gouvernement du Canada, pour tous les domaines relevant du Parlement, y compris ceux qui concernent le territoire du Yukon et les territoires du Nord-Ouest ;

    (*b*) à la législature et au gouvernement de chaque province, pour tous les domaines relevant de cette législature.

(2) Par dérogation au paragraphe (1), l'article 15 n'a d'effet que trois ans après l'entrée en vigueur du présent article. Restriction

33.—(1) Le Parlement ou la législature d'une province peut adopter une loi où il est expressément déclaré que celle-ci ou une de ses dispositions a effet indépendamment d'une disposition donnée de l'article 2 ou des articles 7 à 15 de la présente charte. Dérogation par déclaration expresse

(2) La loi ou la disposition qui fait l'objet d'une déclaration conforme au présent article et en vigueur a l'effet qu'elle aurait sauf la disposition en cause de la charte. Effet de la dérogation

(3) La déclaration visée au paragraphe (1) cesse d'avoir effet à la date qui y est précisée ou, au plus tard, cinq ans après son entrée en vigueur. Durée de validité

(4) Le Parlement ou une législature peut adopter de nouveau une déclaration visée au paragraphe (1). Nouvelle adoption

(5) Le paragraphe (3) s'applique à toute déclaration adoptée sous le régime du paragraphe (4). Durée de validité

Titre

34. Titre de la présente partie : *Charte canadienne des droits et libertés.* Titre

PART II

RIGHTS OF THE ABORIGINAL PEOPLES OF CANADA

Recognition of existing aboriginal and treaty rights

35.—(1) The existing aboriginal and treaty rights of the aboriginal peoples of Canada are hereby recognized and affirmed.

Definition of "aboriginal peoples of Canada"

(2) In this Act, "aboriginal peoples of Canada" includes the Indian, Inuit and Métis peoples of Canada.

PART III

EQUALIZATION AND REGIONAL DISPARITIES

Commitment to promote equal opportunities

36.—(1) Without altering the legislative authority of Parliament or of the provincial legislatures, or the rights of any of them with respect to the exercise of their legislative authority, Parliament and the legislatures, together with the government of Canada and the provincial governments, are committed to

(*a*) promoting equal opportunities for the well-being of Canadians ;

(*b*) furthering economic development to reduce disparity in opportunities ; and

(*c*) providing essential public services of reasonable quality to all Canadians.

Commitment respecting public services

(2) Parliament and the government of Canada are committed to the principle of making equalization payments to ensure that provincial governments have sufficient revenues to provide reasonably comparable levels of public services at reasonably comparable levels of taxation.

PART IV

CONSTITUTIONAL CONFERENCE

Constitutional conference

37.—(1) A constitutional conference composed of the Prime Minister of Canada and the first ministers of the provinces shall be convened by the Prime Minister of Canada within one year after this Part comes into force.

Participation of aboriginal peoples

(2) The conference convened under subsection (1) shall have included in its agenda an item respecting constitutional matters that directly affect the aboriginal peoples of Canada, including the identification and definition of the rights of those peoples to be included in the Constitution of Canada, and the Prime Minister of Canada shall invite representatives of those peoples to participate in the discussions on that item.

Participation of territories

(3) The Prime Minister of Canada shall invite elected representatives of the governments of the Yukon Territory and the Northwest Territories to participate in the discussions on any item on the agenda of the conference convened under subsection (1) that, in the opinion of the Prime Minister, directly affects the Yukon Territory and the Northwest Territories.

PARTIE II

DROITS DES PEUPLES AUTOCHTONES DU CANADA

35.—(1) Les droits existants—ancestraux ou issus de traités—des peuples autochtones du Canada sont reconnus et confirmés.

Confirmation des droits existants des peuples autochtones

(2) Dans la présente loi, " peuples autochtones du Canada " s'entend notamment des Indiens, des Inuit et des Métis du Canada.

Définition de " peuples autochtones du Canada "

PARTIE III

PÉRÉQUATION ET INÉGALITÉS RÉGIONALES

36.—(1) Sous réserve des compétences législatives du Parlement et des législatures et de leur droit de les exercer, le Parlement et les législatures, ainsi que les gouvernements fédéral et provinciaux, s'engagent à :

Engagements relatifs à l'égalité des chances

(*a*) promouvoir l'égalité des chances de tous les Canadiens dans la recherche de leur bien-être ;

(*b*) favoriser le développement économique pour réduire l'inégalité des chances ;

(*c*) fournir à tous les Canadiens, à un niveau de qualité acceptable, les services publics essentiels.

(2) Le Parlement et le gouvernement du Canada prennent l'engagement de principe de faire des paiements de péréquation propres à donner aux gouvernements provinciaux des revenus suffisants pour les mettre en mesure d'assurer les services publics à un niveau de qualité et de fiscalité sensiblement comparables.

Engagement relatif aux services publics

PARTIE IV

CONFÉRENCE CONSTITUTIONNELLE

37.—(1) Dans l'année suivant l'entrée en vigueur de la présente partie, le premier ministre du Canada convoque une conférence constitutionnelle réunissant les premiers ministres provinciaux et lui-même.

Conférence constitutionnelle

(2) Sont placées à l'ordre du jour de la conférence visée au paragraphe (1) les questions constitutionnelles qui intéressent directement les peuples autochtones du Canada, notamment la détermination et la définition des droits de ces peuples à inscrire dans la Constitution du Canada. Le premier ministre du Canada invite leurs représentants à participer aux travaux relatifs à ces questions.

Participation des peuples autochtones

(3) Le premier ministre du Canada invite des représentants élus des gouvernements du territoire du Yukon et des territoires du Nord-Ouest à participer aux travaux relatifs à toute question placée à l'ordre du jour de la conférence visée au paragraphe (1) et qui, selon lui, intéresse directement le territoire du Yukon et les territoires du Nord-Ouest.

Participation des territoires

Part V

Procedure for amending Constitution of Canada

General procedure for amending Constitution of Canada

38.—(1) An amendment to the Constitution of Canada may be made by proclamation issued by the Governor General under the Great Seal of Canada where so authorized by

> (a) resolutions of the Senate and House of Commons ; and
>
> (b) resolutions of the legislative assemblies of at least two-thirds of the provinces that have, in the aggregate, according to the then latest general census, at least fifty per cent. of the population of all the provinces.

Majority of members

(2) An amendment made under subsection (1) that derogates from the legislative powers, the proprietary rights or any other rights or privileges of the legislature or government of a province shall require a resolution supported by a majority of the members of each of the Senate, the House of Commons and the legislative assemblies required under subsection (1).

Expression of dissent

(3) An amendment referred to in subsection (2) shall not have effect in a province the legislative assembly of which has expressed its dissent thereto by resolution supported by a majority of its members prior to the issue of the proclamation to which the amendment relates unless that legislative assembly, subsequently, by resolution supported by a majority of its members, revokes its dissent and authorizes the amendment.

Revocation of dissent

(4) A resolution of dissent made for the purposes of subsection (3) may be revoked at any time before or after the issue of the proclamation to which it relates.

Restriction on proclamation

39.—(1) A proclamation shall not be issued under subsection 38(1) before the expiration of one year from the adoption of the resolution initiating the amendment procedure thereunder, unless the legislative assembly of each province has previously adopted a resolution of assent or dissent.

Idem

(2) A proclamation shall not be issued under subsection 38(1) after the expiration of three years from the adoption of the resolution initiating the amendment procedure thereunder.

Compensation

40. Where an amendment is made under subsection 38(1) that transfers provincial legislative powers relating to education or other cultural matters from provincial legislatures to Parliament, Canada shall provide reasonable compensation to any province to which the amendment does not apply.

Amendment by unanimous consent

41. An amendment to the Constitution of Canada in relation to the following matters may be made by proclamation issued by the Governor General under the Great Seal of Canada only where authorized by resolutions of the Senate and House of Commons and of the legislative assembly of each province :

Partie V

Procédure de Modification de la Constitution du Canada

38.—(1) La Constitution du Canada peut être modifiée par pro-clamation du gouverneur général sous le grand sceau du Canada, autorisée à la fois : Procédure normale de modification

 (*a*) par des résolutions du Sénat et de la Chambre des communes ;

 (*b*) par des résolutions des assemblées législatives d'au moins deux tiers des provinces dont la population confondue représente, selon le recensement général le plus récent à l'époque, au moins cinquante pour cent de la population de toutes les provinces.

(2) Une modification faite conformément au paragraphe (1) mais dérogatoire à la compétence législative, aux droits de propriété ou à tous autres droits ou privilèges d'une législature ou d'un gouvernement provincial exige une résolution adoptée à la majorité des sénateurs, des députés fédéraux et des députés de chacune des assemblées législatives du nombre requis de provinces. Majorité simple

(3) La modification visée au paragraphe (2) est sans effet dans une province dont l'assemblée législative a, avant la prise de la proclamation, exprimé son désaccord par une résolution adoptée à la majorité des députés, sauf si cette assemblée, par résolution également adoptée à la majorité, revient sur son désaccord et autorise la modification. Désaccord

(4) La résolution de désaccord visée au paragraphe (3) peut être révoquée à tout moment, indépendamment de la date de la proclamation à laquelle elle se rapporte. Levée du désaccord

39.—(1) La proclamation visée au paragraphe 38(1) ne peut être prise dans l'année suivant l'adoption de la résolution à l'origine de la procédure de modification que si l'assemblée législative de chaque province a préalablement adopté une résolution d'agrément ou de désaccord. Restriction

(2) La proclamation visée au paragraphe 38(1) ne peut être prise que dans les trois ans suivant l'adoption de la résolution à l'origine de la procédure de modification. Idem

40. Le Canada fournit une juste compensation aux provinces auxquelles ne s'applique pas une modification faite conformément au paragraphe 38(1) et relative, en matière d'éducation ou dans d'autres domaines culturels, à un transfert de compétences législatives provinciales au Parlement. Compensation

41. Toute modification de la Constitution du Canada portant sur les questions suivantes se fait par proclamation du gouverneur général sous le grand sceau du Canada, autorisée par des résolutions du Sénat, de la Chambre des communes et de l'assemblée législative de chaque province : Consentemen unanime

D

(a) the office of the Queen, the Governor General and the Lieutenant Governor of a province ;

(b) the right of a province to a number of members in the House of Commons not less than the number of Senators by which the province is entitled to be represented at the time this Part comes into force ;

(c) subject to section 43, the use of the English or the French language ;

(d) the composition of the Supreme Court of Canada ; and

(e) an amendment to this Part.

Amendment by general procedure

42.—(1) An amendment to the Constitution of Canada in relation to the following matters may be made only in accordance with subsection 38(1):

(a) the principle of proportionate representation of the provinces in the House of Commons prescribed by the Constitution of Canada ;

(b) the powers of the Senate and the method of selecting Senators ;

(c) the number of members by which a province is entitled to be represented in the Senate and the residence qualifications of Senators ;

(d) subject to paragraph 41(d), the Supreme Court of Canada ;

(e) the extension of existing provinces into the territories ; and

(f) notwithstanding any other law or practice, the establishment of new provinces.

Exception

(2) Subsections 38(2) to (4) do not apply in respect of amendments in relation to matters referred to in subsection (1).

Amendment of provisions relating to some but not all provinces

43. An amendment to the Constitution of Canada in relation to any provision that applies to one or more, but not all, provinces, including

(a) any alteration to boundaries between provinces, and

(b) any amendment to any provision that relates to the use of the English or the French language within a province,

may be made by proclamation issued by the Governor General under the Great Seal of Canada only where so authorized by resolution of the Senate and House of Commons and of the legislative assembly of each province to which the amendment applies.

Amendments by Parliament

44. Subject to sections 41 and 42, Parliament may exclusively make laws amending the Constitution of Canada in relation to the executive government of Canada or the Senate and House of Commons.

Amendments by provincial legislatures

45. Subject to section 41, the legislature of each province may exclusively make laws amending the constitution of the province.

(*a*) la charge de Reine, celle de gouverneur général et celle de lieutenant-gouverneur ;

(*b*) le droit d'une province d'avoir à la Chambre des communes un nombre de députés au moins égal à celui des sénateurs par lesquels elle est habilitée à être représentée lors de l'entrée en vigueur de la présente partie ;

(*c*) sous réserve de l'article 43, l'usage du français ou de l'anglais ;

(*d*) la composition de la Cour suprême du Canada ;

(*e*) la modification de la présente partie.

42.—(1) Toute modification de la Constitution du Canada portant sur les questions suivantes se fait conformément au paragraphe 38(1) : Procédure normale de modification

(*a*) le principe de la représentation proportionnelle des provinces à la Chambre des communes prévu par la Constitution du Canada ;

(*b*) les pouvoirs du Sénat et le mode de sélection des sénateurs ;

(*c*) le nombre des sénateurs par lesquels une province est habilitée à être représentée et les conditions de résidence qu'ils doivent remplir ;

(*d*) sous réserve de l'alinéa 41(*d*), la Cour suprême du Canada ;

(*e*) le rattachement aux provinces existantes de tout ou partie des territoires ;

(*f*) par dérogation à toute autre loi ou usage, la création de provinces.

(2) Les paragraphes 38(2) à (4) ne s'appliquent pas aux questions mentionnées au paragraphe (1). Exception

43. Les dispositions de la Constitution du Canada applicables à certaines provinces seulement ne peuvent être modifiées que par proclamation du gouverneur général sous le grand sceau du Canada, autorisée par des résolutions du Sénat, de la Chambre des communes et de l'assemblée législative de chaque province concernée. Le présent article s'applique notamment : Modification à l'égard de certaines provinces

(*a*) aux changements du tracé des frontières interprovinciales ;

(*b*) aux modifications des dispositions relatives à l'usage du français ou de l'anglais dans une province.

44. Sous réserve des articles 41 et 42, le Parlement a compétence exclusive pour modifier les dispositions de la Constitution du Canada relatives au pouvoir exécutif fédéral, au Sénat ou à la Chambre des communes. Modification par le Parlement

45. Sous réserve de l'article 41, une législature a compétence exclusive pour modifier la constitution de sa province. Modification par les législatures

Initiation of
amendment
procedures

46.—(1) The procedures for amendment under sections 38, 41, 42 and 43 may be initiated either by the Senate or the House of Commons or by the legislative assembly of a province.

Revocation of
authorization

(2) A resolution of assent made for the purposes of this Part may be revoked at any time before the issue of a proclamation authorized by it.

Amendments
without Senate
resolution

47.—(1) An amendment to the Constitution of Canada made by proclamation under section 38, 41, 42 or 43 may be made without a resolution of the Senate authorizing the issue of the proclamation if, within one hundred and eighty days after the adoption by the House of Commons of a resolution authorizing its issue, the Senate has not adopted such a resolution and if, at any time after the expiration of that period, the House of Commons again adopts the resolution.

Computation of
period

(2) Any period when Parliament is prorogued or dissolved shall not be counted in computing the one hundred and eighty day period referred to in subsection (1).

Advice to issue
proclamation

48. The Queen's Privy Council for Canada shall advise the Governor General to issue a proclamation under this Part forthwith on the adoption of the resolutions required for an amendment made by proclamation under this Part.

Constitutional
conference

49. A constitutional conference composed of the Prime Minister of Canada and the first ministers of the provinces shall be convened by the Prime Minister of Canada within fifteen years after this Part comes into force to review the provisions of this Part.

PART VI

AMENDMENT TO THE CONSTITUTION ACT, 1867

Amendment to
*Constitution
Act 1867*

50. The *Constitution Act, 1867* (formerly named the *British North America Act, 1867*) is amended by adding thereto, immediately after section 92 thereof, the following heading and section:

" *Non-Renewable Natural Resources, Forestry Resources and Electrical Energy*

Laws respecting
non-renewable
natural
resources,
forestry
resources and
electrical
energy

92A.—(1) In each province, the legislature may exclusively make laws in relation to

(*a*) exploration for non-renewable natural resources in the province;

(*b*) development, conservation and management of non-renewable natural resources and forestry resources in the province, including laws in relation to the rate of primary production therefrom; and

(*c*) development, conservation and management of sites and facilities in the province for the generation and production of electrical energy.

46.—(1) L'initiative des procédures de modification visées aux articles 38, 41, 42 and 43 appartient au Sénat, à la Chambre des communes ou à une assemblée législative.
Initiative des procédures

(2) Une résolution d'agrément adoptée dans le cadre de la présente partie peut être révoquée à tout moment avant la date de la proclamation qu'elle autorise.
Possibilité de révocation

47.—(1) Dans les cas visés à l'article 38, 41, 42 ou 43, il peut être passé outre au défaut d'autorisation du Sénat si celui-ci n'a pas adopté de résolution dans un délai de cent quatre-vingts jours suivant l'adoption de celle de la Chambre des communes et si cette dernière, après l'expiration du délai, adopte une nouvelle résolution dans le même sens.
Modification sans résolution du Sénat

(2) Dans la computation du délai visé au paragraphe (1), ne sont pas comptées les périodes pendant lesquelles le Parlement est prorogé ou dissous.
Computation du délai

48. Le Conseil privé de la Reine pour le Canada demande au gouverneur général de prendre, conformément à la présente partie, une proclamation dès l'adoption des résolutions prévues par cette partie pour une modification par proclamation.
Demande de proclamation

49. Dans les quinze ans suivant l'entrée en vigueur de la présente partie, le premier ministre du Canada convoque une conférence constitutionnelle réunissant les premiers ministres provinciaux et lui-même, en vue du réexamen des dispositions de cette partie.
Conférence constitutionnelle

PARTIE VI

Modification de la loi Constitutionnelle de 1867

50. La *Loi constitutionnelle de 1867* (antérieurement désignée sous le titre : *Acte de l'Amérique du Nord britannique, 1867*) est modifiée par insertion, après l'article 92, de la rubrique et de l'article suivants :
Modification de la *Loi constitution-nelle de 1867*

" *Ressources naturelles non renouvelables, ressources forestières et énergie électrique*

    92A.—(1) La législature de chaque province a compétence exclusive pour légiférer dans les domaines suivants :
Compétence provinciale

    (*a*) prospection des ressources naturelles non renouvelables de la province ;

    (*b*) exploitation, conservation et gestion des ressources naturelles non renouvelables et des ressources forestières de la province, y compris leur rythme de production primaire ;

    (*c*) aménagement, conservation et gestion des emplacements et des installations de la province destinés à la production d'énergie électrique.

Export from
provinces of
resources

(2) In each province, the legislature may make laws in relation to the export from the province to another part of Canada of the primary production from non-renewable natural resources and forestry resources in the province and the production from facilities in the province for the generation of electrical energy, but such laws may not authorize or provide for discrimination in prices or in supplies exported to another part of Canada.

Authority of
Parliament

(3) Nothing in subsection (2) derogates from the authority of Parliament to enact laws in relation to the matters referred to in that subsection and, where such a law of Parliament and a law of a province conflict, the law of Parliament prevails to the extent of the conflict.

Taxation of
resources

(4) In each province, the legislature may make laws in relation to the raising of money by any mode or system of taxation in respect of

(*a*) non-renewable natural resources and forestry resources in the province and the primary production therefrom, and

(*b*) sites and facilities in the province for the generation of electrical energy and the production therefrom,

whether or not such production is exported in whole or in part from the province, but such laws may not authorize or provide for taxation that differentiates between production exported to another part of Canada and production not exported from the province.

" Primary
production "

(5) The expression " primary production " has the meaning assigned by the Sixth Schedule.

Existing powers
or rights

(6) Nothing in subsections (1) to (5) derogates from any powers or rights that a legislature or government of a province had immediately before the coming into force of this section."

Idem

51. The said Act is further amended by adding thereto the following Schedule:

" THE SIXTH SCHEDULE

Primary Production from Non-Renewable Natural Resources and Forestry Resources

1. For the purposes of section 92A of this Act,

(*a*) production from a non-renewable natural resource is primary production therefrom if

(i) it is in the form in which it exists upon its recovery or severance from its natural state, or

(ii) it is a product resulting from processing or refining the resource, and is not a manufactured product or a product resulting from

(2) La législature de chaque province a compétence _{Exportation} pour légiférer en ce qui concerne l'exportation, hors de la _{provinces} province, à destination d'une autre partie du Canada, de la production primaire tirée des ressources naturelles non renouvelables et des ressources forestières de la province, ainsi que de la production d'énergie électrique de la province, sous réserve de ne pas adopter de lois autorisant ou prévoyant des disparités de prix ou des disparités dans les exportations destinées à une autre partie du Canada.

(3) Le paragraphe (2) ne porte pas atteinte au pouvoir Pouvoir du du Parlement de légiférer dans les domaines visés à ce Parlement paragraphe, les dispositions d'une loi du Parlement adoptée dans ces domaines l'emportant sur les dispositions incompatibles d'une loi provinciale.

(4) La législature de chaque province a compétence Taxation des pour prélever des sommes d'argent par tout mode ou ressources système de taxation:

(*a*) des ressources naturelles non renouvelables et des ressources forestières de la province, ainsi que de la production primaire qui en est tirée ;

(*b*) des emplacements et des installations de la province destinés à la production d'énergie électrique, ainsi que de cette production même.

Cette compétence peut s'exercer indépendamment du fait que la production en cause soit ou non, en totalité ou en partie, exportée hors de la province, mais les lois adoptées dans ces domaines ne peuvent autoriser ou prévoir une taxation qui établisse une distinction entre la production exportée à destination d'une autre partie du Canada et la production non exportée hors de la province.

(5) L'expression " production primaire " a le sens qui "Production lui est donné dans la sixième annexe. primaire"

(6) Les paragraphes (1) à (5) ne portent pas atteinte Pouvoirs ou aux pouvoirs ou droits détenus par la législature ou le droits existants gouvernement d'une province lors de l'entrée en vigueur du présent article."

51. Ladite loi est en outre modifiée par adjonction de l'annexe Idem suivante:

" SIXIÈME ANNEXE

Production primaire tirée des ressources naturelles non renouvelables et des ressources forestières

1. Pour l'application de l'article 92A :

(*a*) on entend par production primaire tirée d'une ressource naturelle non renouvelable :

(i) soit le produit qui se présente sous la même forme que lors de son extraction du milieu naturel,

(ii) soit le produit non manufacturé de la transformation, du raffinage ou de l'affinage d'une ressource, à l'exception du produit du

D 4

> refining crude oil, refining upgraded heavy
> crude oil, refining gases or liquids derived
> from coal or refining a synthetic equivalent
> of crude oil ; and
>
> (*b*) production from a forestry resource is primary
> production therefrom if it consists of sawlogs,
> poles, lumber, wood chips, sawdust or any other
> primary wood product, or wood pulp, and is
> not a product manufactured from wood."

PART VII

GENERAL

Primacy of
Constitution of
Canada

52.—(1) The Constitution of Canada is the supreme law of
Canada, and any law that is inconsistent with the provisions of the
Constitution is, to the extent of the inconsistency, of no force or
effect.

Constitution of
Canada

(2) The Constitution of Canada includes

(*a*) the *Canada Act 1982*, including this Act ;

(*b*) the Acts and orders referred to in the schedule ; and

(*c*) any amendment to any Act or order referred to in paragraph
(*a*) or (*b*).

Amendments to
Constitution of
Canada

(3) Amendments to the Constitution of Canada shall be made only
in accordance with the authority contained in the Constitution of
Canada.

Repeals and
new names

53.—(1) The enactments referred to in Column I of the schedule
are hereby repealed or amended to the extent indicated in Column
II thereof and, unless repealed, shall continue as law in Canada
under the names set out in Column III thereof.

Consequential
amendments

(2) Every enactment, except the *Canada Act 1982*, that refers to an
enactment referred to in the schedule by the name in Column I thereof
is hereby amended by substituting for that name the corresponding
name in Column III thereof, and any British North America Act
not referred to in the schedule may be cited as the *Constitution Act*
followed by the year and number, if any, of its enactment.

Repeal and
consequential
amendments

54. Part IV is repealed on the day that is one year after this Part
comes into force and this section may be repealed and this Act
renumbered, consequentially upon the repeal of Part IV and this
section, by proclamation issued by the Governor General under the
Great Seal of Canada.

French version
of Constitution
of Canada

55. A French version of the portions of the Constitution of Canada
referred to in the schedule shall be prepared by the Minister of
Justice of Canada as expeditiously as possible and, when any portion
thereof sufficient to warrant action being taken has been so prepared, it shall be put forward for enactment by proclamation issued
by the Governor General under the Great Seal of Canada pursuant
to the procedure then applicable to an amendment of the same provisions of the Constitution of Canada.

raffinage du pétrole brut, du raffinage du pétrole brut lourd amélioré, du raffinage des gaz ou des liquides dérivés du charbon ou du raffinage d'un équivalent synthétique du pétrole brut ;

(*b*) on entend par production primaire tirée d'une ressource forestière la production constituée de billots, de poteaux, de bois d'œuvre, de copeaux, de sciure ou d'autre produit primaire du bois, ou de pâte de bois, à l'exception d'un produit manufacturé en bois."

PARTIE VII
DISPOSITIONS GÉNÉRALES

52.—(1) La Constitution du Canada est la loi suprême du Canada ; elle rend inopérantes les dispositions incompatibles de toute autre règle de droit. Primauté de la Constitution du Canada

(2) La Constitution du Canada comprend : Constitution du Canada
    (*a*) la *Loi de 1982 sur le Canada*, y compris la présente loi ;
    (*b*) les textes législatifs et les décrets figurant à l'annexe ;
    (*c*) les modifications des textes législatifs et des décrets mentionnés aux alinéas (*a*) ou (*b*).

(3) La Constitution du Canada ne peut être modifiée que conformément aux pouvoirs conférés par elle. Modification

53.—(1) Les textes législatifs et les décrets énumérés à la colonne I de l'annexe sont abrogés ou modifiés dans la mesure indiquée à la colonne II. Sauf abrogation, ils restent en vigueur en tant que lois du Canada sous les titres mentionnés à la colonne III. Abrogation et nouveaux titres

(2) Tout texte législatif ou réglementaire, sauf la *Loi de 1982 sur le Canada*, qui fait mention d'un texte législatif ou décret figurant à l'annexe par le titre indiqué à la colonne I est modifié par substitution à ce titre du titre correspondant mentionné à la colonne III ; tout Acte de l'Amérique du Nord britannique non mentionné à l'annexe peut être cité sous le titre de *Loi constitutionnelle* suivi de l'indication de l'année de son adoption et éventuellement de son numéro. Modifications corrélatives

54. La partie IV est abrogée un an après l'entrée en vigueur de la présente partie et le gouverneur général peut, par proclamation sous le grand sceau du Canada, abroger le présent article et apporter en conséquence de cette double abrogation les aménagements qui s'imposent à la présente loi. Abrogation et modifications qui en découlent

55. Le ministre de la Justice du Canada est chargé de rédiger, dans les meilleurs délais, la version française des parties de la Constitution du Canada qui figurent à l'annexe ; toute partie suffisamment importante est, dès qu'elle est prête, déposée pour adoption par proclamation du gouverneur général sous le grand sceau du Canada, conformément à la procédure applicable à l'époque à la modification des dispositions constitutionnelles qu'elle contient. Version française de certains textes constitutionnels

English and
French versions
of certain
constitutional
texts

56. Where any portion of the Constitution of Canada has been or is enacted in English and French or where a French version of any portion of the Constitution is enacted pursuant to section 55, the English and French versions of that portion of the Constitution are equally authoritative.

English and
French versions
of this Act

57. The English and French versions of this Act are equally authoritative.

Commence-
ment

58. Subject to section 59, this Act shall come into force on a day to be fixed by proclamation issued by the Queen or the Governor General under the Great Seal of Canada.

Commencement of
paragraph 23(1)(a)
in respect of
Quebec

59.—(1) Paragraph 23(1)(a) shall come into force in respect of Quebec on a day to be fixed by proclamation issued by the Queen or the Governor General under the Great Seal of Canada.

Authorization
of Quebec

(2) A proclamation under subsection (1) shall be issued only where authorized by the legislative assembly or government of Quebec.

Repeal of this
section

(3) This section may be repealed on the day paragraph 23(1)(a) comes into force in respect of Quebec and this Act amended and renumbered, consequentially upon the repeal of this section, by proclamation issued by the Queen or the Governor General under the Great Seal of Canada.

Short title and
citations

60. This Act may be cited as the *Constitution Act, 1982,* and the Constitution Acts 1867 to 1975 (No. 2) and this Act may be cited together as the *Constitution Acts, 1867 to 1982.*

56. Les versions française et anglaise des parties de la Constitution du Canada adoptées dans ces deux langues ont également force de loi. En outre, ont également force de loi, dès l'adoption, dans le cadre de l'article 55, d'une partie de la version française de la Constitution, cette partie et la version anglaise correspondante. Versions française et anglaise de certains textes constitutionnels

57. Les versions française et anglaise de la présente loi ont également force de loi. Versions française et anglaise de la présente loi

58. Sous réserve de l'article 59, la présente loi entre en vigueur à la date fixée par proclamation de la Reine ou du gouverneur général sous le grand sceau du Canada. Entrée en vigueur

59.—(1) L'alinéa 23(1)(*a*) entre en vigueur pour le Québec à la date fixée par proclamation de la Reine ou du gouverneur général sous le grand sceau du Canada. Entrée en vigueur de l'alinéa 23(1)(*a*) pour le Québec

(2) La proclamation visée au paragraphe (1) ne peut être prise qu'après autorisation de l'assemblée législative ou du gouvernement du Québec. Autorisation du Québec

(3) Le présent article peut être abrogé à la date d'entrée en vigueur de l'alinéa 23(1)(*a*) pour le Québec, et la présente loi faire l'objet, dès cette abrogation, des modifications et changements de numérotation qui en découlent, par proclamation de la Reine ou du gouverneur général sous le grand sceau du Canada. Abrogation du présent article

60. Titre abrégé de la présente loi: *Loi constitutionnelle de 1982*; titre commun des lois constitutionnelles de 1867 à 1975 (n° 2) et de la présente loi: *Lois constitutionnelles de 1867 à 1982*. Titres

SCHEDULE

to the

CONSTITUTION ACT, 1982

MODERNIZATION OF THE CONSTITUTION

Item	Column I Act Affected	Column II Amendment	Column III New Name
1	British North America Act, 1867, 30-31 Vict., c. 3 (U.K.)	(1) Section 1 is repealed and the following substituted therefor: "1. This Act may be cited as the *Constitution Act, 1867*." (2) Section 20 is repealed. (3) Class 1 of section 91 is repealed. (4) Class 1 of section 92 is repealed.	Constitution Act, 1867
2	An Act to amend and continue the Act 32-33 Victoria chapter 3; and to establish and provide for the Government of the Province of Manitoba, 1870, 33 Vict., c. 3 (Can.)	(1) The long title is repealed and the following substituted therefor: " *Manitoba Act, 1870.* " (2) Section 20 is repealed.	Manitoba Act, 1870
3	Order of Her Majesty in Council admitting Rupert's Land and the North-Western Territory into the Union, dated the 23rd day of June, 1870		Rupert's Land and North-Western Territory Order
4	Order of Her Majesty in Council admitting British Columbia into the Union, dated the 16th day of May, 1871		British Columbia Terms of Union
5	British North America Act, 1871, 34-35 Vict., c. 28 (U.K.)	Section 1 is repealed and the following substituted therefor: "1. This Act may be cited as the *Constitution Act, 1871*."	Constitution Act, 1871
6	Order of Her Majesty in Council admitting Prince Edward Island into the Union, dated the 26th day of June, 1873		Prince Edward Island Terms of Union
7	Parliament of Canada Act, 1875, 38-39 Vict., c. 38 (U.K.)		Parliament of Canada Act, 1875

ANNEXE

de la

LOI CONSTITUTIONNELLE DE 1982

ACTUALISATION DE LA CONSTITUTION

	Colonne I Loi visée	Colonne II Modification	Colonne III Nouveau titre
1	Acte de l'Amérique du Nord britannique, 1867, 30-31 Vict., c. 3 (R.-U.)	(1) L'article 1 est abrogé et remplacé par ce qui suit: "1. Titre abrégé: *Loi constitutionnelle de 1867.*" (2) L'article 20 est abrogé. (3) La catégorie 1 de l'article 91 est abrogée. (4) La catégorie 1 de l'article 92 est abrogée.	Loi constitutionnelle de 1867
2	Acte pour amender et continuer l'acte trente-deux et trente-trois Victoria, chapitre trois, et pour établir et constituer le gouvernement de la province de Manitoba, 1870, 33 Vict., c. 3 (Canada)	(1) Le titre complet est abrogé et remplacé par ce qui suit: "*Loi de 1870 sur le Manitoba.*" (2) L'article 20 est abrogé.	Loi de 1870 sur le Manitoba
3	Arrêté en conseil de Sa Majesté admettant la Terre de Rupert et le Territoire du Nord-Ouest, en date du 23 juin 1870		Décret en conseil sur la terre de Rupert et le territoire du Nord-Ouest
4	Arrêté en conseil de Sa Majesté admettant la Colombie-Britannique, en date du 16 mai 1871		Conditions de l'adhésion de la Colombie-Britannique
5	Acte de l'Amérique du Nord britannique, 1871, 34–35 Vict., c. 28 (R.-U.)	L'article 1 est abrogé et remplacé par ce qui suit: "1. Titre abrégé: *Loi constitutionnelle de 1871.*"	Loi constitutionnelle de 1871
6	Arrêté en conseil de Sa Majesté admettant l'Île-du-Prince-Édouard, en date du 26 juin 1873		Conditions de l'adhésion de l'Île-du-Prince-Édouard
7	Acte du Parlement du Canada, 1875, 38-39 Vict., c. 38 (R.-U.)		**Loi de 1875 sur le Parlement du Canada**

Item	Column I Act Affected	Column II Amendment	Column III New Name
8	Order of Her Majesty in Council admitting all British possessions and Territories in North America and islands adjacent thereto into the Union, dated the 31st day of July, 1880		Adjacent Territories Order
9	British North America Act, 1886, 49–50 Vict., c. 35 (U.K.)	Section 3 is repealed and the following substituted therefor: "3. This Act may be cited as the *Constitution Act, 1886*."	Constitution Act, 1886
10	Canada (Ontario Boundary) Act, 1889, 52-53 Vict., c. 28 (U.K.)		Canada (Ontario Boundary) Act, 1889
11	Canadian Speaker (Appointment of Deputy) Act, 1895, 2nd Sess., 59 Vict., c. 3 (U.K.)	The Act is repealed.	
12	The Alberta Act, 1905, 4-5 Edw. VII, c. 3 (Can.)		Alberta Act
13	The Saskatchewan Act, 1905, 4-5 Edw. VII, c. 42 (Can.)		Saskatchewan Act
14	British North America Act, 1907, 7 Edw. VII, c. 11 (U.K.)	Section 2 is repealed and the following substituted therefor: "2. This Act may be cited as the *Constitution Act, 1907*."	Constitution Act, 1907
15	British North America Act, 1915, 5-6 Geo. V, c. 45 (U.K.)	Section 3 is repealed and the following substituted therefor: "3. This Act may be cited as the *Constitution Act, 1915*."	Constitution Act, 1915
16	British North America Act, 1930, 20-21 Geo. V, c. 26 (U.K.)	Section 3 is repealed and the following substituted therefor: "3. This Act may be cited as the *Constitution Act, 1930*."	Constitution Act, 1930

Colonne I Loi visée	Colonne II Modification	Colonne III Nouveau titre
8 Arrêté en conseil de Sa Majesté admettant dans l'Union tous les territoires et possessions britanniques dans l'Amérique du Nord, et les îles adjacentes à ces territoires et possessions, en date du 31 juillet 1880		Décret en conseil sur les territoires adjacents
9 Acte de l'Amérique du Nord britannique, 1886, 49-50 Vict., c. 35 (R.-U.)	L'article 3 est abrogé et remplacé par ce qui suit: "3. Titre abrégé: *Loi constitutionnelle de 1886.*"	Loi constitutionnelle de 1886
10 Acte du Canada (limites d'Ontario) 1889, 52-53 Vict., c. 28 (R.-U.)		Loi de 1889 sur le Canada (frontières de l'Ontario)
11 Acte concernant l'Orateur canadien (nomination d'un suppléant) 1895, 2e session, 59 Vict., c. 3 (R.-U.)	La loi est abrogée.	
12 Acte de l'Alberta, 1905, 4-5 Ed. VII, c. 3 (Canada)		Loi sur l'Alberta
13 Acte de la Saskatchewan, 1905, 4-5 Ed. VII, c. 42 (Canada)		Loi sur la Saskatchewan
14 Acte de l'Amérique du Nord britannique, 1907, 7 Ed. VII, c. 11 (R.-U.)	L'article 2 est abrogé et remplacé par ce qui suit: "2. Titre abrégé: *Loi constitutionnelle de 1907.*"	Loi constitutionnelle de 1907
15 Acte de l'Amérique du Nord britannique, 1915, 5-6 Geo. V, c. 45 (R.-U.)	L'article 3 est abrogé et remplacé par ce qui suit: "3. Titre abrégé: *Loi constitutionnelle de 1915.*"	Loi constitutionnelle de 1915
16 Acte de l'Amérique du Nord britannique, 1930, 20-21 Geo. V c. 26 (R.-U.)	L'article 3 est abrogé et remplacé par ce qui suit: "3. Titre abrégé: *Loi constitutionnelle de 1930.*"	Loi constitutionnelle de 1930

Item	Column I Act Affected	Column II Amendment	Column III New Name
17	Statute of Westminster, 1931, 22 Geo. V, c. 4 (U.K.)	In so far as they apply to Canada, (*a*) section 4 is repealed; and (*b*) subsection 7(1) is repealed.	Statute of Westminster, 1931
18	British North America Act, 1940, 3-4 Geo. VI, c. 36 (U.K.)	Section 2 is repealed and the following substituted therefor: "2. This Act may be cited as the *Constitution Act, 1940*."	Constitution Act, 1940
19	British North America Act, 1943, 6-7 Geo. VI, c. 30 (U.K.)	The Act is repealed.	
20	British North America Act, 1946, 9-10 Geo. VI, c. 63 (U.K.)	The Act is repealed.	
21	British North America Act, 1949, 12-13 Geo. VI, c. 22 (U.K.)	Section 3 is repealed and the following substituted therefor: "3. This Act may be cited as the *Newfoundland Act*."	Newfoundland Act
22	British North America (No. 2) Act, 1949, 13 Geo. VI, c. 81 (U.K.).	The Act is repealed.	
23	British North America Act, 1951, 14-15 Geo. VI, c. 32 (U.K.)	The Act is repealed.	
24	British North America Act, 1952, 1 Eliz. II, c. 15 (Can.)	The Act is repealed.	
25	British North America Act, 1960, 9 Eliz. II, c. 2 (U.K.)	Section 2 is repealed and the following substituted therefor: "2. This Act may be cited as the *Constitution Act, 1960*."	Constitution Act, 1960
26	British North America Act, 1964, 12-13 Eliz. II, c. 73 (U.K.)	Section 2 is repealed and the following substituted therefor: "2. This Act may be cited as the *Constitution Act, 1964*."	Constitution Act, 1964

		Colonne I Loi visée	Colonne II Modification	Colonne III Nouveau titre
17		Statut de Westminster, 1931, 22 Geo. V, c. 4 (R.-U.)	Dans la mesure où ils s'appliquent au Canada: *a)* l'article 4 est abrogé; *b)* le paragraphe 7(1) est abrogé.	Statut de Westminster de 1931
18		Acte de l'Amérique du Nord britannique, 1940, 3-4 Geo. VI, c. 36 (R.-U.)	L'article 2 est abrogé et remplacé par ce qui suit: "2. Titre abrégé: *Loi constitutionnelle de 1940.*"	Loi constitutionnelle de 1940
19		Acte de 'Amérique du Nord britannique, 1943, 6-7 Geo. VI, c. 30 (R.-U.)	La loi est abrogée.	
20		Acte de l'Amérique du Nord britannique, 1946, 9-10 Geo. VI, c. 63 (R.-U.)	La loi est abrogée.	
21		Acte de l'Amérique du Nord britannique, 1949, 12-13 Geo. VI, c. 22 (R.-U.)	L'article 3 est abrogé et remplacé par ce qui suit: "3. Titre abrégé: *Loi sur Terre-Neuve.*"	Loi sur Terre-Neuve
22		Acte de l'Amérique du Nord britannique (n° 2), 1949, 13 Geo. VI, c. 81 (R.-U.)	La loi est abrogée.	
23		Acte de l'Amérique du Nord britannique, 1951, 14-15 Geo. VI, c. 32 (R.-U.)	La loi est abrogée.	
24		Acte de 'Amérique du Nord britannique, 1952, 1 Eliz. II, c. 15 (Canada)	La loi est abrogée.	
25		Acte de l'Amérique du Nord britannique, 1960, 9 Eliz. II, c. 2 (R.-U.)	L'article 2 est abrogé et remplacé par ce qui suit: "2. Titre abrégé: *Loi constitutionnelle de 1960.*"	Loi constitutionnelle de 1960
26		Acte de l'Amérique du Nord britannique, 1964, 12-13 Eliz. II, c. 73 (R.-U.)	L'article 2 est abrogé et remplacé par ce qui suit: "2. Titre abrégé: *Loi constitutionnelle de 1964.*"	Loi constitutionnelle de 1964

Item	Column I Act Affected	Column II Amendment	Column III New Name
27	British North America Act, 1965, 14 Eliz. II, c. 4, Part I (Can.)	Section 2 is repealed and the following substituted therefor: "2. This Part may be cited as the *Constitution Act, 1965*."	Constitution Act, 1965
28	British North America Act, 1974, 23 Eliz. II, c. 13, Part I (Can.)	Section 3, as amended by 25-26 Eliz. II, c. 28, s. 38(1) (Can.), is repealed and the following substituted therefor: "3. This Part may be cited as the *Constitution Act, 1974*."	Constitution Act, 1974
29	British North America Act, 1975, 23-24 Eliz. II, c. 28, Part I (Can.)	Section 3, as amended by 25-26 Eliz. II, c. 28, s. 31 (Can.), is repealed and the following substituted therefor: "3. This Part may be cited as the *Constitution Act (No. 1), 1975*."	Constitution Act (No. 1), 1975
30	British North America Act (No. 2), 1975, 23-24 Eliz. II, c. 53 (Can.)	Section 3 is repealed and the following substituted therefor: "3. This Act may be cited as the *Constitution Act (No. 2), 1975*."	Constitution Act (No. 2), 1975

	Colonne I Loi visée	Colonne II Modification	Colonne III Nouveau titre
27	Acte de l'Amérique du Nord britannique, 1965, 14 Eliz. II, c. 4, Partie I (Canada)	L'article 2 est abrogé et remplacé par ce qui suit: "2. Titre abrégé de la présente partie: *Loi constitutionnelle de 1965.*"	Loi constitutionnelle de 1965
28	Acte de l'Amérique du Nord britannique, 1974, 23 Eliz. II, c. 13, Partie I (Canada)	L'article 3, modifié par le paragraphe 38(1) de la loi 25-26 Elizabeth II, c. 28 (Canada), est abrogé et remplacé par ce qui suit: "3. Titre abrégé de la présente partie: *Loi constitutionnelle de 1974.*"	Loi constitutionnelle de 1974
29	Acte de l'Amérique du Nord britannique, 1975, 23-24 Eliz. II, c. 28, Partie I (Canada)	L'article 3, modifié par l'article 31 de la loi 25-26 Elizabeth II, c. 28 (Canada), est abrogé et remplacé par ce qui suit: "3. Titre abrégé de la présente partie: *Loi constitutionnelle n° 1 de 1975.*"	Loi constitutionnelle n° 1 de 1975
30	Acte de l'Amérique du Nord britannique, n° 2, 1975, 23-24 Eliz. II, c. 53 (Canada)	L'article 3 est abrogé et remplacé par ce qui suit: "3. Titre abrégé: *Loi constitutionnelle n° 2 de 1975.*"	Loi constitutionnelle n° 2 de 1975

Travel Concessions (London) Act 1982

1982 CHAPTER 12

An Act to confer on the Greater London Council the same powers in respect of travel concessions as those exercisable by the councils of London boroughs and the Common Council of the City of London.

[29th March 1982]

BE IT ENACTED by the Queen's most Excellent Majesty, by and with the advice and consent of the Lords Spiritual and Temporal, and Commons, in this present Parliament assembled, and by the authority of the same, as follows:—

Travel concessions in London.
1968 c. 73.

1969 c. 35.

1.—(1) The Greater London Council shall have the same powers under section 138 of the Transport Act 1968 (travel concessions) as the councils of London boroughs and the Common Council of the City of London; and accordingly in section 40(*a*) of the Transport (London) Act 1969 (by virtue of which section 138 has effect as if " local authority " in that section included the council of a London borough and the Common Council) after the word " included " there shall be inserted the words " the Council, ".

(2) There shall be defrayed out of moneys provided by Parliament any increase attributable to this section in the sums payable out of moneys so provided by way of rate support grants.

Short title.

2. This Act may be cited as the Travel Concessions (London) Act 1982.

Fire Service College Board (Abolition) Act 1982

1982 CHAPTER 13

An Act to repeal section 23(2) of the Fire Services Act 1947, to abolish the Fire Service College Board established thereunder and for connected purposes.

[7th April 1982]

BE IT ENACTED by the Queen's most Excellent Majesty, by and with the advice and consent of the Lords Spiritual and Temporal, and Commons, in this present Parliament assembled, and by the authority of the same, as follows:—

1. On the day on which this Act comes into force—

   (*a*) subsection (2) of section 23 of the Fire Services Act 1947 (which requires the central training institution established under that section to be under the general direction of a board) shall cease to have effect; and

   (*b*) the board known as the Fire Service College Board established under that subsection shall cease to exist;

and on and after that day the general direction of the institution shall be a function of the Secretary of State under that section.

Abolition of the Fire Service College Board.

1947 c. 41.

2.—(1) This Act may be cited as the Fire Service College Board (Abolition) Act 1982.

(2) This Act shall come into force at the expiration of the period of one month beginning with the day on which it is passed.

(3) This Act does not extend to Northern Ireland.

Short title, commencement and extent.

Reserve Forces
Act 1982

1982 CHAPTER 14

An Act to change the name of the Territorial and Army Volunteer Reserve and to amend the Reserve Forces Act 1980.   [7th April 1982]

B E IT ENACTED by the Queen's most Excellent Majesty, by and with the advice and consent of the Lords Spiritual and Temporal, and Commons, in this present Parliament assembled, and by the authority of the same, as follows:—

Change of name of Territorial and Army Volunteer Reserve.

1980 c. 9.

1.—(1) The Territorial and Army Volunteer Reserve shall, instead of being so known, be known as the Territorial Army.

(2) Accordingly—

(*a*) in subsection (1) of section 5 of the Reserve Forces Act 1980 (under which Her Majesty may maintain the Territorial and Army Volunteer Reserve), for the words from " maintain " onwards there shall be substituted the words " maintain the Territorial Army ", and in subsection (1) of section 156 of that Act (interpretation) the definition of " Territorial Army " shall be omitted; and

(*b*) a reference to the Territorial and Army Volunteer Reserve in any other Act or in any instrument shall be construed, so far as may be necessary in consequence of the change of name made by subsection (1) above, as a reference to the Territorial Army.

(3) In sub-paragraph (2) of paragraph 5 of Schedule 8 to the said Act of 1980 (which, among other things, provides that references to the Territorial Army shall continue to be construed as references to the Territorial and Army Volunteer Reserve) the words "Territorial Army and the", "respectively", "the Territorial and Army Volunteer Reserve and" and "army or" shall be omitted.

2.—(1) Paragraph (*b*) of subsection (1) of section 98 of the Reserve Forces Act 1980 (which requires a man of the Territorial Army or Royal Auxiliary Air Force to pay a levy if he is discharged before the end of his term) is hereby repealed; and, accordingly, in subsection (2) of that section (under which all or any of the conditions mentioned in the said subsection (1) may be dispensed with), for the words "all or any" there shall be substituted the words "one or both".

Miscellaneous amendments of the Reserve Forces Act 1980. 1980 c. 9.

(2) In subsection (1) of section 150 of the said Act of 1980 (which provides that the Secretary of State may make regulations with respect to the matters falling to be prescribed under the provisions of that Act listed in that subsection), after paragraph (*d*) there shall be inserted the following paragraph:—

"(*dd*) section 36(1),".

(3) Section 153 of the said Act of 1980 (which makes provision with respect to provisions of that Act deriving from Acts passed before the commencement of the Statutory Instruments Act 1946) is hereby repealed.

1946 c. 36.

(4) In paragraph 1 of Schedule 6 to the said Act of 1980 (general provisions as to evidence in proceedings under Parts IV and V of that Act) after sub-paragraph (7) there shall be inserted the following sub-paragraph:—

"(7A) Sections 198A and 198B of the Army Act 1955 or, as the case requires, of the Air Force Act 1955 (which, as inserted by the Armed Forces Act 1981, make provision with respect to evidence derived from computer records) shall apply, with the omission in each case of subsection (7) of section 198A, in relation to proceedings under Part IV or Part V of this Act as they apply in relation to the proceedings mentioned in those sections.".

(5) Subsection (4) above shall not affect any proceedings begun before whichever is the later of—

(*a*) the expiration of the period of one month beginning with the passing of this Act; and

(*b*) the coming into force of section 9 of the Armed Forces Act 1981 (which gives effect to the provisions applied by virtue of that subsection).

1981 c. 55.

Citation and
extent.

3.—(1) This Act may be cited as the Reserve Forces Act 1982.

(2) This Act extends to Northern Ireland.

1980 c. 9.

(3) Section 158(3) of the Reserve Forces Act 1980 (under which provisions of that Act may be extended to the Isle of Man) shall apply in relation to the provisions of this Act as it applies in relation to the provisions of that Act; but, save as aforesaid, nothing in this Act shall affect the Reserve Forces Act 1980 in its application to the Isle of Man.

Coal Industry Act 1982

1982 CHAPTER 15

An Act to increase the limit on the borrowing powers of the National Coal Board; and to make further provision with respect to grants and payments by the Secretary of State in connection with the coal industry.

[7th April 1982]

BE IT ENACTED by the Queen's most Excellent Majesty, by and with the advice and consent of the Lords Spiritual and Temporal, and Commons, in this present Parliament assembled, and by the authority of the same, as follows:—

1. In section 1(3) of the Act of 1965 (which, as amended by section 1(1) of the Act of 1980, provides for a limit, which may be increased by order, on the borrowing of the Board and their wholly-owned subsidiaries), for " £3,400 million " (the initial limit) substitute " £4,500 million " and for " £4,200 million " (the highest limit which may be set by order) substitute " £5,000 million ". *Borrowing powers.*

2.—(1) In section 3 of the Act of 1980 (under which the Secretary of State may make grants in respect of group deficits of the Board and their subsidiaries for financial years of the Board up to and including 1982–83), at the end of subsection (1) add " or for the financial year of the Board ending in March 1984 ". *Deficit and operating grants.*

(2) In subsection (3) of section 4 of the Act of 1980 (which provides for a limit on the aggregate amount of grants under section 3 of that Act together with certain other grants), for " £525 million " substitute " £1,000 million "; and in subsection (4) of that section (which enables the limit to be increased by order, subject to a maximum) for " £590 million " substitute " £1,750 million ".

Reimburse-
ment of
certain
payments in
respect of
loss of
superannua-
tion and
employment
prospects.

3.—(1) The Secretary of State may out of money provided by Parliament make payments to the Board reimbursing them the amount of payments made by them in respect of loss of super-annuation and employment prospects of persons becoming eligible on or after 11th March 1981 to receive payments under a scheme under section 7 of the Act of 1977 (payments to redundant workers).

(2) The amount of any payments qualifying for reimbursement under subsection (1) shall be determined in such manner as may be agreed between the Secretary of State and the Board with the approval of the Treasury and shall be certified by the Board's auditors.

(3) In Schedule 2 to the Act of 1977 (definition of " relevant expenditure " for the purposes of grants under section 6 of that Act), after sub-paragraph (1) of paragraph 1 insert—

" (1A) Head (ii) above shall not include payments in respect of loss of superannuation and employment prospects where those payments are reimbursed by the Secretary of State under section 3 of the Coal Industry Act 1982.".

Grants and
payments in
connection
with pit
closures and
redundancies.

4.—(1) In section 6 of the Act of 1977 (grants by the Secretary of State in connection with pit closures), in subsection (5) (which, as amended by section 6(1) of the Act of 1980, provides for a single limit on the aggregate amount of such grants) for " £170 million " substitute " £200 million ".

(2) In section 7 of the Act of 1977 (payments by the Secretary of State to or in respect of redundant workers), in subsection (5) (which, as substituted by section 7(3) of the Act of 1980, provides for a single limit on the aggregate amount of such payments) for " £220 million " substitute " £300 million ".

Interpretation.

1965 c. 82.

1977 c. 39.

1980 c. 50.

5. In this Act—

" the Act of 1965 " means the Coal Industry Act 1965;
" the Act of 1977 " means the Coal Industry Act 1977;
" the Act of 1980 " means the Coal Industry Act 1980;
" the Board " means the National Coal Board.

Citation and
extent.

6.—(1) This Act may be cited as the Coal Industry Act 1982, and the Coal Industry Acts 1946 to 1980 and this Act may be cited together as the Coal Industry Acts 1946 to 1982.

(2) This Act does not extend to Northern Ireland.

Civil Aviation
Act 1982

1982 CHAPTER 16

An Act to consolidate certain enactments relating to civil aviation. [27th May 1982]

B E IT ENACTED by the Queen's most Excellent Majesty, by and with the advice and consent of the Lords Spiritual and Temporal, and Commons, in this present Parliament assembled, and by the authority of the same, as follows:—

PART I

ADMINISTRATION

The Secretary of State

1.—(1) The Secretary of State shall continue to be charged with the general duty of organising, carrying out and encouraging measures for— {Functions of Secretary of State.}

   (*a*) the development of civil aviation ;

   (*b*) the designing, development and production of civil aircraft ;

   (*c*) the promotion of safety and efficiency in the use thereof ; and

   (*d*) research into questions relating to air navigation.

(2) Subsection (1) above shall not authorise the production of civil aircraft by the Secretary of State.

PART I

(3) The acquisition and disposal of aircraft, aero-engines and aviation equipment in discharge of the Secretary of State's duty under subsection (1) above shall be subject to the approval of the Treasury.

Constitution and functions of CAA

Constitution of CAA.

2.—(1) There shall continue to be a body corporate called the Civil Aviation Authority (in this Act referred to as " the CAA "), which shall be constituted in accordance with the following provisions of this section.

(2) The CAA shall consist of not less than six nor more than twelve persons appointed by the Secretary of State to be members of the CAA ; and the Secretary of State—

    (a) shall appoint one member to be the chairman of the CAA ; and

    (b) may appoint not more than two other members to be deputy chairmen of the CAA.

(3) Schedule 1 to this Act shall have effect with respect to the CAA.

(4) It is hereby declared that the CAA is not to be regarded as the servant or agent of the Crown or as enjoying any status, privilege or immunity of the Crown or as exempt from any tax, duty, rate, levy or other charge whatsoever, whether general or local, and that its property is not to be regarded as property of, or held on behalf of, the Crown.

Functions of CAA.

3. The functions of the CAA shall be—

    (a) the functions conferred on it by the following provisions of this Part of this Act ;

    (b) the functions conferred on it by or under this Act with respect to the licensing of air transport, the licensing of the provision of accommodation in aircraft, the provision of air navigation services, the operation of aerodromes and the provision of assistance and information ;

    (c) such functions as are for the time being conferred on it by or under Air Navigation Orders with respect to the registration of aircraft, the safety of air navigation and aircraft (including airworthiness), the control of air traffic, the certification of operators of aircraft and the licensing of air crews and aerodromes ;

(*d*) such other functions as are for the time being conferred on it by virtue of this Act or any other enactment ;

and nothing in this Act relating to the CAA shall be construed as derogating from any power exercisable by virtue of any enactment whatsoever (including an enactment contained in this Act) to make an Order in Council or other instrument conferring a function on the CAA.

Regulation of performance by CAA of its functions

4.—(1) It shall be the duty of the CAA to perform the functions conferred on it otherwise than by this section in the manner which it considers is best calculated— General objectives.

(*a*) to secure that British airlines provide air transport services which satisfy all substantial categories of public demand (so far as British airlines may reasonably be expected to provide such services) at the lowest charges consistent with a high standard of safety in operating the services and an economic return to efficient operators on the sums invested in providing the services and with securing the sound development of the civil air transport industry of the United Kingdom ; and

(*b*) to further the reasonable interests of users of air transport services.

(2) In subsection (1) above " British airline " means an undertaking having power to provide air transport services and appearing to the CAA to have its principal place of business in the United Kingdom, the Channel Islands or the Isle of Man and to be controlled by persons who either are United Kingdom nationals or are for the time being approved by the Secretary of State for the purposes of this subsection.

5.—(1) Subject to section 4 above, it shall be the duty of the CAA, in exercising any aerodrome licensing function in relation to any aerodrome to which this section applies, to have regard to the need to minimise so far as reasonably practicable— Duty of CAA to consider environmental factors when licensing certain aerodromes.

(*a*) any adverse effects on the environment, and

(*b*) any disturbance to the public,

from noise, vibration, atmospheric pollution or any other cause attributable to the use of aircraft for the purpose of civil aviation.

(2) The reference in subsection (1) above to an aerodrome licensing function of the CAA is a reference to any function conferred on it by or under an Air Navigation Order with respect to the licensing of aerodromes.

(3) This section applies to any aerodrome in the United Kingdom specified in an order made by the Secretary of State for the purposes of this section; but the Secretary of State may not specify in any such order an aerodrome which is designated for the purposes of section 78 below.

Secretary
of State's
directions
in national
interest, etc.

6.—(1) Without prejudice to subsection (2)(*a*) below, the Secretary of State may, after consultation with the CAA, give it such directions of a general character as to the performance of its functions as he thinks it appropriate to give in the interests of national security; and in so far as any directions given in pursuance of this subsection conflict with the requirements of any enactment or instrument relating to the CAA, except section 63 below, those requirements shall be disregarded.

(2) The Secretary of State may, after consultation with the CAA, give it directions to do a particular thing which it has power to do or refrain from doing a particular thing, if the Secretary of State considers it appropriate to give such directions—

(*a*) in the interests of national security; or

(*b*) in connection with any matter appearing to him to affect the relations of the United Kingdom with a country or territory outside the United Kingdom; or

(*c*) in order to discharge or facilitate the discharge of an obligation binding on the United Kingdom by virtue of its being a member of an international organisation or a party to an international agreement; or

(*d*) in order to attain or facilitate the attainment of any other object the attainment of which is in his opinion appropriate in view of the fact that the United Kingdom is a member of an international organisation or a party to an international agreement; or

(*e*) in order to enable the United Kingdom to become a member of an international organisation or a party to an international agreement; or

(*f*) in order to prevent or deal with noise, vibration, pollution or other disturbance attributable to aircraft used for the purpose of civil aviation;

and in so far as any directions given in pursuance of this subsection conflict with the requirements of any enactment or instrument relating to the CAA, except section 63 below, those
requirements shall be disregarded.

7.—(1) Such functions of the CAA as may be prescribed for Special
the purposes of this subsection shall not be performed on behalf provisions
of the CAA by any other person ; and regulations made by the as respects
Secretary of State may provide that for the purpose of perform- functions.
ing a function prescribed in pursuance of this subsection the
quorum of the CAA shall be such as may be prescribed.

(2) Regulations made by the Secretary of State may provide
for regulating the conduct of the CAA and other persons, including the procedure to be followed by them, in connection
with the performance by the CAA of such of its functions as
may be prescribed for the purposes of this subsection ; and,
without prejudice to the generality of the preceding provisions of
this subsection, regulations made in pursuance of this subsection
may include provision—

> (*a*) requiring or entitling the CAA, notwithstanding any
> rule of law, to withhold from any person (hereafter in
> this paragraph referred to as " the prospective
> recipient ") information which is furnished to the CAA
> by another person in connection with any function so
> prescribed and which in the opinion of the CAA relates
> to the commercial or financial affairs of the other person
> and cannot be disclosed to the prospective recipient
> without disadvantage to the other person which, by
> comparison with the advantage to the public and the
> prospective recipient of its disclosure to him, is
> unwarranted ;
>
> (*b*) for the imposition on summary conviction of a fine of
> an amount not exceeding £100 for any contravention of
> the regulations.

(3) The Tribunals and Inquiries Act 1971 shall have effect as 1971 c. 62.
if—

> (*a*) the CAA were a tribunal specified in Part I of Schedule
> 1 to that Act (which lists the tribunals of which among
> other things the workings and constitutions are to be
> kept under review and reported on by the Council on
> Tribunals) ; and
>
> (*b*) section 8 of that Act (under which certain consents are
> required for the removal of members of tribunals) did
> not apply to the CAA ; and
>
> (*c*) the functions of the CAA were confined to those pre-
> scribed for the purposes of subsection (2) above.

PART I

General
financial
duties.

Financial provisions in relation to CAA

8.—(1) It shall be the duty of the CAA so to conduct its affairs as to secure that its revenue (including any grant towards revenue made to it in pursuance of section 12(1) below is not less than sufficient to meet charges properly chargeable to revenue account, taking one year with another.

(2) Subject to subsection (3) below, it shall be the duty of the CAA—

    (*a*) in framing and carrying out proposals involving substantial outlay on capital account, and

    (*b*) in framing and carrying out proposals involving the taking on hire of any equipment the purchase of which at the time of taking on hire would involve such an outlay,

to act on lines settled from time to time with the approval of the Secretary of State ; and it shall also be the duty of the CAA to secure that any subsidiary of the CAA acts on those lines in framing and carrying out either description of proposals.

(3) Subsection (2)(*b*) above shall not apply to proposals by the CAA, or one of its subsidiaries, involving the taking on hire of equipment from a subsidiary or another of the subsidiaries of the CAA or from the CAA itself, as the case may be.

(4) The Secretary of State may, with the approval of the Treasury, give the CAA a direction as to any matter relating to the establishment or management of reserves or the carrying of sums to the credit of any reserves or the application of any reserves for the purposes of the CAA.

The initial
debt.
1971 c. 75.

9.—(1) In this Act " the initial debt " means the debt which was assumed by the CAA on 16th November 1973 under section 7 of the Civil Aviation Act 1971 as a debt to the Secretary of State and which was subsequently reduced under subsection (5) of that section to £27,073,104.

(2) The rate of interest payable on the initial debt, the arrangements for paying off the principal and the other terms of the debt shall be such as the Secretary of State may from time to time determine with the approval of the Treasury.

(3) Any sums received by the Secretary of State by way of interest on or repayment of the initial debt shall be paid into the National Loans Fund.

Borrowing
powers.

10.—(1) Subject to the following provisions of this section, the CAA shall have power to borrow such sums as it may require for performing its functions.

(2) The CAA's power to borrow sums in sterling otherwise than by way of temporary loan shall be limited to borrowing from the Secretary of State, or with the consent of the Secretary of State from the Commission of the European Communities or the European Investment Bank, any sums which the CAA may require for capital purposes or for fulfilling a guarantee entered into by the CAA.

(3) Except as provided by subsection (2) above, the CAA may borrow any sums it has power to borrow under subsection (1) above from the Secretary of State or, with the consent of, or in accordance with a general authorisation given by, the Secretary of State, from any other person (and whether in sterling or in a currency other than sterling).

(4) The Secretary of State shall not give any consent or authorisation for the purposes of subsection (2) or (3) above except with the approval of the Treasury.

(5) A statement in writing by the Secretary of State to the effect that the approval of the Treasury has been given for any such consent or authorisation shall be conclusive evidence of that fact in any legal proceedings.

(6) The aggregate amount outstanding in respect of the principal of any money borrowed by the CAA under this section and the initial debt shall not exceed £200 million.

11.—(1) The CAA may, after consultation with the Secretary of State, make a scheme for determining the charges which are to be paid to the CAA in respect of the performance of such of its functions as are specified in the scheme; and a scheme under this section may as respects any of those functions—

(*a*) specify the amount of the charge or a scale of charges by reference to which that amount is to be ascertained or provide that the charges shall be of such amount, not exceeding that specified in the scheme, as may be decided by the CAA, having regard to the expense incurred by the CAA in performing the function in question and to such other factors (if any) as may be so specified;

(*b*) provide for different charges for cases of such different descriptions as may be so specified;

(*c*) specify the manner in which, the time at which and the person by whom any charge is to be paid.

(2) A scheme under this section shall come into force on such day as may be specified in the scheme, not being earlier than the expiration of the period of sixty days beginning with the

day on which the scheme is published in the prescribed manner; and a scheme made under this section may vary or revoke a previous scheme so made.

(3) Regulations made by the Secretary of State may make provision for determining the charges which are to be paid to the CAA, or for securing that no charge is payable to the CAA, in respect of such of its functions as may be prescribed; and regulations for determining the said charges may—

    (*a*) prescribe the amount of a charge or the maximum or minimum amount of a charge or a scale of charges by reference to which those amounts are to be ascertained;

    (*b*) prescribe the manner in which, the time at which and the person by whom a charge is to be paid.

(4) In so far as a scheme and regulations under this section make different provision with respect to the same matter the provision made by the scheme shall be disregarded.

(5) Where as respects any function of the CAA provision for a charge to be paid is made by virtue of this section it shall be the duty of the CAA to charge accordingly, except that it may, if it thinks fit to do so in a particular case, waive the whole or part of the charge.

(6) Nothing in the preceding provisions of this section shall be construed as derogating from the power of the CAA to enter into an agreement for the payment to it of charges of such amounts as may be determined in pursuance of the agreement in respect of the performance by it of any of its functions, other than a function in respect of which provision is made in pursuance of those provisions for the making of a charge or of no charge.

(7) Charges shall not be determined in pursuance of this section in respect of the provision of air navigation services; and provision shall not be made by or under an Air Navigation Order for the payment of fees to the CAA.

Grants and loans by Secretary of State.

12.—(1) The Secretary of State may—

    (*a*) make the CAA grants of such amounts as he thinks fit;

    (*b*) give the CAA a direction providing that the whole or part of a grant made in pursuance of paragraph (*a*) above is not to be used by the CAA otherwise than for the purposes of such of the CAA's functions as are specified in the direction.

(2) The Secretary of State may, with the approval of the Treasury, lend the CAA any sums which the CAA has power to borrow from him by virtue of section 10 above.

(3) Any loan which the Secretary of State makes in pursuance of subsection (2) above shall be repaid to him at such times and by such methods, and interest on the loan shall be paid to him at such rates and at such times, as the Secretary of State may with the approval of the Treasury from time to time determine.

(4) The Treasury may issue out of the National Loans Fund to the Secretary of State such sums as are necessary to enable him to make loans in pursuance of subsection (2) above; and any sums received by the Secretary of State in pursuance of subsection (3) above shall be paid into that Fund.

13.—(1) Any excess of the revenues of the CAA for any accounting year over the total sums properly chargeable by the CAA to revenue account for that year shall be applied by the CAA in such manner as the Secretary of State may direct with the approval of the Treasury and after consultation with the CAA; and the direction may require the whole or part of the excess to be paid to the Secretary of State.

(2) The Secretary of State may, with the approval of the Treasury and after consultation with the CAA, direct the CAA to pay to the Secretary of State the whole or part of the sums for the time being standing to the credit of any of its reserves.

14.—(1) The Treasury may guarantee, in such manner and on such conditions as they think fit, the repayment of the principal of, and the payment of interest on, any sums which the CAA borrows from a person other than the Secretary of State.

(2) Immediately after a guarantee is given under this section the Treasury shall lay a statement of the guarantee before each House of Parliament; and where any sum is issued for fulfilling a guarantee so given the Treasury shall, as soon as possible after the end of each financial year (beginning with that in which the sum is issued and ending with that in which all liability in respect of the principal of the sum and in respect of interest thereon is finally discharged), lay before each House of Parliament a statement relating to that sum.

(3) Any sums required by the Treasury for fulfilling a guarantee under this section shall be charged on and issued out of the Consolidated Fund.

(4) If any sums are issued in fulfilment of a guarantee given under this section, the CAA shall make to the Treasury, at such times and in such manner as the Treasury may from time to time direct, payments of such amounts as the Treasury so

Marginal notes:

Part I

Payments to Secretary of State.

Guarantees.

PART I

direct in or towards repayment of the sums so issued and payments of interest, at such rate as the Treasury so direct, on what is outstanding for the time being in respect of sums so issued.

Accounts and audit.

15.—(1) It shall be the duty of the CAA—

   (a) to keep proper accounts and proper records in relation to the accounts ;

   (b) to prepare in respect of each accounting year a statement of accounts, in such form as the Secretary of State may direct with the approval of the Treasury, showing the state of affairs and the profit or loss of the CAA ; and

   (c) to send copies of the statement to the Secretary of State and the Comptroller and Auditor General before the end of the month of November next following the accounting year to which the statement relates.

(2) The Comptroller and Auditor General shall examine, certify and report on each statement received by him in pursuance of subsection (1) above and shall lay copies of the statement and of his report on it before each House of Parliament.

(3) The Secretary of State may by order made with the consent of the Treasury modify or repeal subsections (1)(c) and (2) above as for the time being in force.

(4) It shall be the duty of the Secretary of State as respects each financial year—

   (a) to prepare, in such form and manner as the Treasury may direct, an account of sums issued to the Secretary of State in pursuance of subsection (4) of section 12 above and of any sums required to be paid into the National Loans Fund in pursuance of that subsection or section 9 above or received by the Secretary of State in pursuance of section 13 above and of the disposal by the Secretary of State of those sums respectively ; and

   (b) to send a copy of the account to the Comptroller and Auditor General not later than the end of the month of November next following that year ;

and the Comptroller and Auditor General shall examine, certify and report on the account and shall lay copies of it and of his report on it before each House of Parliament.

Assistance, information, etc. to be given by CAA

Provision by CAA of assistance, etc. for Secretary of State and others.

16.—(1) Subject to subsection (3) below, it shall be the duty of the CAA to provide such assistance and advice as the Secretary of State may require it to provide for him or any other person in connection with any of the Secretary of State's functions relating to civil aviation.

(2) Without prejudice to subsection (1) above, it shall also be the duty of the CAA—

    (*a*) to consider what aerodromes are in its opinion likely to be required from time to time in the United Kingdom in addition to, or in place of, or by way of alteration of, existing aerodromes ; and

    (*b*) to make recommendations to the Secretary of State arising out of its consideration of that matter ;

and it shall be the duty of the Secretary of State to publish the recommendations (except any of them of which the publication appears to him unnecessary) in such manner as he considers appropriate for bringing them to the notice of the public.

(3) Where in pursuance of subsection (1) above the Secretary of State requires the CAA to provide assistance or advice for a person other than the Secretary of State but does not undertake to pay the CAA the cost of doing so, the CAA shall be entitled to refuse to do so until the other person pays it—

    (*a*) in so far as provision is made in pursuance of section 11 above for charges in respect of the assistance or advice, those charges ; and

    (*b*) in so far as provision is not so made, such reasonable charges in respect of the assistance or advice as it may determine.

(4) The CAA shall be entitled to recover from the Secretary of State a sum equal to any expense reasonably incurred by it in providing him with assistance or advice in pursuance of subsection (1) above and in performing the duty imposed on it by subsection (2) above.

(5) Without prejudice to subsection (1) above, the CAA may provide for any person technical assistance and advice, including research services, with respect to any matter in which it has skill or experience.

17.—(1) It shall be the duty of the CAA—

    (*a*) to furnish the Secretary of State with such information as he may specify and the CAA has or can reasonably be expected to obtain with respect to such matters relating to it or to civil aviation as the Secretary of State may specify ;

    (*b*) to permit the Secretary of State to have access to all documents which are under its control and relate to matters specified in pursuance of paragraph (*a*) above ;

    (*c*) if it comes to its notice that a body which is the holder of an air transport licence is proposing to merge or has merged with another body, to give the Secretary of State notice in writing of the proposal or merger ;

(*d*) if it appears to the CAA that any matter which it is dealing with, or has dealt with, is likely—

(i) to affect the relations of the United Kingdom with any other country or territory or any international organisation, or

(ii) to be of special interest to the Secretary of State by reason of the fact that the matter involves or may involve noise, vibration, pollution or other disturbance attributable to aircraft used for the purpose of civil aviation,

to give notice in writing of the matter to the Secretary of State.

(2) Nothing in subsection (1) above shall be construed as prejudicing the generality of section 16(1) above, and nothing in subsection (1)(*c*) or (*d*) above shall be construed as prejudicing the generality of subsection (1)(*a*) above.

(3) The CAA shall be entitled to recover from the Secretary of State a sum equal to any expense reasonably incurred by it in furnishing information in pursuance of subsection (1) above.

Supplemental provisions in relation to CAA

Official secrets.

1911 c. 28.

18.—(1) For the purposes of section 2 of the Official Secrets Act 1911 (which among other things relates to the wrongful communication of information) a member and an employee of the CAA shall be deemed to hold an office under Her Majesty and a contract with the CAA shall be deemed to be a contract with Her Majesty.

(2) For the purposes of section 3(*c*) of the said Act of 1911 (under which the Secretary of State may by order declare any place belonging to Her Majesty to be a prohibited place for the purposes of that Act) a place belonging to or used for the purposes of the CAA shall be deemed to be a place belonging to Her Majesty.

(3) Subject to subsection (4) below, no person shall, except with the consent of and in accordance with any conditions imposed by the CAA, be entitled to exercise any right of entry (whether arising by virtue of a statutory provision or otherwise) upon a place which by virtue of subsection (2) above is a prohibited place for the purposes of the said Act of 1911.

(4) Subsection (3) above shall not apply to—

(*a*) a constable acting in the course of his duty as such; or

(*b*) an officer of customs and excise or inland revenue acting in the execution of his duty as such; or (*c*) an officer of any government department specially authorised for the purpose by or on behalf of a Minister of the Crown ;

and if the CAA refuses consent for or imposes conditions on the exercise by any person of a right of entry upon such a place as is mentioned in subsection (3) above and that person applies to the Secretary of State for an authorisation to exercise the right, the Secretary of State may if he thinks fit authorise that person to exercise it subject to such conditions, if any, as the Secretary of State may determine.

19.—(1) The CAA shall be a public body for the purposes of the Prevention of Corruption Acts 1889 to 1916, and accordingly the expressions " public body " and " such public body " in those Acts shall include the CAA.

(2) Schedule 2 to this Act shall have effect as respects the application of the enactments mentioned in that Schedule (which relate to statutory undertakers, statutory undertakings and related matters).

(3) For the purposes of the law relating to rating, the undertaking of the CAA shall be treated as not being a public utility undertaking.

20.—(1) The CAA—

(*a*) shall, without prejudice to its powers apart from this paragraph but subject to paragraph (*b*) below, have power to do anything which is calculated to facilitate, or is conducive or incidental to, the performance of any of its functions (including a function conferred on it by virtue of this paragraph) ; but

(*b*) shall not without the consent in writing of the Secretary of State promote the formation of, acquire or acquire a financial interest in a body corporate or lend money to or enter into a guarantee for the benefit of a body corporate ;

and it is hereby declared that the CAA has power to do elsewhere than in the United Kingdom such things as it considers appropriate for the purpose of performing any of its functions.

(2) Notwithstanding anything in section 2(4) above, the CAA shall act on behalf of the Crown—

(*a*) in performing any function which the CAA is authorised by an Air Navigation Order to perform and which

E 4

in pursuance of, or of an Annex to, or of an amendment for the time being in force of, the Chicago Convention falls to be performed on behalf of the Crown ; and

(b) in performing such of its other functions as Her Majesty may by Order in Council require it to perform on behalf of the Crown as being functions appearing to Her Majesty in Council to relate to the exercise of powers or the discharge of obligations of the United Kingdom under an international agreement.

(3) It shall be the duty of the CAA to comply with any direction given to it by the Secretary of State in pursuance of any provision of this Act.

(4) Provision may be made by regulations made by the Secretary of State as to the mode of giving evidence of—

(a) any instrument made by the CAA ; and

(b) the publication by the CAA of any matter.

Annual
report.

21.—(1) It shall be the duty of the CAA to make to the Secretary of State, as soon as possible after the end of each accounting year, a report on the performance of its functions during that year.

(2) The report for any accounting year—

(a) shall set out any direction given to the CAA in pursuance of section 6, 63(3) or 72 (2) of this Act during that year except a direction or part of a direction as to which the Secretary of State has notified the CAA that in his opinion it is against the national interest to set it out in the report ;

(b) shall incorporate any statements published by the CAA under section 69 below during that year ;

(c) shall include particulars of any case in which during that year the CAA has decided not to proceed in accordance with advice given to it in pursuance of section 85(2)(a)(i) below ; and

(d) shall include such information as the Secretary of State may from time to time specify with respect to the plans and the past and present activities of the CAA and its financial position.

(3) The Secretary of State shall lay before each House of Parliament a copy of every report made to him in pursuance of this section.

22. Schedule 3 to this Act shall have effect with respect to   PART I
the matters there dealt with, being matters arising out of the   Matters
transfer by virtue of paragraph 1 of Schedule 2 to the Civil   arising in
Aviation Act 1971 to the CAA of the aerodromes mentioned in   connection
the said Schedule 2 and of the other property, rights and liabilities   with original
there mentioned and out of the transfer of staff to the CAA.   transfer
to CAA of
property, staff
etc.
1971 c. 75.

Disclosure of information

23.—(1) Subject to subsection (4) below, no information which   Disclosure of
relates to a particular person and has been furnished to the CAA   information.
in pursuance of any provision of this Act to which this section
applies or of an Air Navigation Order shall be disclosed by the
CAA, or a member or employee of the CAA unless—

(a) the person aforesaid has consented in writing to disclosure of the information ; or

(b) the CAA, after affording that person an opportunity
to make representations about the information and
considering any representation then made by that person
about it, determines that the information may be disclosed ; or

(c) that person is an individual who is dead, or is a body
corporate that has ceased to exist or, whether an individual or a body corporate, cannot be found after all
reasonable inquiries have been made, and the CAA
determines that the information may be disclosed ; or

(d) the CAA determines that the information is of the same
kind as other information as respects which it has
made a determination in pursuance of paragraph (b)
or (c) above.

(2) Subsection (1) above shall apply in relation to the disclosure by an officer of the Secretary of State of information
furnished to the Secretary of State in pursuance of any provision
of this Act to which this section applies or of an Air Navigation Order as it applies in relation to disclosure by the CAA or
a member or employee of the CAA of information so furnished
to the CAA, but with the substitution for references to the
CAA in paragraphs (b) to (d) of references to the Secretary of
State.

(3) For the purposes of subsection (1) above, all reasonable
inquiries to find a body corporate shall be deemed to have been
made if—

(a) in the case of a company within the meaning of the

Companies Act 1948 or the Companies Act (Northern Ireland) 1960, inquiries have been made at its registered office ; or

(b) in the case of a company incorporated outside the United Kingdom and having a place of business within the United Kingdom, inquiries have been made at every address registered in respect of that company for the purposes of section 407(1)(c) of the said Act of 1948, or section 356(1)(c) of the said Act of 1960 (addresses for service of overseas companies).

(4) Nothing in subsection (1) above prohibits the disclosure of any information—

(a) by the CAA or a member or employee of the CAA to the Secretary of State or an officer of his or, with the consent of the Secretary of State, to an international organisation of which the United Kingdom is a member ;

(b) by an officer of the Secretary of State to the CAA or a member or employee of the CAA or to such an organisation or, in accordance with directions given by the Secretary of State—

(i) to an officer of any government department ; or

(ii) in connection with negotiations conducted by officers of the Secretary of State with representatives of the government of any country or territory outside the United Kingdom ; or

(iii) in connection with the discharge of any obligation of the United Kingdom under international arrangements ;

(c) to a person to whom the information in question is required to be disclosed by regulations made in pursuance of section 7(2) above ;

(d) in pursuance of section 67(2) or (4) below ;

(e) by the CAA for the purpose of complying with any duty imposed on it by section 85(1) below;

(f) with a view to the institution of, or otherwise for the purposes of, any criminal proceedings arising out of any enactment relating to civil aviation or for the purposes of any investigation undertaken in pursuance of regulations made by virtue of section 75 below.

(5) If the CAA or a member or employee of the CAA or an officer of the Secretary of State discloses any information in contravention of subsection (1) above, it or he shall be liable—

(a) on summary conviction, to a fine not exceeding the statutory maximum ; and

   (*b*) on conviction on indictment, to a fine or, except in the   Part I
      case of the CAA, to imprisonment for a term not
      exceeding two years or to both.

(6) This section applies to the following provisions of this Act, that is to say, sections 16, 17, 28 and 29, section 36 (so far only as it relates to aerodromes owned or managed by the CAA) sections 64 to 72 (except section 69), sections 78 to 80 and sections 84 and 85.

Eurocontrol

24. Schedule 4 to this Act shall have effect in relation to   Eurocontrol. the European Organisation for the Safety of Air Navigation established by the International Convention relating to co-operation for the safety of air navigation (entitled Eurocontrol) concluded at Brussels on 13th December 1960 (copies of which Convention were laid before Parliament by Command of Her Majesty on 13th June 1961) ; and in this Act—

    " Eurocontrol " means that organisation, including, except where the context otherwise requires, the Permanent Commission for the Safety of Air Navigation and the Air Traffic Services Agency comprised in that Organisation ; and

    " the Eurocontrol Convention " means that Convention and includes any amendment of the Convention which may be agreed upon between the contracting parties thereto.

Part II

Aerodromes and Other Land

Secretary of State's aerodromes

25.—(1) The Secretary of State may for the purposes of civil   Secretary of aviation establish and maintain aerodromes and provide and   State's power maintain in connection therewith roads, approaches, apparatus,   to provide equipment and buildings and other accommodation.   aerodromes.

(2) The Secretary of State shall appoint for each aerodrome vested in him an officer who shall be responsible to the Secretary of State for all services (including signalling services, flying control services and services connected with the execution of works) provided on the aerodrome on the Secretary of State's behalf.

26. In the management and administration of any aerodrome   Consultation vested in him the Secretary of State shall make such provision   with local as he thinks necessary to ensure that adequate facilities for con-   bodies. sultation are provided for—

    (*a*) the local authorities in whose areas the aerodrome or any part thereof is situated ;

(*b*) other local authorities whose areas are in the neighbourhood of the aerodrome ; and

(*c*) other organisations representing the interests of persons
concerned with the locality in which the aerodrome is
situated.

Byelaws at
Secretary
of State's
aerodromes.

27.—(1) The Secretary of State may, in respect of any aerodrome owned or managed by him, make byelaws for regulating
the use and operation of the aerodrome and the conduct of all
persons while within the aerodrome, and in particular byelaws—

(*a*) for securing the safety of aircraft, vehicles and persons
using the aerodrome and preventing danger to the
public arising from the use and operation of the aerodrome ;

(*b*) for controlling the operation of aircraft within or directly
above the aerodrome for the purpose of limiting or
mitigating the effect of noise, vibration and atmospheric
pollution caused by aircraft using the aerodrome ;

(*c*) for preventing obstruction within the aerodrome ;

(*d*) for regulating vehicular traffic anywhere within the
aerodrome, except on roads therein to which the road
traffic enactments apply, and in particular (with that
exception) for imposing speed limits on vehicles
therein and for restricting or regulating the parking of
vehicles or their use for any purpose or in any manner
specified in the byelaws ;

(*e*) for prohibiting waiting by hackney carriages except at
standings appointed by such person as may be specified
in the byelaws ;

(*f*) for prohibiting or restricting access to any part of the
aerodrome ;

(*g*) for preserving order within the aerodrome and preventing damage to property therein ;

(*h*) for regulating or restricting advertising within the aerodrome ;

(*i*) for requiring any person, if so requested by a constable
or aerodrome official, to leave the aerodrome or any
particular part of it, or to state his name and address
and the purpose of his being on the aerodrome ;

(*j*) for restricting the area which is to be taken as constituting the aerodrome for the purposes of the byelaws.

(2) In paragraph (*d*) of subsection (1) above " the road traffic
enactments " means the enactments (whether passed before or
after this Act) relating to road traffic, including the lighting and
parking of vehicles, and any order or other instrument having
effect by virtue of any such enactment

(3) In paragraph (*i*) of subsection (1) above " aerodrome official " means a person authorised by the person who is the owner
or has the management of the aerodrome ; and any such
official shall not exercise any power under a byelaw made by
virtue of that paragraph (including a byelaw so made by virtue
of section 29(1), 32(1) or 33(1) below) without producing written
evidence of his authority if required to do so.

(4) The power to make byelaws under this section shall be
exercisable by statutory instrument.

(5) Before making any byelaws under this section the Secretary of State shall take such steps as appear to him to be appropriate for giving public notice of the proposed byelaws and for
affording an opportunity for representations to be made with respect to them ; and the Secretary of State shall have regard to any
such representations and may then make the byelaws in the form
proposed or in that form with such modifications as he thinks
fit.

CAA's aerodromes

28.—(1) The CAA shall not establish any aerodrome and shall
not acquire any aerodrome in addition to those owned by it by
virtue of paragraph 1 of Schedule 2 to the Civil Aviation Act
1971 ; but the CAA may with the consent in writing of the Secretary of State undertake the management of any aerodrome
(whether in the United Kingdom or elsewhere) which it does not
own and to which the consent extends.

(2) The CAA shall not discontinue the use of any aerodrome
owned or managed by it except with the consent in writing of
the Secretary of State.

(3) It shall be the duty of the CAA to provide at the aerodromes in the United Kingdom which are owned or managed by
it such services and facilities as it considers are necessary or
desirable for their operation ; and in carrying out that duty the
CAA shall have regard to the development of air transport and
to efficiency, economy and safety of operation.

(4) Subject to section 78 below, it shall also be the duty
of the CAA to secure that, at all times when an aerodrome in the
United Kingdom which is owned or managed by it is available
for the landing or departure of aircraft, it is so available to all
persons on equal terms.

(5) Notwithstanding anything in section 7 above, the CAA may,
with the consent in writing of the Secretary of State, appoint
another person to manage on its behalf any aerodrome which is
owned or is being managed by it ; and any reference in this Act
to an aerodrome managed by the CAA includes a reference to
an aerodrome managed by a person appointed in pursuance of
this subsection.

29.—(1) The CAA may, in respect of any aerodrome in the United Kingdom which is owned or managed by it, make bye-laws for regulating the use and operation of the aerodrome and the conduct of all persons while within the aerodrome, and in particular byelaws with respect to any of the matters mentioned in paragraphs (*a*) to (*j*) of section 27(1) above.

(2) Byelaws made in relation to any aerodrome under this section may include provision for securing the safe custody and re-delivery of any property which while not in proper custody is found on that aerodrome or in an aircraft on that aerodrome ; and any such byelaws may in particular—

(*a*) provide for requiring charges to be paid in respect of any such property before it is re-delivered ; and

(*b*) provide for authorising the disposal of any such property if it is not re-delivered before the expiration of such period as may be specified in the byelaws.

(3) Byelaws made under this section shall not have effect until they are confirmed by the Secretary of State, and Schedule 5 to this Act shall apply to any such byelaws.

Aerodromes and facilities at aerodromes provided by local authorities

Provision of
aerodrome
and facilities at
aerodromes
by local
authorities.

30.—(1) A local authority, other than a district council in Scotland, may do one or both of the following things, namely—

(*a*) with the consent of the Secretary of State and subject to such conditions as he may impose, establish and maintain aerodromes ;

(*b*) make arrangements with the person owning or managing an aerodrome in Great Britain whereby the local authority provide and maintain facilities for civil aviation at that aerodrome ;

and a district council in Scotland may do as mentioned in paragraph (*b*) above.

(2) A local authority, other than a district council in Scotland, may in connection with—

(*a*) the establishment and maintenance by them of aerodromes in pursuance of subsection (1)(*a*) above, or

(*b*) any aerodrome in respect of which the local authority have made such an arrangement as is mentioned in subsection (1)(*b*) above,

provide and maintain roads, approaches, apparatus, equipment and buildings and other accommodation.

(3) Nothing in subsection (1)(*a*) or (2) above shall authorise the execution of any works on, over or under tidal lands below high-water mark of ordinary spring tides, except in accordance

with plans and sections previously approved in writing by the
Secretary of State and subject to such conditions as he may
impose.

(4) Without prejudice to any power conferred otherwise than
by this Act, a local authority may, for the purpose of exercising
any of the powers conferred on them by subsections (1)(*a*) and
(2) above, acquire land by agreement or be authorised by the
Secretary of State to purchase land compulsorily.

(5) In relation to the compulsory purchase of land under this
section—

(*a*) if the land is in England and Wales, the Acquisition of 1981 c. 67.
Land Act 1981, and

(*b*) if the land is in Scotland, the Acquisition of Land 1947 c. 42.
(Authorisation Procedure) (Scotland) Act 1947,

shall apply and, in the latter case, shall apply as if this Act
had been in force immediately before the commencement of that
Act.

(6) For the avoidance of doubt, it is hereby declared that
one of the purposes for which a local authority may acquire
land under this section is the purpose of securing that the
land adjacent to the site of an aerodrome which the local
authority have established, or are about to establish, shall not
be used in such manner as to cause interference with, or danger
or damage to, aircraft at, approaching or leaving the aerodrome.

(7) Without prejudice to any power conferred otherwise than
by virtue of this Act, the powers conferred on a local authority
by subsections (1)(*a*), (2) and (4) above shall be exercisable by
that authority outside, as well as within, their area.

(8) For the purpose of the purchase of land by agreement
under this section—

(*a*) if the land is in England and Wales, the provisions of 1965 c. 65.
Part I of the Compulsory Purchase Act 1965 (so far as
applicable) other than sections 4 to 8, section 10 and
section 31 shall apply ; and

(*b*) if the land is in Scotland, the Lands Clauses Acts,
except the provisions of those Acts with respect to the
purchase and taking of land otherwise than by agreement, shall be incorporated with this Act.

31.—(1) If the Secretary of State is satisfied with respect to Power to carry
any local authority aerodrome that it is necessary or expedient on ancillary
that the local authority maintaining the aerodrome should be business.
empowered to carry on in connection with the aerodrome any
ancillary business which the authority would not otherwise have
power to carry on, he may make an order authorising that

PART II   local authority, subject to such conditions (if any) as may be specified in the order, to carry on that business in connection with the aerodrome.

(2) In this section—

" ancillary business " means any business which appears to the Secretary of State to be ancillary to the maintaining of an aerodrome ; and

" local authority aerodrome " means—

(a) any aerodrome maintained by a local authority under section 30 above ; or

(b) so much of any other aerodrome as consists of buildings or other works maintained by a local authority by virtue of that section.

Byelaws at local authority aerodromes.
32.—(1) A local authority with a local authority aerodrome, not being a district council in Scotland, may, in respect of that aerodrome, make byelaws for regulating the use and operation of the aerodrome and the conduct of all persons while within the aerodrome, and in particular byelaws with respect to any of the matters mentioned in paragraphs (a) to (j) of section 27(1) above.

(2) Byelaws made in relation to any aerodrome under this section may include provision for securing the safe custody and re-delivery of any property which while not in proper custody is found on that aerodrome or in an aircraft on that aerodrome ; and any such byelaws may in particular—

(a) provide for requiring charges to be paid in respect of any such property before it is re-delivered ; and

(b) provide for authorising the disposal of any such property if it is not re-delivered before the expiration of such period as may be specified in the byelaws.

(3) The confirming authority in relation to byelaws made under this section shall be the Secretary of State.

1972 c. 70.
1973 c. 65.
(4) Section 236(9) of the Local Government Act 1972 and section 202(13) of the Local Government (Scotland) Act 1973 (notice of byelaws made by one local authority to be given to another) and section 237 of the said Act of 1972 and section 203 of the said Act of 1973 (penalties) shall not apply to byelaws made under this section.

(5) The Secretary of State may, after consultation with any local authority which appears to him to be concerned, by order repeal any enactment in a local Act which appears to him to be unnecessary having regard to the provisions of this section or to be inconsistent therewith.

(6) In this section " local authority aerodrome ", in relation to a local authority, means—

(a) an aerodrome owned or managed by the authority; or

(b) so much of any other aerodrome as consists of buildings or other works maintained by the authority by virtue of section 30 above.

Other aerodromes

33.—(1) The Secretary of State may by order designate for the purposes of this section any private aerodrome (that is to say any aerodrome not owned or managed by the Secretary of State, the CAA, the BAA or a local authority), and the proprietor of any aerodrome so designated shall have power to make byelaws for regulating the use and operation of the aerodrome and the conduct of all persons while within the aerodrome, and in particular byelaws with respect to any of the matters mentioned in paragraphs (a) to (j) of section 27(1) above.

Byelaws at certain private aerodromes.

(2) Byelaws made in relation to any aerodrome under this section may include provision for securing the safe custody and re-delivery of any property which while not in proper custody is found on that aerodrome or in an aircraft on that aerodrome ; and any such byelaws may in particular—

(a) provide for requiring charges to be paid in respect of any such property before it is re-delivered ; and

(b) provide for authorising the disposal of any such property if it is not re-delivered before the expiration of such period as may be specified in the byelaws.

(3) Byelaws made under this section shall not have effect until they are confirmed by the Secretary of State and Schedule 5 to this Act (which governs the making and confirmation of byelaws by the CAA) shall apply also, subject to any necessary modifications, to byelaws made under this section.

Miscellaneous provisions as to aerodromes

34.—(1) Subject to subsection (2) below, the Secretary of State may, with the approval of the Treasury, make grants or loans—

Financial assistance for certain aerodromes.

(a) in respect of any expenses incurred or to be incurred by any person—

(i) in investigating the need for, or for the expansion of, an aerodrome in any part of Great Britain ;

(ii) in establishing or expanding any such aerodrome ;

(iii) in maintaining any such aerodrome or in providing or maintaining, in connection therewith, roads, approaches, apparatus, equipment, buildings or other accommodation ;

(*b*) for making good any losses incurred by any person in the operation of, or in the provision of any services at, any such aerodrome.

(2) No grant or loan shall be made under this section in respect of, or in connection with, any of the aerodromes which were transferred to the BAA by the Airports Authority Act 1965.

(3) Any loan made under this section shall be repaid to the Secretary of State at such times and by such methods, and (except in the case of a loan made free of interest) interest thereon shall be paid to the Secretary of State at such rates and at such times, as he may with the approval of the Treasury from time to time direct.

Facilities for consultation at certain aerodromes.

35.—(1) This section applies to any aerodrome which is managed by a person other than the BAA and is designated for the purposes of this section by an order made by the Secretary of State.

(2) The person having the management of any aerodrome to which this section applies shall provide—

(*a*) for users of the aerodrome,

(*b*) for any local authority (or, if the person having the management of the aerodrome is a local authority, for any other local authority) in whose area the aerodrome or any part thereof is situated or whose area is in the neighbourhood of the aerodrome, and

(*c*) for any other organisation representing the interests of persons concerned with the locality in which the aerodrome is situated,

adequate facilities for consultation with respect to any matter concerning the management or administration of the aerodrome which affects their interests.

Health control at Secretary of State's aerodromes and aerodromes of CAA.

36.—(1) Without prejudice to his general duties under any Act of Parliament or otherwise, it shall be the duty of the Secretary of State to make such arrangements as appear to him to be necessary—

(*a*) for preventing danger to public health from aircraft arriving at any aerodrome which is vested in or under the control of the Secretary of State or at any aerodrome in the United Kingdom which is owned or managed by the CAA ; and

(*b*) for preventing the spread of infection by means of any aircraft leaving any aerodrome mentioned in paragraph (*a*) above, so far as may be expedient for the purpose of carrying out any treaty, convention, arrangement or engagement with any country ;

and in relation to aerodromes in the United Kingdom owned or managed by the CAA it shall also, to such extent as the Secretary of State may direct, be the CAA's duty to make such arrangements as appear to him to be so necessary.

(2) A relevant authority may, and shall if the Secretary of State so requires, undertake duties in connection with the execution of any such arrangements as are mentioned in subsection (1) above, and the Secretary of State shall make to the relevant authority such payments as the relevant authority may reasonably require in respect of expenses incurred by the relevant authority in the performance of those duties.

(3) In the application of subsections (1) and (2) above to Northern Ireland, for references to the Secretary of State (except the reference in paragraph (*a*) of subsection (1) above) there shall be substituted references to the Department of Health and Social Services for Northern Ireland.

(4) In subsection (2) above " relevant authority " means—

(*a*) in relation to England and Wales, any local authority for the purposes of the Public Health Act 1936, any 1936 c 49. county council and any port health authority and any joint board of which all the constituent authorities are authorities or councils as aforesaid;

(*b*) in relation to Scotland, any islands or district council and any port local authority as defined in section 172 of the Public Health (Scotland) Act 1897 ; and 1897 c. 38.

(*c*) in relation to Northern Ireland, such authority as the Department of Health and Social Services for Northern Ireland may designate for the purposes of that subsection.

(5) Section 143 of the Public Health Act 1936 (which authorises the making of health regulations) shall have effect in relation to relevant aerodromes and in relation to persons and aircraft arriving at or departing from such aerodromes subject to the following modifications, that is to say—

(*a*) in subsection (1), the proviso shall be omitted ;

(*b*) in subsection (3), for the words from " shall specify " to " executed " there shall be substituted the words " may provide for their enforcement and execution by officers designated for that purpose by the Secretary of State ", and paragraphs (i) and (ii) of the proviso shall be omitted ;

(*c*) in subsection (4), for the words " Authorised officers of any such authority " there shall be substituted the words " Officers designated as aforesaid ".

PART II

(6) In subsection (5) above " relevant aerodromes " means aerodromes for the time being vested in or under the control of the Secretary of State and aerodromes in Great Britain which are owned or managed by the CAA.

(7) Without prejudice to the generality of the power conferred by the said section 143, regulations made thereunder may provide for requiring persons alighting from aircraft to answer questions pertaining to their state of health or their contact with infection.

1936 c. 49.

1945 c. 15
(9 & 10 Geo. 6).

(8) In the application of subsections (5) to (7) above to Scotland any reference to section 143 of the Public Health Act 1936 shall have effect as if it were a reference to section 1 of the Public Health (Scotland) Act 1945, and in subsection (5), paragraph (*a*) and in paragraph (*b*) the words from " and paragraphs " onwards shall be omitted.

(9) Her Majesty may by Order in Council direct that any regulations made under the said section 143, as that section has effect by virtue of subsections (5) and (7) above in relation to aerodromes vested in or under the control of the Secretary of State, shall extend with such modifications, if any, as may be specified in the Order, to any of the Channel Islands or to the Isle of Man ; and for the purposes of this subsection, subsections (4) and (5) of that section shall be deemed to form part of those regulations.

Control of
road traffic
at Secretary
of State's
aerodromes
and local
authority
aerodromes.

37.—(1) Subject to the provisions of this section, the road traffic enactments shall apply in relation to roads which are within a designated aerodrome but to which the public does not have access as they apply in relation to roads to which the public has access.

(2) The Secretary of State may by order direct that in their application to roads within such an aerodrome the road traffic enactments shall have effect subject to such modifications as appear to him necessary or expedient for the purpose or in consequence of conferring—

(*a*) on the person owning or managing the aerodrome functions exercisable under those enactments by a highway authority or local authority ; and

(*b*) on the chief officer of any aerodrome constabulary functions so exercisable by a chief officer of police.

(3) An order under this section may exempt from the application of the road traffic enactments particular roads or lengths of roads to which the public does not have access and may in the case of an aerodrome owned or managed by a local authority require that authority to indicate the roads or lengths of roads so exempted in such manner as may be specified in the order.

(4) Before making an order under this section in respect of any aerodrome owned or managed by a local authority the Secretary of State shall consult that authority.

(5) In this section—

" designated aerodrome " means any aerodrome which is owned or managed by the Secretary of State or a local authority and is designated for the purposes of this section by an order made by the Secretary of State ;

" the road traffic enactments " has the same meaning as in section 27(1)(*d*) above ;

" aerodrome constabulary " means, in relation to an aerodrome owned or managed by the Secretary of State, the special constables appointed under section 57 below and, in relation to an aerodrome owned or managed by a local authority, any body of constables which the authority have power to maintain at that aerodrome.

38.—(1) Without prejudice to any power of any aerodrome authority to enter into an agreement on such terms as it thinks fit, an aerodrome authority may, for the purpose of encouraging the use of quieter aircraft and of diminishing inconvenience from aircraft noise, fix its charges by reference, among other things, to any fact or matter relevant to—

(*a*) the amount of noise caused by the aircraft in respect of which the charges are made ; or

(*b*) the extent or nature of any inconvenience resulting from such noise.

(2) Without prejudice to section 60(3)(*o*) below, the Secretary of State may by order direct specified aerodrome authorities to fix their charges in exercise of the power conferred by subsection (1) above ; and any such order may contain directions as to the manner in which those charges are to be so fixed.

(3) In this section—

" aerodrome authority " means a person owning or managing an aerodrome licensed under an Air Navigation Order ; and

" charges ", in relation to an aerodrome authority, means the charges the authority makes for the use of an aerodrome so licensed which is owned or managed by the **authority.**

39.—(1) Subject to subsection (2) below, if any person trespasses on any land forming part of an aerodrome licensed in pursuance of an Air Navigation Order, he shall be liable on summary conviction to a fine not exceeding £25.

(2) No person shall be liable under this section unless it is proved that, at the material time, notices warning trespassers of their liability under this section were posted so as to be readily seen and read by members of the public, in such positions on or near the boundary of the aerodrome as appear to the court to be proper.

40.—(1) Any person contravening any byelaws made under sections 27, 29, 32 or 33 above shall be liable on summary conviction to a fine not exceeding such amount as may be specified by the byelaws in question in relation to the contravention, but no amount so specified shall exceed—

　(*a*) in a case not falling within paragraph (*b*) below, £100 ;

　(*b*) where the byelaws in question are made under any of those sections by virtue of paragraph (*b*) of section 27(1) above, £500.

(2) Where any person has in relation to any aerodrome made any byelaw under section 29, 32 or 33 above by virtue of paragraph (*b*) of section 27(1) above, the Secretary of State may, after consultation with that person, by order—

　(*a*) revoke or vary that byelaw if the Secretary of State considers it appropriate to do so by reason of his having designated the aerodrome for the purposes of section 78 below ; or

　(*b*) revoke or vary that byelaw to the extent that it appears to the Secretary of State to be inconsistent with the safety of persons or vehicles using the aerodrome, of aircraft or of the general public or with any international obligation binding on the United Kingdom.

Powers in relation to land exercisable in connection with civil aviation

41.—(1) The Secretary of State may, for any purpose connected with the exercise of his functions relating to civil aviation, acquire land by agreement or be authorised to acquire land compulsorily.

(2) The Acquisition of Land Act 1981—

　(*a*) shall have effect, without Part VI, with respect to the compulsory purchase of land in England and Wales by the Secretary of State under this section ; and

(*b*) may, for the purpose of the compulsory purchase under
    subsection (1) above by the Secretary of State of land
    in Northern Ireland, be extended by Order in Council
    to Northern Ireland subject to any modifications which
    may be provided for by the Order.

(3) The Secretary of State shall have power to manage, sell,
let or exchange any land vested in him and to pay or receive
money in respect of equality of exchange ; but nothing in this
subsection shall be taken to affect the operation of section 5 of
the Defence of the Realm (Acquisition of Land) Act 1916 1916 c. 63.
(which confers on a person from whom land was acquired under
that Act a right of pre-emption in the case of the subsequent
sale of the land) as respects any land acquired under that Act.

(4) The Secretary of State shall have power to manage and
(subject to the terms of the lease) to sublet any land taken on
lease by him or assign the lease.

42.—(1) The CAA may be authorised by the Secretary of Acquisition of
State to acquire land in Great Britain compulsorily for any pur- land by CAA.
pose connected with the performance of the CAA's functions
and the following enactments, that is to say—

(*a*) if the land is in England and Wales, the Acquisition of 1981 c. 67.
    Land Act 1981, other than Part VI, and

(*b*) if the land is in Scotland, the Acquisition of Land 1947 c. 42.
    (Authorisation Procedure) (Scotland) Act 1947, except
    section 3 of that Act,

shall apply in relation to the compulsory purchase of land
by the CAA and, in the case of the latter Act, shall so apply as
if the CAA were a local authority and as if this subsection were
contained in an Act in force immediately before the commencement of that Act.

(2) Where the CAA proposes to acquire, otherwise than by
agreement, any land in Northern Ireland required by it for any
purpose connected with the performance of its functions,
or as to which it can reasonably be foreseen that it will be so
required, it may apply to the Secretary of State for an order
vesting that land in it, and the Secretary of State shall have
power to make such an order.

(3) Schedule 6 to the Local Government Act (Northern Ire- 1972 c. 9
land) 1972 shall, subject to the modifications specified in Sched- (N.I.).
ule 6 to this Act, apply for the purposes of the acquisition of
land by means of an order under subsection (2) above as it
applies to the acquisition of land by means of a vesting order
under that Act.

(4) For the purpose of the acquisition by the CAA of land in Great Britain by agreement the following provisions shall apply, that is to say—

    (*a*) if the land is in England and Wales, the provisions of Part I of the Compulsory Purchase Act 1965 (so far as applicable), other than sections 4 to 8, 27 and 31 ; and

    (*b*) if the land is in Scotland, the provisions of the Lands Clauses Consolidation (Scotland) Act 1845 (so far as applicable), other than sections 120 to 125, 127, 142 and 143.

(5) Any land vested in the CAA by virtue of this section shall be deemed for all purposes to have been acquired by the CAA for the purposes of its undertaking.

(6) In subsections (2) and (3) above, " land " has the meaning assigned to it by section 45(1)(*a*) of the Interpretation Act (Northern Ireland) 1954.

43.—(1) Subject to section 55 below, where any person having an interest in land (in this section referred to as " the grantor ") grants or agrees to grant any relevant right in or in relation to that land—

    (*a*) for any purpose connected with the exercise by the Secretary of State of his functions relating to civil aviation, to the Secretary of State, or

    (*b*) to the CAA,

the grant or agreement shall, to the same extent that it is binding upon the grantor, be binding upon any person deriving title or otherwise claiming under the grantor, notwithstanding that it would not have been binding upon that person apart from the provisions of this subsection.

(2) In this section " relevant right " means any right, whether in perpetuity or for any other period and whether or not capable of subsisting as a legal estate (or, in Scotland, as an estate), in or in relation to land, including the following rights, that is to say—

    (*a*) a right to enter upon that land ;

    (*b*) a right to carry out and maintain works on that land ;

    (*c*) a right to install or maintain structures or apparatus on, under, over or across that land ; and

    (*d*) a right restrictive of the user of that land.

44.—(1) The Secretary of State may make an order under this section if he is satisfied that it is expedient to do so in order—

> (a) to secure the safe and efficient use for civil aviation purposes of any land which is vested in a relevant authority or which such an authority proposes to acquire ; or
>
> (b) to secure the provision of any services required in relation to any such land ; or
>
> (c) to secure that civil aircraft may be navigated with safety and efficiency.

(2) Such an order may provide for the creation—

> (a) if it is made by virtue of paragraph (a) or (b) of subsection (1) above, in favour of the relevant authority in question or, where that authority is Eurocontrol, either of Eurocontrol or of the Secretary of State, or
>
> (b) if it is made by virtue of paragraph (c) of that subsection, in favour of the Secretary of State,

of easements or servitudes over land or of other rights in or in relation to land, including rights to carry out and maintain works on any land and to install and maintain structures and apparatus on, under, over or across any land.

(3) Any such order may contain such consequential, incidental and supplemental provisions as appear to the Secretary of State to be necessary or expedient for the purposes of the order, including, in particular, provisions for authorising persons to enter upon land for the purpose of carrying out, installing, maintaining or removing any works, structures or apparatus.

(4) Subject to subsection (5) below, no person shall, in the exercise of a power conferred by any such order, enter upon land which is occupied, unless, not less than seven days before the day upon which the entry is made, there has been served upon the occupier of the land a notice—

> (a) stating that an entry will be made upon the land upon that day in the exercise of powers conferred by the order ; and
>
> (b) specifying the purposes for which the entry will be made.

(5) Nothing in subsection (4) above shall restrict the right of any person to enter upon land in a case of emergency or for the purpose of performing any functions which are required to be performed from time to time in connection with the maintenance or use of any works, structures or apparatus.

(6) Where any land is damaged in the exercise of any power of entry conferred by any such order, then—

    (*a*) if the relevant authority in whose favour the order was made is the Secretary of State or Eurocontrol, the Secretary of State, and

    (*b*) if the relevant authority in whose favour the order was made is the CAA, the CAA,

shall pay such compensation to the persons interested in the land as may be just ; and where any dispute arises as to whether compensation is payable under this subsection, or as to the amount of any such compensation, or as to the persons to whom it is payable, the dispute shall be referred to and determined by the Lands Tribunal.

(7) The ownership of anything shall not be affected by reason only that it is placed on or under, or affixed to, any land in pursuance of any such order ; and, so long as any such order is in force, no person shall, except with the consent of the Secretary of State, or, if the relevant authority in whose favour the order is made is the CAA, of the Secretary of State or the CAA, wilfully interfere with any works carried out on any land in pursuance of the order, or with anything installed on, under, over or across any land in pursuance of the order.

(8) Subject to the special provisions of this Part of this Act relating to statutory undertakers, Schedule 7 to this Act shall have effect with respect to orders under this section.

(9) Where an order under this section provides for the creation of an easement or servitude over land held by a statutory undertaker for the purposes of the carrying on of his undertaking, or of any other right in or in relation to such land, then, if on a representation made to the Secretary of State before the expiration of the time within which objections to the order may be made the Secretary of State is satisfied that the easement, servitude or right could not be enjoyed without serious detriment to the carrying on of the undertaking, and certifies accordingly, the order shall be subject to special parliamentary procedure.

(10) If any person contravenes the provisions of subsection (7) above he shall be liable, on summary conviction, to imprisonment for a term not exceeding three months or to a fine not exceeding £500 or to both ; and every person who wilfully obstructs any person in the exercise of any power of entry conferred by an order under this section shall be liable, on summary conviction, to a fine not exceeding £100.

(11) Proceedings for an offence under this section shall not be instituted—

    (*a*) in England and Wales, except by or with the consent of the Secretary of State or by or with the consent of the Director of Public Prosecutions ;

(*b*) in Northern Ireland, except by or with the consent of the Secretary of State or by the Attorney General for Northern Ireland ;

except that in England and Wales and in Northern Ireland such proceedings may be instituted by the CAA without such consent if the relevant authority in whose favour the order in question was made is the CAA.

(12) The following are relevant authorities for the purposes of this section, that is to say—

(*a*) the Secretary of State ;

(*b*) Eurocontrol ; and

(*c*) the CAA ;

and in this section and in Schedule 7 to this Act as it has effect with respect to orders under this section, references to land vested in or proposed to be acquired by a relevant authority shall include references to land occupied or, as the case may be, proposed to be occupied by Eurocontrol.

45.—(1) Subject to subsection (2) below, the Secretary of State may by order impose such prohibitions or restrictions on the use of any area of land or water as a place for the arrival and departure of civil aircraft as he thinks expedient for the purpose of securing that aircraft may arrive and depart with safety at any aerodrome vested in him or under his control or at any aerodrome in the United Kingdom owned or managed by the CAA.

Power to restrict use of land for purpose of securing safety at aerodromes.

(2) Nothing in subsection (1) above shall authorise the imposition of any such prohibition or restriction in relation to tidal waters beyond those of the territorial waters adjacent to the United Kingdom.

(3) Part I of Schedule 7 to this Act shall have effect in relation to any order made under this section other than an order for the imposition of prohibitions or restrictions on the use of water ; and in the case of an order for the imposition of prohibitions or restrictions on the use of water the Secretary of State—

(*a*) shall, before making the order, publish notice of his intention to make the order in such manner as he thinks best calculated to bring his intention to the notice of persons who will be affected thereby ; and

(*b*) shall, immediately after the order has been made, publish in one or more newspapers circulating in the locality to which the order relates a notice stating that the order has been made and naming a place where a copy of the order may be seen at all reasonable hours, and shall serve a like notice upon any person who in his opinion will be affected thereby.

(4) Part II of Schedule 7 to this Act and Schedule 8 to this Act shall have effect with respect to orders under this section; but where any aerodrome was first established as such after 31st July 1946 no compensation shall be payable by reason of the imposition under this section of prohibitions or restrictions upon the use of that aerodrome unless it was so established with the consent of the Secretary of State.

(5) Any person who contravenes the provisions of any order under this section shall be liable in respect of each offence—

   (a) on summary conviction to a fine which shall not exceed the statutory maximum or to imprisonment for a term not exceeding three months or to both; and

   (b) on conviction on indictment to a fine or to imprisonment for a term not exceeding two years or to both.

(6) Any offence against any order under this section committed on tidal waters outside the ordinary jurisdiction of a court of summary jurisdiction may be tried and punished by such a court as if it had been committed in the nearest part of the United Kingdom which is within the ordinary jurisdiction of such a court; but nothing in this subsection shall in its application to Scotland be construed as conferring jurisdiction on any court of summary jurisdiction other than the sheriff court.

(7) Proceedings for an offence against any order under this section shall not be instituted—

   (a) in England and Wales, except by or with the consent of the Secretary of State or by or with the consent of the Director of Public Prosecutions;

   (b) in Northern Ireland, except by or with the consent of the Secretary of State or by the Attorney General for Northern Ireland;

except that in England and Wales and in Northern Ireland such proceedings may be instituted by the CAA without such consent if the order in question is made in respect of an aerodrome owned or managed by the CAA.

(8) In this section "aerodrome" includes part of an aerodrome; and, without prejudice to section 105(3) below, the reference in subsection (4) above to the Secretary of State shall, in relation to any time before the passing of this Act, have effect as a reference to whoever at that time was charged with exercising the functions which by virtue of this section are vested in the Secretary of State.

46.—(1) The Secretary of State may, if he is satisfied that it is necessary to do so in order to secure the safe and efficient use for civil aviation purposes (including the testing of aircraft designed for civil aviation) of any land, structures, works or apparatus vested in a relevant authority or which such an authority proposes to acquire or install, by order declare that any area of land specified in the order shall be subject to control by directions given in accordance with the provisions of this section ; and in this Part of this Act that authority, in relation to the making of such an order, is referred to as the person in respect of whom the order is or, as the case may be, is to be made.

(2) Where an order under subsection (1) above is in force, the Secretary of State may, in pursuance of any general or special authority given by the order, give directions—

(a) for requiring the total or partial demolition of any building or structure within the area to which the order relates ;

(b) for restricting the height of trees upon any land within the area, or for requiring any tree upon any such land to be cut down or reduced in height ;

(c) for extinguishing any private right of way over land within the area ;

(d) for restricting the installation of cables, mains, pipes, wires or other apparatus upon, across, under or over any land within the area ;

(e) for extinguishing, at the expiration of such period as may be determined by the directions, any subsisting right of installing or maintaining any such apparatus as aforesaid upon, across, under or over any land within the area ;

(f) for requiring that, before the expiration of such period as may be determined by the directions, any such apparatus shall be removed from any land within the area.

(3) An order under subsection (1) above may contain such consequential, incidental and supplemental provisions, as appear to the Secretary of State to be necessary or expedient for the purposes of the order, including, in particular, provisions for empowering any person authorised for the purpose by the Secretary of State, to remove, pull down, cut down, or alter so as to bring into conformity with the requirements of any directions given under the order, any building, structure, tree or apparatus which contravenes those requirements.

(4) An order under subsection (1) above, other than an order relating to land in Northern Ireland, shall be subject to special parliamentary procedure.

(5) Before making any order under this section, the Secretary of State shall consult every local authority within the area of which the whole or any part of the area of land to which the proposed order will relate is situated.

(6) Notwithstanding anything in section 2(1) of the Statutory Orders (Special Procedure) Act, 1945, the duty of the Secretary of State to comply with the requirements of subsection (5) above in relation to England and Wales shall not excuse him from the duty of complying with the requirements of Schedule 1 to that Act.

(7) Subject to the special provisions of this Part of this Act relating to statutory undertakers, Schedule 9 to this Act shall have effect with respect to directions given under an order made under this section.

(8) The powers of the Secretary of State under this section shall not prejudice his power to acquire land for the purpose of securing the observance of any requirement or restriction which might have been imposed in relation to the land under this section.

(9) The Secretary of State may, after consultation with any local authority which appears to him to be concerned, by order repeal or amend any enactment in a local Act which appears to him to be unnecessary having regard to, or to be inconsistent with, the provisions of this Part of this Act relating to orders made or to be made under subsection (1) above in respect of a relevant authority falling within paragraph (*d*) of subsection (10) below.

(10) The following are relevant authorities for the purposes of this section, that is to say—

(*a*) the Secretary of State ;

(*b*) Eurocontrol ;

(*c*) the CAA ; and

(*d*) the licensee of any aerodrome licensed under an Air Navigation Order ;

and in this section and in Schedule 9 to this Act, references to land, structures, works or apparatus vested in or proposed to be acquired or installed by a relevant authority shall include references to land, structures, works or apparatus occupied or, as the case may be, proposed to be occupied by Eurocontrol.

47.—(1) Subject to the provisions of this section, if the Secretary of State is satisfied with respect to any building, structure or erection in the vicinity of a licensed aerodrome that, in order to avoid danger to aircraft flying in that vicinity in darkness or conditions of poor visibility, provision ought to be made (whether by lighting or otherwise) for giving to such aircraft warning of the presence of that building, structure or erection, he may by order authorise (subject to any conditions specified in the order) the proprietor of the aerodrome, and any person acting under the proprietor's instructions—

PART II
Warning of presence of obstructions near licensed aerodromes.

(a) to execute, install, maintain, operate and, as occasion requires, to repair and alter, such works and apparatus as may be necessary for enabling such warning to be given in the manner specified in the order ; and

(b) so far as may be necessary for exercising any of the powers conferred by the order to enter upon and pass over (with or without vehicles) any such land as may be specified in the order.

(2) An order shall not be made under this section in relation to any building, structure or erection if it appears to the Secretary of State that there have been made, and are being carried out, satisfactory arrangements for the giving of such warning as aforesaid of the presence of the building, structure or erection.

(3) The Secretary of State shall, before making an order under this section—

(a) cause to be published, in such manner as he thinks best for informing persons concerned, notice of the proposal to make the order and of the place where copies of the draft order may be obtained free of charge ; and

(b) take into consideration any representations with respect to the order which may, within such period not being less than two months after the publication of the notice as may be specified therein, be made to him by any person appearing to him to have an interest in any land which would be affected by the order ;

and at the end of that period the order may, subject to the provisions of this section, be made with such modifications (if any) of the original draft as the Secretary of State thinks proper.

(4) Every order under this section shall provide—

(a) that, except in a case of emergency, no works shall be executed on any land in pursuance of the order, unless, at least fourteen days previously, the proprietor of the aerodrome to which the order relates has served in the manner specified in the order on the occupier of that land, and on every other person known by the proprietor to have an interest therein, a written notice containing such particulars of the nature of the proposed works, and the manner in which and the time at which it is proposed to execute them, as may be specified in or in accordance with the order ; and

(b) that if, within fourteen days after service of the said notice on any person having such an interest, the proprietor of the aerodrome receives a written intimation of objection on the part of that person to the proposals contained in the notice, being an intimation which specifies the grounds of objection, then, unless and except in so far as the objection is withdrawn, no steps shall be taken in pursuance of the notice without the specific sanction of the Secretary of State ;

and shall also provide for requiring the proprietor of the aerodrome to which the order relates to pay to any person having an interest in any land affected by the order such compensation for any loss or damage which that person may suffer in consequence of the order as may, in default of agreement, be determined from time to time by a single arbitrator appointed by the Lord Chief Justice or, in Scotland, by a single arbiter appointed by the Lord President of the Court of Session.

(5) For the purposes of subsection (4) above, any expense reasonably incurred in connection with the lawful removal of any apparatus installed in pursuance of an order under this section, and so much of any expense incurred in connection with the repair, alteration, demolition or removal of any building, structure or erection to which such an order relates as is attributable to the operation of the order, shall be deemed to be loss or damage suffered in consequence of the order.

(6) The ownership of anything shall not be taken to be affected by reason only that it is placed in, or affixed to, any land in pursuance of an order under this section ; and (subject to the provisions of subsection (8) below) so long as any such order in respect of an aerodrome is in force, no person shall, except with the consent of the proprietor of the aerodrome, wilfully interfere with any works or things which, to the knowledge of that person, are works or things executed or placed, in, on or over any land in pursuance of the order.

(7) If any person contravenes the provisions of subsection (6) above, he shall be liable, on summary conviction, to imprisonment for a term not exceeding six months or to a fine not exceeding £200 or to both ; and every person who wilfully obstructs a person in the exercise of any of the powers conferred by an order under this section shall be liable, on summary conviction, to a fine not exceeding £50.

(8) Nothing in this section shall operate, in relation to any building, structure or erection, so as to restrict the doing of any work for the purpose of repairing, altering, demolishing or removing the building, structure or erection if—

(*a*) notice of the doing of that work is given as soon as may be to the proprietor of the aerodrome ; and

(*b*) the giving of warning of the presence of the building, structure or erection in the manner provided by any order under this section in force in relation thereto is not interrupted.

(9) The following provisions shall have effect, without prejudice to the general application of subsections (4) and (5) above, for the protection of statutory undertakers—

(*a*) any order made under this section affecting any property held by such undertakers for the purposes of their undertaking shall be so framed as to avoid interference with the proper carrying on of the undertaking ;

(*b*) no person shall, except in a case of emergency, enter, in pursuance of such an order, upon any land held by such undertakers for the purposes of their undertaking, unless he has given to the undertakers at least three clear days' notice of his intention so to do, and any person so entering on any such land shall comply with any reasonable directions given to him by or on behalf of the undertakers for preventing interference with the proper carrying on of the undertaking ;

(*c*) if any such undertakers show that, by reason of the operation of such an order, they have been obliged to take special measures for the purpose of ensuring the safety of persons so entering on any such land or otherwise acting under the order in relation to any property of the undertakers, the amount of any expenses reasonably incurred by the undertakers in taking such measures shall be paid to them by the proprietor of the aerodrome to which the order relates, and any dispute as to whether any sum is payable under this paragraph, or as to the amount of any sum so payable, shall, unless the parties otherwise agree, be referred for determination to a single arbitrator appointed by the Lord Chief Justice or, in Scotland, to a single arbiter appointed by the Lord President of the Court of Session.

(10) In this section—

" licensed aerodrome " means any premises which, by virtue of an Air Navigation Order, are for the time being licensed as an aerodrome for public use, but does not include any premises belonging to the Secretary of State ;

" proprietor of the aerodrome " means, in relation to any premises used or appropriated for use as an aerodrome, the person carrying on or entitled to carry on the business of an aerodrome in those premises ;

and nothing in section 104(1) below shall affect the construction of the reference in the definition in this subsection of " licensed aerodrome " to premises belonging to the Secretary of State.

Power of Secretary of State to stop up and divert highways etc. in interests of civil aviation.

48.—(1) Subject to subsection (2) below, the Secretary of State may if he is satisfied that it is necessary to do so in order to secure the safe and efficient use for civil aviation purposes (including the testing of aircraft designed for civil aviation) of any land vested in the Secretary of State or the CAA, or of any land which the Secretary of State or the CAA proposes to acquire, by order authorise the stopping-up or diversion of any highway.

(2) The power conferred by subsection (1) above shall, in Northern Ireland, be exercisable by the Department of the Environment for Northern Ireland (in this section referred to as " the Department ") instead of by the Secretary of State, and notwithstanding anything in section 104(1) below, the reference in subsection (1) above to land which is vested in the Secretary of State or which the Secretary of State proposes to acquire shall include a reference to land which is vested in him, or which he proposes to acquire, as the case may be, in connection with the exercise of the following functions, that is to say—

1975 c. 9.

(*a*) his functions under the Supply Powers Act 1975 ; and

1939 S.R. & O. No. 877.

(*b*) the related functions which by virtue of the Ministry of Supply (Transfer of Powers) (No. 1) Order 1939 became exercisable by the Minister of Supply and which have subsequently become vested in the Secretary of State.

(3) An order under subsection (1) above may provide for all or any of the following matters, that is to say—

(*a*) for securing the provision or improvement of any highway so far as the Secretary of State or, as the case may be, the Department thinks such provision or improvement necessary or desirable in consequence of any such stopping-up or diversion as aforesaid ;

(*b*) for directing that any highway to be provided or improved in pursuance of the order shall—

1980 c. 66.

(i) in England and Wales, be a highway which for the purposes of the Highways Act 1980 is maintainable at public expense ;

(ii) in Scotland, be maintained and managed by a regional, islands or district council ; and

S.I. 1980/1085 (N.I. 11).

(iii) in Northern Ireland be a public road within the meaning of the Roads (Northern Ireland) Order 1980 ;

(c) for specifying—

(i) in England and Wales or Northern Ireland, the highway authority which is to be the highway authority for any highway to be provided or improved in pursuance of the order ; and

(ii) in Scotland, the council which is to be responsible for the maintenance and management referred to in paragraph (b)(ii) above ;

(d) for directing that any highway to be provided or improved in consequence of the stopping-up or diversion of a trunk road under the order shall itself be a trunk road for all or any of the purposes of the enactments relating to trunk roads ;

(e) for the retention or removal of any cables, mains, pipes, wires or similar apparatus placed along, across, over or under any highway stopped up or diverted under the order, and for the extinguishment, modification or preservation of any rights as to the use or maintenance of that apparatus ;

(f) if any highway is to be provided or improved under the order, for authorising or requiring the provision of any such apparatus as aforesaid along, across, over or under that highway, in lieu of any apparatus removed from a highway in pursuance of the order, and for conferring rights as to the use or maintenance of apparatus so provided ;

(g) for requiring the Secretary of State or the Department or any other specified authority or person—

(i) to pay, or to make contributions in respect of, the cost of doing any work provided for by the order or any increased expenditure to be incurred which is ascribable to the doing of any such work ; or

(ii) to repay, or to make contributions in respect of, any compensation paid by a highway authority in England and Wales or Scotland in respect of restrictions imposed under section 1 or 2 of the Restriction of Ribbon Development Act 1935 as 1935 c. 47. respects any highway stopped up or diverted under the order.

(4) An order under subsection (1) above may contain such consequential, incidental and supplemental provisions as appear to the Secretary of State or, as the case may be, the Department to be necessary or expedient for the purposes of the order.

F 2

(5) An order under subsection (1) above shall, if made in respect of land in England and Wales or Scotland, be subject to special parliamentary procedure ; and—

    (*a*) if the order was made in respect of land in England and Wales, Schedule 1 to the Statutory Orders (Special Procedure) Act 1945 (which sets out the notices to be given and the other requirements to be complied with before an order is made), and

1945 c. 18
(9 & 10 Geo. 6.)

    (*b*) if the order was made in respect of land in Scotland, section 2 of that Act (which contains comparable provision for Scotland), as that section applies by virtue of section 10 of that Act to Scotland,

shall apply in relation to the order, but in their application in relation thereto, shall have effect as if paragraph 1 of the said Schedule 1 or subsection (1) of the said section 2, as the case may be, included the provisions set out in subsection (6) below.

(6) The said provisions are provisions—

    (*a*) requiring notice of the order as proposed to be made to be displayed in a prominent position at the ends of so much of any highway as is proposed to be stopped up or diverted under the order ;

    (*b*) requiring notice of the order as proposed to be made to be sent to every local authority in whose area any highway to be stopped up or diverted under the order, or any highway to be provided or improved under the order, is or will be situated ; and

    (*c*) requiring notice of the order as proposed to be made to be served upon any water, gas or electricity undertakers having any cables, mains, pipes or wires laid along, across, under or over any highway to be stopped up or diverted under the order.

(7) In subsection (6) above—

    (*a*) the reference in paragraph (*b*) to a local authority shall include a reference to a parish council in England, to a parish meeting of a parish in England not having a separate parish council, to a council of a community in Wales and to the community in the case of a community in Wales without a council ; and

    (*b*) the reference in paragraph (*c*) to electricity undertakers shall be deemed to include references to the Post Office and British Telecommunications.

(8) The powers of the Secretary of State and of the Department under subsection (1) above shall include power to make an order authorising the stopping-up or diversion of any highway

which is temporarily stopped up or diverted under any other
enactment ; and the provisions of this section shall not prejudice
any power conferred upon the Secretary of State or the Department by any other enactment to authorise the stopping-up or
diversion of a highway.

(9) The following provisions (which relate to telegraphic
lines of British Telecommunications affected by the stopping-up,
diversion or improvement of a highway), that is to say—

> (a) in England and Wales, subsections (1) and (2) of section
> 220 of the Town and Country Planning Act 1971 ; 1971 c. 78.

> (b) in Scotland, subsections (1) and (2) of section 209 of the
> Town and Country Planning (Scotland) Act 1972 ; and 1972 c. 52.

> (c) in Northern Ireland, paragraphs 2 and 3 of Schedule 7 S.I. 1980/1085.
> to the Roads (Northern Ireland) Order 1980.   (N.I. 11).

shall have effect as if references in those subsections to an order
under section 209 of the said Act of 1971 and to an order under
section 198 of the said Act of 1972 and in those paragraphs to
an order under Article 40 of the said Order of 1980 included
references to an order made under subsection (1) above in
relation to land which is vested in the CAA or which the CAA
proposes to acquire.

49.—(1) The Secretary of State may be authorised to purchase Power to
land in Great Britain compulsorily for the purpose of providing acquire land
or improving any highway which is to be provided or improved in connection
in pursuance of an order under section 48(1) above or for any under s. 48.
other purpose for which land is required in connection with
such an order.

(2) The Acquisition of Land Act 1981 shall apply, in relation 1981 c. 67.
to land in England and Wales, to a compulsory purchase under
subsection (1) above.

(3) The CAA's power of acquiring land compulsorily under
this Act may be exercised for the purpose of providing
or improving any highway which is to be provided or improved
in pursuance of an order made under section 48(1) above in
relation to land which is vested in the CAA or which the CAA
proposes to acquire or for any other purpose for which land is
required in connection with such an order.

(4) The powers of compulsory acquisition of land exercisable
by the Department of the Environment for Northern Ireland
under paragraph (3) of Article 53 of the Roads (Northern
Ireland) Order 1980 shall include the power to acquire lands
compulsorily in accordance with the provisions of that Article for
the purpose of providing or improving any highway which is to be
provided or improved in pursuance of an order under section

48(1) above or for any other purpose for which land is required in connection with such an order ; and the said Order of 1980 shall have effect accordingly.

(5) The powers conferred on the Department of the Environment for Northern Ireland by subsection (4) above shall be exercisable in relation to any land notwithstanding that the land is the property of a statutory undertaker or is declared by any other enactment to be inalienable

Power of
entry for
purposes of
survey.

50.—(1) This section applies—

(a) where the Secretary of State has confirmed or is considering the confirmation of an order authorising the CAA to acquire land in Great Britain compulsorily ;

(b) where the CAA proposes to acquire land in Northern Ireland compulsorily ;

(c) where the Secretary of State has made or has under consideration the making of an order under section 44 above providing for the creation in favour of the CAA of easements or servitudes over land or of other rights in or in relation to land ;

(d) where the Secretary of State has made, or has under consideration the making of, an order under section 46(1) above in respect of the CAA or the licensee of an aerodrome licensed under an Air Navigation Order, being an order declaring that an area of land shall be subject to control by directions ; and

(e) in any case not falling within paragraphs (a) to (d) above where the Secretary of State has made, or has under consideration the making of, an order under or in pursuance of this Part of this Act, being—

(i) an order authorising the compulsory purchase of land ; or

(ii) an order providing for the creation in favour of a particular person of easements or servitudes over land or of other rights in or in relation to land ; or

(iii) an order declaring that an area of land shall be subject to control by directions.

(2) Where this section applies any person authorised in writing by the Secretary of State may at all reasonable times on producing if so required evidence of his authority for the purpose enter upon any of the land in question in order to make a relevant survey.

(3) In subsection (2) above " a relevant survey " means—

(a) in a case falling within subsection (1)(*a*) above, any survey which the Secretary of State or the CAA requires to be made for the purpose of any steps to be taken in consequence of the order, or, as the case may be, for the purpose of determining whether the order should be confirmed ;

(b) in a case falling within subsection (1)(*b*) above, any survey which the Secretary of State or the CAA requires to be made for the purpose of ascertaining whether the land would be suitable for the purposes for which it is proposed to acquire it ;

(c) in a case falling within subsection (1)(*c*) above, any survey which the Secretary of State or the CAA requires to be made for the purpose of any steps to be taken in consequence of the order or, as the case may be, for the purpose of determining whether the order should be made ;

(d) in a case falling within subsection (1)(*d*) above, any survey which the Secretary of State or the person in respect of whom the order under the said section 46(1) has been, or is to be, made requires to be made for the purpose of any steps to be taken in consequence of that order or, as the case may be, for the purpose of determining whether the order should be made ;

(e) in a case falling within subsection (1)(*e*) above, any survey which the Secretary of State requires to be made for the purpose of any steps to be taken in consequence of the order in question or, as the case may be, for the purpose of determining whether the order should be made.

(4) Admission shall not, by virtue of subsection (2) above, be demanded as of right to any land which is occupied unless the following notice of the intended entry has been served on the occupier, that is to say—

(a) in a case falling within subsection (1) (*a*) to (*d*) above, eight days' notice ; and

(b) in a case falling within subsection (1)(*e*) above, twenty-four hours' notice.

(5) If any person obstructs a person authorised as mentioned in subsection (2) above in the exercise of any power conferred by this section he shall be liable on summary conviction to a fine not exceeding £50.

F 4

(6) Proceedings for an offence under this section shall not be instituted—

    (*a*) in England and Wales, except by or with the consent of the Secretary of State or by or with the consent of the Director of Public Prosecutions ;

    (*b*) in Northern Ireland, except by or with the consent of the Secretary of State or by the Attorney General for Northern Ireland,

except that in England and Wales and in Northern Ireland such proceedings may be instituted without such consent, in a case falling within subsection (1)(*a*) to (*c*) above, by the CAA and, in a case falling within subsection (1)(*d*) above, by the person in respect of whom the order in question has been, or is to be, made.

(7) Where any land is damaged in the exercise of a power of entry conferred in pursuance of an authority given under this section, or in the making of any survey for the purpose of which any such power of entry has been conferred—

    (*a*) in a case falling within subsection (1)(*a*) to (*c*) above, the CAA,

    (*b*) in a case falling within subsection (1)(*d*) above, the person in respect of whom the order in question has been, or is to be, made,

    (*c*) in a case falling within subsection(1)(*e*) above, the Secretary of State,

shall pay such compensation to the persons interested in the land as may be just ; and where any dispute arises as to whether compensation is payable under this subsection, or as to the amount of any such compensation or as to the persons to whom it is payable, the dispute shall be referred to and determined by the Lands Tribunal.

Supplemental

Special provisions relating to statutory undertakers.

51.—(1) Subject to the provisions of this section, the compensation to be paid to a statutory undertaker—

    (*a*) in respect of the compulsory purchase in pursuance of this Part of this Act, otherwise than under section 30, of any land held by the undertaker for the purposes of the carrying on of his undertaking,

    (*b*) in respect of the creation, by virtue of an order made under this Part of this Act, otherwise than under section 30 above, of any easement or servitude over any such land or of any other right in or in relation to any such land,

(*c*) in respect of any direction under section 46 above
which affects any building, structure or apparatus held
or used by him for the purposes of his undertaking,
or which affects any of his rights to install or maintain
apparatus for those purposes or which affects any
right of way enjoyed by him for those purposes,

shall, in default of agreement, be assessed by the Lands
Tribunal ; but this subsection shall not apply to any compensation payable by virtue of section 42 above.

(2) Subject to those provisions, the amount of any compensation payable as mentioned in subsection (1) above shall be an
amount calculated in accordance with the following enactments,
that is to say—

(*a*) if the land is in England and Wales, section 238(2), (3),
(5) and (6) of the Town and Country Planning Act 1971 c. 78.
1971 ; and

(*b*) if the land is in Scotland, section 227(2), (3), (5) and (6)
of the Town and Country Planning (Scotland) Act 1972 c. 52.
1972.

(3) Subsection (4) below applies in relation to compensation
payable as so mentioned in respect of a compulsory purchase.

(4) If, before the expiration of two months from the date
on which notice to treat is served in respect of the interest of the
person by whom the statutory undertaking is carried on, that
person gives notice in writing to the Secretary of State that he
elects that as respects all or any of the land comprised in the
purchase the compensation shall be ascertained in accordance
with the enactments, other than Rule (5) of the Rules set out
in section 5 of the Land Compensation Act 1961 and section 1961 c. 33.
12(1) of the Land Compensation (Scotland) Act 1963, which 1963 c. 51.
would be applicable apart from subsection (2) above, the compensation shall be so ascertained.

(5) Subsections (2), (3), (5) and (6) of the said sections 238
and 227 shall have effect for the purposes of this section with
the following modifications, that is to say—

(*a*) in subsection (2)(*c*) of the said section 238 the words
" is under section 237(2) of this Act and " and in
subsection (2)(*c*) of the said section 227 the words " is
under section 226(2) of this Act and " shall be
omitted ;

(*b*) after subsection (2)(*c*) of each of the said sections there
shall be inserted the following paragraph : —

" (*d*) in respect of the imposition of a requirement
to demolish a building or structure either wholly or
in part, any expense reasonably incurred by the

person carrying on the undertaking in complying with the requirement, reduced by the value to that person of any materials derived from the demolished building or structure, or from the demolished part of the building or structure, as the case may be ; " ;

(c) in subsection (6) of each of the said sections any reference to the imposition of a requirement shall include a reference to anything which may be done by virtue of an order made, otherwise than by virtue of section 42 above, under this Part of this Act.

(6) The preceding provisions of this section as to the assessment of compensation shall not have effect—

(a) in the case of the compulsory purchase of land, unless the Secretary of State has, upon a representation made to him before the expiration of the time within which objections may be made to the compulsory purchase order, certified that the land is in respect of its nature or situation of such a kind that it is comparable less with the generality of land than with land held for the purpose of the carrying on of statutory undertakings ;

(b) in the case of the creation of any easement or servitude over land or any other right in or in relation to land, unless the Secretary of State has, upon a representation made to him before the expiration of the time within which objections may be made to the order providing for the creation of that easement, servitude or right, certified that the land in question is of such a kind as aforesaid ; and

(c) in the case of any direction which affects a building or structure, unless the Secretary of State has, upon a representation made to him before the expiration of the time within which an application may be made to the court with respect to the direction in accordance with the provisions of Part II of Schedule 7 to this Act, certified that the building or structure is in respect of its nature or situation comparable less with the generality of buildings or structures than with buildings or structures held for the purpose of the carrying on of statutory undertakings.

1971 c. 78.

1972 c. 52.
(7) Schedule 10 to this Act (which broadly corresponds to sections 233 to 235 of the Town and Country Planning Act 1971 and sections 222 to 224 of the Town and Country Planning (Scotland) Act 1972) shall have effect for the purpose of making any adjustments of the functions of statutory undertakers which may be necessary in consequence of the provisions

of this Part of this Act; but in that Schedule references to an order made or proposed to be made in pursuance of this Part of this Act—

(*a*) shall, in relation to an order for the compulsory purchase of land by the CAA, have effect as references to an order confirmed or, as the case may be, proposed to be confirmed by the Secretary of State; but

(*b*) shall be deemed not to include a reference to an order made or, as the case may be, proposed to be made in pursuance of section 30 above or under any enactment conferring a power exercisable by statutory instrument.

52.—(1) This section applies where—

(*a*) the Secretary of State has acquired land for purposes connected with the exercise of his functions relating to civil aviation;

(*b*) the Secretary of State (in a case not falling within paragraph (*a*) above) or the Department of the Environment for Northern Ireland has acquired land in pursuance of this Part of this Act;

(*c*) the CAA has acquired land for purposes connected with the discharge of its functions; or

(*d*) the Secretary of State gives a direction in relation to any land in pursuance of an order made under section 46(1) above;

and the use of the land by the person who has acquired it for the purposes for which he acquired it or, as the case may be, the execution of the direction will involve the displacement of persons residing in premises on the land.

(2) Where this section applies, the following, that is to say—

(*a*) in a case falling within paragraph (*a*), (*b*) or (*c*) of subsection (1) above, the person who has acquired the land,

(*b*) in a case falling within paragraph (*d*) of that subsection where the person in respect of whom the order was made is the Secretary of State or Eurocontrol, the Secretary of State, and

(*c*) in any other case falling within the said paragraph (*d*), the person in respect of whom the order was made,

shall be under a duty, in so far as there is no other residential accommodation available on reasonable terms to the persons who require it in consequence of the displacement, being residential accommodation suitable to the reasonable requirements of those persons, to secure the provision of such accommodation.

PART II

(3) A person required under subsection (2) above to secure the provision of accommodation shall secure its provision in advance of the displacement unless—

    (*a*) in a case falling within paragraph (*a*), (*c*) or (*d*) of sub-section (1) above, the Secretary of State is satisfied that for reasons of exceptional public importance it is essential that the displacement should be effected before such accommodation as aforesaid can be found ; or

    (*b*) in a case falling within paragraph (*b*) of that subsection, the Secretary of State or, as the case may be, the Department of the Environment for Northern Ireland is so satisfied.

Compensation in respect of planning decisions relating to safety of aerodromes, etc.

1971 c. 78.
1972 c. 52.

53.—(1) A local planning authority (in this section referred to as " a planning authority ") shall be entitled to recover from the CAA a sum equal to any compensation which the planning authority has become liable to pay, if—

    (*a*) it has become so liable under section 164, 165, 169, 187(2) or 237(1) of the Town and Country Planning Act 1971 or section 153, 154, 158, 176(2) or 226(1) of the Town and Country Planning (Scotland) Act 1972 (which relate to compensation for certain planning restrictions, for purchase notices which do not take effect and in respect of undertakers' operational land) ; **and**

    (*b*) the liability is attributable to a planning decision which would not have been taken, or, in the case of compensation under the said section 164 or the said section 153 to an order under section 45 of the said Act of 1971 or section 42 of the said Act of 1972 which would not have been made, but for the need—

        (i) to secure the safe and efficient operation of an aerodrome owned by the CAA ; or

        (ii) to prevent persons or buildings from being struck by aircraft using such an aerodrome ; or

        (iii) to secure the safe and efficient operation of apparatus owned by the CAA and provided for the purpose of assisting air traffic control or as an aid to air navigation.

(2) Where a sum equal to any compensation is payable or paid to a planning authority in pursuance of subsection (1) above, the planning authority shall pay the CAA any amount received by the planning authority in respect of the compensation under section 168 of the said Act of 1971 or section 157 of the said Act of 1972 (which relate to the recovery of compensation on subsequent development).

(3) Where a purchase notice is served under section 180 of the said Act of 1971 or section 169 of the said Act of 1972 in respect of a planning decision which would not have been taken but for such a need as aforesaid in respect of an aerodrome or apparatus owned by the CAA, any local authority who are deemed under section 181(2) or 186(1) of the said Act of 1971 or section 170(2) or 175(1) of the said Act of 1972 to have served a notice to treat in respect of the interest to which the purchase notice relates may, by notice in writing given to the CAA not later than one month from the time when the amount of compensation payable by the local authority for the interest is agreed or determined, require the CAA to purchase the interest from the local authority for a sum equal to the amount of compensation so agreed or determined.

(4) Where a notice in writing is given to the CAA under subsection (3) above, the CAA shall, subject to any agreement between it and the local authority, be deemed to have contracted with the local authority to purchase the interest at that price.

(5) Any dispute as to whether a planning decision would not have been taken or an order under the said section 45 or the said section 42 would not have been made but for such a need as is mentioned in subsection (1) above shall be referred to and determined by the Secretary of State.

(6) In the preceding provisions of this section " planning decision " means a decision made on an application under Part III of the said Act of 1971 or Part III of the said Act of 1972 ; and references in those provisions to a local planning authority include, in relation to England and Wales, references to any authority to whom functions of a local planning authority are delegated.

(7) Where by reason of a planning decision taken under the Planning Acts (Northern Ireland) 1931 and 1944 by a planning authority in Northern Ireland or under the Planning (Northern Ireland) Order 1972 by the Department of the Environment for Northern Ireland or the Planning Appeals Commission—

S.I. 1972/1634 (N.I. 17).

(a) the Department of the Environment for Northern Ireland becomes liable to pay compensation to any person :

and

(b) the decision would not have been taken but for the need to secure the safe and efficient operation of apparatus owned by the CAA and provided for the purpose of assisting air traffic control or as an aid to air navigation,

the Department shall be entitled to recover from the CAA a sum equal to that compensation.

(8) Where a sum equal to any compensation is payable or paid to the said Department in pursuance of subsection (7) above, the Department shall pay the CAA any amount received by the Department in respect of the compensation under section 24 of the Land Development Values (Compensation) Act (Northern Ireland) 1965 (which relates to the recovery of compensation on subsequent development).

1965 c. 23.
(N.I.).

(9) In subsection (7) above, " planning decision " includes a revocation or modification of planning permission under section 3 of the Planning (Interim Development) Act (Northern Ireland) 1944.

1944 c. 3
(N.I.).

Consecrated
land and
burial grounds.

1971 c. 78.
1972 c. 52.

54.—(1) Subject to subsection (2) below, section 128 of the Town and Country Planning Act 1971 and section 118 of the Town and Country Planning (Scotland) Act 1972 (consecrated land and burial grounds) shall have effect in relation—

    (a) to land acquired by the Secretary of State for purposes connected with the exercise of his functions relating to civil aviation, and

    (b) to land acquired by the Secretary of State in pursuance of this Part of this Act and otherwise than as mentioned in paragraph (a) above,

as if the Secretary of State had acquired that land under Part VI of the said Act of 1971 or, as the case may be, Part VI of the said Act of 1972.

(2) The said sections 128 and 118 shall have effect in relation to any land acquired by the CAA as they have effect in relation to land acquired by statutory undertakers under Part VI of the said Act of 1971 or, as the case may be, Part VI of the said Act of 1972.

Registration
of orders, etc.
under Part II.

55.—(1) The following shall be local land charges in England and Wales:—

    (a) a right in or in relation to land granted or agreed to be granted on or after 25th October 1968 and enforceable by virtue of section 43 above;

    (b) the following instruments when operative that is to say

        (i) an order under section 44 above;

        (ii) an order under section 45 above, other than an order for the imposition of prohibitions or restrictions on the use of water; and

        (iii) an order under section 46(1) above or any direction given under such an order.

(2) A grant or agreement made as respects land in Scotland shall not be enforceable by virtue of section 43 above against a third party who shall have in good faith and for value acquired a right (whether completed by infeftment or not) to the land prior to the grant or agreement being registered in the Land Register of Scotland or against any person deriving title from such third party.

(3) In Scotland where any such instrument as is mentioned in subsection (1)(*b*) above becomes operative it shall be registered as a deed in the said Land Register, and on being so registered shall be enforceable against any person having or subsequently acquiring any estate or interest in the land to which the order or direction relates.

(4) For the purposes of the recording of a deed in the Register of Sasines under section 8 of the Land Registration (Scotland) Act 1979 or of the application of subsection (2) or (3) above in relation to any area in respect of which section 29(2) of that Act (modification of references to Register of Sasines) is not yet in force, any reference in subsections (2) and (3) above to the registration of any grant, agreement or instrument in the Land Register of Scotland shall have effect as a reference to the recording of the grant, agreement or instrument in the Register of Sasines. 1979 c. 33.

(5) A right in or in relation to land in Northern Ireland granted or agreed to be granted to the CAA shall not be enforceable by virtue of section 43 above against a purchaser for money or money's worth of any estate or interest in the land to which the grant or agreement in question relates unless before the completion of the purchase the grant or agreement is registered in the Statutory Charges Register pursuant to Part X of the Land Registration Act (Northern Ireland) 1970; and accordingly such a grant or agreement shall be included among the matters which are required to be registered in that Register. 1970 c. 18 (N.I.).

(6) Where any such instrument as is mentioned in subsection (1)(*b*) above adversely affects land in Northern Ireland, then—

    (*a*) if the land is registered land to which the Land Registration Act (Northern Ireland) 1970 applies, the instrument on the lodgment by the relevant authority of a copy thereof with the Registrar of Titles shall, notwithstanding anything in the said Act or rules made thereunder, be registered as a burden affecting the land and created after the first registration of the land, and may be so registered without the concurrence of the registered owner of the land or the production of the land certificate, without prejudice, however, to the power of the registering authority to order the production of the land certificate ; and (*b*) if the land is not registered land to which that Act applies, the instrument shall, on lodgment by the relevant authority of a copy thereof with the Registrar of Deeds for Northern Ireland, be registered in the Registry of Deeds, Northern Ireland, as an instrument affecting the lands to which the instrument relates.

(7) In subsection (6) above " the relevant authority " means—

(*a*) in the case of an order under section 44 above—

(i) if the order is made in favour of the Secretary of State or Eurocontrol, the Secretary of State ; and

(ii) if the order is made in favour of the CAA, the CAA ; and

(*b*) in the case of an order under section 45 above—

(i) if the order is made in respect of an aerodrome owned or managed by the CAA, the CAA ; and

(ii) in any other case, the Secretary of State ; and

(*c*) in the case of an order under section 46(1) above or of a direction given under such an order—

(i) if the order is made in respect of the CAA, the CAA ; and

(ii) in any other case, the Secretary of State.

56.—(1) Any notice required to be served on any person for the purposes of any provision to which this section applies may be served on him either by delivering it to him or by leaving it at his proper address, or by post, so however that the notice shall not be duly served by post unless it is sent by registered letter or by the recorded delivery service.

(2) Any such notice required to be served upon an incorporated company or body shall be duly served if it is served on the secretary or clerk of the company or body.

(3) For the purposes of this section and of section 7 of the Interpretation Act 1978, the proper address of any person upon whom any such notice is to be served shall, in the case of the secretary or clerk of any incorporated company or body, be that of the registered or principal office of the company or body and in any other case be the last known address of the person to be served, except that, where the person to be served has furnished an address for service, that address shall be his proper address for those purposes.

(4) If it is not practicable after reasonable inquiry to ascertain the name or address of any owner, lessee or occupier of land on whom any such notice is to be served, the notice may be

served by addressing it to him by the description of " owner ",
" lessee " or " occupier " of the land (describing it) to which the
notice relates, and by delivering it to some person on the
premises or, if there is no person on the premises to whom it
can be delivered, by affixing it, or a copy of it, to some conspicuous part of the premises.

(5) In the application to Scotland of any provision to which
this section applies and which requires notice to be served on
the owners, lessees or occupiers of any land, that requirement
shall be deemed to be complied with if notice is served on all the
persons appearing from the valuation roll to have an interest in
the land, and any reference in this Part of this Act to " owners ",
" lessees " or " occupiers " shall be construed accordingly.

(6) Service of a notice under subsection (5) above on any
person appearing from the valuation roll to have an interest in
land may be effected by sending the notice either—

(*a*) in a registered letter addressed to him at his address as
entered in that roll ; or

(*b*) by the recorded delivery service to him at that address.

(7) This section applies to any provision of this Part of this
Act except section 42 above and so much of section 50 above as
relates to the service of a notice under the said section 50 otherwise than by the Secretary of State.

(8) In this section " owner "—

(*a*) in relation to any land in England and Wales, means a
person, other than a mortgagee not in possession, who
is for the time being entitled to dispose of the fee
simple of the land, whether in possession or in reversion,
and includes also a person holding or entitled to the
rents and profits under a lease or agreement, the unexpired term whereof exceeds three years ;

(*b*) in relation to any land in Scotland or Northern Ireland,
includes any person who under the Lands Clauses Acts
would be enabled to sell and convey the land to the
promotors of an undertaking and includes also a
lessee under a lease the unexpired period of which
exceeds three years.

57.—(1) Any two justices of the peace may appoint such Power to
persons as may be nominated for the purpose by the Secretary appoint
of State to be special constables on any premises for the time special
being vested in or under the control of the Secretary of State. constables.

(2) Every person so appointed shall be sworn in by the justices duly to execute the office of a constable on those premises and when so sworn in shall, on those premises, have the powers and privileges and be liable to the duties and responsibilities of a constable.

(3) Special constables appointed under this section shall be under the exclusive control of the Secretary of State, and the Secretary of State shall have power to suspend or terminate the appointment of any such special constable.

(4) In the application of this section to Scotland references to two justices of the peace shall be construed as references to a single justice of the peace, and references to swearing in shall be construed as references to making a declaration in the terms prescribed under section 16 of the Police (Scotland) Act 1967.

1967 c. 77.

Lost property.

58.—(1) The Secretary of State may by regulations make provision for securing the safe custody and redelivery of any property which, while not in proper custody, is found on any premises belonging to him or under his control or in any aircraft on any such premises ; and any such regulations may in particular—

    (a) provide for requiring charges to be paid in respect of any such property before it is redelivered ; and

    (b) provide for authorising the disposal of any such property if it is not redelivered before the expiration of such period as may be specified in the regulations.

1980 c. 60.

(2) Until the appointed day within the meaning of Part I of the Civil Aviation Act 1980, subsection (1) above shall have effect as if after the word " control " there were inserted the words " or on any premises occupied by the British Airways Board ".

Expenses and stamp duty.

59.—(1) Any expenses incurred by the Department of the Environment for Northern Ireland under this Part of this Act shall, to such extent as the Treasury may direct, be defrayed by the Secretary of State.

(2) Stamp duty shall not be payable on any conveyance of land, or on any instrument creating or disposing of any right in or in relation to land being a conveyance or instrument to which the Secretary of State is a party if he certifies that the duty would fall to be defrayed as part of his expenses and either—

    (a) that the expenses as part of which the duty would fall to be defrayed are his expenses in connection with the performance of his functions relating to civil aviation ; or (*b*) in a case not falling within paragraph (*a*) above of a conveyance of land, that the conveyance is made for the purpose of this Part of this Act.

(3) Stamp duty shall not be payable on any conveyance of land to which the Department of the Environment for Northern Ireland is a party if that Department certifies that the conveyance is made for the purpose of this Part of this Act and that the duty would fall to be defrayed as part of that Department's expenses.

PART III

REGULATION OF CIVIL AVIATION

General

60.—(1) Subject to section 11(7) above, Her Majesty may by Order in Council under this section (in this Act referred to as " an Air Navigation Order ") make such provision as is auth- orised by subsections (2) and (3) below or otherwise by this Act or any other enactment.

Power to give effect to Chicago Convention and to regulate air navigation, etc.

(2) An Air Navigation Order may contain such provision as appears to Her Majesty in Council to be requisite or expedient—

(*a*) for carrying out the Chicago Convention, any Annex thereto relating to international standards and recom- mended practices (being an Annex adopted in accord- ance with the Convention) and any amendment of the Convention or any such Annex made in accordance with the Convention ; or

(*b*) generally for regulating air navigation.

(3) Without prejudice to the generality of subsection (2) above or to any other provision of this Act, an Air Navigation Order may contain provision—

(*a*) as to the registration of aircraft in the United Kingdom ;

(*b*) for prohibiting aircraft from flying unless certificates of airworthiness issued or validated under the Order are in force with respect to them and except upon com- pliance with such conditions as to maintenance or repair as may be specified in the Order ;

(*c*) for the licensing, inspection and regulation of aero- dromes, for access to aerodromes and places where aircraft have landed, for access to aircraft factories for the purpose of inspecting work therein carried on in relation to aircraft or parts thereof and for prohibiting or regulating the use of unlicensed aerodromes ;

(d) for prohibiting persons from engaging in, or being employed in or (except in the maintenance at unlicensed aerodromes of aircraft not used for or in connection with commercial, industrial or other gainful purposes) in connection with, air navigation in such capacities as may be specified in the Order except in accordance with provisions in that behalf contained in the Order, and for the licensing of those employed at aerodromes licensed under the Order in the inspection or supervision of aircraft ;

(e) as to the conditions under which, and in particular the aerodromes to or from which, aircraft entering or leaving the United Kingdom may fly, and as to the conditions under which aircraft may fly from one part of the United Kingdom to another ;

(f) as to the conditions under which passengers and goods may be carried by air and under which aircraft may be used for other commercial, industrial or gainful purposes, and for prohibiting the carriage by air of goods of such classes as may be specified in the Order ;

(g) for minimizing or preventing interference with the use or effectiveness of apparatus used in connection with air navigation, and for prohibiting or regulating the use of such apparatus as aforesaid and the display of signs and lights liable to endanger aircraft ;

(h) generally for securing the safety, efficiency and regularity of air navigation and the safety of aircraft and of persons and property carried therein, for preventing aircraft endangering other persons and property and, in particular, for the detention of aircraft for any of the purposes specified in this paragraph ;

(i) for requiring persons engaged in, or employed in or in connection with, air navigation to supply meteorological information for the purposes of air navigation ;

(j) for regulating the making of signals and other communications by or to aircraft and persons carried therein ;

(k) for regulating the use of the civil air ensign and any other ensign established by Her Majesty in Council for purposes connected with air navigation ;

(l) for prohibiting aircraft from flying over such areas in the United Kingdom as may be specified in the Order ;

(*m*) for applying, adapting or modifying the enactments for the time being in force relating to customs or excise in relation to aerodromes and to aircraft and to persons and property carried therein and for preventing smuggling by air, and for permitting in connection with air navigation, subject to such conditions as appear to Her Majesty in Council to be requisite or expedient for the protection of the revenue, the importation of goods into the United Kingdom without payment of duty;

(*n*) as to the manner and conditions of the issue, validation, renewal, extension or variation of any certificate, licence or other document required by the Order (including the examinations and tests to be undergone), and as to the form, custody, production, cancellation, suspension, endorsement and surrender of any such document;

(*o*) for regulating the charges that may be made for the use of, and for services provided at, an aerodrome licensed under the Order or so much of any aerodrome (whether or not so licensed) as consists of buildings or other works maintained by a local authority by virtue of section 30 above at an aerodrome which is not an aerodrome maintained by that authority;

(*p*) for specifying, subject to the consent of the Treasury, the fees to be paid in respect of the issue, validation, renewal, extension or variation of any certificate, licence or other document or the undergoing of any examination or test required by the Order and in respect of any other matters in respect of which it appears to Her Majesty in Council to be expedient for the purpose of the Order to charge fees:

(*q*) for exempting from the provisions of the Order or any of them any aircraft or persons or classes of aircraft or persons;

(*r*) for prohibiting aircraft from taking off or landing in the United Kingdom unless there are in force in respect of those aircraft such certificates of compliance with standards as to noise as may be specified in the Order and except upon compliance with the conditions of those certificates; and

(*s*) for regulating or prohibiting the flight of aircraft over the United Kingdom at speeds in excess of Flight Mach 1.

(4) An Air Navigation Order may make different provision with respect to different classes of aircraft, aerodromes, persons or property and with respect to different circumstances and with

PART III

respect to different parts of the United Kingdom but shall, so far as practicable, be so framed as not to discriminate in like circumstances between aircraft registered in the United Kingdom operated on charter terms by one air transport undertaking and such aircraft so operated by another such undertaking.

(5) The powers conferred by the preceding provisions of this section may be exercised so as to provide for the licensing of any aerodrome in Northern Ireland notwithstanding that the aerodrome is owned or managed by a Northern Ireland department and so as to impose duties on any such department as licensee of any such aerodrome, including duties as to the charges which may be made for the use of, or for services provided at, any such aerodrome.

(6) In this section a reference to goods shall include a reference to mails or animals.

Air
Navigation
Orders etc.:
supplemental.

61.—(1) An Air Navigation Order may, for the purpose of securing compliance with its provisions, provide—

(a) subject to subsection (2) below, for persons to be guilty of offences in such circumstances as may be specified in the Order and to be liable on conviction of those offences to such penalties as may be so specified ; and

(b) in the case of a provision having effect by virtue of paragraph (*l*) of subsection (3) of section 60 above, for the taking of such steps (including firing on aircraft) as may be specified in the Order.

(2) The power conferred by virtue of subsection (1)(a) above shall not include power—

(a) to provide for offences to be triable only on indictment ;

(b) to authorise the imposition, on summary conviction of any offence, of any term of imprisonment or of a fine exceeding the statutory maximum ;

(c) to authorise the imposition, on conviction on indictment of an offence, of a term of imprisonment exceeding two years.

1980 c. 43.
S.I. 1981/1675
(N.I. 26).

(3) Without prejudice to section 127(2) of the Magistrates' Courts Act 1980 or to Article 19(2) of the Magistrates' Courts (Northern Ireland) Order 1981 (no time limit for offences triable either way), summary proceedings for an offence against an Air Navigation Order, or any regulations made by virtue of such an Order, may be instituted at any time within twelve months from the commission of the offence if—

(a) it was committed in connection with the flight of an aircraft in the course of which an accident occurred ; **and** (*b*) not more than six months after the commission of the offence—

 (i) public notice has been given that an investigation into the accident is being carried out in accordance with regulations under section 75 below ; or

 (ii) the Secretary of State (acting alone or with any government department) has directed that a public inquiry into the accident be held in accordance with those regulations.

(4) In subsection (3) above " accident " has the same meaning as it has for the time being for the purposes of section 75 below ; and for the purposes of that subsection, the flight of an aircraft shall be deemed to include any period from the moment when the power is applied for the purpose of the aircraft taking off on a flight until the moment when the landing run (if any) at the termination of that flight ends.

(5) The fact that any such direction as is mentioned in subsection (3)(*b*)(ii) above has been given on any date may be proved by the production of a certificate to that effect purporting to be signed by an officer of the Secretary of State.

(6) The Secretary of State may, after consultation with any local authority which appears to him to be concerned, by order repeal any enactment in a local Act which appears to him to be unnecessary having regard to the provisions of paragraph (*o*) of subsection (3) of section 60 above in relation to so much of an aerodrome as consists of buildings or other works maintained as mentioned in that paragraph or to be inconsistent with those provisions.

(7) There shall be paid out of moneys provided by Parliament—

(*a*) any sums payable by Her Majesty's Government in the United Kingdom by way of contribution to the expenses of the International Civil Aviation Organisation under the Chicago Convention ;

(*b*) such expenses of any delegate, representative or nominee of Her Majesty's Government in the United Kingdom appointed for any purposes connected with the Chicago Convention as may be approved by the Treasury ; and

(*c*) any expenses incurred by Her Majesty's Government in the United Kingdom for the purposes of Chapter XV of the Chicago Convention (which relates to the provision of airports and other air navigation facilities).

(8) There shall be paid into the Consolidated Fund—

> (*a*) all sums received by Her Majesty's Government in the United Kingdom by way of repayment of expenses incurred for the purposes of the said Chapter XV ; and

> (*b*) all sums received by way of fees paid under an Air Navigation Order.

War and emergencies

Control of aviation in time of war or emergency.

62.—(1) In time of war, whether actual or imminent, or of great national emergency, the Secretary of State—

> (*a*) may by order regulate or prohibit, either absolutely or subject to such conditions as may be contained in the order and notwithstanding the provisions of any enactment relating to civil aviation or any Order in Council or regulations made thereunder, the navigation of all or any descriptions of aircraft over the United Kingdom or any portion thereof or over any area of sea specified in the order ; and

> (*b*) may by order provide for taking possession of and using for the purposes of Her Majesty's naval, military or air forces any aerodrome, or any aircraft, machinery, plant, material or things found therein or thereon, and for regulating or prohibiting the use, erection, building, maintenance or establishment of any aerodrome, or flying school, or any class or description thereof.

(2) An order under this section may make, for the purposes of the order, such provision as an Air Navigation Order may make by virtue of subsection (1) of section 61 above for the purpose of securing compliance with provisions thereof having effect by virtue of paragraph (*l*) of subsection (3) of section 60 above.

(3) Any person who suffers direct injury or loss, owing to the operation of an order of the Secretary of State under this section, shall be entitled to receive compensation from the Secretary of State, the amount thereof to be fixed in default of agreement by the Lands Tribunal.

(4) The principles of the Land Compensation Act shall, with the necessary modifications, apply for the purpose of subsection (3) above where possession is taken of any land ; but no compensation shall be payable by reason of the operation of a general order under this section prohibiting flying in the United Kingdom or any part thereof or over any area of sea.

Control of CAA and air transport undertakings in time of war or emergency.

63.—(1) In time of war, whether actual or imminent, or of great national emergency, the Secretary of State may by order require that—

> (*a*) all or any property or rights of or under the control of the CAA,

(*b*) the whole or any part of the relevant undertaking of any British air transport business,

(*c*) all or any property or rights of or under the control of any such business which appertain to that under-taking,

shall be placed at the disposal of the Secretary of State.

(2) References in this section to a British air transport busi-ness are references to any person or body appearing to the Secretary of State to have his or its principal place of business in the United Kingdom whose business includes the provision of commercial air transport services ; and in relation to any such business " the relevant undertaking " in subsection (1)(*b*) above means that part of its undertaking which consists of the provision of commercial air transport services.

In this subsection " commercial air transport services " means services for the carriage by air of passengers or cargo for hire or reward.

(3) While an order under this section is in force with respect to the CAA—

(*a*) the Secretary of State may give the CAA such directions as he thinks fit ; and

(*b*) in so far as any directions given in pursuance of this subsection conflict with the requirements of any enact-ment or instrument relating to the CAA, apart from the preceding provisions of this section, those requirements shall be disregarded.

(4) While an order under this section is in force with respect to any British air transport business, the Secretary of State may give to the persons managing that business such directions as he thinks fit for conducting, managing or dealing with any part of its undertaking, or any property or rights, placed at his disposal by virtue of the order ; and it shall be the duty of those persons to comply with those directions.

(5) An order under this section may, for the purpose of securing compliance with its provisions, provide for the impo-sition—

(*a*) on summary conviction of a fine not exceeding the statutory maximum ; and

(*b*) on conviction on indictment of a fine or imprisonment for a term not exceeding two years or both.

(6) Any person who suffers direct injury or loss owing to the operation of an order under this section shall be entitled to receive compensation from the Secretary of State of which the amount shall be fixed, in default of agreement, by the Lands

Tribunal; and the principles of the Land Compensation Act shall, with the necessary modifications, apply where possession is taken of any land.

Air transport, etc.

Restriction of
unlicensed
carriage by air
for reward.

64.—(1) No aircraft shall be used for the carriage for reward of passengers or cargo on a flight to which this subsection applies unless—

> (a) the operator of the aircraft holds a licence granted to him by the CAA in pursuance of section 65 below (in this Act referred to as an "air transport licence") authorising him to operate aircraft on such flights as the flight in question ; and
>
> (b) the terms of the licence are complied with so far as they relate to that flight and fall to be complied with before or during the flight.

(2) Subsection (1) above applies to any flight in any part of the world by an aircraft registered in the United Kingdom and to any flight beginning or ending in the United Kingdom by an aircraft registered in a relevant overseas territory or an associated state, except that it does not apply to—

> (a) a flight of a description specified in an instrument made by the CAA for the purposes of this paragraph and in force in accordance with subsection (3) below ;
>
> (b) a particular flight or series of flights specified in an instrument made by the CAA for the purposes of this paragraph ;
>
> (c) a flight by an aircraft of which the CAA is the operator.

(3) An instrument made in pursuance of paragraph (a) of subsection (2) above shall not come into force until it is published in the prescribed manner, and it shall be the duty of the CAA forthwith after making an instrument in pursuance of paragraph (b) of that subsection to publish the instrument in the prescribed manner ; and an instrument made in pursuance of paragraph (a) or (b) of that subsection may be revoked or varied by a subsequent instrument made in pursuance of that paragraph.

(4) Where an aircraft is used for the carriage of passengers or cargo in pursuance of an arrangement made between a member of an incorporated or unincorporated body of persons and that body or another member of it, then, if by reason of relationships arising from membership of the body the carriage is not apart from this subsection carriage for reward, it shall be treated for the purposes of this section as carriage for reward.

(5) Where an aircraft is used on a flight in contravention of subsection (1) above or, after an aircraft has been used in pursuance of an air transport licence on a flight to which that

subsection applies, any term of the licence relating to the flight
and falling to be complied with at or after the end of the flight
by the operator of the aircraft or by another person who made
available such accommodation as is mentioned in paragraph (*b*)
of this subsection is contravened, then—

(*a*) if before the flight began the operator of the aircraft
knew or ought to have known that the use of the aircraft on that flight was likely to be in contravention of
that subsection or, as the case may be, that the term
in question was likely to be contravened, he shall be
guilty of an offence under this subsection ; and

(*b*) if any other person, either by negotiating a contract
or otherwise howsoever, made available accommodation for the carriage of passengers or cargo on the
aircraft on the flight when he knew or ought to have
known before the flight began that the accommodation was likely to be provided on an aircraft when
used on a flight in contravention of the said subsection
(1) or, as the case may be, that such a term as the
term in question was likely to be contravened, that
person shall be guilty of an offence under this subsection ;

but a person shall not (except in pursuance of section 99(1)
below or the law relating to persons who aid, abet, counsel or
procure the commission of offences) be guilty of an offence
by virtue of paragraph (*b*) above in consequence of the contravention by another person of a term of a licence.

(6) For the purpose of determining in pursuance of subsection
(5) above whether an offence relating to a flight has been
committed by the operator of the aircraft used on the flight, it is
immaterial that the relevant contravention mentioned in that
subsection occurred outside the United Kingdom if when it
occurred the operator—

(*a*) was a United Kingdom national, or

(*b*) was a body incorporated under the law of any part of
the United Kingdom or the law of a relevant overseas
territory or an associated state, or

(*c*) was a person (other than a United Kingdom national or
such a body) maintaining a place of business in the
United Kingdom ;

and for the purpose of determining in pursuance of
that subsection whether an offence relating to a flight
has been committed by a person who made available such
accommodation as is mentioned in that subsection it is
immaterial that the relevant contravention there mentioned
occurred outside the United Kingdom and that at any relevant
time that person was not a United Kingdom national or such

a body as aforesaid if any part of the negotiations resulting in the making available of the accommodation in question took place, whether by means of the post or otherwise, in the United Kingdom.

(7) Where the CAA has reason to believe that an aircraft is intended to be used in contravention of subsection (1) above on a particular flight beginning in the United Kingdom or that any term of an air transport licence relating to such a flight and falling to be complied with at or after the end of the flight may not be complied with, the CAA may—

> (a) give to the person appearing to it to be in command of the aircraft a direction that he shall not permit the aircraft to take off until it has informed him that the direction is cancelled ;
>
> (b) whether or not it has given such a direction, detain the aircraft until it is satisfied that the aircraft will not be used on the flight in contravention of the said subsection (1) or, as the case may be, that the term aforesaid will be complied with ;

and a person who fails to comply with a direction given to him in pursuance of this subsection shall be guilty of an offence under this subsection.

(8) A person guilty of an offence under subsection (5) or (7) above shall be liable—

> (a) on summary conviction, to a fine not exceeding the statutory maximum ; and
>
> (b) on conviction on indictment, to a fine or to imprisonment for a term not exceeding two years or to both.

Grant and refusal of air transport licences.

65.—(1) An application for the grant of an air transport licence must be made in writing to the CAA and contain such particulars with respect to such matters as the CAA may specify in a notice published in the prescribed manner ; and where an application is made for the grant of an air transport licence the CAA shall either grant a licence to the applicant in the terms requested in the application or in those terms with such modifications as the CAA thinks fit or refuse to grant a licence.

(2) The CAA shall refuse to grant an air transport licence in pursuance of an application if it is not satisfied that—

> (a) the applicant is, having regard to—
>
>> (i) his and his employees' experience in the field of aviation and his and their past activities generally, and
>>
>> (ii) where the applicant is a body corporate, the experience in the field of aviation and the past activities generally of the persons appearing to the CAA to control that body,

a fit person to operate aircraft under the authority of the licence which, apart from this subsection, the CAA considers should be granted to him in pursuance of the application ; or

(*b*) the resources of the applicant and the financial arrangements made by him are adequate for discharging his actual and potential obligations in respect of the business activities in which he is engaged (if any) and in which he may be expected to engage if he is granted the licence which, apart from this subsection, the CAA considers should be granted to him in pursuance of the application.

(3) If the CAA is not satisfied that an applicant for an air transport licence is—

(*a*) a United Kingdom national ; or

(*b*) a body which is incorporated under the law of any part of the United Kingdom or the law of a relevant overseas territory or an associated state and is controlled by United Kingdom nationals,

it shall refuse to grant a licence in pursuance of his application unless the Secretary of State consents to the grant of the licence ; and where the CAA proposes to refuse to grant a licence by reason only of the preceding provisions of this subsection it shall be the duty of the CAA to give the Secretary of State notice of the proposal and to postpone its decision on the application until the Secretary of State's consent is given or refused.

(4) Nothing in the provisions of subsections (2) and (3) above shall be construed as prejudicing the CAA's power in its discretion to refuse an air transport licence otherwise than in pursuance of any of those provisions.

(5) An air transport licence may contain such terms as the CAA thinks fit ; and (without prejudice to the generality of the CAA's power to decide those terms) the terms may—

(*a*) be or include terms settled by a person other than the CAA and include provision for any of the terms to have effect with such modifications as the CAA or another person may from time to time determine ; and

(*b*) include terms as to the charges which are to be made and the goods, services and other benefits which are and are not to be furnished by any person whatsoever under or in connection with any contract which includes provision for the making available of accommodation on flights to which the licence relates.

(6) If the holder of a current air transport licence applies for the grant of another air transport licence in continuation of or in substitution for the current licence and does so not later than

such time before the expiration of the term of the current licence as the CAA may specify in a notice published in the prescribed manner, then, unless the application is withdrawn and without prejudice to the CAA's power to revoke, suspend or vary the current licence, the current licence shall not cease to be in force by reason only of the expiration of that term—

> (a) until the CAA gives its decision on the application;
>
> (b) if in pursuance of the application the CAA decides to refuse a licence or to grant a licence otherwise than in the terms requested in the application, until the expiration of the time during which an appeal to the Secretary of State against the decision may be brought in pursuance of regulations made by virtue of section 67(5) below and, if such an appeal is brought, until the appeal is determined or abandoned;
>
> (c) if such an appeal against a decision to refuse a licence or to grant one otherwise than in the terms aforesaid is successful, until the date when the licence granted in consequence of the appeal comes into force.

(7) A notice published in pursuance of subsection (1) or subsection (6) above may be altered or cancelled by subsequent notice published in pursuance of that subsection.

Revocation, suspension and variation of air transport licences.
66.—(1) An application for the revocation, suspension or variation of an air transport licence may be made to the CAA at any time by a person of a prescribed description.

(2) The CAA may at any time revoke, suspend or vary an air transport licence if it considers it appropriate to do so, whether or not an application with respect to the licence has been made in pursuance of subsection (1) above.

(3) It shall be the duty of the CAA to revoke or suspend or vary an air transport licence (whichever it thinks appropriate in the circumstances) if it is not or is no longer satisfied—

> (a) that the holder of the licence is, having regard to—
>
>> (i) his and his employees' experience in the field of aviation and his and their past activities generally, and
>>
>> (ii) where the holder of the licence is a body corporate, the experience in the field of aviation and the past activities generally of the persons appearing to the CAA to control that body,
>
> a fit person to operate aircraft under the authority of the licence; or
>
> (b) that the resources of the holder of the licence and the financial arrangements made by him are adequate for discharging his actual and potential obligations in

respect of the business activities in which he is engaged ;

and if the CAA has reason to believe that the holder of a licence
is neither a United Kingdom national nor such a body as is
mentioned in paragraph (*b*) of subsection (3) of section 65 above
it shall be the duty of the CAA to inform the Secretary of State
accordingly and, if he so directs, to revoke the licence.

(4) The provisions of subsections (2) and (3) above conferring
on the CAA power to suspend an air transport licence shall be
construed as conferring on the CAA power to provide, by a
notice in writing served in the prescribed manner on the holder
of the licence, that subject to subsection (5) below the licence
shall not be effective during a period specified in the notice ; and
while a licence is ineffective by virtue of such a notice the CAA
may, by a further notice in writing served in the prescribed
manner on the holder of the licence, provide that the licence
shall be effective on and after a date specified in the further
notice, but the further notice shall not prejudice the CAA's
powers to suspend the licence again or to revoke or vary it.

(5) Subject to subsection (6) below, if a licence is revoked,
suspended or varied by the CAA otherwise than on the application of the holder of the licence and otherwise than in consequence of a direction given in pursuance of subsection (3) above,
the revocation, suspension or variation shall not take effect before
the expiration of the period prescribed in pursuance of subsection (5) of section 67 below for the bringing of an appeal
against the CAA's decision nor, if such an appeal is brought
during that period, before the determination or abandonment of
the appeal.

(6) Notwithstanding anything in subsection (5) above, the
CAA may—

(*a*) direct that so much of the variation of a licence as
relates to any tariff provision of the licence,

(*b*) with the consent of the holder of the licence, direct
that so much of the variation of a licence as relates to
any other matter,

shall to a specified extent take effect on a specified day earlier
than is permitted by that subsection.

In this subsection " tariff provision " means, in relation to any
licence, any term of that licence being a term such as is
mentioned in section 65(5)(*b*) above.

67.—(1) Regulations made by the Secretary of State may
make provision as to the circumstances in which an air transport
licence shall or may be transferred or treated as if granted to
a person other than the person to whom it was granted.

Supplementary
provisions
relating to
air transport
licensing.

(2) Where the CAA takes a decision to grant, refuse to grant, vary, suspend or revoke an air transport licence it shall be the duty of the CAA, subject to subsection (3) below, to furnish a statement of its reasons for the decision to the applicant for the licence or, as the case may be, to the holder or former holder of it and to any other person who in accordance with regulations made by the Secretary of State has entered an objection in the case or requested such a statement, so however that no statement of reasons need be furnished in pursuance of this subsection in a case in which—

(a) no such objection has been entered and no such request has been made ; and

(b) the decision is taken in pursuance of, and is in the terms requested in, an application for the grant of a licence or an application by the holder of a licence for the variation, suspension or revocation of it.

(3) If the CAA has reason to believe that the furnishing of a statement of reasons in pursuance of subsection (2) above might be contrary to the interests of national security or might affect adversely the relations of the United Kingdom with any other country or territory, it shall be the duty of the CAA to give notice of the case to the Secretary of State and, if he so directs, to refrain from furnishing the statement in question or to exclude from the statement such matter as is specified in the direction ; and the CAA may—

(a) refrain from furnishing a statement of reasons in pursuance of subsection (2) above to a person (hereafter in this subsection referred to as a " relevant person ") who is an applicant for or holder or former holder of an air transport licence or has in accordance with regulations made by the Secretary of State entered an objection in the case or requested such a statement, or

(b) exclude matter from a statement furnished in pursuance of that subsection to a relevant person,

if the CAA considers it necessary to do so for the purpose of withholding from the relevant person information which in the opinion of the CAA relates to the commercial or financial affairs of another person and cannot be disclosed to the relevant person without disadvantage to the other person which, by comparison with the advantage to the public and the relevant person of its disclosure to him, is unwarranted.

(4) The CAA may publish in such manner as it thinks fit particulars of, and of its reasons for, any decision taken by it with respect to an air transport licence or an application for such a licence.

(5) The Secretary of State shall make regulations—

  (a) conferring on persons of prescribed descriptions a right to appeal to the Secretary of State from any decision of the CAA with respect to or to an application for an air transport licence ;

  (b) authorising the Secretary of State on such an appeal to direct the CAA to reverse or vary the decision in question and in consequence to do or refrain from doing such other things as may be specified in the direction ; and

  (c) containing such provisions as the Secretary of State thinks fit with respect to such an appeal, which (without prejudice to the generality of the preceding provisions of this paragraph) may include provisions as to—

    (i) the time within which an appeal must be brought,

    (ii) the persons in addition to the appellant who are to be parties to an appeal, and

    (iii) the liability of any of the parties in respect of costs or expenses incurred in connection with an appeal ;

and the Secretary of State shall, when considering whether to give a direction in pursuance of regulations made by virtue of paragraph (b) of this subsection and when considering the terms of any such direction, have regard in particular to the duties imposed on the CAA by section 4 above and section 68 below.

(6) A person who, for the purpose of obtaining for himself or another person either an air transport licence or a variation of an air transport licence or the cancellation of the suspension of an air transport licence, knowingly or recklessly furnishes the CAA or the Secretary of State with any information which is false in a material particular shall be guilty of an offence and liable—

  (a) on summary conviction, to a fine not exceeding the statutory maximum ; and

  (b) on conviction on indictment, to a fine or to imprisonment for a term not exceeding two years or to both.

68.—(1) It shall be the duty of the CAA to perform its air transport licensing functions in the manner which it considers is best calculated to ensure that British airlines compete as effectively as possible with other airlines in providing air transport services on international routes ; and in performing those functions the CAA shall also have regard— *General duties in relation to air transpor licensing functions of CAA.*

  (a) to any advice received from the Secretary of State with respect to the likely outcome of negotiations with the government of any other country or territory for the purpose of securing any right required for the operation by a British airline of any air transport services outside the United Kingdom ; and

(b) to the need to secure the most effective use of airports within the United Kingdom.

(2) In considering whether to grant any air transport licence, it shall be the duty of the CAA to have regard to the effect on existing air transport services provided by British airlines of authorising any new services the applicant proposes to provide under the licence, and in any case where those existing services are similar (in terms of route) to the proposed new services or where two or more applicants have applied for licences under which each proposes to provide similar services, the CAA shall have regard in particular to any benefits which may arise from enabling two or more airlines to provide the services in question.

(3) Subject to section 4 above and to subsections (1) and (2) above, it shall be the duty of the CAA in performing its air transport licensing functions to have regard to the need to minimise so far as reasonably practicable—

(a) any adverse effects on the environment, and

(b) any disturbance to the public,

from noise, vibration, atmospheric pollution or any other cause attributable to the use of aircraft for the purpose of civil aviation.

(4) In addition to the duties with respect to particular matters imposed on the CAA by the preceding provisions of this section, it shall be the duty of the CAA to perform its air transport licensing functions in the manner which it considers is best calculated to impose on the civil air transport industry of the United Kingdom and on the services it provides for users of air transport services the minimum restrictions consistent with the performance by the CAA of its duties under sections 4, 65 and 66 above and the preceding provisions of this section.

(5) In this section—

(a) references to the air transport licensing functions of the CAA are references to its functions under sections 64 to 66 above and any functions conferred on it by regulations made under subsection (1) of section 67 above ; and

(b) " British airline " has the same meaning as in section 4(1) above.

69.—(1) It shall be the duty of the CAA to publish from time to time a statement of the policies it intends to adopt in performing its functions under sections 64 to 68 above.

(2) If the Secretary of State considers it appropriate to do so, he may by notice in writing require the CAA to publish a statement of the policy it intends to adopt with respect to any particular matter in performing the functions mentioned in subsection (1) above (or any of them) ; and it shall be the duty of the CAA to publish any statement required by a notice under this subsection within six months of the date of the notice.

(3) Before publishing any statement under this section the CAA shall consult such persons as appear to it to be representative respectively—

    (a) of the civil air transport industry of the United Kingdom ; and

    (b) of users of air transport services.

(4) The manner of publication of any statement under this section shall be as the CAA may determine.

70. In the application of sections 4(1) and 68(1) and (2) above in relation to the performance by the CAA of its functions under sections 64 to 68 above with respect to authorising the operation of aircraft on flights—

Modification
of CAA's
duties with
respect to
British airlines
in relation to
certain air
transport
services.

    (a) between the United Kingdom and any relevant overseas territory other than the Channel Islands or the Isle of Man, or

    (b) between the United Kingdom and any associated state,

the CAA shall treat any undertaking appearing to the CAA to have its principal place of business in that territory or state as a British airline if it would fall to be so treated but for the situation of its principal place of business.

71.—(1) Provision may be made by regulations made by the Secretary of State for securing that a person does not in the United Kingdom—

    (a) make available, as a principal or an agent, accommodation for the carriage of persons or cargo on flights in any part of the world, or (*b*) hold himself out as a person who, either as a principal or an agent or without disclosing his capacity, may make such accommodation available,

unless he is the operator of the relevant aircraft or holds and complies with the terms of a licence issued in pursuance of the regulations or is exempted by or under the regulations from the need to hold such a licence.

(2) Regulations made by the Secretary of State for the purposes of subsection (1) above may contain such provisions as the Secretary of State, after consultation with the CAA, considers appropriate for those purposes and may, without prejudice to the generality of the preceding provisions of this subsection, include provision—

(*a*) as to the circumstances in which licences shall or shall not be issued in pursuance of the regulations;

(*b*) as to the terms of licences, which may include terms as to the minimum charges which are to be made and the goods, services and other benefits which are or are not to be furnished by any person whatsoever under or in connection with any contract which includes provision for the making available of accommodation on flights to which the licences in question relate;

(*c*) for the variation, suspension and revocation of licences;

(*d*) for appeals against refusals, variations, suspensions or revocations of licences to lie to a prescribed body or person (which may be a court, a Minister of the Crown, a body or person constituted or appointed by or under the regulations or such other body or person as the Secretary of State thinks fit) and for applying the provisions of any enactment, with or without modifications, in relation to such appeals;

(*e*) for imposing penalties for contraventions of the regulations not exceeding in the case of each contravention a fine of the statutory maximum on summary conviction and a fine and imprisonment for a term not exceeding two years on conviction on indictment;

(*f*) for repealing, either wholly or in relation to prescribed cases, so much of subsection (5) of section 64 of this Act as begins with the word " and " at the end of paragraph (*a*) and in subsection (6) of that section the words from " and for the purpose " onwards.

Air navigation services

Duty of CAA to provide air navigation services.

72.—(1) It shall be the duty of the CAA to provide air navigation services—

(*a*) in the United Kingdom, and

(b) for any area outside the United Kingdom for which the United Kingdom has, in pursuance of international arrangements, undertaken to provide air navigation services,

to the extent to which it appears to the CAA that such services are necessary and are not being provided by it (either alone or jointly with another person) or by some other person.

(2) It shall be the duty of the CAA to join with the Secretary of State, in such manner as may be specified in directions given to the CAA by the Secretary of State—

(a) in providing such air navigation services in respect of such areas (whether in the United Kingdom or elsewhere) as may be specified in the directions ; and

(b) in defraying the cost of providing the services so specified ; and

(c) without prejudice to the generality of paragraph (b) above, in discharging any liability to a third party which is incurred by the CAA and the Secretary of State or either of them in providing the services so specified.

(3) Without prejudice to any right of action in respect of an act or omission which takes place in the course of providing air navigation services in pursuance of this section, no action shall lie in respect of a failure by the CAA to perform the duty imposed on it by subsection (1) or (2) above.

73.—(1) The Secretary of State may make regulations— Charges for air navigation services etc.

(a) for requiring the payment to him or the CAA or Eurocontrol of charges, of such amounts and in such currencies as may be prescribed, in respect of air navigation services which, either in pursuance of international arrangements or otherwise, are provided for aircraft by him, the CAA, Eurocontrol or any other person or by any persons jointly ;

(b) for requiring the payment to any international organisation other than Eurocontrol or to any government outside the United Kingdom of charges of such amounts as may be prescribed in respect of air navigation services provided for aircraft, being services provided by that international organisation or government, as the case may be, in pursuance of an agreement to which the United Kingdom is a party.

(2) The Secretary of State may make regulations—

(a) providing for the payment of an annual charge of such amount as may be prescribed to the CAA in respect of any aircraft for which there is in force at the time the charge becomes payable a certificate of airworthiness ; and

    (*b*) requiring the CAA to refund so much of any such payment made in respect of an aircraft by any person as is equal to the amount which that person becomes liable (whether by virtue of regulations under this section or otherwise) to pay to Eurocontrol in respect of so much of any flight made by that aircraft as is made over the United Kingdom during the period of twelve months commencing with the date on which the payment to the CAA became due.

(3) The liability for any charges payable by virtue of regulations under subsection (1) above may be imposed upon the operators or owners of aircraft for which the air navigation services in question are available (whether or not they are actually used or could be used with the equipment installed in the aircraft) or upon those operators and owners or upon the managers of aerodromes used by such aircraft, or partly upon those operators or owners or operators and owners and partly upon those managers.

(4) Regulations under subsection (1) above may provide for charges payable by virtue of the regulations to be so payable elsewhere than in the United Kingdom and to be recoverable in the United Kingdom wherever they are payable (without prejudice to their recovery elsewhere) ; and liability for any charges payable by virtue of regulations under that subsection may be imposed upon the operator of any aircraft whether or not it is registered in the United Kingdom, whether or not it is in or over the United Kingdom at the time when the services to which the charges relate are provided and whether or not those services are provided from a place in the United Kingdom.

(5) Regulations under subsection (2) above may—

    (*a*) impose liability for any charges payable by virtue of the regulations upon the operators or owners of the aircraft in respect of which the charge is payable ; and

    (*b*) impose that liability whether or not the aircraft is registered in the United Kingdom and whether or not it is in the United Kingdom during the year in respect of which the charge is payable.

(6) The charges to be prescribed under this section shall—

    (*a*) in the case of charges payable to the Secretary of State or the CAA, be at such rates or of such amounts as the Secretary of State may, with the consent of the Treasury, determine ;

(b) in the case of charges payable to Eurocontrol, be at
such rates as the Secretary of State may determine in
pursuance of tariffs which are either—

(i) approved under any international agreement to
which the United Kingdom is a party ; or

(ii) in the opinion of the Secretary of State likely
to be approved before or within one month after
the date when the regulations come into force, under
any international agreement to which the United
Kingdom is likely to be party before or within one
month after that date ;

(c) in the case of charges payable to an international
organisation other than Eurocontrol or to a government
outside the United Kingdom, be at such rates as the
Secretary of State may determine in pursuance of tariffs
which are either—

(i) approved under the relevant international
agreement with the United Kingdom ; or

(ii) in the opinion of the Secretary of State likely
to be approved under that agreement before or
within one month after the date when the regulations come into force ;

and the regulations may prescribe different charges in respect
of aircraft of different classes or descriptions or in respect of
aircraft used in different circumstances, may provide for the
payment, with any charges or separately, of interest on the
charges in respect of any period during which the charges were
due but unpaid and may dispense with charges in such cases
as may be prescribed by or determined under the regulations.

(7) For the purpose of facilitating the assessment and collection of charges payable by virtue of regulations under this
section, the regulations may make provision for requiring
operators of aircraft or managers of aerodromes—

(a) to make such records of the movements of aircraft, and
of such other particulars relating to aircraft, as may
be prescribed, and to preserve those records for such
period as may be prescribed ;

(b) to produce for inspection at such times as may be
prescribed and—

(i) in the case of charges payable by virtue of
regulations made under subsection (1)(a) or (2) above,
by such officers of the Secretary of State or of the
CAA or of Eurocontrol as may be prescribed, and

(ii) in the case of charges payable by virtue of
regulations made under subsection (1)(b) above, by
such officers of the international organisation or

government, as the case may be, to whom the charges are payable or of the Secretary of State or of the CAA as may be prescribed,

any records which are required by the regulations or an Air Navigation Order to be preserved by those operators or managers ;

(c) to furnish such particulars of any such records as may be prescribed—

(i) in the case of charges payable by virtue of regulations made under subsection (1)(a) or (2) above, to the Secretary of State or to the CAA or to Eurocontrol ; and

(ii) in the case of charges payable by virtue of regulations made under subsection (1)(b) above, to the international organisation or government, as the case may be, to whom the charges are payable or to the Secretary of State or the CAA.

(8) The requirements mentioned in subsection (7) above may be imposed upon the operator of any aircraft whether or not it is registered in the United Kingdom, whether or not it is in or over the United Kingdom at the time when the services to which the charges relate are provided and whether or not those services are provided from a place in the United Kingdom.

(9) Regulations under this section may contain provision for regulating the disposal by the CAA of sums received by it by virtue of the regulations.

(10) In this section—

" manager ", in relation to an aerodrome, means a person who is in charge of it or holds a licence granted in respect of it by virtue of section 60 above ;

" record " includes, in addition to a record in writing—

(a) any disc, tape, sound-track or other device in which sounds or signals are embodied so as to be capable (with or without the aid of some other instrument) of being reproduced therefrom ;

(b) any film, tape or other device in which visual images are embodied so as to be capable (as aforesaid) of being reproduced therefrom ; and

(c) any photograph ;

and any reference to a copy of a record includes in the case of a record falling within paragraph (a) only of this definition, a transcript of the sounds or signals embodied therein, in the case of a record falling within paragraph (b) only of this definition, a still reproduction

of the images embodied therein, and in the case of a
record falling within both those paragraphs, such a
transcript together with such a still reproduction.

74.—(1) Any person who, without reasonable cause, fails to
comply with any requirement of regulations made by virtue of
subsection (7) of section 73 above shall be liable on summary
conviction to a fine not exceeding £100.

(2) Any person who, being in possession of information furnished to or obtained by him in pursuance of regulations under
the said subsection (7), discloses that information otherwise
than—

(*a*) with the consent of the person by whom it was furnished
or from whom it was obtained, or

(*b*) for the purposes of the regulations, or

(*c*) for the purposes of any proceedings arising out of section
73 above, of proceedings brought by virtue of paragraph 3 of Schedule 4 to this Act or of any criminal
proceedings whether or not arising out of this Act, or

(*d*) for the purposes of any public inquiry or Inspector's
investigation held or carried out in pursuance of regulations made under section 75 below, or

(*e*) for the purpose of any report of any such proceedings,
inquiry or investigation as aforesaid,

shall be liable on summary conviction to a fine not exceeding
£100 or to imprisonment for a term not exceeding three months
or to both.

(3) Any person who, in furnishing in pursuance of such regulations any such particulars as are described in paragraph (*c*) of
the said subsection (7), furnishes any particulars which to his
knowledge are false in any material particular, or recklessly
furnishes any particulars which are false in any material particular, shall be liable—

(*a*) on summary conviction, to a fine not exceeding the
statutory maximum or to imprisonment for a term not
exceeding three months or to both ; and

(*b*) on conviction on indictment, to a fine or to imprisonment for a term not exceeding two years or to both.

(4) Without prejudice to paragraph 4 of Part III of Schedule
13 to this Act, regulations under section 73 above may make
provision—

(*a*) in the case of default in the payment of any charge
payable by an operator under the regulations, for authorising the detention, pending payment, of the aircraft

in respect of which the charge was incurred or of any other aircraft of which the person in default is the operator at the time when the detention begins ;

(b) in the case of default in complying with any requirement imposed by the regulations on the operators of aircraft with respect to the production for inspection, or the furnishing of particulars, of any records, for authorising the detention, pending compliance, of any aircraft of which the person in default is the operator at the time when the detention begins ;

and such regulations may make such further provision as appears to the Secretary of State to be necessary or expedient for securing such detention.

(5) Regulations in pursuance of subsection (4) above may make, in relation to aircraft detained for non-payment of any charge payable by virtue of regulations under section 73 above, provision corresponding to any provision made by or under section 88 below.

(6) A court in any part of the United Kingdom shall have jurisdiction to hear and determine a claim for charges or interest payable to the Secretary of State or the CAA or Eurocontrol by virtue of regulations under section 73 above, notwithstanding that the person against whom the claim is made is not resident within the jurisdiction of the court.

(7) In this section " record " has the same meaning as in section 73 above.

Investigation of accidents

Investigation of accidents.

75.—(1) Without predudice to section 60 above, the Secretary of State may by regulations under this section make such provision as appears to him to be requisite or expedient—

(a) for the investigation of any accident arising out of or in the course of air navigation and either occurring in or over the United Kingdom or occurring elsewhere to aircraft registered in the United Kingdom ; and

(b) for carrying out any Annex to the Chicago Convention (being an Annex adopted in accordance with the Convention and relating to the investigation of accidents involving aircraft) as it has effect from time to time with anv amendment made in accordance with the Convention (hereafter in this section referred to as " the Annex ").

(2) Without prejudice to the generality of subsection (1)(*b*) above, the provision there authorised includes provision with respect to any of the following matters, that is to say—

(*a*) the definition of "accident" for the purposes of this section so as to correspond to the meaning adopted for the time being in the Annex ;

(*b*) the participation of any persons authorised for the purpose in accordance with the regulations in any investigation held in accordance with the requirements of the Annex by the competent authorities of any other state ; and

(*c*) the investigation of any accident other than one to which subsection (1)(*a*) above applies for the purpose of securing any information, articles or other material which it is the duty of the United Kingdom in accordance with any requirements of the Annex to furnish to any other state.

(3) Without prejudice to the generality of subsection (1) above, regulations under this section may contain provisions—

(*a*) requiring notice to be given of any such accident as is mentioned in subsection (1)(*a*) above in such manner and by such persons as may be specified in the regulations ;

(*b*) applying any of the provisions of section 3 of the Notice 1894 c. 28. of Accidents Act 1894 (with or without modifications) for the purposes of any investigations held in accordance with the regulations or any inquiries undertaken in accordance with the regulations with a view to determining whether any such investigation should be held ;

(*c*) prohibiting, pending investigation, access to or interference with aircraft to which an accident has occurred, and authorising any person so far as may be necessary for the purposes of an investigation, or for the purpose of determining whether an investigation should be held, to have access to, examine, remove, test, take measures for the preservation of, or otherwise deal with, any such aircraft and any other aircraft ;

(*d*) authorising or requiring the cancellation, suspension, endorsement or surrender of any licence or certificate granted under an Air Navigation Order or an order under section 62 above where it appears on an investigation that the licence or certificate ought to be cancelled, suspended, endorsed or surrendered and requiring the production of any such licence or certificate for the purpose of being so dealt with.

(4) Without prejudice to subsection (2)(*a*) above, in this section " accident " shall be construed as including any fortuitous or unexpected event by which the safety of an aircraft or any person is threatened.

(5) If any person contravenes or fails to comply with any regulations under this section he shall be liable on summary conviction to a fine not exceeding £1,000 or to imprisonment for a term not exceeding three months.

(6) Nothing in this section shall limit the powers of any authority under sections 530 to 537 of the Merchant Shipping Act 1894 or any enactment amending those sections.

Trespass by aircraft and aircraft nuisance, noise, etc.

76.—(1) No action shall lie in respect of trespass or in respect of nuisance, by reason only of the flight of an aircraft over any property at a height above the ground which, having regard to wind, weather and all the circumstances of the case is reasonable, or the ordinary incidents of such flight, so long as the provisions of any Air Navigation Order and of any orders under section 62 above have been duly complied with and there has been no breach of section 81 below.

(2) Subject to subsection (3) below, where material loss or damage is caused to any person or property on land or water by, or by a person in, or an article, animal or person falling from, an aircraft while in flight, taking off or landing, then unless the loss or damage was caused or contributed to by the negligence of the person by whom it was suffered, damages in respect of the loss or damage shall be recoverable without proof of negligence or intention or other cause of action, as if the loss or damage had been caused by the wilful act, neglect, or default of the owner of the aircraft.

(3) Where material loss or damage is caused as aforesaid in circumstances in which—

(*a*) damages are recoverable in respect of the said loss or damage by virtue only of subsection (2) above, and

(*b*) a legal liability is created in some person other than the owner to pay damages in respect of the said loss or damage,

the owner shall be entitled to be indemnified by that other person against any claim in respect of the said loss or damage.

(4) Where the aircraft concerned has been bona fide demised, let or hired out for any period exceeding fourteen days to any other person by the owner thereof, and no pilot, commander, navigator or operative member of the crew of the aircraft is in the employment of the owner, this section shall have effect as if

for references to the owner there were substituted references to
the person to whom the aircraft has been so demised, let or
hired out.

77.—(1) An Air Navigation Order may provide for regulating Nuisance
the conditions under which noise and vibration may be caused caused by
by aircraft on aerodromes and may provide that subsection (2) aircraft on
below shall apply to any aerodrome as respects which provision aerodromes.
as to noise and vibration caused by aircraft is so made.

(2) No action shall lie in respect of nuisance by reason only
of the noise and vibration caused by aircraft on an aerodrome
to which this subsection applies by virtue of an Air Navigation
Order, as long as the provisions of any such Order are duly
complied with.

78.—(1) The Secretary of State may by a notice published in Regulation
the prescribed manner provide that it shall be the duty of the of noise and
person who is the operator of an aircraft which is to take off or vibration
land at a designated aerodrome to secure that, after the aircraft from aircraft.
takes off or, as the case may be, before it lands at the aerodrome,
such requirements as are specified in the notice are complied with
in relation to the aircraft, being requirements appearing to the
Secretary of State to be appropriate for the purpose of limiting
or of mitigating the effect of noise and vibration connected with
the taking off or landing of aircraft at the aerodrome.

(2) If it appears to the Secretary of State that any requirement
specified in relation to a designated aerodrome in a notice published in pursuance of subsection (1) above has not been complied
with as respects any aircraft he may, after affording to the person
who at the relevant time was the operator of the aircraft an
opportunity of making representations to him with respect to the
matter and after considering any representations then made
by that person, give to the person managing the aerodrome a
direction requiring him to secure that, until the Secretary of
State revokes the direction, facilities for using the aerodrome are
withheld to the extent specified in the direction from aircraft of
which the person aforesaid is the operator and from his servants ;
and it shall be the duty of the person for the time being managing the aerodrome to comply with the direction.

(3) If the Secretary of State considers it appropriate, for the
purpose of avoiding, limiting or mitigating the effect of noise and
vibration connected with the taking-off or landing of aircraft at
a designated aerodrome, to prohibit aircraft from taking off or
landing, or limit the number of occasions on which they may
take off or land, at the aerodrome during certain periods, he may

PART III   by a notice published in the prescribed manner do all or any of
the following, that is to say—

    (a) prohibit aircraft of descriptions specified in the notice
from taking off or landing at the aerodrome (otherwise
than in an emergency of a description so specified)
during periods so specified;

    (b) specify the maximum number of occasions on which
aircraft of descriptions so specified may be permitted to
take off or land at the aerodrome (otherwise than as
aforesaid) during periods so specified;

    (c) determine the persons who shall be entitled to arrange
for aircraft of which they are the operators to take off
or land at the aerodrome during the periods specified
under paragraph (b) above and, as respects each of
those persons, the number of occasions on which aircraft of a particular description of which he is the
operator may take off or land at the aerodrome during
those periods;

and subject to subsection (4) below and paragraphs (e) and (f) of
subsection (5) below it shall be the duty of the person for the
time being managing the aerodrome to secure that the prohibitions or restrictions relating to the aerodrome which are imposed
by the notice are complied with.

(4) Without prejudice to subsection (5)(f) below, a particular
occasion or series of occasions on which aircraft take off or land
at an aerodrome shall be disregarded for the purposes of any
notice under subsection (3) above in respect of that aerodrome
if—

    (a) on that occasion or series of occasions the aircraft take
off or land in circumstances specified for the purposes
of this subsection in relation to that aerodrome by the
Secretary of State in a notice published in the prescribed manner; and

    (b) the person for the time being managing the aerodrome
or a person authorised by him for the purpose, determines that that occasion or series of occasions should
be so disregarded,

but it shall be the duty of the first-mentioned person to notify
the Secretary of State in writing, within one week from its
occurring, of any occasion (whether a single occasion or one
of a series of occasions) to which this subsection applies.

(5) The following supplementary provisions shall have effect
for the purposes of subsection (3) above, that is to say—

    (a) it shall be the duty of the Secretary of State, before he
makes a determination in respect of an aerodrome in
pursuance of paragraph (c) of that subsection, to

consult any body appearing to him to be representative
of operators of aircraft using the aerodrome ;

(*b*) a notice under that subsection may make, in relation to
a designated aerodrome, provision as respects any
period notwithstanding that the period is included in
or that there is included in the period, any other period
as respects which provision relating to the aerodrome
is made by the notice or by another notice under that
subsection ;

(*c*) if it appears to the Secretary of State that an aircraft
is about to take off in contravention of any prohibition
or restriction imposed in pursuance of that subsection,
then, without prejudice to the powers exercisable by
virtue of that subsection by the person managing the
relevant aerodrome, any person authorised by the Secretary of State for the purpose may detain the aircraft
for such period as that person considers appropriate
for preventing the contravention and may, for the purpose of detaining the aircraft, enter upon any land ;

(*d*) if it appears to a person authorised for the purpose
by the person for the time being managing the relevant
aerodrome that an aircraft is about to take off in contravention of any prohibition or restriction imposed in
pursuance of that subsection, then without prejudice
to paragraph (*c*) above or the powers mentioned
therein, the first-mentioned person, or a person authorised by him for the purpose, may detain the aircraft
for such period as the first-mentioned person considers
appropriate for preventing the contravention and may,
for the purpose of detaining the aircraft, enter upon
any land ;

(*e*) nothing in that subsection requires a person managing
an aerodrome to prevent an aircraft from landing at
the aerodrome ; and

(*f*) the Secretary of State may, by a notice given in the
prescribed manner to the person managing an aerodrome to which a notice under that subsection relates,
determine that a particular occasion or series of occasions on which aircraft take off or land at the aerodrome shall be disregarded for the purposes of the
notice under that subsection.

(6) The Secretary of State may give to the person managing
a designated aerodrome such directions as the Secretary of
State considers appropriate for the purpose of avoiding, limiting, or mitigating the effect of, noise and vibration connected
with the taking-off or landing of aircraft at the aerodrome ; and

it shall be the duty of the person for the time being managing the aerodrome to comply with the directions.

(7) The duties imposed by subsections (1) to (3) and (6) above in relation to aerodromes in Scotland shall be enforceable by order of the Court of Session on an application by or on behalf of the Secretary of State under section 91 of the Court of Session Act 1868.

(8) The Secretary of State may, after consultation with the person managing a designated aerodrome, by order require him at his own expense—

(*a*) to provide in an area and within a period specified in the order, and to maintain and operate in accordance with any instructions so specified, such equipment for measuring noise in the vicinity of the aerodrome as is so specified ; and

(*b*) to make to the Secretary of State such reports as are so specified with respect to the noise measured by the equipment and to permit any person authorised by the Secretary of State for the purpose to inspect the equipment on demand at any time ;

and it shall be the duty of the person for the time being managing the aerodrome to comply with the requirements of the order.

(9) If a person fails to perform any duty imposed on him by subsection (8) above the Secretary of State may, after affording him an opportunity of making representations to the Secretary of State with respect to the matter and after considering any representations then made by him—

(*a*) take such steps as the Secretary of State considers appropriate for remedying the failure, which may include steps to secure the provision, maintenance and operation of equipment by the Secretary of State or the CAA ; and

(*b*) recover in any court of competent jurisdiction from the person aforesaid any expense attributable to the taking of those steps which is incurred by the Secretary of State from time to time ;

and if a person fails to perform any duty imposed on him by virtue of paragraph (*b*) of subsection (8) above, then without prejudice to the preceding provisions of this subsection he shall—

(i) be guilty of an offence and liable on summary conviction to a fine not exceeding £50 ; and

(ii) if the failure continues after his conviction of an offence under this subsection arising from the failure, be guilty of a separate offence under this subsection on each day on which the failure continues thereafter and liable to be fined accordingly.

(10) Paragraph (*b*) of subsection (9) above is without prejudice to the Secretary of State's power apart from that paragraph to recover the expenses mentioned therein.

(11) The Secretary of State may, after consultation with any local authority appearing to him to be concerned, by order repeal any provision of a local Act which he considers is unnecessary having regard to the provisions of this section and of section 79 below.

(12) Any notice published in pursuance of subsection (1), (3) or (4) above may contain such incidental or supplementary provisions as the Secretary of State considers appropriate for the purposes of that subsection and may be varied or revoked by a subsequent notice published in pursuance of that subsection.

79.—(1) If it appears to the Secretary of State that buildings near a designated aerodrome require protection from noise and vibration attributable to the use of the aerodrome, he may by statutory instrument make a scheme requiring the person for the time being managing the aerodrome (hereafter in this section referred to as " the relevant manager ") to make grants towards the cost of insulating such buildings or parts of such buildings against noise ; but a scheme under this section need apply only to such classes of buildings as the Secretary of State thinks fit. *Grants towards cost of sound-proofing buildings.*

(2) A scheme under this section shall specify the area or areas in which buildings must be situated for the grants to be payable, and the persons to whom, the expenditure in respect of which and the rate at which the grants are to be paid, and may make the payment of any grant dependent upon compliance with such conditions as may be specified in the scheme.

(3) A scheme under this section may require the relevant manager, in any case where an application for a grant is refused, to give the applicant at his request a written statement of the relevant manager's reasons for the refusal.

(4) A scheme under this section may authorise or require local authorities to act as agents of the relevant manager in dealing with applications for and payments of grants and may provide for the making by the relevant manager of payments to local authorities in respect of anything done by them as such agents.

(5) A scheme under this section may make different provision with respect to different areas or different circumstances.

PART III

(6) Before making a scheme under this section relating to an aerodrome the Secretary of State shall consult the relevant manager.

(7) In this section " local authority " in relation to England and Wales does not include the council of a county.

(8) A statutory instrument containing a scheme under this section shall be subject to annulment in pursuance of a resolution of either House of Parliament.

Designation of aerodromes for purposes of ss. 78 and 79.

80. In sections 78 and 79 above " designated aerodrome " means any aerodrome in Great Britain which is designated for the purposes of the section in which the expression is used by an order made by the Secretary of State ; and the Secretary of State may designate an aerodrome for the purposes of either or both of those sections.

Dangerous flying.

81.—(1) Where an aircraft is flown in such a manner as to be the cause of unnecessary danger to any person or property on land or water, the pilot or the person in charge of the aircraft, and also the owner thereof, unless he proves to the satisfaction of the court that the aircraft was so flown without his actual fault or privity, shall be liable on summary conviction to a fine not exceeding £200 or to imprisonment for a term not exceeding six months or to both.

(2) In this section the expression " owner " in relation to an aircraft includes any person by whom the aircraft is hired at the time of the offence.

(3) The provisions of this section shall be in addition to and not in derogation of the powers conferred on Her Majesty in Council by section 60 above.

Prohibition of aerial advertising and propaganda.

82.—(1) Save in such circumstances as may be prescribed, no aircraft while in the air over any part of the United Kingdom shall be used, whether wholly or partly for emitting or displaying any advertisement or other communication in such a way that the advertisement or communication is audible or visible from the ground.

(2) Any person who uses an aircraft, or knowingly causes or permits an aircraft to be used, in contravention of subsection (1) above shall be guilty of an offence and liable on summary conviction—

(a) in the case of a first conviction of an offence under this section, to a fine not exceeding £100 ;

(b) in any other case, to a fine not exceeding £200 or to imprisonment for a term not exceeding three months or to both ;

but (without prejudice to section 105(3) below) a previous con-   PART III
viction of an offence under section 7 of the Civil Aviation 1960 c. 38.
(Licensing) Act 1960 shall be treated as a conviction of an offence under this section for the purposes of determining whether
a conviction of an offence under this section is a first such conviction.

Records and provision of information, etc.

83.—(1) The Secretary of State may by regulations provide Recording and
for requiring such persons as may be specified in the regulations registration of
to keep records and make returns to the CAA—   births and
                                                                deaths, etc.

    (*a*) of births and deaths occurring in any part of the world
        in any aircraft registered in the United Kingdom ; and

    (*b*) of the death, outside the United Kingdom, of any per-
        son who, being a traveller on such an aircraft, is killed
        on the journey in consequence of an accident ;

and for the keeping by the CAA of a record of any returns made
to it in accordance with any such requirement as aforesaid.

(2) Any person who fails to comply with any such requirement
shall be liable on summary conviction to a fine not exceeding
£50.

(3) Proceedings for an offence under this section shall not be
instituted—

    (*a*) in England and Wales, except by or with the consent
        of the Secretary of State or by or with the consent of
        the Director of Public Prosecutions ;

    (*b*) in Northern Ireland, except by or with the consent of
        the Secretary of State or by the Attorney General for
        Northern Ireland.

(4) Where regulations made under subsection (1) above provide for the keeping of records by the CAA in accordance with
that subsection they shall also provide for the transmission of
certified copies of those records to the Registrar General of
Births, Deaths and Marriages in England and Wales, the Registrar General of Births, Deaths and Marriages in Scotland, or
the Registrar General for Northern Ireland, as the case may
require.

(5) The Registrar General to whom any such certified copies
are sent shall cause them to be filed and preserved in a book to
be kept by him for the purpose, and to be called the Air Register
Book of Births and Deaths.

(6) Regulations made under subsection (1) above shall provide
for the rectification of any records kept by the CAA in pursuance
of the regulations and for the transmission of certified copies of
any corrected entry in the records to the Registrar General of
Births, Deaths and Marriages in England and Wales, the

PART III
Registrar General of Births, Deaths and Marriages in Scotland, or the Registrar General for Northern Ireland, as the case may require.

(7) The Registrar General to whom a certified copy of any such corrected entry is sent in accordance with the regulations shall cause the corrected entry to be substituted for the corresponding entry for the time being made in the Air Register Book of Births and Deaths.

(8) The enactments relating to the registration of births and deaths in England and Wales, Scotland and Northern Ireland shall have effect as if the Air Register Book of Births and Deaths were a certified copy or duplicate register transmitted to the Registrar General in accordance with those enactments.

(9) The Secretary of State may by regulations provide—

(a) for the keeping by the CAA of a record of persons reported to him as missing, being persons with respect to whom there are reasonable grounds for believing that they have died in consequence of an accident to an aircraft registered in the United Kingdom;

(b) for the rectification of any such record; and

(c) for the transmission of information as to the matters for the time being entered on the record to the Registrar General of Births, Deaths and Marriages in England and Wales, the Registrar General of Births, Deaths and Marriages in Scotland or the Registrar General for Northern Ireland, as the case may require.

Provision by others of information for the CAA and Secretary of State.
84.—(1) The CAA may, by a notice in writing served in the prescribed manner on a person of any of the following descriptions, that is to say—

(a) a holder of a licence issued by the CAA under this Act or a licence or certificate issued by the CAA under an Air Navigation Order,

(b) a recipient of an approval given by the CAA under an Air Navigation Order,

(c) a person who in the United Kingdom has, at any time during the period of two years ending with the date of service of the notice, held himself out as one who may as a principal or otherwise enter into a contract to make available accommodation for the carriage of persons or cargo on flights in any part of the world in aircraft of which he is not the operator,

(d) a person carrying on business in the United Kingdom as a manufacturer of aircraft or engines or other equipment for aircraft or as an insurer of aircraft,

require him to furnish to the CAA, in such form and at such PART III
times as may be specified in the notice, information of such
descriptions as may be so specified, being—

    (i) in the case of such a holder or recipient as aforesaid
(other than the holder of an aerodrome licence), descriptions of information which relates to his past, present
or future activities as the holder or recipient of the
licence, certificate or approval in question or his past
activities as the holder or recipient of any similar
licence, certificate or approval or is of a kind which
the CAA considers that it requires for the purpose
of reviewing the licence, certificate or approval in
question,

    (ii) in the case of such a person as is mentioned in paragraph
(c) of this subsection, descriptions of information which
relates to his past, present or future activities in the
United Kingdom connected with the making available
of accommodation so mentioned,

    (iii) in the case of such a person as is mentioned in para-
graph (d) of this subsection or the holder of an aerodrome licence, descriptions of information which relates
to his past, present or future activities (including, in the
case of the holder of an aerodrome licence, information
as to the numbers of aircraft and passengers and the
quantity of cargo passing and expected to pass through
the relevant aerodrome) and is of a kind which the
CAA considers that it requires for the purpose of performing any of its functions.

In this subsection " aerodrome licence " means a licence to
operate an aerodrome issued by the CAA under an Air Navigation Order.

(2) Without prejudice to the generality of subsection (1) above,
the information relating to the activities of the holder of an air
transport licence which the CAA may require him to furnish
in pursuance of that subsection includes particulars of any contract or arrangement—

    (a) to which he is or was at any time a party and, if he is
not or was not then an operator of aircraft registered
in the United Kingdom or a relevant overseas territory
or an associated state, to which such an operator is or
was then a party ; and

    (b) which constitutes or relates to an agreement or under-
standing between operators of aircraft or such operators
and other persons with respect to any of the following
matters, that is to say—

        (i) the provision of flights or of accommodation
in aircraft,

(ii) the sharing or transfer of revenue from flights on particular routes,

(iii) the sale by a party to the contract or arrangement of tickets for flights in aircraft operated by another party to it,

(iv) the making available by a party to the contract or arrangement of staff, equipment or other facilities for use by another party to it.

(3) Provision may be made by regulations made by the Secretary of State for requiring a person of any description specified in subsection (1) above to furnish the Secretary of State, in such form and at such times as may be prescribed, with information of such descriptions as may be prescribed, being descriptions of information relating to civil aviation which the Secretary of State considers that he requires for the purpose of performing any of his functions or descriptions of information which he considers that he requires in order to facilitate the performance by the CAA of any of its functions.

(4) If a person required to furnish information by virtue of any of the preceding provisions of this section fails to comply with the requirement or in purported compliance with the requirement knowingly or recklessly furnishes information which is false in a material particular, then—

(*a*) in the case of a failure to comply with the requirement he shall be guilty of an offence and liable on summary conviction to a fine of an amount not exceeding £100 ; and

(*b*) in any other case he shall be guilty of an offence and liable on summary conviction to a fine not exceeding the statutory maximum and on conviction on indictment to a fine or to imprisonment for a term not exceeding two years or to both ; and

(*c*) if the requirement was made by virtue of subsection (1) or (2) above, the CAA may, whether or not any proceedings in respect of the requirement have been brought in pursuance of paragraph (*a*) or (*b*) of this subsection, revoke any licence or certificate or approval which was issued or given by the CAA and to which the requirement related ;

and a person who fails to comply with a requirement imposed on him in pursuance of this section shall be guilty of an offence by virtue of paragraph (*a*) of this subsection notwithstanding that at any relevant time he is outside the United Kingdom and is neither a United Kingdom national nor a body incorporated under the law of a part of the United Kingdom or of a relevant overseas territory or an associated state.

Part IV

Aircraft

Design, construction and maintenance of aircraft

85.—(1) It shall be the duty of the CAA to consult the board referred to in subsection (2) below on all matters appearing to the CAA to be of significance as respects the standards of design, construction and maintenance by reference to which certificates of airworthiness for aircraft are to be granted or renewed in pursuance of Air Navigation Orders and to consult the said board as to whether an aircraft of a new type satisfies the standards of design and construction required for the issue of such a certificate for the aircraft ; and— *Design, construction and maintenance of aircraft.*

> (*a*) any question whether a matter is one on which consultations are required by virtue of this subsection shall be decided by the CAA ;

> (*b*) it shall be the duty of the CAA to consider all advice given to it by the said board in pursuance of this section ;

> (*c*) if the CAA decides not to proceed in accordance with any advice given to it by the said board it shall be the duty of the CAA to inform the board in writing of its reasons for the decision and, if the advice was given in consequence of consultations required by virtue of this subsection, to publish particulars of the case forthwith in the prescribed manner.

(2) There shall continue to be a body of persons, to be known as the Airworthiness Requirements Board (and hereinafter in this section referred to as " the board "), of which the functions shall be—

> (*a*) to give advice to the CAA on—

>> (i) all matters on which the CAA consults the board in pursuance of subsection (1) above ; and

>> (ii) any other matters which appear to the board to relate to the standards mentioned in that subsection and on which the board considers it appropriate to give advice to the CAA ;

> (*b*) to consult such persons as the board considers appropriate for the purposes of giving such advice as aforesaid.

(3) The board shall consist of not less than twelve nor more than twenty persons appointed by the CAA of whom—

> (*a*) four shall be appointed on the nomination of any body or persons appearing to the CAA to be representative—

>> (i) as to one of the four, of manufacturers of aircraft,

    (ii) as to another of them, of operators of aircraft,

    (iii) as to another of them, of insurers of aircraft,

    (iv) as to the other of them, of pilots of aircraft ;

  (b) more than half the persons for the time being so appointed shall be representative members (and in this paragraph " representative member " means a person appointed to be a member of the board on the nomination of any body or persons appearing to the CAA to be representative of manufacturers or operators or insurers or pilots of aircraft) ; and

  (c) the remainder may include one or more members of the CAA ;

and the CAA shall designate as the chairman of the board a member of it nominated by the board.

(4) Schedule 11 to this Act shall have effect with respect to the board.

Rights etc. in relation to aircraft

86.—(1) Her Majesty may by Order in Council make provision for the mortgaging of aircraft registered in the United Kingdom or capable of being so registered.

(2) Without prejudice to the generality of the powers conferred by subsection (1) above, an Order in Council under this section may, in particular—

  (a) include provisions which correspond (subject to such modifications as appear to Her Majesty in Council to be necessary or expedient) to any of the provisions of the Merchant Shipping Act 1894 relating to the mortgaging of ships ;

  (b) make provision as respects the rights and liabilities of mortgagors and mortgagees of such aircraft as are mentioned in subsection (1) above, and as respects the priority inter se of such rights and the relationship of such rights to other rights in or over such aircraft, including possessory liens for work done to such aircraft and rights under section 88 below or under regulations made by virtue of section 74(4) above ;

  (c) make provision as respects the operation, in relation to such aircraft as aforesaid, of any of the enactments in force in any part of the United Kingdom relating to bills of sale or the registration of charges on the property or undertaking of companies ;

  (d) provide for the rights of mortgagees of such aircraft to be exercisable, in such circumstances as may be specified in the Order, in relation to payments for the use of the aircraft ;

(e) confer on courts in the United Kingdom powers in respect of any register maintained in pursuance of the Order and in respect of transactions affecting aircraft registered therein ;

(f) make provision for enabling the mortgage of an aircraft to extend to any store of spare parts for that aircraft and for applying, for that purpose, to any such spare parts provisions such as are mentioned in the preceding paragraphs of this subsection ;

(g) make provision specifying, subject to the consent of the Treasury, the fees to be paid in respect of the making or deletion of entries in any such register as aforesaid and in respect of any other matters in respect of which it appears to Her Majesty in Council to be expedient for the purposes of the Order to charge fees ;

(h) provide for the imposition of penalties in respect of the making of false statements in connection with matters dealt with in the Order and in respect of the forgery of documents relating to such matters.

87.—(1) Any services rendered in assisting, or in saving life Application of from, or in saving the cargo or apparel of, an aircraft in, on or law of wreck over the sea or any tidal water, or on or over the shores of the and salvage sea or any tidal water, shall be deemed to be salvage services to aircraft. in all cases in which they would have been salvage services if they had been rendered in relation to a vessel.

(2) Where salvage services are rendered by an aircraft to any property or person, the owner of the aircraft shall be entitled to the same reward for those services as he would have been entitled to if the aircraft had been a vessel.

(3) Subsections (1) and (2) above shall have effect notwithstanding that the aircraft concerned is a foreign aircraft and notwithstanding that the services in quesion are rendered elsewhere than within the limits of the territorial waters adjacent to any part of Her Majesty's dominions.

(4) Her Majesty may by Order in Council direct that any provisions of any Act for the time being in force which relate to wreck, to salvage of life or property or to the duty of rendering assistance to vessels in distress shall, with such modifications, if any, as may be specified in the Order apply in relation to aircraft as those provisions apply in relation to vessels.

(5) For the purposes of this section—

(a) any provisions of an Act which relate to vessels laid by or neglected as unfit for sea service shall be deemed to be provisions relating to wreck ; and (*b*) " Act " shall include any local or special Act and any provisions of the Harbours, Docks and Piers Clauses Act 1847, as incorporated with any local or special Act, whenever passed.

Detention
and sale of
aircraft for
unpaid airport
charges.

88.—(1) Where default is made in the payment of airport charges incurred in respect of any aircraft at an aerodrome to which this section applies, the aerodrome authority may, subject to the provisions of this section—

(*a*) detain, pending payment, either—

(i) the aircraft in respect of which the charges were incurred (whether or not they were incurred by the person who is the operator of the aircraft at the time when the detention begins) ; or

(ii) any other aircraft of which the person in default is the operator at the time when the detention begins ; and

(*b*) if the charges are not paid within 56 days of the date when the detention begins, sell the aircraft in order to satisfy the charges.

(2) An aerodrome authority shall not detain or continue to detain an aircraft under this section by reason of any alleged default in the payment of airport charges if the operator of the aircraft or any other person claiming an interest therein—

(*a*) disputes that the charges, or any of them, are due or, if the aircraft is detained under subsection (1)(*a*)(i) above, that the charges in question were incurred in respect of that aircraft ; and

(*b*) gives to the authority, pending the determination of the dispute, sufficient security for the payment of the charges which are alleged to be due.

(3) An aerodrome authority shall not sell an aircraft under this section without the leave of the court ; and the court shall not give leave except on proof—

(*a*) that a sum is due to the authority for airport charges ;

(*b*) that default has been made in the payment thereof ; and

(*c*) that the aircraft which the authority seek leave to sell is liable to sale under this section by reason of the default.

(4) An aerodrome authority proposing to apply for leave to sell an aircraft under this section shall take such steps as may be prescribed—

(*a*) for bringing the proposed application to the notice of persons whose interests may be affected by the determination of the court thereon ; and (*b*) for affording to any such person an opportunity of becoming a party to the proceedings on the application ;

and, if leave is given, the aerodrome authority shall secure that the aircraft is sold for the best price that can reasonably be obtained.

5) Failure to comply with any requirement of subsection (4) above in respect of any sale, while actionable as against the aerodrome authority concerned at the suit of any person suffering loss in consequence thereof, shall not, after the sale has taken place, be a ground for impugning its validity.

(6) The proceeds of any sale under this section shall be applied as follows, and in the following order, that is to say—

(*a*) in payment of any duty (whether of customs or excise) chargeable on imported goods or value added tax which is due in consequence of the aircraft's having been brought into the United Kingdom ;

(*b*) in payment of the expenses incurred by the aerodrome authority in detaining, keeping and selling the aircraft, including their expenses in connection with the application to the court ;

(*c*) in payment of the airport charges which the court has found to be due ;

(*d*) in payment of any charge in respect of the aircraft which is due by virtue of regulations under section 73 above ;

and the surplus, if any, shall be paid to or among the person or persons whose interests in the aircraft have been divested by reason of the sale.

(7) The power of detention and sale conferred by this section in respect of an aircraft extends to the equipment of the aircraft and any stores for use in connection with its operation (being equipment and stores carried in the aircraft) whether or not the property of the person who is its operator, and references to the aircraft in subsections (2) to (6) above include, except where the context otherwise requires, references to any such equipment and stores.

(8) The power of detention conferred by this section in respect of an aircraft extends to any aircraft documents carried in it, and any such documents may, if the aircraft is sold under this section, be transferred by the aerodrome authority to the purchaser.

(9) The power conferred by this section to detain an aircraft in respect of which charges have been incurred may be exercised on the occasion on which the charges have been incurred

or on any subsequent occasion when the aircraft is on the aerodrome on which those charges were incurred or on any other aerodrome owned or managed by the aerodrome authority concerned.

(10) This section applies to any aerodrome owned or managed by any government department, the BAA or a local authority, other than a district council in Scotland, and to any other aerodrome designated for the purposes of this section by an order made by the Secretary of State ; and in this section—

> " aerodrome authority " in relation to any aerodrome, means the person owning or managing it ;

> " airport charges " means charges payable to an aerodrome authority for the use of, or for services provided at, an aerodrome but does not include charges payable by virtue of regulations under section 73 above ;

> " aircraft documents ", in relation to any aircraft, means any certificate of registration, maintenance or airworthiness of that aircraft, any log book relating to the use of that aircraft or its equipment and any similar document ;

> " the court " means—

>> (a) as respects England and Wales, the High Court; and

>> (b) as respects Scotland, the Court of Session.

(11) The Secretary of State may, after consultation with any local authority which appears to him to be concerned, by order repeal any enactment in a local Act which appears to the Secretary of State to be unnecessary having regard to the provisions of this section or to be inconsistent therewith.

(12) Nothing in this section shall prejudice any right of an aerodrome authority to recover any charges, or any part thereof, by action.

Exemption of aircraft and parts thereof from seizure on patent claims.

89.—(1) Any lawful entry into the United Kingdom or any lawful transit across the United Kingdom, with or without landings, of an aircraft to which this section applies shall not entail any seizure or detention of the aircraft or any proceedings being brought against the owner or operator thereof or any other interference therewith by or on behalf of any person in the United Kingdom, on the ground that the construction, mechanism, parts, accessories or operation of the aircraft is or are an infringement of any patent, design or model.

(2) Subject to subsection (3) below, the importation into, and storage in, the United Kingdom of spare parts and spare equipment for an aircraft to which this section applies and the use and installation thereof in the repair of such an aircraft shall not

entail any seizure or detention of the aircraft or of the spare parts or spare equipment or any proceedings being brought against the owner or operator of the aircraft or the owner of the spare parts or spare equipment or any other interference with the aircraft by or on behalf of any person in the United Kingdom on the ground that the spare parts or spare equipment or their installation are or is an infringement of any patent, design or model.

(3) Subsection (2) above shall not apply in relation to any spare parts or spare equipment which are sold or distributed in the United Kingdom or are exported from the United Kingdom for sale or distribution.

(4) This section applies—

(*a*) to an aircraft other than an aircraft used in military, customs or police services, registered in any country or territory in the case of which there is for the time being in force a declaration made by Her Majesty by Order in Council with a view to the fulfilment of the provisions of the Chicago Convention to which this section relates, that the benefits of those provisions apply to that country or territory ; and

(*b*) to such other aircraft as Her Majesty may by Order in Council specify.

(5) Schedule 12 to this Act shall have effect with respect to detention on patent claims in respect of foreign aircraft other than aircraft to which this section applies.

90.—(1) Her Majesty may by Order in Council make such provision as appears to Her Majesty in Council to be necessary or expedient for giving effect to the Convention on the International Recognition of Rights in Aircraft which was signed at Geneva on behalf of the United Kingdom on 19th June 1948.

Power to give effect to Convention on rights in aircraft.

(2) Without prejudice to the generality of the powers conferred by subsection (1) above, an Order in Council under this section may, in particular, make provision—

(*a*) for the recognition in the United Kingdom of rights of the kind specified in the Convention in or over aircraft registered in other states party to the Convention, being rights registered or recorded in those states in accordance with the Convention and recognised as valid by the law of the state party to the Convention in which the aircraft in question was registered when the rights were constituted ;

(*b*) for subordinating to any such rights as aforesaid, to such extent as may be required under the Convention, any other rights in or over such aircraft as aforesaid, including possessory liens for work done to such aircraft and rights under section 88 above or under regulations made by virtue of section 74(4) above ;

(c) as respects the operation, in relation to such aircraft as aforesaid, of any of the enactments in force in any part of the United Kingdom relating to bills of sale or the registration of charges on the property or undertaking of companies ;

(d) for prohibiting the sale in execution of any such aircraft as aforesaid without an order of a court, and otherwise for safeguarding in the case of such a sale any such rights as are mentioned in paragraph (a) above ;

(e) for the recognition in the United Kingdom, in priority to other rights in or over any such aircraft as aforesaid or any aircraft registered in the United Kingdom or a relevant overseas territory, of any charge consequent on salvage or similar operations in respect of the aircraft, being a charge arising in accordance with the law of any other state party to the Convention in which those operations terminated ;

(f) for the application, in accordance with the Convention, of provisions corresponding to those made by virtue of paragraphs (a) to (d) above to cases where a right such as is mentioned in the said paragraph (a) (being a right created as security for the payment of indebtedness) extends to any store of spare parts for the aircraft in question.

Jurisdiction, etc.

Jurisdiction in civil matters.

91. Her Majesty may by Order in Council make provision as to the courts in which proceedings may be taken for enforcing any claim in respect of aircraft, and in particular may provide—

(a) for conferring jurisdiction in any such proceedings on any court exercising Admiralty jurisdiction ; and

(b) for applying to such proceedings any rules of practice or procedure applicable to proceedings in Admiralty.

Application of criminal law to aircraft.

92.—(1) Any act or omission taking place on board a British-controlled aircraft while in flight elsewhere than in or over the United Kingdom which, if taking place in, or in a part of, the United Kingdom, would constitute an offence under the law in force in, or in that part of, the United Kingdom shall constitute that offence ; but this subsection shall not apply to any act or omission which is expressly or impliedly authorised by or under that law when taking place outside the United Kingdom.

(2) Subject to any provision to the contrary in any Act passed after 14th July 1967, no proceedings for any offence under the law in force in, or in a part of, the United Kingdom committed on board an aircraft while in flight elsewhere than in or over the United Kingdom (other than an offence under, or under any instrument made under, any of the air navigation enactments) shall be instituted—

   (*a*) in England and Wales, except by or with the consent of the Director of Public Prosecutions ; or

   (*b*) in Northern Ireland, except by or with the consent of the Attorney General for Northern Ireland ;

but, unless the Attorney General for Northern Ireland otherwise directs, paragraph (*b*) above shall be deemed to be complied with as respects the institution of any proceedings if the Director of Public Prosecutions for Northern Ireland gives his consent to the institution or carrying on of the proceedings.

(3) For the purpose of conferring jurisdiction, any offence under the law in force in, or in a part of, the United Kingdom committed on board an aircraft in flight shall be deemed to have been committed in any place in the United Kingdom (or, as the case may be, in that part thereof) where the offender may for the time being be.

(4) For the purposes of this section the period during which an aircraft is in flight shall be deemed to include any period from the moment when power is applied for the purpose of the aircraft taking off on a flight until the moment when the landing run (if any) at the termination of that flight ends ; and any reference in this section to an aircraft in flight shall include a reference to an aircraft during any period when it is on the surface of the sea or land but not within the territorial limits of any country.

(5) In this section, except where the context otherwise requires—

   " aircraft " means any aircraft, whether or not a British-controlled aircraft, other than—

      (*a*) a military aircraft ; or

      (*b*) subject to section 101(1)(*b*) below, an aircraft which, not being a military aircraft, belongs to or is exclusively employed in the service of Her Majesty in right of the United Kingdom ;

   " the air navigation enactments " mean the enactments contained in sections 60 to 62, 72 to 77, 81 to 83, 87 and 97 of this Act ;

   " British-controlled aircraft " means an aircraft—

      (*a*) which is for the time being registered in the United Kingdom ; or

PART IV

(*b*) which is not for the time being registered in any country but in the case of which either the operator of the aircraft or each person entitled as owner to any legal or beneficial interest in it satisfies the following requirements, namely—

    (i) that he is a person qualified to be the owner of a legal or beneficial interest in an aircraft registered in the United Kingdom ; and

    (ii) that he resides or has his principal place of business in the United Kingdom ; or

(*c*) which, being for the time being registered in some other country, is for the time being chartered by demise to a person who, or to persons each of whom, satisfies the requirements aforesaid ;

" military aircraft " means—

(*a*) an aircraft of the naval, military or air forces of any country ; or

(*b*) any other aircraft in respect of which there is in force a certificate issued in accordance with any Order in Council in force under section 60, 87, 89, 91, 101(1)(*a*) or 107(2) of this Act that the aircraft is to be treated for the purposes of that Order in Council as a military aircraft ;

and a certificate of the Secretary of State that any aircraft is or is not a military aircraft for the purposes of this section shall be conclusive evidence of the fact certified.

(6) In subsection (2) above, the words from " but " onwards shall (notwithstanding their enactment in this Act) have effect subject to any question arising as to the validity, in relation to any such provision as is re-enacted in the preceding provisions of that subsection, of the provisions from which the words derive, that is to say, Article 7 of the Prosecution of Offences (Northern Ireland) Order 1972 and paragraphs 67 and 68 of Part II of Schedule 1 to the Criminal Justice (Northern Ireland) Order 1980.

S.I. 1972/538 (N.I. 1).
S.I. 1980/704 (N.I. 6).

Provisions as to extradition.
1870 c. 52.

93.—(1) For the purposes of the application of the Extradition Act 1870 to crimes committed on board an aircraft in flight, any aircraft registered in a Convention country shall at any time while that aircraft is in flight be deemed to be within the jurisdiction of that country, whether or not it is for the time being also within the jurisdiction of any other country.

(2) Paragraphs (1) to (3) of section 16 of the said Act of 1870 (which have effect where a person's surrender is sought in respect of a crime committed on board a vessel on the high seas which

comes into any port of the United Kingdom) shall have effect also where a person's surrender is sought in respect of a crime committed on board an aircraft in flight which lands in the United Kingdom, but as if in the said paragraph (3) for references to the port where the vessel lies there were substituted references to the place at which the person whose surrender is sought is disembarked.

(3) Subsections (4) and (5) of section 92 above shall apply for the purposes of this section as they apply for the purposes of that section.

(4) Sections 17 and 22 of the said Act of 1870 (which relate to the extent of that Act) shall apply to the preceding provisions of this section as if those provisions were included in that Act.

Powers of commander of aircraft

94.—(1) The provisions of subsections (2) to (5) below shall have effect for the purposes of any proceedings before any court in the United Kingdom.

Powers of commander of aircraft.

(2) If the commander of an aircraft in flight, wherever that aircraft may be, has reasonable grounds to believe in respect of any person on board the aircraft—

  (*a*) that the person in question has done or is about to do any act on the aircraft while it is in flight which jeopardises or may jeopardise—

    (i) the safety of the aircraft or of persons or property on board the aircraft, or

    (ii) good order and discipline on board the aircraft, or

  (*b*) that the person in question has done on the aircraft while in flight any act which in the opinion of the commander is a serious offence under any law in force in the country in which the aircraft is registered, not being a law of a political nature or based on racial or religious discrimination,

then, subject to subsection (4) below, the commander may take with respect to that person such reasonable measures, including restraint of his person, as may be necessary—

  (i) to protect the safety of the aircraft or of persons or property on board the aircraft ; or

  (ii) to maintain good order and discipline on board the aircraft ; or

  (iii) to enable the commander to disembark or deliver that person in accordance with subsection (5) below,

and for the purposes of paragraph (*b*) of this subsection any British-controlled aircraft shall be deemed to be registered in the United Kingdom whether or not it is in fact so registered and whether or not it is in fact registered in some other country.

Part I   H

(3) Any member of the crew of an aircraft and any other person on board the aircraft may, at the request or with the authority of the commander of the aircraft, and any such member shall if so required by that commander, render assistance in restraining any person whom the commander is entitled under subsection (2) above to restrain; and at any time when the aircraft is in flight any such member or other person may, without obtaining the authority of the commander, take with respect to any person on board the aircraft any measures such as are mentioned in that subsection which he has reasonable grounds to believe are immediately necessary to protect the safety of the aircraft or of persons or property on board the aircraft.

(4) Any restraint imposed on any person on board an aircraft under the powers conferred by the preceding provisions of this section shall not be continued after the time when the aircraft first thereafter ceases to be in flight unless before or as soon as is reasonably practicable after that time the commander of the aircraft causes notification of the fact that a person on board the aircraft is under restraint and of the reasons therefor to be sent to an appropriate authority of the country in which the aircraft so ceases to be in flight, but subject to such notification may be continued after that time—

(a) for any period (including the period of any further flight) between that time and the first occasion thereafter on which the commander is able with any requisite consent of the appropriate authorities to disembark or deliver the person under restraint in accordance with subsection (5) below; or

(b) if the person under restraint agrees to continue his journey under restraint on board that aircraft.

(5) The commander of an aircraft—

(a) if in the case of any person on board the aircraft he has reasonable grounds—

(i) to believe as mentioned in subsection (2)(a) above, and

(ii) to believe that it is necessary so to do in order to protect the safety of the aircraft or of persons or property on board the aircraft or to maintain good order and discipline on board the aircraft,

may disembark that person in any country in which that aircraft may be; and

(b) if in the case of any person on board the aircraft he has reasonable grounds to believe as mentioned in subsection (2)(b) above, may deliver that person—

(i) in the United Kingdom, to a constable or immigration officer; or

(ii) in any other country which is a Convention country, to an officer having functions corresponding to the functions in the United Kingdom either of a constable or of an immigration officer.

(6) The commander of an aircraft—

(*a*) if he disembarks any person in pursuance of subsection (5)(*a*) above, in the case of a British-controlled aircraft, in any country or, in the case of any other aircraft, in the United Kingdom, shall report the fact of, and the reasons for, that disembarkation to—

(i) an appropriate authority in the country of disembarkation ; and

(ii) the appropriate diplomatic or consular office of the country of nationality of that person ;

(*b*) if he intends to deliver any person in accordance with subsection (5)(*b*) above in the United Kingdom or, in the case of a British-controlled aircraft, in any other country which is a Convention country, shall before or as soon as reasonably practicable after landing give notification of his intention and of the reasons therefor—

(i) where the country in question is the United Kingdom, to a constable or immigration officer or, in the case of any other country, to an officer having functions corresponding to the functions in the United Kingdom either of a constable or of an immigration officer ;

(ii) in either case to the appropriate diplomatic or consular office of the country of nationality of that person ;

and any commander of an aircraft who without reasonable cause fails to comply with the requirements of this subsection shall be liable on summary conviction to a fine not exceeding £100.

(7) In this section—

" commander " in relation to an aircraft, means the member of the crew designated as commander of that aircraft by the operator thereof, or, failing such a person, the person who is for the time being the pilot in command of the aircraft ; and

" pilot in command " in relation to an aircraft, means a person who for the time being is in charge of the piloting of the aircraft without being under the direction of any other pilot in the aircraft ;

and, subject to subsection (8) below, subsections (4) and (5) of section 92 above shall apply for the purposes of this section as they apply for the purposes of that section.

H 2

(8) The time during which an aircraft is in flight shall, for the purposes of this section, be deemed to include, in addition to such a period as is mentioned in subsection (4) of section 92 above—

> (a) any further period from the moment when all external doors, if any, of the aircraft are closed following embarkation for a flight until the moment when any such door is opened for disembarkation after that flight ; and

> (b) if the aircraft makes a forced landing, any period thereafter until the time when competent authorities of the country in which the forced landing takes place take over the responsibility for the aircraft and for the persons and property on board the aircraft (being, if the forced landing takes place in the United Kingdom, the time when a constable arrives at the place of landing).

Evidence, etc.

Provisions as to evidence in connection with aircraft.

95.—(1) Where in any proceedings before a court in the United Kingdom for an offence committed on board an aircraft the testimony of any person is required and the court is satisfied that the person in question cannot be found in the United Kingdom, there shall be admissible in evidence before that court any deposition relating to the subject matter of those proceedings previously made on oath by that person outside the United Kingdom which was so made—

> (a) in the presence of the person charged with the offence ; and

1981 c. 61.

> (b) before a judge or magistrate of a country such as is mentioned in Schedule 3 to the British Nationality Act 1981 as for the time being in force or which was part of Her Majesty's dominions at the time the deposition was made or in which Her Majesty had jurisdiction at that time, or before a consular officer of Her Majesty's Government in the United Kingdom.

(2) Any such deposition shall be authenticated by the signature of the judge, magistrate or consular officer before whom it was made who shall certify that the person charged with the offence was present at the taking of the deposition.

(3) It shall not be necessary in any proceedings to prove the signature or official character of the person appearing so to have authenticated any such deposition or to have given such a certificate, and such a certificate shall, unless the contrary is proved, be sufficient evidence in any proceedings that the person charged with the offence was present at the making of the deposition.

(4) If a complaint is made to such a consular officer as aforesaid that any offence has been committed on a British-controlled aircraft while in flight elsewhere than in or over the United Kingdom, that officer may inquire into the case upon oath.

(5) In this section—

"deposition" includes any affidavit, affirmation or statement made upon oath ; and

"oath" includes an affirmation or declaration in the case of persons allowed by law to affirm or declare instead of swearing ;

and subsections (4) and (5) of section 92 above shall apply for the purposes of this section as they apply for the purposes of that section.

(6) Nothing in this section shall prejudice the admission as evidence of any deposition which is admissible in evidence apart from this section.

96.—(1) In any legal proceedings—

    (*a*) a document purporting to be certified by such authority or person as may be designated for the purpose by regulations made by the Secretary of State as being, or being a true copy of, or of part of, a document issued or record kept in pursuance of—

        (i) an Air Navigation Order, or

        (ii) the Civil Aviation (Licensing) Act 1960,

by, or by the Minister in charge of, a government department, by an official of a government department specified for the purpose in an Air Navigation Order or by the Air Registration Board or the Air Transport Licensing Board, or

    (*b*) a document printed by either Her Majesty's Stationery Office or the CAA and purporting to be the publication known as the "United Kingdom Air Pilot" or a publication of the series known as "Notam—United Kingdom",

shall be evidence, and in Scotland sufficient evidence, of the matters appearing from the document.

(2) In any legal proceedings any record made by any such authority or person as may be designated for the purposes of this subsection by regulations made by the Secretary of State, or by a person acting under the control of such an authority or person, being a record purporting to show—

    (*a*) the position of an aircraft at any material time, or

Use of records and documentary evidence.

1960 c. 38.

H 3

> (*b*) the terms or content of any message or signal trans-
> mitted to any aircraft, either alone or in common with
> other aircraft, or received from any aircraft, by the first-
> mentioned authority or person, or by a person acting
> under the control of that authority or person,

shall, if produced from the custody of that authority or person,
be evidence, and in Scotland sufficient evidence, of the matters
appearing from the record.

(3) The references in subsection (2) above to a record made
by or under the control of any authority or person include
references to a document or article purporting to be a copy of a
record so made, and certified to be a true copy by or on behalf
of that authority or person ; and in relation to such a copy that
subsection shall have effect as if the words " if produced from
the custody of that authority or person " were omitted.

(4) Any person who wilfully certifies any document or article
to be a true copy of any such record as is mentioned in subsection (2) above knowing it not to be a true copy shall be
liable—

> (*a*) on summary conviction, to a fine not exceeding the
> statutory maximum or to imprisonment for a term not
> exceeding three months or to both ; and
>
> (*b*) on conviction on indictment to a fine or to imprisonment
> for a term not exceeding two years or to both.

(5) In this section " record " has the same meaning as in
section 73 above.

Seaplanes

Seaplanes.
1894 c. 60.   **97.**—(1) The power of Her Majesty in Council under subsection (1) of section 418 of the Merchant Shipping Act 1894 to
make regulations for the prevention of collisions at sea shall include power to make regulations for the prevention of collisions
at sea—

> (*a*) between seaplanes on the surface of the water ; and
>
> (*b*) between vessels and seaplanes on the surface of the
> water ;

and accordingly sections 418, 419, 421 and 424 of the said Act
of 1894 shall apply in relation to seaplanes on the surface of the
water as they apply in relation to ships or vessels, except that—

> (i) for the purposes of subsection (2) of the said section 418
> and for the purposes of the said section 424, sections
> 418, 419, 421 and 424 of the said Act of 1894 shall be
> deemed to be the only provisions of Part V of that
> Act relating to the collision regulations or otherwise
> relating to collisions ; and

(ii) any reference in the said section 419 to the master or PART IV
to the person in charge of the deck shall be construed
as a reference to the pilot or other person on duty in
charge of the seaplane.

In this subsection " vessels " has the same meaning as in the
said Act of 1894.

(2) For the purpose of the Dockyard Ports Regulation Act 1865 c. 125.
1865 seaplanes when on the surface of the water shall be deemed
to be vessels.

(3) In section 28 of the Harbours, Docks and Piers Clauses Act 1847 c. 27.
1847 (which relates to the exemption of certain vessels from
harbour rates) as incorporated with any statutory provision, the
expression " vessel " shall be deemed to include any aircraft on
the surface of the water, being an aircraft which is designed to
float or manoeuvre on water.

(4) Subject to subsection (5) below, any enactment which
confers or imposes on a conservancy or harbour authority any
power or duty to make byelaws for the regulation of ships or
vessels shall be construed as if the power or duty so conferred
or imposed included a power or duty to make byelaws for the
regulation of seaplanes when on the surface of the water,
and also a power to include in the byelaws provisions authorising
the harbour master or other officer of the authority to exercise,
as respects seaplanes on the surface of the water, all or any of
the functions which he is authorised by the enactment in question
to exercise as respects ships or vessels.

(5) Byelaws made by virtue of subsection (4) above shall not
in any circumstances require, or authorise a harbour master or
other officer to require, the dismantling of a seaplane or any
part thereof or the making of any alteration whatever of the structure or equipment of a seaplane.

(6) Where any enactment, whether by virtue of subsection (4)
above or not, confers or imposes on a conservancy or harbour
authority a power or duty to make byelaws for the regulation
of seaplanes when on the surface of the water, or to include in
the byelaws such provisions as are mentioned in that subsection,
the following provisions shall have effect—

(a) in the case where the enactment provides that the byelaws shall not come into force unless they have been
confirmed or approved by some government department, byelaws made thereunder in relation to seaplanes shall not be confirmed or approved by that
department except after consultation with the Secretary of State ;

H 4

PART IV

(*b*) in a case where the enactment in question does not provide as aforesaid, byelaws made thereunder in relation to seaplanes shall not, except in a case where they are required to be allowed or approved by a court or a judge, come into force unless they have been confirmed by the Secretary of State ;

(*c*) in a case where the enactment in question provides that the byelaws shall not come into force unless they have been allowed or approved by a court or a judge, the conservancy or harbour authority shall, before making application to that court or judge for the allowance of the byelaws, forward a copy thereof to the Secretary of State, and the court or judge shall, before allowing or approving the byelaws, take into consideration any representations made with respect thereto by or on behalf of the Secretary of State.

(6) In this section—

" byelaws " includes rules and regulations ;

" conservancy authority " and " harbour authority " shall have the meanings assigned to them by section 742 of the Merchant Shipping Act 1894 ;

1894 c. 60.

" enactment " includes any provisional order for the time being in force (whether or not it has been confirmed by an Act) ;

" seaplane " includes a flying boat and any other aircraft designed to manoeuvre on the water ;

and, for the purposes of this section, seaplanes taking off from or alighting on the water shall be deemed to be on the surface of the water while in contact therewith.

Supplemental

Construction of certain provisions of Part IV.

98. If the Secretary of State is satisfied that the requirements of Article 18 of the Tokyo Convention have been satisfied (which Article makes provision as to the country which is to be treated as the country of registration of certain aircraft operated by joint air transport organisations or international operating agencies established by two or more Convention countries) the Secretary of State may by order provide that for the purposes of sections 92 to 95 above such aircraft as may be specified in the order shall be treated as registered in such Convention country as may be so specified.

PART V

MISCELLANEOUS AND GENERAL

99.—(1) Where an offence to which this subsection applies Offences. has been committed by a body corporate and is proved to have been committed with the consent or connivance of or to be attributable to any neglect on the part of any director, manager, secretary or other similar officer of the body corporate or any person who was purporting to act in any such capacity, he as well as the body corporate shall be guilty of that offence and be liable to be proceeded against and punished accordingly.

(2) Where the affairs of a body corporate are managed by its members subsection (1) above shall apply in relation to the acts and defaults of a member in connection with his functions of management as if he were a director of the body corporate.

(3) Any offence to which this subsection applies shall, for the purpose of conferring jurisdiction, be deemed to have been committed in any place where the offender may for the time being be.

(4) Subsection (1) above applies to any offence under section 44, 45, 50, 64(5), 67(6), 82, 83 or 84(4) above or under regulations made by virtue of section 7(2)(*b*) or 71 above.

(5) Subsection (3) above applies to any offence under any provision made by or under this Act, except, without prejudice to section 92(3) above—

   (*a*) an offence consisting in a contravention of a byelaw made by virtue of section 27, 32 or 33 above ;

   (*b*) an offence under section 44, 45, 50, 83 or 94(6) above ;

   (*c*) an offence consisting in a contravention of an order made under section 62 above ;

   (*d*) an offence consisting in a convention of an order made under section 63 above with respect to a British air transport undertaking ;

   (*e*) an offence consisting in a contravention of an Order in Council under section 86 above.

100. The enactments and instruments with respect to which Application provision may be made by Order in Council in pursuance of of Act to section 1(1)(*h*) of the Hovercraft Act 1968 (power to apply hovercraft. enactments and instruments in relation to hovercraft etc.) shall 1968 c. 59. include this Act and any instrument made under it.

PART V
Power to
apply certain
provisions to
Crown
aircraft.

101.—(1) Her Majesty may by Order in Council—

(a) apply to any aircraft belonging to or exclusively employed in the service of Her Majesty, with or without modification, any of the provisions of this Act mentioned in subsection (2) below (being provisions which do not otherwise apply to such aircraft) or any Orders in Council, orders or regulations under those provisions ;

(b) apply the provisions of sections 92 to 95 above, with or without modifications, to aircraft such as are excluded from the definition of " aircraft " in subsection (5) of the said section 92 by paragraph (b) of the **definition.**

(2) The provisions of this Act referred to in subsection (1)(a) above are sections 60 to 62, 73 to 77, 81, 87, 89, 91, 96 and 97 and Part III of Schedule 13.

Powers to
make Orders
in Council,
orders and
regulations.

102.—(1) Any power conferred on the Secretary of State by this Act to make an order or regulations, other than a power conferred by a provision of this Act specified in Part I of Schedule 13 to this Act, shall be exercisable by statutory instrument.

(2) The powers to make Orders in Council, orders and regulations which are conferred by virtue of the provisions of this Act specified in column 1 of Part II of the said Schedule 13 (being the Orders in Council, orders and regulations a general description of which is given in column 2 of that Part)—

(a) are, to the extent specified in column 3 of that Part, conferred subject to subsections (3) and (4) below ; and

(b) shall, to the extent specified in column 4 of that Part, include the powers conferred by virtue of Part III of that Schedule.

(3) Where an entry in column 3 of the said Part II specifies that a power to make an Order in Council is subject to the affirmative resolution procedure, the Order shall not be submitted to Her Majesty in Council unless a draft of the Order has been laid before Parliament and approved by a resolution of each House.

(4) Where an entry in the said column 3 specifies that a power to make an Order in Council, order or regulations is subject to the negative resolution procedure, the Order in Council, order or regulations, as the case may be, shall be subject to annulment in pursuance of a resolution of either House of Parliament.

(5) Any power to make an order which is conferred by a provision of this Act specified in Part I of Schedule 13, except the power to make a vesting order under section 42(2) above, shall be construed as including a power exercisable in the like manner and subject to the like provisions (if any) to vary or revoke the order.

103. For the purposes of the application of this Act to Scotland, any inquiry in relation to an order which by virtue of any provision of this Act is subject to special parliamentary procedure, shall, if the Secretary of State so directs, be held by Commissioners under the Private Legislation Procedure (Scotland) Act 1936, and where any direction has been so given—

Special parliamentary procedure: Scotland.

1936 c. 52.

(a) it shall be deemed to have been so given under section 2 as read with section 10 of the Statutory Orders (Special Procedure) Act 1945 ; and

1945 c. 18.

(b) nothing in section 267 of the Town and Country Planning (Scotland) Act 1972, as applied by virtue of paragraph 4 or paragraph 8 of Schedule 10 to this Act, shall apply to such inquiry.

1972 c. 52.

104.—(1) Except where the context otherwise requires, nothing in this Act applying (in whatever terms) in relation to property (including any aerodrome) which is owned or managed or controlled by the Secretary of State or which he proposes to acquire shall apply in relation to such property unless, as the case may be, he owns, manages, controls or proposes to acquire the property in connection with the exercise of his functions relating to civil aviation.

Construction of provisions relating to property.

(2) Any reference in this Act to the carrying out of works on land shall be construed as including a reference to the making of excavations on the land or to the carrying out of levelling operations on the land ; and references to the maintenance of works or to interference with works shall be construed accordingly.

105.—(1) In this Act, except where the context otherwise requires—

General interpretation.

" accounting year ", in relation to the CAA, means the period of twelve months ending with 31st March in any year ;

" aerodrome " means any area of land or water designed, equipped, set apart or commonly used for affording facilities for the landing and departure of aircraft and includes any area or space, whether on the ground, on the roof of a building or elsewhere, which is designed, equipped or set apart for affording facilities for the landing and departure of aircraft capable of descending or climbing vertically ;

" Air Navigation Order " means an Order in Council under section 60 above ;

" air navigation services " includes information, directions and other facilities furnished, issued or provided in connection with the navigation or movement of aircraft, and includes the control of movement of vehicles in any part of an aerodrome used for the movement of aircraft ;

" air transport licence " has the meaning given by section 64(1)(*a*) above ;

" air transport service " means a service for the carriage by air of passengers or cargo ;

" the BAA " means the British Airports Authority ;

" the CAA " means the Civil Aviation Authority ;

" cargo " includes mail ;

" the Chicago Convention " means the convention on International Civil Aviation which was, on 7th December 1944, signed on behalf of the Government of the United Kingdom at the International Civil Aviation Conference held at Chicago ;

" Convention country " means a country in which the Tokyo Convention is for the time being in force ; and Her Majesty may by Order in Council certify that any country specified in the Order is for the time being a Convention country and any such Order in Council for the time being in force shall be conclusive evidence that the country in question is for the time being a Convention country ;

" enactment " includes any enactment contained in an Act of the Parliament of Northern Ireland, an Order in Council under section 1(3) of the Northern Ireland (Temporary Provisions) Act 1972 or a Measure of the Northern Ireland Assembly ;

1972 c. 22.

" Eurocontrol " and " the Eurocontrol Convention " have the meanings given by section 24 above ;

" flight " means a journey by air beginning when the aircraft in question takes off and ending when it next lands ;

" functions " includes powers and duties ;

" the initial debt " has the meaning given by section 9(1) above ;

" the Land Compensation Act "—

> (*a*) in relation to England and Wales, means the Land Compensation Act 1961 ; 1961 c. 33.

> (*b*) in relation to Scotland, means the Land Compensation (Scotland) Act 1963 ; and 1963 c. 51.

> (*c*) in relation to Northern Ireland, means, subject to subsection (7) below, the Acquisition of Land (Assessment of Compensation) Act 1919 ; 1919 c. 57.

" the Lands Tribunal " shall be construed subject to subsection (5) below ;

" local authority "—

> (*a*) in relation to England and Wales, means a county council, the Greater London Council, the council of a district or London borough or the Common Council of the City of London ;

> (*b*) in relation to Scotland, means a regional, islands or district council ;

> (*c*) in relation to Northern Ireland, means a district council established under the Local Government Act (Northern Ireland) 1972 ; 1972 c. 9 (N.I.).

" loss or damage " includes, in relation to persons, loss of life and personal injury ;

" modifications " includes additions, omissions and amendments, and " modify " shall be construed accordingly ;

" operator ", in relation to an aircraft, means the person having the management of the aircraft for the time being or, in relation to a time, at that time ;

" prescribed " means prescribed by regulations made by the Secretary of State ;

" relevant overseas territory " means any of the Channel Islands, the Isle of Man, any colony and any country or place outside Her Majesty's dominions in which for the time being Her Majesty has jurisdiction ;

" reward ", in relation to a flight, includes any form of consideration received or to be received wholly or partly in connection with the flight irrespective of the person by whom or to whom the consideration has been or is to be given ;

" the statutory maximum " means—

> (*a*) in England and Wales and Northern Ireland, the prescribed sum within the meaning of section 32

of the Magistrates' Courts Act 1980 (that is to say,
£1,000 or another sum fixed by order under section
143 of that Act to take account of changes in the
value of money) ;

(b) in Scotland, the prescribed sum within the
meaning of section 289B of the Criminal Procedure
(Scotland) Act 1975 (that is to say £1,000 or another
sum fixed by order under section 289D of that Act
for that purpose) ;

"statutory undertaker" means the CAA, the Post Office,
British Telecommunications or any person (including
a local authority) authorised by any Act (whether
public general or local) or by any order or scheme
made under or confirmed by any Act to construct,
work or carry on—

(a) any railway, light railway, tramway, road
transport, water transport, canal, inland navigation,
dock, harbour, pier or lighthouse undertaking ;

(b) any undertaking for the supply of electricity,
gas or hydraulic power ;

(c) any undertaking for the supply of water ;

and "statutory undertaking" shall be construed
accordingly ;

"subsidiary" shall be construed in accordance with section
154 of the Companies Act 1948 ; and

"Tokyo Convention" means the Convention on Offences
and certain other Acts Committed on board Aircraft,
which was signed at Tokyo on 14th September 1963 ;

"United Kingdom national" means an individual who is—

(a) a British citizen, a British Dependent Territories citizen or a British Overseas citizen ;

(b) a person who under the British Nationality
Act 1981 is a British subject ; or

(c) a British protected person (within the meaning
of that Act).

(2) Except where the context otherwise requires, any reference
in this Act to the provisions of an Order in Council shall, if
paragraph 3 of Part III of Schedule 13 to this Act (power to
authorise making of regulations) applies to the power to make the
Order in question, include a reference to the provisions of any
regulations made, or directions given, under the Order in
Council.

(3) Without prejudice to any transitional or transitory provision made by this Act or to section 17(2) of the Interpretation Act 1978 (repeal and re-enactment), any reference in any enactment contained in this Act (including a reference to a provision of that enactment or to any other enactment so contained) to a provision which is a re-enactment of a repealed enactment or to things done or falling to be done under such a provision shall, so far as the context permits, be construed as including, in relation to times, circumstances and purposes in relation to which the repealed enactment had effect, a reference to, or to things done or falling to be done under, that repealed enactment; and where the repealed enactment was itself a re-enactment of an earlier provision the reference shall extend in the same way to that earlier provision, and so on.

PART V
1978 c. 30.

(4) Any reference in this Act to the re-enactment of a provision includes a reference to its re-enactment with modifications.

(5) In the application of this Act to Scotland and to Northern Ireland references to the Lands Tribunal shall have effect as references respectively to the Lands Tribunal for Scotland and to the Lands Tribunal for Northern Ireland.

(6) Except where the context otherwise requires, any reference in this Act to an Act of Parliament shall include a reference to an Act of the Parliament of Northern Ireland, an Order in Council under section 1(3) of the Northern Ireland (Temporary Provisions) Act 1972 and a Measure of the Northern Ireland Assembly.

1972 c. 22.

(7) In the application of this Act to Northern Ireland, references in this Act to provisions of the Acquisition of Land (Assessment of Compensation) Act 1919 shall, in relation to any matter about which the Parliament of Northern Ireland had power to make laws, have effect as references to the corresponding provisions of the Land Compensation (Northern Ireland) Order 1982.

1919 c. 57.

(8) For the purposes of the application to Northern Ireland of the definition in subsection (1) above of " the statutory maximum ", the provisions of the Magistrates' Courts Act 1980 which relate to the sum mentioned in paragraph (*a*) of that definition shall extend to Northern Ireland.

1980 c. 43.

106.—(1) Except where the context otherwise requires, in any provision of this Act to which this section applies a reference to a country or territory or to the territorial limits of any country shall be construed as including a reference to the territorial waters of the country or territory, as the case may be; and a reference to a part of the United Kingdom shall be construed as including a reference to so much of the territorial waters of the United Kingdom as are adjacent to that part.

Application of Act to territorial waters.

(2) This section applies to Parts III and IV of this Act, except sections 63 to 74 and 84.

(3) Nothing in this section shall prejudice the construction of any provision of this Act to which this section does not apply.

Application of Act to Northern Ireland.

107.—(1) The following provisions of this Act, that is to say, sections 27, 30 to 35, 37, 44(9), 51, 54 and 88, paragraph 12 of Schedule 7 and paragraph 10 of Schedule 9 and Schedule 10 shall not extend to Northern Ireland.

(2) Her Majesty may by Order in Council direct that any of the provisions of sections 39, 47 and 97 of this Act (except subsection (3) of section 97) and any of the provisions of this Part of this Act so far as it relates to those sections shall, in the application of that provision to Northern Ireland, have effect subject to such adaptations as may be specified in the Order.

Extension of provisions of Act outside United Kingdom.

108.—(1) Her Majesty may by Order in Council direct that any of the provisions of this Act, other than the provisions of sections 27, 32 to 35, 37, 61(3) to (5), 82, and 88 of this Act, shall extend, with such modifications (if any) as may be specified in the Order to any relevant overseas territory.

(2) Her Majesty may by Order in Council direct that—

(*a*) any provision of this Act, other than a provision of sections 92 to 95 ; or

(*b*) any provision of any Order in Council or regulations made by virtue of section 60, 73, 75, 86, 87 or 89 above,

shall apply in relation to an aircraft registered in any relevant overseas territory as that provision applies to an aircraft registered in the United Kingdom, but with such modifications (if any) as may be specified in the Order.

Transitional provisions, consequential amendments, repeals, etc.

1978 c. 30.

109.—(1) Schedule 14 to this Act (which contains transitional and transitory provisions and savings) shall have effect ; and the provisions of that Schedule are without prejudice to sections 16 and 17 of the Interpretation Act 1978 (which relate to repeals).

(2) The enactments specified in Schedule 15 to this Act shall have effect subject to the amendments there specified, being amendments consequential on the provisions of this Act.

(3) Subject to the provisions of the said Schedule 14, the enactments and instruments specified in Schedule 16 to this Act are hereby repealed to the extent specified in the third column of the said Schedule 16.

110.—(1) This Act may be cited as the Civil Aviation Act 1982.

(2) This Act shall come into force at the expiration of the period of three months beginning with its passing.

SCHEDULES

SCHEDULE 1

ADDITIONAL PROVISIONS RELATING TO CONSTITUTION, ETC. OF CAA

Appointment and tenure of members

1. It shall be the duty of the Secretary of State—

   (*a*) to satisfy himself, before he appoints a person to be a member, that that person will have no such financial or other interest as is likely to affect prejudicially the performance of his functions as a member ; and

   (*b*) to satisfy himself from time to time with respect to each member that the member has no such interest ;

and a person who is a member or whom the Secretary of State proposes to appoint as a member shall, whenever requested by the Secretary of State to do so, furnish him with such information as he may specify with a view to carrying out his duty under this paragraph.

2. Subject to the following provisions of this Schedule, a person shall hold and vacate office as a member or the chairman or a deputy chairman in accordance with the terms of the instrument appointing him to that office.

3. A person may at any time resign his office as a member or the chairman or a deputy chairman by giving to the Secretary of State a notice in writing signed by that person and stating that he resigns that office.

4.—(1) If a member becomes or ceases to be the chairman or a deputy chairman the Secretary of State may vary the terms of the instrument appointing him to be a member so as to alter the date on which he is to vacate office as a member.

(2) If the chairman or a deputy chairman ceases to be a member, he shall cease to be the chairman or a deputy chairman, as the case may be.

5.—(1) If the Secretary of State is satisfied that a member—

   (*a*) has been absent from meetings of the CAA for a period longer than three consecutive months without the permission of the CAA, or

   (*b*) has become bankrupt or made an arrangement with his creditors, or

   (*c*) is incapacitated by physical or mental illness, or

   (*d*) is otherwise unable or unfit to discharge the functions of a member,

the Secretary of State may declare his office as a member to be vacant and shall notify the declaration in such manner as he thinks fit ; and thereupon the office shall become vacant.

(2) In the application of sub-paragraph (1) above to Scotland, for the references in paragraph (*b*) to a member's having become bankrupt and to a member's having made an arrangement with his creditors there shall be substituted respectively references to sequestration of a member's estate having been awarded and to a member's having made a trust deed for behoof of his creditors or a composition contract.

Remuneration etc. of members

6. The CAA shall pay each member such remuneration as the Secretary of State may determine with the consent of the Treasury.

7.—(1) The CAA shall make such provision as may be determined by the Secretary of State with the consent of the Treasury for the payment of pensions, allowances or gratuities to or in respect of such members as may be so determined.

(2) The Secretary of State shall as soon as possible after making a determination in pursuance of sub-paragraph (1) above lay before each House of Parliament a statement containing particulars of the determination.

8. Where a person ceases to be a member otherwise than on the expiry of his term of office and it appears to the Secretary of State that there are special circumstances which make it right for that person to receive compensation, the Secretary of State may with the consent of the Treasury direct the CAA to make that person a payment of such amount as the Secretary of State may determine with the consent of the Treasury.

Proceedings

9. Subject to section 7 of this Act, the quorum of the CAA and the arrangements relating to its meetings shall be such as it may determine.

10.—(1) A member who is in any way directly or indirectly interested in a contract made or proposed to be made by the CAA, or in any other matter whatsoever which falls to be considered by the CAA, shall disclose the nature of his interest at a meeting of the CAA and the disclosure shall be recorded in the minutes of the meeting ; and the member shall not—

(*a*) in the case of a contract, take part in any deliberation or decision of the CAA with respect to the contract ; and

(*b*) in the case of any other matter, take part in any deliberation or decision of the CAA with respect to the matter if the CAA decides that the interest in question might affect prejudicially the member's consideration of the matter.

(2) A notice given by a member at a meeting of the CAA to the effect that he is a member of a specified company or firm and is to be regarded as interested in any contract which is made after the date of the notice with the company or firm shall, for the purposes of sub-paragraph (1) above, be a sufficient disclosure of his interest in relation to any contract so made.

(3) A member need not attend in person at a meeting of the CAA in order to make a disclosure which he is required to make under this paragraph if he takes reasonable steps to secure that the disclosure is made by a notice which is taken into consideration and read at such a meeting.

11. The validity of any proceedings of the CAA shall not be affected by any vacancy among the members or by any defect in the appointment of a member or by any failure to comply with the requirements of paragraph 10 above.

Staff

12. The CAA may appoint such officers and servants as it may determine ; and any reference in this Act to an employee of the CAA is a reference to a person appointed in pursuance of this paragraph or employed by the CAA in pursuance of paragraph 14 of Schedule 1 to the Civil Aviation Act 1971 (existing employees to whom CAA obliged to offer employment).

13.—(1) The CAA shall, in the case of such of its employees as it may determine, pay such pensions, allowances or gratuities to or in respect of them as it may determine, make such payments towards the provision of such pensions, allowances or gratuities as it may determine or provide and maintain such schemes (whether contributory or not) for the payment of such pensions, allowances or gratuities as it may determine.

(2) If an employee of the CAA becomes a member and was by reference to his employment by the CAA a participant in a pension scheme maintained by the CAA for the benefit of any of its employees, the CAA may determine that his service as a member shall be treated for the purposes of the scheme as service as an employee of the CAA ; and the benefits payable to or in respect of a person by virtue of the preceding provisions of this sub-paragraph shall be in addition to the benefits, if any, which are payable to or in respect of him by virtue of paragraph 7 above.

14. It shall be the duty of the CAA, except so far as it is satisfied that adequate machinery exists for achieving the purpose of this paragraph, to seek consultation with any organisation appearing to the CAA to be appropriate with a view to the conclusion between the CAA and that organisation of such agreements as appear to the parties to be desirable with respect to the establishment and maintenance of machinery for—

(a) the settlement by negotiation of terms and conditions of employment of employees of the CAA, with provision for reference to arbitration in default of such a settlement in such cases as may be determined by or under the agreements ; and

(b) the promotion and encouragement of measures affecting the safety, health and welfare of employees of the CAA and the discussion of other matters of mutual interest to the CAA and its employees, including efficiency in the performance of the CAA's functions.

Performance of functions

15. Subject to section 7(1) of this Act, the CAA may authorise any member or employee of the CAA and, except so far as regulations made by the Secretary of State provide otherwise, any other person to perform on behalf of the CAA such of its functions (including the function conferred on it by this paragraph) as are specified in the authorisation.

Instruments and contracts

16. The fixing of the common seal of the CAA shall be authenticated by the signature of the secretary of the CAA or some other person authorised by the CAA to act for that purpose.

17. A document purporting to be duly executed under the seal of the CAA shall be received in evidence and shall, unless the contrary is proved, be deemed to be so executed.

Interpretation

18. In this Schedule " the chairman ", " a deputy chairman " and " a member " mean respectively the chairman, a deputy chairman and a member of the CAA and " gratuities " includes a refund of contributions to a pension fund with or without interest on, or any other addition to, the contributions.

SCHEDULE 2

Section 19.

APPLICATION OF ENACTMENTS RELATING TO STATUTORY UNDERTAKERS, ETC.

1.—(1) Section 39(3) of the Public Health Act 1936 (which exempts buildings belonging to statutory undertakers from certain drainage requirements) shall apply in relation to the CAA as it applies in relation to statutory undertakers but as if in the proviso to the said section 39(3) (which excludes from the exemption houses and buildings used as offices or showrooms) the references to offices or showrooms did not include offices or showrooms on any aerodrome owned by the CAA.

1936 c. 49.

(2) Section 330 of the said Act of 1936 (power of certain undertakers in England and Wales to alter sewers), section 333 of that Act (protection of certain undertakings in England and Wales from works executed under that Act) and section 107 of the Public Health (Scotland) Act 1897 (protection of certain undertakings in Scotland from works connected with sewers) shall apply in relation to the CAA and any property owned by the CAA as they apply in relation to a railway company and its railway.

1897 c. 38.

2. The CAA shall be deemed to be public utility undertakers and its undertaking a public utility undertaking for the purposes of the provisions of the Civil Defence Act 1939 other than paragraphs (*a*) to (*c*) of section 7(6) and section 9(4) ; and in that Act " appropriate department " shall, in relation to the CAA, mean the Secretary of State.

1939 c. 31.

SCH. 2
1945 c. 42.
1980 c. 45.

3.—(1) Section 93 of Schedule 3 to the Water Act 1945 and section 45 of Schedule 4 to the Water (Scotland) Act 1980 (which relate to the protection of certain statutory undertakers) shall apply with the necessary modifications in relation to any works along, upon or under any property owned by the CAA which statutory water undertakers propose to execute, whether or not the said section 93 or the said section 45 has been applied to the undertakers by an order under the said Act of 1945 or the said Act of 1980.

(2) In sub-paragraph (1) above " statutory water undertakers " means—

1973 c. 37.

(a) in relation to England and Wales, statutory water under-takers within the meaning of the Water Act 1973 and includes a person authorised to construct works by an order under section 23 of the Water Act 1945 ; and

(b) in relation to Scotland, a water authority within the meaning of the Water (Scotland) Act 1980.

4. The CAA shall be deemed to be statutory undertakers and its undertaking a statutory undertaking for the purposes of the follow-ing enactments, that is to say—

1947 c. 42.

the Acquisition of Land (Authorisation Procedure) (Scotland) Act 1947 ;

1948 c. 17.

section 4 of the Requisitioned Land and War Works Act 1948 ;

1949 c. 97.

the National Parks and Access to the Countryside Act 1949 ;

1951 c. 65.

the Reserve and Auxiliary Forces (Protection of Civil Interests) Act 1951 ;

1954 c. 56.

the Landlord and Tenant Act 1954 ;

1957 c. 56.

Part III of the Housing Act 1957 ;

1958 c. 69.

section 39(6)(b) of the Opencast Coal Act 1958 ;

1961 c. 33.

section 11 of the Land Compensation Act 1961 ;

1961 c. 41.

section 3(4) of the Flood Prevention (Scotland) Act 1961 ;

1962 c. 58.

the Pipe-lines Act 1962 ;

1963 c. 51.

section 18 of the Land Compensation (Scotland) Act 1963 ;

1981 c. 56.
1964 c. 40.

Schedule 3 and (pending the coming into force of its repeal by the Transport Act 1981) Schedule 5 to the Harbours Act 1964 ;

1965 c. 36.

Schedule 6 to the Gas Act 1965 ;

1965 c. 46.

section 10(4) of the Highlands and Islands Development (Scot-land) Act 1965 ;

1967 c. 86.

sections 11(5)(f), 54(6) and 75(4) of, and Schedule 3 to, the Countryside (Scotland) Act 1967 ;

1968 c. 16.

the New Towns (Scotland) Act 1968 ;

1968 c. 41.

paragraph 6 of Schedule 2 to the Countryside Act 1968 ;

1968 c. 47.

section 22 of the Sewerage (Scotland) Act 1968 ;

1970 c. 20.

section 39 of the Roads (Scotland) Act 1970 ;

sections 22, 40, 48, 49, 118(2), 127 to 129, 149, 165(3), 181 to 183,   Sch. 2
186, 192, 206(6), 209(3)(*b*), 210(2), 213(3), 216, 223, 225 to
241 (except section 230 as applied by section 13 of the
Opencast Coal Act 1958), 245(7)(*b*), 255, 281(6)(*b*) of, and 1958 c. 69.
Schedule 10, paragraphs 1 to 3 of Schedule 19, and Schedule
20 to, the Town and Country Planning Act 1971 ;   1971 c. 78.

sections 19, 37, 45, 46, 108(2), 117, 118, 119, 138, 154(3), 170 to
172, 175, 181, 195(6), 198(3)(*b*), 199(2), 202(3), 205, 212, 214
to 230, 233(7), 242, 266(6)(*b*) of, and Schedules 8 and 9,
paragraphs 1 to 3 of Schedule 17, and Schedule 18 to, the
Town and Country Planning (Scotland) Act 1972,   1972 c. 52.

5. In the following enactments, that is to say—

section 13 of the Pipe-lines Act 1962,   1962 c. 58.

the New Towns (Scotland) Act 1968,   1968 c. 16.

sections 149(3), 165(3) and 225 to 241 of, and Schedule 10 to,
the Town and Country Planning Act 1971,

sections 138(3), 154(3) and 214 to 230 of, and Schedule 8 to, the
Town and Country Planning (Scotland) Act 1972,

the New Towns Act 1981,   1981 c. 64.

" operational land " shall, in relation to the CAA, mean land of the
CAA's of any such class as may be prescribed ; and—

(*a*) the definition of a class of land for the purposes of regulations made in pursuance of this paragraph may be framed
by reference to any circumstances whatsoever ; and

(*b*) without prejudice to paragraph 1 of Part III of Schedule 13
to this Act, regulations so made may prescribe different
classes of land for the purposes of different enactments
mentioned in the preceding provisions of this paragraph ;
and

(*c*) if any question arises whether land of the CAA's falls within
a class prescribed in pursuance of this paragraph, it shall
be determined by the Secretary of State.

6.—(1) Where an interest in land is held by the CAA, section 223
of the Town and Country Planning Act 1971 shall not apply for the
purpose of determining whether the land is operational land in
relation to the CAA for the purposes of that Act.

(2) Section 225(2)(*b*) of the said Act of 1971 (which specifies the
circumstances in which special provisions relating to planning applications and appeals by statutory undertakers are to apply to land
which is not operational land of the undertakers) shall have effect
in relation to the CAA as if for the reference to development
involving the use of the land for the purpose of carrying on the
CAA's undertaking there were substituted a reference to development
involving the use of the land for such of the purposes of carrying
on that undertaking as may be prescribed.

7.—(1) Where an interest in land is held by the CAA, section 212
of the Town and Country Planning (Scotland) Act 1972 shall not
apply for the purpose of determining whether the land is operational
land in relation to the CAA for the purposes of that Act.

Sch. 2   (2) Section 214(2)(*b*) of the said Act of 1972 (which specifies the circumstances in which special provisions relating to planning applications and appeals by statutory undertakers are to apply to land which is not operational land of the undertakers) shall have effect in relation to the CAA as if for the reference to development involving the use of the land for the purpose of carrying on the CAA's undertaking there were substituted a reference to development involving the use of the land for such of the purposes of carrying on that undertaking as may be prescribed.

Section 22.

SCHEDULE 3

Matters Arising out of Transfer to CAA of Aerodromes and Other Property, Rights and Liabilities and Staff

1. A certificate issued by the Secretary of State and stating that any property, rights or liabilities of the Crown or a government department were or were not transferred to the CAA by paragraph 1 1971 c. 75. of Schedule 2 to the Civil Aviation Act 1971 shall be conclusive evidence that the property, rights and liabilities in question were or were not so transferred.

2.—(1) Any agreement and any provision in a document which is not an agreement shall, so far as may be necessary for or in consequence of the transfers effected by the said Schedule 2, continue to have effect as if references to, or to an officer of, the Crown or a government department were, or as the case may be included, references to or to an employee of the CAA.

(2) Without prejudice to sub-paragraph (1) above, any agreement to which the Crown or a government department was a party, whether in writing or not and whether or not of such a nature that rights and liabilities under it could be assigned, shall continue to have effect, so far as may be necessary for or in consequence of the transfers effected by that Schedule, as if the CAA had been a party to the agreement.

(3) Without prejudice to sub-paragraph (1) above, where by the operation of that Schedule any right or liability has become a right or liability of the CAA, the CAA and all other persons shall have the same rights, powers and remedies (and in particular the same rights, powers and remedies as to taking or resisting legal proceedings or the making or resisting of applications to any authority) for ascertaining, perfecting or enforcing the right or liability as they would have had if it had at all times been a right or liability of the CAA.

1968 c. 3.
1971 c. 69.

1970 c. 10.   3. For the purposes of the Capital Allowances Act 1968 and Chapter I of Part III of the Finance Act 1971 (which confer relief from income tax in respect of certain capital expenditure) and Chapter II of Part XI of the Income and Corporation Taxes Act 1970 (which relates to companies' capital gains) the transfer by the said Schedule 2, of any assets shall be deemed to be a sale of those assets by the Secretary of State to the CAA in the open market at a price equal to so much of the initial debt as is determined by the Secretary of State to relate to those assets ; but no initial allowance or first year allowance shall be made under the said Act of 1968 or the said Act of 1971 in respect of any of those assets.

SCH. 3

4. The Secretary of State shall, before making a determination or issuing a certificate under any of the preceding provisions of this Schedule, consult the CAA and shall after making the determination or issuing the certificate send a copy of it to the CAA.

5.—(1) Where after any land was transferred to the CAA under the said Schedule 2, a government department or a person acting on behalf of the Crown retained possession of any document relating to the title to that land, the department or person shall be assumed to have given to the CAA an acknowledgment in writing of the right of the CAA to the production of that document and to delivery of copies of it ; and as respects land in England and Wales section 64 of the Law of Property Act 1925 and as respects land in Northern Ireland section 9 of the Conveyancing Act 1881 (which relate to the production and safe custody of documents) shall have effect accordingly and as if the acknowledgment did not contain any such expression of a contrary intention as is mentioned in the said section 64 or section 9.

1925 c. 20.
1881 c. 41.

(2) In the application of sub-paragraph (1) above to Scotland, for the words from " an acknowledgment " onwards there shall be substituted the words " an undertaking to produce those documents to the CAA (on a proper receipt and undertaking to re-deliver) for the purpose of enabling the CAA to maintain and defend its rights in respect of that part of the land which has vested in it ".

6.—(1) Where a person entered the employment of the CAA on 1st April 1972 and immediately before that date was occupied in employment to which this paragraph applies, then, for the purpose of ascertaining the length of the period of his employment for the purposes of sections 49 and 50 and Part VI of the Employment Protection (Consolidation) Act 1978, Schedule 13 to that Act shall have effect—

1978 c. 44.

(a) as if, in a case where he was so occupied otherwise than under a contract of service, employment of his to which this paragraph applies in which he was occupied otherwise than as aforesaid before the said 1st April had been employment within the meaning of the said Act of 1978, and, while he was occupied therein, he had been an employee within the meaning of that Act, but as if for paragraph 4 of that Schedule there were substituted the following paragraph—

" 4. Any week during the whole or part of which the terms of his employment normally involve employment for sixteen hours or more weekly shall count in computing a period of employment." ;

and

(b) as if, in any case, subject to sub-paragraph (2) below, the period, ending immediately before the said 1st April, of employment of his to which this paragraph applies counted

Sch. 3

as a period of employment with the CAA (if, apart from this provision, it would not so count) and his transfer to employment with the CAA did not break the continuity of the period of employment (if, apart from this provision, the transfer would have done so).

(2) Where, before the said 1st April, a person's employment to which this paragraph applies was terminated and a payment made to him in respect of the termination in accordance with the Superannuation Act 1965 or any enactment repealed by that Act or in accordance with a scheme made under section 1 of the Superannuation Act 1972, or under such arrangements as were mentioned (before it was repealed) in section 41(3) of the Redundancy Payments Act 1965, then, whether or not he was re-employed in employment to which this paragraph applies immediately following the termination, Schedule 13 to the said Act of 1978 shall have effect as if the period of his employment before that termination in employment to which this paragraph applies did not count as a period of employment with the CAA.

1965 c. 74.

1972 c. 11.

1965 c. 62.

(3) In the application of paragraph 10 of Schedule 14 to the said Act of 1978 (calculation of rates of remuneration) to a person in whose case sub-paragraph (1) above applies, references in that paragraph to a former employer and a period of employment with a former employer shall be construed in accordance with the preceding sub-paragraphs, and the reference in that paragraph to Schedule 13 to that Act shall be construed as a reference to that Schedule as it has effect by virtue of sub-paragraph (1) above.

(4) Section 7 of the said Act of 1978 (power to vary number of weekly hours of employment necessary to qualify for rights) shall have effect as if references to paragraph 4 of Schedule 13 to that Act included references to the paragraph substituted for that paragraph by sub-paragraph (1) above and to sub-paragraph (5) below.

(5) This paragraph applies to employment of a person in the civil service of the State, and to employment of a person therein in part-time service, where he gives personal service of at least twenty-one hours a week and the remuneration in respect thereof is defrayed entirely out of money provided by Parliament.

(6) This paragraph applies notwithstanding the provisions of section 99 of the said Act of 1978.

7.—(1) Where a person entered the employment of the CAA on 1st April 1972 and immediately before that date was occupied in employment to which this paragraph applies, then, for the purpose of ascertaining the length of the period of his employment for the purposes of sections 1 and 2 of the Contracts of Employment and Redundancy Payments Act (Northern Ireland) 1965 (in this paragraph referred to as " the Act of 1965 "), Schedule 1 to that Act shall have effect—

1965 c. 19
(N.I.).

    (a) as if, in a case where he was so occupied otherwise than under a contract of service, employment of his to which this paragraph applies in which he was occupied otherwise

than as aforesaid before the said 1st April had been employment within the meaning of the Act of 1965, and, while he
was occupied therein, he had been an employee within
the meaning of that Act, but as if, for paragraph 4 of that
Schedule, there were substituted the following paragraph—

> " 4. Any week during the whole or part of which the
> terms of his employment normally involve employment
> for twenty-one hours or more weekly shall count in
> computing a period of employment." ;

and

(b) as if, in any case, subject to sub-paragraph (2) below, the
period, ending immediately before the said 1st April, of
employment of his to which this paragraph applies counted
as a period of employment with the CAA (if, apart from
this provision, it would not so count) and his transfer to
employment with the CAA did not break the continuity
of the period of employment (if, apart from this provision,
the transfer would have done so).

(2) Where, before the said 1st April, a person's employment to
which this paragraph applies was terminated and a payment made
to him in respect of the termination in accordance with the Super- 1965 c. 74.
annuation Act 1965 or any enactment repealed by that Act or in
accordance with a scheme made under section 1 of the Super- 1972 c. 11.
annuation Act 1972, or under such arrangements as were mentioned
(before it was repealed) in section 41(3) of the Redundancy Pay- 1965 c. 62.
ments Act 1965, then, whether or not he was re-employed in
employment to which this paragraph applies immediately following
that termination, Schedule 1 to the Act of 1965 shall have effect as
if the period of his employment before that termination in employment to which this paragraph applies did not count as a period of
employment with the CAA.

(3) In the application of paragraph 8 of Schedule 2 to the Indus- S.I. 1976/1043
trial Relations (Northern Ireland) Order 1976 (calculation of rates (N.I. 16).
of remuneration) to a person in whose case sub-paragraph (1) above
applies, references in that paragraph to a former employer and a
period of employment with a former employer shall be construed
in accordance with the preceding sub-paragraphs, and the reference
in that paragraph to Schedule 1 to the Act of 1965 shall be construed
as a reference to that Schedule as it has effect by virtue of sub-
paragraph (1) above.

(4) Section 7 of the Act of 1965 (power to vary number of weekly
hours of employment necessary to qualify for rights) shall have
effect as if the reference therein to paragraph 4 of Schedule 1 to
that Act included a reference to the paragraph substituted for that
paragraph by sub-paragraph (1) above and to sub-paragraph (7)
below.

(5) For the purpose of computing, for the purposes of the Act
of 1965, a period of employment of a person in whose case sub-
paragraph (1) above applies, any reference in that Act to Schedule

Sch. 3
S.I. 1976/1043
(N.I. 16).

1 to that Act or to Schedule 2 to the Industrial Relations (Northern Ireland) Order 1976 shall, in relation to employment of his to which this paragraph applies being employment before the said 1st April, be construed as a reference to the said Schedule 1 or the said Schedule 2, as the case may be, as it has effect by virtue of sub-paragraphs (1) to (4) above.

(6) Where a person entered the employment of the CAA on the said 1st April and, immediately before that date, was occupied in employment to which this paragraph applies, then, for the purpose of computing a period of employment for the purposes of the said Schedule 1 as applied by Schedule 3 to the Act of 1965, a period in which he was occupied in employment to which this paragraph applies shall, notwithstanding the provisions of section 26(3) of the Act of 1965 (which excludes the application of section 11 of that Act to a person in respect of certain employment), be treated as if it had been a period in respect of which section 11 of that Act had applied.

(7) This paragraph applies to employment of a person in the civil service of the State and to employment of a person therein in part-time service where he gives personal service of at least twenty-one hours a week and the remuneration in respect thereof is defrayed entirely out of money provided by Parliament.

1978 c. 44.

1971 c. 75.
1949 c. 67.

8.—(1) For the purposes of section 94(1) of and paragraph 17(2) of Schedule 13 to the Employment Protection (Consolidation) Act 1978 (which relate to changes of ownership of businesses), there shall be deemed to have been transferred to the CAA on the said 1st April the business of any body which by virtue of section 27(1) of the Civil Aviation Act 1971 ceased to have functions conferred on it in pursuance of section 7 of the Civil Aviation Act 1949 ; and a body whose business is deemed for those purposes to have been transferred by virtue of this paragraph shall on the said 1st April be deemed for the purposes of the said section 94(1) to have terminated in connection with the transfer its contracts of employment with persons employed by it immediately before the said 1st April.

(2) In the application of the preceding sub-paragraph to Northern Ireland, for the reference to the said paragraph 17(2) and the references to the said section 94(1) there shall be substituted respectively a reference to paragraph 10(2) of Schedule 1 to the Contracts of Employment and Redundancy Payments Act (Northern Ireland) 1965 and references to section 23(1) of that Act.

1965 c. 19
(N.I.).

9. It is hereby declared that in this Schedule " property " includes land.

Section 24.

SCHEDULE 4

Eurocontrol

1.—(1) Eurocontrol shall have the legal capacity of a body corporate ; and anything which may be required or authorised by law to be done by or to Eurocontrol may be done by or to the Agency on behalf of Eurocontrol.

(2) Eurocontrol shall be entitled to the exemptions and reliefs described in paragraphs 3 to 5 of Schedule 1 to the International Organisations Act 1968 (rates and taxes, import duties and import and export restrictions).

(3) Subject to sub-paragraph (4) below, any rule of law relating to the inviolability of the official archives and premises of an envoy of a foreign sovereign Power accredited to Her Majesty shall extend to the official archives of Eurocontrol, and to premises occupied by Eurocontrol wholly or mainly for the housing of its installations ; and without prejudice to the foregoing provisions, no judgment or order of any court shall be enforced by the levying of execution or by diligence upon anything forming part of any such installations.

(4) Sub-paragraph (3) above (except so far as it relates to execution or diligence) shall not preclude access to any premises or the inspection of any record or document—

> (*a*) by a constable or other person acting in the execution of a warrant or other legal process ;
>
> (*b*) by a court of Inquiry or an Inspector of Accidents acting in pursuance of regulations made under section 75 of this Act ; or
>
> (*c*) by a constable having reason to believe that an offence has been or is being or is about to be committed on the premises.

(5) In this paragraph—

> " the Agency " means the Air Traffic Services Agency comprised in Eurocontrol ;
>
> " installations " means apparatus for locating, directing, affording navigational aid to, or otherwise communicating with, aircraft in flight, including apparatus for recording or processing material received or transmitted by such apparatus, and any other apparatus for use in connection with any such apparatus as aforesaid ;
>
> " record " has the same meaning as in section 73 of this Act.

2.—(1) The Secretary of State may from time to time pay to Eurocontrol such sums on account of its expenses as he may with the consent of the Treasury determine, being sums for the payment of which Her Majesty's Government in the United Kingdom are liable under the Eurocontrol Convention.

(2) The Secretary of State may provide for Eurocontrol any land, premises, installations, equipment or services (including the services of personnel), whether within or without the United Kingdom which may be required for the purposes of or in connection with the functions of Eurocontrol under the Eurocontrol Convention.

(3) Any sums received from Eurocontrol by the Secretary of State in consideration of anything done under this paragraph shall be paid into the Consolidated Fund.

3.—(1) Subject to sub-paragraph (2) below, a court in any part of the United Kingdom shall have jurisdiction to hear and determine a claim against Eurocontrol for damages in respect of any wrongful

Sch. 4   act, neglect or default, notwithstanding that the act, neglect or default did not take place within the jurisdiction of the court or that Eurocontrol is not present within the jurisdiction of the court.

(2) A court shall not have jurisdiction by virtue of sub-paragraph (1) above in respect of damage or injury sustained wholly within or over a country to which the provisions of this Act relating to Euro control do not extend.

Sections 29 and 33.

SCHEDULE 5

Byelaws Made by CAA or Proprietor of Private Aerodrome

1. The byelaws shall be made under the common seal of the CAA.

2. At least one month before application for confirmation of the byelaws is made, notice of the intention to apply for confirmation shall be given by the CAA in one or more local newspapers circulating in the locality in which the aerodrome to which the byelaws relate is situated or, if the byelaws relate to more than one aerodrome, circulating respectively in the several localities in which those aerodromes are situated ; and the notice shall specify a period of not less than one month during which representations on the byelaws may be made to the Secretary of State.

3. For at least one month before application for confirmation is made a copy of the byelaws shall be deposited at the offices of the CAA at each aerodrome to which the byelaws relate and shall at all reasonable hours be open to public inspection free of charge.

4. The CAA shall, on application made by any person before the byelaws are confirmed, furnish him with a copy of the byelaws or of any part of them on payment of such sum, not exceeding 5p for every hundred words contained in the copy, as the CAA may determine.

5. The Secretary of State may confirm with or without modifications, or refuse to confirm, any byelaw submitted to him for confirmation, and may fix the date on which a byelaw confirmed by him is to come into operation ; and if no date is so fixed the byelaw shall come into operation at the expiration of one month beginning with the day on which it is confirmed.

6. A copy of the byelaws, when confirmed, shall be printed and deposited at the offices of the CAA at each aerodrome to which the byelaws relate and shall at all reasonable hours be open to public inspection free of charge ; and a copy of the byelaws shall on application be furnished to any person on payment of such sum, not exceeding 10p for every copy, as the CAA may determine.

7. The production of a printed copy of a byelaw purporting to be made by the CAA upon which is endorsed a certificate purporting to be signed by a person authorised for the purpose by the CAA stating—

(*a*) that the byelaw was made by the CAA,

(*b*) that the copy is a true copy of the byelaw,

(*c*) that on a specified date the byelaw was confirmed by the Secretary of State, and

(*d*) the date, if any, fixed by the Secretary of State for the coming into operation of the byelaw,

shall be evidence, and in Scotland sufficient evidence, of the facts stated in the certificate, without proof of the handwriting or authorisation of the person by whom it purports to be signed.

SCHEDULE 6

Section 42.

MODIFICATIONS OF SCHEDULE 6 TO THE LOCAL GOVERNMENT ACT (NORTHERN IRELAND) 1972

1. For references to the department concerned there shall be substituted references to the Secretary of State.

2. For references to a district council there shall be substituted references to the Civil Aviation Authority.

3. References to Schedule 6 to the Local Government Act (Northern Ireland) 1972 shall be construed as references to that Schedule as modified by this Schedule. 1972 c. 9 (N.I.).

4. For paragraph 1 there shall be substituted the following paragraph—

" 1. An application by the Civil Aviation Authority to the Secretary of State for a vesting order shall be in the prescribed **form**.".

5. For sub-paragraph (2) of paragraph 6 there shall be substituted the following sub-paragraph—

" (2) To the extent to which compensation is payable in accordance with the provisions of this Schedule, as from the date of vesting the rights and claims of all persons in respect of any land acquired by the vesting order shall be transferred and attached to the funds of the Civil Aviation Authority (in this Schedule referred to as " the compensation fund ") and shall be discharged by payments made by the Civil Aviation Authority.".

6. In paragraph 12(2) for the words " the clerk of the council " there shall be substituted the words " such person as may be designated for the purposes of this Schedule by the Civil Aviation Authority ".

7. Paragraph 20(2) shall be omitted.

SCHEDULE 7

PROVISIONS RELATING TO CERTAIN ORDERS UNDER PART II

Sections 44, 45 and 51 and Schedules 8 and 9.

PART I

1.—(1) Before making the order, the Secretary of State shall, unless the order is to be made on the application of the CAA—

(*a*) publish in one or more newspapers circulating in the locality in which the land is situated, and

(b) serve on every owner, lessee and occupier of any of the land and upon every local authority within whose area any of the land is situated,

a notice stating that the Secretary of State proposes to make the order and the effect thereof, and specifying the time (not being less than 28 days from the service of the notice) within which, and the manner in which, objections to the making of the order may be made.

(2) Before making an application for an order, the CAA shall—

(a) publish in one or more newspapers circulating in the locality in which the land is situated, and

(b) serve on every owner, lessee and occupier of any of the land and upon every local authority within whose area any of the land is situated,

a notice stating that the CAA proposes to apply for the order and the effect thereof and specifying the time (not being less than 42 days from service of the notice) within which, and the manner in which, objections to the making of the order may be made.

2. If no objection is duly made by any such local authority, owner, lessee or occupier as is mentioned in paragraph 1 above or if all objections so made are withdrawn, the Secretary of State may, if he thinks fit, make the order.

3. If any objection duly made as aforesaid is not withdrawn, the Secretary of State shall, before making the order, either cause a public local inquiry to be held or afford to any person by whom any objection has been duly made as aforesaid and not withdrawn an opportunity of appearing before and being heard by a person appointed by the Secretary of State for the purpose, and after considering the objection and the report of the person who held the inquiry or the person appointed as aforesaid, may, if he thinks fit, make the order.

4. Notwithstanding anything in paragraphs 2 and 3 above, the Secretary of State may require any person who has made an objection to state in writing the grounds of his objection, and may disregard the objection for the purposes of those paragraphs if he is satisfied that the objection relates exclusively to matters which can be dealt with by the tribunal by whom the compensation is to be assessed.

5.—(1) Immediately after the order has been made the appropriate person shall publish in one or more newspapers circulating in the locality in which the land is situated a notice stating that the order has been made and naming a place where a copy of the order may be seen at all reasonable hours, and shall serve a like notice on every person who, having duly objected to the order, has not withdrawn his objection.

(2) In this paragraph " the appropriate person " means—

(a) the CAA in the case of an order under section 44 of this Act made in favour of the CAA or in the case of an order under section 45 of this Act made in respect of an aerodrome owned or managed by the CAA ; and (*b*) the Secretary of State in any other case.

6. In this Part of this Schedule " owner " has the same meaning as in section 56 of this Act.

PART II

7. If any person aggrieved by the order desires to question the validity thereof, or of any provision contained therein, on the ground that it is not within the powers of the Secretary of State or that any requirement of this Act has not been complied with in relation to the order, he may, within six weeks from the time when notice that the order has been made is first published in accordance with the requirements of this Act, make an application to the High Court or in Scotland to the Court of Session ; and on any such application the court—

(*a*) may by interim order suspend the operation of the order or of any provision contained therein, either generally or in so far as it affects the applicant, until the final determination of the proceedings ; and

(*b*) if satisfied that the order or any provision contained therein is not within the powers of the Secretary of State, or that the interests of the applicant have been substantially prejudiced by any requirement of this Act not having been complied with, may quash the order or any provision contained therein, either generally or in so far as it affects the applicant.

8. Subject to the provisions of paragraph 7 above, the order shall not, either before or after it has been made, be questioned in any legal proceedings whatsoever, and shall become operative on the expiration of six weeks from the date on which notice of the making of the order is first published in accordance with the requirements of this Act.

9.—(1) Subject to sub-paragraph (2) below, this Part of this Schedule shall have effect in relation to an order to which the Statutory Orders (Special Procedure) Act 1945 applies—

1945 c. 18.

(*a*) as if in paragraph 7, for the reference to the time when notice that the order has been made is first published in accordance with the requirements of this Act there were substituted a reference to the time when the order becomes operative under that Act ; and

(*b*) as if in paragraph 8, the words from " and shall become operative " to the end were omitted.

(2) This Part of this Schedule shall not apply to an order which is confirmed by Act of Parliament under—

(*a*) section 6 of the said Act of 1945 ; or

(*b*) under section 2(4) of that Act in its application (as set out in section 10 of that Act) to orders extending to Scotland only.

Part III

10.—(1) Any person having an interest in land the value of which is diminished in consequence of the coming into operation of the order shall be entitled to recover compensation for the diminution from the appropriate person ; and the provisions of the Land Compensation Act shall have effect accordingly.

(2) In this paragraph " the appropriate person " has the same meaning as in paragraph 5 above.

11.—(1) Where any interest in land is subject to a mortgage or, in Scotland, to a heritable security—

    (*a*) any compensation payable under the preceding provisions of this Schedule in respect of the diminution in the value of the interest shall be assessed as if the interest were not subject to the mortgage or heritable security ;

    (*b*) a claim for any such compensation may be made by any mortgagee of the interest or, in Scotland, by any creditor in a heritable security of the interest, but without prejudice to the making of a claim by the person entitled to the interest ;

    (*c*) a mortgagee or, in Scotland, a creditor in a heritable security shall not be entitled to claim compensation under the said provisions in respect of his interest as such ; and

    (*d*) the compensation payable in respect of the interest subject to the mortgage or heritable security may be paid to such of the claimants as the Secretary of State thinks proper, and shall be applied by that claimant in such manner as the parties interested may agree, or, in default of such agreement, as may be determined by arbitration.

(2) In this paragraph—

    " mortgage " includes an equitable charge and any other encumbrance, and includes a sub-mortgage, and the expression " mortgagee " shall be construed accordingly ;

1924 c. 27.   " heritable security " means a heritable security within the meaning of the Conveyancing (Scotland) Act 1924, exclusive of a security by way of ground annual and a real burden ad factum praestandum, but inclusive of a security constituted by ex facie absolute disposition.

12.—(1) Where the order provides for the creation of any easement or servitude over land in England and Wales or Scotland held by a statutory undertaker for the purposes of the carrying on of his undertaking, or of any right in or in relation to such land, the undertaker shall be entitled to recover compensation in accordance with the special provisions of Part II of this Act relating to statutory undertakers in any case in which those provisions apply ; and shall not, in any such case, be entitled to recover compensation under the preceding paragraphs of this Schedule.

(2) Compensation recoverable by virtue of sub-paragraph (1) above shall be recoverable—

(a) from the Secretary of State in the case of an order made otherwise than in favour of the CAA ;

(b) from the CAA in the case of an order made in favour of the CAA.

SCHEDULE 8

Provisions Relating to Orders Under Section 45

1. Any person having an interest in land to which the order relates shall, if the value of the interest is diminished by the coming into operation of the order, be entitled to recover compensation for the diminution—

(a) from the Secretary of State, if the order is made in respect of an aerodrome vested in or under the control of the Secretary of State ; and

(b) from the CAA, if it is made in respect of an aerodrome owned or managed by the CAA.

2. Paragraph 11 of Schedule 7 to this Act shall have effect in relation to any compensation payable under paragraph 1 above as it has effect in relation to any such compensation as is mentioned in the said paragraph 11.

3. Any person who sustains damage by being disturbed in the use of land or water by reason of the coming into operation of the order (not being damage which consists of the diminution in the value of an interest in land) shall be entitled to recover compensation for the damage—

(a) from the Secretary of State, if the order is made in respect of an aerodrome vested in or under the control of the Secretary of State ; and

(b) from the CAA, if it is made in respect of an aerodrome owned or managed by the CAA.

4. For the purpose of assessing compensation under this Schedule, in so far as it is payable in respect of the diminution in the value of an interest in land, section 5 of the Land Compensation Act 1961, section 12 of the Land Compensation (Scotland) Act 1963 or section 2 of the Acquisition of Land (Assessment of Compensation) Act 1919 (which contain rules for assessing compensation) shall (according as the land is in England and Wales, Scotland or Northern Ireland), so far as applicable and subject to any necessary modifications, have effect as it has effect for the purpose of assessing compensation for the compulsory acquisition of land.

5. Where any dispute arises as to whether compensation is payable under this Schedule, or as to the amount of any such compensation or as to the persons to whom it is payable, the dispute shall be referred to and determined by the Lands Tribunal.

SCHEDULE 9

PROVISIONS RELATING TO DIRECTIONS UNDER SECTION 46

PART I

1.—(1) Immediately after the Secretary of State has given the direction, the appropriate person shall publish in one or more newspapers circulating in the locality a notice stating that the direction has been given, and shall also serve notice of the direction upon the persons mentioned in sub-paragraph (2) below.

(2) The said persons are—

    (*a*) in the case of a direction given for the purpose specified in paragraph (*c*) of subsection (2) of section 46 of this Act, every owner, lessee and occupier of any land to which the right of way is appurtenant or, in Scotland, of the dominant tenement and every local authority in whose area any of that land is situated ;

    (*b*) in the case of a direction given for any other purpose specified in that subsection, every owner, lessee and occupier of the land to which the direction relates and every local authority in whose area any of that land is situated ;

    (*c*) in the case of a direction restricting the installation of apparatus or extinguishing rights to install or maintain apparatus, every person whose rights to install or maintain apparatus are affected by the direction ; and

    (*d*) in the case of a direction requiring the removal of any apparatus, the person entitled to maintain the apparatus required to be removed under the direction.

(3) Any notice given with respect to any direction for the purpose of complying with the requirements of this paragraph shall state the effect of the direction.

2. The provisions of Part II of Schedule 7 to this Act shall, with the necessary modifications, have effect in relation to the direction as they have effect in relation to orders made under section 44 of this Act.

PART II

3. Any person having an interest in land the value of which is diminished in consequence of the coming into operation of the direction shall be entitled to recover compensation for the diminution from the appropriate person.

4. Paragraph 11 of Schedule 7 to this Act shall have effect in relation to any compensation payable under paragraph 3 of this Schedule as it has effect in relation to any such compensation as is mentioned in the said paragraph 11.

5. Any person who sustains damage by being disturbed in the enjoyment of any right in or over land in consequence of the coming into operation of the direction (not being damage which consists of

the diminution in the value of an interest in land) shall be entitled to recover compensation from the appropriate person in respect of that damage.

6. The appropriate person shall pay compensation in respect of any expenditure reasonably incurred by any person for the purpose of carrying out work which is required to be carried out by the direction.

7. The compensation payable to any person by virtue of the preceding provisions of this Schedule shall be reduced by the value to him of any timber, apparatus or other materials removed for the purposes of complying with the direction.

8. For the purpose of assessing compensation under this Schedule, in so far as it is payable in respect of the diminution in the value of an interest in land, section 5 of the Land Compensation Act 1961, section 12 of the Land Compensation (Scotland) Act 1963 or section 2 of the Acquisition of Land (Assessment of Compensation) Act 1919 (which contain rules for assessing compensation) shall (according as the land is in England and Wales, Scotland or Northern Ireland), so far as applicable and subject to any necessary modifications, have effect as it has effect for the purpose of assessing compensation for the compulsory acquisition of land.

9. Where any dispute arises as to whether compensation is payable under this Schedule, or as to the amount of any such compensation, or as to the persons to whom it is payable, the dispute shall be referred to and determined by the Lands Tribunal.

10. Where the direction affects any building, structure, or apparatus held or used by a statutory undertaker for the purposes of his undertaking, or affects any of the rights of a statutory undertaker to install or maintain apparatus for those purposes, or affects any right of way enjoyed by a statutory undertaker for those purposes, the undertaker shall be entitled to recover compensation from the appropriate person in accordance with the special provisions of Part II of this Act relating to statutory undertakers in any case in which those provisions apply, and shall not, in any such case, be entitled to recover compensation under the preceding paragraphs of this Schedule.

PART III

11. In this Schedule—

" the appropriate person " means—

      (*a*) except where the order was made in respect of Eurocontrol, the person in respect of whom the order was made ; and

      (*b*) where the order was made in respect of Eurocontrol, the Secretary of State ;

" the order ", in relation to a direction, means the order in pursuance of which the direction is given ;

" owner " has the same meaning as in section 56 of this Act.

SCHEDULE 10

ADJUSTMENTS OF THE FUNCTIONS OF STATUTORY UNDERTAKERS

PART I

1. Where it appears to the Secretary of State, upon a representation made by the person carrying on a statutory undertaking, that in order to facilitate any adjustment of the carrying on of the undertaking necessitated by any order made or proposed to be made under or in pursuance of Part II of this Act, or by any direction given or proposed to be given in pursuance of the said Part II, it is expedient that the powers and duties of the said person in relation to the carrying on of the undertaking should be extended or modified, the Secretary of State may by order provide for such extension or modification of the said powers and duties as appears to him to be requisite for facilitating the adjustment.

2. Without prejudice to the generality of paragraph 1 above, an order under this Part of this Schedule may provide—

    (*a*) for empowering the person carrying on the undertaking to acquire, whether compulsorily or by agreement, any land specified in the order and to erect or construct any buildings or works so specified ;

    (*b*) for applying in relation to the acquisition of such land and the construction of such works enactments relating to the acquisition of land and the construction of works ;

and for such incidental and supplemental matters as appear to the Secretary of State to be expedient for the purposes of the order.

3. As soon as may be after the making of a representation under this Part of this Schedule, the person carrying on the undertaking shall publish, in such form and manner as may be directed by the Secretary of State, a notice giving such particulars as may be so directed of the matters to which the representation relates and specifying the time within which, and the manner in which, objections to the making of an order on the representation may be made, and shall also, if it is so directed by the Secretary of State, serve a like notice on such persons, or persons of such classes, as may be so directed.

4. The provisions of section 236 of the Town and Country Planning Act 1971 and section 225 of the Town and Country Planning (Scotland) Act 1972 shall have effect as if—

    (*a*) references in the said section 236 to section 233 of the said Act of 1971,

    (*b*) references in the said section 225 to section 222 of the said Act of 1972, and

    (*c*) references in either the said section 236 or the said section 225 to the section under which the order is proposed to be made,

1971 c. 78.
1972 c. 52.

included references to this Part of this Schedule; and subject to those provisions in a case in which they have effect, the Secretary of State may, if he thinks fit, make an order.

5. An order under this Part of this Schedule shall be subject to special parliamentary procedure.

PART II

6. Where on a representation made for the purpose by the person carrying on a statutory undertaking the Secretary of State is satisfied that the making of any order under or in pursuance of Part II of this Act or the giving of any direction in pursuance of the said Part II has rendered impracticable the fulfilment of any obligation of that person incurred in connection with the carrying on of the undertaking, the Secretary of State may by order direct that that person shall be relieved of the fulfilment of the obligation either absolutely or to such extent as may be specified in the order.

7. As soon as may be after the making of a representation to the Secretary of State under paragraph 6 above the person carrying on the undertaking in question shall, as may be directed by the Secretary of State, do one or both of the following, that is to say—

    (*a*) publish, in such manner as may be so directed, a notice giving such particulars as may be so directed of the matters to which the representation relates and specifying the time within which, and the manner in which, objections to the making of an order on the representation may be made; and

    (*b*) serve such a notice on such persons, or persons of such classes, as may be so directed.

8. The provisions of section 236 of the Town and Country Planning Act 1971 and section 225 of the Town and Country Planning (Scotland) Act 1972 shall have effect as if—

    (*a*) references in the said section 236 to section 235 of the said Act of 1971,

    (*b*) references in the said section 225 to section 224 of the said Act of 1972, and

    (*c*) references in either the said section 236 or the said section 225 to the section under which the order is proposed to be made,

included references to this Part of this Schedule; and, subject to those provisions in a case in which they have effect, the Secretary of State may, if he thinks fit, make an order.

9. If any objection to the making of an order under this Part of this Schedule is made and is not withdrawn before the making of the order, the order shall be subject to special parliamentary procedure.

SCHEDULE 11

ADDITIONAL PROVISIONS RELATING TO AIRWORTHINESS REQUIREMENTS BOARD

Tenure of members

1.—(1) A person shall hold and vacate office as a member or the chairman in accordance with the terms of the instrument appointing him to that office.

(2) A person may at any time resign his office as a member or the chairman by giving the CAA a notice in writing signed by him and stating that he resigns that office.

(3) If the CAA is satisfied that a member—

  (a) has been absent from meetings of the board for a period longer than three consecutive months without the permission of the board, or

  (b) has become bankrupt or made an arrangement with his creditors, or

  (c) is incapacitated by physical or mental illness, or

  (d) is otherwise unable or unfit to discharge the functions of a member,

the CAA may declare his office as a member to be vacant and shall notify the declaration in such manner as it thinks fit ; and thereupon the office shall become vacant.

(4) In the application of sub-paragraph (3) above to Scotland, for the references in paragraph (b) to a member's having become bankrupt and to a member's having made an arrangement with his creditors there shall be substituted respectively references to sequestration of a member's estate having been awarded and to a member's having made a trust deed for behoof of his creditors or a composition contract.

2. If the chairman ceases to be a member he shall also cease to be the chairman.

Procedure

3. The procedure of the board (including the quorum) shall be such as the board may determine.

Supplemental

4. It shall be the duty of the CAA—

  (a) to provide the board with such staff and other facilities as the CAA after consultation with the board considers appropriate for enabling the board to perform its functions ; and

  (b) to pay any member such travelling and subsistence allowances as the CAA considers appropriate in connection with his functions as a member.

5. In this Schedule—

" the board " means the Airworthiness Requirements Board ;

" the chairman " means the chairman of the board ; and

" member " means member of the board.

SCHEDULE 12

Patent Claims Against Aircraft not Protected Under Chicago Convention

1. Where it is alleged by any person interested that a foreign aircraft which is not an aircraft to which section 89 of this Act applies, and which is making a passage through or over the United Kingdom, infringes in itself or in any part of it any invention, design or model which is entitled to protection in the United Kingdom, it shall be lawful, subject to and in accordance with rules of court, to detain the aircraft until the owner thereof deposits or secures in respect of the alleged infringement a sum (in this Schedule referred to as " the deposited sum ") ; and thereupon the aircraft shall not during the continuance or in the course of the passage be subject to any lien, arrest, detention or prohibition (whether by order of a court or otherwise) in respect or on account of the alleged infringement.

2. The deposited sum shall be such sum as may be agreed between the parties interested or, in default of agreement, fixed by the Secretary of State or some person duly authorised on his behalf ; and payment thereof shall be made or secured to the Secretary of State in such manner as the Secretary of State shall approve.

3. The deposited sum shall be dealt with by such tribunal and in accordance with such procedure as may be specified by rules of court, and such rules may provide generally for carrying this Schedule into effect.

4. For the purposes of this Schedule—

" owner " shall include the actual owner of an aircraft and any person claiming through or under him ; and

" passage " shall include all reasonable landings and stoppages in the course or for the purpose of the passage.

SCHEDULE 13

SUBORDINATE INSTRUMENTS

PART I

POWERS NOT EXERCISABLE BY STATUTORY INSTRUMENT

Section 31 (order authorising local authority to carry on ancillary business).

Section 42(2) (order vesting land in CAA).

Section 44 (order for creation of rights over land).

Section 45 (order restricting use of land).

Section 46 (order for control of land).

Section 47 (order requiring warnings on land).

Section 48(1) (order for stopping-up or diversion of a highway).

Part I or Part II of Schedule 10 (orders with respect to functions of a statutory undertaker).

PART II

PROVISIONS APPLYING TO CERTAIN POWERS

Provision of Act	General description	Parliamentary control	Supplemental powers
Section 5(3).	Orders designating aerodromes for purposes of section 5.	Subject to the negative resolution procedure.	Paragraphs 1 and 2 of Part III apply.
Section 7.	Regulations with respect to performance of CAA's functions.	Subject to the negative resolution procedure.	Paragraphs 1 and 2 of Part III apply.
Section 11(2).	Regulations prescribing manner of publishing scheme for charges.	Subject to the negative resolution procedure.	Paragraphs 1 and 2 of Part III apply.
Section 11(3).	Regulations for determining charges to be paid to CAA.	Subject to the negative resolution procedure.	Paragraphs 1 and 2 of Part III apply.
Section 15(3).	Order modifying or repealing section 15(1)(c) and (2).	Subject to the negative resolution procedure.	Paragraphs 1 and 2 of Part III apply.
Section 20(4).	Regulations about mode of giving evidence of instruments and publications of CAA.	Subject to the negative resolution procedure.	Paragraphs 1 and 2 of Part III apply.
Section 32(5).	Order repealing local enactment.	Subject to the negative resolution procedure.	Paragraph 2 of Part III applies.
Section 33(1).	Order designating aerodrome as aerodrome in respect of which byelaws may be made.	Subject to the negative resolution procedure.	—
Section 35(1).	Order designating aerodrome for purposes of requiring consultation.	Subject to the negative resolution procedure where the order revokes or amends a previous order under section 35(1).	—
Section 37.	Order designating aerodrome or applying road traffic enactments to designated aerodrome.	Subject to the negative resolution procedure.	—
Section 38(2).	Order directing aerodrome authority to fix charges by reference to noise factors.	Subject to the negative resolution procedure.	Paragraph 2 of Part III applies.
Section 40(2).	Order revoking or varying byelaws.	Subject to the negative resolution procedure.	Paragraph 2 of Part III applies.
Section 41(2)(b).	Order in Council extending Acquisition of Land Act 1981 to Northern Ireland.	Subject to the negative resolution procedure.	Paragraphs 2 and 3 of Part III apply.
Section 46(9).	Order repealing or amending local enactment.	Subject to the negative resolution procedure.	Paragraph 2 of Part III applies.

Provision of Act	General description	Parliamentary control	Supplemental powers
Section 60.	An Air Navigation Order.	Subject to the affirmative resolution procedure where the Order makes provision for any such matter as is mentioned in section 60(3)(r) and subject to the negative resolution procedure in any other case.	Paragraphs 2, 3, 4 and 6 of Part III apply.
Section 61(6).	Order repealing local enactment.	Subject to the negative resolution procedure.	Paragraph 2 of Part III applies.
Section 62.	Orders controlling air navigation in time of war or emergency.	—	Paragraph 4 of Part III applies.
Section 63.	Order in time of war or emergency for control of CAA's undertaking or other air transport undertaking.	Subject to the negative resolution procedure in the case of an order with respect to the CAA.	Paragraphs 1 and 2 of Part III apply in the case of an order with respect to the CAA and paragraph 4 applies in any case.
Section 64(3).	Regulations prescribing manner of publishing instruments under section 64(2)(a) and (b).	Subject to the negative resolution procedure.	Paragraphs 1 and 2 of Part III apply.
Section 65(1) or (6).	Regulations prescribing manner of publishing certain notices.	Subject to the negative resolution procedure.	Paragraphs 1 and 2 of Part III apply.
Section 66(1).	Regulations prescribing persons who may apply for revocation, suspension or variation of an air transport licence.	Subject to the negative resolution procedure.	Paragraphs 1 and 2 of Part III apply.
Section 66(4).	Regulations prescribing manner of serving certain notices.	Subject to the negative resolution procedure.	Paragraphs 1 and 2 of Part III apply.
Section 67.	Regulations making supplementary provision in respect of air transport licensing.	Subject to the negative resolution procedure.	Paragraphs 1 and 2 of Part III apply.
Section 71.	Regulations with respect to provision of accommodation in aircraft.	Subject to the negative resolution procedure.	Paragraphs 1 and 2 of Part III apply.
Section 73.	Regulations with respect to charges for air navigation services.	Subject to the negative resolution procedure.	Paragraphs 2, 4 and 6 of Part III apply.
Section 75.	Regulations with respect to the investigation of aircraft accidents.	—	Paragraphs 4 and 6 of Part III apply.
Section 78(1), (3), (4) or (5).	Regulations prescribing manner of publishing certain notices.	Subject to the negative resolution procedure.	Paragraphs 1 and 2 of Part III apply.

Provision of Act	General description	Parliamentary control	Supplemental powers
Section 78(8).	Order requiring provision and maintenance of noise measuring equipment etc.	Subject to the negative resolution procedure.	Paragraphs 1 and 2 of Part III apply.
Section 78(11).	Order repealing local enactment.	Subject to the negative resolution procedure.	Paragraphs 1 and 2 of Part III apply.
Section 80.	Order designating aerodrome for purposes of noise, etc. provisions.	Subject to the negative resolution procedure.	Paragraphs 1 and 2 of Part III apply.
Section 82(1).	Regulations permitting aerial advertising.	Subject to the negative resolution procedure.	Paragraphs 1 and 2 of Part III apply.
Section 84.	Regulations with respect to supply of information.	Subject to the negative resolution procedure.	Paragraphs 1 and 2 of Part III apply.
Section 85(1)(c).	Regulations prescribing manner of publishing certain particulars.	Subject to the negative resolution procedure.	Paragraphs 1 and 2 of Part III apply.
Section 86.	Order in Council making provision with respect to mortgaging of aircraft.	Subject to the affirmative resolution procedure.	Paragraphs 2 and 5 of Part III apply.
Section 87.	Order in Council applying law of wreck or salvage to aircraft.	Subject to the negative resolution procedure.	Paragraphs 2, 3, 4 and 6 of Part III apply.
Section 88(10).	Order designating aerodrome for purposes of section 88.	Subject to the negative resolution procedure.	—
Section 88(11).	Order repealing local enactment.	Subject to the negative resolution procedure.	Paragraph 2 of Part III applies.
Section 89(4).	Order in Council with respect to seizure of aircraft on patent claims.	Subject to the negative resolution procedure.	Paragraphs 2, 3, 4 and 6 of Part III apply.
Section 90.	Order in Council giving effect to Convention on rights in aircraft.	Subject to the affirmative resolution procedure.	Paragraphs 2 and 5 of Part III apply.
Section 91.	Order in Council with respect to civil jurisdiction in proceedings involving aircraft.	Subject to the negative resolution procedure.	Paragraphs 2, 3, 4 and 6 of Part III apply.
Section 96.	Regulations designating person for purposes of section 96(1) or (2).	Subject to the negative resolution procedure.	—
Section 101.	Order in Council extending provisions of Act to Crown aircraft.	Subject to the negative resolution procedure in the case of an Order made by virtue of section 101(1)(a).	Paragraphs 2, 3, 4 and 6 of Part III apply in the case of an Order made by virtue of section 101(1)(a).
Section 107(2).	Order in Council adapting provisions of Act in their application to Northern Ireland.	Subject to the negative resolution procedure.	Paragraphs 2, 3, 4 and 6 of Part III apply.

Provision of Act	General description	Parliamentary control	Supplemental powers
Section 108(1).	Order in Council extending provisions of Act to relevant overseas territory.	—	Paragraph 2 of Part III applies.
Section 108(2).	Order in Council extending provisions of Act to aircraft registered in a relevant overseas territory.	—	Paragraphs 1 and 2 of Part III apply.
Paragraph 15 of Schedule 1.	Regulations with respect to the sub-delegation of the CAA's functions.	Subject to the negative resolution procedure.	Paragraphs 1 and 2 of Part III apply.
Schedule 2.	Regulations in connection with the application of enactments relating to statutory undertakers.	Subject to the negative resolution procedure.	Paragraphs 1 and 2 of Part III apply.

PART III

SUPPLEMENTAL POWERS

Different provision for different cases

1.—(1) A power to which this paragraph applies shall include power to make different provision for different circumstances.

(2) Sub-paragraph (1) above is without prejudice to the generality of any provision of this Act conferring a power to which this paragraph does not apply.

Incidental supplementary and transitional provision

2. A power to which this paragraph applies shall include power to make such incidental, supplementary or transitional provision as the authority exercising the power thinks fit.

Power to authorise making of regulations

3.—(1) An Order in Council made in pursuance of a power to which this paragraph applies may authorise the Secretary of State to make regulations for carrying out the purposes of the Order in respect of such matters as may be specified in the Order.

(2) Paragraphs 2, 4 and 6 of this Part of this Schedule apply to any power to make regulations conferred by virtue of sub-paragraph (1) above.

Power to provide for detention of aircraft

4.—(1) Any Order in Council, order or regulations made, in relation to aircraft, in pursuance of any power to which this paragraph applies may provide for the detention of aircraft to secure compliance with the Order in Council, order or regulations, as the case may be, or with any enactment which is mentioned in sub-paragraph (2) below, and in connection with which the Order in Council, order or regulations is or are made, and may make such further provision as appears to the authority exercising the power to be necessary or expedient for securing such detention.

(2) The enactments referred to in sub-paragraph (1) above are the enactments contained in sections 73, 74, 76, 81, 89 and 97 of this Act and the enactments conferring powers to which this paragraph applies.

Crown aircraft

5. Without prejudice to section 101 of this Act, an Order in Council made in pursuance of a power to which this paragraph applies may apply in such cases and to such extent as appears to Her Majesty in Council to be expedient to aircraft belonging to or employed in the service of Her Majesty.

Extra-territorial provisions

6.—(1) Notwithstanding that an Order in Council or regulation made in pursuance of a power to which this paragraph applies has effect only as part of the law of the United Kingdom, no provision contained in the Order or regulation shall, on the ground

Sch. 13
that it would have extra-territorial operation, be deemed to be invalid in so far as it applies to aircraft registered in the United Kingdom, wherever they may be, or prohibits, requires or regulates—

> (a) the doing of anything by persons in, or any of the personnel of, such aircraft, wherever they may be ; or
>
> (b) the doing of anything in relation to such aircraft by other persons, being Commonwealth citizens, or citizens of the Republic of Ireland, wherever they may be.

1948 c. 56.
(2) Nothing in sub-paragraph (1) above shall affect subsection (1) of section 3 of the British Nationality Act 1948 (which limits the criminal liability of certain persons).

(3) For the purposes of sub-paragraph (1) above, the personnel of an aircraft shall be deemed to include the commander or other person in charge of the aircraft and all other members of the crew of the aircraft.

(4) Without prejudice to sub-paragraph (5) below, in the application of this paragraph to the power to make an Air Navigation Order or to make regulations by virtue of paragraph 3 above under such an Order, the references in sub-paragraph (1) above to aircraft registered in the United Kingdom shall have effect as if they included references to any aircraft which is not so registered but is for the time being under the management of a person who, or of persons each of whom, is qualified to be the owner of a legal or beneficial interest in an aircraft registered in the United Kingdom.

1971 c. 61.
(5) So far as relates to any provision of an Order in Council or regulation concerning aircraft on or in the neighbourhood of offshore installations, within the meaning of the Mineral Workings (Offshore Installations) Act 1971, this paragraph shall apply to all aircraft and not only to aircraft registered in the United Kingdom and shall apply to the doing of anything in relation to any aircraft by any person irrespective of nationality or, in the case of a body corporate, of the law under which it was incorporated.

(6) Sub-paragraph (5) above shall apply to installations notwithstanding that they are for the time being in transit.

Section 109.

SCHEDULE 14

Transitional and Transitory Provisions and Savings

General

1. Where any enactment has been repealed (whether by this Act or otherwise) but, by virtue of any provision of the Act making the repeal (including a provision delaying the coming into force of the repeal), continues on and after the operative date to have effect for any purpose, then any other enactment repealed by this Act which, but for its repeal, would have effect for the purpose of construing or otherwise giving effect to the first mentioned enactment shall, notwithstanding its repeal, continue to have effect in relation to that provision for that purpose.

2.—(1) Subject to sub-paragraph (2) below, where any period of time specified in an enactment re-enacted by this Act is current on the operative date, this Act shall have effect as if the provision of this Act re-enacting that enactment had been in force when that period began to run.

(2) A person shall not, by virtue of sub-paragraph (1) above, be liable in respect of any offence which continues or continued during any period beginning before the operative date to any penalty greater than that which might have been imposed on him apart from this Act; and accordingly the maximum penalty for such an offence shall be determined in accordance with the law in force immediately before the operative date.

3. Where anything was done before the operative date for the purposes of any enactment which is re-enacted by any provision of this Act the doing of that thing shall, on and after that date, have effect so far as may be necessary for giving the doing of that thing continuing effect as if that provision had been in force when the thing was done and as if the thing had been done for the purposes of that provision.

Extra-territorial provisions

4.—(1) The repeals made by this Act shall not affect the law in force in any country or territory which is outside the United Kingdom and is not a relevant overseas territory.

(2) The provisions of this Act, including the repeal of any power by Order in Council to extend any enactment to a relevant overseas territory or of any enactment which has been so extended, do not extend to any such territory except in so far as they are extended to that territory by an Order in Council under section 108(1) of this Act.

(3) Subsection (2) of section 59 of the Civil Aviation Act 1949 shall continue to have effect for the purposes of any Order in Council made under that subsection and in force before the coming into operation of Schedule 1 to the Civil Aviation (Amendment) Act 1982, and for the purpose of varying or revoking such an Order. 1949 c. 67.

1982 c. 1.

Byelaws

5.—(1) Byelaws having effect by virtue of subsection (4) of section 31 of the Civil Aviation Act 1971 as if made and confirmed under that section shall, on and after the operative date, continue to have effect with the modifications mentioned in that subsection (being the modifications made necessary by the transfer to the CAA of aerodromes to which the byelaws relate), but shall so have effect as if made and confirmed under section 29 of this Act. 1971 c. 75.

(2) Section 97(6)(*b*) of this Act shall not affect the validity of any byelaws made before the end of July 1936.

Section 6 of the Civil Aviation Act 1949

6. Notwithstanding the repeal of section 6 of the Civil Aviation Act 1949, a certificate under subsection (3) of that section shall continue to be conclusive of the matters certified.

Lighthouse authorities

7. The rights, powers and privileges of any general or local lighthouse authority shall not be prejudiced by, or by an instrument under, any of the following provisions of this Act, that is to say, sections 39, 41, 43, 47, 60, 62, 73 to 77, 81, 87, 89, 96, 97 and 107(2).

The Hovercraft Act 1968

1968 c. 59.

8. The enactments and instruments with respect to which provision may be made by Order in Council in pursuance of section 1(1)(*h*) of the Hovercraft Act 1968 shall, notwithstanding the repeal by this Act of paragraph 49 of Schedule 1 to the Civil Aviation (Amendment) Act 1982, continue to include the Civil Aviation Act 1980 and any instrument made under that Act.

1982 c. 1.
1980 c. 60.

Schedule 9 to the Civil Aviation Act 1971

1971 c. 75.

9. The repeal by this Act of Schedule 9 to the Civil Aviation Act 1971 shall not affect the validity of—

(*a*) any alteration in a valuation list made in consequence of paragraph 5 of that Schedule ; or

1968 c. 73.

(*b*) any operator's licence issued under Part V of the Transport Act 1968 in pursuance of an application in relation to which paragraph 8 of that Schedule applied ;

and notwithstanding that repeal, the valuation roll and valuation lists to which paragraphs 6(1) and 7 respectively of that Schedule applied shall continue to have effect as modified by virtue of those paragraphs.

Section 1 of the Civil Aviation Act 1978

10. Notwithstanding the repeal by this Act of paragraph 45 of Schedule 1 to the Civil Aviation (Amendment) Act 1982, section 1(4) of the Civil Aviation Act 1978 shall continue to have effect as amended by that paragraph.

1978 c. 8.

Section 7 of the Civil Aviation Act 1978

11. The repeal by this Act of section 7 of the Civil Aviation Act 1978 (which made retrospective provision in respect of certain agreements) shall not affect the validity of any agreement entered into before the operative date.

The British Nationality Act 1981

1981 c. 61.

12.—(1) Until the commencement of the British Nationality Act 1981—

(*a*) section 95(1)(*b*) of this Act shall have effect as if for the reference to Schedule 3 to the said Act of 1981 there

were substituted a reference to section 1(3) of the British
Nationality Act 1948 ;

(b) section 105(1) of this Act shall have effect as if for the definition of " United Kingdom national " there were substituted the definition specified in sub-paragraph (2) below ; and

(c) paragraph 6(1) of Part III of Schedule 13 to this Act shall have effect as if for the reference to Commonwealth citizens there were substituted a reference to British subjects.

(2) The definition referred to in sub-paragraph (1)(b) above is as follows : —

" United Kingdom national " means an individual who is—

(a) a citizen of the United Kingdom and Colonies ; or

(b) a British subject by virtue of section 2 of the British Nationality Act 1948 ; or

(c) a British subject without citizenship by virtue of section 13 or 16 of the said Act of 1948 ; or

(d) a British subject by virtue of the British Nationality 1965 c. 34. Act 1965 ; or

(e) a British protected person within the meaning of the said Act of 1948.

Interpretation

13. In this Schedule " the operative date " means the date of the coming into force of this Act.

SCHEDULE 15

Consequential Amendments

The Law of Property Act 1925

1. For paragraph (b) of section 84(11) of the Law of Property Act 1925 there shall be substituted the following paragraph : —

" (b) for civil aviation purposes under the powers of the Air 1920 c. 80. Navigation Act 1920, of section 19 or 23 of the Civil 1949 c. 67. Aviation Act 1949 or of section 30 or 41 of the Civil Aviation Act 1982.".

The Acquisition of Land (Authorisation Procedure) (Scotland) 1947 c. 42. *Act 1947*

2.—(1) In section 1(1) of the Acquisition of Land (Authorisation Procedure) (Scotland) Act 1947, for paragraphs (b) and (c) there shall be substituted the following paragraph : —

" (b) by the Secretary of State under section 41 or 49 of the Civil Aviation Act 1982 ".

SCH. 15   (2) In section 3(7) of that Act, for the words from " by the " onwards there shall be substituted the words " by the Secretary of State under section 41 of the Civil Aviation Act 1982.".

1958 c. 51.   *The Public Records Act 1958*

3. The Table at the end of paragraph 3 of Schedule 1 to the Public Records Act 1958 shall continue to have effect with the inclusion in the second column of Part I after the entry relating to the Air Registration Board of the following entries—

" Airworthiness Requirements Board,
Civil Aviation Authority."

1964 c. 40.   *The Harbours Act 1964*

4. In section 37 of the Harbours Act 1964—

1949 c. 67.   (a) for the words " section 8(2) of the Civil Aviation Act 1949 " there shall be substituted the words " section 60 of the Civil Aviation Act 1982 " ; and

(b) for the words " that subsection " there shall be substituted the words " subsection (3) of that section ".

1966 c. 34.   *The Industrial Development Act 1966*

5. Schedule 2 to the Industrial Development Act 1966 shall continue to have effect as if the CAA and, until the appointed day
1980 c. 60.   within the meaning of Part I of the Civil Aviation Act 1980, the British Airways Board were included among the bodies there specified.

1967 c. 52.   *The Tokyo Convention Act 1967*

6. In section 7(1) of the Tokyo Convention Act, for the definitions of " aircraft " and " British-controlled aircraft " there shall be substituted the following definition—

" ' aircraft ' has the same meaning as in section 92 of the Civil Aviation Act 1982 ; and for the purposes of this definition section 101 of that Act shall apply to this Act as it applies to the said section 92 ; ",

and the definition of " modifications " shall continue to have effect notwithstanding the repeal by this Act of paragraph 27 of Schedule
1982 c. 1.   1 to the Civil Aviation (Amendment) Act 1982.

1968 c. 32.   *The Industrial Expansion Act 1968*

7. In section 12 of the Industrial Expansion Act 1968, for the words " The proviso to subsection (1) of section 1 of the Civil Aviation Act 1949 " there shall be substituted the words " Section 1(2) of the Civil Aviation Act 1982 ".

1970 c. 18   *The Land Registration Act (Northern Ireland) 1970*
(N.I.).
8. In Schedule 11 to the Land Registration Act (Northern Ireland) 1970, for paragraph (24) there shall be substituted the following paragraph : —

" 24. A grant or agreement referred to in section 55(5) of Civil Aviation Act 1982."

The Rolls Royce (Purchase) Act 1971   SCH. 15

9. In section 1(2) of the Rolls Royce (Purchase) Act 1971, for the 1971 c. 9.
words " Section 1(1) proviso of the Civil Aviation Act 1949 " there 1949 c. 67.
shall be substituted the words " Section 1(2) of the Civil Aviation
Act 1982 ".

The Hijacking Act 1971   1971 c. 70.

10. In section 2 of the Hijacking Act 1971, for the words " section
1 of the Tokyo Convention Act 1967 " there shall be substituted 1967 c. 52.
the words " section 92 of the Civil Aviation Act 1982 ".

The Local Government Act 1972   1972 c. 70.

11. In section 236(2) of the Local Government Act 1972, for the
words " section 31 of the Civil Aviation Act 1971 " there shall 1971 c. 75.
be substituted the words " section 29 of the Civil Aviation Act
1982 ".

The Land Compensation Act 1973   1973 c. 26.

12.—(1) In section 1(6) of the Land Compensation Act 1973, for
the words " section 41(2) of the Civil Aviation Act 1949 " there shall
be substituted the words " section 77(2) of the Civil Aviation Act
1982 ".

(2) In section 4(3)(*a*) of that Act, after the words " section 29A of
the Civil Aviation Act 1971 " there shall be inserted the words
", section 79 of the Civil Aviation Act 1982 ".

(3) In section 87(1) of that Act, for the definition of " aerodrome "
there shall be substituted the following definition—

" ' aerodrome ' has the same meaning as in the Civil Aviation
    Act 1982 ; ".

The Protection of Aircraft Act 1973   1973 c. 47.

13. In section 26(1) of the Protection of Aircraft Act 1973—

(*a*) in the definition of " aerodrome ", for the words " section
     28(3) of the Civil Aviation Act 1968 " there shall be sub- 1968 c. 61.
     stituted the words " section 105(1) of the Civil Aviation
     Act 1982 " ; and

(*b*) in the definition of " operator ", for the words " Civil
     Aviation Act 1971 " there shall be substituted the words
     " Civil Aviation Act 1982 ".

The Land Compensation (Scotland) Act 1973   1973 c. 56.

14.—(1) In section 1(6) of the Land Compensation (Scotland) Act
1973, for the words " section 41(2) of the Civil Aviation Act 1949 "
there shall be substituted the words " section 77(2) of the Civil
Aviation Act 1982 ".

SCH. 15
1971 c. 75.

(2) In section 4(3)(*a*) of that Act, after the words " section 29A of the Civil Aviation Act 1971 " there shall be inserted the words " section 79 of the Civil Aviation Act 1982 ".

(3) In section 80(1) of that Act, for the definition of " aerodrome " there shall be substituted the following definition—

" ' aerodrome ' has the same meaning as in the Civil Aviation Act 1982 ; ".

1974 c. 41.

The Policing of Airports Act 1974

1968 c. 61.

15. In section 5(1) of the Policing of Airports Act 1974, for the words " section 1 of the Civil Aviation Act 1968 " there shall be substituted the words " section 37 of the Civil Aviation Act 1982 ".

1975 c. 36.

The Air Travel Reserve Fund Act 1975

16. In the Air Travel Reserve Fund Act 1975—

(*a*) in subsections (6)(*b*), (9) and (10) of section 2 and in subsection (1) of section 4, for the words " section 26 of the Civil Aviation Act 1971 " there shall be substituted the words " section 71 of the Civil Aviation Act 1982 " ;

(*b*) in subsections (2), (3) and (4) of section 4 for the words " section 26 " there shall be substituted the words " section 71 "

(*c*) at the end of the said subsection (3) of section 4 there shall be inserted the words " ; and a statutory instrument of which a draft has been approved in accordance with this subsection by a resolution of each House of Parliament shall not be subject to annulment in accordance with section 102(4) of the said Act of 1982." ;

(*d*) in section 6 after the word " order " there shall be inserted the words " made by statutory instrument " and at the end there shall be inserted the words " An order under this section shall be subject to annulment in pursuance of a resolution of either House of Parliament, and paragraphs 1 and 2 of Part III of Schedule 13 to the Civil Aviation Act 1982 (which confer supplemental powers) shall apply to the power to make an order under this section." ;

(*e*) in subsection (1) of section 7 for the words " the Civil Aviation Act 1971 " there shall be substituted the words " the Civil Aviation Act 1982 " ; and

(*f*) for subsections (2) and (3) of section 7 there shall be substituted the following subsections—

" (2) Sections 4 and 11 of the said Act of 1982 (which provide for the general objectives of the Authority in respect of the performance of its functions and for charges by the Authority in respect of the performance of its functions) do not apply in relation to the functions conferred on the Authority by this Act.

(3) Subsection (1) of section 108 of the said Act of   Sᴄʜ. 15
1982 (which provides for the extension of that Act to
certain overseas territories) shall apply to the provisions
of this Act as it applies to the provisions mentioned in
that subsection.".

The Airports Authority Act 1975   1975 c. 78.

17.—(1) In section 2(3) of the Airports Authority Act 1975, for
the words from " or of " onwards there shall be substituted the words
" or of any duty imposed on it by virtue of section 78 or 79 of the
Civil Aviation Act 1982 ".

(2) In section 5(4)(*b*) of the said Act of 1975, after the words
" section 12 of the Civil Aviation Act 1968 " there shall be inserted 1968 c. 61.
the words " or section 34 of the Civil Aviation Act 1982.".

(3) In section 16 of the said Act of 1975 for the words " Section
56 of the Civil Aviation Act 1949 " there shall be substituted the 1949 c. 67.
words " Section 58 of the Civil Aviation Act 1982 ".

(4) In section 17 of the said Act of 1975—

(*a*) for subsections (3) and (4) there shall be substituted the
following subsections : —

" (3) The provisions of the Civil Aviation Act 1982
which are specified in subsection (4) below shall apply in
relation to the Authority as they apply in Great Britain
in relation to the Civil Aviation Authority and, in the
case of Schedule 10 to that Act, as if references to an
order made or proposed to be made under Part II of that
Act or to the making of such an order included an order
for the compulsory purchase of land by the Authority
which the Secretary has confirmed or proposes to confirm
or as the case may be, to the confirmation of such an
order.

(4) The provisions of the Civil Aviation Act 1982 mentioned in subsection (3) above are—

section 44 (power to obtain rights over land) ;

section 45 (power to restrict use of land for purpose
of securing safety at aerodromes);

section 46 (power to exercise control of land in
interests of civil aviation) ;

section 48, except subsection (9), (power to stop up
and divert highways) ;

section 50 (power of entry for purposes of survey) ;

section 52 (displacements from land) ;

Schedules 7 to 10 (supplemental provisions and provisions relating to statutory undertakers)." ;

(*b*) in subsection (5) for the words " the said section 28 " there
shall be substituted the words " the said section 48 ".

(5) In section 20(1) of the said Act of 1975—

(*a*) in paragraph (*a*), for the words " section 24 or 26 of the Civil Aviation Act 1949 " there shall be substituted the words " section 44 or 46 of the Civil Aviation Act 1982 " ; and

(*b*) in paragraph (*b*), for the words " section 28 " there shall be substituted the words " section 48 ".

The Aircraft and Shipbuilding Industries Act 1977

18. In subsection (1) of section 56 of the Aircraft and Shipbuilding Industries Act 1977, in the definition of " works ", for the words " section 64(1) of the Civil Aviation Act 1971 " there shall be substituted the words " section 105(1) of the Civil Aviation Act 1982 ".

The Patents Act 1977

19. In section 60(7) of the Patents Act 1977, in the definition of " exempted aircraft " for the words " section 53 of the Civil Aviation Act 1949 " there shall be substituted the words " section 89 of the Civil Aviation Act 1982 ".

The Civil Aviation Act 1978

20.—(1) In section 8 of the Civil Aviation Act 1978—

(*a*) in subsection (3) for the words from " section 5 " onwards there shall be substituted the words " the said section 9) " ;

(*b*) in paragraph (*a*) of subsection (4) for the words from " an " onwards there shall be substituted the words " for the purposes of section 78 of the Civil Aviation Act 1982 (regulation of noise and vibration from aircraft) ".

(2) After subsection (1) of section 13 of the said Act of 1978 there shall be inserted the following subsection—

" (2) Any power conferred by this Act to make an order or to make regulations shall include power to make such incidental, supplemental or transitional provision as the authority exercising the power thinks fit."

(3) After subsection (3) of section 16 of the said Act of 1978, there shall be inserted the following subsection—

" (4) Subsection (1) of section 108 of the Civil Aviation Act 1982 (which provides for the extension of that Act outside the United Kingdom) shall apply to the provisions of this Act as it applies to the provisions mentioned in that subsection.".

The Suppression of Terrorism Act 1978

21. In subsection (7) of section 4 of the Suppression of Terrorism Act 1978, for the words from " and section " onwards there shall be substituted the words " and subsection (4) of section 92 of the Civil Aviation Act 1982 (definition of ' in flight ' or, as applied to

hovercraft, 'in journey') shall apply for the purposes of this sub-section as it applies for the purposes of that section."

The National Health Service (Scotland) Act 1978

22. In paragraph 19 of Schedule 1 to the National Health Service (Scotland) Act 1978—

    (*a*) for the words "paragraph 1 of Schedule 9 to the Civil Aviation Act 1971" there shall be substituted the words "paragraph 6 of Schedule 3 to the Civil Aviation Act 1982", and

    (*b*) for the words "the said paragraph 1" there shall be substituted the words "the said paragraph 6".

The Customs and Excise Management Act 1979

23. In section 21(7) of the Customs and Excise Management Act 1979 for the words "section 8 of the Civil Aviation Act 1949" there shall be substituted the words "section 60 of the Civil Aviation Act 1982".

The Highlands and Islands Air Services (Scotland) Act 1980

24. In section 3 of the Highlands and Islands Air Services (Scotland) Act 1980, in the definition of "air services" for the words from "or under" to "that Act" there shall be substituted the words "or section 65 of the Civil Aviation Act 1982 or under the authority of an instrument made under section 21(2) of the said Act of 1971 or section 64(2) of the said Act of 1982".

The Supreme Court Act 1981

25. In subsections (2)(*j*) and (6) of section 20 of the Supreme Court Act 1981, for the words "section 51 of the Civil Aviation Act 1949" there shall be substituted the words "section 87 of the Civil Aviation Act 1982".

The New Towns Act 1981

26. In section 79(3)(*b*) of the New Towns Act 1981, for the words "paragraph 7 of Schedule 5 to the Civil Aviation Act 1971" there shall be substituted the words "paragraph 5 of Schedule 2 to the Civil Aviation Act 1982".

The Acquisition of Land Act 1981

27. In section 32(8) of the Acquisition of Land Act 1981, for the words from "section 23(3)" to "1971" there shall be substituted the words "section 41 or 42 of the Civil Aviation Act 1982".

SCHEDULE 16

REPEALS

Chapter or number	Short title	Extent of repeal
12, 13 & 14 Geo. 6. c. 67.	The Civil Aviation Act 1949.	Section 1. Section 6. Sections 8 to 11. Section 16(1) and (2). Sections 17 to 20. Sections 23 to 35. Sections 37 to 41. Section 49. Sections 51 to 53. Sections 55 to 58. Section 59(1). Sections 60 to 65. Sections 69 to 71. Schedules 1 to 4. Schedules 8 and 9. Schedule 11.
2 & 3 Eliz. 2. c. 64.	The Transport Charges &c. (Miscellaneous Provisions) Act 1954.	Section 7(4).
8 & 9 Eliz. 2. c. 38.	The Civil Aviation (Licensing) Act 1960.	Section 5(3) and (4). Section 6(6), (6A) and (7). Section 7. Section 10. Section 12.
10 & 11 Eliz. 2. c. 8.	The Civil Aviation (Eurocontrol) Act 1962.	Sections 1 to 4. Section 5(1) and (3). Sections 6 to 10.
10 & 11 Eliz. 2. c. 38.	The Town and Country Planning Act 1962.	In Schedule 12, the entry relating to the Civil Aviation Act 1949.
1965 c. 56.	The Compulsory Purchase Act 1965.	In Schedule 6, the entry relating to the Civil Aviation Act 1949.
1967 c. 52.	The Tokyo Convention Act 1967.	Sections 1 to 3. Sections 5 and 6. In section 7, in subsection (1) the definitions of "commander", "Convention country", "military aircraft", "operator", "pilot in command" and "Tokyo Convention", subsection (2), in subsection (3) the words from "and references" onwards and subsection (4). In section 8(1), the words "other than section 2". Section 9(2).
1968 c. 48.	The International Organisations Act 1968.	In section 12, subsection (1).

Chapter or number	Short title	Extent of repeal
1968 c. 61.	The Civil Aviation Act 1968.	Sections 1 to 6. Section 8. Section 12. Section 13(2) and (3). Sections 14 to 23. Sections 26 to 28.
1969 c. 48.	The Post Office Act 1969.	In Schedule 4, paragraph 46 and in paragraph 93 sub-paragraphs (1)(ix) and (2)(*e*).
1969 c. 59.	The Law of Property Act 1969.	Section 28(8).
1971 c. 61.	The Mineral Workings (Offshore Installations) Act 1971.	Section 8(4).
1971 c. 68.	The Finance Act 1971.	In Schedule 8, paragraph 16(10).
1971 c. 75.	The Civil Aviation Act 1971.	Sections 1 to 36. Sections 61 to 70. Schedules 1 to 7. Schedules 9 to 11.
1971 c. 78.	The Town and Country Planning Act 1971.	In Part II of Schedule 23, the entry relating to the Civil Aviation Act 1949 and the entry relating to the Civil Aviation Act 1971.
1972 c. 11.	The Superannuation Act 1972.	In Schedule 6, paragraphs 94 and 95.
1972 c. 52.	The Town and Country Planning (Scotland) Act 1972.	In Part II of Schedule 21, the entry relating to the Civil Aviation Act 1949 and the entry relating to the Civil Aviation Act 1971.
1973 c. 65.	The Local Government (Scotland) Act 1973.	Section 152. In Part II of Schedule 27, paragraphs 97, 98, 188 to 190 and 201.
1975 c. 76.	The Local Land Charges Act 1975.	In Schedule 1, the entry relating to the Civil Aviation Act 1949, the entry relating to the Civil Aviation Act 1968 and the entry relating to the Civil Aviation Act 1971.
1975 c. 78.	The Airports Authority Act 1975.	In section 25, subsection (1). Schedule 3. In Schedule 5, Part I and in Part II paragraph 4.

Chapter or number	Short title	Extent of repeal
1978 c. 8.	The Civil Aviation Act 1978.	Sections 6 and 7. In section 8, in subsection (2) paragraphs (*a*) to (*d*). Sections 9 to 11. In section 14, in subsection (1) paragraph (*b*) and the word " and " immediately preceding it and subsection (3). In section 15, subsection (1). In Schedule 1, in Part I paragraphs 1 to 3, 6 and 7(2) and Part II.
1978 c. 44.	The Employment Protection (Consolidation) Act 1978.	In Schedule 16, paragraph 12.
1979 c. 2.	The Customs and Excise Management Act 1979.	In Schedule 4, in Part I of the table in paragraph 12, the entry relating to the Civil Aviation Act 1949 and the entry relating to the Civil Aviation Act 1968.
1979 c. 33.	The Land Registration (Scotland) Act 1979.	In section 28(1), in the definition of " deed ", the words from " and includes " to " 1949 ".
1980 c. 45.	The Water (Scotland) Act 1980.	In Schedule 10, the entry relating to the Civil Aviation Act 1971.
1980 c. 60.	The Civil Aviation Act 1980.	Sections 11 to 19. Section 21. Section 26.
1981 c. 38.	The British Telecommunications Act 1981.	In Schedule 3, paragraphs 10(1)(*e*), 11(1)(*c*) and 29.
1981 c. 61.	The British Nationality Act 1981.	In Schedule 7, the entry relating to the Civil Aviation Act 1971.
1981 c. 64.	The New Towns Act 1981.	In Schedule 12, paragraph 6.
1981 c. 67.	The Acquisition of Land Act 1981.	In Schedule 4, paragraphs 6 and 20.
1982 c. 1.	The Civil Aviation (Amendment) Act 1982.	Section 4. Schedules 1 and 2.
S.I. 1973 No. 2095.	The Local Government Reorganisation (Consequential Provisions) (Northern Ireland) Order 1973.	In Schedule 1, paragraph 11.
S.I. 1980 No. 1085 (N.I. 11).	The Roads (Northern Ireland) Order 1980.	In the table in paragraph 3 of Schedule 8, the entry relating to the Civil Aviation Act 1949.

Harbours (Scotland)

Act 1982

1982 CHAPTER 17

An Act to make provision for Scotland for establishing harbour trusts to hold, manage and maintain harbours and for the transfer of harbours held and maintained by the Secretary of State to such trusts; and for connected purposes.   [27th May 1982]

BE IT ENACTED by the Queen's most Excellent Majesty, by and with the advice and consent of the Lords Spiritual and Temporal, and Commons, in this present Parliament assembled, and by the authority of the same, as follows:—

1.—(1) The Secretary of State may by order establish a trust to hold, manage and maintain a harbour transferred to it under subsection (2) below.

(2) The Secretary of State may by order transfer to a harbour trust a harbour (or part thereof) which is held and maintained by him and with that harbour all such rights enjoyed by and liabilities incumbent on him in relation thereto as he considers should be so transferred.

(3) A transfer made by the Secretary of State under subsection (2) above shall be subject to such terms and conditions as the Secretary of State may decide and may be made either with or without any valuable consideration being paid in respect of the transfer.

(4) A harbour trust shall be the harbour authority in relation to a harbour transferred to it under subsection (2) above.

Establishing of harbour trusts and transfer of harbours to them.

Orders.

2. An order made under section 1 of this Act shall be made by statutory instrument subject to annulment in pursuance of a resolution of either House of Parliament and may contain such transitional, incidental, supplementary and consequential provisions as the Secretary of State may consider necessary or expedient.

Interpretation.

3. In this Act—

1972 c. 64.

" harbour " has the same meaning as in section 1 of the Harbours Development (Scotland) Act 1972;

1964 c. 40.

" harbour authority " has the same meaning as in the Harbours Act 1964; and

" harbour trust " means a trust established under section 1(1) of this Act.

Citation and extent.

4.—(1) This Act may be cited as the Harbours (Scotland) Act 1982.

(2) This Act extends to Scotland only.

Industry Act 1982

1982 CHAPTER 18

An Act to raise the limits imposed on the Secretary of State's financial assistance to industry under section 8(7) and (8) of the Industry Act 1972.   [27th May 1982]

BE IT ENACTED by the Queen's most Excellent Majesty, by and with the advice and consent of the Lords Spiritual and Temporal, and Commons, in this present Parliament assembled, and by the authority of the same, as follows:—

1.—(1) In section 8 of the Industry Act 1972 (power of Secretary of State to give selective financial assistance), in subsection (7), for the first sentence (limit on assistance not relating to foreign currency guarantees is £600 million with power to make four increases of up to £250 million each) there shall be substituted—

> " The said limit shall be £1,900 million but the Secretary of State may, on not more than four occasions, by order made with the consent of the Treasury increase or further increase that limit by a sum specified in the order, being a sum not exceeding £200 million."

(2) In subsection (8) of that section (assistance, other than by foreign currency guarantees, in respect of any one project not to exceed £5 million, unless excess authorised by resolution of House of Commons), for " £5 million " (in both places) there shall be substituted " £10 million ".

(3) The Industry (Amendment) Act 1976 (which raised the limits imposed under section 8(7) of the Industry Act 1972 with the proviso that the Secretary of State should not use any of the

Limits on Secretary of State's financial assistance to industry.
1972 c. 63.

1976 c. 73.

1972 c. 63.

money for the acquisition or assistance of banks or insurance companies) is hereby repealed; and at the end of section 8(2) of the Industry Act 1972 (assistance under section may be given in any of the ways set out in section 7(3)) there shall be added " but the Secretary of State shall not under this section use any money for the acquisition or assistance of banks or insurance companies ".

Short title
and extent.

2.—(1) This Act may be cited as the Industry Act 1982.

(2) This Act extends to Northern Ireland.

Deer (Amendment) (Scotland) Act 1982

1982 CHAPTER 19

An Act to amend the Deer (Scotland) Act 1959 and certain related enactments.   [28th June 1982]

BE IT ENACTED by the Queen's most Excellent Majesty, by and with the advice and consent of the Lords Spiritual and Temporal, and Commons, in this present Parliament assembled, and by the authority of the same, as follows:—

Functions of the Red Deer Commission

1.—(1) In sections 1(1) (with the exception of the reference to "the Red Deer Commission"), 3(1) and 4 of the Deer (Scotland) Act 1959 after the words "red deer" wherever they occur there shall be inserted the words "or sika deer or such other deer as may be specified from time to time by direction of the Secretary of State".

Alteration of general functions of the Red Deer Commission.
1959 c. 40.

(2) In sections 5(1), 7(1) and (2), 8(1) and (3), 11(1), 12(1), 14, 15(1) and 19 of the said Act of 1959 after the words "red deer" wherever they occur there shall be inserted the words "or sika deer".

(3) In section 4(*a*) of the said Act of 1959 the words "in the interests of conservation" shall be deleted.

(4) In section 20 of the said Act of 1959 at the end there shall be inserted the following—

"" sika deer " means deer of the species *cervus nippon* ;

and any reference to "red deer" or "sika deer" includes any deer which is a hybrid of those species.".

Part I   K

Composition and operation of the Red Deer Commission

Observers and
research.

2.—(1) At the end of section 2(1) of the said Act of 1959 there shall be inserted the words ", and the Commission may appoint a member of the Commission or a member of the Commission's staff to act as observer to the panel for the purpose of sitting with the panel at any meeting and of taking part in their discussions and of informing the Commission of information arising during and decisions taken at such meetings ; such an observer shall not be a member of the panel.".

(2) At the end of section 4 of the said Act of 1959 there shall be inserted the words " (*c*) to support and to engage in research on questions of practical or scientific importance relating to red deer or sika deer or such other deer as may be specified from time to time by direction of the Secretary of State.".

Power of
Commission
to deal with
marauding
deer.

3. Section 6 of the said Act of 1959 shall be amended as follows—

    (*a*) for subsection (1) there shall be substituted the following subsection—

" (1) Subject to the following provisions of this section, where the Commission are satisfied—

    (*a*) that red deer or sika deer are, on any agricultural land, woodland or garden ground—

    (i) causing serious damage to forestry or to agricultural production, including any crops or foodstuffs ; or

    (ii) causing injury to farm animals (including serious overgrazing of pastures and competing with them for supplementary feeding) ; and

    (*b*) that the killing of the deer is necessary to prevent further such damage or injury,

they shall authorise in writing, subject to such conditions as may be specified in the authorisation, any person who in their opinion is competent to do so to follow and kill on any land mentioned in the authorisation such red deer or sika deer as appear to that person to be causing the damage or injury." ;

    (*b*) in subsection (4) for the word " fourteen " there shall be substituted the word " 28 ".

4. The following section shall be inserted after section 6 of the said Act of 1959— Further power of Commission to deal with marauding deer.

"Further power of Commission to deal with marauding deer. 6A.—(1) Where the Commission are satisfied that deer of species other than red deer or sika deer are causing serious damage to agricultural land or to woodland and that the killing of the deer is necessary for the prevention of further such damage, they shall be entitled by their servants with the consent of the occupier of the agricultural land or woodland to kill such deer as such servants may encounter in the course of their duties.

(2) The Commission shall give to the owner of the agricultural land or woodland concerned such notice of their intention to kill deer under this section as may be practicable.

(3) Sections 21 and 23(1) of this Act shall not apply to the power conferred by subsection (1) above.".

5. In Schedule 1 to the said Act of 1959 there shall be inserted after paragraph 2 the following new paragraphs— Chairman of Commission.

"2A. If the Secretary of State is satisfied that the chairman of the Commission—

(*a*) has had his estate sequestrated or has made a trust deed for behoof of his creditors or a composition contract with his creditors;

(*b*) is incapacitated by reason of physical or mental illness;

(*c*) has been absent from meetings of the Commission for a period of more than 3 consecutive months without the permission of the Commission or of the Secretary of State; or

(*d*) is otherwise unable or unfit to discharge the functions of a member of the Commission, or is unsuitable to continue as the chairman,

the Secretary of State shall have power to remove him from his said office.

2B. Where a person ceases to be chairman of the Commission otherwise than on the expiry of his term of office and it appears to the Secretary of State that there are special circumstances which make it right for that person to receive compensation, the Secretary of State may make to that person a payment of such amount as the Secretary of State may, with the approval of the Treasury, determine.

K 2

2C. The Secretary of State may make such provision, if any, as he may, with the approval of the Treasury, determine for the payment of pensions to or in respect of chairmen of the Commission.".

Miscellaneous

Unlawful taking, killing and injury of deer, and removal of carcases.

6. The said Act of 1959 shall be amended as follows—

(*a*) in sections 21(1) and 23(2) after the word " kill " there shall be inserted the words " or injure " ;

(*b*) for subsection (2) of section 21 there shall be substituted the following subsection—

" (2) The Secretary of State may by order fix a period in each year during which no person shall take or wilfully kill or injure—

(*a*) any species of deer named in the order other than red deer ; or

(*b*) any hybrid of any species of deer named in the order,

and he may fix a different period for males and females of the species or, as the case may be, of the hybrid so named." ;

(*c*) in section 22 at the end there shall be added the following new subsection—

" (2) Subject to section 33 of this Act, if any person without legal right to take or kill deer on any land or without permission from a person having such right removes any deer carcase from that land, he shall be guilty of an offence and liable on summary conviction to a fine not exceeding £500 for each carcase in respect of which the offence was committed or to imprisonment for a term not exceeding three months or to both and to the forfeiture of any carcase illegally removed by him or in his possession at the time of the offence." ; and

(*d*) in sections 22 and 23(1) after the word " kills " there shall be inserted the words " or injures ".

Deer farming.

7. After subsection (5) of section 21 of the said Act of 1959 there shall be inserted the following new subsection—

" (5A) This section does not apply to the killing of deer by any person who keeps those deer by way of business on land enclosed by a deer-proof barrier for the production of meat or foodstuffs, or skins or other by-products, or as breeding stock (or to such killing of deer by the servant or agent of any such person authorised by him for that purpose) ; provided that the deer are conspicuously marked to demonstrate that they are so kept.".

8.—(1) After subsection (2) of section 23 of the said Act of 1959 there shall be inserted the following new subsections—

" (2A) Subject to subsection (2B) below and section 33(1) of this Act, if any person—

    (*a*) discharges any firearm, or discharges or projects any missile, from any aircraft at any deer ; or

    (*b*) notwithstanding the provisions of section 23(5) of this Act uses any aircraft for the purpose of transporting any live deer other than in the interior of the aircraft,

he shall be guilty of an offence.

(2B) Nothing in subsection (2A)(*b*) above shall make unlawful anything done by, or under the supervision of, a veterinary surgeon or practitioner.

(2C) In subsection (2B) above " veterinary practitioner " means a person who is for the time being registered in the supplementary register, and " veterinary surgeon " means a person who is for the time being registered in the register of veterinary surgeons ".

(2) In subsection (3) of section 23 of the said Act of 1959 for the words " subsections (1) or (2) " there shall be substituted the words " subsection (1), (2) or (2A) ".

9. After section 23(3) of the said Act of 1959 there shall be inserted the following new subsection—

" (3A) Any person who uses a vehicle to drive deer on unenclosed land with the intention of taking, killing or injuring them shall be guilty of an offence and liable on summary conviction to a fine not exceeding £500 or to imprisonment for a term not exceeding 3 months or to both.".

10.—(1) After section 23 of the said Act of 1959 there shall be inserted the following new section—

" Firearms and ammunition.   23A.—(1) The Secretary of State shall have power to make such order as he thinks fit regarding the classes of firearms, ammunition, sights and other equipment which may lawfully be used in connection with killing or taking deer, and the circumstances in which any class of firearms, ammunition, sights or other equipment may be so used.

(2) Before making an order under subsection (1) above the Secretary of State shall consult any organisations which in his opinion represent persons likely to be interested in or affected by the order.

(3) Any person who fails to comply with an order under subsection (1) above shall be guilty of an offence and liable on summary conviction to a fine not exceeding £500 in relation to each deer taken or killed or to imprisonment for a term not exceeding three months, or to both.

(4) No order shall be made under this section unless a draft of the order has been laid before Parliament and approved by a resolution of each House of Parliament.

(5) If any person uses any firearm or any ammunition for the purpose of wilfully injuring any deer, he shall be guilty of an offence and liable on summary conviction to a fine not exceeding £500 for each deer in respect of which the offence was committed or to imprisonment for a term not exceeding three months, or to both.".

(2) In section 24 of the said Act of 1959, for " either of the two " there shall be substituted " any of the three ".

Licensing of dealing in venison

Licensing of dealing in venison.

11. After Part III of the said Act of 1959 there shall be inserted the following new Part—

" PART IIIA

LICENSING OF DEALING IN VENISON

Licences to deal in venison.

25A.—(1) An islands or district council may grant to any person whom they consider fit a licence to deal in venison (to be known as a " venison dealer's licence ").

(2) The Secretary of State shall have power by order to regulate applications for venison dealers' licences and the manner in which they are to be dealt with (including power to authorise islands and district councils to charge fees in respect of such applications); and also to regulate the procedure by which venison dealers' licences may be surrendered, and the procedure for handing in of licences where a court has ordered their forfeiture or the holders have ceased to deal in venison; and in that regard he may apply any provision of Schedule 1 to the Civic Government (Scotland) Act 1982, as he thinks fit.

(3) A venison dealer's licence shall be valid for 3 years (unless the dealer has been disqualified from holding a licence by reason of his conviction of an

offence under this Act), and may be renewed provided that he is not at the time of application subject to such disqualification.

(4) Every islands or district council which grants a venison dealer's licence shall cause to be sent to the Commission as soon as may be a copy of the licence.

(5) Every islands or district council by whom venison dealers' licences are granted shall, as soon as may be after the first day of January in each year, make a return to the Commission of the names and addresses of the persons who on that day held venison dealers' licences issued by the council.

Records. 25B.—(1) Every licensed venison dealer shall keep a book wherein shall be entered records in the prescribed form of all purchases and receipts of venison by him and shall enter in such book forthwith the prescribed particulars of such purchases and receipts.

(2) Any person authorised in writing in that behalf by the Secretary of State or by the Commission and showing his written authority when so requested, or any constable, may inspect any book kept in pursuance of this section and it shall be the duty of the dealer to produce for inspection by such authorised person or constable such book and also all venison in the dealer's possession or under his control, or on premises or in vehicles under his control, together with all invoices, consignment notes, receipts and other documents (including copies thereof where the originals are not available) which may be required to verify any entry in such book, and to allow such authorised person or constable to take copies of such book or document or extracts therefrom.

(3) Every book kept in pursuance of subsection (1) above shall be kept until the end of the period of three years beginning with the day on which the last entry was made in the book and any such documents as are mentioned in subsection (2) above shall be kept for a period of three years beginning with the date of the entry to which they refer.

(4) For the purposes of this section " prescribed " means prescribed by order.

K 4

Reciprocal
provisions.

1980 c. 49.

25C. A licensed venison dealer who has purchased or received venison from another licensed venison dealer or from a licensed game dealer within the meaning of section 2(4) of the Deer Act 1980 shall be deemed to have complied with the requirements of the preceding section of this Act if he has recorded in his record book—

(a) that the venison was so purchased or received ;

(b) the name and address of the other licensed venison dealer or of the licensed game dealer concerned ;

(c) the date when the venison was so purchased or received ;

(d) the number of carcases and sex of the venison ; and

(e) the species of deer, provided that it is possible to identify it.

Offences.

25D.—(1) It shall be an offence for any person to sell, offer or expose for sale or have in his possession, transport or cause to be transported for the purpose of sale at any premises any venison unless he is a licensed venison dealer or he does so for the purpose of selling to a licensed venison dealer, or he has purchased the venison from a licensed venison dealer.

(2) A person who is guilty of an offence under subsection (1) above shall be liable on summary conviction to a fine not exceeding £200.

(3) If any person sells, offers or exposes for sale, or has in his possession for the purpose of sale at any premises, or transports for the purpose of sale, or purchases or offers to purchase or receives, the carcase or any part of the carcase of a deer which he knows or has reason to believe has been killed unlawfully, he shall be guilty of an offence.

(4) A person who is guilty of an offence under subsection (3) above shall be liable on summary conviction to a fine not exceeding £500 or to imprisonment for a term not exceeding 3 months or to both.

(5) Any licensed venison dealer who fails to comply with any provision of section 25B of this Act, or who knowingly or recklessly makes in any book or

document which he is required to keep under that section an entry which is false or misleading in any material particular, shall be guilty of an offence and liable on summary conviction to a fine not exceeding £50.

(6) Any person who obstructs a person entitled under section 25B(2) of this Act to inspect any book or document or other thing in the making of such inspection shall be guilty of an offence and liable on summary conviction to a fine not exceeding £200.

(7) The court by which any person is convicted of an offence under Part III or IIIA of this Act may disqualify him from holding or obtaining a venison dealer's licence for such period as the court thinks fit.

(8) In subsection (1) above " licensed venison dealer " means the holder of a venison dealer's licence granted by the islands or district council within whose area the sale, offer or exposure for sale takes place, or where the premises concerned are situated.

Transitional provision.

25E. Notwithstanding the coming into force of section 11 of the Deer (Amendment) (Scotland) Act 1982, sections 25B and 25C and subsections (1), (2), (5), (6) and (8) of section 25D of this Act shall not apply to a registered venison dealer within the meaning of the Sale of Venison (Scotland) Act 1968 until whichever is the earlier of—

1968 c. 38.

(a) the date on which a venison dealer's licence is granted to that dealer ;

(b) the expiry of 12 months after the commencement of the said section 11,

and the said Act of 1968 shall continue to have effect in relation to such a registered venison dealer during the said period notwithstanding its repeal by the said Act of 1982.

Interpretation of Part III A.

25F. In this Part of this Act—

" deer " means deer of any species ;

" sale " includes barter, exchange, and any other transaction by which venison is disposed of for value ;

" venison " means the carcase or any edible part of the carcase of a deer.".

General

12. In section 33(1) of the said Act of 1959 after the word " calf " there shall be inserted the words ", fawn or kid ".

13.—(1) For section 33(3) and (4) of the said Act of 1959 there shall be substituted the following subsections—

" (3) Notwithstanding section 21 of this Act (close season shooting) or any order made thereunder, or anything in any agreement between an occupier of agricultural land or of enclosed woodlands and the owner thereof, it shall be lawful for—

(*a*) the owner in person, provided that he is duly authorised in writing by the occupier for that purpose ;

(*b*) the owner's servants in his ordinary service, provided that they are duly authorised in writing by the occupier for that purpose ;

(*c*) the occupier in person ;

(*d*) the servants of the occupier in his ordinary service on the land or other persons normally resident on the land provided that they are duly authorised in writing by the occupier for that purpose ; or

(*e*) any other person approved in writing by the Commission as a fit and competent person for the purpose who has been duly authorised in writing by the occupier for that purpose

to take or kill, and to sell or otherwise dispose of the carcases of, any deer found on any arable land, garden grounds or land laid down in permanent grass (other than moorland and unenclosed land) and forming part of that land or on enclosed woodland, as the case may be, provided that the occupier has reasonable grounds for believing that serious damage will be caused to crops, pasture, trees or human or animal foodstuffs on that land if the deer are not killed.

(3A) Any authority given under subsection (3) above shall expire—

(*a*) at the end of such period as the occupier may specify in it ;

(*b*) when a person to whom paragraph (*b*) or (*d*) of that subsection applies ceases to be normally resident or in the owner's or, as the case may be, occupier's ordinary service ;

(*c*) where paragraph (*e*) of that subsection applies, at
the end of the period specified in the Commission's
approval ; or

(*d*) if the occupier revokes the authority.

(3B) Notwithstanding section 21 of this Act (close season
shooting) or any order made thereunder it shall be lawful
for any person authorised in writing for the purpose by
the Secretary of State to take or kill deer during the close
season for any scientific purpose.

(4) Notwithstanding section 23(1) of this Act (night
shooting) or anything contained in any agreement between
an occupier of agricultural land or of enclosed woodlands
and the owner thereof, it shall be lawful for the occupier in
person to carry out night shooting of red deer or sika
deer on such land or woodlands, provided that the occupier
has reasonable grounds for believing that serious damage
will be caused to crops, pasture, trees or human or animal
foodstuffs on that land if the deer are not killed.

(4A) Notwithstanding anything contained in section 23(1)
of this Act the Commission may authorise in writing
(subject to such conditions as they may specify) any person
nominated by the occupier of agricultural land or enclosed
woodlands to shoot deer of any species on that land or
woodlands during the period specified in the said section
23(1), provided that the Commission are satisfied—

(*a*) that the shooting is necessary to prevent serious
damage to crops, pasture, trees or human or
animal foodstuffs ; and

(*b*) that no other method of control which might reasonably be adopted in the circumstances would
be adequate ; and

(*c*) that the person concerned is a fit and competent
person to receive such authorisation.

(4B) Such authorisation as is mentioned in subsection
(4A) above shall be valid for such period as the Commission
may specify therein.

(4C) The owner of the agricultural land or enclosed woodlands may at any time request the occupier to inform him of
the numbers of red deer or sika deer shot by virtue of subsection (3), (4) or (4A) above within the period of 12 months
immediately preceding the request and the occupier shall
comply with any such request as soon as may be.

(4D) The Commission shall prepare and publish (with
power to prepare and publish a revised version from time to

time) a code of practice for night shooting to which they shall have regard when exercising their powers under subsection (4A) above and it shall be a condition of any authorisation under the said subsection that the person concerned complies with the relevant provisions of the code.

(4E) In this section—

"red deer" means deer of the species *cervus elaphus* and "sika deer" means deer of the species *cervus nippon*;

and any reference to "red deer" or "sika deer" includes any deer which is a hybrid of those species.".

1948 c. 45.   (2) Section 43(1) of the Agriculture (Scotland) Act 1948 is repealed.

Penalties and enforcement.   **14.**—(1) The provisions of the said Act of 1959 specified in column 1 of Schedule 1 to this Act, which relate to the penalties or maximum penalties for the offences mentioned in those provisions, shall be amended in accordance with the amendments specified in column 2 of that Schedule; and in that Schedule column 3 shows the penalties or, as the case may be, maximum penalties in force immediately before the commencement of this section and column 4 shows the penalties or, as the case may be, maximum penalties resulting from the amendments.

(2) Section 23(4) of the said Act of 1959 is repealed.

(3) In section 27 of the said Act of 1959, in subsections (2) and (4) for the words " section twenty-four " there shall be substituted the words " Part III or section 25D(1) or (3) ".

Minor amendments and repeals.   **15.**—(1) The minor and consequential amendments contained in Schedule 2 to this Act shall have effect.

(2) The provisions mentioned in column 1 of Schedule 3 to this Act are repealed to the extent provided for in column 3 of that Schedule.

Citation, commencement and extent.   **16.**—(1) This Act may be cited as the Deer (Amendment) (Scotland) Act 1982.

(2) With the exception of section 15(1) of this Act insofar as it refers to paragraph 4 of Schedule 2 to this Act and that paragraph, which extend to England and Wales only, this Act extends only to Scotland.

(3) This Act except the provisions mentioned in subsection (4) below shall come into force one month after it is passed.

(4) Section 11 of this Act and the repeal in Schedule 3 to this Act of the Sale of Venison (Scotland) Act 1968 shall come into force at such date as the Secretary of State may by order pre- scribe, and different orders may be made in respect of different provisions.

1968 c. 38.

SCHEDULES

SCHEDULE 1

PENALTIES

Section 14.

Enactment 1	Amendment 2	Present penalty 3	New penalty 4
Section 5(2) (offences relating to returns of deer killed).	For the words from " twenty pounds " to " fifty pounds " substitute the words " £200 ".	(a) for a first offence, £20; (b) for a second or subsequent offence, £50 or 3 months or both.	£200 or 3 months or both.
Section 9(2) (failure to comply with requirements of control scheme).	For the words from " fifty pounds " to " one hundred pounds " substitute the words " £500 ".	(a) for a first offence, £50; (b) for a second or subsequent offence, £100 or 3 months or both.	£500 or 3 months or both.
Section 17 (obstructing an authorised person).	For the words from " fifty pounds " to " one hundred pounds " substitute the words " £200 ".	(a) for a first offence, £50; (b) for a second or subsequent offence, £100 or 3 months or both.	£200 or 3 months or both.
Section 21(5) (killing or injuring deer in close season).	For the words from " twenty pounds " to " fifty pounds " substitute the words " £500 for each deer in respect of which the offence was committed ", and at the end add the words " and to the forfeiture of any deer in respect of which the offence was committed ".	(a) for a first offence, £20; (b) for a second or subsequent offence, £50 or 3 months or both.	£500 per deer or 3 months or both, and forfeiture of deer.
Section 22 (poaching).	For the words " twenty pounds " substitute the words " £500 for each deer in respect of which the offence was committed or to imprisonment for a term not exceeding three months, or to both ", and after the word " illegally " insert the words " taken or ".	£20 and forfeiture of deer.	£500 per deer or 3 months or both, and forfeiture of deer.
Section 23(3) (unlawful taking, killing or injuring of deer).	For the words from " twenty pounds " to " fifty pounds " substitute the words " £500 for each deer in respect of which the offence was committed ", and at the end add " and to the forfeiture of any deer illegally taken or killed by him or in his possession at the time of the offence ".	(a) for a first offence, £20; (b) for a second or subsequent offence, £50 or 3 months or both.	£500 per deer or 3 months or both, and forfeiture of deer.

Enactment 1	*Amendment* 2	*Present penalty* 3	*New penalty* 4
Section 24 (unlawful taking, killing or injuring of deer, or breach of firearms order, by 2 or more persons).	In paragraph (a), for the words from "fifty pounds," to "one hundred pounds," substitute the words "in respect of each deer taken or killed the statutory maximum, which in this section means the prescribed sum within the meaning of section 289B(6) of the Criminal Procedure (Scotland) Act 1975". In paragraph (b), delete the words "not exceeding five hundred pounds". At the end of the section, add the words "and on any conviction to the forfeiture of any deer illegally taken or killed by him or in his possession at the time of the offence".	On summary conviction— (a) for a first offence, £50 or 3 months; (b) for a second or subsequent offence, £100 or 6 months or both. On conviction on indictment, £500 or 2 years or both.	On summary conviction in respect of each deer taken or killed "the statutory maximum" (presently £1,000) or 6 months or both, and forfeiture of deer. On conviction on indictment, an unlimited fine or 2 years or both, and forfeiture of deer.
Section 26 (attempts to commit offences).	At the end of the section, add the words "; except that in the case of preparatory acts, the penalty shall be a fine not exceeding £500 or imprisonment for a term not exceeding three months or both.".	As for offence.	As for offence, except for preparatory acts, where it is £500 or 3 months or both.

Section 15.   SCHEDULE 2

MINOR AND CONSEQUENTIAL AMENDMENTS

Deer (Scotland) Act 1959 (c. 40)

1. After section 28 of the Deer (Scotland) Act 1959 there shall be inserted the following new section—

" Can-   28A.—(1) In any case where a person is convicted of an
cellation of   offence provided for by any of sections 22 to 25 of this Act
firearms   the court shall have power (in addition to any other power)
certificates. to cancel any firearm or shotgun certificate held by him.

(2) Where the court cancels a firearm or shotgun certificate under subsection (1) above—

    (*a*) the court shall cause notice in writing of that fact to be sent to the chief constable by whom the certificate was granted; and

    (*b*) the chief constable shall by notice in writing require the holder of the certificate to surrender it; and

    (*c*) if the holder fails to surrender the certificate within twenty-one days from the date of that requirement, he shall be guilty of an offence and liable on summary conviction to a fine not exceeding £50.".

2. In section 27(1) of the said Act of 1959, for the words " in pursuance of " there shall be substituted the words " on conviction of an offence under ".

3. In section 35(1) of the said Act of 1959, at the beginning there shall be inserted the words " Subject to section 23A(4) of this Act,".

Deer Act 1980 (c. 49)

4. In section 3(3) of the Deer Act 1980, after the word " 1968 " insert the words " or licensed under Part IIIA of the Deer (Scotland) Act 1959 ".

SCHEDULE 3
REPEALS

Column 1	Column 2	Column 3
1948 c. 45.	Agriculture (Scotland) Act 1948.	Sections 39 to 42 so far as relating to sika deer within the meaning of the Deer (Amendment) (Scotland) Act 1982 or to any hybrid mentioned in section 1(4) of that Act.
1959 c. 40.	Deer (Scotland) Act 1959.	Section 43(1). In section 4(*a*) the words " in the interests of conservation ". In section 12, the word " such ". Section 23(4). In section 24(*b*), the words " not exceeding five hundred pounds ". Section 29.
1968 c. 38.	Sale of Venison (Scotland) Act 1968.	The whole Act.

Children's Homes Act 1982

1982 CHAPTER 20

An Act to provide for the registration, inspection and conduct of certain homes and other institutions for the accommodation of children in the care of local authorities; and for connected purposes.   [28th June 1982]

B E IT ENACTED by the Queen's most Excellent Majesty, by and with the advice and consent of the Lords Spiritual and Temporal, and Commons, in this present Parliament assembled, and by the authority of the same, as follows:—

1.—(1) For the purposes of this Act a children's home is a home or other institution providing accommodation and mainte- nance wholly or mainly for children, other than an institution excluded by subsection (2) below.

Children's homes to which the Act applies.

(2) The institutions excluded by this subsection are—

  (a) community homes provided under section 32 of the Child Care Act 1980 ;

  1980 c. 5.

  (b) voluntary homes as defined by section 56 of that Act ;

  (c) homes registered under the Nursing Homes Act 1975 or the Residential Homes Act 1980 ;

  1975 c. 37.
1980 c. 7.

  (d) any health service hospital within the meaning of the National Health Service Act 1977 and any accom- modation provided by a local authority and used as a hospital by or on behalf of the Secretary of State ;

  1977 c. 49.

(e) homes and other premises managed by a government department or provided by a local authority ; and

(f) subject to subsection (3) below, any school within the meaning of the Education Act 1944.

1944 c. 31.

(3) An independent school within the meaning of that Act is not excluded by subsection (2) above (and is accordingly a children's home for the purposes of this Act) if the school provides accommodation for fifty children or less and is not for the time being approved by the Secretary of State under section 11(3)(a) of the Education Act 1981.

1981 c. 60.

Children in care not to be accommodated in unregistered children's homes.

2.—(1) A local authority shall not place a child in their care in a children's home, or allow such a child to remain in a children's home, unless it is a home for the time being registered under this Act (in this Act referred to as a " registered home ").

(2) Any person who carries on a children's home which is not a registered home but in which are accommodated one or more children in the care of a local authority shall be guilty of an offence and liable on summary conviction to a fine not exceeding £1,000.

Registration of children's homes.

3.—(1) An application for the registration of a children's home under this Act shall be made by the person carrying on, or intending to carry on, the home and shall be made to the local authority for the area in which the home is or is to be situated.

(2) An application for registration shall be made in the prescribed manner and shall be accompanied by—

(a) such particulars as may be prescribed ; and

(b) such reasonable fee as the local authority may determine.

(3) If a local authority are satisfied that a children's home in respect of which an application has been made in accordance with this section complies or (as the case may be) will comply—

(a) with such requirements as may be prescribed, and

(b) with such other requirements (if any) as appear to the authority to be appropriate,

the authority shall grant the application, either unconditionally or subject to conditions imposed under section 4 below, and shall give to the applicant notice that the home has been registered by the authority under this Act as from such date as may be specified in the notice.

(4) If the local authority are not satisfied as mentioned in subsection (3) above, they shall refuse the application, and shall give to the applicant notice of their refusal of the application and of the grounds on which they have refused it.

(5) For the purposes of this Act an application under this section which has not been granted or refused by a local authority within the period of twelve months beginning with the date when the application is served on them shall be deemed to have been refused by them, and the applicant shall be deemed to have been notified of their refusal at the end of that period.

(6) Where an application for the registration of a children's home is made to a local authority in accordance with this section, the home shall, as from the date when the application is served on the authority, be treated for the purposes of this Act as if it were registered thereunder—

> (a) until the home becomes registered under subsection (3) above, or

> (b) if the authority refuse the application, until the expiry of a period of twenty-eight days beginning with the date when the applicant is notified of their refusal.

(7) Where a school to which section 1(3) above applies is registered under subsection (3) above it shall not cease to be a children's home registered under this Act by reason only of a subsequent change in the number of children for whom it provides accommodation.

(8) Where an application for the registration of a home is refused, no further application for the registration of the home may be made under this section within the period of six months beginning with the date when the applicant is notified of the refusal.

4.—(1) A local authority may grant an application for the registration of a children's home subject to such conditions relating to the conduct of the home as they think fit. Conditions imposed on registration.

(2) Where a local authority grant an application subject to conditions they shall, at the time of giving notice to the applicant of the registration of the home, also give notice of those conditions ; but the conditions shall not take effect before the expiry of the period of twenty-eight days beginning with the date on which the applicant is so notified.

(3) If any condition imposed under this section is not complied with, the person carrying on the home shall be guilty of

an offence and liable on summary conviction to a fine not exceeding £500.

5.—(1) A local authority which have registered a children's home (in this Act referred to, in relation to the home, as " the responsible authority ") shall at the end of the period of twelve months beginning with the date of registration, and annually thereafter, review the registration of the home for the purpose of determining whether the registration should continue in force or be cancelled under section 6(2) below.

(2) If on any such annual review the responsible authority are satisfied that a home is being carried on in accordance with the relevant requirements they shall determine that, subject to subsection (3) below, the registration of the home should continue in force.

(3) The responsible authority shall give to the person carrying on the home notice of their determination under subsection (2) above, and the notice shall require him to pay to the authority in respect of the carrying out of the annual review in question such reasonable fee as the authority may determine ; and it shall be a condition of the home's continued registration that the fee is so paid before the expiry of the period of twenty-eight days beginning with the date on which the notice is received by the person carrying on the home.

(4) In this section " the relevant requirements " means any requirements of this Act and of any regulations made under section 8 below, and any conditions imposed under section 4 above.

6.—(1) The person carrying on a registered home may at any time make an application, in such manner and including such particulars as may be prescribed, for the cancellation by the responsible authority of the registration of the home ; and, if the authority are satisfied either—

(a) that no child in the care of a local authority is for the time being accommodated in the home, or

(b) in the case of a school registered by virtue of section 1(3) above, that it is no longer a school to which that provision applies,

the authority shall give to the person carrying on the home notice that the registration of the home has been cancelled by the authority as from the date of the notice.

(2) If on any annual review under section 5 above, or at any other time, it appears to the responsible authority that a registered home is being carried on otherwise than in accordance

with the relevant requirements, they may determine that the registration of the home should be cancelled.

(3) The responsible authority may at any time determine that the registration of a home should be cancelled on the ground that the person carrying on the home has been convicted of an offence under this Act or any regulations made under section 8 below, or on the ground that any other person has been convicted of such an offence in relation to the home.

(4) Where a local authority have determined under subsection (2) or (3) above that the registration of a home should be cancelled, they shall give to the person carrying on the home either—

(*a*) a notice that they propose to cancel the registration on such date as may be specified in the notice, being a date at least twenty-eight days after the date of the notice, or

(*b*) a notice that they propose to cancel it on such a date as aforesaid unless the person carrying on the home has previously complied, to their satisfaction, with any relevant requirement specified in the notice,

and any such notice shall state the grounds on which the authority propose to cancel the registration of the home ; and the authority shall accordingly cancel its registration on the date specified in the notice unless, in the case of a notice under paragraph (*b*), there has been such previous compliance as is mentioned in that paragraph.

(5) Where the registration of a home is cancelled under subsection (2) or (3) above, no application for the registration of the home shall be made under section 3 above within the period of six months beginning with the date of cancellation.

(6) In this section " the relevant requirements " has the same meaning as in section 5 above.

7.—(1) Where a person is notified by a local authority that Appeals. they have refused his application for registration, have imposed any condition or propose to cancel the registration of a home, he may, within the period of twenty-eight days beginning with the date on which he is so notified, appeal against that refusal, condition or proposal by a notice given to the local authority and requiring them to refer that matter to an appeal tribunal constituted in accordance with Schedule 3 to the Child Care 1980 c. 5. Act 1980.

(2) Subsections (4) to (6) of section 58 of that Act (procedure and expenses of tribunals) shall, with the necessary modifications, apply in relation to appeal tribunals constituted in accordance with that Schedule for the purposes of this section as they apply in relation to appeal tribunals so constituted for the purposes of section 58.

(3) Where an appeal is brought under this section against the refusal of an application for registration, then—

(a) the home shall continue to be treated for the purposes of this Act as if it were registered thereunder until such time as the appeal is determined or abandoned (in this section referred to, in relation to any appeal under this section, as " the relevant time ") ; and

(b) the period of six months mentioned in section 3(8) above shall, instead of beginning as there provided, begin at the relevant time ;

and the appeal tribunal may on any such appeal either confirm the refusal of the application or direct that the home shall be registered.

(4) Where an appeal is brought under this section against the imposition of a condition, that condition shall not take effect before the relevant time ; and the appeal tribunal may on any such appeal either confirm the imposition of the condition or direct that it shall not apply or that some other condition or conditions specified by the tribunal shall apply instead.

(5) Where an appeal is brought under this section against a proposal to cancel the registration of any home—

(a) the cancellation shall not take effect before the relevant time ; and

(b) the period of six months mentioned in section 6(5) above shall, instead of beginning as there provided, begin at the relevant time ;

and the appeal tribunal may on any such appeal either confirm the proposal to cancel the registration of the home or direct that it shall not be cancelled.

(6) A local authority shall comply with any directions given by an appeal tribunal under this section.

Regulations as to registered homes.

8.—(1) The Secretary of State may make regulations as to the registration of children's homes, as to the conduct of registered homes, and for securing the welfare of the children in registered homes.

(2) Regulations under this section may in particular—

(a) make provision as to the carrying out of annual reviews under section 5 above ;

(*b*) impose requirements as to the accommodation, staff and equipment to be provided in registered homes and as to the arrangements for medical (including psychiatric) and dental care which are to be made for protecting the health of children in such homes ;

(*c*) make provision for children accommodated in registered homes to receive a religious upbringing appropriate to the religious persuasion to which they belong ;

(*d*) authorise the responsible authority to limit the number of children who may be accommodated in any particular registered home ;

(*e*) impose requirements as to the keeping of records and giving of notices in respect of such children ;

(*f*) require notice to be given to the responsible authority of any change of the person carrying on a registered home or of the premises used by such a home.

(3) Regulations under this section may make different provision for different cases.

(4) Regulations under this section may provide that a contravention of or failure to comply with any specified provision of the regulations shall be an offence against the regulations ; and any person guilty of such an offence shall be liable on summary conviction to a fine not exceeding £500.

(5) Any regulations under this section shall be made by statutory instrument, which shall be subject to annulment in pursuance of a resolution of either House of Parliament.

9.—(1) Any person authorised in that behalf by the responsible authority may at all reasonable times enter and inspect any registered home or any premises which he has reasonable cause to believe are being used as part of such a home. Inspection of registered homes.

(2) Any person inspecting a home under this section may in particular—

(*a*) inspect any child accommodated in the home ; and

(*b*) require the production of, and inspect, any records required to be kept in accordance with regulations made under section 8 above.

(3) A person who proposes to exercise any power conferred by this section shall, if so required, produce some duly authenticated document showing his authority to exercise the power.

(4) Any person who without reasonable cause obstructs any person in the exercise of any power conferred by this section shall be guilty of an offence and liable on summary conviction to a fine not exceeding £500.

1933 c. 12.

(5) A refusal to allow any such person as is referred to in subsection (1) above to enter a registered home or such premises as are there mentioned shall be deemed, for the purposes of section 40 of the Children and Young Persons Act 1933 (search warrants), to be a reasonable cause to suspect that a child in the home or premises is being neglected in a manner likely to cause him unnecessary suffering or injury to health.

Persons disqualified from carrying on, or being employed in, registered homes.

1975 c. 21.

10.—(1) This section applies to any person who has been convicted of any offence specified in Schedule 1 to the Children and Young Persons Act 1933 or in Schedule 1 to the Criminal Procedure (Scotland) Act 1975, or has been placed on probation or discharged absolutely or conditionally for any such offence.

(2) A person to whom this section applies shall not carry on or be otherwise concerned in the management of, or have any financial interest in, a registered home unless he has—

 (a) disclosed to the responsible authority the fact that he has been convicted or otherwise dealt with as mentioned in subsection (1) above, and

 (b) obtained their written consent.

(3) A person shall not employ in a registered home a person to whom this section applies unless he, the employer, has—

 (a) disclosed to the responsible authority the fact that that person has been convicted or otherwise dealt with as mentioned in subsection (1) above, and

 (b) obtained their written consent.

(4) Any person who—

 (a) contravenes subsection (2) above, or

 (b) knowingly employs a person to whom this section applies in contravention of subsection (3) above,

shall be guilty of an offence and liable on summary conviction to imprisonment for a term not exceeding six months or to a fine not exceeding £1,000 or to both.

Provisions as to offences.

11.—(1) A local authority may institute proceedings for an offence under this Act or any regulations made under it.

(2) Where any such offence committed by a body corporate is proved to have been committed with the consent or connivance of or to be attributable to any neglect on the part of any director, manager, secretary or other similar officer of the body corporate, or any person who was purporting to act in any such capacity, he as well as the body corporate shall be guilty of the offence and shall be liable to be proceeded against and punished accordingly.

(3) Where a person is charged with an offence under section 2(2) or 4(3) above or under regulations made under section 8 above, it shall be a defence to prove that he took all reasonable precautions and exercised all due diligence to avoid the commission of the offence by himself or any person under his control.

12.—(1) Any notice required to be given under this Act— Notices.

    (*a*) shall be given in writing ; and

    (*b*) may be given by post.

(2) Where any such notice is required to be given to the person carrying on a children's home and more than one person is for the time being carrying it on, the notice may be given to any one of them ; and for the purposes of section 7 of the Interpretation Act 1978 (references to " service by post ") a 1978 c. 30. letter enclosing a notice under this Act to any such person or persons shall be deemed to be properly addressed if it is addressed to him or them at the home.

13. There shall be paid out of money provided by Parliament Expenses. any increase attributable to this Act in the sums so payable under any other Act.

14.—(1) In this Act— Interpretation.

    " child " means a person under the age of 18 years and any person who has attained that age and is the subject of a care order within the meaning of the Children and Young Persons Act 1969 ; 1969 c. 54.

    " children's home " shall be construed in accordance with section 1 above ;

    " local authority " means, except in section 1(2)(*d*) and (*e*) above, the council of a non-metropolitan county, metropolitan district or London borough, or the Common Council of the City of London, and in those provisions means a local authority within the meaning of the Local Government Act 1972 ; 1972 c. 70.

    " prescribed " means prescribed by regulations made under section 8 above ;

    " registered home " means a children's home registered under this Act, and " registration " means registration thereunder ;

    " responsible authority ", in relation to a registered home, means the local authority which registered it under this Act.

(2) References in this Act to a child in the care of a local authority are references to a child in the care of a local authority under or by virtue of any enactment, but do not include any child who is for the time being boarded out in accordance with

any regulations made or having effect as if made under section 22 of the Child Care Act 1980.

15.—(1) At the end of Schedule 1 to the Local Authority Social Services Act 1970 (list of enactments conferring functions assigned to the social services committee of a local authority) there shall be added—

" Children's Homes Act 1982. Registration of children's homes ; supervision of registered homes."

(2) In Part I of Schedule 1 to the Tribunals and Inquiries Act 1971 (tribunals under direct supervision of Council on Tribunals), for paragraph 4 there shall be substituted—

" Children's homes.   4. Appeal tribunals constituted in accordance with Schedule 3 to the Child Care Act 1980 (c.5) for the purposes of section 58 of that Act or of section 7 of the Children's Homes Act 1982 (c. 20)."

(3) In section 21(1) of the Child Care Act 1980 (methods of providing for accommodation and maintenance of children in care), at the end of paragraph (*c*) there shall be added " or

(*d*) by maintaining him in a children's home registered under the Children's Homes Act 1982 ; ".

(4) Paragraph 33 of Schedule 5 to the Child Care Act 1980 is hereby repealed.

16.—(1) This Act may be cited as the Children's Homes Act 1982.

(2) This Act shall come into force on such day as the Secretary of State may appoint by an order made by statutory instrument, and different days may be appointed for, or for different purposes of, different provisions of this Act.

(3) This Act extends to England and Wales only.

Planning Inquiries (Attendance of Public) Act 1982

1982 CHAPTER 21

An Act to require that evidence at planning inquiries held under the Town and Country Planning Act 1971 be given in public, subject to certain exceptions.

[28th June 1982]

BE IT ENACTED by the Queen's most Excellent Majesty, by and with the advice and consent of the Lords Spiritual and Temporal, and Commons, in this present Parliament assembled, and by the authority of the same, as follows:—

1.—(1) Subject to subsection (2) below, at any planning inquiry oral evidence shall be heard in public and documentary evidence shall be open to public inspection.

(2) Subject to subsection (3) below, the Secretary of State may, in the case of any planning inquiry, direct that evidence of any description indicated in the direction shall not be heard or (as the case may be) open to inspection at that inquiry by anyone other than such persons or persons of such descriptions as he may specify in that direction.

Planning inquiries to be held in public, subject to certain exceptions.

(3) The Secretary of State may give a direction under subsection (2) above only if he is satisfied—

  (*a*) that giving evidence of the description indicated or (as the case may be) making it available for inspection would be likely to result in the disclosure of information as to any of the matters mentioned in subsection (4) below; and (*b*) that the public disclosure of that information would be contrary to the national interest.

(4) The matters referred to in subsection (3)(*a*) above are—

(*a*) national security; and

(*b*) the measures taken or to be taken to ensure the security of any premises or property.

(5) In this section " planning inquiry " means any local inquiry held under—

1971 c. 78.

(*a*) section 49(3) of the Town and Country Planning Act 1971 (inquiry held by a Planning Inquiry Commission);

(*b*) section 282(1) of that Act (inquiry held for purpose of discharging functions of Secretary of State); or

(*c*) paragraph 5 of Schedule 9 to that Act (inquiry held by person appointed by Secretary of State to determine appeal).

Short title and extent.   **2.**—(1) This Act may be cited as the Planning Inquiries (Attendance of Public) Act 1982.

(2) This Act extends to England and Wales only.

Gaming (Amendment) Act 1982

1982 CHAPTER 22

An Act to amend the law with respect to the times of year at which applications may be made relating to the licensing of premises or the registration of clubs or institutes under section 10 of the Gaming Act 1845 or Part II of the Gaming Act 1968 and otherwise with respect to the procedure to be followed in connection with such applications; to empower the Secretary of State to make provision by order as to the fees payable in connection with licences under the said section 10; and to repeal certain spent or obsolete enactments relating to the matters aforesaid.   [28th June 1982]

BE IT ENACTED by the Queen's most Excellent Majesty, by and with the advice and consent of the Lords Spiritual and Temporal, and Commons, in this present Parliament assembled, and by the authority of the same, as follows:—

1. The Gaming Act 1968 shall have effect with the amendments specified in Schedule 1 to this Act.

The purpose of those amendments is—

   (*a*) to enable an application to be made at any time of year for the grant of a licence under that Act, for the registration under Part II of that Act in England or Wales of a members' club or miners' welfare institute or for the renewal of such a licence or registration ;

   (*b*) to make minor changes in the procedure to be followed in connection with such applications ; and

   (*c*) to repeal spent provisions.

Amendments of the Gaming Act 1968.
1968 c. 65.

Amendments
relating to
billiard
licences.

1845 c. 109.

1872 c. 94.

1964 c. 26.

2. The Gaming Act 1845 and the Licensing Act 1872 shall have effect with the amendments specified in Schedule 2 to this Act.

The purpose of those amendments is—

(*a*) to enable an application for the grant or transfer of a billiard licence under section 10 of the Gaming Act 1845 to be made at any licensing sessions held under the Licensing Act 1964 ;

(*b*) to empower the Secretary of State to make provision by order as to the fees payable for the grant or transfer of such licences ; and

(*c*) to replace or repeal obsolete provisions.

Short title,
commence-
ment, savings
and extent.

3.—(1) This Act may be cited as the Gaming (Amendment) Act 1982.

(2) The provisions of this Act come into force at the end of the period of two months beginning with the day on which it is passed.

(3) The amendments made by this Act do not affect—

(*a*) the duration or validity of a licence or registration in force immediately before the commencement of this Act ; or

(*b*) the procedure for granting, transferring or renewing a licence or registration in a case where the application was made before the commencement of this Act.

(4) This Act does not extend to Northern Ireland.

SCHEDULES

SCHEDULE 1

AMENDMENTS OF THE GAMING ACT 1968

Meetings of licensing authority

1.—(1) In Schedule 2 (which relates to the grant, renewal, cancellation and transfer of licences), insert the following paragraph after paragraph 2—

" 2A.—(1) Each licensing authority shall for each year fix a day in each of the months of—

(a) January, April, July and October if the authority is in England or Wales ; or

(b) January, March, June and October if the authority is in Scotland,

as a day on which, subject to paragraphs 7 and 13 of this Schedule, they will hold a meeting for the purpose of considering any application for the grant or renewal of a licence under this Act then awaiting consideration.

(2) In addition to any meeting on a day fixed in pursuance of the preceding sub-paragraph, a licensing authority may hold a meeting on any other day for the purpose of considering such applications as are mentioned in that sub-paragraph.".

(2) In paragraph 2 of Schedule 3 (which applies in relation to the registration of members' clubs and miners' welfare institutes in England and Wales certain of the introductory provisions of Schedule 2), for " Paragraph 2 " substitute " Paragraphs 2 and 2A " and for " that paragraph " substitute " those paragraphs ".

Application for Gaming Board consent

2. In paragraph 4 of Schedule 2 (application for Gaming Board consent to licence application), omit sub-paragraph (3) (which in paragraph (b) requires such applications to be made before the end of October, and is otherwise spent).

Application for grant of licence or registration

3. In paragraph 5 of Schedule 2 (application for grant of licence), for sub-paragraph (1) (which requires such applications to be made in January or February) substitute—

" (1) An application for the grant of a licence under this Act may be made at any time.".

4.—(1) Paragraph 6 of Schedule 2 (publication of notices in connection with an application for the grant of a licence) is amended as follows.

(2) In sub-paragraph (1) (advertisement giving notice of application to be published in local newspaper), for " At any time in March in the year in which such an application is made " substitute " Not

Part I   L

later than fourteen days after the making of any such application to the licensing authority ".

(3) In sub-paragraph (2) (which requires the notice to contain specified particulars and to invite objections by 15th April), for " before 15th April " substitute " before such date (not being earlier than fourteen days after the publication of the advertisement) as may be specified in the notice ".

(4) For sub-paragraph (3) (which requires a like notice to be displayed outside the relevant premises during the period 1st to 14th April) substitute—

"(3) Not later than fourteen days before the date specified in the notice in accordance with the preceding sub-paragraph the applicant shall cause a like notice to be displayed outside the entrance to the relevant premises ; and the applicant shall take such steps as he reasonably can to keep that notice so displayed until that date.".

5.—(1) Paragraph 7 of Schedule 2 (further steps preparatory to the hearing of an application for the grant of a licence) is amended as follows.

(2) In sub-paragraph (1) (which requires the applicant to send a copy of the newspaper containing the required advertisement to the clerk to the authority and prohibits the authority from considering the application before the beginning of May), for " before the beginning of May " substitute " earlier than fourteen days after the date specified in the advertisement ".

(3) In sub-paragraph (2) (which requires the clerk to the authority to give notice, after the expiry of the period for objecting to the application, of the date fixed for its consideration), for " On or after 15th April " substitute " On or after the date so specified ".

6.—(1) Omit paragraphs 8 to 11 of Schedule 2 (which, although also applied for certain other purposes, primarily relate to applications made in the initial period following the commencement of the 1968 Act and are in that connection spent).

(2) In paragraph 14 of Schedule 2 (proceedings on an application for the grant of a licence), in sub-paragraph (2)(*b*) (which relates to the right of objectors to be heard), omit " or paragraph 11(2) ".

(3) In paragraph 59 of Schedule 2 (which applies in relation to an application for the transfer of a licence certain procedural provisions relating to an application for the grant of a licence)—

(*a*) for " Paragraphs 10 and 11 of this Schedule " substitute " Paragraphs 6 and 7 of this Schedule " ; and

(*b*) omit " made during the initial period ".

(4) In paragraph 3 of Schedule 3 (which applies in relation to the registration of clubs and institutes in England and Wales the provisions of Schedule 2 relating to applications for licences)—

(*a*) in the opening words, for " Paragraphs 5 to 11 " substitute " Paragraphs 5 to 7 " ;

(b) in sub-paragraph (a), for " paragraphs 6(2) and 10(2) " substitute " paragraph 6(2) " ;

(c) in sub-paragraph (b), for " paragraphs 6(3) and 10(3) " substitute " paragraph 6(3) " ; and

(d) in the closing words, omit the words from " and in paragraph 8 " to the end.

(5) In paragraph 4 of Schedule 4 (which applies in relation to the registration of clubs and institutes in Scotland certain provisions of Schedule 2 relating to applications for licences) for " Paragraph 10 of Schedule 2 " substitute " Paragraph 6 of Schedule 2 " ; and in paragraph 5(1) of that Schedule (which specifies the further steps to be taken on such an application) for " paragraph 10 of Schedule 2 " substitute " paragraph 6 of Schedule 2 ".

Application for renewal of licence or registration

7.—(1) Paragraph 12 of Schedule 2 (application for renewal of licence) is amended as follows.

(2) In sub-paragraph (1) (which requires such applications to be made in January or February, subject to sub-paragraph (2)), for " in January or February in the year in which the licence is due to expire " substitute " not earlier than five or later than two months before the date on which the licence is due to expire ".

(3) In sub-paragraph (2) (which enables the licensing authority to consider a late application if the failure to apply in time was due to inadvertence)—

(a) for " after the end of February " substitute " later than is required by the last preceding sub-paragraph " ; and

(b) for " before the end of that month " substitute " in time ".

8. For paragraph 13 of Schedule 2 (steps preparatory to the hearing by the licensing authority of an application for renewal of a licence) substitute—

" 13.—(1) Not later than seven days after the date on which an application for the renewal of a licence under this Act is made, the applicant shall send a copy of the application—

(a) to the Board ;

(b) to the appropriate officer of police ;

(c) to the appropriate local authority ;

(d) to the appropriate fire authority, if that authority is not the same body as the appropriate local authority ; and

(e) to the appropriate collector of duty.

(2) Not later than fourteen days after the making of any such application, the clerk to the licensing authority shall cause notice of the making of the application to be published by means of an advertisement in a newspaper circulating in the licensing authority's area.

(3) A notice published in pursuance of the preceding sub-paragraph shall state that any person who desires to object to the renewal by the licensing authority of the licence should send to the clerk to the licensing authority, before such date (not being earlier than fourteen days after the publication of the advertisement) as may be specified in the notice, two copies of a brief statement in writing of the grounds of his objection.

(4) On or after the date so specified, but not less than seven days before the day appointed for the consideration of the application, the clerk to the licensing authority shall send notice in writing of the date, time and place of the meeting of the authority at which the application will be considered—

> (a) to the applicant ;
>
> (b) to all the persons and bodies specified in sub-paragraph (1) of this paragraph ; and
>
> (c) if the clerk has received from any other person an objection in writing which has not been withdrawn and the address of that person is known to the clerk, to that person.

(5) With the notice sent to the applicant in accordance with the preceding sub-paragraph there shall be enclosed a copy of any objection to the renewal of the licence which has been received by the clerk to the licensing authority and which has not been withdrawn.".

9. In paragraph 14 of Schedule 2 (proceedings on an application for the renewal of a licence), in sub-paragraph (2)(b) (which relates to the right of objectors to be heard) for " paragraph 13(3) (b) " substitute " paragraph 13(5) ".

10. For paragraphs 4 and 5 of Schedule 3 (which provide for the making of applications for renewal of registration and for the steps to be taken preparatory to the hearing of such applications by the licensing authority) substitute—

> " 4. Paragraphs 12 and 13 of Schedule 2 to this Act shall have effect in relation to any application for renewal of the registration of a club or institute under Part II of this Act as they have effect in relation to applications for the renewal of licences under this Act, but as if in paragraph 13(1) of that Schedule the references to the appropriate local authority and the appropriate fire authority were omitted.".

Duration of licence or registration

11.—(1) Paragraph 52 of Schedule 2 (duration of licences) is amended as follows.

(2) In sub-paragraph (1) (of which paragraph (a) relates to the expiry of licences which have not been renewed and paragraph (b) to the expiry of licences which have been renewed)—

(*a*) in paragraph (*a*) for "the end of the month of May in the
year following that in which it was granted" substitute
"the end of the period of one year beginning with the date
on which it was granted"; and

(*b*) in paragraph (*b*) for "the end of the month of May in the
year following that in which it was last renewed" substitute "the end of the period of one year from the
date on which it would otherwise have expired".

(3) Omit sub-paragraph (2) (which is spent).

12.—(1) Paragraph 19 of Schedule 3 (duration of registration) is
amended as follows.

(2) In sub-paragraph (1), in paragraph (*a*) (which relates to the
expiry of a registration which has not been renewed) for "the
end of the month of May in the year following that in which it was
effected" substitute "the end of the period of one year beginning
with the date on which it was effected".

(3) Omit sub-paragraph (2) (which is spent).

13. In paragraph 21 of Schedule 3 (which permits an application
for renewal of registration to be made in a year when the registration is not due to expire, for the purpose of securing the cancellation or variation of a restriction imposed under paragraph 11
as to the parts of the premises in which gaming may take place),
in sub-paragraph (2) for "as if it were due to expire at the end of
the month of May in that year" substitute "as if it were due to
expire on the day before the anniversary of the date on which it was
renewed or last renewed".

14. In paragraph 17 of Schedule 4 (duration of registration), omit
sub-paragraph (2) (which is spent).

SCHEDULE 2   Section 2.

AMENDMENTS RELATING TO BILLIARD LICENCES

Replacement of main licensing provision

1. For section 10 of the Gaming Act 1845 (grant and transfer of 1845 c. 109.
billiard licences) substitute the following section—

"Billiard   10.—(1) The licensing justices for any licensing dis-
licences.   trict may at any licensing sessions held by them in
pursuance of section 2(3) of the Licensing Act 1964—

    (*a*) grant billiard licences to such persons as the
justices shall in their discretion deem fit and
proper persons to keep public billiard tables
and bagatelle boards or instruments used in
any game of the like kind;

L 3

SCH. 2

(*b*) transfer such billiard licences to such other persons as they in their discretion shall deem fit and proper to continue to hold the same.

(2) The provisions of Part II of Schedule 1 to the Licensing Act 1964 (which relate to the holding of licensing sessions) and the provisions of Schedule 2 to that Act (which relate to the procedure to be followed in connection with applications for justices' licences) shall apply in relation to applications for the grant or transfer of billiard licences as they apply to applications for the grant or transfer of a justices' on-licence under that Act.

(3) A billiard licence shall be in the form given in the Third Schedule annexed to this Act and shall have effect for a period of one year beginning with such date as may be specified in the licence.

(4) There may be charged by justices' clerks in respect of the grant or transfer of billiard licences such fees as may be provided for by order of the Secretary of State ; and the fee so provided for in relation to the grant of a licence may be different from that provided for in relation to the transfer of a licence.

(5) An order under subsection (4) shall be made by statutory instrument which shall be subject to annulment in pursuance of a resolution of either House of Parliament.".

Form of licence

1845 c. 109.   2. In the Third Schedule to the Gaming Act 1845 (which sets out the form of a billiard licence under section 10 of that Act)—

(*a*) for " general licensing annual meeting [or an adjournment of the general annual licensing meeting, or at a special petty session] " substitute " licensing sessions " ;

(*b*) for " division [or liberty, &c., as the case may be,] " and " county [or liberty, &c., as the case may be,] " substitute " licensing district " ; and

(*c*) for " the said session " substitute " the said sessions ".

Consequential repeal

1872 c. 94.   3. In the proviso to section 75 of the Licensing Act 1872, omit the words from " in the case of persons intending to apply for billiard licences " to " or as near thereto as the circumstances admit ; and " (which provide for the giving of notices by persons intending to apply for the grant or transfer of a billiard licence).

Oil and Gas (Enterprise) Act 1982

1982 CHAPTER 23

An Act to make further provision with respect to the British National Oil Corporation; to abolish the National Oil Account; to make further provision with respect to the British Gas Corporation; to make provision for and in connection with the supply of gas through pipes by persons other than the Corporation; to amend the Petroleum (Production) Act 1934 and to make further provision about licences to search for and get petroleum; to repeal and re-enact with amendments sections 2 and 3 of the Continental Shelf Act 1964; to extend the application of the Mineral Workings (Offshore Installations) Act 1971 and the Offshore Petroleum Development (Scotland) Act 1975; to amend the Miscellaneous Financial Provisions Act 1968, the Petroleum and Submarine Pipe-lines Act 1975 and the Participation Agreements Act 1978; and for connected purposes.   [28th June 1982]

B E IT ENACTED by the Queen's most Excellent Majesty, by and with the advice and consent of the Lords Spiritual and Temporal, and Commons, in this present Parliament assembled, and by the authority of the same, as follows:—

PART I

OIL

The British National Oil Corporation

1.—(1) Without prejudice to any powers conferred on it by any other enactment, the British National Oil Corporation (in this Act referred to as "the Oil Corporation") shall, subject to

Oil Corporation's powers of disposal.

L 4

PART I   subsection (2) below, have power to provide for the disposal, in such manner as it thinks fit, of any shares of an equity oil subsidiary.

(2) The Oil Corporation shall not, and shall secure that each other member of the group does not, dispose of any shares of an equity oil subsidiary except with the consent of the Secretary of State and in accordance with any conditions specified in the instrument signifying his consent ; and the Secretary of State shall not give any such consent except with the approval of the Treasury.

(3) In exercising its powers under subsection (1) above the Oil Corporation may, with the consent of the Secretary of State, provide for employees' share schemes to be established in respect of equity oil subsidiaries ; and any such scheme may provide for the transfer of shares without consideration.

(4) In this section and sections 2 and 3 below—

" equity oil subsidiary " means a relevant subsidiary which has as its principal object searching and boring for and getting petroleum ;

" group " means the Oil Corporation and all relevant subsidiaries taken together ;

1975 c. 74.   " petroleum " has the same meaning as in Part I of the Petroleum and Submarine Pipe-lines Act 1975 (in this Act referred to as " the 1975 Act ") ;

and in this Part "subsidiary " and " relevant subsidiary " have the same meanings as in the 1975 Act.

Provisions supplementary to section 1.   **2.**—(1) For the purpose of facilitating the eventual disposal under section 1(1) above of—

(*a*) any part of the undertaking of the Oil Corporation, or any part of the undertaking of a relevant subsidiary which is not an equity oil subsidiary, being (in either case) a part which is concerned with searching and boring for and getting petroleum, or any property rights or liabilities comprised in such a part ; or

(*b*) the whole or any part of the undertaking of, or any property, rights or liabilities of, an equity oil subsidiary,

the Corporation may exercise its powers to establish subsidiaries, to secure increases in the capital of subsidiaries and to transfer property, rights and liabilities to subsidiaries, notwithstanding the provisions of any enactment which may be taken to limit the purposes for which those powers may be exercised.

(2) The Oil Corporation may also, for the said purpose, make schemes for the transfer, between the Corporation and a relevant subsidiary or between one such subsidiary and another, of—

(a) any prescribed property, rights or liabilities ;

(b) all property, rights and liabilities comprised in, or in a prescribed part of, the transferor's undertaking.

(3) A scheme under subsection (2) above may—

(a) provide that any prescribed rights or liabilities of the transferor shall be enforceable either by or against either party or by or against both ;

(b) for the purpose of dealing with matters arising out of or related to the transfer, confer or impose on either party rights or liabilities which are to be enforceable against or by the other ;

(c) provide that for the purposes of section 6 of the 1975 Act (borrowing limits) any aggregate amount there mentioned shall be determined as if any money borrowed or debt assumed by the transferor the liability to repay which is transferred were (in either case) money borrowed by the transferee ;

and may contain such other supplementary, incidental and consequential provisions (including provisions as to the construction of agreements, licences and other documents) as may appear to the Oil Corporation to be necessary or expedient.

(4) A scheme under subsection (2) above may also provide that—

(a) prescribed securities of the transferee shall be issued to the transferor in consideration of the transfer and shall be credited as fully paid up ;

(b) for the purposes of section 56 of the Companies Act 1948 c. 38. 1948 (share premium account) and of any statutory accounts of the transferee, the value of any asset and the amount of any liability transferred shall be taken to be the value or (as the case may be) the amount which would have been assigned to that asset or liability for the purposes of the statutory accounts prepared by the transferor in respect of its last accounting period ending before the transfer date if that period had ended immediately before that date ;

(c) a prescribed amount not exceeding the accumulated realised profits of the transferor at the transfer date shall be treated by the transferee as a reserve which represents its profits available for distribution (within the meaning of Part III of the Companies Act 1980) ; 1980 c. 22.

(*d*) in ascertaining for the purposes of the said section 56 what amount (if any) falls to be treated as a premium received on the issue of any shares in pursuance of any provision made by virtue of paragraph (*a*) above, the amount of the net assets transferred shall be taken to be reduced by an amount corresponding to the amount of any reserve for which provision is made by virtue of paragraph (*c*) above ;

(*e*) subject to any provision made by virtue of the preceding provisions of this subsection, for the purposes of any statutory accounts of the transferee the amount to be included in respect of any item shall be determined as if any relevant thing done by the transferor (whether by way of acquiring, revaluing or disposing of any asset or incurring, revaluing or discharging any liability, or by carrying any amount to any provision or reserve, or otherwise) had been done by the transferee.

(5) A scheme under subsection (2) above shall not come into force until it is approved by the Secretary of State or until such date as the Secretary of State may in giving his approval specify ; and the Secretary of State may approve a scheme either without modifications or with such modifications as, after consultation with the Oil Corporation, he thinks fit.

(6) On the coming into force of a scheme under subsection (2) above—

(*a*) the property, rights and liabilities to be transferred shall, subject to subsection (7) below, be transferred and vest in accordance with the scheme ; and

(*b*) any provision made by virtue of subsection (3) or (4) above shall have effect in accordance with the scheme notwithstanding any rule of law and the provisions of any enactment.

(7) Schedule 1 to this Act shall apply to any transfer under paragraph (*a*) of subsection (6) above and that paragraph shall have effect subject to the provisions of that Schedule.

(8) In this section " statutory accounts " means—

(*a*) in relation to the Oil Corporation, a statement of accounts prepared by the Corporation in accordance with section 10 of the 1975 Act ;

(*b*) in relation to any other party, accounts prepared by that party for the purposes of any provision of the Companies Acts 1948 to 1981 (including group accounts) ;

and in this section and in Schedule 1 to this Act " prescribed ", in relation to a scheme under subsection (2) above, means specified or described in or determined in accordance with the scheme.

3.—(1) The Secretary of State may, after consultation with the Oil Corporation, give directions to the Corporation requiring it to exercise its powers under sections 1 and 2 above (including the powers extended by section 2(1) above) for such purposes and in such manner as may be specified in the directions.

PART I

Powers of Secretary of State as respects disposals by Oil Corporation.

(2) For the purpose of facilitating a disposal under section 1(1) above, the Secretary of State may by order provide that, in its application to any equity oil subsidiary specified in the order, Part I of the 1975 Act shall have effect with such modifications as may be so specified.

(3) Except in so far as the Secretary of State, after consultation with the Oil Corporation, otherwise directs, the Corporation shall pay to the Secretary of State any sums received by it or a relevant subsidiary on a disposal on or after the commencement date of any shares of an equity oil subsidiary.

(4) The Secretary of State may by order transfer to himself or a nominee of his any shares of a company which is or has been an equity oil subsidiary, being shares held by or on behalf of one or more members of the group; and any shares transferred by an order under this subsection shall vest in the Secretary of State or the nominee by virtue of the order.

(5) If an order under subsection (4) above so provides, the Secretary of State shall pay to the transferor such sum by way of consideration for the shares as may be specified in the order.

(6) In determining for the purposes of the 1975 Act or this Part whether any subsidiary of the Oil Corporation is a relevant subsidiary, any shares of the subsidiary held by the Secretary of State or a nominee of his shall be treated as held by the Corporation.

(7) The Secretary of State shall not give any direction or make any order under this section except with the approval of the Treasury; and except as aforesaid neither the Secretary of State nor a nominee of his shall dispose of any shares held by virtue of this section.

(8) Any sums required by the Secretary of State for making payments under subsection (5) above shall be paid out of money provided by Parliament; and any sums received by the Secretary of State under subsection (3) above and any dividends or other sums received by the Secretary of State or a nominee of his in right of, on the disposal of, or otherwise in connection with, any shares held by virtue of this section shall be paid into the Consolidated Fund.

4.—(1) On and after the commencement date no further sums shall be paid out of the National Oil Account (in this section referred to as " the Account ") under section 40(3)(a) or (c) of the 1975 Act (sums needed by the Oil Corporation or wholly owned subsidiaries of the Corporation and sums payable to Ministers in respect of revenue accruing in respect of certain services) ; and on and after that date no further sums shall be paid into the Account under any of the following provisions of that Act, namely—

(a) section 7(2) (sums lent to the Corporation by the Secretary of State) ;

(b) section 14(4)(b) (sums received by wholly owned subsidiaries of the Corporation) ; and

(c) section 40(2)(a) and (c) (sums received by the Corporation and sums payable to the Corporation in respect of certain services).

(2) On the commencement date the Oil Corporation shall assume a debt due to the Secretary of State (in this section referred to as " the Oil Corporation's commencing debt ") of such amount as may be determined by the Secretary of State, with the approval of the Treasury and after consultation with the Corporation, to be the excess of the aggregate of the sums paid out of the Account under section 40(3)(a) of the 1975 Act over the aggregate of the sums paid into the Account under sections 14(4)(b) and 40(2)(a) and (c) of that Act, or such other amount as may be so determined.

(3) The Treasury shall be deemed to have issued under section 7(4) of the 1975 Act to the Secretary of State out of the National Loans Fund on the commencement date a sum equal to the amount of the Oil Corporation's commencing debt.

(4) The rate of interest payable on so much of the principal of the Oil Corporation's commencing debt as is for the time being outstanding, the date from which interest is to begin to accrue, the arrangements for paying off the principal of the debt and the other terms of the debt shall be such as the Secretary of State may, with the approval of the Treasury, from time to time determine ; and different rates and dates may be determined under this subsection with respect to different portions of the commencing debt.

(5) Any sums received by the Secretary of State by way of interest on or repayment of the Oil Corporation's commencing debt shall be paid into the National Loans Fund.

(6) In consequence of subsection (1) above section 7(2), section 14(4)(b) and section 40(2)(a) and (c) and (3)(a) and (c) of the 1975 Act shall cease to have effect.

5.—(1) If for any accounting year there is an excess of the revenue of the Oil Corporation or any relevant subsidiary over the total sums required by it to meet expenditure properly chargeable to revenue account, the Secretary of State may, with the approval of the Treasury and after consultation with the Corporation, give the Corporation directions requiring it to pay, or cause to be paid, the whole or part of the excess to the Secretary of State.

PART I

Payments by Oil Corporation to Secretary of State.

(2) The Secretary of State may, with the approval of the Treasury and after consultation with the Oil Corporation, direct the Corporation to pay, or cause to be paid, to the Secretary of State the whole or part of any sum which is or, in the opinion of the Secretary of State, ought to be standing to the credit of a reserve of the Corporation or a relevant subsidiary.

(3) Any sums received by the Secretary of State in pursuance of this section shall be paid into the Consolidated Fund.

(4) In this section " accounting year " has the same meaning as in Part I of the 1975 Act.

6.—(1) The Secretary of State with the approval of the Treasury may, out of money provided by Parliament, make grants to the Oil Corporation or a relevant subsidiary towards expenditure incurred by the Corporation or subsidiary in or in connection with the exercise of the power conferred on the Corporation by section 2(1)(*e*) of the 1975 Act (power to enter into, and give effect to, participation agreements).

Grants by Secretary of State to Oil Corporation.

(2) Grants under this section may be made subject to such conditions as the Secretary of State with the approval of the Treasury may determine.

7. For subsections (3) and (4) of section 6 of the 1975 Act (borrowing powers etc.) there shall be substituted the following subsections—

Borrowing powers etc. of Oil Corporation.

" (3) The aggregate amount outstanding at any time in respect of the principal of any money borrowed temporarily by the Corporation and relevant subsidiaries shall not exceed such amount as is for the time being specified by the Secretary of State ; and the aggregate amount outstanding at any time in respect of the principal of—

(*a*) any money borrowed by the Corporation or a relevant subsidiary from an outside person ;

(*b*) any sums for the repayment of which by an outside person the Corporation or a relevant subsidiary is surety or guarantor ; and

(*c*) the Corporation's commencing debt,

shall not exceed £600 million or such larger amount, not

exceeding £800 million, as is for the time being specified by an order made by the Secretary of State.

(4) In applying subsection (3) above, any money borrowed temporarily by the Corporation or a relevant subsidiary for the purpose of repaying, before the due date, any money borrowed by it otherwise than by way of temporary loan shall be disregarded

(5) Where the Corporation or a relevant subsidiary sells petroleum on terms such that any of the petroleum will or may fall to be delivered more than twelve months after the payment of the price therefor, the price of so much of the petroleum as has not been delivered at any time after the payment shall be treated for the purposes of subsection (3) above as money borrowed by the Corporation or subsidiary from the purchaser.

(6) Where any person makes to the Corporation or a relevant subsidiary a payment which is to be appropriated to purchases of petroleum by that person from the Corporation or subsidiary, then, unless the terms of the payment are such that the whole of it may reasonably be expected to be so appropriated within twelve months after the making of the payment, so much of the payment as has not been so appropriated at any time shall be treated for the purposes of subsection (3) above as money borrowed by the Corporation or subsidiary from the purchaser.

(7) Where the Corporation or a relevant subsidiary purchases property on terms such that any part of the price will or may fall to be paid more than twelve months after the transfer of the property, so much of the price as has not been paid at any time after the transfer shall be treated for the purposes of subsection (3) above as money borrowed by the Corporation or subsidiary from the vendor.

(8) In applying subsection (7) above, any part of the price which may fall to be paid more than twelve months after the transfer of the property and which, if it did, would fall to be calculated by reference to the amount by which the value of the property exceeded its estimated value, or any income derived from the property exceeded the estimated amount of that income, shall be disregarded.

(9) Where in any case to which subsection (7) above applies any part of the price cannot be ascertained at the time of the transfer, that subsection shall have effect in relation to that part of the price as if—

    (*a*) the amount thereof ; and

    (*b*) the extent to which it has not been paid at any
       time,

were such amount or extent as the Secretary of State, with the approval of the Treasury and after consultation with the Corporation, may determine.

(10) Where at any time a company ceases to be a relevant subsidiary, the Secretary of State may by order provide that subsection (3) above shall have effect as if for the amounts there specified there were substituted such lower amounts as he may consider appropriate having regard, in particular, to the aggregate amount outstanding at that time in respect of the principal of—

> (*a*) any money borrowed by that company ; and
>
> (*b*) any sums for the repayment of which by an outside person that company was at that time surety or guarantor.

(11) In this section—

> ' the Corporation's commencing debt ' means the debt assumed by the Corporation under section 4(2) of the Oil and Gas (Enterprise) Act 1982 ;
>
> ' outside person ' means a person other than the Corporation or a relevant subsidiary ;
>
> ' sell ' includes barter and exchange and ' purchase ', ' price ' and ' payment ' shall be construed accordingly."

The National Oil Account

8.—(1) The National Oil Account (in this section referred to as " the Account ") shall cease to exist and the amount standing to the credit of the Account shall be paid into the Consolidated Fund.

Abolition of the National Oil Account.

(2) In consequence of subsection (1) above, the 1975 Act shall be amended as follows—

> (*a*) in sections 25(3) and 40(2)(*b*) (certain sums received by the Secretary of State to be paid into the Account) for references to the Account there shall be substituted references to the Consolidated Fund ; and
>
> (*b*) in sections 40(3)(*b*) and 41(4) (certain sums payable by the Secretary of State to be paid out of the Account) for references to the Account there shall be substituted references to money provided by Parliament.

(3) Also in consequence of subsection (1) above, section 40(1) and (4) of that Act and, in section 40(3), the words " and when " onwards (establishment of the Account, accounts and audit and payment of excess amount into the Consolidated Fund) shall cease to have effect.

(4) Nothing in this section shall affect the operation of the said section 40(4) (accounts and audit) in relation to the financial year ending 31st March next before the commencement date.

(5) If the commencement date is other than a 1st April, the said section 40(4) and subsection (4) above shall have effect in relation to the period beginning with the immediately preceding 1st April and ending with the date immediately preceding the commencement date as they apply with respect to the financial year mentioned in subsection (4) above subject, however, in the case of the said section 40(4), to the modification that a copy of the account mentioned in that subsection shall be sent to the Comptroller and Auditor General as soon as possible.

PART II

GAS

The British Gas Corporation

Gas
Corporation's
powers of
disposal.

9.—(1) Without prejudice to any powers conferred on it by any other enactment, the British Gas Corporation (in this Act referred to as " the Gas Corporation ") shall, subject to subsection (2) below, have power to provide for the disposal, in such manner as it thinks fit, of—

(*a*) any shares of a relevant subsidiary ;

(*b*) the whole or any part of the undertaking of, or any property, rights or liabilities of, a relevant subsidiary ; **or**

(*c*) any part of the undertaking of, or any property, rights or liabilities of, the Corporation.

(2) The Gas Corporation shall not, and shall secure that each member of the group does not, dispose of any shares of a relevant subsidiary except with the consent of the Secretary of State and in accordance with any conditions specified in the instrument signifying his consent ; and the Secretary of State shall not give any such consent except with the approval of the Treasury.

(3) In exercising its powers under subsection (1)(*a*) above the Gas Corporation may, with the consent of the Secretary of State, provide for employees' share schemes to be established in respect of subsidiaries of the Corporation ; and any such scheme may provide for the transfer of shares without consideration.

(4) In determining for the purposes of this Part whether any subsidiary of the Gas Corporation is a relevant subsidiary, any shares of the subsidiary which cease or have ceased to be held by or on behalf of one or more members of the group after

17th December 1981 and before the coming into force of subsection (2) above shall be treated as continuing to be so held.

(5) In this section and sections 10 and 11 below—

" group " means the Gas Corporation and all relevant
subsidiaries taken together ;

" relevant subsidiary " means a wholly owned subsidiary of
the Corporation ;

" subsidiary " and " wholly owned subsidiary " have the
same meanings as in the Gas Act 1972 (in this Act 1972 c. 60.
referred to as " the 1972 Act ").

10.—(1) For the purpose of facilitating the eventual disposal Provisions
under section 9(1)(*a*) above of— supplementary
to section 9.

(*a*) any part of the undertaking of, or any property, rights
or liabilities of, the Gas Corporation ; or

(*b*) the whole or any part of the undertaking of, or any
property, rights or liabilities of, a relevant subsidiary,

the Corporation may exercise its powers to establish subsidiaries,
to secure increases in the capital of subsidiaries and to transfer
property, rights and liabilities to subsidiaries, notwithstanding
the provisions of any enactment which may be taken to limit
the purposes for which those powers may be exercised.

(2) The Gas Corporation may also, for the said purpose, make
schemes for the transfer, between the Corporation and a relevant
subsidiary or between one such subsidiary and another, of—

(*a*) any prescribed property, rights or liabilities ;

(*b*) all property, rights and liabilities comprised in, or in
a prescribed part of, the transferor's undertaking.

(3) A scheme under subsection (2) above may—

(*a*) provide that any prescribed rights or liabilities of the
transferor shall be enforceable either by or against either
party or by or against both ;

(*b*) for the purpose of dealing with matters arising out of
or related to the transfer, confer or impose on either
party rights or liabilities which are to be enforceable
against or by the other ;

(*c*) provide that for the purposes of section 19 of the 1972
Act (borrowing limit) the aggregate there mentioned
shall be determined as if any money borrowed by the
transferor the liability to repay which is transferred
were money borrowed by the transferee ;

and may contain such other supplementary, incidental and
consequential provisions (including provisions as to the construction of agreements, licences and other documents) as may
appear to the Gas Corporation to be necessary or expedient.

(4) A scheme under subsection (2) above may also provide that—

   (a) prescribed securities of the transferee shall be issued to the transferor in consideration of the transfer and shall be credited as fully paid up ;

   (b) for the purposes of section 56 of the Companies Act 1948 (share premium account) and of any statutory accounts of the transferee, the value of any asset and the amount of any liability transferred shall be taken to be the value or (as the case may be) the amount which would have been assigned to that asset or liability for the purposes of the statutory accounts prepared by the transferor in respect of its last accounting period ending before the transfer date if that period had ended immediately before that date ;

   (c) a prescribed amount not exceeding the accumulated realised profits of the transferor at the transfer date shall be treated by the transferee as a reserve which represents its profits available for distribution (within the meaning of Part III of the Companies Act 1980) ;

   (d) in ascertaining for the purposes of the said section 56 what amount (if any) falls to be treated as a premium received on the issue of any shares in pursuance of any provision made by virtue of paragraph (a) above, the amount of the net assets transferred shall be taken to be reduced by an amount corresponding to the amount of any reserve for which provision is made by virtue of paragraph (c) above ;

   (e) subject to any provision made by virtue of the preceding provisions of this subsection, for the purposes of any statutory accounts of the transferee the amount to be included in respect of any item shall be determined as if any relevant thing done by the transferor (whether by way of acquiring, revaluing or disposing of any asset or incurring, revaluing or discharging any liability, or by carrying any amount to any provision or reserve, or otherwise) had been done by the transferee.

(5) A scheme under subsection (2) above shall not come into force until it is approved by the Secretary of State or until such date as the Secretary of State may in giving his approval specify ; and the Secretary of State may approve a scheme either without modifications or with such modifications as, after consultation with the Gas Corporation, he thinks fit.

(6) On the coming into force of a scheme under subsection (2) above—

   (a) the property, rights and liabilities to be transferred shall, subject to subsection (7) below, be transferred and vest in accordance with the scheme ; and

(*b*) any provision made by virtue of subsection (3) or (4) above shall have effect in accordance with the scheme, notwithstanding any rule of law and the provisions of any enactment.

(7) Schedule 1 to this Act shall apply to any transfer under paragraph (*a*) of subsection (6) above and that paragraph shall have effect subject to the provisions of that Schedule.

(8) In this section " statutory accounts " means—

(*a*) in relation to the Gas Corporation, a statement of accounts prepared by the Corporation in accordance with section 23 of the 1972 Act ;

(*b*) in relation to any other party, accounts prepared by that party for the purposes of any provision of the Companies Acts 1948 to 1981 (including group accounts) ;

and in this section and in Schedule 1 to this Act " prescribed ", in relation to a scheme under subsection (2) above, means specified or described in or determined in accordance with the scheme.

11.—(1) The Secretary of State may, after consultation with the Gas Corporation, give directions to the Corporation requiring it to exercise its powers under sections 9 and 10 above (including the powers extended by section 10(1) above) for such purposes and in such manner as may be specified in the directions.

(2) The matters to which the Secretary of State shall have regard in exercising his powers under subsection (1) above shall include, in particular, the need to secure that the public is so far as practicable protected from any personal injury, fire, explosion or other dangers arising from the transmission or distribution of gas through pipes, or from the use of gas supplied through pipes.

(3) For the purpose of facilitating a disposal under section 9(1)(*a*) above, the Secretary of State may by order provide that, in its application to any relevant subsidiary specified in the order, the 1972 Act shall have effect with such modifications as may be so specified.

(4) If and to the extent that the Secretary of State, after consultation with the Gas Corporation, so directs, the Corporation shall pay to the Secretary of State any sums received by it or a relevant subsidiary on a disposal of—

(*a*) any shares of a relevant subsidiary ;

(*b*) the whole or any part of the undertaking of, or any property, rights or liabilities of, a relevant subsidiary ; or

(*c*) any part of the undertaking of, or any property, rights or liabilities of, the Corporation,

being a disposal effected on or after the commencement date or in pursuance of a direction given under section 7(2) of the 1972 Act.

(5) The Secretary of State may by order transfer to himself or a nominee of his any shares of a company which is or has been a relevant subsidiary of the Gas Corporation, being shares held by or on behalf of one or more members of the group ; and any shares transferred by an order under this subsection shall vest in the Secretary of State or the nominee by virtue of the order.

(6) If an order under subsection (5) above so provides, the Secretary of State shall pay to the transferor such sum by way of consideration for the shares as may be specified in the order.

(7) In determining for the purposes of the 1972 Act or this Part whether any company is a relevant subsidiary or a subsidiary of the Gas Corporation, any shares of the company held by the Secretary of State or a nominee of his shall be treated as held by the Corporation.

(8) The Secretary of State shall not give any direction or make any order under this section except with the approval of the Treasury ; and except as aforesaid neither the Secretary of State nor a nominee of his shall dispose of any shares held by virtue of this section.

(9) Any sums required by the Secretary of State for making payments under subsection (6) above shall be paid out of money provided by Parliament ; and any sums received by the Secretary of State under subsection (4) above and any dividends or other sums received by the Secretary of State or a nominee of his in right of, on the disposal of, or otherwise in connection with, any shares held by virtue of this section shall be paid into the Consolidated Fund.

Supply of gas by persons other than Gas Corporation

Supply of gas by other persons.

12.—(1) For section 29 of the 1972 Act there shall be substituted the following sections—

" Restrictions on supply by other persons.

29.—(1) Subject to section 29A below, the Secretary of State's consent is required for gas to be supplied through pipes to any premises, except supply by or to the Corporation.

(2) Consent is not to be given to the supply of gas by any person to premises situated within 25

yards from a distribution main of the Corporation PART II
unless either—

>   (*a*) the Secretary of State is of the opinion that
>   the rate of supply to those premises would
>   be likely to exceed 25,000 therms a year ;
>   or

>   (*b*) the Corporation, having been given the
>   opportunity to do so, have not objected
>   to the giving of consent.

(3) The Secretary of State's consent may be
given—

>   (*a*) either unconditionally or subject to condi-
>   tions ; and

>   (*b*) either with reference to particular cases or
>   by means of orders of general application.

(4) A specific consent given to any person (that
is to say, consent given to him otherwise than by
order of general application) is irrevocable and may
be given for a specified period or indefinitely.

(5) Where consent has been given by an order of
general application, any person who proposes to
undertake a supply which is covered by that general
consent may notify the Secretary of State of his
proposal (in the manner specified by the order),
whereupon subsection (4) above applies as if specific consent either unlimited in duration or, if the
order so provides, for the period there specified
had been given to him for that supply.

(6) For the purposes of this section—

>   (*a*) a person providing gas for his own use shall
>   not in so doing be deemed to supply gas,
>   and gas provided by a company for the use
>   of any subsidiary or holding company of
>   that company, or of any subsidiary of a
>   holding company of that company, shall be
>   deemed to be provided for the use of that
>   company ;

>   (*b*) a person providing, for use in a flat or part
>   of a building let by him, gas supplied to
>   him shall not in so doing be deemed to be
>   supplying gas.

Exceptions   29A.—(1) Where a person (in this section referred
to section 29. to as a supplier) notifies the Secretary of State that
he proposes to undertake a supply of gas to any
premises at a rate in excess of 2,000,000 therms a

year (in this section referred to as 'the required rate '), the Secretary of State's consent under section 29 above is not required for that supply unless, within six weeks of receiving the notification, the Secretary of State notifies the supplier either—

(a) that he is of the opinion that the rate of supply to those premises would be unlikely to exceed the required rate ; or

(b) that he is unable to form an opinion as to whether the rate of supply to those premises would or would not be likely to exceed the required rate.

(2) Where a supplier has given the Secretary of State a notification under subsection (1) above and—

(a) the rate of supply to the premises to which the notification relates fails to exceed the required rate for three successive periods of twelve months ;

(b) the supplier fails to furnish the Secretary of State with such information as he may require for the purpose of determining whether the condition in paragraph (a) above is fulfilled ; or

(c) the supplier fails to afford the Secretary of State with such facilities as he may require for the purpose of verifying any information furnished in pursuance of such a requirement as is mentioned in paragraph (b) above,

the Secretary of State may direct that the supplier's notification shall be treated as invalid for the purposes of that subsection except as regards gas previously supplied."

1976 c. 76.   (2) Section 4 of the 1934 Act and section 8 of the Energy Act 1976 (which are superseded by this section) shall cease to have effect.

(3) Each of the following, namely—

(a) an authorisation given by the Secretary of State under the said section 4 ;

(b) a consent given by him or by the Gas Corporation under the said section 8 ; and

(c) a consent given by the Corporation under section 29 of the 1972 Act either as originally enacted or as amended by the said section 8,

shall have effect as if it were a consent given by the Secretary of State under the said section 29 as substituted by this section.

13.—(1) After section 29A of the 1972 Act there shall be inserted the following section—

" *Standards of quality*

Power to
prescribe
standards.

29B.—(1) The Secretary of State shall after consultation with the Corporation prescribe standards of pressure, purity and uniformity of calorific value to be complied with by the Corporation in supplying gas through pipes, and may after such consultation prescribe other standards with respect to the properties, condition and composition of gas so supplied.

(2) The Secretary of State shall after consultation with such persons and organisations as he considers appropriate prescribe standards of pressure and purity to be complied with by persons other than the Corporation in supplying gas through pipes, and may after such consultation prescribe standards of uniformity of calorific value and other standards with respect to the properties, condition and composition of gas so supplied.

(3) The Secretary of State shall appoint competent and impartial persons to carry out tests of gas supplied through pipes for the purpose of ascertaining whether it conforms with the standards prescribed under this section and (in the case of gas supplied by the Corporation) whether it is of the declared calorific value.

(4) Regulations may provide—

(*a*) for determining the places at which such tests are to be carried out,

(*b*) for requiring premises, apparatus and equipment to be provided and maintained by persons supplying gas through pipes (in this section referred to as suppliers) for the purpose of carrying out such tests,

(*c*) for persons representing the supplier concerned to be present during the carrying out of such tests,

(*d*) for the manner in which the results of such tests are to be made available to the public,

(*e*) for conferring powers of entry on property of suppliers for the purpose of deciding where tests are to be carried out and otherwise for the purposes of this section, and

(*f*) for any other matters supplementary or incidental to the matters aforesaid for which provision appears to the Secretary of State to be necessary or expedient.

(5) There shall be paid out of money provided by Parliament to the persons appointed under subsection (3) above such remuneration and such allowances as may be determined by the Secretary of State with the approval of the Treasury, and such pensions as may be so determined may be paid out of money provided by Parliament to or in respect of those persons.

(6) Every person who is a supplier during any period shall pay to the Secretary of State such proportion as the Secretary of State may determine of—

> (a) any sums paid by him under subsection (5) above in respect of that period ; and

> (b) such part of his other expenses for that period as he may with the consent of the Treasury determine to be attributable to his functions in connection with the testing of gas for the purposes of this section ;

and any liability under this subsection to pay to the Secretary of State sums on account of pensions (whether paid by him under subsection (5) above or otherwise) shall, if the Secretary of State so determines, be satisfied by way of contributions calculated, at such rate as may be determined by the Treasury, by reference to remuneration.

(7) The reference in subsection (6) above to expenses of the Secretary of State includes a reference to expenses incurred by any government department in connection with the Department of Energy, and to such sums as the Treasury may determine in respect of the use for the purposes of that Department of any premises belonging to the Crown."

(2) Section 26 of the 1972 Act (which is superseded by this section) shall cease to have effect.

Safety regulations.

14. For section 31 of the 1972 Act there shall be substituted the following section—

"Power to make safety regulations

31.—(1) The Secretary of State may make such regulations as he thinks fit for the purpose of securing that the public is so far as practicable protected from any personal injury, fire, explosion or other dangers arising from the transmission or distribution of gas through pipes, or from the use of gas supplied through pipes.

(2) Without prejudice to the generality of subsection (1) above, any regulations made under this

section may make provision for empowering any officer authorised by the relevant authority, with such other persons (if any) as may be necessary,—

(a) to enter any premises in which there is a service pipe connected with gas mains, for the purpose of inspecting any gas fitting on the premises, any flue or means of ventilation used in connection with any such gas fitting, or any service pipe or other apparatus (not being a gas fitting) which is on the premises and is used for the supply of gas or is connected with gas mains,

(b) where he so enters any such premises, to examine or apply any test to any such object as is mentioned in paragraph (a) above and (where the object is a gas fitting) to verify what supply of air is available for it, with a view to ascertaining whether the provisions of any regulations made under this section have been complied with or whether the object is in such a condition, or (in the case of a gas fitting) the supply of air available for it is so inadequate, that it (or, in the case of a flue or means of ventilation, the gas fitting in connection with which it is used) is likely to constitute a danger to any person or property, and

(c) where in his opinion it is necessary to do so for the purpose of averting danger to life or property, and notwithstanding any contract previously existing, to disconnect and seal off any gas fitting or any part of the gas supply system on the premises, or cut off the supply of gas to the premises or, if no such supply is being given, to signify the refusal of the relevant authority to give or, as the case may be, allow such a supply.

(3) Where any regulations under this section confer any power in accordance with paragraph (c) of subsection (2) above, the regulations shall also include provision—

(a) for securing that, where any such power is exercised, the consumer will be notified as to the nature of the defect or other circumstances in consequence of which it has been exercised,

(b) for enabling any consumer so notified to appeal to the Secretary of State on the grounds that the defect or other circumstances in question did not constitute a danger such as to justify the action taken in the exercise of the power, or did not exist or have ceased to exist, and

(c) for enabling the Secretary of State to give such directions as may in accordance with the regulations be determined by him to be appropriate in consequence of any such appeal.

(4) Regulations made under this section may make provision for prohibiting any person, except with the consent of the relevant authority or in pursuance of any directions given by the Secretary of State as mentioned in subsection (3)(c) above, from—

(a) reconnecting any gas fitting or part of any gas supply system which has been disconnected by or on behalf of the relevant authority in exercise of a power conferred by the regulations, or

(b) restoring the supply of gas to any premises where it has been cut off by or on behalf of the relevant authority in the exercise of any such power, or

(c) causing gas from gas mains to be supplied to any premises where in pursuance of the regulations the refusal of the relevant authority to give or, as the case may be, allow a supply to those premises has been signified and that refusal has not been withdrawn.

(5) Where in pursuance of any powers conferred by regulations made under this section, entry is made on any premises by an officer authorised by the relevant authority, the officer shall ensure that the premises are left not less secure by reason of the entry; and the relevant authority shall make good, or pay compensation for, any damage caused by the officer, or by any person accompanying him in entering the premises, in taking any action therein authorised by the regulations, or in making the premises secure.

(6) If any person wilfully obstructs any officer exercising powers conferred by regulations made under this section, he shall be guilty of an offence and liable on summary conviction to a fine not exceeding £200.

(7) The Rights of Entry (Gas and Electricity
Boards) Act 1954 (entry under a justice's warrant)
shall apply in relation to any powers of entry conferred by regulations made under this section as if—

> (*a*) any reference to the Corporation were a
> reference to the relevant authority, and
>
> (*b*) any reference to an employee of the Cor-
> poration were a reference to an officer auth-
> orised by the relevant authority.

(8) Any local enactment which is inconsistent with
or rendered redundant by any regulations made under
this section shall cease to have effect as from the
date on which those regulations come into operation.

(9) In this section ' the relevant authority '—

> (*a*) in relation to dangers arising from the distri-
> bution of gas by the Corporation, or from
> the use of gas supplied by the Corporation,
> means the Corporation, and
>
> (*b*) in relation to dangers arising from the dis-
> tribution of gas by a person other than the
> Corporation, or from the use of gas sup-
> plied by such a person, means the Secre-
> tary of State."

Use by other persons of pipe-lines belonging to Gas Corporation

15.—(1) The Gas Corporation shall not at any time execute Construction
any works for the construction of a high pressure pipe-line of pipe-lines
unless, not less than two years (or such shorter period as the by Gas
Secretary of State may allow) before that time, it has given Corporation.
notice to the Secretary of State stating that it intends to execute
the works.

(2) A notice under subsection (1) above shall—

> (*a*) specify the points between which the proposed pipe-line
> is to run and be accompanied by a map (drawn to a
> scale not less than 1 : 1,500,000) on which is delineated
> the route which it is proposed to take ;
>
> (*b*) specify the length, diameter and capacity of the pro-
> posed pipe-line, the kind of gas which it is designed
> to convey and the quantities of gas which the Gas Cor-
> poration requires or expects to require to be con-
> veyed by the pipe-line in order to secure the perform-
> ance by the Corporation of its statutory duties and
> contractual obligations ; and
>
> (*c*) contain such other particulars (if any) as may be pres-
> cribed by regulations made by the Secretary of State.

(3) The Secretary of State shall cause to be published in such publication or publications as he considers appropriate notice of the receipt by him of any notice under subsection (1) above; and a notice so published shall—

   (a) specify the points between which the proposed pipe-line is to run;

   (b) name a place or places where a copy of the notice under subsection (1) above (and of the map accompanying it) may be inspected free of charge, and copies thereof may be obtained at a reasonable charge, at all reasonable hours; and

   (c) specify the time within which, and the manner in which, representations may be made as to the matters mentioned in paragraphs (a) and (b) of subsection (4) below.

(4) Where in the light of any such representations duly made the Secretary of State is satisfied—

   (a) that a demand exists or is likely to arise for the conveyance of gas of, or of a kind similar to, the kind specified in the notice under subsection (1) above; and

   (b) that the routes along which the gas will require to be conveyed will severally be, as to the whole or any part thereof, the same or substantially the same as the route or any part of the route so specified,

then, subject to subsection (6) and section 17(4) below, the Secretary of State may give directions to the Corporation in accordance with subsection (5) below.

(5) Directions under subsection (4) above may—

   (a) require the Gas Corporation to secure that the pipe-line, or any length of it specified in the directions, shall be so constructed as to be capable of conveying quantities so specified of gas of, or of a kind similar to, the kind specified in the notice under subsection (1) above;

   (b) specify the sums or the method of determining the sums which the Secretary of State considers should be paid to the Corporation by such of the persons who made representations to the Secretary of State as are specified in the directions for the purpose of defraying so much of the cost of constructing the pipe-line as is attributable to that requirement;

   (c) specify the arrangements which the Secretary of State considers should be made by each of those persons, within a period specified in that behalf in the directions, for the purpose of securing that those sums will be paid to the Corporation if it constructs the pipe-line in accordance with that requirement;

(*d*) provide that the Corporation may, if such arrangements are not made by any of those persons within the period aforesaid, elect in the manner specified in the directions that the requirement shall have effect with such modifications as are so specified with a view to eliminating the consequences of the representations made by that person.

(6) The Secretary of State shall not give directions under subsection (4) above without first giving the Gas Corporation particulars of the requirement he proposes to specify in the directions and an opportunity of being heard about the matter; and the said particulars must be given to the Corporation within six months of the Secretary of State receiving the notice under subsection (1) above.

(7) If, after a notice under subsection (1) above has been given to the Secretary of State, the execution of the works to which the notice relates has not been substantially begun at the expiration of three years from the date on which it was given to him, or at the expiration of any extension of that period which he may allow, the notice shall be treated as invalid for the purposes of that subsection except as regards works previously executed.

(8) This section shall not apply as respects works for the completion of a pipe-line of which the construction was begun before the commencement date or, if the Secretary of State so directs in the case of any works, within three years of that date.

(9) In this section and sections 16 and 17 below—

"gas" has the same meaning as in Part III of the 1972 Act;

"high pressure pipe-line" means any pipe-line which—

 (*a*) has a design operating pressure exceeding 7 bars; or

 (*b*) is of a class specified in an order made by the Secretary of State;

"pipe-line" has the same meaning as in the Pipe-lines Act 1962;   1962 c. 58.

"statutory duties", in relation to the Gas Corporation, means the duties imposed on the Corporation by section 2(1) of and paragraph 2 of Schedule 4 to the 1972 Act.

16.—(1) If in the case of a pipe-line belonging to the Gas Corporation it appears to the Secretary of State, on the application of a person other than the Corporation—

 (*a*) that the pipe-line can and should be modified by installing in it a junction through which another pipe-line may be connected to the pipe-line; or

Increase of capacity etc. of pipe-lines belonging to Gas Corporation.

PART II

(b) in the case of a high pressure pipe-line, that the capacity of the pipe-line can and should be increased by modifying apparatus and works associated with the pipe-line,

then, subject to section 17(4) below, the Secretary of State may, after giving to the Corporation an opportunity of being heard about the matter, give directions to the Corporation in accordance with subsection (2) below in consequence of the application.

(2) Directions under this section may—

(a) specify the modifications which the Secretary of State considers should be made in consequence of the application ;

(b) specify the sums or the method of determining the sums which the Secretary of State considers should be paid to the Gas Corporation by the applicant for the purpose of defraying the cost of the modifications ;

(c) specify the arrangements which the Secretary of State considers should be made by the applicant, within a period specified in that behalf in the directions, for the purpose of securing that those sums will be paid to the Corporation if it carries out the modifications ;

(d) require the Corporation, if the applicant makes those arrangements within the period aforesaid, to carry out the modifications within a period specified in that behalf in the directions.

(3) References in subsections (1) and (2) above to modifications include, in the case of modifications to any apparatus and works, references to changes in, substitutions for and additions to the apparatus and works ; and the reference in subsection (1) above to apparatus and works associated with a pipe-line shall be construed in accordance with section 65(2) of the Pipe-lines Act 1962.

1962 c. 58.

Acquisition of rights to use pipe-lines belonging to Gas Corporation.

17.—(1) If a person applies to the Secretary of State for directions under this section which enable the applicant to secure a right to have conveyed, by a pipe-line belonging to the Gas Corporation, during a period specified in the application quantities so specified of gas which is of a kind so specified and is of, or of a kind similar to, the kind which the pipe-line is designed to convey, it shall be the duty of the Secretary of State—

(a) to decide whether the application is to be considered further or rejected ;

(b) to serve notice of his decision on the applicant ; and

(c) in the case of a decision that the application is to be considered further, to give the Corporation notice that it is to be so considered and an opportunity of being heard about the matter.

(2) Where, after further considering an application under sub-section (1) above, the Secretary of State is satisfied that the giving of directions under this section would not prejudice the conveyance by the pipe-line of—

(a) the quantities of gas which the Gas Corporation requires or may reasonably be expected to require to be conveyed by the pipe-line in order to secure the performance by the Corporation of its statutory duties and contractual obligations; and

(b) the quantities of gas which any person who has a right to have gas conveyed by the pipe-line is entitled to require to be so conveyed in the exercise of that right,

the Secretary of State may give such directions to the Corporation.

(3) Directions under this section may—

(a) specify the terms on which the Secretary of State considers the Gas Corporation should enter into an agreement with the applicant for all or any of the following purposes—

(i) for securing to the applicant the right to have conveyed by the pipe-line during the period specified in the directions the quantities so specified of gas which is of the kind so specified;

(ii) for securing that the exercise of that right is not prevented or impeded;

(iii) for regulating the charges which may be made for the conveyance of gas by virtue of that right;

(iv) for securing to the applicant the right to have a pipe-line of his connected to the pipe-line by the Corporation;

(b) specify the sums or the method of determining the sums which the Secretary of State considers should be paid by way of consideration for any such right; and

(c) require the Corporation, if the applicant pays or agrees to pay those sums within a period specified in that behalf in the directions, to enter into an agreement with him on the terms so specified.

(4) Where the Secretary of State proposes to give directions to the Gas Corporation under section 15(4) or 16 above, it shall be his duty before doing so—

(a) in the case of directions under section 15(4) above, to give to any person whom he proposes to specify in the

PART II

directions particulars of the requirement he proposes so
to specify and an opportunity of making an application
under subsection (1) above in respect of the proposed
pipe-line ; and

(b) in the case of directions under section 16 above, to give
to the applicant particulars of the modifications he
proposes to specify in the directions and an opportunity
of making such an application in respect of the pipe-
line ;

and subsections (1) to (3) above shall have effect in relation to
such an application made by virtue of this subsection as if for
references to a pipe-line there were substituted references to the
proposed pipe-line or, as the case may be, the pipe-line as it
would be with those modifications.

(5) Any reference in this section to a right to have a quantity
of gas of any kind conveyed by a pipe-line is a reference to a
right—

(a) to introduce that quantity of gas of that kind at one
point in the pipe-line ; and

(b) to take off such quantity as may be appropriate of gas
of, or of a kind similar to, that kind at another point
in the pipe-line.

(6) Any reference in a deed or other instrument or document
to the functions of the Gas Corporation shall be taken to include
a reference to any obligations arising under an agreement entered
into by the Corporation in pursuance of directions given under
this section.

PART III

PETROLEUM LICENCES

Amendment
of enabling
powers etc.
1934 c. 36.

18.—(1) The Petroleum (Production) Act 1934 (in this Act
referred to as " the 1934 Act ") shall have effect, and be deemed
always to have had effect, as if subsection (2) of section 1
(vesting of property in petroleum) were renumbered as subsection (4) of that section and for subsection (1) of that section there
were substituted the following subsections—

" (1) The property in petroleum to which subsection (2)
of this section applies at the commencement of this Act, so
far as it is not already so vested, is hereby vested in His
Majesty ; and His Majesty shall at any time have the exclusive right of searching and boring for and getting petroleum to which that subsection applies at that time.

(2) Subject to subsection (3) of this section, this subsection applies at any time to petroleum which at that time

exists in its natural condition in strata in Great Britain or   PART III
beneath the territorial waters of the United Kingdom adjacent to Great Britain ; and it so applies notwithstanding
that the land in which any such petroleum so exists belongs
to His Majesty or the Duchy of Cornwall, belongs to a
government department or is held in trust for His Majesty
for the purposes of a government department.

(3) Subsection (2) of this section does not apply to petroleum which at the commencement of this Act may be lawfully gotten under a licence in force under the Petroleum 1918 c. 52.
(Production) Act 1918, being a licence specified in the
Schedule to this Act, so long as that licence remains in
force."

(2) The 1934 Act shall also have effect, and be deemed always
to have had effect, as if in subsection (1) of section 2 (power to
grant licences) after the word " shall " there were inserted the
words " at any time " and at the end of that subsection there
were added the words " to which subsection (2) of section 1 of
this Act applies at that time ".

19.—(1) Where a licence granted under section 2 of the 1934 Modification
Act before the coming into force of section 20 below in- of model
corporates— clauses in
existing
   (*a*) the model clauses set out in Part II of Schedule 2 to the licences.
        1975 Act (clauses relating to production licences for
        seaward areas) ;
   (*b*) the model clauses set out in Part II of Schedule 3 to
        that Act (clauses relating to production licences for
        landward areas) ;
   (*c*) the model clauses set out in Schedule 4 to the Petroleum S.I. 1976/1129.
        (Production) Regulations 1976 (clauses relating to pro-
        duction licences for landward areas) ;
   (*d*) the model clauses set out in Schedule 5 to the said
        Regulations of 1976 as originally made or as amended
        by the Petroleum (Production) (Amendment) S.I. 1978/929.
        Regulations 1978 (clauses relating to production
        licences for seaward areas) ; or
   (*e*) the model clauses set out in Schedule 5 to the said
        Regulations of 1976 as amended by the said Regulations
        of 1978 and the Petroleum (Production) (Amendment) S.I. 1980/721.
        Regulations 1980,
those model clauses as so incorporated shall have effect with the
amendments provided for by whichever is appropriate of paragraphs 1 to 5 of Schedule 2 to this Act.

(2) It is hereby declared that any provisions of a licence
which are amended by subsection (1) above may be altered

Part I   M

PART III   or deleted by an instrument under seal executed by the Secretary of State and the licensee.

(3) Any reference in any document to provisions of a licence which are amended by subsection (1) above shall, except so far as the nature of the document or the context otherwise requires, be construed as a reference to those provisions as so amended.

Modification of model clauses for incorporation in future licences.

20. The following model clauses, namely—

(a) the model clauses set out in Schedule 4 to the said Regulations of 1976 ; and

(b) the model clauses set out in Schedule 5 to those regulations as amended by the said Regulations of 1978 and the said Regulations of 1980,

shall have effect with the amendments provided for by paragraphs 3 and 5 respectively of Schedule 2 to this Act.

PART IV

OFFSHORE ACTIVITIES

Safety zones around installations.

21.—(1) The Secretary of State may by order establish a safety zone around any installation which, or part of which, is maintained, or is in the course of being assembled or dismantled, in waters to which this section applies.

(2) A safety zone shall not extend more than five hundred metres from the installation to which it relates but, subject to that, may extend to waters outside waters to which this section applies.

(3) A vessel shall not enter or remain in a safety zone except under and in accordance with the terms of an order made or consent given by the Secretary of State.

(4) If a vessel enters or remains in a safety zone in contravention of subsection (3) above, then, subject to subsection (5) below, its owner and its master shall each be liable—

(a) on summary conviction, to a fine not exceeding the statutory maximum ; and

(b) on conviction on indictment, to imprisonment for a term not exceeding two years or to a fine or to both.

(5) It shall be a defence for a person charged with an offence under this section to prove that the establishment of the safety zone was not, and would not on reasonable enquiry have become, known to the master.

(6) Where the commission by any person of an offence under this section is due to the act or default of some other person,

that other person, as well as the first-mentioned person, shall be
guilty of that offence and shall be liable to be proceeded against
and punished accordingly.

(7) Where a body corporate is guilty of an offence under this
section and that offence is proved to have been committed with
the consent or connivance of, or to be attributable to any neglect
on the part of, any director, manager, secretary or other similar
officer of the body corporate, or any person who was purporting
to act in any such capacity, he, as well as the body corporate,
shall be guilty of that offence and shall be liable to be proceeded
against and punished accordingly.

Where the affairs of a body corporate are managed by its
members this subsection shall apply in relation to the acts and
defaults of a member in connection with his functions of management as if he were a director of the body corporate.

(8) Proceedings for an offence under this section may be
taken, and the offence may for all incidental purposes be treated
as having been committed, in any place in the United Kingdom.

(9) The waters to which this section applies are—

  (a) tidal waters and parts of the sea in or adjacent to the
      United Kingdom up to the seaward limits of territorial
      waters ; and

  (b) waters in any area designated under section 1(7) of the
      Continental Shelf Act 1964 (in this Act referred to as
      " the 1964 Act ").   1964 c. 29.

(10) In this section " installation " does not include any part
of a pipe-line within the meaning of section 33 of the 1975 Act
other than apparatus or works which are by virtue of that
section to be treated as associated with a pipe or system of
pipes for the purposes of Part III of that Act.

(11) Section 2 of the 1964 Act (which is superseded by this
section) shall cease to have effect.

22.—(1) Her Majesty may by Order in Council provide that, Application
in such cases and subject to such exceptions as may be prescribed of criminal
by the Order, any act or omission which—   law etc.

  (a) takes place on, under or above an installation in waters
      to which this section applies or any waters within five
      hundred metres of any such installation ; and

  (b) would, if taking place in any part of the United King-
      dom, constitute an offence under the law in force in
      that part,

shall be treated for the purposes of that law as taking place
in that part.

(2) Her Majesty may by Order in Council provide that, in such cases and subject to such exceptions as may be prescribed by the Order, a constable shall on, under or above any installation in waters to which this section applies or any waters within five hundred metres of such an installation have all the powers, protection and privileges which he has in the area for which he acts as constable.

This subsection is without prejudice to any other enactment or rule of law affording any power, protection or privilege to constables.

(3) Subsections (7) and (8) of section 21 above shall apply in relation to anything that is an offence by virtue of an Order in Council under this section as they apply in relation to an offence under that section.

(4) The waters to which this section applies are—

(a) territorial waters of the United Kingdom ;

(b) waters in any area designated under section 1(7) of the 1964 Act ; and

(c) waters in any area specified under subsection (5) below.

(5) Her Majesty may from time to time by Order in Council specify any area which—

(a) is in a foreign sector of the continental shelf ; and

(b) comprises any part of a cross-boundary field,

as an area as respects which the powers conferred by this section and section 23 below are exercisable.

(6) In this section—

" cross-boundary field " means a field that extends across the boundary between an area designated under section 1(7) of the 1964 Act and a foreign sector of the continental shelf ;

" field " means a geological structure identified as such by Order in Council under subsection (5) above.

(7) This section and section 23 below shall apply to installations notwithstanding that they are for the time being in transit.

(8) Section 3 of the 1964 Act (which is superseded by this section and section 23 below) shall cease to have effect

Application of civil law.

23.—(1) Her Majesty may by Order in Council—

(a) provide that, in such cases and subject to such exceptions as may be prescribed by the Order, questions arising out of acts or omissions taking place on, under or above waters to which this section applies in connection with any activity mentioned in subsection (2)

below shall be determined in accordance with the law
in force in such part of the United Kingdom as may be
specified in the Order ; and

(b) make provision for conferring jurisdiction with respect
to such questions on courts in any part of the United
Kingdom so specified.

(2) The activities referred to in subsection (1) above are—

(a) activities connected with the exploration of, or the
exploitation of the natural resources of, the shore or
bed of waters to which this section applies or the subsoil
beneath it ; and

(b) without prejudice to the generality of paragraph (a)
above, activities carried on from, by means of or on, or
for purposes connected with, installations to which subsection (3) below applies.

(3) This subsection applies to any installation which is or
has been maintained, or is intended to be established, for the
carrying on of any of the following activities, namely—

(a) the exploitation or exploration of mineral resources in
or under the shore or bed of waters to which this
section applies ;

(b) the storage of gas in or under the shore or bed of such
waters or the recovery of gas so stored ;

(c) the conveyance of things by means of a pipe, or system
of pipes, constructed or placed on, in or under the
shore or bed of such waters ; and

(d) the provision of accommodation for persons who work
on or from an installation which is or has been maintained, or is intended to be established, for the carrying
on of an activity falling within paragraph (a), (b) or (c)
above or this paragraph.

(4) The fact that an installation has been maintained for the
carrying on of an activity falling within subsection (3) above shall
be disregarded for the purposes of that subsection if, since it
was so maintained, it has been outside waters to which this
section applies or has been maintained for the carrying on of
an activity not falling within that subsection.

(5) Any jurisdiction conferred on any court under this section
shall be without prejudice to any jurisdiction exercisable apart
from this section by that or any other court.

(6) The waters to which this section applies are—

(a) tidal waters and parts of the sea in or adjacent to the
United Kingdom up to the seaward limits of territorial
waters ;

M 3

    (*b*) waters in any area designated under section 1(7) of the 1964 Act;

    (*c*) waters in any area specified under section 22(5) above; and

    (*d*) in relation to installations which are or have been maintained, or are intended to be established, in waters falling within paragraph (*a*), (*b*) or (*c*) above, waters in a foreign sector of the continental shelf which are adjacent to such waters.

Extended meaning of " offshore installation" in the 1971 Act.
1971 c. 61.

24. For section 1 of the Mineral Workings (Offshore Installations) Act 1971 (in this Act referred to as " the 1971 Act ") there shall be substituted the following section—

" Application of Act.

    1.—(1) This Act shall apply to any activity mentioned in subsection (2) below which is carried on from, by means of or on an installation which is maintained in the water, or on the foreshore or other land intermittently covered with water, and is not connected with dry land by a permanent structure providing access at all times and for all purposes.

    (2) The activities referred to in subsection (1) above are—

        (*a*) the exploitation or exploration of mineral resources in or under the shore or bed of controlled waters;

        (*b*) the storage of gas in or under the shore or bed of controlled waters or the recovery of gas so stored;

        (*c*) the conveyance of things by means of a pipe, or system of pipes, constructed or placed on, in or under the shore or bed of controlled waters; and

        (*d*) the provision of accommodation for persons who work on or from an installation which is or has been maintained, or is intended to be established, for the carrying on of an activity falling within paragraph (*a*), (*b*) or (*c*) above or this paragraph.

    (3) Her Majesty may by Order in Council provide that, in such cases and subject to such exceptions and modifications as may be prescribed by the Order, this Act shall have effect as if—

        (*a*) any reference to controlled waters included a reference to waters in any area specified under section 22(5) of the Oil and Gas (Enterprise) Act 1982; and (*b*) in relation to installations which are or have been maintained, or are intended to be established, in controlled waters, any reference in subsection (2) above to controlled waters included a reference to waters in a foreign sector of the continental shelf which are adjacent to such waters.

(4) In this Act—

'controlled waters' means—

(*a*) tidal waters and parts of the sea in or adjacent to the United Kingdom up to the seaward limits of territorial waters ;

(*b*) waters in any area designated under section 1(7) of the Continental Shelf Act 1964 ; and 1964 c. 29.

(*c*) such inland waters as may for the time being be specified for the purposes of this paragraph by Order in Council ;

'foreign sector of the continental shelf' means an area which is outside the territorial waters of any state and within which rights are exercisable by a state other than the United Kingdom with respect to the sea bed and subsoil and their natural resources ;

'offshore installation' means any installation which is or has been maintained, or is intended to be established, for the carrying on of any activity to which this Act applies.

(5) In this section—

'exploration' means exploration with a view to exploitation ;

'inland waters' means waters within the United Kingdom other than tidal waters and parts of the sea ;

'installation' includes—

(*a*) any floating structure or device maintained on a station by whatever means ; and

(*b*) in such cases and subject to such exceptions as may be prescribed by Order in Council, any apparatus or works which are by virtue of section 33 of the Petroleum and Submarine Pipe-lines Act 1975 c. 74. 1975 to be treated as associated with a

M 4

pipe or system of pipes for the purposes of Part III of that Act,

but, subject to paragraph (*b*) above, does not include any part of a pipe-line within the meaning of that section ;

' modifications' includes additions, omissions and alterations.

(6) The fact that an installation has been maintained for the carrying on of an activity falling within subsection (2) above shall be disregarded for the purposes of this section if, since it was so maintained, the installation—

(*a*) has been outside controlled waters or, where it was so maintained in a part of a foreign sector of the continental shelf adjacent to those waters, the area consisting of those waters and that part ; or

(*b*) has been maintained for the carrying on of an activity not falling within that subsection.

(7) Orders in Council made under this section may be varied or revoked by a subsequent Order so made ; and any statutory instrument containing an Order under subsection (3) above shall be subject to annulment in pursuance of a resolution of either House of Parliament."

Extended
meaning of
" pipe-line "
etc. in the 1975
Act.

25.—(1) In section 33(1) of the 1975 Act (meaning of pipe-line etc.), after paragraph (*a*) there shall be inserted the following paragraph—

" (*aa*) any apparatus for treating or cooling any thing which is to flow through, or through part of, the pipe or system ; ".

(2) In section 22(1) of that Act (compulsory increases in capacity etc. of pipe-lines)—

(*a*) for the words " a pipe " in paragraph (*b*) there shall be substituted the words " another pipe-line " ; and

(*b*) the words " connected with the pipe-line " in paragraph (i) shall be omitted.

(3) In section 23(3)(*d*) of that Act (acquisition by persons of right to use pipe-lines belonging to others) for the words " a pipe and apparatus " there shall be substituted the words " a pipe-line ".

(4) Any pipe-line in relation to which there is in force an

authorisation which has been granted under Part III of that Act before the coming into force of subsection (1) above shall not be regarded for the purposes of—

(*a*) section 24(4) of that Act (termination of authorisations) ; or

(*b*) section 25(1) of that Act (vesting of pipe-lines on termination of authorisations),

as comprising any such associated apparatus as is mentioned in paragraph (*aa*) of section 33(1) of that Act.

(5) In subsection (3)(*a*) of section 26 of that Act (safety regulations) sub-paragraphs (i) and (ii) (exclusion of pipe-lines forming part of offshore installations etc.) shall cease to have effect.

26.—(1) In section 1 of the Offshore Petroleum Development (Scotland) Act 1975 (acquisition of land in connection with offshore petroleum)—

Extended application of the Offshore Petroleum Development (Scotland) Act 1975.
1975 c. 8.

(*a*) at the end of subsection (1) there shall be inserted the words " or the storage of gas in or under the sea bed or the recovery of gas so stored " ;

(*b*) at the end of subsection (2)(*a*) there shall be inserted the words " or the storage of gas in or under the sea bed or the recovery of gas so stored " ;

(*c*) at the end of subsection (2)(*b*) there shall be inserted the words " or conveying gas to or from the places in or under the sea bed where it is stored or to be stored " ; and

(*d*) in subsection (2)(*c*) after the word " despatch " there shall be inserted the words " or for the reception of gas and for its storage or onward despatch to or from the places in or under the sea bed where it is stored or to be stored and any treatment incidental thereto ".

(2) In section 20(2) of that Act (interpretation)—

(*a*) after the definition of " harbour authority " there shall be inserted the following definition—

" ' installation ' includes any floating structure or device maintained on a station by whatever means ; " ; and

(*b*) in the definition of " relevant operations " after the word " petroleum " there shall be inserted the words " or the storage of gas in or under the sea bed or the recovery of gas so stored ".

27.—(1) Subject to subsection (2) below, this section has effect as respects—

Prosecutions.

(*a*) any offence alleged to have been committed on, under

or above an installation in waters to which section 22 above applies, or any waters within five hundred metres of such an installation ;

(*b*) any offence under the 1971 Act alleged to have been committed elsewhere than in the United Kingdom ;

(*c*) any offence committed on or as respects an aircraft which is not registered in the United Kingdom, being an offence created by virtue of paragraph 6(5) of Part III of Schedule 13 to the Civil Aviation Act 1982 ; and

(*d*) any offence under section 21 above alleged to have been committed elsewhere than in the United Kingdom.

(2) An offence shall not be one within subsection (1) above if it is an offence under, or under any provision having effect under—

(*a*) the Merchant Shipping Acts 1894 to 1979, or any enactment to be construed as one with the Merchant Shipping Act 1894 ;

(*b*) the Prevention of Oil Pollution Act 1971, or any enactment to be construed as one with that Act ;

(*c*) Part I of the Finance Act 1972, or any enactment to be construed as one with that Part ;

(*d*) Part III of the 1975 Act ;

(*e*) the Customs and Excise Acts 1979, or any enactment to be construed as one with those Acts or any of them ; or

(*f*) except where it is created by virtue of paragraph 6(5) of Part III of Schedule 13 to the Civil Aviation Act 1982, that Act or any enactment to be construed as one with that Act.

(3) No proceedings shall be instituted in England and Wales for an offence within subsection (1) above except—

(*a*) in the case of an offence under the 1971 Act or under section 21 above, by the Secretary of State or by a person authorised in that behalf by the Secretary of State ; or

(*b*) in the case of any offence, by or with the consent of the Director of Public Prosecutions ;

but this subsection shall not apply to an offence if prosecution of that offence in England and Wales requires the consent of the Attorney General.

(4) No proceedings shall be instituted in Northern Ireland for any offence within subsection (1) above except—

(*a*) in the case of an offence under the 1971 Act or under

section 21 above, by the Secretary of State or by a
person authorised in that behalf by the Secretary of
State ; or

   (*b*) in the case of any offence, by or with the consent of
      the Director of Public Prosecutions for Northern
      Ireland ;

but this subsection shall not apply to an offence if prosecution
of that offence in Northern Ireland requires the consent of the
Attorney General for Northern Ireland.

(5) Section 3 of the Territorial Waters Jurisdiction Act 1878 1878 c. 73.
(consents required for prosecutions) shall not apply to any
proceedings for an offence within subsection (1) above.

(6) Any reference in this section to an offence under the 1971
Act includes a reference to an offence under regulations made
under that Act.

(7) Section 10 of the 1971 Act (which is superseded by this
section) shall cease to have effect.

28.—(1) In this Part—   Interpretation
                                                 of Part IV.
   " foreign sector of the continental shelf " means an area
      which is outside the territorial waters of any state and
      within which rights are exercisable by a state other
      than the United Kingdom with respect to the sea bed
      and subsoil and their natural resources ;

   " installation " includes any floating structure or device
      maintained on a station by whatever means ;

   " statutory maximum ", in relation to a fine on summary
      conviction, means—

         (*a*) in England, Wales and Northern Ireland, the
      prescribed sum within the meaning of section 32 of
      the Magistrates' Courts Act 1980 (at the passing of 1980 c. 45.
      this Act £1,000) ; and

         (*b*) in Scotland, the prescribed sum within the
      meaning of section 289B of the Criminal Procedure 1975 c. 21.
      (Scotland) Act 1975 (at the passing of this Act
      £1,000) ;

      and for the purpose of the application of this definition
      in Northern Ireland the provisions of the said Act of
      1980 which relate to the sum mentioned in paragraph
      (*a*) above shall extend to Northern Ireland ;

   " submersible apparatus " has the same meaning as in
      section 16(2) of the Merchant Shipping Act 1974 ;   1974 c. 43.

   " vessel " includes a hovercraft, submersible apparatus and
      an installation which is in transit and " master "—
         (*a*) in relation to a hovercraft, means the captain ;

(*b*) in relation to submersible apparatus, means the person in charge of the apparatus ; and

(*c*) in relation to an installation which is in transit, means the person in charge of the transit operation.

(2) It is hereby declared that, notwithstanding that this Part may affect individuals or bodies corporate outside the United Kingdom, it applies to any individual whether or not he is a British subject, and to any body corporate whether or not incorporated under the law of any part of the United Kingdom.

PART V
MISCELLANEOUS AND GENERAL

Northern
Ireland and
Isle of Man
shares of
petroleum
revenue.
1968 c. 75.

29.—(1) Where petroleum is delivered to the Secretary of State under the terms of a licence granted under section 2 of the 1934 Act as applied by section 1(3) of the 1964 Act, then, for the purposes of section 2 of the Miscellaneous Financial Provisions Act 1968 (Northern Ireland and Isle of Man shares of revenue from the continental shelf), the proceeds from the licence shall be taken to include the proceeds of the sale of the petroleum less—

(*a*) any sums paid by the Secretary of State in respect of the petroleum or the delivery or treatment of the petroleum ; and

(*b*) any expenses incurred by the Secretary of State in connection with the sale.

(2) In this section and section 30 below " petroleum " has the same meaning as in the 1934 Act.

Payments to
petroleum
production
licence
holders etc.

30.—(1) Where for any chargeable period for the purposes of a licence granted under section 2 of the 1934 Act any person has been required to deliver petroleum to the Secretary of State under the terms of that licence, subsection (3) of section 41 of the 1975 Act (repayment of royalty payments to facilitate or maintain the development of the petroleum resources of the United Kingdom) shall have effect as if for that period that person had paid to the Secretary of State by way of royalty such sum, or (where he has been required to deliver some but not all of the petroleum which he could have been required to deliver) such additional sum, as he would have been required to pay under the terms of the licence if he had not been required to deliver the petroleum.

(2) Subsections (1) and (2) of the said section 41 (payments in pursuance of participation agreements) and, in subsection (4) of that section, the words " or an order made by virtue of this section " shall cease to have effect.

31. In section 1(3) of the Participation Agreements Act 1978 (meaning of " participation agreement ") after the word " petroleum ", in the first place where it occurs, there shall be inserted the words " existing in its natural condition in strata in the United Kingdom or ".

PART V
Participation
agreements
as respects
onshore
petroleum.
1978 c. 1.

32.—(1) Any power conferred by this Act to make regulations or orders and the power conferred by section 11(1) above to give directions shall be exercisable by statutory instrument.

(2) Any statutory instrument containing an Order in Council under this Act, an order under section 3(2) or 11(3) or (5) above or a direction under section 11(1) above shall be subject to annulment in pursuance of a resolution of either House of Parliament.

(3) Where the Secretary of State gives directions—

    (*a*) to the Oil Corporation under any provision of Part I of this Act ; or

    (*b*) to the Gas Corporation under any provision of Part II of this Act.

it shall be the duty of that Corporation (notwithstanding any duty imposed on it by or under any enactment) to comply with the directions.

33.—(1) Stamp duty shall not be chargeable on any instrument which is certified to the Commissioners of Inland Revenue by the Oil Corporation or the Gas Corporation as having been made or executed for both of the following purposes, namely—

    (*a*) to facilitate such an eventual disposal as is mentioned in section 2(1) or, as the case may be, section 10(1) above ; and

    (*b*) to comply with a direction given by the Secretary of State under section 3(1) or, as the case may be, section 11(1) above ;

but no such instrument shall be deemed to be duly stamped unless it is stamped with the duty to which it would but for this subsection be liable or it has, in accordance with the provisions of section 12 of the Stamp Act 1891, been stamped with a particular stamp denoting that it is not chargeable with any duty or that it is duly stamped.

(2) Stamp duty shall not be chargeable under section 47 of the Finance Act 1973 in respect of—

    (*a*) the formation of a subsidiary of either Corporation ; or

    (*b*) any increase in the capital of such a subsidiary,

if the transaction concerned is certified by the Treasury as satisfying the requirements of subsection (3) below.

(3) A transaction satisfies the requirements of this subsection if—

> (a) it is effected for both of the purposes mentioned in subsection (1) above ; and
>
> (b) it is entered into in connection with one or more transfers to be effected under section 2 or 10 above and does not give rise to an excess of capital.

(4) For the purposes of subsection (3) above a transaction gives rise to an excess of capital if—

> (a) in a case falling within subsection (2)(a) above, the total issued capital of the subsidiary exceeds, on the date of the transaction, the total value of the assets less liabilities transferred ; or
>
> (b) in a case falling within subsection (2)(b) above, the aggregate amount of the increase of issued capital of the subsidiary exceeds, on that date, that total value ;

and in this subsection " issued capital " means issued share capital or loan capital.

34.—(1) For the purpose of applying paragraph 3(b) of Part IV of Schedule 1 to the Trustee Investments Act 1961 (which provides that shares and debentures of a company shall not count as wider-range and narrower-range investments respectively within the meaning of that Act unless the company has paid dividends in each of the five years immediately preceding that in which the investment is made) in relation to investment in shares or debentures of a company to which this section applies during the first investment year or during any year following that year, the company shall be deemed to have paid a dividend as there mentioned—

> (a) in any year preceding the first investment year which is included in the relevant five years ; and
>
> (b) in the first investment year, if that year is included in the relevant five years and the company does not in fact pay such a dividend in that year.

(2) This section applies to any company of which shares have been transferred to the Secretary of State or a nominee of his by an order under section 3(4) or 11(5) above.

(3) In this section—

> " the first investment year ", in relation to a company to which this section applies, means the calendar year in which the relevant order or, as the case may be, the first such order was made ; and
>
> " the relevant five years " means the five years immediately preceding the calendar year in which the investment in question is made or is proposed to be made.

35.—(1) There shall be paid out of money provided by Parliament—

    (*a*) any administrative expenses of the Secretary of State ; and

    (*b*) any increase attributable to the provisions of this Act in the sums which under any other enactment are paid out of money so provided.

(2) There shall be paid into the Consolidated Fund any increase attributable to this Act in the sums which under any other enactment are payable into that Fund.

36. In this Act—

" the 1934 Act " means the Petroleum (Production) Act 1934 ;

" the 1964 Act " means the Continental Shelf Act 1964 ;

" the 1971 Act " means the Mineral Workings (Offshore Installations) Act 1971 ;

" the 1972 Act " means the Gas Act 1972 ;

" the 1975 Act " means the Petroleum and Submarine Pipelines Act 1975 ;

" the commencement date ", in relation to any provision of this Act, means the date of the coming into force of that provision ;

" employees' share scheme " means a scheme for encouraging or facilitating the holding of shares or debentures in a company by or for the benefit of—

    (*a*) the bona fide employees or former employees of the company or of a subsidiary of the company ; or

    (*b*) the wives, husbands, widows, widowers or children or step-children under the age of 18 of such employees or former employees ;

" the Gas Corporation " means the British Gas Corporation ;

" modifications " includes additions, omissions and alterations ;

" the Oil Corporation " means the British National Oil Corporation ;

" securities " includes shares, debentures, debenture stock, bonds and other securities of the company concerned, whether or not constituting a charge on the assets of the company ;

" shares " includes stock ;

" statutory provision ", except in relation to Northern Ireland, has the same meaning as in section 57(1) of the

PART V
1964 c. 40.
1954 c. 33.
(N.I.).

Harbours Act 1964 and, in relation to Northern Ireland, has the same meaning as in section 1(*f*) of the Interpretation Act (Northern Ireland) 1954.

Amendments and repeals.

37.—(1) The enactments specified in Schedule 3 to this Act shall have effect subject to the amendments specified in that Schedule (being minor amendments or amendments consequential on the preceding provisions of this Act).

(2) The enactments specified in Schedule 4 to this Act are hereby repealed to the extent specified in the third column of that Schedule.

Short title, commencement and extent.

38.—(1) This Act may be cited as the Oil and Gas (Enterprise) Act 1982.

(2) This Act shall come into force on such day as the Secretary of State may by order appoint, and different days may be so appointed for different provisions or different purposes.

(3) This Act, except Parts II and III and Schedule 2, extends to Northern Ireland.

SCHEDULES

SCHEDULE 1

PROVISIONS AS TO TRANSFERS OF PROPERTY, RIGHTS AND LIABILITIES

Allocation of property, rights and liabilities

1.—(1) The provisions of this paragraph and paragraph 2 below shall have effect where a transfer to which this Schedule applies is a transfer of all property, rights and liabilities comprised in a pre-scribed part of the transferor's undertaking, but shall not apply to any such rights or liabilities under a contract of employment.

(2) Any property, right or liability comprised partly in the part of the transferor's undertaking which is transferred to the transferee and partly in the part of that undertaking which is retained by the transferor shall, where the nature of the property, right or liability permits, be divided or apportioned between the transferor and the transferee in such proportions as may be appropriate ; and, where any estate or interest in land falls to be so divided—

    (*a*) any rent payable under a lease in respect of that estate or interest ; and

    (*b*) any rent charged on that estate or interest,

shall be correspondingly apportioned or divided so that the one part is payable in respect of, or charged on, only one part of the estate or interest and the other part is payable in respect of, or charged on, only the other part of the estate or interest.

(3) Sub-paragraph (2) above shall apply, with any necessary modifications, in relation to any feuduty payable in respect of an estate or interest in land in Scotland as it applies in relation to any rents charged on an estate or interest in land.

(4) Any property, right or liability comprised as mentioned in sub-paragraph (2) above the nature of which does not permit its division or apportionment as so mentioned shall be transferred to the transferee or retained by the transferor according to—

    (*a*) in the case of an estate or interest in land, whether on the transfer date the transferor or the transferee appears to be in greater need of the security afforded by that estate or interest or, where neither appears to be in greater need of that security, whether on that date the transferor or the transferee appears likely to make use of the land to the greater extent ;

    (*b*) in the case of any other property or any right or liability, whether on the transfer date the transferor or the trans-feree appears likely to make use of the property, or as the case may be to be affected by the right or liability, to the greater extent,

subject (in either case) to such arrangements for the protection of the other of them as may be agreed between them.

2.—(1) It shall be the duty of the transferor and the transferee, whether before or after the transfer date, so far as practicable to arrive at such written agreements and to execute such other instruments as are necessary or expedient to identify or define the property, rights and liabilities transferred to the transferee or retained by the transferor and as will—

(a) afford to the transferor and the transferee as against one another such rights and safeguards as they may require for the proper discharge of their respective functions ; and

(b) make as from such date, not being earlier than the transfer date, as may be specified in the agreement or instrument such clarification and modifications of the division of the transferor's undertaking as will best serve the proper discharge of the respective functions of the transferor and the transferee.

(2) Any such agreement shall provide so far as it is expedient—

(a) for the granting of leases and for the creation of other liabilities and rights over land whether amounting in law to interests in land or not, and whether involving the surrender of any existing interest or the creation of a new interest or not ;

(b) for the granting of indemnities in connection with the severance of leases and other matters ; and

(c) for responsibility for registration of any matter in any statutory register.

(3) If the transferor or the transferee represents to the Secretary of State, or if it appears to the Secretary of State without such a representation, that it is unlikely in the case of any matter on which agreement is required under sub-paragraph (1) above that such agreement will be reached, the Secretary of State may, whether before or after the transfer date, give a direction determining that matter and may include in the direction any provision which might have been included in an agreement under sub-paragraph (1) above ; and any property, rights or liabilities required by the direction to be transferred to the transferee shall be regarded as having been transferred by the scheme to, and by virtue thereof vested in, the transferee accordingly.

Rights and liabilities under contracts of employment

3.—(1) The provisions of this paragraph shall have effect where a transfer to which this Schedule applies is a transfer of all property, rights and liabilities comprised in a prescribed part of the transferor's undertaking and it falls to be determined whether the rights and liabilities transferred include rights and liabilities under a particular contract of employment.

(2) Rights and liabilities under the contract of employment shall be transferred only if immediately before the transfer date the employee is employed wholly or mainly for the purposes of the part of the transferor's undertaking which is transferred.

(3) The transferor, the transferee or the employee may apply to the Secretary of State to determine whether or not rights and liabilities in respect of the employee's services under the contract of employment are transferred, and the Secretary of State's decision on the application shall be final.

Right to production of documents of title

4. Where on any transfer to which this Schedule applies the transferor is entitled to retain possession of any documents relating in part to the title to, or to the management of, any land or other property transferred to the transferee, the transferor shall be deemed to have given to the transferee an acknowledgment in writing of the right of the transferee to production of that document and to delivery of copies thereof ; and section 64 of the Law of Property Act 1925 shall have effect accordingly, and on the basis that the acknowledgment did not contain any such expression of contrary intention as is mentioned in that section.

1925 c. 20.

Perfection of vesting of certain property or rights

5. Where in the case of any transfer to which this Schedule applies any property, right or liability which falls to be transferred to the transferee cannot be properly vested in the transferee by virtue of the scheme because transfers thereof are governed otherwise than by the law of a part of the United Kingdom, the transferor and the transferee shall take all practicable steps for the purpose of securing that the transfer of the property, right or liability is effective under the relevant foreign law.

Proof of title by certificate

6. In the case of any transfer to which this Schedule applies, a joint certificate by or on behalf of the transferor and the transferee that any property specified in the certificate, or any such interest in or right over any such property as may be so specified, or any right or liability so specified, is by virtue of the scheme for the time being vested in such one of them as may be so specified, shall be conclusive evidence for all purposes of that fact ; and if on the expiration of one month after a request from either of them for the preparation of such a joint certificate as respects any property, interest, right or liability they have failed to agree on the terms of the certificate, they shall refer the matter to the Secretary of State and issue the certificate in such terms as he may direct.

Restrictions on dealing with certain land

7. If the Secretary of State is satisfied on the representation of the transferor or the transferee that, in consequence of a transfer to which this Schedule applies, different interests in land, whether the same or different land, are held by the transferor and by the transferee and that the circumstances are such that this paragraph should have effect, the Secretary of State may direct that this paragraph

SCH. 1   shall apply to such of that land as may be specified in the direction,
and while that direction remains in force—

(*a*) neither the transferor nor the transferee shall dispose of any
interest to which they may respectively be entitled in any
of the specified land except with the consent of the Secretary
of State ;

(*b*) if in connection with any proposal to dispose of any interest
of either the transferor or the transferee in any of the
specified land it appears to the Secretary of State to be
necessary or expedient for the protection of either of them,
he may—

(i) require either the transferor or the transferee to
dispose of any interest to which it may be entitled in any
of the specified land to such person and in such manner
as may be specified in the requirement ;

(ii) require either the transferor or the transferee to
acquire from the other any interest in any of the specified
land to which that other is entitled ; or

(iii) consent to the proposed disposal subject to compliance with such conditions as the Secretary of State may
see fit to impose ;

but a person other than the transferor and the transferee dealing with,
or with a person claiming under, either the transferor or the transferee shall not be concerned to see or enquire whether this paragraph
applies or has applied in relation to any land to which the dealing
relates or as to whether the provisions of this paragraph have been
complied with in connection with that or any other dealing with
that land, and no transaction between persons other than the transferor and the transferee shall be invalid by reason of any failure to
comply with those provisions.

Construction of agreements, licences, statutory provisions and documents

8.—(1) This paragraph applies where in the case of any transfer
to which this Schedule applies any rights or liabilities transferred are
rights or liabilities under an agreement or licence to which the transferor was a party immediately before the transfer date, whether in
writing or not, and whether or not of such nature that rights and
liabilities thereunder could be assigned by the transferor.

(2) So far as relating to property, rights or liabilities transferred to
the transferee, the agreement or licence shall have effect on and after
the transfer date as if—

(*a*) the transferee had been the party thereto ;

(*b*) for any reference (whether express or implied and, if express,
however worded) to the transferor there were substituted,
as respects anything falling to be done on or after the
transfer date, a reference to the transferee ;

(*c*) any reference (whether express or implied and, if express,
however worded) to a person employed by, or engaged in
the business of, the transferor and holding a specified office

or serving in a specified capacity were, as respects anything
falling to be done on or after the transfer date, a reference
to such person as the transferee may appoint or, in default
of appointment, to a person employed by, or engaged in
the business of, the transferee who corresponds as nearly
as may be to the first-mentioned person ;

(*d*) any reference in general terms (however worded) to persons
employed by, persons engaged in the business of, or agents
of, the transferor were, as respects anything to be done
on or after the transfer date, a reference to persons
employed by, persons engaged in the business of, or agents
of, the transferee.

9. Except as otherwise provided in any provision of this Act
(whether expressly or by necessary implication) paragraph 8 above
shall, so far as applicable, apply in relation to any statutory provision, any provision of an agreement or licence to which the transferor was not a party and any provision of a document other than
an agreement or licence, if and so far as the provision in question
relates to any of the transferred rights and liabilities, as it applies
in relation to an agreement or licence to which the transferor was a
party, and, in relation to any such statutory or other provision as
aforesaid, references in sub-paragraph (2)(*b*), (*c*) and (*d*) of that paragraph to the transferor and to any persons employed by, persons
engaged in the business of, or agents of, the transferor include references made by means of a general reference to a class of persons of
which the transferor is one, without the transferor itself being specifically referred to.

10. Without prejudice to the generality of the provisions of paragraphs 8 and 9 above, the transferee under a transfer to which this
Schedule applies and any other person shall, as from the transfer
date, have the same rights, powers and remedies (and in particular
the same rights and powers as to the taking or resisting of legal
proceedings or the making or resisting of applications to any authority) for ascertaining, perfecting or enforcing any right or liability
vested in the transferee by virtue of the scheme as he would have had
if that right or liability had at all times been a right or liability of the
transferee, and any legal proceedings or applications to any authority
pending on the transfer date by or against the transferor in so far
as they relate to any property, right or liability vested in the transferee by virtue of the scheme, or to any agreement or enactment
relating to any such property, right or liability, shall be continued
by or against the transferee to the exclusion of the transferor.

11. The provisions of paragraphs 8 to 10 above shall have effect
for the interpretation of agreements, licences, statutory provisions and
other instruments subject to the context, and shall not apply where
the context otherwise requires.

Third parties affected by vesting provisions

12.—(1) Without prejudice to the provisions of paragraphs 8 to
11 above, any transaction effected between the transferor and the

transferee in pursuance of paragraph 2(1) above or of a direction under paragraph 2(3) above shall be binding on all other persons, and notwithstanding that it would, apart from this sub-paragraph, have required the consent or concurrence of any other person.

(2) It shall be the duty of the transferor and the transferee if they effect any transaction in pursuance of paragraph 2(1) above or a direction under paragraph 2(3) above to notify any person who has rights or liabilities which thereby become enforceable as to part by or against the transferor and as to part by or against the transferee, and if, within 28 days of being notified, such a person applies to the Secretary of State and satisfies him that the transaction operated unfairly against him the Secretary of State may give such directions to the transferor and the transferee as appear to him appropriate for varying the transaction.

(3) If in consequence of a transfer to which this Schedule applies or of anything done in pursuance of the provisions of this Schedule the rights or liabilities of any person other than the transferor and the transferee which were enforceable against or by the transferor become enforceable as to part against or by the transferor and as to part against or by the transferee, and the value of any property or interest of that person is thereby diminished, such compensation as may be just shall be paid to that person by the transferor, the transferee or both, and any dispute as to whether and if so how much compensation is so payable, or as to the person to or by whom it shall be paid, shall be referred to and determined by an arbitrator appointed by the Lord Chancellor or, where the proceedings are to be held in Scotland, by an arbiter appointed by the Lord President of the Court of Session.

(4) Where in the case of a transfer to which this Schedule applies the transferor or the transferee purports by any conveyance or transfer to transfer to some person other than the transferor or the transferee for consideration any land or any other property transferred which before the transfer date belonged to the transferor or which is an interest in property which before that date belonged to the transferor, the conveyance or transfer shall be as effective as if both the transferor and the transferee had been parties thereto and had thereby conveyed or transferred all their interests in the property conveyed or transferred.

(5) If in the case of any transfer to which this Schedule applies it appears to the court, at any stage in any court proceedings to which the transferor or the transferee and a person other than the transferor or the transferee are parties, that the issues in the proceedings depend on the identification or definition of any of the property, rights or liabilities transferred which the transferor and the transferee have not yet effected, or to raise a question of construction on the relevant provisions of this Act which would not arise if the transferor and the transferee constituted a single person, the court may, if it thinks fit on the application of a party to the proceedings other than the transferor and the transferee, hear and determine the proceedings on the footing that such one of the transferor and the

transferee as is a party to the proceedings represents and is answerable for the other of them, and that the transferor and the transferee constitute a single person, and any judgment or order given by the court shall bind both the transferor and the transferee accordingly.

(6) In the case of any transfer to which this Schedule applies it shall be the duty of the transferor and the transferee to keep one another informed of any case where either of them may be prejudiced by sub-paragraph (4) or (5) above, and if either the transferor or the transferee claims that it has been so prejudiced and that the other of them ought to indemnify or make a repayment to it on that account and has unreasonably failed to meet that claim, it may refer the matter to the Secretary of State for determination by him.

SCHEDULE 2

Petroleum Production Licences: Modification of Model Clauses

Part II of Schedule 2 to the 1975 Act

1.—(1) In paragraph (1) of clause 9 of the model clauses set out in Part II of Schedule 2 to the 1975 Act for the words " clause 10 " there shall be substituted the words " clauses 10 and 11A ".

(2) In paragraph (6) of clause 10 of those clauses after the words " for tax purposes " there shall be inserted the words " and a sum has been ascertained in pursuance of paragraph (7) of clause 9 of this licence in respect of the cost of conveying and treating the petroleum " and for the words " clause 9 of this licence " there shall be substituted the words " that clause ".

(3) In paragraph (7) of that clause for the words " the amount specified in the previous notice " there shall be substituted the words " the total amount already paid by the Licensee in pursuance of this clause in respect of that period ".

(4) In paragraph (9) of that clause for the words " falls to be " there shall be substituted the word " is ".

(5) After paragraph (10) of that clause there shall be inserted the following paragraph—

" (11) For the purposes of this clause any amount paid by the Licensee or the Minister on account of a prospective liability under paragraph (5), (6) or (7) of this clause shall be treated as paid in pursuance of that paragraph."

(6) In paragraph (3) of clause 11 of those clauses—

(*a*) in sub-paragraph (*c*) from " crude oil " onwards there shall be substituted the words " crude oil, condensate, natural gas and natural gas liquids, in each case of a quality or composition or of each quality or composition determined in the manner specified in the notice " ; and

(*b*) in sub-paragraph (*d*) for the word " specify " there shall be substituted the words " contain provisions with respect to ".

(7) In paragraph (4) of that clause for sub-paragraph (*c*) there shall be substituted the following sub-paragraph—

" (*c*) shall not specify, or enable to be specified, as a place at which delivery is to be made in pursuance of the notice a place which is neither a point at sea at which the Licensee normally loads, nor a point on land at which the Licensee normally lands, petroleum of any kind from the licensed area."

(8) Paragraph (5) of that clause shall be omitted.

(9) After that clause there shall be inserted the following clause—

" Cost of delivery and treatment of petroleum.

11A.—(1) Where petroleum or petroleum of any kind is delivered to the Minister in pursuance of a notice served by virtue of clause 11(1) of this licence, the Minister shall pay to the Licensee a sum in respect of the cost of the delivery and treatment of the petroleum ; and clause 9(7) of this licence shall apply for the purpose of ascertaining that sum as if for the reference to paragraph (5)(*b*) of that clause there were substituted a reference to this paragraph.

(2) Where, in any chargeable period, petroleum or petroleum of any kind is delivered to the Minister as mentioned in paragraph (1) of this clause, the Licensee shall, within two months after the end of that period, deliver to the Minister, in such form as the Minister may specify, a statement of the amount which the Licensee estimates is payable by the Minister in pursuance of this clause in respect of that period ; and where the amount specified in the statement is larger or smaller than the total amount (if any) already paid by the Minister in pursuance of this clause in respect of that period, then—

(*a*) if it is larger the difference shall be paid forthwith by the Minister to the Licensee ; and

(*b*) if it is smaller the difference shall be paid forthwith by the Licensee to the Minister.

(3) The Minister may from time to time, after a statement in respect of any chargeable period has been delivered to him in pursuance of paragraph (2) of this clause and before he has given to the Licensee a notice in pursuance of paragraph (4) of this clause in respect of that period, give a notice in writing to the Licensee specifying the amount which the Minister estimates is payable by him in pursuance of this clause in respect of that period ; and where the amount specified in the notice is larger or smaller than the total amount already paid by the Minister in pursuance of this clause in respect of that period, then—

(*a*) if it is larger the difference shall be paid forthwith by the Minister to the Licensee ; and

(*b*) if it is smaller the difference shall be paid forthwith by the Licensee to the Minister.

(4) When it appears to the Minister that the amount payable by him in pursuance of this clause in respect of any chargeable period has been finally ascertained, he may give to the Licensee a notice in writing specifying the amount which the Minister considers is so payable ; and where the amount specified in the notice is larger or smaller than the total amount already paid by the Minister in pursuance of this clause in respect of that period, then, subject to paragraph (5) of this clause—

SCH. 2

    (*a*) if it is larger the difference shall be paid forthwith by the Minister to the Licensee ; and

    (*b*) if it is smaller the difference shall be paid forthwith by the Licensee to the Minister.

(5) A decision made by the Minister for the purposes of paragraph (3) or (4) of this clause shall not be called in question by the Licensee except that any dispute between the Minister and the Licensee as to whether an amount specified in a notice given in pursuance of the said paragraph (4) is payable in pursuance of this clause may be referred to arbitration in the manner provided by clause 40 of this licence.

(6) Where any payment is made by the Minister or the Licensee in pursuance of paragraph (3) or (4) of this clause, an amount in respect of interest on the payment shall also be payable by him to the recipient of the payment and that amount shall be calculated in such manner as the Minister may specify from time to time in a notice in writing given by him to the Licensee ; but—

    (*a*) a notice in pursuance of this paragraph shall provide for amounts by way of interest to be calculated by applying a rate of interest which is for the time being a commercial rate of interest ; and

    (*b*) any such amount in respect of interest shall be disregarded in calculating for the purposes of the said paragraph (3) or (4) any amount already paid by the Minister in pursuance of this clause.

(7) For the purposes of this clause any amount paid by the Minister or the Licensee on account of a prospective liability under paragraph (3) or (4) of this clause shall be treated as paid in pursuance of that paragraph."

Part II of Schedule 3 to the 1975 Act

2.—(1) In paragraph (6) of clause 10 of the model clauses set out in Part II of Schedule 3 to the 1975 Act after the words " for tax purposes " there shall be inserted the words " and a sum has been ascertained in pursuance of paragraph (7) of clause 9 of this licence in respect of the cost of conveying and treating the petroleum " and for the words " clause 9 of this licence " there shall be substituted the words " that clause ".

SCH. 2

(2) In paragraph (7) of that clause for the words "the amount specified in the previous notice" there shall be substituted the words "the total amount already paid by the Licensee in pursuance of this clause in respect of that period".

(3) In paragraph (9) of that clause for the words "falls to be" there shall be substituted the word "is".

(4) After paragraph (10) of that clause there shall be inserted the following paragraph—

"(11) For the purposes of this clause any amount paid by the Licensee or the Minister on account of a prospective liability under paragraph (5), (6) or (7) of this clause shall be treated as paid in pursuance of that paragraph."

(5) In paragraph (1) of clause 11 of those clauses the words "at the place where it was won" shall be omitted.

(6) In paragraph (3) of that clause—

(*a*) in sub-paragraph (*c*) for the words from "crude oil" onwards there shall be substituted the words "crude oil, condensate, natural gas and natural gas liquids, in each case of a quality or composition or of each quality or composition determined in the manner specified in the notice"; and

(*b*) in sub-paragraph (*d*) for the word "specify" there shall be substituted the words "contain provisions with respect to".

(7) In paragraph (4) of that clause there shall be inserted at the end the following sub-paragraph—

"(*c*) shall not specify, or enable to be specified, as a place at which delivery is to be made in pursuance of the notice a place which is not a point at which the Licensee normally delivers petroleum of any kind from the licensed area."

(8) Paragraph (5) of that clause shall be omitted.

(9) After that clause there shall be inserted the following clause—

"Cost of delivery and treatment of petroleum.

11A.—(1) Where petroleum or petroleum of any kind is delivered to the Minister in pursuance of a notice served by virtue of clause 11(1) of this licence, the Minister shall pay to the Licensee a sum in respect of the cost of the delivery and treatment of the petroleum; and clause 9(7) of this licence shall apply for the purpose of ascertaining that sum as if for the reference to paragraph (5)(*b*) of that clause there were substituted a reference to this paragraph.

(2) Where, in any chargeable period, petroleum or petroleum of any kind is delivered to the Minister as mentioned in paragraph (1) of this clause, the Licensee shall, within two months after the end of that period, deliver to the Minister, in such form as the Minister may specify, a statement of the amount which the Licensee estimates is payable by the Minister in pursuance of this clause in respect of that period; and where the

amount specified in the statement is larger or smaller than the total amount (if any) already paid by the Minister in pursuance of this clause in respect of that period, then—

> (*a*) if it is larger the difference shall be paid forthwith by the Minister to the Licensee ; and

> (*b*) if it is smaller the difference shall be paid forthwith by the Licensee to the Minister.

(3) The Minister may from time to time, after a statement in respect of any chargeable period has been delivered to him in pursuance of paragraph (2) of this clause and before he has given to the Licensee a notice in pursuance of paragraph (4) of this clause in respect of that period, give a notice in writing to the Licensee specifying the amount which the Minister estimates is payable by him in pursuance of this clause in respect of that period ; and where the amount specified in the notice is larger or smaller than the total amount already paid by the Minister in pursuance of this clause in respect of that period, then—

> (*a*) if it is larger the difference shall be paid forthwith by the Minister to the Licensee ; and

> (*b*) if it is smaller the difference shall be paid forthwith by the Licensee to the Minister.

(4) When it appears to the Minister that the amount payable by him in pursuance of this clause in respect of any chargeable period has been finally ascertained, he may give to the Licensee a notice in writing specifying the amount which the Minister considers is so payable ; and where the amount specified in the notice is larger or smaller than the total amount already paid by the Minister in pursuance of this clause in respect of that period, then, subject to paragraph (5) of this clause—

> (*a*) if it is larger the difference shall be paid forthwith by the Minister to the Licensee ; and

> (*b*) if it is smaller the difference shall be paid forthwith by the Licensee to the Minister.

(5) A decision made by the Minister for the purposes of paragraph (3) or (4) of this clause shall not be called in question by the Licensee except that any dispute between the Minister and the Licensee as to whether an amount specified in a notice given in pursuance of the said paragraph (4) is payable in pursuance of this clause may be referred to arbitration in the manner provided by clause 38 of this licence.

(6) Where any payment is made by the Minister or the Licensee in pursuance of paragraph (3) or (4) of this clause, an amount in respect of interest on the payment shall also be payable by him to the recipient of the payment and that amount shall be calculated in such manner

as the Minister may specify from time to time in a notice in writing given by him to the Licensee ; but—

> (*a*) a notice in pursuance of this paragraph shall provide for amounts by way of interest to be calculated by applying a rate of interest which is for the time being a commercial rate of interest ; and
>
> (*b*) any such amount in respect of interest shall be disregarded in calculating for the purposes of the said paragraph (3) or (4) any amount already paid by the Minister in pursuance of this clause.

(7) For the purposes of this clause any amount paid by the Minister or the Licensee on account of a prospective liability under paragraph (3) or (4) of this clause shall be treated as paid in pursuance of that paragraph.

(8) In this clause ' chargeable period ' has the same meaning as in clause 9 of this licence."

Schedule 4 to the 1976 Regulations

3.—(1) In paragraph (6) of clause 10 of the model clauses set out in Schedule 4 to the Petroleum (Production) Regulations 1976 for the words " the amount specified in the previous notice " there shall be substituted the words " the total amount already paid by the Licensee in pursuance of this clause in respect of that period ".

(2) In paragraph (8) of that clause for the words " falls to be " there shall be substituted the word " is ".

(3) After paragraph (9) of that clause there shall be inserted the following paragraph—

> " (10) For the purposes of this clause any amount paid by the Licensee or the Minister on account of a prospective liability under paragraph (4), (5) or (6) of this clause shall be treated as paid in pursuance of that paragraph."

(4) In paragraph (1) of clause 11 of those clauses the words " at the place where it was won " shall be omitted.

(5) In paragraph (3) of that clause—

> (*a*) in sub-paragraph (*c*) for the words from " crude oil " onwards there shall be substituted the words " crude oil, condensate, natural gas and natural gas liquids, in each case of a quality or composition or of each quality or composition determined in the manner specified in the notice " ; and
>
> (*b*) in sub-paragraph (*d*) for the word " specify " there shall be substituted the words " contain provisions with respect to ".

(6) In paragraph (4) of that clause there shall be inserted at the end the following sub-paragraph—

> " (*c*) shall not specify, or enable to be specified, as a place at which delivery is to be made in pursuance of the notice a place which is not a point at which the Licensee normally delivers petroleum of any kind from the licensed area."

Schedule 5 to the 1976 Regulations as originally made or   Sch. 2
as amended by the 1978 Regulations

4.—(1) In paragraph (6) of clause 10 of the model clauses set out
in Schedule 5 to the Petroleum (Production) Regulations 1976 as S.I. 1976/1129.
originally made or as amended by the Petroleum (Production) S.I. 1978/929.
(Amendment) Regulations 1978 for the words " the amount specified
in the previous notice " there shall be substituted the words " the
total amount already paid by the Licensee in pursuance of this clause
in respect of that period ".

(2) In paragraph (8) of that clause for the words " falls to be "
there shall be substituted the word " is ".

(3) After paragraph (9) of that clause there shall be inserted the
following paragraph—

" (10) For the purposes of this clause any amount paid by the
Licensee or the Minister on account of a prospective liability
under paragraph (4), (5) or (6) of this clause shall be treated as
paid in pursuance of that paragraph."

(4) In paragraph (3) of clause 11 of those clauses—

(*a*) in sub-paragraph (*c*) for the words from " crude oil " onwards there shall be substituted the words " crude oil,
condensate, natural gas and natural gas liquids, in each
case of a quality or composition or of each quality or
composition determined in the manner specified in the
notice " ; and

(*b*) in sub-paragraph (*d*) for the word " specify " there shall be
substituted the words " contain provisions with respect to ".

(5) In paragraph (4) of that clause for sub-paragraph (*c*) there shall
be substituted the following sub-paragraph—

" (*c*) shall not specify, or enable to be specified, as a place at
which delivery is to be made in pursuance of the notice a
place which is neither a point at sea at which the Licensee
normally loads, nor a point on land at which the Licensee
normally lands, petroleum of any kind from the licensed
area."

Schedule 5 to the 1976 Regulations
as amended by the 1978 and 1980 Regulations

5.—(1) In paragraph (4) of clause 10 of the model clauses set out
in Schedule 5 to the Petroleum (Production) Regulations 1976 as S.I. 1976/1129.
amended by the Petroleum (Production) (Amendment) Regulations S.I. 1978/929.
1978 and the Petroleum (Production) (Amendment) Regulations 1980 S.I. 1980/721.
after the words " of this clause " there shall be inserted the words
" and before he has given to the Licensee a notice in pursuance of
paragraph (5) of this clause in respect of that period ".

(2) In paragraph (6) of that clause for the words " the amount
specified in the previous notice " there shall be substituted the words
" the total amount already paid by the Licensee in pursuance of this
clause in respect of that period ".

(3) In paragraph (8) of that clause the words " or on account of a
prospective liability under " shall be omitted.

Sch. 2   (4) After paragraph (9) of that clause there shall be inserted the following paragraph—

" (10) For the purposes of this clause any amount paid by the Licensee or the Minister on account of a prospective liability under paragraph (4), (5) or (6) of this clause shall be treated as paid in pursuance of that paragraph."

(5) In paragraph (3) of clause 11 of those clauses, in sub-paragraph (c) for the words from " crude oil " onwards there shall be substituted the words " crude oil, condensate, natural gas and natural gas liquids, in each case of a quality or composition or of each quality or composition determined in the manner specified in the notice ".

Section 37.

SCHEDULE 3

MINOR AND CONSEQUENTIAL AMENDMENTS

The Continental Shelf Act 1964

1. At the end of section 1(7) of the 1964 Act (designated areas) there shall be inserted the words " ; and the power to make Orders under this subsection shall include power to revoke Orders for the purpose of consolidating them."

2. In section 6 (wireless telegraphy) and section 7 (radioactive substances) of that Act for the words " section 3 of this Act " there shall be substituted the words " section 23 of the Oil and Gas (Enterprise) Act 1982 ".

3. In section 11(1) of that Act for the words from " under this Act (including " to " section 3(1) of this Act) " there shall be substituted the words " under another Act as applied by or under this Act ".

4. After section 11 of that Act there shall be inserted the following section—

"Interpre-   11A. In this Act ' installation ' includes any floating
tation.   structure or device maintained on a station by whatever means."

The General Rate Act 1967

1967 c. 9.   5.—(1) In subsection (3) of section 33 of the General Rate Act 1967 (British Gas Corporation) for the words from " the Corporation ", in the first place where they occur, to the end of paragraph (c) there shall be substituted the following paragraphs—

" (a) the Corporation—

(i) supplied gas to consumers in that area ; or

(ii) manufactured gas in that area ; or

(iii) produced gas in that area by the application to gas purchased by them of any process not consisting only of purification, or of blending with other gases, or of both purification and such blending ; or

(b) private suppliers (within the meaning of section 33A of this Act) supplied to consumers in that area gas which had been conveyed (whether within or outside that area) by pipe-lines belonging to the Corporation,".

(2) In subsection (7) of that section for the words " includes gas in a liquid state " there shall be substituted the words " has the same meaning as in Part I of the Gas Act 1972 ".

6. After that section there shall be inserted the following section—

" Other suppliers of gas.　　33A.—(1) The Secretary of State may by order provide that, in such cases and subject to such exceptions and modifications as may be prescribed by the order, section 33 of and Part II of Schedule 6 to this Act shall apply to premises occupied by private suppliers for or in connection with the supply of gas through pipes to consumers' premises.

(2) In this section—

' gas ' has the same meaning as in Part III of the Gas Act 1972 ;

' private supplier ' means a person authorised by a consent given under section 29 of that Act, or by section 29A of that Act, to supply gas through pipes to consumers' premises.

(3) Any statutory instrument containing an order under this section shall be subject to annulment in pursuance of a resolution of either House of Parliament.".

The Mineral Workings (Offshore Installations) Act 1971

7.—(1) In section 3(4) of the 1971 Act (construction and survey regulations for offshore installations) for the words " the concession owner ", in both places where they occur, there shall be substituted the words " every person who, in relation to the installation, is a concession owner ".

8. In sections 3(4), 4(1), 6(1) and 9(2) of that Act, for the words " waters to which this Act applies ", wherever they occur, there shall be substituted the words " controlled waters ".

9. In section 5(2) of that Act (masters of offshore installations, further provisions) for the words " an installation " there shall be substituted the words " an offshore installation ".

10. In section 6(2) of that Act (safety regulations) the word " and " immediately following paragraph (c) shall be omitted and after that paragraph there shall be inserted the following paragraph—

" (cc) vessels on which accommodation is provided for persons who work on or from installations, and ".

11.—(1) In subsection (1) of section 12 of that Act (interpretation)—

(a) for the definition of " concession owner " there shall be substituted the following definition—

" ' controlled waters ' has the meaning given by section 1(4) of this Act," ;

(*b*) after the definition of "designated area" there shall be inserted the following definition—

"'foreign sector of the continental shelf' has the meaning given by section 1(4) of this Act," ;

(*c*) for the definition of "offshore installation" there shall be substituted the following definition—

"'offshore installation' has the meaning given by section 1(4) of this Act," ; and

(*d*) the definitions of "underwater exploitation" and "underwater exploration" shall be omitted.

(2) For subsections (2) and (3) of that section there shall be substituted the following subsections—

"(2) A person who has the right to exploit or explore mineral resources in any area, or to store gas in any area and to recover gas so stored, shall be a concession owner for the purposes of this Act in relation to any offshore installation at any time if, at that time, there is carried on from, by means of or on the installation any of the following activities, namely—

(*a*) the exploitation or exploration of mineral resources, or the storage or recovery of gas, in the exercise of that right ;

(*b*) the conveyance in that area by means of a pipe or system of pipes, of minerals gotten, or gas being stored or recovered, in the exercise of that right ; and

(*c*) the provision of accommodation for persons who work on or from an installation which is or has been maintained, or is intended to be established, for the carrying on of an activity falling within paragraph (*a*) or (*b*) above or this paragraph.

(3) The fact that an installation has been maintained for the carrying on of an activity falling within subsection (2) above shall be disregarded for the purposes of paragraph (*c*) of that subsection if, since it was so maintained, the installation—

(*a*) has been outside controlled waters or, where it was so maintained in a part of a foreign sector of the continental shelf adjacent to those waters, the area consisting of those waters and that part ; or

(*b*) has been maintained for the carrying on of an activity not falling within that subsection."

The Gas Act 1972

12. In section 7(2) of the 1972 Act (general powers of Secretary of State to give directions to Gas Corporation)—

(*a*) the words "to dispose of any part of their undertaking or of any assets held by them" and the words "to dispose of any part of its undertaking or of any assets held by it" shall be omitted ; and

(*b*) for the words from "the Corporation shall" onwards there shall be substituted the words "it shall be the duty of the Corporation (notwithstanding any duty imposed on them by or under any enactment) to give effect to any such direction".

13. In section 24 of that Act (duty of Gas Corporation to avoid undue preference) the following subsection shall be inserted after subsection (2)—

 " (3) In this section ' consumer ' means any person who—

  (*a*) is the owner or occupier of premises situated within 25 yards from any distribution main of the Corporation ; and

  (*b*) is there supplied with gas by the Corporation at a rate not exceeding 25,000 therms a year."

SCH. 3

14.—(1) After section 31 of that Act there shall be inserted the following section—

" Supplementary

Relief to suppliers in emergency conditions.

 31A.—(1) Without prejudice to any other provision of this Act or the provisions of any regulations thereunder, in any proceedings against any person supplying gas through pipes for or arising out of a failure by him to comply with any duty with respect to the supply of gas imposed on him by or under any enactment (including any duty with respect to pressure of supply), it shall be a defence for that person to prove that circumstances existed by reason of which compliance with the duty would or might have involved danger to the public, and that he took all such steps as it was reasonable for him to take both to prevent the circumstances from occurring and to prevent them from having that effect."

(2) Section 28 of that Act (which is superseded by this paragraph) shall be omitted.

15. Section 30(8) of that Act (provisions as to testing and stamping of meters not to apply in relation to the supply of gas under certain agreements made by the Gas Corporation) shall be omitted.

16. In section 45(4) of that Act (provisions as to regulations and orders) after the words " an order appointing a day " there shall be inserted the words " , an order under section 29(3) above ".

17. In section 48(1) of that Act (interpretation)—

 (*a*) after the definition of " the Corporation " there shall be inserted the following definition—

  " ' distribution main ', in relation to the Corporation, means any main of the Corporation through which the Corporation are for the time being distributing gas and which is not used only for the purpose of giving a separate supply of gas for industrial purposes, or of conveying gas in bulk ; " ; and

 (*b*) after the definition of " functions " there shall be inserted the following definition—

  " ' gas ' means—

   (*a*) any substance which consists wholly or mainly of—

    (i) methane, ethane, propane, butane, hydrogen or carbon monoxide ;

(ii) a mixture of two or more of those gases ; or

(iii) a combustible mixture of one or more of those gases and air ; and

(*b*) any other substance which is gaseous at a temperature of 15°C and a pressure of 1013.25 millibars and is specified in an order made by the Secretary of State,

except that, in Part III of this Act, that expression does not include any substance which is not in a gaseous state."

18. At the end of paragraph 1 of Schedule 2 to that Act (powers of acquisition) there shall be added the words " (including any enactment passed or made after the passing of this Act) ".

19. In paragraph 2(1) of Schedule 4 to that Act (obligation to supply gas) for the words " any main of the Corporation through which the Corporation are for the time being distributing gas " there shall be substituted the words " any distribution main of the Corporation ", and the proviso shall be omitted.

The Local Government Act 1974

1974 c. 7.

20. In Schedule 3 to the Local Government Act 1974 (hereditaments to which section 19(1) of that Act applies) after paragraph 3 there shall be inserted the following paragraphs—

" 3A.—(1) Any hereditament which a private supplier is to be treated as occupying in a rating area by virtue of section 33(3) of the principal Act as applied by order under section 33A of that Act.

(2) In this paragraph and paragraph 3B below—

1972 c. 60.

' gas ' has the same meaning as in Part III of the Gas Act 1972 ;

' private supplier ' means a person authorised by a consent given under section 29 of that Act, or by section 29A of that Act, to supply gas through pipes to consumers' premises.

3B. Any hereditament occupied for or in connection with the conveyance of gas through pipes other than one which—

(*a*) is occupied by the British Gas Corporation ; or

(*b*) is occupied by a private supplier for or in connection with the supply of gas through pipes to consumers' premises."

The Social Security Act 1975

1975 c. 14.

21. In section 132(2) of the Social Security Act 1975 (meaning of " continental shelf operations ") for the words from " the exploitation " onwards there shall be substituted the words " any activities which, if paragraphs (*a*) and (*d*) of subsection (6) of section 23 of the Oil and Gas (Enterprise) Act 1982 (application of civil law to certain offshore activities) were omitted, would nevertheless fall within subsection (2) of that section."

The Oil Taxation Act 1975

22. In paragraph 2A(4) of Schedule 3 to the Oil Taxation Act 1975 c. 22. 1975—

   (*a*) in paragraph (*a*) for the words " section 8 or 9 of that Act " there shall be substituted the words " section 29 of the Gas 1972 c. 60. Act 1972 " and the words " or use " and " and to the use of the gas supplied under it " shall be omitted ; and

   (*b*) in paragraph (*b*) for the words " those sections " there shall be substituted the words " that section " and the words " or use " shall be omitted.

The Local Government (Scotland) Act 1975

23. After paragraph 3 of Schedule 1 to the Local Government 1975 c. 30. (Scotland) Act 1975 (certain lands and heritages of the Gas Corporation to be valued by formula for rating) there shall be inserted the following paragraphs—

" 3A.—(1) Any lands and heritages occupied by a private supplier for or in connection with the supply of gas through pipes to consumers' premises, other than—

   (*a*) lands and heritages occupied and used as a dwelling house ;

   (*b*) a shop, room or other place occupied and used by a private supplier wholly or mainly for the sale, display or demonstration of apparatus or accessories for use by consumers of gas :

      Provided that in determining whether any such shop, room or other place is wholly or mainly occupied and used as aforesaid, use for the receipt of payments for gas consumed shall be disregarded ;

   (*c*) lands and heritages held by a private supplier under a lease for a period not exceeding 21 years ;

   (*d*) premises which are—

      (i) occupied by a private supplier ;

      (ii) used wholly or mainly as an office or for office purposes (within the meaning of paragraph 2 of this Schedule) ; and

      (iii) situated on land which, in respect of its nature and situation, is comparable rather with land in general than with land used for the purpose of supplying gas through pipes ; or

   (*e*) lands and heritages occupied and used by a private supplier wholly or mainly for the manufacture of plant or gas fittings.

(2) In this paragraph and paragraph 3B below—

   ' gas ' has the same meaning as in Part III of the Gas Act 1972 ;

   ' private supplier ' means a person authorised by a consent given under section 29 of that Act, or by section 29A of that Act, to supply gas through pipes to consumers' premises.

3B. Any lands and heritages occupied for or in connection with the conveyance of gas through pipes other than lands and heritages which—

(a) are occupied by the British Gas Corporation ;

(b) are occupied by a private supplier for or in connection with the supply of gas through pipes to consumers' premises ; or

(c) are occupied and used as a dwelling house."

The Sex Discrimination Act 1975

24. In section 10(5) of the Sex Discrimination Act 1975 (employment at establishment in Great Britain)—

(a) for the words from " exploration " to " natural resources " there shall be substituted the words " any activity falling within section 23(2) of the Oil and Gas (Enterprise) Act 1982 " ; and

(b) after " 1964 " there shall be inserted the words " or specified under section 22(5) of the Oil and Gas (Enterprise) Act 1982 ".

The Employment Protection Act 1975

25. For subsection (2) of section 127 of the Employment Protection Act 1975 (power to extend employment legislation) there shall be substituted the following subsection—

" (2) This section applies to employment for the purposes of—

(a) any activities in the territorial waters of the United Kingdom ; or

(b) any activities which, if paragraphs (a) and (d) of subsection (6) of section 23 of the Oil and Gas (Enterprise) Act 1982 (application of civil law to certain offshore activities) were omitted, would nevertheless fall within subsection (2) of that section."

The Petroleum and Submarine Pipe-lines Act 1975

26. In section 1 of the 1975 Act (constitution of the Oil Corporation)—

(a) in subsection (2) (number of members) for the words " not less than eight and not more than twenty " there shall be substituted the words " not less than five and not more than twelve " ; and

(b) subsection (3)(c) (two members to be civil servants) shall be omitted.

27. In section 2 of that Act (general powers of the Oil Corporation)—

(a) in subsection (1) for paragraph (e) there shall be substituted the following paragraph—

"(e) without prejudice to the generality of the preceding paragraphs, to enter into participation agreements
(within the meaning of the Participation Agreements Act 1978) and to do anything required for the purpose of

giving effect to such arrangements, including agreements entered into by persons other than the Corporation ; " ; and

(b) in subsection (4)(d) the words " or lend " shall be omitted and for the word " guarantee " there shall be substituted the words " give any surety or guarantee for ".

28. In section 3 of that Act (general duties of the Oil Corporation) subsection (3) (duty to tender advice to the Secretary of State) shall be omitted.

29. At the beginning of subsection (2) of section 37 of that Act (inspectors) there shall be inserted the words " Subject to subsection (3) of this section " and after that subsection there shall be inserted the following subsection—

" (3) The powers conferred on an inspector by paragraph (a) or (b) of the preceding subsection shall not be exercisable as respects any refinery or land unless not less than 7 days' notice has been given to a person having control of that refinery or land."

30. In section 44 of that Act (extension of the 1971 Act) subsections (1) to (4) shall be omitted.

31. In section 45(3) of that Act (exclusion of Dumping at Sea Act 1974) the words " or any such other installation as is mentioned in section 44(1) of this Act " shall be omitted.

32. In section 46 of the 1975 Act (orders and regulations), in subsections (1) and (2), after the words " section 6(3) " there shall be inserted the words " or (10) ".

33. In paragraph 14 of Schedule 1 to that Act (constitution etc. of the Oil Corporation) for the words from " appointed " onwards there shall be substituted the words " who is employed in the civil service of the State ".

The Fatal Accidents and Sudden Deaths Inquiry (Scotland) Act 1976

34. In section 9 of the Fatal Accidents and Sudden Deaths Inquiry (Scotland) Act 1976 (application to continental shelf) for the words from " the exploration " to " resources " there shall be substituted the words " any activity falling within subsection (2) of section 23 of the Oil and Gas (Enterprise) Act 1982 " and for the words " section 3(2) of the Continental Shelf Act 1964 " there shall be substituted the words " subsection (1) of that section ". 1976 c. 14.

1964 c. 29.

The Fair Employment (Northern Ireland) Act 1976

35. In section 49(3) of the Fair Employment (Northern Ireland) Act 1976 (employment at establishment in Northern Ireland)— 1976 c. 25.

(a) for the words from " the exploration " to " natural resources " there shall be substituted the words " any activity falling within section 23(2) of the Oil and Gas (Enterprise) Act 1982 " ; and

(b) after " 1964 " there shall be inserted the words " or specified under section 22(5) of the Oil and Gas (Enterprise) Act 1982 ".

The Race Relations Act 1976

36. In section 8(5) (employment at establishment in Great Britain) and section 9(3) (exception for seamen recruited abroad) of the Race Relations Act 1976—

(*a*) for the words from " exploration " to " natural resources " there shall be substituted the words " any activity falling within section 23(2) of the Oil and Gas (Enterprise) Act 1982 " ; and

(*b*) after " 1964 " there shall be inserted the words " or specified under section 22(5) of the Oil and Gas (Enterprise) Act 1982 ".

The Energy Act 1976

37.—(1) For sections 9 to 11 of the Energy Act 1976 (which impose restrictions on the use and liquefaction of offshore natural gas) there shall be substituted the following section—

"Lique-
faction of
offshore
natural
gas.
9.—(1) The Secretary of State's consent is required for offshore natural gas to be subjected in Great Britain to any process of liquefaction which results in the production of liquid methane or ethane except such small quantities of liquid methane or ethane as may be produced in the course of providing a supply with consent under section 29 of the Gas Act 1972 and in compliance with any conditions subject to which that consent was given, or providing a supply for which such consent is not required.

(2) The Secretary of State's consent under subsection (1) above may be given either with reference to particular cases or by means of orders of general application.

(3) A specific consent given to any person under subsection (1) above (that is to say, a consent given to him otherwise than by an order of general application) is irrevocable and may be given for a specified period or indefinitely.

(4) Where consent under that subsection has been given by an order of general application, any person who proposes to undertake a process of liquefaction which is covered by that general consent may notify the Secretary of State of his proposal (in the manner specified in the order), whereupon subsection (3) above applies as if specific consent either unlimited in duration or, if the order so provides, for the period there specified, had been given to him for that process of liquefaction.

(5) The consent of the Secretary of State under subsection (1) above may in any case be made subject to conditions which may, in particular, be framed by reference to the description or origin of the gas.

(6) In this section—

" offshore natural gas " means natural gas won under the authority of licences under the Petroleum (Production) Act 1934, as applied by

section 1(3) of the Continental Shelf Act 1964,   Sch. 3
but does not include gas derived from offshore 1964 c. 29.
crude otherwise than as a by-product of crude
stabilisation ;

" offshore crude " means crude liquid petroleum won
under such authority ;

" crude stabilisation " means the treating of offshore
crude to enable it to be safely stored or transported.".

(2) In section 17(1) of that Act for the words " 10 or " there shall
be substituted the words " 9 or ".

The Sex Discrimination (Northern Ireland) Order 1976

38. In section 13(5) of the Sex Discrimination (Northern Ireland) S.I. 1976/1042
Order 1976 (employment at establishment in Northern Ireland)— (N.I. 15).

(*a*) for the words from " exploration " to " natural resources "
there shall be substituted the words " any activity falling
within section 23(2) of the Oil and Gas (Enterprise) Act
1982 " ; and

(*b*) after " 1964 " there shall be inserted the words " or specified under section 22(5) of the Oil and Gas (Enterprise) Act
1982 ".

The Patents Act 1977

39. In section 132(4) of the Patents Act 1977 (application of Act) 1977 c. 37.
for the words from " in connection " to " resources " there shall be
substituted the words " or specified by Order under section 22(5) of
the Oil and Gas (Enterprise) Act 1982 in connection with any
activity falling within section 23(2) of that Act ".

The Employment Protection (Consolidation) Act 1978

40.—(1) For subsection (2) of section 137 of the Employment 1978 c. 44.
Protection (Consolidation) Act 1978 (extension of employment protection legislation) there shall be substituted the following subsection—

" (2) This section applies to employment for the purposes
of—

(*a*) any activities in the territorial waters of the United Kingdom ; or

(*b*) any activities which, if paragraphs (*a*) and (*d*) of subsection
(6) of section 23 of the Oil and Gas (Enterprise) Act 1982
(application of civil law to certain offshore activities) were
omitted, would nevertheless fall within subsection (2) of that
section."

(2) Subsection (5) of that section shall be omitted.

N 4

The Wages Councils Act 1979

41.—(1) For subsection (2) of section 27 of the Wages Councils Act 1979 (extension of Act) there shall be substituted the following subsection—

" (2) This section applies to employment for the purposes of—

(*a*) any activities in the territorial waters of the United Kingdom ; or

(*b*) any activities which, if paragraphs (*a*) and (*d*) of subsection (6) of section 23 of the Oil and Gas (Enterprise) Act 1982 (application of civil law to certain offshore activities) were omitted, would nevertheless fall within subsection (2) of that section ".

(2) Subsection (5) of that section shall be omitted.

The Civil Jurisdiction and Judgments Act 1982

42. In paragraph 9 of Schedule 5 to the Civil Jurisdiction and Judgments Act 1982 (proceedings excluded from Schedule 4 to that Act) for the words " section 3 of the Continental Shelf Act 1964 " there shall be substituted the words " section 23 of the Oil and Gas (Enterprise) Act 1982 ".

43. In paragraph 10 of Schedule 9 to that Act (proceedings excluded from Schedule 8 to that Act) for the words " section 3 of the Continental Shelf Act 1964 " there shall be substituted the words " section 23 of the Oil and Gas (Enterprise) Act 1982 ".

The Social Security and Housing Benefits Act 1982

44. In section 22(3) of the Social Security and Housing Benefits Act 1982 (meaning of " continental shelf operations ") for the words from " the exploitation " onwards there shall be substituted the words " any activities which, if paragraphs (*a*) and (*d*) of subsection (6) of section 23 of the Oil and Gas (Enterprise) Act 1982 (application of civil law to certain offshore activities) were omitted, would nevertheless fall within subsection (2) of that section ".

SCHEDULE 4

REPEALS

Chapter	Short Title	Extent of Repeal
24 & 25 Geo. 5. c. 36.	The Petroleum (Production) Act 1934.	Section 4. Section 10(1).
1964 c. 29.	The Continental Shelf Act 1964.	Sections 2 and 3. Section 11(3).
1971 c. 61.	The Mineral Workings (Offshore Installations) Act 1971.	In section 6(2), the word " and " immediately following paragraph (c). Section 8. Section 9(5). Section 10. In section 12(1) the definitions of " underwater exploitation " and " underwater exploration ".
1972 c. 60.	The Gas Act 1972.	In section 7(2), the words " to dispose of any part of their undertaking or of any assets held by them " and the words " to dispose of any part of its undertaking or of any assets held by it ". Section 26. Section 28. Section 30(8). In Schedule 4— in paragraph 2(1), the proviso; in paragraph 10, in sub-paragraph (1) the words " Subject to sub-paragraph (2) below " and sub-paragraph (2); in paragraph 26 the words " or by regulations made under section 31 of this Act "; in paragraph 27 the words " or under any regulations made under section 31 of this Act "; and in paragraph 28 the words "and any regulations under section 31 of this Act ". In Schedule 6, paragraph 2.
1975 c. 22.	The Oil Taxation Act 1975.	In Schedule 3, in paragraph 2A(4) in paragraph (a) the words " or use " and " and to the use of gas supplied under it " and, in paragraph (b), the words " or use ".

Chapter	Short Title	Extent of Repeal
1975 c. 74.	The Petroleum and Sub-marine Pipe-lines Act 1975.	Section 1(3)(*c*). In section 2(4)(*d*) the words " or lend ". Section 3(3). Section 7(2). Section 14(4)(*b*) In section 22(1)(i), the words " connected with the pipe-line ". In section 26(3)(*a*), sub-paragraphs (i) and (ii). In section 40, subsections (1) and (4), in subsection (2), paragraphs (*a*) and (*c*) and, in subsection (3), paragraphs (*a*) and (*c*) and the words " and when " onwards. In section 41, subsections (1) and (2) and, in subsection (4), the words " or an order made by virtue of this section ". Section 44(1) to (4). In section 45(3) the words " or any such other installation as is mentioned in section 44(1) of this Act ".
1976 c. 76.	The Energy Act 1976.	Section 8. In section 18(2)(*a*) and (3)(*a*) the word " 8,".
1978 c. 44.	The Employment Protection (Consolidation) Act 1978.	Section 137(5).
1978 c. 46.	The Employment (Continental Shelf) Act 1978.	The whole Act.
1979 c. 2.	The Customs and Excise Management Act 1979.	In Schedule 4, in Part I, the entry relating to the Mineral Workings (Offshore Installations) Act 1971.
1979 c. 12.	The Wages Councils Act 1979.	Section 27(5).
1980 c. 37.	The Gas Act 1980.	In section 1(2) the words from " and nothing " to the end.

Social Security and Housing Benefits Act 1982

1982 CHAPTER 24

An Act to make provision for the payment of statutory sick pay by employers; to make new provision with respect to the grant of, and the payment of subsidies in respect of, rate rebates, rent rebates and rent allowances; to amend the law relating to social security and war pensions; to amend section 44 of the National Assistance Act 1948; and for connected purposes.

[28th June 1982]

BE IT ENACTED by the Queen's most Excellent Majesty, by and with the advice and consent of the Lords Spiritual and Temporal, and Commons, in this present Parliament assembled, and by the authority of the same, as follows:—

PART I

STATUTORY SICK PAY

1.—(1) Where an employee has a day of incapacity for work in relation to his contract of service with an employer, that employer shall, if the conditions set out in sections 2 to 4 of this Act are satisfied, be liable to make to him, in accordance with the following provisions of this Part, a payment (to be known as " statutory sick pay ") in respect of that day. Employer's liability.

(2) Any agreement shall be void to the extent that it purports—

    (*a*) to exclude, limit or otherwise modify any provision of this Part ; or

    (*b*) to require an employee to contribute (whether directly or indirectly) towards any costs incurred by his employer under this Part.

(3) For the purposes of this Part a day shall not be treated as a day of incapacity for work in relation to any contract of service unless on that day the employee concerned is, or is deemed in accordance with regulations to be, incapable by reason of some specific disease or bodily or mental disablement of doing work which he can reasonably be expected to do under that contract.

(4) In any case where an employee has more than one contract of service with the same employer the provisions of this Part shall, except in such cases as may be prescribed and subject to the following provisions of this Part, have effect as if the employer were a different employer in relation to each contract of service.

The qualifying conditions

Period of incapacity for work.

2.—(1) The first condition is that the day in question forms part of a period of incapacity for work.

(2) In this Part " period of incapacity for work " means any period of four or more consecutive days, each of which is a day of incapacity for work in relation to the contract of service in question.

(3) Any two periods of incapacity for work which are separated by a period of not more than two weeks shall be treated as a single period of incapacity for work.

(4) No day of the week shall be disregarded in calculating any period of consecutive days for the purposes of this section.

(5) A day may be a day of incapacity for work in relation to a contract of service, and so form part of a period of incapacity for work, notwithstanding that—

    (*a*) it falls before the making of the contract or after the contract expires or is brought to an end ; or

    (*b*) it is not a day on which the employee concerned would be required by that contract to be available for work.

Period of entitlement.

3.—(1) The second condition is that the day in question falls within a period which is, as between the employee and his employer, a period of entitlement.

(2) For the purposes of this Part a period of entitlement, as between an employee and his employer, is a period beginning with the commencement of a period of incapacity for work and ending with whichever of the following first occurs—

    (*a*) the termination of that period of incapacity for work ;

    (*b*) the day on which the employee reaches, as against the employer concerned, his maximum entitlement to statutory sick pay (determined in accordance with section 5 of this Act) ;

(c) the day on which the employee's contract of service with the employer concerned expires or is brought to an end ;

(d) in the case of an employee who is, or has been, pregnant, the day immediately preceding the beginning of the disqualifying period.

(3) Schedule 1 to this Act has effect for the purpose of specifying circumstances in which a period of entitlement does not arise in relation to a particular period of incapacity for work.

(4) A period of entitlement as between an employee and an employer of his may also be, or form part of, a period of entitlement as between him and another employer of his.

(5) Regulations may provide, in relation to prescribed cases, for a period of entitlement to end otherwise than in accordance with subsection (2) above.

(6) In a case where the employee's contract of service first takes effect on a day which falls within a period of incapacity for work, the period of entitlement begins with that day.

(7) Regulations shall make provision as to an employer's liability under this Part to pay statutory sick pay to an employee in any case where the employer's contract of service with that employee has been brought to an end by the employer solely, or mainly, for the purpose of avoiding liability for statutory sick pay.

(8) Subsection (2)(d) above does not apply in relation to an employee who has been pregnant if her pregnancy terminated, before the beginning of the disqualifying period, otherwise than by confinement.

(9) In this section—

" confinement " has the same meaning as in section 23 of the principal Act ;

" disqualifying period " means the period of eighteen weeks beginning with the eleventh week before the expected week of confinement ; and

" expected week of confinement " has the same meaning as in section 22 of the principal Act.

4.—(1) The third condition is that the day in question is a qualifying day. Qualifying days.

(2) The days which are, for the purposes of this Part, to be qualifying days as between an employee and an employer of his (that is to say those days of the week on which he is required by his contract of service with that employer to be available for work or which are chosen to reflect the terms of that contract)

shall be such day, or days, as may be agreed between the employee and his employer or, failing such agreement, determined in accordance with regulations.

(3) In any case where qualifying days are determined by agreement between an employee and his employer there shall, in each week (beginning with Sunday), be at least one qualifying day.

(4) A day which is a qualifying day as between an employee and an employer of his may also be a qualifying day as between him and another employer of his.

Limitations on entitlement, etc.

Limitations on entitlement. **5.**—(1) Statutory sick pay shall not be payable for the first three qualifying days in any period of entitlement.

(2) An employee shall not be entitled, as against any one employer, to an aggregate amount of statutory sick pay in respect of any one period of entitlement, or tax year, which exceeds his maximum entitlement.

(3) The maximum entitlement as against any one employer is reached on the day on which the amount to which the employee has become entitled by way of statutory sick pay during the period of entitlement in question or, as the case may be, the aggregate amount to which he has become so entitled during the tax year in question first reaches or passes the entitlement limit.

(4) The entitlement limit is an amount equal to eight times the appropriate weekly rate set out in section 7 of this Act.

(5) Regulations may make provision for calculating the entitlement limit in any case where an employee's entitlement to statutory sick pay is calculated by reference to different weekly rates in the same tax year or period of entitlement.

Notification of incapacity for work. **6.**—(1) Regulations shall prescribe the manner in which, and the time within which, notice of any day of incapacity for work is to be given by or on behalf of an employee to his employer.

(2) An employer who would, apart from this section, be liable to pay an amount of statutory sick pay to an employee in respect of a qualifying day (the " day in question ") shall be entitled to withhold payment of that amount if—

    (*a*) the day in question is one in respect of which he has not been duly notified in accordance with regulations under subsection (1) above ; or

(b) he has not been so notified in respect of any of the first three qualifying days in a period of entitlement (a " waiting day ") and the day in question is the first qualifying day in that period of entitlement in respect of which the employer is not entitled to withhold payment—

    (i) by virtue of paragraph (a) above ; or

    (ii) in respect of an earlier waiting day by virtue of this paragraph.

(3) Where an employer withholds any amount of statutory sick pay under this section—

    (a) the period of entitlement in question shall not be affected ; and

    (b) for the purposes of calculating his maximum entitlement in accordance with section 5 of this Act, the employee shall not be taken to have become entitled to the amount so withheld.

Rate of payment, etc.

7.—(1) Statutory sick pay shall be payable by an employer at the weekly rate of— Rate of payment.

    (a) £37, in a case where the employee's normal weekly earnings under his contract of service with that employer are not less than £60 ;

    (b) £31, in a case where those earnings are less than £60 but not less than £45 ; or

    (c) £25, in any other case.

(2) The amount of statutory sick pay payable by any one employer in respect of any day shall be the weekly rate applicable on that day divided by the number of days which are, in the week (beginning with Sunday) in which that day falls, qualifying days as between that employer and the employee concerned.

(3) The Secretary of State shall in the tax year 1982-1983, and in each subsequent tax year, review the sums specified in subsection (1)(a), (b) and (c) above for the purpose of determining whether they have retained their value in relation to the general level of prices obtaining in Great Britain.

(4) For the purposes of any such review the Secretary of State shall estimate the general level of prices in such manner as he thinks fit.

(5) Following any such review the Secretary of State may, in the tax year in which the review is carried out, prepare and lay before Parliament the draft of an order increasing one or more of the sums by such amount as he considers appropriate.

(6) If a draft order laid before Parliament in pursuance of this section is approved by resolution of each House, the Secretary of State shall make an order in the form of the draft.

(7) If on a review under this section the Secretary of State concludes that the general level of prices in Great Britain has risen during the period under review, but decides—

> (*a*) not to prepare and lay before Parliament the draft of an order increasing one or more of the sums ; or
>
> (*b*) to prepare, and so lay, the draft of an order which provides for no increase in any one or more of the sums, or for an increase in any of them which differs from the appropriate amount ;

he shall, unless in his opinion the amount by which that general level has risen, or, as the case may be, the amount by which an increase differs from the appropriate amount, is inconsiderable, lay before Parliament a report explaining his reasons for so deciding.

(8) If on a review under this section the Secretary of State concludes that the general level of prices in Great Britain has not risen during the period under review but decides to prepare and lay before Parliament the draft of an order increasing one or more of the sums, he shall lay before Parliament a report explaining his reasons for so deciding.

(9) In subsection (7) above " appropriate amount " means the amount which would, in the opinion of the Secretary of State, reflect the amount by which the general level of prices in Great Britain has risen during the period under review.

(10) A draft order prepared under subsection (5) above shall be framed so as to bring the increases in the sums to which it relates into force on the first day of the tax year beginning after the tax year in which the order is laid before Parliament in draft ; and shall make such transitional provision as the Secretary of State considers expedient in respect of periods of entitlement running at that date.

8.—(1) Regulations may prescribe the manner in which statutory sick pay may, and may not, be paid.

(2) Regulations may prescribe, in relation to any case where—

> (*a*) a decision has been made by an insurance officer, local tribunal or Commissioner in proceedings under this Part that an employee is entitled to an amount of statutory sick pay ; and
>
> (*b*) the time for bringing an appeal against the decision has expired and either—
>
> > (i) no such appeal has been brought ; or

(ii) such an appeal has been brought and has been finally disposed of ;

the time within which that amount of statutory sick pay is to be paid.

(3) Regulations may make provision—

(a) enabling a person to be appointed to exercise, on behalf of an employee who may be or become unable for the time being to act, any right or power which the employee may be entitled to exercise under this Part ;

(b) authorising a person so appointed to receive and deal with, on behalf of the employee, any sum payable by way of statutory sick pay ;

(c) in connection with an employee's death—

(i) enabling proceedings on a question as to, or arising under this Part in connection with, entitlement to statutory sick pay to be begun or continued in his name ;

(ii) authorising payment or distribution of statutory sick pay to or amongst persons claiming as his personal representatives, legatees, next of kin, or creditors (or, in any case where a deceased employed earner was illegitimate, to or amongst others) ; and

(iii) dispensing with strict proof of the title of persons so claiming ; and

(d) adjusting amounts payable by way of statutory sick pay so as to avoid fractional amounts or facilitate computation.

(4) In subsection (3)(c)(ii) above " next of kin " means the persons who would take beneficially (or who, in Scotland, would be entitled to the moveable estate of the deceased) on an intestacy.

9.—(1) Regulations shall make provision—

(a) entitling, except in prescribed circumstances, any employer who has made a payment of statutory sick pay to recover the amount so paid by making one or more deductions from his contributions payments ; and

(b) for the payment, in prescribed circumstances, by or on behalf of the Secretary of State of sums to employers who are unable so to recover the whole, or any part, of any payments of statutory sick pay which they have made.

Recovery by employers of amounts paid by way of statutory sick pay.

(2) In subsection (1)(*a*) above, " contributions payments ", in relation to an employer, means any payments (other than payments arising under the National Insurance Surcharge Act 1976) which the employer is required, by or under any enactment, to make in discharge of any liability in respect of primary or secondary Class 1 contributions.

(3) Regulations under this section may, in particular,—

(*a*) require employers who have made payments of statutory sick pay to furnish to the Secretary of State such documents and information, at such times, as may be prescribed ; and

(*b*) provide for any deduction made in accordance with the regulations to be disregarded for prescribed purposes.

(4) The power to make regulations conferred by paragraph 5 of Schedule 1 to the principal Act (power to combine collection of contributions with collection of income tax) shall include power to make such provision as the Secretary of State considers expedient in consequence of any provision made by or under this section.

(5) Provision made in regulations under paragraph 5 of Schedule 1, by virtue of subsection (4) above, may in particular require the inclusion—

(*a*) in returns, certificates and other documents ; or

(*b*) in any other form of record ;

which the regulations require to be kept or produced or to which those regulations otherwise apply, of such particulars relating to statutory sick pay as may be prescribed by those regulations.

(6) Where, in accordance with any provision of regulations made under this section, an amount has been deducted from an employer's contributions payments, the amount so deducted shall (except in such cases as may be prescribed) be treated for the purposes of any provision made by or under any enactment in relation to primary or secondary Class 1 contributions as having been—

(*a*) paid (on such date as may be determined in accordance with the regulations) ; and

(*b*) received by the Secretary of State ;

towards discharging the liability mentioned in subsection (2) above.

(7) Any sums paid under regulations made by virtue of subsection (1)(*b*) above shall be paid out of the National Insurance Fund.

(8) Any employer who, in purporting to comply with any requirement imposed by regulations under this section—

   (*a*) produces or furnishes, or causes or knowingly allows to be produced or furnished, any document or information which he knows to be false in a material particular ; or

   (*b*) recklessly produces or furnishes any document or information which is false in a material particular ;

shall be guilty of an offence.

(9) A person guilty of an offence under subsection (8) above shall be liable, on summary conviction—

   (*a*) in the case of an offence under paragraph (*a*), to a fine not exceeding £1,000 or to imprisonment for a term of not more than three months or to both; or

   (*b*) in the case of an offence under paragraph (*b*), to a fine not exceeding £500.

(10) Subsections (8) and (9) above shall apply, in place of the provision made by section 98(2) of the Taxes Management Act 1970 c. 9. 1970 (penalties for providing false information etc.) as applied by paragraph 5(2) of Schedule 1 to the principal Act, in relation to such requirements of the regulations made under paragraph 5 of Schedule 1 by virtue of subsection (4) above as may be specified in those regulations.

Relationship with benefits and other payments, etc.

10. Schedule 2 to this Act has effect with respect to the Relationship relationship between statutory sick pay and certain benefits with benefits and payments and for the purpose of modifying other enact- and other ments. payments, etc.

Determination of questions

11.—(1) Any question arising under any provision of this Determination Part, or of regulations under this Part, as to— of questions by

   (*a*) whether a person is, or was, an employee or employer Secretary of of another ; State.

   (*b*) whether an employer is entitled to make any deduction from his contributions payments, in accordance with regulations under section 9 of this Act ;

   (*c*) whether a payment falls to be made to an employer in accordance with those regulations ;

   (*d*) the amount that falls to be so deducted or paid ; or

   (*e*) whether two or more employers or two or more contracts of service are, by virtue of regulations made under section 26(5) of this Act, to be treated as one ;

shall be determined by the Secretary of State on a reference to him under this section made in accordance with regulations.

(2) Regulations under subsection (1) above may, in particular—

(*a*) provide for questions to be referred to the Secretary of State under this section only by prescribed persons or classes of person ; and

(*b*) make provision as to the manner in which, and time within which, references are to be made.

(3) The Secretary of State may, if he thinks fit, before determining any question under this section, appoint a person to hold an inquiry into, and to report on, the question or any matter arising in connection with it.

(4) A question of law arising in connection with the determination by the Secretary of State of any question under this section may, if he thinks fit, be referred for decision to the appropriate court, that is to say the High Court or, in Scotland, the Court of Session.

(5) Any person aggrieved by the decision of the Secretary of State on any such question of law which is not so referred may appeal from that decision to the appropriate court.

(6) If the Secretary of State determines to refer any question of law to the appropriate court, he shall give notice in writing of his intention to do so to any person appearing to him to be concerned with that question.

(7) On any such reference or appeal—

(*a*) the Secretary of State shall be entitled to appear and be heard ;

(*b*) the court may order him to pay the costs (in Scotland, the expenses) of any other person, whether or not the decision is in that other person's favour and whether or not the Secretary of State has appeared on the reference or appeal ;

(*c*) the decision of the court shall be final.

(8) Rules of court may include provision for regulating references and appeals under this section and for limiting the time within which such appeals may be brought.

Determination by insurance officer or local tribunal.
12.—(1) Any question arising under any provision of this Part, or of regulations under this Part, as to, or in connection with, entitlement to statutory sick pay shall, unless it is for determination—

(*a*) by the Secretary of State under section 11 of this Act ; or

(*b*) by a local tribunal on a reference under subsection (2) or (4) below ;

be determined by an insurance officer on a reference to him PART I
under this subsection.

(2) Regulations may prescribe cases in which any such question
is to be determined by a local tribunal on a reference to the tribunal under this subsection.

(3) An insurance officer to whom a question is referred under
subsection (1) above shall, so far as is practicable, dispose of it
within fourteen days of the making of the reference.

(4) An insurance officer may, instead of determining a question
referred to him under subsection (1) above, refer it to a local
tribunal.

(5) Any reference under this section shall be made in accordance with regulations.

(6) Regulations under subsection (5) above may, in particular—

> (a) provide for questions to be referred under this section
> only by the Secretary of State or prescribed persons or
> classes of person ; and

> (b) make provision as to the manner in which, and time
> within which, references are to be made.

(7) Where an insurance officer refers a question to a local
tribunal under subsection (4) above, notice of the reference shall
be given in writing by the Secretary of State to those appearing
to him to be concerned with the question.

(8) Where an insurance officer determines a question referred
to him under subsection (1) above, notice—

> (a) of the insurance officer's decision and of the reasons for
> it ; and

> (b) of the right of appeal given by section 13(1) of this Act ;

shall be given in writing by the Secretary of State to those
appearing to him to be concerned with the question.

13.—(1) Where an insurance officer has determined a question Appeals.
referred to him under section 12(1) of this Act any person
aggrieved by his decision may appeal to a local tribunal ; but
where—

> (a) there has arisen a question for determination by the
> Secretary of State under section 11 of this Act ;

> (b) that question has been determined ; and

> (c) the insurance officer certifies that the decision on that
> question is the sole ground of his decision ;

no appeal lies under this section without leave of the chairman
of the local tribunal.

(2) Where a local tribunal has taken any decision in respect of a question referred to it under section 12(2) or (4) of this Act or on an appeal brought under subsection (1) above, an insurance officer or any person aggrieved by the decision may, subject to section 15 of the Social Security Act 1980 (leave required for appeal from local tribunal to Commissioner), appeal to a Commissioner.

(3) An appeal to a local tribunal under subsection (1) above shall be brought by giving notice of appeal at a local office before the expiry of the period of 28 days beginning with the date on which notice of the insurance officer's decision was given to the appellant in accordance with section 12(8) of this Act or within such further time as the chairman of the local tribunal may for good cause allow.

(4) An appeal to a Commissioner under subsection (2) above shall be brought by giving notice of appeal at a local office before the expiry of the period of three months beginning—

   (*a*) in a case where leave to appeal is required, with the date on which leave was given for the appeal ; or

   (*b*) in any other case, with the date on which notice of the tribunal's decision was given to the appellant ;

or within such further time as a Commissioner may for special reasons allow.

(5) A notice of appeal under subsection (3) or (4) above shall be in writing and shall contain a statement of the grounds upon which the appeal is made ; and regulations may provide for copies of the notice to be sent by the Secretary of State to prescribed persons.

Review of decisions.

14.—(1) Regulations may make provision for requiring or enabling, in prescribed circumstances—

   (*a*) the Secretary of State to review any determination of his under this Part ; and

   (*b*) an insurance officer or (on a reference from an insurance officer) a local tribunal to review any other determination under this Part, whether made by an insurance officer or by a local tribunal or Commissioner ;

and as to the consequences of any such review.

(2) Regulations under this section may in particular provide for any decision on a review carried out in accordance with the regulations to be subject to appeal in such circumstances and in such manner as may be prescribed.

15.—(1) If, in determining any question under this Part, it appears to an insurance officer that a question arises for deter-mination by the Secretary of State under section 11 of this Act the insurance officer shall refer that question to the Secretary of State for determination.

(2) An insurance officer may, in any case, postpone the refer-ence, or determination, of any question until any other question has been determined (whether by him or by a local tribunal or Commissioner).

(3) Subsections (1) and (2) above apply to a local tribunal and a Commissioner as they apply to an insurance officer except that a tribunal or Commissioner shall, instead of referring a question to the Secretary of State in accordance with subsection (1), direct it to be so referred by an insurance officer.

(4) Where a question for determination under this Part (other than one for determination by the Secretary of State under sec-tion 11) first arises in the course of an appeal to a local tribunal or Commissioner, the tribunal or Commissioner may proceed to determine the question notwithstanding that it has not been considered by an insurance officer.

(5) Regulations may make provision as to the procedure to be followed in connection with the determination of questions under this Part ; and any such regulations may, in particular, make any provision of a kind mentioned in Schedule 3 to this Act.

16.—(1) This section applies to any case where—

(*a*) a decision of an insurance officer, local tribunal or Commissioner in proceedings under this Part is that an employee is entitled to an amount of statutory sick pay ; and

(*b*) the requirements of regulations made under section 8(2) of this Act (time within which statutory sick pay to be paid) have not been satisfied in respect of the whole or any part of that amount.

(2) In a case to which this section applies—

(*a*) any amount payable in pursuance of the decision shall, if the county court so orders, be recoverable by execu-tion issued from the county court or otherwise as if it were payable under an order of that court ;

(*b*) the decision (or a copy of the decision certified by the person who, or chairman of the tribunal which, made it) may be enforced in like manner as an extract registered decree arbitral bearing a warrant for execu-tion issued by the sheriff court of any sheriffdom in Scotland.

(3) Regulations may, in relation to cases to which this section applies, make provision for payments to be made by the Secretary of State to employees in prescribed circumstances in connection with court fees (including sheriff officers' and messengers-at-arms' fees for doing diligence) incurred, or likely to be incurred, by those employees in seeking to enforce decisions by virtue of subsection (2) above.

(4) The regulations may, in particular, make provision for the recovery of payments made under the regulations from persons to whom such payments are made ; and any sum so recoverable may, without prejudice to any other method of recovery, be recovered by deduction from prescribed benefits (" benefits " having the meaning given by the regulations).

(5) Any payment made by the Secretary of State under the regulations shall be paid out of the National Insurance Fund, and any sums recovered by him under the regulations shall be paid into that Fund.

Provision of
information:
general.

17.—(1) Where the Secretary of State considers that it is reasonable for information held by him to be disclosed to an employer, for the purpose of enabling that employer to determine the duration of a period of entitlement in respect of an employee, or whether such a period exists, he may disclose the information to that employer.

(2) Any employee who claims to be entitled to statutory sick pay from his employer shall, if so required by his employer, provide such information as may reasonably be required for the purpose of determining the duration of the period of entitlement in question or whether a period of entitlement exists as between them.

(3) Where an employee asks an employer of his to provide him with a written statement, in respect of a period before the request is made, of one or more of the following—

(a) the days within that period which the employer regards as days in respect of which he is liable to pay statutory sick pay to that employee ;

(b) the reasons why the employer does not so regard the other days in that period ;

(c) the employer's opinion as to the amount of statutory sick pay to which the employee is entitled in respect of each of those days ;

the employer shall, to the extent to which the request was reasonable, comply with it within a reasonable time.

(4) Regulations may require employers to maintain such records in connection with statutory sick pay as may be prescribed and may provide for—

> (*a*) any person claiming to be entitled to statutory sick pay ; or
>
> (*b*) any other person who is a party to proceedings arising under this Part ;

to furnish to the Secretary of State, within a prescribed period, any information required for the determination of any question arising in connection therewith.

18.—(1) Regulations may make provision requiring an employer, in a case falling within subsection (3) below, to furnish information in connection with the making, by a person who is, or has been, an employee of that employer, of a claim for— Claims for sickness and other benefits: provision of information by employers.

> (*a*) sickness benefit ;
>
> (*b*) a maternity allowance ;
>
> (*c*) an invalidity pension ;
>
> (*d*) industrial injuries benefit ; or
>
> (*e*) a non-contributory invalidity pension.

(2) Regulations under this section shall prescribe—

> (*a*) the kind of information to be furnished in accordance with the regulations ;
>
> (*b*) the person to whom information of the prescribed kind is to be furnished ; and
>
> (*c*) the manner in which, and period within which, it is to be furnished.

(3) The cases are—

> (*a*) where, by virtue of paragraph 2 of Schedule 1 to this Act or of regulations made under paragraph 1 of that Schedule, a period of entitlement does not arise in relation to a period of incapacity for work ;
>
> (*b*) where a period of entitlement has come to an end but the period of incapacity for work which was running immediately before the period of entitlement came to an end continues ; and
>
> (*c*) where a period of entitlement has not come to an end but, on the assumption that—
>
>> (i) the period of incapacity for work in question continues to run for a prescribed period ; and
>>
>> (ii) there is no material change in circumstances,
>
> the period of entitlement will have ended on or before the end of the prescribed period.

PART I
Inspections.

1970 c. 55.
1976 c. 71.

Inspections and offences

19.—(1) Every appointment of an inspector under section 144 of the principal Act shall be an appointment for the purposes of this Part as well as for the purposes of the principal Act, the Family Income Supplements Act 1970, and the Supplementary Benefits Act 1976.

(2) Accordingly, the principal Act shall have effect as if—

    (*a*) in sections 144(2) to (5) and 145 references to that Act included references to this Part ; and

    (*b*) in section 145—

        (i) in subsection (1)(*b*) the reference to benefit included a reference to statutory sick pay ;

        (ii) in subsection (2)(*b*) the reference to any person who is or has been employing another included a reference to any person who is or has been an employer (within the meaning of this Part) ; and

        (iii) in subsection (2)(*e*) the reference to any person who is or has been liable to pay contributions included a reference to any person who is or has been an employee (within the meaning of this Part).

(3) The following provisions of sections 144 and 145 (which among other things relate to injuries and diseases and to contributions and premiums) shall not apply for the purposes of this Part—

    (*a*) in section 144, subsection (2)(*b*)(ii) and (*d*) and so much of subsection (2)(*c*) as relates to contributions and premiums ;

    (*b*) in section 145, subsection (1)(*a*).

Offences and
penalties.

20. Regulations may provide for contravention of, or failure to comply with, any provision contained in regulations made under section 8(2), 9(3)(*a*), 17(4) or 18 of this Act to be an offence under this Part and for the recovery, on summary conviction of any such offence, of penalties not exceeding—

    (*a*) for any one offence, £200 ; or

    (*b*) for an offence of continuing any such contravention or failure after conviction, £20 for each day on which it is so continued.

General
provisions
as to
prosecutions.

21.—(1) Proceedings in England and Wales for an offence under this Part shall not be instituted except—

    (*a*) by or with the consent of the Secretary of State ; or

    (*b*) by an inspector or other officer authorised for that purpose by special or general directions of the Secretary of State.

(2) An inspector or other officer so authorised may, although not of counsel or a solicitor, prosecute or conduct before a magistrates' court any proceedings for such an offence.

(3) Notwithstanding any enactment prescribing the period within which summary proceedings may be commenced, proceedings for an offence under this Part may in England and Wales be commenced at any time within whichever of the following periods expires the later—

(a) the period of three months from the date on which evidence, sufficient in the opinion of the Secretary of State to justify a prosecution for the offence, comes to his knowledge ;

(b) the period of 12 months after the commission of the offence.

(4) In Scotland, proceedings for an offence under this Part may be commenced at any time within whichever of the following periods expires the later—

(a) the period of three months from the date on which evidence, sufficient in the opinion of the Secretary of State to justify a report to the Lord Advocate with a view to consideration of the question of prosecution, comes to the knowledge of the Secretary of State ;

(b) the period of 12 months after the commission of the offence.

Section 331(3) of the Criminal Procedure (Scotland) Act 1975 (time limits) shall apply for the purposes of this subsection as it applies for the purposes of that section. 1975 c. 21.

(5) For the purposes of subsections (3) and (4) above, a certificate purporting to be signed by or on behalf of the Secretary of State as to the date on which the evidence in question came to his knowledge is conclusive evidence of the date on which it did so.

(6) In proceedings for an offence under this Part, the wife or husband of the accused—

(a) is competent to give evidence, whether for or against the accused ;

(b) is not compellable either to give evidence or, in giving evidence, to disclose any communication made to her or him by the accused during the marriage.

(7) Where an offence under this Part which has been committed by a body corporate is proved to have been committed with the consent or connivance of, or to be attributable to any neglect on the part of, a director, manager, secretary or other similar officer of the body corporate, or any person who was purporting to act in any such capacity, he, as well as the body

corporate, shall be guilty of that offence and be liable to be proceeded against accordingly.

Where the affairs of a body corporate are managed by its members, this subsection applies in relation to the acts and defaults of a member in connection with his functions of management as if he were a director of the body corporate.

1965 c. 20.

(8) For the purposes of section 1 of the Criminal Evidence Act 1965 (admissibility of statements contained in certain business records) as it applies in relation to proceedings for any offence under this Part " business " shall include the activities of the Secretary of State.

Miscellaneous

Modification of provisions of Part I.

22.—(1) The Secretary of State may make regulations modifying provisions of this Part, in such manner as he thinks proper, in their application to any person who is, has been or is to be—

(a) employed on board any ship, vessel, hovercraft or aircraft ;

(b) outside Great Britain at any prescribed time or in any prescribed circumstances ; or

(c) in prescribed employment in connection with continental shelf operations.

(2) Regulations under subsection (1) above may in particular provide—

(a) for any provision of this Part to apply to any such person, notwithstanding that it would not otherwise apply ;

(b) for any provision of this Part not to apply to any such person, notwithstanding that it would otherwise apply ;

(c) for excepting any such person from the application of any such provision where he neither is domiciled nor has a place of residence in any part of Great Britain ;

(d) for the taking of evidence, for the purposes of the determination of any question arising under this Part, in a country or territory outside Great Britain, by a British consular official or such other person as may be prescribed.

1964 c. 29.

(3) " Continental shelf operations " means the exploitation of resources mentioned in section 1(1) of the Continental Shelf Act 1964 or the exploration of the seabed and subsoil in any area designated under section 1(7) of that Act.

Statutory sick pay to count as remuneration for principal Act.

23. For the purposes of section 3 of the principal Act (meaning of " earnings "), any sums paid to, or for the benefit of, a person in satisfaction (whether in whole or in part) of any entitlement of his to statutory sick pay shall be treated as remuneration derived from an employed earner's employment.

24.—(1) Regulations may make provision for the payment to an employer, by the Secretary of State and in prescribed circumstances, of an amount calculated in accordance with the regulations in any case where—

  (a) a payment purporting to be a payment of statutory sick pay (the " payment wrongly made ") has been made by that employer to a person (the " recipient ") ; and

  (b) that employer was not liable to make that payment under this Part.

(2) Regulations may make provision, in relation to such a case, for the recovery by the Secretary of State from the recipient, in prescribed circumstances, of an amount calculated in accordance with the regulations.

(3) Regulations under this section may make such incidental and supplemental provision in relation to any payment made, or amount recovered, by the Secretary of State under the regulations as he considers expedient and may, in particular, provide—

  (a) for any such payment to be treated as discharging, or in prescribed circumstances as partially discharging, any liability of the recipient to repay to the employer the payment wrongly made ;

  (b) for any such payment to be treated, in prescribed circumstances, as a payment to the recipient of a prescribed benefit (" benefit " having the meaning given by the regulations).

(4) In this section " employer " includes a person believing himself to be an employer of the recipient in question.

(5) Any payment made by the Secretary of State in accordance with regulations under this section shall be paid out of the National Insurance Fund and any amount recovered by him in accordance with the regulations shall be paid by him into that Fund.

25.—(1) No obligation as to secrecy imposed by statute or otherwise on persons employed in relation to the Inland Revenue shall prevent information obtained in connection with the assessment or collection of income tax under Schedule E from being disclosed to the Secretary of State, or the Department of Health and Social Services for Northern Ireland, or to an officer of either of them authorised to receive such information, in connection with the operation of this Part or of any corresponding enactment of Northern Ireland legislation.

(2) Subsection (1) above extends only to disclosure by or under the authority of the Inland Revenue ; and information

which is the subject of disclosure to any person by virtue of that subsection shall not be further disclosed to any other person, except where the further disclosure is made—

>   (*a*) to a person to whom disclosure could by virtue of this section have been made by or under the authority of the Inland Revenue ; or

>   (*b*) for the purposes of any proceedings (civil or criminal) in connection with the operation of this Part or of any corresponding enactment of Northern Ireland legislation.

Interpretation of Part I and supplementary provisions.

26.—(1) In this Part—

" Commissioner " means a Social Security Commissioner and includes a tribunal of Commissioners constituted under section 116 of the principal Act ;

" contract of service " (except in paragraph (*a*) of the definition below of " employee ") includes any arrangement providing for the terms of appointment of an employee ;

" employed earner's employment " has the same meaning as in the principal Act ;

" employee " means a person who is—

>   (*a*) gainfully employed in Great Britain either under a contract of service or in an office (including elective office) with emoluments chargeable to income tax under Schedule E ; and

>   (*b*) over the age of 16 ;

but subject to regulations, which may provide for cases where any such person is not to be treated as an employee for the purposes of this Part and for cases where any person who would not otherwise be an employee for those purposes is to be treated as an employee for those purposes ;

" employer ", in relation to an employee and a contract of service of his, means the secondary contributor (within the meaning of section 4 of the principal Act) in relation to any earnings paid, or to be paid, to or for the benefit of that employee under that contract ;

" insurance officer " means an officer appointed under section 97(1) of the principal Act ;

" local office " means any office appointed by the Secretary of State as a local office for the purposes of this Part ;

" local tribunal " means a tribunal established under section 97(2) of the principal Act ;

" maternity allowance " means an allowance payable under section 22 of the principal Act ;

" pensionable age " means, in the case of a man, 65 or, in
the case of a woman, 60 ;

" period of entitlement " has the meaning given by section
3 of this Act ;

" period of incapacity for work " has the meaning given
by section 2 of this Act ;

" period of interruption of employment " has the same
meaning as it has in the principal Act by virtue of
section 17(1)(*d*) ;

" prescribed " means prescribed by regulations ;

" primary Class 1 contributions " and " secondary Class 1
contributions " have the same meaning as in the
principal Act ;

" qualifying day " has the meaning given by section 4 of this
Act ;

" week " means any period of seven days.

(2) For the purposes of this Part an employee's normal
weekly earnings shall, subject to subsection (4) below, be taken
to be his average weekly earnings in the relevant period under
his contract of service with the employer in question.

(3) For the purposes of subsection (2) above, the expressions
" earnings " and " relevant period " shall have the meaning given
to them by regulations.

(4) In such cases as may be prescribed an employee's normal
weekly earnings shall be calculated in accordance with regulations.

(5) Without prejudice to any other power to make regulations
under this Part, regulations may specify cases in which, for the
purposes of this Part or of such provisions of this Part as may
be prescribed—

(*a*) two or more employers are to be treated as one ;

(*b*) two or more contracts of service in respect of which the
same person is an employee are to be treated as one.

(6) Regulations may provide for periods of work which begin
on one day and finish on the following day to be treated, for
purposes of this Part, as falling solely within one or other of
those days.

(7) In this Part any reference to Great Britain includes a
reference to the territorial waters of the United Kingdom adjacent
to Great Britain.

27.—(1) Subject to subsection (2) below, the provisions of this Crown
Part apply in relation to persons employed by or under the employment.
Crown as they apply in relation to persons employed otherwise
than by or under the Crown.

(2) The provisions of this Part do not apply in relation to persons serving as members of Her Majesty's forces, in their capacity as such.

PART II

HOUSING BENEFITS

The statutory schemes.

28.—(1) The Secretary of State may by regulations make, with the consent of the Treasury—

(*a*) a scheme (in this Part referred to as " the statutory rate rebate scheme ") for the grant, by rating authorities to persons who occupy as their homes dwellings in respect of which they are liable to make payments by way of rates (whether to those authorities or to other persons), of rebates from those payments (in this Part referred to as rate rebates) ;

(*b*) a scheme (in this Part referred to as " the statutory rent rebate scheme ") for the grant, by housing authorities to persons who occupy as their homes dwellings in respect of which they are liable to make to those authorities payments otherwise than by way of rates, of rebates from those payments (in this Part referred to as rent rebates) ; and

(*c*) a scheme (in this Part referred to as " the statutory rent allowance scheme ") for the grant, by local authorities to persons who occupy as their homes dwellings in the areas of those authorities in respect of which they are liable to make payments not falling within paragraph (*a*) or (*b*) above, of allowances towards those payments (in this Part referred to as rent allowances),

being (in each case) rebates or allowances determined in accordance with the provisions of the scheme by reference to the needs and resources of those persons.

(2) Regulations under subsection (1) above may in particular provide—

(*a*) for treating any person who, without being liable to do so, makes payments in respect of a dwelling as if he were so liable ;

(*b*) for treating any person who occupies a dwelling otherwise than as his home as if he occupied it as his home ;

(*c*) for treating any one or more of the joint occupiers of a dwelling as if he or they were the only occupiers ;

(d) for treating as included in a dwelling any land used
for the purposes of the dwelling ;

(e) for enabling any rate rebate or rent allowance to be
so applied as to discharge, in whole or in part, the
liability to which it relates ;

(f) for enabling any rebate or allowance granted to a person not entitled to it to be recovered by the authority
or the Secretary of State, and to be so recovered by
deduction from a prescribed benefit ; and

(g) for enabling any person to exercise a discretion in dealing with any matter ;

and may make such transitional provision as appears to the
Secretary of State to be necessary or expedient.

(3) References in this section to payments in respect of dwellings do not include mortgage payments or, in Scotland, payments
under heritable securities but, subject to that, they include any
payments in respect of dwellings including, in particular—

(a) payments under tenancies of dwellings or licences or, in
Scotland, rights or permissions to occupy dwellings ;
and

(b) payments for services performed or facilities provided
for, or rights made available to, the occupiers of dwellings.

(4) In this section—

" dwelling " means any residential accommodation, whether
or not consisting of the whole or part of a building
and whether or not comprising separate and self-
contained premises ;

" prescribed " means specified in or determined in accordance with regulations.

(5) The provisions of this section and section 30 below
have effect in substitution for the following enactments, namely—

(a) Part II of and Schedules 3 and 4 to the Housing Finance   1972 c. 47.
Act 1972, sections 11 to 14 of the Local Government   1974 c. 7.
Act 1974 and section 20 of the Development of Rural   1976 c. 75.
Wales Act 1976 (which make provision, in relation
to England and Wales, for rent rebates, rent allowances
and rate rebates) ; and

(b) Part II of and Schedules 2 and 3 to the Housing   1972 c. 46.
(Financial Provisions) (Scotland) Act 1972 and sections
112 to 114 of the Local Government (Scotland) Act   1973 c. 65.
1973 (which make corresponding provision in relation
to Scotland) ;

and those enactments are accordingly repealed.

Part I   O

29.—(1) In each review period the Secretary of State shall review, for the purpose of determining whether they have retained their value, both the main and housing elements of any needs allowances specified in regulations made under section 28(1) above.

(2) Following the reviews for any review period the Secretary of State may prepare and lay before Parliament a draft of regulations under section 28(1) above increasing one or more needs allowances by such amount as he considers appropriate ; and any draft regulations so prepared shall be framed so as to bring the increases in the needs allowances to which they relate into force before the end of the review period.

(3) If draft regulations laid before Parliament in pursuance of this section are approved by a resolution of each House, the Secretary of State shall make regulations in the form of the draft.

(4) If after completing the reviews for any review period the Secretary of State considers that the main or housing elements of any needs allowances will not have retained their value at the end of that period, but decides—

(a) not to prepare and lay before Parliament a draft of regulations increasing one or more of those allowances ; or

(b) to prepare and so lay the draft of regulations which provide for no increase in any one or more of those allowances, or for an increase in any of them which is less than the appropriate amount,

he shall, unless in his opinion the amount by which those elements will not have retained their value or, as the case may be, the amount by which the increase is less than the appropriate amount is inconsiderable, lay before Parliament a report explaining his reasons for so deciding.

(5) In this section—

" appropriate amount ", in relation to a needs allowance, means the amount by which the allowance would, in the opinion of the Secretary of State, have to be increased in order to restore the value at the end of the review period of such of its main and housing elements as, in his opinion, will not have retained their value at the end of that period ;

" housing element " and " main element ", in relation to a needs allowance, mean respectively—

(a) the part of that allowance which, in the opinion of the Secretary of State, represents housing costs ; and

(b) the remaining part of that allowance ;

" needs allowance " means an amount to be allowed, in the determination of rebates or allowances, for the needs of an occupier and (where appropriate) the needs of any other person or persons whose needs fall to be aggregated with his ;

" prices " does not include housing costs ;

" review period " means a period of twelve months ending with 30th November in the year 1983 or any subsequent year ;

" value "—

(*a*) in relation to the main element of a needs allowance, means value in relation to the general level of prices obtaining in Great Britain ; and

(*b*) in relation to the housing element of such an allowance, means value in relation to the general level of housing costs so obtaining.

(6) For the purpose of carrying out the reviews for any review period the Secretary of State shall estimate the general level of prices obtaining in Great Britain and the general level of housing costs so obtaining in such manner as he thinks fit.

30.—(1) Subject to the following provisions of this section—   Local schemes.

(*a*) a rating authority may by resolution provide that, in its application to the authority, the statutory rate rebate scheme shall have effect with the modifications specified in the resolution ;

(*b*) a housing authority may by resolution provide that, in its application to the authority, the statutory rent rebate scheme shall have effect with the modifications specified in the resolution ; and

(*c*) a local authority may by resolution provide that, in its application to the authority, the statutory rent allowance scheme shall have effect with the modifications specified in the resolution ;

and in this Part " local rate rebate scheme ", " local rent rebate scheme " and " local rent allowance scheme " mean (in each case) the corresponding statutory scheme as so modified.

(2) The power to modify a statutory scheme under this section shall be subject to any exceptions specified in the scheme ; but nothing in such a scheme shall preclude the making of modifications which secure that, in determining the resources of any person (whether the occupier or any other person whose resources fall to be aggregated with his), any war disablement pension or war widow's pension payable to that person shall be disregarded.

In this subsection " war disablement pension " and " war widow's pension " have the same meanings as in the Pensioners' Payments and Social Security Act 1979.

(3) No modifications under this section shall be such that a person to whom the statutory scheme would otherwise apply receives a rebate or allowance less than that which he would have received under that scheme ; and where a local authority make modifications of either statutory rent scheme, they shall also make such modifications (if any) of the other statutory rent scheme as appear to them to correspond to those modifications.

(4) Modifications under this section shall be so framed as to secure that, in the estimate of the authority, the total of the rebates or allowances which will be granted by the authority under the local scheme in any year will not exceed the permitted total of rebates or allowances for that year.

(5) Modifications under this section may be revoked or varied by a further resolution of the authority.

(6) In relation to a local scheme, the permitted total of rebates or allowances for any year shall be an amount calculated, in the manner prescribed by regulations made by the Secretary of State with the consent of the Treasury, by reference to the rebates or allowances which, if—

(a) the local scheme had not been in force ; and

(b) the statutory scheme had had effect with such modifications (if any) as may be prescribed by the regulations,

would have been granted by the authority under the statutory scheme during that year.

Publicity for schemes.
31.—(1) Every authority granting rebates or allowances under a statutory or local scheme shall—

(a) take such steps as may appear to them appropriate for the purpose of securing that the provisions of the scheme come to the notice of any persons who may be entitled to a rebate or allowance under the scheme ;

(b) make copies of the scheme available for public inspection at their principal office at all reasonable hours without payment ; and

(c) in the case of a local scheme, furnish a copy to any person on payment of such reasonable sum as the authority may determine.

(2) If it appears to the Secretary of State that the steps taken by such an authority are inadequate for the purpose mentioned in subsection (1)(a) above, he may give to the authority directions requiring them to take such steps for that purpose as are specified in the directions.

32.—(1) For the initial year and each subsequent year the
Secretary of State shall pay out of money provided by Parliament—

    (*a*) a subsidy to be known as " rate rebate subsidy " to each
        rating authority ;

    (*b*) a subsidy to be known as " rent rebate subsidy " to each
        housing authority ; and

    (*c*) a subsidy to be known as " rent allowance subsidy " to
        each local authority.

(2) Subject to subsection (3) below, an authority's subsidy
for any year shall be of an amount calculated, in the manner
prescribed by an order made by the Secretary of State with the
consent of the Treasury, by reference to—

    (*a*) in the case of an authority granting rebates or allowances
        under the statutory scheme during that year or any part
        of it, the rebates or allowances so granted or, if the
        order so provides, the rebates or allowances which, if
        the scheme had had effect with the modifications
        prescribed by the order, would have been granted by
        the authority under the scheme during that year or, as
        the case may be, that part of it ;

    (*b*) in the case of an authority granting rebates or allowances
        under a local scheme during that year or any part of
        it, the rebates or allowances which, if—

           (i) the local scheme had not been in force ; and

           (ii) the statutory scheme had had effect with
        such modifications (if any) as may be prescribed by
        the order,

        would have been granted by the authority under the
        statutory scheme during that year or, as the case may
        be, that part of it ; and

    (*c*) in any case, such of the costs of administering rebates
        or allowances incurred by the authority during the
        year as may be determined in the manner prescribed
        by the order.

(3) The amount of an authority's subsidy for any year shall
not be less than the aggregate of—

    (*a*) in the case of an authority falling within paragraph (*a*)
        of subsection (2) above, 90 per cent. of the rebates or
        allowances mentioned in that paragraph ;

    (*b*) in the case of an authority falling within paragraph (*b*)
        of that subsection, 90 per cent. of the rebates or
        allowances mentioned in that paragraph ; and

    (*c*) in any case, the costs mentioned in paragraph (*c*) of that
        subsection.

(4) Rent rebate subsidy shall be payable—

(*a*) in the case of a local authority in England and Wales or the Greater London Council,—

(i) for the credit of their Housing Revenue Account to the extent that it is calculated by reference to Housing Revenue Account rebates and the costs of administering such rebates ; and

(ii) for the credit of their general rate fund to the extent that it is not so calculated :

(*b*) in the case of a local authority in Scotland, for the credit of their rent rebate account ;

(*c*) in the case of a new town corporation in England and Wales or the Development Board for Rural Wales, for the credit of their housing account ; and

(*d*) in the case of a new town corporation in Scotland or the Scottish Special Housing Association, for the credit of the account to which rent rebates granted by them are debited.

(5) Rent allowance subsidy shall be payable—

(*a*) in the case of a local authority in England and Wales, for the credit of their general rate fund ; and

(*b*) in the case of a local authority in Scotland, for the credit of their rent allowance account.

(6) In this section " initial year " means the period of twelve months ending with 31st March 1983.

(7) The provisions of this section and sections 33 and 34 below have effect in substitution for the following enactments, namely—

1974 c. 7.
1975 c. 6.
1976 c. 75.
1980 c. 51.

(*a*) section 8(1) of the Local Government Act 1974, section 3 of the Housing Rents and Subsidies Act 1975, section 19 of the Development of Rural Wales Act 1976 and section 117 of the Housing Act 1980 (which make provision, in relation to England and Wales, for rate rebate grants and rent rebate and rent allowance subsidies) ; and

1972 c. 46.
1973 c. 65.

(*b*) sections 5, 6 and 11 of the Housing (Financial Provisions) (Scotland) Act 1972 and section 115 of the Local Government (Scotland) Act 1973 (which make corresponding provision for Scotland) ;

and those enactments are accordingly repealed.

Administration
of subsidies.

33.—(1) Any subsidy under section 32 above shall be payable by the Secretary of State at such times and in such manner as the Treasury may direct, but subject to such conditions as to records, certificates, audit or otherwise as the Secretary of State may, with the approval of the Treasury, impose.

(2) Without prejudice to the generality of subsection (1) above, the making of any such payment shall be subject to the making of a claim for it in such form and containing such particulars as the Secretary of State may from time to time determine.

(3) The amount of any subsidy payable to an authority under section 32 above shall be calculated to the nearest pound, by disregarding an odd amount of 50 pence or less and by treating an odd amount exceeding 50 pence as a whole pound.

34.—(1) Every local authority and the Greater London Council shall make for each year a rate fund contribution to their Housing Revenue Account of an amount equal to the difference between so much of their rent rebate subsidy for the year as is credited to that Account and the total of the Housing Revenue Account rebates granted, and the costs of administering such rebates incurred, by the authority or Council during the year.

Rate fund contributions and rate support grant.

(2) If an order made by the Secretary of State with the consent of the Treasury so provides, the items mentioned in subsection (3) below, or such proportion thereof as may be calculated in the manner prescribed by the order, shall not count as relevant expenditure for the purposes of section 54 of the Local Government, Planning and Land Act 1980 (rate support grant).

1980 c. 65.

(3) The items referred to in subsection (2) above are—

(a) the costs of administering rate rebates incurred by a rating authority during any year ;

(b) the rate fund contribution under subsection (1) above made by a local authority or the Greater London Council for any year ;

(c) the costs of administering rent rebates (other than Housing Revenue Account rebates) incurred by a local authority or the Greater London Council during any year ;

(d) the rent allowances granted, and the costs of administering such allowances incurred, by a local authority during any year.

(4) In this section " rate fund contribution " means a contribution made by a local authority or the Greater London Council out of their general rate fund.

(5) This section extends to England and Wales only.

35.—(1) In this Part, unless the context otherwise requires—

" housing authority " means a local authority, a new town corporation, the Greater London Council, the Scottish Special Housing Association or the Development Board for Rural Wales ;

" Housing Revenue Account rebate ", in relation to a local authority in England and Wales or the Greater London Council, means a rent rebate granted to a tenant of a Housing Revenue Account dwelling (within the meaning of the Housing Finance Act 1972) of that authority or Council and includes, unless the context otherwise requires,—

1972 c. 47.

    (*a*) a rent rebate which, on the assumptions stated in section 32(2) above, would have been granted to such a tenant ; and

    (*b*) a rent rebate which is to be so granted ;

" local authority " means—

    (*a*) in relation to England and Wales, the council of a district or London borough, the Common Council of the City of London or the Council of the Isles of Scilly ; and

    (*b*) in relation to Scotland, an islands or district council ;

" local rate rebate scheme ", " local rent rebate scheme " and " local rent allowance scheme " have the meanings given by section 30 above and " local scheme " and " local rent scheme " shall be construed accordingly ;

" new town corporation " means—

1981 c. 64.

    (*a*) in relation to England and Wales, a development corporation established under the New Towns Act 1981 or the Commission for the New Towns ; and

1968 c. 16.

    (*b*) in relation to Scotland, a development corporation established under the New Towns (Scotland) Act 1968 ;

" rate rebate ", " rent rebate " and " rent allowance " shall be construed in accordance with section 28 above ;

" rates " and " rating authority "—

1967 c. 9.

    (*a*) in relation to England and Wales, have the same meanings as in the General Rate Act 1967 ; and

1947 c. 43.
1973 c. 65.

    (*b*) in relation to Scotland, have respectively the same meanings as " rate " has in section 379 of the Local Government (Scotland) Act 1947 and " rating authority " has in section 109 of the Local Government (Scotland) Act 1973 ;

" statutory rate rebate scheme ", " statutory rent rebate scheme " and " statutory rent allowance scheme " have the meanings given by section 28 above and " statutory scheme " and " statutory rent scheme " shall be construed accordingly.

(2) References in this Part to the general rate fund of an authority shall be construed—

(*a*) in relation to the Greater London Council or the Council of the Isles of Scilly, as references to their general fund ; and

(*b*) in relation to the Common Council of the City of London, as references to their general rate.

36.—(1) Before making—

Other supplementary provisions.

(*a*) regulations under section 28(1) above other than regulations of which the effect is to increase any amount specified in regulations previously made ;

(*b*) regulations under section 30(6) above ; or

(*c*) an order under section 32(2) above,

the Secretary of State shall consult with organisations appearing to him to be representative of the authorities concerned.

(2) Where, in consequence of the foregoing provisions of this Part, regulations under the Supplementary Benefits Act 1976 contain provisions excluding any items from those to which housing requirements for the purposes of Schedule 1 to that Act relate, the regulations may also contain such provision as the Secretary of State considers appropriate for dealing with transitional matters connected with or arising out of the coming into force of that provision.

1976 c. 71.

(3) Authorities shall supply the Secretary of State with such information in their possession as may be required to give effect to the said Act of 1976 ; and the Secretary of State shall supply authorities with such information concerning claims for and payments of supplementary benefits (within the meaning of that Act) as authorities may require to give effect to statutory and local schemes.

(4) In order to assist authorities to give effect to statutory and local schemes, where a rent is registered under Part IV of the Rent Act 1977, there shall be noted on the register the amount (if any) of the registered rent which, in the opinion of the rent officer or rent assessment committee, is fairly attributable to the provision of services, but excepting any amount which in the opinion of the rent officer or, as the case may be, the rent assessment committee is negligible.

1977 c. 42.

PART III

MISCELLANEOUS

Sick pay to
count as
remuneration
for principal
Act.

37.—(1) In section 3 of the principal Act (meaning of " earnings ") there are inserted, after subsection (1), the following subsections—

" (1A) For the purposes of this section there shall be treated as remuneration derived from an employed earner's employment any sickness payment made—

(*a*) to or for the benefit of the employed earner ; and

(*b*) in accordance with arrangements under which the person who is the secondary contributor in relation to the employment concerned has made or remains liable to make payments towards the provision of that sickness payment.

(1B) Where the funds for making sickness payments under arrangements of the kind mentioned in subsection (1A)(*b*) above are attributable in part to contributions to those funds made by the employed earner, regulations may make provision for disregarding, for the purposes of subsection (1A) above, the prescribed part of any sum paid as a result of the arrangements.

(1C) In this section—

' sickness payment ' means any payment made in respect of absence from work due to incapacity for work (within the meaning of section 17 of this Act) ; and

' secondary contributor ' has the meaning given by section 4 of this Act.".

(2) In Schedule 1 to the principal Act (supplementary provisions relating to contributions) the following paragraph is inserted at the end—

" *Sickness payments counting as remuneration*

9.—(1) Regulations may make provision as to the manner in which, and the person through whom, any sickness payment which, by virtue of section 3(1A) of this Act, is to be treated as remuneration derived from employed earner's employment is to be made.

(2) In any case where regulations made under sub-paragraph (1) above have the effect of requiring a registered

friendly society (within the meaning of the Friendly Societies Act 1974) to make amendments to its rules, the amendments may, notwithstanding any provision of those rules, be made in accordance with the procedure prescribed by regulations made by the Chief Registrar of Friendly Societies for the purposes of this paragraph.

(3) Regulations made under sub-paragraph (2) above shall be subject to annulment in pursuance of a resolution of either House of Parliament.".

38.—(1) For section 5 of the Supplementary Benefits Act 1976 (right to supplementary allowance) there is substituted the following section—

" Supplementary allowance: conditions.
     5.—(1) The right of any person to a supplementary allowance is subject—

> (a) except in prescribed cases, to the condition that he is available for employment; and
>
> (b) in prescribed cases only, to the further condition that he is registered in the prescribed manner for employment.

(2) Regulations may make provision as to—

> (a) what is and is not to be treated as employment for the purposes of this section ; and
>
> (b) the circumstances in which a person is or is not to be treated for those purposes as available for employment.".

(2) In section 10 of the Act of 1976 (modification of right to supplementary allowance in certain cases) for paragraph (a) of subsection (1) there is substituted—

> " (a) in a case in which the condition mentioned in section 5(1)(a) of this Act applies, a person claims or is in receipt of supplementary allowance and is not receiving unemployment benefit under the Social Security Act 1975 ; and ".

39.—(1) Injury benefit is hereby abolished ; and accordingly sections 50(2)(a) and 56 of the principal Act (which make provision for injury benefit) are hereby repealed.

(2) In section 57 of the principal Act, for subsection (4) (period in respect of which disablement benefit is not payable) there is substituted the following subsection—

> " (4) Disablement benefit shall not be available to a person until after the expiry of the period of ninety days (disregarding Sundays) beginning with the day of the relevant accident.".

(3) In section 14 of the principal Act (sickness benefit) the following subsection is inserted after subsection (2)—

" (2A) Subsection (1) above is subject to the provision made by section 50A of this Act in relation to entitlement to sickness benefit in cases of industrial injury.".

(4) After section 50 of the principal Act there is inserted the following section—

" Sickness
benefit in
respect of
industrial
injury.

50A.—(1) In any case where—

    (a) an employed earner is incapable of work as a result of a personal injury of a kind mentioned in section 50(1) of this Act ; and

    (b) the contribution conditions are not satisfied in respect of him ;

those conditions shall be taken to be satisfied for the purposes of paragraph (a) or, as the case may be, (b) of section 14(2) of this Act as that paragraph applies in relation to sickness benefit.

(2) In the case of a person who—

    (a) is entitled, by virtue of this section, to sickness benefit under subsection (2)(b) of section 14 ; and

    (b) is not also entitled to sickness benefit under subsection (2)(c) of that section ;

the weekly rate at which sickness benefit is payable shall be determined in accordance with regulations.

(3) In subsection (1) above ' contribution conditions ' means—

    (a) in the case of a person who is under pensionable age, the contribution conditions specified for sickness benefit in Schedule 3, Part I, paragraph 1 ; and

    (b) in the case of a person who has attained pensionable age but has not retired from regular employment, the contribution conditions for a Category A retirement pension specified in Schedule 3, Part I, paragraph 5."

(5) Regulations may make such transitional or saving provision as the Secretary of State considers necessary or expedient in connection with the provisions of this section.

40. In the Social Security Pensions Act 1975 the following section is inserted after section 51—

PART III

Refusal and cancellation of contracting-out certificates.

1975 c. 60.

" Refusal and cancellation of contracting-out certificates.

51A.—(1) This subsection applies in any case where—

(a) a contracting-out certificate (the ' first certificate ') has been surrendered by an employer or cancelled by the Occupational Pensions Board ; and

(b) at any time before the expiry of the period of twelve months beginning with the date of the surrender or cancellation, that or any connected employer, with a view to the issue of a further contracting-out certificate, makes an election in respect of any employment which was specified by virtue of section 31(1)(a) of this Act in the first certificate.

(2) This subsection applies in any case where—

(a) a contracting-out certificate (the ' first certificate ') has been surrendered by an employer or cancelled by the Board ;

(b) a further contracting-out certificate has been issued, after the surrender or cancellation of the first certificate but before the expiry of the period of twelve months beginning with the date of the surrender or cancellation, in respect of any employment which was specified by virtue of section 31(1)(a) of this Act in the first certificate ; and

(c) the Board have formed the opinion that had they been aware of all the circumstances of the case at the time when the further contracting-out certificate was issued they would have been prevented by subsection (4) below from issuing it.

(3) Subsections (1) and (2) above apply whether or not the occupational pension scheme by reference to which the employment concerned was contracted-out employment by virtue of the first certificate is the same as the scheme by reference to which the employment—

(a) would be contracted-out employment if the further contracting-out certificate were issued ; or

(b) is contracted-out employment by virtue of the further contracting-out certificate.

(4) In a case to which subsection (1) above applies, the Board shall not give effect to the election referred to in that subsection by issuing a further contracting-out certificate unless they consider that, in all the circumstances of the case, it would be reasonable to do so.

(5) In a case to which subsection (2) above applies, the Board may, before the expiry of the period of twelve months beginning with the date on which the further contracting-out certificate was issued, cancel the further contracting-out certificate.

(6) Where a contracting-out certificate is cancelled under subsection (5) above the provisions of this Act and of any regulations and orders made under it shall have effect as if the certificate had never been issued.

(7) This section does not apply in any case where the surrender or cancellation of the first certificate occurred before 22nd July 1981.

(8) Where the further contracting-out certificate referred to in paragraph (*b*) of subsection (2) above was issued before the commencement of this section, then—

(*a*) paragraph (*c*) of that subsection shall have effect as if this section had been in force at the time when the further contracting-out certificate was issued ; and

(*b*) subsection (5) above shall have effect as if the reference to the date of issue of that certificate were a reference to the commencement of this section.

(9) Regulations may make such supplemental provision in relation to cases falling within subsection (1) or (2) above as the Secretary of State considers necessary or expedient.

(10) Without prejudice to subsection (9) above, regulations may make provision, in relation to any case in which the Board have cancelled a contracting-out certificate under subsection (5) above, preventing the recovery by the employer concerned (whether by deduction from emoluments or otherwise) of such arrears which he is required to pay to the Secretary of State in respect of an earner's liability under section 4(3) of the principal Act as may be prescribed.

(11) For the purposes of subsections (1) and (2) above an employment (the ' second employment ') in respect of which—

> (a) an election of the kind referred to in sub-section (1)(b) above has been made ; or
>
> (b) a further contracting-out certificate of the kind referred to in subsection (2)(b) above has been issued ;

and an employment (the ' first employment ') which was specified by virtue of section 31(1)(a) of this Act in the first certificate shall be treated as one employment if, in the opinion of the Board,—

> (i) they are substantially the same, however described ; or
>
> (ii) the first employment falls wholly or partly within the description of the second employment or the second employment falls wholly or partly within the description of the first employment.

(12) Regulations shall prescribe the cases in which employers are to be treated as connected for the purposes of this section.

(13) Where the Secretary of State proposes to make regulations under subsection (10) above, section 10(1) of the Social Security Act 1980 (duty of Secretary of State to refer proposed regulations to the Social Security Advisory Committee) shall apply in relation to those proposals.".

1980 c. 30.

41.—(1) In section 8 of the Family Income Supplements Act 1970 (prevention of double payments and recovery of overpayments) the following subsections are inserted after subsection (4)—

Recovery of sums due to Secretary of State.

1970 c. 55.

" (5) Any sum which is, by virtue of regulations under subsection (3) above or section 10(2)(ii) of this Act, recoverable by the Secretary of State in pursuance of a decision made by a supplement officer, the Appeal Tribunal or a Social Security Commissioner shall, if the person from whom that sum is recoverable resides in England and Wales and the county court so orders, be recoverable by execution issued from the county court or otherwise as if it were payable under an order of that court.

(6) Any such decision may, if the person from whom the sum in question is recoverable resides in Scotland, be enforced in like manner as an extract registered decree arbitral bearing a warrant for execution issued by the sheriff court of any sheriffdom in Scotland.".

(2) In section 119 of the principal Act (effect of adjudication on payment and recovery) the following subsections are inserted after subsection (4)—

"(5) Any sum which is, by virtue of this section or regulations under subsection (3) above, required to be repaid to the Secretary of State in pursuance of a decision made by an insurance officer, local tribunal or Commissioner shall, if the person required to repay that sum resides in England and Wales and the county court so orders, be recoverable by execution issued from the county court or otherwise as if it were payable under an order of that court.

(6) Any such decision may, if the person required to repay the sum in question resides in Scotland, be enforced in like manner as an extract registered decree arbitral bearing a warrant for execution issued by the sheriff court of any sheriffdom in Scotland.".

(3) In section 20 of the Supplementary Benefits Act 1976 (recovery in cases of misrepresentation or non-disclosure) the following subsections are inserted after subsection (5)—

"(6) Any sum which is, by virtue of this section or regulations under section 14(2)(*dd*) of this Act, recoverable by the Secretary of State in pursuance of a decision made by a benefit officer, the Appeal Tribunal or a Social Security Comissioner shall, if the person from whom that sum is recoverable resides in England and Wales and the county court so orders, be recoverable by execution issued from the county court or otherwise as if it were payable under an order of that court.

(7) Any such decision may, if the person from whom the sum in question is recoverable resides in Scotland, be enforced in like manner as an extract registered decree arbitral bearing a warrant for execution issued by the sheriff court of any sheriffdom in Scotland.".

Up-rating regulations.

42.—(1) In paragraph 8 of Schedule 16 to the principal Act (exemption in respect of up-rating regulations from requirement to consult Industrial Injuries Advisory Council) for the words from "section" to the end there are substituted the words "one or more of the following sections of this Act, that is to say sections 120, 122, 124 and 126A.".

(2) In paragraph 12(2) of Schedule 3 to the Social Security Act 1980 (exemption in respect of up-rating regulations from requirement to consult Social Security Advisory Committee) for the words from "section 120" to "that Act" there are substituted the words "one or more of the following sections of the principal Act, that is to say sections 120, 122, 124 and 126A (up-rating regulations)".

(3) Neither section 139 nor section 141 of the principal Act PART III
(consultation with the Council and with the Committee) shall
be taken to have applied in relation to any regulations contained in the Social Security Benefits Up-rating Regulations 1979 S.I. 1979/1278.
or the Social Security Benefits Up-rating Regulations 1980. S.I. 1980/1505.

43.—(1) In section 6 of the Pensions Appeal Tribunals Act War pensions.
1943 (setting aside of Tribunal's decision and rehearing of 1943 c. 39.
appeal), after the words " Minister's decision " in subsection (2A)
there are inserted the words " (the ' original decision ') " and
after subsection (2B) there are inserted the following subsections—

" (2C) Where a direction for a rehearing is given under
subsection (2A) above, the Minister may, before the expiry
of the period of two months beginning with the date of
the direction, review the original decision.

(2D) If, on any such review, the Minister is of the opinion
that there are grounds for revising the original decision he
shall—

(*a*) notify the appellant of his opinion and of the revision which he proposes to make ; and

(*b*) if the appellant withdraws his appeal against the
original decision, revise it accordingly.".

(2) In any case where, before the commencement of this
section, an award has been made in respect of a claim for a war
pension, the validity of that award shall not be called into
question on the ground that it was made—

(*a*) in consequence of the review of a decision made in
respect of the claim (whether or not following an appeal
against that decision) ; and

(*b*) at a time when there was no provision in force authorising that review.

(3) The Secretary of State may by order make provision for
determining the date from which any award made before the
commencement of this section in respect of a claim for a war
pension is to be taken to have had effect in a case where—

(*a*) at the time when the award was made there was no
provision in force for determining that date ; or

(*b*) the award was made following—

(i) an appeal to the High Court, Court of Session
or Court of Appeal ; or

(ii) the rehearing of any appeal ;

and the date from which payment under the award
was first made was later than the date from which payment was, by virtue of any provision in force at the

time when the award was made, required to be first made.

(4) An order under subsection (3) above may provide that in any case where the date from which an award is, by virtue of the order, to be taken to have had effect is earlier than the date from which payment under the award was first made, any arrears due to a person in respect of the award shall be limited to those payable in respect of a specified period of not more than six years.

(5) In this section " war pension " means—

1977 c. 5.

(*a*) such pensions and other benefits as are referred to in section 12 of the Social Security (Miscellaneous Provisions) Act 1977 (exercise by Order in Council of existing powers relating to benefits for death or disablement through service in the armed forces) ;

1939 c. 82.
1939 c. 83.

1947 c. 19.

(*b*) any pension or benefit awarded under the Personal Injuries (Emergency Provisions) Act 1939, the Pensions (Navy, Army, Air Force and Mercantile Marine) Act 1939 or the Polish Resettlement Act 1947 ; and

(*c*) such other pensions and benefits as may be specified in an order made by the Secretary of State for the purposes of this section.

Application of social security legislation in relation to territorial waters.
1970 c. 55.
1975 c. 16.
1975 c. 61.
1976 c. 71.
1979 c. 48.

44.—(1) The following enactments are referred to in this section as the " listed enactments "—

(*a*) the Family Income Supplements Act 1970 ;

(*b*) the principal Act ;

(*c*) the Industrial Injuries and Diseases (Old Cases) Act 1975 ;

(*d*) the Child Benefit Act 1975 ;

(*e*) the Supplementary Benefits Act 1976 ;

(*f*) the Pensioners' Payments and Social Security Act 1979.

(2) The listed enactments shall have effect, and be deemed always to have had effect, as if—

(*a*) any reference to Great Britain included a reference to the territorial waters of the United Kingdom adjacent to Great Britain ;

(*b*) in any reference to the presence or residence of a person in the United Kingdom (however expressed) the reference to the United Kingdom included a reference to the territorial waters of the United Kingdom ; and

(*c*) in any reference to a person residing or being in Northern Ireland (however expressed) the reference to Northern Ireland included a reference to the territorial waters of the United Kingdom adjacent to Northern Ireland.

(3) Where any of the listed enactments is derived from an
earlier enactment (whether directly or indirectly) anything done
under or by virtue of a provision of, or made under, that earlier
enactment which contained a reference of a kind mentioned in
paragraph (*a*), (*b*) or (*c*) of subsection (2) above shall have effect
as if that reference had at the material time been the extended
reference provided for by that paragraph.

PART III

(4) The Secretary of State may by regulations make such
provision in respect of any enactment (including a listed enactment) as he considers necessary or expedient in connection with
the operation of that enactment in relation to the territorial
waters of the United Kingdom.

45.—(1) Subsections (2), (3) and (5) of section 166 of the
principal Act (which among other things make provision about
the extent of powers to make orders and regulations) shall apply
to any power to make orders or regulations conferred by this
Act as they apply to any power to make orders or regulations
conferred by that Act; and any power to make orders or regulations conferred by Part II of this Act shall include power to make
different provision for different areas.

Regulations.

(2) Any power of the Secretary of State to make orders or
regulations under this Act shall be exercisable by statutory instrument which, except in the case of —

(*a*) an order under section 7 or 48(3) of this Act;
(*b*) the first regulations under section 28(1)(*a*), (*b*) or (*c*)
or 30(6) of this Act; or
(*c*) regulations under section 28(1) made in pursuance of
section 29 of this Act;

shall be subject to annulment in pursuance of a resolution of
either House of Parliament.

(3) The Secretary of State shall not make the first regulations
under section 28(1)(*a*), (*b*) or (*c*) or 30(6) of this Act unless a
draft of the regulations has been laid before and approved by
a resolution of each House of Parliament.

46.—(1) There shall be paid out of money provided by Parliament—

Expenses.

(*a*) any administrative expenses of the Secretary of State
incurred under this Act; and
(*b*) any increase attributable to this Act in the sums payable out of money so provided under any other Act.

(2) The administrative expenses referred to in subsection (1)
(*a*) above include those in connection with any inquiry undertaken on behalf of the Secretary of State with a view to obtaining statistics relating to the operation of Part I.

PART III

(3) There shall be paid out of the National Insurance Fund into the Consolidated Fund, at such time and in such manner as the Treasury may direct, such sums as the Secretary of State may estimate (in accordance with any directions given by the Treasury) to be the amount of the administrative expenses incurred by the Secretary of State under Part I of this Act, excluding—

(a) any category of expenses which the Treasury may direct, or any enactment may require, to be excluded from the Secretary of State's estimate under this subsection ; and

(b) any expenses incurred under paragraphs 7 to 10 of Schedule 2 to this Act.

Interpretation.

47. In this Act—

" benefit ", except in Part II and section 43, has the same meaning as in the principal Act ;

1975 c. 14.

" principal Act " means the Social Security Act 1975 ;

" regulations " means regulations made by the Secretary of State ;

" tax year " means the period of twelve months beginning with 6th April in any year.

Short title etc.

48.—(1) This Act may be cited as the Social Security and Housing Benefits Act 1982, and Parts I and III of this Act and the Social Security Acts 1975 to 1981 may be cited together as the Social Security Acts 1975 to 1982.

1974 c. 28.

(2) An Order in Council under paragraph 1(1)(b) of Schedule 1 to the Northern Ireland Act 1974 (legislation for Northern Ireland in the interim period) which states that it is made only for purposes corresponding to those of Parts I and III of this Act—

(a) shall not be subject to paragraph 1(4) and (5) of that Schedule (affirmative resolution of both Houses of Parliament) ; but

(b) shall be subject to annulment in pursuance of a resolution of either House.

(3) The following provisions come into force on the passing of this Act—

(a) sections 7, 26, 40, 42 and 44 to 47 ;

(b) paragraphs 1 to 4, 7, 11, 14(1) and (3), 16, 21, 23 to 25, 30 to 34, 37 and 38 of Schedule 4 ; and

(c) subsections (1) to (4) and (7) of this section and subsection (5) of this section so far as it relates to the provisions mentioned in paragraph (b) above ;

and the other provisions of this Act come into force on such day as the Secretary of State may appoint by order made by statutory instrument ; and different days may be appointed for different provisions, different purposes or different areas.

(4) An order under subsection (3) above may make such transitional provision as appears to the Secretary of State to be necessary or expedient in connection with the provisions thereby brought into force.

(5) The enactments mentioned in Part I of Schedule 4 to this Act shall have effect subject to the minor and consequential amendments specified in that Part ; and the transitional provisions in Part II of that Schedule shall have effect.

(6) The enactments mentioned in Schedule 5 to this Act (which include some that are spent) are hereby repealed to the extent specified in the third column of that Schedule.

(7) This Act, except sections 42(2), 43 and 45 and this section and paragraphs 2 and 30, 32 and 33 of Schedule 4, does not extend to Northern Ireland.

SCHEDULES

SCHEDULE 1

CIRCUMSTANCES IN WHICH PERIODS OF ENTITLEMENT DO NOT ARISE

1. A period of entitlement does not arise in relation to a particular period of incapacity for work in any of the circumstances set out in paragraph 2 below or in such other circumstances as may be prescribed.

2. The circumstances are that—

   (*a*) at the relevant date the employee is over pensionable age ;

   (*b*) the employee's contract of service was entered into for a specified period of not more than three months ;

   (*c*) at the relevant date the employee's normal weekly earnings are less than the lower earnings limit then in force under section 4(1)(*a*) of the principal Act ;

   (*d*) the employee had—

      (i) in the period of 57 days ending immediately before the relevant date, at least one day which formed part of a period of interruption of employment ; and

      (ii) at any time during that period of interruption of employment, an invalidity pension day (whether or not the day referred to in sub-paragraph (i) above) ;

   (*e*) in the period of 57 days ending immediately before the relevant date the employee had at least one day on which—

      (i) he was entitled to sickness benefit (or on which he would have been so entitled if he had satisfied the contribution conditions for sickness benefit mentioned in section 14(2)(*a*) of the principal Act) ; or

      (ii) she was entitled to a maternity allowance ;

   (*f*) the employee has done no work for his employer under his contract of service ;

   (*g*) on the relevant date there is, within the meaning of section 19 of the principal Act, a stoppage of work due to a trade dispute at the employee's place of employment ;

   (*h*) before the relevant date the employee has reached his maximum entitlement to statutory sick pay as against the employer concerned, in the tax year in question ; and

   (*i*) the employee is, or has been, pregnant and the relevant date falls within the disqualifying period (within the meaning of section 3(9) of this Act).

3. In this Schedule " relevant date " means the date on which a period of entitlement would begin in accordance with section 3 of this Act if this Schedule did not prevent it arising.

4.—(1) Paragraph 2(*b*) above does not apply in any case where—

   (*a*) at the relevant date the contract of service has become a contract for a period exceeding three months ; or

(*b*) the contract of service (the "current contract") was pre-   SCH. 1
ceded by a contract of service entered into by the employee
with the same employer (the " previous contract ") and—

(i) the interval between the date on which the previous contract ceased to have effect and that on which
the current contract came into force was not more than
eight weeks ; and

(ii) the aggregate of the period for which the previous
contract had effect and the period specified in the current contract (or, where that period has been extended,
the specified period as so extended) exceeds thirteen
weeks.

(2) For the purposes of sub-paragraph (1)(*b*)(ii) above, in any case
where the employee entered into more than one contract of service
with the same employer before the current contract, any of those
contracts which came into effect not more than eight weeks after the
date on which an earlier one of them ceased to have effect shall be
treated as one with the earlier contract.

5.—(1) In paragraph 2(*d*) above " invalidity pension day " means
a day—

(*a*) for which the employee in question was entitled to an
invalidity pension or a non-contributory invalidity pension ;
or

(*b*) for which he was not so entitled but which was the last
day of the invalidity pension qualifying period.

(2) In sub-paragraph (1)(*b*) above the " invalidity pension qualifying
period " means the period mentioned in section 15(1) of the principal
Act or, as the case may be, section 15(2) or 16(2) of the Social   1975 c. 60.
Security Pensions Act 1975 as falling within the period of interruption of employment referred to in that section.

6. For the purposes of paragraph 2(*f*) above, if an employee
enters into a contract of service which is to take effect not more
than eight weeks after the date on which a previous contract of
service entered into by him with the same employer ceased to have
effect, the two contracts shall be treated as one.

7. Paragraph 2(*g*) above does not apply in the case of an employee
who proves that at no time on or before the relevant date did he
participate in, or have a direct interest in, the trade dispute in question.

8. Paragraph 2(*i*) above does not apply in relation to an employee
who has been pregnant if her pregnancy terminated, before the beginning of the disqualifying period, otherwise than by confinement
(within the meaning of section 3(9) of this Act).

SCHEDULE 2   Section 10.
RELATIONSHIP WITH BENEFITS
AND OTHER PAYMENTS, ETC.
The general principle

1. Any day which—

(*a*) is a day of incapacity for work in relation to any contract of
service ; and

    (*b*) falls within a period of entitlement (whether or not it is also a qualifying day) ;

shall not be treated, for the purposes of the principal Act or the Social Security Pensions Act 1975, as a day of incapacity for work for the purposes of determining whether a period is a period of interruption of employment.

Contractual remuneration

2.—(1) Subject to sub-paragraphs (2) and (3) below, any entitlement to statutory sick pay shall not affect any right of an employee in relation to remuneration under any contract of service (" contractual remuneration ").

(2) Subject to sub-paragraph (3) below—

    (*a*) any contractual remuneration paid to an employee by an employer of his in respect of a day of incapacity for work shall go towards discharging any liability of that employer to pay statutory sick pay to that employee in respect of that day ; and

    (*b*) any statutory sick pay paid by an employer to an employee of his in respect of a day of incapacity for work shall go towards discharging any liability of that employer to pay contractual remuneration to that employee in respect of that day.

(3) Regulations may make provision as to payments which are, and those which are not, to be treated as contractual remuneration for the purposes of sub-paragraph (1) or (2) above.

Sickness and unemployment benefit

3.—(1) This paragraph applies in any case where—

    (*a*) a period of entitlement as between an employee and an employer of his comes to an end ; and

    (*b*) the first day immediately following the day on which the period of entitlement came to an end—

        (i) is a day of incapacity for work in relation to that employee ; and

        (ii) is not prevented by paragraph 1 above from being treated as a day of incapacity for work for the purposes of determining whether a period is a period of interruption of employment.

(2) In a case to which this paragraph applies, the day of incapacity for work mentioned in sub-paragraph (1)(*b*) above shall, except in prescribed cases, be or as the case may be form part of a period of interruption of employment notwithstanding section 17(1)(*d*)(ii) of the principal Act (which requires a period of interruption of employment to consist of four or more consecutive days of incapacity for work).

(3) Where each of the first two consecutive days, or the first three consecutive days, following the day on which the period of entitlement came to an end is a day falling within sub-paragraphs (i) and (ii) of sub-paragraph (1)(*b*) above, sub-paragraph (2) above shall have

effect in relation to the second day or, as the case may be, the   SCH. 2
second and third days, as it has effect in relation to the first day.

(4) Any day which is, by virtue of section 17(1)(*e*) of the principal
Act, to be disregarded in computing any period of consecutive days
for the purposes of that Act shall be disregarded in determining,
for the purposes of this paragraph, whether a day is the first day
following the end of a period of entitlement or, as the case may be,
the second or third consecutive such day.

4.—(1) This paragraph applies in any case where—

(*a*) a period of entitlement as between an employee and an
employer of his comes to an end ; and

(*b*) that employee has a day of incapacity for work which—

(i) is, or forms part of, a period of interruption of
employment ; and

(ii) falls within the period of 57 days immediately
following the day on which the period of entitlement
came to an end.

(2) In a case to which this paragraph applies, section 14(3) of the
principal Act (which provides for no entitlement to unemployment
or sickness benefit for the first three days of any period of interruption of employment) shall not apply in relation to a day of incapacity
for work of a kind mentioned in sub-paragraph (1)(*b*) above or to
any later day in the period of interruption of employment concerned.

Invalidity pension

5.—(1) This paragraph applies in any case where—

(*a*) a period of entitlement as between an employee and an
employer of his (the " first period ") comes to an end ;

(*b*) the first period, or another period of entitlement as between
the employee and an employer of his which came to an end
while the first period was running, came to an end by virtue
of section 3(2)(*b*) of this Act ; and

(*c*) the employee has a day of incapacity for work which—

(i) is, or forms part of, a period of interruption of
employment ; and

(ii) falls within the period of 57 days immediately
following the day on which the first period came to an
end.

(2) In a case to which this paragraph applies, sections 15(1) of the
principal Act (entitlement to invalidity pension) and 15(2) and 16(2)
of the Social Security Pensions Act 1975 (entitlement to invalidity   1975 c. 60.
pension for, respectively, widow and widower) shall have effect, in
relation to the period of interruption of employment mentioned in
sub-paragraph (1)(*c*)(i) above, as if for the references to 168 days there
were substituted references to 120 days.

Unemployability supplement

6. Paragraph 1 above does not apply in relation to section 59
of the principal Act (increases in unemployability supplement) and

accordingly the references in that section to a period of interruption of employment shall be construed as if this Part had not been enacted.

Supplementary benefit

7.—(1) This paragraph applies in any case where—

(a) for any period an amount has been paid by way of supplementary benefit to or in respect of an employee ; and

(b) it appears to the Secretary of State that the whole, or some part, of that amount might not have been so paid if an employer who was liable to make to that employee one or more payments of statutory sick pay had made that payment or, as the case may be, those payments.

(2) In this paragraph and in paragraphs 8 and 9 below " sickness payment " means—

(a) any payment by way of statutory sick pay ; and

(b) any payment, of a prescribed kind, made to an employee in respect of his incapacity for work.

(3) In any case to which this paragraph applies, the Secretary of State may serve on the employer concerned, in a prescribed form and manner, a notice—

(a) informing him that an amount has been paid by way of supplementary benefit to or in respect of the employee and of the period for which the payment was made ;

(b) requiring him to inform the Secretary of State in writing, within such period as may be specified in the notice—

(i) whether or not he is, or has at any time been, liable to make any sickness payment to the employee in respect of any day specified in the notice ;

(ii) of the amount of any such liability in respect of statutory sick pay ;

(iii) of the amount of any such liability in respect of any other sickness payment ; and

(iv) if any such liability has been discharged in whole or in part, of the extent to which it has been, and the date on which it was, discharged ; and

(c) requiring him to comply with sub-paragraph (4) below if he has been liable as mentioned in paragraph (b)(i) above, in respect of statutory sick pay, and at the time when he receives the notice—

(i) that liability ; or

(ii) if he has also been so liable in respect of any other sickness payment, his liability for that other sickness payment ;

has not been wholly discharged.

(4) Where an employer is required to comply with this sub-paragraph he shall—

(a) calculate, in accordance with regulations, the net payment for the purposes of paragraph 8 below ;

(b) inform the Secretary of State, in writing and before the expiry of the period mentioned in sub-paragraph (3)(b) above, of the amount of the net payment, as calculated by him ; and

(c) withhold, until such time as it is determined whether or not the employer is to be required to make a payment to the Secretary of State under paragraph 8(2) below, so much of the sickness payment, or part, in question as is equal to the net payment.

(5) In any case where an employer who is required by sub-paragraph (4) above to calculate the net payment to be made in his case—

(a) fails to inform the Secretary of State as required by sub-paragraph (4)(b) above ; or

(b) in the opinion of the Secretary of State, has in purporting to calculate that payment failed to do so in accordance with the relevant regulations ;

the Secretary of State may make the calculation for him ; and this and the following paragraph shall have effect as if a calculation made by the Secretary of State under this sub-paragraph had been duly made by the employer concerned.

8.—(1) This paragraph applies in any case where—

(a) a notice has been served on an employer under paragraph 7(3) above and the employer has been required to comply with paragraph 7(4) above ; and

(b) a benefit officer appointed under section 27 of the Supplementary Benefits Act 1976 determines that the whole, or a specified part, of the amount paid by way of supplementary benefit would not have been paid if the employer had paid to the employee concerned, on or before a date determined in accordance with regulations, an amount equal to the net payment, or the aggregate of the net payments, attributable to the sickness payment or payments in question. **1976 c. 71.**

(2) In a case to which this paragraph applies, the employer concerned shall, if the Secretary of State so requires, pay to the Secretary of State, within the prescribed period, whichever is the lesser of the following—

(a) the amount determined in accordance with sub-paragraph (1)(b) above ;

(b) an amount equal to the net payment, or the aggregate of the net payments, required to be withheld by virtue of paragraph 7(4)(c) above.

(3) Any sum paid to the Secretary of State under this paragraph shall be paid by him into the Consolidated Fund.

(4) For the purposes of regulations made under section 14(2)(d) (provision for review of determinations) of the Act of 1976 a determination by a benefit officer made for the purposes of this paragraph shall be treated as if it had been made under that Act ; and

for the purposes of section 15 of that Act (right of appeal) the employee shall be treated as a person to whom section 15 gives a right of appeal against the determination (including a determination to refuse to review a determination).

9.—(1) Regulations shall provide—

   (a) for the extent to which, and purposes for which, an employer who has made a payment to the Secretary of State under paragraph 8 above is to be treated as having discharged his liability to make the sickness payment or payments to which the payment under paragraph 8 is attributable ; and

   (b) for an amount, calculated in accordance with the regulations, to be treated in a case to which sub-paragraph (2) below applies and for prescribed purposes as having been paid to the employee concerned as remuneration derived from an employed earner's employment.

(2) This sub-paragraph applies to any case (other than one of a prescribed class) where an employer is required by virtue of paragraph 7(4)(c) above to withhold the whole or any part of a sickness payment.

(3) Regulations made by virtue of sub-paragraph (1)(b) above may make provision for determining the date on which any payment treated as mentioned in that sub-paragraph is to be taken as having been made.

10. Nothing in paragraphs 7 to 9 above shall be taken to prejudice the right of the Secretary of State, under any other enactment, to recover the amount of any supplementary benefit from any person.

Benefit paid when statutory sick pay due

11.—(1) This paragraph applies in any case where—

   (a) in respect of any period, an amount has been paid to a person by way of benefit ;

   (b) as a result of any appeal heard, or review conducted, under any enactment it has been determined that the recipient of the benefit was not entitled to it ; and

   (c) the recipient was entitled, in respect of that period, to payment by an employer of his of an amount of statutory sick pay.

(2) In any case to which this paragraph applies, the Secretary of State may serve on the employer concerned, in a prescribed form and manner, a notice—

   (a) informing him that an amount has been paid to the recipient by way of benefit and of the period in respect of which the payment was made ;

   (b) requiring him to inform the Secretary of State in writing within such period as may be specified in the notice—

       (i) of the amount of any statutory sick pay which he was liable to pay to the employee in respect of the period mentioned in sub-paragraph (1)(c) above ;

(ii) of the amount of any other sickness payment for which he was so liable ; and

(iii) if any such liability has been discharged in whole or in part, of the extent to which it has been, and the date on which it was, discharged ; and

(c) requiring him to comply with sub-paragraph (3) below if, at the time when he receives the notice, any liability of his falling within paragraph (b)(i) or (ii) above has not been wholly discharged.

(3) Where an employer is required to comply with this sub-paragraph he shall—

(a) calculate, in accordance with regulations, the net payment for the purposes of sub-paragraph (5) below ;

(b) inform the Secretary of State, in writing and before the expiry of the period mentioned in sub-paragraph (2)(b) above, of the amount of the net payment, as calculated by him ; and

(c) withhold, pending a decision by the Secretary of State as to whether to require payment under sub-paragraph (5) below, so much of the sickness payment, or part, in question as is equal to the net payment.

(4) In any case where an employer who is required by sub-paragraph (3) above to calculate the net payment to be made in his case—

(a) fails to inform the Secretary of State as required by sub-paragraph (3)(b) above ; or

(b) in the opinion of the Secretary of State, has in purporting to calculate that payment failed to do so in accordance with the relevant regulations ;

the Secretary of State may make the calculation for him ; and this paragraph shall have effect as if a calculation made by the Secretary of State under this sub-paragraph had been duly made by the employer concerned.

(5) Where the Secretary of State has served a notice under sub-paragraph (2) above, and the employer concerned has been required to comply with sub-paragraph (3) above, that employer shall, if the Secretary of State so requires, pay to the Secretary of State within the prescribed period whichever is the lesser of the following—

(a) the amount mentioned in sub-paragraph (2)(a) above ;

(b) an amount equal to the net payment, or the aggregate of the net payments, required to be withheld by virtue of sub-paragraph (3)(c) above.

(6) In this paragraph " sickness payment " has the same meaning as in paragraph 7 above.

(7) Regulations shall provide—

(a) for the extent to which, and purposes for which, an employer who has made a payment to the Secretary of State under

SCH. 2

this paragraph is to be treated as having discharged his liability to make the sickness payment or payments to which the payment under this paragraph is attributable ; and

(b) for an amount, calculated in accordance with the regulations, to be treated in a case to which sub-paragraph (8) below applies and for prescribed purposes as having been paid to the employee concerned as remuneration derived from an employed earner's employment.

(8) This sub-paragraph applies to any case (other than one of a prescribed class) where an employer is required by virtue of sub-paragraph (3)(c) above to withhold the whole or any part of a sickness payment.

(9) Regulations made by virtue of sub-paragraph (7)(b) above may make provision for determining the date on which any payment treated as mentioned in that sub-paragraph is to be taken as having been made.

(10) Subject to regulations made under sub-paragraph (11) below, nothing in this paragraph shall be taken to prejudice the right of the Secretary of State, under any enactment, to recover any amount paid to a person by way of benefit.

(11) Regulations may provide for the modification of section 119 of the principal Act (effect of adjudication on payment and recovery of benefit) in relation to any case to which this paragraph applies ; and any such regulations may, in particular—

(a) make provision pending a determination whether or not a case is one to which this paragraph applies ; and

(b) provide for section 119 to have effect as if subsection (2) (no recovery of benefit where no lack of due care and diligence) were omitted.

(12) Any sum paid to the Secretary of State under this paragraph shall be paid by him into the National Insurance Fund.

Employment Protection (Consolidation) Act 1978 (c. 44)

12. In section 121 of the Employment Protection (Consolidation) Act 1978 (priority of certain debts on insolvency) the following paragraph is inserted at the end of subsection (2)—

" (e) statutory sick pay, payable under Part I of the Social Security and Housing Benefits Act 1982.".

13. In paragraphs 2(2) and 3(3) of Schedule 3 to the Act of 1978 (sick pay etc. treated as discharging employer's liability towards employee in period of notice terminating contract of employment), in each case, after the words " sick pay " there are inserted the words " statutory sick pay ".

Section 15(5).

SCHEDULE 3

DETERMINATION OF QUESTIONS : PROCEDURE

1. The following are the kinds of provision referred to in section 15(5) of this Act.

2. Provision as to the form which is to be used for any document, the evidence which is to be required and the circumstances in which any official record or certificate is to be sufficient or conclusive evidence.

3. Provision as to the time to be allowed for producing any evidence.

4. Provision for summoning persons to attend to give evidence or produce documents and for authorising the administration of oaths to witnesses.

5. Provision for the award of costs or expenses.

6. Provision for authorising a local tribunal consisting of two or more members to proceed with any case, with the consent of the prescribed person, in the absence of any member.

7. Provision for giving the chairman or acting chairman of a local tribunal consisting of two or more members a second or casting vote where the number of members present is an even number.

8. Provision for empowering the Secretary of State, an insurance officer, a local tribunal or a Commissioner to refer to a medical practitioner for examination and report any question arising for his or their decision.

9. Provision that in such cases as may be prescribed, one or more medical practitioners shall sit with a local tribunal or Commissioner either as additional members or as assessors.

10. Provision for the appointment by the Secretary of State of medical practitioners to act for the purposes of this Part of this Act either generally or for such cases and for such adjudicators as the Secretary of State may determine.

In this paragraph "adjudicators" means insurance officers, local tribunals, Commissioners and the Secretary of State.

11. Provision for extending and defining the functions of assessors for the purposes of this Part of this Act.

12. Provision for withholding from a person the particulars of any medical advice or medical evidence given or submitted in connection with the determination of any question if, in the opinion of the prescribed authority (being the person or tribunal, or the chairman of the tribunal, by whom that determination falls to be made), disclosure of those particulars to that person would be undesirable in his interests.

SCHEDULE 4

Amendments and Transitional Provisions

Part I

Minor and Consequential Amendments

National Assistance Act 1948 (c. 29)

1. In section 44 of the National Assistance Act 1948 (affiliation orders)—

    (*a*) in subsection (4) for the words "the mother or a person

SCH. 4

appointed to have the custody of the child" there are substituted the words " a person entitled thereunder " ; and

(*b*) in subsection (6) for the words from " the mother or a person " to the end there are substituted the words " a person entitled as mentioned in subsection (4) above ".

Maintenance Orders Act 1950 (c. 37)

2. In section 16(2)(*b*)(viii) of the Maintenance Orders Act 1950 (orders to which enforcement provisions of Part II apply) for the words " section 19(8)(*b*) " there are substituted the words " section 18 or 19(8) ".

Industrial Training Act 1964 (c. 16)

3. Section 10 of the Industrial Training Act 1964 (accidents in connection with training), as it applies otherwise than in relation to the Agricultural Training Board, shall have effect as if after the word " board " in subsection (1) and in each place where it occurs in subsection (3) there were inserted the words " the Commission or the Minister ".

Family Income Supplements Act 1970 (c. 55)

4.—(1) Section 10 of the Family Income Supplements Act 1970 (regulation-making powers) is amended as follows.

(2) After paragraph (*i*), in subsection (2), there is inserted the following paragraph—

" (*ii*) as respects matters arising in connection with the making of interim payments (including provision for the recovery of such payments in whole or in part) ; ".

(3) After subsection (5) there are inserted the following subsections—

" (6) Where any amount is recoverable under regulations made by virtue of subsection (2)(*ii*) above it may, without prejudice to any other method of recovery, be recovered by deduction from any family income supplement or from any benefit under the Social Security Act 1975 or the Child Benefit Act 1975.

1975 c. 14.
1975 c. 61.

(7) In subsection (2)(*ii*) above " interim payments " means payments made—

(*a*) otherwise than in accordance with this Act, under arrangements made by the Secretary of State with the consent of the Treasury ; and

(*b*) pending the determination, whether in the first instance or on an appeal or reference and whether originally or on review, of any claim to family income supplement.".

Housing (Financial Provisions) (Scotland) Act 1972 (c. 46)

5.—(1) In section 24(1)(*a*) of the Housing (Financial Provisions) (Scotland) Act 1972 (amount to be carried to credit of rent rebate account) for the words " under section 5 of this Act " there are substituted the words " under section 32 of the Social Security and Housing Benefits Act 1982 ".

(2) In section 25(1)(*a*) of that Act (amount to be carried to credit of rent allowance account) for the words " under section 6 of this Act " there are substituted the words " under section 32 of the Social Security and Housing Benefits Act 1982 ".

Housing Finance Act 1972 (c. 47)

6. (1) In paragraph 1(1)(*a*) of Schedule 1 to the Housing Finance Act 1972 (the Housing Revenue Account) the words " or water rates or charges " are hereby repealed.

(2) For paragraph 1(1)(*c*) of that Schedule there is substituted the following—

" (*c*) any of the following subsidies payable to the local authority for that year, namely—

(i) housing subsidy under the Housing Rents and Subsidies Act 1975 ;

(ii) expanding towns subsidy under that Act ; and

(iii) rent rebate subsidy under the Social Security and Housing Benefits Act 1982 to the extent that it is calculated by reference to Housing Revenue Account rebates (within the meaning of Part II of that Act) and the cost of administering such rebates.".

(3) In paragraph 3(2) of that Schedule after the words " other than " there are inserted the words " water rates or charges or ".

(4) In paragraph 6(*a*) of that Schedule, for the words " under section 3 of the Housing Rents and Subsidies Act 1975 " there are substituted the words " under section 32 of the Social Security and Housing Benefits Act 1982 ".

National Insurance Act 1974 (c. 14)

7. In section 6(1) of the National Insurance Act 1974 (power to make regulations providing, amongst other things, for the correction of accidental errors in decisions or records of decisions under relevant enactments) there are added, at the end, the words " or the Social Security and Housing Benefits Act 1982 ".

Social Security Act 1975 (c. 14)

8. In section 3 of the principal Act (meaning of " earnings ") there is inserted, at the end, the following subsection—

" (4) For the purposes of this section, regulations may make provision for treating as remuneration derived from an employed earner's employment any payment made by a body corporate to or for the benefit of any of its directors where that payment would, when made, not be earnings for the purposes of this Act.".

9. In section 14 of the principal Act (unemployment and sickness benefit), in subsection (4), after the words " subsection (2)(*a*) above " there are inserted the words " (including a person entitled by virtue of that subsection and section 50A of this Act) ".

10. In section 15 of the principal Act (invalidity pension) the following subsection is inserted at the end—

" (6) Regulations may make provision in relation to entitlement to invalidity pension—

(a) corresponding to that made by or under section 50A of this Act in relation to sickness benefit for persons who have attained pensionable age but have not retired from regular employment ;

(b) restricting entitlement to invalidity pension in cases where in respect of one or more of the 168 days mentioned in subsection (1) above the person claiming invalidity pension (whether or not he has attained pensionable age) would not have been entitled to sickness benefit but for the provisions of section 50A(1) of this Act.".

11. For subsection (2) of section 48 of the principal Act (priority of reductions under earnings rules) there are substituted the following subsections—

" (2) Sections 45 and 46 above, as they relate to the amount of the increase of a Category A retirement pension, have effect subject to section 30(1) above (earnings rule).

(3) In any case where a reduction in the amount of a Category A retirement pension falls to be made under section 30(1), then—

(a) if a reduction in an increase in that pension under section 45 or 46 above falls to be made under section 45(3) or, as the case may be, under regulations made under section 46(4), the reduction under section 30(1) shall be made first ;

(b) the reduction under section 30(1) shall be made, so far as is necessary—

(i) initially against so much of the pension (other than any increase falling within sub-paragraph (ii) or (iii) below) as is subject to section 30(1) ;

(ii) then against any increase in the pension under section 45 or, as the case may be, 46 ; and

(iii) finally against any increase in the pension under section 41 above.".

12.—(1) Section 50 of the principal Act (descriptions of industrial injuries benefits) is amended as follows.

(2) For subsection (4) there is substituted the following subsection—

" (4) Regulations may make provision as to the day which, in the case of night workers and other special cases, is to be treated for the purposes of industrial injuries benefit as the day of the accident.".

(3) The following subsection is inserted at the end—

" (6) In this Chapter ' work ', in the contexts ' incapable of work ' and ' incapacity for work ', means work which the person in question can reasonably be expected to do.".

13. In section 60(1) of the principal Act (increase of disablement pension for special hardship) for the words " injury benefit period " there are substituted the words " period of ninety days referred to in section 57(4) of this Act ".

14.—(1) Section 79 of the principal Act is amended as follows.

(2) In subsection (3)(*a*) (regulations about claims for benefits) for the words " non-contributory invalidity pension or injury benefit " there are substituted the words " or non-contributory invalidity pension ".

(3) In subsection (3)(*b*) (award of benefit in respect of period after date of claim) for the words " 13 weeks " there are substituted the words " 26 weeks ".

15. In section 91(1)(*b*)(i) of the principal Act (regulations as to adjusting injury benefit in certain circumstances) for the word " either " there are substituted the words " that benefit ".

16. In section 141 of the principal Act (Industrial Injuries Advisory Council) the following subsection is inserted at the end—

" (4) The Council may also give advice to the Secretary of State on any other matter relating to industrial injuries benefit or its administration."

17. In paragraph 4 of Schedule 8 to the principal Act (period to be taken into account in assessing extent of disablement for purposes of industrial injuries benefit) for the words " injury benefit period " there are substituted the words " period of ninety days referred to in section 57(4) of this Act ".

Industrial Injuries and Diseases (Old Cases) Act 1975 (c. 16)

18.—(1) Section 7 of the Industrial Injuries and Diseases (Old Cases) Act 1975 (nature and amount of benefit under industrial diseases benefit schemes) is amended as follows.

(2) In subsection (3), in paragraph (*a*), for the words " 55 " and " 55 and 56 " there are substituted respectively " 58 " and " 58 and 59 " ; and that paragraph shall have effect as if it had been enacted as so amended.

(3) In subsection (3), for paragraphs (*c*) and (*d*) there are substituted the following paragraphs—

" (*c*) where the person is entitled to child benefit in respect of a child or children, by an amount equal to any increase which would be payable under section 41 of that Act in respect of that child or those children if he were entitled to sickness benefit ;

(*d*) where the person is treated under the provisions of the scheme as residing with his wife or contributing at a weekly rate of not less than the relevant amount towards her maintenance, by the relevant amount (that is to say

Sch. 4
an amount equal to any increase which would be payable under section 44 of that Act in respect of her if he were entitled to sickness benefit).".

(4) For subsection (4) there is substituted the following subsection—

" (4) Where under this section an allowance comprises such an increase as is mentioned in paragraph (*a*) of subsection (3) above, that subsection shall have effect as if for paragraphs (*c*) and (*d*) there were substituted the following paragraphs—

' (*c*) where the person is entitled to child benefit in respect of a child or children, by an amount equal to any increase which would be payable under section 64 of that Act in respect of that child or those children if he were entitled to disablement pension plus unemployability supplement ;

(*d*) where the person is treated under the provisions of the scheme as residing with his wife or contributing at a weekly rate of not less than the relevant amount towards her maintenance, by the relevant amount (that is to say an amount equal to any increase which would be payable under section 66 of that Act in respect of her if he were entitled to disablement pension plus unemployability supplement).'.".

Local Government (Scotland) Act 1975 (c. 30)

19. In section 8(4) of the Local Government (Scotland) Act 1975 (payment of rates by instalments) for the words from " the standard " to " that Act " there are substituted the words " section 28(1)(*a*) of the Social Security and Housing Benefits Act 1982 (whether or not modified under section 30(1)(*a*) of that Act) ".

Social Security Pensions Act 1975 (c. 60)

20. In section 32 of the Social Security Pensions Act 1975 (contracted-out schemes) the following subsection is added at the end—

" (7) An occupational pension scheme which—

(*a*) at any time before the coming into operation of the first regulations made under paragraph (*a*) of subsection (2) above did not satisfy that paragraph ; but

(*b*) would have satisfied it if those regulations had then been in operation ;

shall, for the purpose of determining whether the scheme satisfied that paragraph, be treated as if those regulations had been in operation at that time."

21. In section 61(2) of the Act of 1975 (duty of Secretary of State to refer proposed regulations to the Occupational Pensions Board) after the words " other than " there are inserted the words " regulations under section 51A(10) above ".

Supplementary Benefits Act 1976 (c. 71)

22. In section 12 of the Supplementary Benefits Act 1976 (prevention of duplication of payments)—

    (*a*) subsection (3) is hereby repealed ; and

    (*b*) in subsection (5) for the words " subsection (1), (2) or (3) " there are substituted the words " subsection (1) or (2) ".

23.—(1) Section 14 of the Act of 1976 (administration of supplementary benefit) is amended as follows.

(2) After paragraph (*d*), in subsection (2), there is inserted the following paragraph—

    " (*dd*) as respects matters arising in connection with the making of interim payments (including provision for the recovery of such payments in whole or in part) ; ".

(3) After subsection (2) there are inserted the following subsections—

    " (2A) Where any amount is recoverable under regulations made by virtue of subsection (2)(*dd*) above, it may, without prejudice to any other method of recovery, be recovered by deduction from prescribed benefits.

    (2B) In subsection (2)(*dd*) above ' interim payments ' means payments made—

        (*a*) otherwise than in accordance with this Act, under arrangements made by the Secretary of State with the consent of the Treasury ; and

        (*b*) pending the determination, whether in the first instance or on an appeal or reference and whether originally or on review, of any claim for supplementary benefit.".

24. In section 15A(4) of the Act of 1976 (powers of Commissioners on hearing appeals from Appeal Tribunals) for paragraph (*b*) there is substituted—

    " (*b*) to refer the case to an Appeal Tribunal, with directions (which may include directions as to the constitution of the tribunal) ; ".

25. In section 19 of the Act of 1976 (affiliation orders)—

    (*a*) in subsection (4) for the words " the mother or a person having custody of the child " there are substituted the words " a person entitled under section 5 of the said Act of 1957 " ; and

    (*b*) in subsection (6) for the words from " the mother or a person " to the end there are substituted the words " a person entitled under section 5 of the said Act of 1957 ".

26. In section 20 of the Act of 1976 (recovery in cases of misrepresentation or non-disclosure), in subsection (5), for the words "subsection (4) " there are substituted the words " subsections (4), (6) and (7) ".

Rating (Disabled Persons) Act 1978 (c. 40)

27. In section 1(6) of the Rating (Disabled Persons) Act 1978 (rebates for hereditaments with special facilities for disabled persons) for the words " section 11 or 12 of the Local Government Act 1974 " there are substituted the words " section 28(1)(*a*) of the Social Security and Housing Benefits Act 1982 (whether or not modified under section 30(1)(*a*) of that Act) ".

28. In section 4(9) of the Act of 1978 (rebates for lands and heritages with special facilities for disabled persons) for the words " section 112 of the Local Government (Scotland) Act 1973 (whether or not varied under section 114 of that Act) " there are substituted the words " section 28(1)(*a*) of the Social Security and Housing Benefits Act 1982 (whether or not modified under section 30(1)(*a*) of that Act) ".

Employment Protection (Consolidation) Act 1978 (c. 44)

29. In section 132(4)(*b*) of the Employment Protection (Consolidation) Act 1978 (which provides that certain provisions of the Supplementary Benefits Act 1976 relating to the recovery of benefit shall not apply to supplementary benefit recouped by virtue of that section) for the words " section 12(1), (2) or (3) " there are substituted the words " section 12(1) or (2) ".

Social Security Act 1980 (c. 30)

30. In section 9 of the Social Security Act 1980 (functions etc. of the Social Security Advisory Committee) in the definition of " relevant enactments " in subsection (7) there are inserted, after the words " Act 1976 ", the words " and Parts I and II of the Social Security and Housing Benefits Act 1982."

31. In section 18(1) of the Act of 1980 (computation of age in Scotland for purposes of certain enactments including the Social Security Acts 1975 to 1979) for the words " 1979 " there are substituted the words " 1982 ".

32.—(1) Part I of Schedule 3 to the Act of 1980 (constitution etc. of Social Security Advisory Committee) is amended as follows.

(2) In paragraph 1 for the words " not less than 8 nor more than 11 " there are substituted the words " not less than 10 nor more than 13 ".

(3) In paragraph 2 for the words from the beginning to " but any member— " there is substituted the following—

" 2.—(1) Each member of the Committee shall be appointed to hold office for such period of not more than 5 years, nor less than 3 years, as the Secretary of State shall determine.

(2) The Secretary of State may, at any time before the expiration of the term of office of any member, extend or further extend that member's term of office ; but no one extension shall be for a period of more than 5 years from the date when the term of office would otherwise expire.

(3) Any member—".

33.—(1) Part II of Schedule 3 to the Act of 1980 (regulations not requiring prior submission to the Committee) is amended as follows.

(2) In paragraph 13(2) after the words " Part III " there are inserted the words " (other than regulations made under section 51A(10) of that Act) ".

(3) After paragraph 15 there is inserted—

" Statutory sick pay

15A. Regulations under section 9 of the Social Security and Housing Benefits Act 1982 and corresponding regulations applying to Northern Ireland.

Housing benefits

15B. Regulations under section 28(1) of the Social Security and Housing Benefits Act 1982 of which the effect is to increase any amount specified in regulations previously made.".

Social Security (No. 2) Act 1980 (c. 39)

34.—(1) Section 5 of the Social Security (No. 2) Act 1980 (abatement of unemployment benefit on account of payments of occupational pension) is amended as follows.

(2) The following subsection is inserted after subsection (1)—

" (1A) Where a reduction in the rate of unemployment benefit payable to a person falls to be made under this section the reduction shall be made, so far as is necessary—

(*a*) initially against so much of the benefit as falls to be paid by virtue of subsection (4) or (6) of section 14 of the principal Act (basic rates) or of regulations under section 33 of that Act (lower rate where contribution conditions partially satisfied) ;

(*b*) then against so much of the benefit as falls to be paid by way of earnings-related supplement under subsection (7) of section 14 ;

(*c*) then against any increase in the benefit payable under section 44 of the principal Act (dependent adults) ; and

(*d*) finally against any increase in the benefit payable under section 41 of the principal Act (dependent children).".

(3) In subsection (2)(*b*) for the words " the preceding subsection " there are substituted the words " subsection (1) above ".

Local Government, Planning and Land Act 1980 (c. 65)

35.—(1) In section 54 of the Local Government, Planning and Land Act 1980 (rate support grant) in subsections (1) and (2) after the words " section 8 of the Local Government Act 1974 " there are inserted the words " and subsidies under section 32(1)(*a*) of the Social Security and Housing Benefits Act 1982 ".

SCH. 4

(2) For paragraph (*d*) of subsection (5) of that section there is substituted—

"(*d*) to subsection (2) of section 34 of the Social Security and Housing Benefits Act 1982 (power to exclude rate fund contributions under subsection (1) of that section and certain other items) ; ".

(3) In subsection (6) of that section (excluded items) paragraph (*c*) and the word " and " immediately preceding that paragraph are hereby repealed.

36. For section 154 of the said Act of 1980 (grant of rent rebates by urban development corporations) there is substituted the following section—

" 154.—(1) If the Secretary of State so provides by order, such of the provisions of Part II of the Social Security and Housing Benefits Act 1982 relating to rent rebates as may be specified in the order shall have effect in relation to an urban development corporation—

(*a*) as if the corporation were a housing authority ; and

(*b*) with such other modifications (if any) as may be so specified.

(2) The power to make an order under this section shall be exercisable by statutory instrument which shall be subject to annulment in pursuance of a resolution of either House of Parliament."

Industrial Training Act 1982 (*c. 10*)

37. In section 18 of the Industrial Training Act 1982 (industrial injuries benefit for accidents in training) after the word " board " in subsection (1) and in each place where it occurs in subsection (3) there shall be inserted the words " , the Commission or the Secretary of State ".

PART II

TRANSITIONALS

38.—(1) Neither section 141(2) of the principal Act nor section 10(1) of the Social Security Act 1980 (duty of Secretary of State to refer proposals for regulations to Industrial Injuries Advisory Council and Social Security Advisory Committee) shall apply to any regulations contained in a statutory instrument which states that it satisfies the requirements of this paragraph.

1980 c. 30.

(2) A statutory instrument satisfies the requirements of this paragraph if it contains only one or more of the following—

(*a*) regulations made under or by virtue of any provision of this Act and before the expiry of the period of six months beginning with the commencement of that provision ;

(*b*) regulations made under any enactment in consequence of a provision of this Act, or in consequence of any provision

made by virtue of a provision of this Act, and before the
expiry of the period of six months beginning with the
commencement of the relevant provision of this Act ;

(c) regulations proposals for which are not subject to the requirements of section 141(2) or section 10(1).

39. Regulations may make provision with respect to the date from
which a period of entitlement is to be taken to have begun in any
case where, on the date on which section 3 of this Act comes into
force, a period of incapacity for work which began before that date
has not come to an end.

SCHEDULE 5

REPEALS

Chapter	Short title	Extent of repeal
1972 c. 46.	The Housing (Financial Provisions) (Scotland) Act 1972.	In section 1(2), the entries relating to rent rebate and rent allowance subsidies. Section 1(3). Sections 5, 6 and 11. Part II. Schedules 2 and 3.
1972 c. 47.	The Housing Finance Act 1972.	In section 1(2), the entry relating to rent allowance subsidy. Section 17(2). Part II. In section 104(1), in the definition of " dwelling " the words " except in Part II of this Act ". In Schedule 1, in paragraph 1(1)(*a*) the words " or water rates or charges ". Schedules 3 and 4.
1973 c. 6.	The Furnished Lettings (Rent Allowances) Act 1973.	The whole Act.
1973 c. 65.	The Local Government (Scotland) Act 1973.	Sections 112 to 115. In Schedule 12, paragraph 23.
1974 c. 7.	The Local Government Act 1974.	In section 8, subsections (1) and (4) and, in subsection (3) the words " subsection (1) or ". Sections 11 to 14.
1974 c. 51.	The Rent Act 1974.	Sections 11 and 12. In Schedule 3, paragraphs 4 to 6.
1975 c. 6.	The Housing Rents and Subsidies Act 1975.	In section 1(1) the words from " but without prejudice " to the end. Section 3. Section 12. In section 16(1), the definitions of " rate fund contribution " and " standard amount of rent rebates ". In Schedule 5, paragraphs 3 to 5 and 8(3).
1975 c. 14.	The Social Security Act 1975.	In section 4(2), the words " Subject to section 6 below ". Section 50(2)(*a*). Section 56. In section 64(1) and (2), paragraph (*a*). In section 65(4) the words " injury benefit or ", " benefit or " and " paragraph 11 or, as the case may be, ".

Chapter	Short title	Extent of repeal
1975 c. 14. —*cont.*	The Social Security Act 1975.—*cont.*	In section 66, in subsection (1), the words " of injury benefit, and " and subsection (2)(*a*). In section 77(2)(*a*) the words " injury benefit and ". Section 78(4)(*a*). In section 81(3) the words " injury benefit ". In section 87(3) the words " injury benefit or ". In section 89(1) the words " injury benefit or ". In section 90, subsection (1), in subsection (2) the words from " disqualifying ", in the first place, to " provide for ", in the second place, and in subsection (4)(*a*) the words " subsection (1) above, or those of ". In section 91(1), in paragraph (*a*) the words from " either " to " or pensions or " and in paragraph (*b*) the words " injury benefit or ". In section 92(2) the words " injury benefit, and ". In Schedule 4, in Part V, paragraphs 1, 9 and 11. In Schedule 11, paragraph 2.
1975 c. 28.	The Housing Rents and Subsidies (Scotland) Act 1975.	In Schedule 3, paragraphs 6 and 8.
1975 c. 60.	The Social Security Pensions Act 1975.	In Schedule 4, paragraph 22.
1975 c. 61.	The Child Benefit Act 1975.	In Schedule 4, paragraph 39.
1976 c. 71	The Supplementary Benefits Act 1976.	Section 12(3). In Schedule 7, paragraphs 26 to 28 and 32.
1976 c. 75.	The Development of Rural Wales Act 1976.	Sections 19 and 20. In section 22 the words " 19 or " and " or of Part II of the Housing Finance Act 1972 (as extended to the Board by section 20 of this Act) ". In Schedule 5, Part III.
1976 c. 80.	The Rent (Agriculture) Act 1976.	Section 32. Schedule 7.
1977 c. 42.	The Rent Act 1977.	In Schedule 23, paragraphs 52 to 54, 56 and 57.
1978 c. 14.	The Housing (Financial Provisions) (Scotland) Act 1978.	Sections 12 and 13. In Schedule 2, paragraphs 8 to 10 and 34 to 36.

Chapter	Short title	Extent of repeal
1980 c. 30.	The Social Security Act 1980.	In Schedule 1, in paragraph 1(1)(*b*) the words " benefit or " and " paragraph 11, or as the case may be, " and in paragraph 6 the words " of injury benefit and ".
1980 c. 39.	The Social Security (No. 2) Act 1980.	Section 3(2).
1980 c. 51.	The Housing Act 1980.	Sections 117 to 119. Schedule 15.
1980 c. 52.	The Tenants' Rights, Etc. (Scotland) Act 1980.	Sections 78 and 79.
1980 c. 65.	The Local Government, Planning and Land Act 1980.	Section 45. In section 54(6), paragraph (*c*) and the word " and " immediately preceding that paragraph.

Iron and Steel Act 1982

1982 CHAPTER 25

An Act to consolidate certain enactments relating to
the British Steel Corporation and the iron and steel
industry.   [13th July 1982]

B E IT ENACTED by the Queen's most Excellent Majesty, by and
with the advice and consent of the Lords Spiritual and
Temporal, and Commons, in this present Parliament
assembled, and by the authority of the same, as follows:—

PART I

THE BRITISH STEEL CORPORATION
AND THEIR SUBSIDIARIES

1.—(1) There shall continue to be a public authority called the
British Steel Corporation (in this Act referred to as "the
Corporation"), which shall have such powers and duties as are
conferred and imposed on them by, or by virtue of, this Act.

The British Steel Corporation.

(2) The Corporation shall be a body corporate.

(3) The Corporation shall consist of a chairman and not less
than seven nor more than twenty other members.

(4) The chairman and the other members of the Corporation
shall be appointed by the Secretary of State from amongst
persons appearing to him to have had wide experience of, and

Part I shown capacity in, the production of iron ore or iron or steel, industrial, commercial or financial matters, applied science, administration or the organisation of workers.

(5) The appointment of a member of the Corporation, other than the chairman, shall not be made by the Secretary of State except after consultation with the chairman.

(6) Schedule 1 to this Act shall have effect in relation to the Corporation.

Powers of the Corporation.

2.—(1) Subject to the provisions of this Act, the Corporation shall have power—

(a) to carry on or promote the carrying on of any iron and steel activities and to sell or promote the sale of iron and steel products (whether within or outside the United Kingdom), and

(b) with the consent of, or in accordance with the terms of any general authority given by, the Secretary of State, to carry on or promote the carrying on of any other activities which any publicly-owned company is for the time being authorised by its memorandum of association or by its charter of incorporation or other charter, as the case may be, to carry on, or which any company that was at any time publicly-owned was at any time so authorised to carry on or to sell or promote the sale of the products of any activities authorised by this paragraph (whether within or outside the United Kingdom),

and may, instead of themselves carrying on any iron and steel or other activities, promote the carrying on of any of those activities to such extent as they think fit by other persons none of whom need be a publicly-owned company.

(2) The Corporation shall not—

(a) acquire by agreement interests in companies or hold interests so acquired, or

(b) form, or take part in forming, companies,

except with the consent of, or in accordance with the terms of any general authority given by, the Secretary of State.

(3) The Corporation shall have power to provide for any group of companies any services which, in the opinion of the Corporation, can conveniently be provided as common services therefor; and for the purposes of this subsection the Corporation shall be entitled to treat themselves as being included in the group.

(4) The Corporation shall have power to do any thing or to enter into any transaction (whether or not involving the expenditure of money, the borrowing of money in accordance with the provisions of this Act, the lending of money, the acquisition of any property or rights or the disposal of any property or rights) which in their opinion is incidental or conducive to the exercise of their powers under the preceding provisions of this section.

(5) Without prejudice to subsection (4) above, the Corporation shall have power to lend to a subsidiary of theirs such sums as that company has power to borrow.

(6) Any reference in this section to interests in a company includes a reference to rights in respect of money lent to the company or guarantees given for the benefit of the company.

(7) The provisions of this section relate only to the capacity of the Corporation as a statutory corporation, and nothing in those provisions shall be construed as authorising the disregard by the Corporation of any enactment or rule of law.

3. The Secretary of State may, after consultation with the Corporation, give to the Corporation directions of a general character as to the exercise by the Corporation of their powers (including the exercise of rights conferred by the holding of interests in companies) in relation to matters which appear to him to affect the national interest ; and the Corporation shall give effect to any directions so given. General directions of the Secretary of State.

4.—(1) It shall be the duty of the Corporation so to exercise their powers as to secure that the carrying on of the activities that have fallen to be carried on under their ultimate control is organised, so far as regards the direction thereof, in the most efficient manner. Organisation of the Corporation's activities.

(2) The Corporation shall not make, or permit to be made, any substantial change in the manner in which the carrying on of the activities that have fallen to be carried on under their ultimate control is organised, so far as regards the direction thereof, except with the consent of the Secretary of State.

(3) In carrying out any measure of reorganisation or any work of development which involves substantial outlay on capital account, and in securing the carrying out by any publicly-owned companies of any such measure or work, the Corporation shall act in accordance with a general programme settled from time to time with the approval of the Secretary of State.

PART I

Dis-
continuance
and
restriction
of the
Corporation's
activities.

5.—(1) Without prejudice to section 3 or 4(3) above but subject as provided in subsection (2) below, the Secretary of State may, after consultation with the Corporation, by order, give to the Corporation directions—

(*a*) to discontinue or restrict any of their activities or to dispose of any of their property, rights, liabilities and obligations ; or

(*b*) to secure the discontinuance or restriction of any of the activities of a publicly-owned company or the disposal of all or any of its property, rights, liabilities and obligations, or the winding up of any such company ;

and the Corporation shall give effect to any directions so given.

(2) The Secretary of State shall not give any direction under subsection (1) above unless he is satisfied that the giving of it will further the public interest.

(3) Subject to subsection (4) below, any direction under subsection (1) above to dispose or secure the disposal of property, rights, liabilities or obligations may in particular include a direction—

(*a*) to form a company for the purpose of acquiring the property or rights and assuming the liabilities or obligations to be transferred in pursuance of the direction ;

(*b*) prohibiting, except with the consent of the Secretary of State, the disposal to, or acquisition from any person by, any company which will acquire property or rights in pursuance of the direction of assets used or capable of use in the production of products of a description, or of products other than products of a description, specified in the direction.

(4) The powers to direct the formation of a company and to restrict the disposal or acquisition of assets are exercisable subject to the following further limitations, that is to say—

(*a*) no company shall be directed to be formed otherwise than as a publicly-owned company ; and

(*b*) no such restriction shall be imposed except on a company which is, or when formed will be, in public ownership or be binding after it ceases to be in public ownership.

(5) So long as a restriction on the disposal or acquisition of assets is binding on the Corporation or a publicly-owned company the provisions of this Act relating to the capacity of the Corporation or the publicly-owned company shall have effect subject to the restriction.

6.—(1) The Corporation shall supply the Secretary of State with such returns, accounts and other information with respect to their property and activities, and the property and activities of any publicly-owned companies, as he may from time to time require.

(2) Without prejudice to subsection (1) above, the Corporation shall, as soon as possible after the end of each financial year of the Corporation, make to the Secretary of State a report on the exercise and performance by the Corporation of their functions during that year and on their policy and programme, and the report shall include a general account of the activities of their subsidiaries.

(3) The report made under subsection (2) above for any year shall set out any direction given by the Secretary of State to the Corporation during that year unless—

    (a) the Secretary of State has notified to the Corporation his opinion that it is against the interests of national security to do so ; or

    (b) the Secretary of State accepts the contention of the Corporation that it is contrary to the commercial interests of the Corporation to do so.

(4) Except as provided in subsection (5) below, the report made under subsection (2) above for any year shall set out any consent given by the Secretary of State to the Corporation during that year under subsection (2) of section 4 above and shall include a general account of the changes in organisation made during that year by virtue of any consent of his given in that or in any earlier year under that subsection.

(5) Paragraphs (a) and (b) of subsection (3) above shall apply in relation to any consent given during the year by the Secretary of State as they apply in relation to any direction given by him and, in relation to changes in organisation made during the year, shall so apply except to such extent as the Secretary of State agrees.

(6) Schedule 2 to this Act shall have effect with respect to the inclusion in reports under subsection (2) above of information respecting business of the Corporation and any publicly-owned companies consisting wholly or mainly in activities other than iron and steel activities.

(7) The Secretary of State shall lay before each House of Parliament a copy of every report made under subsection (2) above.

(8) Without prejudice to section 17 of the Interpretation Act 1978 (repeal and re-enactment), in relation to any financial year of the Corporation which began before the commencement of

this Act, the references in subsection (4) above to any consent given under subsection (2) of section 4 above shall include references to any consent given under subsection (2) of section 4A of the Iron and Steel Act 1975.

Machinery for
settling terms
and conditions
of
employment.

7.—(1) Except as provided in subsections (2) and (3) below, it shall be the duty of the Corporation to seek consultation with any organisation appearing to them to be appropriate with a view to the making of such agreements between the Corporation and that organisation as appear to the parties to be desirable with respect to the establishment and maintenance of machinery, for operation at national level or works level or any level falling between those levels which appears to the Corporation to be appropriate, for the purposes of—

(a) the settlement by negotiation of terms and conditions of employment of persons employed by the Corporation and by any publicly-owned companies with provision for reference to arbitration in default of a settlement in such cases as may be determined by or under the agreements ; and

(b) the promotion and encouragement of measures affecting efficiency, in any respect, in the carrying on by the Corporation and by any publicly-owned companies of their activities ; and

(c) the promotion and encouragement of measures affecting the safety, health and welfare of persons employed by the Corporation and by any publicly-owned companies.

(2) The duty to seek consultation with any organisation under subsection (1) above may be performed by the Corporation either directly, or indirectly by exercising control over any publicly-owned companies ; and, if the Corporation so decide, such consultation may be sought with a view to the making of such agreements as are referred to in that subsection between any publicly-owned companies and any organisation.

(3) The Corporation are not required to seek consultation with any organisation under subsection (1) above in so far as they are satisfied that adequate machinery, for operation at any such level as is referred to in that subsection, exists for achieving the purposes specified in that subsection.

(4) The Corporation shall send to the Secretary of State copies of any such agreement as aforesaid and of any instrument varying the terms of any such agreement.

(5) Where it falls to the Corporation or a publicly-owned company to participate in the operation of machinery established under this section, and the operation involves discussion of a

subject by other persons participating therein, the Corporation or the publicly-owned company, as the case may be, shall make available to those persons, at a reasonable time before the discussion is to take place, such information in their possession relating to the subject as, after consultation with those persons, appears to the Corporation or the publicly-owned company, as the case may be, to be necessary to enable those persons to participate effectively in the discussion.

(6) Nothing in this section shall be construed as prohibiting the Corporation or a publicly-owned company from taking part, together with other employers, or organisations of employers, in the establishment and maintenance of machinery for the settlement of terms and conditions of employment and the promotion and encouragement of measures affecting the safety, health and welfare of persons employed by them, and in the discussion of other matters of mutual interest to them and persons employed by them.

8.—(1) Schedule 3 to this Act shall have effect with respect Pension rights. to the provision of pensions to, or in respect of, persons employed or formerly employed by the Corporation and other bodies corporate, including provision for the making by the Secretary of State of regulations for those purposes.

(2) The Secretary of State shall not make regulations under the said Schedule 3 except after consultation with the Corporation and such organisations as appear to him to be representative of the persons concerned.

9.—(1) Subject to subsection (2) below, the Secretary of State Compulsory may authorise the Corporation to purchase compulsorily any purchase of land required for the exercise and performance of their functions land. or the carrying on of any activity by a publicly-owned company ; and the Acquisition of Land Act shall apply.

(2) The Secretary of State shall not under this section authorise the acquisition by the Corporation of any land for the purpose of the carrying on by them or any publicly-owned company of any activity, other than the working and getting of iron ore, if that land is being used wholly or mainly by any other person for the purpose of carrying on the same activity or for purposes incidental to the carrying on of that activity.

(3) In this section " the Acquisition of Land Act " means—

> (*a*) in the application of this section to England and Wales, the Acquisition of Land Act 1981 ; 1981 c. 67.

    (*b*) in the application of this section to Scotland, the Acquisition of Land (Authorisation Procedure) (Scotland) Act 1947 ;

and the said Act of 1947 shall have effect for the purposes of subsection (1) above as if the Corporation were a local authority within the meaning of that Act and as if this Act had been in force immediately before the commencement of the said Act of 1947.

10. The Corporation may, with the consent of the Secretary of State, promote Bills in Parliament or orders under the Private Legislation Procedure (Scotland) Act 1936 and may, without any such consent, oppose any Bill in Parliament or any such order.

11.—(1) A publicly-owned company shall not, except with the consent of, or in accordance with the terms of any general authority given by, the Secretary of State, acquire by agreement interests in a company or form, or take part in forming, a company.

(2) Schedule 4 to this Act shall have effect with respect to the constitution and proceedings of any publicly-owned company that is a private company and shall so have effect for as long as the company remains in public ownership and notwithstanding any enactment or other instrument applicable to the company.

(3) When any company comes into public ownership or ceases to be in public ownership, the Corporation shall, as soon as possible thereafter, publish that fact in the London and Edinburgh Gazettes.

(4) The Corporation shall keep at their principal office a list, which shall be available for inspection during business hours, of the companies which are for the time being publicly-owned companies and of the other companies, to be shown separately, in which shares are for the time being held by the Corporation, and shall supply a copy of the list to any person on demand and on the payment of such reasonable charge as the Corporation may require.

(5) If any sum required by any judgment or order to be paid by a company which at the time of the judgment or order is a publicly-owned company, or has at any time since the cause of action arose been a publicly-owned company, is not paid by the company within fourteen days from the date on which execution becomes leviable to enforce the judgment or order, the Corporation shall be liable to pay that sum, and that judgment or order shall be enforceable against the Corporation accordingly.

(6) Where any such sum as is referred to in subsection (5) above is required to be paid in respect of a liability arising under a contract made by the company, the cause of action shall be deemed, for the purposes of that subsection, to have arisen at the time when the contract was made.

12.—(1) The Secretary of State may, with respect to a publicly-owned company which was in public ownership on 30th April 1969, by order, vest all or any of its property, rights, liabilities and obligations in the Corporation.

(2) An order under subsection (1) above may make such provision as appears to the Secretary of State to be requisite or expedient in connection with, or in consequence of, the vesting.

(3) If at any time it appears to the Secretary of State that a publicly-owned company which was in public ownership on 30th April 1969 is void of property, rights, liabilities and obligations, he may, by order, dissolve it.

13.—(1) Except as provided in this section, nothing in this Act exempts the Corporation from liability for any tax, duty, rate, levy or other charge whatsoever, whether general or local.

(2) Where a company is formed by the Corporation or the amount of the capital of a subsidiary of the Corporation is increased, then, if the Treasury are satisfied that the formation of the company or the increase of capital, as the case may be, is—

(a) for the purpose of giving effect to a direction given by the Secretary of State under section 5(1) above, or

(b) for the purpose of making a change in organisation for which the Secretary of State has given his consent under section 4(2) above, or

(c) for purposes that include either of those purposes,

stamp duty shall not be chargeable under section 47 of the Finance Act 1973 on any document relating to a chargeable transaction consisting of the formation of the company or the increase of capital except to the extent to which, in the opinion of the Treasury, the transaction goes beyond what is necessary for achieving that purpose.

(3) Where, in accordance with arrangements approved by the Secretary of State for the purposes of section 9 of the Iron and Steel Act 1969, section 13(3) of the Iron and Steel Act 1975 or this subsection, a publicly-owned company which was in public ownership on 30th April 1969 ceases to carry on a trade and the Corporation begin to carry on activities of that trade

as part of their trade, section 252(3) of the Income and Corporation Taxes Act 1970 (company reconstructions without change of ownership) shall, in its application to the company and the Corporation, have effect as if, after the words " carrying on the trade ", there were inserted the words " or any trade of which it has come to form part ".

(4) In the event of the dissolution of a company which was in public ownership both on 30th April 1969 and immediately before its dissolution, the Corporation shall be entitled to relief from corporation tax under section 265(1) of the Income and Corporation Taxes Act 1970 (computation of chargeable gains) for any amount for which the company, had it not been dissolved, would have been entitled to claim relief in respect of allowable losses.

PART II

FINANCE

General
financial
duties of the
Corporation.

14.—(1) Subject as provided in subsection (6) below, it shall be the duty of the Corporation so to exercise and perform their functions under this Act as to secure that the combined revenues of the Corporation and all their subsidiaries taken together are not less than sufficient to meet their combined charges properly chargeable to revenue account, taking one year with another.

(2) The Corporation shall—

(*a*) charge to revenue account in every year all charges which are proper to be made to revenue account including, in particular, proper provision for the depreciation or renewal of assets and proper allocations to general reserve ; and

(*b*) secure that their subsidiaries charge to revenue account in every year all charges which are proper to be made to revenue account including, in particular, proper provision for the depreciation or renewal of assets ;

and in this section " charges properly chargeable to revenue account " shall be construed in accordance with this subsection.

(3) If in any financial year of the Corporation the revenues of the Corporation or (where any companies are in public ownership) the combined revenues of the Corporation and all the publicly-owned companies taken together (as shown in the statement prepared pursuant to section 24(1)(*b*) below) exceed their charges or (as the case may be) their combined charges properly chargeable to revenue account for that year (as so shown), it shall be incumbent on the Corporation to secure that the excess is, to such extent (if any) as the Secretary of State may direct,

applied for such purposes of the Corporation or (as the case may be) of the Corporation and of the said companies as he may direct and, subject to that, is applied for such of those purposes as the Corporation may determine.

(4) The Secretary of State may from time to time determine, with the approval of the Treasury and after consultation with the Corporation, as respects such period as the Secretary of State may so determine, the rate of return on net assets (as for the time being defined by the Secretary of State for the purposes of this subsection) which the Secretary of State considers it is reasonable for the Corporation to achieve in that period ; and the Secretary of State may, with the like approval and after such consultation as aforesaid, vary a determination under this subsection as respects any period by a further determination.

(5) The Secretary of State shall give notice to the Corporation of any determination under subsection (4) above.

(6) The Corporation shall conduct their affairs during any period as respects which a determination has been made under subsection (4) above with a view to achieving in that period a rate of return on net assets not less than that specified by the determination as for the time being in force, and the operation of subsection (1) above shall be suspended during any such period.

(7) The Secretary of State may, by order—

(*a*) substitute for the duty imposed by subsection (6) above a financial duty expressed otherwise than by reference to a rate of return on net assets ; and

(*b*) for that purpose direct that subsections (4) to (6) above shall have effect subject to such modifications as may be specified in the order and make such other incidental and transitional provisions as appear to the Secretary of State to be necessary or expedient.

15.—(1) Without prejudice to the Corporation's power to establish specific reserves, they shall establish and maintain a general reserve.

General reserve.

(2) The management by the Corporation of their general reserve and the sums to be carried from time to time to the credit of, and the application of moneys comprised in, that general reserve shall, subject to the following provisions of this section, be as the Corporation may determine.

(3) None of the moneys comprised in the Corporation's general reserve shall be applied otherwise than for the purposes of the Corporation or of their subsidiaries.

(4) The power to give directions to the Corporation under section 3 above shall, notwithstanding the limitation therein to the giving of directions of a general character, extend to the giving to them, with the approval of the Treasury, of directions of a general or specific character as to any matter relating to the establishment or management of the Corporation's general reserve or the carrying of sums to the credit of, or the application of the moneys comprised in, that general reserve.

16.—(1) The Corporation may borrow temporarily, by way of overdraft or otherwise, either from the Secretary of State or, with the consent of the Secretary of State and the approval of the Treasury, from any other person, such sums in sterling as the Corporation may require for—

> (a) meeting their obligations or exercising and performing their functions under this Act ; or

> (b) lending money temporarily to a subsidiary of theirs.

(2) The Corporation may borrow (otherwise than by way of temporary loan) from the Secretary of State, or, with his consent and the approval of the Treasury, from the Commission of the European Communities or the European Investment Bank, such sums in sterling as they may require for all or any of the following purposes—

> (a) the provision of money for meeting any expenses incurred by the Corporation or a subsidiary of theirs in connection with any works the cost of which is properly chargeable to capital ;

> (b) the provision of working capital required by the Corporation or a subsidiary of theirs ;

> (c) the acquisition under section 2 above of any interests in, or property or rights of, a company or the formation under that section of a company ;

> (d) the lending of money to a subsidiary of the Corporation (otherwise than by way of temporary loan) ;

> (e) the repayment of any money borrowed by the Corporation ;

> (f) any other purpose for which capital moneys are properly applicable.

(3) The Corporation may, with the consent of the Secretary of State (which shall require the approval of the Treasury), borrow any sum in a currency other than sterling which they have power to borrow in sterling from the Secretary of State.

(4) Without prejudice to the preceding provisions of this section, the Corporation may, without obtaining the consent of the

Secretary of State or the approval of the Treasury under this section— PART II

(a) borrow temporarily, by way of overdraft or otherwise, from a subsidiary of the Corporation such sums in any currency as the Corporation may require for—

   (i) meeting their obligations or exercising and performing their functions under this Act ; or

   (ii) lending money temporarily to another subsidiary of the Corporation ;

(b) borrow (otherwise than by way of temporary loan) from a subsidiary of the Corporation such sums in any currency as the Corporation may require for all or any of the purposes mentioned in subsection (2) above.

(5) A power to borrow any sum under this section is subject to the limit imposed by section 19 below, and the Corporation shall not have power to borrow money except in accordance with this section.

(6) The Corporation shall secure that no publicly-owned company borrows money otherwise than from the Corporation or from another publicly-owned company except with the consent of the Secretary of State and the approval of the Treasury.

17.—(1) The Secretary of State may, with the approval of the Treasury, lend to the Corporation any sums which the Corporation have power to borrow under subsection (1) or (2) of section 16 above. Loans by the Secretary of State to the Corporation.

(2) Any loans which the Secretary of State makes under this section shall be repaid to him at such times and by such methods, and interest thereon shall be paid to him at such rates and at such times, as he may, with the approval of the Treasury, from time to time direct.

(3) The Treasury may issue out of the National Loans Fund to the Secretary of State such sums as are necessary to enable him to make loans under this section.

(4) Any sums received by the Secretary of State under subsection (2) above shall be paid into the National Loans Fund.

18.—(1) Subject to the limit imposed by section 19 below, the Secretary of State may, with the approval of the Treasury, pay to the Corporation such sums as he thinks fit. Other public investment in the Corporation.

(2) Any sums required by the Secretary of State for making payments under subsection (1) above shall be defrayed out of moneys provided by Parliament.

(3) Without prejudice to the following provisions of this section, the sum which at the commencement of this Act is treated as having been paid by the Secretary of State to the Corporation under section 18(1) of the Iron and Steel Act 1975 shall thereafter be treated as having been so paid under subsection (1) above.

(4) Once in each of the Corporation's financial years the Secretary of State may, after consultation with the Corporation and with the approval of the Treasury, direct that a specified sum shall be treated as having been paid by him to the Corporation under subsection (1) above, but any sum so specified in a direction given in any financial year shall not exceed the aggregate of the reserves, at the end of the Corporation's immediately preceding financial year, of the Corporation and any companies that were then in public ownership.

(5) The Corporation shall, as respects each of their financial years, be under an obligation either—

(a) to make to the Secretary of State (within such reasonable period as he may determine beginning with the day on which a copy of the statement of the Corporation's accounts in respect of the year is sent to him in compliance with section 24(4) of this Act) a proposal for the payment by them to him of a dividend at a specified rate per cent. in respect of that year on the aggregate of any sums paid by the Secretary of State to the Corporation under subsection (1) above (including the sums treated, under subsection (3) or (4) above, as having been so paid), or

(b) to satisfy him, within that period, that no dividend in respect of that year ought to be paid on that aggregate ;

and, if the Corporation do not within that period make a proposal under paragraph (a) above, or such a proposal acceptable to the Secretary of State and the Treasury, and do not within that period satisfy the Secretary of State that no dividend in respect of that year ought to be paid on that aggregate, he may, with the approval of the Treasury and after consultation with the Corporation, direct them to pay to him such a dividend as aforesaid at such rate per cent. as he specifies.

(6) Where a proposal made in satisfaction of the obligation imposed by subsection (5) above is accepted by the Secretary of State or a direction is given under that subsection by him, a dividend on the aggregate to which the proposal or direction relates at the rate proposed or directed shall become payable by the Corporation to the Secretary of State on the expiration of the period of seven days beginning with the day immediately following that on which written notice of acceptance of the proposal

is given to the Corporation or the direction is communicated to them in writing, as the case may be.

(7) If the Secretary of State so provides by an order made so as to come into force no later than the end of 1982, the aggregate of—

> (*a*) the sums paid under subsection (1) above, and
>
> (*b*) so much of the sum treated as so paid as represents sums paid under section 18(1) of the Iron and Steel Act 1975 c. 64. 1975,

shall be treated as reduced by the sum specified in the order ; and on the coming into force of the order any entitlement of the Secretary of State and any liability of the Corporation in respect of those sums shall be correspondingly reduced.

(8) The sum specified in an order under subsection (7) above shall not exceed £1,000 million and, if more than one order is made under subsection (7) above or if an order has been made under subsection (3) of section 4 of the Iron and Steel Act 1981, 1981 c. 46. the aggregate of the sums specified in all orders under the said subsection (7) or the said subsection (3) shall not exceed £1,000 million.

(9) Any sums received by the Secretary of State under subsection (6) above shall be paid into the Consolidated Fund.

(10) Without prejudice to paragraph 1 of Schedule 6 to this Act, in relation to any financial year beginning before the commencement of this Act, the reference in subsection (5)(*a*) above to section 24(4) of this Act shall include a reference to section 24(4) of the Iron and Steel Act 1975.

19.—(1) The aggregate of the following shall not at any time Limit on exceed the limit imposed by or by virtue of subsection (2) borrowing by below— and investment in

> (*a*) the amount outstanding in respect of the principal of the any money borrowed by the Corporation under section Corporation. 16 above, section 16 of the Iron and Steel Act 1975 1967 c. 17. or section 19 of the Iron and Steel Act 1967, other than money borrowed by them for the payment off of any part of their commencing capital debt, being the debt of £133,988,359·20 which the Corporation were treated as having assumed on 28th July 1967 and other than money borrowed by them from a publicly-owned company ;
>
> (*b*) any sums actually paid by the Secretary of State to the Corporation under subsection (1) of section 18 above together with the sum referred to in subsection

(3) of that section, other than so much of it as represents any sum which was treated by virtue of subsection (3) or (4) of section 18 of the Iron and Steel Act 1975 (the £500 million deemed to have been paid on 28th July 1967 and sums specified in a direction equivalent to a direction under section 18(4) above) as having been paid by the Secretary of State under that section ; and

(c) the amount outstanding in respect of the principal of any money borrowed by any publicly-owned company, other than money borrowed from the Corporation or another publicly-owned company.

(2) The said limit is £3,500 million or such other sum as the Secretary of State may specify by order made with the consent of the Treasury.

(3) The specified sum may be greater than the one it replaces, but shall not exceed £4,500 million and where an order is made so as to come into force before the end of 1982, the specified sum may be less than the one it replaces, but shall not be less than £2,500 million.

Accounts of the Secretary of State.

20.—(1) The Secretary of State shall, as respects each financial year, prepare in such form and manner as the Treasury may direct an account of—

(a) sums received by him under subsection (2) of section 17 above and subsection (6) of section 18 above,

(b) sums issued to him under subsection (3) of the said section 17,

(c) the disposal by him of any such sums respectively, and

(d) the sums which by virtue of paragraph (b) of subsection (1) of section 19 above are to be taken into account for the purposes of that subsection,

and shall send the account to the Comptroller and Auditor General not later than the end of November in the following year ; and the Comptroller and Auditor General shall examine, certify and report on the account and lay copies of it, together with his report, before each House of Parliament.

1978 c. 30.

(2) Without prejudice to section 17 of the Interpretation Act 1978 (repeal and re-enactment), in relation to any financial year beginning before the commencement of this Act, the references in subsection (1) above to sections 17 and 18 above shall include references to sections 17 and 18 respectively of the Iron and Steel Act 1975.

1975 c. 64.

Treasury guarantees.

21.—(1) The Treasury may guarantee, in such manner and on such conditions as they may think fit, the repayment of the principal of, and the payment of interest on, any sums which

the Corporation borrow from a person other than the Secretary
of State.

(2) Immediately after such a guarantee is given, the Treasury shall lay a statement of the guarantee before each House of Parliament, and where any sum is issued for fulfilling such a guarantee the Treasury shall, as soon as possible after the end of each financial year beginning with that in which the sum is issued and ending with that in which all liability in respect of the principal of the sum and in respect of interest thereon is finally discharged, lay before each House of Parliament a statement relating to that sum.

(3) Any sums required by the Treasury for fulfilling any such guarantee shall be charged on, and issued out of, the Consolidated Fund.

(4) If any sums are issued in fulfilment of any such guarantee, the Corporation shall make to the Treasury, at such times and in such manner as the Treasury may from time to time direct, payments of such amounts as the Treasury may so direct in or towards repayment of the sums so issued, and payments of interest on what is outstanding for the time being in respect of sums so issued at such rate as the Treasury may so direct.

(5) Any sums received by the Treasury under subsection (4) above shall be paid into the Consolidated Fund.

22.—(1) Any sums in the hands of the Corporation which are not immediately required for the purposes of their business may be invested in such manner as the Corporation think proper. Investment powers of the Corporation.

(2) Nothing in subsection (1) above shall be taken to authorise the Corporation to do, without the consent of, or otherwise than in accordance with the terms of any general authority given by, the Secretary of State, anything which may be done by them under section 2 above only with such consent or in accordance with the terms of any such authority.

23. Each of the Corporation's financial years shall, unless a different period is prescribed by order made by the Secretary of State, be a period beginning with the end of the immediately preceding financial year and ending— The Corporation's financial year.

(a) if the last day of the following March is a Saturday, with that day ; or

(b) if not, with the Saturday which (whether falling in March or April) falls nearest to the last day of the following March.

24.—(1) The Corporation shall keep proper accounts and other records and shall prepare in such form as the Secretary of State may, with the approval of the Treasury, direct—

(*a*) in respect of each financial year, a statement of the accounts of the Corporation ;

(*b*) in respect of each financial year, a consolidated statement of accounts dealing with the state of affairs and profit or loss of the Corporation and their subsidiaries or, if the Secretary of State so directs in respect of any financial year, of the Corporation and their subsidiaries other than any subsidiary (not being a publicly-owned company) specified in the direction ; and

(*c*) in respect of a financial year as to which the Secretary of State, with the approval of the Treasury, directs that this paragraph shall have effect, a consolidated statement of accounts dealing with the state of affairs and profit or loss of the Corporation and such companies as were in public ownership during any part of the year.

(2) The Secretary of State may make regulations—

(*a*) requiring that there shall be stated in, or in a note on or statement annexed to, the statement referred to in subsection (1)(*a*) above, such information as may be specified in the regulations relating to—

(i) bodies which, at a time so specified, are subsidiaries of the Corporation ; and

(ii) assets of the Corporation consisting of shares in, or amounts owing (whether on account of a loan or otherwise) from, such bodies ;

(*b*) requiring that there shall be so stated such information as may be so specified relating to—

(i) bodies corporate that are not at such time as aforesaid subsidiaries of the Corporation, in which shares are, at that time, to such extent as may be so specified, held by the Corporation ; and

(ii) assets of the Corporation consisting of shares in, or amounts owing (whether on account of a loan or otherwise) from, those bodies corporate ;

(*c*) requiring that there shall be so stated, in such form as may be so specified, the information supplied by the Corporation's subsidiaries in compliance with any provision of the enactments for the time being in force relating to companies imposing on a company a requirement to supply information corresponding to any that may be required to be supplied by the Corporation by virtue of paragraph (*b*) above ;

(*d*) determining the circumstances in which, for the purposes of any requirement imposed by virtue of paragraph (*a*) or (*b*) above, shares in, or amounts owing
from, a body corporate are to be treated as being held
by, or owing to, the Corporation ;

(*e*) granting exemption in circumstances so specified from a
requirement imposed by virtue of paragraph (*a*) or (*b*)
above ;

(*f*) making such provision supplementary to any requirement imposed by virtue of paragraph (*a*) or (*b*) above
as the Secretary of State thinks necessary or expedient.

(3) The accounts of the Corporation shall be audited by
auditors appointed by the Secretary of State, and a person shall
not be qualified to be so appointed unless he is a member of one
or more of the following bodies—

The Institute of Chartered Accountants in England and
Wales ;

The Institute of Chartered Accountants of Scotland ;

The Association of Certified Accountants ;

The Institute of Chartered Accountants in Ireland ;

any other body of accountants established in the United
Kingdom and for the time being recognised for the
purposes of section 161(1)(*a*) of the Companies Act   1948 c. 38.
1948 by the Secretary of State ;

but a Scottish firm may be so appointed if each of the partners
is qualified to be so appointed.

(4) As soon as the accounts of the Corporation for a financial
year have been audited, the Corporation shall send to the Secretary of State—

(*a*) a copy of the statement referred to in subsection (1)(*a*)
above and of any note or statement required by virtue
of subsection (2) above to be placed thereon or annexed
thereto, together with a copy of any report made by the
auditors on the statement so referred to ;

(*b*) copies of the accounts of such companies as were in
public ownership during any part of the year prepared in accordance with the Companies Act 1948
(as amended by any subsequent enactment, whether
passed before or after the passing of this Act) and a
copy of the report of the directors of each such company, but so that where group accounts within the
meaning of that Act are prepared by any company
it shall not be necessary for a copy of the accounts

of any subsidiary dealt with in those group accounts or of the report of the directors of the subsidiary to be sent to the Secretary of State ;

(c) a copy of the consolidated statement referred to in subsection (1)(b) above, together with a copy of any report made by the auditors on that statement ; and

(d) if the first-mentioned accounts are in respect of a financial year in respect of which the Corporation are required to prepare a consolidated statement of accounts under subsection (1)(c) above, a copy of that consolidated statement, together with a copy of any report made by the auditors on that statement.

(5) In subsection (4) above any reference to the report of the directors of a company is a reference to any report of the directors of the company which, under section 157 of the Companies Act 1948, is required to be attached to a balance sheet of the company.

(6) The Secretary of State shall lay a copy of every such statement, note, account and report before each House of Parliament.

(7) The Corporation shall keep at their principal office copies, which shall be available for inspection during business hours, of any statement of information supplied by the Corporation in compliance with a requirement imposed by virtue of subsection (2) above and shall supply a copy of the statement to any person on demand and on payment of such reasonable charge as the Corporation may require.

PART III

IRON AND STEEL ARBITRATION TRIBUNAL

Iron and Steel Arbitration Tribunal.

25.—(1) There shall continue to be a tribunal called the Iron and Steel Arbitration Tribunal (in this Act referred to as " the arbitration tribunal ") for the purpose of determining any question or dispute which under, or by virtue of, any provision of this Act, or of any regulations made under any such provision, is expressly required to be determined by arbitration under this Act or any matter in respect of which jurisdiction is given to the arbitration tribunal by virtue of any such provision.

(2) The arbitration tribunal shall, subject to subsection (9) below, hear and determine every question, dispute or matter referred to in subsection (1) above.

(3) Where any question, dispute or matter referred to in sub-section (1) above arises out of, or in connection with, the transfer of the securities of any company, or in connection with the recovery of assets of any company, or in connection with any transaction of any company then, if the principal place of business of the company, or the principal place at which the works comprised in the business are situated, as the case may be, is in Scotland, the proceedings before the arbitration tribunal in respect of that question, dispute or matter shall, subject to the provisions of this section, be Scottish proceedings ; and the provisions of this Part of this Act relating to Scottish proceedings shall have effect accordingly.

(4) The arbitration tribunal shall, as the Lord Chancellor may direct, either sit as a single tribunal or sit in two or more divisions, and shall, for the hearing of any proceedings, be constituted as follows—

    (*a*) one member, who shall be the president of the arbitration tribunal, shall be a barrister or solicitor, except that, in the case of Scottish proceedings, he shall be an advocate or solicitor who has practised in Scotland ;

    (*b*) there shall be two other members of whom one shall be a person of experience in business and the other shall be a person of experience in finance.

(5) The members of the arbitration tribunal shall be appointed by the Lord Chancellor, except that any member or members appointed for the hearing of Scottish proceedings shall be appointed by the Lord President of the Court of Session.

(6) Any member appointed by the Lord President of the Court of Session shall act only in relation to Scottish proceedings.

(7) The members of the arbitration tribunal shall hold office for such period as may be determined at the time of their respective appointments and shall be eligible for reappointment, but—

    (*a*) a member may at any time by not less than one month's notice in writing to the Lord Chancellor, or the Lord President of the Court of Session, as the case may be, resign his office ;

    (*b*) the Lord Chancellor, or the Lord President of the Court of Session, as the case may be, may declare the office of any member vacant on the ground that he is unfit to continue in his office ;

    (*c*) if any member becomes bankrupt or makes a composition with his creditors his office shall thereupon become vacant.

PART III   (8) If by reason of illness or other infirmity any member of the arbitration tribunal becomes temporarily incapable of performing the duties of his office, the Lord Chancellor, or the Lord President of the Court of Session, as the case may be, shall appoint some other fit person to discharge his duties for any period not exceeding six months at one time, and the person so appointed shall, during that period, have the same powers as the person in whose place he was appointed.

(9) The arbitration tribunal may, at any stage in any proceedings before them, refer to a person or persons appointed by them for the purpose, for inquiry and report, any question arising in the proceedings, not being a question which in the opinion of the tribunal is primarily one of law, and the report of any such person or persons may be adopted wholly or partly by the tribunal and, if so adopted, may be incorporated in an order of the tribunal.

Procedure and enforcement of orders.   **26.**—(1) The arbitration tribunal shall be a court of record and have an official seal, which shall be judicially noticed, and any order of the tribunal shall be enforceable in England and Wales as if it were an order of the High Court.

1950 c. 27.   (2) The provisions of the Arbitration Act 1950 with respect to—

> (*a*) the administration of oaths and the taking of affirmations ;
>
> (*b*) the correction in awards of mistakes and errors ;
>
> (*c*) the summoning, attendance and examination of witnesses and the production of documents ; and
>
> (*d*) the costs of the reference and award ;

shall, with any necessary modifications, apply in respect of any proceedings before the arbitration tribunal, but except as provided in this subsection that Act shall not apply to any such proceedings.

(3) The arbitration tribunal may, and, if so ordered by the Court of Appeal, shall, state in the form of a special case for determination by the Court of Appeal any question of law which may arise before them.

(4) Subject to the provisions of this section, the procedure in, or in connection with, any proceedings before the arbitration tribunal shall be such as may be determined by rules to be made by the Lord Chancellor.

(5) In relation to Scottish proceedings, this section shall have effect subject to the following modifications—

(*a*) for subsections (2) and (3) there shall be substituted the following subsections—

" (2) The arbitration tribunal shall have the like powers for securing the attendance of witnesses and the production of documents, and with regard to the examination of witnesses on oath and the awarding of expenses, as if the arbitration tribunal were an arbiter under a submission.

(2A) An order of the arbitration tribunal may be recorded for execution in the books of Council and Session and may be enforced accordingly.

(3) The arbitration tribunal may, and, if so directed by the Court of Session, shall, state a case for the opinion of that Court on any question of law arising in the proceedings.

(3A) An appeal shall lie, with the leave of the Court of Session or of the House of Lords, from any decision of the Court of Session under subsection (3) above, and that leave may be given on such terms as to costs or otherwise as the Court of Session or the House of Lords may determine." ;

(*b*) in subsection (4) for the reference to the Lord Chancellor there shall be substituted a reference to the Lord Advocate ;

and in the case of any such proceedings, the tribunal shall, except in so far as for special reasons they think fit not to do so, sit in Scotland.

27.—(1) If, at any stage in any proceedings before the arbitration tribunal which would not otherwise fall to be treated as Scottish proceedings, the tribunal are satisfied that, by reason of the fact that questions of Scottish law arise or for any other reason, the proceedings ought thereafter to be treated as Scottish proceedings, the tribunal may order that they shall thereafter be so treated, and the provisions of this Part of this Act shall have effect accordingly.

Transfer of proceedings between England and Scotland.

(2) If, at any stage in any proceedings before the arbitration tribunal which would otherwise be treated as Scottish proceedings, the tribunal are satisfied that, by reason of the fact that questions of English law arise or for any other reason, the proceedings ought not to be treated as Scottish proceedings, they may make an order that the proceedings shall thereafter not be treated as Scottish proceedings, and the provisions of this Part of this Act shall have effect accordingly.

Part III

Staff and
expenses of
the
arbitration
tribunal.

28.—(1) The arbitration tribunal may, subject to the consent of the Treasury as to numbers, appoint such officers as they consider necessary for assisting them in the proper execution of their duties.

(2) There shall be paid to the members of the arbitration tribunal and to any such officer as aforesaid such remuneration (whether by way of salaries or fees) and such allowances as the Secretary of State may, with the approval of the Treasury, determine.

(3) There shall be paid to any person to whom proceedings are referred by the arbitration tribunal under section 25(9) above for inquiry and report such remuneration (whether by way of salary or fees) and such allowances as the tribunal may, with the approval of the Treasury, determine.

(4) Any remuneration and allowances payable under subsection (2) or (3) above and any other expenses of the arbitration tribunal shall be defrayed in the first instance by the Secretary of State out of moneys provided by Parliament, but the amounts from time to time so paid by him shall be repaid on demand to the Secretary of State by the Corporation and shall be paid by him into the Consolidated Fund.

Part IV

Miscellaneous and General

Power of the
Secretary of
State to
extend
definition of
iron and steel
activities.

29.—(1) If it appears to the Secretary of State that the processing of iron or steel by a process which, on 22nd March 1967, was not being applied by persons carrying on business in Great Britain, or was not, in his opinion, being so applied to a substantial extent, ought to be treated as included in Schedule 5 to this Act, he may, by order, provide that the processing of iron or steel by that process shall be deemed, for the purposes of this Act, to be included in that Schedule.

(2) An order under subsection (1) above with respect to a process shall not be made by the Secretary of State except after consultation with—

(*a*) the Corporation ;

(*b*) such organisations as appear to him to be representative of the interests of persons carrying on business in Great Britain who apply that process ; and

(*c*) such organisations as appear to him to be representative of the interests of persons employed in Great Britain in applying that process.

30. In planning and carrying out, or securing the planning and carrying out of, any programme of capital development or reorganisation of activities relating to carbonisation, the Corporation shall consult with the National Coal Board ; and, in planning and carrying out any such programme in respect of their activities relating to carbonisation, the National Coal Board shall consult with the Corporation.

PART IV

Consultation with respect to carbonisation development between the Corporation and the National Coal Board.

31.—(1) For the purpose of obtaining forecasts reasonably required by him for the exercise and performance of his functions under this Act, the Secretary of State may, by notice in writing served on the producer, require an iron and steel producer (other than the Corporation or a publicly-owned company) to supply the Secretary of State with such forecasts with respect to his output of, and capacity to produce, such iron and steel products as may be specified in the notice ; and any such notice may require any forecasts specified therein to be supplied in such manner and within such time as may be specified in the notice, and either periodically or on one occasion or more.

Power of the Secretary of State to require information from iron and steel producers.

(2) A person who fails to satisfy an obligation to which he is subject by, or by virtue of, subsection (1) above shall, unless he proves that he had reasonable excuse for the failure, be guilty of an offence and liable, on summary conviction, to a fine not exceeding £50, or, in the case of a second or subsequent conviction, or if he has previously been convicted of an offence under section 41 of the Iron and Steel Act 1967 or section 31(2) of the Iron and Steel Act 1975, to a fine not exceeding £200.

1967 c. 17.
1975 c. 64.

32.—(1) A person shall be guilty of an offence if—

False information.

(a) in purported compliance with a requirement imposed under any provision of this Act or of regulations under this Act to supply information, he supplies any information which he knows to be false in a material particular or recklessly supplies any information which is so false ; or

(b) in purported compliance with a requirement so imposed to supply a copy of, or extract from, a book of account, record or document, he supplies a document purporting to be such a copy or extract but which he knows to differ in a material particular from the book, record or document of which it purports to be a copy or, as the case may be, from the passage in which it purports to consist, or recklessly supplies a document purporting to be such a copy or extract but which so differs.

(2) A person guilty of an offence under subsection (1) above shall be liable—

(a) on summary conviction, to imprisonment for a term not exceeding three months or to a fine not exceeding the statutory maximum, or to both;

(b) on conviction on indictment, to imprisonment for a term not exceeding two years or to a fine, or to both.

Restriction of disclosure of information.

33.—(1) No information obtained under this Act or any of its predecessors shall be disclosed except—

(a) with the consent of the person by whom it was supplied or, as the case may be, carrying on the undertaking or business to which the books, records or other documents from which it was obtained related; or

(b) in the form of a summary of information supplied by, or obtained from documents relating to undertakings or businesses carried on by, a number of persons, being a summary so framed as not to enable particulars relating to the business of individual persons to be ascertained therefrom; or

(c) for the purpose of enabling the Corporation or the Secretary of State to discharge their or his functions under this Act; or

(d) with a view to the institution of, or otherwise for the purposes of, any criminal proceedings pursuant to, or arising out of, this Act or any of its predecessors.

(2) Nothing contained in a forecast obtained under this Act or any of its predecessors shall be disclosed except—

(a) with the consent of the person by whom the forecast was supplied;

(b) in the form of a summary of forecasts supplied by a number of persons, being a summary framed as mentioned in subsection (1)(b) above;

(c) for such a purpose as is mentioned in subsection (1)(c) above; or

(d) as mentioned in subsection (1)(d) above.

(3) If a disclosure is made by a person in contravention of subsection (1) or (2) above he shall be guilty of an offence and liable—

(a) on summary conviction, to imprisonment for a term not exceeding three months or to a fine not exceeding the statutory maximum, or to both;

(b) on conviction on indictment, to imprisonment for a term not exceeding two years or to a fine, or to both.

(4) For the purposes of this section the predecessors of this Act are the Iron and Steel Act 1949, the Iron and Steel Act 1953, the Iron and Steel Act 1967 and the Iron and Steel Act 1975.

34.—(1) Where an offence under section 32 or 33 above Offences by which has been committed by a body corporate is proved to bodies have been committed with the consent or connivance of, or to corporate. be attributable to any neglect on the part of, a director, manager, secretary or other similar officer of the body corporate, or any person who was purporting to act in any such capacity, he, as well as the body corporate, shall be guilty of that offence and shall be liable to be proceeded against accordingly.

(2) In subsection (1) above " director ", in relation to the Corporation or any other body corporate established by or under an enactment for the purpose of carrying on under national ownership an industry or part of an industry or under-taking, being a body corporate the affairs of which are managed by its members, means a member of the Corporation or that other body corporate, as the case may be.

35. Any notice authorised to be served under section 31 above, Service of or any other document required or authorised to be given, documents. delivered or served by or under any regulations made under or having effect by virtue of this Act may, without prejudice to any provisions in that behalf of any such regulations, be given, de-livered or served either—

(*a*) by delivering it to the person to whom it is to be given or delivered or on whom it is to be served ; or

(*b*) by leaving it at the usual or last known address of that person ; or

(*c*) by sending it in a prepaid letter addressed to that person at his usual or last known address ; or

(*d*) in the case of an incorporated company or body or the arbitration tribunal, by delivering it to the secretary or clerk of the company, body or tribunal at their registered or principal office or sending it in a prepaid letter addressed to the secretary or clerk of the com-pany, body or tribunal at that office ; or

(*e*) if it is not practicable after reasonable enquiry to ascer-tain the name or address of a person to whom it should be given or delivered, or on whom it should be served, as being a person having any interest in premises, by addressing it to him by the description of the person having that interest in the premises (naming them) to which it relates, and delivering it to some responsible person on the premises, or affixing it, or a copy of it, to some conspicuous part of the premises.

PART IV
Regulations,
orders and
rules.

36.—(1) Any power conferred by this Act to make regulations, any power conferred on the Secretary of State by this Act to make an order, and the power conferred by section 26(4) above to make rules shall be exercisable by statutory instrument.

(2) A statutory instrument which contains an order under section 5(1) or 23 above, or any regulations or rules (except regulations under Schedule 3 to this Act), shall be subject to annulment in pursuance of a resolution of either House of Parliament.

(3) No order shall be made under section 14(7) or 29(1) above unless a draft of the order has been laid before Parliament and has been approved by resolution of each House of Parliament.

(4) No order shall be made under section 18(7) or 19(2) above unless a draft of the order has been laid before, and approved by a resolution of, the House of Commons.

1978 c. 30.

(5) No order shall be made under section 12 above unless a draft of the order has been laid before Parliament; and section 14 of the Intepretation Act 1978 (implied power to amend or revoke) shall not apply to the power to make an order under section 12 above.

Interpretation.

37.—(1) In this Act—

"the arbitration tribunal" has the meaning assigned by section 25(1) above;

1948 c. 38.

"company" means a company within the meaning of the Companies Act 1948 and a body incorporated by royal charter;

"the Corporation" has the meaning assigned by section 1(1) above;

"financial year"—

(*a*) in relation to the Corporation, means the period prescribed by or under section 23 above; and

(*b*) in relation to any publicly-owned company, means the period for which the accounts of the company are made up for the purpose of being laid before its annual meeting, whether that period is a year or not;

"iron and steel activities" means the activities described in Schedule 5 to this Act;

"iron and steel producer" means a person carrying on in Great Britain a business comprising any iron and steel activities;

"iron and steel products" means products of any iron and steel activities;

" iron ore " means ore containing not less than one fifth part by weight of iron ;

" pension ", in relation to any person, means a pension whether contributory or not, of any kind whatsoever payable to, or in respect of, him, and includes a gratuity so payable and a return of contributions to a pension fund, with or without interest thereon or any other addition thereto ;

" products ", in relation to any activities, means the direct products of those activities and does not include any by-products thereof ;

" publicly-owned company " means a company which for the time being qualifies for inclusion in any group of bodies corporate as respects which the following conditions are for the time being fulfilled—

> (a) every body corporate of the group is either the Corporation or a subsidiary of the Corporation ; and

> (b) every member of every company in the group is either the Corporation or another company in the group or a nominee of the Corporation or of a company in the group ;

> and " public ownership ", in relation to any company, shall be construed accordingly ;

" Scottish proceedings " has the meaning assigned by section 25(3) above ;

" the statutory maximum " means—

> (a) in England and Wales, the prescribed sum within the meaning of section 32 of the Magistrates' Courts Act 1980 (that is to say £1,000 or another sum fixed by order under section 143 of that Act to take account of changes in the value of money) ; and

1980 c. 43.

> (b) in Scotland, the prescribed sum within the meaning of section 289B of the Criminal Procedure (Scotland) Act 1975 (that is to say £1,000 or another sum fixed by order under section 289D of that Act for that purpose) ;

1975 c. 21.

" subsidiary " shall be construed in accordance with section 154 of the Companies Act 1948 ;

1948 c. 38.

" works " means—

> (a) any factory (within the meaning of the Factories Act 1961) ;

1961 c. 34.

> (b) any mine or quarry ; or

> (c) any premises used by way of trade or business for the purposes of the storage, transport or distribution of any articles or for the supply of electricity or other forms of power ;

PART IV

together with any machinery or equipment installed in any factory, mine, quarry or premises as aforesaid and any land occupied for the purposes thereof, but does not include any factory, mine, quarry, premises or land outside Great Britain.

(2) References in this Act to a person employed by a company do not include references to a director of the company whose functions are not substantially those of a managing director or an employee.

Consequential provisions etc. and repeals.

1978 c. 30.

38.—(1) Schedule 6 to this Act (which contains consequential and transitional provisions and savings) shall have effect, and the provisions of that Schedule are without prejudice to sections 16 and 17 of the Interpretation Act 1978 (which relate to repeals).

(2) Subject to the provisions of the said Schedule 6, the enactments specified in Schedule 7 to this Act are hereby repealed to the extent specified in the third column of Schedule 7.

Short title, commencement and extent.

39.—(1) This Act may be cited as the Iron and Steel Act 1982.

(2) This Act shall come into force on the expiration of the period of three months beginning with its passing.

(3) Without prejudice to the capacity of the Corporation under section 2 above, the following provisions only of this Act shall extend to Northern Ireland, that is to say, sections 12(1) and (2), 13(3) and (4), 36(1) and (5), 37, section 38 so far as it relates to paragraph 6 of Schedule 6 and to Schedule 7 and this section.

SCHEDULES

SCHEDULE 1

Section 1.

PROVISIONS AS TO THE CORPORATION

Deputy chairmen

1. The Secretary of State may appoint one or more members of the Corporation to be deputy chairman or deputy chairmen of the Corporation.

Terms of office of members

2.—(1) Every member of the Corporation shall hold and vacate his office in accordance with the terms of his appointment and shall, on ceasing to be a member, be eligible for re-appointment.

(2) Any member may at any time by notice in writing to the Secretary of State resign his office.

3.—(1) Before appointing a person to be a member of the Corporation, the Secretary of State shall satisfy himself that that person will have no such financial or other interest as is likely to affect prejudicially the exercise or performance by him of his functions as a member of the Corporation.

(2) The Secretary of State shall from time to time satisfy himself with respect to every member of the Corporation that he has no such interest as is referred to in sub-paragraph (1) above.

(3) Any person whom the Secretary of State proposes to appoint as, and who has consented to be, a member of the Corporation, and any member of the Corporation, shall, whenever requested by the Secretary of State to do so, supply him with such information as the Secretary of State considers necessary for the performance by the Secretary of State of his duties under this paragraph.

4.—(1) A member of the Corporation who is in any way directly or indirectly interested in a contract made or proposed to be made by the Corporation, or in any contract made or proposed to be made by a subsidiary of the Corporation, which is brought up for consideration by the Corporation, shall, as soon as possible after the relevant circumstances have come to his knowledge, declare the nature of his interest—

 (*a*) if he is the chairman, to the Secretary of State ;

 (*b*) if he is not the chairman, to the chairman ;

 (*c*) in any case, at a meeting of the Corporation.

(2) After a member has made a declaration under sub-paragraph (1) above in respect of any contract he shall not take part in any deliberation or decision of the Corporation with respect to the contract.

(3) A declaration made in pursuance of sub-paragraph (1)(*c*) above shall be recorded in the minutes of the Corporation.

Meetings and proceedings

5. The Corporation may act notwithstanding a vacancy among their members.

6.—(1) The quorum of the Corporation shall be such number as the Corporation may from time to time determine, being—

(*a*) not less than five if the number of the members of the Corporation exceeds ten ; and

(*b*) not less than three if the number of the members does not exceed ten.

(2) Where any member is disqualified from taking part in any deliberation or decision of the Corporation with respect to any matter he shall be disregarded for the purpose of constituting a quorum of the Corporation for deliberating on or deciding that matter.

(3) Subject to the preceding provisions of this paragraph, the Corporation may regulate their own procedure.

Remuneration, pensions, etc. of members

7. The Corporation—

(*a*) shall pay to their members such remuneration (whether by way of salaries or fees) and such allowances as the Secretary of State may, with the approval of the Treasury, determine ; and

(*b*) as regards any members in whose case the Secretary of State may, with the approval of the Treasury, so determine, shall make provision for, or pay to or in respect of them, such pensions as may be so determined.

Compensation for loss of office

8. Where a person ceases, otherwise than on the expiry of his term of office, to be a member of the Corporation, and it appears to the Secretary of State that there are special circumstances which make it right that that person should receive compensation, the Secretary of State may, with the approval of the Treasury, require the Corporation to make to that person a payment of such amount as may be determined by the Secretary of State with the like approval.

Officers

9. The Corporation shall appoint a secretary and may appoint such other officers and such servants as they may determine.

Sealing of instruments

10. The fixing of the seal of the Corporation shall be authenticated by the signature of the secretary of the Corporation or of some other person authorised, either generally or specially, by the Corporation to act for that purpose.

11. Every document purporting to be an instrument issued by the Corporation and to be sealed as aforesaid or signed on behalf of the Corporation shall be received in evidence and be deemed to be such an instrument without further proof unless the contrary is shown.

SCHEDULE 2

Information Respecting Classes of Business

1. This Schedule applies to business of a kind which consists wholly or mainly in activities other than iron or steel activities and, for the purposes of this Schedule, classes of business that do not differ substantially from each other shall be treated as one class of business.

2.—(1) If a body in the group consisting of the Corporation and any publicly-owned companies has, in the course of a financial year of the body ending after such date as the Secretary of State may determine for the purposes of this paragraph, carried on business of a kind to which this Schedule applies or business of that kind of two or more classes, the Corporation shall determine the amount of the turnover of the body for that financial year in respect of business of that kind or of each of those classes, as the case may be.

(2) Where the amount of that turnover in respect of business of that kind or of any of those classes, as the case may be, is determined by the Corporation to have exceeded £250,000, there shall be contained, in the report which the Corporation are required to make under section 6(2) of this Act (being, if the body referred to in subparagraph (1) above is the Corporation, the report which they are so required to make next after the end of the financial year therein referred to and, if the body is a publicly-owned company, the report which the Corporation are so required to make next after the end of the financial year of the Corporation with or within which the first-mentioned financial year ends), a statement of—

(*a*) the amount of that turnover ;

(*b*) the extent or approximate extent (expressed, in either case, in monetary terms), as determined by the Corporation, to which the carrying on by the body of business of that kind or class, as the case may be, contributed to, or restricted, the profit or loss of the body for the financial year of the body before taxation ;

(*c*) the extent or approximate extent, as so determined, to which capital moneys were, in the course of that financial year, employed in the carrying on by the body of business of that kind or class, as the case may be ; and

(*d*) such further information, if any, relating to the carrying on by the body of business of that kind or class, as the case may be, as the Secretary of State may from time to time direct.

3.—(1) If, in the course of a financial year of the Corporation ending after such date as the Secretary of State may determine for the purposes of this paragraph, any two or more bodies in the group consisting of the Corporation and any publicly-owned companies have carried on business of a kind to which this Schedule applies or business of that kind of two or more classes, the 'Corporation shall determine the amount of the turnover of those bodies as a whole for that financial year in respect of business of that kind or of each of those classes, as the case may be.

(2) Where the amount of that turnover in respect of business of that kind or of any of those classes, as the case may be, is determined by the Corporation to have exceeded £1,000,000, there shall be contained, in the report which the Corporation are required to make under section 6(2) of this Act next after the end of the financial year referred to in sub-paragraph (1) above, a statement of—

    (*a*) the amount of that turnover ;

    (*b*) the extent or approximate extent (expressed, in either case, in monetary terms), as determined by the Corporation, to which the carrying on by the bodies therein referred to of business of that kind or class, as the case may be, contributed to or restricted the profit or loss of the Corporation and the publicly-owned companies as a whole for that financial year ;

    (*c*) the extent or approximate extent, as so determined, to which capital moneys were, in the course of that year, employed in the carrying on by those bodies as a whole of business of that kind or class, as the case may be ;

    (*d*) such further information, if any, relating to the carrying on by those bodies of business of that kind or class, as the case may be, as the Secretary of State may from time to time direct.

4. Each report made by the Corporation under section 6(2) of this Act after they are required to make a determination in pursuance of paragraph 2 or 3 above shall contain a statement of the method or, if more than one method is used, of each method, by which turnover is determined by the Corporation for the purposes of that paragraph ; and, in any such report containing a statement made in pursuance of either of those paragraphs, there shall be stated with respect to each matter involving a determination by the Corporation (other than the determination of an amount of turnover) the method by which that determination is arrived at.

5. The method used in arriving at a determination in any case for the purposes of paragraph 2(2)(*c*) above, and that used in arriving at a determination in any case for the purposes of paragraph 3(2)(*c*) above, shall be such as, when examined in conjunction with the determination made, in the first-mentioned case, in pursuance of paragraph 2(2)(*b*) above and that made, in the second-mentioned case, in pursuance of paragraph 3(2)(*b*) above, will give a true and fair view of the relationship in those cases respectively between capital employed and profits made or loss incurred.

6. The Corporation shall not be required, by virtue of this Schedule, to supply information which is supplied in any statement, note, account or report sent by the Corporation to the Secretary of State in pursuance of section 24(4) of this Act.

7. The Secretary of State may from time to time direct that this Schedule or a provision thereof shall not apply to business of a class or description specified in the direction ; and if the Secretary of State gives a direction under this paragraph, that fact, and the class or description of business to which the direction relates, shall be stated in each report made under section 6(2) of this Act so long as that direction is in force.

8. The Secretary of State may from time to time vary the amount by reference to which it is to be determined, under paragraph 2 or 3 above, whether a statement is to be contained in a report, and may fix different amounts under this paragraph for different purposes.

SCHEDULE 3

PENSION RIGHTS OF EMPLOYEES

1.—(1) The Secretary of State may make regulations for all or any of the following purposes—

(a) for providing pensions to, or in respect of, persons who are or have been employed by the Corporation or the Iron and Steel Board or a company which has come into public ownership ;

(b) for the establishment and administration of pension schemes and pension funds for the purposes of paragraph (a) above ;

(c) for the continuance, amendment, repeal or revocation of existing pension schemes relating to the like purposes, whatever the date on which they came into force, and of enactments relating thereto and of trust deeds, rules or other instruments made for the purposes thereof ;

(d) for the transfer in whole or in part, or for the extinguishment, of liabilities under any such existing pension schemes ;

(e) for the transfer in whole or in part, or winding up, of pension funds held for the purposes of any such existing pension schemes ; and

(f) for making any provision consequential on any such provision as aforesaid, including provision for the dissolution or winding up of bodies, whether incorporated or not, whose continued existence is unnecessary having regard to the regulations.

(2) Nothing in sub-paragraph (1)(b) to (e) above shall be taken to authorise the diversion of any funds referred to therein to purposes other than those of sub-paragraph (1)(a) above.

2.—(1) Where provision is made by any regulations under this Schedule for—

(*a*) the amendment, repeal or revocation of any existing pension scheme, or of any enactment relating thereto, or any trust deed, rules or other instrument made for the purposes thereof ; or

(*b*) for the transfer or extinguishment of any liability under any pension scheme ; or

(*c*) for the transfer or winding up of any pension fund held for the purposes of any such scheme ;

the regulations shall be so framed as to secure that persons having pension rights under the scheme, whether or not they are persons mentioned in paragraph 1(1)(*a*) above, are not placed in any worse position by reason of the amendment, repeal, revocation, transfer, extinguishment or winding up.

1949 c. 72.
1967 c. 17.

(2) Sub-paragraph (1) above shall have effect subject to such limitations as the Secretary of State may by regulations prescribe for meeting cases in which, in connection with any provision made by the Iron and Steel Act 1949 or the Iron and Steel Act 1967, or in anticipation of the making of any provision by the said Act of 1967, pension rights were created otherwise than in the ordinary course.

(3) Regulations made under this Schedule shall not be invalid by reason that they do not secure that persons having pension rights are not placed in any worse position by reason of any such amendment, repeal, revocation, transfer, extinguishment or winding up as is mentioned in sub-paragraph (1) above, but if the Secretary of State is satisfied, or it is determined as hereinafter mentioned, that any such regulations have failed to secure that result, the Secretary of State shall as soon as possible make the necessary amending regulations.

(4) Any dispute arising as to whether or not the said result has been secured by any regulations made under this Schedule shall be referred to, and determined by, an industrial tribunal.

(5) Where, by reason of any such amendment, repeal, revocation, transfer, extinguishment or winding up as is mentioned in sub-paragraph (1) above, loss is suffered by any person (not being a publicly-owned company) liable as an employer to make contributions, or to pay pensions, under the existing pension scheme in question, the Corporation shall pay compensation to that person in respect of that loss, and the amount thereof shall, in default of agreement between the Corporation and that person, be determined by arbitration under this Act.

3. Without prejudice to the generality of the preceding provisions of this Schedule, regulations made under this Schedule may contain provisions authorising the treatment of any person who, being a participant in any pension scheme to which the regulations relate, becomes a member of the Corporation as if his service as a member of the Corporation were service as an employee of the Corporation,

and the pension rights of any such person resulting from the operation
of any such provision shall not be affected by the provisions of paragraph 7(*b*) of Schedule 1 to this Act which require that the pensions,
if any, which are to be paid in the case of certain members of the
Corporation are to be determined by the Secretary of State with the
approval of the Treasury.

SCH. 3

4.—(1) Regulations made under this Schedule may contain such
supplementary and consequential provisions as the Secretary of State
thinks necessary, including provisions as to the manner in which
questions arising under the regulations are to be determined and
provisions adapting, modifying or repealing enactments, whether of
general or special application.

(2) Regulations made under this Schedule may be made so as to
have effect from a date prior to their being made, but so much of any
regulations as provides that any provision is to have effect from
such a prior date shall not place any person, other than the Corporation or a publicly-owned company, in a worse position than he
would have been in if the regulations had been made to have effect
only as from the date on which they were made.

5. In this Schedule—

" pension fund " means a fund established for the purposes of
paying pensions ;

" pension rights " includes, in relation to any person, all forms
of right to, or eligibility for, the present or future payment
of a pension to, or in respect of, that person, and any
expectation of the accruer of a pension to, or in respect of
that person under any customary practice, and includes a
right of allocation in respect of the present or future payment of a pension ;

" pension scheme " includes any form of arrangements for the
payment of pensions, whether subsisting by virtue of an Act,
trust, contract, or otherwise, and includes any customary
practice under which pensions are paid.

SCHEDULE 4

Section 11.

CONSTITUTION AND PROCEEDINGS OF PUBLICLY-OWNED COMPANIES THAT ARE PRIVATE COMPANIES

Private companies

1. This Schedule applies to any publicly-owned company that is a
private company within the meaning of the Companies Acts 1948
to 1980 (in this Schedule referred to as " a relevant company ").

Meetings

2. Notwithstanding anything in section 134 of the Companies Act
1948, or the company's articles of association, the Corporation may
call a meeting of a relevant company, and there shall be deemed to
be a quorum present at any meeting of such a company at which
the Corporation is represented.

1948 c. 38.

Sch. 4   3.—(1) The provisions of this paragraph apply in respect of any relevant company all of whose securities are held by the Corporation.

1948 c. 38.   (2) The obligation of the company under the Companies Act 1948, or under the company's articles of association or otherwise, to hold an annual meeting may be discharged by the holding of a meeting of the Corporation summoned and held in such manner, and after such notice, as may be determined by the Corporation in regulating their procedure.

(3) Any power of the company which is by the Companies Act 1948, or by the company's articles of association or otherwise, required to be exercised by the company in general meeting (including a power required to be so exercised by special resolution, extraordinary resolution or a resolution requiring special notice), may be exercised by the Corporation at a meeting summoned and held as aforesaid.

(4) Where any power is exercised by the company in a case where, apart from this paragraph, special notice would be required and a copy of the notice would have to be sent to any person, the company shall give notice in writing to that person not less than twenty-eight days before exercising that power.

(5) Section 143 of the Companies Act 1948 (which provides for the registration of certain resolutions and agreements) shall apply to any resolution of the company which, but for this paragraph, would be a resolution to which that section applied.

1967 c. 81.   (6) Section 14(7) of the Companies Act 1967 (which entitles auditors of a company to attend and be heard at general meetings of the company and to receive notice thereof) shall apply to meetings of the Corporation held for the purpose of exercising their powers under this paragraph with respect to the affairs of the company.

Directors

4. Any provision in the memorandum or articles of association of a relevant company requiring a director to hold a specified share qualification shall not have effect in the case of a relevant company.

5. The power conferred on a company by section 184 of the Companies Act 1948 to remove a director before the expiration of his period of office notwithstanding anything in its articles of association or in any agreement between it and him, shall, in the case of a relevant company, be extended so as to be exercisable notwithstanding anything in any agreement between the company and any person other than the director, and the proviso to subsection (1) of that section (which contains a saving for directors of private companies holding office for life on 18th July 1945) shall not apply to directors of relevant companies.

Alteration of memorandum

6. A relevant company shall not, without the consent in writing of the Secretary of State, so alter the provisions of its memorandum of association or, as the case may be, charter of incorporation or other charter as to increase the activities which it is authorised to carry on.

7. The power conferred by subsection (1) of section 23 of the Companies Act 1948 (which provides that a company may alter by special resolution any conditions contained in its memorandum which could lawfully have been contained in articles of association instead of in the memorandum) shall, in the case of a relevant company, be exercisable notwithstanding the provisions of subsection (2) of that section (which provides that that section shall not apply where the memorandum itself provides for, or prohibits, the alteration of all or any of the said conditions and shall not authorise any variation or abrogation of the special rights of any class of members). 1948 c. 38.

Reduction of capital

8. The power conferred by section 66 of the Companies Act 1948 on a company to reduce its share capital may, in the case of a relevant company, be exercised by ordinary resolution, and any reduction so made shall not be subject to confirmation by the court, and in any such case—

    (a) section 69 of the Companies Act 1948 shall apply with the modification that, for any reference to an order of the court confirming the reduction of the share capital of a company, there shall be substituted a reference to a copy of the resolution of the company for reducing its share capital, and, for the reference to a minute approved by the court showing the particulars mentioned in that section, there shall be substituted a reference to a minute showing those particulars to the satisfaction of the registrar of companies ;

    (b) section 69(3) and (4) of the Companies Act 1948 shall not apply, but notice of the registration of the resolution by the registrar of companies shall be published in the London and Edinburgh Gazettes and the registrar shall certify under his hand the registration of the resolution, and his certificate shall be conclusive evidence that the share capital of the company is such as is stated in the resolution ; and

    (c) sections 67, 68, 70 and 71 of the Companies Act 1948 shall not apply.

Number of members

9. No petition shall be presented for the winding up of a relevant company on the ground that the number of its members is less than the number required by law, nor shall any person be liable on that ground as a member of the company for the payment of any of its debts.

SCH. 4
1948 c. 38.

10. In this Schedule " special resolution ", " extraordinary resolution " and " special notice " have the same meanings as in the Companies Act 1948.

Sections 29
and 37.

SCHEDULE 5

IRON AND STEEL ACTIVITIES

1. The quarrying or mining of iron ore or the treatment or preparation of iron ore for smelting.

2. The smelting of iron ore in a blast furnace with or without other metalliferous materials, or the production of iron by any other process.

3. The production of steel by any process.

4. The casting of iron or steel by any process.

5. The rolling, with or without heat, of any iron and steel products for the purpose of reducing the cross-sectional area thereof.

6. The production, with or without heat, of iron or steel forgings, but not including—
   (a) smiths' hand forging ;
   (b) the production of bolts, nuts, screws, rivets or springs ;
   (c) drop forging or any other stamping or pressing involving the use either of a die conforming to the shape of the final product of the stamping or pressing, or of a series of dies one of which so conforms ;
   (d) the hammering or pressing of any part or component of plant or machinery carried out incidentally to, and by the persons engaged in, the manufacture or repair of the plant or machinery in which the part or component is to be incorporated.

7. The production from iron or steel of bright bars or of hot-finished tubes or of hot-finished pipes.

8. The production of tinplate or terneplate.

Note : The production of pig iron and the production of steel in the form of ingots, slabs, blooms or billets shall be deemed not to fall within paragraph 4 of this Schedule but to fall within paragraph 2 or 3 thereof, as the case may be.

Section 38.

SCHEDULE 6

CONSEQUENTIAL AND TRANSITIONAL PROVISIONS AND SAVINGS

Periods running at commencement

1. Where any period of time specified in any provision repealed by this Act is current at the commencement of this Act, this Act shall have effect as if the corresponding provision of this Act had been in force when the period began to run.

The Mineral Workings Act 1951

2. In subsection (1) of section 15 of the Mineral Workings Act 1951 c. 60. 1951, for the words " the Iron and Steel Act 1975 " there shall be 1975 c. 64. substituted the words " the Iron and Steel Act 1982 " ; and nothing in this Act shall affect the continuance in force of that subsection with the reference in paragraph (*a*) thereof to the Corporation.

The Building Control Act 1966 1966 c. 27.

3. The Building Control Act 1966 shall continue to have effect as if the Corporation and any publicly-owned companies were included amongst the bodies mentioned in the Schedule to that Act.

Fair trading

4. The repeal by this Act of paragraph 8 of Schedule 6 to the Iron and Steel Act 1975 shall not affect the application of the Restrictive Trade Practices Act 1976 in relation to any agreement which has 1976 c. 34. not been registered in accordance with the provisions of that paragraph ; and the period within which particulars of the variation or determination of any agreement to which that paragraph applied are to be furnished in accordance with section 24(2) of the said Act of 1976 to the Director General of Fair Trading shall be the period of three months beginning with the date of the variation or determination.

The Tribunals and Inquiries Act 1971 1971 c. 62.

5. In Part I of Schedule 1 to the Tribunals and Inquiries Act 1971, for the entry relating to Iron and Steel there shall be substituted the following entry—

" Iron and Steel ... ... 11. The Iron and Steel Arbitration Tribunal continued in existence under section 25 of the Iron and Steel Act 1982."

Investment grants

6.—(1) Where in pursuance of an order under section 12(1) of this Act or of arrangements approved for the purposes of this paragraph any asset of a company which was in public ownership on the 30th April 1969 vests in the Corporation, the Secretary of State or, as the case may be, the Department of Commerce for Northern Ireland may make a grant to the Corporation of the same amount as any grant which the Secretary of State or that Department might have made to the company in respect of that asset under section 1, 2 or 6 1966 c. 34. of the Industrial Development Act 1966 or section 1, 2, 5 or 7 of 1966 c. 41 the Industrial Investment (General Assistance) Act (Northern Ireland) (N.I.). 1966 if—

    (*a*) the asset had not vested in the Corporation ; and

    (*b*) in a case in which capital expenditure has been incurred, or is incurred, by the Corporation with reference to the asset, that expenditure had been incurred by the company.

SCH. 6

1975 c. 64.

(2) Where immediately before the commencement of this Act the Secretary of State or the said Department had power to make a grant to the Corporation under paragraph 9 or 10 of Schedule 6 to the Iron and Steel Act 1975 (investment grants) the Secretary of State or, as the case may be, that Department may make that grant after the commencement of this Act notwithstanding the repeal of those paragraphs.

1966 c. 34.
1966 c. 41
(N.I.).

(3) Section 8 of the Industrial Development Act 1966 and section 10 of the Industrial Investment (General Assistance) Act (Northern Ireland) 1966 (conditions) shall apply in relation to grants under sub-paragraph (1) or (2) above, and grants made before the commencement of this Act by virtue of the said paragraph 9 or 10, as they apply in relation to the corresponding grants under those Acts.

Functions transferred to the Corporation

7. The repeal by this Act of Schedule 6 to the Iron and Steel Act 1975 shall not affect—

1953 c. 15.

   (*a*) the continuance in force, or the effect of, any regulations made under section 24 of the Iron and Steel Act 1953 ;

   (*b*) the power to amend or revoke such regulations ;

   (*c*) anything which immediately before the commencement of this Act has effect or is continuing subject to, or to modifications in consequence of, the substitution of the Corporation for any other person or body.

Compensation regulations

1981 c. 46.

8. The repeal by this Act of subsection (6) of section 2 of the Iron and Steel Act 1981 shall not affect the continuance in force after the commencement of this Act of any regulations under paragraph 2 of Schedule 4 to the Iron and Steel Act 1975 (duty to make regulations providing compensation to employees of certain nationalised companies or of the Iron and Steel Board) which were in force by virtue of that subsection immediately before the commencement of this Act.

Section 38.

SCHEDULE 7

REPEALS

Chapter	Short title	Extent of repeal
1975 c. 64.	The Iron and Steel Act 1975.	The whole Act.
1976 c. 41.	The Iron and Steel (Amendment) Act 1976.	The whole Act.
1980 c. 22.	The Companies Act 1980.	In Schedule 3, paragraph 47.
1981 c. 46.	The Iron and Steel Act 1981.	The whole Act.
1981 c. 67.	Acquisition of Land Act 1981.	In Schedule 4, paragraph 24.

ELIZABETH II

Food and Drugs (Amendment) Act 1982

1982 CHAPTER 26

An Act to amend the Food and Drugs Act 1955 by altering certain penalties; by enabling offences to be tried on indictment as well as summarily; by extending in certain circumstances the time limits for prosecution; and for purposes connected therewith. [13th July 1982]

BE IT ENACTED by the Queen's most Excellent Majesty, by and with the advice and consent of the Lords Spiritual and Temporal, and Commons, in this present Parliament assembled, and by the authority of the same, as follows:—

Trial of and penalties for offences under principal Act

1. The following section shall be substituted for section 106 of the Food and Drugs Act 1955 (in this Act referred to as " the principal Act ")— *Offences made triable either way.*

1955 c. 16. (4 & 5 Eliz. 2)

" Offences triable either way.

106.—(1) A person guilty of an offence to which this section applies shall be liable—

> (*a*) on summary conviction, to a fine not exceeding the statutory maximum ; and

> (*b*) on conviction on indictment, to a fine or imprisonment for a term not exceeding two years or both.

(2) This section applies to any offence under this Act except—

> (*a*) an offence under section 5(3) of this Act; **and**

(*b*) an offence under any provision of this Act specified in section 106A(3) of this Act.".

2. The following section shall be inserted after section 106 of the principal Act—

106A.—(1) Any offence to which this section applies shall be triable summarily.

(2) The offences to which this section applies are—

(*a*) an offence under any provision of this Act specified in subsection (3) of this section ;

(*b*) an offence under regulations made under this Act other than an offence which by virtue of the regulations is triable either on indictment or summarily ;

(*c*) an offence under byelaws made under this Act ; and

(*d*) an offence under an order made under section 5 of this Act.

(3) The provisions of this Act mentioned in subsection (2)(*a*) of this section are—

(*a*) section 18(4) ;

(*b*) section 22(1) ;

(*c*) section 23(1) ;

(*d*) section 23(3) ;

(*e*) section 27(1) ;

(*f*) section 52(4) ;

(*g*) section 55(1) ;

(*h*) section 57(1) ;

(*j*) section 100(5) ;

(*k*) section 105(1) ;

(*l*) section 105(3).".

Time limits

3. The following subsections shall be substituted for section 108(1) of the principal Act—

" (1) No prosecution for an offence under this Act or regulations under it which is triable either on indictment or summarily shall be begun after the expiration of three years from the commission of the offence or one year from its discovery by the prosecutor, whichever is the earlier.

(1A) Where a sample has been procured under this Act, no prosecution in respect of the article or substance sampled shall be begun after the expiration of the following period, beginning with the date on which the sample was procured, that is to say—

(i) in the case of a sample of milk, twenty-eight days,

(ii) in any other case, two months,

unless the justice of the peace before whom the information is laid, on being satisfied on oath that having regard to the circumstances of the particular case it was not practicable to lay the information at an earlier date, gives a certificate to that effect ; and, if the prosecution is in respect of a sample of milk, it shall not in any case be begun after the expiration of forty-two days beginning with the said date.".

Trial of and penalties for offences under regulations

4.—(1) The following paragraphs shall be substituted for paragraph (*e*) of section 123(1) of the principal Act (which specifies certain provisions that may be included in regulations under Part I of the Act, Milk and Dairies Regulations and Milk (Special Designation) Regulations)—

" (*e*) provide that an offence under the regulations shall be triable either on indictment or summarily ;

(*ea*) include provisions under which a person guilty of an offence under the regulations which is so triable is liable on summary conviction to a fine not exceeding the statutory maximum or such smaller amount as may be specified in the regulations and on conviction on indictment to either or both of the following—

(i) a fine not exceeding an amount specified in the regulations or of an indefinite amount ;

(ii) imprisonment for a term not exceeding two years or such shorter term as may be specified in the regulations ;

(*eb*) include provisions under which a person guilty of an offence under the regulations which is triable only summarily is liable on conviction to a fine not exceeding £1,000 or such smaller amount as may be specified in the regulations.".

(2) In section 123(2) of the principal Act (which applies subsection (1) of that section to orders requiring particulars of food ingredients) after the word " section ", in the first place where it occurs, there shall be inserted the words ", other than paragraphs (*e*) and (*ea*).".

Powers to provide in regulations for mode of trial and penalties.

Obstruction of execution of principal Act

Abolition of
imprisonment
for
obstruction.

5. In the proviso to section 105(1) of the principal Act (by virtue of which, if a court is satisfied that a person guilty of an offence of obstruction under that subsection committed it with intent to prevent the discovery of some other offence under the Act, or has within the twelve months last preceding been convicted of an offence under the subsection, he may be sentenced to imprisonment for a term not exceeding one month) the words " or to imprisonment for a term not exceeding one month " shall cease to have effect.

Supplementary provisions relating to subordinate legislation

Abolition
of certain
penalties.

6. There shall be omitted from any regulations under the principal Act any provision under which a person guilty of an offence created by them is liable—

    (*a*) to imprisonment on summary conviction ; or

    (*b*) to a further fine for each day during which the offence continues after conviction.

Pre-1956
subordinate
legislation.

7. In Schedule 12 to the principal Act—

    (*a*) paragraph 1(2) ; and

    (*b*) in paragraph 2(3), the words from " (subject " to " effect ", in the second place where it occurs,

(the effect of which is that certain offences against subordinate legislation made before the commencement of the Act are treated as offences under the Act) are hereby repealed.

Northern Ireland

Application
to Northern
Ireland.

8.—(1) Paragraph 1(*b*) of Schedule 10 to the principal Act shall have effect as if the enactments listed in it included section 106A.

(2) In the Table in paragraph 2 of that Schedule the fourth paragraph of the entry relating to section 123(1) is hereby repealed.

Supplementary

Meaning of
" statutory
maximum ".

1980 c. 43.

9. The following definition shall be inserted in section 135(1) of the principal Act after the definition of " slaughterhouse "—

    " statutory maximum " means the prescribed sum within the meaning of section 32 of the Magistrates' Courts Act 1980 (£1,000 or another sum fixed by order under section 143 of that Act to take account of changes in the value of money) ; ".

10. Nothing in this Act— Offences
committed
(a) shall render a person liable to be prosecuted for an before
offence which was committed before 1st January 1983 commence-
after the end of the period during which he could have ment.
been prosecuted for the offence if this Act had not been
passed ; or

(b) shall affect the mode of trial or the punishment for an
offence committed before 1st January 1983.

11.—(1) The following sections of this Act extend to England Extent.
and Wales only—

section 1 ;
section 5 ; and
section 7.

(2) Section 8 above extends to Northern Ireland only.

(3) Subject to subsections (1) and (2) above, this Act extends
to England and Wales and Northern Ireland.

12.—(1) Sections 4 and 9 above shall come into force on 1st Commence-
November 1982. ment.

(2) Subject to subsection (1) above, this Act shall come into
force on 1st January 1983.

13. This Act may be cited as the Food and Drugs (Amend- Citation.
ment) Act 1982, and the principal Act, the Food and Drugs 1976 c. 37.
(Control of Food Premises) Act 1976, the Food and Drugs 1981 c. 26.
(Amendment) Act 1981 and this Act may be cited together as
the Food and Drugs Acts 1955 to 1982.

Civil Jurisdiction and Judgments Act 1982

1982 CHAPTER 27

An Act to make further provision about the jurisdiction of courts and tribunals in the United Kingdom and certain other territories and about the recognition and enforcement of judgments given in the United Kingdom or elsewhere; to provide for the modification of certain provisions relating to legal aid; and for connected purposes.   [13th July 1982]

B E IT ENACTED by the Queen's most Excellent Majesty, by and with the advice and consent of the Lords Spiritual and Temporal, and Commons, in this present Parliament assembled, and by the authority of the same, as follows:—

PART I

IMPLEMENTATION OF THE CONVENTIONS

Main implementing provisions

1.—(1) In this Act—

"the 1968 Convention" means the Convention on jurisdiction and the enforcement of judgments in civil and commercial matters (including the Protocol annexed to that Convention), signed at Brussels on 27th September 1968;

"the 1971 Protocol" means the Protocol on the interpretation of the 1968 Convention by the European Court, signed at Luxembourg on 3rd June 1971;

Interpretation of references to the Conventions and Contracting States.

" the Accession Convention " means the Convention on the accession to the 1968 Convention and the 1971 Protocol of Denmark, the Republic of Ireland and the United Kingdom, signed at Luxembourg on 9th October 1978 ;

" the Conventions " means the 1968 Convention, the 1971 Protocol and the Accession Convention.

(2) In this Act, unless the context otherwise requires—

(*a*) references to, or to any provision of, the 1968 Convention or the 1971 Protocol are references to that Convention, Protocol or provision as amended by the Accession Convention ; and

(*b*) any reference to a numbered Article is a reference to the Article so numbered of the 1968 Convention, and any reference to a sub-division of a numbered Article shall be construed accordingly.

(3) In this Act " Contracting State " means—

(*a*) one of the original parties to the 1968 Convention (Belgium, the Federal Republic of Germany, France, Italy, Luxembourg and the Netherlands) ; or

(*b*) one of the parties acceding to that Convention under the Accession Convention (Denmark, the Republic of Ireland and the United Kingdom),

being a state in respect of which the Accession Convention has entered into force in accordance with Article 39 of that Convention.

The Conventions to have the force of law.

2.—(1) The Conventions shall have the force of law in the United Kingdom, and judicial notice shall be taken of them.

(2) For convenience of reference there are set out in Schedules 1, 2 and 3 respectively the English texts of—

(*a*) the 1968 Convention as amended by Titles II and III of the Accession Convention ;

(*b*) the 1971 Protocol as amended by Title IV of the Accession Convention ; and

(*c*) Titles V and VI of the Accession Convention (transitional and final provisions),

being texts prepared from the authentic English texts referred to in Articles 37 and 41 of the Accession Convention.

Interpretation of the Conventions.

3.—(1) Any question as to the meaning or effect of any provision of the Conventions shall, if not referred to the European Court in accordance with the 1971 Protocol, be determined in accordance with the principles laid down by and any relevant decision of the European Court.

(2) Judicial notice shall be taken of any decision of, or ex- pression of opinion by, the European Court on any such question.

(3) Without prejudice to the generality of subsection (1), the following reports (which are reproduced in the Official Journal of the Communities), namely—

 (a) the reports by Mr. P. Jenard on the 1968 Convention O.J. 1979 and the 1971 Protocol ; and   No. C59/1 and

 (b) the report by Professor Peter Schlosser on the Accession 66. Convention,   O.J. 1979 No. C59/71.

may be considered in ascertaining the meaning or effect of any provision of the Conventions and shall be given such weight as is appropriate in the circumstances.

Supplementary provisions as to recognition and enforcement of judgments

4.—(1) A judgment, other than a maintenance order, which is Enforcement the subject of an application under Article 31 for its enforcement of judgments in any part of the United Kingdom shall, to the extent that its other than enforcement is authorised by the appropriate court, be registered maintenance in the prescribed manner in that court. orders.

In this subsection " the appropriate court " means the court to which the application is made in pursuance of Article 32 (that is to say, the High Court or the Court of Session).

(2) Where a judgment is registered under this section, the reasonable costs or expenses of and incidental to its registration shall be recoverable as if they were sums recoverable under the judgment.

(3) A judgment registered under this section shall, for the purposes of its enforcement, be of the same force and effect, the registering court shall have in relation to its enforcement the same powers, and proceedings for or with respect to its enforcement may be taken, as if the judgment had been originally given by the registering court and had (where relevant) been entered.

(4) Subsection (3) is subject to Article 39 (restriction on enforcement where appeal pending or time for appeal unexpired), to section 7 and to any provision made by rules of court as to the manner in which and conditions subject to which a judgment registered under this section may be enforced.

5.—(1) The function of transmitting to the appropriate court Recognition an application under Article 31 for the recognition or enforce- and ment in the United Kingdom of a maintenance order shall be dis- enforcement charged— of maintenance

 (a) as respects England and Wales and Scotland, by the orders. Secretary of State ;

 (b) as respects Northern Ireland, by the Lord Chancellor.

In this subsection " the appropriate court " means the magistrates' court or sheriff court having jurisdiction in the matter in accordance with the second paragraph of Article 32.

(2) Such an application shall be determined in the first instance by the prescribed officer of that court.

(3) Where on such an application the enforcement of the order is authorised to any extent, the order shall to that extent be registered in the prescribed manner in that court.

(4) A maintenance order registered under this section shall, for the purposes of its enforcement, be of the same force and effect, the registering court shall have in relation to its enforcement the same powers, and proceedings for or with respect to its enforcement may be taken, as if the order had been originally made by the registering court.

(5) Subsection (4) is subject to Article 39 (restriction on enforcement where appeal pending or time for appeal unexpired), to section 7 and to any provision made by rules of court as to the manner in which and conditions subject to which an order registered under this section may be enforced.

(6) A maintenance order which by virtue of this section is enforceable by a magistrates' court in England and Wales or Northern Ireland shall be enforceable in the same manner as an affiliation order made by that court.

(7) The payer under a maintenance order registered under this section in a magistrates' court in England and Wales or Northern Ireland shall give notice of any change of address to the clerk of that court.

A person who without reasonable excuse fails to comply with this subsection shall be guilty of an offence and liable on summary conviction to a fine not exceeding £50.

6.—(1) The single further appeal on a point of law referred to in Article 37, second paragraph and Article 41 in relation to the recognition or enforcement of a judgment other than a mainten-ance order lies—

(*a*) in England and Wales or Northern Ireland, to the Court of Appeal or to the House of Lords in accordance with Part II of the Administration of Justice Act 1969 (appeals direct from the High Court to the House of Lords) ;

(*b*) in Scotland, to the Inner House of the Court of Session.

(2) Paragraph (*a*) of subsection (1) has effect notwithstanding section 15(2) of the Administration of Justice Act 1969 (exclusion of direct appeal to the House of Lords in cases where no appeal to that House lies from a decision of the Court of Appeal).

(3) The single further appeal on a point of law referred to in Article 37, second paragraph and Article 41 in relation to the recognition or enforcement of a maintenance order lies—

> (a) in England and Wales, to the High Court by way of case stated in accordance with section 111 of the Magis- 1980 c. 43. trates' Courts Act 1980;
>
> (b) in Scotland, to the Inner House of the Court of Session;
>
> (c) in Northern Ireland, to the Court of Appeal.

7.—(1) Subject to subsection (4), where in connection with an application for registration of a judgment under section 4 or 5 the applicant shows—

Interest on registered judgments.

> (a) that the judgment provides for the payment of a sum of money; and
>
> (b) that in accordance with the law of the Contracting State in which the judgment was given interest on that sum is recoverable under the judgment from a particular date or time,

the rate of interest and the date or time from which it is so recoverable shall be registered with the judgment and, subject to any provision made under subsection (2), the debt resulting, apart from section 4(2), from the registration of the judgment shall carry interest in accordance with the registered particulars.

(2) Provision may be made by rules of court as to the manner in which and the periods by reference to which any interest payable by virtue of subsection (1) is to be calculated and paid, including provision for such interest to cease to accrue as from a prescribed date.

(3) Costs or expenses recoverable by virtue of section 4(2) shall carry interest as if they were the subject of an order for the payment of costs or expenses made by the registering court on the date of registration.

(4) Interest on arrears of sums payable under a maintenance order registered under section 5 in a magistrates' court in England and Wales or Northern Ireland shall not be recoverable in that court, but without prejudice to the operation in relation to any such order of section 2A of the Maintenance Orders Act 1958 or section 11A of the Maintenance and Affiliation Orders Act (Northern Ireland) 1966 (which enable interest to be re- covered if the order is re-registered for enforcement in the High Court).

1958 c. 39.
1966 c. 35
(N.I.).

(5) Except as mentioned in subsection (4), debts under judg- ments registered under section 4 or 5 shall carry interest only as provided by this section.

PART I
Currency of
payment under
registered
maintenance
orders.

8.—(1) Sums payable in the United Kingdom under a maintenance order by virtue of its registration under section 5, including any arrears so payable, shall be paid in the currency of the United Kingdom.

(2) Where the order is expressed in any other currency, the amounts shall be converted on the basis of the exchange rate prevailing on the date of registration of the order.

(3) For the purposes of this section, a written certificate purporting to be signed by an officer of any bank in the United Kingdom and stating the exchange rate prevailing on a specified date shall be evidence, and in Scotland sufficient evidence, of the facts stated.

Other supplementary provisions

Provisions
supplementary
to Title VII of
1968 Convention.

9.—(1) The provisions of Title VII of the 1968 Convention (relationship between that convention and other conventions to which Contracting States are or may become parties) shall have effect in relation to—

> (a) any statutory provision, whenever passed or made, implementing any such other convention in the United Kingdom ; and
>
> (b) any rule of law so far as it has the effect of so implementing any such other convention,

as they have effect in relation to that other convention itself.

(2) Her Majesty may by Order in Council declare a provision of a convention entered into by the United Kingdom to be a provision whereby the United Kingdom assumed an obligation of a kind provided for in Article 59 (which allows a Contracting State to agree with a third State to withhold recognition in certain cases from a judgment given by a court in another Contracting State which took jurisdiction on one of the grounds mentioned in the second paragraph of Article 3).

Allocation
within U.K.
of
jurisdiction
with respect
to trusts and
consumer
contracts.

10.—(1) The provisions of this section have effect for the purpose of allocating within the United Kingdom jurisdiction in certain proceedings in respect of which the 1968 Convention confers jurisdiction on the courts of the United Kingdom generally and to which section 16 does not apply.

(2) Any proceedings which by virtue of Article 5(6) (trusts) are brought in the United Kingdom shall be brought in the courts of the part of the United Kingdom in which the trust is domiciled.

(3) Any proceedings which by virtue of the first paragraph of Article 14 (consumer contracts) are brought in the United Kingdom by a consumer on the ground that he is himself domiciled there shall be brought in the courts of the part of the United Kingdom in which he is domiciled.

11.—(1) For the purposes of the 1968 Convention—

Proof and admissibility of certain judgments and related documents.

(a) a document, duly authenticated, which purports to be a copy of a judgment given by a court of a Contracting State other than the United Kingdom shall without further proof be deemed to be a true copy, unless the contrary is shown ; and

(b) the original or a copy of any such document as is mentioned in Article 46(2) or 47 (supporting documents to be produced by a party seeking recognition or enforcement of a judgment) shall be evidence, and in Scotland sufficient evidence, of any matter to which it relates.

(2) A document purporting to be a copy of a judgment given by any such court as is mentioned in subsection (1)(a) is duly authenticated for the purposes of this section if it purports—

(a) to bear the seal of that court ; or

(b) to be certified by any person in his capacity as a judge or officer of that court to be a true copy of a judgment given by that court.

(3) Nothing in this section shall prejudice the admission in evidence of any document which is admissible apart from this section.

12. Rules of court may make provision for enabling any interested party wishing to secure under the 1968 Convention the recognition or enforcement in another Contracting State of a judgment given by a court in the United Kingdom to obtain, subject to any conditions specified in the rules—

Provision for issue of copies of, and certificates in connection with, U.K. judgments.

(a) a copy of the judgment ; and

(b) a certificate giving particulars relating to the judgment and the proceedings in which it was given.

13.—(1) Her Majesty may by Order in Council provide that—

Modifications to cover authentic instruments and court settlements.

(a) any provision of this Act relating to the recognition or enforcement in the United Kingdom or elsewhere of judgments to which the 1968 Convention applies ; and

(b) any other statutory provision, whenever passed or made, so relating,

PART I

shall apply, with such modifications as may be specified in the Order, in relation to documents and settlements within Title IV of the 1968 Convention (authentic instruments and court settlements enforceable in the same manner as judgments) as if they were judgments to which that Convention applies.

(2) An Order in Council under this section may make different provision in relation to different descriptions of documents and settlements.

(3) Any Order in Council under this section shall be subject to annulment in pursuance of a resolution of either House of Parliament.

Modifications consequential on revision of the Conventions.

14.—(1) If at any time it appears to Her Majesty in Council that Her Majesty's Government in the United Kingdom have agreed to a revision of any of the Conventions, including in particular any revision connected with the accession to the 1968 Convention of one or more further states, Her Majesty may by Order in Council make such modifications of this Act or any other statutory provision, whenever passed or made, as Her Majesty considers appropriate in consequence of the revision.

(2) An Order in Council under this section shall not be made unless a draft of the Order has been laid before Parliament and approved by a resolution of each House of Parliament.

(3) In this section "revision" means an omission from, addition to or alteration of any of the Conventions and includes replacement of any of the Conventions to any extent by another convention, protocol or other description of international agreement.

Interpretation of Part I and consequential amendments.

15.—(1) In this Part, unless the context otherwise requires—

"judgment" has the meaning given by Article 25;

"maintenance order" means a maintenance judgment within the meaning of the 1968 Convention;

"payer", in relation to a maintenance order, means the person liable to make the payments for which the order provides;

"prescribed" means prescribed by rules of court.

(2) References in this Part to a judgment registered under section 4 or 5 include, to the extent of its registration, references to a judgment so registered to a limited extent only.

(3) Anything authorised or required by the 1968 Convention or this Part to be done by, to or before a particular magistrates' court may be done by, to or before any magistrates' court acting for the same petty sessions area (or, in Northern Ireland, petty sessions district) as that court.

(4) The enactments specified in Part I of Schedule 12 shall
have effect with the amendments specified there, being amendments consequential on this Part.

PART II

JURISDICTION, AND RECOGNITION AND ENFORCEMENT OF JUDGMENTS, WITHIN UNITED KINGDOM

16.—(1) The provisions set out in Schedule 4 (which contains
a modified version of Title II of the 1968 Convention) shall have
effect for determining, for each part of the United Kingdom,
whether the courts of law of that part, or any particular court
of law in that part, have or has jurisdiction in proceedings
where—

Allocation
within U.K.
of jurisdiction
in certain
civil
proceedings.

> (*a*) the subject-matter of the proceedings is within the scope
>   of the 1968 Convention as determined by Article 1
>   (whether or not the Convention has effect in relation to
>   the proceedings) ; and
>
> (*b*) the defendant or defender is domiciled in the United
>   Kingdom or the proceedings are of a kind mentioned
>   in Article 16 (exclusive jurisdiction regardless of domi-
>   cile).

(2) In Schedule 4 modifications of Title II of the 1968 Convention are indicated as follows—

> (*a*) modifications by way of omission are indicated by dots ;
>   and
>
> (*b*) within each Article words resulting from modifications
>   by way of addition or substitution are printed in heavy
>   type.

(3) In determining any question as to the meaning or effect
of any provision contained in Schedule 4—

> (*a*) regard shall be had to any relevant principles laid down
>   by the European Court in connection with Title II of
>   the 1968 Convention and to any relevant decision of
>   that court as to the meaning or effect of any provision
>   of that Title ; and
>
> (*b*) without prejudice to the generality of paragraph (*a*), the
>   reports mentioned in section 3(3) may be considered
>   and shall, so far as relevant, be given such weight as is
>   appropriate in the circumstances.

(4) The provisions of this section and Schedule 4 shall have
effect subject to the 1968 Convention and to the provisions of
section 17.

R 3

(5) In section 15(1)(*a*) of the Maintenance Orders Act 1950 (domestic proceedings in which initial process may be served in another part of the United Kingdom), after sub-paragraph (v) there shall be added—

" (vi) Article 5(2) of Schedule 4 to the Civil Jurisdiction and Judgments Act 1982 ; or ".

17.—(1) Schedule 4 shall not apply to proceedings of any description listed in Schedule 5 or to proceedings in Scotland under any enactment which confers jurisdiction on a Scottish court in respect of a specific subject-matter on specific grounds.

(2) Her Majesty may by Order in Council—

(*a*) add to the list in Schedule 5 any description of proceedings in any part of the United Kingdom ; and

(*b*) remove from that list any description of proceedings in any part of the United Kingdom (whether included in the list as originally enacted or added by virtue of this subsection).

(3) An Order in Council under subsection (2)—

(*a*) may make different provisions for different descriptions of proceedings, for the same description of proceedings in different courts or for different parts of the United Kingdom ; and

(*b*) may contain such transitional and other incidental provisions as appear to Her Majesty to be appropriate.

(4) An Order in Council under subsection (2) shall not be made unless a draft of the Order has been laid before Parliament and approved by a resolution of each House of Parliament.

18.—(1) In relation to any judgment to which this section applies—

(*a*) Schedule 6 shall have effect for the purpose of enabling any money provisions contained in the judgment to be enforced in a part of the United Kingdom other than the part in which the judgment was given ; and

(*b*) Schedule 7 shall have effect for the purpose of enabling any non-money provisions so contained to be so enforced.

(2) In this section " judgment " means any of the following (references to the giving of a judgment being construed accordingly)—

(*a*) any judgment or order (by whatever name called) given or made by a court of law in the United Kingdom ;

(b) any judgment or order not within paragraph (a) which
has been entered in England and Wales or Northern
Ireland in the High Court or a county court ;

(c) any document which in Scotland has been registered
for execution in the Books of Council and Session or
in the sheriff court books kept for any sheriffdom ;

(d) any award or order made by a tribunal in any part of
the United Kingdom which is enforceable in that part
without an order of a court of law ;

(e) an arbitration award which has become enforceable in
the part of the United Kingdom in which it was given
in the same manner as a judgment given by a court of
law in that part ;

and, subject to the following provisions of this section, this
section applies to all such judgments.

(3) Subject to subsection (4), this section does not apply to—

(a) a judgment given in proceedings in a magistrates' court
in England and Wales or Northern Ireland ;

(b) a judgment given in proceedings other than civil proceedings ;

(c) a judgment given in proceedings relating to—

(i) bankruptcy ; or

(ii) the winding up of a corporation or association ; or

(iii) the obtaining of title to administer the estate
of a deceased person.

(4) This section applies, whatever the nature of the proceedings in which it is made, to—

(a) a decree issued under section 13 of the Court of Ex- 1856 c. 56.
chequer (Scotland) Act 1856 (recovery of certain rent-
charges and penalties by process of the Court of
Session) ;

(b) an order which is enforceable in the same manner as a
judgment of the High Court in England and Wales by
virtue of section 16 of the Contempt of Court Act 1981 1981 c. 49.
or section 140 of the Supreme Court Act 1981 (which 1981 c. 54.
relate to fines for contempt of court and forfeiture of
recognisances).

(5) This section does not apply to so much of any judgment
as—

(a) is an order to which section 16 of the Maintenance 1950 c. 37.
Orders Act 1950 applies (and is therefore an order
for whose enforcement in another part of the United
Kingdom provision is made by Part II of that Act) ;

R 4

(*b*) concerns the status or legal capacity of an individual ;

(*c*) relates to the management of the affairs of a person not capable of managing his own affairs ;

(*d*) is a provisional (including protective) measure other than an order for the making of an interim payment ;

and except where otherwise stated references to a judgment to which this section applies are to such a judgment exclusive of any such provisions.

(6) The following are within subsection (5)(*b*), but without prejudice to the generality of that provision—

(*a*) a decree of judicial separation or of separation ;

(*b*) any provision relating to guardianship or custody.

(7) This section does not apply to a judgment of a court outside the United Kingdom which falls to be treated for the purposes of its enforcement as a judgment of a court of law in the United Kingdom by virtue of registration under Part II of the Administration of Justice Act 1920, Part I of the Foreign Judgments (Reciprocal Enforcement) Act 1933, Part I of the Maintenance Orders (Reciprocal Enforcement) Act 1972 or section 4 or 5 of this Act.

1920 c. 81.
1933 c. 13.
1972 c. 18.

(8) A judgment to which this section applies, other than a judgment within paragraph (*e*) of subsection (2), shall not be enforced in another part of the United Kingdom except by way of registration under Schedule 6 or 7.

Recognition of U.K. judgments in other parts of U.K.

19.—(1) A judgment to which this section applies given in one part of the United Kingdom shall not be refused recognition in another part of the United Kingdom solely on the ground that, in relation to that judgment, the court which gave it was not a court of competent jurisdiction according to the rules of private international law in force in that other part.

(2) Subject to subsection (3), this section applies to any judgment to which section 18 applies.

(3) This section does not apply to—

(*a*) the documents mentioned in paragraph (*c*) of the definition of " judgment " in section 18(2) ;

(*b*) the awards and orders mentioned in paragraphs (*d*) and (*e*) of that definition ;

(*c*) the decrees and orders referred to in section 18(4) ;

PART III

JURISDICTION IN SCOTLAND

Rules as to jurisdiction in Scotland.

20.—(1) Subject to Parts I and II and to the following provisions of this Part, Schedule 8 has effect to determine in what

circumstances a person may be sued in civil proceedings in the
Court of Session or in a sheriff court.

(2) Nothing in Schedule 8 affects the competence as respects
subject-matter or value of the Court of Session or of the sheriff
court.

(3) Section 6 of the Sheriff Courts (Scotland) Act 1907 shall 1907 c. 51.
cease to have effect to the extent that it determines jurisdiction
in relation to any matter to which Schedule 8 applies.

(4) In Schedule 8—

   (*a*) words resulting from modifications of Title II of the 1968
      Convention, by way of addition or substitution, and
      provisions not derived from that Title are printed in
      heavy type ; and

   (*b*) the marginal notes show, where appropriate, of which
      provision of Title II a provision of Schedule 8 is a
      modified version.

(5) In determining any question as to the meaning or effect
of any provision contained in Schedule 8 and derived to any
extent from Title II of the 1968 Convention—

   (*a*) regard shall be had to any relevant principles laid down
      by the European Court in connection with Title II
      of the 1968 Convention and to any relevant decision
      of that court as to the meaning or effect of any pro-
      vision of that Title ; and

   (*b*) without prejudice to the generality of paragraph (*a*),
      the reports mentioned in section 3(3) may be con-
      sidered and shall, so far as relevant, be given such
      weight as is appropriate in the circumstances.

21.—(1) Schedule 8 does not affect—   Continuance
   (*a*) the operation of any enactment which confers jurisdic-   of certain
      tion on a Scottish court in respect of a specific subject-   existing
      matter on specific grounds ;   jurisdictions.

   (*b*) without prejudice to the foregoing generality, the juris-
      diction of any court in respect of any matter mentioned
      in Schedule 9.

(2) Her Majesty may by Order in Council—

   (*a*) add to the list in Schedule 9 any description of proceed-
      ings ; and

   (*b*) remove from that list any description of proceedings
      (whether included in the list as originally enacted or
      added by virtue of this subsection).

PART III

(3) An Order in Council under subsection (2) may—

(a) make different provision for different descriptions of proceedings or for the same description of proceedings in different courts ; and

(b) contain such transitional and other incidental provisions as appear to Her Majesty to be appropriate.

(4) An Order in Council under subsection (2) shall not be made unless a draft of the Order has been laid before Parliament and approved by a resolution of each House of Parliament.

Supplementary provisions.

22.—(1) Nothing in Schedule 8 shall prevent a court from declining jurisdiction on the ground of *forum non conveniens*.

(2) Nothing in Schedule 8 affects the operation of any enactment or rule of law under which a court may decline to exercise jurisdiction because of the prorogation by parties of the jurisdiction of another court.

(3) For the avoidance of doubt, it is declared that nothing in Schedule 8 affects the *nobile officium* of the Court of Session.

(4) Where a court has jurisdiction in any proceedings by virtue of Schedule 8, that court shall also have jurisdiction to determine any matter which—

(a) is ancillary or incidental to the proceedings ; or

(b) requires to be determined for the purposes of a decision in the proceedings.

Savings and consequential amendments.

23.—(1) Nothing in Schedule 8 shall affect—

(a) the power of any court to vary or recall a maintenance order granted by that court ;

1950 c. 37.

(b) the power of a sheriff court under section 22 of the Maintenance Orders Act 1950 (discharge and variation of maintenance orders registered in sheriff courts) to vary or discharge a maintenance order registered in that court under Part II of that Act ; or

1972 c. 18.

(c) the power of a sheriff court under section 9 of the Maintenance Orders (Reciprocal Enforcement) Act 1972 (variation and revocation of maintenance orders registered in United Kingdom courts) to vary or revoke a registered order within the meaning of Part I of that Act.

(2) The enactments specified in Part II of Schedule 12 shall have effect with the amendments specified there, being amendments consequential on Schedule 8.

Part IV

Miscellaneous Provisions

Provisions relating to jurisdiction

24.—(1) Any power of a court in England and Wales or Interim relief
Northern Ireland to grant interim relief pending trial or pending and
the determination of an appeal shall extend to a case where— protective
measures in

   (*a*) the issue to be tried, or which is the subject of the cases of
      appeal, relates to the jurisdiction of the court to enter- doubtful
      tain the proceedings ; or jurisdiction.

   (*b*) the proceedings involve the reference of any matter to
      the European Court under the 1971 Protocol.

(2) Any power of a court in Scotland to grant protective
measures pending the decision of any hearing shall apply to a
case where—

   (*a*) the subject of the proceedings includes a question as to
      the jurisdiction of the court to entertain them ; or

   (*b*) the proceedings involve the reference of a matter to the
      European Court under the 1971 Protocol.

(3) Subsections (1) and (2) shall not be construed as restricting
any power to grant interim relief or protective measures which a
court may have apart from this section.

25.—(1) The High Court in England and Wales or Northern Interim relief
Ireland shall have power to grant interim relief where— in England
and Wales

   (*a*) proceedings have been or are to be commenced in a and Northern
      Contracting State other than the United Kingdom or Ireland in the
      in a part of the United Kingdom other than that in absence of
      which the High Court in question exercises jurisdic- substantive
      tion ; and proceedings.

   (*b*) they are or will be proceedings whose subject-matter
      is within the scope of the 1968 Convention as deter-
      mined by Article 1 (whether or not the Convention has
      effect in relation to the proceedings).

(2) On an application for any interim relief under subsection (1)
the court may refuse to grant that relief if, in the opinion of the
court, the fact that the court has no jurisdiction apart from this
section in relation to the subject-matter of the proceedings in
question makes it inexpedient for the court to grant it.

(3) Her Majesty may by Order in Council extend the power
to grant interim relief conferred by subsection (1) so as to make
it exercisable in relation to proceedings of any of the following
descriptions, namely—

   (*a*) proceedings commenced or to be commenced otherwise
      than in a Contracting State ;

PART IV

(b) proceedings whose subject-matter is not within the scope of the 1968 Convention as determined by Article 1 ;

(c) arbitration proceedings.

(4) An Order in Council under subsection (3)—

(a) may confer power to grant only specified descriptions of interim relief ;

(b) may make different provision for different classes of proceedings, for proceedings pending in different countries or courts outside the United Kingdom or in different parts of the United Kingdom, and for other different circumstances ; and

(c) may impose conditions or restrictions on the exercise of any power conferred by the Order.

(5) An Order in Council under subsection (3) which confers power to grant interim relief in relation to arbitration proceedings may provide for the repeal of any provision of section 12(6) of the Arbitration Act 1950 or section 21(1) of the Arbitration Act (Northern Ireland) 1937 to the extent that it is superseded by the provisions of the Order.

1950 c. 27.
1937 c. 8
(N.I.).

(6) Any Order in Council under subsection (3) shall be subject to annulment in pursuance of a resolution of either House of Parliament.

(7) In this section " interim relief ", in relation to the High Court in England and Wales or Northern Ireland, means interim relief of any kind which that court has power to grant in proceedings relating to matters within its jurisdiction, other than—

(a) a warrant for the arrest of property ; or

(b) provision for obtaining evidence.

Security in
Admiralty
proceedings
in England
and Wales or
Northern
Ireland in
case of stay,
etc.

26.—(1) Where in England and Wales or Northern Ireland a court stays or dismisses Admiralty proceedings on the ground that the dispute in question should be submitted to arbitration or to the determination of the courts of another part of the United Kingdom or of an overseas country, the court may, if in those proceedings property has been arrested or bail or other security has been given to prevent or obtain release from arrest—

(a) order that the property arrested be retained as security for the satisfaction of any award or judgment which—

(i) is given in respect of the dispute in the arbitration or legal proceedings in favour of which those proceedings are stayed or dismissed ; and

(ii) is enforceable in England and Wales or, as the case may be, in Northern Ireland ; or (*b*) order that the stay or dismissal of those proceedings be conditional on the provision of equivalent security for the satisfaction of any such award or judgment.

(2) Where a court makes an order under subsection (1), it may attach such conditions to the order as it thinks fit, in particular conditions with respect to the institution or prosecution of the relevant arbitration or legal proceedings.

(3) Subject to any provision made by rules of court and to any necessary modifications, the same law and practice shall apply in relation to property retained in pursuance of an order made by a court under subsection (1) as would apply if it were held for the purposes of proceedings in that court.

27.—(1) The Court of Session may, in any case to which this subsection applies—

(*a*) subject to subsection (2)(*c*), grant a warrant for the arrestment of any assets situated in Scotland ;

(*b*) subject to subsection (2)(*c*), grant a warrant of inhibition over any property situated in Scotland ; and

(*c*) grant interim interdict.

Provisional and protective measures in Scotland in the absence of substantive proceedings.

(2) Subsection (1) applies to any case in which—

(*a*) proceedings have been commenced but not concluded, or, in relation to paragraph (*c*) of that subsection, are to be commenced, in another Contracting State or in England and Wales or Northern Ireland ;

(*b*) the subject-matter of the proceedings is within the scope of the 1968 Convention as determined by Article 1 ; and

(*c*) in relation to paragraphs (*a*) and (*b*) of subsection (1), such a warrant could competently have been granted in equivalent proceedings before a Scottish court ;

but it shall not be necessary, in determining whether proceedings have been commenced for the purpose of paragraph (*a*) of this subsection, to show that any document has been served on or notice given to the defender.

(3) Her Majesty may by Order in Council confer on the Court of Session power to do anything mentioned in subsection (1) or in section 28 in relation to proceedings of any of the following descriptions, namely—

(*a*) proceedings commenced otherwise than in a Contracting State ;

(*b*) proceedings whose subject-matter is not within the scope of the 1968 Convention as determined by Article 1 ;

(*c*) arbitration proceedings ;

(*d*) in relation to subsection (1)(*c*) or section 28, proceedings which are to be commenced otherwise than in a Contracting State.

(4) An Order in Council under subsection (3)—

    (*a*) may confer power to do only certain of the things mentioned in subsection (1) or in section 28 ;

    (*b*) may make different provision for different classes of proceedings, for proceedings pending in different countries or courts outside the United Kingdom or in different parts of the United Kingdom, and for other different circumstances ; and

    (*c*) may impose conditions or restrictions on the exercise of any power conferred by the Order.

(5) Any Order in Council under subsection (3) shall be subject to annulment in pursuance of a resolution of either House of Parliament.

Application of s. 1 of Administration of Justice (Scotland) Act 1972.

1972 c. 59.

28. When any proceedings have been brought, or are likely to be brought, in another Contracting State or in England and Wales or Northern Ireland in respect of any matter which is within the scope of the 1968 Convention as determined in Article 1, the Court of Session shall have the like power to make an order under section 1 of the Administration of Justice (Scotland) Act 1972 as if the proceedings in question had been brought, or were likely to be brought, in that court.

Service of county court process outside Northern Ireland.

S.I. 1980/397 (N.I. 3).

29. The County Court Rules Committee established by Article 46 of the County Courts (Northern Ireland) Order 1980 may make county court rules with respect to the service of process outside Northern Ireland and the conditions subject to which process may be so served ; and accordingly in Article 48 of that Order (powers of Rules Committee), after paragraph (*e*) there shall be added—

    " (*f*) the service of process outside Northern Ireland, and the conditions subject to which process may be so served.".

Proceedings in England and Wales or Northern Ireland for torts to immovable property.

30.—(1) The jurisdiction of any court in England and Wales or Northern Ireland to entertain proceedings for trespass to, or any other tort affecting, immovable property shall extend to cases in which the property in question is situated outside that part of the United Kingdom unless the proceedings are principally concerned with a question of the title to, or the right to possession of, that property.

(2) Subsection (1) has effect subject to the 1968 Convention and to the provisions set out in Schedule 4.

Provisions relating to recognition and enforcement of judgments

31.—(1) A judgment given by a court of an overseas country against a state other than the United Kingdom or the state to which that court belongs shall be recognised and enforced in the United Kingdom if, and only if—

(a) it would be so recognised and enforced if it had not been given against a state ; and

(b) that court would have had jurisdiction in the matter if it had applied rules corresponding to those applicable to such matters in the United Kingdom in accordance with sections 2 to 11 of the State Immunity Act 1978.

(2) References in subsection (1) to a judgment given against a state include references to judgments of any of the following descriptions given in relation to a state—

(a) judgments against the government, or a department of the government, of the state but not (except as mentioned in paragraph (c)) judgments against an entity which is distinct from the executive organs of government ;

(b) judgments against the sovereign or head of state in his public capacity ;

(c) judgments against any such separate entity as is mentioned in paragraph (a) given in proceedings relating to anything done by it in the exercise of the sovereign authority of the state.

(3) Nothing in subsection (1) shall affect the recognition or enforcement in the United Kingdom of a judgment to which Part I of the Foreign Judgments (Reciprocal Enforcement) Act 1933 applies by virtue of section 4 of the Carriage of Goods by Road Act 1965, section 17(4) of the Nuclear Installations Act 1965, section 13(3) of the Merchant Shipping (Oil Pollution) Act 1971, section 5 of the Carriage by Railway Act 1972 or section 5 of the Carriage of Passengers by Road Act 1974. 1933 c. 13.
1965 c. 37.
1965 c. 57.
1971 c. 59.
1972 c. 33.
1974 c. 35.

(4) Sections 12, 13 and 14(3) and (4) of the State Immunity Act 1978 (service of process and procedural privileges) shall apply to proceedings for the recognition or enforcement in the United Kingdom of a judgment given by a court of an overseas country (whether or not that judgment is within subsection (1) of this section) as they apply to other proceedings.

(5) In this section " state ", in the case of a federal state, includes any of its constituent territories.

PART IV
Overseas
judgments
given in
proceedings
brought in
breach of
agreement for
settlement
of disputes.

32.—(1) Subject to the following provisions of this section, a judgment given by a court of an overseas country in any proceedings shall not be recognised or enforced in the United Kingdom if—

(a) the bringing of those proceedings in that court was contrary to an agreement under which the dispute in question was to be settled otherwise than by proceedings in the courts of that country ; and

(b) those proceedings were not brought in that court by, or with the agreement of, the person against whom the judgment was given ; and

(c) that person did not counterclaim in the proceedings or otherwise submit to the jurisdiction of that court.

(2) Subsection (1) does not apply where the agreement referred to in paragraph (a) of that subsection was illegal, void or unenforceable or was incapable of being performed for reasons not attributable to the fault of the party bringing the proceedings in which the judgment was given.

(3) In determining whether a judgment given by a court of an overseas country should be recognised or enforced in the United Kingdom, a court in the United Kingdom shall not be bound by any decision of the overseas court relating to any of the matters mentioned in subsection (1) or (2).

(4) Nothing in subsection (1) shall affect the recognition or enforcement in the United Kingdom of—

(a) a judgment which is required to be recognised or enforced there under the 1968 Convention ;

1933 c. 13.

1965 c. 37.
1965 c. 57.
1971 c. 59.
1972 c. 33.
1974 c. 35.
1974 c. 43.

(b) a judgment to which Part I of the Foreign Judgments (Reciprocal Enforcement) Act 1933 applies by virtue of section 4 of the Carriage of Goods by Road Act 1965, section 17(4) of the Nuclear Installations Act 1965, section 13(3) of the Merchant Shipping (Oil Pollution) Act 1971, section 5 of the Carriage by Railway Act 1972, section 5 of the Carriage of Passengers by Road Act 1974 or section 6(4) of the Merchant Shipping Act 1974.

Certain steps
not to amount
to submission
to jurisdiction
of overseas
court.

33.—(1) For the purposes of determining whether a judgment given by a court of an overseas country should be recognised or enforced in England and Wales or Northern Ireland, the person against whom the judgment was given shall not be regarded as having submitted to the jurisdiction of the court by reason only of the fact that he appeared (conditionally or otherwise) in the proceedings for all or any one or more of the following purposes, namely—

(a) to contest the jurisdiction of the court ;

(b) to ask the court to dismiss or stay the proceedings on
the ground that the dispute in question should be
submitted to arbitration or to the determination of
the courts of another country ;

(c) to protect, or obtain the release of, property seized or
threatened with seizure in the proceedings.

(2) Nothing in this section shall affect the recognition or
enforcement in England and Wales or Northern Ireland of a
judgment which is required to be recognised or enforced there
under the 1968 Convention.

34. No proceedings may be brought by a person in England
and Wales or Northern Ireland on a cause of action in respect
of which a judgment has been given in his favour in proceedings
between the same parties, or their privies, in a court in another
part of the United Kingdom or in a court of an overseas country,
unless that judgment is not enforceable or entitled to recognition in England and Wales or, as the case may be, in Northern
Ireland.

Certain
judgments a
bar to further
proceedings
on the same
cause of
action.

35.—(1) The Foreign Judgments (Reciprocal Enforcement)
Act 1933 shall have effect with the amendments specified in
Schedule 10, being amendments whose main purpose is to enable
Part I of that Act to be applied to judgments of courts other
than superior courts, to judgments providing for interim pay-
ments and to certain arbitration awards.

Minor
amendments
relating to
overseas
judgments.
1933 c. 13.

(2) For section 10 of the Administration of Justice Act 1920
(issue of certificates of judgments obtained in the United Kingdom) there shall be substituted—

1920 c. 81.

" 10.—(1) Where—

(a) a judgment has been obtained in the High Court in
England or Northern Ireland, or in the Court of
Session in Scotland, against any person ; and

(b) the judgment creditor wishes to secure the enforcement of the judgment in a part of Her Majesty's
dominions outside the United Kingdom to which
this Part of this Act extends,

the court shall, on an application made by the judgment
creditor, issue to him a certified copy of the judgment.

PART IV

(2) The reference in the preceding subsection to Her Majesty's dominions shall be construed as if that subsection had come into force in its present form at the commencement of this Act. ".

1920 c. 81.

(3) In section 14 of the Administration of Justice Act 1920 (extent of Part II of that Act), after subsection (2) there shall be inserted—

" (3) Her Majesty may by Order in Council under this section consolidate any Orders in Council under this section which are in force when the consolidating Order is made.".

Registration of maintenance orders in Northern Ireland.
1950 c. 37.

36.—(1) Where—

(a) a High Court order or a Court of Session order has been registered in the High Court of Justice in Northern Ireland (" the Northern Ireland High Court ") under Part II of the Maintenance Orders Act 1950 ; or

(b) a county court order, a magistrates' court order or a sheriff court order has been registered in a court of summary jurisdiction in Northern Ireland under that Part,

an application may be made to the original court for the registration of the order in, respectively, a court of summary jurisdiction in Northern Ireland or the Northern Ireland High Court.

(2) In subsection (1) " the original court ", in relation to an order, means the court by which the order was made.

1958 c. 39.

(3) Section 2 (except subsection (6A)) and section 2A of the Maintenance Orders Act 1958 shall have effect for the purposes of an application under subsection (1), and subsections (2), (3), (4) and (4A) of section 5 of that Act shall have effect for the purposes of the cancellation of a registration made on such an application, as if—

(a) " registration " in those provisions included registration in the appropriate Northern Ireland court (" registered " being construed accordingly) ;

(b) any reference in those provisions to a High Court order or a magistrates' court order included, respectively, a Court of Session order or a sheriff court order ; and

(c) any other reference in those provisions to the High Court or a magistrates' court included the Northern Ireland High Court or a court of summary jurisdiction in Northern Ireland.

1966 c. 35 (N.I.).

(4) Where an order is registered in Northern Ireland under this section, Part II of the Maintenance and Affiliation Orders Act (Northern Ireland) 1966, except sections 11, 11A and 14(2) and (3), shall apply as if the order had been registered in accordance with the provisions of that Part.

(5) A court of summary jurisdiction in Northern Ireland shall have jurisdiction to hear a complaint by or against a person residing outside Northern Ireland for the discharge or variation of an order registered in Northern Ireland under this section ; and where such a complaint is made against a person residing outside Northern Ireland, then, if he resides in England and Wales or Scotland, section 15 of the Maintenance Orders Act 1950 (which relates to the service of process on persons residing in those countries) shall have effect in relation to the complaint as it has effect in relation to the proceedings therein mentioned.

1950 c. 37.

(6) The enactments specified in Part III of Schedule 12 shall have effect with the amendments specified there, being amendments consequential on this section.

37.—(1) The enactments specified in Schedule 11 shall have effect with the amendments specified there, being amendments whose main purpose is as follows—

Minor amendments relating to maintenance orders.

> Part I—to extend certain enforcement provisions to lump sum maintenance orders ;
>
> Part II—to provide for the recovery of interest according to the law of the country of origin in the case of maintenance orders made in other jurisdictions and registered in the High Court ;
>
> Part III—to extend the Maintenance Orders (Reciprocal Enforcement) Act 1972 to cases where the payer under a maintenance order is not resident within the jurisdiction but has assets there.

1972 c. 18.

(2) In section 27(1) of the Maintenance Orders (Reciprocal Enforcement) Act 1972 (application by person in convention country for recovery of maintenance in England and Wales or Northern Ireland to be treated as a complaint), after " as if it were a complaint " there shall be inserted " made at the time when the application was received by the Secretary of State or the Lord Chancellor ".

38.—(1) Section 7 of the Protection of Trading Interests Act 1980 (which enables provision to be made by Order in Council for the enforcement in the United Kingdom on a reciprocal basis of overseas judgments directed to counteracting a judgment for multiple damages given in a third country) shall be amended as follows.

Overseas judgments counteracting an award of multiple damages.

1980 c. 11.

(2) In subsection (1) for " judgments given under any provision of the law of that country corresponding to that section " there shall be substituted " judgments of any description specified in the Order which are given under any provision of the law of that

PART IV   country relating to the recovery of sums paid or obtained pursuant to a judgment for multiple damages within the meaning of section 5(3) above, whether or not that provision corresponds to section 6 above ".

(3) After subsection (1) there shall be inserted—

" (1A) Such an Order in Council may, as respects judgments to which it relates—

(a) make different provisions for different descriptions of judgment ; and

(b) impose conditions or restrictions on the enforcement of judgments of any description.".

Jurisdiction, and recognition and enforcement of judgments, as between United Kingdom and certain territories

Application of provisions corresponding to 1968 Convention in relation to certain territories.

39.—(1) Her Majesty may by Order in Council make provision corresponding to the provision made by the 1968 Convention as between the Contracting States to that Convention, with such modifications as appear to Her Majesty to be appropriate, for regulating, as between the United Kingdom and any of the territories mentioned in subsection (2), the jurisdiction of courts and the recognition and enforcement of judgments.

(2) The territories referred to in subsection (1) are—

(a) the Isle of Man ;

(b) any of the Channel Islands ;

(c) Gibraltar ;

(d) the Sovereign Base Areas of Akrotiri and Dhekelia (that is to say the areas mentioned in section 2(1) of the Cyprus Act 1960).

1960 c. 52.

(3) An Order in Council under this section may contain such supplementary and incidental provisions as appear to Her Majesty to be necessary or expedient, including in particular provisions corresponding to or applying any of the provisions of Part I with such modifications as may be specified in the Order.

(4) Any Order in Council under this section shall be subject to annulment in pursuance of a resolution of either House of Parliament.

Legal aid

Power to modify enactments relating to legal aid etc.

1974 c. 4.

40.—(1) In section 20 of the Legal Aid Act 1974 (power of Lord Chancellor to make regulations), after subsection (4) there shall be inserted as subsection (4A)—

" (4A) Without prejudice to the preceding provisions of this section or any other provision of this Part of this Act

authorising the making of regulations, regulations may also
modify the provisions of, or of any instrument having effect
under, this Part of this Act (including so much of any of
those provisions as specifies a sum of money) for the purposes of the application of those provisions—

> (*a*) in cases where their modification appears to the
> Lord Chancellor necessary for the purpose of ful-
> filling any obligation imposed on the United King-
> dom or Her Majesty's government therein by any
> international agreement ; or
>
> (*b*) in relation to proceedings for securing the recog-
> nition or enforcement in England and Wales of
> judgments given outside the United Kingdom for
> whose recognition or enforcement in the United
> Kingdom provision is made by any international
> agreement.".

(2) In section 15 of the Legal Aid (Scotland) Act 1967 (power   1967 c. 43.
of Secretary of State to make regulations), after subsection (4)
there shall be inserted as subsection (4A)—

" (4A) Without prejudice to the preceding provisions of
this section or any other provision of this Act authorising
the making of regulations, regulations may also modify
the provisions of, or of any instrument having effect under,
this Act (including so much of any of those provisions as
specifies a sum of money) for the purposes of the application
of those provisions—

> (*a*) in cases where their modification appears to the
> Secretary of State necessary for the purpose of
> fulfilling any obligation imposed on the United
> Kingdom or Her Majesty's government therein by
> any international agreement ; or
>
> (*b*) in relation to proceedings for securing the recogni-
> tion or enforcement in Scotland of judgments given
> outside the United Kingdom for whose recogni-
> tion or enforcement in the United Kingdom pro-
> vision is made by any international agreement.".

(3) In Article 22 of the Legal Aid, Advice and Assistance   S.I. 1981/228
(Northern Ireland) Order 1981 (power of Lord Chancellor to   (N.I. 8).
make regulations), after paragraph (4) there shall be inserted
as paragraph (4A)—

" (4A) Without prejudice to the preceding provisions of
this Article or any other provision of this Part authorising
the making of regulations, regulations may also modify the
provisions of, or of any instrument having effect under,
this Part (including so much of any of those provisions as
specifies a sum of money) for the purposes of the application of those provisions—

> (*a*) in cases where their modification appears to the
> Lord Chancellor necessary for the purpose of

PART IV

fulfilling any obligation imposed on the United Kingdom or Her Majesty's government therein by any international agreement ; or

(b) in relation to proceedings for securing the recognition or enforcement in Northern Ireland of judgments given outside the United Kingdom for whose recognition or enforcement in the United Kingdom provision is made by any international agreement.".

PART V

SUPPLEMENTARY AND GENERAL PROVISIONS

Domicile

Domicile of individuals.

41.—(1) Subject to Article 52 (which contains provisions for determining whether a party is domiciled in a Contracting State), the following provisions of this section determine, for the purposes of the 1968 Convention and this Act, whether an individual is domiciled in the United Kingdom or in a particular part of, or place in, the United Kingdom or in a state other than a Contracting State.

(2) An individual is domiciled in the United Kingdom if and only if—

(a) he is resident in the United Kingdom ; and

(b) the nature and circumstances of his residence indicate that he has a substantial connection with the United Kingdom.

(3) Subject to subsection (5), an individual is domiciled in a particular part of the United Kingdom if and only if—

(a) he is resident in that part ; and

(b) the nature and circumstances of his residence indicate that he has a substantial connection with that part.

(4) An individual is domiciled in a particular place in the United Kingdom if and only if he—

(a) is domiciled in the part of the United Kingdom in which that place is situated ; and

(b) is resident in that place.

(5) An individual who is domiciled in the United Kingdom but in whose case the requirements of subsection (3)(b) are not satisfied in relation to any particular part of the United Kingdom shall be treated as domiciled in the part of the United Kingdom in which he is resident.

(6) In the case of an individual who—

(a) is resident in the United Kingdom, or in a particular part of the United Kingdom ; and

(b) has been so resident for the last three months or more,

the requirements of subsection (2)(b) or, as the case may be, subsection (3)(b) shall be presumed to be fulfilled unless the contrary is proved.

(7) An individual is domiciled in a state other than a Contracting State if and only if—

(a) he is resident in that state ; and

(b) the nature and circumstances of his residence indicate that he has a substantial connection with that state.

42.—(1) For the purposes of this Act the seat of a corporation or association (as determined by this section) shall be treated as its domicile.

(2) The following provisions of this section determine where a corporation or association has its seat—

(a) for the purpose of Article 53 (which for the purposes of the 1968 Convention equates the domicile of such a body with its seat) ; and

(b) for the purposes of this Act other than the provisions mentioned in section 43(1)(b) and (c).

(3) A corporation or association has its seat in the United Kingdom if and only if—

(a) it was incorporated or formed under the law of a part of the United Kingdom and has its registered office or some other official address in the United Kingdom ; or

(b) its central management and control is exercised in the United Kingdom.

(4) A corporation or association has its seat in a particular part of the United Kingdom if and only if it has its seat in the United Kingdom and—

(a) it has its registered office or some other official address in that part ; or

(b) its central management and control is exercised in that part ; or

(c) it has a place of business in that part.

(5) A corporation or association has its seat in a particular place in the United Kingdom if and only if it has its seat in the part of the United Kingdom in which that place is situated and—

(a) it has its registered office or some other official address in that place ; or

(b) its central management and control is exercised in that place ; or

(c) it has a place of business in that place.

(6) Subject to subsection (7), a corporation or association has its seat in a state other than the United Kingdom if and only if—

    (a) it was incorporated or formed under the law of that state and has its registered office or some other official address there ; or

    (b) its central management and control is exercised in that state.

(7) A corporation or association shall not be regarded as having its seat in a Contracting State other than the United Kingdom if it is shown that the courts of that state would not regard it as having its seat there.

(8) In this section—

    " business " includes any activity carried on by a corporation or association, and " place of business " shall be construed accordingly ;

    " official address ", in relation to a corporation or association, means an address which it is required by law to register, notify or maintain for the purpose of receiving notices or other communications.

Seat of
corporation or
association for
purposes of
Article 16(2)
and related
provisions.

43.—(1) The following provisions of this section determine where a corporation or association has its seat for the purposes of—

    (a) Article 16(2) (which confers exclusive jurisdiction over proceedings relating to the formation or dissolution of such bodies, or to the decisions of their organs) ;

    (b) Articles 5A and 16(2) in Schedule 4 ; and

    (c) Rules 2(12) and 4(1)(b) in Schedule 8.

(2) A corporation or association has its seat in the United Kingdom if and only if—

    (a) it was incorporated or formed under the law of a part of the United Kingdom ; or

    (b) its central management and control is exercised in the United Kingdom.

(3) A corporation or association has its seat in a particular part of the United Kingdom if and only if it has its seat in the United Kingdom and—

    (a) subject to subsection (5), it was incorporated or formed under the law of that part ; or

    (b) being incorporated or formed under the law of a state other than the United Kingdom, its central management and control is exercised in that part.

(4) A corporation or association has its seat in a particular place in Scotland if and only if it has its seat in Scotland and—

   (*a*) it has its registered office or some other official address in that place ; or

   (*b*) it has no registered office or other official address in Scotland, but its central management and control is exercised in that place.

(5) A corporation or association incorporated or formed under—

   (*a*) an enactment forming part of the law of more than one part of the United Kingdom ; or

   (*b*) an instrument having effect in the domestic law of more than one part of the United Kingdom,

shall, if it has a registered office, be taken to have its seat in the part of the United Kingdom in which that office is situated, and not in any other part of the United Kingdom.

(6) Subject to subsection (7), a corporation or association has its seat in a Contracting State other than the United Kingdom if and only if—

   (*a*) it was incorporated or formed under the law of that state ; or

   (*b*) its central management and control is exercised in that state.

(7) A corporation or association shall not be regarded as having its seat in a Contracting State other than the United Kingdom if—

   (*a*) it has its seat in the United Kingdom by virtue of subsection (2)(*a*) ; or

   (*b*) it is shown that the courts of that other state would not regard it for the purposes of Article 16(2) as having its seat there.

(8) In this section " official address " has the same meaning as in section 42.

44.—(1) This section applies to—

   (*a*) proceedings within Section 3 of Title II of the 1968 Convention (insurance contracts), and

   (*b*) proceedings within Section 4 of that Title (consumer contracts).

Persons deemed to be domiciled in the United Kingdom for certain purposes.

(2) A person who, for the purposes of proceedings to which this section applies arising out of the operations of a branch, agency or other establishment in the United Kingdom, is deemed for the purposes of the 1968 Convention to be domiciled in the United Kingdom by virtue of—

   (*a*) Article 8, second paragraph (insurers) ; or

PART V   (*b*) Article 13, second paragraph (suppliers of goods, services or credit to consumers),

shall, for the purposes of those proceedings, be treated for the purposes of this Act as so domiciled and as domiciled in the part of the United Kingdom in which the branch, agency or establishment in question is situated.

Domicile of trusts.

45.—(1) The following provisions of this section determine, for the purposes of the 1968 Convention and this Act, where a trust is domiciled.

(2) A trust is domiciled in the United Kingdom if and only if it is by virtue of subsection (3) domiciled in a part of the United Kingdom.

(3) A trust is domiciled in a part of the United Kingdom if and only if the system of law of that part is the system of law with which the trust has its closest and most real connection.

Domicile and seat of the Crown.

46.—(1) For the purposes of this Act the seat of the Crown (as determined by this section) shall be treated as its domicile.

(2) The following provisions of this section determine where the Crown has its seat—

(*a*) for the purposes of the 1968 Convention (in which Article 53 equates the domicile of a legal person with its seat) ; and

(*b*) for the purposes of this Act.

(3) Subject to the provisions of any Order in Council for the time being in force under subsection (4)—

(*a*) the Crown in right of Her Majesty's government in the United Kingdom has its seat in every part of, and every place in, the United Kingdom ; and

(*b*) the Crown in right of Her Majesty's government in Northern Ireland has its seat in, and in every place in, Northern Ireland.

(4) Her Majesty may by Order in Council provide that, in the case of proceedings of any specified description against the Crown in right of Her Majesty's government in the United Kingdom, the Crown shall be treated for the purposes of the 1968 Convention and this Act as having its seat in, and in every place in, a specified part of the United Kingdom and not in any other part of the United Kingdom.

(5) An Order in Council under subsection (4) may frame a description of proceedings in any way, and in particular may do so by reference to the government department or officer of the Crown against which or against whom they fall to be instituted.

(6) Any Order in Council made under this section shall be subject to annulment in pursuance of a resolution of either House of Parliament.

(7) Nothing in this section applies to the Crown otherwise than in right of Her Majesty's government in the United Kingdom or Her Majesty's government in Northern Ireland.

Other supplementary provisions

47.—(1) Her Majesty may by Order in Council—

Modifications occasioned by decisions of European Court as to meaning or effect of Conventions.

(*a*) make such provision as Her Majesty considers appropriate for the purpose of bringing the law of any part of the United Kingdom into accord with the Conventions as affected by any principle laid down by the European Court in connection with the Conventions or by any decision of that court as to the meaning or effect of any provision of the Conventions ; or

(*b*) make such modifications of Schedule 4 or Schedule 8, or of any other statutory provision affected by any provision of either of those Schedules, as Her Majesty considers appropriate in view of any principle laid down by the European Court in connection with Title II of the 1968 Convention or of any decision of that court as to the meaning or effect of any provision of that Title.

(2) The provision which may be made by virtue of paragraph (*a*) of subsection (1) includes such modifications of this Act or any other statutory provision, whenever passed or made, as Her Majesty considers appropriate for the purpose mentioned in that paragraph.

(3) The modifications which may be made by virtue of paragraph (*b*) of subsection (1) include modifications designed to produce divergence between any provision of Schedule 4 or Schedule 8 and a corresponding provision of Title II of the 1968 Convention as affected by any such principle or decision as is mentioned in that paragraph.

(4) An Order in Council under this section shall not be made unless a draft of the Order has been laid before Parliament and approved by a resolution of each House of Parliament.

48.—(1) Rules of court may make provision for regulating the procedure to be followed in any court in connection with any provision of this Act or the Conventions.

Matters for which rules of court may provide.

(2) Rules of court may make provision as to the manner in which and the conditions subject to which a certificate or judgment registered in any court under any provision of this Act

PART V   may be enforced, including provision for enabling the court or, in Northern Ireland the Enforcement of Judgments Office, subject to any conditions specified in the rules, to give directions about such matters.

(3) Without prejudice to the generality of subsections (1) and (2), the power to make rules of court for magistrates' courts, and in Northern Ireland the power to make Judgment Enforcement Rules, shall include power to make such provision as the rule-making authority considers necessary or expedient for the purposes of the provisions of the Conventions and this Act relating to maintenance proceedings and the recognition and enforcement of maintenance orders, and shall in particular include power to make provision as to any of the following matters—

(a) authorising the service in another Contracting State of process issued by or for the purposes of a magistrates' court and the service and execution in England and Wales or Northern Ireland of process issued in another Contracting State;

(b) requesting courts in other parts of the United Kingdom or in other Contracting States to take evidence there for the purposes of proceedings in England and Wales or Northern Ireland;

(c) the taking of evidence in England and Wales or Northern Ireland in response to similar requests received from such courts;

(d) the circumstances in which and the conditions subject to which any powers conferred under paragraphs (a) to (c) are to be exercised;

(e) the admission in evidence, subject to such conditions as may be prescribed in the rules, of statements contained in documents purporting to be made or authenticated by a court in another part of the United Kingdom or in another Contracting State, or by a judge or official of such a court, which purport—

(i) to set out or summarise evidence given in proceedings in that court or to be documents received in evidence in such proceedings or copies of such documents; or

(ii) to set out or summarise evidence taken for the purposes of proceedings in England and Wales or Northern Ireland, whether or not in response to any such request as is mentioned in paragraph (b); or

(iii) to record information relating to the payments made under an order of that court;

(f) the circumstances and manner in which a magistrates' court may or must vary or revoke a maintenance order

registered in that court, cancel the registration of, or
refrain from enforcing, such an order or transmit such
an order for enforcement in another part of the United
Kingdom ;

(*g*) the cases and manner in which courts in other parts of
the United Kingdom or in other Contracting States are
to be informed of orders made, or other things done,
by or for the purposes of a magistrates' court ;

(*h*) the circumstances and manner in which a magistrates'
court may communicate for other purposes with such
courts ;

(*i*) the giving of notice of such matters as may be prescribed
in the rules to such persons as may be so prescribed
and the manner in which such notice is to be given.

(4) Nothing in this section shall be taken as derogating from
the generality of any power to make rules of court conferred by
any other enactment.

49. Nothing in this Act shall prevent any court in the
United Kingdom from staying, sisting, striking out or dismis-
sing any proceedings before it, on the ground of *forum non
conveniens* or otherwise, where to do so is not inconsistent with
the 1968 Convention.

Saving for
powers to
stay, sist,
strike out or
dismiss
proceedings.

General

50. In this Act, unless the context otherwise requires—

Interpretation:
general.

" the Accession Convention " has the meaning given by
section 1(1) ;

" Article " and references to sub-divisions of numbered
Articles are to be construed in accordance with section
1(2)(*b*) ;

" association " means an unincorporated body of persons ;

" Contracting State " has the meaning given by section
1(3) ;

" the 1968 Convention " has the meaning given by section
1(1), and references to that Convention and to provi-
visions of it are to be construed in accordance with
section 1(2)(*a*) ;

" the Conventions " has the meaning given by section 1(1) ;

" corporation " means a body corporate, and includes a
partnership subsisting under the law of Scotland ;

" court ", without more, includes a tribunal ;

" court of law ", in relation to the United Kingdom, means any of the following courts, namely—

(*a*) the House of Lords,

(*b*) in England and Wales or Northern Ireland, the Court of Appeal, the High Court, the Crown Court, a county court and a magistrates' court,

(*c*) in Scotland, the Court of Session and a sheriff court ;

" the Crown " is to be construed in accordance with section 51(2) ;

" enactment " includes an enactment comprised in Northern Ireland legislation ;

" judgment ", subject to sections 15(1) and 18(2) and to paragraph 1 of Schedules 6 and 7, means any judgment or order (by whatever name called) given or made by a court in any civil proceedings ;

" magistrates' court ", in relation to Northern Ireland, means a court of summary jurisdiction ;

" modifications " includes additions, omissions and alterations ;

" overseas country " means any country or territory outside the United Kingdom ;

" part of the United Kingdom " means England and Wales, Scotland or Northern Ireland ;

" the 1971 Protocol " has the meaning given by section 1(1), and references to that Protocol and to provisions of it are to be construed in accordance with section 1(2)(*a*) ;

" rules of court ", in relation to any court, means rules, orders or regulations made by the authority having power to make rules, orders or regulations regulating the procedure of that court, and includes—

(*a*) in Scotland, Acts of Sederunt ;

(*b*) in Northern Ireland, Judgment Enforcement Rules ;

" statutory provision " means any provision contained in an Act, or in any Northern Ireland legislation, or in—

1978 c. 30.

(*a*) subordinate legislation (as defined in section 21(1) of the Interpretation Act 1978) ; or

(*b*) any instrument of a legislative character made under any Northern Ireland legislation ;

" tribunal "—

(*a*) means a tribunal of any description other than a court of law ;

(*b*) in relation to an overseas country, includes, as
regards matters relating to maintenance within the
meaning of the 1968 Convention, any authority
having power to give, enforce, vary or revoke a maintenance order.

PART V

51.—(1) This Act binds the Crown.

(2) In this section and elsewhere in this Act references to the
Crown do not include references to Her Majesty in Her private
capacity or to Her Majesty in right of Her Duchy of Lancaster
or to the Duke of Cornwall.

Application to
Crown.

52.—(1) This Act extends to Northern Ireland.

(2) Without prejudice to the power conferred by section 39,
Her Majesty may by Order in Council direct that all or any of
the provisions of this Act apart from that section shall extend,
subject to such modifications as may be specified in the Order,
to any of the following territories, that is to say—

Extent.

(*a*) the Isle of Man ;

(*b*) any of the Channel Islands ;

(*c*) Gibraltar ;

(*d*) the Sovereign Base Areas of Akrotiri and Dhekelia
(that is to say the areas mentioned in section 2(1) of
the Cyprus Act 1960).

1960 c. 52.

53.—(1) This Act shall come into force in accordance with
the provisions of Part I of Schedule 13.

(2) The transitional provisions and savings contained in Part
II of that Schedule shall have effect in relation to the commencement of the provisions of this Act mentioned in that Part.

Commence-
ment,
transitional
provisions and
savings.

54. The enactments mentioned in Schedule 14 are hereby repealed to the extent specified in the third column of that Schedule.

Repeals.

55. This Act may be cited as the Civil Jurisdiction and
Judgments Act 1982.

Short title.

SCHEDULES

SCHEDULE 1

Text of 1968 Convention, as Amended

ARRANGEMENT OF PROVISIONS

CONVENTION ON JURISDICTION AND THE ENFORCEMENT OF JUDGMENTS IN CIVIL AND COMMERCIAL MATTERS

Preamble

The High Contracting Parties to the Treaty establishing the European Economic Community,

Desiring to implement the provisions of Article 220 of that Treaty by virtue of which they undertook to secure the simplification of formalities governing the reciprocal recognition and enforcement of judgments of courts or tribunals;

Anxious to strengthen in the Community the legal protection of persons therein established;

Considering that it is necessary for this purpose to determine the international jurisdiction of their courts, to facilitate recognition and to introduce an expeditious procedure for securing the enforcement of judgments, authentic instruments and court settlements;

Have decided to conclude this Convention and to this end have designated as their Plenipotentiaries:

(Designations of Plenipotentiaries of the original six Contracting States)

Who, meeting within the Council, having exchanged their Full Powers, found in good and due form,

Have agreed as follows:

TITLE I
SCOPE
ARTICLE 1

This Convention shall apply in civil and commercial matters whatever the nature of the court or tribunal. It shall not extend, in particular, to revenue, customs or administrative matters.

The Convention shall not apply to:

(1) the status or legal capacity of natural persons, rights in property arising out of a matrimonial relationship, wills and succession;

(2) bankruptcy, proceedings relating to the winding-up of insolvent companies or other legal persons, judicial arrangements, compositions and analogous proceedings;

(3) social security;

(4) arbitration.

Part I

S

TITLE II

JURISDICTION

Section 1

General provisions

ARTICLE 2

Subject to the provisions of this Convention, persons domiciled in a Contracting State shall, whatever their nationality, be sued in the courts of that State.

Persons who are not nationals of the State in which they are domiciled shall be governed by the rules of jurisdiction applicable to nationals of that State.

ARTICLE 3

Persons domiciled in a Contracting State may be sued in the courts of another Contracting State only by virtue of the rules set out in Sections 2 to 6 of this Title.

In particular the following provisions shall not be applicable as against them:

—in Belgium:	Article 15 of the civil code (*Code civil—Burgerlijk Wetboek*) and Article 638 of the Judicial code (*Code judiciaire—Gerechtelijk Wetboek*);
—in Denmark:	Article 248(2) of the law on civil procedure (*Lov om rettens pleje*) and Chapter 3, Article 3 of the Greenland law on civil procedure (*Lov for Grønland om rettens pleje*);
—in the Federal Republic of Germany:	Article 23 of the code of civil procedure (*Zivilprozessordnung*);
—in France:	Articles 14 and 15 of the civil code (*Code civil*);
—in Ireland:	the rules which enable jurisdiction to be founded on the document instituting the proceedings having been served on the defendant during his temporary presence in Ireland;
—in Italy:	Article 2 and Article 4, Nos 1 and 2 of the code of civil procedure (*Codice di procedura civile*);
—in Luxembourg:	Articles 14 and 15 of the civil code (*Code civil*);

| —in the Netherlands: | Article 126(3) and Article 127 of the code of civil procedure *(Wetboek van Burgerlijke Rechtsvordering)*; |

—in the United Kingdom:

the rules which enable jurisdiction to be founded on:

(a) the document instituting the proceedings having been served on the defendant during his temporary presence in the United Kingdom; or

(b) the presence within the United Kingdom of property belonging to the defendant; or

(c) the seizure by the plaintiff of property situated in the United Kingdom.

ARTICLE 4

If the defendant is not domiciled in a Contracting State, the jurisdiction of the courts of each Contracting State shall, subject to the provisions of Article 16, be determined by the law of that State.

As against such a defendant, any person domiciled in a Contracting State may, whatever his nationality, avail himself in that State of the rules of jurisdiction there in force, and in particular those specified in the second paragraph of Article 3, in the same way as the nationals of that State.

Section 2

Special jurisdiction

ARTICLE 5

A person domiciled in a Contracting State may, in another Contracting State, be sued:

(1) in matters relating to a contract, in the courts for the place of performance of the obligation in question;

(2) in matters relating to maintenance, in the courts for the place where the maintenance creditor is domiciled or habitually resident or, if the matter is ancillary to proceedings concerning the status of a person, in the court which, according to its own law, has jurisdiction to entertain those proceedings, unless that jurisdiction is based solely on the nationality of one of the parties;

(3) in matters relating to tort, delict or quasi-delict, in the courts for the place where the harmful event occurred;

S 2

(4) as regards a civil claim for damages or restitution which is based on an act giving rise to criminal proceedings, in the court seised of those proceedings, to the extent that that court has jurisdiction under its own law to entertain civil proceedings ;

(5) as regards a dispute arising out of the operations of a branch, agency or other establishment, in the courts for the place in which the branch, agency or other establishment is situated ;

(6) in his capacity as settlor, trustee or beneficiary of a trust created by the operation of a statute, or by a written instrument, or created orally and evidenced in writing, in the courts of the Contracting State in which the trust is domiciled ;

(7) as regards a dispute concerning the payment of remuneration claimed in respect of the salvage of a cargo or freight, in the court under the authority of which the cargo or freight in question:

(a) has been arrested to secure such payment, or

(b) could have been so arrested, but bail or other security has been given ;

provided that this provision shall apply only if it is claimed that the defendant has an interest in the cargo or freight or had such an interest at the time of salvage.

ARTICLE 6

A person domiciled in a Contracting State may also be sued:

(1) where he is one of a number of defendants, in the courts for the place where any one of them is domiciled ;

(2) as a third party in an action on a warranty or guarantee or in any other third party proceedings, in the court seised of the original proceedings, unless these were instituted solely with the object of removing him from the jurisdiction of the court which would be competent in his case ;

(3) on a counterclaim arising from the same contract or facts on which the original claim was based, in the court in which the original claim is pending.

ARTICLE 6A

Where by virtue of this Convention a court of a Contracting State has jurisdiction in actions relating to liability arising from the use or operation of a ship, that court, or any other court substituted for this purpose by the internal law of that State, shall also have jurisdiction over claims for limitation of such liability.

Section 3

Jurisdiction in matters relating to insurance

ARTICLE 7

In matters relating to insurance, jurisdiction shall be determined by this Section, without prejudice to the provisions of Articles 4 and 5(5).

ARTICLE 8

An insurer domiciled in a Contracting State may be sued:

(1) in the courts of the State where he is domiciled, or

(2) in another Contracting State, in the courts for the place where the policy-holder is domiciled, or

(3) if he is a co-insurer, in the courts of a Contracting State in which proceedings are brought against the leading insurer.

An insurer who is not domiciled in a Contracting State but has a branch, agency or other establishment in one of the Contracting States shall, in disputes arising out of the operations of the branch, agency or establishment, be deemed to be domiciled in that State.

ARTICLE 9

In respect of liability insurance or insurance of immovable property, the insurer may in addition be sued in the courts for the place where the harmful event occurred. The same applies if movable and immovable property are covered by the same insurance policy and both are adversely affected by the same contingency.

ARTICLE 10

In respect of liability insurance, the insurer may also, if the law of the court permits it, be joined in proceedings which the injured party has brought against the insured.

The provisions of Articles 7, 8 and 9 shall apply to actions brought by the injured party directly against the insurer, where such direct actions are permitted.

If the law governing such direct actions provides that the policy-holder or the insured may be joined as a party to the action, the same court shall have jurisdiction over them.

ARTICLE 11

Without prejudice to the provisions of the third paragraph of Article 10, an insurer may bring proceedings only in the courts of the Contracting State in which the defendant is domiciled, irrespective of whether he is the policy-holder, the insured or a beneficiary.

SCH. 1   The provisions of this Section shall not affect the right to bring a counterclaim in the court in which, in accordance with this Section, the original claim is pending.

ARTICLE 12

The provisions of this Section may be departed from only by an agreement on jurisdiction:

(1) which is entered into after the dispute has arisen, or

(2) which allows the policy-holder, the insured or a beneficiary to bring proceedings in courts other than those indicated in this Section, or

(3) which is concluded between a policy-holder and an insurer, both of whom are at the time of conclusion of the contract domiciled or habitually resident in the same Contracting State, and which has the effect of conferring jurisdiction on the courts of that State even if the harmful event were to occur abroad, provided that such an agreement is not contrary to the law of that State, or

(4) which is concluded with a policy-holder who is not domiciled in a Contracting State, except in so far as the insurance is compulsory or relates to immovable property in a Contracting State, or

(5) which relates to a contract of insurance in so far as it covers one or more of the risks set out in Article 12A.

ARTICLE 12A

The following are the risks referred to in Article 12(5):

(1) Any loss of or damage to

(*a*) sea-going ships, installations situated offshore or on the high seas, or aircraft, arising from perils which relate to their use for commercial purposes,

(*b*) goods in transit other than passengers' baggage where the transit consists of or includes carriage by such ships or aircraft;

(2) Any liability, other than for bodily injury to passengers or loss of or damage to their baggage,

(*a*) arising out of the use or operation of ships, installations or aircraft as referred to in (1)(*a*) above in so far as the law of the Contracting State in which such aircraft are registered does not prohibit agreements on jurisdiction regarding insurance of such risks,

(*b*) for loss or damage caused by goods in transit as described in (1)(*b*) above;

(3) Any financial loss connected with the use or operation of ships, installations or aircraft as referred to in (1)(*a*) above, in particular loss of freight or charter-hire;

(4) Any risk or interest connected with any of those referred to in (1) to (3) above.

Section 4

Jurisdiction over consumer contracts

ARTICLE 13

In proceedings concerning a contract concluded by a person for a purpose which can be regarded as being outside his trade or profession, hereinafter called the " consumer ", jurisdiction shall be determined by this Section, without prejudice to the provisions of Articles 4 and 5(5), if it is :

(1) a contract for the sale of goods on instalment credit terms, or

(2) a contract for a loan repayable by instalments, or for any other form of credit, made to finance the sale of goods, or

(3) any other contract for the supply of goods or a contract for the supply of services and

   (*a*) in the State of the consumer's domicile the conclusion of the contract was preceded by a specific invitation addressed to him or by advertising, and

   (*b*) the consumer took in that State the steps necessary for the conclusion of the contract.

Where a consumer enters into a contract with a party who is not domiciled in a Contracting State but has a branch, agency or other establishment in one of the Contracting States, that party shall, in disputes arising out of the operations of the branch, agency or establishment, be deemed to be domiciled in that State.

This Section shall not apply to contracts of transport.

ARTICLE 14

A consumer may bring proceedings against the other party to a contract either in the courts of the Contracting State in which that party is domiciled or in the courts of the Contracting State in which he is himself domiciled.

Proceedings may be brought against a consumer by the other party to the contract only in the courts of the Contracting State in which the consumer is domiciled.

SCH. 1   These provisions shall not affect the right to bring a counter-claim in the court in which, in accordance with this Section, the original claim is pending.

ARTICLE 15

The provisions of this Section may be departed from only by an agreement:

(1) which is entered into after the dispute has arisen,
or

(2) which allows the consumer to bring proceedings in courts other than those indicated in this Section,
or

(3) which is entered into by the consumer and the other party to the contract, both of whom are at the time of conclusion of the contract domiciled or habitually resident in the same Contracting State, and which confers jurisdiction on the courts of that State, provided that such an agreement is not contrary to the law of that State.

Section 5

Exclusive jurisdiction

ARTICLE 16

The following courts shall have exclusive jurisdiction, regardless of domicile:

(1) in proceedings which have as their object rights *in rem* in, or tenancies of, immovable property, the courts of the Contracting State in which the property is situated;

(2) in proceedings which have as their object the validity of the constitution, the nullity or the dissolution of companies or other legal persons or associations of natural or legal persons, or the decisions of their organs, the courts of the Contracting State in which the company, legal person or association has its seat;

(3) in proceedings which have as their object the validity of entries in public registers, the courts of the Contracting State in which the register is kept;

(4) in proceedings concerned with the registration or validity of patents, trade marks, designs, or other similar rights required to be deposited or registered, the courts of the Contracting State in which the deposit or registration has been applied for, has taken place or is under the terms of an international convention deemed to have taken place;

(5) in proceedings concerned with the enforcement of judgments, the courts of the Contracting State in which the judgment has been or is to be enforced.

Section 6

Prorogation of jurisdiction

ARTICLE 17

If the parties, one or more of whom is domiciled in a Contracting State, have agreed that a court or the courts of a Contracting State are to have jurisdiction to settle any disputes which have arisen or which may arise in connection with a particular legal relationship, that court or those courts shall have exclusive jurisdiction. Such an agreement conferring jurisdiction shall be either in writing or evidenced in writing or, in international trade or commerce, in a form which accords with practices in that trade or commerce of which the parties are or ought to have been aware. Where such an agreement is concluded by parties, none of whom is domiciled in a Contracting State, the courts of other Contracting States shall have no jurisdiction over their disputes unless the court or courts chosen have declined jurisdiction.

The court or courts of a Contracting State on which a trust instrument has conferred jurisdiction shall have exclusive jurisdiction in any proceedings brought against a settlor, trustee or beneficiary, if relations between these persons or their rights or obligations under the trust are involved.

Agreements or provisions of a trust instrument conferring jurisdiction shall have no legal force if they are contrary to the provisions of Articles 12 or 15, or if the courts whose jurisdiction they purport to exclude have exclusive jurisdiction by virtue of Article 16.

If an agreement conferring jurisdiction was concluded for the benefit of only one of the parties, that party shall retain the right to bring proceedings in any other court which has jurisdiction by virtue of this Convention.

ARTICLE 18

Apart from jurisdiction derived from other provisions of this Convention, a court of a Contracting State before whom a defendant enters an appearance shall have jurisdiction. This rule shall not apply where appearance was entered solely to contest the jurisdiction, or where another court has exclusive jurisdiction by virtue of Article 16.

Section 7

Examination as to jurisdiction and admissibility

ARTICLE 19

Where a court of a Contracting State is seised of a claim which is principally concerned with a matter over which the courts of another Contracting State have exclusive jurisdiction by virtue of Article 16, it shall declare of its own motion that it has no jurisdiction.

ARTICLE 20

Where proceedings involving the same cause of action and sued in a court of another Contracting State and does not enter an appearance, the court shall declare of its own motion that it has no jurisdiction unless its jurisdiction is derived from the provisions of this Convention.

The court shall stay the proceedings so long as it is not shown that the defendant has been able to receive the document instituting the proceedings or an equivalent document in sufficient time to enable him to arrange for his defence, or that all necessary steps have been taken to this end.

The provisions of the foregoing paragraph shall be replaced by those of Article 15 of the Hague Convention of 15 November 1965 on the Service Abroad of Judicial and Extrajudicial Documents in Civil or Commercial Matters, if the document instituting the proceedings or notice thereof had to be transmitted abroad in accordance with that Convention.

Section 8

Lis Pendens—Related actions

ARTICLE 21

Where proceedings involving the same cause of action and between the same parties are brought in the courts of different Contracting States, any court other than the court first seised shall of its own motion decline jurisdiction in favour of that court.

A court which would be required to decline jurisdiction may stay its proceedings if the jurisdiction of the other court is contested.

ARTICLE 22

Where related actions are brought in the courts of different Contracting States, any court other than the court first seised may, while the actions are pending at first instance, stay its proceedings.

A court other than the court first seised may also, on the application of one of the parties, decline jurisdiction if the law of that court permits the consolidation of related actions and the court first seised has jurisdiction over both actions.

For the purposes of this Article, actions are deemed to be related where they are so closely connected that it is expedient to hear and determine them together to avoid the risk of irreconcilable judgments resulting from separate proceedings.

ARTICLE 23

Where actions come within the exclusive jurisdiction of several courts, any court other than the court first seised shall decline jurisdiction in favour of that court.

Section 9

Provisional, including protective, measures

ARTICLE 24

Application may be made to the courts of a Contracting State for such provisional, including protective, measures as may be available under the law of that State, even if, under this Convention, the courts of another Contracting State have jurisdiction as to the substance of the matter.

TITLE III

RECOGNITION AND ENFORCEMENT

ARTICLE 25

For the purposes of this Convention, "judgment" means any judgment given by a court or tribunal of a Contracting State, whatever the judgment may be called, including a decree, order, decision or writ of execution, as well as the determination of costs or expenses by an officer of the court.

Section 1

Recognition

ARTICLE 26

A judgment given in a Contracting State shall be recognised in the other Contracting States without any special procedure being required.

Any interested party who raises the recognition of a judgment as the principal issue in a dispute may, in accordance with the procedures provided for in Sections 2 and 3 of this Title, apply for a decision that the judgment be recognised.

If the outcome of proceedings in a court of a Contracting State depends on the determination of an incidental question of recognition that court shall have jurisdiction over that question.

ARTICLE 27

A judgment shall not be recognised:

(1) if such recognition is contrary to public policy in the State in which recognition is sought;

(2) where it was given in default of appearance, if the defendant was not duly served with the document which instituted the proceedings or with an equivalent document in sufficient time to enable him to arrange for his defence;

(3) if the judgment is irreconcilable with a judgment given in a dispute between the same parties in the State in which recognition is sought;

(4) if the court of the State in which the judgment was given, in order to arrive at its judgment, has decided a preliminary question concerning the status or legal capacity of natural persons, rights in property arising out of a matrimonial relationship, wills or succession in a way that conflicts with a rule of the private international law of the State in which the recognition is sought, unless the same result would have been reached by the application of the rules of private international law of that State;

(5) if the judgment is irreconcilable with an earlier judgment given in a non-Contracting State involving the same cause of action and between the same parties, provided that this latter judgment fulfils the conditions necessary for its recognition in the State addressed.

ARTICLE 28

Moreover, a judgment shall not be recognised if it conflicts with the provisions of Sections 3, 4 or 5 of Title II, or in a case provided for in Article 59.

In its examination of the grounds of jurisdiction referred to in the foregoing paragraph, the court or authority applied to shall be bound by the findings of fact on which the court of the State in which the judgment was given based its jurisdiction.

Subject to the provisions of the first paragraph, the jurisdiction of the court of the State in which the judgment was given may not be reviewed; the test of public policy referred to in Article 27(1) may not be applied to the rules relating to jurisdiction.

ARTICLE 29

Under no circumstances may a foreign judgment be reviewed as to its substance.

ARTICLE 30

A court of a Contracting State in which recognition is sought of a judgment given in another Contracting State may stay the proceedings if an ordinary appeal against the judgment has been lodged.

A court of a Contracting State in which recognition is sought of a judgment given in Ireland or the United Kingdom may stay the proceedings if enforcement is suspended in the State in which the judgment was given by reason of an appeal.

Section 2

Enforcement

ARTICLE 31

A judgment given in a Contracting State and enforceable in that State shall be enforced in another Contracting State when, on the application of any interested party, the order for its enforcement has been issued there.

However, in the United Kingdom, such a judgment shall be enforced in England and Wales, in Scotland, or in Northern Ireland when, on the application of any interested party, it has been registered for enforcement in that part of the United Kingdom.

ARTICLE 32

The application shall be submitted:

— in Belgium, to the *tribunal de première instance* or *rechtbank van eerste aanleg;*

— in Denmark, to the *underret;*

— in the Federal Republic of Germany, to the presiding judge of a chamber of the *Landgericht;*

— in France, to the presiding judge of the *tribunal de grande instance;*

— in Ireland, to the High Court;

— in Italy, to the *corte d'appello;*

— in Luxembourg, to the presiding judge of the *tribunal d'arrondissement;*

— in the Netherlands, to the presiding judge of the *arrondissementsrechtbank;*

— in the United Kingdom:

(1) in England and Wales, to the High Court of Justice, or in the case of a maintenance judgment to the Magistrates' Court on transmission by the Secretary of State ;

(2) in Scotland, to the Court of Session, or in the case of a maintenance judgment to the Sheriff Court on transmission by the Secretary of State ;

(3) in Northern Ireland, to the High Court of Justice, or in the case of a maintenance judgment to the Magistrates' Court on transmission by the Secretary of State.

The jurisdiction of local courts shall be determined by reference to the place of domicile of the party against whom enforcement is sought. If he is not domiciled in the State in which enforcement is sought, it shall be determined by reference to the place of enforcement.

ARTICLE 33

The procedure for making the application shall be governed by the law of the State in which enforcement is sought.

The applicant must give an address for service of process within the area of jurisdiction of the court applied to. However, if the law of the State in which enforcement is sought does not provide for the furnishing of such an address, the applicant shall appoint a representative *ad litem*.

The documents referred to in Articles 46 and 47 shall be attached to the application.

ARTICLE 34

The court applied to shall give its decision without delay; the party against whom enforcement is sought shall not at this stage of the proceedings be entitled to make any submissions on the application.

The application may be refused only for one of the reasons specified in Articles 27 and 28.

Under no circumstances may the foreign judgment be reviewed as to its substance.

ARTICLE 35

The appropriate officer of the court shall without delay bring the decision given on the application to the notice of the applicant in accordance with the procedure laid down by the law of the State in which enforcement is sought.

ARTICLE 36

If enforcement is authorised, the party against whom enforcement is sought may appeal against the decision within one month of service thereof.

If that party is domiciled in a Contracting State other than Sch. 1
that in which the decision authorising enforcement was given,
the time for appealing shall be two months and shall run from
the date of service, either on him in person or at his residence.
No extension of time may be granted on account of distance.

Article 37

An appeal against the decision authorising enforcement shall
be lodged in accordance with the rules governing procedure in
contentious matters :

— in Belgium, with the *tribunal de première instance* or *rechtbank van eerste aanleg ;*

— in Denmark, with the *landsret ;*

— in the Federal Republic of Germany, with the *Oberlandesgericht ;*

— in France, with the *cour d'appel ;*

— in Ireland, with the High Court ;

— in Italy, with the *corte d'appello ;*

— in Luxembourg, with the *Cour supérieure de Justice* sitting
as a court of civil appeal ;

— in the Netherlands, with the *arrondissementsrechtbank ;*

— in the United Kingdom:

(1) in England and Wales, with the High Court of Justice,
or in the case of a maintenance judgment with the
Magistrates' Court ;

(2) in Scotland, with the Court of Session, or in the case
of a maintenance judgment with the Sheriff Court ;

(3) in Northern Ireland, with the High Court of Justice,
or in the case of a maintenance judgment with the
Magistrates' Court.

The judgment given on the appeal may be contested only:

— in Belgium, France, Italy, Luxembourg and the Netherlands, by an appeal in cassation ;

—in Denmark, by an appeal to the *højesteret*, with the leave
of the Minister of Justice ;

— in the Federal Republic of Germany, by a *Rechtsbesch-
werde ;*

— in Ireland, by an appeal on a point of law to the Supreme
Court ;

—in the United Kingdom, by a single further appeal on a
point of law.

ARTICLE 38

The court with which the appeal under the first paragraph of Article 37 is lodged may, on the application of the appellant, stay the proceedings if an ordinary appeal has been lodged against the judgment in the State in which that judgment was given or if the time for such an appeal has not yet expired ; in the latter case, the court may specify the time within which such an appeal is to be lodged.

Where the judgment was given in Ireland or the United Kingdom, any form of appeal available in the State in which it was given shall be treated as an ordinary appeal for the purposes of the first paragraph.

The court may also make enforcement conditional on the provision of such security as it shall determine.

ARTICLE 39

During the time specified for an appeal pursuant to Article 36 and until any such appeal has been determined, no measures of enforcement may be taken other than protective measures taken against the property of the party against whom enforcement is sought.

The decision authorising enforcement shall carry with it the power to proceed to any such protective measures.

ARTICLE 40

If the application for enforcement is refused, the applicant may appeal:

— in Belgium, to the *cour d'appel* or *hof van beroep ;*

— in Denmark, to the *landsret ;*

— in the Federal Republic of Germany, to the *Oberlandesgericht ;*

— in France, to the *cour d'appel ;*

— in Ireland, to the High Court ;

— in Italy, to the *corte d'appello* ;

— in Luxembourg, to the *Cour supérieure de Justice* sitting as a court of civil appeal ;

— in the Netherlands, to the *gerechtshof ;*

— in the United Kingdom:

   (1) in England and Wales, to the High Court of Justice, or in the case of a maintenance judgment to the Magistrates' Court ;

   (2) in Scotland, to the Court of Session, or in the case of a maintenance judgment to the Sheriff Court ;

(3) in Northern Ireland, to the High Court of Justice,
or in the case of a maintenance judgment to the
Magistrates' Court.

The party against whom enforcement is sought shall be summoned to appear before the appellate court. If he fails to appear,
the provisions of the second and third paragraphs of Article 20
shall apply even where he is not domiciled in any of the
Contracting States.

ARTICLE 41

A judgment given on an appeal provided for in Article 40
may be contested only:

— in Belgium, France, Italy, Luxembourg and the Netherlands, by an appeal in cassation ;

— in Denmark, by an appeal to the *højesteret*, with the leave
of the Minister of Justice ;

— in the Federal Republic of Germany, by a *Rechtbesch-
werde ;*

— in Ireland, by an appeal on a point of law to the Supreme
Court ;

— in the United Kingdom, by a single further appeal on a
point of law.

ARTICLE 42

Where a foreign judgment has been given in respect of
several matters and enforcement cannot be authorised for all
of them, the court shall authorise enforcement for one or more
of them.

An applicant may request partial enforcement of a judgment.

ARTICLE 43

A foreign judgment which orders a periodic payment by way
of a penalty shall be enforceable in the State in which enforcement is sought only if the amount of the payment has been
finally determined by the courts of the State in which the
judgment was given.

ARTICLE 44

An applicant who, in the State in which the judgment was
given, has benefited from complete or partial legal aid or exemption from costs or expenses, shall be entitled, in the procedures
provided for in Articles 32 to 35, to benefit from the most
favourable legal aid or the most extensive exemption from costs
or expenses provided for by the law of the State addressed.

An applicant who requests the enforcement of a decision
given by an administrative authority in Denmark in respect of a

maintenance order may, in the State addressed, claim the benefits referred to in the first paragraph if he presents a statement from the Danish Ministry of Justice to the effect that he fulfils the economic requirements to qualify for the grant of complete or partial legal aid or exemption from costs or expenses.

Article 45

No security, bond or deposit, however described, shall be required of a party who in one Contracting State applies for enforcement of a judgment given in another Contracting State on the ground that he is a foreign national or that he is not domiciled or resident in the State in which enforcement is sought.

Section 3

Common provisions

Article 46

A party seeking recognition or applying for enforcement of a judgment shall produce :

(1) a copy of the judgment which satisfies the conditions necessary to establish its authenticity ;

(2) in the case of a judgment given in default, the original or a certified true copy of the document which establishes that the party in default was served with the document instituting the proceedings or with an equivalent document.

Article 47

A party applying for enforcement shall also produce :

(1) documents which establish that, according to the law of the State in which it has been given, the judgment is enforceable and has been served ;

(2) where appropriate, a document showing that the applicant is in receipt of legal aid in the State in which the judgment was given.

Article 48

If the documents specified in Article 46(2) and Article 47(2) are not produced, the court may specify a time for their production, accept equivalent documents or, if it considers that it has sufficient information before it, dispense with their production.

If the court so requires, a translation of the documents shall be produced ; the translation shall be certified by a person qualified to do so in one of the Contracting States.

Article 49

No legalisation or other similar formality shall be required in respect of the documents referred to in Articles 46 or 47 or the second paragraph of Article 48, or in respect of a document appointing a representative *ad litem.*

TITLE IV
AUTHENTIC INSTRUMENTS AND COURT SETTLEMENTS
ARTICLE 50

A document which has been formally drawn up or registered as an authentic instrument and is enforceable in one Contracting State shall, in another Contracting State, have an order for its enforcement issued there, on application made in accordance with the procedures provided for in Article 31 *et seq.* The application may be refused only if enforcement of the instrument is contrary to public policy in the State in which enforcement is sought.

The instrument produced must satisfy the conditions necessary to establish its authenticity in the State of origin.

The provisions of Section 3 of Title III shall apply as appropriate.

ARTICLE 51

A settlement which has been approved by a court in the course of proceedings and is enforceable in the State in which it was concluded shall be enforceable in the State in which enforcement is sought under the same conditions as authentic instruments.

TITLE V
GENERAL PROVISIONS
ARTICLE 52

In order to determine whether a party is domiciled in the Contracting State whose courts are seised of the matter, the court shall apply its internal law.

If a party is not domiciled in the State whose courts are seised of the matter, then, in order to determine whether the party is domiciled in another Contracting State, the court shall apply the law of that State.

The domicile of a party shall, however, be determined in accordance with his national law if, by that law, his domicile depends on that of another person or on the seat of an authority.

ARTICLE 53

For the purposes of this Convention, the seat of a company or other legal person or association of natural or legal persons shall be treated as its domicile. However, in order to determine that seat, the court shall apply its rules of private international law.

In order to determine whether a trust is domiciled in the Contracting State whose courts are seised of the matter, the court shall apply its rules of private international law.

TITLE VI
TRANSITIONAL PROVISIONS
ARTICLE 54

The provisions of this Convention shall apply only to legal proceedings instituted and to documents formally drawn up or registered as authentic instruments after its entry into force.

However, judgments given after the date of entry into force of this Convention in proceedings instituted before that date shall be recognised and enforced in accordance with the provisions of Title III if jurisdiction was founded upon rules which accorded with those provided for either in Title II of this Convention or in a convention concluded between the State of origin and the State addressed which was in force when the proceedings were instituted.

TITLE VII
RELATIONSHIP TO OTHER CONVENTIONS
ARTICLE 55

Subject to the provisions of the second paragraph of Article 54, and of Article 56, this Convention shall, for the States which are parties to it, supersede the following conventions concluded between two or more of them:

— the Convention between Belgium and France on Jurisdiction and the Validity and Enforcement of Judgments, Arbitration Awards and Authentic Instruments, signed at Paris on 8 July 1899;

— the Convention between Belgium and the Netherlands on Jurisdiction, Bankruptcy, and the Validity and Enforcement of Judgments, Arbitration Awards and Authentic Instruments, signed at Brussels on 28 March 1925;

— the Convention between France and Italy on the Enforcement of Judgments in Civil and Commercial Matters, signed at Rome on 3 June 1930;

— the Convention between the United Kingdom and the French Republic providing for the Reciprocal Enforcement of Judgments in Civil and Commercial Matters, with Protocol, signed at Paris on 18 January 1934;

— the Convention between the United Kingdom and the Kingdom of Belgium providing for the Reciprocal Enforcement of Judgments in Civil and Commercial Matters, with Protocol, signed at Brussels on 2 May 1934;

— the Convention between Germany and Italy on the Recognition and Enforcement of Judgments in Civil and Commercial matters, signed at Rome on 9 March 1936;

— the Convention between the Federal Republic of Germany and the Kingdom of Belgium on the Mutual Recognition and Enforcement of Judgments, Arbitration Awards and Authentic Instruments in Civil and Commercial Matters, signed at Bonn on 30 June 1958 ;

— the Convention between the Kingdom of the Netherlands and the Italian Republic on the Recognition and Enforcement of Judgments in Civil and Commercial Matters, signed at Rome on 17 April 1959 ;

— the Convention between the United Kingdom and the Federal Republic of Germany for the Reciprocal Recognition and Enforcement of Judgments in Civil and Commercial Matters, signed at Bonn on 14 July 1960 ;

— the Convention between the Kingdom of Belgium and the Italian Republic on the Recognition and Enforcement of Judgments and other Enforceable Instruments in Civil and Commercial Matters, signed at Rome on 6 April 1962 ;

— the Convention between the Kingdom of the Netherlands and the Federal Republic of Germany on the Mutual Recognition and Enforcement of Judgments and other Enforceable Instruments in Civil and Commercial Matters, signed at The Hague on 30 August 1962 ;

— the Convention between the United Kingdom and the Republic of Italy for the Reciprocal Recognition and Enforcement of Judgments in Civil and Commercial Matters, signed at Rome on 7 February 1964, with amending Protocol signed at Rome on 14 July 1970 ;

— the Convention between the United Kingdom and the Kingdom of the Netherlands providing for the Reciprocal Recognition and Enforcement of Judgments in Civil Matters, signed at The Hague on 17 November 1967,

and, in so far as it is in force:

— the Treaty between Belgium, the Netherlands and Luxembourg on Jurisdiction, Bankruptcy, and the Validity and Enforcement of Judgments, Arbitration Awards and Authentic Instruments, signed at Brussels on 24 November 1961.

ARTICLE 56

The Treaty and the conventions referred to in Article 55 shall continue to have effect in relation to matters to which this Convention does not apply.

They shall continue to have effect in respect of judgments given and documents formally drawn up or registered as authentic instruments before the entry into force of this Convention.

ARTICLE 57

This Convention shall not affect any conventions to which the Contracting States are or will be parties and which, in relation to particular matters, govern jurisdiction or the recognition or enforcement of judgments.

This Convention shall not affect the application of provisions which, in relation to particular matters, govern jurisdiction or the recognition or enforcement of judgments and which are or will be contained in acts of the Institutions of the European Communities or in national laws harmonised in implementation of such acts.

(*Article* 25(2) *of the Accession Convention provides* :

" With a view to its uniform interpretation, paragraph 1 of Article 57 shall be applied in the following manner :

(*a*) The 1968 Convention as amended shall not prevent a court of a Contracting State which is a party to a convention on a particular matter from assuming jurisdiction in accordance with that convention, even where the defendant is domiciled in another Contracting State which is not a party to that convention. The court shall, in any event, apply Article 20 of the 1968 Convention as amended.

(*b*) A judgment given in a Contracting State in the exercise of jurisdiction provided for in a convention on a particular matter shall be recognised and enforced in the other Contracting States in accordance with the 1968 Convention as amended.

Where a convention on a particular matter to which both the State of origin and the State addressed are parties lays down conditions for the recognition or enforcement of judgments, those conditions shall apply. In any event, the provisions of the 1968 Convention as amended which concern the procedures for recognition and enforcement of judgments may be applied.")

ARTICLE 58

This Convention shall not affect the rights granted to Swiss nationals by the Convention concluded on 15 June 1869 between France and the Swiss Confederation on Jurisdiction and the Enforcement of Judgments in Civil Matters.

ARTICLE 59

This Convention shall not prevent a Contracting State from assuming, in a convention on the recognition and enforcement of judgments, an obligation towards a third State not to recognise judgments given in other Contracting States against defendants domiciled or habitually resident in the third State where, in cases provided for in Article 4, the judgment could only be founded on a ground of jurisdiction specified in the second paragraph of Article 3.

However, a Contracting State may not assume an obligation towards a third State not to recognise a judgment given in another Contracting State by a court basing its jurisdiction on the presence within that State of property belonging to the defendant, or the seizure by the plaintiff of property situated there:

(1) if the action is brought to assert or declare proprietary or possessory rights in that property, seeks to obtain authority to dispose of it, or arises from another issue relating to such property, or,

(2) if the property constitutes the security for a debt which is the subject-matter of the action.

TITLE VIII

FINAL PROVISIONS

ARTICLE 60

This Convention shall apply to the European territories of the Contracting States, including Greenland, to the French overseas departments and territories, and to Mayotte.

The Kingdom of the Netherlands may declare at the time of signing or ratifying this Convention or at any later time, by notifying the Secretary-General of the Council of the European Communities, that this Convention shall be applicable to the Netherlands Antilles. In the absence of such declaration, proceedings taking place in the European territory of the Kingdom as a result of an appeal in cassation from the judgment of a court in the Netherlands Antilles shall be deemed to be proceedings taking place in the latter court.

Notwithstanding the first paragraph, this Convention shall not apply to:

(1) the Faroe Islands, unless the Kingdom of Denmark makes a declaration to the contrary,

(2) any European territory situated outside the United Kingdom for the international relations of which the United Kingdom is responsible, unless the United Kingdom makes a declaration to the contrary in respect of any such territory.

Such declarations may be made at any time by notifying the Secretary-General of the Council of the European Communities.

Proceedings brought in the United Kingdom on appeal from courts in one of the territories referred to in subparagraph (2) of the third paragraph shall be deemed to be proceedings taking place in those courts.

Proceedings which in the Kingdom of Denmark are dealt with under the law on civil procedure for the Faroe Islands (*lov for Faerøerne om rettens pleje*) shall be deemed to be proceedings taking place in the courts of the Faroe Islands.

ARTICLE 61

This Convention shall be ratified by the signatory States. The instruments of ratification shall be deposited with the Secretary-General of the Council of the European Communities.

ARTICLE 62

This Convention shall enter into force on the first day of the third month following the deposit of the instrument of ratification by the last signatory State to take this step.

ARTICLE 63

The Contracting States recognise that any State which becomes a member of the European Economic Community shall be required to accept this Convention as a basis for the negotiations between the Contracting States and that State necessary to ensure the implementation of the last paragraph of Article 220 of the Treaty establishing the European Economic Community.

The necessary adjustments may be the subject of a special convention between the Contracting States of the one part and the new Member State of the other part.

ARTICLE 64

The Secretary-General of the Council of the European Communities shall notify the signatory States of:

(a) the deposit of each instrument of ratification;

(b) the date of entry into force of this Convention;

(c) any declaration received pursuant to Article 60;

(d) any declaration received pursuant to Article IV of the Protocol;

(e) any communication made pursuant to Article VI of the Protocol.

ARTICLE 65

The Protocol annexed to this Convention by common accord of the Contracting States shall form an integral part thereof.

ARTICLE 66

This Convention is concluded for an unlimited period.

ARTICLE 67

Any Contracting State may request the revision of this Convention. In this event, a revision conference shall be convened by the President of the Council of the European Communities.

ARTICLE 68

This Convention, drawn up in a single original in the Dutch, French, German and Italian languages, all four texts being equally authentic, shall be deposited in the archives of the

Secretariat of the Council of the European Communities. The Secretary-General shall transmit a certified copy to the Government of each signatory State.

(*Signatures of Plenipotentiaries of the original six Contracting States*)

ANNEXED PROTOCOL

Article I

Any person domiciled in Luxembourg who is sued in a court of another Contracting State pursuant to Article 5(1) may refuse to submit to the jurisdiction of that court. If the defendant does not enter an appearance the court shall declare of its own motion that it has no jurisdiction.

An agreement conferring jurisdiction, within the meaning of Article 17, shall be valid with respect to a person domiciled in Luxembourg only if that person has expressly and specifically so agreed.

Article II

Without prejudice to any more favourable provisions of national laws, persons domiciled in a Contracting State who are being prosecuted in the criminal courts of another Contracting State of which they are not nationals for an offence which was not intentionally committed may be defended by persons qualified to do so, even if they do not appear in person.

However, the court seised of the matter may order appearance in person; in the case of failure to appear, a judgment given in the civil action without the person concerned having had the opportunity to arrange for his defence need not be recognised or enforced in the other Contracting States.

Article III

In proceedings for the issue of an order for enforcement, no charge, duty or fee calculated by reference to the value of the matter in issue may be levied in the State in which enforcement is sought.

Article IV

Judicial and extrajudicial documents drawn up in one Contracting State which have to be served on persons in another Contracting State shall be transmitted in accordance with the procedures laid down in the conventions and agreements concluded between the Contracting States.

Unless the State in which service is to take place objects by declaration to the Secretary-General of the Council of the European Communities, such documents may also be sent by the appropriate public officers of the State in which the document has been drawn up directly to the appropriate public officers of the State in which the addressee is to be found. In this case the officer of the State of origin shall send a copy of the document to the officer of the State addressed who is competent to forward it to the addressee. The document shall be forwarded in the manner specified by the law of the State addressed. The forwarding shall be recorded by a certificate sent directly to the officer of the State of origin.

ARTICLE V

The jurisdiction specified in Article 6(2) and Article 10 in actions on a warranty or guarantee or in any other third party proceedings may not be resorted to in the Federal Republic of Germany. In that State, any person domiciled in another Contracting State may be sued in the courts in pursuance of Articles 68, 72, 73 and 74 of the code of civil procedure (*Zivilprozessordnung*) concerning third-party notices.

Judgments given in the other Contracting States by virtue of Article 6(2) or Article 10 shall be recognised and enforced in the Federal Republic of Germany in accordance with Title III. Any effects which judgments given in that State may have on third parties by application of Articles 68, 72, 73 and 74 of the code of civil procedure (*Zivilprozessordnung*) shall also be recognised in the other Contracting States.

ARTICLE V A

In matters relating to maintenance, the expression " court " includes the Danish administrative authorities.

ARTICLE V B

In proceedings involving a dispute between the master and a member of the crew of a sea-going ship registered in Denmark or in Ireland, concerning remuneration or other conditions of service, a court in a Contracting State shall establish whether the diplomatic or consular officer responsible for the ship has been notified of the dispute. It shall stay the proceedings so long as he has not been notified. It shall of its own motion decline jurisdiction if the officer, having been duly notified, has exercised the powers accorded to him in the matter by a consular convention, or in the absence of such a convention, has, within the time allowed, raised any objection to the exercise of such jurisdiction.

ARTICLE V C

Articles 52 and 53 of this Convention shall, when applied by Article 69(5) of the Convention for the European Patent for the Common Market, signed at Luxembourg on 15 December 1975, to the provisions relating to " residence " in the English text of that Convention, operate as if " residence " in that text were the same as " domicile " in Articles 52 and 53.

ARTICLE V D

Without prejudice to the jurisdiction of the European Patent Office under the Convention on the Grant of European Patents, signed at Munich on 5 October 1973, the courts of each Contracting State shall have exclusive jurisdiction, regardless of domicile, in proceedings concerned with the registration or validity of any European patent granted for that State which is not a Community patent by virtue of the provisions of Article 86 of the Convention for the European Patent for the Common Market, signed at Luxembourg on 15 December 1975.

ARTICLE VI

The Contracting States shall communicate to the Secretary-General of the Council of the European Communities the text of any provisions of their laws which amend either those articles of their laws mentioned in the Convention or the lists of courts specified in Section 2 of Title III of the Convention.

SCHEDULE 2

TEXT OF 1971 PROTOCOL, AS AMENDED

ARTICLE 1

The Court of Justice of the European Communities shall have jurisdiction to give rulings on the interpretation of the Convention on Jurisdiction and the Enforcement of Judgments in Civil and Commercial Matters and of the Protocol annexed to that Convention, signed at Brussels on 27 September 1968, and also on the interpretation of the present Protocol.

The Court of Justice of the European Communities shall also have jurisdiction to give rulings on the interpretation of the Convention on the Accession of the Kingdom of Denmark, Ireland and the United Kingdom of Great Britain and Northern Ireland to the Convention of 27 September 1968 and to this Protocol.

ARTICLE 2

The following courts may request the Court of Justice to give preliminary rulings on questions of interpretation:

(1) — in Belgium: *la Cour de Cassation—het Hof van Cassatie* and *le Conseil d'Etat—de Raad van State,*

    — in Denmark: *højesteret,*

    — in the Federal Republic of Germany: *die obersten Gerichtshöfe des Bundes,*

    — in France: *la Cour de Cassation* and *le Conseil d'Etat,*

    — in Ireland: the Supreme Court,

    — in Italy: *la Corte Suprema di Cassazione,*

— in Luxembourg: *la Cour supérieure de Justice* when sitting as *Cour de Cassation,*

— in the Netherlands: *de Hoge Raad,*

— in the United Kingdom: the House of Lords and courts to which application has been made under the second paragraph of Article 37 or under Article 41 of the Convention ;

(2) the courts of the Contracting States when they are sitting in an appellate capacity ;

(3) in the cases provided for in Article 37 of the Convention, the courts referred to in that Article.

ARTICLE 3

(1) Where a question of interpretation of the Convention or of one of the other instruments referred to in Article 1 is raised in a case pending before one of the courts listed in Article 2(1), that court shall, if it considers that a decision on the question is necessary to enable it to give judgment, request the Court of Justice to give a ruling thereon.

(2) Where such a question is raised before any court referred to in Article 2(2) or (3), that court may, under the conditions laid down in paragraph (1), request the Court of Justice to give a ruling thereon.

ARTICLE 4

(1) The competent authority of a Contracting State may request the Court of Justice to give a ruling on a question of interpretation of the Convention or of one of the other instruments referred to in Article 1 if judgments given by courts of that State conflict with the interpretation given either by the Court of Justice or in a judgment of one of the courts of another Contracting State referred to in Article 2(1) or (2). The provisions of this paragraph shall apply only to judgments which have become *res judicata.*

(2) The interpretation given by the Court of Justice in response to such a request shall not affect the judgments which gave rise to the request for interpretation.

(3) The Procurators-General of the Courts of Cassation of the Contracting States, or any other authority designated by a Contracting State, shall be entitled to request the Court of Justice for a ruling on interpretation in accordance with paragraph (1).

(4) The Registrar of the Court of Justice shall give notice of the request to the Contracting States, to the Commission and to the Council of the European Communities ; they shall then be entitled within two months of the notification to submit statements of case or written observations to the Court.

(5) No fees shall be levied or any costs or expenses awarded in respect of the proceedings provided for in this Article.

ARTICLE 5

(1) Except where this Protocol otherwise provides, the provisions of the Treaty establishing the European Economic Community and those of the Protocol on the Statute of the Court of Justice annexed thereto, which are applicable when the Court is requested to give a preliminary ruling, shall also apply to any proceedings for the interpretation of the Convention and the other instruments referred to in Article 1.

(2) The Rules of Procedure of the Court of Justice shall, if necessary, be adjusted and supplemented in accordance with Article 188 of the Treaty establishing the European Economic Community.

ARTICLE 6

This Protocol shall apply to the European territories of the Contracting States, including Greenland, to the French overseas departments and territories, and to Mayotte.

The Kingdom of the Netherlands may declare at the time of signing or ratifying this Protocol or at any later time, by notifying the Secretary-General of the Council of the European Communities, that this Protocol shall be applicable to the Netherlands Antilles.

Notwithstanding the first paragraph, this Protocol shall not apply to:

(1) the Faroe Islands, unless the Kingdom of Denmark makes a declaration to the contrary,

(2) any European territory situated outside the United Kingdom for the international relations of which the United Kingdom is responsible, unless the United Kingdom makes a declaration to the contrary in respect of any such territory.

Such declarations may be made at any time by notifying the Secretary-General of the Council of the European Communities.

ARTICLE 7

This Protocol shall be ratified by the signatory States. The instruments of ratification shall be deposited with the Secretary-General of the Council of the European Communities.

ARTICLE 8

This Protocol shall enter into force on the first day of the third month following the deposit of the instrument of ratification by the last signatory State to take this step; provided that

SCH. 2   it shall at the earliest enter into force at the same time as the Convention of 27 September 1968 on Jurisdiction and the Enforcement of Judgments in Civil and Commercial Matters.

ARTICLE 9

The Contracting States recognise that any State which becomes a member of the European Economic Community, and to which Article 63 of the Convention on Jurisdiction and the Enforcement of Judgments in Civil and Commercial Matters applies, must accept the provisions of this Protocol, subject to such adjustments as may be required.

ARTICLE 10

The Secretary-General of the Council of the European Communities shall notify the signatory States of:

(*a*) the deposit of each instrument of ratification;

(*b*) the date of entry into force of this Protocol;

(*c*) any designation received pursuant to Article 4(3);

(*d*) any declaration received pursuant to Article 6.

ARTICLE 11

The Contracting States shall communicate to the Secretary-General of the Council of the European Communities the texts of any provisions of their laws which necessitate an amendment to the list of courts in Article 2(1).

ARTICLE 12

This Protocol is concluded for an unlimited period.

ARTICLE 13

Any Contracting State may request the revision of this Protocol. In this event, a revision conference shall be convened by the President of the Council of the European Communities.

ARTICLE 14

This Protocol, drawn up in a single original in the Dutch, French, German and Italian languages, all four texts being equally authentic, shall be deposited in the archives of the Secretariat of the Council of the European Communities. The Secretary-General shall transmit a certified copy to the Government of each signatory State.

SCHEDULE 3

TEXT OF TITLES V AND VI OF ACCESSION CONVENTION

TITLE V

TRANSITIONAL PROVISIONS

ARTICLE 34

(1) The 1968 Convention and the 1971 Protocol, with the amendments made by this Convention, shall apply only to legal proceedings instituted and to authentic instruments formally drawn up or registered after the entry into force of this Convention in the State of origin and, where recognition or enforcement of a judgment or authentic instrument is sought, in the State addressed.

(2) However, as between the six Contracting States to the 1968 Convention, judgments given after the date of entry into force of this Convention in proceedings instituted before that date shall be recognised and enforced in accordance with the provisions of Title III of the 1968 Convention as amended.

(3) Moreover, as between the six Contracting States to the 1968 Convention and the three States mentioned in Article 1 of this Convention, and as between those three States, judgments given after the date of entry into force of this Convention between the State of origin and the State addressed in proceedings instituted before that date shall also be recognised and enforced in accordance with the provisions of Title III of the 1968 Convention as amended if jurisdiction was founded upon rules which accorded with the provisions of Title II, as amended, or with provisions of a convention concluded between the State of origin and the State addressed which was in force when the proceedings were instituted.

ARTICLE 35

If the parties to a dispute concerning a contract had agreed in writing before the entry into force of this Convention that the contract was to be governed by the law of Ireland or of a part of the United Kingdom, the courts of Ireland or of that part of the United Kingdom shall retain the right to exercise jurisdiction in the dispute.

ARTICLE 36

For a period of three years from the entry into force of the 1968 Convention for the Kingdom of Denmark and Ireland respectively, jurisdiction in maritime matters shall be determined in these States not only in accordance with the provisions of that

Convention but also in accordance with the provisions of paragraphs (1) to (6) following. However, upon the entry into force of
the International Convention relating to the Arrest of Sea-going
Ships, signed at Brussels on 10 May 1952, for one of these States,
these provisions shall cease to have effect for that State.

(1) A person who is domiciled in a Contracting State may be
sued in the courts of one of the States mentioned above in respect
of a maritime claim if the ship to which the claim relates or any
other ship owned by him has been arrested by judicial process
within the territory of the latter State to secure the claim, or
could have been so arrested there but bail or other security has
been given, and either:

(a) the claimant is domiciled in the latter State; or

(b) the claim arose in the latter State; or

(c) the claim concerns the voyage during which the arrest
was made or could have been made; or

(d) the claim arises out of a collision or out of damage
caused by a ship to another ship or to goods or persons
on board either ship, either by the execution or non-
execution of a manoeuvre or by the non-observance of
regulations; or

(e) the claim is for salvage; or

(f) the claim is in respect of a mortgage or hypothecation
of the ship arrested.

(2) A claimant may arrest either the particular ship to which
the maritime claim relates, or any other ship which is owned by
the person who was, at the time when the maritime claim arose,
the owner of the particular ship. However, only the particular
ship to which the maritime claim relates may be arrested in respect of the maritime claims set out in subparagraphs (o), (p) or
(q) of paragraph (5) of this Article.

(3) Ships shall be deemed to be in the same ownership when all
the shares therein are owned by the same person or persons.

(4) When in the case of a charter by demise of a ship the
charterer alone is liable in respect of a maritime claim relating
to that ship, the claimant may arrest that ship or any other ship
owned by the charterer, but no other ship owned by the owner
may be arrested in respect of such claim. The same shall apply
to any case in which a person other than the owner of a ship
is liable in respect of a maritime claim relating to that ship.

(5) The expression " maritime claim " means a claim arising
out of one or more of the following:

(a) damage caused by any ship either in collision or otherwise;

(b) loss of life or personal injury caused by any ship or   Sch. 3
occurring in connection with the operation of any ship ;

(c) salvage ;

(d) agreement relating to the use or hire of any ship whether
by charterparty or otherwise ;

(e) agreement relating to the carriage of goods in any ship
whether by charterparty or otherwise ;

(f) loss of or damage to goods including baggage carried
in any ship ;

(g) general average ;

(h) bottomry ;

(i) towage ;

(j) pilotage ;

(k) goods or materials wherever supplied to a ship for her
operation or maintenance ;

(l) construction, repair or equipment of any ship or dock
charges and dues ;

(m) wages of masters, officers or crew ;

(n) master's disbursements, including disbursements made
by shippers, charterers or agents on behalf of a ship or
her owner ;

(o) dispute as to the title to or ownership of any ship ;

(p) disputes between co-owners of any ship as to the ownership, possession, employment or earnings of that ship ;

(q) the mortgage or hypothecation of any ship.

(6) In Denmark, the expression " arrest " shall be deemed as
regards the maritime claims referred to in subparagraphs (o)
and (p) of paragraph (5) of this Article, to include a *forbud,*
where that is the only procedure allowed in respect of such a
claim under Articles 646 to 653 of the law on civil procedure
(*lov om rettens pleje*).

TITLE VI

FINAL PROVISIONS

Article 37

The Secretary-General of the Council of the European Communities shall transmit a certified copy of the 1968 Convention
and of the 1971 Protocol in the Dutch, French, German and
Italian languages to the Governments of the Kingdom of Denmark, Ireland and the United Kingdom of Great Britain and
Northern Ireland.

The texts of the 1968 Convention and the 1971 Protocol, drawn up in the Danish, English and Irish languages, shall be annexed to this Convention. The texts drawn up in the Danish, English and Irish languages shall be authentic under the same conditions as the original texts of the 1968 Convention and the 1971 Protocol.

ARTICLE 38

This Convention shall be ratified by the signatory States. The instruments of ratification shall be deposited with the Secretary-General of the Council of the European Communities.

ARTICLE 39

This Convention shall enter into force, as between the States which shall have ratified it, on the first day of the third month following the deposit of the last instrument of ratification by the original Member States of the Community and one new Member State.

It shall enter into force for each new Member State which subsequently ratifies it on the first day of the third month following the deposit of its instrument of ratification.

ARTICLE 40

The Secretary-General of the Council of the European Communities shall notify the signatory States of:

(*a*) the deposit of each instrument of ratification,

(*b*) the dates of entry into force of this Convention for the Contracting States.

ARTICLE 41

This Convention, drawn up in a single original in the Danish, Dutch, English, French, German, Irish and Italian languages, all seven texts being equally authentic, shall be deposited in the archives of the Secretariat of the Council of the European Communities. The Secretary-General shall transmit a certified copy to the Government of each signatory State.

Section 16.

SCHEDULE 4

TITLE II OF 1968 CONVENTION AS MODIFIED FOR ALLOCATION OF JURISDICTION WITHIN U.K.

TITLE II

JURISDICTION

Section 1

General Provisions

ARTICLE 2

Subject to the provisions of this **Title,** persons domiciled in **a part of the United Kingdom** shall . . . be sued in the courts of **that part.**

. . . .

ARTICLE 3

Persons domiciled in a **part of the United Kingdom** may be sued in the courts of another **part of the United Kingdom** only by virtue of the rules set out in Sections 2, **4, 5 and** 6 of this Title.

. . . .

Section 2

Special jurisdiction

ARTICLE 5

A person domiciled in a **part of the United Kingdom** may, in another **part of the United Kingdom,** be sued:

(1) in matters relating to a contract, in the courts for the place of performance of the obligation in question ;

(2) in matters relating to maintenance, in the courts for the place where the maintenance creditor is domiciled or habitually resident or, if the matter is ancillary to proceedings concerning the status of a person, in the court which, according to its own law, has jurisdiction to entertain those proceedings, unless that jurisdiction is based solely on the nationality of one of the parties ;

(3) in matters relating to tort, delict or quasi-delict, in the **courts** for the place where the harmful event occurred **or in the case of a threatened wrong is likely to occur** ;

T 2

(4) as regards a civil claim for damages or restitution which is based on an act giving rise to criminal proceedings, in the court seised of those proceedings, to the extent that that court has jurisdiction under its own law to entertain civil proceedings ;

(5) as regards a dispute arising out of the operations of a branch, agency or other establishment, in the courts for the place in which the branch, agency or other establishment is situated ;

(6) in his capacity as a settlor, trustee or beneficiary of a trust created by the operation of a statute, or by a written instrument, or created orally and evidenced in writing, in the courts of the **part of the United Kingdom** in which the trust is domiciled ;

(7) as regards a dispute concerning the payment of remuneration claimed in respect of the salvage of a cargo or freight, in the court under the authority of which the cargo or freight in question

   (*a*) has been arrested to secure such payment, or

   (*b*) could have been so arrested, but bail or other security has been given ;

provided that this provision shall apply only if it is claimed that the defendant has an interest in the cargo or freight or had such an interest at the time of salvage ;

(8) **in proceedings—**

   (a) **concerning a debt secured on immovable property ; or**

   (b) **which are brought to assert, declare or determine proprietary or possessory rights, or rights of security, in or over movable property, or to obtain authority to dispose of movable property,**

in the courts of the part of the United Kingdom in which the property is situated.

ARTICLE 5A

Proceedings which have as their object a decision of an organ of a company or other legal person or of an association of natural or legal persons may, without prejudice to the other provisions of this Title, be brought in the courts of the part of the United Kingdom in which that company, legal person or association has its seat.

ARTICLE 6

A person domiciled in a **part of the United Kingdom** may, **in another part of the United Kingdom,** also be sued :

(1) where he is one of a number of defendants, in the courts for the place where any one of them is domiciled;

(2) as a third party in an action on a warranty or guarantee or
in any other third party proceedings, in the court seised of
the original proceedings, unless these were instituted solely
with the object of removing him from the jurisdiction of
the court which would be competent in his case ;

(3) on a counterclaim arising from the same contract or facts on
which the original claim was based, in the court in which the
original claim is pending.

ARTICLE 6A

Where by virtue of this **Title** a court of a **part of the United Kingdom** has jurisdiction in actions relating to liability arising from the
use or operation of a ship, that court, or any other court substituted
for this purpose by the internal law of that **part,** shall also have jurisdiction over claims for limitation of such liability.

. . . .

Section 4

Jurisdiction over consumer contracts

ARTICLE 13

In proceedings concerning a contract concluded by a person for
a purpose which can be regarded as being outside his trade or profession, hereinafter called " the consumer ", jurisdiction shall be
determined by this Section, without prejudice to the provisions
of Articles . . . 5(5) **and (8)(b),** if it is :

(1) a contract for the sale of goods on instalment credit terms,
or

(2) a contract for a loan repayable by instalments, or for any
other form of credit, made to finance the sale of goods, or

(3) any other contract for the supply of goods or a contract for
the supply of services and . . . the consumer took in **the part
of the United Kingdom in which he is domiciled** the steps
necessary for the conclusion of the contract.

. . . .

This Section shall not apply to contracts of transport **or insurance.**

ARTICLE 14

A consumer may bring proceedings against the other party to a
contract either in the courts of the **part of the United Kingdom** in

SCH. 4   which that party is domiciled or in the courts of the **part of the United Kingdom** in which he is himself domiciled.

Proceedings may be brought against a consumer by the other party to the contract only in the courts of the **part of the United Kingdom** in which the consumer is domiciled.

These provisions shall not affect the right to bring a counterclaim in the court in which, in accordance with this Section, the original claim is pending.

ARTICLE 15

The provisions of this Section may be departed from only by an agreement:

(1) which is entered into after the dispute has arisen,
    or

(2) which allows the consumer to bring proceedings in courts other than those indicated in this Section,
    or

(3) which is entered into by the consumer and the other party to the contract, both of whom are at the time of conclusion of the contract domiciled or habitually resident in the same **part of the United Kingdom,** and which confers jurisdiction on the courts of that **part,** provided that such an agreement is not contrary to the law of that **part.**

Section 5

Exclusive jurisdiction

ARTICLE 16

The following courts shall have exclusive jurisdiction, regardless of domicile:

(1) in proceedings which have as their object rights *in rem* in, or tenancies of, immovable property, the courts of the **part of the United Kingdom** in which the property is situated ;

(2) in proceedings which have as their object the validity of the constitution, the nullity or the dissolution of companies or other legal persons or associations of natural or legal persons . . . the courts of the **part of the United Kingdom** in which the company, legal person or association has its seat ;

(3) in proceedings which have as their object the validity of entries in public registers, the courts of the **part of the United Kingdom** in which the register is kept ;

. . . .

(5) in proceedings concerned with the enforcement of judgments, the courts of the **part of the United Kingdom** in which the judgment has been or is to be enforced.

Section 6

Prorogation of jurisdiction

ARTICLE 17

If the parties . . . have agreed that a court or the courts of a **part of the United Kingdom** are to have jurisdiction to settle **any** disputes which have arisen or which may arise in connection with a particular legal relationship, **and, apart from this Schedule, the agreement would be effective to confer jurisdiction under the law of that part,** that court or those courts shall have . . . jurisdiction . . .

The court or courts of a **part of the United Kingdom** on which a trust instrument has conferred jurisdiction shall have . . . jurisdiction in any proceedings brought against a settlor, trustee or beneficiary, if relations between these persons or their rights or obligations under the trust are involved.

Agreements or provisions of a trust instrument conferring jurisdiction shall have no legal force if they are contrary to the provisions of Article . . . 15, or if the courts whose jurisdiction they purport to exclude have exclusive jurisdiction by virtue of Article 16.

. . . .

ARTICLE 18

Apart from jurisdiction derived from other provisions of this **Title,** a court of a **part of the United Kingdom** before whom **a** defendant enters an appearance shall have jurisdiction. This rule shall not apply where appearance was entered solely to contest the jurisdiction, or where another court has exclusive jurisdiction by virtue of Article 16.

Section 7

Examination as to jurisdiction and admissibility

ARTICLE 19

Where a court of a **part of the United Kingdom** is seised of a claim which is principally concerned with a matter over which the courts of another **part of the United Kingdom** have exclusive jurisdiction by virtue of Article 16, it shall declare of its own motion that it has no jurisdiction.

ARTICLE 20

Where a defendant domiciled in one **part of the United Kingdom** is sued in a court of another **part of the United Kingdom** and does not enter an appearance, the court shall declare of its own motion that it has no jurisdiction unless its jurisdiction is derived from the provisions of this **Title.**

The court shall stay the proceedings so long as it is not shown that the defendant has been able to receive the document instituting the proceedings or an equivalent document in sufficient time to enable him to arrange for his defence, or that all necessary steps have been taken to this end.

. . . .

SCH. 4

Section 9

Provisional, including protective, measures

ARTICLE 24

Application may be made to the courts of a **part of the United Kingdom** for such provisional, including protective, measures as may be available under the law of that **part,** even if, under this **Title,** the courts of another **part of the United Kingdom** have jurisdiction as to the substance of the matter.

Section 17.

SCHEDULE 5

PROCEEDINGS EXCLUDED FROM SCHEDULE 4

Proceedings under the Companies Acts

1948 c. 38.
1960 c. 22
(N.I.).

1. Proceedings for the winding up of a company under the Companies Act 1948 or the Companies Act (Northern Ireland) 1960, or proceedings relating to a company as respects which jurisdiction is conferred on the court having winding up jurisdiction under either of those Acts.

Patents, trade marks, designs and similar rights

2. Proceedings concerned with the registration or validity of patents, trade marks, designs or other similar rights required to be deposited or registered.

Protection of Trading Interests Act 1980

1980 c. 11.

3. Proceedings under section 6 of the Protection of Trading Interests Act 1980 (recovery of sums paid or obtained pursuant to a judgment for multiple damages).

Appeals etc. from tribunals

4. Proceedings on appeal from, or for review of, decisions of tribunals.

Maintenance and similar payments to local and other public authorities

5. Proceedings for, or otherwise relating to, an order under any of the following provisions—

1980 c. 5.
1968 c. 49.
1968 c. 34
(N.I.).

(*a*) section 47 or 51 of the Child Care Act 1980, section 80 of the Social Work (Scotland) Act 1968 or section 156 of the Children and Young Persons Act (Northern Ireland) 1968 (contributions in respect of children in care, etc.) ;

(*b*) section 49 or 50 of the Child Care Act 1980, section 81 of the Social Work (Scotland) Act 1968 or section 159 of the Children and Young Persons Act (Northern Ireland) 1968 (applications for, or for variation of, affiliation orders in respect of children in care, etc.) ;

(c) section 43 of the National Assistance Act 1948, section 18 SCH. 5
of the Supplementary Benefits Act 1976, Article 101 of the 1948 c. 29.
Health and Personal Social Services (Northern Ireland) 1976 c. 21.
Order 1972 or Article 23 of the Supplementary Benefits S.I. 1972/1265
(N.I. 14).
(Northern Ireland) Order 1977 (recovery of cost of assistance S.I. 1977/2156
or benefit from person liable to maintain the assisted (N.I. 27).
person) ;

(d) section 44 of the National Assistance Act 1948, section 19 of
the Supplementary Benefits Act 1976, Article 102 of the
Health and Personal Social Services (Northern Ireland)
Order 1972 or Article 24 of the Supplementary Benefits
(Northern Ireland) Order 1977 (applications for, or for variation of, affiliation orders in respect of children for whom
assistance or benefit provided).

Proceedings under certain conventions, etc.

6. Proceedings brought in any court in pursuance of—

(a) any statutory provision which, in the case of any convention
to which Article 57 applies (conventions relating to specific
matters which override the general rules in the 1968 Convention), implements the convention or makes provision with
respect to jurisdiction in any field to which the convention
relates ; and

(b) any rule of law so far as it has the effect of implementing
any such convention.

Certain Admiralty proceedings in Scotland

7. Proceedings in Scotland in an Admiralty cause where the jurisdiction of the Court of Session or, as the case may be, of the sheriff
is based on arrestment *in rem* or *ad fundandam jurisdictionem* of a
ship, cargo or freight.

Register of aircraft mortgages

8. Proceedings for the rectification of the register of aircraft mortgages kept by the Civil Aviation Authority.

Continental Shelf Act 1964

9. Proceedings brought in any court in pursuance of an order 1964 c. 29.
under section 3 of the Continental Shelf Act 1964.

SCHEDULE 6   Section 18.

ENFORCEMENT OF U.K. JUDGMENTS (MONEY PROVISIONS)

Preliminary

1. In this Schedule—

" judgment " means any judgment to which section 18 applies
and references to the giving of a judgment shall be construed
accordingly ;

" money provision " means a provision for the payment of one or more sums of money ;

" prescribed " means prescribed by rules of court.

Certificates in respect of judgments

2.—(1) Any interested party who wishes to secure the enforcement in another part of the United Kingdom of any money provisions contained in a judgment may apply for a certificate under this Schedule.

(2) The application shall be made in the prescribed manner to the proper officer of the original court, that is to say—

(a) in relation to a judgment within paragraph (a) of the definition of " judgment " in section 18(2), the court by which the judgment or order was given or made ;

(b) in relation to a judgment within paragraph (b) of that definition, the court in which the judgment or order is entered ;

(c) in relation to a judgment within paragraph (c) of that definition, the court in whose books the document is registered ;

(d) in relation to a judgment within paragraph (d) of that definition, the tribunal by which the award or order was made ;

(e) in relation to a judgment within paragraph (e) of that definition, the court which gave the judgment or made the order by virtue of which the award has become enforceable as mentioned in that paragraph.

3. A certificate shall not be issued under this Schedule in respect of a judgment unless under the law of the part of the United Kingdom in which the judgment was given—

(a) either—

(i) the time for bringing an appeal against the judgment has expired, no such appeal having been brought within that time ; or

(ii) such an appeal having been brought within that time, that appeal has been finally disposed of ; and

(b) enforcement of the judgment is not for the time being stayed or suspended, and the time available for its enforcement has not expired.

4.—(1) Subject to paragraph 3, on an application under paragraph 2 the proper officer shall issue to the applicant a certificate in the prescribed form—

(a) stating the sum or aggregate of the sums (including any costs or expenses) payable under the money provisions contained in the judgment, the rate of interest, if any, payable thereon and the date or time from which any such interest began to accrue ;

(b) stating that the conditions specified in paragraph 3(a) and (b) are satisfied in relation to the judgment ; and

(c) containing such other particulars as may be prescribed.

(2) More than one certificate may be issued under this Schedule (simultaneously or at different times) in respect of the same judgment.

Registration of certificates

5.—(1) Where a certificate has been issued under this Schedule in any part of the United Kingdom, any interested party may, within six months from the date of its issue, apply in the prescribed manner to the proper officer of the superior court in any other part of the United Kingdom for the certificate to be registered in that court.

(2) In this paragraph "superior court" means, in relation to England and Wales or Northern Ireland, the High Court and, in relation to Scotland, the Court of Session.

(3) Where an application is duly made under this paragraph to the proper officer of a superior court, he shall register the certificate in that court in the prescribed manner.

General effect of registration

6.—(1) A certificate registered under this Schedule shall, for the purposes of its enforcement, be of the same force and effect, the registering court shall have in relation to its enforcement the same powers, and proceedings for or with respect to its enforcement may be taken, as if the certificate had been a judgment originally given in the registering court and had (where relevant) been entered.

(2) Sub-paragraph (1) is subject to the following provisions of this Schedule and to any provision made by rules of court as to the manner in which and the conditions subject to which a certificate registered under this Schedule may be enforced.

Costs or expenses

7. Where a certificate is registered under this Schedule, the reasonable costs or expenses of and incidental to the obtaining of the certificate and its registration shall be recoverable as if they were costs or expenses stated in the certificate to be payable under a money provision contained in the original judgment.

Interest

8.—(1) Subject to any provision made under sub-paragraph (2), the debt resulting, apart from paragraph 7, from the registration of the certificate shall carry interest at the rate, if any, stated in the certificate from the date or time so stated.

(2) Provision may be made by rules of court as to the manner in which and the periods by reference to which any interest payable by virtue of sub-paragraph (1) is to be calculated and paid, including provision for such interest to cease to accrue as from a prescribed date.

(3) All such sums as are recoverable by virtue of paragraph 7 carry interest as if they were the subject of an order for costs or expenses made by the registering court on the date of registration of the certificate.

(4) Except as provided by this paragraph sums payable by virtue of the registration of a certificate under this Schedule shall not carry interest.

Stay or sisting of enforcement in certain cases

9. Where a certificate in respect of a judgment has been registered under this Schedule, the registering court may, if it is satisfied that any person against whom it is sought to enforce the certificate is entitled and intends to apply under the law of the part of the United Kingdom in which the judgment was given for any remedy which would result in the setting aside or quashing of the judgment, stay (or, in Scotland, sist) proceedings for the enforcement of the certificate, on such terms as it thinks fit, for such period as appears to the court to be reasonably sufficient to enable the application to be disposed of.

Cases in which registration of a certificate must or may be set aside

10. Where a certificate has been registered under this Schedule, the registering court—

    (*a*) shall set aside the registration if, on an application made by any interested party, it is satisfied that the registration was contrary to the provisions of this Schedule ;

    (*b*) may set aside the registration if, on an application so made, it is satisfied that the matter in dispute in the proceedings in which the judgment in question was given had previously been the subject of a judgment by another court or tribunal having jurisdiction in the matter.

SCHEDULE 7

Enforcement of U.K. Judgments (Non-Money Provisions)

Preliminary

1. In this Schedule—

    " judgment " means any judgment to which section 18 applies and references to the giving of a judgment shall be construed accordingly ;

    " non-money provision " means a provision for any relief or remedy not requiring payment of a sum of money ;

    " prescribed " means prescribed by rules of court.

Certified copies of judgments

2.—(1) Any interested party who wishes to secure the enforcement in another part of the United Kingdom of any non-money provisions contained in a judgment may apply for a certified copy of the judgment.

(2) The application shall be made in the prescribed manner to the proper officer of the original court, that is to say—

    (*a*) in relation to a judgment within paragraph (*a*) of the definition of " judgment " in section 18(2), the court by which the judgment or order was given or made ;

(*b*) in relation to a judgment within paragraph (*b*) of that definition, the court in which the judgment or order is entered ;

(*c*) in relation to a judgment within paragraph (*c*) of that definition, the court in whose books the document is registered ;

(*d*) in relation to a judgment within paragraph (*d*) of that definition, the tribunal by which the award or order was made ;

(*e*) in relation to a judgment within paragraph (*e*) of that definition, the court which gave the judgment or made the order by virtue of which the award has become enforceable as mentioned in that paragraph.

3. A certified copy of a judgment shall not be issued under this Schedule unless under the law of the part of the United Kingdom in which the judgment was given—

(*a*) either—

    (i) the time for bringing an appeal against the judgment has expired, no such appeal having been brought within that time ; or

    (ii) such an appeal having been brought within that time, that appeal has been finally disposed of ; and

(*b*) enforcement of the judgment is not for the time being stayed or suspended, and the time available for its enforcement has not expired.

4.—(1) Subject to paragraph 3, on an application under paragraph 2 the proper officer shall issue to the applicant—

(*a*) a certified copy of the judgment (including any money provisions or excepted provisions which it may contain) ; and

(*b*) a certificate stating that the conditions specified in paragraph 3(*a*) and (*b*) are satisfied in relation to the judgment.

(2) In sub-paragraph (1)(*a*) " excepted provision " means any provision of a judgment which is excepted from the application of section 18 by subsection (5) of that section.

(3) There may be issued under this Schedule (simultaneously or at different times)—

(*a*) more than one certified copy of the same judgment ; and

(*b*) more than one certificate in respect of the same judgment.

Registration of judgments

5.—(1) Where a certified copy of a judgment has been issued under this Schedule in any part of the United Kingdom, any interested party may apply in the prescribed manner to the superior court in any other part of the United Kingdom for the judgment to be registered in that court.

(2) In this paragraph " superior court " means, in relation to England and Wales or Northern Ireland, the High Court and, in relation to Scotland, the Court of Session.

(3) An application under this paragraph for the registration of a judgment must be accompanied by—

   (*a*) a certified copy of the judgment issued under this Schedule ; and

   (*b*) a certificate issued under paragraph 4(1)(*b*) in respect of the judgment not more than six months before the date of the application.

(4) Subject to sub-paragraph (5), where an application under this paragraph is duly made to a superior court, the court shall order the whole of the judgment as set out in the certified copy to be registered in that court in the prescribed manner.

(5) A judgment shall not be registered under this Schedule by the superior court in any part of the United Kingdom if compliance with the non-money provisions contained in the judgment would involve a breach of the law of that part of the United Kingdom.

General effect of registration

6.—(1) The non-money provisions contained in a judgment registered under this Schedule shall, for the purposes of their enforcement, be of the same force and effect, the registering court shall have in relation to their enforcement the same powers, and proceedings for or with respect to their enforcement may be taken, as if the judgment containing them had been originally given in the registering court and had (where relevant) been entered.

(2) Sub-paragraph (1) is subject to the following provisions of this Schedule and to any provision made by rules of court as to the manner in which and conditions subject to which the non-money provisions contained in a judgment registered under this Schedule may be enforced.

Costs or expenses

7.—(1) Where a judgment is registered under this Schedule, the reasonable costs or expenses of and incidental to—

   (*a*) the obtaining of the certified copy of the judgment and of the necessary certificate under paragraph 4(1)(*b*) in respect of it ; and

   (*b*) the registration of the judgment,

shall be recoverable as if on the date of registration there had also been registered in the registering court a certificate under Schedule 6 in respect of the judgment and as if those costs or expenses were costs or expenses stated in that certificate to be payable under a money provision contained in the judgment.

(2) All such sums as are recoverable by virtue of sub-paragraph (1) shall carry interest as if they were the subject of an order for costs or expenses made by the registering court on the date of registration of the judgment.

Stay or sisting of enforcement in certain cases

8. Where a judgment has been registered under this Schedule, the registering court may, if it is satisfied that any person against whom it is sought to enforce the judgment is entitled and intends to apply under the law of the part of the United Kingdom in which the judgment was given for any remedy which would result in the setting aside or quashing of the judgment, stay (or, in Scotland, sist) proceedings for the enforcement of the judgment, on such terms as it thinks fit, for such period as appears to the court to be reasonably sufficient to enable the application to be disposed of.

Cases in which registered judgment must or may be set aside

9. Where a judgment has been registered under this Schedule, the registering court—

(a) shall set aside the registration if, on an application made by any interested party, it is satisfied that the registration was contrary to the provisions of this Schedule ;

(b) may set aside the registration if, on an application so made, it is satisfied that the matter in dispute in the proceedings in which the judgment was given had previously been the subject of a judgment by another court or tribunal having jurisdiction in the matter.

SCHEDULE 8

Section 20.

RULES AS TO JURISDICTION IN SCOTLAND

General

1. Subject to the **following Rules,** persons shall be sued in the courts **for the place where they are domiciled.** [Article 2]

Special jurisdiction

2. Subject to Rules 3 (jurisdiction over consumer contracts), 4 (exclusive jurisdiction) and 5 (prorogation) a person may **also** be sued— [Article 5]

(1) **where he has no fixed residence, in a court within whose jurisdiction he is personally cited ;**

(2) in matters relating to a contract, in the courts for the place of performance of the obligation in question ; [Article 5(1)]

(3) in matters relating to delict or quasi-delict, in the courts for the place where the harmful event occurred ; [Article 5(3)]

(4) as regards a civil claim for damages or restitution which is based on an act giving rise to criminal proceedings, in the court seised of those proceedings to the extent that that court has jurisdiction to entertain civil proceedings ; [Article 5(4)]

(5) in matters relating to maintenance, in the courts for the place where the maintenance creditor is domiciled or habitually resident or, if the matter is ancillary to proceedings concerning the status of a person, in the court which has [Article 5(2)]

SCH. 8

jurisdiction to entertain those proceedings, **provided that an action for adherence and aliment or of affiliation and aliment shall be treated as a matter relating to maintenance which is not ancillary to proceedings concerning the status of a person, and provided also that—**

1948 c. 29.

1968 c. 49.

(a) where a local authority exercises its power to raise an action under section 44(7)(a) of the National Assistance Act 1948 or under section 81(1) of the Social Work (Scotland) Act 1968 ; and

1976 c. 71.

(b) where the Secretary of State exercises his power to raise an action under section 19(8)(a) of the Supplementary Benefits Act 1976 ;

this Rule shall apply as if the reference to the maintenance creditor were a reference to the mother of the child ;

[Article 5(5)]

(6) as regards a dispute arising out of the operations of a branch, agency or other establishment, in the courts for the place in which the branch, agency or other establishment is situated ;

Article 5(6)]

(7) in his capacity as settlor, trustee or beneficiary of a trust **domiciled in Scotland** created by the operation of a statute, or by a written instrument, or created orally and evidenced in writing, in the **Court of Session, or the appropriate sheriff court within the meaning of section 24A of the Trusts (Scotland) Act 1921 ;**

1921 c. 58.

(8) **where he is not domiciled in the United Kingdom, in the courts for any place where—**

(a) any moveable property belonging to him has been arrested ; or

(b) any immoveable property in which he has any beneficial interest is situated ;

(9) **in proceedings which are brought to assert, declare or determine proprietary or possessory rights, or rights of security, in or over moveable property, or to obtain authority to dispose of moveable property, in the courts for the place where the property is situated ;**

(10) **in proceedings for interdict, in the courts for the place where it is alleged that the wrong is likely to be committed ;**

(11) **in proceedings concerning a debt secured over immoveable property, in the courts for the place where the property is situated ;**

(12) **in proceedings which have as their object a decision of an organ of a company or other legal person or of an association of natural or legal persons, in the courts for the place where that company, legal person or association has its seat ;**

(13) **in proceedings concerning an arbitration which is conducted in Scotland or in which the procedure is governed by Scots law, in the Court of Session ;**

(14) **in proceedings principally concerned with the registration in the United Kingdom or the validity in the United Kingdom of patents, trade marks, designs or other similar rights required to be deposited or registered, in the Court of Session ;**

(15) (*a*) where he is one of a number of **defenders,** in the courts for the place where any one of them is domiciled ; [Article 6]

    (*b*) as a third party in an action on a warranty or guarantee or in any other third party proceedings; in the court seised of the original proceedings, unless these were instituted solely with the object of removing him from the jurisdiction of the court which would be competent in his case ;

    (*c*) on a counterclaim arising from the same contract or facts on which the original claim was based, in the court in which the original claim is pending.

Jurisdiction over consumer contracts

3.—(1) In proceedings concerning a contract concluded by a person for a purpose which can be regarded as being outside his trade or profession, hereinafter called the " consumer ", **subject to Rule 4 (exclusive jurisdiction),** jurisdiction shall be determined by this **Rule** if it is— [Article 13]

    (*a*) a contract for the sale of goods on instalment credit terms ; or

    (*b*) a contract for a loan repayable by instalments, or for any other form of credit, made to finance the sale of goods ; or

    (*c*) any other contract for the supply of goods or a contract for the supply of services, **if**—

        (i) the consumer took in **Scotland** the steps necessary for the conclusion of the contract ; **or**

        (ii) **proceedings are brought in Scotland by virtue of section 10(3).**

(2) This **Rule** shall not apply to contracts of transport **or contracts of insurance.**

(3) A consumer may bring proceedings against the other party to a contract **only** in— [Article 14]

    (*a*) the courts **for the place** in which that party is domiciled ;

    (*b*) the courts **for the place** in which he is himself domiciled ; **or**

    (*c*) **any court having jurisdiction by virtue of Rule 2(6) or (9).**

(4) Proceedings may be brought against a consumer by the other party to the contract only in the courts **for the place where** the consumer is domiciled **or any court having jurisdiction under Rule 2(9).**

(5) **Nothing in this Rule** shall affect the right to bring a counterclaim in the court in which, **in accordance with this Rule,** the original claim is pending.

SCH. 8
[Article 15(1)
and (2)]

(6) The provisions of this **Rule** may be departed from only by an agreement—

    (*a*) which is entered into after the dispute has arisen ; or

    (*b*) which allows the consumer to bring proceedings in **a court** other than **a court** indicated in this **Rule.**

Exclusive jurisdiction

[Article 16]

4.—(1) **Notwithstanding anything contained in any of Rules 1 to 3 above or 5 to 8 below,** the following courts shall have exclusive jurisdiction—

[Article 16(1)]

    (*a*) in proceedings which have as their object rights *in rem* in, or tenancies of, immoveable property, the courts **for the place where** the property is situated ;

[Article 16(2)]

    (*b*) in proceedings which have as their object the validity of the constitution, the nullity or the dissolution of companies or other legal persons or associations of natural or legal persons, the courts **for the place where** the company, legal person or association has its seat ;

[Article 16(3)]

    (*c*) in proceedings which have as their object the validity of entries in public registers, the courts **for the place where** the register is kept ;

[Article 16(5)]

    (*d*) in proceedings concerned with the enforcement of judgements, the courts **for the place where** the judgement has been or is to be enforced.

(2) **Nothing in paragraph (1)(c) above affects jurisdiction in any proceedings concerning the validity of entries in registers of patents, trade marks, designs, or other similar rights required to be deposited or registered.**

(3) **No court shall exercise jurisdiction in a case where immoveable property, the seat of a body mentioned in paragraph (1)(b) above, a public register or the place where a judgement has been or is to be enforced is situated outside Scotland and where paragraph (1) above would apply if the property, seat, register or, as the case may be, place of enforcement were situated in Scotland.**

Prorogation of jurisdiction

[Article 17(1)]

5.—(1) If the parties have agreed that a court is to have jurisdiction to settle any disputes which have arisen or which may arise in connection with a particular legal relationship, that court shall have exclusive jurisdiction.

[Article 17(1)]

(2) Such an agreement conferring jurisdiction shall be either in writing or evidenced in writing or, in trade or commerce, in a form which accords with practices in that trade or commerce of which the parties are or ought to have been aware.

[Article 17(2)]

(3) The court on which a trust instrument has conferred jurisdiction shall have exclusive jurisdiction in any proceedings brought against a settlor, trustee or beneficiary, if relations between these persons or their rights or obligations under the trust are involved.

(4) **Where an agreement or a trust instrument confers jurisdiction on the courts of the United Kingdom or of Scotland, proceedings to which paragraph (1) or, as the case may be, (3) above applies may be brought in any court in Scotland.**

(5) Agreements or provisions of a trust instrument conferring [Article 17(3)] jurisdiction shall have no legal force if the courts whose jurisdiction they purport to exclude have exclusive jurisdiction by virtue of **Rule 4 or where Rule 4(3) applies.**

6.—(1) Apart from jurisdiction derived from other provisions of [Article 18] this **Schedule,** a court before whom a defender enters an appearance shall have jurisdiction.

(2) This Rule shall not apply where appearance was entered solely to contest jurisdiction, or where another court has exclusive jurisdiction by virtue of **Rule 4 or where Rule 4(3) applies.**

Examination as to jurisdiction and admissibility

7. Where a court is seised of a claim which is principally concerned [Article 19] with a matter over which **another court has** exclusive jurisdiction by virtue of **Rule 4, or where it is precluded from exercising jurisdiction by Rule 4(3),** it shall declare of its own motion that it has no jurisdiction.

8. Where **in any case a court has no jurisdiction which is com-** [Article 20] **patible with this Act, and the defender** does not enter an appearance, the court shall declare of its own motion that it has no jurisdiction.

SCHEDULE 9

PROCEEDINGS EXCLUDED FROM SCHEDULE 8

1. Proceedings concerning the status or legal capacity of natural persons (including proceedings for separation) other than proceedings which consist solely of proceedings for adherence and aliment or of affiliation and aliment.

2. Proceedings for regulating the custody of children.

3. Proceedings relating to tutory and curatory and all proceedings relating to the management of the affairs of persons who are incapable of managing their own affairs.

4. Proceedings in respect of sequestration in bankruptcy; or the winding up of a company or other legal person; or proceedings in respect of a judicial arrangement or judicial composition with creditors.

5. Proceedings relating to a company where, by any enactment, jurisdiction in respect of those proceedings is conferred on the court having jurisdiction to wind it up.

6. Admiralty causes in so far as the jurisdiction is based on arrestment *in rem* or *ad fundandam jurisdictionem* of a ship, cargo or freight.

Sch. 9 7. Commissary proceedings.

8. Proceedings for the rectification of the register of aircraft mortgages kept by the Civil Aviation Authority.

1962 c. 8. 9. Proceedings under section 7(3) of the Civil Aviation (Eurocontrol) Act 1962 (recovery of charges for air navigation services and proceedings for damages against Eurocontrol).

1964 c. 29. 10. Proceedings brought in pursuance of an order under section 3 of the Continental Shelf Act 1964.

1980 c. 11. 11. Proceedings under section 6 of the Protection of Trading Interests Act 1980 (recovery of sums paid or obtained pursuant to a judgment for multiple damages).

12. Appeals from or review of decisions of tribunals.

13. Proceedings which are not in substance proceedings in which a decree against any person is sought.

14. Proceedings brought in any court in pursuance of—

(*a*) any statutory provision which, in the case of any convention to which Article 57 applies (conventions relating to specific matters which override the general rules in the 1968 Convention), implements the convention ; and

(*b*) any rule of law so far as it has the effect of implementing any such convention.

Section 35(1).
SCHEDULE 10
1933 c. 13.
Amendments of Foreign Judgments (Reciprocal Enforcement) Act 1933

1.—(1) Section 1 (power to extend Part I to foreign countries giving reciprocal treatment) is amended as follows.

(2) For subsections (1) and (2) substitute—

" (1) If, in the case of any foreign country, Her Majesty is satisfied that, in the event of the benefits conferred by this Part of this Act being extended to, or to any particular class of, judgments given in the courts of that country or in any particular class of those courts, substantial reciprocity of treatment will be assured as regards the enforcement in that country of similar judgments given in similar courts of the United Kingdom, She may by Order in Council direct—

(*a*) that this Part of this Act shall extend to that country ;

(*b*) that such courts of that country as are specified in the Order shall be recognised courts of that country for the purposes of this Part of this Act ; and

(*c*) that judgments of any such recognised court, or such judgments of any class so specified, shall, if within subsection (2) of this section, be judgments to which this Part of this Act applies.

(2) Subject to subsection (2A) of this section, a judgment of a recognised court is within this subsection if it satisfies the following conditions, namely—

> (*a*) it is either final and conclusive as between the judgment debtor and the judgment creditor or requires the former to make an interim payment to the latter ; and

> (*b*) there is payable under it a sum of money, not being a sum payable in respect of taxes or other charges of a like nature or in respect of a fine or other penalty ; and

> (*c*) it is given after the coming into force of the Order in Council which made that court a recognised court.

(2A) The following judgments of a recognised court are not within subsection (2) of this section—

> (*a*) a judgment given by that court on appeal from a court which is not a recognised court ;

> (*b*) a judgment or other instrument which is regarded for the purposes of its enforcement as a judgment of that court but which was given or made in another country ;

> (*c*) a judgment given by that court in proceedings founded on a judgment of a court in another country and having as their object the enforcement of that judgment.".

(3) After subsection (4) add—

> " (5) Any Order in Council made under this section before its amendment by the Civil Jurisdiction and Judgments Act 1982 which deems any court of a foreign country to be a superior court of that country for the purposes of this Part of this Act shall (without prejudice to subsection (4) of this section) have effect from the time of that amendment as if it provided for that court to be a recognised court of that country for those purposes, and for any final and conclusive judgment of that court, if within subsection (2) of this section, to be a judgment to which this Part of this Act applies.".

2. In section 9 (power to make foreign judgments unenforceable in United Kingdom if no reciprocity), in subsection (1) omit " superior " in both places where it occurs.

3. For section 10 (issue of certificates of judgments obtained in the United Kingdom) substitute—

" Provision for issue of copies of, and certificates in connection with, U.K. judgments.

10.—(1) Rules may make provision for enabling any judgment creditor wishing to secure the enforcement in a foreign country to which Part I of this Act extends of a judgment to which this subsection applies, to obtain, subject to any conditions specified in the rules—

> (*a*) a copy of the judgment ; and

> (*b*) a certificate giving particulars relating to the judgment and the proceedings in which it was given.

(2) Subsection (1) applies to any judgment given by a court or tribunal in the United Kingdom under which a

SCH. 10

sum of money is payable, not being a sum payable in respect of taxes or other charges of a like nature or in respect of a fine or other penalty.

(3) In this section " rules "—

   (*a*) in relation to judgments given by a court, means rules of court ;

   (*b*) in relation to judgments given by any other tribunal, means rules or regulations made by the authority having power to make rules or regulations regulating the procedure of that tribunal.".

4. After section 10 insert—

"Arbitration awards.   10A. The provisions of this Act, except sections 1(5) and 6, shall apply, as they apply to a judgment, in relation to an award in proceedings on an arbitration which has, in pursuance of the law in force in the place where it was made, become enforceable in the same manner as a judgment given by a court in that place.".

5.—(1) Section 11(1) (interpretation) is amended as follows.

(2) After the definition of " Country of the original court " insert—

   " " Court ", except in section 10 of this Act, includes a tribunal ; ".

(3) Omit the definition of " Judgments given in the superior courts of the United Kingdom ".

Section 37(1).

SCHEDULE 11

MINOR AMENDMENTS RELATING TO MAINTENANCE ORDERS

PART I

ENFORCEMENT OF LUMP SUM ORDERS

Maintenance Orders Act 1950 *(c. 37)*

1. In section 18(3A) of the Maintenance Orders Act 1950 (order not to be enforced by registering court under that Act if re-registered for enforcement in another court), for " whilst it is registered " substitute " to the extent that it is for the time being registered ".

Maintenance Orders Act 1958 *(c. 39)*

2.—(1) Section 2 of the Maintenance Orders Act 1958 (registration of orders) is amended as follows.

(2) In subsection (3) (registration of magistrates' court order for enforcement in the High Court), for the words from " shall " onwards (which require the court to be satisfied that not less than a certain number of periodical payments are in arrears) substitute " may, if it thinks fit, grant the application ".

(3) After subsection (3) insert—

" (3A) Without prejudice to subsection (3) of this section, where a magistrates' court order provides both for the payment of a lump sum and for the making of periodical payments, a person entitled to receive a lump sum under the order who considers that, so far as it relates to that sum, the order could be more effectively enforced if it were registered may apply to the original court for the registration of the order so far as it so relates, and the court may, if it thinks fit, grant the application.

(3B) Where an application under subsection (3A) of this section is granted in the case of a magistrates' court order, the provisions of this Part of this Act shall have effect in relation to that order as if so far as it relates to the payment of a lump sum it were a separate order.".

Maintenance and Affiliation Orders Act (Northern Ireland) 1966 (c. 35) (N.I.)

3.—(1) Section 11 of the Maintenance and Affiliation Orders Act (Northern Ireland) 1966 (registration of orders) is amended as follows.

(2) In subsection (3) (registration of order made by court of summary jurisdiction for enforcement in the High Court), for the words from " shall " onwards (which require the court to be satisfied that not less than a certain number of periodical payments are in arrears) substitute " may, if it thinks fit, grant the application ".

(3) After subsection (3) insert—

" (3A) Without prejudice to subsection (3), where an order made by a court of summary jurisdiction provides both for the payment of a lump sum and for the making of periodical payments, a person entitled to receive a lump sum under the order who considers that, so far as it relates to that sum the order could be more effectively enforced if it were registered may apply to the original court for the registration of the order so far as it so relates, and the court may, if it thinks fit, grant the application.

(3B) Where an application under subsection (3A) is granted in the case of an order made by a court of summary jurisdiction, the provisions of this Part shall have effect in relation to that order as if so far as it relates to the payment of a lump sum it were a separate order.".

Maintenance Orders (Reciprocal Enforcement) Act 1972 (c. 18)

4.—(1) In section 9 of the Maintenance Orders (Reciprocal Enforcement) Act 1972 (variation and revocation of orders), after subsection (1) insert—

" (1A) The powers conferred by subsection (1) above are not exercisable in relation to so much of a registered order as provides for the payment of a lump sum.".

SCH. 11   (2) In section 21 of that Act (interpretation of Part I)—
    (*a*) in paragraph (*a*) of the definition of " maintenance order "
        in subsection (1) ; and
    (*b*) in subsection (2),
for " periodical payment of sums of money " substitute " payment
of a lump sum or the making of periodical payments ".

PART II

RECOVERY OF INTEREST ON ARREARS

Maintenance Orders Act 1950 *(c. 37)*

5. In section 18 of the Maintenance Orders Act 1950 (enforcement
of registered orders), after subsection (1) (orders to be enforced in
the same manner as orders made by the court of registration), insert—

    " (1A) A maintenance order registered under this Part of this
    Act in a court of summary jurisdiction in England or Northern
    Ireland shall not carry interest ; but where a maintenance order
    so registered is registered in the High Court under Part I of
    the Maintenance Orders Act 1958 or section 36 of the Civil
    Jurisdiction and Judgments Act 1982, this subsection shall not
    prevent any sum for whose payment the order provides from
    carrying interest in accordance with section 2A of the said Act
    of 1958 or section 11A of the Maintenance and Affiliation
    Orders Act (Northern Ireland) 1966.

    (1B) A maintenance order made in Scotland which is regis-
    tered under this Part of this Act in the Supreme Court in
    England or Northern Ireland shall, if interest is by the law of
    Scotland recoverable under the order, carry the like interest in
    accordance with subsection (1) of this section.".

Maintenance Orders Act 1958 *(c. 39)*

6.—(1) The Maintenance Orders Act 1958 is amended as follows.

(2) After section 2 insert—

" Interest on   2A.—(1) Where, in connection with an application
sums recover- under section 2(3) of this Act for the registration of a
able under
certain orders magistrates' court order, the applicant shows in accor-
registered   dance with rules of court—
in the High
Court.   (*a*) that the order, though deemed for the purposes
                    of section 1 of this Act to have been made by
                    a magistrates' court in England, was in fact
                    made in another part of the United Kingdom or
                    in a country or territory outside the United
                    Kingdom ; and
                (*b*) that, as regards any sum for whose payment the
                    order provides, interest on that sum at a parti-
                    cular rate is, by the law of that part or of that
                    country or territory, recoverable under the order
                    from a particular date or time.

then, if the original court grants the application and causes a certified copy of the order to be sent to the prescribed officer of the High Court under section 2(4)(*c*) of this Act, it shall also cause to be sent to him a certificate in the prescribed form showing, as regards that sum, the rate of interest so recoverable and the date or time from which it is so recoverable.

(2) The officer of the court who receives a certificate sent to him under the preceding subsection shall cause the certificate to be registered in that court together with the order to which it relates.

(3) Where an order is registered together with a certificate under this section, then, subject to any provision made under the next following subsection, sums payable under the order shall carry interest at the rate specified in the certificate from the date or time so specified.

(4) Provision may be made by rules of court as to the manner in which and the periods by reference to which any interest payable by virtue of subsection (3) is to be calculated and paid, including provision for such interest to cease to accrue as from a prescribed date.

(5) Except as provided by this section sums payable under registered orders shall not carry interest.".

(3) In section 3(1) of that Act (enforcement of registered orders), after " Subject to the provisions of " insert " section 2A of this Act and ".

Maintenance and Affiliation Orders Act (Northern Ireland) 1966
(c. 35) (N.I.)

7.—(1) The Maintenance and Affiliation Orders Act (Northern Ireland) 1966 is amended as follows.

(2) After section 11 insert—

" Interest on sums recoverable under certain orders registered in the High Court.

11A.—(1) Where, in connection with an application under section 11(3) for the registration of an order made by a court of summary jurisdiction, the applicant shows in accordance with rules of court—

    (*a*) that the order, though deemed for the purposes of this Part to have been made by a court of summary jurisdiction in Northern Ireland, was in fact made in a country or territory outside the United Kingdom ; and

    (*b*) that, as regards any sum for whose payment the order provides, interest on that sum at a particular rate is, by the law of that country or territory, recoverable under the order from a particular date or time,

then, if the original court grants the application and causes a certified copy of the order to be sent to the prescribed officer of the High Court under section 11(4)(*c*) it shall also cause to be sent to him a certificate in the prescribed form showing, as regards that sum, the rate of interest so recoverable and the date or time from which it is so recoverable.

(2) The officer of a court who receives a certificate sent to him under subsection (1) shall cause the certificate to be registered in that court together with the order to which it relates.

(3) Where an order is registered together with a certificate under this section, then, subject to any provision made under subsection (4), sums payable under the order shall carry interest at the rate specified in the certificate from the date or time so specified.

(4) Provision may be made by rules of court as to the manner in which and the periods by reference to which any interest payable by virtue of subsection (3) is to be calculated and paid, including provision for such interest to cease to accrue as from a prescribed date.

(5) Except as provided by this section sums payable under registered orders shall not carry interest.".

(3) In section 12(1) (enforcement of registered orders), after " Subject to the provisions of " insert " section 11A and ".

(4) In section 16(2) of that Act (construction of " rules of court ") at the end add " and in section 11A(4) shall be construed as including a reference to Judgment Enforcement Rules made under Article 141 of the Judgments Enforcement (Northern Ireland) Order 1981 ".

PART III

RECIPROCAL ENFORCEMENT FOUNDED ON PRESENCE OF ASSETS

Maintenance Orders (Reciprocal Enforcement) Act 1972 *(c. 18)*

8. The Maintenance Orders (Reciprocal Enforcement) Act 1972 is amended as follows.

9. In section 2 (transmission of United Kingdom order for enforcement in reciprocating country)—

　　(*a*) in subsections (1) and (4), after " residing " insert " or has assets " ; and

　　(*b*) in subsection (4), after " whereabouts of the payer ", in both places where it occurs, insert " and the nature and location of his assets in that country ".

10. In section 6 (registration in United Kingdom of order made in reciprocating country)—

　　(*a*) in subsection (2), after " residing " insert " or has assets " ; and (*b*) in subsection (4)—

(i) after " is residing " insert " or has assets " ;

(ii) for " so residing " substitute " residing and has no assets within the jurisdiction of the court " ; and

(iii) at the end insert " and the nature and location of his assets ".

11. In section 8(5) (duty of magistrates' court and its officers to take prescribed steps for enforcing registered orders), after " enforcing " insert " or facilitating the enforcement of ".

12. In section 9 (variation and revocation of orders), after the subsection (1A) inserted by paragraph 4(1) of this Schedule, insert—

"(1B) The registering court shall not vary or revoke a registered order if neither the payer nor the payee under the order is resident in the United Kingdom.".

13.—(1) Section 10 (cancellation of registration and transfer of orders) is amended as follows.

(2) In subsection (2), for " has ceased to reside within the jurisdiction of that court," substitute " is not residing within the jurisdiction of that court and has no assets within that jurisdiction against which the order can be effectively enforced,".

(3) In subsection (3), after " residing " insert " or has assets ".

(4) In subsection (5), for " still residing " substitute " residing or has assets ".

(5) In subsection (6)—

(*a*) after " is residing " insert " or has assets " ; and

(*b*) for " so residing " insert " residing and has no assets within the jurisdiction of the court ".

(6) In subsection (7)(*b*), after " payer " insert " and the nature and location of his assets ".

14. In section 11(1) (steps to be taken where payer is not residing in the United Kingdom)—

(*a*) before " it appears " insert " at any time " ;

(*b*) for the words from " in the United Kingdom " to " therein, " substitute " and has no assets in the United Kingdom," ; and

(*c*) after " payer " in paragraph (*c*) insert " and the nature and location of his assets ".

15. In section 21(1) (interpretation of Part I), in the definition of " the appropriate court "—

(i) after " residing ", in the first and second places where it occurs, insert " or having assets " ;

SCH. 11

(ii) for " the sheriff court " substitute " a sheriff court " ; and

(iii) after " residing ", where it last occurs, insert " or has assets ".

1920 c. 33.

16. In section 24 (application of Part I to certain orders and proceedings under Maintenance Orders (Facilities for Enforcement) Act 1920), in paragraph (*a*)(i) and (ii), after " residing " insert " or having assets ".

17. In section 40 (power to apply Act with modifications by Order in Council)—

(*a*) in paragraph (*a*), omit " against persons in that country or territory " ; and

(*b*) in paragraph (*b*), omit " against persons in the United Kingdom ".

18. In section 47 (interpretation), in subsection (3) (construction of references to a court's jurisdiction), after " the reference is " insert " to assets being located or " and omit the words " or having ceased to reside ".

Sections 15(4),
23(2) and 36(6).

SCHEDULE 12

CONSEQUENTIAL AMENDMENTS

PART I

AMENDMENTS CONSEQUENTIAL ON
PART I OF THIS ACT

Army Act 1955 (c. 18) and Air Force Act 1955 (c. 19)

1. In section 150 of the Army Act 1955 and in section 150 of the Air Force Act 1955 (enforcement of maintenance and other orders by deduction from pay), in subsection (5), after " Part I of the Maintenance Orders (Reciprocal Enforcement) Act 1972 " insert " or Part I of the Civil Jurisdiction and Judgments Act 1982 ".

Naval Discipline Act 1957 (c. 53)

2. In section 101 of the Naval Discipline Act 1957 (service of process in maintenance and other proceedings), in subsection (5), after " Part I of the Maintenance Orders (Reciprocal Enforcement) Act 1972 " insert " or Part I of the Civil Jurisdiction and Judgments Act 1982 ".

Maintenance Orders Act 1958 (c. 39)

3. In section 1 of the Maintenance Orders Act 1958 (scope of application of Part I), in subsection (4), for the words from " within the meaning " to " the said Part I " substitute " which is registered in a magistrates' court under Part I of the Maintenance Orders (Reciprocal Enforcement) Act 1972 or Part I of the Civil Jurisdiction and Judgments Act 1982 ".

Maintenance and Affiliation Orders Act (Northern Ireland)
1966 (c. 35) (N.I.)

4. In section 10 of the Maintenance and Affiliation Orders Act
(Northern Ireland) 1966 (orders to which Part II of that Act applies),
in subsections (2) and (5), after " Part I of the Maintenance Orders
(Reciprocal Enforcement) Act 1972 " insert " or Part I of the Civil
Jurisdiction and Judgments Act 1982 ".

Administration of Justice Act 1970 (c. 31)

5. In Schedule 8 to the Administration of Justice Act 1970 (orders
which are " maintenance orders " for the purposes of Part II of that
Act and Part II of the Maintenance Orders Act 1958), after para- 1958 c. 39.
graph 12 insert—

" 13. A maintenance order within the meaning of Part I of
the Civil Jurisdiction and Judgments Act 1982 which is registered
in a magistrates' court under that Part.".

Attachment of Earnings Act 1971 (c. 32)

6. In Schedule 1 to the Attachment of Earnings Act 1971 (orders
which are " maintenance orders " for the purposes of that Act),
after paragraph 12 insert—

" 13. A maintenance order within the meaning of Part I of the
Civil Jurisdiction and Judgments Act 1982 which is registered
in a magistrates' court under that Part.".

Magistrates' Courts Act 1980 (c. 43)

7. In section 65 of the Magistrates' Courts Act 1980 (definition
of " domestic proceedings " for the purposes of that Act)—

(*a*) in subsection (1), after paragraph (*l*) insert—

" (*m*) Part I of the Civil Jurisdiction and Judgments Act
1982, so far as that Part relates to the recognition or
enforcement of maintenance orders ; " ;

(*b*) in subsection (2)(*a*), after " (*k*) " insert " and (*m*) ".

Magistrates' Courts (Northern Ireland) Order 1981
(S.I. 1981/1675 (N.I. 26))

8.—(1) In Article 88 of the Magistrates' Courts (Northern Ireland)
Order 1981 (definition of " domestic proceedings " for the purposes
of that Order), in paragraph (*a*), after " Part I of the Maintenance
Orders (Reciprocal Enforcement) Act 1972 " insert " or under Part I
of the Civil Jurisdiction and Judgments Act 1982 so far as that Part
relates to the recognition and enforcement of maintenance orders ".

(2) In Article 98 of that Order (enforcement of orders for periodical payment of money), in sub-paragraph (*b*) of paragraph (11), after
" Part I of the Maintenance Orders (Reciprocal Enforcement) Act
1972 " insert " or Part I of the Civil Jurisdiction and Judgments
Act 1982 ".

Part II

Amendments Consequential on Schedule 8

Law Reform (Miscellaneous Provisions) (Scotland) Act 1940 (c. 42)

1. In the Law Reform (Miscellaneous Provisions) (Scotland) Act 1940 after section 4(2) there shall be inserted the following subsection—

" (3) This section does not apply—

    (*a*) in the case of an agreement entered into after the dispute in respect of which the agreement is intended to have effect has arisen ; or

    (*b*) where the contract is one referred to in Rule 3 of Schedule 8 to the Civil Jurisdiction and Judgments Act 1982.".

Maintenance Orders Act 1950 (c. 37)

2. In section 15(1)(*b*) of the Maintenance Orders Act 1950 for the words " for separation and aliment " there shall be substituted the words " which contains a conclusion for aliment not falling within the scope of paragraph (*a*)(i) above ".

Maintenance Orders (Reciprocal Enforcement) Act 1972 (c. 18)

3.—(1) In section 4 of the Maintenance Orders (Reciprocal Enforcement) Act 1972 (power of the sheriff to make a provisional maintenance order against a person residing in a reciprocating country) the following subsection shall be substituted for subsections (1) and (2)—

" (1) In any action where the sheriff has jurisdiction by virtue of Rule 2(5) of Schedule 8 to the Civil Jurisdiction and Judgments Act 1982 and the defender resides in a reciprocating country, any maintenance order granted by the sheriff shall be a provisional order.".

(2) In subsections (3), (4) and (5) of that section for the words " in which the sheriff has jurisdiction by virtue of " there shall be substituted in each place where they occur the words " referred to in ".

Consumer Credit Act 1974 (c. 39)

4. In section 141 of the Consumer Credit Act 1974 the following subsections shall be substituted for subsection (3)—

" (3) In Scotland the sheriff court shall have jurisdiction to hear and determine any action referred to in subsection (1) and such an action shall not be brought in any other court.

(3A) Subject to subsection (3B) an action which is brought in the sheriff court by virtue of subsection (3) shall be brought only in one of the following courts, namely—

    (*a*) the court for the place where the debtor or hirer is domiciled (within the meaning of section 41 or 42 of the Civil Jurisdiction and Judgments Act 1982) ;

(*b*) the court for the place where the debtor or hirer carries on business ; and

(*c*) where the purpose of the action is to assert, declare or determine proprietary or possessory rights, or rights of security, in or over moveable property, or to obtain authority to dispose of moveable property, the court for the place where the property is situated.

(3B) Subsection (3A) shall not apply—

(*a*) where Rule 3 of Schedule 8 to the said Act of 1982 applies ; or

(*b*) where the jurisdiction of another court has been prorogated by an agreement entered into after the dispute has arisen.".

Part III

Amendments Consequential on Section 36

Maintenance Orders Act 1950 (*c.*37)

1.—(1) The Maintenance Orders Act 1950 is amended as follows.

(2) In section 18 (enforcement of registered orders), after subsection (3A) insert—

" (3B) Notwithstanding subsection (1) above, no court in Northern Ireland in which a maintenance order is registered under this Part of this Act shall enforce that order to the extent that it is for the time being registered in another court in Northern Ireland under section 36 of the Civil Jurisdiction and Judgments Act 1982.".

(3) In section 21(2) (evidence admissible before court where order registered)—

(*a*) in paragraph (*a*) after " 1958 " insert " or under section 36 of the Civil Jurisdiction and Judgments Act 1982 " ;

(*b*) after " that Act " (twice) insert " of 1958 " ;

(*c*) after paragraph (*b*) insert—

" (*c*) registered in a court in Northern Ireland under section 36 of the Civil Jurisdiction and Judgments Act **1982** ".

(4) In section 24(3) (notice of cancellation of order to be given to other courts interested), after " Part I of the Maintenance Orders Act 1958 " insert " or section 36 of the Civil Jurisdiction and Judgments Act 1982 ".

Maintenance Orders Act 1958 (*c.* 39)

2. In section 23(2) of the Maintenance Orders Act 1958 (provisions which extend to Scotland and Northern Ireland) after " section 2 " insert " section 2A ".

Maintenance and Affiliation Orders Act (Northern Ireland)
1966 (c. 35) (N.I.)

3.—(1) The Maintenance and Affiliation Orders Act (Northern Ireland) 1966 is amended as follows.

(2) At the beginning of section 9 (introductory provisions relating to registration in one court of maintenance order made by another) insert " Without prejudice to section 36 of the Civil Jurisdiction and Judgments Act 1982,".

(3) In section 10 (orders to which Part II applies), after subsection (1) insert—

" (1A) This Part, except sections 11, 11A and 14(2) and (3), also applies in accordance with section 36 of the Civil Jurisdiction and Judgments Act 1982 to maintenance orders made by a court in England and Wales or Scotland and registered in Northern Ireland under Part II of the Maintenance Orders Act 1950.".

(4) In section 13 (variation of orders registered in courts of summary jurisdiction), after subsection (7) insert—

"(7A) No application for any variation in respect of a registered order shall be made to any court in respect of an order made by the High Court of Justice in England or the Court of Session and registered in that court under section 36 of the Civil Jurisdiction and Judgments Act 1982.".

Judgments Enforcement (Northern Ireland)
Order 1981 (S.I. 1981/266 (N.I. 6))

4. In Article 98 of the Judgments Enforcement (Northern Ireland) Order 1981, (powers of courts to make attachment of earnings orders), in sub-paragraph (iv) of paragraph (*a*) at the end add " but not subsequently registered in a court of summary jurisdiction under section 36 of the Civil Jurisdiction and Judgments Act 1982 ".

Magistrates' Courts (Northern Ireland)
Order 1981 (S.I. 1981/1675 (N.I. 26))

5.—(1) In Article 88 of the Magistrates' Courts (Northern Ireland) Order 1981 (definition of " domestic proceedings " for the purposes of that Order)—

(*a*) in paragraph (*a*), delete the words " or the Maintenance Orders Act 1950 " ;

(*b*) after paragraph (*a*) insert—

" (*aa*) in relation to maintenance orders registered in a court of summary jurisdiction under the Maintenance Orders Act 1950 or Part II of the Maintenance and Affiliation Orders Act (Northern Ireland) 1966 or section 36 of the Civil Jurisdiction and Judgments Act 1982, under that Act of 1950 or Part II of that Act of 1966 ".

(2) In Article 98 of that Order (enforcement of orders for periodical payment of money), in sub-paragraph (*d*) of paragraph (11), at the end add—

" or under section 36 of the Civil Jurisdiction and Judgments Act 1982 ".

SCHEDULE 13
COMMENCEMENT, TRANSITIONAL PROVISIONS AND SAVINGS

PART I
COMMENCEMENT

Provisions coming into force on Royal Assent

1. The following provisions come into force on Royal Assent:

Provision	*Subject-matter*
section 53(1) and Part I of this Schedule.	Commencement.
section 55	Short title.

Provisions coming into force six weeks after Royal Assent

2. The following provisions come into force at the end of the period of six weeks beginning with the day on which this Act is passed:

Provision	*Subject-matter*	
section 24(1)(*a*), (2)(*a*) and (3).	Interim relief and protective measures in cases of doubtful jurisdiction.	
section 29	Service of county court process outside Northern Ireland.	
section 30	Proceedings in England and Wales or Northern Ireland for torts to immovable property.	
section 31	Overseas judgments given against states.	
section 32	Overseas judgments given in breach of agreement for settlement of disputes.	
section 33	Certain steps not to amount to submission to jurisdiction of overseas court.	
section 34	Certain judgments a bar to further proceedings on the same cause of action.	
section 35(3)	Consolidation of Orders in Council under section 14 of the Administration of Justice Act 1920.	1920 c. 81.
section 38	Overseas judgments counteracting an award of multiple damages.	
section 40	Power to modify enactments relating to legal aid, etc.	
section 49	Saving for powers to stay, sist, strike out or dismiss proceedings.	
section 50	Interpretation: general.	
section 51	Application to Crown.	
section 52	Extent.	

Provision	Subject-matter
paragraphs 7 to 10 of Part II of this Schedule and section 53(2) so far as relates to those paragraphs.	Transitional provisions and savings.
section 54 and Schedule 14 so far as relating to the repeal of provisions in section 4 of the Foreign Judgments (Reciprocal Enforcement) Act 1933.	Repeals consequential on sections 32 and 33.

1933 c. 13.

Provisions coming into force on a day to be appointed

3.—(1) The other provisions of this Act come into force on such day as the Lord Chancellor and the Lord Advocate may appoint by order made by statutory instrument.

(2) Different days may be appointed under this paragraph for different purposes.

Part II

Transitional Provisions and Savings

Section 16 *and Schedule* 4

1.—(1) Section 16 and Schedule 4 shall not apply to any proceedings begun before the commencement of that section.

(2) Nothing in section 16 or Schedule 4 shall preclude the bringing of proceedings in any part of the United Kingdom in connection with a dispute concerning a contract if the parties to the dispute had agreed before the commencement of that section that the contract was to be governed by the law of that part of the United Kingdom.

Section 18 *and Schedule* 6 *and associated repeals*

2.—(1) In relation to a judgment a certificate whereof has been registered under the 1868 Act or the 1882 Act before the repeal of that Act by this Act, the 1868 Act or, as the case may be, the 1882 Act shall continue to have effect notwithstanding its repeal.

(2) Where by virtue of sub-paragraph (1) the 1882 Act continues to have effect in relation to an order to which section 47 of the Fair Employment (Northern Ireland) Act 1976 (damages etc. for unfair discrimination) applies, that section shall continue to have effect in relation to that order notwithstanding the repeal of that section by this Act.

1976 c. 25.

(3) A certificate issued under Schedule 6 shall not be registered under that Schedule in a part of the United Kingdom if the judgment to which that certificate relates is the subject of a certificate registered in that part under the 1868 Act or the 1882 Act.

(4) In this paragraph— Sch. 13

"the 1868 Act" means the Judgments Extension Act 1868 ; 1868 c. 54.

"the 1882 Act" means the Inferior Courts Judgments Extension Act 1882 ; 1882 c. 31.

"judgment" has the same meaning as in section 18.

Section 18 *and Schedule* 7

3. Schedule 7 and, so far as it relates to that Schedule, section 18 shall not apply to judgments given before the coming into force of that section.

Section 19

4. Section 19 shall not apply to judgments given before the commencement of that section.

Section 20 *and Schedule* 8

5. Section 20 and Schedule 8 shall not apply to any proceedings begun before the commencement of that section.

Section 26

6. The power conferred by section 26 shall not be exercisable in relation to property arrested before the commencement of that section or in relation to bail or other security given—

   (*a*) before the commencement of that section to prevent the arrest of property ; or

   (*b*) to obtain the release of property arrested before the commencement of that section ; or

   (*c*) in substitution (whether directly or indirectly) for security given as mentioned in sub-paragraph (*a*) or (*b*).

Section 31

7. Section 31 shall not apply to any judgment—

   (*a*) which has been registered under Part II of the Administration of Justice Act 1920 or Part I of the Foreign Judgments (Reciprocal Enforcement) Act 1933 before the time when that section comes into force ; or 1920 c. 81.
1933 c. 13.

   (*b*) in respect of which proceedings at common law for its enforcement have been finally determined before that time.

Section 32 *and associated repeal*

8.—(1) Section 32 shall not apply to any judgment—

   (*a*) which has been registered under Part II of the Administration of Justice Act 1920, Part I of the Foreign Judgments (Reciprocal Enforcement) Act 1933 or Part I of the Maintenance Orders (Reciprocal Enforcement) Act 1972 before the time when that section comes into force ; or 1972 c. 18.

   (*b*) in respect of which proceedings at common law for its enforcement have been finally determined before that time.

U 2

SCH. 13
1933 c. 13.

(2) Section 4(3)(*b*) of the Foreign Judgments (Reciprocal Enforcement) Act 1933 shall continue to have effect, notwithstanding its repeal by this Act, in relation to a judgment registered under Part I of that Act before the commencement of section 32.

Section 33 and associated repeal

9.—(1) Section 33 shall not apply to any judgment—

1920 c. 81.

(*a*) which has been registered under Part II of the Administration of Justice Act 1920 or Part I of the Foreign Judgments (Reciprocal Enforcement) Act 1933 before the time when that section comes into force ; or

(*b*) in respect of which proceedings at common law for its enforcement have been finally determined before that time.

(2) The repeal by this Act of words in section 4(2)(*a*)(i) of the Foreign Judgments (Reciprocal Enforcement) Act 1933 shall not affect the operation of that provision in relation to a judgment registered under Part I of that Act before the commencement of section 33.

Section 34

10. Section 34 shall not apply to judgments given before the commencement of that section.

Section 54.

SCHEDULE 14

REPEALS

Chapter	Short title	Extent of repeal
41 Geo. 3. c. 90.	Crown Debts Act 1801.	The preamble. Sections 1 to 8.
5 Geo. 4. c. 111.	Crown Debts Act 1824.	The whole Act.
22 & 23 Vict. c. 21.	Queen's Remembrancer Act 1859.	Section 24.
31 & 32 Vict. c. 54.	Judgments Extension Act 1868.	The whole Act.
31 & 32 Vict. c. 96.	Ecclesiastical Buildings and Glebes (Scotland) Act 1868.	In section 4, the words " of the county in which the parish concerned is situated " and the words from " provided " to the end.
45 & 46 Vict. c. 31.	Inferior Courts Judgments Extension Act 1882.	The whole Act.
7 Edw. 7. c. 51.	Sheriff Courts (Scotland) Act 1907.	In section 5, the words from the first " Provided " to " that jurisdiction ".
14 & 15 Geo. 5. c. 27.	Conveyancing (Scotland) Act 1924.	In section 23(6) the words from " of the county " to " is situated ".

Chapter	Short title	Extent of repeal
23 & 24 Geo. 5. c. 13.	Foreign Judgments (Reciprocal Enforcement) Act 1933.	In section 4(2)(*a*)(i), the words from " otherwise " to " that court ". Section 4(3)(*b*). In section 9(1), the word " superior " in both places where it occurs. In section 11(1), the definition of " Judgments given in the superior courts of the United Kingdom ". In section 12, in paragraph (*a*) the words from " (except " to " this Act) ", and paragraph (*d*). In section 13(*b*), the words " and section two hundred and thirteen ", " respectively " and " and 116 ".
14 Geo. 6. c. 37.	Maintenance Orders Act 1950.	Section 6. Section 8. Section 9(1)(*a*). In section 16(2)(*b*)(v), the words from the beginning to " or ".
4 & 5 Eliz. 2. c. 46.	Administration of Justice Act 1956.	Section 51(*a*).
1963 c. 22.	Sheriff Courts (Civil Jurisdiction and Procedure) (Scotland) Act 1963.	Section 3(2).
1965 c. 2.	Administration of Justice Act 1965.	In Schedule 1, the entry relating to the Crown Debts Act 1801.
1971 c. 55.	Law Reform (Jurisdiction in Delict) (Scotland) Act 1971.	The whole Act.
1972 c. 18.	Maintenance Orders (Reciprocal Enforcement) Act 1972.	In section 40— (*a*) in paragraph (*a*), the words " against persons in that country or territory "; and (*b*) in paragraph (*b*), the words " against persons in the United Kingdom ". In section 47(3), the words " or having ceased to reside ". In the Schedule, paragraph 4.
1976 c. 25.	Fair Employment (Northern Ireland) Act 1976.	Section 47.
1978 c. 23.	Judicature (Northern Ireland) Act 1978.	In Part II of Schedule 5— (*a*) the entry relating to the Crown Debts Act 1801; and (*b*) in the entry relating to the Foreign Judgments (Reciprocal Enforcement) Act 1933, the word " respectively ", where last occurring, and the words " and 116 ".

Chapter	Short title	Extent of repeal
1981 c. 54	Supreme Court Act 1981.	In Schedule 5, paragraph 2 of the entry relating to the Foreign Judgments (Reciprocal Enforcement) Act 1933

ELIZABETH II

Taking of Hostages Act 1982

1982 CHAPTER 28

An Act to implement the International Convention against the Taking of Hostages; and for connected purposes.
[13th July 1982]

BE IT ENACTED by the Queen's most Excellent Majesty, by and with the advice and consent of the Lords Spiritual and Temporal, and Commons, in this present Parliament assembled, and by the authority of the same, as follows:—

1.—(1) A person, whatever his nationality, who, in the United Kingdom or elsewhere,—

Hostage-taking.

    (*a*) detains any other person ("the hostage"), and

    (*b*) in order to compel a State, international governmental organisation or person to do or abstain from doing any act, threatens to kill, injure or continue to detain the hostage,

commits an offence.

(2) A person guilty of an offence under this Act shall be liable, on conviction on indictment, to imprisonment for life.

2.—(1) Proceedings for an offence under this Act shall not be instituted—

Prosecution of offences.

    (*a*) in England and Wales, except by or with the consent of the Attorney General; and

    (*b*) in Northern Ireland, except by or with the consent of the Attorney General for Northern Ireland.

U 4

(2) As respects Scotland, for the purpose of conferring on the sheriff jurisdiction to entertain proceedings for an offence under this Act, any such offence shall, without prejudice to any jurisdiction exercisable apart from this subsection, be deemed to have been committed in any place in Scotland where the offender may for the time being be.

1978 c. 5.   (3) In Part I of Schedule 4 to the Northern Ireland (Emergency Provisions) Act 1978 (scheduled offences for the purposes of that Act) after paragraph 19 there shall be inserted the following paragraph—

" *Taking of Hostages Act 1982*
19A. Offences under the Taking of Hostages Act 1982.".

Extradition.   **3.**—(1) There shall be deemed to be included—

(*a*) in the list of extradition crimes in Schedule 1 to the
1870 c. 52.   Extradition Act 1870, and

(*b*) among the description of offences set out in Schedule 1
1967 c. 68.   to the Fugitive Offenders Act 1967,

any offence under this Act.

1978 c. 26.   (2) In Schedule 1 to the Suppression of Terrorism Act 1978 (offences not to be regarded as of a political character) after paragraph 11 there shall be inserted the following paragraph—

" *Taking of hostages*
11A. An offence under the Taking of Hostages Act 1982.".

(3) Where no such arrangement as is mentioned in section 2 of the Extradition Act 1870 has been made with a State which is a party to the Convention, an Order in Council applying the Act of 1870 may be made under that section as if the Convention were such an arrangement with that State; but where the Act of 1870 is so applied it shall have effect as if the only extradition crimes within the meaning of that Act were offences under this Act and attempts to commit such offences.

(4) For the purposes of the Act of 1870 any act, wherever committed, which—

(*a*) is an offence under this Act or an attempt to commit such an offence, and

(*b*) is an offence against the law of any State in the case of which that Act is applied by an Order in Council under section 2 of that Act,

shall be deemed to be an offence committed within the jurisdiction of that State.

(5) In subsection (3) above " the Convention " means the International Convention against the Taking of Hostages opened for signature at New York on 18th December 1979.

4. In the Fugitive Offenders Act 1967 the following section shall be inserted after section 4—

Further provisions as to extradition.

"Restriction on return: hostage-taking.

4A.—(1) A person shall not be returned under this Act to a designated Commonwealth country which is party to the Convention referred to in subsection (3) below, or committed to or kept in custody for the purposes of such return, if it appears to the Secretary of State, to the court of committal or to the High Court or High Court of Justiciary on an application for habeas corpus or for review of the order of committal—

1967 c. 68.

(*a*) that he might, if returned, be prejudiced at his trial by reason of the impossibility of effecting communications between him and the appropriate authorities of the State entitled to exercise rights of protection in relation to him ; and

(*b*) that the act or omission constituting the offence of which he has been accused or convicted also constituted an offence under section 1 of the Taking of Hostages Act 1982 or an attempt to commit such an offence.

(2) Where the Secretary of State certifies that a country is a party to the Convention the certificate shall, in any proceedings under this Act, be conclusive evidence of that fact.

(3) The Convention mentioned in subsections (1) and (2) above is the International Convention against the Taking of Hostages opened for signature at New York on 18th December 1979.".

5.—(1) Sections 17 and 22 of the Extradition Act 1870 and sections 16 and 17 of the Fugitive Offenders Act 1967 (application to Channel Islands, Isle of Man and colonies) shall extend respectively to the provisions of this Act amending those Acts.

Application to Channel Islands, Isle of Man, etc.
1870 c. 52.

(2) Her Majesty may by Order in Council make provision for extending the other provisions of this Act, with such exceptions, adaptations or modifications as may be specified in the Order, to any of the Channel Islands, the Isle of Man or any colony.

6.—(1) This Act may be cited as the Taking of Hostages Act 1982.

Short title and commencement.

(2) This Act shall come into force on such day as Her Majesty may by Order in Council appoint.

ELIZABETH II

Supply of Goods and Services Act 1982

1982 CHAPTER 29

An Act to amend the law with respect to the terms to be implied in certain contracts for the transfer of the property in goods, in certain contracts for the hire of goods and in certain contracts for the supply of a service; and for connected purposes.   [13th July 1982]

BE IT ENACTED by the Queen's most Excellent Majesty, by and with the advice and consent of the Lords Spiritual and Temporal, and Commons, in this present Parliament assembled, and by the authority of the same, as follows:—

PART I

SUPPLY OF GOODS

Contracts for the transfer of property in goods

1.—(1) In this Act a "contract for the transfer of goods" means a contract under which one person transfers or agrees to transfer to another the property in goods, other than an excepted contract.

The contracts concerned.

(2) For the purposes of this section an excepted contract means any of the following:—

(*a*) a contract of sale of goods;

(*b*) a hire-purchase agreement;

(*c*) a contract under which the property in goods is (or is to be) transferred in exchange for trading stamps on their redemption;

(*d*) a transfer or agreement to transfer which is made by deed and for which there is no consideration other than the presumed consideration imported by the deed ;

(*e*) a contract intended to operate by way of mortgage, pledge, charge or other security.

(3) For the purposes of this Act a contract is a contract for the transfer of goods whether or not services are also provided or to be provided under the contract, and (subject to subsection (2) above) whatever is the nature of the consideration for the transfer or agreement to transfer.

Implied terms about title, etc.

2.—(1) In a contract for the transfer of goods, other than one to which subsection (3) below applies, there is an implied condition on the part of the transferor that in the case of a transfer of the property in the goods he has a right to transfer the property and in the case of an agreement to transfer the property in the goods he will have such a right at the time when the property is to be transferred.

(2) In a contract for the transfer of goods, other than one to which subsection (3) below applies, there is also an implied warranty that—

(*a*) the goods are free, and will remain free until the time when the property is to be transferred, from any charge or encumbrance not disclosed or known to the transferee before the contract is made, and

(*b*) the transferee will enjoy quiet possession of the goods except so far as it may be disturbed by the owner or other person entitled to the benefit of any charge or encumbrance so disclosed or known.

(3) This subsection applies to a contract for the transfer of goods in the case of which there appears from the contract or is to be inferred from its circumstances an intention that the transferor should transfer only such title as he or a third person may have.

(4) In a contract to which subsection (3) above applies there is an implied warranty that all charges or encumbrances known to the transferor and not known to the transferee have been disclosed to the transferee before the contract is made.

(5) In a contract to which subsection (3) above applies there is also an implied warranty that none of the following will disturb the transferee's quiet possession of the goods, namely—

(*a*) the transferor ;

(*b*) in a case where the parties to the contract intend that the transferor should transfer only such title as a third person may have, that person ;

(c) anyone claiming through or under the transferor or that third person otherwise than under a charge or encumbrance disclosed or known to the transferee before the contract is made.

3.—(1) This section applies where, under a contract for the transfer of goods, the transferor transfers or agrees to transfer the property in the goods by description.

(2) In such case there is an implied condition that the goods will correspond with the description.

(3) If the transferor transfers or agrees to transfer the property in the goods by sample as well as by description it is not sufficient that the bulk of the goods corresponds with the sample if the goods do not also correspond with the description.

(4) A contract is not prevented from falling within subsection (1) above by reason only that, being exposed for supply, the goods are selected by the transferee.

4.—(1) Except as provided by this section and section 5 below and subject to the provisions of any other enactment, there is no implied condition or warranty about the quality or fitness for any particular purpose of goods supplied under a contract for the transfer of goods.

(2) Where, under such a contract, the transferor transfers the property in goods in the course of a business, there is (subject to subsection (3) below) an implied condition that the goods supplied under the contract are of merchantable quality.

(3) There is no such condition as is mentioned in subsection (2) above—

    (a) as regards defects specifically drawn to the transferee's attention before the contract is made ; or

    (b) if the transferee examines the goods before the contract is made, as regards defects which that examination ought to reveal.

(4) Subsection (5) below applies where, under a contract for the transfer of goods, the transferor transfers the property in goods in the course of a business and the transferee, expressly or by implication, makes known—

    (a) to the transferor, or

    (b) where the consideration or part of the consideration for the transfer is a sum payable by instalments and the goods were previously sold by a credit-broker to the transferor, to that credit-broker,

any particular purpose for which the goods are being acquired.

PART I

(5) In that case there is (subject to subsection (6) below) an implied condition that the goods supplied under the contract are reasonably fit for that purpose, whether or not that is a purpose for which such goods are commonly supplied.

(6) Subsection (5) above does not apply where the circumstances show that the transferee does not rely, or that it is unreasonable for him to rely, on the skill or judgment of the transferor or credit-broker.

(7) An implied condition or warranty about quality or fitness for a particular purpose may be annexed by usage to a contract for the transfer of goods.

(8) The preceding provisions of this section apply to a transfer by a person who in the course of a business is acting as agent for another as they apply to a transfer by a principal in the course of a business, except where that other is not transferring in the course of a business and either the transferee knows that fact or reasonable steps are taken to bring it to the transferee's notice before the contract concerned is made.

(9) Goods of any kind are of merchantable quality within the meaning of subsection (2) above if they are as fit for the purpose or purposes for which goods of that kind are commonly supplied as it is reasonable to expect having regard to any description applied to them, the price (if relevant) and all the other relevant circumstances.

Implied terms where transfer is by sample.

5.—(1) This section applies where, under a contract for the transfer of goods, the transferor transfers or agrees to transfer the property in the goods by reference to a sample.

(2) In such a case there is an implied condition—

(a) that the bulk will correspond with the sample in quality ; and

(b) that the transferee will have a reasonable opportunity of comparing the bulk with the sample ; and

(c) that the goods will be free from any defect, rendering them unmerchantable, which would not be apparent on reasonable examination of the sample.

(3) In subsection (2)(c) above " unmerchantable " is to be construed in accordance with section 4(9) above.

(4) For the purposes of this section a transferor transfers or agrees to transfer the property in goods by reference to a sample where there is an express or implied term to that effect in the contract concerned.

Contracts for the hire of goods

6.—(1) In this Act a " contract for the hire of goods " means a contract under which one person bails or agrees to bail goods to another by way of hire, other than an excepted contract.

The contracts concerned.

(2) For the purposes of this section an excepted contract means any of the following:—

    (*a*) a hire-purchase agreement;

    (*b*) a contract under which goods are (or are to be) bailed in exchange for trading stamps on their redemption.

(3) For the purposes of this Act a contract is a contract for the hire of goods whether or not services are also provided or to be provided under the contract, and (subject to subsection (2) above) whatever is the nature of the consideration for the bailment or agreement to bail by way of hire.

7.—(1) In a contract for the hire of goods there is an implied condition on the part of the bailor that in the case of a bailment he has a right to transfer possession of the goods by way of hire for the period of the bailment and in the case of an agreement to bail he will have such a right at the time of the bailment.

Implied terms about right to transfer possession, etc.

(2) In a contract for the hire of goods there is also an implied warranty that the bailee will enjoy quiet possession of the goods for the period of the bailment except so far as the possession may be disturbed by the owner or other person entitled to the benefit of any charge or encumbrance disclosed or known to the bailee before the contract is made.

(3) The preceding provisions of this section do not affect the right of the bailor to repossess the goods under an express or implied term of the contract.

8.—(1) This section applies where, under a contract for the hire of goods, the bailor bails or agrees to bail the goods by description.

Implied terms where hire is by description.

(2) In such a case there is an implied condition that the goods will correspond with the description.

(3) If under the contract the bailor bails or agrees to bail the goods by reference to a sample as well as a description it is not sufficient that the bulk of the goods corresponds with the sample if the goods do not also correspond with the description.

(4) A contract is not prevented from falling within subsection (1) above by reason only that, being exposed for supply, the goods are selected by the bailee.

9.—(1) Except as provided by this section and section 10 below and subject to the provisions of any other enactment, there is no implied condition or warranty about the quality or fitness for any particular purpose of goods bailed under a contract for the hire of goods.

(2) Where, under such a contract, the bailor bails goods in the course of a business, there is (subject to subsection (3) below) an implied condition that the goods supplied under the contract are of merchantable quality.

(3) There is no such condition as is mentioned in subsection (2) above—

    (*a*) as regards defects specifically drawn to the bailee's attention before the contract is made ; or

    (*b*) if the bailee examines the goods before the contract is made, as regards defects which that examination ought to reveal.

(4) Subsection (5) below applies where, under a contract for the hire of goods, the bailor bails goods in the course of a business and the bailee, expressly or by implication, makes known—

    (*a*) to the bailor in the course of negotiations conducted by him in relation to the making of the contract, or

    (*b*) to a credit-broker in the course of negotiations conducted by that broker in relation to goods sold by him to the bailor before forming the subject matter of the contract,

any particular purpose for which the goods are being bailed.

(5) In that case there is (subject to subsection (6) below) an implied condition that the goods supplied under the contract are reasonably fit for that purpose, whether or not that is a purpose for which such goods are commonly supplied.

(6) Subsection (5) above does not apply where the circumstances show that the bailee does not rely, or that it is unreasonable for him to rely, on the skill or judgment of the bailor or credit-broker.

(7) An implied condition or warranty about quality or fitness for a particular purpose may be annexed by usage to a contract for the hire of goods.

(8) The preceding provisions of this section apply to a bailment by a person who in the course of a business is acting as agent for another as they apply to a bailment by a principal in the course of a business, except where that other is not bailing in the course of a business and either the bailee knows that fact or reasonable steps are taken to bring it to the bailee's notice before the contract concerned is made.

(9) Goods of any kind are of merchantable quality within the meaning of subsection (2) above if they are as fit for the purpose or purposes for which goods of that kind are commonly supplied as it is reasonable to expect having regard to any description applied to them, the consideration for the bailment (if relevant) and all the other relevant circumstances.

10.—(1) This section applies where, under a contract for the hire of goods, the bailor bails or agrees to bail the goods by reference to a sample.

(2) In such a case there is an implied condition—

    (*a*) that the bulk will correspond with the sample in quality; and

    (*b*) that the bailee will have a reasonable opportunity of comparing the bulk with the sample ; and

    (*c*) that the goods will be free from any defect, rendering them unmerchantable, which would not be apparent on reasonable examination of the sample.

(3) In subsection (2)(*c*) above " unmerchantable " is to be construed in accordance with section 9(9) above.

(4) For the purposes of this section a bailor bails or agrees to bail goods by reference to a sample where there is an express or implied term to that effect in the contract concerned.

Exclusion of implied terms, etc.

11.—(1) Where a right, duty or liability would arise under a contract for the transfer of goods or a contract for the hire of goods by implication of law, it may (subject to subsection (2) below and the 1977 Act) be negatived or varied by express agreement, or by the course of dealing between the parties, or by such usage as binds both parties to the contract.

(2) An express condition or warranty does not negative a condition or warranty implied by the preceding provisions of this Act unless inconsistent with it.

(3) Nothing in the preceding provisions of this Act prejudices the operation of any other enactment or any rule of law whereby any condition or warranty (other than one relating to quality or fitness) is to be implied in a contract for the transfer of goods or a contract for the hire of goods.

PART II

SUPPLY OF SERVICES

The contracts concerned.

12.—(1) In this Act a " contract for the supply of a service " means, subject to subsection (2) below, a contract under which a person (" the supplier ") agrees to carry out a service.

(2) For the purposes of this Act, a contract of service or apprenticeship is not a contract for the supply of a service.

(3) Subject to subsection (2) above, a contract is a contract for the supply of a service for the purposes of this Act whether or not goods are also—

(a) transferred or to be transferred, or

(b) bailed or to be bailed by way of hire,

under the contract, and whatever is the nature of the consideration for which the service is to be carried out.

(4) The Secretary of State may by order provide that one or more of sections 13 to 15 below shall not apply to services of a description specified in the order, and such an order may make different provision for different circumstances.

(5) The power to make an order under subsection (4) above shall be exercisable by statutory instrument subject to annulment in pursuance of a resolution of either House of Parliament.

Implied term about care and skill.

13. In a contract for the supply of a service where the supplier is acting in the course of a business, there is an implied term that the supplier will carry out the service with reasonable care and skill.

Implied term about time for performance.

14.—(1) Where, under a contract for the supply of a service by a supplier acting in the course of a business, the time for the service to be carried out is not fixed by the contract, left to be fixed in a manner agreed by the contract or determined by the course of dealing between the parties, there is an implied term that the supplier will carry out the service within a reasonable time.

(2) What is a reasonable time is a question of fact.

Implied term about consideration.

15.—(1) Where, under a contract for the supply of a service, the consideration for the service is not determined by the contract, left to be determined in a manner agreed by the contract or determined by the course of dealing between the parties, there is an implied term that the party contracting with the supplier will pay a reasonable charge.

(2) What is a reasonable charge is a question of fact.

16.—(1) Where a right, duty or liability would arise under
a contract for the supply of a service by virtue of this Part of Exclusion of
this Act, it may (subject to subsection (2) below and the 1977 implied terms,
Act) be negatived or varied by express agreement, or by the etc.
course of dealing between the parties, or by such usage as binds
both parties to the contract.

(2) An express term does not negative a term implied by this
Part of this Act unless inconsistent with it.

(3) Nothing in this Part of this Act prejudices—

> (*a*) any rule of law which imposes on the supplier a duty
> stricter than that imposed by section 13 or 14 above ;
> or

> (*b*) subject to paragraph (*a*) above, any rule of law whereby
> any term not inconsistent with this Part of this Act
> is to be implied in a contract for the supply of a
> service.

(4) This Part of this Act has effect subject to any other enactment which defines or restricts the rights, duties or liabilities
arising in connection with a service of any description.

PART III

SUPPLEMENTARY

17.—(1) In section 10(2) of the 1973 Act, as originally enacted Minor and
and as prospectively substituted by paragraph 35 of Schedule 4 consequential
to the 1974 Act (implied condition in hire-purchase agreement amendments.
that goods are of merchantable quality), after " implied condition
that the goods " there shall be inserted " supplied under the
agreement ".

(2) The following subsection shall be inserted after section
7(3) of the 1977 Act:—

> " (3A) Liability for breach of the obligations arising
> under section 2 of the Supply of Goods and Services Act
> 1982 (implied terms about title etc. in certain contracts for
> the transfer of the property in goods) cannot be excluded
> or restricted by reference to any such term."

(3) In consequence of subsection (2) above, in section 7(4)
of the 1977 Act, after " cannot " there shall be inserted " (in
a case to which subsection (3A) above does not apply) ".

18.—(1) In the preceding provisions of this Act and this Interpretation:
section— general.

> " bailee ", in relation to a contract for the hire of goods
> means (depending on the context) a person to whom the

goods are bailed under the contract, or a person to whom they are to be so bailed, or a person to whom the rights under the contract of either of those persons have passed ;

" bailor ", in relation to a contract for the hire of goods, means (depending on the context) a person who bails the goods under the contract, or a person who agrees to do so, or a person to whom the duties under the contract of either of those persons have passed ;

" business " includes a profession and the activities of any government department or local or public authority ;

" credit-broker " means a person acting in the course of a business of credit brokerage carried on by him ;

" credit brokerage " means the effecting of introductions—

(a) of individuals desiring to obtain credit to persons carrying on any business so far as it relates to the provision of credit ; or

(b) of individuals desiring to obtain goods on hire to persons carrying on a business which comprises or relates to the bailment of goods under a contract for the hire of goods ; or

(c) of individuals desiring to obtain credit, or to obtain goods on hire, to other credit-brokers ;

" enactment " means any legislation (including subordinate legislation) of the United Kingdom or Northern Ireland ;

" goods " include all personal chattels (including emblements, industrial growing crops, and things attached to or forming part of the land which are agreed to be severed before the transfer or bailment concerned or under the contract concerned), other than things in action and money ;

" hire-purchase agreement " has the same meaning as in the 1974 Act ;

" property ", in relation to goods, means the general property in them and not merely a special property ;

" quality ", in relation to goods, includes their state or condition ;

" redemption ", in relation to trading stamps, has the same meaning as in the Trading Stamps Act 1964 or, as respects Northern Ireland, the Trading Stamps Act (Northern Ireland) 1965 ;

" trading stamps " has the same meaning as in the said Act of 1964 or, as respects Northern Ireland, the said Act of 1965 ;

" transferee ", in relation to a contract for the transfer of
goods, means (depending on the context) a person to
whom the property in the goods is transferred under
the contract, or a person to whom the property is to be
so transferred, or a person to whom the rights under
the contract of either of those persons have passed ;

" transferor ", in relation to a contract for the transfer
of goods, means (depending on the context) a person
who transfers the property in the goods under the contract, or a person who agrees to do so, or a person to
whom the duties under the contract of either of those
persons have passed.

(2) In subsection (1) above, in the definitions of bailee, bailor,
transferee and transferor, a reference to rights or duties passing
is to their passing by assignment, operation of law or otherwise.

19. In this Act—   Interpretation:

" the 1973 Act " means the Supply of Goods (Implied   references to Acts.
Terms) Act 1973 ;   1973 c. 13.

" the 1974 Act " means the Consumer Credit Act 1974 ;   1974 c. 39.

" the 1977 Act " means the Unfair Contract Terms Act   1977 c. 50.
1977 ; and

" the 1979 Act " means the Sale of Goods Act 1979.   1979 c. 54.

20.—(1) This Act may be cited as the Supply of Goods and   Citation,
Services Act 1982.   transitional provisions,

(2) The transitional provisions in the Schedule to this Act shall   commence-
have effect.   ment and extent.

(3) Part I of this Act together with section 17 and so much
of sections 18 and 19 above as relates to that Part shall not
come into operation until 4th January 1983 ; and Part II of this
Act together with so much of sections 18 and 19 above as relates
to that Part shall not come into operation until such day as
may be appointed by an order made by the Secretary of State.

(4) The power to make an order under subsection (3) above
shall be exercisable by statutory instrument.

(5) No provision of this Act applies to a contract made before
the provision comes into operation.

(6) This Act extends to Northern Ireland but not to Scotland.

SCHEDULE

TRANSITIONAL PROVISIONS

1.—(1) If section 4 of this Act comes into operation before the day appointed for the purposes of section 14(7) of and paragraph 5 of Schedule 1 to the 1979 Act, then until that day, section 4 of this Act shall have effect with the modifications set out in sub-paragraphs (2) to (4) below.

(2) For subsection (4) substitute:—

" (4) Subsection (5) below applies where, under a contract for the transfer of goods, the transferor transfers the property in goods in the course of a business and the transferee, expressly or by implication, makes known to the transferor any particular purpose for which the goods are being acquired."

(3) In subsection (6) omit " or credit-broker ".

(4) After subsection (9) insert:—

" (10) In the application of subsections (4) to (6) above to a contract for the transfer of goods under which the consideration or part of the consideration for the transfer is a sum payable by instalments any reference to the transferor includes a reference to the person by whom any antecedent negotiations are conducted.

1965 c. 66.   (11) Section 58(3) and (5) of the Hire-Purchase Act 1965 (meaning of antecedent negotiations and related expressions) apply, with the appropriate modifications, in relation to subsection (10) above as in relation to that Act."

2.—(1) If section 9 of this Act comes into operation before paragraph 35 of Schedule 4 to the 1974 Act (which, among other things, amends section 10(3) of the 1973 Act so as to make it refer to credit-brokers), then, until the paragraph comes into operation, section 9 of this Act shall have effect with the modifications set out in sub-paragraphs (2) to (4) below.

(2) For subsection (4) substitute:—

" (4) Subsection (5) below applies where, under a contract for the hire of goods, the bailor bails goods in the course of a business and the bailee, expressly or by implication, makes known to the bailor or the person by whom any antecedent negotiations are conducted any particular purpose for which the goods are being bailed."

(3) In subsection (6), for " credit-broker " substitute " person by whom the antecedent negotiations are conducted ".

(4) After subsection (9) insert:—

" (10) Section 58(3) and (5) of the Hire-Purchase Act 1965 (meaning of antecedent negotiations and related expressions) apply, with the appropriate modifications, in relation to subsections (4) to (6) above as in relation to that Act."

ELIZABETH II

Local Government (Miscellaneous Provisions) Act 1982

1982 CHAPTER 30

An Act to make amendments for England and Wales of
provisions of that part of the law relating to local
authorities or highways which is commonly amended
by local Acts; to make provision for the control of
sex establishments; to make further provision for the
control of refreshment premises and for consultation
between local authorities in England and Wales and
fire authorities with regard to fire precautions for
buildings and caravan sites; to repeal the Theatrical
Employers Registration Acts 1925 and 1928; to make
further provision as to the enforcement of section 8 of
the Public Utilities Street Works Act 1950 and sections
171 and 174 of the Highways Act 1980; to make
provision in connection with the computerisation of
local land charges registers; to make further provision
in connection with the acquisition of land and rights
over land by boards constituted in pursuance of
section 1 of the Town and Country Planning Act 1971
or reconstituted in pursuance of Schedule 17 to the
Local Government Act 1972; to exclude from the
definition of " construction or maintenance work " in
section 20 of the Local Government, Planning and
Land Act 1980 work undertaken by local authorities
and development bodies pursuant to certain agreements with the Manpower Services Commission which
specify the work to be undertaken and under which the

Commission agrees to pay the whole or part of the cost of the work so specified; to define " year " for the purposes of Part III of the said Act of 1980; to amend section 140 of the Local Government Act 1972 and to provide for the insurance by local authorities of persons voluntarily assisting probation committees; to make provision for controlling nuisance and disturbance on educational premises; to amend section 137 of the Local Government Act 1972; to make further provision as to arrangements made by local authorities under the Employment and Training Act 1973; to extend the duration of certain powers to assist industry or employment conferred by local Acts; to make corrections and minor improvements in certain enactments relating to the local administration of health and planning functions; and for connected purposes.

[13th July 1982]

B E IT ENACTED by the Queen's most Excellent Majesty, by and with the advice and consent of the Lords Spiritual and Temporal, and Commons, in this present Parliament assembled, and by the authority of the same, as follows:—

PART I

LICENSING OF PUBLIC ENTERTAINMENTS

Licensing of public entertainments.

1.—(1) Subject to subsection (2) below, Schedule 1 to this Act shall have effect with respect to the licensing outside Greater London of the public entertainments referred to in that Schedule.

(2) Paragraphs 3 and 4 of the Schedule shall not have effect in the area of a local authority unless the authority so resolve.

(3) If a local authority do so resolve, those paragraphs shall come into force in their area on the day specified in that behalf in the resolution (which must not be before the expiration of the period of one month beginning with the day on which the resolution is passed).

(4) A local authority shall publish notice that they have passed a resolution under this section in two consecutive weeks in a local newspaper circulating in their area.

(5) The first publication shall not be later than 28 days before the day specified in the resolution for the coming into force of the paragraphs in the local authority's area.

(6) The notice shall state the general effect of the paragraphs.

(7) The enactments specified in Schedule 2 to this Act shall
have effect subject to the amendments specified in that Schedule,
being amendments consequential on subsections (1) to (6) above.

(8) In Schedule 12 to the London Government Act 1963—

    (*a*) in paragraph 10(3) (penalties for offences relating to
    entertainments held without licences or contravening
    licences) for " five hundred pounds " there shall be
    substituted " £1,000 " ; and

    (*b*) in paragraph 12(3) (penalty for refusal to permit entry to
    or inspection of premises) for " twenty pounds " there
    shall be substituted " £200 ".

(9) Subsection (8) above has effect only in relation to offences
committed after 1st January 1983.

(10) So much of any local enactment passed before 1974 as
relates to the regulation by means of licensing of public entertainments of any description referred to in Schedule 1 to this
Act shall cease to have effect.

(11) In this section " local authority " means—

    (*a*) the council of a district ; and

    (*b*) the Council of the Isles of Scilly.

(12) This section shall come into force on 1st January 1983.

PART II

CONTROL OF SEX ESTABLISHMENTS

2.—(1) A local authority may resolve that Schedule 3 to this Control of sex
Act is to apply to their area ; and if a local authority do so establish-
resolve, that Schedule shall come into force in their area on the ments.
day specified in that behalf in the resolution (which must not
be before the expiration of the period of one month beginning
with the day on which the resolution is passed).

(2) A local authority shall publish notice that they have passed
a resolution under this section in two consecutive weeks in a
local newspaper circulating in their area.

(3) The first publication shall not be later than 28 days before
the day specified in the resolution for the coming into force
of Schedule 3 to this Act in the local authority's area.

(4) The notice shall state the general effect of that Schedule.

(5) In this Part of this Act " local authority " means—

    (*a*) the council of a district ;

    (*b*) the council of a London borough ; and

    (*c*) the Common Council of the City of London.

Part III
Street Trading

Power of district council to adopt Schedule 4.

3. A district council may resolve that Schedule 4 to this Act shall apply to their district and, if a council so resolve, that Schedule shall come into force in their district on such day as may be specified in the resolution.

Part IV
Control of Refreshment Premises
Take-away food shops

Closing hours for take-away food shops.

4.—(1) A district council may make an order under this sub-section (in this Part of this Act referred to as a " closing order ") with respect to any premises in their district where meals or refreshments are supplied for consumption off the premises, other than—

1969 c. 53.

    (*a*) any premises that are a late night refreshment house, as defined in section 1 of the Late Night Refreshment Houses Act 1969 ; and

    (*b*) any premises that are exempt licensed premises as defined in that section,

if they are satisfied that it is desirable to make such an order to prevent residents in the neighbourhood of the premises being unreasonably disturbed either by persons resorting to the premises or by the use of the premises for the supply of meals or refreshments.

(2) A closing order shall be an order specifying individual premises and prohibiting the use of the premises for the supply of meals and refreshments to the public between such hours as may be specified in the order.

(3) The hours specified in a closing order shall commence not earlier than midnight and finish not later than 5 o'clock in the morning.

(4) A closing order may prohibit the use of the premises to which it relates for the supply of meals and refreshments to the public between different hours on different days of the week.

(5) A district council may vary a closing order by an order under this subsection (in this Part of this Act referred to as a " variation order ").

(6) A district council may revoke a closing order by an order under this subsection (in this Part of this Act referred to as a " revocation order ").

(7) A variation order or a revocation order may be made
on the written application of the keeper of the premises to
which the closing order relates, or without such an application.

(8) Subject to subsection (9) below, a closing order shall
cease to have effect 3 years from the date on which it was made,
but without prejudice to the power of the district council to
make a further closing order.

(9) Subsection (8) above shall have effect in relation to a
closing order which has been varied as if the reference to the
date on which it was made were a reference to the date on
which it was last varied.

(10) In this Part of this Act " the keeper ", in relation to any
premises, means the person having the conduct or management
of the premises.

(11) Until section 7(1) and (2) below come into force this section shall have effect as if the following paragraph were substituted for subsection (1)(*b*) above—

> " (*b*) a house, room, shop or building which is licensed for
> the sale of beer, cider, wine or spirits,".

5.—(1) A district council shall take all relevant circumstances   Closing
into consideration when determining whether to make—   orders etc.—
    procedure
    (*a*) a closing order ; or   and appeals.

    (*b*) a variation order which varies a closing order or a
    previous variation order by specifying—

> (i) an hour later than that specified in the order
> which it varies as the hour at which the use of the
> premises for the supply of meals and refreshments
> to the public may begin ; or

> (ii) an hour earlier than that so specified as the
> hour at which their use for that purpose is to end,

but a council may not make a closing order or such a variation
order unless residents in the neighbourhood of the premises to
which the order, if made, would relate have complained of disturbance such as is mentioned in section 4(1) above.

(2) If a district council propose—

    (*a*) to make a closing order ; or

    (*b*) to make such a variation order as is mentioned in sub-
    section (1)(*b*) above,

they shall first serve a notice in accordance with subsections (12)
to (15) below—

> (i) giving their reasons for seeking to make the order ; and

> (ii) stating that within 28 days of service of the notice the

keeper of the premises to which the order, if made, would relate may in writing require them to give him an opportunity to make representations to them concerning the matter.

(3) Where a notice has been served under subsection (2) above, the district council shall not determine the matter until either—

 (a) the keeper has made representations to them concerning it ; or

 (b) the period during which he could have required them to give him an opportunity to make representations has elapsed without his requiring them to give him such an opportunity ; or

 (c) the conditions specified in subsection (4) below are satisfied.

(4) The conditions mentioned in subsection (3) above are—

 (a) that the keeper has required the district council to give him an opportunity to make representations to them ;

 (b) that the council have allowed him a reasonable period for making his representations ; and

 (c) that he has failed to make them within that period.

(5) Representations may be made, at the keeper's option, either in writing or orally.

(6) If the keeper informs the council that he desires to make oral representations, they shall give him an opportunity of appearing before and of being heard by a committee or sub-committee of the council.

(7) The council shall not reveal to the keeper the name or address of any person who has made a complaint concerning the premises, unless they have first obtained the consent of the person who made the complaint.

(8) Where the keeper of any premises has applied for a variation order or a revocation order, the council shall be deemed to have refused the application if they fail to determine the matter within 8 weeks from the date on which the application was made.

(9) When a council make an order under section 4 above, they shall serve a copy in accordance with subsections (12) to (15) below.

(10) A closing order and any such variation order as is mentioned in subsection (1)(b) above shall come into force 21 days after the date of service.

(11) A variation order other than a variation order such as is mentioned in subsection (1)(b) above and a revocation order shall come into force on such date as may be specified in it.

(12) Any document required to be served under this section shall be served on the keeper of the premises to which it relates and, subject to subsection (13) below, may be served on him by post.

(13) Service of any such document by post may only be effected by sending it in a pre-paid registered letter or by the recorded delivery service.

(14) For the purposes of service any such document may be addressed to the keeper at the premises to which it relates.

(15) The keeper may be addressed either by name or by the description of " the keeper " of the premises (describing them).

(16) An appeal—

(a) against a closing order or a variation order ; or

(b) against a refusal by the district council to make a variation order or a revocation order,

may be brought to a magistrates' court by the keeper of the premises to which the order relates or would relate.

(17) No appeal against an order may be brought after it has come into force, and if an appeal is brought against an order, the order shall not come into force until the appeal has been determined or abandoned.

(18) No appeal against a refusal to make a variation order or a revocation order may be brought after the expiry of the period of 21 days from the date on which the keeper was notified of the refusal.

(19) An appeal against a decision of a magistrates' court under this section may be brought to the Crown Court.

(20) On an appeal to the magistrates' court or the Crown Court under this section relating to any premises the court may confirm an order relating to the premises made under section 4 above or set it aside or give directions to the district council as to the making of such an order relating to the premises.

(21) Subject to subsection (22) below, it shall be the duty of the district council to comply with any directions under subsection (20) above.

(22) The district council need not comply with any directions given by the magistrates' court if they bring an appeal against the decision of the magistrates' court to the Crown Court under subsection (19) above within 21 days of the date of the decision.

6.—(1) In the event of a contravention of any of the provisions of a closing order, whether as originally made or as varied by a variation order, the keeper of the premises to which the order relates shall be guilty of an offence.

(2) It shall be a defence for a person charged with an offence under this section to prove that he took all reasonable precautions and exercised all due diligence to avoid commission of the offence by himself or by any person under his control.

(3) A person guilty of an offence under this section shall be liable on summary conviction to a fine not exceeding £500.

(4) Where an offence under this section which has been committed by a body corporate is proved to have been committed with the consent or connivance of, or to be attributable to any neglect on the part of, a director, manager, secretary or other similar officer of the body corporate, or any person who was purporting to act in any such capacity, he, as well as the body corporate, shall be guilty of that offence and be liable to be proceeded against and punished accordingly.

Late night refreshment houses

Refreshments etc. on licensed premises.
1969 c. 53.

7.—(1) In section 1 of the Late Night Refreshment Houses Act 1969 (meaning of " late night refreshment house ") for the words from " a house ", in the second place where those words occur, to the end of the section there shall be substituted the words " exempt licensed premises ".

(2) The said section 1, as amended by subsection (1) above, shall be renumbered so as to become section 1(1) of the said Act ; and at the end of the resulting subsection (1) there shall be added as subsections (2) and (3)—

"(2) In subsection (1) above " exempt licensed premises " means a house, room, shop or building which—

(i) is licensed for the sale of beer, cider, wine or spirits ; and

(ii) is not kept open for public refreshment, resort and entertainment at any time between normal evening closing time and 5 o'clock of the following morning.

(3) In subsection (2) above " normal evening closing time " means—

(a) in relation to premises with permitted hours in the evening, a time thirty minutes after the end of those hours ; and

(b) in relation to premises without permitted hours in the evening, 10 o'clock at night ;

1964 c. 26.

and in this subsection " permitted hours " means the hours specified in section 60 of the Licensing Act 1964 as modified by any other provision of that Act.".

(3) Subsections (1) and (2) above shall come into force at the expiration of the period of three months beginning with the date on which this Act is passed.

(4) Nothing in this section affects premises in Greater London.

PART V
FIRE PRECAUTIONS
Provisions as to consultation

8.—(1) In the Public Health Act 1936— Consultation

    (*a*) in section 59 (exits, entrances &c, in the case of certain public and other buildings)—
        (i) in subsections (1) and (2), the words ", after consultation with the fire authority, deem satisfactory, regard being had " shall be substituted for the words "deem satisfactory, regard being had by them " ; and
        (ii) in subsection (4), after the word " authority " there shall be inserted the words " after consultation with the fire authority," ;

    (*b*) in subsection (1) of section 60 (means of escape from fire in the case of certain high buildings) after the word " authority "—
        (i) in the first place where it occurs, there shall be inserted the words ", after consultation with the fire authority," ; and
        (ii) in the second place where it occurs, there shall be inserted the words ", after such consultation " ; and

    (*c*) in section 343 (interpretation) the following definition shall be inserted after the definition of " factory "—
        " " fire authority " has the meaning assigned to it by section 43(1) of the Fire Precautions Act 1971." 1971 c. 40.

[margin note: between authorities. 1936 c. 49.]

(2) In the Caravan Sites and Control of Development Act 1960— 1960 c. 62.

    (*a*) the following subsections shall be inserted after subsection (3) of section 5 (power of local authority to attach conditions to site licences)—
        " (3A) The local authority shall consult the fire authority as to the extent to which any model standards relating to fire precautions which have been specified under subsection (6) of this section are appropriate to the land.
        (3B) If—
            (*a*) no such standards have been specified ; or

(b) any standard that has been specified appears to the fire authority to be inappropriate to the land,

the local authority shall consult the fire authority as to what conditions relating to fire precautions ought to be attached to the site licence instead." ;

(b) the following subsections shall be added after subsection (6) of that section—

" (7) The duty imposed on a local authority by subsection (6) of this section to have regard to standards specified under that subsection is to be construed, as regards standards relating to fire precautions which are so specified, as a duty to have regard to them subject to any advice given by the fire authority under subsection (3A) or (3B) of this section.

(8) In this section " fire precautions " means precautions to be taken for any of the purposes specified in paragraph (e) of subsection (1) of this section for which conditions may be imposed by virtue of that subsection." ;

(c) the following subsection shall be added at the end of section 8 (powers of local authority to alter conditions attached to site licences)—

" (5) The local authority shall consult the fire authority before exercising the powers conferred upon them by subsection (1) of this section in relation to a condition attached to a site licence for the purposes set out in section 5(1)(e) of this Act." ;

(d) the following subsection shall be inserted after subsection (2) of section 24 (power of local authorities to provide sites for caravans)—

" (2A) Before exercising the power to provide a site conferred on them by subsection (1) of this section the local authority shall consult the fire authority, if they are not themselves the fire authority,—

(a) as to measures to be taken for preventing and detecting the outbreak of fire on the site ; and

(b) as to the provision and maintenance of means of fighting fire on it." ; and

(e) the following definition shall be inserted in section 29 (interpretation of Part I) after the definition of " existing site "—

" " fire authority ", in relation to any land, means the authority discharging in the area in which the

land is situated the functions of fire authority under
the Fire Services Act 1947 ; ".

Firemen's switches

9.—(1) A fire authority may resolve that section 10 below is Application
to apply to their area ; and if a fire authority do so resolve, of section 10.
that section shall come into force in their area on the day
specified in that behalf in the resolution (which must not be
before the expiration of the period of 42 days beginning with
the day on which the resolution is passed).

(2) A fire authority shall publish notice that they have passed
a resolution under this section in two consecutive weeks in a
local newspaper circulating in their area.

(3) Any such notice shall state the general effect of section 10
below.

(4) In this section and section 10 below " fire authority " means
an authority discharging the functions of fire authority under
the Fire Services Act 1947.

10.—(1) This section applies to apparatus consisting of lumi- Firemen's
nous tube signs designed to work at a voltage normally exceed- switches for
ing 650 volts, or other equipment so designed, and references luminous
in this section to a cut-off switch are, in a case where a trans- tube signs.
former is provided to raise the voltage to operate the apparatus,
references to a cut-off switch on the low-voltage side of the
transformer.

(2) No apparatus to which this section applies shall be installed unless it is provided with a cut-off switch.

(3) Subject to subsection (4) below, the cut-off switch shall be
so placed, and coloured or marked, as to satisfy such reasonable
requirements as the fire authority may impose to secure that it
shall be readily recognisable by and accessible to firemen.

(4) If a cut-off switch complies in position, colour and marking
with the current regulations of the Institution of Electrical Engineers for a firemen's emergency switch, the fire authority may
not impose any further requirements in respect of it under subsection (3) above.

(5) Not less than 42 days before work is begun to install
apparatus to which this section applies, the owner or occupier
of the premises where the apparatus is to be installed shall give
notice to the fire authority showing where the cut-off switch
is to be placed and how it is to be coloured or marked.

(6) Where notice has been given to the fire authority as required by subsection (5) above, the proposed position, colouring
or marking of the switch shall be deemed to satisfy the require-

ments of the fire authority unless, within 21 days from the date of the service of the notice, the fire authority have served on the owner or occupier a counter-notice stating that their requirements are not satisfied.

(7) Where apparatus to which this section applies has been installed in premises before the day specified in a resolution under section 9(1) above as the day on which this section is to come into force in the area in which the premises are situated, the owner or occupier of the premises shall, not more than 21 days after that day, give notice to the fire authority stating whether the apparatus is already provided with a cut-off switch and, if so, where the switch is placed and how it is coloured or marked.

(8) Subject to subsection (9) below, where apparatus to which this section applies has been installed in premises before the day specified in a resolution under section 9(1) above as the day on which this section is to come into force in the area in which the premises are situated, the fire authority may serve on the owner or occupier of the premises a notice—

(*a*) in the case of apparatus already provided with a cut-off switch, stating that they are not satisfied with the position, colouring or marking of the switch and requiring him, within such period as may be specified in the notice, to take such steps as will secure that the switch will be so placed and coloured or marked as to be readily recognisable by, and accessible to, firemen in accordance with the reasonable requirements of the fire authority ; or

(*b*) in the case of apparatus not already provided with a cut-off switch, requiring him, within such period as may be specified in the notice, to provide such a cut-off switch in such a position and so coloured or marked as to be readily recognisable by, and accessible to, firemen in accordance with the reasonable requirements of the fire authority.

(9) If a cut-off switch complies in position, colour and marking with the current regulations of the Institution of Electrical Engineers for a firemen's emergency switch, the fire authority may not serve a notice in respect of it under subsection (8) above.

1936 c. 49.   (10) Section 290 of the Public Health Act 1936 shall apply to notices given by a fire authority under this section as it applies to the notices mentioned in subsection (1) of that section as if the references in that section to a local authority included references to a fire authority.

(11) This section shall not apply to apparatus installed or proposed to be installed on or in premises in respect of which

a licence under the Cinematograph Acts 1909 and 1952 is for the
time being in force.

(12) The following persons, namely—

(*a*) any owner and any occupier of premises where apparatus to which this section applies is installed who without reasonable excuse fails to ensure that it complies
with subsection (2) above ;

(*b*) any owner and any occupier of premises who without
reasonable excuse fails to comply with subsection (3)
above ;

shall each be guilty of an offence and liable on summary conviction to a fine not exceeding £200 and to a daily fine not
exceeding £20.

(13) In proceedings for an offence under subsection (12) above,
it shall be a defence for either the owner or the occupier to
show that it would have been equitable for the prosecution to
be brought only against the other.

(14) A person charged shall not be entitled to rely on the
defence set out in subsection (13) above unless within a period
ending 7 clear days before the hearing he has served on the
prosecutor notice in writing of his intention so to do.

(15) Any person who without reasonable excuse fails to give
a notice required by subsection (5) or (7) above shall be guilty
of an offence and liable on summary conviction to a fine not
exceeding £200 unless he establishes that some other person
duly gave the notice in question.

(16) Any owner or occupier of premises who without reasonable excuse fails to comply with a notice served on him under
subsection (8) above within the period specified in it for compliance with it shall be guilty of an offence and liable on summary conviction to a fine not exceeding £200 and to a daily
fine not exceeding £20.

(17) It shall be a defence for a person charged with an offence
under this section to prove that he took all reasonable precautions and exercised all due diligence to avoid commission
of the offence.

PART VI

ABOLITION OF REGISTRATION OF THEATRICAL EMPLOYERS

11.—(1) The Theatrical Employers Registration Acts 1925
and 1928 (which require theatrical employers to be registered
with certain local authorities) shall cease to have effect.

(2) This section extends to Scotland.

Repeal of
Theatrical
Employers
Registration
Acts 1925 and
1928.

X 2

PART VII
BYELAWS

General
provisions
relating to
byelaws.
1936 c. 49.
1875 c. 55.

12.—(1) Notwithstanding anything in section 298 of the Public Health Act 1936 or section 253 of the Public Health Act 1875 or any other enactment, a constable may take proceedings in respect of an offence against a byelaw made by a relevant local authority under any enactment without the consent of the Attorney General.

(2) In subsection (1) above "relevant local authority" means—

1972 c. 70.

> (a) a local authority, as defined in section 270 of the Local Government Act 1972 ; and

> (b) any body that was the predecessor of a local authority as so defined.

(3) It is immaterial for the purposes of this section that a byelaw was made after the passing of this Act.

PART VIII
ACUPUNCTURE, TATTOOING, EAR-PIERCING AND ELECTROLYSIS

Application
of Part VIII.

13.—(1) The provisions of this Part of this Act, except this section, shall come into force in accordance with the following provisions of this section.

(2) A local authority may resolve that the provisions of this Part of this Act which are mentioned in paragraph (a), (b) or (c) of subsection (3) below are to apply to their area; and if a local authority do so resolve, the provisions specified in the resolution shall come into force in their area on the day specified in that behalf in the resolution (which must not be before the expiration of the period of one month beginning with the day on which the resolution is passed).

(3) The provisions that may be specified in a resolution under subsection (2) above are—

> (a) sections 14, 16 and 17 below ; or

> (b) sections 15 to 17 below ; or

> (c) sections 14 to 17 below.

(4) A resolution which provides that section 15 below is to apply to the area of a local authority need not provide that it shall apply to all the descriptions of persons specified in subsection (1) of that section ; and if such a resolution does not provide that section 15 below is to apply to persons of all of those descriptions, the reference in subsection (2) above to the coming into force of provisions specified in the resolution shall be construed, in its application to section 15 below, and to

section 16 below so far as it has effect for the purposes of section 15 below, as a reference to the coming into force of those sections only in relation to persons of the description or descriptions specified in the resolution.

(5) If a resolution provides for the coming into force of section 15 below in relation to persons of more than one of the descriptions specified in subsection (1) of that section, it may provide that that section, and section 16 below so far as it has effect for the purposes of that section, shall come into force on different days in relation to persons of each of the descriptions specified in the resolution.

(6) A local authority shall publish notice that they have passed a resolution under this section in two consecutive weeks in a local newspaper circulating in their area.

(7) The first publication shall not be later than 28 days before the day specified in the resolution for the coming into force of the provisions specified in it in the local authority's area.

(8) The notice shall state which provisions are to come into force in that area.

(9) The notice shall also—

    (a) if the resolution provides for the coming into force of section 14 below, explain that that section applies to persons carrying on the practice of acupuncture ; and

    (b) if it provides for the coming into force of section 15 below, specify the descriptions of persons in relation to whom that section is to come into force.

(10) Any such notice shall state the general effect, in relation to persons to whom the provisions specified in the resolution will apply, of the coming into force of those provisions.

(11) In this Part of this Act " local authority " means—

    (a) the council of a district ;

    (b) the council of a London borough ; and

    (c) the Common Council of the City of London.

14.—(1) A person shall not in any area in which this section *Acupuncture.* is in force carry on the practice of acupuncture unless he is registered by the local authority for the area under this section.

(2) A person shall only carry on the practice of acupuncture in any area in which this section is in force in premises registered by the local authority for the area under this section ; but a person who is registered under this section does not contravene this

PART VIII

subsection merely because he sometimes visits people to give them treatment at their request.

(3) Subject to section 16(8)(*b*) below, on application for registration under this section a local authority shall register the applicant and the premises where he desires to practise and shall issue to the applicant a certificate of registration.

(4) An application for registration under this section shall be accompanied by such particulars as the local authority may reasonably require.

(5) The particulars that the local authority may require include, without prejudice to the generality of subsection (4) above,—

    (*a*) particulars as to the premises where the applicant desires to practise ; and

    (*b*) particulars of any conviction of the applicant under section 16 below,

but do not include information about individual people to whom the applicant has given treatment.

(6) A local authority may charge such reasonable fees as they may determine for registration under this section.

(7) A local authority may make byelaws for the purpose of securing—

    (*a*) the cleanliness of premises registered under this section and fittings in such premises ;

    (*b*) the cleanliness of persons so registered and persons assisting persons so registered in their practice ;

    (*c*) the cleansing and, so far as is appropriate, the sterilisation of instruments, materials and equipment used in connection with the practice of acupuncture.

(8) Nothing in this section shall extend to the practice of acupuncture by or under the supervision of a person who is registered as a medical practitioner or a dentist or to premises on which the practice of acupuncture is carried on by or under the supervision of such a person.

Tattooing, ear-piercing and electrolysis.

15.—(1) A person shall not in any area in which this section is in force carry on the business—

    (*a*) of tattooing ;

    (*b*) of ear-piercing ; or

    (*c*) of electrolysis,

unless he is registered by the local authority for the area under this section.

(2) A person shall only carry on a business mentioned in subsection (1) above in any area in which this section is in force in premises registered under this section for the carrying on of that business ; but a person who carries on the business of tattooing, ear-piercing or electrolysis and is registered under this section as carrying on that business does not contravene this subsection merely because he sometimes visits people at their request to tattoo them or, as the case may be, to pierce their ears or give them electrolysis.

(3) Subject to section 16(8)(*b*) below, on application for registration under this section a local authority shall register the applicant and the premises where he desires to carry on his business and shall issue to the applicant a certificate of registration.

(4) An application for registration under this section shall be accompanied by such particulars as the local authority may reasonably require.

(5) The particulars that the local authority may require include, without prejudice to the generality of subsection (4) above,—

　　(*a*) particulars as to the premises where the applicant desires to carry on his business ; and

　　(*b*) particulars of any conviction of the applicant under section 16 below,

but do not include information about individual people whom the applicant has tattooed or given electrolysis or whose ears he has pierced.

(6) A local authority may charge such reasonable fees as they may determine for registration under this section.

(7) A local authority may make byelaws for the purposes of securing—

　　(*a*) the cleanliness of premises registered under this section and fittings in such premises ;

　　(*b*) the cleanliness of persons so registered and persons assisting persons so registered in the business in respect of which they are registered ;

　　(*c*) the cleansing and, so far as is appropriate, the sterilisation of instruments, materials and equipment used in connection with a business in respect of which a person is registered under this section.

(8) Nothing in this section shall extend to the carrying on of a business such as is mentioned in subsection (1) above by or under the supervision of a person who is registered as a medical practitioner or to premises on which any such business is carried on by or under the supervision of such a person.

16.—(1) Any person who contravenes—

    (*a*) section 14(1) or (2) above ; or

    (*b*) section 15(1) or (2) above,

shall be guilty of an offence and liable on summary conviction to a fine not exceeding £200.

(2) Any person who contravenes a byelaw made—

    (*a*) under section 14(7) above ; or

    (*b*) under section 15(7) above,

shall be guilty of an offence and liable on summary conviction to a fine not exceeding £200.

(3) If a person registered under section 14 above is found guilty of an offence under subsection (2)(*a*) above, the court, instead of or in addition to imposing a fine under subsection (2) above, may order the suspension or cancellation of his registration.

(4) If a person registered under section 15 above is found guilty of an offence under subsection (2)(*b*) above, the court, instead of or in addition to imposing a fine under subsection (2) above, may order the suspension or cancellation of his registration.

(5) A court which orders the suspension or cancellation of a registration by virtue of subsection (3) or (4) above may also order the suspension or cancellation of any registration under section 14 or, as the case may be, 15 above of the premises in which the offence was committed, if they are occupied by the person found guilty of the offence.

(6) Subject to subsection (7) below, a court ordering the suspension or cancellation of registration by virtue of subsection (3) or (4) above may suspend the operation of the order until the expiration of the period prescribed by Crown Court Rules for giving notice of appeal to the Crown Court.

(7) If notice of appeal is given within the period so prescribed, an order under subsection (3) or (4) above shall be suspended until the appeal is finally determined or abandoned.

(8) Where the registration of any person under section 14 or 15 above is cancelled by order of the court under this section—

    (*a*) he shall within 7 days deliver up to the local authority the cancelled certificate of registration, and, if he fails to do so, he shall be guilty of an offence and liable on summary conviction to a fine not exceeding £50 and thereafter to a daily fine not exceeding £5 ; and

    (*b*) he shall not again be registered by the local authority under section 14 or, as the case may be, 15 above except with the consent of the magistrates' court which convicted him.

(9) A person registered under this Part of this Act shall keep a copy—

> (*a*) of any certificate of registration issued to him under this Part of this Act ; and
>
> (*b*) of any byelaws under this Part of this Act relating to the practice or business in respect of which he is so registered,

prominently displayed at the place where he carries on that practice or business.

(10) A person who contravenes subsection (9) above shall be guilty of an offence and liable on summary conviction to a fine not exceeding £50.

(11) It shall be a defence for a person charged with an offence under subsection (1), (2), (8) or (10) above to prove that he took all reasonable precautions and exercised all due diligence to avoid commission of the offence.

(12) Nothing in this Part of this Act applies to anything done to an animal.

17.—(1) Subject to subsection (2) below, an authorised officer of a local authority may enter any premises in the authority's area if he has reason to suspect that an offence under section 16 above is being committed there.

(2) The power conferred by this section may be exercised by an authorised officer of a local authority only if he has been granted a warrant by a justice of the peace.

(3) A justice may grant a warrant under this section only if he is satisfied—

> (*a*) that admission to any premises has been refused, or that refusal is apprehended, or that the case is one of urgency, or that an application for admission would defeat the object of the entry ; and
>
> (*b*) that there is reasonable ground for entry under this section.

(4) A warrant shall not be granted unless the justice is satisfied either that notice of the intention to apply for a warrant has been given to the occupier, or that the case is one of urgency, or that the giving of such notice would defeat the object of the entry.

(5) A warrant shall continue in force—

> (*a*) for seven days ; or
>
> (*b*) until the power conferred by this section has been exercised in accordance with the warrant,

whichever period is the shorter.

(6) Where an authorised officer of a local authority exercises the power conferred by this section, he shall produce his authority if required to do so by the occupier of the premises.

(7) Any person who without reasonable excuse refuses to permit an authorised officer of a local authority to exercise the power conferred by this section shall be guilty of an offence and shall for every such refusal be liable on summary conviction to a fine not exceeding £200.

Part IX

Sale of Food by Hawkers

Application of section 19.

18.—(1) A local authority may resolve that section 19 below is to apply to their area; and if a local authority do so resolve, that section shall come into force in their area on the day specified in that behalf in the resolution (which must not be before the expiration of the period of one month beginning with the day on which the resolution is passed).

(2) A local authority shall publish notice that they have passed a resolution under this section in two consecutive weeks in a local newspaper circulating in their area.

(3) The first publication shall not be later than 28 days before the day specified in the resolution for the coming into force of section 19 below in the local authority's area.

(4) The notice shall state the general effect of that section.

(5) In this Part of this Act " local authority " has the meaning assigned to it by section 85 of the Food and Drugs Act 1955.

1955 c. 16
(4 & 5 Eliz. 2).

Registration of hawkers of food and premises.

19.—(1) Subject to subsection (11) below, in any area in which this section is in force—

(a) no person shall hawk food unless he is registered by the local authority for the area under this section; and

(b) no premises shall be used as storage accommodation for any food intended for hawking unless the premises are so registered.

(2) For the purposes of this section a person hawks food if for private gain—

(a) he goes from place to place selling food or offering or exposing food for sale; or

(b) he sells food in the open air or offers or exposes food for sale in the open air,

unless he does so as part of, or as an activity ancillary to, a trade or business carried on by him or some other person on identifiable property.

(3) Subsection (1) above applies to a person who hawks food as an assistant to a person registered under this section unless—

(*a*) he is normally supervised when so doing ; or

(*b*) he assists only as a temporary replacement.

(4) Any person who without reasonable excuse contravenes subsection (1) above shall be guilty of an offence and liable on summary conviction to a fine not exceeding £200.

(5) It shall be a defence for a person charged with an offence under subsection (4) above to prove that he took all reasonable precautions and exercised all due diligence to avoid commission of the offence.

(6) An application for registration under this section shall be accompanied by such particulars as the local authority may reasonably require.

(7) The particulars that the local authority may require include, without prejudice to the generality of subsection (6) above, particulars as to any vehicle to be used by the applicant in connection with food hawking.

(8) A local authority may charge such reasonable fees as they may determine for registration under this section.

(9) An application for premises to be registered under this section shall be made by the person intending to use them as storage accommodation.

(10) On application for registration under this section the local authority shall register the applicant and, if the application is for the registration of premises, those premises, and shall issue to the applicant a certificate of registration.

(11) This section shall not apply—

(*a*) to the sale or offer or exposure for sale of food—

(i) at a market or fair the right to hold which was acquired by virtue of a grant (including a presumed grant) or acquired or established by virtue of an enactment or order ;

(ii) at a notified temporary market ; or

(iii) at a notified pleasure fair ; or

(*b*) to the sale or offer or exposure for sale of food in or from premises exempt from registration by section 16(3A) of the Food and Drugs Act 1955 or of food prepared or manufactured on such premises ; or   1955 c. 16
(4 & 5 Eliz. 2).

(*c*) to the sale or offer or exposure for sale of food by way of street trading at any place in the area of a local authority by a person whom the local authority have authorised under any enactment to engage in such trading in their area (whether or not they have authorised him to trade at the place where the food was sold or offered or exposed for sale) or by a person acting as an assistant to a person so authorised ; or

(d) to premises used as storage accommodation for food prepared for sale as mentioned in paragraphs (a) to (c) above ; or

(e) to the sale or offer or exposure for sale of food in containers of such materials and so closed as to exclude all risks of contamination.

(12) In this section—

" food " means food and ingredients of food for human consumption, including—

(a) drink (other than water) ;

(b) chewing gum and like products,

but does not include—

(i) milk and cream ;

(ii) live animals or birds ;

(iii) articles or substances used only as drugs ;

1961 c. 64.
" notified pleasure fair " means a pleasure fair, as defined in subsection (2)(a) of section 75 of the Public Health Act 1961, notice of which has been given to the local authority in accordance with byelaws under that section ;

" notified temporary market " means a temporary market notice of which has been given to the local authority in accordance with section 37(2) below or any other enactment regulating such markets.

PART X

HIGHWAYS

Highway amenities.
20. The enactments specified in Schedule 5 to this Act shall have effect subject to the amendments there specified, being amendments concerning amenities for certain highways.

Prosecutions for offences, relating to works in street.
1950 c. 39.
21.—(1) In section 30 of the Public Utilities Street Works Act 1950 (enforcement)—

(a) in subsection (2), for the words " Proceedings for the enforcement of " there shall be substituted the words " Subject to subsection (2A) of this section, proceedings for an offence under " ; and

(*b*) the following subsection shall be inserted after that sub-
     section—

>   " (2A) A constable may take proceedings for an
>   offence under section 8 of this Act without the
>   consent of the Attorney General.".

(2) In section 312 of the Highways Act 1980 (restriction on   1980 c. 66.
institution of proceedings)—

(*a*) in subsection (1), for the word " Proceedings " there
     shall be substituted the words " Subject to subsection (3)
     below, proceedings " ; and

(*b*) the following subsection shall be inserted after subsec-
     tion (2)—

>   " (3) A constable may take proceedings—
>
>>   (*a*) for an offence under paragraph (*b*) of section
>>   171(6) above ; or
>>
>>   (*b*) for an offence under paragraph (*c*) of that
>>   subsection consisting of failure to perform
>>   a duty imposed by section 171(5)(*a*) above ;
>>   or
>>
>>   (*c*) for an offence under section 174 above,
>
>   without the consent of the Attorney General.".

22.—(1) The following paragraph shall be substituted for the   Control of
first paragraph of subsection (1) of section 179 of the Highways   construction
Act 1980 (by virtue of which no person may construct a vault,   under streets.
arch or cellar under any street in Greater London or the carriage-
way of any street outside Greater London without the consent
of the appropriate authority)—

>   " No person shall construct works to which this section
>   applies under any part of a street without the consent of
>   the appropriate authority, and the authority may by notice
>   served on a person who has constructed such works in
>   contravention of this section require him to remove them,
>   or to alter or deal with them in such a manner as may be
>   specified in the notice.".

(2) The words " works to which this section applies " shall be
substituted for the words " a vault, arch or cellar " where
occurring in subsections (3) and (4) of that section.

(3) The following subsections shall be substituted for subsection (5) of that section—

>   " (5) As soon as may be after an authority consent to
>   the construction of works to which this section applies
>   under a street they shall give notice of their consent to

PART X

any public utility undertakers having any apparatus under the street.

(6) Subject to subsection (7) below, the works to which this section applies are—

    (*a*) any part of a building ; and

    (*b*) without prejudice to the generality of paragraph (*a*) above, a vault, arch or cellar, whether forming part of a building or not.

1950 c. 39.

(7) This section does not apply to code-regulated works, as defined in section 1(5) of the Public Utilities Street Works Act 1950.".

Control of road-side sales.

1980 c. 66.

23. The following section shall be inserted after section 147 of the Highways Act 1980—

" Road-side sales.

147A.—(1) Subject to subsection (4) below, no person shall, for the purpose of selling anything, or offering or exposing anything for sale, use any stall or similar structure or any container or vehicle, kept or placed on—

    (*a*) the verge of a trunk road or a principal road ;

    (*b*) a lay-by on any such road ; or

    (*c*) unenclosed land within 15 metres of any part of any such road,

where its presence or its use for that purpose causes or is likely to cause danger on the road or interrupts or is likely to interrupt any user of the road.

(2) Any person who contravenes this section shall be guilty of an offence and liable on summary conviction to a fine not exceeding £200.

(3) It shall be a defence for a person charged with an offence under this section to prove that he took all reasonable precautions and exercised all due diligence to avoid commission of the offence.

(4) This section does not apply—

    (*a*) to the sale or offer or exposure for sale of things from or on a vehicle which is used only for the purposes of itinerant trading with the occupiers of premises, or is used only for that purpose and for purposes other than trading ;

    (*b*) to the sale or offer or exposure for sale of newspapers ;

    (*c*) to anything done at a market in respect

of which tolls, stallages or rents are payable ; or

(*d*) to the sale or offer or exposure for sale of anything by way of street trading which has been authorised under Schedule 4 to the Local Government (Miscellaneous Provisions) Act 1982 or under any local enactment which makes provision similar to that made by that Schedule, either by the person so authorised or by a person acting as assistant to the person so authorised.".

PART XI

PUBLIC HEALTH, ETC.

24. The following section shall be substituted for section 56 of the Public Health Act 1936—

Paving of yards and passages.
1936 c. 49.

" Yards and passages to be paved and drained.   **56.**—(1) If any court or yard appertaining to, or any passage giving access to, buildings to which this section applies is not so formed, flagged, asphalted or paved or is not provided with such works on, above, or below its surface, as to allow of the satisfactory drainage of its surface or subsoil to a proper outfall, the local authority may by notice require any person who is the owner of any of the buildings to execute all such works as may be necessary to remedy the defect.

(2) The buildings to which this section applies are houses and industrial and commercial buildings.

(3) The provisions of Part XII of this Act with respect to appeals against and the enforcement of notices requiring the execution of works shall apply in relation to any notice given under subsection (1) of this section.

(4) This section shall apply in relation to any court, yard or passage which is used in common by the occupiers of two or more houses, or a house and a commercial or industrial building but which is not a highway maintainable at the public expense.".

25.—(1) The following subsections shall be substituted for subsections (1) and (2) of section 64 of the Public Health Act 1936 (passing or rejection of plans, and power to retain plans, etc.)—

Building regulations.

" (1) Where plans of any proposed work are, in accordance with building regulations, deposited with a local authority, it shall be the duty of the local authority, subject to the provisions of any other section of this Act which expressly requires or authorises them in certain cases to reject plans, to pass the plans unless they either are defective or show that the proposed work would contravene any of the building regulations.

(1A) If the plans—

(a) are defective ; or

(b) show that the proposed work would contravene any of the building regulations,

the local authority—

(i) may reject the plans ; or

(ii) subject to subsection (1C) below, may pass them subject to either or both of the conditions set out in subsection (1B) below.

(1B) The conditions mentioned in subsection (1A) above are—

(a) that such modifications as the local authority may specify shall be made in the deposited plans ; and

(b) that such further plans as they may specify shall be deposited.

(1C) A local authority may only pass plans subject to a condition such as is specified in subsection (1B) above if the person by whom or on whose behalf they were deposited—

(a) has requested them to do so ; or

(b) has consented to their doing so.

(1D) A request or consent under subsection (1C) above must be in writing.

(2) The authority shall within the prescribed period from the deposit of the plans give notice to the person by whom or on whose behalf they were deposited whether they have been passed or rejected.

(2A) A notice that plans have been rejected shall specify the defects on account of which, or the regulation or section of this Act for non-conformity with which, or under the authority of which, they have been rejected.

(2B) A notice that plans have been passed—

(a) shall specify any condition subject to which they have been passed ; and

(b) shall state that the passing of the plans operates as an approval of them only for the purposes of the requirements of the regulations and of any such section of this Act as is referred to in subsection (1) above.".

(2) In section 65(4) of that Act (by virtue of which, among other things, in any case where plans were deposited, a local authority may not give a notice requiring the pulling down, removal etc. of the work if the plans were passed by the authority) after the word " deposited " there shall be inserted the words " and the work was shown on them ".

(3) This section, and section 47 below, so far as it relates to section 63 of the Health and Safety at Work etc. Act 1974, shall come into operation on such day as the Secretary of State may by order made by statutory instrument appoint.

26.—(1) In section 92(1)(*d*) of the Public Health Act 1936 (by virtue of which statutory nuisances include any dust or effluvia caused by any trade, business, manufacture or process, being prejudicial to the health of, or a nuisance to, the inhabitants of the neighbourhood) for the words from " being " to " neighbourhood " there shall be substituted the words " injurious, or likely to cause injury, to the public health or a nuisance ".

(2) In section 16(1) of the Clean Air Act 1956 (by virtue of which smoke of certain descriptions is deemed to be a statutory nuisance for the purposes of Part III of the Public Health Act 1936 if it is a nuisance to the inhabitants of the neighbourhood) for the words " a nuisance to the inhabitants of the neighbourhood " there shall be substituted the words " injurious, or likely to cause injury, to the public health or a nuisance ".

27.—(1) The following section shall be substituted for sections 17 and 18 of the Public Health Act 1961—

" Powers to repair drains etc. and to remedy stopped-up drains etc.

17.—(1) If it appears to a local authority that a drain, private sewer, water-closet, waste pipe or soil pipe—

> (*a*) is not sufficiently maintained and kept in good repair, and
>
> (*b*) can be sufficiently repaired at a cost not exceeding £250,

the local authority may, after giving not less than seven days notice to the person or persons concerned, cause the drain, private sewer, water-closet or pipe to be repaired and, subject to subsections (7) and (8) below, recover the expenses reasonably incurred in so doing, so far as they do not exceed £250, from the person or persons concerned, in such proportions, if there is more than one such person, as the local authority may determine.

(2) In subsection (1) above " person concerned " means—

> (a) in relation to a water-closet, waste pipe or soil pipe, the owner or occupier of the premises on which it is situated, and
>
> (b) in relation to a drain or private sewer, any person owning any premises drained by means of it and also, in the case of a sewer, the owner of the sewer.

(3) If it appears to a local authority that on any premises a drain, private sewer, water-closet, waste pipe or soil pipe is stopped up, they may by notice in writing require the owner or occupier of the premises to remedy the defect within forty-eight hours from the service of the notice.

(4) If a notice under subsection (3) of this section is not complied with, the local authority may themselves carry out the work necessary to remedy the defect and, subject to subsections (7) and (8) below, may recover the expenses reasonably incurred in so doing from the person on whom the notice was served.

(5) Where the expenses recoverable by a local authority under subsection (1) or (4) of this section do not exceed £10, the local authority may, if they think fit, remit the payment of the expenses.

(6) In proceedings to recover expenses under this section—

> (a) where the expenses were incurred under subsection (1) of this section, the court—
>
> > (i) shall inquire whether the local authority were justified in concluding that the drain, private sewer, water-closet, waste pipe or soil pipe was not sufficiently maintained and kept in good repair ; and
> >
> > (ii) may inquire whether any apportionment of expenses by the local authority under that subsection was fair ;
>
> (b) where the expenses were incurred under subsection (4) of this section, the court may inquire—
>
> > (i) whether any requirement contained in a notice served under subsection (3) of this section was reasonable ; and

(ii) whether the expenses ought to be borne wholly or in part by some person other than the defendant in the proceedings.

(7) Subject to subsection (8) below, the court may make such order concerning the expenses or their apportionment as appears to the court to be just.

(8) Where the court determines that the local authority were not justified in concluding that a drain, private sewer, water-closet, waste pipe or soil pipe was not sufficiently maintained and kept in good repair, the local authority shall not recover expenses incurred by them under subsection (1) of this section.

(9) The court shall not revise an apportionment unless it is satisfied that all persons affected by the apportionment or by an order made by virtue of subsection (6)(*b*)(ii) above have had notice of the proceedings and an opportunity of being heard.

(10) Subject to subsection (11) of this section, the provisions of subsection (1) of this section shall not authorise a local authority to carry out works on land which belongs to any statutory undertakers and is held or used by them for the purposes of their undertaking.

(11) Subsection (10) of this section does not apply to houses, or to buildings used as offices or showrooms, other than buildings so used which form part of a railway station.

(12) The Secretary of State may by order made by statutory instrument increase any amount specified in this section.

(13) Nothing in an order made under subsection (12) of this section shall apply to a notice given under this section before the commencement of the order.

(14) A statutory instrument containing an order under subsection (12) of this section shall be subject to annulment in pursuance of a resolution of either House of Parliament.

(15) The provisions of this section shall be without prejudice to section 39 of the Public Health Act 1936 (which empowers a local authority to serve notices as regards defective drains).". 1936 c. 49.

(2) Section 24 of the Greater London Council (General Powers) Act 1967 (which makes certain modifications to sections 17 and 18 of the Public Health Act 1961 in their application to Greater London) is hereby repealed. 1967 c. xx.

1961 c. 64.

PART XI
Control of
demolitions.
1961 c. 64.

1957 c. 56.

1967 c. 9.

28.—(1) The following sections shall be substituted for section 29 of the Public Health Act 1961 (powers of local authority in relation to demolitions)—

" Duty to
give local
authority
notice of
intended
demolition.

29.—(1) This section applies to any demolition of the whole or part of a building except—

    (*a*) a demolition in pursuance of a demolition order made under the Housing Act 1957 ; and

    (*b*) a demolition—

        (i) of an internal part of a building where the building is occupied, and it is intended that it should continue to be occupied ; or

        (ii) of a building which has a cubic content (as ascertained by external measurement) of not more than 1750 cubic feet, or, where a greenhouse, conservatory, shed or prefabricated garage forms part of a larger building, of that greenhouse, conservatory, shed or prefabricated garage ; or

        (iii) without prejudice to sub-paragraph (ii) above, of an agricultural building (as defined in section 26 of the General Rate Act 1967) unless it is contiguous to another building which is not itself an agricultural building or a building of a kind mentioned in that sub-paragraph.

(2) No person shall begin a demolition to which this section applies unless—

    (*a*) he has given the local authority notice of his intention to do so ; and

    (*b*) either—

        (i) the local authority have served a notice on him under section 29A of this Act ; or

        (ii) the relevant period (as defined in that section) has expired.

(3) A notice under this section shall be in writing and shall specify the building to which it relates and the works of demolition intended to be carried out, and it shall be the duty of a person giving such a notice to a local authority to send or give a copy of it—

    (*a*) to the occupier of any building adjacent to the building ;

(b) to the British Gas Corporation ; and

(c) to the Area Electricity Board in whose area the building is situated.

(4) A person who contravenes subsection (2) above shall be guilty of an offence and liable on summary conviction to a fine not exceeding £500.

29A.—(1) A local authority may serve a notice under this section—

Power of
local
authority
to serve
notice
concerning
demolition.

(a) on any person on whom a demolition order has been served under the Housing Act 1957 ; 1957 c. 56.

(b) on any person who appears to them not to be intending to comply with an order made under section 58 of the Public Health Act 1936 or a notice served under section 27 of this Act ; and 1936 c. 49.

(c) on any person who appears to them to have begun or to be intending to begin a demolition to which section 29 above otherwise applies.

(2) Nothing contained in a notice under this section shall prejudice or affect the operation of any of the relevant statutory provisions, as defined in section 53(1) of the Health and Safety at Work etc. Act 1974 ; and accordingly, if any requirement of such a notice is inconsistent with any requirement imposed by or under the said Act of 1974, the latter requirement shall prevail. 1974 c. 37.

(3) Where—

(a) a person has given a notice under section 29 of this Act ; or

(b) the local authority have served a demolition order on a person under the Housing Act 1957,

a notice under this section may only be served on the person in question within the relevant period.

(4) In this section and section 29 of this Act " the relevant period " means—

(a) in a case such as is mentioned in paragraph (a) of subsection (3) above, six weeks from the giving of the notice under section 29 of this Act, or such longer period as the person who gave that notice may in writing allow ; and (*b*) in a case such as is mentioned in paragraph (*b*) of that subsection, seven days after the local authority served a copy of the demolition order in accordance with the Housing Act 1957, or such longer period as the person on whom the copy was served may in writing allow.

(5) It shall be the duty of the local authority to send or give a copy of a notice under this section to the owner and occupier of any building adjacent to the building to which the notice relates.

(6) It shall also be the duty of the local authority to send or give a copy of a notice under this section—

(*a*) if it contains a requirement such as is specified in paragraph (*h*) of section 29B(1) of this Act, to the statutory undertakers concerned ; and

(*b*) if it contains any such requirement as is specified in paragraph (*j*) of that section—

(i) to the fire authority, if they are not themselves the fire authority ; and

(ii) to the Health and Safety Executive, if the premises are special premises.

(7) In this section and section 29B of this Act—

" fire authority " has the meaning assigned to it by section 43(1) of the Fire Precautions Act 1971 ; and

" special premises " means premises for which a fire certificate is required by virtue of regulations under the Health and Safety at Work etc. Act 1974.

Contents of notices under section 29A.

29B.—(1) A notice under section 29A(1) of this Act may require the person on whom it is served—

(*a*) to shore up any building adjacent to the building to which the notice relates ;

(*b*) to weatherproof any surfaces of an adjacent building which are exposed by the demolition ;

(*c*) to repair and make good any damage to an adjacent building caused by the demolition or by the negligent act or omission of any person engaged in it ;

(*d*) to remove material or rubbish resulting from the demolition and clearance of the site ;

(*e*) to disconnect and seal, at such points as the local authority may reasonably require, any sewer or drain in or under the building ;

(*f*) to remove any such sewer or drain and seal any sewer or drain with which the sewer or drain to be removed is connected ;

(*g*) to make good to the satisfaction of the local authority the surface of the ground disturbed by anything done under paragraph (*e*) or paragraph (*f*) of this subsection ;

(*h*) to make arrangements with the relevant statutory undertakers for the disconnection of the supply of gas, electricity and water to the building ;

(*j*) to make such arrangements with regard to the burning of structures or materials on the site as may be reasonably required—

　(i) if the building is or forms part of special premises, by the Health and Safety Executive and the fire authority ; and

　(ii) in any other case, by the fire authority ; and

(*k*) to take such steps relating to the conditions subject to which the demolition is to be undertaken and the condition in which the site is to be left on completion of the demolition as the local authority may consider reasonably necessary for the protection of the public and the preservation of public amenity.

(2) No one shall be required under paragraph (*c*), (*e*) or (*f*) of subsection (1) of this section to carry out any work in land outside the premises on which the works of demolition are being carried out if he has no right to carry out that work, but, subject to the provisions of Part XII of the Public Health Act 1936 with respect to the breaking open of streets, the person undertaking the demolition, or the local authority acting in his default, may break open any street for the purpose of complying with any such requirement.

(3) Nothing in subsection (1) or (2) of this section shall be construed as authorising any interference with apparatus or works of statutory undertakers authorised by any enactment to carry on an undertaking for the supply of electricity, gas or water.

(4) Without prejudice to the generality of subsection (3) of this section, nothing in subsection (1) or (2) of this section shall be construed as exempting any person—

(a) from the obligation to obtain any consent required under section 67 of Schedule 3 to the Water Act 1945 (which relates to interference with valves and other apparatus) or section 68 of that Schedule (which relates to alterations to supply pipes and other apparatus) ; or

(b) from criminal liability under any enactment relating to the supply of gas or electricity ; or

(c) from the requirements of regulations under section 31 of the Gas Act 1972 (public safety).

(5) Before a person complies with any requirement under paragraph (e) or paragraph (f) of subsection (1) of this section he shall give at least 48 hours notice to the local authority, and before he complies with paragraph (g) of that subsection he shall give at least 24 hours notice to the local authority ; and a person who fails to comply with this subsection shall be liable on summary conviction to a fine not exceeding £50.

29C.—(1) The provisions of Part XII of the Public Health Act 1936 with respect to appeals against and the enforcement of notices requiring the execution of works shall apply in relation to any notice given under section 29A of this Act.

(2) Among the grounds on which an appeal may be brought under section 290(3) of the Public Health Act 1936 against such a notice shall be—

(a) in the case of a notice requiring an adjacent building to be shored up, that the owner of the building is not entitled to the support of that building by the building which is being demolished, and ought to pay, or contribute towards, the expenses of shoring it up ; and

(b) in the case of a notice requiring any surfaces of an adjacent building to be weatherproofed, that the owner of the adjacent building ought to pay, or contribute towards, the expenses of weatherproofing those surfaces.

(3) Where the grounds on which an appeal under
the said section 290 is brought include any ground
specified in subsection (2) of this section, the appellant shall serve a copy of his notice of appeal on
the person or persons referred to in that ground of
appeal, and on the hearing of the appeal the court
may make such order as it thinks fit in respect of
the payment of, or contribution towards, the cost
of the works by any such person, or as to how any
expenses which may be recoverable by the local
authority are to be borne between the appellant
and any such person.".

(2) Section 29 of the Public Health Act 1961 shall continue 1961 c. 64.
to have effect as if this section had not been enacted in a case
where a notice under subsection (1) of that section was served
before the commencement of this section.

29.—(1) The section applies where it appears to a local autho- Protection of
rity— buildings.

   (*a*) that any building in their area is unoccupied ; or

   (*b*) that the occupier of a building in their area is tempor-
      arily absent from it.

(2) Where this section applies and it appears to the local
authority that the building—

   (*a*) is not effectively secured against unauthorised entry ; or

   (*b*) is likely to become a danger to public health,

the local authority may undertake works in connection with the
building for the purpose of preventing unauthorised entry to it,
or, as the case may be, for the purpose of preventing it becoming a danger to public health.

(3) In this section and sections 30 and 32 " building " includes
structure.

(4) Subject to subsection (5) below, in this section, the
sections mentioned in subsection (3) above and section 31 below
" local authority " means a district council, a London borough
council and the Common Council of the City of London.

(5) This section and the other sections mentioned in subsection (4) above shall have effect, in relation to a building in
respect of which—

   (*a*) an undertaking that it shall not be used for human
      habitation is in force by virtue of section 16(4) of the
      Housing Act 1957 or paragraph 5 of Schedule 24 to 1957 c. 56.
      the Housing Act 1980 ; or 1980 c. 51.

   (*b*) a closing order is in force by virtue of section 17, 26
      or 35 of the Housing Act 1957, section 26 of the

Housing Act 1961 or paragraph 6 of Schedule 24 to the Housing Act 1980,

and which is situated in an area which in pursuance of section 40 of the Housing Act 1969 or section 49 of the Housing Act 1974 is for the time being declared by the Greater London Council to be a general improvement area or a housing action area, as if for the words " the local authority ", in each place where they occur, there were substituted the words " the Greater London Council ".

(6) Subject to subsection (8) below, before undertaking any works under subsection (2) above, other than works on land to which section 30 below applies, a local authority shall serve a notice that they propose to undertake works under this section in connection with the building on each owner or occupier of the building.

(7) A notice under subsection (6) above shall specify the works in connection with the building which the local authority propose to undertake.

(8) A local authority need not give any such notice where they consider—

(a) that it is necessary to undertake works immediately in order to secure the building against unauthorised entry or to prevent it from becoming a danger to public health ; or

(b) that it is not reasonably practicable to ascertain the name and address of an owner or to trace the whereabouts of an occupier who is absent from the building.

(9) A local authority shall not undertake works specified in a notice under subsection (6) above before the expiry of the period of 48 hours from the service of the notice.

(10) For the purpose of exercising the power conferred on a local authority by this section any person duly authorised in writing by the authority may enter—

(a) the building in connection with which works are to be undertaken ;

(b) any land that appears to the local authority to be appurtenant to the building ; and

(c) any other land if—

(i) it appears to the local authority to be unoccupied ; and

(ii) it would be impossible to undertake the works without entering it.

(11) Where the local authority undertake any works under subsection (2) above, they may recover the expenses reasonably incurred in so doing from any person to whom notice was given

under subsection (6) above or subsection (2) of section 30 below
or to whom notice would have been required to be given but
for subsection (8) of this section or subsection (4) of that section.

(12) Section 293 of the Public Health Act 1936 shall have 1936 c. 49.
effect in relation to the recovery of expenses under this section as
it has effect in relation to the recovery of a sum which a council
are entitled to recover under that Act and with respect to the
recovery of which provision is not made by any other section of
that Act.

(13) In proceedings to recover expenses under this section the
court may inquire whether the expenses ought to be borne wholly
or in part by some person other than the defendant in the proceedings, and the court may make such order concerning the
expenses of their apportionment as appears to the court to be
just.

30.—(1) This section applies to operational land—   Buildings on
    (*a*) of the British Railways Board (in this section referred to operational
        as " the Board ") ; or   land of
British
    (*b*) of persons (in this section referred to as " the statutory Railways
        undertakers ") authorised by any enactment to carry on Board and
        an undertaking for the generation or supply of electricity certain
        or the supply of gas or water.   statutory
undertakers.

(2) Subject to subsection (4) below, before undertaking any
works under section 29(2) above on land to which this section
applies a local authority shall serve notice that they propose to
undertake works under that section in connection with the
building—
    (*a*) on the Board, if the works which they propose to under-
        take will be undertaken on operational land of the
        Board ; and
    (*b*) in any other case, on the statutory undertakers on whose
        operational land the works will be undertaken.

(3) A notice under subsection (2) above shall specify the works
which the local authority propose to undertake.

(4) A local authority need not give any such notice where they
consider that it is necessary to undertake works immediately in
order to secure a building against unauthorised entry or to prevent it from becoming a danger to public health.

(5) A local authority shall not undertake works specified in a
notice under subsection (2) above before the expiry of the period
of 48 hours from the service of the notice on the Board or the
statutory undertakers.

(6) In carrying out any works under section 29(2) above on
land to which this section applies a local authority shall comply

with any reasonable requirement which the Board or, as the case may be, the statutory undertakers may impose for the protection or safety of their undertaking.

(7) In this section " operational land " means, in relation to the Board or the statutory undertakers—

    (*a*) land which is used for the purpose of carrying on their undertaking ; and

    (*b*) land in which an interest is held for that purpose,

not being land which, in respect of its nature and situation, is comparable rather with land in general than with land which is used, or in which interests are held, for the purpose of carrying on such undertakings.

31. (1) A person on whom a notice is served under section 29 or 30 above may appeal against the notice to the county court.

(2) No such appeal may be brought after the expiry of the period of 21 days from the date on which the notice was served.

(3) The ground of any such appeal may be—

    (*a*) that the works specified in the notice were not authorised by section 29 above ; or

    (*b*) that they were unnecessary ; or

    (*c*) that it was otherwise unreasonable for the local authority to undertake them.

(4) If such an appeal is brought, the local authority—

    (*a*) shall cease from any works specified in the notice which they have commenced ; and

    (*b*) shall not commence any further works so specified except as provided by subsection (7) below.

(5) The court may make an order confirming or quashing the notice or varying it in such manner as it thinks fit.

(6) An order under subsection (5) above may make such provision as to the recovery of expenses arising in connection with the works specified in the notice as the court thinks fit.

(7) Upon the confirmation or variation of a notice the local authority may commence or recommence the works authorised by the notice as originally served or, as the case may be, as varied by the order of the court.

32.—(1) If a local authority seek to recover expenses incurred in undertaking works under section 29(2) above in connection with a building—

    (*a*) where the building is on land to which section 30 above applies, from the Board or the statutory undertakers ; or

(b) in any other case, from an occupier of the building ; and

(c) they did not serve notice of their proposal to undertake the works under section 29(6) or 30(2) above on the Board or, as the case may be, the statutory undertakers or that occupier,

the person from whom they seek to recover the expenses may apply to the county court for a declaration—

    (i) that the works undertaken in connection with the building were unnecessary ; or

    (ii) that it was otherwise unreasonable for the local authority to undertake them.

(2) No such application may be made after the expiry of the period of 21 days from the date on which the local authority first requested payment of the expenses.

(3) If the court makes a declaration under subsection (1) above, it may make such order as it thinks fit in respect of the payment of the expenses incurred in connection with the works.

PART XII

MISCELLANEOUS

33.—(1) The provisions of this section shall apply if a principal council (in the exercise of their powers under section 111 of the Local Government Act 1972 or otherwise) and any other person are parties to an instrument under seal which—

    (a) is executed for the purpose of securing the carrying out of works on or facilitating the development or regulating the use of land in the council's area in which the other person has an interest ; or

    (b) is executed for the purpose of facilitating the development or regulating the use of land outside the council's area in which the other person has an interest ; or

    (c) is otherwise connected with land in or outside the council's area in which the other person has an interest.

Enforceability by local authorities of certain covenants relating to land.
1972 c. 70.

(2) If, in a case where this section applies,—

    (a) the instrument contains a covenant on the part of any person having an interest in land, being a covenant to carry out any works or do any other thing on or in relation to that land, and

    (b) the instrument defines the land to which the covenant relates, being land in which that person has an interest at the time the instrument is executed, and

        (c) the covenant is expressed to be one to which this section or section 126 of the Housing Act 1974 (which is superseded by this section) applies,

the covenant shall be enforceable (without any limit of time) against any person deriving title from the original covenantor in respect of his interest in any of the land defined as mentioned in paragraph (b) above and any person deriving title under him in respect of any lesser interest in that land as if that person had also been an original covenanting party in respect of the interest for the time being held by him.

(3) Without prejudice to any other method of enforcement of a covenant falling within subsection (2) above, if there is a breach of the covenant in relation to any of the land to which the covenant relates, then, subject to subsection (4) below, the principal council who are a party to the instrument in which the covenant is contained may—

        (a) enter on the land concerned and carry out the works or do anything which the covenant requires to be carried out or done or remedy anything which has been done and which the covenant required not to be done ; and

        (b) recover from any person against whom the covenant is enforceable (whether by virtue of subsection (2) above or otherwise) any expenses incurred by the council in exercise of their powers under this subsection.

(4) Before a principal council exercise their powers under subsection (3)(a) above they shall give not less than 21 days notice of their intention to do so to any person—

        (a) who has for the time being an interest in the land on or in relation to which the works are to be carried out or other thing is to be done ; and

        (b) against whom the covenant is enforceable (whether by virtue of subsection (2) above or otherwise).

(5) If a person against whom a covenant is enforceable by virtue of subsection (2) above requests the principal council to supply him with a copy of the covenant, it shall be their duty to do so free of charge.

(6) The Public Health Act 1936 shall have effect as if any reference to that Act in—

        (a) section 283 of that Act (notices to be in writing ; forms of notices, etc.),

        (b) section 288 of that Act (penalty for obstructing execution of Act), and

(c) section 291 of that Act (certain expenses recoverable from owners to be a charge on the premises ; power to order payment by instalments),

included a reference to subsections (1) to (4) above and as if any reference in those sections of that Act—

    (i) to a local authority were a reference to a principal council ; and

    (ii) to the owner of the premises were a reference to the holder of an interest in land.

(7) Section 16 of the Local Government (Miscellaneous Provisions) Act 1976 shall have effect as if references to a local authority and to functions conferred on a local authority by any enactment included respectively references to such a board as is mentioned in subsection (9) below and to functions of such a board under this section. *1976 c. 57.*

(8) In its application to a notice or other document authorised to be given or served under subsection (4) above or by virtue of any provision of the Public Health Act 1936 specified in subsection (6) above, section 233 of the Local Government Act 1972 (service of notices by local authorities) shall have effect as if any reference in that section to a local authority included a reference to the Common Council of the City of London and such a board as is mentioned in the following subsection. *1936 c. 49.* *1972 c. 70.*

(9) In this section—

    (a) " principal council " means the council of a county, district or London borough, a board constituted in pursuance of section 1 of the Town and Country Planning Act 1971 or reconstituted in pursuance of Schedule 17 to the Local Government Act 1972, the Common Council of the City of London or the Greater London Council ; and *1971 c. 78.*

    (b) " area " in relation to such a board means the district for which the board is constituted or reconstituted.

(10) Section 126 of the Housing Act 1974 (which is superseded by this section) shall cease to have effect ; but in relation to a covenant falling within subsection (2) of that section, section 1(1)(d) of the Local Land Charges Act 1975 shall continue to have effect as if the reference to the commencement of that Act had been a reference to the coming into operation of the said section 126. *1974 c. 44.* *1975 c. 76.*

34. In the Local Land Charges Act 1975—

    (a) the following subsection shall be substituted for subsection (3) of section 3 (which provides for the keeping

Local land charges registers— computerisation etc.

of local land charges registers and indexes of such registers)—

" (3) Neither a local land charges register nor an index such as is mentioned in subsection (2)(*b*) above need be kept in documentary form.";

(*b*) the following subsection shall be inserted after subsection (1) of section 8 (personal searches)—

" (1A) If a local land charges register is kept otherwise than in documentary form, the entitlement of a person to search in it is satisfied if the registering authority makes the portion of it which he wishes to examine available for inspection in visible and legible form.";

(*c*) in subsection (2) of that section, for the words " subsection (1) " there shall be substituted the words " subsections (1) and (1A) ";

(*d*) in section 10(1) (compensation)—

(i) the following paragraph shall be inserted after paragraph (*a*)—

" (*aa*) in a case where the appropriate local land charges register is kept otherwise than in documentary form and a material personal search of that register was made in respect of the land in question before the relevant time, if the entitlement to search in that register conferred by section 8 above was not satisfied as mentioned in subsection (1A) of that section ; or " ; and

(ii) the words " in consequence " shall be substituted for the words from " by reason " onwards ; and

(*e*) the following subsection shall be inserted after subsection (1) of section 16 (interpretation)—

" (1A) Any reference in this Act to an office copy of an entry includes a reference to the reproduction of an entry in a register kept otherwise than in documentary form.".

Acquisition of land etc. by Planning Boards.
1980 c. 65.

1971 c. 78.

1972 c. 70.

35. In section 119 of the Local Government, Planning and Land Act 1980—

(*a*) in subsection (1), for the words " The Peak Park Joint Planning Board and the Lake District Special Planning Board " there shall be substituted the words " A board constituted in pursuance of section 1 of the Town and Country Planning Act 1971 or reconstituted in pursuance of Schedule 17 to the Local Government Act 1972."

(*b*) in subsection (2), for the words " The Boards " there
shall be substituted the words " Any such board " ;

(*c*) in subsection (3), for the words " the Boards were local
authorities " there shall be substituted the words " any
such board were a local authority " ; and

(*d*) the following subsection shall be added after that subsection—

" (4) On being authorised to do so by the Secretary
of State any such board shall have, for any purpose
for which by virtue of this section they may acquire
land compulsorily, the power to purchase compulsorily rights over land not in existence when their
compulsory purchase is authorised which section 13
of the Local Government (Miscellaneous Provisions) 1976 c. 57.
Act 1976 confers on the local authorities to whom
subsection (1) of that section applies, and subsections
(2) to (5) of that section shall accordingly apply to
the purchase of rights under this subsection as they
apply to the purchase of rights under the said subsection (1).".

36. In the Town and Country Planning Act 1971— Control of
fly-posting.
(*a*) the following section shall be inserted after section 109— 1971 c. 78.
" Power to **109A.**—(1) Subject to subsections (2) and (3) of
remove or
obliterate this section, the council of a district or a London
placards borough may remove or obliterate any placard or
and
posters. poster—

(*a*) which is displayed in their area ; and

(*b*) which, in their opinion, is so displayed in
contravention of the advertisement regulations.

(2) Subsection (1) of this section does not authorise
the removal or obliteration of a placard or poster
displayed within a building to which there is no
public right of access.

(3) Subject to subsection (4) of this section, a
council shall not exercise any power conferred by
subsection (1) of this section where a placard or
poster identifies the person who displayed it or
caused it to be displayed unless they have first
given him notice in writing—

(*a*) that in their opinion it is displayed in contravention of the advertisement regulations ;
and

(*b*) that they intend to remove or obliterate it on the expiry of a period specified in the notice.

(4) A council may exercise a power conferred by subsection (1) of this section without giving the person who displayed the placard or poster notice under subsection (3) of this section if the placard or poster does not give his address and the council do not know it and are unable to ascertain it after reasonable inquiry.

(5) The period to be specified in a notice under subsection (3) of this section shall be a period of not less than two days from the date of service of the notice.

(6) In this section " the advertisement regulations " means regulations made or having effect as if made under section 63 of this Act." ;

(*b*) in section 269(2) (provisions specified in Part III of Schedule 21 to have effect as if the Isles of Scilly were a district and the Council of the Isles were its council) after the word " Schedule " there shall be inserted the words " and section 109A of this Act " ;

(*c*) the following subsection shall be inserted after subsection (4) of section 280 (rights of entry)—

" (4A) Any person duly authorised in writing by the council of a district or a London borough may at any reasonable time enter any land for the purpose of exercising a power conferred on the council by section 109A above if—

(*a*) the land is unoccupied ; and

(*b*) it would be impossible to exercise the power without entering the land." ; and

(*d*) in Part I of Schedule 21 (provisions that may be applied to the Isles of Scilly as if they were a separate county) for the words " Sections 104 to 111 " there shall be substituted the words—

" Sections 104 to 109.
Sections 110 and 111.".

Temporary markets.

37.—(1) The council of a district or a London borough may resolve that the following provisions of this section shall apply to their district or borough ; and if a council so resolve and within 14 days of the passing of the resolution give notice of the resolution by advertising in a local newspaper circulating in their area, those provisions shall come into force in their district or borough on the day specified in the resolution.

(2) Subject to subsection (3) below, any person intending to hold a temporary market in a district or London borough where the provisions of this section have come into force, and any occupier of land in such a district or borough who intends to permit the land to be used as the site of a temporary market or for purposes of that market, shall give the council of the district or the borough not less than one month before the date on which it is proposed to hold the market notice of his intention to hold it or to permit the land to be so used, as the case may be.

(3) No notice is required under subsection (2) above if the proceeds of the temporary market are to be applied solely or principally for charitable, social, sporting or political purposes.

(4) Any notice given under subsection (2) above shall state—

(a) the full name and address of the person intending to hold the market;

(b) the day or days on which it is proposed that the market shall be held and its proposed opening and closing times;

(c) the site on which it is proposed that it shall be held;

(d) the full name and address of the occupier of that site, if he is not the person intending to hold the market.

(5) A person who without giving the notice required by subsection (2) above holds a temporary market or permits land occupied by him to be used as the site of a temporary market shall be guilty of an offence and liable on summary conviction to a fine not exceeding £500.

(6) In this section " temporary market " means a concourse of buyers and sellers of articles held otherwise than in a building or on a highway, and comprising not less than five stalls, stands, vehicles (whether movable or not) or pitches from which articles are sold, but does not include—

(a) a market or fair the right to hold which was acquired by virtue of a grant (including a presumed grant) or acquired or established by virtue of an enactment or order; or

(b) a sale by auction of farm livestock or deadstock.

(7) A person holds a temporary market for the purposes of this section if—

(a) he is entitled to payment for any space or pitch hired or let on the site of the market to persons wishing to trade in the market; or

(b) he is entitled, as a person promoting the market, or as the agent, licensee or assignee of a person promoting the market, to payment for goods sold or services rendered to persons attending the market.

PART XII

1971 c. 78.

(8) This section does not apply to a market held on any land in accordance with planning permission granted on an application made under Part III of the Town and Country Planning Act 1971.

Work undertaken by local authorities and development bodies under certain agreements with Manpower Services Commission.

1980 c. 65.

38.—(1) The following subsection shall be added at the end of section 20 of the Local Government, Planning and Land Act 1980—

" (4) Notwithstanding anything in subsection (1) above, in this Act " construction or maintenance work " does not include work undertaken by a local authority or a development body pursuant to an agreement made with the Manpower Services Commission on or after 1st April 1982 which specifies the work to be undertaken by the authority or body and under which the Commission has agreed to pay the whole or part of the cost of the work so specified.".

(2) The words " to (4) " shall accordingly be substituted for the words " and (3) " in the definition of " construction or maintenance work " in subsection (1) of that section.

(3) This section extends to Scotland.

Insurance etc. of local authority members and persons voluntarily assisting local authorities and probation committees.

1972 c. 70.
1981 c. 31.

39.—(1) In section 140 of the Local Government Act 1972 (insurance by local authorities against accidents to members)—

(a) the following subsection shall be substituted for subsection (1)—

" (1) A local authority may enter into a contract of insurance of Class 1 in Part I of Schedule 2 to the Insurance Companies Act 1981 against risks of any member of the authority meeting with a personal accident, whether fatal or not, while engaged on the business of the authority." ; and

(b) the words in subsection (3) from " but " to the end shall cease to have effect.

(2) The following sections shall be inserted after that section—

" Insurance of voluntary assistants of local authorities.

140A.—(1) A local authority may enter into a contract of insurance of a relevant class against risks of any voluntary assistant of the authority meeting with a personal accident, whether fatal or not, while engaged as such, or suffering from any disease or sickness, whether fatal or not, as the result of being so engaged.

(2) In this section—

" local authority " includes—

(a) a board constituted in pursuance of section 1 of the Town and Country Planning Act 1971 or reconstituted in pursuance of Schedule 17 to this Act ;

(*b*) the Common Council of the City of London ; and

(*c*) the Council of the Isles of Scilly ; and

" voluntary assistant " means a person who, at the request of the local authority or an authorised officer of the local authority, performs any service or does anything otherwise than for payment by the local authority (except by way of reimbursement of expenses), for the purposes of, or in connection with, the carrying out of any of the functions of the local authority.

Insurance of voluntary assistants of probation committees.

140B.—(1) A county council and the Greater London Council may enter into a contract of insurance of a relevant class against risks of any voluntary assistant of a relevant probation committee meeting with a personal accident, whether fatal or not, while engaged as such, or suffering from any disease or sickness, whether fatal or not, as the result of being so engaged.

(2) In this section—

" relevant probation committee " means—

(*a*) in relation to a county council, a probation committee for a probation area wholly or partly within the county ; and

(*b*) in relation to Greater London, a probation committee for a probation area wholly or partly within an outer London borough (within the meaning of section 1 of the 1963 Act) ; and

" voluntary assistant " means a person who, at the request of an authorised officer of the probation committee, performs any service or does anything otherwise than for payment by the committee (except by way of reimbursement of expenses), for the purposes of, or in connection with, the carrying out of any of the functions of the committee.

Y 3

Provisions supplementary to sections 140A and 140B.

140C.—(1) The relevant classes of contracts of insurance for the purposes of sections 140A and 140B above are—

> (*a*) class IV in Schedule 1 to the Insurance Companies Act 1981 (permanent health insurance) ; and
>
> (*b*) class 1 in Part I of Schedule 2 to that Act (accident insurance).

(2) Any sum received under a contract of insurance made by virtue of section 140A or 140B above shall, after deduction of any expenses incurred in the recovery thereof, be paid by the authority receiving it to, or to the personal representatives of, the voluntary assistant who suffered the accident, disease or sickness in respect of which the sum is received or to such other person as the authority consider appropriate having regard to the circumstances of the case ; and a sum paid to any person other than the assistant or his personal representatives shall be applied by that person in accordance with any directions given by the authority for the benefit of any dependant of the voluntary assistant.

1774 c. 48.

(3) The provisions of the Life Assurance Act 1774 shall not apply to any such contract.

(4) Section 119 above shall apply to any sum which is due by virtue of subsection (2) above and does not exceed the amount for the time being specified in section 119(1) above.".

(3) In the entry relating to Class 1 in Part I of Schedule 2 to the Insurance Companies Act 1981, after the words " the person insured " there shall be inserted the words " or, in the case of a contract made by virtue of section 140, 140A or 140B of the Local Government Act 1972, a person for whose benefit the contract is made ".

1972 c. 70.

Nuisance and disturbance on educational premises.

40.—(1) Any person who without lawful authority is present on premises to which this section applies and causes or permits nuisance or disturbance to the annoyance of persons who lawfully use those premises (whether or not any such persons are present at the time) shall be guilty of an offence and shall be liable on summary conviction to a fine not exceeding £50.

(2) This section applies to premises, including playgrounds, playing fields and other premises for outdoor recreation—

> (*a*) of a school maintained by a local education authority ; or
>
> (*b*) of a further education establishment provided by such an authority.

(3) If—

(*a*) a police constable ; or

(*b*) subject to subsection (5) below, a person whom a local education authority have authorised to exercise the power conferred by this subsection,

has reasonable cause to suspect that any person is committing or has committed an offence under this section, he may remove him from the premises.

(4) The power conferred by subsection (3) above may also be exercised, in relation to premises of an aided or special agreement school, by a person whom the school governors have authorised to exercise it.

(5) A local education authority may not authorise a person to exercise the power conferred by subsection (3) above in relation to premises of a voluntary school without first obtaining the consent of the school governors.

(6) Except as provided by subsection (7) below, no proceedings under this section shall be brought by any person other than—

(*a*) a police constable ; or

(*b*) subject to subsection (8) below, a local education authority.

(7) Proceedings under this section for an offence committed on premises of an aided or special agreement school may be brought by a person whom the school governors have authorised to bring such proceedings.

(8) A local education authority may not bring proceedings under this section for an offence committed on premises of a voluntary school without first obtaining the consent of the school governors.

(9) Expressions used in this section and in the Education Act 1944 c. 31. 1944 have the meanings assigned to them by that Act.

(10) This section shall come into force on the expiry of the period of two months beginning with the date on which this Act is passed.

41.—(1) This section has effect where—   Lost and uncollected property.

(*a*) property comes into the possession of a local authority after being found on buildings or premises owned or managed by them ; or

(*b*) property which has been deposited with a local authority is not collected from them in accordance with the terms under which it was deposited.

(2) Where—

(*a*) property is found on any building or premises owned or managed by a local authority ; and

Y 4

(*b*) it is subsequently handed over to the authority,

any right of possession of the property which was vested in a person by virtue of its having been found is extinguished.

(3) If—

    (*a*) the local authority gives the owner or, as the case may be, the depositor of the property notice in writing—

        (i) that they require him to collect the property by a date specified in the notice ; and

        (ii) that if he does not do so the property will vest in the local authority on that date ; and

    (*b*) he fails to comply with the notice,

the property shall vest in the local authority on the specified date.

(4) The date to be specified in a notice under subsection (3) above shall be not less than one month from the date of the notice.

(5) Where it appears to the local authority, on the date when property comes into their possession as mentioned in paragraph (*a*) of subsection (1) above, that it is impossible to serve a notice under subsection (3) above, the property shall vest in the authority one month from that date.

(6) Where the local authority are satisfied after reasonable inquiry that it is impossible to serve a notice under subsection (3) above in relation to any property, it shall vest in them six months from the relevant date.

(7) Where—

    (*a*) any property is of a perishable nature ; or

    (*b*) to look after it adequately would involve the local authority in unreasonable expense or inconvenience,

the authority may sell or otherwise dispose of it at such time and in such manner as they think fit.

(8) Where property is sold or otherwise disposed of under subsection (7) above—

    (*a*) any person to whom the property is transferred shall have a good title to it ; and

    (*b*) any proceeds of sale shall vest in the local authority on the day when the property would have vested in them under this section if it had not been sold.

(9) Where any property which came into the possession of a local authority as mentioned in paragraph (*a*) of subsection (1) above vests in the authority under this section, the authority may give the whole or any part of the property to the person through whom it came into their possession.

(10) Where the proceeds of sale of property which came into the possession of a local authority as mentioned in the said paragraph (*a*) vest in the authority under this section, the authority may make a payment not exceeding the value of the property to the person through whom it came into their possession.

(11) Where property is claimed by its owner or depositor before it vests in a local authority under this section, he may collect it on payment to the local authority of any sum which they require him to pay in respect of costs incurred by them—

(*a*) in making inquiries for the purposes of this section or serving any notice under subsection (3) above ; and

(*b*) in looking after the property adequately.

(12) This section shall not apply to any property which is found—

(*a*) on an aerodrome or in an aircraft on an aerodrome ;

(*b*) in a public service vehicle ; or

(*c*) on any premises belonging to the London Transport Executive or under the control of that Executive.

(13) In this section—

" aerodrome " has the meaning assigned to it by section 28(1) of the Civil Aviation Act 1968 ;   1968 c. 61.

" local authority " means—

(*a*) a local authority as defined in section 270(1) of the Local Government Act 1972 ; and   1972 c. 70.

(*b*) a board constituted in pursuance of section 1 of the Town and Country Planning Act 1971 or re- 1971 c. 78. constituted in pursuance of Schedule 17 to the Local Government Act 1972 ; and

(*c*) the Common Council of the City of London ;

" public service vehicle " has the meaning assigned to it by section 1 of the Public Passenger Vehicles Act 1981 ;   1981 c. 14.

" the relevant date " means—

(*a*) in relation to property which came into the possession of a local authority as mentioned in paragraph (*a*) of subsection (1) above, the date when it came into their possession ; and

(*b*) in relation to uncollected property,—

(i) the date when the local authority accepted custody of it ; or

(ii) the date when the period for which it was deposited with them expired,

whichever is the later.

PART XII
Port health
districts and
port health
authorities.
1936 c. 49.

42.—(1) In section 2(2) of the Public Health Act 1936 (constitution of port health district under port health authority)—

(a) for the words " (i) constitute a port health district consisting of the whole or part of a port " there shall be substituted the words " constitute a port health district consisting of any area, being a port or part of a port, or of two or more such areas, or consisting of such an area or two or more such areas together with so much (being either the whole or any part or parts) of the district or districts of one or more riparian authorities as (not being comprised in that area or any of those areas, as the case may be) is specified in the order " ; and

(b) paragraph (ii) shall be omitted.

(2) In section 3(1)(a) of that Act (which specifies the waters and land over which a port health authority is to have jurisdiction) for the words from " waters " to " so specified " there shall be substituted the words " waters and land within the port health district ".

(3) In section 41 of the London Government Act 1963 (port health authority for the Port of London)—

(a) in subsection (1), after the words " Port of London " there shall be inserted the words " together with so much (being either the whole or any part or parts) of the district or districts of one or more riparian authorities as (not being comprised in the Port of London) may be specified in an order made by the Secretary of State " ;

(b) in paragraph (a) of that subsection, for the words from " waters " to the end of the paragraph there shall be substituted the words " waters and land within that port health district " ;

(c) in paragraph (c) of that subsection, for the words from " mentioned in paragraph (a) " to " so mentioned " there shall be substituted the words " and land within that port health district " ; and

(d) at the end of the section there shall be added the following subsection—

" (4) In this section " riparian authority " means a riparian authority within the meaning of Part I of the Public Health Act 1936 as amended by subsection (3) of this section.".

(4) The amendments made by subsections (1) to (3) above shall not affect the validity of any order made under section 2(2)

of the Public Health Act 1936, or under section 41 of the London Part XII Government Act 1963, before the passing of this Act ; but the power conferred by section 9(2) of the said Act of 1936, or by section 90 of the said Act of 1963, to amend or vary orders shall include power to amend or vary any order so made so as to have effect in accordance with the provisions of the Act in question as amended by this section.

1936 c. 49.
1963 c. 33.

43. In section 3 of the Local Authorities (Land) Act 1963— Advances for

   (*a*) the following subsection shall be substituted for sub-section (1)—

> " (1) Where a local authority are satisfied that it would be for the benefit or improvement of their area, they may, subject to the provisions of this section, advance money to any person for the purpose of enabling him—

>> (*a*) to acquire land ; or

>> (*b*) to erect any building or carry out any work on land." ; and

   (*b*) the following subsections shall be substituted for sub-section (3)—

> " (3) The amount of the principal of an advance made under subsection (1)(*a*) of this section shall not exceed nine-tenths of the value of the land.

> (3A) The amount of the principal of an advance made under subsection (1)(*b*) of this section shall not exceed nine-tenths of the value which it is estimated the mortgaged security will bear upon the completion of the building or other works in respect of which the advance is made.".

Advances for acquisition of land, erection of buildings or carrying out of works.
1963 c. 29.

44. In section 137 of the Local Government Act 1972 (which gives local authorities power to incur expenditure for certain purposes not otherwise authorised, but limits the expenditure which it authorises)—

   (*a*) the following subsections shall be inserted after sub-section (2)—

> "(2A) Without prejudice to the generality of sub-section (1) above, the power of a local authority to incur expenditure under that subsection includes power to incur expenditure in giving financial assistance to persons carrying on commercial or industrial undertakings.

Definition of certain local authority expenditure etc.
1972 c. 70.

(2B) Financial assistance under subsection (2A) above may be given by lending or guarantee, or by making grants. " ;

(b) the following subsections shall be inserted after subsection (4)—

" (4A) For the purpose of determining whether a local authority have exceeded the limit set out in subsection (4) above, their expenditure in any financial year under this section shall be taken to be the difference between their gross expenditure under this section for that year and the aggregate of the amounts specified in subsection (4B) below.

(4B) The amounts mentioned in subsection (4A) above are—

(a) any grant paid to the local authority for that year under the Local Government Grants (Social Need) Act 1969, in so far as the grant is in respect of an activity in relation to which the authority have incurred expenditure in that year under this section ;

(b) the amount of any repayment in that year of the principal of a loan for the purpose of financing expenditure under this section in any year ;

(c) so much of any amount raised by public subscription as is spent in that year for a purpose for which the authority are authorised by this section to incur expenditure ;

(d) any grant received by the authority for that year out of the European Regional Development Fund or the Social Fund of the European Economic Community, in so far as the grant is in respect of an activity in relation to which the authority incurred expenditure in that year under this section ;

(e) the amount of any repayment in that year of a loan under this section made by the authority in any year ; and

(f) the amount of any expenditure—

(i) which is incurred by the authority in that year in circumstances specified in an order made by the Secretary of State ; or

(ii) which is incurred by the authority in that year and is of a description so specified ; or

(iii) which is defrayed by any grant
or other payment to the authority which
is made in or in respect of that year and
is of a description so specified."; and

(c) in subsection (5), for the words " subsection (4) above "
there shall be substituted the words " this section ".

45.—(1) A local authority to whom this section applies shall Arrangements
have power and shall be deemed always to have had power to under
enter into arrangements with the Manpower Services Commission and Training
or the Secretary of State under any provision of the Employment Act 1973.
and Training Act 1973. 1973 c. 50.

(2) The local authorities to whom this section applies are—

(a) a local authority as defined in section 270(1) of the
Local Government Act 1972 ; 1972 c. 70.

(b) a board constituted in pursuance of section 1 of the
Town and Country Planning Act 1971 or reconstituted 1971 c. 78.
in pursuance of Schedule 17 to the Local Government
Act 1972 ; and

(c) the Common Council of the City of London.

46.—(1) In each of the enactments to which this subsection Extension of
applies " 1986 " shall be substituted for " 1984 ". duration of
local Act

(2) The enactments to which subsection (1) above applies are— powers to
assist
(a) section 62A of the Isle of Wight County Council Act industry etc.
1971, so far as it relates to sections 18 to 20 of that Act ; 1971 c. lxxi.

(b) section 11(2) of the County of South Glamorgan Act 1976 c. xxxv.
1976 ;

(c) section 52 of the Tyne and Wear Act 1976 ; 1976 c. xxxvi.

(d) section 9 of the County of Merseyside Act 1980 ; 1980 c. x.

(e) section 122(2) of the West Midlands County Council 1980 c. xi.
Act 1980 ;

(f) section 4 of the Cheshire County Council Act 1980 ; 1980 c. xiii.

(g) section 8 of the West Yorkshire Act 1980 ; and 1980 c. xiv.

(h) section 9 of the Greater Manchester Act 1981. 1981 c. ix.

PART XIII

SUPPLEMENTARY

47.—(1) The enactments specified in Schedule 6 to this Act Minor
shall have effect subject to the amendments specified in that amendments
Schedule. and repeals.

PART XIII   (2) The enactments specified in Schedule 7 to this Act are repealed to the extent specified in the third column of that Schedule.

(3) So far as subsection (2) above relates to Parts I and II of Schedule 7 to this Act, it shall come into force on 1st January 1983.

(4) Subsection (2) above extends to Scotland in so far as it relates to any enactment contained in Part IV of Schedule 7 to this Act which so extends.

Consequential repeal or amendment of local statutory provisions.

48.—(1) The Secretary of State may by order—

(a) repeal any provision of a local Act passed before or in the same Session as this Act or of an order or other instrument made under or confirmed by any Act so passed if it appears to him that the provision is inconsistent with or has become unnecessary in consequence of any provision of this Act ; and

(b) amend any provision of such a local Act, order or instrument if it appears to him that the provision requires amendment in consequence of any provision contained in this Act or any repeal made by virtue of paragraph (a) above.

(2) An order under subsection (1) above may contain such incidental or transitional provisions as the Secretary of State considers appropriate in connection with the order.

(3) It shall be the duty of the Secretary of State, before he makes an order under subsection (1) above repealing or amending any provision of a local Act, to consult each local authority which he considers would be affected by the repeal or amendment of that provision.

(4) A statutory instrument containing an order under subsection (1) above shall be subject to annulment in pursuance of a resolution of either House of Parliament.

Citation and extent.

49.—(1) This Act may be cited as the Local Government (Miscellaneous Provisions) Act 1982.

(2) Subject to sections 11(2), 38(3) and 47(4) above, and to paragraph 8(2) of Schedule 6 to this Act, this Act extends to England and Wales only.

SCHEDULES

SCHEDULE 1

LICENSING OF PUBLIC ENTERTAINMENTS

Grant, renewal and transfer of entertainments licences

1.—(1) An entertainment to which this paragraph applies shall not be provided in any place except under and in accordance with the terms of a licence granted under this paragraph by the appropriate authority.

(2) Subject to sub-paragraph (3) below, this paragraph applies to public dancing or music or any other public entertainment of a like kind.

(3) This paragraph does not apply—

(*a*) to any music—

(i) in a place of public religious worship ; or

(ii) performed as an incident of a religious meeting or service ;

(*b*) to an entertainment held in a pleasure fair ; or

(*c*) to an entertainment which takes place wholly or mainly in the open air.

(4) The appropriate authority may grant to any applicant, and from time to time renew, a licence for the use of any place specified in it for all or any of the entertainments to which this paragraph applies on such terms and conditions and subject to such restrictions as may be so specified.

(5) The appropriate authority may grant a licence under this paragraph in respect of such one or more particular occasions only as may be specified in the licence.

2.—(1) An entertainment to which this paragraph applies shall not be provided in any place except under and in accordance with the terms of a licence granted under this paragraph by the appropriate authority.

(2) Subject to sub-paragraph (3) below, this paragraph applies to any entertainment which consists of, or includes, any public contest, exhibition or display of boxing, wrestling, judo, karate or any similar sport.

(3) This paragraph does not apply—

(*a*) to an entertainment held in a pleasure fair ; or

(*b*) to an entertainment which takes place wholly or mainly in the open air.

(4) The appropriate authority may grant to any applicant, and from time to time renew, a licence for the use of any place specified in it for all or any of the entertainments to which this paragraph

applies on such terms and conditions and subject to such restrictions as may be so specified.

(5) The appropriate authority may grant a licence under this paragraph in respect of such one or more particular occasions only as may be specified in the licence.

3.—(1) This paragraph applies to any public musical entertainment which is held—

> (a) in an area in which this paragraph and paragraph 4 below have effect; and
>
> (b) wholly or mainly in the open air; and
>
> (c) at a place on private land.

(2) For the purposes of this paragraph and paragraph 4 below—

> (a) an entertainment is musical if music is a substantial ingredient; and
>
> (b) land is private if the public has access to it (whether on payment or otherwise) only by permission of the owner, occupier or lessee.

(3) This paragraph does not apply—

> (a) to a garden fete, bazaar, sale of work, sporting or athletic event, exhibition, display or other function or event of a similar character, whether limited to one day or extending over two or more days; or
>
> (b) to a religious meeting or service,

merely because music is incidental to it.

(4) This paragraph does not apply to an entertainment held in a pleasure fair.

4.—(1) An entertainment to which paragraph 3 above applies shall not be provided except under and in accordance with the terms of a licence granted under this paragraph by the appropriate authority.

(2) The appropriate authority may grant to any applicant, and from time to time renew, a licence for the use of any place specified in it for any entertainment to which paragraph 3 above applies.

(3) The appropriate authority may grant a licence under this paragraph in respect of such one or more particular occasions only as may be specified in the licence.

(4) A licence under this paragraph may be granted—

> (a) on terms and conditions; and
>
> (b) subject to restrictions,

imposed for all or any of the following purposes, but no others,—

> (i) for securing the safety of performers at the entertainment for which the licence is granted and other persons present at the entertainment;

(ii) without prejudice to the generality of paragraph (i) above, for securing adequate access for fire engines, ambulances, police cars or other vehicles that may be required in an emergency ;

(iii) for securing the provision of adequate sanitary appliances and things used in connection with such appliances ;

(iv) for preventing persons in the neighbourhood being unreasonably disturbed by noise.

5.—(1) Subject to paragraphs 8 and 17 below, any entertainments licence other than a licence in respect of one or more particular occasions only shall, unless previously cancelled under paragraph 10 or revoked under paragraph 12(4) below, remain in force for one year or for such shorter period specified in the licence as the appropriate authority may think fit.

(2) Where an entertainments licence has been granted to any person, the appropriate authority may, if they think fit, transfer that licence to any other person on the application of that other person or the holder of the licence.

6.—(1) An applicant for the grant, renewal or transfer of an entertainments licence in respect of any place shall give not less than 28 days' notice of his intention to make the application to—

(*a*) the appropriate authority ;

(*b*) the chief officer of police ; and

(*c*) the fire authority.

(2) The appropriate authority may in such cases as they think fit, after consulting with the chief officer of police and the fire authority, grant an application for the grant, renewal or transfer of an entertainments licence notwithstanding the fact that the applicant has failed to give notice in accordance with sub-paragraph (1) above.

(3) An applicant for the grant, renewal or transfer of an entertainments licence shall furnish such particulars and give such other notices as the appropriate authority may by regulation prescribe.

(4) In considering any application for the grant, renewal or transfer of an entertainments licence, the appropriate authority shall have regard to any observations submitted to them by the chief officer of police and by the fire authority.

7.—(1) Subject to sub-paragraphs (2) and (3) below, an applicant for the grant, renewal or transfer of an entertainments licence shall pay a reasonable fee determined by the appropriate authority.

(2) No fee shall be payable if the application is for a licence for an entertainment—

(*a*) at a church hall, chapel hall or other similar building occupied in connection with a place of public religious worship ; or

(*b*) at a village hall, parish or community hall or other similar building.

(3) The appropriate authority may remit the whole or any part of the fee that would otherwise be payable for the grant, renewal or transfer of an entertainments licence, where in the opinion of the authority the entertainment in question—

    (*a*) is of an educational or other like character ; or

    (*b*) is given for a charitable or other like purpose.

8.—(1) Where, before the date of expiry of an entertainments licence, an application has been made for its renewal, it shall be deemed to remain in force notwithstanding that the date has passed until the withdrawal of the application or its determination by the appropriate authority.

(2) Where, before the date of expiry of an entertainments licence, an application has been made for its transfer, it shall be deemed to remain in force with any necessary modifications until the withdrawal of the application or its determination notwithstanding that the date has passed or that the person to whom the licence is to be transferred if the application is granted is carrying on at the place in respect of which the licence was granted the functions to which it relates.

Transmission and cancellation of entertainments licences

9. In the event of the death of the holder of an entertainments licence, the person carrying on at the place in respect of which the licence was granted the functions to which the licence relates shall be deemed to be the holder of the licence unless and until—

    (*a*) a legal personal representative of the deceased has been duly constituted ; or

    (*b*) the licence is transferred to some other person.

10. The appropriate authority may, at the written request of the holder of an entertainments licence, cancel the licence.

Power to prescribe standard terms, conditions and restrictions

11.—(1) The appropriate authority may make regulations prescribing standard conditions applicable to all, or any class of, entertainments licences, that is to say terms, conditions and restrictions on or subject to which such licences, or licences of that class, are in general to be granted, renewed or transferred by them.

(2) Regulations relating to entertainments to which paragraph 3 above applies may only prescribe standard conditions for the purposes specified in paragraph 4(4) above.

(3) Where the appropriate authority have made regulations under sub-paragraph (1) above, every such licence granted, renewed or transferred by them shall be presumed to have been so granted, renewed or transferred subject to any standard conditions applicable to it unless they have been expressly excluded or varied.

(4) Where the appropriate authority have made regulations under sub-paragraph (1) above, they shall, if so requested by any person,

supply him with a copy of the regulations on payment of such
reasonable fee as the authority may determine.

(5) In any legal proceedings the production of a copy of any
regulations made by the appropriate authority under sub-paragraph
(1) above purporting to be certified as a true copy by an officer of
the authority authorised to give a certificate for the purposes of
this paragraph shall be prima facie evidence of such regulations,
and no proof shall be required of the handwriting or official position
or authority of any person giving such a certificate.

Enforcement

12.—(1) If any entertainment to which paragraph 1, 2 or 3 above
applies is provided at any place in respect of which a licence under
the relevant paragraph is not in force, then, subject to sub-paragraph
(3) below—

(*a*) any person concerned in the organisation or management of
that entertainment ; and

(*b*) any other person who, knowing or having reasonable cause
to suspect that such an entertainment would be so provided at the place,—

(i) allowed the place to be used for the provision of
that entertainment ; or

(ii) let the place, or otherwise made it available, to
any person by whom an offence in connection with that
use of the place has been committed,

shall be guilty of an offence and liable on summary conviction to
a fine not exceeding £1,000.

(2) If any place in respect of which a licence under paragraph
1, 2 or 4 above is in force is used for any entertainment otherwise
than in accordance with the terms, conditions or restrictions on or
subject to which the licence is held, then, subject to sub-paragraph
(3) and to paragraph 13 below,—

(*a*) the holder of the licence ; and

(*b*) any other person who, knowing or having reasonable cause
to suspect that the place would be so used,—

(i) allowed the place to be so used ; or

(ii) let the place, or otherwise made it available, to
any person by whom an offence in connection with that
use of the place has been committed,

shall be guilty of an offence and liable on summary conviction
to a fine not exceeding £1,000.

(3) It shall be a defence for a person charged with an offence
under this paragraph to prove that he took all reasonable precautions
and exercised all due diligence to avoid commission of the offence.

(4) Subject to paragraph 17 below, the authority by whom an
entertainments licence was granted may revoke it if its holder is
convicted of an offence under sub-paragraph (2)(*a*) above.

13. Where—

    (*a*) a special order of exemption has been granted in respect of premises under section 74(4) of the Licensing Act 1964 ; and

    (*b*) the premises form all or part of a place in respect of which a licence under paragraph 1 above is for the time being in force,

no person shall be guilty of an offence under paragraph 12(2) above by reason only of those premises being kept open on that special occasion for any of the purposes authorised by the licence after the latest hour so authorised but not later than the hour specified in that special order of exemption as the hour for closing.

14.—(1) Where—

    (*a*) a constable ; or

    (*b*) an authorised officer of the appropriate authority ; or

    (*c*) an authorised officer of the fire authority,

has reason to believe that an entertainment to which paragraph 1, 2 or 3 above applies is being, or is about to be, given in any place in respect of which an entertainments licence is for the time being in force, he may enter the place with a view to seeing whether the terms, conditions or restrictions on or subject to which the licence is held are complied with.

(2) An authorised officer of the fire authority may, on giving not less than 24 hours' notice to the occupier of any place in respect of which an entertainments licence is for the time being in force, enter the place for the purpose of—

    (*a*) inspecting the place to ensure that there are adequate fire precautions ; and

    (*b*) seeing whether the terms, conditions or restrictions relating to fire precautions on or subject to which the licence is held are being complied with.

(3) A constable or authorised officer of the appropriate authority may enter any place in respect of which he has reason to suspect that an offence under paragraph 12 above is being committed if authorised to do so by a warrant granted by a justice of the peace.

(4) Where an authorised officer of the appropriate authority or of the fire authority enters any place in exercise of any power under this paragraph he shall, if required to do so by the occupier, produce to him his authority.

(5) Any person who without reasonable excuse refuses to permit a constable or officer to enter or inspect any place in accordance with the provisions of this paragraph shall be guilty of an offence and shall for every such refusal be liable on summary conviction to a fine not exceeding £200.

Provisional grant of licences

15.—(1) Where application is made to the appropriate authority for the grant of an entertainments licence in respect of premises

which are to be, or are in the course of being, constructed, extended   SCH. 1
or altered and the authority are satisfied that the premises would,
if completed in accordance with plans deposited in accordance with
the requirements of the authority, be such that they would grant
the licence, the authority may grant the licence subject to a condition
that it shall be of no effect until confirmed by them.

(2) The authority shall confirm any licence granted by virtue of
the foregoing sub-paragraph if and when they are satisfied that the
premises have been completed in accordance with the plans referred
to in sub-paragraph (1) above or in accordance with those plans as
modified with the approval of the authority, and that the licence is
held by a fit and proper person.

Variation of licences

16.—(1) The holder of an entertainments licence may at any time
apply to the appropriate authority for such variations of the terms,
conditions or restrictions on or subject to which the licence is held
as may be specified in the application.

(2) An authority to whom an application under sub-paragraph
(1) above is made may—

(a) make the variations specified in the application ;

(b) make such variations as they think fit, including, subject to
paragraph 4(4) above, the imposition of terms, conditions or
restrictions other than those so specified ; or

(c) refuse the application.

Appeals

17.—(1) Any of the following persons, that is to say—

(a) an applicant for the grant, renewal or transfer of an entertainments licence in respect of any place whose application
is refused ;

(b) an applicant for the variation of the terms, conditions or
restrictions on or subject to which any such licence is held
whose application is refused ;

(c) a holder of any such licence who is aggrieved by any term,
condition or restriction on or subject to which the licence
is held ; or

(d) a holder of any such licence whose licence is revoked under
paragraph 12(4) above,

may at any time before the expiration of the period of 21 days
beginning with the relevant date appeal to the magistrates' court
acting for the petty sessions area in which the place is situated.

(2) In this paragraph " the relevant date " means the date on which
the person in question is notified of the refusal of his application, the
imposition of the term, condition or restriction by which he is
aggrieved or the revocation of his licence, as the case may be.

(3) An appeal against the decision of a magistrates' court under
this paragraph may be brought to the Crown Court.

(4) On an appeal to the magistrates' court or the Crown Court under this paragraph the court may make such order as it thinks fit.

(5) Subject to sub-paragraphs (6) to (9) below, it shall be the duty of the appropriate authority to give effect to an order of the magistrates' court or the Crown Court.

(6) The appropriate authority need not give effect to the order of the magistrates' court until the time for bringing an appeal under sub-paragraph (3) above has expired and, if such an appeal is duly brought, until the determination or abandonment of the appeal.

(7) Where any entertainments licence is revoked under paragraph 12(4) above or an application for the renewal of such a licence is refused, the licence shall be deemed to remain in force—

(*a*) until the time for bringing an appeal under this paragraph has expired and, if such an appeal is duly brought, until the determination or abandonment of the appeal ; and

(*b*) where an appeal relating to the refusal of an application for such a renewal is successful and no further appeal is available, until the licence is renewed by the appropriate authority.

(8) Where—

(*a*) the holder of an entertainments licence makes an application under paragraph 16 above ; and

(*b*) the appropriate authority impose any term, condition or restriction other than one specified in the application,

the licence shall be deemed to be free of it until the time for bringing an appeal under this paragraph has expired.

(9) Where an appeal is brought under this paragraph against the imposition of any such term, condition or restriction, the licence shall be deemed to be free of the term, condition or restriction until the determination or abandonment of the appeal.

Miscellaneous

18. Where a place in respect of which an entertainments licence has been granted constitutes a roller skating rink within the meaning of section 75(2)(*b*) of the Public Health Act 1961, it shall not be subject to any byelaws made under section 75 for so long as the licence is in force.

1961 c. 64.

Savings and transitional provisions

19.—(1) Any licence relating to public entertainments which was granted under an enactment repealed by this Act and which is in force immediately before the commencement date—

(*a*) shall have effect as from the commencement date as if granted under this Act by the appropriate authority on and subject to terms, conditions and restrictions corresponding to those on and subject to which it is held immediately before the commencement date ; and

(b) in the case of a licence granted or renewed for a specified   SCH. 1
period, shall remain in force, subject to paragraphs 10, 12(4)
and 16(2) of this Schedule, for so much of that period as
falls on or after the commencement date.

(2) Where an appeal under any enactment mentioned in sub-
paragraph (1) above has been brought in respect of a licence before
the commencement date but has not been determined or abandoned
before that date, the provisions of paragraph 17 above shall apply
to proceedings relating to the appeal as if the appeal had been
brought under that paragraph.

20.—(1) Nothing in this Schedule shall affect—

(a) the application of the Private Places of Entertainment (Licen-   1967 c. 19.
sing) Act 1967 to any area in respect of which an adoption
has been made under section 1 of that Act ; or

(b) the validity of any licence granted under that Act before the
commencement date.

(2) Where by virtue of such an adoption made before the commencement date the Private Places of Entertainment (Licensing) Act
1967 applies to part only of a district, the district council may adopt
that Act in respect of the remaining part of that district.

21. Nothing in this Schedule shall affect—

(a) section 3 of the Sunday Entertainments Act 1932 ;   1932 c. 51.
(b) section 7 of the Cinematograph Act 1952 ;   1952 c. 68.
(c) paragraph 1 of Schedule 3 to the Revision of the Army and   1955 c. 20.
Air Force Acts (Transitional Provisions) Act 1955 ;
(d) section 182(1) of the Licensing Act 1964 ;   1964 c. 26.
(e) section 12 of the Theatres Act 1968 ; or   1968 c. 54.
(f) section 31 of the Fire Precautions Act 1971.   1971 c. 40.

Supplemental

22. In this Schedule—

" the appropriate authority " means—

(i) in relation to any place in England and Wales, the
district council for the area in which the place is situated ; or

(ii) in relation to any place situated in the Isles of
Scilly, the Council of the Isles of Scilly ;

" the chief officer of police ", in relation to any place, means
the chief officer of police for the police area in which the
place is situated ;

" the commencement date " means 1st January 1983 ;

" an entertainments licence " means a licence granted under
this Schedule ;

Sch. 1

1947 c. 41.
" fire authority ", in relation to any place, means the authority discharging in the area in which the place is situated the functions of fire authority under the Fire Services Act 1947 ;

1914 c. 91.
" place of public religious worship " means a place of public religious worship which belongs to the Church of England or to the Church in Wales (within the meaning of the Welsh Church Act 1914), or which is for the time being certified as required by law as a place of religious worship ;

1961 c. 64.
" pleasure fair " has the meaning assigned to it by section 75(2)(*a*) of the Public Health Act 1961.

Section 1.

SCHEDULE 2

Amendments Consequential on Section 1

Hypnotism Act 1952 (c. 46)

1. For section 2(4) of the Hypnotism Act 1952 (control of demonstrations of hypnotism at places not licensed for public entertainment) there shall be substituted the following subsection—

" (4) In this section, the expression " controlling authority " in relation to a place in any area means the authority having power to grant licences of the kind mentioned in section 1 above in that area.".

Private Places of Entertainment (Licensing) Act 1967 (c. 19)

2. In section 1(1) of the Private Places of Entertainment (Licensing) Act 1967 (power to adopt that Act in certain areas) for the words from " in which any " to the end there shall be substituted the words " specified in the first column of Part I of the Schedule to this Act.".

3. In section 2 of that Act (certain private places of entertainment to require licences)—

(*a*) in subsection (1)(*a*) for the words from " public " to " area " there shall be substituted the words " a public entertainment " ; and

1963 c. 33.
(*b*) in subsection (2)(*a*) for the words " any enactment mentioned in section 1(1) of this Act " there shall be substituted the words " paragraph 1 of Schedule 12 to the London Government Act 1963 (which provides for the licensing of premises used for public music or dancing in London) or paragraph 1 or 4 of Schedule 1 to the Local Government (Miscellaneous Provisions) Act 1982 (which taken together make similar provision for other areas in England and Wales)".

4. For Part I of the Schedule to that Act there shall be substituted   Sch. 2
the following—

" Part I

Adopting and Licensing Authorities

Area	Authority which may adopt this Act	Licensing authority
A district.	The council of the district.	The council of the district.
A London borough.	The Greater London Council acting with the consent of the council of the borough.	The Greater London Council.
The City of London.	The Greater London Council acting with the consent of the Common Council.	The Greater London Council.
The Isles of Scilly.	The Council of the Isles of Scilly.	The Council of the Isles of Scilly ".

Licensing Act 1964 (*c.* 26)

5. In section 79(1) of the Licensing Act 1964 (licensing authority's certificate of suitability of club premises for music and dancing) for the words from " and which are " to " those regulations " there shall be substituted the words " , the licensing authority under the statutory regulations for music and dancing ".

6. In section 201(1) of that Act for the words after the word " means " in the definition of " statutory regulations for music and dancing " there shall be substituted—

" (i) Schedule 12 to the London Government Act 1963 ; or   1963 c. 33.

(ii) Schedule 1 to the Local Government (Miscellaneous Provisions) Act 1982 ; ".

SCHEDULE 3   Section 2.

Control of Sex Establishments

Saving for existing law

1. Nothing in this Schedule—

   (*a*) shall afford a defence to a charge in respect of any offence at common law or under an enactment other than this Schedule ; or

   (*b*) shall be taken into account in any way—

      (i) at a trial for such an offence ; or

      (ii) in proceedings for forfeiture under section 3 of the Obscene Publications Act 1959 or section 5 of the 1959 c. 66.
Protection of Children Act 1978 ; or   1978 c. 37.

      (iii) in proceedings for condemnation under Schedule 3 to the Customs and Excise Management Act 1979 of 1979 c. 2.
goods which section 42 of the Customs Consolidation Act 1876 c. 36.
1876 prohibits to be imported or brought into the United Kingdom as being indecent or obscene ; or

SCH. 3

(c) shall in any way limit the other powers exercisable under any of those Acts.

Meaning of " sex establishment "

2. In this Schedule " sex establishment " means a sex cinema or a sex shop.

Meaning of " sex cinema "

3.—(1) In this Schedule, " sex cinema " means any premises, vehicle, vessel or stall used to a significant degree for the exhibition of moving pictures, by whatever means produced, which—

(a) are concerned primarily with the portrayal of, or primarily deal with or relate to, or are intended to stimulate or encourage—

   (i) sexual activity ; or

   (ii) acts of force or restraint which are associated with sexual activity ; or

(b) are concerned primarily with the portrayal of, or primarily deal with or relate to, genital organs or urinary or excretory functions,

but does not include a dwelling-house to which the public is not admitted.

(2) No premises shall be treated as a sex cinema by reason only—

1909 c. 30.

(a) if they are licensed under the Cinematograph Act 1909, of their use for a purpose for which a licence under that Act is required ; or

1952 c. 68.

(b) of their use for an exempted exhibition as defined in section 5 of the Cinematograph Act 1952 (which relates to exemptions from the requirements of that Act for non-commercial organisations) by an exempted organisation within the meaning of section 5(4) of that Act.

Meaning of " sex shop " and " sex article "

4.—(1) In this Schedule " sex shop " means any premises, vehicle, vessel or stall used for a business which consists to a significant degree of selling, hiring, exchanging, lending, displaying or demonstrating—

(a) sex articles ; or

(b) other things intended for use in connection with, or for the purpose of stimulating or encouraging—

   (i) sexual activity ; or

   (ii) acts of force or restraint which are associated with sexual activity.

(2) No premises shall be treated as a sex shop by reason only of their use for the exhibition of moving pictures by whatever means produced.

(3) In this Schedule " sex article " means—

(a) anything made for use in connection with, or for the purpose of stimulating or encouraging—

   (i) sexual activity ; or

(ii) acts of force or restraint which are associated with sexual activity ; and

(*b*) anything to which sub-paragraph (4) below applies.

(4) This sub-paragraph applies—

(*a*) to any article containing or embodying matter to be read or looked at or anything intended to be used, either alone or as one of a set, for the reproduction or manufacture of any such article ; and

(*b*) to any recording of vision or sound,
which—

     (i) is concerned primarily with the portrayal of, or primarily deals with or relates to, or is intended to stimulate or encourage, sexual activity or acts of force or restraint which are associated with sexual activity ; or

     (ii) is concerned primarily with the portrayal of, or primarily deals with or relates to, genital organs, or urinary or excretory functions.

Miscellaneous definitions

5.—(1) In this Schedule—

" the appropriate authority " means, in relation to any area for which a resolution has been passed under section 2 above, the local authority who passed it ;

" the chief officer of police ", in relation to any locality, means the chief officer of police for the police area in which the locality is situated ; and

" vessel " includes any ship, boat, raft or other apparatus constructed or adapted for floating on water.

(2) This Schedule applies to hovercraft as it applies to vessels.

Requirement for licences for sex establishments

6.—(1) Subject to the provisions of this Schedule, no person shall in any area in which this Schedule is in force use any premises, vehicle, vessel or stall as a sex establishment except under and in accordance with the terms of a licence granted under this Schedule by the appropriate authority.

(2) Sub-paragraph (1) above does not apply to the sale, supply or demonstration of articles which—

(*a*) are manufactured for use primarily for the purposes of birth control ; or

(*b*) primarily relate to birth control.

7.—(1) Any person who—

(*a*) uses any premises, vehicle, vessel or stall as a sex establishment ; or

(*b*) proposes to do so,

may apply to the appropriate authority for them to waive the requirement of a licence.

(2) An application under this paragraph may be made either as part of an application for a licence under this Schedule or without any such application.

(3) An application under this paragraph shall be made in writing and shall contain the particulars specified in paragraph 10(2) to (5) below and such particulars as the appropriate authority may reasonably require in addition.

(4) The appropriate authority may waive the requirement of a licence in any case where they consider that to require a licence would be unreasonable or inappropriate.

(5) A waiver may be for such period as the appropriate authority think fit.

(6) Where the appropriate authority grant an application for a waiver, they shall give the applicant for the waiver notice that they have granted his application.

(7) The appropriate authority may at any time give a person who would require a licence but for a waiver notice that the waiver is to terminate on such date not less than 28 days from the date on which they give the notice as may be specified in the notice.

Grant, renewal and transfer of licences for sex establishments

8. Subject to paragraph 12(1) below, the appropriate authority may grant to any applicant, and from time to time renew, a licence under this Schedule for the use of any premises, vehicle, vessel or stall specified in it for a sex establishment on such terms and conditions and subject to such restrictions as may be so specified.

9.—(1) Subject to paragraphs 11 and 27 below, any licence under this Schedule shall, unless previously cancelled under paragraph 16 or revoked under paragraph 17(1) below, remain in force for one year or for such shorter period specified in the licence as the appropriate authority may think fit.

(2) Where a licence under this Schedule has been granted to any person, the appropriate authority may, if they think fit, transfer that licence to any other person on the application of that other person.

10.—(1) An application for the grant, renewal or transfer of a licence under this Schedule shall be made in writing to the appropriate authority.

(2) An application made otherwise than by or on behalf of a body corporate or an unincorporated body shall state—

    (*a*) the full name of the applicant ;

    (*b*) his permanent address ; and

    (*c*) his age.

(3) An application made by a body corporate or an unincorporated body shall state—

    (*a*) the full name of the body ;

(*b*) the address of its registered or principal office ; and

(*c*) the full names and private addresses of the directors or other persons responsible for its management.

(4) An application relating to premises shall state the full address of the premises.

(5) An application relating to a vehicle, vessel or stall shall state where it is to be used as a sex establishment.

(6) Every application shall contain such particulars as the appropriate authority may reasonably require in addition to any particulars required under sub-paragraphs (2) to (5) above.

(7) An applicant for the grant, renewal or transfer of a licence under this Schedule shall give public notice of the application.

(8) Notice shall in all cases be given by publishing an advertisement in a local newspaper circulating in the appropriate authority's area.

(9) The publication shall not be later than 7 days after the date of the application.

(10) Where the application is in respect of premises, notice of it shall in addition be displayed for 21 days beginning with the date of the application on or near the premises and in a place where the notice can conveniently be read by the public.

(11) Every notice under this paragraph which relates to premises shall identify the premises.

(12) Every such notice which relates to a vehicle, vessel or stall shall specify where it is to be used as a sex establishment.

(13) Subject to sub-paragraphs (11) and (12) above, a notice under this paragraph shall be in such form as the appropriate authority may prescribe.

(14) An applicant for the grant, renewal or transfer of a licence under this Schedule shall, not later than 7 days after the date of the application, send a copy of the application to the chief officer of police.

(15) Any person objecting to an application for the grant, renewal or transfer of a licence under this Schedule shall give notice in writing of his objection to the appropriate authority, stating in general terms the grounds of the objection, not later than 28 days after the date of the application.

(16) Where the appropriate authority receive notice of any objection under sub-paragraph (15) above, the authority shall, before considering the application, give notice in writing of the general terms of the objection to the applicant.

(17) The appropriate authority shall not without the consent of the person making the objection reveal his name or address to the applicant.

(18) In considering any application for the grant, renewal or transfer of a licence the appropriate authority shall have regard to any

SCH. 3

observations submitted to them by the chief officer of police and any objections of which notice has been sent to them under sub-paragraph (15) above.

(19) The appropriate authority shall give an opportunity of appearing before and of being heard by a committee or sub-committee of the authority—

(a) before refusing to grant a licence, to the applicant ;

(b) before refusing to renew a licence, to the holder ; and

(c) before refusing to transfer a licence, to the holder and the person to whom he desires that it shall be transferred.

(20) Where the appropriate authority refuse to grant, renew or transfer a licence, they shall, if required to do so by the applicant or holder of the licence, give him a statement in writing of the reasons for their decision within 7 days of his requiring them to do so.

11.—(1) Where, before the date of expiry of a licence, an application has been made for its renewal, it shall be deemed to remain in force notwithstanding that the date has passed until the withdrawal of the application or its determination by the appropriate authority.

(2) Where, before the date of expiry of a licence, an application has been made for its transfer, it shall be deemed to remain in force with any necessary modifications until the withdrawal of the application or its determination, notwithstanding that the date has passed or that the person to whom the licence is to be transferred if the application is granted is carrying on the business of the sex establishment.

Refusal of licences

12.—(1) A licence under this Schedule shall not be granted—

(a) to a person under the age of 18 ; or

(b) to a person who is for the time being disqualified under paragraph 17(3) below ; or

(c) to a person, other than a body corporate, who is not resident in the United Kingdom or was not so resident throughout the period of six months immediately preceding the date when the application was made ; or

(d) to a body corporate which is not incorporated in the United Kingdom ; or

(e) to a person who has, within a period of 12 months immediately preceding the date when the application was made, been refused the grant or renewal of a licence for the premises, vehicle, vessel or stall in respect of which the application is made, unless the refusal has been reversed on appeal.

(2) Subject to paragraph 27 below, the appropriate authority may refuse—

(a) an application for the grant or renewal of a licence on one or more of the grounds specified in sub-paragraph (3) below ;

(*b*) an application for the transfer of a licence on either or both of the grounds specified in paragraphs (*a*) and (*b*) of that sub-paragraph.

(3) The grounds mentioned in sub-paragraph (2) above are—

(*a*) that the applicant is unsuitable to hold the licence by reason of having been convicted of an offence or for any other reason ;

(*b*) that if the licence were to be granted, renewed or transferred the business to which it relates would be managed by or carried on for the benefit of a person, other than the applicant, who would be refused the grant, renewal or transfer of such a licence if he made the application himself ;

(*c*) that the number of sex establishments in the relevant locality at the time the application is made is equal to or exceeds the number which the authority consider is appropriate for that locality ;

(*d*) that the grant or renewal of the licence would be inappropriate, having regard—

(i) to the character of the relevant locality ; or

(ii) to the use to which any premises in the vicinity are put ; or

(iii) to the layout, character or condition of the premises, vehicle, vessel or stall in respect of which the application is made.

(4) Nil may be an appropriate number for the purposes of sub-paragraph (3)(*c*) above.

(5) In this paragraph " the relevant locality " means—

(*a*) in relation to premises, the locality where they are situated ; and

(*b*) in relation to a vehicle, vessel or stall, any locality where it is desired to use it as a sex establishment.

Power to prescribe standard conditions

13.—(1) Subject to the provisions of this Schedule, the appropriate authority may make regulations prescribing standard conditions applicable to licences for sex establishments, that is to say, terms, conditions and restrictions on or subject to which licences under this Schedule are in general to be granted, renewed or transferred by them.

(2) Regulations under sub-paragraph (1) above may make different provision—

(*a*) for sex cinemas and sex shops ; and

(*b*) for different kinds of sex cinemas and sex shops.

(3) Without prejudice to the generality of sub-paragraphs (1) and (2) above, regulations under this paragraph may prescribe conditions regulating—

(*a*) the hours of opening and closing of sex establishments ;

(*b*) displays or advertisements on or in such establishments ;

(c) the visibility of the interior of sex establishments to passers-by ; and

(d) any change of a sex cinema to a sex shop or a sex shop to a sex cinema.

(4) Where the appropriate authority have made regulations under sub-paragraph (1) above, every such licence granted, renewed or transferred by them shall be presumed to have been so granted, renewed or transferred subject to any standard conditions applicable to it unless they have been expressly excluded or varied.

(5) Where the appropriate authority have made regulations under sub-paragraph (1) above, they shall, if so requested by any person, supply him with a copy of the regulations on payment of such reasonable fee as the authority may determine.

(6) In any legal proceedings the production of a copy of any regulations made by the appropriate authority under sub-paragraph (1) above purporting to be certified as a true copy by an officer of the authority authorised to give a certificate for the purposes of this paragraph shall be prima facie evidence of such regulations, and no proof shall be required of the handwriting or official position or authority of any person giving such certificate.

Copies of licences and standard conditions

14.—(1) The holder of a licence under this Schedule shall keep exhibited in a suitable place to be specified in the licence a copy of the licence and any regulations made under paragraph 13(1) above which prescribe standard conditions subject to which the licence is held.

(2) The appropriate authority shall send a copy of any licence granted under this Schedule to the chief officer of police for the area where the sex establishment is situated.

Transmission and cancellation of licences

15.—In the event of the death of the holder of a licence granted under this Schedule, that licence shall be deemed to have been granted to his personal representatives and shall, unless previously revoked, remain in force until the end of the period of 3 months beginning with the death and shall then expire ; but the appropriate authority may from time to time, on the application of those representatives, extend or further extend the period of three months if the authority are satisfied that the extension is necessary for the purpose of winding up the deceased's estate and that no other circumstances make it undesirable.

16. The appropriate authority may, at the written request of the holder of a licence, cancel the licence.

Revocation of licences

17.—(1) The appropriate authority may, after giving the holder of a licence under this Schedule an opportunity of appearing before and being heard by them, at any time revoke the licence—

(a) on any ground specified in sub-paragraph (1) of paragraph 12 above ; or

    (*b*) on either of the grounds specified in sub-paragraph (3)(*a*)   Sch 3.
and (*b*) of that paragraph.

(2) Where a licence is revoked, the appropriate authority shall, if
required to do so by the person who held it, give him a statement in
writing of the reasons for their decision within 7 days of his requiring them to do so.

(3) Where a licence is revoked, its holder shall be disqualified
from holding or obtaining a licence in the area of the appropriate
authority for a period of 12 months beginning with the date of
revocation.

Variation of licences

18.—(1) The holder of a licence under this Schedule may at any
time apply to the appropriate authority for any such variation of
the terms, conditions or restrictions on or subject to which the licence
is held as may be specified in the application.

(2) The appropriate authority—

    (*a*) may make the variation specified in the application ; or

    (*b*) may make such variations as they think fit ; or

    (*c*) may refuse the application.

(3) The variations that an authority may make by virtue of sub-
paragraph (2)(*b*) above include, without prejudice to the generality
of that sub-paragraph, variations involving the imposition of terms,
conditions or restrictions other than those specified in the application.

Fees

19. An applicant for the grant, renewal or transfer of a licence
under this Schedule shall pay a reasonable fee determined by the
appropriate authority.

Enforcement

20.—(1) A person who—

    (*a*) knowingly uses, or knowingly causes or permits the use of,
        any premises, vehicle, vessel or stall contrary to paragraph 6
        above ; or

    (*b*) being the holder of a licence for a sex establishment, employs
        in the business of the establishment any person known to
        him to be disqualified from holding such a licence ; or

    (*c*) being the holder of a licence under this Schedule, without
        reasonable excuse knowingly contravenes, or without reason-
        able excuse knowingly permits the contravention of, a term,
        condition or restriction specified in the licence ; or

    (*d*) being the servant or agent of the holder of a licence under
        this Schedule, without reasonable excuse knowingly con-
        travenes, or without reasonable excuse knowingly permits the
        contravention of, a term, condition or restriction specified
        in the licence,

shall be guilty of an offence.

21. Any person who, in connection with an application for the grant, renewal or transfer of a licence under this Schedule, makes a false statement which he knows to be false in any material respect or which he does not believe to be true, shall be guilty of an offence.

22.—(1) A person guilty of an offence under paragraph 20 or 21 above shall be liable on summary conviction to a fine not exceeding £10,000.

(2) A person who, being the holder of a licence under this Schedule, fails without reasonable excuse to comply with paragraph 14(1) above shall be guilty of an offence and liable on summary conviction to a fine not exceeding £200.

Offences relating to persons under 18

23.—(1) A person who, being the holder of a licence for a sex establishment—

> (a) without reasonable excuse knowingly permits a person under 18 years of age to enter the establishment ; or
>
> (b) employs a person known to him to be under 18 years of age in the business of the establishment,

shall be guilty of an offence.

(2) A person guilty of an offence under this paragraph shall be liable on summary conviction to a fine not exceeding £10,000.

Powers of constables and local authority officers

24. If a constable has reasonable cause to suspect that a person has committed an offence under paragraph 20 or 23 above, he may require him to give his name and address, and if that person refuses or fails to do so, or gives a name or address which the constable reasonably suspects to be false, the constable may arrest him without warrant.

25.—(1) A constable may, at any reasonable time, enter and inspect any sex establishment in respect of which a licence under this Schedule is for the time being in force, with a view to seeing—

> (i) whether the terms, conditions or restrictions on or subject to which the licence is held are complied with ;
>
> (ii) whether any person employed in the business of the establishment is disqualified from holding a licence under this Schedule ;
>
> (iii) whether any person under 18 years of age is in the establishment ; and
>
> (iv) whether any person under that age is employed in the business of the establishment.

(2) Subject to sub-paragraph (4) below, a constable may enter and inspect a sex establishment if he has reason to suspect that an offence

under paragraph 20, 21 or 23 above has been, is being, or is about to be committed in relation to it.

(3) An authorised officer of a local authority may exercise the powers conferred by sub-paragraphs (1) and (2) above in relation to a sex establishment in the local authority's area.

(4) No power conferred by sub-paragraph (2) above may be exercised by a constable or an authorised officer of a local authority unless he has been authorised to exercise it by a warrant granted by a justice of the peace.

(5) Where an authorised officer of a local authority exercises any such power, he shall produce his authority if required to do so by the occupier of the premises or the person in charge of the vehicle, vessel or stall in relation to which the power is exercised.

(6) Any person who without reasonable excuse refuses to permit a constable or an authorised officer of a local authority to exercise any such power shall be guilty of an offence and shall for every such refusal be liable on summary conviction to a fine not exceeding £1,000.

Offences by bodies corporate

26.—(1) Where an offence under this Schedule committed by a body corporate is proved to have been committed with the consent or connivance of, or to be attributable to any neglect on the part of, any director, manager, secretary or other similar officer of the body corporate, or any person who was purporting to act in any such capacity, he, as well as the body corporate, shall be guilty of the offence.

(2) Where the affairs of a body corporate are managed by its members sub-paragraph (1) above shall apply to the acts and defaults of a member in connection with his function of management as if he were a director of the body corporate.

Appeals

27.—(1) Subject to sub-paragraphs (2) and (3) below, any of the following persons, that is to say—

- (a) an applicant for the grant, renewal or transfer of a licence under this Schedule whose application is refused ;
- (b) an applicant for the variation of the terms, conditions or restrictions on or subject to which any such licence is held whose application is refused ;
- (c) a holder of any such licence who is aggrieved by any term, condition or restriction on or subject to which the licence is held ; or
- (d) a holder of any such licence whose licence is revoked,

may at any time before the expiration of the period of 21 days beginning with the relevant date appeal to the magistrates' court acting for the relevant area.

Z 2

(2) An applicant whose application for the grant or renewal of a licence is refused, or whose licence is revoked, on any ground specified in paragraph 12(1) above shall not have a right to appeal under this paragraph unless the applicant seeks to show that the ground did not apply to him.

(3) An applicant whose application for the grant or renewal of a licence is refused on either ground specified in paragraph 12(3)(*c*) or (*d*) above shall not have the right to appeal under this paragraph.

(4) In this paragraph—

" the relevant area " means—

    (*a*) in relation to premises, the petty sessions area in which they are situated ; and

    (*b*) in relation to a vehicle, vessel or stall, the petty sessions area in which it is used or, as the case may be, desired to be used as a sex establishment ; and

" the relevant date " means the date on which the person in question is notified of the refusal of his application, the imposition of the term, condition or restriction by which he is aggrieved or the revocation of his licence, as the case may be.

(5) An appeal against the decision of a magistrates' court under this paragraph may be brought to the Crown Court.

1981 c. 54.

(6) Where an appeal is brought to the Crown Court under sub-paragraph (5) above, the decision of the Crown Court shall be final : and accordingly in section 28(2)(*b*) of the Supreme Court Act 1981 for the words " or the Gaming Act 1968 " there shall be substituted the words " , the Gaming Act 1968 or the Local Government (Miscellaneous Provisions) Act 1982 ".

(7) On an appeal to the magistrates' court or the Crown Court under this paragraph the court may make such order as it thinks fit.

(8) Subject to sub-paragraphs (9) to (12) below, it shall be the duty of the appropriate authority to give effect to an order of the magistrates' court or the Crown Court.

(9) The appropriate authority need not give effect to the order of the magistrates' court until the time for bringing an appeal under sub-paragraph (5) above has expired and, if such an appeal is duly brought, until the determination or abandonment of the appeal.

(10) Where a licence is revoked or an application for the renewal of a licence is refused, the licence shall be deemed to remain in force—

    (*a*) until the time for bringing an appeal under this paragraph has expired and, if such an appeal is duly brought, until the determination or abandonment of the appeal ; and

    (*b*) where an appeal relating to the refusal of an application for such a renewal is successful and no further appeal is available, until the licence is renewed by the appropriate authority.

(11) Where—

    (*a*) the holder of a licence makes an application under paragraph 18 above ; and

    (*b*) the appropriate authority impose any term, condition or restriction other than one specified in the application,

the licence shall be deemed to be free of it until the time for bringing an appeal under this paragraph has expired.

(12) Where an appeal is brought under this paragraph against the imposition of any such term, condition or restriction, the licence shall be deemed to be free of it until the determination or abandonment of the appeal.

Provisions relating to existing premises

28.—(1) Without prejudice to any other enactment it shall be lawful for any person who—

    (*a*) was using any premises, vehicle, vessel or stall as a sex establishment immediately before the date of the first publication under subsection (2) of section 2 above of a notice of the passing of a resolution under that section by the local authority for the area ; and

    (*b*) had before the appointed day duly applied to the appropriate authority for a licence for the establishment,

to continue to use the premises, vehicle, vessel or stall as a sex establishment until the determination of his application.

(2) In this paragraph and paragraph 29 below " the appointed day ", in relation to any area, means the day specified in the resolution passed under section 2 above as the date upon which this Schedule is to come into force in that area.

29.—(1) This paragraph applies to an application for the grant of a licence under this Schedule made before the appointed day.

(2) A local authority shall not consider any application to which this paragraph applies before the appointed day.

(3) A local authority shall not grant any application to which this paragraph applies until they have considered all such applications.

(4) In considering which of several applications to which this paragraph applies should be granted a local authority shall give preference over other applicants to any applicant who satisfies them—

    (*a*) that he is using the premises, vehicle, vessel or stall to which the application relates as a sex establishment ; and

    (*b*) that some person was using the premises, vehicle, vessel or stall as a sex establishment on 22nd December 1981 ; and

    (*c*) that—

        (i) he is that person ; or

        (ii) he is a successor of that person in the business or activity which was being carried on there on that date.

Commencement of Schedule

30.—(1) So far as it relates to sex cinemas, this Schedule shall come into force on such day as the Secretary of State may by order made by statutory instrument appoint, and accordingly, until the day so appointed, this Schedule shall have effect—

(*a*) with the omission—

(i) of paragraph 3 above ; and

(ii) of paragraph 13(3)(*d*) above ;

(*b*) as if any reference to a sex establishment were a reference only to a sex shop ; and

(*c*) as if for paragraphs (*a*) and (*b*) of paragraph 13(2) above there were substituted the words " for different kinds of sex shops ".

(2) Subject to sub-paragraph (1) above, this Schedule shall come into force on the day on which this Act is passed.

(3) Where, in relation to any area, the day appointed under sub-paragraph (1) above falls after the day specified in a resolution passed under section 2 above as the day upon which this Schedule is to come into force in that area, the day so appointed shall, for the purposes of paragraphs 28 and 29 above, be the appointed day in relation to sex cinemas in the area.

Section 3.

SCHEDULE 4

STREET TRADING

Interpretation

1.—(1) In this Schedule—

" consent street " means a street in which street trading is prohibited without the consent of the district council ;

" licence street " means a street in which street trading is prohibited without a licence granted by the district council ;

" principal terms ", in relation to a street trading licence, has the meaning assigned to it by paragraph 4(3) below ;

" prohibited street " means a street in which street trading is prohibited ;

" street " includes—

(*a*) any road, footway, beach or other area to which the public have access without payment ; and

1980 c. 66. (*b*) a service area as defined in section 329 of the Highways Act 1980,

and also includes any part of a street ;

" street trading " means, subject to sub-paragraph (2) below, the selling or exposing or offering for sale of any article (including a living thing) in a street ; and

" subsidiary terms ", in relation to a street trading licence, has the meaning assigned to it by paragraph 4(4) below.

(2) The following are not street trading for the purposes of this SCH. 4
Schedule—

   (*a*) trading by a person acting as a pedlar under the authority of a pedlar's certificate granted under the Pedlars Act 1871 c. 96. 1871 ;

   (*b*) anything done in a market or fair the right to hold which was acquired by virtue of a grant (including a presumed grant) or acquired or established by virtue of an enactment or order.

   (*c*) trading in a trunk road picnic area provided by the Secretary of State under section 112 of the Highways Act 1980 c. 66. 1980 ;

   (*d*) trading as a news vendor ;

   (*e*) trading which—

      (i) is carried on at premises used as a petrol filling station ; or

      (ii) is carried on at premises used as a shop or in a street adjoining premises so used and as part of the business of the shop ;

   (*f*) selling things, or offering or exposing them for sale, as a roundsman ;

   (*g*) the use for trading under Part VIIA of the Highways Act 1980 of an object or structure placed on, in or over a highway ;

   (*h*) the operation of facilities for recreation or refreshment under Part VIIA of the Highways Act 1980 ;

   (*j*) the doing of anything authorised by regulations made under section. 5 of the Police, Factories, etc. (Miscellaneous Provisions) Act 1916. 1916 c. 31.

(3) The reference to trading as a news vendor in sub-paragraph (2)(*d*) above is a reference to trading where—

   (*a*) the only articles sold or exposed or offered for sale are newspapers or periodicals ; and

   (*b*) they are sold or exposed or offered for sale without a stall or receptacle for them or with a stall or receptacle for them which does not—

      (i) exceed one metre in length or width or two metres in height ;

      (ii) occupy a ground area exceeding 0·25 square metres ; or

      (iii) stand on the carriageway of a street.

Designation of streets

2.—(1) A district council may by resolution designate any street in their district as—

   (*a*) a prohibited street ;

   (*b*) a licence street ; or

   (*c*) a consent street.

(2) If a district council pass such a resolution as is mentioned in sub-paragraph (1) above, the designation of the street shall take effect on the day specified in that behalf in the resolution (which must not be before the expiration of the period of one month beginning with the day on which the resolution is passed).

(3) A council shall not pass such a resolution unless—

(*a*) they have published notice of their intention to pass such a resolution in a local newspaper circulating in their area ;

(*b*) they have served a copy of the notice—

(i) on the chief officer of police for the area in which the street to be designated by the resolution is situated ; and

(ii) on any highway authority responsible for that street ; and

(*c*) where sub-paragraph (4) below applies, they have obtained the necessary consent.

(4) This sub-paragraph applies—

(*a*) where the resolution relates to a street which is owned or maintainable by a relevant corporation ; and

(*b*) where the resolution designates as a licence street any street maintained by a highway authority ;

and in sub-paragraph (3) above " necessary consent " means—

(i) in the case mentioned in paragraph (*a*) above, the consent of the relevant corporation ; and

(ii) in the case mentioned in paragraph (*b*) above, the consent of the highway authority.

(5) The following are relevant corporations for the purposes of this paragraph—

(*a*) the British Railways Board ;

(*b*) the Commission for the New Towns ;

(*c*) a development corporation for a new town ;

(*d*) an urban development corporation established under the Local Government, Planning and Land Act 1980 ; and

(*e*) the Development Board for Rural Wales.

1980 c. 65.

(6) The notice referred to in sub-paragraph (3) above—

(*a*) shall contain a draft of the resolution ; and

(*b*) shall state that representations relating to it may be made in writing to the council within such period, not less than 28 days after publication of the notice, as may be specified in the notice.

(7) As soon as practicable after the expiry of the period specified under sub-paragraph (6) above, the council shall consider any representations relating to the proposed resolution which they have received before the expiry of that period.

(8) After the council have considered those representations, they may, if they think fit, pass such a resolution relating to the street as is mentioned in sub-paragraph (1) above.

(9) The council shall publish notice that they have passed such a   SCH. 4
resolution in two consecutive weeks in a local newspaper circulating
in their area.

(10) The first publication shall not be later than 28 days before the
day specified in the resolution for the coming into force of the
designation.

(11) Where a street is designated as a licence street, the council
may resolve—

    (*a*) in the resolution which so designates the street ; or

    (*b*) subject to sub-paragraph (12) below, by a separate resolution
        at any time,

that a street trading licence is not to be granted to any person who
proposes to trade in the street for a number of days in every week
less than a number specified in the resolution.

(12) Sub-paragraphs (3)(*a*) and (6) to (10) above shall apply in
relation to a resolution under sub-paragraph (11)(*b*) above as they
apply in relation to a resolution under sub-paragraph (1) above.

(13) Any resolution passed under this paragraph may be varied
or rescinded by a subsequent resolution so passed.

Street trading licences

3.—(1) An application for a street trading licence or the renewal
of such a licence shall be made in writing to the district council.

(2) The applicant shall state—

    (*a*) his full name and address ;

    (*b*) the street in which, days on which and times between which
        he desires to trade ;

    (*c*) the description of articles in which he desires to trade and
        the description of any stall or container which he desires to
        use in connection with his trade in those articles ; and

    (*d*) such other particulars as the council may reasonably require.

(3) If the council so require, the applicant shall submit two
photographs of himself with his application.

(4) A street trading licence shall not be granted—

    (*a*) to a person under the age of 17 years ; or

    (*b*) for any trading in a highway in relation to which a control
        order under section 7 of the Local Government (Miscel-   1976 c. 57.
        laneous Provisions) Act 1976 (road-side sales) is in force,
        other than trading to which the control order does not
        apply.

(5) Subject to sub-paragraph (4) above, it shall be the duty of the
council to grant an application for a street trading licence or the
renewal of such a licence unless they consider that the application
ought to be refused on one or more of the grounds specified in
sub-paragraph (6) below.

(6) Subject to sub-paragraph (8) below, the council may refuse an application on any of the following grounds—

    (*a*) that there is not enough space in the street for the applicant to engage in the trading in which he desires to engage without causing undue interference or inconvenience to persons using the street ;

    (*b*) that there are already enough traders trading in the street from shops or otherwise in the goods in which the applicant desires to trade ;

    (*c*) that the applicant desires to trade on fewer days than the minimum number specified in a resolution under paragraph 2(11) above ;

    (*d*) that the applicant is unsuitable to hold the licence by reason of having been convicted of an offence or for any other reason ;

    (*e*) that the applicant has at any time been granted a street trading licence by the council and has persistently refused or neglected to pay fees due to them for it or charges due to them under paragraph 9(6) below for services rendered by them to him in his capacity as licence-holder ;

    (*f*) that the applicant has at any time been granted a street trading consent by the council and has persistently refused or neglected to pay fees due to them for it ;

    (*g*) that the applicant has without reasonable excuse failed to avail himself to a reasonable extent of a previous street trading licence.

(7) If the council consider that grounds for refusal exist under sub-paragraph (6)(*a*), (*b*) or (*g*) above, they may grant the applicant a licence which permits him—

    (*a*) to trade on fewer days or during a shorter period in each day than specified in the application ; or

    (*b*) to trade only in one or more of the descriptions of goods specified in the application.

(8) If—

    (*a*) a person is licensed or otherwise authorised to trade in a street under the provisions of any local Act ; and

    (*b*) the street becomes a licence street ; and

    (*c*) he was trading from a fixed position in the street immediately before it became a licence street ; and

    (*d*) he applied for a street trading licence to trade in the street, his application shall not be refused on any of the grounds mentioned in sub-paragraph (6)(*a*) to (*c*) above.

4.—(1) A street trading licence shall specify—

    (*a*) the street in which, days on which and times between which the licence-holder is permitted to trade ; and

    (*b*) the description of articles in which he is permitted to trade.

(2) If the district council determine that a licence-holder is to confine his trading to a particular place in the street, his street trading licence shall specify that place.

(3) Matters that fall to be specified in a street trading licence by virtue of sub-paragraph (1) or (2) above are referred to in this Schedule as the " principal terms " of the licence.

(4) When granting or renewing a street trading licence, the council may attach such further conditions (in this Schedule referred to as the "subsidiary terms" of the licence) as appear to them to be reasonable.

(5) Without prejudice to the generality of sub-paragraph (4) above, the subsidiary terms of a licence may include conditions—

(a) specifying the size and type of any stall or container which the licence-holder may use for trading ;

(b) requiring that any stall or container so used shall carry the name of the licence-holder or the number of his licence or both ; and

(c) prohibiting the leaving of refuse by the licence-holder or restricting the amount of refuse which he may leave or the places in which he may leave it.

(6) A street trading licence shall, unless previously revoked or surrendered, remain valid for a period of 12 months from the date on which it is granted or, if a shorter period is specified in the licence, for that period.

(7) If a district council resolve that the whole or part of a licence street shall be designated a prohibited street, then, on the designation taking effect, any street trading licence issued for trading in that street shall cease to be valid so far as it relates to the prohibited street.

5.—(1) A district council may at any time revoke a street trading licence if they consider—

(a) that, owing to circumstances which have arisen since the grant or renewal of the licence, there is not enough space in the street for the licence-holder to engage in the trading permitted by the licence without causing undue inter- ference or inconvenience to persons using the street ;

(b) that the licence-holder is unsuitable to hold the licence by reason of having been convicted of an offence or for any other reason ;

(c) that, since the grant or renewal of the licence, the licence- holder has persistently refused or neglected to pay fees due to the council for it or charges due to them under para- graph 9(6) below for services rendered by them to him in his capacity as licence-holder ; or

(d) that, since the grant or renewal of the licence, the licence- holder has without reasonable excuse failed to avail himself of the licence to a reasonable extent.

(2) If the council consider that they have ground for revoking a licence by virtue of sub-paragraph (1)(a) or (d) above, they may, instead of revoking it, vary its principal terms—

(a) by reducing the number of days or the period in any one day during which the licence-holder is permitted to trade ; or (*b*) by restricting the descriptions of goods in which he is permitted to trade.

(3) A licence-holder may at any time surrender his licence to the council and it shall then cease to be valid.

6.—(1) When a district council receive an application for the grant or renewal of a street trading licence, they shall within a reasonable time—

(*a*) grant a licence in the terms applied for ; or

(*b*) serve notice on the applicant under sub-paragraph (2) below.

(2) If the council propose—

(*a*) to refuse an application for the grant or renewal of a licence ; or

(*b*) to grant a licence on principal terms different from those specified in the application ; or

(*c*) to grant a licence confining the applicant's trading to a particular place in a street ; or

(*d*) to vary the principal terms of a licence ; or

(*e*) to revoke a licence,

they shall first serve a notice on the applicant or, as the case may be, the licence-holder—

(i) specifying the ground or grounds on which their decision would be based ; and

(ii) stating that within 7 days of receiving the notice he may in writing require them to give him an opportunity to make representations to them concerning it.

(3) Where a notice has been served under sub-paragraph (2) above, the council shall not determine the matter until either—

(*a*) the person on whom it was served has made representations to them concerning their decision ; or

(*b*) the period during which he could have required them to give him an opportunity to make representations has elapsed without his requiring them to give him such an opportunity ; or

(*c*) the conditions specified in sub-paragraph (4) below are satisfied.

(4) The conditions mentioned in sub-paragraph (3)(*c*) above are—

(*a*) that the person on whom the notice under sub-paragraph (2) above was served has required the council to give him an opportunity to make representations to them concerning it, as provided by sub-paragraph (2)(ii) above ;

(*b*) that the council have allowed him a reasonable period for making his representations ; and

(*c*) that he has failed to make them within that period.

(5) A person aggrieved—

(*a*) by the refusal of a council to grant or renew a licence, where—

(i) they specified in their notice under sub-paragraph (2) above one of the grounds mentioned in paragraph

    3(6)(*d*) to (*g*) above as the only ground on which their decision would be based ; or

      (ii) they specified more than one ground in that notice but all the specified grounds were grounds mentioned in those paragraphs ; or

(*b*) by a decision of a council to grant him a licence with principal terms different from those of a licence which he previously held, where they specified in their notice under sub-paragraph (2) above the ground mentioned in paragraph 3(6)(*g*) above as the only ground on which their decision would be based ; or

(*c*) by a decision of a council—

      (i) to vary the principal terms of a licence ; or

      (ii) to revoke a licence,

in a case where they specified in their notice under sub-paragraph (2) above one of the grounds mentioned in paragraph 5(1)(*b*) to (*d*) above as the only ground on which their decision would be based or they specified more than one ground in that notice but all the specified grounds were grounds mentioned in those paragraphs,

may, at any time before the expiration of the period of 21 days beginning with the date upon which he is notified of the refusal or decision, appeal to the magistrates' court acting for the petty sessions area in which the street is situated.

(6) An appeal against the decisions of a magistrates' court under this paragraph may be brought to the Crown Court.

(7) On an appeal to the magistrates' court or the Crown Court under this paragraph the court may make such order as it thinks fit.

(8) Subject to sub-paragraphs (9) to (11) below, it shall be the duty of the council to give effect to an order of the magistrates' court or the Crown Court.

(9) The council need not give effect to the order of the magistrates' court until the time for bringing an appeal under sub-paragraph (6) above has expired and, if such an appeal is duly brought, until the determination or abandonment of the appeal.

(10) If a licence-holder applies for renewal of his licence before the date of its expiry, it shall remain valid—

(*a*) until the grant by the council of a new licence with the same principal terms ; or

(*b*) if—

      (i) the council refuse renewal of the licence or decide to grant a licence with principal terms different from those of the existing licence, and

      (ii) he has a right of appeal under this paragraph,

until the time for bringing an appeal has expired or, where an appeal is duly brought, until the determination or abandonment of the appeal ; or (*c*) if he has no right of appeal under this paragraph, until the council either grant him a new licence with principal terms different from those of the existing licence or notify him of their decision to refuse his application.

(11) Where—
(*a*) a council decide—
(i) to vary the principal terms of a licence ; or
(ii) to revoke a licence ; and
(*b*) a right of appeal is available to the licence-holder under this paragraph,

the variation or revocation shall not take effect until the time for bringing an appeal has expired or, where an appeal is duly brought, until the determination or abandonment of the appeal.

Street trading consents

7.—(1) An application for a street trading consent or the renewal of such a consent shall be made in writing to the district council.

(2) Subject to sub-paragraph (3) below, the council may grant a consent if they think fit.

(3) A street trading consent shall not be granted—
(*a*) to a person under the age of 17 years ; or
(*b*) for any trading in a highway to which a control order under section 7 of the Local Government (Miscellaneous Provisions) Act 1976 is in force, other than trading to which the control order does not apply.

1976 c. 57.

(4) When granting or renewing a street trading consent the council may attach such conditions to it as they consider reasonably necessary.

(5) Without prejudice to the generality of sub-paragraph (4) above, the conditions that may be attached to a street trading consent by virtue of that sub-paragraph include conditions to prevent—
(*a*) obstruction of the street or danger to persons using it ; or
(*b*) nuisance or annoyance (whether to persons using the street or otherwise).

(6) The council may at any time vary the conditions of a street trading consent.

(7) Subject to sub-paragraph (8) below, the holder of a street trading consent shall not trade in a consent street from a van or other vehicle or from a stall, barrow or cart.

(8) The council may include in a street trading consent permission for its holder to trade in a consent street—
(*a*) from a stationary van, cart, barrow or other vehicle ; or
(*b*) from a portable stall.

(9) If they include such a permission, they may make the consent subject to conditions—
(*a*) as to where the holder of the street trading consent may trade by virtue of the permission ; and

(*b*) as to the times between which or periods for which he may so trade.

(10) A street trading consent may be granted for any period not exceeding 12 months but may be revoked at any time.

(11) The holder of a street trading consent may at any time surrender his consent to the council and it shall then cease to be valid.

General

8. The holder of a street trading licence or a street trading consent may employ any other person to assist him in his trading without a further licence or consent being required.

9.—(1) A district council may charge such fees as they consider reasonable for the grant or renewal of a street trading licence or a street trading consent.

(2) A council may determine different fees for different types of licence or consent and, in particular, but without prejudice to the generality of this sub-paragraph, may determine fees differing according—

(*a*) to the duration of the licence or consent ;

(*b*) to the street in which it authorises trading ; and

(*c*) to the descriptions of articles in which the holder is authorised to trade.

(3) A council may require that applications for the grant or renewal of licences or consents shall be accompanied by so much of the fee as the council may require, by way of a deposit to be repaid by the council to the applicant if the application is refused.

(4) A council may determine that fees may be paid by instalments.

(5) Where a consent is surrendered or revoked, the council shall remit or refund, as they consider appropriate, the whole or a part of any fee paid for the grant or renewal of the consent.

(6) A council may recover from a licence-holder such reasonable charges as they may determine for the collection of refuse, the cleansing of streets and other services rendered by them to him in his capacity as licence-holder.

(7) Where a licence—

(*a*) is surrendered or revoked ; or

(*b*) ceases to be valid by virtue of paragraph 4(7) above,

the council may remit or refund, as they consider appropriate, the whole or a part—

    (i) of any fee paid for the grant or renewal of the licence ; or

    (ii) of any charges recoverable under sub-paragraph (6) above.

(8) The council may determine—

(*a*) that charges under sub-paragraph (6) above shall be included in a fee payable under sub-paragraph (1) above ; or (*b*) that they shall be separately recoverable.

(9) Before determining charges to be made under sub-paragraph (6) above or varying the amount of such charges the council—

    (*a*) shall give notice of the proposed charges to licence-holders ; and

    (*b*) shall publish notice of the proposed charges in a local newspaper circulating in their area.

(10) A notice under sub-paragraph (9) above shall specify a reasonable period within which representations concerning the proposed charges may be made to the council.

(11) It shall be the duty of a council to consider any such representations which are made to them within the period specified in the notice.

Offences

10.—(1) A person who—

    (*a*) engages in street trading in a prohibited street ; or

    (*b*) engages in street trading in a licence street or a consent street without being authorised to do so under this Schedule ; or

    (*c*) contravenes any of the principal terms of a street trading licence ; or

    (*d*) being authorised by a street trading consent to trade in a consent street, trades in that street—

        (i) from a stationary van, cart, barrow or other vehicle ; or

        (ii) from a portable stall,

    without first having been granted permission to do so under paragraph 7(8) above ; or

    (*e*) contravenes a condition imposed under paragraph 7(9) above,

shall be guilty of an offence.

(2) It shall be a defence for a person charged with an offence under sub-paragraph (1) above to prove that he took all reasonable precautions and exercised all due diligence to avoid commission of the offence.

(3) Any person who, in connection with an application for a street trading licence or for a street trading consent, makes a false statement which he knows to be false in any material respect, or which he does not believe to be true, shall be guilty of an offence.

(4) A person guilty of an offence under this paragraph shall be liable on summary conviction to a fine not exceeding £200.

Savings

11. Nothing in this Schedule shall affect—

1847 c. 14.   (*a*) section 13 of the Markets and Fairs Clauses Act 1847 (prohibition of sales elsewhere than in market or in shops etc.) as applied by any other Act ;

(*b*) section 55 of the Food and Drugs Act 1955 (prohibition of certain sales during market hours).

Sch. 4
1955 c. 16
(4 & 5 Eliz. 2).

SCHEDULE 5

Section 20.

Highway Amenities

Part I

Addition of Part VIIA to Highways Act 1980

1. The following shall be inserted after section 115 of the Highways Act 1980— 1980 c. 66.

"Part VIIA

Provision of Amenities on Certain Highways

Scope of Part VIIA.
115A.—(1) This Part of this Act applies—

(*a*) to a highway in relation to which a pedestrian planning order is in force ;

(*b*) to a bridleway ;

(*c*) to a footpath (including a walkway as defined in section 35(2) above) ;

(*d*) to a footway ;

(*e*) to a subway constructed under section 69 above ;

(*f*) to a footbridge constructed under section 70 above ;

(*g*) to a highway of a description not mentioned in any of the preceding paragraphs of this definition whose use by vehicular traffic is prohibited by a traffic order but whose use by other traffic is not prohibited or restricted or regulated by such an order ; and

(*h*) to a local Act walkway.

(2) In this Part of this Act—

"local Act walkway" means a way or place which is declared in pursuance of a local enactment to be a walkway, city walkway or pedestrian way ;

"pedestrian planning order" means an order made under section 212(2) of the Town and Country Planning Act 1971 ; and 1971 c. 78.

"traffic order" means an order made under section 1 or 6 of the Road Traffic Regulation Act 1967 (traffic regulation orders) or under section 9 of that Act (experimental traffic orders) ; and 1967 c. 76.

"walkway consent" means—

(*a*) in relation to a walkway as defined in section 35(2) above, the consent—

(i) of any person who is an occupier of the building in which the walkway subsists and to whom subsection (3) below applies ; **and**

(ii) of the persons whose agreement would be needed for the creation of the walkway if it did not already subsist ; and

(*b*) in relation to a local Act walkway, the consent—

(i) of any person who is an owner or occupier of premises adjoining the walkway and to whom subsection (3) below applies ; and

(ii) of the owner of the land on, under or above which the walkway subsists.

(3) The persons to whom this subsection applies are persons who, in the opinion of a council, are likely to be materially affected—

(*a*) by the exercise of a power which the council may not exercise until they have first obtained walkway consent ; or

(*b*) by a grant of permission which the council may not grant unless they have first obtained walkway consent.

(4) In the following provisions of this Part of this Act " walkway " includes both a walkway as defined in section 35(2) above and a local Act walkway.

(5) Any reference in this Part of this Act to a highway to which this Part of this Act applies includes a reference to a local Act walkway which but for this subsection—

(*a*) is not a highway ; or

(*b*) is a highway only for certain purposes.

(6) The use of a highway by vehicular traffic is to be taken as prohibited for the purposes of this Part of this Act where its use by such traffic is prohibited over the whole width of the highway even if the prohibition is contained in a traffic order which does not prohibit certain vehicles or certain classes of vehicle using the highway or part of it or using the highway or part of it at certain times or on certain days or during certain periods.

(7) In this Part of this Act " frontagers " means the owners and occupiers of any premises adjoining the part of a highway on, in or over which an object or structure would be placed or on which facilities for recreation or refreshment or both have been, are being or would be provided ; but frontagers have an interest under this Part of this Act only in proposals to place objects or structures or provide or operate facilities wholly or partly between their premises and the centre of the highway.

(8) References to a council in this Part of this Act include references to the Council of the Isles of Scilly.

Provision
etc. of
services and
amenities by
councils.

115B.—(1) Subject to subsections (4), (5) and (7) below, a council shall have power—

(*a*) to carry out works on, in or over a highway to which this Part of this Act applies ; and

(*b*) to place objects or structures on, in or over such a highway,

for the purpose—

(i) of giving effect to a pedestrian planning order ;

(ii) of enhancing the amenity of the highway and its immediate surroundings ; or

(iii) of providing a service for the benefit of the public or a section of the public.

(2) A council shall have power to maintain—

(*a*) any works carried out under paragraph (*a*) of subsection (1) above ; and

(*b*) any objects or structures placed on, in or over a highway under paragraph (*b*) of that subsection.

(3) Without prejudice to the generality of this section, the amenity of a highway may be enhanced by providing lawns, trees, shrubs or flowers.

(4) A council may not exercise the powers conferred by this section on, in or over a walkway unless they have first obtained walkway consent.

(5) Where subsection (6) below applies, a council may not, in the exercise of the power conferred by subsection (1)(*b*) above, place an object or structure on, in or over a highway—

(*a*) for a purpose which will result in the production of income ; or

(*b*) for the purpose of providing a centre for advice or information,

unless they have first obtained the consent of the frontagers with an interest—

(i) to the placing of the object or structure ; and

(ii) to the purpose for which it is to be placed.

(6) This subsection applies where the object or structure would be placed—

(*a*) on, in or over a footpath ;

(*b*) on, in or over a bridleway ; or

(*c*) on, in or over a footway in relation to which no pedestrian planning order or traffic order is in force.

(7) Where a council propose—

    (*a*) to place an object or structure on, in or over a highway to which this Part of this Act applies—

        (i) for a purpose which will result in the production of income ; or

        (ii) for the purpose of providing a centre for advice or information ; and

    (*b*) to grant a person permission under section 115E below to use the object or structure,

they may not exercise the power conferred by subsection (1)(*b*) above unless they have first obtained the consent of the frontagers with an interest—

        (i) to the placing of the object or structure ;

        (ii) to the purpose for which it would be placed ; and

        (iii) to the proposed grant of permission.

Provision of recreation and refreshment facilities by councils.

115C.—(1) Subject to subsections (2) and (3) below, a council shall have power to provide, maintain and operate facilities for recreation or refreshment or both on a highway to which this Part of this Act applies.

(2) A council may not exercise the powers conferred by this section on a walkway unless they have first obtained walkway consent.

(3) Where subsection (4) below applies, a council may not exercise the powers conferred by this section unless they have first obtained the consent of the frontagers with an interest.

(4) This subsection applies where the facilities are to be provided—

    (*a*) on a footpath ; or

    (*b*) on a bridleway ; or

    (*c*) on a footway in relation to which no pedestrian planning order or traffic order is in force.

Limits of powers under ss. 115B and 115C.

115D. A council may exercise their powers under section 115B or 115C above to restrict the access of the public to any part of a highway to which this Part of this Act applies, but shall not so exercise them—

    (*a*) as to prevent traffic, other than vehicular traffic,—

        (i) entering the highway at any place where such traffic could enter it before, as the case may be, the making of a pedestrian planning order or a traffic order in relation to it or the exercise in relation to it of a power conferred by this Part of this Act ; or

        (ii) passing along it ; or

          (iii) having normal access to premises ad-
joining it ; or

    (*b*) as to prevent any use of vehicles which is per-
mitted by a pedestrian planning order or which
is not prohibited by a traffic order ; or

    (*c*) as to prevent statutory undertakers or sewerage
authorities having access to any apparatus
of theirs under, in, on or over the highway.

Execution
of works
and use of
objects etc.
by persons
other than
councils.

115E.—(1) Subject to subsections (2) to (4) below, a
council may grant a person permission—

    (*a*) to do on, in or over a highway to which this Part
of this Act applies anything which the council
could do on, in or over such a highway under
section 115B(1) to (3) or 115C above ; or

    (*b*) to use objects or structures on, in or over a
highway to which this Part of this Act applies—

          (i) for a purpose which will result in the
production of income ;

          (ii) for the purpose of providing a centre
for advice or information ; or

          (iii) for the purpose of advertising.

(2) A council may not grant a person permission under
subsection (1)(*a*) above to place an object or structure on,
in or over a highway to which this Part of this Act
applies—

    (*a*) for a purpose which will result in the production
of income ; or

    (*b*) for the purpose of providing a centre for advice
or information,

unless they have first obtained the consent of the frontagers with an interest—

          (i) to the placing of the object or struc-
ture ;

          (ii) to the purpose for which it would be
placed ; and

          (iii) to the proposed grant of permission.

(3) A council may not grant a person permission to
do anything which the council could only do under
section 115C above unless they have first obtained the
consent of the frontagers with an interest.

(4) A council may not grant a person permission—

    (*a*) to carry out works on, in or over a walkway ;

    (*b*) to place an object or structure on, in or over a
walkway ; or

    (*c*) to provide, maintain or operate facilities for re-
creation or refreshment or both on a walkway,

unless they have first obtained walkway consent.

Sch. 5

Power to impose conditions on permissions under section 115E.

115F.—(1) Subject to subsections (2) to (4) below, a council may grant a permission under section 115E above upon such conditions as they think fit, including conditions requiring the payment to the council of such reasonable charges as they may determine.

(2) Except where the council are the owners of the subsoil beneath the part of the highway in relation to which the permission is granted, the charges may not exceed the standard amount.

(3) In subsection (2) above, "the standard amount" means—

(a) in relation to permission to use an object or structure provided by a council, the aggregate—

(i) of the cost of providing it ; and

(ii) of such charges as will reimburse the council their reasonable expenses in connection with granting the permission ;

(b) in relation to permission to operate facilities provided by a council for recreation or refreshment or both, the aggregate—

(i) of the cost of providing them ; and

(ii) of such charges as will reimburse the council their reasonable expenses in connection with granting the permission ; and

(c) in any other case, such charges as will reimburse the council their reasonable expenses in connection with granting the permission.

(4) Nothing in this section shall prejudice the right of a council to require an indemnity against any claim in respect of injury, damage or loss arising out of the grant of the permission ; but this subsection is not to be taken as requiring any person to indemnify a council against any claim in respect of injury, damage or loss which is attributable to the negligence of the council.

Notices to be given before exercise of powers under Part VIIA.

115G.—(1) Subject to subsection (4) below, a council shall not—

(a) exercise any power conferred by section 115B or 115C above ; or

(b) grant any permission under section 115E above unless they have first published a notice under this section.

(2) A council shall publish a notice under this section—

(a) by affixing it in a conspicuous position at or near the place to which the proposal relates ; and

(b) by serving a copy of the notice on the owner and occupier of any premises appearing to the council to be likely to be materially affected.

(3) A notice under this section—

    (*a*) shall give details of the proposal ; and

    (*b*) shall specify a period (being not less than 28 days after the publication of the notice) during which representations regarding the proposal may be made to the council.

(4) No notice under this section is required where a council propose to exercise a power conferred by section 115B or 115C above in relation to a highway in relation to which a pedestrian planning order or a traffic order has been made.

(5) Where a council have published a notice under this section, they shall not exercise the power or grant the permission to which the notice relates until they have taken into consideration all representations made to them in connection with the proposal within the period specified in the notice.

Duties to consult or obtain consent of other authorities.

115H.—(1) Subject to subsections (2) and (3) below, a council shall not—

    (*a*) exercise any power conferred by section 115B or 115C above ; or

    (*b*) grant any permission under section 115E above, in relation to a highway unless they have consulted—

        (i) any authority other than themselves who are the highway authority for the highway ; and

        (ii) any authority other than themselves who are a local planning authority, as defined in the Town and Country Planning Act 1971, 1971 c. 78. for the area in which, as the case may be, they propose to exercise the power or to which the proposed permission would relate.

(2) Where a highway to which this Part of this Act applies is situated in Greater London, subsection (1) above shall have effect in relation to the highway as if the requirement to consult the highway authority and the local planning authority were a requirement to obtain their consent to the exercise of the power or the granting of the permission.

(3) Where—

    (*a*) a highway to which this Part of this Act applies is situated outside Greater London ; and

    (*b*) there is no pedestrian planning order in force in relation to it,

subsection (1) above shall have effect in relation to the highway as if the requirement to consult the highway authority were a requirement to obtain their consent to the exercise of the power or the granting of the permission.

(4) Where a highway to which this Part of this Act applies is maintained by the British Railways Board or the London Transport Executive, a council shall not exercise any power conferred by section 115B or 115C above or grant a permission in relation to it under section 115E above except with the consent of the Board or, as the case may be, the Executive.

Consents not to be unreasonably withheld.

115J.—(1) Consent to which this section applies is not to be unreasonably withheld but may be given subject to any reasonable conditions.

(2) Without prejudice to the generality of subsection (1) above, it may be reasonable for consent to which this section applies to be given for a specified period of time or subject to the payment of a reasonable sum.

(3) Consent is to be treated as unreasonably withheld for the purposes of this section if—

(a) the council have served a notice asking for consent on the person whose consent is required ; and

(b) he fails within 28 days of the service of the notice to give the council notice of his consent or his refusal to give it.

(4) Any question whether consent is unreasonably withheld or is given subject to reasonable conditions shall be referred to and determined by an arbitrator to be appointed, in default of agreement, by the President of the Chartered Institute of Arbitrators.

(5) If—

(a) the arbitrator determines that consent has been unreasonably withheld ; but

(b) it appears to him that there are conditions subject to which it would be reasonable to give it,

he may direct that it shall be treated as having been given subject to those conditions.

(6) If—

(a) the arbitrator determines that any condition subject to which consent has been given is unreasonable ; but

(b) it appears to him that there are conditions subject to which it would have been reasonable to give it,

he may direct that it shall be treated as having been given subject to those conditions.

(7) Subject to subsection (8) below, the expenses and remuneration of the arbitrator shall be paid by the council seeking the consent.

SCH. 5

(8) Where the arbitration concerns the consent of the British Railways Board or the London Transport Executive under section 115H(4) above, the arbitrator may give such directions as he thinks fit as to the payment of his expenses and remuneration.

(9) This section applies to consent required under any provision of this Part of this Act except section 115H(1) above.

Failure to comply with terms of permission.

115K.—(1) If it appears to a council that a person to whom they have granted a permission under section 115E above has committed any breach of the terms of that permission, they may serve a notice on him requiring him to take such steps to remedy the breach as are specified in the notice within such time as is so specified.

(2) If a person on whom a notice is served under subsection (1) above fails to comply with the notice, the council may take the steps themselves.

(3) Where a council have incurred expenses in the exercise of the power conferred on them by subsection (2) above, those expenses, together with interest at such reasonable rate as the council may determine from the date of service of a notice of demand for the expenses, may be recovered by the council from the person on whom the notice under subsection (1) above was served.".

PART II

AMENDMENTS OF TOWN AND COUNTRY PLANNING ACT 1971

2. In section 212 of the Town and Country Planning Act 1971 (order extinguishing right to use vehicles on highway) the following subsection shall be inserted after subsection (8)— 1971 c. 78.

" (8A) An order under subsection (8) of this section may make provision requiring the removal of any obstruction of a highway resulting from the exercise of powers under Part VIIA of the Highways Act 1980.". 1980 c. 66.

3. Section 213 of that Act (provision of amenity for highway reserved to pedestrians) shall cease to have effect, and " 212 " shall accordingly be substituted for " 213 " in Part II of Schedule 21.

SCHEDULE 6

Section 47.

MINOR AMENDMENTS

Health

1. In subsection (1)(*b*) of section 3 of the Public Health Act 1936 (jurisdiction, powers, etc. of port health authority) for the words from " contained " onwards there shall be substituted the words " relating to public health, waste disposal or the control of pollution, whether passed before or after, or contained in, this Act ". 1936 c. 49.

2. In subsection (1)(*c*) of section 169 of that Act (provision for removal to hospital of persons suffering from notifiable disease where

Sch. 6   serious risk of infection) after the word " hospital " there shall be inserted the words " vested in the Secretary of State,".

3. In section 160(3) of that Act (which provides in certain cases for the recovery of a sum in respect of disinfecting a public conveyance) for the words " in a summary manner " there shall be substituted the words " summarily as a civil debt ".

4. In section 267 of that Act (application to ships and boats of certain provisions of Act), in paragraph (*a*) of subsection (3), after the words " county, of the " there shall be inserted the words " port health authority or " ; and at the end of that section there shall be added the following subsection—

" (6) In determining for the purposes of subsection (1) above what provisions of this Act specified in subsection (4) above are provisions for the execution of which local authorities are responsible, no account shall be taken of any enactment (whether contained in this Act or not) relating to port health authorities or joint boards or to any particular port health authority or joint board or of any instrument made under any such enactment ".

5. In section 346(1)(*c*) of that Act (by virtue of which, among other things, an order, rule or regulation which was made under any enactment repealed by that Act but which could have been made under a corresponding provision of that Act has effect as if it had been made under that corresponding provision) after the word " regulation," there shall be inserted the word " byelaw,".

1968 c. 46.   6. In section 48(2)(*b*)(iii) of the Health Services and Public Health Act 1968 (which requires a copy of a certificate to be sent in certain cases to the proper officer of the relevant port health
1936 c. 49.   authority constituted in pursuance of section 2 of the Public Health Act 1936) the words " constituted in pursuance of section 2 of the Public Health Act 1936 " shall be omitted.

Planning

1971 c. 78.   7. The Town and Country Planning Act 1971 shall be amended—

(*a*) by inserting the words " and paragraph 8 of Schedule 16
1972 c. 70.   to the Local Government Act 1972 " after the word " Act " in section 10(7) ; and

(*b*) in the provisions specified in the first column of the Table below, by substituting the corrected text set out in the third column for the portion of the text indicated in the second column.

TABLE

Provision of 1971 *Act*	Text to be corrected	Corrected text
Section 7(4)	(3)(*a*)	(1A)(*a*)
Section 15(3)	The words from the beginning to " the provisions of "	Subject to subsection (4) of this section and to section 15A of this Act,
Section 15A(6)	mentioned in subsection (4)	specified in subsection (7)
Section 15A(7)	(3) above	(6) of this section
Section 23(9)	served	issued
Section 177(2)(*a*)	88(1)	88(2)
Section 242(3)(*f*)	section 88(5)(*a*) of this Act	paragraph (*a*) of section 88B(1) of this Act or to discharge a condition or limitation under paragraph (*b*) of that subsection.
Section 242(3)(*h*)	The words from " under subsection (5)(*a*) " onwards.	to grant listed building consent under paragraph (*a*) of section 97A(4) of this Act or to discharge a condition or limitation under paragraph (*b*) of that subsection.
Schedule 4, paragraph 12(2)	15A(3)	15A(6)

Direct labour

8.—(1) The following subsection shall be added at the end of section 21 of the Local Government, Planning and Land Act 1980 1980 c. 65. (which exempts small direct labour organisations from the requirements of Part III of that Act)—

" (8) In this section " year " means a financial year.".

(2) This paragraph extends to Scotland.

SCHEDULE 7

Section 47.

REPEALS

PART I

REPEALS IN PUBLIC GENERAL ACTS IN CONSEQUENCE OF SECTION 1

Chapter	Short title	Extent of repeal
53 & 54 Vict. c. 59.	Public Health Acts Amendment Act 1890.	Section 51.
16 & 17 Geo. 5. c. 31.	Home Counties (Music and Dancing) Licensing Act 1926.	The whole Act.

Chapter	Short title	Extent of repeal
12, 13 & 14 Geo. 6. c. 101.	Justices of the Peace Act 1949.	In section 41, in subsection (1), the words " or music and dancing licence ", in subsection (4) the words from " and the " to the end and subsection (5).
1964 c. 26.	Licensing Act 1964.	In section 77 the words from " in any area " to " dancing ". In section 78 the words from "and which are" to "dancing". Section 79(7).
1966 c. 42.	Local Government Act 1966.	In Schedule 3, in Part II, paragraphs 10 and 27.
1967 c. 19.	Private Places of Entertainment (Licensing) Act 1967.	Section 6.
1967 c. 80.	Criminal Justice Act 1967.	In Schedule 3, in Part I, the entries relating to the Public Health Acts Amendment Act 1890 and the Home Counties (Music and Dancing) Licensing Act 1926.
1972 c. 70.	Local Government Act 1972.	Section 204(7). In Schedule 14, in Part II, paragraph 24(*c*), paragraph 25(2) (*b*) and paragraph 26(*b*). In Schedule 25, in Part II, paragraphs 10 to 12. In Schedule 29, paragraph 27.
1974 c. 7.	Local Government Act 1974.	In Schedule 6, paragraph 3.
1980 c. 43.	Magistrates' Courts Act 1980.	In Schedule 6, in Part III, paragraph 2.

Part II

Repeals in Local Acts in Consequence of Section 1

Chapter	Short title	Extent of repeal
1976 c. xxxi.	Royal County of Berkshire (Public Entertainment) Provisional Order Confirmation Act 1976.	The whole Act.
1976 c. xxxv.	County of South Glamorgan Act 1976.	Sections 15 to 23. In section 24, the words " this Part of this Act or ". In section 66(2)(*b*), the words " Part IV (Music and dancing licences in Cardiff); ". In Schedule 3, in Part I, the words " Section 19 (Fines under Part IV of Act); ".
1979 c. xxiii.	Greater London Council (General Powers) Act 1979.	Paragraph (*b*) of section 3.

Chapter	Short title	Extent of repeal
1980 c. x.	County of Merseyside Act 1980.	Sections 73 to 80. In section 81(1) the words " of an entertainment licence, or ". In section 137(2), the words " Section 76 (Offences under Part XI); ".
1980 c. xi.	West Midlands County Council Act 1980.	Sections 59 to 66. In section 67(1), the words " of an entertainment licence or ". Section 93. In section 116(2), the words " Section 62 (Offences under Part VIII); ".
1980 c. xiii.	Cheshire County Council Act 1980.	Sections 32 to 39. In section 40(1), the words " of an entertainment licence or ". In section 108(2), the words " Section 35 (Offences under Part VII); ".
1980 c. xiv.	West Yorkshire Act 1980.	Sections 25 to 32. In section 33(1), the words " of an entertainment licence or ". In Schedule 3, the words " Section 28 (Offences under Part VII); ".
1980 c. xxxvii.	South Yorkshire Act 1980.	Section 48.
1981 c. ix.	Greater Manchester Act 1981.	Sections 107 to 114. In section 115(1), the words " of an entertainment licence or ". In section 179(2), the words " Section 110 (Offences under Part XIII); ".
1981 c. xviii.	County of Kent Act 1981.	Sections 63 to 70. In section 71(1), the words " of an entertainment licence or ". In section 128(2) the words " Section 66 (Offences under Part X); ".
1981 c. xxv.	East Sussex Act 1981.	Section 30.

PART III

REPEAL IN LOCAL ACT IN CONSEQUENCE OF SECTION 8

Chapter	Short title	Extent of repeal
1980 c. xi.	West Midlands County Council Act 1980.	Section 51.

PART IV

REPEALS IN PUBLIC GENERAL ACTS IN CONSEQUENCE OF SECTION 11

Chapter	Short title	Extent of repeal
15 & 16 Geo. 5. c. 50.	Theatrical Employers Registration Act 1925.	The whole Act.
18 & 19 Geo. 5. c. 46.	Theatrical Employers Registration (Amendment) Act 1928.	The whole Act.
1968 c. 54.	Theatres Act 1968.	In Schedule 2, the entry relating to the Theatrical Employers Registration Act 1925.
1971 c. 23.	Courts Act 1971.	In Schedule 9, the entry relating to the Theatrical Employers Registration Act 1925.
1972 c. 70.	Local Government Act 1972.	In section 204(6), the words from " and in the definition " to the end.
1972 c. 71.	Criminal Justice Act 1972.	In Schedule 5, the entry relating to the Theatrical Employers Registration Act 1925.
1973 c. 65.	Local Government (Scotland) Act 1973.	In Schedule 24, in Part III, paragraph 35.
1980 c. 65.	Local Government, Planning and Land Act 1980.	In Schedule 6, paragraphs 2 and 3.

PART V

REPEALS IN LOCAL ACTS IN CONSEQUENCE OF SECTION 12

Chapter	Short title	Extent of repeal
1980 c. x.	County of Merseyside Act 1980.	Section 29.
1980 c. xiii.	Cheshire County Council Act 1980.	Section 31.
1980 c. xxxvii.	South Yorkshire Act 1980.	Section 44.
1981 c. ix.	Greater Manchester Act 1981.	Section 57.
1981 c. xviii.	County of Kent Act 1981.	Section 26.
1981 c. xxv.	East Sussex Act 1981.	Section 91.
1982 c. iii.	Humberside Act 1982.	Section 46.

PART VI

REPEALS IN LOCAL ACTS IN CONSEQUENCE OF SECTION 20

Chapter	Short title	Extent of repeal
1976 c. xxxv.	County of South Glamorgan Act 1976.	Section 56.
1979 c. xxiii.	Greater London Council (General Powers) Act 1979.	Section 5. Section 9.

Chapter	Short title	Extent of repeal
1980 c. x.	County of Merseyside Act 1980.	Sections 11 and 12.
1980 c. xi.	West Midlands County Council Act 1980.	Sections 7 and 8.
1980 c. xiii.	Cheshire County Council Act 1980.	Section 10.
1980 c. xiv.	West Yorkshire Act 1980.	Sections 13 and 14.
1980 c. xv.	Isle of Wight Act 1980.	Sections 11 and 12.
1980 c. xxxvii.	South Yorkshire Act 1980.	Sections 11 and 12.
1980 c. xliii.	Tyne and Wear Act 1980.	Sections 7 to 9.
1981 c. ix.	Greater Manchester Act 1981.	Sections 17 to 19.
1981 c. xviii.	County of Kent Act 1981.	Sections 8 and 9.
1981 c. xxv.	East Sussex Act 1981.	Sections 4 and 5.
1982 c. iii.	Humberside Act 1982.	Sections 31 to 33.
1982 c. iv.	County of Avon Act 1982.	Sections 4 and 35.

PART VII

REPEALS IN LOCAL ACTS IN CONSEQUENCE OF SECTION 22

Chapter	Short title	Extent of repeal
1980 c. x.	County of Merseyside Act 1980.	Section 14.
1980 c. xi.	West Midlands County Council Act 1980.	Section 10.
1980 c. xiii.	Cheshire County Council Act 1980.	Section 9.
1980 c. xv.	Isle of Wight Act 1980.	Section 51.
1980 c. xxxvii.	South Yorkshire Act 1980.	Section 13.
1981 c. ix.	Greater Manchester Act 1981.	Section 20.
1981 c. xviii.	County of Kent Act 1981.	Section 11.
1981 c. xix.	South Yorkshire Act 1981.	In the Table, the entries relating to section 13(1) and (2) of the South Yorkshire Act 1980.
1981 c. xxv.	East Sussex Act 1981.	Section 6.

PART VIII

REPEALS IN LOCAL ACTS IN CONSEQUENCE OF SECTION 24

Chapter	Short title	Extent of repeal
1980 c. xi.	West Midlands County Council Act 1980.	Section 17.
1980 c. xiii.	Cheshire County Council Act 1980.	Section 24.
1980 c. xxxvii.	South Yorkshire Act 1980.	Section 35.
1981 c. xxxiv.	Derbyshire Act 1981.	Section 18.
1982 c. iii.	Humberside Act 1982.	Section 38.
1982 c. iv.	County of Avon Act 1982.	Section 24.

PART IX

REPEALS IN LOCAL ACTS IN CONSEQUENCE OF SECTION 26

Chapter	Short title	Extent of repeal
1980 c. xiv.	West Yorkshire Act 1980.	Section 45.
1980 c. xxxvii.	South Yorkshire Act 1980.	Section 23.
1980 c. xliii.	Tyne and Wear Act 1980.	Section 14.
1981 c. ix.	Greater Manchester Act 1981.	Section 33.
1981 c. xxv.	East Sussex Act 1981.	Section 16.

PART X

REPEALS IN LOCAL ACTS IN CONSEQUENCE OF SECTION 27

Chapter	Short title	Extent of repeal
1967 c. xx.	Greater London Council (General Powers) Act 1967.	Section 24.
1980 c. xiv.	West Yorkshire Act 1980.	Section 10.
1980 c. xxxvii.	South Yorkshire Act 1980.	Section 40.
1980 c. xliii.	Tyne and Wear Act 1980.	Section 15.
1981 c. ix.	Greater Manchester Act 1981.	Section 46.
1981 c. xviii.	County of Kent Act 1981.	Sections 24 and 25.
1981 c. xxv.	East Sussex Act 1981.	Section 15.
1982 c. iv.	County of Avon Act 1982.	Section 26.

Part XI

Repeals in Local Acts in Consequence of Section 28

Chapter	Short title	Extent of repeal
1976 c. xxxv.	County of South Glamorgan Act 1976.	Section 28.
1980 c. x.	County of Merseyside Act 1980.	Section 17.
1980 c. xiii.	Cheshire County Council Act 1980.	Section 26.
1980 c. xxxvii.	South Yorkshire Act 1980.	Section 30.
1980 c. xliii.	Tyne and Wear Act 1980.	Section 20.
1981 c. ix.	Greater Manchester Act 1981.	Section 39.
1981 c. xviii.	County of Kent Act 1981.	Section 27.
1981 c. xxxiv.	Derbyshire Act 1981.	Section 17.
1982 c. iii.	Humberside Act 1982.	Section 43.

Part XII

Repeals in Local Acts in Consequence of Section 33

Chapter	Short title	Extent of repeal
1980 c. xiii.	Cheshire County Council Act 1980.	Section 94.
1980 c. xv.	Isle of Wight Act 1980.	Section 17.
1981 c. xviii.	County of Kent Act 1981.	Section 4.
1982 c. iii.	Humberside Act 1982.	Section 50.
1982 c. iv.	County of Avon Act 1982.	Section 46.

Part XIII

Repeals in Local Acts in Consequence of Section 34

Chapter	Short title	Extent of repeal
1980 c. xiv.	West Yorkshire Act 1980.	Section 82.
1980 c. xxxvii.	South Yorkshire Act 1980.	Section 90.
1981 c. xxv.	East Sussex Act 1981.	Section 90.

PART XIV

REPEALS IN LOCAL ACTS IN CONSEQUENCE OF SECTION 36

Chapter	Short title	Extent of repeal
1980 c. xxxvii.	South Yorkshire Act 1980.	Section 94.
1980 c. xliii.	Tyne and Wear Act 1980.	Section 22.
1981 c. xviii.	County of Kent Act 1981.	Section 31.

PART XV

REPEALS IN LOCAL ACTS IN CONSEQUENCE OF SECTION 39

Chapter	Short title	Extent of repeal
1980 c. xi.	West Midlands County Council Act 1980.	Section 68.
1980 c. xiv.	West Yorkshire Act 1980.	Section 52.
1980 c. xv.	Isle of Wight Act 1980.	Section 47.
1980 c. xxxvii.	South Yorkshire Act 1980.	Section 83.
1981 c. ix.	Greater Manchester Act 1981.	Section 95.
1982 c. iii.	Humberside Act 1982.	Section 54.

PART XVI

MISCELLANEOUS REPEALS IN PUBLIC GENERAL ACTS

Chapter	Short title	Extent of repeal
1936 c. 49.	Public Health Act 1936.	In section 2(2), paragraph (ii).
1971 c. 78.	Town and Country Planning Act 1971.	Section 213.
1972 c. 70.	Local Government Act 1972.	In section 140(3), the words from " but " to the end. In Schedule 16, paragraph 9(2).
1974 c. 37.	Health and Safety at Work etc. Act 1974.	Section 63(1) to (4).
1974 c. 44.	Housing Act 1974.	Section 126.
1975 c. 76.	Local Land Charges Act 1975.	In Schedule 1, in the entry relating to the Housing Act 1974, paragraph (*e*).
1976 c. 57.	Local Government (Miscellaneous Provisions) Act 1976.	Section 8. Section 43.
1980 c. 65.	Local Government, Planning and Land Act 1980.	In section 88(2)(*b*), the words from " in ", in the second place where it occurs, to " proposed) " and the words " in each subsection ". In Schedule 14, paragraph 11(a).

ELIZABETH II

Firearms Act 1982

1982 CHAPTER 31

An act to apply the provisions of the Firearms Act 1968 (with certain exceptions) to imitation firearms which are readily convertible into firearms to which section 1 of that Act applies. [13th July 1982]

B E IT ENACTED by the Queen's most Excellent Majesty, by and with the advice and consent of the Lords Spiritual and Temporal, and Commons, in this present Parliament assembled, and by the authority of the same, as follows:—

1.—(1) This Act applies to an imitation firearm if—

    (*a*) it has the appearance of being a firearm to which section 1 of the 1968 Act (firearms requiring a firearm certificate) applies; and

    (*b*) it is so constructed or adapted as to be readily convertible into a firearm to which that section applies.

Control of imitation firearms readily convertible into firearms to which section 1 of the 1968 Act applies.

(2) Subject to section 2(2) of this Act and the following provisions of this section, the 1968 Act shall apply in relation to an imitation firearm to which this Act applies as it applies in relation to a firearm to which section 1 of that Act applies.

(3) Subject to the modifications in subsection (4) below, any expression given a meaning for the purposes of the 1968 Act has the same meaning in this Act.

(4) For the purposes of this section and the 1968 Act, as it applies by virtue of this section—

    (*a*) the definition of air weapon in section 1(3)(*b*) of that Act (air weapons excepted from requirement of firearm certificate) shall have effect without the exclusion of any type declared by rules made by the Secretary of

2 A 2

State under section 53 of that Act to be specially dangerous; and

(b) the definition of firearm in section 57(1) of that Act shall have effect without paragraphs (b) and (c) of that subsection (component parts and accessories).

(5) In any proceedings brought by virtue of this section for an offence under the 1968 Act involving an imitation firearm to which this Act applies, it shall be a defence for the accused to show that he did not know and had no reason to suspect that the imitation firearm was so constructed or adapted as to be readily convertible into a firearm to which section 1 of that Act applies.

(6) For the purposes of this section an imitation firearm shall be regarded as readily convertible into a firearm to which section 1 of the 1968 Act applies if—

(a) it can be so converted without any special skill on the part of the person converting it in the construction or adaptation of firearms of any description; and

(b) the work involved in converting it does not require equipment or tools other than such as are in common use by persons carrying out works of construction and maintenance in their own homes.

Provisions supplementary to section 1.
2.—(1) Subject to subsection (2) below, references in the 1968 Act, and in any order made under section 6 of that Act (orders prohibiting movement of firearms or ammunition) before this Act comes into force—

(a) to firearms (without qualification); or

(b) to firearms to which section 1 of that Act applies;

shall be read as including imitation firearms to which this Act applies.

(2) The following provisions of the 1968 Act do not apply by virtue of this Act to an imitation firearm to which this Act applies, that is to say—

(a) section 4(3) and (4) (offence to convert anything having appearance of firearm into a firearm and aggravated offence under section 1 involving a converted firearm); and

(b) the provisions of that Act which relate to, or to the enforcement of control over, the manner in which a firearm is used or the circumstances in which it is carried;

but without prejudice, in the case of the provisions mentioned in paragraph (b) above, to the application to such an imitation firearm of such of those provisions as apply to imitation firearms apart from this Act.

(3) The provisions referred to in subsection (2)(*b*) above are sections 16 to 20 and section 47.

3. An Order in Council under paragraph 1(1)(*b*) of Schedule 1 to the Northern Ireland Act 1974 (legislation for Northern Ireland in the interim period) which contains a statement that it is made only for purposes corresponding to the purposes of this Act— Corresponding provision for Northern Ireland. 1974 c. 28.

(*a*) shall not be subject to paragraph 1(4) and (5) of that Schedule (affirmative resolution of both Houses of Parliament); but

(*b*) shall be subject to annulment in pursuance of a resolution of either House of Parliament.

4.—(1) This Act may be cited as the Firearms Act 1982, and this Act and the 1968 Act may be cited together as the Firearms Acts 1968 and 1982. Citation, interpretation, commencement and extent. 1968 c. 27.

(2) In this Act " the 1968 Act " means the Firearms Act 1968.

(3) This Act shall come into force on such day as the Secretary of State may by order made by statutory instrument appoint.

(4) This Act, except section 3, does not extend to Northern Ireland.

ELIZABETH II

Local Government
Finance Act 1982

1982 CHAPTER 32

An Act to abolish supplementary rates and supplementary
precepts; to require rates and precepts to be made or
issued for complete financial years; to provide for the
making of substituted rates and the issue of substituted
precepts; to regulate proceedings for challenging the
validity of rates and precepts; to make further provision with respect to the borrowing powers of local
authorities and with respect to relief from rates in
enterprise zones; to amend the provisions relating to
block grant; to make new provision for auditing the
accounts of local authorities and other public bodies;
and for connected purposes.   [13th July 1982]

BE IT ENACTED by the Queen's most Excellent Majesty, by and
with the advice and consent of the Lords Spiritual and
Temporal, and Commons, in this present Parliament
assembled, and by the authority of the same, as follows:—

PART I

RATES, PRECEPTS AND BORROWING

1. A rating authority shall not have power—   Limitation
 of rating
   (*a*) to make a supplementary rate ; or   powers.
   (*b*) to make a rate for any period other than a financial
   year.

2 A 4

2. A precepting authority shall not have power—

   (*a*) to issue a supplementary precept ; or

   (*b*) to issue a precept in respect of any period other than a financial year.

3.—(1) Subject to subsection (2) below—

   (*a*) a rating authority may make a rate for a financial year in substitution for a rate previously made by it for that year ; and

   (*b*) a precepting authority may issue a precept in respect of a financial year in substitution for a precept previously issued by it in respect of that year.

(2) The estimated product of a substituted rate or precept shall not exceed the estimated product of the rate or precept for which it is substituted (the " original " rate or precept) ; and for the purposes of this subsection the product of a substituted rate or precept shall be estimated by reference to the same gross rateable value as the product of the original rate or precept.

(3) Section 12(6) of the General Rate Act 1967 (which requires a precept to be issued or notified before the beginning of a financial year) shall not apply to a precept issued by virtue of subsection (1)(*b*) above.

(4) Where a precept is substituted by virtue of this section any authority which has made a rate by reference to the original precept—

   (*a*) shall under subsection (1)(*a*) above make a substituted rate by reference to the substituted precept ; and

   (*b*) shall be entitled to recover from the precepting authority—

      (i) its administrative expenses in making repayments and allowing credits under subsections (5) and (6) below in respect of the original rate ; and

      (ii) any increase attributable to paragraph (*a*) above in its rate collection expenses for the financial year ;

and in relation to the substituted rate made pursuant to paragraph (*a*) above the estimated product of the original rate shall for the purposes of subsection (2) above be treated as reduced by the difference (if any) between the estimated products of the original and the substituted precepts.

(5) Where a rate or precept is substituted by virtue of this section any sum paid to the rating or precepting authority in

respect of the original rate or precept (including any sum paid by way of an instalment or other part payment) shall—

> (*a*) to the extent to which it would have been payable if the original rate or precept had corresponded to the substituted rate or precept, be treated as paid in respect of the substituted rate or precept ; and
>
> (*b*) as to any excess, be repaid if the ratepayer by whom that sum was paid or, as the case may be, the authority to which the precept was issued so requires.

(6) Where repayment of any amount is not required under subsection (5)(*b*) above that amount shall, as the rating or precepting authority may determine, either be repaid or—

> (*a*) in the case of an amount paid in respect of a rate, be credited against any subsequent liability of the ratepayer for rates in respect of the hereditament in question ;
>
> (*b*) in the case of an amount paid in respect of a precept, be credited against any subsequent liability of the authority to which the precept was issued in respect of precepts issued to it by the precepting authority.

(7) Where a person as tenant or licensee of any premises—

> (*a*) is liable to make payments (whether as part of his rent or otherwise) which vary or may vary according to the rates chargeable in respect of those premises ; or
>
> (*b*) is entitled to make deductions from his rent in respect of those rates,

he shall, where a rate affecting those premises is substituted by virtue of this section, be entitled to recover or, as the case may be, liable to make good so much of any payment or deduction as he would not have been liable or entitled to make if the original rate had corresponded to the substituted rate ; and any sum which he is entitled to recover as aforesaid may, without prejudice to any other method of recovery, be deducted by him from any rent payable by him to the person by whom that sum was received.

(8) This section applies whether or not the original rate or precept was validly made or issued but shall not be construed as authorising the substitution of a rate or precept for one made or issued after the passing of this Act in contravention of section 1 or 2 above.

4.—(1) The validity of a precept shall not be questioned Proceedings in respect of rates and precepts. except by an application for judicial review ; and the validity of a rate shall not be questioned except as aforesaid on any of the grounds mentioned in subsection (2) below.

PART I

(2) The grounds referred to in subsection (1) above in the case of a rate are—

(a) that any part of it was made for financing expenditure which the rating authority could not lawfully incur ;

(b) that it was made by reference to a precept which was wholly or partly invalid ; or

(c) any other ground not based on facts relating to a particular hereditament or to the inclusion or exclusion of any particular person in or from the rate.

(3) If on an application for judicial review the court decides to grant relief in respect of a rate on any of the grounds mentioned in subsection (2) above or in respect of a precept it shall quash the rate or precept whether the ground of invalidity relates to the whole or only to a part of it.

(4) Subsection (1) above is without prejudice to the making of an application for judicial review in any case in which it could be made apart from that subsection.

1967 c. 9.

(5) Section 7 of the General Rate Act 1967 (appeal against rate) shall have effect subject to the foregoing provisions of this section, and accordingly the court shall not under that section amend or quash a rate except in relation to a particular hereditament.

Borrowing powers.
1972 c. 70.

5.—(1) After paragraph 11(2) of Schedule 13 to the Local Government Act 1972 (security for money borrowed by local authority) there shall be inserted—

" (2A) The reference in sub-paragraph (1) above to money borrowed by a local authority includes a reference to the interest for the time being payable in respect of that money."

(2) The Greater London Council may, with the approval of the Secretary of State and in accordance with any conditions subject to which the approval is given, borrow money for any purpose other than the purposes mentioned in paragraph 29 of

1963 c. 33.

Schedule 2 to the London Government Act 1963 (capital expenditure and lending to other persons).

(3) Subsection (2) above is without prejudice to any borrowing powers of the Greater London Council existing apart from that subsection.

Rate relief in enterprise zones.
1980 c. 65.

6.—(1) At the end of paragraph 27(1) of Schedule 32 to the Local Government, Planning and Land Act 1980 (exemption from rates of certain hereditaments situated in areas designated as enterprise zones) there shall be added the words " or in respect of any part of an exempt hereditament as regards any period

during which the area in which that part is situated is so designated."

(2) In paragraph 28 of the said Schedule 32 (mixed hereditaments)—

> (*a*) in sub-paragraph (2) (mixed hereditament to be rated
> as a dwelling of the appropriate rateable value), for the
> word " dwelling " there shall be substituted the word
> " dwelling-house " ; and
>
> (*b*) for sub-paragraph (3)(*b*) (extension of power to make
> regulations about appeals) there shall be substituted—
>
>> " (*b*) the reference to the occupier or person
>> treated as occupier of the hereditament being dis-
>> satisfied by the view taken by the rating authority
>> included a reference to the occupier, the person
>> aforesaid or the rating authority being dissatisfied by
>> the view taken by the valuation officer ; and ".

(3) After the said paragraph 28 there shall be inserted—

" Hereditaments partially within enterprise zones

28A.—(1) As regards any period during which part only
of an exempt hereditament (within the meaning of paragraph 27 above) is situated in an area designated as an
enterprise zone, the valuation officer shall determine the
portion of the rateable value of the hereditament attributable to the part of the hereditament situated outside the
enterprise zone.

(2) Where a determination in respect of a hereditament
has been made under sub-paragraph (1) above, the amount
of any rates payable in respect of the hereditament shall
(subject to sub-paragraph (3)(*b*) below) be the amount
which would be payable in respect of it if its rateable value
were equal to the portion of the rateable value which was
determined under sub-paragraph (1) above.

(3) Where the hereditament in respect of which a determination has been so made is a mixed hereditament—

> (*a*) the valuation officer shall also determine the portion
> of the rateable value of the hereditament attribut-
> able to any part of it which is used for the purposes
> of a private dwelling or private dwellings and is
> situated within the enterprise zone ; and
>
> (*b*) if such a determination is made, the amount of any
> rates payable in respect of the hereditament shall
> be the aggregate of the following amounts,
> namely—
>
>> (i) the amount payable under sub-paragraph
>> (2) above, and

(ii) the amount which would be payable in respect of it if it were a dwelling-house of a rateable value equal to the portion of the rateable value determined under paragraph (a) above.

(4) Section 48(6) of the 1967 Act shall, with modifications corresponding to those contained in paragraph 28(3) above, apply also in relation to questions as to the portions mentioned in sub-paragraphs (1) and (3)(a) above."

7.—(1) In this Part of this Act—

" financial year " means a period of twelve months beginning with 1st April ;

" gross rateable value ", in relation to a rating or precepting authority, means the aggregate of the rateable values of the hereditaments in the authority's area ;

" precepting authority " means an authority having power to issue a precept either to a rating authority or to a county council ;

" rate " means a general rate except that—

 (a) in the case of the City of London, it includes the poor rate ; and

 (b) in the case of the Inner Temple and the Middle Temple, it means any rate in the nature of a general rate levied in the Inner Temple or the Middle Temple, as the case may be ;

" rating authority " means any authority having power to make a rate under section 1 of the General Rate Act 1967 ;

" supplementary precept " means a precept which is issued by a precepting authority—

 (a) in respect of (or of part of) a financial year in respect of which it has already issued a precept ; and

 (b) by way of addition to and not in substitution for that previous precept.

(2) Sections 1 to 3 and 6(1) and (3) above have effect in relation to any financial year beginning on or after 1st April 1982.

(3) Schedule 1 to this Act shall have effect in connection with the coming into force of sections 1 and 2 above.

PART II
BLOCK GRANT

8.—(1) In subsection (6) of section 59 of the Local Government, Planning and Land Act 1980 (purposes for which the

amount of block grant payable to a local authority may be
adjusted under that section) after paragraph (c) there shall be
inserted—

> " (cc) making, in the amount of block grant payable to an
> authority, adjustments by reference to guidance issued
> by the Secretary of State and designed to achieve any
> reduction in the level of local authority expenditure
> (or any restriction on increases in that level) which he
> thinks necessary having regard to general economic
> conditions ; and ".

(2) After subsection (11) of the said section 59 there shall be
inserted—

> " (11A) Any guidance issued for the purposes of sub-
> section (6)(cc) above shall be framed by reference to princi-
> ples applicable to all local authorities ; and before issuing
> any guidance for those purposes the Secretary of State
> shall consult such associations of local authorities as appear
> to him to be concerned and any local authority with whom
> consultation appears to him to be desirable."

(3) The powers conferred by the said section 59 and by
paragraph 8 of Schedule 11 to the said Act of 1980 (which
makes corresponding provision in relation to authorities wholly
or partly within the Metropolitan Police District)—

> (a) shall not be exercised for the purpose specified in para-
> graph (a) of subsection (6) of that section so as to
> decrease the amount of block grant payable to a local
> authority unless the Secretary of State is satisfied that
> there will be an unreasonable increase, unless he
> exercises the power, in the amount of block grant
> payable to that authority for a year compared with
> the amount payable to them for the previous year ;
> (b) shall not be exercised for the purpose specified in para-
> graph (b) or (c) of that subsection so as to decrease
> the amount of block grant payable to a local auth-
> ority ; and
> (c) shall be exercisable for the purpose specified in para-
> graph (cc) of that subsection so as to increase or de-
> crease the amount of block grant payable to a local
> authority according to whether or the extent to which
> they have or have not complied (or have or have not
> taken steps to comply) with the guidance referred to in
> that paragraph.

(4) If representations in that behalf are made to him by any
association of local authorities or by any local authority the
Secretary of State may—

> (a) in the Rate Support Grant Report made for any year
> under section 60 of the said Act of 1980 ; or

(*b*) in a supplementary report made for any year under section 61 of that Act,

provide that expenditure of any description or amount shall be disregarded for the purposes of paragraph (*cc*) of subsection (6) of the said section 59 and in determining under subsection (3)(*c*) above whether or the extent to which local authorities have or have not complied (or have or have not taken steps to comply) with the guidance referred to in that paragraph.

(5) Subsections (2) and (3) of the said section 59 and sub-paragraphs (3) and (4) of the said paragraph 8 (which are super-seded by subsection (3) above) shall be omitted ; and the refer-ence to the said subsection (3) in section 59(12) and to the said sub-paragraph (4) in paragraph 8(13) shall be construed as re-ferences to subsection (3)(*a*) above.

(6) The powers conferred by the said section 59 and para-graph 8 shall not be exercised for the purpose specified in sub-section (6)(*cc*) of that section except in accordance with prin-ciples to be applied to all local authorities ; and accordingly subsections (5)(*a*)(ii) and (7) of that section and sub-paragraphs (9) to (11) of that paragraph shall not apply to any exercise of those powers for that purpose.

(7) A supplementary report made for any year under section 61 of the said Act of 1980 may specify a determination under the said section 59 or paragraph 8 in relation to a local authority notwithstanding that no such determination was specified in relation to that authority in the Rate Support Grant Report made for that year under section 60 of that Act.

(8) No determination made for the purpose specified in sub-section (6)(*cc*) of the said section 59 and specified by virtue of subsection (7) above in a supplementary report shall be such as to decrease the amount of block grant payable to a local authority in any year to any greater extent than is permissible in accordance with principles specified in that behalf in the Rate Support Grant Report made for that year.

(9) Where by virtue of subsection (7) above a determination is specified in a supplementary report—

(*a*) the principles in accordance with which the power to make the determination are exercised ; and

(*b*) the considerations leading the Secretary of State to make the determination,

shall be specified in the supplementary report except that para-graph (*a*) above shall not apply to any determination which is subject to subsection (8) above.

(10) This section has effect in relation to block grant for any year beginning on or after 1st April 1981 except that so much of

subsection (2) above as relates to consultation and subsection
(8) above do not apply to any year beginning before 1st April
1983.

(11) In relation to the year beginning on 1st April 1981 or
1st April 1982 references in this section to guidance issued by
the Secretary of State include references to guidance issued by
him before the passing of this Act and, as respects any determination under the said section 59 or paragraph 8, the requirements of subsection (5) of section 60 of the said Act of 1980
and of that subsection as applied by section 61(2) of that Act
may be satisfied by consultation before the passing of this Act.

9.—(1) The Secretary of State shall have power to require any Information
information submitted to him by a local authority under section for purposes
65(1) of the Local Government, Planning and Land Act 1980 of block grant.
(information for purposes of block grant) to be certified under 1980 c. 65.
arrangements made by the Audit Commission established under
Part III of this Act.

(2) The said section 65(1) shall have effect with the substitution for the words " the total expenditure to be incurred "
of the words " the expenditure incurred or to be incurred " and
as if section 8 above were included in the provisions there mentioned.

(3) Subsection (2) above has effect in relation to any year
beginning on or after 1st April 1981.

10.—(1) Schedule 2 to this Act shall have effect for enabling Block grant
block grant to be paid to the Receiver for the Metropolitan for Receiver
Police District. for the
Metropolitan
(2) This section has effect for any year beginning on or after Police
1st April 1983. District.

PART III

ACCOUNTS AND AUDIT

The Audit Commission

11.—(1) For the purposes of this Part of this Act there shall Establishment
be a body to be known as the Audit Commission for Local of Audit
Authorities in England and Wales. Commission.

(2) The Commission shall consist of not less than thirteen
nor more than seventeen members appointed by the Secretary
of State after consultation with—

    (*a*) such associations of local authorities as appear to him
        to be concerned ; and

    (*b*) such bodies of accountants, such bodies representing
        local authority employees, and such other organisations
        or persons as appear to him to be appropriate.

A 4

(3) The Secretary of State shall, after the like consultation, appoint one of the members to be chairman and another to be deputy chairman.

(4) Schedule 3 to this Act shall have effect with respect to the Commission.

Audit of accounts

Accounts subject to audit.

12.—(1) All accounts to which this section applies shall be made up yearly to 31st March or such other date as the Secretary of State may generally or in any special case direct and shall be audited in accordance with this Part of this Act by an auditor or auditors appointed by the Commission.

(2) This section applies to all accounts of—

    (*a*) a local authority ;

    (*b*) a parish meeting of a parish not having a separate parish council ;

    (*c*) a committee of a local authority, including a joint committee of two or more such authorities ;

    (*d*) the Council of the Isles of Scilly ;

1972 c. 70.

    (*e*) any charter trustees constituted under section 246 of the Local Government Act 1972 ;

    (*f*) a port health authority ;

    (*g*) a combined police authority ;

    (*h*) a fire authority constituted by a combination scheme ;

    (*i*) a licensing planning committee ;

    (*j*) an internal drainage board ;

    (*k*) a children's regional planning committee ; and

    (*l*) a probation and after-care committee.

(3) This section also applies to the accounts of the rate fund and superannuation fund of the City, that is to say—

    (*a*) the accounts relating to the levy and collection of the poor rate and general rate made by the Common Council and to the income and expenditure which falls to be credited in aid of, or to be met out of, the poor rate or the general rate ; and

    (*b*) the accounts relating to the superannuation fund established and administered by the Common Council under the Local Government Superannuation Regulations 1974 as amended by the Local Government Superannuation (City of London) Regulations 1977 ;

S.I. 1974/520.
S.I. 1977/1341.

and any reference in this Part of this Act to the accounts of a body shall be construed, in relation to the Common Council, as a reference to the accounts of the rate fund and superannuation fund of the City.

(4) References in any statutory provision or document to district audit, to audit by a district auditor, to audit in accordance
with Part VIII of the Local Government Act 1972 or to profes- 1972 c. 70.
sional audit shall be construed, in relation to the accounts of a
local authority or other public body, as references to audit as
mentioned in subsection (1) above.

13.—(1) An auditor appointed by the Commission to audit Appointment
the accounts of any body whose accounts are required to be of auditors.
audited in accordance with this Part of this Act may be an
officer of the Commission, an individual who is not such an
officer or a firm of such individuals.

(2) Where two or more auditors are appointed in relation to
the accounts of any body, some but not others may be officers
of the Commission and they may be appointed to act jointly,
to act separately in relation to different parts of the accounts
or to discharge different functions in relation to the audit.

(3) Before appointing any auditor or auditors to audit the
accounts of any body the Commission shall consult that body.

(4) For the purpose of assisting the Commission in deciding
on the appointment of an auditor or auditors in relation to the
accounts of any body the Commission may require that body to
make available for inspection by or on behalf of the Commission such documents relating to any accounts of the body as
the Commission may reasonably require for that purpose.

(5) A person shall not be appointed by the Commission as an
auditor unless he is a member of one or more of the bodies
mentioned in subsection (6) below or has such other qualifications
as may be approved for the purposes of this section by the
Secretary of State ; and a firm shall not be so appointed unless
each of its members is a member of one or more of those bodies.

(6) The bodies referred to in subsection (5) above are—

(a) the Institute of Chartered Accountants in England and
Wales ;

(b) the Institute of Chartered Accountants of Scotland ;

(c) the Association of Certified Accountants ;

(d) the Chartered Institute of Public Finance and Accountancy ;

(e) the Institute of Chartered Accountants in Ireland ; and

(f) any other body of accountants established in the United
Kingdom and for the time being approved by the Secretary of State for the purposes of this section.

(7) The appointment by the Commission of an auditor who
is not an officer of the Commission shall be on such terms and
for such period as the Commission may determine.

(8) Arrangements may be approved by the Commission, either generally or in any particular case, for a person or persons to assist an auditor appointed by the Commission by carrying out such of his functions under this Part of this Act as may be specified in the arrangements; and references in the following provisions of this Part of this Act to an auditor include, in relation to any function of an auditor, a reference to any person carrying out that function under arrangements approved under this subsection.

(9) Subsection (8) above applies whether or not the auditor is an officer of the Commission.

Code of audit practice.

14.—(1) The Commission shall prepare, and keep under review, a code of audit practice prescribing the way in which auditors are to carry out their functions under this Part of this Act.

(2) The code shall embody what appears to the Commission to be the best professional practice with respect to the standards, procedures and techniques to be adopted by auditors.

(3) The code shall not come into force until approved by a resolution of each House of Parliament, and its continuation in force shall be subject to its being so approved at intervals of not more than five years.

(4) Subsection (3) above shall not preclude alterations to the code being made by the Commission in the intervals between its being approved as aforesaid.

(5) The Commission shall send copies of the code and of any alterations made to the code to the Secretary of State who shall lay them before Parliament; and the Commission shall from time to time publish the code as for the time being in force.

(6) Before preparing the code or making any alteration in it the Commission shall consult such associations of local authorities as appear to it to be concerned and such bodies of accountants as appear to it to be appropriate.

General duties of auditors.

15.—(1) In auditing any accounts required to be audited in accordance with this Part of this Act, an auditor shall by examination of the accounts and otherwise satisfy himself—

(a) that the accounts are prepared in accordance with regulations made under section 23 below and comply with the requirements of all other statutory provisions applicable to the accounts;

(b) that proper practices have been observed in the compilation of the accounts; and

(c) that the body whose accounts are being audited has made proper arrangements for securing economy, efficiency and effectiveness in its use of resources.

(2) The auditor shall comply with the code of audit practice as for the time being in force.

(3) The auditor shall consider whether, in the public interest, he should make a report on any matter coming to his notice in the course of the audit in order that it may be considered by the body concerned or brought to the attention of the public, and shall consider whether the public interest requires any such matter to be made the subject of an immediate report rather than of a report to be made at the conclusion of the audit.

16.—(1) An auditor shall have a right of access at all reasonable times to all such documents relating to a body whose accounts are required to be audited in accordance with this Part of this Act as appear to him necessary for the purposes of the audit and shall be entitled to require from any person holding or accountable for any such document such information and explanation as he thinks necessary for those purposes and, if he thinks it necessary, to require any such person to attend before him in person to give the information or explanation or to produce any such document.

Auditor's right to obtain documents and information.

(2) Without prejudice to subsection (1) above, the auditor shall be entitled to require any officer or member of a body whose accounts are required to be audited in accordance with this Part of this Act to give him such information or explanation as he thinks necessary for the purposes of the audit and, if he thinks it necessary, to require any such officer or member to attend before him in person to give the information or explanation.

(3) Without prejudice to subsections (1) and (2) above, every body whose accounts are required to be audited in accordance with this Part of this Act shall provide the auditor with every facility and all information which he may reasonably require for the purposes of the audit.

(4) Any person who without reasonable excuse fails to comply with any requirement of an auditor under subsection (1) or (2) above shall be liable on summary conviction to a fine not exceeding £200 and to an additional fine not exceeding £20 for each day on which the offence continues after conviction thereof.

(5) Any expenses incurred by an auditor in connection with proceedings for an offence under subsection (4) above alleged to have been committed in relation to the audit of the accounts of any body shall, so far as not recovered from any other source, be recoverable from that body.

PART III
Public
inspection of
accounts and
right of
challenge.

17.—(1) At each audit by an auditor under this Part of this Act any persons interested may inspect the accounts to be audited and all books, deeds, contracts, bills, vouchers and receipts relating to them and make copies of all or any part of the accounts and those other documents.

(2) At the request of a local government elector for any area to which those accounts relate, the auditor shall give the elector, or any representative of his, an opportunity to question the auditor about the accounts.

(3) Subject to subsection (4) below, any local government elector for any area to which those accounts relate, or any representative of his, may attend before the auditor and make objections—

> (a) as to any matter in respect of which the auditor could take action under section 19 or 20 below ; or
>
> (b) as to any other matter in respect of which the auditor could make a report under section 15(3) above.

(4) No objection may be made under subsection (3) above by or on behalf of a local government elector unless the auditor has previously received written notice of the proposed objection and of the grounds on which it is to be made.

(5) Where an elector sends a notice to an auditor for the purposes of subsection (4) above he shall at the same time send a copy of the notice to the body whose accounts are the subject of the audit.

Auditor's
reports.

18.—(1) When an auditor has concluded his audit of the accounts of any body under this Part of this Act—

> (a) a certificate that he has completed the audit in accordance with this Part of this Act ; and
>
> (b) his opinion on the relevant statement of accounts prepared pursuant to regulations under section 23 below (or, where no such statement is required to be prepared, on the accounts),

shall, subject to subsection (2) below, be entered by him on the statement (or, as the case may be, on the accounts).

(2) Where an auditor makes a report to the body concerned under section 15(3) above at the conclusion of the audit, the certificate and opinion referred to in subsection (1) above may be included by him in that report.

(3) Any report under section 15(3) above shall be sent by the auditor to the body concerned or, in the case of a parish meeting, to the chairman, and (except in the case of an immediate report) shall be so sent not later than fourteen days after the conclusion

of the audit, and that body shall take the report into considera- PART III
tion as soon as practicable after they have received it.

(4) A copy of any such report shall be sent by the auditor to
the Commission forthwith, if the report is an immediate report,
and otherwise not later than fourteen days after the conclusion
of the audit.

(5) The agenda supplied to the members of a body for the
meeting of the body at which they take into consideration a
report of an auditor sent to them under subsection (3) above
shall be accompanied by that report, and the report shall not be
excluded from the matter supplied for the benefit of any newspaper under section 1(4)(*b*) of the Public Bodies (Admission to 1960 c. 67.
Meetings) Act 1960 (supply of agenda of meetings and related
documents to newspapers).

19.—(1) Where it appears to the auditor carrying out the audit Declaration
of any accounts under this Part of this Act that any item of that item of
account is contrary to law he may apply to the court for a account is
declaration that the item is contrary to law except where it is unlawful.
sanctioned by the Secretary of State.

(2) On an application under this section the court may make
or refuse to make the declaration asked for, and where the court
makes that declaration, then, subject to subsection (3) below,
it may also—

(*a*) order that any person responsible for incurring or
authorising any expenditure declared unlawful shall
repay it in whole or in part to the body in question
and, where two or more persons are found to be
responsible, that they shall be jointly and severally
liable to repay it as aforesaid ;

(*b*) if any such expenditure exceeds £2,000 and the person
responsible for incurring or authorising it is, or was
at the time of his conduct in question, a member of a
local authority, order him to be disqualified for being
a member of a local authority for a specified period ;
and

(*c*) order rectification of the accounts.

(3) The court shall not make an order under subsection
(2)(*a*) or (*b*) above if the court is satisfied that the person
responsible for incurring or authorising any such expenditure
acted reasonably or in the belief that the expenditure was
authorised by law, and in any other case shall have regard to
all the circumstances, including that person's means and ability
to repay that expenditure or any part of it.

(4) Any person who has made an objection under section 17(3)(*a*) above and is aggrieved by a decision of an auditor not to apply for a declaration under this section may—

>   (*a*) not later than six weeks after he has been notified of the decision, require the auditor to state in writing the reasons for his decision ; and

>   (*b*) appeal against the decision to the court,

and on any such appeal the court shall have the like powers in relation to the item of account to which the objection relates as if the auditor had applied for the declaration.

(5) On an application or appeal under this section relating to the accounts of a body, the court may make such order as the court thinks fit for the payment by that body of expenses incurred in connection with the application or appeal by the auditor or the person to whom the application or appeal relates or by whom the appeal is brought, as the case may be.

(6) The court having jurisdiction for the purposes of this section shall be the High Court except that, if the amount of the item of account alleged to be contrary to law does not exceed the amount over which county courts have jurisdiction in actions founded on contract, the county court shall have concurrent jurisdiction with the High Court.

(7) In this section " local authority " includes the Common Council and the Council of the Isles of Scilly.

20.—(1) Where it appears to the auditor carrying out the audit of any accounts under this Part of this Act—

>   (*a*) that any person has failed to bring into account any sum which should have been so included and that the failure has not been sanctioned by the Secretary of State ; or

>   (*b*) that a loss has been incurred or deficiency caused by the wilful misconduct of any person,

he shall certify that the sum or, as the case may be, the amount of the loss or the deficiency is due from that person and, subject to subsections (3) and (5) below, both he and the body in question (or, in the case of a parish meeting, the chairman of the meeting) may recover that sum or amount for the benefit of that body ; and if the auditor certifies under this section that any sum or amount is due from two or more persons, they shall be jointly and severally liable for that sum or amount.

(2) Any person who—

>   (*a*) has made an objection under section 17(3)(*a*) above and is aggrieved by a decision of an auditor not to certify under this section that a sum or amount is due from another person ; or

(*b*) is aggrieved by a decision of an auditor to certify under
this section that a sum or amount is due from him,

may not later than six weeks after he has been notified of the
decision require the auditor to state in writing the reasons for
his decision.

(3) Any such person who is aggrieved by such a decision
may appeal against the decision to the court and—

(*a*) in the case of a decision to certify that any sum or
amount is due from any person, the court may confirm,
vary or quash the decision and give any certificate which
the auditor could have given ;

(*b*) in the case of a decision not to certify that any sum
or amount is due from any person, the court may
confirm the decision or quash it and give any certificate which the auditor could have given ;

and any certificate given under this subsection shall be treated
for the purposes of subsection (1) above and the following
provisions of this section as if it had been given by the auditor
under subsection (1) above.

(4) If a certificate under this section relates to a loss or
deficiency caused by the wilful misconduct of a person who is,
or was at the time of such misconduct, a member of a local
authority and the amount certified to be due from him exceeds
£2,000, that person shall be disqualified for being a member of
a local authority for the period of five years beginning on the
ordinary date on which the period allowed for bringing an appeal
against a decision to give the certificate expires or, if such an
appeal is brought, the date on which the appeal is finally disposed
of or abandoned or fails for non-prosecution.

(5) A sum or other amount certified under this section to be
due from any person shall be payable within fourteen days after
the date of the issue of the certificate or, if an appeal is brought,
within fourteen days after the appeal is finally disposed of or
abandoned or fails for non-prosecution.

(6) In any proceedings for the recovery of any sum or amount
due from any person under this section a certificate signed by an
auditor appointed by the Commission stating that that sum or
amount is due from a person specified in the certificate to a body
so specified shall be conclusive evidence of that fact ; and any
certificate purporting to be so signed shall be taken to have been
so signed unless the contrary is proved.

(7) On an appeal under this section relating to the accounts
of a body, the court may make such order as the court thinks
fit for the payment by that body of expenses incurred in connection with the appeal by the auditor or the person to whom
the appeal relates or by whom the appeal is brought, as the case
may be.

(8) Any expenses incurred by an auditor in recovering a sum or other amount certified under this section to be due in connection with the accounts of a body shall, so far as not recovered from any other source, be recoverable from that body unless the court otherwise directs.

(9) The court having jurisdiction for the purposes of this section shall be the High Court except that, if the sum or amount alleged to be due does not exceed the amount over which county courts have jurisdiction in actions founded on contract, the county court shall have concurrent jurisdiction with the High Court.

(10) In this section " local authority " includes the Common Council and the Council of the Isles of Scilly.

Fees for audit.

21.—(1) The Commission shall prescribe a scale or scales of fees in respect of the audit of accounts which are required to be audited in accordance with this Part of this Act.

(2) Before prescribing any scale of fees under subsection (1) above the Commission shall consult such associations of local authorities as appear to it to be concerned and such bodies of accountants as appear to it to be appropriate.

(3) A body whose accounts are audited in accordance with this Part of this Act shall, subject to subsection (4) below, pay to the Commission the fee applicable to the audit in accordance with the appropriate scale.

(4) If it appears to the Commission that the work involved in a particular audit was substantially more or less than that envisaged by the appropriate scale, the Commission may charge a fee which is larger or smaller than that referred to in subsection (3) above.

(5) For the purpose of determining the fee payable for an audit, a body whose accounts are being audited (or, in the case of the accounts of a parish meeting, the chairman of the meeting) shall complete a statement containing such information as the Commission may require and submit it to the auditor who shall send it to the Commission on the conclusion of the audit with a certificate that the statement is correct to the best of his knowledge and belief ; and, in addition, the body shall furnish the Commission with such further information as it may at any time require for the said purpose.

(6) The fee payable for an audit shall be the same whether the audit is carried out by an auditor who is an officer of the Commission or by an auditor who is not such an officer.

(7) If the Secretary of State considers it necessary or desirable to do so, he may by regulations prescribe a scale or scales of fees to have effect, for such period as is specified in the

regulations, in place of any scale or scales prescribed by the Commission and, if he does so, references in subsections (3) and (4) above to the appropriate scale shall, as respects that period, be construed as references to the appropriate scale prescribed by the Secretary of State.

PART III

22.—(1) The Commission may direct an auditor or auditors appointed by it to hold an extraordinary audit of the accounts of any body whose accounts are required to be audited in accordance with this Part of this Act if—

Extraordinary audit.

(a) an application in that behalf is made by a local government elector for the area of that body ; or

(b) it appears to the Commission to be desirable to do so in consequence of a report made under this Part of this Act by an auditor or for any other reason.

(2) If it appears to the Secretary of State that it is desirable in the public interest that there should be an extraordinary audit of the accounts of any such body as aforesaid he may require the Commission to direct such an audit by an auditor or auditors appointed by it.

(3) The provisions of sections 13 and 15 to 20 above, except subsections (1) and (2) of section 17, shall apply to an extraordinary audit under this section as they apply to an ordinary audit under this Part of this Act.

(4) An extraordinary audit under this section may be held after three clear days notice in writing given to the body whose accounts are to be audited or, in the case of the accounts of a parish meeting, to the chairman of the meeting.

(5) The expenditure incurred in holding an extraordinary audit of the accounts of any body shall be defrayed in the first instance by the Commission but it may, if it thinks fit, recover the whole or any proportion of that expenditure from that body.

23.—(1) The Secretary of State may by regulations applying to bodies whose accounts are required to be audited in accordance with this Part of this Act make provision with respect to—

Regulations as to accounts.

(a) the keeping of accounts ;

(b) the form, preparation and certification of accounts and of statements of accounts ;

(c) the deposit of the accounts of any body at the offices of the body or at any other place ;

(d) the publication of information relating to accounts and the publication of statements of accounts ;

(e) the exercise of any rights of inspection or objection conferred by section 17 above or section 24 below and the steps to be taken by any body for informing local government electors for the area of that body of those rights.

(2) Regulations under this section may make different provision in relation to bodies of different descriptions.

(3) Any person who without reasonable excuse contravenes any provision of regulations under this section, the contravention of which is declared by the regulations to be an offence, shall be liable on summary conviction to a fine not exceeding £200.

(4) Any expenses incurred by an auditor in connection with proceedings in respect of an offence under subsection (3) above alleged to have been committed in relation to the accounts of any body shall, so far as not recovered from any other source, be recoverable from that body.

Right to
inspect
statements of
accounts and
auditor's
reports.

24.—(1) Any local government elector for the area of a body whose accounts are required to be audited in accordance with this Part of this Act shall be entitled—

(*a*) to inspect and make copies of any statement of accounts prepared by the body pursuant to regulations under section 23 above and any report made to the body by an auditor ; and

(*b*) to require copies of any such statement or report to be delivered to him on payment of a reasonable sum for each copy.

(2) Any document which a person is entitled to inspect under this section may be inspected by him at all reasonable times and without payment.

(3) Any person having the custody of any such document who—

(*a*) obstructs a person in the exercise of any right under this section to inspect or make copies of the document ; or

(*b*) refuses to give copies of the document to a person entitled under this section to obtain them,

shall be liable on summary conviction to a fine not exceeding £200.

(4) References in this section to copies of a document include references to copies of any part of it.

Audit of
accounts of
officers.

25. Where an officer of a body whose accounts are required to be audited in accordance with this Part of this Act receives any money or other property on behalf of that body or receives any money or other property for which he ought to account to that body the accounts of the officer shall be audited by the auditor

of the accounts of that body and sections 12(1) and **15 to 24** PART III
above shall with the necessary modifications apply accordingly
to the accounts and audit.

Miscellaneous and supplementary

26.—(1) The Commission shall undertake or promote com- Studies for
parative and other studies designed to enable it to make recom- improving
mendations for improving economy, efficiency and effectiveness in services.
in the provision of local authority services and of other services
provided by bodies whose accounts are required to be audited
in accordance with this Part of this Act, and for improving the
financial or other management of such bodies.

(2) The Commission may undertake or promote other studies
relating to the provision by such bodies of their services besides
the studies referred to in subsection (1) above and section 27
below.

(3) The Commission shall publish or otherwise make available
its recommendations and the results of any studies under this
section.

(4) Before undertaking or promoting any study under this
section the Commission shall consult such associations of local
authorities or other bodies whose accounts are required to be
audited in accordance with this Part of this Act as appear to
it to be concerned and such associations of employees as appear
to it to be appropriate.

27.—(1) In addition to the studies referred to in section Reports on
26(1) above, the Commission shall undertake or promote studies impact of
designed to enable it to prepare reports as to the impact— statutory
provisions
    (*a*) of the operation of any particular statutory provision or etc.
        provisions ; or

    (*b*) of any directions or guidance given by a Minister of the
        Crown (whether pursuant to any such provision or
        otherwise),

on economy, efficiency and effectiveness in the provision of local
authority services and of other services provided by bodies whose
accounts are required to be audited in accordance with this Part
of this Act, or on the financial management of such bodies.

(2) The Commission shall publish or otherwise make available
its report of the results of any study under this section, and shall
send a copy of any such report to the Comptroller and Auditor
General.

(3) Where the Comptroller and Auditor General has received
a copy of any such report he may require the Commission to
furnish him with any information obtained by it in connection

with the preparation of the report, and for that purpose the Commission shall permit any person authorised by him to inspect and make copies of any documents containing any such information ; but no information shall be required by the Comptroller and Auditor General under this section in respect of any particular body.

(4) The Comptroller and Auditor General shall from time to time lay before the House of Commons a report of any matters which, in his opinion, arise out of any studies of the Commission under this section and ought to be drawn to the attention of that House.

(5) Before undertaking or promoting any study under this section the Commission shall consult—

 (a) the Comptroller and Auditor General ;

 (b) any Minister of the Crown who appears to it to be concerned ; and

 (c) such associations of local authorities or other bodies whose accounts are required to be audited in accordance with this Part of this Act as appear to it to be concerned and such associations of employees as appear to it to be appropriate.

Furnishing of information and documents to Commission. **28.**—(1) Without prejudice to any other provision of this Part of this Act, the Commission may require any body whose accounts are required to be audited in accordance with this Part of this Act, and any officer or member of any such body, to furnish the Commission or any person authorised by it with all such information as the Commission or that person may reasonably require for the discharge of the functions under this Part of this Act of the Commission or of that person, including the carrying out of any study under section 26 or 27 above.

(2) For the purpose of assisting the Commission to maintain proper standards in the auditing of the accounts of any such body the Commission may require that body to make available for inspection by or on behalf of the Commission the accounts concerned and such other documents relating to the body as might reasonably be required by an auditor for the purposes of the audit.

(3) Subsections (4) and (5) of section 16 above shall apply in relation to a requirement imposed on any officer or member of a body under subsection (1) above as they apply in relation to a requirement imposed under that section.

Miscellaneous functions of Commission. **29.**—(1) The Commission shall, if so required by the body concerned, make arrangements—

 (a) for certifying claims and returns in respect of grants or subsidies made or paid by any Minister of the Crown to any body whose accounts are required to be audited in accordance with this Part of this Act ; or

(b) for certifying any account submitted by any such body to any such Minister with a view to obtaining payment under a contract between that body and the Minister.

(2) The Commission may, at the request of the body concerned, promote or undertake studies designed to improve economy, efficiency and effectiveness in the management or operations of any body whose accounts are required to be audited in accordance with this Part of this Act, but before making a request under this subsection a body shall consult such associations of employees as appear to the body to be appropriate.

(3) The Commission may, with the consent of the Secretary of State and by agreement with the body concerned, undertake the audit of the accounts of any body other than one whose accounts are required to be so audited, being a body which appears to the Secretary of State to be connected with local government.

(4) Without prejudice to any applicable statutory provision, any audit carried out pursuant to subsection (3) above shall be carried out in such a manner as the Commission and the body in question may agree ; and references in the foregoing provisions of this Part of this Act to an audit carried out thereunder accordingly do not include an audit carried out pursuant to that subsection.

(5) The Commission shall charge the body concerned such fees for services provided under this section as will cover the full cost of providing them.

30.—(1) No information relating to a particular body or other person and obtained by the Commission or an auditor, or by a person acting on behalf of the Commission or an auditor, pursuant to any provision of this Part of this Act or in the course of any audit or study thereunder shall be disclosed except—

(a) with the consent of the body or person to whom the information relates ; or

(b) for the purposes of any functions of the Commission or an auditor under this Part of this Act ; or

(c) for the purposes of any criminal proceedings.

(2) Any person who discloses any information in contravention of subsection (1) above shall be guilty of an offence and liable—

(a) on summary conviction, to imprisonment for a term not exceeding six months or to a fine not exceeding the prescribed sum (as defined in section 32(9) of the Magistrates' Courts Act 1980) or to both ; or (*b*) on conviction on indictment, to imprisonment for a term not exceeding two years or to a fine or to both.

Passenger
transport
executives and
their
subsidiaries.

    31.—(1) The foregoing provisions of this Part of this Act shall apply in relation to a Passenger Transport Executive and the London Transport Executive as they apply in relation to a body to which section 12 above applies, but subject to the following modifications—

    (*a*) the Commission shall under section 13(3) consult the relevant authority instead of the Executive ;

    (*b*) the reference in sections 17(2) and (3), 22(1)(*a*), 23(1)(*e*) and 24(1) to a local government elector for any such area as is there mentioned shall be construed as a reference to a local government elector for the area of the relevant authority ;

    (*c*) the requirements of subsection (3) of section 18 shall apply in relation to the relevant authority as well as the Executive, but subsection (5) of that section shall apply only to the relevant authority ;

    (*d*) the notice required to be given by section 22(4) shall be given to the relevant authority as well as the Executive.

    (2) In subsection (1) above " the relevant authority "—

    (*a*) in relation to a Passenger Transport Executive, means the Passenger Transport Authority for the area for which the Executive is established ; and

    (*b*) in relation to the London Transport Executive, means the Greater London Council.

1968 c. 73.
1969 c. 35.

    (3) Section 14(1)(*a*) of the Transport Act 1968 and section 10(1)(*a*) of the Transport (London) Act 1969 (which provide for the keeping of proper accounts and other records) shall have effect subject to any regulations made under section 23 above.

    (4) The Secretary of State may, if it appears to him expedient to do so, by regulations provide—

    (*a*) for the provisions of this Part of this Act to apply in relation to subsidiaries of the Executives mentioned in subsection (1) above with such modifications, additions and omissions as may be prescribed in the regulations ; and

    (*b*) for any statutory provision which would otherwise apply in relation to the auditing of the accounts of those subsidiaries to cease to apply.

1948 c. 38.

    (5) In this section " subsidiary " means, subject to subsection (6) below, a subsidiary within the meaning of section 154 of the Companies Act 1948.

(6) Where a company would, if an Executive and any other body or bodies whose accounts are required to be audited in accordance with this Part of this Act were a single body corporate, be a subsidiary of that body corporate, the company shall be treated for the purposes of subsection (4) above as a subsidiary of the Executive.

32. Schedule 3 to the Water Act 1973 shall have effect with the substitution for paragraphs 38 and 39 of that Schedule (accounts and audit of water authorities and National Water Council) of the paragraphs set out in Schedule 4 to this Act.

Part III

Water authorities and National Water Council.
1973 c. 37.

33.—(1) The Commission shall come into existence on such day (" the first appointed day ") as may be appointed by an order made by the Secretary of State.

(2) The provisions of this Part of this Act relating to the audit of accounts shall have effect in relation to accounts for any period beginning on or after such later date (" the second appointed day ") as may be appointed by an order made by the Secretary of State ; and the amendments made by section 32 and Schedule 4 to this Act shall have effect in relation to any such period.

(3) The Secretary of State may by regulations provide for any statutory provision not contained in this Part of this Act to continue to apply on and after the second appointed day in relation to accounts for any period beginning before that day of bodies falling within subsection (4) below with such modifications, additions and omissions as may be prescribed in the regulations ; and different provision may be made by such regulations in relation to the accounts of bodies of different descriptions and in relation to their accounts for different periods.

(4) The bodies referred to in subsection (3) above are—

(a) the bodies to which section 12 above applies ;

(b) Passenger Transport Executives and the London Transport Executive ; and

(c) water authorities and the National Water Council.

(5) The expenses incurred by the Commission between the first and second appointed days shall be paid by the Secretary of State ; and in the two years beginning with the second appointed day the Secretary of State may, with the consent of the Treasury, make to the Commission grants for the purpose of providing it with working capital.

Commencement of Part III and transitional provisions.

PART III
Consequential
amendments.

34.—(1) The enactments mentioned in Schedule 5 to this Act shall have effect with the amendments there specified, being amendments consequential on the provisions of this Part of this Act.

(2) The amendments made by that Schedule do not affect any enactment in its application—

(a) to accounts for any period beginning before the second appointed day ; or

(b) to a person disqualified under any enactment in its application to any such accounts.

Orders and
regulations.

35.—(1) Any power conferred by this Part of this Act to make orders or regulations shall be exercisable by statutory instrument.

(2) Any regulations made under this Part of this Act shall be subject to annulment in pursuance of a resolution of either House of Parliament.

(3) Before making any regulations under section 21(7) or 23 above the Secretary of State shall consult the Commission, such associations of local authorities as appear to him to be concerned and such bodies of accountants as appear to him to be appropriate.

Interpretation
of Part III.

36.—(1) In this Part of this Act—

" the first appointed day " and " the second appointed day " have the meaning given by section 33 above ;

" auditor ", in relation to the accounts of any body, means the person or any of the persons appointed by the Commission to act as auditor in relation to those accounts and, to the extent provided by section 13(8) above, includes a person assisting an auditor under arrangements approved under that provision ;

" the Commission " means the Audit Commission for Local Authorities in England and Wales ;

" statutory provision " means any provision contained in or having effect under any enactment.

1972 c. 70.

(2) Section 270 of the Local Government Act 1972 (general interpretation) shall apply for the interpretation of this Part of this Act.

PART IV

SUPPLEMENTARY

Expenses.

37. There shall be paid out of moneys provided by Parliament—

(a) any expenses under this Act of the Secretary of State ; and (*b*) any increase attributable to this Act in the sums payable out of such moneys under any other Act.

38.—(1) The enactments mentioned in Schedule 6 to this Act are hereby repealed to the extent specified in the third column of that Schedule.

(2) The repeals in Part I of that Schedule have effect for financial years beginning on or after 1st April 1982.

(3) The repeals in Part II of that Schedule have effect for financial years beginning on or after 1st April 1981.

(4) The repeals in Part III of that Schedule have effect for financial years beginning on or after 1st April 1983.

(5) The repeals in Part IV of that Schedule do not affect any enactment in its application to accounts for any period beginning before the second appointed day referred to in section 33 above or any disqualification to which a person is subject immediately before the coming into force of the repeals.

(6) Any regulations in force under section 166 of the Local Government Act 1972 immediately before the repeal of that section shall have effect as if made under section 23 above.

39.—(1) This Act may be cited as the Local Government Finance Act 1982.

(2) This Act extends to England and Wales only.

SCHEDULES

Section 7(3).

SCHEDULE 1

RATES AND PRECEPTS: TRANSITIONAL PROVISIONS

1. The following provisions of this Schedule apply where before the passing of this Act and whether before or after 1st April 1982—

   (*a*) a rating authority or precepting authority has made or issued—

      (i) a supplementary rate or supplementary precept for or in respect of a period beginning on or after that date ; or

      (ii) a rate or precept for or in respect of any such period other than a financial year ; or

   (*b*) a rating authority has made a rate (other than a supplementary rate or rate falling within sub-paragraph (*a*) above) by reference to a supplementary precept or precept falling within that sub-paragraph.

2. No rate or precept shall by virtue of section 3 of this Act be substituted for a supplementary rate or precept falling within paragraph 1(*a*)(i) above.

3. Where a rating authority has made a supplementary rate falling within paragraph 1(*a*)(i) above any sum paid by a ratepayer to the rating authority in respect of the supplementary rate (or so much of any sum so paid in respect of rates generally as is attributable to the supplementary rate)—

   (*a*) shall be repaid if the ratepayer so requires ; or

   (*b*) if repayment is not required shall, as the rating authority may determine, either be repaid to him or credited against any liability of his for rates in respect of the hereditament in question.

4. Where a person as tenant or licensee of any premises—

   (*a*) is liable to make payments (whether as part of his rent or otherwise) which vary or may vary according to the rates chargeable in respect of those premises ; or

   (*b*) is entitled to make deductions from his rent in respect of those rates,

he shall, where a rating authority has made a supplementary rate falling within paragraph 1(*a*)(i) above which affects those premises, be entitled to recover or, as the case may be, liable to make good any payment or deduction which he would not have been liable or entitled to make if that rate had not been made ; and any sum which he is entitled to recover as aforesaid may, without prejudice to any other method of recovery, be deducted by him from any rent payable by him to the person by whom that sum was received.

5. Where a precepting authority has issued a supplementary precept falling within paragraph 1(*a*)(i) above any sum paid to that

authority in respect of the precept shall be repaid if the authority to which the precept was issued so requires or, if repayment is not required, credited or otherwise dealt with as may be agreed between those authorities.

6. A rating or precepting authority which has made a rate or issued a precept falling within paragraph 1(*a*)(ii) above shall under section 3 of this Act make a rate or issue a precept in substitution for that rate or precept as if it were a rate or precept for a financial year but the estimated product of that rate or precept shall for the purposes of subsection (2) of that section be adjusted in such manner as the Secretary of State may direct.

7.—(1) A rating authority which has made a rate falling within paragraph 1(*b*) above shall under section 3 of this Act make a rate in substitution for the rate falling within that paragraph.

(2) Where the precept by reference to which the original rate was made fell within paragraph 1(*a*)(i) above, the estimated product of the original rate shall for the purposes of subsection (2) of that section be calculated without reference to the precept.

(3) Where the precept by reference to which the original rate was made fell within paragraph 1(*a*)(ii) above—

(*a*) the rate substituted under the said section 3 shall be made by reference to the precept substituted pursuant to paragraph 6 above ; and

(*b*) the estimated product of the original rate shall for the purposes of subsection (2) of that section be adjusted in such manner as the Secretary of State may direct.

(4) Where the precept by reference to which the original rate was made fell within paragraph 1(*a*)(ii) above and was issued under section 150(4) of the Local Government Act 1972 (expenses of parish and community councils) sub-paragraph (1) above shall not require the rating authority to make a substituted rate unless it considers that a substituted rate will be required for meeting the precept substituted pursuant to paragraph 6 above.

1972 c. 70.

8.—(1) Where a rating authority has made a supplementary rate falling within paragraph 1(*a*)(i) above by reference to a supplementary precept falling within that provision it shall be entitled to recover from the precepting authority—

(*a*) its administrative expenses in making repayments or allowing credits under paragraph 3 above in respect of the supplementary rate ; and

(*b*) its rate collection expenses in respect of that rate.

(2) Where a rating authority has made a rate falling within sub-paragraph (*a*)(ii) or (*b*) of paragraph 1 above by reference to a supplementary precept or precept falling within sub-paragraph (1)(*a*) of that paragraph it shall be entitled to recover from the precepting authority—

(*a*) its administrative expenses in making repayments or allowing credits under section 3(5) and (6) of this Act in respect of that rate : and (*b*) any increase attributable to paragraph 6 or 7(1) above in its rate collection expenses for the financial year.

9. In this Schedule any expression which is also used in Part I of this Act has the same meaning as in that Part.

SCHEDULE 2

BLOCK GRANT: RECEIVER FOR THE METROPOLITAN POLICE
DISTRICT

Interpretation

1.—(1) In this Schedule—

"gross rateable value", in relation to the Metropolitan Police District, means the aggregate of the rateable values of the hereditaments in that District;

"the principal Act" means the Local Government, Planning and Land Act 1980;

"rateable values", in relation to hereditaments in that District, means, subject to sub-paragraphs (2) and (3) below, rateable values ascribed to them in the valuation lists on a date to be specified in each year in the Rate Support Grant Report;

"the Receiver" means the Receiver for the Metropolitan Police District;

"Receiver's grant-related poundage" means a poundage determined by the Secretary of State and related—

(*a*) to a given ratio between the Receiver's total expenditure and the Receiver's grant-related expenditure; or

(*b*) to a given difference between his total expenditure divided by the population of the Metropolitan Police District and his grant-related expenditure so divided;

"Receiver's total expenditure" means that part of the Receiver's expenditure for a year which falls to be defrayed out of the Metropolitan Police Fund and which is not met by any such grant as is mentioned in section 54(7)(*a*) or (*b*) of the principal Act but reduced by the amount of any payments of such descriptions as the Secretary of State may specify which fall to be paid for that year into the Metropolitan Police Fund;

"Receiver's grant-related expenditure" means a sum determined by the Secretary of State as being the aggregate for the year of the Receiver's notional expenditure having regard to his functions.

(2) The reference to hereditaments in the definition of "rateable values" in sub-paragraph (1) above includes a reference to a notional hereditament which a body is treated as occupying by virtue of any enactment.

(3) A Rate Support Grant Report may provide that for the year to which it relates the rateable values of hereditaments in the Metropolitan Police District falling within any class of hereditaments shall

be ascertained for the purposes of this Schedule otherwise than by reference to the values ascribed to them in the valuation lists.

Payment of block grant

2. In section 53(1) and (8) of the principal Act, so far as relating to block grant, references to local authorities or a local authority shall include references to the Receiver.

Aggregate amount of rate support grants

3. In subsection (1) of section 54 of the principal Act the reference to local authorities shall include a reference to the Receiver, " relevant expenditure " as defined in subsection (5) of that section shall include the Receiver's total expenditure and the reference in subsection (6)(a) of that section to sums falling to be paid to another local authority shall include a reference to sums falling to be paid to the Receiver.

Calculation of block grant

4.—(1) The amount of block grant payable to the Receiver is to be calculated by deducting from the Receiver's total expenditure for the year the product arrived at by multiplying the Receiver's grant-related poundage by the gross rateable value of the Metropolitan Police District.

(2) Sub-paragraph (1) above has effect subject to subsection (7) of section 56 of the principal Act in which the reference to a local authority shall include a reference to the Receiver.

Adjustment of distribution of block grant

5.—(1) Subject to the following provisions of this paragraph, the Secretary of State may provide in a Rate Support Grant Report that the amount of block grant payable to the Receiver for a year shall be calculated by deducting from his total expenditure, instead of the product of his grant-related poundage and the gross rateable value of the Metropolitan Police District, the product of those sums multiplied by a multiplier determined by the Secretary of State.

(2) In paragraphs (a) and (b) of subsection (6) of section 59 of the principal Act references to a local authority shall include references to the Receiver and the power conferred by this paragraph may only be exercised—

(a) for the purposes specified in either of those paragraphs or in paragraph (c) or (d) of that subsection ; or

(b) for the purpose of preventing or limiting any change in the amount of block grant payable to the Receiver that would otherwise result from any fresh determination of his grant-related poundage in a supplementary report made under section 61 of the principal Act.

(3) In Section 8(3) and (7) of this Act references to section 59 of the principal Act and to a local authority shall include references to this paragraph and to the Receiver.

SCH. 2

(4) If the Secretary of State exercises the power conferred by this paragraph the principles on which he exercises it shall, subject to section 8(9) of this Act, be specified in the Rate Support Grant Report.

Rate Support Grant Reports

6. In subsection (6)(*a*) of section 60 of the principal Act the reference to Part VI of that Act shall include a reference to this Schedule and in subsection (9) of that section the reference to a local authority shall include a reference to the Receiver.

Supplementary Reports

7. In the application of section 61 of the principal Act to the Receiver's grant-related poundage and the Receiver's grant-related expenditure subsection (5) shall be omitted.

Adjustment of block grant total

8.—(1) In subsections (1) and (2) of section 62 of the principal Act references to a local authority or local authorities shall include references to the Receiver.

(2) The Secretary of State may, for the purpose of the adjustment required by that section, make a fresh calculation of the entitlement of the Receiver to block grant, substituting the total of the Receiver's expenditure actually defrayed out of the Metropolitan Police Fund for the figure calculated as his total expenditure under paragraph 4(1) above.

Information

9. In section 65(1) of the principal Act for the words " sections 53 to 64 above and to Schedule 11 to this Act " there shall be substituted the words " sections 53 to 63 above ".

Estimates and calculations

10. In section 66 of the principal Act, so far as relating to block grant, references to a local authority shall include references to the Receiver.

Section 11(4).

SCHEDULE 3

THE AUDIT COMMISSION

Status

1. The Commission shall be a body corporate.

2. The Commission shall not be regarded as acting on behalf of the Crown and neither the Commission nor its members, officers or servants shall be regarded as Crown servants.

Functions of Secretary of State in relation to Commission

3.—(1) The Secretary of State may give the Commission directions as to the discharge of its functions and the Commission shall give effect to any such directions.

(2) The Commission shall furnish the Secretary of State with such information relating to the discharge of its functions as he may require and for that purpose shall permit any person authorised by him to inspect and make copies of any accounts or other documents of the Commission and shall afford such explanation of them as that person or the Secretary of State may require.

(3) No direction shall be given by the Secretary of State and no information shall be required by him under this paragraph in respect of any particular body whose accounts are required to be audited in accordance with Part III of this Act ; and before giving any direction under this paragraph the Secretary of State shall consult the Commission, such associations of local authorities as appear to him to be concerned and such bodies of accountants as appear to him to be appropriate.

(4) The Secretary of State shall publish any direction given by him under this paragraph.

Tenure of office of members

4.—(1) Subject to the provisions of this paragraph, every member of the Commission shall hold and vacate his office in accordance with the terms of his appointment.

(2) Any member may resign by notice in writing to the Secretary of State, and the chairman or deputy chairman may by a like notice resign his office as such.

(3) The Secretary of State may remove a member from office if that member—

    (*a*) has become bankrupt or made an arrangement with his creditors ;

    (*b*) is incapacitated by physical or mental illness ;

    (*c*) has been absent from meetings of the Commission for a period of six months otherwise than for a reason approved by the Secretary of State ; or

    (*d*) is in the opinion of the Secretary of State otherwise unable or unfit to discharge the functions of a member.

(4) If the chairman or deputy chairman ceases to be a member he shall also cease to be chairman or deputy chairman.

Remuneration etc. of members

5.—(1) The Commission shall pay to each member such remuneration and allowances (if any) as the Secretary of State may determine.

(2) As regards any member in whose case the Secretary of State may so determine, the Commission shall pay or make provision for the payment of such sums by way of pension, allowances and gratuities to or in respect of him as the Secretary of State may determine.

(3) Where a person ceases to be a member otherwise than on the expiration of his term of office and it appears to the Secretary of State that there are special circumstances which make it right for him to receive compensation, the Commission shall pay as compensation to that person such amount as the Secretary of State may determine.

(4) Any determination by the Secretary of State under this paragraph shall require the consent of the Treasury.

House of Commons disqualification

6. In Part III of Schedule 1 to the House of Commons Disqualification Act 1975 (disqualifying offices) there shall be inserted at the appropriate place in alphabetical order—

" Any member of the Audit Commission for Local Authorities in England and Wales in receipt of remuneration ".

Staff

7.—(1) The Commission shall appoint a chief officer who shall be known as the Controller of Audit and his appointment shall require the approval of the Secretary of State.

(2) The Commission shall appoint such other officers and servants as it considers necessary for the discharge of its functions.

(3) The Commission's officers and servants (in this paragraph referred to as employees) shall be appointed at such remuneration and on such other terms and conditions as the Commission may determine.

(4) The Commission may pay such pensions, allowances or gratuities as it may determine to or in respect of any of its employees, make such payments as it may determine towards the provision of pensions, allowances or gratuities to or in respect of any of its employees or provide and maintain such schemes as it may determine (whether contributory or not) for the payment of pensions, allowances or gratuities to or in respect of any of its employees.

(5) The references in sub-paragraph (4) above to pensions, allowances or gratuities to or in respect of any employees include references to pensions, allowances or gratuities by way of compensation to or in respect of employees who suffer loss of office or employment.

(6) If an employee becomes a member of the Commission and was by reference to his employment by the Commission a participant in a pension scheme maintained by the Commission for the benefit of any of its employees, the Commission may determine that his service as a member shall be treated for the purposes of the scheme as service as an employee of the Commission whether or not any benefits are payable to or in respect of him by virtue of paragraph 5 above.

(7) Notwithstanding sub-paragraphs (1) and (3) above, the first Controller of Audit shall be appointed by the Secretary of State who shall determine the terms and conditions on which he is to be employed by the Commission.

8.—(1) It shall be the duty of the Commission to make, by such   SCH. 3
date as the Secretary of State may determine, an offer of employment by the Commission to each person employed in the civil
service of the State as a district auditor, assistant to a district
auditor or otherwise in the district audit service whose name is
notified to the Commission by the Secretary of State for the purposes
of this paragraph ; and the terms of the offer must be such that
they are, taken as a whole, not less favourable to the person to
whom the offer is made than the terms on which he is employed on
the date on which the offer is made.

(2) An offer made in pursuance of this paragraph shall not be
revocable during the period of three months beginning with the date
on which it is made.

(3) Where a person becomes an officer or servant of the Commission in consequence of this paragraph, then, for the purposes of
the Employment Protection (Consolidation) Act 1978, his period   1978 c. 44.
of employment in the civil service of the State shall count as a period
of employment by the Commission and the change of employment
shall not break the continuity of the period of employment.

(4) Where a person ceases to be employed as mentioned in sub-
paragraph (1) above—

    (*a*) on becoming an officer or servant of the Commission in con-
        sequence of this paragraph ; or

    (*b*) having unreasonably refused an offer made to him in pur-
        suance of this paragraph,

he shall not, on ceasing to be so employed, be treated for the
purposes of any scheme under section 1 of the Superannuation Act   1972 c. 11.
1972 as having been retired on redundancy.

Financial provisions

9. It shall be the duty of the Commission so to manage its
affairs that its income from fees and otherwise will, taking one year
with another, be not less than its expenditure properly chargeable to
its income and expenditure account.

10.—(1) The Commission may borrow—

    (*a*) from the Secretary of State ; or

    (*b*) temporarily (by way of overdraft or otherwise) and with
        his consent, from any other person,

such sums as it may require for the purpose of meeting its obligations
and discharging its functions.

(2) The aggregate amount outstanding in respect of the principal
of any sums borrowed by the Commission under sub-paragraph (1)
above shall not exceed £4 million or such greater sum, not exceeding
£20 million, as the Secretary of State may from time to time by
order specify ; and no such order shall be made unless a draft of
the order has been approved by a resolution of the House of Commons.

(3) The Secretary of State may lend to the Commission any sums which it has power to borrow under sub-paragraph (1)(*a*) above ; and the Treasury may issue to the Secretary of State out of the National Loans Fund any sums necessary to enable him to make loans under this sub-paragraph.

(4) Loans made under sub-paragraph (3) above shall be repaid to the Secretary of State at such times and by such methods, and interest on the loans shall be paid to him at such times and at such rates, as he may from time to time determine.

(5) All sums received by the Secretary of State under sub-paragraph (4) above shall be paid into the National Loans Fund.

(6) The Secretary of State shall prepare, in respect of each financial year and in such form as the Treasury may direct, an account—

(*a*) of any sums issued to him under sub-paragraph (3) above or received by him under sub-paragraph (4) above ; and

(*b*) of the disposal by him of any sums so received,

and shall send the account to the Comptroller and Auditor General not later than the end of the month of November following the financial year to which it relates ; and the Comptroller and Auditor General shall examine, certify and report on the account and lay copies of it and of his report before each House of Parliament.

(7) Any consent, loan or determination by the Secretary of State under this paragraph shall require the approval of the Treasury.

11.—(1) The Treasury may guarantee, in such manner and on such conditions as they think fit, the repayment of the principal of and the payment of interest on any sums which the Commission borrows from a person other than the Secretary of State.

(2) Immediately after a guarantee is given under this paragraph, the Treasury shall lay a statement of the guarantee before each House of Parliament ; and where any sum is issued for fulfilling a guarantee so given, the Treasury shall lay before each House of Parliament a statement relating to that sum as soon as possible after the end of each financial year beginning with that in which the sum is issued and ending with that in which all liability in respect of the principal sum and in respect of interest on it is finally discharged.

(3) Any sums required by the Treasury for fulfilling a guarantee under this paragraph shall be charged on and issued out of the Consolidated Fund.

(4) If any sums are issued in fulfilment of a guarantee given under this paragraph, the Commission shall make to the Treasury, at such times and in such manner as the Treasury may from time to time direct, payments of such amounts as the Treasury so direct in or towards repayment of the sums so issued and payments of interest, at such rates as the Treasury so direct, on what is outstanding for the time being in respect of sums so issued.

(5) Any sums received by the Treasury in pursuance of sub-para- SCH. 3
graph (4) above shall be paid into the Consolidated Fund.

12.—(1) The Commission shall keep proper accounts and other
records in relation to its accounts and shall prepare in respect of
each financial year a statement of account in such form as the
Secretary of State may, with the approval of the Treasury, direct.

(2) The statement of account prepared by the Commission in
respect of each financial year shall be submitted to the Secretary
of State before such date as he may, with the approval of the
Treasury, direct.

(3) The Secretary of State shall, on or before 30th November in
each year, transmit to the Comptroller and Auditor General the
statement of account prepared by the Commission for the financial
year last ended.

(4) The Comptroller and Auditor General shall examine and
certify the statement of account transmitted to him under sub-
paragraph (3) above and shall lay before Parliament copies of that
statement together with his report thereon.

Proceedings

13.—(1) The Commission shall regulate its own proceedings.

(2) The validity of any proceedings of the Commission shall not be
affected by any vacancy among its members or by any defect in the
appointment of any of its members.

14.—(1) The application of the seal of the Commission shall be
authenticated by the signature of the chairman or of some other
member authorised either generally or specially by the Commission
for that purpose.

(2) Any document purporting to be a document duly executed
under the seal of the Commission shall be received in evidence and
shall, unless the contrary is proved, be deemed to be so executed.

Annual report

15.—(1) The Commission shall publish an annual report on the discharge of its functions.

(2) Copies of each annual report shall be sent by the Commission
to the Secretary of State who shall lay copies of it before each
House of Parliament.

SCHEDULE 4

Section 32.

NEW PARAGRAPHS FOR SCHEDULE 3 TO THE WATER ACT 1973

Accounts of water authorities and Council

38.—(1) It shall be the duty of a water authority and of the
Council—

    (a) to keep proper accounts and proper records in relation to the
        accounts ; and

(*b*) to prepare in respect of each accounting year a statement of accounts giving a true and fair view of the state of affairs and profit or loss of the body preparing the state- ment.

(2) Every statement of accounts prepared by a body in accordance with this paragraph shall comply with any requirement which the Ministers have, with the consent of the Treasury, notified in writing to that body and which relates to any of the following matters, namely—

(*a*) the information to be contained in the statement;

(*b*) the manner in which that information is to be presented;

(*c*) the methods and principles according to which the state- ment is to be prepared.

(3) Subject to any requirement notified to it under sub-paragraph (2) above, in preparing any statement of accounts in accordance with this paragraph a body shall follow, with respect to each of the matters referred to in that sub-paragraph, such course as may be for the time being approved by the Ministers with the consent of the Treasury.

(4) Without prejudice to the foregoing provisions of this paragraph, the Minister may direct a water authority to keep such accounts and records and to prepare such statements with regard to money ex- pended in the performance of their land drainage functions as he may think fit.

(5) In this paragraph " accounting year ", in relation to a water authority or the Council, means, subject to sub-paragraph (6) below, a period of twelve months ending on 31st March.

(6) If the Ministers so direct in relation to any accounting year of a water authority or the Council, that accounting year shall end on such other date as may be specified in the direction.

Audit of water authorities and Council

39.—(1) The accounts of a water authority or the Council, includ- ing all statements prepared by them under paragraph 38 above, shall be audited in accordance with this Schedule by auditors ap- pointed for each accounting year (within the meaning of that para- graph) by the Secretary of State.

(2) A person shall not be qualified for appointment under this paragraph unless he is—

(*a*) a member of a body of accountants established in the United Kingdom and recognised for the purposes of section 161(1) (*a*) of the Companies Act 1948; or

1948 c. 38.

(*b*) a member of the Chartered Institute of Public Finance and Accountancy;

but a firm may be so appointed if each of its members is quali- fied to be so appointed.

General duties of auditors

39A.—(1) In auditing any accounts in accordance with this Schedule, an auditor shall by examination of the accounts and otherwise satisfy himself that the body concerned has complied with the requirements of paragraph 38 above.

(2) The auditor shall consider whether, in the public interest, he should make a report on any matter coming to his notice in the course of the audit in order that it may be considered by the body concerned or brought to the attention of the public, and shall consider whether the public interest requires any such matter to be made the subject of an immediate report rather than of a report to be made at the conclusion of the audit.

Auditor's right to obtain documents and information

39B.—(1) An auditor shall have a right of access at all reasonable times to all such documents relating to a body whose accounts are required to be audited in accordance with this Schedule as appear to him necessary for the purposes of the audit and shall be entitled to require from any person holding or accountable for any such document such information and explanation as he thinks necessary for those purposes and, if he thinks it necessary, to require any such person to attend before him in person to give the information or explanation or to produce any such document.

(2) Without prejudice to sub-paragraph (1) above, the auditor shall be entitled to require any officer or member of the body concerned to give him such information or explanation as he thinks necessary for the purposes of the audit and, if he thinks it necessary, to require any such officer or member to attend before him in person to give the information or explanation.

(3) Without prejudice to sub-paragraphs (1) and (2) above, the body concerned shall provide the auditor with every facility and all information which he may reasonably require for the purposes of the audit.

(4) Any person who without reasonable excuse fails to comply with any requirement of an auditor under sub-paragraph (1) or (2) above shall be liable on summary conviction to a fine not exceeding £200 and to an additional fine not exceeding £20 for each day on which the offence continues after conviction thereof.

(5) Any expenses incurred by an auditor in connection with proceedings for an offence under sub-paragraph (4) above alleged to have been committed in relation to the audit of the accounts of any body shall, so far as not recovered from any other source, be recoverable from that body.

Public inspection of accounts and right to make representations

39C.—(1) At each audit of the accounts of a water authority under this Schedule any local government elector for any area to which the accounts to be audited relate may inspect those accounts and all books, deeds, contracts, bills, vouchers and receipts relating to them and make copies of all or any part of the accounts and those other documents.

(2) At the request of any such local government elector, the auditor shall give the elector, or any representative of his, an opportunity to question the auditor about those accounts or to draw the auditor's attention to any matter on which he could make a report under paragraph 39A above.

Transmission of documents to Ministers and local authorities

39D.—(1) As soon as the audit of the accounts of any body under this Schedule has been concluded a copy of any statement prepared by the body for the accounting year in question under paragraph 38 above, together with a copy of any report made by the auditor on the statement or on the accounts, shall be sent by the body—

    (*a*) to the Ministers ; and

    (*b*) in the case of a water authority, in addition to every local authority whose area is wholly or partly situated in the area of the water authority.

(2) The Ministers shall lay a copy of every statement and report of which a copy is received by them in pursuance of sub-paragraph (1) above before each House of Parliament.

Right to inspect statements of accounts and auditor's reports

39E.—(1) Any person, on application to a water authority or to the Council, shall be entitled—

    (*a*) to inspect and make copies of any statement prepared by them under paragraph 38 above and any report made by an auditor on the statement or on their accounts ; and

    (*b*) to be furnished with copies of any such statement or report on payment of such reasonable sum as the authority or the Council may determine.

(2) Any document which a person is entitled to inspect under this paragraph may be inspected by him at all reasonable times and without payment.

Regulations as to accounts

39F.—(1) The Ministers may by regulations applying to water authorities and the Council make regulations with respect to—

    (*a*) the deposit of the accounts of a water authority or the Council at their offices or at any other place ;

    (*b*) the publication of information relating to accounts and the publication of statements of accounts ;

    (*c*) the exercise of any rights of inspection or making representations conferred by paragraph 39C or 39E above, and the steps to be taken for informing persons entitled to exercise them of those rights.

(2) Regulations under this paragraph may make different provision in relation to water authorities and the Council respectively.

(3) The power to make regulations under this paragraph shall be exercisable by statutory instrument subject to annulment in pursuance of a resolution of either House of Parliament.   Sch. 4

Restriction on disclosure of information

39G.—(1) No information relating to a particular body or other person and obtained by any auditor, or by a person acting on behalf of an auditor, in the course of any audit under this Schedule shall be disclosed except—

(a) with the consent of the body or person to whom the information relates ; or

(b) for the purposes of any functions of an auditor under this Schedule ; or

(c) for the purposes of any criminal proceedings.

(2) Any person who discloses any information in contravention of sub-paragraph (1) above shall be guilty of an offence and liable—

(a) on summary conviction, to imprisonment for a term not exceeding six months or to a fine not exceeding the prescribed sum (as defined in section 32(9) of the Magistrates' Courts 1980 c. 43. Act 1980) or to both ; or

(b) on conviction on indictment, to imprisonment for a term not exceeding two years or to a fine or to both.

SCHEDULE 5   Section 34

CONSEQUENTIAL AMENDMENTS

The Public Health Act 1875

1. In section 265 of the Public Health Act 1875, for the words 1875 c. 55. from " make any payment " onwards there shall be substituted the words " make any payment in pursuance of section 19 or 20 of the Local Government Finance Act 1982 ".

The Police Act 1964

2. In section 8(3) of the Police Act 1964 for the words " Part VIII 1964 c. 48. of the Local Government Act 1972 " there shall be substituted the 1972 c. 70. words " Part III of the Local Government Finance Act 1982 ".

The Transport Act 1968

3. For section 14(3) of the Transport Act 1968 there shall be sub- 1968 c. 73. stituted—

" (3) As soon as the accounts of the Executive for any accounting period have been audited in accordance with Part III of the Local Government Finance Act 1982 they shall send a copy of any statement of accounts prepared by them for that period pursuant to regulations under section 23 of that Act to the Minister, to the Authority for the designated area and to each of the councils of the constituent areas, together with a copy of the auditor's opinion on that statement."

The Transport (London) Act 1969

4. For section 15(2)(*a*) of the Transport (London) Act 1969 there shall be substituted—

"(*a*) any statement of accounts prepared by the Executive for that period pursuant to regulations under section 23 of the Local Government Finance Act 1982, together with the auditor's opinion on that statement ; and ".

The Local Government Act 1972

1972 c. 70.

5.—(1) In section 80(1)(*e*) of the Local Government Act 1972, for the words " Part VIII below " there shall be substituted the words " Part III of the Local Government Finance Act 1982 ".

(2) In section 86(*b*) of that Act, for the words " by virtue of an order under Part VIII below, a surcharge ", there shall be substituted the words " under Part III of the Local Government Finance Act 1982 or by virtue of ".

(3) In section 87(1)(*d*) of that Act—

(*a*) for the words " by virtue of an order under Part VIII below or a surcharge or " there shall be substituted the words " under Part III of the Local Government Finance Act 1982 or by virtue of a " ; and

(*b*) for the words " order, surcharge or ", there shall be substituted the words " relevant order or decision under that Part of that Act or (as the case may be) that ".

(4) In section 137(7) of that Act, for the words from " and section " onwards there shall be substituted the words " and section 24 of the Local Government Finance Act 1982 (rights of inspection) shall apply in relation to any such separate account of a local authority as it applies in relation to any statement of accounts prepared by them pursuant to regulations under section 23 of that Act."

(5) In section 246(15) of that Act, for the words " Sections 154 to 168 above " there shall be substituted the words " Section 168 above ".

The Water Act 1973

1973 c. 37.

6.—(1) In paragraphs 6(1)(*c*) and 9(1)(*e*) of Schedule 3 to the Water Act 1973, for the words " Part VIII of the 1972 Act " there shall be substituted the words " Part III of the Local Government Finance Act 1982 ".

(2) For paragraph 40(1) of that Schedule there shall be substituted—

"(1) There shall be made to the Ministers—

(*a*) by each water authority and the Council as soon as possible after the end of each accounting year (within the meaning of paragraph 38 above) ; and

(*b*) by the Water Space Amenity Commission as soon as possible after 31st March in each year,

a report on the discharge by them of their functions during that year and of their policy and programme."

The Land Drainage Act 1976

7. In paragraphs 5(1)(*c*) and 8(1)(*e*) of Schedule 1 to the Land Drainage Act 1976, for the words " Part VIII of the Local Government Act 1972 " there shall be substituted the words " Part III of the Local Government Finance Act 1982 ".

The Local Government, Planning and Land Act 1980

8.—(1) In section 2(7) of the Local Government, Planning and 1980 c. 65. Land Act 1980, for paragraph (*b*) there shall be substituted—

" (*b*) its inclusion in a statement of accounts prepared by an authority to which this section applies in accordance with regulations under section 23 of the Local Government Finance Act 1982 or in an abstract of accounts prepared by such an authority in accordance with regulations under section 105 of the Local Government (Scotland) Act 1973 ; 1973 c. 65. or ".

(2) In section 14(1) of that Act for the words " section 166 of the Local Government Act 1972 " there shall be substituted the words " section 23 of the Local Government Finance Act 1982 ".

(3) In section 80(2) of that Act, for the words from " section " onwards there shall be substituted the words " section 19 of the Local Government Finance Act 1982 (declaration that item of account is unlawful)."

Section 38.

SCHEDULE 6

Repeals

Part I

Chapter	Short title	Extent of repeal
1967 c. 9.	The General Rate Act 1967.	In section 2(4)(*b*) the words ", or any part of the year,". In section 3, in subsection (3) the words " Subject to subsection (5) of this section " and the words from " and ending " onwards, in subsection (4) the words " Where a rate is made for a period exceeding three months " and subsection (5). In section 7, in subsection (5) the words from " but " onwards and subsection (6). In section 12, in subsections (6) and (9), the words " or half-year, as the case may be," wherever they occur and in subsection (9)(*b*) the words " or half-year " in the second place where they occur. Section 48(2). In section 115(1), in the definition of " rate period " the words " or part of a year, being a year or part ". In Schedule 6, in paragraph 10(*b*) the words " or comprising ". In Schedule 7, in paragraph 14(*b*) the words " or comprising ". In Schedule 10, in paragraph 5 the words from the beginning of sub-paragraph (*a*) to " in every case " in sub-paragraph (*c*).
1972 c. 70.	The Local Government Act 1972.	In section 149(1) the words from " and may at any time " onwards.
1976 c. 70.	The Land Drainage Act 1976.	Section 46(4). Section 49(4).
1980 c. 65.	The Local Government, Planning and Land Act 1980.	Section 33(3).

Part II

Chapter	Short title	Extent of repeal
1980 c. 65.	The Local Government, Planning and Land Act 1980.	In section 59, subsections (2) and (3) and in subsection (6)(*c*) the word " and ". In Schedule 11, paragraph 8(3) and (4).

Part III

Chapter	Short title	Extent of repeal
1980 c. 65.	The Local Government, Planning and Land Act 1980.	In section 56(8), in the definition of " grant-related poundage " the words " subject to paragraph 6 of Schedule 11 below". Section 64. Schedule 11.
1982 c. 32.	The Local Government Finance Act 1982.	In section 8, in subsection (3) the words from " and by paragraph 8 " to " District) ", in subsection (5) the words " and sub-paragraphs (3) and (4) of the said paragraph 8 " and the words following the semi-colon, in subsection (6) the words " and paragraph 8 " and " and sub-paragraphs (9) to (11) of that paragraph ", in subsection (7) the words " or paragraph 8 " and subsection (11).

Part IV

Chapter	Short title	Extent of repeal
10 & 11 Geo. 6 c. 41.	The Fire Services Act 1947.	Section 8(5).
1964 c. 48.	The Police Act 1964.	In section 8(3) the words from " and the accounts of every combined police authority " onwards.
1968 c. 73.	The Transport Act 1968.	In section 14, in subsection (1), paragraph (*b*) and the word " and " preceding it, and subsection (2).
1969 c. 35.	The Transport (London) Act 1969.	In section 10, in subsection (1), paragraph (*b*) and the word " and " preceding it, and subsection (2).

Chapter	Short title	Extent of repeal
1972 c. 70.	The Local Government Act 1972.	In section 80, subsection (1)(*c*) and, in subsection (5), the words " (*c*) and ", " surcharge or " (in both places), and " as the case may be ". Sections 154 to 167. Section 197(4). Section 228(4). In Schedule 24, paragraph 3. In Schedule 29, paragraph 7.
1973 c. 37.	The Water Act 1973.	In Schedule 3, in paragraph 9, sub-paragraph (1)(*c*) and, in sub-paragraph (4), the words " (*c*) and ", " surcharge or " (in both places), and " as the case may be ".
1976 c. 57.	The Local Government (Miscellaneous Provisions) Act 1976.	Section 27(2). In section 39(1) the words " as amended by section 27(2) of this Act ".
1976 c. 70.	The Land Drainage Act 1976.	In Schedule 1, in paragraph 8, sub-paragraph (1)(*c*) and, in sub-paragraph (4), the words " (*c*) and ", " surcharge or " (in both places), and " as the case may be ". In Schedule 2, paragraph 19.
1980 c. 5.	The Child Care Act 1980.	In Schedule 1, in paragraph 6, the words following paragraph (*b*).

Cinematograph
(Amendment) Act 1982

1982 CHAPTER 33

An Act to extend and amend the Cinematograph Acts
1909 and 1952.   [13th July 1982]

BE IT ENACTED by the Queen's most Excellent Majesty, by and
with the advice and consent of the Lords Spiritual and
Temporal, and Commons, in this present Parliament
assembled, and by the authority of the same, as follows:—

1. Subject to the provisions of—
    (a) section 7 (application of Act to special premises) of the
     Cinematograph Act 1909 (in this Act referred to as
     " the 1909 Act ") ; and
    (b) section 5 (exemption for non-commercial exhibitions)
     of the Cinematograph Act 1952 (in this Act referred to
     as " the 1952 Act "),

the 1909 Act and (except so far as they otherwise provide) any
regulations made under it shall apply as respects all exhibitions
of moving pictures which are produced otherwise than by the
simultaneous reception and exhibition of television programmes
broadcast by the British Broadcasting Corporation or the Independent Broadcasting Authority or distributed by a system
licensed by the Secretary of State under section 89 of the Post
Office Act 1969.

Margin notes:
Extension of
1909 Act to
certain other
exhibitions
of moving
pictures.
1909 c. 30.
1925 c. 68.

1969 c. 48.

Exclusion of
exhibitions
promoted for
private gain
from certain
exemptions
under the
1909 and 1952
Acts.

2.—(1) Subject to subsection (2) below, an exhibition which is promoted for private gain shall be excluded—

(*a*) from the exhibitions to which section 7(4) of the 1909 Act (exhibitions in private dwelling houses) applies ; and

(*b*) from the exhibitions which are exempted exhibitions for the purposes of section 5 of the 1952 Act.

(2) Subsection (1) above does not apply to an exhibition the sole or main purpose of which is to demonstrate any product, to advertise any goods or services or to provide information, education or instruction.

(3) An exhibition is promoted for private gain if, and only if,—

(*a*) any proceeds of the exhibition, that is to say, any sums paid for admission to the exhibition ; or

(*b*) any other sums (whenever paid) which, having regard to all the circumstances, can reasonably be regarded as paid wholly or partly for admission to the exhibition ; or

(*c*) where the exhibition is advertised (whether to the public or otherwise), any sums not falling within paragraph (*b*) above which are paid for facilities or services provided for persons admitted to the exhibition,

are applied wholly or partly for purposes of private gain.

(4) If in proceedings for an offence under section 7(1) below any question arises whether an exhibition was promoted for private gain and it is proved—

(*a*) that any sums were paid for admission to the exhibition or to the premises at which it was given and that the exhibition was advertised to the public ; or

(*b*) that any sums were paid for facilities or services provided for persons admitted to the exhibition and that the exhibition was advertised (whether to the public or otherwise) ; or

(*c*) that the amount of any payment falling to be made in connection with the promotion of the exhibition was determined wholly or partly by reference to the proceeds of the exhibition or any facilities or services provided for persons admitted to it,

the exhibition shall be deemed to have been promoted for private gain unless the contrary is shown.

(5) Where an exhibition is promoted by a society which is established and conducted wholly for purposes other than purposes of any commercial undertaking and sums falling

within subsection (3) above are applied for any purpose calculated to benefit the society as a whole, the exhibition shall not be held to be promoted for private gain by reason only that the application of those sums for that purpose results in benefit to any person as an individual.

(6) In subsection (5) above " society " includes any club, institution, organisation or association of persons, by whatever name called.

3.—(1) An applicant for the grant, renewal or transfer of a licence shall give to— Applications for grant, renewal or transfer of licence or consent.

(a) the licensing authority ;

(b) the fire authority ; and

(c) the chief officer of police,

not less than 28 days' notice of his intention to make the application.

(2) The licensing authority may in such cases as they think fit, after consulting with the fire authority and the chief officer of police, grant an application for the grant, renewal or transfer of a licence notwithstanding the fact that the applicant has failed to give notice in accordance with subsection (1) above.

(3) In considering any application for the grant, renewal or transfer of a licence, the licensing authority shall have regard to any observations submitted to them by the fire authority or by the chief officer of police.

(4) Where, before the date of expiry of a licence, an application has been made for its renewal or transfer, the licence shall be deemed to remain in force or, as the case may require, to have effect with any necessary modifications until the determination of the application by the licensing authority or the withdrawal of the application.

(5) In this Act, unless the contrary intention appears, " licence " means a licence under section 2 of the 1909 Act or a consent under section 4 of the 1952 Act, and references to a licence of either kind shall be construed accordingly.

4.—(1) Any person aggrieved— Appeals against decisions of licensing authority.

(a) by the refusal or revocation of a licence ;

(b) by any terms, conditions or restrictions on or subject to which a licence is granted ; or

(c) by the refusal of a renewal or transfer of a licence,

may appeal to the Crown Court or, in Scotland, to the sheriff.

(2) Where the decision against which an appeal under this section is brought was given on an application of which (in

accordance with section 3(1) above) notice was required to be given to a fire authority and a chief officer of police, any notice of appeal under this section against that decision shall be given to that authority and that officer as well as to any other person to whom it is required to be given apart from this subsection.

(3) Where a licence is revoked it shall be deemed to remain in force during the period within which an appeal under this section may be brought and, if such an appeal is brought, until the determination or abandonment of the appeal.

(4) Where an application for the renewal or transfer of a licence is refused, the licence shall be deemed to remain in force or, as the case may require, to have effect with any necessary modifications—

    (*a*) during any period within which an appeal under this section may be brought and, if such an appeal is brought, until the determination or abandonment of the appeal ; and

    (*b*) where such an appeal is successful, until the licence is renewed or transferred by the licensing authority.

Powers of entry.

5.—(1) Where a constable or an authorised officer of the licensing authority or of the fire authority has reasonable cause to believe that—

    (*a*) any premises in respect of which a licence of either kind is in force are being or are about to be used for an exhibition which requires a licence of that kind ;

    (*b*) any premises in respect of which a licence under section 2 of the 1909 Act is in force are being or are about to be used for an exempted exhibition ; or

    (*c*) any premises in respect of which notice has been given under subsection (2) (occasional exhibitions) or subsection (3) (exhibitions in moveable buildings or structures) of section 7 of that Act are being or are about to be used for an exhibition which, but for that subsection, would require a licence under section 2 of that Act,

he may enter and inspect the premises with a view to seeing whether the relevant provisions are being complied with.

(2) An authorised officer of the fire authority may, on giving not less than 24 hours' notice—

    (*a*) to the occupier of any premises in respect of which a licence is in force ; or

    (*b*) to the occupier of any premises in respect of which notice has been given under section 7(2) or (3) of the 1909 Act,

enter and inspect the premises for the purpose of ensuring that there are adequate fire precautions and of seeing whether the relevant provisions, so far as relating to fire precautions, are being complied with.

(3) A constable or authorised officer of the licensing authority may enter and search any premises in respect of which he has reason to suspect that an offence under section 7(1) below has been, is being or is about to be committed if authorised to do so by a warrant granted by a justice of the peace or, in Scotland, by a sheriff, stipendiary magistrate or justice of the peace.

(4) Where an authorised officer of the licensing authority or of the fire authority enters any premises in the exercise of any power under this section he shall, if required to do so by the occupier, produce to the occupier his authority.

(5) Any person who intentionally obstructs the exercise of any power conferred by this section shall be guilty of an offence and liable on summary conviction to a fine not exceeding £200.

(6) In this section " relevant provisions " means—

    (*a*) in a case falling within subsection (1)(*a*) or (2)(*a*) above, regulations under the 1909 Act and the terms, conditions and restrictions on or subject to which the licence is held ;

    (*b*) in a case falling within subsection (1)(*b*) above, regulations under the 1909 Act making such provision as is mentioned in paragraph (*a*) of section 2(1) of the 1952 Act and the conditions and restrictions on or subject to which the licence is held so far as relating to the matters specified in that paragraph ;

    (*c*) in a case falling within subsection (1)(*c*) or (2)(*b*) above, regulations under the 1909 Act and any conditions notified in writing by the licensing authority to the occupier of the premises ;

and in relation to any premises in respect of which notice has been given under section 7(3) of the 1909 Act any reference to the occupier shall be construed as a reference to the owner.

6.—(1) If a constable has reasonable cause to suspect that a person has committed an offence under this Act he may require him to give his name and address, and if that person refuses or fails to do so or gives a name or address which the constable reasonably suspects to be false, the constable may arrest him without warrant. Powers of arrest and seizure.

This subsection does not extend to Scotland.

(2) A constable or authorised officer of the licensing authority who enters and searches any premises under the authority of a warrant issued under section 5(3) above may seize and remove any apparatus or equipment or other thing whatsoever found on

the premises which he has reasonable cause to believe may be liable to be forfeited under section 7(5) below.

Penalties and forfeitures.

7.—(1) If—

(a) any premises in respect of which a licence under section 2 of the 1909 Act is not in force are used for an exhibition which requires such a licence ;

(b) any premises in respect of which a consent under section 4 of the 1952 Act is not in force are used for an exhibition which requires such a consent ;

(c) any premises in respect of which a licence of either kind is in force are used for an exhibition which requires a licence of that kind and are so used otherwise than in accordance with the terms, conditions or restrictions on or subject to which the licence is held ;

(d) any premises in respect of which a licence under section 2 of the 1909 Act is in force are used for an exempted exhibition and are so used otherwise than in accordance with the conditions or restrictions on or subject to which the licence is held, so far as relating to the matters specified in section 2(1)(a) of the 1952 Act ; or

(e) any premises are used for an exhibition to which regulations made under the 1909 Act apply and are so used in contravention of those regulations,

then, subject to subsection (3) below, each of the persons mentioned in subsection (2) below shall be guilty of an offence.

(2) The persons referred to in subsection (1) above are—

(a) any person concerned in the organisation or management of the exhibition ;

(b) where a licence of either kind is in force in respect of the premises and the exhibition requires a licence of that kind or a licence under section 2 of the 1909 Act is in force in respect of the premises and the exhibition is an exempted exhibition, the holder of the licence ; and

(c) any other person who, knowing or having reasonable cause to suspect that the premises would be used as mentioned in that subsection—

(i) allowed the premises to be so used ; or

(ii) let the premises, or otherwise made them available, to any person by whom an offence in connection with that use of the premises has been committed.

(3) It shall be a defence for a person charged with an offence under subsection (1) above to prove that he took all reasonable

precautions and exercised all due diligence to avoid the commission of the offence.

(4) A person guilty of an offence under subsection (1) above shall be liable on summary conviction to a fine not exceeding—

    (a) in the case of an offence under paragraph (a) of that subsection, £10,000 ;

    (b) in any other case, £1,000.

(5) Subject to subsection (6) below, the court by or before which a person is convicted of an offence under subsection (1)(a) above may order any thing produced to the court, and shown to the satisfaction of the court to relate to the offence, to be forfeited and dealt with in such manner as the court may order.

(6) The court shall not order any thing to be forfeited under subsection (5) above, where a person claiming to be the owner of or otherwise interested in it applies to be heard by the court, unless an opportunity has been given to him to show cause why the order should not be made.

(7) If the holder of a licence is convicted of an offence under subsection (1) above, the licensing authority may revoke the licence.

8.—(1) Where an offence under this Act committed by a body corporate is proved to have been committed with the consent or connivance of, or to be attributable to any neglect on the part of, any director, manager, secretary or other officer of the body corporate, or any person who was purporting to act in any such capacity, he as well as the body corporate shall be guilty of that offence and shall be liable to be proceeded against and punished accordingly.

Offences by
bodies
corporate.

(2) Where the affairs of a body corporate are managed by its members, subsection (1) above shall apply in relation to the acts and defaults of a member in connection with his functions of management as if he were a director of the body corporate.

9.—(1) In this Act—

Interpretation.

    " the 1909 Act " means the Cinematograph Act 1909 ;

1909 c. 30.

    " the 1952 Act " means the Cinematograph Act 1952 ;

1952 c. 68.

    " chief officer of police ", in relation to any premises, means the chief officer of police for the police area in which the premises are situated ;

    " exempted exhibition " means an exhibition which, by virtue only of section 5 of the 1952 Act, does not require a licence under section 2 of the 1909 Act ;

1947 c. 41.

" fire authority ", in relation to any premises, means the authority discharging in the area in which the premises are situated the functions of fire authority under the Fire Services Act 1947 ;

" licence " and references to a licence of either kind shall be construed in accordance with section 3(5) above ;

" licensing authority ", in relation to any premises, means the authority having power to grant licences for the premises.

(2) Any reference in this Act to an exhibition which requires a licence under section 2 of the 1909 Act is a reference to an exhibition to which section 1(1) of that Act (premises not to be used for certain exhibitions unless a licence is in force in respect of the premises) applies ; and any reference in this Act to an exhibition which requires a consent under section 4 of the 1952 Act (premises not to be used for certain exhibitions unless a consent is in force in respect of the premises) is a reference to an exhibition to which that section applies.

Amendments
and repeals.

10.—(1) The enactments mentioned in Schedule 1 to this Act shall have effect subject to the amendments specified in that Schedule, being minor amendments and amendments consequential on the foregoing provisions of this Act.

(2) The enactments mentioned in Schedule 2 to this Act are hereby repealed to the extent specified in the third column of that Schedule.

1971 c. 40.

(3) On the coming into force of section 12(11) of the Fire Precautions Act 1971 (regulations relating to fire precautions to be made under that Act), there shall cease to have effect section 7(2)(*b*) and (3)(*b*)(ii) of the 1909 Act and the following provisions of this Act, namely—

(*a*) in section 3—

(i) in subsection (1), paragraph (*b*) ;

(ii) in subsection (2) the words " the fire authority and " ;

(iii) in subsection (3) the words " by the fire authority or " ;

(*b*) in section 4, in subsection (2), the words " a fire authority and " and the words " that authority and " ;

(*c*) in section 5—

(i) in subsections (1) and (4) the words " or of the fire authority " ;

(ii) subsection (1)(*b*) and (2) ;

(iii) in subsection (6), in the definition of " relevant provisions ", in paragraph (*a*) the words " or (2)(*a*) ", paragraph (*b*) and in paragraph (*c*) the words " or (2)(*b*) " ;

(*d*) in section 7, subsection (1)(*d*) and, in subsection (2)(*b*), the words from " or " to " exempted exhibition " ; and

(*e*) in section 9, the definitions of " exempted exhibition " and " fire authority ".

11.—(1) This Act may be cited as the Cinematograph (Amendment) Act 1982.

(2) The Cinematograph Acts 1909 and 1952 and this Act may be cited together as the Cinematograph Acts 1909 to 1982.

Short title, citation, commencement and extent.

(3) This Act shall come into force on the expiry of the period of three months beginning with the day on which this Act is passed.

(4) This Act does not extend to Northern Ireland.

SCHEDULES

SCHEDULE 1

MINOR AND CONSEQUENTIAL AMENDMENTS

Cinematograph Act 1909

1. For section 1 of the 1909 Act there shall be substituted the following section—

1952 c. 68.

" Provision against cinematograph exhibition except in licensed premises.

1.—(1) Subject to the provisions of section 7 of this Act and of section 5 of the Cinematograph Act 1952, no premises shall be used for a cinematograph exhibition unless they are licensed for the purpose in accordance with this Act.

(2) Subject to those provisions, no cinematograph exhibition shall be given unless the regulations made by the Secretary of State under this Act are complied with.

(3) In this Act ' cinematograph exhibition ' means any exhibition of moving pictures which is produced otherwise than by the simultaneous reception and exhibition of television programmes broadcast by the British Broadcasting Corporation or the Independent Broadcasting Authority or distributed by a system licensed by the Secretary of State under section 89 of the Post Office Act 1969."

1969 c. 48.

2.—(1) In subsection (1) of section 2 of that Act (grant of licences) for the words " the premises " there shall be substituted the words " any premises in their area ".

(2) In subsection (2) of that section (duration of licences) for the words " revoked as herein-after provided " there shall be substituted the words " revoked as provided by section 7(7) of the Cinematograph (Amendment) Act 1982 ".

3.—(1) In subsection (2) of section 7 of that Act (occasional exhibitions)—

(a) for the words " to the county council and to the chief officer of police of the police area " (as originally enacted) there shall be substituted the following paragraphs—

" (a) to the local authority in whose area the premises are situated ;

(b) to the authority discharging in the area in which the premises are situated the functions of fire authority under the Fire Services Act 1947 ; and

1947 c. 41.

(c) to the chief officer of police for the police area in which the premises are situated ; " ; and

(b) for the words " by the county council " (as originally enacted) there shall be substituted the words " by that local authority ".

(2) In subsection (3) of that section (moveable buildings or structures—

    (*a*) for the words " the council of the county in which " (as originally enacted) there shall be substituted the words " the local authority in whose area " ;

    (*b*) in paragraph (*a*), for the words from " the council of the county " to " this Act " (as originally enacted) there shall be substituted the words " the local authority in whose area he ordinarily resides " ;

    (*c*) in paragraph (*b*), for the words " to the council of the county and to the chief officer of police of the police area in which it is proposed to give the exhibition " (as originally enacted) there shall be substituted the following sub-paragraphs—

        " (i) to the local authority in whose area it is proposed to give the exhibition ;

        (ii) to the authority discharging in the area in which it is proposed to give the exhibition the functions of fire authority under the Fire Services Act 1947 ; and   1947 c. 41.

        (iii) to the chief officer of police of the police area in which it is proposed to give the exhibition ; " ; and

    (*d*) in paragraph (*c*), for the words " the county council " (as originally enacted) there shall be substituted the words " the local authority in whose area it is proposed to give the exhibition ".

(3) For subsection (4) of that section (exhibitions in private dwelling-houses) there shall be substituted the following subsections—

    " (4) The following exemptions shall have effect in relation to any cinematograph exhibition to which this subsection applies, that is to say—

    (*a*) neither a licence under section 2 of this Act nor a consent under section 4 of the Cinematograph Act 1952 c. 68. 1952 shall be required by reason only of the giving of the exhibition ;

    (*b*) where the exhibition is given in premises in respect of which such a licence or consent is in force, no condition or restriction on or subject to which the licence or consent was granted shall apply to the exhibition ;

    (*c*) regulations under this Act shall not apply to the exhibition ; and

    (*d*) for the purposes of subsection (2) of this section the giving of the exhibition shall be disregarded.

    (5) Subsection (4) of this section applies to any cinematograph exhibition which—

    (*a*) is given in a private dwelling-house ; and

    (*b*) is one to which the public are not admitted.

    (6) In this section ' local authority ' means—

    (*a*) in England and Wales, the Greater London Council or a district council ;

    (*b*) in Scotland, an islands or district council.".

Sunday Entertainments Act 1932

4. In section 1(2) of the Sunday Entertainments Act 1932 for the words " section four of the Cinematograph Act, 1909 " there shall be substituted the words " section 5 of the Cinematograph (Amendment) Act 1982 " and for the words " that Act " there shall be substituted the words " the Cinematograph Act 1909 ".

Public Health Act 1936

5. In section 226(3) of the Public Health Act 1936 after the words " cinematograph exhibitions " there shall be inserted the words " (within the meaning of the Cinematograph Act 1909) " and for the words " the Cinematograph Act, 1909," there shall be substituted the words " that Act ".

Shops Act 1950

6. In section 74(1) of the Shops Act 1950, in the definition of " theatre ", for the words from " the exhibition " to " suitable apparatus " there shall be substituted the words " cinematograph exhibitions (within the meaning of the Cinematograph Act 1909) ".

Cinematograph Act 1952

7.—(1) For subsection (4) of section 5 of the 1952 Act (exempted organisations) there shall be substituted the following subsections—

" (4) In the last foregoing subsection the expression ' exempted organisation ' means a society, institution, committee or other organisation as respects which there is in force at the time of the exhibition in question a certificate given by the Secretary of State certifying that he is satisfied that the organisation is not conducted or established for profit ; and there shall be paid to the Secretary of State in respect of the giving of such a certificate such reasonable fee as he may determine.

(5) The Secretary of State shall not give such a certificate with respect to any organisation—

(a) the activities of which appear to him to consist of or include the giving of cinematograph exhibitions promoted for private gain ; or

(b) the objects of which do not appear to him to consist of or include the giving of cinematograph exhibitions to which the public are admitted ;

and the Secretary of State may revoke such a certificate at any time if it appears to him that, since the certificate was given, the activities or the organisation have consisted of or included the giving of cinematograph exhibitions promoted for private gain.".

(2) Any certificate given by the Commissioners of Customs and Excise under that subsection before the commencement of this Act shall have effect as if given by the Secretary of State.

8. In section 9(1) of that Act for the definition of " cinematograph exhibition " there shall be substituted—

" ' cinematograph exhibition ' has the same meaning as in the Act of 1909 ; ".

Obscene Publications Act 1959

9. In section 2(7) of the Obscene Publications Act 1959 for the 1959 c. 66. words from " means " to the end there shall be substituted the words " has the same meaning as in the Cinematograph Act 1909.".

London Government Act 1963

10. In paragraph 19(5) of Schedule 12 to the London Government 1963 c. 33. Act 1963 for the words " Section 6 of the Cinematograph Act 1952 " there shall be substituted the words " Section 4 of the Cinematograph (Amendment) Act 1982 ".

Sunday Cinema Act 1972

11. In section 2 of the Sunday Cinema Act 1972 for the words 1972 c. 19. " section 6 of the Cinematograph Act 1952 " there shall be substituted the words " section 4 of the Cinematograph (Amendment) Act 1982 ".

Indecent Displays (Control) Act 1981

12. In section 1(4) of the Indecent Displays (Control) Act 1981 for 1981 c. 42. the words " the Cinematograph Act 1952 ", in the first place where they occur, there shall be substituted the words " the Cinematograph Act 1909 ".

SCHEDULE 2
REPEALS

Section 10.

Chapter	Short title	Extent of repeal
9 Edw. 7. c. 30.	The Cinematograph Act 1909.	In section 2, in subsection (1) the words " (as defined in the Cinematograph Act 1952) " and subsection (4). Sections 3 and 4.
15 & 16 Geo. 6. & 1 Eliz. 2. c. 68.	The Cinematograph Act 1952.	Section 1. In section 4(3), the words from " and sections three and four" to the end. Section 6. In the Schedule, the entries relating to sections 1, 3 and 4 of the Cinematograph Act 1909.
1967 c. 80.	The Criminal Justice Act 1967.	In Schedule 3, in Part I, the entry relating to section 3 of the Cinematograph Act 1909.
1971 c. 23.	The Courts Act 1971.	In Schedule 9, in Part I, the entry relating to section 6 of the Cinematograph Act 1952.
1972 c. 70.	The Local Government Act 1972.	Section 204(5)(*b*).
1973 c. 65.	The Local Government (Scotland) Act 1973.	In Schedule 24, in paragraph 33, the words from " in section 7(3) " to " islands area or district "

Chapter	Short title	Extent of repeal
1975 c. 21.	The Criminal Procedure (Scotland) Act 1975.	In Schedule 7D, paragraph 4.
	The Criminal Justice Act 1982.	In Schedule 3, the entry relating to section 3 of the Cinematograph Act 1909.

Forfeiture Act 1982

1982 CHAPTER 34

An Act to provide for relief for persons guilty of unlawful killing from forfeiture of inheritance and other rights; to enable such persons to apply for financial provision out of the deceased's estate; to provide for the question whether pension and social security benefits have been forfeited to be determined by the Social Security Commissioners; and for connected purposes.

[13th July 1982]

BE IT ENACTED by the Queen's most Excellent Majesty, by and with the advice and consent of the Lords Spiritual and Temporal, and Commons, in this present Parliament assembled, and by the authority of the same, as follows:—

1.—(1) In this Act, the " forfeiture rule " means the rule of public policy which in certain circumstances precludes a person who has unlawfully killed another from acquiring a benefit in consequence of the killing. *The " forfeiture rule ".*

(2) References in this Act to a person who has unlawfully killed another include a reference to a person who has unlawfully aided, abetted, counselled or procured the death of that other and references in this Act to unlawful killing shall be interpreted accordingly.

2.—(1) Where a court determines that the forfeiture rule has precluded a person (in this section referred to as " the offender ") who has unlawfully killed another from acquiring any interest in property mentioned in subsection (4) below, the court may make an order under this section modifying the effect of that rule. *Power to modify the rule.*

(2) The court shall not make an order under this section modifying the effect of the forfeiture rule in any case unless it is satisfied that, having regard to the conduct of the offender and of the deceased and to such other circumstances as appear to the court to be material, the justice of the case requires the effect of the rule to be so modified in that case.

(3) In any case where a person stands convicted of an offence of which unlawful killing is an element, the court shall not make an order under this section modifying the effect of the forfeiture rule in that case unless proceedings for the purpose are brought before the expiry of the period of three months beginning with his conviction.

(4) The interests in property referred to in subsection (1) above are—

    (*a*) any beneficial interest in property which (apart from the forfeiture rule) the offender would have acquired—

        (i) under the deceased's will (including, as respects Scotland, any writing having testamentary effect) or the law relating to intestacy or by way of ius relicti, ius relictae or legitim;

        (ii) on the nomination of the deceased in accordance with the provisions of any enactment;

        (iii) as a donatio mortis causa made by the deceased; or

        (iv) under a special destination (whether relating to heritable or moveable property); or

    (*b*) any beneficial interest in property which (apart from the forfeiture rule) the offender would have acquired in consequence of the death of the deceased, being property which, before the death, was held on trust for any person.

(5) An order under this section may modify the effect of the forfeiture rule in respect of any interest in property to which the determination referred to in subsection (1) above relates and may do so in either or both of the following ways, that is—

    (*a*) where there is more than one such interest, by excluding the application of the rule in respect of any (but not all) of those interests; and

    (*b*) in the case of any such interest in property, by excluding the application of the rule in respect of part of the property.

(6) On the making of an order under this section, the forfeiture rule shall have effect for all purposes (including purposes relating to anything done before the order is made) subject to the modifications made by the order.

(7) The court shall not make an order under this section modifying the effect of the forfeiture rule in respect of any interest in property which, in consequence of the rule, has been acquired before the coming into force of this section by a person other than the offender or a person claiming through him.

(8) In this section—

" property " includes any chose in action or incorporeal moveable property; and

" will " includes codicil.

3.—(1) The forfeiture rule shall not be taken to preclude any person from making any application under a provision mentioned in subsection (2) below or the making of any order on the application.

Application for financial provision not affected by the rule.

(2) The provisions referred to in subsection (1) above are—

(*a*) any provision of the Inheritance (Provision for Family and Dependants) Act 1975; and 1975 c. 63.

(*b*) sections 31(6) (variation etc. of periodical payments orders) and 36(1) (variation of maintenance agreements) of the Matrimonial Causes Act 1973 and section 5(4) of the Divorce (Scotland) Act 1976 (variation etc. of periodical allowances). 1973 c. 18. 1976 c. 39.

4.—(1) Where a question arises as to whether, if a person were otherwise entitled to or eligible for any benefit or advantage under a relevant enactment, he would be precluded by virtue of the forfeiture rule from receiving the whole or part of the benefit or advantage, that question shall (notwithstanding anything in any relevant enactment) be determined by a Commissioner.

Commissioner to decide whether rule applies to social security benefits.

(2) Regulations under this section may make such provision as appears to the Secretary of State to be necessary or expedient for carrying this section into effect; and (without prejudice to the generality of that) the regulations may, in relation to the question mentioned in subsection (1) above or any determination under that subsection—

(*a*) apply any provision of any relevant enactment, with or without modifications, or exclude or contain provision corresponding to any such provision; and

(*b*) make provision for purposes corresponding to those for which provision may be made by regulations under section 115 of the Social Security Act 1975 (matters relating to adjudication). 1975 c. 14.

(3) The power to make regulations under this section shall be exercisable by statutory instrument which shall be subject to

annulment in pursuance of a resolution of either House of Parliament.

(4) Section 166(2) and (3) of the Social Security Act 1975 (provision about extent of power to make regulations) shall apply to the power to make regulations conferred by this section as it applies to the power to make regulations conferred by that Act, but as if for references to that Act there were substituted references to this section.

(5) In this section—

" Commissioner " has the same meaning as in the Social Security Act 1975; and

" relevant enactment " means any provision of the following and any instrument made by virtue of such a provision:

<table>
<tr><td>1939 c. 82.</td><td>the Personal Injuries (Emergency Provisions) Act 1939,</td></tr>
<tr><td>1939 c. 83.</td><td>the Pensions (Navy, Army, Air Force and Mercantile Marine) Act 1939,</td></tr>
<tr><td>1947 c. 19.</td><td>the Polish Resettlement Act 1947,</td></tr>
<tr><td>1970 c. 55.</td><td>the Family Income Supplements Act 1970,</td></tr>
<tr><td>1975 c. 14.</td><td>the Social Security Act 1975,</td></tr>
<tr><td>1975 c. 60.</td><td>Part II of the Social Security Pensions Act 1975,</td></tr>
<tr><td>1975 c. 61.</td><td>the Child Benefit Act 1975,</td></tr>
<tr><td>1976 c. 71.</td><td>Part I of the Supplementary Benefits Act 1976,</td></tr>
<tr><td>1977 c. 5.</td><td>section 12 of the Social Security (Miscellaneous Provisions) Act 1977,</td></tr>
<tr><td>1980 c. 30.</td><td>section 14 of the Social Security Act 1980,</td></tr>
</table>

and any other enactment relating to pensions or social security prescribed by regulations under this section.

Exclusion of murderers.

5. Nothing in this Act or in any order made under section 2 or referred to in section 3(1) of this Act shall affect the application of the forfeiture rule in the case of a person who stands convicted of murder.

Corresponding provision for Northern Ireland.

1974 c. 28.

6. An Order in Council under paragraph 1(1)(*b*) of Schedule 1 to the Northern Ireland Act 1974 (legislation for Northern Ireland in the interim period) which contains a statement that it is made only for purposes corresponding to the purposes of this Act—

(*a*) shall not be subject to paragraph 1(4) and (5) of that Schedule (affirmative resolution of both Houses of Parliament); but

(*b*) shall be subject to annulment in pursuance of a resolution of either House.

7.—(1) This Act may be cited as the Forfeiture Act 1982.   Short title, etc.

(2) Section 4 of this Act shall come into force on such day as the Secretary of State may appoint by order made by statutory instrument; and sections 1 to 3 and 5 of this Act shall come into force on the expiry of the period of three months beginning with the day on which it is passed.

(3) This Act, except section 6, does not extend to Northern Ireland.

(4) Subject to section 2(7) of this Act, an order under section 2 of this Act or an order referred to in section 3(1) of this Act and made in respect of a person who has unlawfully killed another may be made whether the unlawful killing occurred before or after the coming into force of those sections.

Copyright Act 1956 (Amendment) Act 1982

1982 CHAPTER 35

An Act to amend section 21 of the Copyright Act 1956 so as to make it an offence to be in possession of an infringing copy of a sound recording or cinematograph film by way of trade.   [13th July 1982]

BE IT ENACTED by the Queen's most Excellent Majesty, by and with the advice and consent of the Lords Spiritual and Temporal, and Commons, in this present Parliament assembled, and by the authority of the same, as follows:—

Amendment of s. 21 of Copyright Act 1956.
1956 c. 74.

1. In section 21 of the Copyright Act 1956 (penalties and summary proceedings in respect of dealings which infringe copyright) after subsection (4) there shall be inserted the following new subsection—

"(4A) Any person who, at a time when copyright subsists in a sound recording or in a cinematograph film, by way of trade has in his possession any article which he knows to be an infringing copy of the sound recording or cinematograph film, as the case may be, shall be guilty of an offence under this subsection.";

and in subsection (7) the word " or " where it first occurs shall be omitted and the words " or subsection (4A) " shall be added after the words " subsection (2) ".

Short title.
2. This Act may be cited as the Copyright Act 1956 (Amendment) Act 1982.

Aviation Security Act 1982

1982 CHAPTER 36

An Act to consolidate certain enactments relating to aviation security.   [23rd July, 1982]

B E IT ENACTED by the Queen's most Excellent Majesty, by and with the advice and consent of the Lords Spiritual and Temporal, and Commons, in this present Parliament assembled, and by the authority of the same, as follows:—

PART I

OFFENCES AGAINST THE SAFETY OF AIRCRAFT ETC.

1.—(1) A person on board an aircraft in flight who unlawfully, Hijacking. by the use of force or by threats of any kind, seizes the aircraft or exercises control of it commits the offence of hijacking, whatever his nationality, whatever the State in which the aircraft is registered and whether the aircraft is in the United Kingdom or elsewhere, but subject to subsection (2) below.

(2) If—

    (*a*) the aircraft is used in military, customs or police service, or

    (*b*) both the place of take-off and the place of landing are in the territory of the State in which the aircraft is registered, subsection (1) above shall not apply unless—

> (i) the person seizing or exercising control of the aircraft is a United Kingdom national ; or

> (ii) his act is committed in the United Kingdom ; or

> (iii) the aircraft is registered in the United Kingdom or is used in the military or customs service of the United Kingdom or in the service of any police force in the United Kingdom.

(3) A person who commits the offence of hijacking shall be liable, on conviction on indictment, to imprisonment for life.

(4) If the Secretary of State by order made by statutory instrument declares—

> (*a*) that any two or more States named in the order have established an organisation or agency which operates aircraft ; and

> (*b*) that one of those States has been designated as exercising, for aircraft so operated, the powers of the State of registration,

the State declared under paragraph (*b*) of this subsection shall be deemed for the purposes of this section to be the State in which any aircraft so operated is registered ; but in relation to such an aircraft subsection (2)(*b*) above shall have effect as if it referred to the territory of any one of the States named in the order.

(5) For the purposes of this section the territorial waters of any State shall be treated as part of its territory.

Destroying, damaging or endangering safety of aircraft.
2.—(1) It shall, subject to subsection (4) below, be an offence for any person unlawfully and intentionally—

> (*a*) to destroy an aircraft in service or so to damage such an aircraft as to render it incapable of flight or as to be likely to endanger its safety in flight ; or

> (*b*) to commit on board an aircraft in flight any act of violence which is likely to endanger the safety of the aircraft.

(2) It shall also, subject to subsection (4) below, be an offence for any person unlawfully and intentionally to place, or cause to be placed, on an aircraft in service any device or substance which is likely to destroy the aircraft, or is likely so to damage it as to render it incapable of flight or as to be likely to endanger its safety in flight ; but nothing in this subsection shall

be construed as limiting the circumstances in which the commission of any act—

    (*a*) may constitute an offence under subsection (1) above, or

    (*b*) may constitute attempting or conspiring to commit, or aiding, abetting, counselling or procuring, or being art and part in, the commission of such an offence.

(3) Except as provided by subsection (4) below, subsections (1) and (2) above shall apply whether any such act as is therein mentioned is committed in the United Kingdom or elsewhere, whatever the nationality of the person committing the act and whatever the State in which the aircraft is registered.

(4) Subsections (1) and (2) above shall not apply to any act committed in relation to an aircraft used in military, customs or police service unless—

    (*a*) the act is committed in the United Kingdom, or

    (*b*) where the act is committed outside the United Kingdom, the person committing it is a United Kingdom national.

(5) A person who commits an offence under this section shall be liable, on conviction on indictment, to imprisonment for life.

(6) In this section " unlawfully "—

    (*a*) in relation to the commission of an act in the United Kingdom, means so as (apart from this Act) to constitute an offence under the law of the part of the United Kingdom in which the act is committed, and

    (*b*) in relation to the commission of an act outside the United Kingdom, means so that the commission of the act would (apart from this Act) have been an offence under the law of England and Wales if it had been committed in England and Wales or of Scotland if it had been committed in Scotland.

(7) In this section " act of violence " means—

    (*a*) any act done in the United Kingdom which constitutes the offence of murder, attempted murder, manslaughter, culpable homicide or assault or an offence under section 18, 20, 21, 22, 23, 24, 28 or 29 of the Offences against the Person Act 1861 or under section 2 of the Explo- 1861 c. 100. sive Substances Act 1883, and 1883 c. 3.

    (*b*) any act done outside the United Kingdom which, if done in the United Kingdom, would constitute such an offence as is mentioned in paragraph (*a*) above.

PART I
Other acts
endangering
or likely to
endanger
safety of
aircraft.

3.—(1) It shall, subject to subsections (5) and (6) below, be an offence for any person unlawfully and intentionally to destroy or damage any property to which this subsection applies, or to interfere with the operation of any such property, where the destruction, damage or interference is likely to endanger the safety of aircraft in flight.

(2) Subsection (1) above applies to any property used for the provision of air navigation facilities, including any land, building or ship so used, and including any apparatus or equipment so used, whether it is on board an aircraft or elsewhere.

(3) It shall also, subject to subsections (4) and (5) below, be an offence for any person intentionally to communicate any information which is false, misleading or deceptive in a material particular, where the communication of the information endangers the safety of an aircraft in flight or is likely to endanger the safety of aircraft in flight.

(4) It shall be a defence for a person charged with an offence under subsection (3) above to prove—

(*a*) that he believed, and had reasonable grounds for believing, that the information was true ; or

(*b*) that, when he communicated the information, he was lawfully employed to perform duties which consisted of or included the communication of information and that he communicated the information in good faith in the performance of those duties.

(5) Subsections (1) and (3) above shall not apply to the commission of any act unless either the act is committed in the United Kingdom, or, where it is committed outside the United Kingdom—

(*a*) the person committing it is a United Kingdom national ; or

(*b*) the commission of the act endangers or is likely to endanger the safety in flight of a civil aircraft registered in the United Kingdom or chartered by demise to a lessee whose principal place of business, or (if he has no place of business) whose permanent residence, is in the United Kingdom ; or

(*c*) the act is committed on board a civil aircraft which is so registered or so chartered ; or

(*d*) the act is committed on board a civil aircraft which lands in the United Kingdom with the person who committed the act still on board.

(6) Subsection (1) above shall also not apply to any act committed outside the United Kingdom and so committed in relation

to property which is situated outside the United Kingdom and is not used for the provision of air navigation facilities in connection with international air navigation, unless the person committing the act is a United Kingdom national.

(7) A person who commits an offence under this section shall be liable, on conviction on indictment, to imprisonment for life.

(8) In this section " civil aircraft " means any aircraft other than an aircraft used in military, customs or police service and " unlawfully " has the same meaning as in section 2 of this Act.

4.—(1) It shall be an offence for any person without lawful authority or reasonable excuse (the proof of which shall lie on him) to have with him—

    (*a*) in any aircraft registered in the United Kingdom, whether at a time when the aircraft is in the United Kingdom or not, or

    (*b*) in any other aircraft at a time when it is in, or in flight over, the United Kingdom, or

    (*c*) in any part of an aerodrome in the United Kingdom, or

    (*d*) in any air navigation installation in the United Kingdom which does not form part of an aerodrome,

any article to which this section applies.

(2) This section applies to the following articles, that is to say—

    (*a*) any firearm, or any article having the appearance of being a firearm, whether capable of being discharged or not ;

    (*b*) any explosive, any article manufactured or adapted (whether in the form of a bomb, grenade or otherwise) so as to have the appearance of being an explosive, whether it is capable of producing a practical effect by explosion or not, or any article marked or labelled so as to indicate that it is or contains an explosive ; and

    (*c*) any article (not falling within either of the preceding paragraphs) made or adapted for use for causing injury to or incapacitating a person or for destroying or damaging property, or intended by the person having it with him for such use, whether by him or by any other person.

(3) For the purposes of this section a person who is for the time being in an aircraft, or in part of an aerodrome, shall be

treated as having with him in the aircraft, or in that part of the aerodrome, as the case may be, an article to which this section applies if—

  (*a*) where he is in an aircraft, the article, or an article in which it is contained, is in the aircraft and has been caused (whether by him or by any other person) to be brought there as being, or as forming part of, his baggage on a flight in the aircraft or has been caused by him to be brought there as being, or as forming part of, any other property to be carried on such a flight, or

  (*b*) where he is in part of an aerodrome (otherwise than in an aircraft), the article, or an article in which it is contained, is in that or any other part of the aerodrome and has been caused (whether by him or by any other person) to be brought into the aerodrome as being, or as forming part of, his baggage on a flight from that aerodrome or has been caused by him to be brought there as being, or as forming part of, any other property to be carried on such a flight on which he is also to be carried,

notwithstanding that the circumstances may be such that (apart from this subsection) he would not be regarded as having the article with him in the aircraft or in a part of the aerodrome, as the case may be.

(4) A person guilty of an offence under this section shall be liable—

  (*a*) on summary conviction, to a fine not exceeding the statutory maximum or to imprisonment for a term not exceeding three months or to both ;

  (*b*) on conviction on indictment, to a fine or to imprisonment for a term not exceeding five years or to both.

(5) Nothing in subsection (3) above shall be construed as limiting the circumstances in which a person would, apart from that subsection, be regarded as having an article with him as mentioned in subsection (1) above.

Jurisdiction of courts in respect of air piracy.

5.—(1) Any court in the United Kingdom having jurisdiction in respect of piracy committed on the high seas shall have jurisdiction in respect of piracy committed by or against an aircraft, wherever that piracy is committed.

1982 c. 16.

(2) In subsection (1) above, " aircraft " has the same meaning as in section 92 of the Civil Aviation Act 1982 (application of criminal law to aircraft) ; and, for the purposes of this definition, section 101 of that Act (Crown aircraft) shall apply to this section as it applies to the said section 92.

6.—(1) Without prejudice to section 92 of the Civil Aviation Act 1982 (application of criminal law to aircraft) or to section 2(1)(*b*) of this Act, where a person (of whatever nationality) does on board any aircraft (wherever registered) and while outside the United Kingdom any act which, if done in the United Kingdom would constitute the offence of murder, attempted murder, manslaughter, culpable homicide or assault or an offence under section 18, 20, 21, 22, 23, 28 or 29 of the Offences against the Person Act 1861 or section 2 of the Explosive Substances Act 1883, his act shall constitute that offence if it is done in connection with the offence of hijacking committed or attempted by him on board that aircraft.

PART I
Ancillary
offences.
1982 c. 16.

1861 c. 100.
1883 c. 3.

(2) It shall be an offence for any person in the United Kingdom to induce or assist the commission outside the United Kingdom of any act which—

    (*a*) would, but for subsection (2) of section 1 of this Act, be an offence under that section ; or

    (*b*) would, but for subsection (4) of section 2 of this Act, be an offence under that section ; or

    (*c*) would, but for subsection (5) or (6) of section 3 of this Act, be an offence under that section.

(3) A person who commits an offence under subsection (2) above shall be liable, on conviction on indictment, to imprisonment for life.

(4) Subsection (2) above shall have effect without prejudice to the operation, in relation to any offence under section 1, 2 or 3 of this Act—

    (*a*) in England and Wales, or in Northern Ireland, of section 8 of the Accessories and Abettors Act 1861 ; or

1861 c. 94.

    (*b*) in Scotland, of any rule of law relating to art and part guilt.

7.—(1) Where a constable has reasonable cause to suspect that a person about to embark on an aircraft in the United Kingdom, or a person on board such an aircraft, intends to commit, in relation to the aircraft, an offence under any of the preceding provisions of this Part of this Act (other than section 4), the constable may prohibit him from travelling on board the aircraft, and for the purpose of enforcing that prohibition the constable—

Powers
exercisable on
suspicion of
intended
offence under
Part I.

    (*a*) may prevent him from embarking on the aircraft or, as the case may be, may remove him from the aircraft ; and (*b*) may arrest him without warrant and detain him for so long as may be necessary for that purpose.

(2) Any person who wilfully obstructs or impedes a person acting in the exercise of a power conferred on him by subsection (1) above shall be guilty of an offence and liable—

(*a*) on summary conviction, to a fine not exceeding the statutory maximum ;

(*b*) on conviction on indictment, to a fine or to imprisonment for a term not exceeding two years or to both.

(3) Subsection (1) above shall have effect without prejudice to the operation in relation to any offence under this Act—

1967 c. 58.

(*a*) in England and Wales, of section 2 of the Criminal Law Act 1967 (which confers power to arrest without warrant) or of section 3 of that Act (use of force in making arrest etc.) ; or

(*b*) in Scotland, of any rule of law relating to power to arrest without warrant ; or

1967 c. 18 (N.I.).

(*c*) in Northern Ireland, of section 2 or 3 of the Criminal Law Act (Northern Ireland) 1967.

Prosecution of offences and proceedings.

8.—(1) Proceedings for an offence under any of the preceding provisions of this Part of this Act (other than sections 4 and 7) shall not be instituted—

(*a*) in England and Wales, except by, or with the consent of, the Attorney General ; and

(*b*) in Northern Ireland, except by, or with the consent of, the Attorney General for Northern Ireland.

(2) As respects Scotland, for the purpose of conferring on the sheriff jurisdiction to entertain proceedings for an offence under or by virtue of section 2, 3 or 6(2)(*b*) or (*c*) of this Act, any such offence shall, without prejudice to any jurisdiction exercisable apart from this subsection, be deemed to have been committed in any place in Scotland where the offender may for the time being be.

Extradition.

9.—(1) There shall be deemed to be included—

1870 c. 52.

(*a*) in the list of extradition crimes contained in Schedule 1 to the Extradition Act 1870 ; and

1967 c. 68.

(*b*) among the descriptions of offences set out in Schedule 1 to the Fugitive Offenders Act 1967 ;

any offence under any of the preceding provisions of this Part of this Act (other than sections 4 and 7).

(2) Where no such arrangement as is mentioned in section 2 of the Extradition Act 1870 has been made with a State which is a party to a relevant Convention, an Order in Council applying that Act may be made under that section as if that Convention were such an arrangement with that State ; but where that Act is so applied it shall have effect as if the only extradition crimes within the meaning of that Act were the offences which are offences in pursuance of that Convention.

(3) For the purposes of subsection (2) above—

(a) the Convention for the Suppression of Unlawful Seizure of Aircraft signed at The Hague on 16th December 1970 is a relevant Convention and the offences which are offences in pursuance of that Convention are the offences under or by virtue of section 1 or 6(1) or (2)(a) of this Act and attempts to commit such offences ; and

(b) the Convention for the Suppression of Unlawful Acts against the Safety of Civil Aviation signed at Montreal on 23rd September 1971 is the only other relevant Convention and the offences which are offences in pursuance of that Convention are the offences under or by virtue of section 2, 3 or 6(2)(b) or (c) of this Act and attempts to commit such offences.

(4) For the purposes of the Extradition Act 1870, any act wherever committed, which—

(a) is an offence under any of the preceding provisions of this Part of this Act (other than sections 4 and 7) or an attempt to commit such an offence, or would be such an offence or attempt but for section 1(2), 2(4), or 3(5) or (6) of this Act, and

(b) is an offence against the law of any State in the case of which that Act has been applied by an Order in Council under section 2 of that Act,

shall be deemed to be an offence committed within the jurisdiction of that State.

PART II

PROTECTION OF AIRCRAFT, AERODROMES AND AIR NAVIGATION INSTALLATIONS AGAINST ACTS OF VIOLENCE

General purposes

10.—(1) The purposes to which this Part of this Act applies Purposes to are the protection against acts of violence—   which Part II

applies.
(a) of aircraft, and of persons or property on board aircraft ;

(*b*) of aerodromes, and of such persons or property as (in the case of persons) are at any time present in any part of an aerodrome or (in the case of property) forms part of an aerodrome or is at any time (whether permanently or temporarily) in any part of an aerodrome ; and

(*c*) of air navigation installations which do not form part of an aerodrome.

(2) In this Part of this Act " act of violence " means any act (whether actual or potential, and whether done or to be done in the United Kingdom or elsewhere) which either—

(*a*) being an act done in Great Britain, constitutes, or

(*b*) if done in Great Britain would constitute,

the offence of murder, attempted murder, manslaughter, culpable homicide or assault, or an offence under section 18, 20, 21, 22, 23, 24, 28 or 29 of the Offences against the Person Act 1861, under section 2 of the Explosive Substances Act 1883 or under section 1 of the Criminal Damage Act 1971 or, in Scotland, the offence of malicious mischief.

1861 c. 100.
1883 c. 3.
1971 c. 48.

Powers of Secretary of State

Power for
Secretary of
State to
require
information.

11.—(1) The Secretary of State may, by notice in writing served on any person who is—

(*a*) the operator of one or more aircraft registered or operating in the United Kingdom, or

(*b*) the manager of an aerodrome in the United Kingdom,

require that person to inform the Secretary of State of the measures, of a description specified in the notice, which are being taken in respect of aircraft registered or operating in the United Kingdom of which he is the operator or in respect of that aerodrome, as the case may be, for purposes to which this Part of this Act applies.

(2) A notice under subsection (1) above shall specify a date (not being earlier than four weeks from the date on which the notice is served) before which the information required by the notice in accordance with subsection (1) above is to be furnished to the Secretary of State.

(3) Any such notice shall also require the person on whom it served, after he has furnished to the Secretary of State the

information required by the notice in accordance with subsection PART II
(1) above, to inform the Secretary of State if at any time—

    (*a*) any further measures, in respect of aircraft registered or
operating in the United Kingdom of which at that time
he is the operator, or in respect of the aerodrome to
which the information so furnished related, as the case
may be, are taken for purposes to which this Part of
this Act applies, either—

        (i) by way of alteration of, or addition to, the meas-
ures specified in any information previously furnished
by him under this section, or

        (ii) by way of applying any measures so specified
to aircraft, or to a part of the aerodrome, not comprised in the previous information ;

    or

    (*b*) any measures taken as mentioned in that subsection or
in paragraph (*a*) of this subsection are discontinued.

(4) In so far as such a notice requires further information to
be furnished to the Secretary of State in accordance with subsection (3) above, it shall require that information to be furnished to him before the end of such period (not being less than
seven days from the date on which the further measures in question are taken or the measures are discontinued, as the case may
be) as is specified in the notice for the purposes of this subsection.

(5) Any person who—

    (*a*) refuses or, without reasonable excuse, fails to comply
with a requirement imposed on him by a notice under
this section, or

    (*b*) in furnishing any information so required, makes a
statement which he knows to be false in a material
particular, or recklessly makes a statement which is
false in a material particular,

shall be guilty of an offence and liable—

        (i) on summary conviction, to a fine not exceeding
the statutory maximum ;

        (ii) on conviction on indictment, to a fine or to
imprisonment for a term not exceeding two years or
to both.

(6) A notice served on a person under subsection (1) above
may at any time be revoked by a further notice served on him
by the Secretary of State.

PART II
Power to
impose
restrictions in
relation to
aircraft.

12.—(1) For purposes to which this Part of this Act applies, the Secretary of State may give a direction in writing to the operator of any one or more aircraft registered or operating in the United Kingdom, or to the manager of any aerodrome in the United Kingdom, requiring him—

(*a*) not to cause or permit persons or property to go or be taken on board any aircraft to which the direction relates, or to come or be brought into proximity to any such aircraft, unless such searches of those persons or that property as are specified in the direction have been carried out by constables or by other persons of a description specified in the direction, or

(*b*) not to cause or permit any such aircraft to fly unless such searches of the aircraft as are specified in the direction have been carried out by constables or by other persons of a description so specified.

(2) Subject to subsection (3) below, the Secretary of State may give a direction in writing to the operator of any one or more aircraft registered in the United Kingdom requiring him not to cause or permit the aircraft to fly unless such modifications or alterations of the aircraft, or of apparatus or equipment installed in the aircraft, as are specified in the direction have first been carried out, or such additional apparatus or equipment as is so specified is first installed in the aircraft.

(3) Before giving any direction under subsection (2) above, the Secretary of State shall inform the Civil Aviation Authority of the modifications, alterations or additional apparatus or equipment proposed to be required, and shall take account of any advice given to him by that Authority with respect to those proposals.

(4) In giving any direction under subsection (2) above, the Secretary of State shall allow, and shall specify in the direction, such period as appears to him to be reasonably required for carrying out the modifications or alterations or installing the additional apparatus or equipment in question ; and the direction shall not take effect before the end of the period so specified.

(5) Subject to the following provisions of this Part of this Act, a direction given to an operator of aircraft under subsection (1) above may be given so as to relate—

(*a*) either to all the aircraft registered or operating in the United Kingdom of which at the time when the direction is given or at any subsequent time he is the operator or only to one or more such aircraft, or to a class of such aircraft, specified in the direction ;

(*b*) either to all persons or only to one or more persons, or persons of one or more descriptions, specified in the direction ; and

(c) either to property of every description or only to particular property, or property of one or more descriptions, specified in the direction;

and a direction given to an operator of aircraft under subsection (2) above may be given so as to relate either to all aircraft registered in the United Kingdom of which at the time when the direction is given or at any subsequent time he is the operator or only to one or more such aircraft, or to a class of such aircraft, specified in the direction.

(6) Subject to the following provisions of this Part of this Act, a direction given to the manager of an aerodrome under subsection (1) above may be given so as to relate—

(a) either to all aircraft which at the time when the direction is given or at any subsequent time are in any part of the aerodrome, or to a class of such aircraft specified in the direction;

(b) either to all persons or only to one or more persons, or persons of one or more descriptions, specified in the direction; and

(c) either to property of every description or only to particular property, or property of one or more descriptions, specified in the direction.

(7) Subject to the following provisions of this Part of this Act, any direction given under this section to any person not to cause or permit anything to be done shall be construed as requiring him to take all such steps as in any particular circumstances are practicable and necessary to prevent that thing from being done.

(8) A direction may be given under this section to a person appearing to the Secretary of State to be about to become—

(a) such an operator as is mentioned in subsection (1) or (2) above; or

(b) such a manager as is mentioned in subsection (1) above;

but a direction given to a person by virtue of this subsection shall not take effect until he becomes such an operator or manager, and, in relation to a direction so given, the preceding provisions of this section shall apply with the necessary modifications.

(9) Any person who refuses or fails to comply with a direction given to him under this section shall be guilty of an offence and liable—

(a) on summary conviction, to a fine not exceeding the statutory maximum;

(b) on conviction on indictment, to a fine or to imprisonment for a term not exceeding two years or to both.

PART II
Power to
require
aerodrome
managers to
promote
searches at
aerodromes.

13.—(1) For purposes to which this Part of this Act applies, the Secretary of State may give a direction in writing to the manager of any aerodrome in the United Kingdom requiring him to use his best endeavours to secure that such searches to which this section applies as are specified in the direction are carried out by constables or by other persons of a description specified in the direction.

(2) The searches to which this section applies, in relation to an aerodrome, are searches—

(*a*) of the aerodrome or any part of it ;

(*b*) of any aircraft which at the time when the direction is given or at any subsequent time is in any part of the aerodrome ; and

(*c*) of persons or property (other than aircraft) which may at any such time be in any part of the aerodrome.

(3) Without prejudice to section 7(1) of this Act, where a direction given under this section to the manager of an aerodrome is for the time being in force, then if a constable, or any other person specified in the direction in accordance with this section, has reasonable cause to suspect that an article to which section 4 of this Act applies is in, or may be brought into, any part of the aerodrome, he may, by virtue of this subsection and without a warrant, search any part of the aerodrome or any aircraft, vehicle, goods or other moveable property of any description which, or any person who, is for the time being in any part of the aerodrome, and for that purpose—

(*a*) may enter any building or works in the aerodrome, or enter upon any land in the aerodrome, if need be by force, and

(*b*) may stop any such aircraft, vehicle, goods, property or person and detain it or him for so long as may be necessary for that purpose.

(4) Any person who—

(*a*) refuses or fails to comply with a direction given to him under this section , or

(*b*) wilfully obstructs or impedes a person acting in the exercise of a power conferred on him by subsection (3) above,

shall be guilty of an offence and liable—

(i) on summary conviction, to a fine not exceeding the statutory maximum ;

(ii) on conviction on indictment, to a fine or to imprisonment for a term not exceeding two years or to both.

(5) Subsection (3) above shall have effect without prejudice to the operation, in relation to any offence under this Act—

    (*a*) in England and Wales, of section 2 of the Criminal Law Act 1967 (which confers power to arrest without warrant) or of section 3 of that Act (use of force in making arrest etc.) ; or

    (*b*) in Scotland, of any rule of law relating to power to arrest without warrant ; or

    (*c*) in Northern Ireland, of section 2 or 3 of the Criminal Law Act (Northern Ireland) 1967.

14.—(1) Subject to the following provisions of this section, the Secretary of State may give a direction in writing to any person who is—

    (*a*) the operator of one or more aircraft registered or operating in the United Kingdom, or

    (*b*) the manager of an aerodrome in the United Kingdom,

requiring him to take, in respect of aircraft registered or operating in the United Kingdom of which he is the operator or in respect of that aerodrome, as the case may be, such measures for purposes to which this Part of this Act applies as are specified in the direction.

(2) Without prejudice to the generality of subsection (1) above, the measures to be specified in a direction given under this section to an operator of aircraft, or to the manager of an aerodrome, may include the provision by the operator or manager of persons charged with the duty (at such times as may be specified in the direction)—

    (*a*) of guarding the aircraft, or

    (*b*) of guarding the aerodrome, or persons or property (including aircraft) in any part of the aerodrome,

against acts of violence.

(3) A direction given under this section may be either of a general or of a specific character, and may require any measures specified in the direction to be taken at such time or within such period as may be so specified.

(4) A direction given under subsection (1) above to an operator of aircraft may be given so as to relate either to all the aircraft registered or operating in the United Kingdom of which at the time when the direction is given or at any subsequent time he is the operator or only to one or more such aircraft, or to a class of such aircraft, specified in the direction.

(5) A direction under this section—

    (*a*) shall not require any search (whether of persons or of property), and

    (*b*) shall not require the modification or alteration of any aircraft, or of any of its apparatus or equipment, or the installation of additional apparatus or equipment, or prohibit any aircraft from being caused or permitted to fly without some modification or alteration of the aircraft or its apparatus or equipment or the installation of additional apparatus or equipment.

(6) A direction may be given under this section to a person appearing to the Secretary of State to be about to become such an operator or manager as is mentioned in paragraph (*a*) or (*b*) of subsection (1) above, but a direction given to a person by virtue of this subsection shall not take effect until he becomes such an operator or manager, and, in relation to a direction so given, the preceding provisions of this section shall apply with the necessary modifications.

(7) Any person—

    (*a*) who refuses or, without reasonable excuse, fails to comply with a direction given to him under this section, or

    (*b*) wilfully interferes with any building constructed or works executed on any land in compliance with a direction under this section or with anything installed on, under, over or across any land in compliance with such a direction,

shall be guilty of an offence and liable—

        (i) on summary conviction, to a fine not exceeding the statutory maximum;

        (ii) on conviction on indictment, to a fine or to imprisonment for a term not exceeding two years or to both.

(8) The ownership of any property shall not be affected by reason only that it is placed on or under, or affixed to, any land in compliance with a direction under this section.

Supplemental provisions with respect to directions

Matters which
may be
included in
directions
under ss. 12
to 14.
    15.—(1) A direction under subsection (1) of section 12 or under section 13 of this Act may specify the minimum number of persons by whom any search to which the direction relates is to be carried out, the qualifications which persons carrying out any such search are to have, the manner in which any such search is to be carried out, and any apparatus, equipment or other aids to be used for the purpose of carrying out any such search.

(2) A direction under subsection (2) of section 12 of this Act may specify the qualifications required to be had by persons carrying out any modifications or alterations, or the installation of any additional apparatus or equipment, to which the direction relates.

(3) Before specifying any qualifications in accordance with subsection (2) above, the Secretary of State shall inform the Civil Aviation Authority of the qualifications proposed to be specified, and shall take account of any advice given to him by that Authority with respect to those proposals.

(4) A direction under section 14 of this Act may specify—

(a) the minimum number of persons to be employed for the purposes of any measures required by the direction to be taken by an operator of aircraft or by the manager of an aerodrome, and the qualifications which persons employed for those purposes are to have, and

(b) any apparatus, equipment or other aids to be used for those purposes.

(5) In so far as a direction under any of the preceding provisions of this Part of this Act requires searches to be carried out, or other measures to be taken, by constables, the direction may require the person to whom it is given to use his best endeavours to secure that constables will be duly authorised to carry, and will carry, firearms when carrying out the searches or taking the measures in question.

(6) Nothing in subsections (1) to (5) above shall be construed as limiting the generality of any of the preceding provisions of this Part of this Act.

(7) In this section " qualifications " includes training and experience.

16.—(1) Without prejudice to subsection (5) of section 15 of this Act, a direction shall not require or authorise any person to carry a firearm.

(2) A direction shall not have effect in relation to any aircraft used in military, customs or police service.

(3) A direction shall not have effect in relation to any aircraft of which the operator is the Government of a country outside the United Kingdom, or is a department or agency of such a Government, except at a time when any such aircraft is being used for the carriage of passengers or cargo for reward or is for the time being allocated by that Government, department or agency for such use.

(4) A direction (except in so far as it requires any building or other works to be constructed, executed, altered, demolished or removed) shall not be construed as requiring or authorising the operator of any aircraft, or the manager of any aerodrome, or any person acting as the servant or agent of such an operator or manager, to do anything which, apart from the direction, would constitute an act of violence ; but nothing in this subsection shall restrict the use of such force as is reasonable in the circumstances (whether at the instance of such an operator or manager or otherwise) by a constable, or its use by any other person in the exercise of a power conferred by section 7(1) or 13(3) of this Act or by any of the following provisions of this Act.

(5) In so far as a direction requires anything to be done or not done at a place outside the United Kingdom—

> (*a*) it shall not have effect except in relation to aircraft registered in the United Kingdom, and

> (*b*) it shall not have effect so as to require anything to be done or not done in contravention of any provision of the law (whether civil or criminal) in force at that place, other than any such provision relating to breach of contract.

(6) In so far as a direction given to the manager of an aerodrome requires any building or other works to be constructed, executed, altered, demolished or removed on land outside the aerodrome, or requires any other measures to be taken on such land, the direction shall not confer on the manager of the aerodrome any rights as against a person having—

> (*a*) an interest in that land, or

> (*b*) a right to occupy that land, or

> (*c*) a right restrictive of its use ;

and accordingly the direction shall not be construed as requiring the manager of the aerodrome to do anything which would be actionable at the suit or instance of such a person in his capacity as a person having that interest or right.

(7) Nothing in this section shall be construed as derogating from any exemption or immunity of the Crown in relation to the provisions of this Part of this Act.

(8) In this section " direction " means a direction under section 12, 13 or 14 of this Act.

General or urgent directions under ss. 12 and 14.

17.—(1) A direction given to any person under section 12 or 14 of this Act need not be addressed to that particular person, but may be framed in general terms applicable to all persons to whom such a direction may be given or to any class of such persons to which that particular person belongs.

(2) If it appears to the Secretary of State that an exception from any direction given under either of those sections is required as a matter of urgency in any particular case he may, by a notification given (otherwise than in writing) to the person for the time being subject to the direction, authorise that person to disregard the requirements of the direction—

(a) in relation to such aircraft or class of aircraft, or in relation to such persons or property or such description of persons or property, and

(b) on such occasion or series of occasions, or for such period,

as he may specify; and the direction shall have effect in that case subject to any exceptions so specified.

(3) Any notification given to any person under subsection (2) above with respect to any direction shall cease to have effect (if it has not already done so)—

(a) if a direction in writing is subsequently given to that person varying or revoking the original direction; or

(b) if no such direction in writing is given within the period of thirty days beginning with the date on which the notification was given, at the end of that period.

(4) Any notification given under subsection (2) above shall be regarded as given to the person to whom it is directed if it is given—

(a) to any person authorised by that person to receive any such direction or notification;

(b) where that person is a body corporate, to the secretary, clerk or similar officer of the body corporate; and

(c) in any other case, to anyone holding a comparable office or position in that person's employment.

18.—(1) This section applies to any direction given under Objections section 14 of this Act which— to certain directions

(a) requires a person to take measures consisting of or under s. 14. including the construction, execution, alteration, demolition or removal of a building or other works; and

(b) does not contain a statement that the measures are urgently required and that accordingly the direction is to take effect immediately.

(2) At any time before the end of the period of thirty days beginning with the date on which a direction to which this section applies is given, the person to whom the direction is given may serve on the Secretary of State a notice in writing objecting to the direction, on the grounds that the measures

PART II   specified in the direction, in so far as they relate to the construction, execution, alteration, demolition or removal of a building or other works—

> (*a*) are unnecessary and should be dispensed with ; or
>
> (*b*) are excessively onerous or inconvenient and should be modified in a manner specified in the notice.

(3) Where the person to whom such a direction is given serves a notice under subsection (2) above objecting to the direction, the Secretary of State shall consider the grounds of the objection and, if so required by the objector, shall afford to him an opportunity of appearing before, and being heard by, a person appointed by the Secretary of State for the purpose, and shall then serve on the objector a notice in writing either—

> (*a*) confirming the direction as originally given ; or
>
> (*b*) confirming it subject to one or more modifications specified in the notice under this subsection ; or
>
> (*c*) withdrawing the direction ;

and the direction shall not take effect until it has been confirmed (with or without modifications) by a notice served under this subsection.

Operation of directions under Part II in relation to rights and duties under other laws.

19.—(1) The following provisions of this section, where they refer to a direction under any of the preceding provisions of this Part of this Act, shall be construed as referring to that direction as it has effect subject to any limitation imposed on its operation——

> (*a*) by section 16 of this Act, or
>
> (*b*) by any exemption or immunity of the Crown ;

and any reference in those provisions to compliance with such a direction shall be construed as a reference to compliance with it subject to any limitation so imposed.

(2) In so far as any such direction requires anything to be done or not done in the United Kingdom, the direction shall have effect notwithstanding anything contained in any contract (whether a United Kingdom contract or not) or contained in, or having effect by virtue of, any other Act or any rule of law ; and accordingly no proceedings (whether civil or criminal) shall lie against any person in any United Kingdom court by reason of anything done or not done by him or on his behalf in compliance with such a direction.

(3) In so far as such a direction requires anything to be done or not done at a place outside the United Kingdom, the direction shall have effect notwithstanding anything contained in any contract (whether a United Kingdom contract or not) ; and accordingly, where such a direction is inconsistent with anything in

such a contract, it shall (without prejudice to any proceedings in a court other than a United Kingdom court) be construed as requiring compliance with the direction notwithstanding that compliance would be in breach of that contract.

(4) No proceedings for breach of contract shall lie against any person in a United Kingdom court by reason of anything done or not done by him or on his behalf at a place outside the United Kingdom in compliance with any such direction, if the contract in question is a United Kingdom contract.

(5) In this section " United Kingdom court " means a court exercising jurisdiction in any part of the United Kingdom under the law of the United Kingdom or of part of the United Kingdom, and " United Kingdom contract " means a contract which is either expressed to have effect in accordance with the law of the United Kingdom or of part of the United Kingdom or (not being so expressed) is a contract of which the proper law is the law of the United Kingdom or of part of the United Kingdom.

20.—(1) For the purpose of enabling the Secretary of State to determine whether to give a direction to any person under any of the preceding provisions of this Part of this Act, or of ascertaining whether any such direction is being or has been complied with, any person authorised in writing by the Secretary of State (in this section referred to as an " authorised person ") shall have power, on production (if required) of his credentials, to inspect— Inspection of aircraft and aerodromes.

    (*a*) any aircraft registered or operating in the United Kingdom, at a time when it is in the United Kingdom, or

    (*b*) any part of any aerodrome in the United Kingdom.

(2) An authorised person inspecting an aircraft or any part of an aerodrome under subsection (1) above shall have power—

    (*a*) to subject any property found by him in the aircraft (but not the aircraft itself or any apparatus or equipment installed in it) or, as the case may be, to subject that part of the aerodrome or any property found by him there, to such tests, or

    (*b*) to require the operator of the aircraft, or the manager of the aerodrome, to furnish to him such information,

as the authorised person may consider necessary for the purpose for which the inspection is carried out.

(3) Subject to subsection (4) below, an authorised person, for the purpose of exercising any power conferred on him by the preceding provisions of this section in relation to an aircraft or in relation to an aerodrome, shall have power—

    (*a*) for the purpose of inspecting an aircraft, to enter it and to take all such steps as are necessary to detain it, or

(b) for the purpose of inspecting any part of an aerodrome, to enter any building or works in the aerodrome or enter upon any land in the aerodrome.

(4) The powers conferred by subsection (3) above shall not include power for an authorised person to use force for the purpose of entering any aircraft, building or works or entering upon any land.

(5) Any person who—

(a) wilfully obstructs or impedes a person acting in the exercise of a power conferred on him by or under this section, or

(b) refuses or, without reasonable excuse, fails to comply with a requirement imposed on him under subsection (2)(b) above, or

(c) in furnishing any information so required, makes a statement which he knows to be false in a material particular, or recklessly makes a statement which is false in a material particular,

shall be guilty of an offence and liable—

(i) on summary conviction, to a fine not exceeding the statutory maximum ;

(ii) on conviction on indictment, to a fine or to imprisonment for a term not exceeding two years or to both.

Air navigation installations

Application of provisions of Part II to air navigation installations.

21.—(1) Sections 11, 13, 14, 15, 16 and 20 of this Act shall have effect in relation to air navigation installations in the United Kingdom in accordance with the following provisions of this section.

(2) In relation to any such air navigation installation which does not form part of an aerodrome, those sections shall have effect, subject to subsection (5) below, as if in them any reference to an aerodrome were a reference to such an air navigation installation and any reference to the manager of an aerodrome were a reference to the authority responsible for such an air navigation installation.

(3) Where an air navigation installation forms part of an aerodrome in the United Kingdom, those sections shall have effect, subject to subsection (5) below, as if in them any reference to an aerodrome were a reference either—

(a) to an aerodrome, or

(b) to an air navigation installation which forms part of an aerodrome, or

(*c*) to so much of an aerodrome as does not consist of an
air navigation installation ;

and accordingly a notice under section 11 of this Act or a
direction under section 13 or 14 of this Act may be served or
given either in respect of the whole of the aerodrome, or in respect of the air navigation installation separately, or in respect
of so much of the aerodrome as does not consist of an air navigation installation.

(4) For the purposes—

(*a*) of the service of a notice or the giving of a direction
under section 11, 13 or 14 of this Act as modified by
subsection (3) above, where the notice is to be served
or the direction given in respect of an air navigation
installation separately, and

(*b*) of the operation of section 16 (6) of this Act in relation
to a direction so given,

any reference in any of those sections to the manager of the
aerodrome shall be construed as a reference to any person
who is either the manager of the aerodrome or the authority
responsible for the air navigation installation.

(5) Subsections (2) and (3) above shall not apply to section
13(3) of this Act ; but where a direction given under section 13
of this Act, as applied or modified by the preceding provisions
of this section, is for the time being in force—

(*a*) if it is a direction given in respect of an air navigation
installation separately (whether that installation forms
part of an aerodrome or not), the said section 13 (3)
shall have effect in relation to that direction as if the
air navigation installation were an aerodrome and,
where the direction was given to the authority responsible for the air navigation installation, as if it had been
given to the manager of that aerodrome ;

(*b*) if it is a direction given in respect of so much of an
aerodrome as does not consist of an air navigation
installation, the said section 13 (3) shall have effect
in relation to that direction as if any air navigation
installation comprised in the aerodrome did not form
part of the aerodrome.

(6) A direction under section 14 of this Act, as applied or
modified by the preceding provisions of this section, may be
given to the authority responsible for one or more air navigation
installations so as to relate either—

(*a*) to all air navigation installations in the United Kingdom
for which it is responsible at the time when the direction is given or at any subsequent time, or

(*b*) only to one or more such air navigation installations, or to a class of such air navigation installations, specified in the direction.

(7) Any reference in section 17, 18 (1) or 19 (1) of this Act to a direction given under a provision therein mentioned shall be construed as including a reference to a direction given under that provision as applied or modified by the preceding provisions of this section.

(8) Notwithstanding anything in subsection (2) (*a*) of section 20 of this Act, a person inspecting an air navigation installation under that section (or under that section as applied or modified by the preceding provisions of this section) shall not be empowered thereby to test any apparatus or equipment which constitutes or forms part of the air navigation installation.

Miscellaneous supplemental provisions

Compensation in respect of certain measures taken under Part II.

22.—(1) The provisions of this section shall have effect where, in compliance with a direction under section 14 of this Act or under that section as applied or modified by section 21 of this Act, the manager of an aerodrome or the authority responsible for an air navigation installation takes any measures consisting of the construction, execution, alteration, demolition or removal of a building or other works on land either within or outside the aerodrome or that air navigation installation, as the case may be.

(2) If the value of any interest in that land to which a person is entitled is depreciated in conseqence of the taking of those measures, or the person having such an interest suffers loss in consequence of them by being disturbed in his enjoyment of any of that land, he shall be entitled to compensation equal to the amount of the depreciation or loss.

(3) If any land other than the land on which the measures are taken is injuriously affected by the taking of those measures, any person having an interest in that other land, who suffers loss in consequence of its being injuriously affected, shall be entitled to compensation equal to the amount of the loss.

(4) Any compensation to which a person is entitled under this section shall be payable to him by the person (whether being a manager of an aerodrome or the authority responsible for an air navigation installation) by whom the measures in question were taken.

(5) The provisions of Schedule 1 to this Act shall have effect for the purposes of this section ; and the preceding provisions of this section shall have effect subject to the provisions of that Schedule.

23.—(1) The Secretary of State shall, on or before 31st January in each year, lay before each House of Parliament a report stating the number of notices served by him under section 11 of this Act and the number of directions given by him under sections 12, 13 and 14 of this Act during the period of twelve months which expired with the preceding December.

PART II

Annual report by Secretary of State as to notices and directions under Part II.

(2) Each such report shall deal separately with notices served under section 11, directions given under section 12, directions given under section 13 and directions given under section 14 of this Act, and, in relation to each of those matters, shall show separately—

(a) the number of notices or directions which, during the period to which the report relates, were served on or given to persons as being, or as appearing to the Secretary of State to be about to become, operators of aircraft;

(b) the number of notices or directions which during that period were served on or given to persons as being, or as appearing to the Secretary of State to be about to become, managers of aerodromes; and

(c) the number of notices or directions which during that period were served on or given to persons as being, or as appearing to the Secretary of State to be about to become, authorities responsible for air navigation installations.

(3) In this section any reference to section 11, 13 or 14 of this Act shall be construed as including a reference to that section as applied or modified by section 21 of this Act.

24. Any notice, any document containing a direction and any other document required or authorised by any provision of this Part of this Act to be served on or given to any person may be served or given—

(a) by delivering it to him, or

(b) by sending it to him by post at his usual or last-known residence or place of business, whether in the United Kingdom or elsewhere, or

(c) in the case of a body corporate, by delivering it to the secretary, clerk or similar officer of the body corporate at its registered or principal office in the United Kingdom (or, if it has no office in the United Kingdom, at its principal office, wherever it may be) or sending it by post to the secretary, clerk or similar officer of that body corporate at that office.

PART III

POLICING OF AIRPORTS

25.—(1) The Secretary of State may by order designate for the purposes of this Part of this Act any aerodrome used for the purposes of civil aviation if he considers that the policing of that aerodrome should, in the interests of the preservation of the peace and the prevention of crime, be undertaken by constables under the direction and control of the chief officer of police for the police area in which the aerodrome is wholly or mainly situated.

(2) Before making an order under subsection (1) above in relation to any aerodrome the Secretary of State shall consult the manager of the aerodrome and the police authority and chief officer of police for the police area in question.

(3) The power to make an order under subsection (1) above shall be exercisable by statutory instrument and—

(*a*) any order containing a statement that it is made with the consent of the manager and the authority mentioned in subsection (2) above shall be subject to annulment in pursuance of a resolution of either House of Parliament ;

(*b*) any order not containing such a statement shall be laid before Parliament in draft and shall not be made unless the draft is approved by resolution of each House of Parliament.

26.—(1) So long as any aerodrome is a designated airport—

(*a*) any relevant constable shall, when acting in the execution of his duty and, in particular, for the purpose of exercising the powers conferred on such a constable by or under the following provisions of this Part of this Act, be entitled as against the manager of the aerodrome to enter any part of the aerodrome ; and

(*b*) no member of any aerodrome constabulary maintained by the manager shall have the powers and privileges or be liable to the duties and responsibilities of a constable on the aerodrome or exercise there any power conferred by or under any enactment on members of that constabulary or on constables generally.

(2) Paragraph (*a*) of subsection (1) above is without prejudice to any right of entry existing apart from that paragraph.

(3) The manager of an aerodrome which is a designated airport shall—

(*a*) make to the police authority for the relevant police area such payments in respect of the policing of the aerodrome, and (*b*) provide, for use in connection with the policing of the aerodrome, such accommodation and facilities,

as the manager and that authority may agree or as may, in default of agreement, be determined by the Secretary of State.

(4) Where the relevant police area is the metropolitan police district, subsection (3) above shall have effect with the substitution for references to the police authority of references to the receiver for that district.

27.—(1) Any relevant constable may in any aerodrome which is a designated airport—

    (*a*) stop, and without warrant search and arrest, any airport employee whom he has reasonable grounds to suspect of having in his possession or of conveying in any manner anything stolen or unlawfully obtained on the aerodrome ; and

    (*b*) if he has reasonable grounds to suspect that anything stolen or unlawfully obtained on the aerodrome may be found in or on any vehicle carrying an airport employee or in or on any aircraft, stop and without warrant search and detain the vehicle or, as the case may be, board and without warrant search the aircraft.

(2) Any relevant constable may—

    (*a*) stop any person who is leaving a cargo area in an aerodrome which is a designated airport and inspect any goods carried by that person ;

    (*b*) stop and search any vehicle or aircraft which is leaving any such area and inspect the vehicle or aircraft and any goods carried on or in it ; and

    (*c*) detain in the area—

        (i) any such goods as aforesaid for which there is not produced a document authorising their removal from the area signed by a person authorised in that behalf by the manager of the aerodrome ; and

        (ii) any such vehicle or aircraft as aforesaid so long as there are on or in it goods liable to detention under this paragraph.

(3) Nothing in subsection (2) above shall be construed as conferring a power to search any person.

(4) In any cargo area in an aerodrome which is a designated airport the powers of a constable under subsection (1)(*b*) above—

    (*a*) extend to any vehicle whether or not it is carrying an airport employee ; and

2 D 2

(*b*) include power, not only to board and search an aircraft, but also to stop and detain it.

(5) In this section " airport employee ", in relation to any aerodrome, means any person in the employment of the manager of the aerodrome and any person employed otherwise than by the manager to work on the aerodrome.

(6) In this section " cargo area " means, subject to subsection (7) below, any area which appears to the Secretary of State to be used wholly or mainly for the storage or handling of cargo in an aerodrome and is designated by an order made by him for the purposes of this section.

(7) Where an aerodrome owned or managed by the British Airports Authority becomes a designated airport at a time when an area in that aerodrome is designated for the purposes of

section 12 of the Airports Authority Act 1975 (which makes provision corresponding to subsections (2) to (4) above) that area shall, unless the Secretary of State by order otherwise directs, be treated as a cargo area for the purposes of this section.

(8) Any power to make an order under this section shall be exercisable by statutory instrument subject to annulment in pursuance of a resolution of either House of Parliament.

(9) The powers conferred by this section on a relevant constable are without prejudice to any powers exercisable by him apart from this section.

28.—(1) So long as any aerodrome is a designated airport any power of the manager of the aerodrome to make aerodrome byelaws shall, if it would not otherwise do so—

(*a*) extend to the making of byelaws in respect of the whole of the aerodrome ; and

(*b*) include power to make byelaws requiring any person, if so requested by a relevant constable, to leave the aerodrome or any particular part of it or to state his name and address and the purpose of his being on the aerodrome.

(2) A relevant constable may remove from any aerodrome which is a designated airport, or from any part of it—

(*a*) any person who, in contravention of any aerodrome byelaws, fails or refuses to leave the aerodrome or part after being requested by the constable to do so ;

(*b*) any vehicle, animal or thing brought to or left within the aerodrome or part in contravention of any aerodrome byelaws and any vehicle, animal or thing likely to cause danger or obstruction.

(3) A relevant constable may without warrant arrest a person within any aerodrome which is a designated airport—

  (*a*) if he has reasonable cause to believe that the person has contravened any aerodrome byelaws and he does not know and cannot ascertain that person's name and address ; or

  (*b*) if that person, in contravention of any aerodrome byelaws, fails or refuses to leave the aerodrome or any particular part of it after being requested by the constable to do so.

29.—(1) So long as any aerodrome is a designated airport, the functions of a chief officer of police under any provisions applying in relation to the aerodrome under section 13(1) to (3) of the Airports Authority Act 1975 or section 37 of the Civil Aviation Act 1982 (application to certain aerodromes of provisions relating to road traffic) shall, notwithstanding any order under those sections, be exercisable by that officer to the exclusion of the chief officer of any aerodrome constabulary ; and for the purposes of any functions of a chief officer of police under those provisions any part of the aerodrome which is not within the relevant police area shall be treated as if it were.

(2) So long as any aerodrome is a designated airport—

  (*a*) traffic wardens appointed by the police authority for the relevant police area (or, if that area is the metropolitan police district, by the commissioner of police of the metropolis) may exercise their functions on the aerodrome and shall be entitled, as against the manager of the aerodrome, to enter the aerodrome accordingly ;

  (*b*) if the aerodrome is owned or managed by the British Airports Authority, no person employed by the Authority shall exercise in relation to the aerodrome any such functions as are mentioned in section 13(4) of the Airports Authority Act 1975 (appointment of traffic wardens by the Authority).

(3) The reference in subsection (1) above to section 13(1) to (3) of the Airports Authority Act 1975 includes a reference to section 13(2) of that Act as extended by section 14(2) thereof (functions as respects abandoned vehicles) ; and subsection (2)(*a*) above has effect whether or not the whole of the aerodrome is in the relevant police area.

30.—(1) The Secretary of State may by order make such provision as appears to him to be necessary or expedient in connection with, or in consequence of, any aerodrome becoming or ceasing to be a designated airport.

(2) Without prejudice to the generality of subsection (1) above and to the preceding provisions of this Part of this Act, any order under this section may in particular—

(a) modify or suspend the operation of any local Act in so far as it makes provision in relation to the policing of the aerodrome ;

(b) amend any aerodrome byelaws for the purpose of transferring to relevant constables any functions conferred thereby on members of an aerodrome constabulary, of extending the byelaws to the whole of the aerodrome or of including in them any such requirement as is mentioned in section 28(1)(b) of this Act ;

(c) make provision for any such transfers of officers and staff as are mentioned in subsection (3) below ;

(d) make provision in respect of the pension rights of officers and staff so transferred, whether by requiring the making of payments, by modifying or revoking, or transferring or extinguishing liabilities or obligations under, any pension scheme, by transferring or winding up any pension fund or otherwise ;

(e) require the manager of the aerodrome to make payments by way of compensation to or in respect of persons who suffer any loss of office or employment or loss or diminution of emoluments which is attributable to the aerodrome becoming a designated airport, being payments of such amount and on such terms and conditions as may be specified by or determined in accordance with the order ;

(f) exclude any part of the aerodrome from the right of entry conferred by section 26(1)(a) or 29(2)(a) of this Act.

(3) The transfers for which provision may be made under this section are transfers, with the consent of the persons to be transferred, of—

(a) members of any aerodrome constabulary maintained by the manager of the aerodrome to the police force for the relevant police area ;

(b) persons employed by the British Airports Authority to discharge such functions as are mentioned in section 13(4) of the Airports Authority Act 1975 to employment as traffic wardens by the police authority for the relevant police area or, if that area is the metropolitan police district, by the commissioner of police of the metropolis ;

(c) other persons employed by the manager of the aerodrome for police purposes to employment by the police

1975 c. 78.

authority for the relevant police area or, if that area is a county, to employment by the police authority or the county council or, if that area is the metropolitan police district, to employment as members of the metropolitan civil staffs.

(4) Any member of an aerodrome constabulary transferred by virtue of an order under this section to the police force for the relevant police area shall be deemed to have been duly appointed as a member of that force and to have been duly attested as such and, unless the order otherwise provides, shall hold in that force the same rank as he held in the aerodrome constabulary.

(5) Any amendment of aerodrome byelaws by an order under this section shall have effect as if duly made by the manager of the aerodrome and confirmed under the enactment authorising the manager of the aerodrome to make aerodrome byelaws.

(6) Before making an order under this section in relation to any aerodrome the Secretary of State shall consult the manager of the aerodrome and the police authority and chief officer of police for the relevant police area.

(7) The power to make an order under this section shall be exercisable by statutory instrument subject to annulment in pursuance of a resolution of either House of Parliament.

31.—(1) In this Part of this Act, subject to the following provisions of this section—

> " aerodrome byelaws " means, in relation to any aerodrome, byelaws having effect under any enactment authorising the manager of the aerodrome to make byelaws in respect of the whole or any part of the aerodrome ;
>
> " aerodrome constabulary " means, in relation to any aerodrome, any body of constables which the manager of the aerodrome has power to maintain at the aerodrome ;
>
> " designated airport " means any aerodrome for the time being designated under section 25 of this Act ;
>
> " members of the metropolitan civil staffs " means persons who are employed under the commissioner of police of the metropolis or the receiver for the metropolitan police district and are not constables and whose salaries are paid out of the metropolitan police fund ;
>
> " relevant police area " and " relevant constable ", in relation to any aerodrome, mean respectively the police

Interpretation and application of Part III to Scotland and Northern Ireland.

area in which the aerodrome is wholly or mainly situated and any constable under the direction and control of the chief officer of police for that area.

(2) In the application of this Part of this Act to Scotland—

(a) references to the police authority shall, where the relevant police area is a combined area, be construed as references to the joint police committee ; and

(b) for the words in paragraph (c) of section 30(3) of this Act from " if that area is a county " to the end of the paragraph there shall be substituted the words " by any local authority exercising functions for that area or any part of that area ".

(3) In the application of this Part of this Act to Northern Ireland—

(a) the references in section 25(1) of this Act and subsection (1) above to constables or any constable under the direction and control of the chief officer of police for the area there mentioned shall be construed as references to members or any member of the Royal Ulster Constabulary or the Royal Ulster Constabulary Reserve ;

(b) references in other provisions to a chief officer of police shall be construed as references to the Chief Constable of the Royal Ulster Constabulary ; and

(c) references in any provision to the police authority or police force for a police area shall be construed respectively as references to the Police Authority for Northern Ireland and the Royal Ulster Constabulary.

PART IV

THE AVIATION SECURITY FUND

The Aviation Security Fund.
32.—(1) There shall continue to be, under the control and management of the Secretary of State, a fund called the Aviation Security Fund out of which payments shall be made in accordance with this section.

(2) The Secretary of State may, out of the Aviation Security Fund, reimburse to any person who is—

(a) the operator of one or more aircraft registered or operating in the United Kingdom, or

(b) the manager of an aerodrome in the United Kingdom, or

(c) the authority responsible for an air navigation installation in the United Kingdom,

the whole or part of any expenses which, for purposes to which
Part II of this Act applies, have at any time on or after 1st
June 1972 been, or may at any time after the commencement
of this Act be, incurred by that person in relation to those aircraft or to that aerodrome or air navigation installation, as the
case may be, whether or not the expenses have been or are
incurred in consequence of a direction given under Part II of
this Act.

(3) For the purposes of this section any expenses incurred in
paying compensation under section 22 of this Act shall be
treated as being expenses incurred as mentioned in subsection
(2) above.

(4) The Secretary of State may, out of the Aviation Security
Fund, reimburse to the manager of an aerodrome such part as
he may determine of—

> (a) any payments made or other expenses incurred by the
> manager under section 26(3) of this Act ;

> (b) any payments made by the manager by virtue of any
> order under section 30 of this Act.

(5) If the Secretary of State certifies that any payment which,
but for this subsection, would be paid out of the Aviation
Security Fund under the preceding provisions of this section is
of an exceptional nature, that payment may, with the consent
of the Treasury, be paid out of money provided by Parliament
instead of out of the Fund.

(6) Any money in the Aviation Security Fund which appears
to the Secretary of the State not to be immediately required for
the purposes of the Fund may be deposited by him with the
Bank of England or with a recognised bank or licensed institution within the meaning of the Banking Act 1979, and any   1979 c. 37.
interest received by the Secretary of State in respect of money
so deposited shall be paid by him into the Fund.

(7) There shall be paid out of the Aviation Security Fund
into the Consolidated Fund sums equal to the amount of any
expenses incurred by the Secretary of State in the management
and control of the first-mentioned Fund.

33.—(1) The Secretary of State may make regulations con-   Contributions
taining such provisions as he considers appropriate for requir-   to the Fund.
ing managers of aerodromes to pay him, in respect of all
aerodromes or of aerodromes of a prescribed class, contributions to the Aviation Security Fund calculated in accordance
with the following provisions of this section.

(2) Those contributions shall be payable in respect of pre-scribed periods and the contribution payable for any aero-drome in respect of each such period shall be one of the follow-ing amounts, or if the regulations so provide, the aggregate of those amounts, that is to say—

(a) an amount ascertained by multiplying a prescribed sum by the number of passengers, or passengers of a prescribed description, who during that period arrived by air at or departed by air from that aerodrome or the number of such passengers in excess of a pre-scribed limit ;

(b) an amount ascertained by multiplying a prescribed sum by the total prescribed units of weight of each aircraft, or aircraft of a prescribed description, which during that period arrived at or departed from that aero-drome.

(3) Without prejudice to the generality of subsection (1) above, regulations under this section may—

(a) prescribe the time when any contribution is to be paid ;

(b) charge interest at a rate prescribed with the consent of the Treasury on so much of any contribution as is overdue ;

(c) require managers of aerodromes, in relation to the aerodromes under their management, to furnish the Secretary of State with such information, to keep such records and to make such returns to him about the matters mentioned in subsection (2) above as may be prescribed ;

(d) provide that contravention of any prescribed provision of the regulations (other than a failure to pay a con-tribution or interest on any overdue contribution) shall be an offence, either triable on indictment or sum-marily or triable only summarily, and punishable in each case with a fine, not exceeding, in the case of a summary conviction—

(i) in Great Britain, the statutory maximum if the offence is also triable on indictment or £1,000 if it is not ;

(ii) in Northern Ireland, £1,000 ;

(e) make such incidental, supplemental and transitional provision as the Secretary of State thinks fit ; and

(f) make different provision for different cases.

(4) The Secretary of State shall pay into the Aviation Security Fund all money received by him by virtue of regulations made under this section.

(5) The power to make regulations under this section shall be exercisable by statutory instrument; and regulations shall not be made under this section unless a draft of the regulations has been laid before Parliament and approved by a resolution of each House of Parliament.

(6) In this section " prescribed " means prescribed by regulations under this section.

34.—(1) The Secretary of State may borrow temporarily by overdraft or otherwise such sums in sterling as he may require for the purposes of the Aviation Security Fund.

(2) The Secretary of State shall pay into the Aviation Security Fund any sum borrowed under subsection (1) above; and the Secretary of State shall make any repayment in respect of the principal of any such sum, and any payment in respect of interest thereon, out of the Fund.

(3) The aggregate amount outstanding by way of principal in respect of sums borrowed by the Secretary of State under subsection (1) above shall not at any time exceed £5 million, or such larger sum, not exceeding £10 million, as the Secretary of State may, by order made by statutory instrument with the consent of the Treasury, determine.

(4) The Treasury may guarantee in such manner and on such conditions as they think fit the repayment of, and the payment of any interest on, any sums borrowed by the Secretary of State under subsection (1) above.

(5) Immediately after any guarantee is given under subsection (4) above, the Treasury shall lay a statement of the guarantee before each House of Parliament.

(6) Any sums required by the Treasury for fulfilling any guarantee given under subsection (4) above shall be charged on and paid out of the Consolidated Fund.

(7) Where any sum is issued out of the Consolidated Fund under subsection (6) above, the Treasury shall, as soon as possible after the end of each financial year (beginning with that in which the sum is issued and ending with that in which all liability in respect of the principal of the sum and in respect of interest thereon is finally discharged) lay before each House of Parliament an account of that sum and of any payments made, during the financial year to which the account relates, by way of repayment of that sum or by way of interest thereon.

(8) Any sum issued for fulfilling a guarantee given under subsection (4) above shall be repaid by the Secretary of State out of the Aviation Security Fund to the Treasury in such

Part IVmanner and over such period and with interest thereon at such rate as the Treasury may determine ; and any sums received by the Treasury under this subsection shall be paid into the Consolidated Fund.

(9) An order shall not be made under this section unless a draft of the order has been laid before the House of Commons and approved by a resolution of that House.

(10) References in this section to the borrowing of any sum under subsection (1) above, the giving of a guarantee under subsection (4) above, or the issuing of any sum out of the Consolidated Fund under subsection (6) above shall, in relation to any time before the commencement of this Act, include references to the borrowing of any sum, the giving of a guarantee or the issuing of any sum out of that Fund under subsection (1), (4) or, as the case may be, (6) of section 3 of the Civil Aviation Act 1978.

1978 c. 8.

Accounts of the Fund.**35.** The Secretary of State shall prepare accounts of the Aviation Security Fund in such form as the Treasury may direct and shall send them to the Comptroller and Auditor General not later than the end of the month of November following the end of the financial year to which the accounts relate ; and the Comptroller and Auditor General shall examine and certify every such account and shall lay copies thereof, together with his report thereon, before Parliament.

Power to wind up the Fund.**36.**—(1) The Secretary of State may at any time by order provide for the winding up of the Aviation Security Fund and, on the completion of the winding up, for the return to each manager of an aerodrome by whom contributions have been made to the Fund of a share of the net assets standing to the credit of the Fund which bears the same proportion to those assets as the manager's contributions to the Fund in the last twelve months during which contributions were made to the Fund bear to the total contributions made by managers of aerodromes to the Fund during those twelve months.

(2) On such day as is declared by the Secretary of State by order to be that on which the winding up was completed sections 32(1), (5), (6) and (7) and 33 of this Act shall cease to have effect, and as from that day subsections (2) and (4) of section 32 of this Act shall have effect as if—

(*a*) all payments under those subsections fell to be defrayed out of money provided by Parliament, instead of out of the Aviation Security Fund ; and

(*b*) the consent of the Treasury were required for all such payments.

(3) The power to make an order under this section—

    (*a*) shall be exercisable by statutory instrument ; and

    (*b*) shall include power to make such incidental, supple-
        mental or transitional provision as the Secretary of
        State thinks fit ;

and a statutory instrument containing an order under this section
shall be subject to annulment in pursuance of a resolution of
either House of Parliament.

PART V

MISCELLANEOUS AND GENERAL

37.—(1) Where an offence under this Act or under regulations Offences by
made under section 33 of this Act has been committed by a bodies
body corporate and is proved to have been committed with the corporate.
consent or connivance of, or to be attributable to any neglect
on the part of, any director, manager, secretary or other similar
officer of the body corporate, or any person who was purporting to act in any such capacity, he as well as the body corporate
shall be guilty of that offence and shall be liable to be proceeded
against and punished accordingly.

(2) Where the affairs of a body corporate are managed by its
members, subsection (1) above shall apply in relation to the acts
and defaults of a member in connection with his functions of
management as if he were a director of the body corporate.

38.—(1) In this Act, except in so far as the context otherwise Interpretation
requires— etc.

    " act of violence " shall be construed in accordance with
        section 2(7) or, as the case may require, section 10(2)
        of this Act ;

    " aerodrome " means the aggregate of the land, buildings
        and works comprised in an aerodrome within the
        meaning of the Civil Aviation Act 1982 and (if and 1982 c. 16.
        so far as not comprised in an aerodrome as defined in
        that Act) any land, building or works situated within
        the boundaries of an area designated, by an order
        made by the Secretary of State which is for the time
        being in force, as constituting the area of an aero-
        drome for the purposes of this Act ;

    " air navigation installation " means any building, works,
        apparatus or equipment used wholly or mainly for the
        purpose of assisting air traffic control or as an aid
        to air navigation, together with any land contiguous

or adjacent to any such building, works, apparatus or equipment and used wholly or mainly for purposes connected therewith;

" aircraft registered or operating in the United Kingdom " means any aircraft which is either—

(a) an aircraft registered in the United Kingdom, or

(b) an aircraft not so registered which is for the time being allocated for use on flights which (otherwise than in exceptional circumstances) include landing at or taking off from one or more aerodromes in the United Kingdom;

" article " includes any substance, whether in solid or liquid form or in the form of a gas or vapour;

" constable " includes any person having the powers and privileges of a constable;

" explosive " means any article manufactured for the purpose of producing a practical effect by explosion, or intended for that purpose by a person having the article with him;

" firearm " includes an airgun or air pistol;

" manager ", in relation to an aerodrome, means the person (whether the British Airports Authority, the Civil Aviation Authority, a local authority or any other person) by whom the aerodrome is managed;

" military service " includes naval and air force service;

" measures " (without prejudice to the generality of that expression) includes the construction, execution, alteration, demolition or removal of buildings or other works and also includes the institution or modification, and the supervision and enforcement, of any practice or procedure;

1982 c. 16.
" operator " has the same meaning as in the Civil Aviation Act 1982;

" property " includes any land, buildings or works, any aircraft or vehicle and any baggage, cargo or other article of any description;

" the statutory maximum " means—

1980 c. 43.
(a) in England and Wales, the prescribed sum within the meaning of section 32 of the Magistrates' Courts Act 1980 (that is to say, £1,000 or another sum fixed by order under section 143 of that Act to take account of changes in the value of money);

(*b*) in Scotland, the prescribed sum within the meaning of section 289B of the Criminal Procedure (Scotland) Act 1975 (that is to say, £1,000 or another sum fixed by order under section 289D of that Act for that purpose) ;

(*c*) in Northern Ireland, £400 ;

" United Kingdom national " means an individual who is—

(*a*) a British citizen, a British Dependent Territories citizen or a British Overseas citizen ;

(*b*) a person who under the British Nationality Act 1981 is a British subject ; or

(*c*) a British protected person (within the meaning of that Act).

(2) For the purposes of this Act—

(*a*) in the case of an air navigation installation provided by, or used wholly or mainly by, the Civil Aviation Authority, that Authority, and

(*b*) in the case of any other air navigation installation, the manager of an aerodrome by whom it is provided, or by whom it is wholly or mainly used,

shall be taken to be the authority responsible for that air navigation installation.

(3) For the purposes of this Act—

(*a*) the period during which an aircraft is in flight shall be deemed to include any period from the moment when all its external doors are closed following embarkation until the moment when any such door is opened for disembarkation, and, in the case of a forced landing, any period until the competent authorities take over responsibility for the aircraft and for persons and property on board ; and

(*b*) an aircraft shall be taken to be in service during the whole of the period which begins with the pre-flight preparation of the aircraft for a flight and ends 24 hours after the aircraft lands having completed that flight, and also at any time (not falling within that period) while, in accordance with the preceding paragraph, the aircraft is in flight,

and anything done on board an aircraft while in flight over any part of the United Kingdom shall be treated as done in that part of the United Kingdom.

(4) For the purposes of this Act the territorial waters adjacent to any part of the United Kingdom shall be treated as included in that part of the United Kingdom.

PART V

(5) Any power to make an order under subsection (1) above shall be exercisable by statutory instrument; and any statutory instrument containing any such order shall be subject to annulment in pursuance of a resolution of either House of Parliament.

(6) Any power to give a direction under any provision of this Act shall be construed as including power to revoke or vary any such direction by a further direction given under that provision.

1978 c. 30.

(7) Subject to section 18 of the Interpretation Act 1978 (which relates to offences under two or more laws), Part I of this Act shall not be construed as—

> (a) conferring a right of action in any civil proceedings in respect of any contravention of this Act, or
>
> (b) derogating from any right of action or other remedy (whether civil or criminal) in proceedings instituted otherwise than under this Act.

(8). References in this Act to enactments (including the reference to Acts in section 30(2)(a) of this Act) shall include references to Northern Ireland enactments, that is to say, to any enactment contained in an Act of the Parliament of Northern Ireland or a Measure of the Northern Ireland Assembly, and without prejudice to the provisions of the Interpretation Act 1978, in the application of this Act to Northern Ireland, any reference to a Northern Ireland enactment or to an enactment which the Parliament of Northern Ireland had power to amend—

> (a) shall be construed as including a reference to any Northern Ireland enactment passed after this Act and re-enacting the said enactment with or without modifications, and
>
> (b) shall, except in so far as the context otherwise requires, be construed as a reference to that enactment as amended by any enactment, whether passed before or after this Act, and as including a reference thereto as extended or applied by or under any other enactment, including this Act.

Extension of Act outside United Kingdom.
1870 c. 52.
1967 c. 68.

39.—(1) Sections 17 and 22 of the Extradition Act 1870 and sections 16 and 17 of the Fugitive Offenders Act 1967 (application to Channel Islands, Isle of Man and United Kingdom dependencies) shall extend respectively to the provisions of this Act amending those Acts.

1967 c. 52.

(2) Section 8 of the Tokyo Convention Act 1967 (application to Channel Islands, Isle of Man and United Kingdom dependancies) shall apply to section 5 of this Act as it applies to section 4 of that Act.

(3) Her Majesty may by Order in Council make provision for extending any of the provisions of this Act (other than the provisions to which subsection (1) or (2) above applies and the provisions of Part III) with such exceptions, adaptations or modifications as may be specified in the Order, to any of the Channel Islands, the Isle of Man, any colony, other than a colony for whose external relations a country other than the United Kingdom is responsible, or any country outside Her Majesty's dominions in which Her Majesty has jurisdiction in right of Her Majesty's Government in the United Kingdom.   Part V

(4) Except in pursuance of subsection (1), (2) or (3) above, the provisions of this Act and, in particular, the repeal of the provisions which those subsections re-enact do not affect the law of any country or territory outside the United Kingdom.

40.—(1) Schedule 2 to this Act (which contains consequential amendments and savings) shall have effect ; and the provisions of that Schedule are without prejudice to sections 16 and 17 of the Interpretation Act 1978 (which relate to repeals).   Consequential amendments, savings and repeals.

1978 c. 30.

(2) Subject to the provisions of Schedule 2 to this Act, the enactments specified in Schedule 3 to this Act are hereby repealed to the extent specified in the third column of Schedule 3.

41.—(1) This Act may be cited as the Aviation Security Act 1982.   Short title and commencement.

(2) This Act shall come into force on the expiration of the period of three months beginning with its passing.

SCHEDULES

SCHEDULE 1

Provisions Relating to Compensation

1. This Schedule applies to compensation under section 22 of this Act (in this Schedule referred to as " the relevant section ").

2. No compensation to which this Schedule applies shall be payable unless the person to whom it is payable in accordance with the relevant section (or in accordance with regulations made under the following provisions of this Schedule) serves on the manager of the aerodrome by whom the measures in question were taken a notice in writing claiming compensation under that section, and that notice is served before the end of the period of two years from the completion of the measures.

3. In relation to any measures taken by the manager of an aerodrome on land outside the aerodrome, any reference in the relevant section to a direction, or to compliance with a direction, shall be construed as if subsection (6) of section 16 of this Act were omitted.

4. In calculating value for any of the purposes of the relevant section—

1961 c. 33.

     (*a*) rules (2) to (4) of the rules set out in section 5 of the Land Compensation Act 1961 shall apply with the necessary modifications, and

     (*b*) if the interest to be valued is subject to a mortgage, it shall be treated as if it were not subject to the mortgage.

5. Regulations made by the Secretary of State by statutory instrument may make provision—

     (*a*) requiring compensation to which this Schedule applies, in such cases as may be specified in the regulations, to be paid to a person other than the person entitled to it in accordance with the relevant section ;

     (*b*) as to the application of any compensation to which this Schedule applies, or any part of it, in cases where the right to claim compensation is exercisable by reference to an interest in land which is subject to a mortgage, or to a rentcharge, or to the trusts of a settlement, or, in Scotland, to a feuduty or ground annual or to the purposes of a trust, or which was so subject at a time specified in the regulations ; or

     (*c*) as to any assumptions to be made, or matters to be taken into or left out of account, for the purpose of assessing any compensation to which this Schedule applies.

6. A statutory instrument containing regulations made under paragraph 5 of this Schedule shall be subject to annulment in pursuance of a resolution of either House of Parliament.

SCH. 1

7. Any dispute arising under the relevant section or under this Schedule, whether as to the right to any compensation or as to the amount of any compensation or otherwise, shall be referred to and determined by the Lands Tribunal.

8. For the purposes of the application of paragraphs 2 to 7 of this Schedule to compensation in respect of measures taken by the authority responsible for an air navigation installation, references in those paragraphs to an aerodrome and to the manager of an aerodrome shall be construed respectively as references to an air navigation installation and to the authority responsible for it.

9. In the application of this Schedule to Scotland—

   (a) the reference in paragraph 4(a) to section 5 of the Land Com- 1961 c. 33. pensation Act 1961 shall be construed as a reference to section 12 of the Land Compensation (Scotland) Act 1963, 1963 c. 51. and

   (b) the reference in paragraph 7 to the Lands Tribunal shall be construed as a reference to the Lands Tribunal for Scotland.

10. In the application of this Schedule to Northern Ireland—

   (a) the reference in paragraph 4(a) to section 5 of the Land Com- 1961 c. 33. pensation Act 1961 shall be construed, notwithstanding paragraph 4 of Schedule 1 to the Land Compensation (Northern S.I. 1982/712 Ireland) Order 1982 (which confines the operation of that (N.I. 9). Order to matters within the legislative competence of the Parliament of Northern Ireland), as a reference to Article 6(1) of that Order ; and

   (b) the reference in paragraph 7 to the Lands Tribunal shall be construed as a reference to the Lands Tribunal for Northern Ireland.

11. In this Schedule " mortgage " includes any charge or lien on any property for securing money or money's worth, and any heritable security within the meaning of section 9(8) of the Conveyancing 1970 c. 35. and Feudal Reform (Scotland) Act 1970.

SCHEDULE 2

Section 40.

CONSEQUENTIAL AMENDMENTS AND SAVINGS

Periods running at commencement

1. Where any period of time specified in or for the purposes of any enactment re-enacted by this Act is current at the commencement of this Act, this Act shall have effect as if the provision of this Act re-enacting that enactment had been in force when that period began to run.

Past offences

2. This Act (and, in particular, the following provisions of this Schedule) shall not affect the law applicable to, or to proceedings in respect of, an offence committed before the commencement of this Act under any enactment repealed by this Act.

The Visiting Forces Act 1952

3. Section 3 of the Visiting Forces Act 1952, as amended by the Protection of Aircraft Act 1973, shall, after the commencement of this Act, continue to have effect as so amended notwithstanding the repeal of the said Act of 1973 but subject to the substitution in subsection (1)—

(*a*) for the words " section 1(4)(*b*) of the Hijacking Act 1971 " of the words " section 6(2)(*a*) of the Aviation Security Act 1982 " ;

(*b*) for the words " section 1 or section 2 of the Protection of Aircraft Act 1973 " of the words " section 2 or section 3 of that Act " ; and

(*c*) for the words " section 3(1) " of the words " section 6(2)(*b*) and (*c*) ".

The Protection of Aircraft Act 1973

4. Where before the commencement of this Act any land, building or works was or were, by virtue of an order under section 26 of the Protection of Aircraft Act 1973, included in an aerodrome for the purposes of that Act, the land, building or works shall, to the extent that that order has effect on or after the commencement of this Act, be treated as included in that aerodrome not only for the purposes of the provisions of this Act re-enacting provisions of that Act but also for the purposes of the other provisions of this Act.

The Criminal Jurisdiction Act 1975

5. In paragraph 11 of Schedule 1 to the Criminal Jurisdiction Act 1975, for the words " the Hijacking Act 1971 " there shall be substituted the words " the Aviation Security Act 1982 ".

The Northern Ireland (Emergency Provisions) Act 1978

6. In paragraph 14 of Schedule 4 to the Northern Ireland (Emergency Provisions) Act 1978, for the words " the Hijacking Act 1971 " there shall be substituted the words " the Aviation Security Act 1982 ".

The Suppression of Terrorism Act 1978

7. For paragraphs 18 and 19 of Schedule 1 to the Suppression of Terrorism Act 1978 there shall be substituted the following paragraph—

" 18. An offence under Part I of the Aviation Security Act 1982 (other than an offence under section 4 or 7 of that Act) ".

The British Nationality Act 1981   <small>SCH. 2</small>

8. Until the commencement of the British Nationality Act 1981 <small>1981 c. 61.</small>
section 38(1) of this Act shall have effect as if for the definition
" United Kingdom national " there were substituted the following
definition—

    " ' United Kingdom national ' means an individual who is—

      (*a*) a citizen of the United Kingdom and Colonies ; or

      (*b*) a British subject by virtue of section 2 of the British <small>1948 c. 56.</small>
         Nationality Act 1948 ; or

      (*c*) a British subject without citizenship by virtue of section
         13 or 16 of the said Act of 1948 ; or

      (*d*) a British subject by virtue of the British Nationality Act <small>1965 c. 34.</small>
         1965 ; or

      (*e*) a British protected person within the meaning of the said
         Act of 1948.".

SCHEDULE 3

REPEALS

Chapter	Short title	Extent of repeal
1967 c. 52.	The Tokyo Convention Act 1967.	In section 4, the words from " and any such court " onwards. In section 7(1), the words from " except where " to " the said section 92 ".
1971 c. 70.	The Hijacking Act 1971.	The whole Act.
1973 c. 47.	The Protection of Aircraft Act 1973.	The whole Act.
1974 c. 41.	The Policing of Airports Act 1974.	The whole Act.
1975 c. 78.	The Airports Authority Act 1975.	In Part II of Schedule 5, paragraph 7.
1978 c. 8.	The Civil Aviation Act 1978.	Sections 1 to 4. In section 13, in subsection (1) the words from " other " to " regulations ", in subsection (2) the words " or to make regulations ". and in subsection (3) the words " (including an Order in Council) ". Section 16(3) and (4).
1980 c. 43.	The Magistrates' Courts Act 1980.	In Schedule 7, paragraph 156.
1980 c. 60.	The Civil Aviation Act 1980.	Sections 22 and 23.
1981 c. 61.	The British Nationality Act 1981.	In Schedule 7, the entries relating to the Hijacking Act 1971 and the Protection of Aircraft Act 1973.
1982 c. 16.	The Civil Aviation Act 1982.	In Schedule 14, paragraph 10. In Schedule 15, in paragraph 6 the words from " for the definitions " to " the said section 92 '; and " and paragraphs 10, 13, 15 and 20(3).

Merchant Shipping (Liner Conferences) Act 1982

1982 CHAPTER 37

An Act to provide for the implementation in the United Kingdom of the Convention on a Code of Conduct for Liner Conferences signed at Geneva on 6th April 1974; and for connected purposes.   [23rd July 1982]

BE IT ENACTED by the Queen's most Excellent Majesty, by and with the advice and consent of the Lords Spiritual and Temporal, and Commons, in this present Parliament assembled, and by the authority of the same, as follows:—

Main implementing provisions

1.—(1) In this Act " the Code " means the Convention on a Code of Conduct for Liner Conferences signed at Geneva on 6th April 1974.

Introductory provisions: the Code and the Contracting Parties to it.

(2) The text of the Code is set out in the Schedule to this Act.

(3) Her Majesty may by Order in Council certify which states are Contracting Parties to the Code, and in respect of what countries they are parties, and an Order in Council under this subsection shall be conclusive evidence of the matters certified by it.

2.—(1) The Secretary of State may by regulations made by statutory instrument make such provision as appears to him appropriate for giving effect to the Code in the United Kingdom, having regard in particular to the reservations made by the United Kingdom when acceding to the Code.

Implementing regulations: the general scheme.

(2) The general scheme of regulations under subsection (1) shall be—

(*a*) that the provisions of Chapters I to V of the Code shall apply—

(i) to a conference which has its seat in the United Kingdom, so far as it serves the trade between states which are Contracting Parties to the Code, and

(ii) to a conference which does not have its seat in the United Kingdom, so far as it serves the trade between the United Kingdom and another state which is a Contracting Party to the Code ;

(*b*) that only such of those provisions as are identified by the regulations as mandatory provisions shall give rise to enforceable duties ;

(*c*) that compliance with those mandatory provisions may be enforced by civil proceedings and not otherwise.

(3) For the purposes of paragraph (*a*) of subsection (2) a conference has its seat in the United Kingdom if, and only if—

(*a*) it is incorporated or formed under the law of a part of the United Kingdom, or

(*b*) its central management and control is exercised in the United Kingdom.

(4) Provisions of regulations under subsection (1) to the effect described in paragraph (*a*) of subsection (2) shall apply as mentioned in that paragraph whether or not the law of a part of the United Kingdom would fall to be applied in accordance with the ordinary rules of private international law.

Matters which may be provided for by regulations.

3.—(1) In this section " regulations " means regulations under section 2(1) and the specific mention of any matter in this section shall not be construed as restricting the generality of that provision.

(2) Regulations may—

(*a*) clarify the meaning of the provisions of the Code ;

(*b*) supplement the provisions of the Code ; and

(*c*) make different provision for different cases and circumstances, as for example for different trades or according to the nationality of the parties involved.

(3) Regulations may specify with respect to any mandatory provision of the Code—

(*a*) the content of the duties expressly or impliedly imposed by that provision ; and

(*b*) the persons owing those duties and the persons to whom those duties are owed.

(4) Regulations may provide that a duty imposed by a mandatory provision of the Code is a statutory duty enforceable at the suit of a person to whom the duty is owed.

(5) Where a duty imposed by a mandatory provision of the Code has effect as between parties to a contract, regulations may provide that it has effect as an implied term of that contract and where a term is so implied—

(a) any agreed terms which are to any extent inconsistent with that term shall to that extent be of no effect ; and

(b) without prejudice to paragraph (a), any agreed provision for the settlement of disputes arising out of the contract shall apply to disputes arising out of that term only if—

(i) the parties to the contract have expressly agreed that that provision shall apply to such disputes ; or

(ii) the parties to the dispute in question agree that it should apply to that dispute.

(6) Regulations may provide with respect to any mandatory provision of the Code that the duties imposed by that provision are owed by or to a conference as such, whether it be incorporated or unincorporated, and where regulations provide that any such duties are owed by an incorporated conference they may also provide that the members of the conference owe to the persons to whom the duties are owed a duty to take all reasonable steps to secure that the conference fulfils its duties.

(7) Regulations may provide for excluding or restricting, in proceedings for the enforcement of a duty arising under a mandatory provision of the Code, liabilities or remedies of any description specified in the regulations.

(8) Regulations may specify—

(a) the conditions for recognition as a United Kingdom shipping line for the purpose of the Code, and

(b) the conditions for recognition of a shippers' organisation by the Secretary of State for the purposes of the Code,

and may empower the Secretary of State to designate for the purposes of Article 11 (consultation machinery) such persons or organisations as are mentioned in paragraph 1 of that Article.

4. Where it appears to the Secretary of State that—   Power to exclude or

(a) a state which is a Contracting Party to the Code has restrict made reservations when becoming a party to the Code operation of the or has materially failed to fulfil its obligations under Code for lack the Code, and   of reciprocity.

(b) the implementation of those reservations or, as the case

> may be, the failure to fulfil those obligations is damaging to or threatens to damage the shipping or trading interests of the United Kingdom,

he may by regulations made by statutory instrument exclude or restrict the operation of all or any of the provisions of Chapters I to V of the Code, as they apply by virtue of regulations under section 2(1), in relation to trade with that state or in relation to persons having any such connection with that state as may be specified in the regulations.

Proceedings arising out of the Code

Liability of members of conference to be in proportion to their responsibility.

5.—(1) Where proceedings arising out of the Code are brought against a member of a conference in respect of damage or loss suffered by any person and other members of the conference are also liable (whether jointly or otherwise) in respect of the same damage or loss, the liability of that member to make good that damage or loss shall be in proportion to his responsibility.

The reference above to the liability of other members of the conference is to any such liability which has been or could be established in proceedings brought before the same court or other tribunal by or on behalf of the person suffering the damage or loss ; and for the purposes of this subsection it is immaterial by reference to what law the issue of liability was or would be determined.

(2) In ascertaining the responsibility of a member of a conference for the purposes of subsection (1), regard shall be had not only to the member's part (if any) in the particular matters giving rise to the proceedings but also to his general involvement in the affairs of the conference as shown, for example, by his share of the conference trade, the nature of pooling arrangements to which he is a party and the extent to which he contributes to the administrative expenses of the conference.

(3) Subsections (1) and (2) apply to any proceedings in the United Kingdom and to proceedings elsewhere in which the extent of the liability of a member of a conference falls to be determined by reference to the law of a part of the United Kingdom.

(4) Where in proceedings arising out of the Code—

  (a) judgment is given against a member of a conference in respect of damage or loss caused to any person, and

  (b) the extent of the member's liability is not determined by reference to subsections (1) and (2),

the member shall not, if it is sought to enforce the judgment in the United Kingdom, be liable to make good any greater proportion of that damage or loss than if the extent of his liability had been determined by reference to those subsections.

(5) A member of an unincorporated conference against which judgment is given, whether in the United Kingdom or elsewhere, in proceedings arising out of the Code in respect of damage or loss caused by any person by a breach of duty by the conference, shall not, by virtue of section 6(3), be liable to make good any greater proportion of that damage or loss than he would have been if the proceedings had been brought against him and the other members of the conference in respect of a duty owed by all the members of the conference and the extent of his liability had been determined by reference to subsections (1) and (2).

(6) Subsections (4) and (5) shall not affect the enforcement in the United Kingdom of a judgment required to be enforced there by virtue of Part I of the Foreign Judgments (Reciprocal 1933 c. 13. Enforcement) Act 1933 (judgments given in countries wth whom reciprocal arrangements exist) or Part I of the Civil Jurisdiction 1982 c. 27. and Judgments Act 1982 (judgments given in other E.E.C. member states).

6.—(1) A conference which is not a body corporate may never- Proceedings by theless sue and be sued in its own name in proceedings arising or against un- out of the Code. incorporated conferences.

(2) Subsection (1) applies to any proceedings in the United Kingdom and to proceedings elsewhere in which the capacity of a conference to sue and be sued in its own name falls to be determined by reference to the law of a part of the United Kingdom.

(3) A judgment given for or against an unincorporated conference in proceedings brought against the conference in its own name, whether in the United Kingdom or elsewhere, shall be binding on the members of the conference, and such a judgment given against a conference shall be enforceable—

    (*a*) against any property held in trust for the purposes of the conference, to the like extent and in the like manner as if the conference were a body corporate ; and

    (*b*) against any member of the conference, subject to section 5(5).

(4) Subsection (3) applies in each part of the United Kingdom to judgments given by a court of that part or which are enforceable or entitled to recognition in that part.

7.—(1) Legal proceedings arising out of a dispute relating to Restrictions the application or operation of the Code may be brought in the on legal United Kingdom only in the High Court or the Court of Session ; proceedings. and in this section " the court " means either of those courts.

(2) Proceedings arising out of a dispute to which Article 23, paragraph 2 applies (disputes to be resolved within the framework of the national jurisdiction concerned) shall not be entertained by the court except as permitted by that paragraph.

(3) The court shall stay proceedings before it if on the application of a party to the proceedings, made after appearance but before delivering any pleadings or taking any other steps in the proceedings, it is shown that the proceedings arise out of a dispute to which Article 23, paragraph 4 applies and that—

(a) the dispute has not been referred to conciliation in accordance with that paragraph or has been so referred and conciliation proceedings are still in progress ; or

(b) the parties to the dispute have made an agreement to which Article 25, paragraph 1 applies (agreed procedures in lieu of conciliation) which is capable of being, or has been, performed.

(4) The court may attach to a stay granted under subsection (3) such conditions as appear to it appropriate, in particular conditions with respect to the institution or prosecution of conciliation or other proceedings ; and the court may remove a stay granted under that subsection if any such condition is not complied with or if at any time it appears to the court that the circumstances are such that a new application for the stay would not be granted.

1950 c. 27.
1937 c. 8 (N.I.).
1975 c. 3.
(5) In relation to an arbitration agreement to which Article 25, paragraph 1 applies, subsections (3) and (4) apply in place of section 4(1) of the Arbitration Act 1950, section 4 of the Arbitration Act (Northern Ireland) 1937 and section 1(1) of the Arbitration Act 1975 (which also provide for the staying of legal proceedings).

(6) In the application of this section to Scotland, for the references to staying proceedings substitute references to sisting proceedings.

Time for bringing legal proceedings.
8.—(1) No legal proceedings arising out of a dispute relating to the application or operation of the Code shall be brought in the United Kingdom after the end of the period of two years from the date on which the cause of action accrued or, if later, the end of the period of six months from the date on which conciliation proceedings relating to the dispute were completed or abandoned.

1980 c. 58.
(2) In England and Wales the following provisions of the Limitation Act 1980 apply to the limitation period prescribed by

subsection (1) as they apply to the limitation periods prescribed
by that Act—

 (a) section 28(1) (extension of period in case of legal dis-
    ability), but with the substitution of " two years " for
    " six years " ;

 (b) section 32(1) (postponement of period in case of fraud,
    concealment or mistake) ;

 (c) section 35 (application to new claims in pending actions).

(3) In Scotland section 6(4) of the Prescription and Limitation 1973 c. 52.
(Scotland) Act 1973 (extension of prescriptive period in case of
fraud, error or legal disability) applies to the limitation period
prescribed by subsection (1) as it applies to the prescriptive
period mentioned in section 6(1) of that Act.

(4) In Northern Ireland the following provisions of the Statute 1958 c. 10
of Limitations Act (Northern Ireland) 1958 apply to the limita- (N.I.).
tion period prescribed by subsection (1) as they apply to the
limitation periods prescribed by that Act—

 (a) section 2 (application to new claims in pending actions) ;

 (b) section 50(1) (extension of period in case of legal dis-
    ability), but with the substitution of " two years " for
    " six years " ;

 (c) section 70(1) (postponement of period in case of fraud,
    concealment or mistake).

9.—(1) Where a recommendation of conciliators has become Recognition
binding as between two or more parties in accordance with and
Article 37, then, subject to subsection (2)— enforcement of
recommenda-
 (a) it shall be recognised in the United Kingdom as con- tions, etc. of
    clusive as between those parties of the dispute to which conciliators.
    it relates ; and

 (b) any of those parties may apply to have the recommenda-
    tion registered for enforcement in the High Court or
    the Court of Session.

(2) A recommendation shall not be so recognised or enforced
if it is affected by any of the matters mentioned in sub-paragraphs (a) to (d) of Article 39, paragraph 2 (disability, fraud,
coercion, public policy or irregularity of composition or procedure of the conciliators), unless the affected part can be severed
as mentioned in Article 39, paragraph 3 and the remainder of the
recommendation recognised and enforced.

(3) Where the costs to be borne by a party to conciliation
proceedings in accordance with Article 43, paragraph 1 (costs of
the conciliation and its administration) have been determined,
the person to whom those costs are to be paid may apply to have

the determination registered for enforcement in the High Court or the Court of Session.

(4) A party in whose favour an award of costs has been made by conciliators under Article 43, paragraph 3 (vexatious or frivolous proceedings) may apply to have the award registered for enforcement in the High Court or the Court of Session.

(5) Provision may be made by rules of court as to—

    (a) the manner in which application is to be made for registration of a recommendation, determination or award under this section ;

    (b) the documents to be produced and the matters to be proved by a person seeking recognition of a recommendation or enforcement of a recommendation, determination or award ;

    (c) the manner in which a recommendation, determination or award is to be registered under this section ;

    (d) the manner in which and the conditions subject to which a recommendation, determination or award so registered may be enforced.

(6) Subject to any provision made under subsection (5)(d), a recommendation, determination or award registered under this section shall, for the purposes of its enforcement, be of the same force and effect, the registering court shall have the same powers in relation to its enforcement, and proceedings for or with respect to its enforcement may be taken, as if the recommendation, determination or award had been a judgment or decree originally given in the registering court and had (where relevant) been entered.

(7) Where a recommendation, determination or award is registered under this section, the reasonable costs or expenses of, and incidental to, its registration are recoverable as if they were sums recoverable under it, except that they carry interest as if they were the subject of an order for the payment of costs or expenses made by the registering court on the date of registration.

Other supplementary provisions

Secretary of
State to be
appropriate
authority in
the U.K.

10.—(1) The appropriate authority in the United Kingdom for the purposes of the Code is the Secretary of State.

(2) Information obtained by the Secretary of State as appropriate authority for the purposes of the Code shall not, without the consent of the person from whom it was obtained, be disclosed except—

    (a) for the purpose of the discharge by the Secretary of

State of his functions in connection with the Code ; or

(*b*) for the purpose of any proceedings arising out of the Code ; or

(*c*) with a view to the institution of, or otherwise for the purposes of, any criminal proceedings, whether under this Act or otherwise ; or

(*d*) to a Community institution in pursuance of a Community obligation ;

and a person who discloses any information in contravention of this subsection shall be guilty of an offence and liable on summary conviction to a fine not exceeding £1,000.

(3) Proceedings in England and Wales for an offence under subsection (2) shall not be brought except by or with the consent of the Director of Public Prosecutions ; and proceedings in Northern Ireland for such an offence shall not be brought except by or with the consent of the Director of Public Prosecutions for Northern Ireland.

11.—(1) No account shall be taken of any restriction to which this section applies for the purposes of the Restrictive Trade Practices Act 1976, and no agreement shall so far as it relates to any such restriction be unenforceable by virtue of any rule of law about unreasonable restraint of trade.

Exclusion of restrictive practices law. 1976 c. 34.

(2) This section applies to restrictions of any of the following descriptions which relate to the trade between states which are Contracting Parties to the Code and are accepted within the framework of a conference, that is to say—

(*a*) restrictions in respect of the provision of international liner services accepted by the operators of such services under an agreement to which two or more such operators are parties ;

(*b*) restrictions in respect of international liner services accepted by operators of such services or persons for whom such services are provided under an agreement to which one or more such operators and one or more such persons are parties ;

(*c*) restrictions in respect of the supply or acquisition of any service in connection with the operation of international liner services accepted by operators of such services or persons in the business of supplying such a service under an agreement to which one or more such operators and one such supplier are parties.

(3) Where a restriction relates only in part to the matters mentioned in subsection (2), this section applies to the restriction so far as it relates to those matters.

(4) For the purposes of paragraph (*a*), (*b*) or (*c*) of subsection (2) it is immaterial that there are other parties to an agreement in addition to those mentioned in that paragraph, except that paragraph (*c*) does not apply where the parties to an agreement include more than one such supplier as is mentioned in that paragraph.

1976 c. 34.

(5) If provision with respect to any such service as is mentioned in subsection (2) is made by order under section 11 or 12 of the Restrictive Trade Practices Act 1976 (under which provision may be made as respects the application of the Act to restrictive agreements or information agreements as to services), provision may also be made by order under that section for such consequential modifications of this section as appear to the Secretary of State to be appropriate.

(6) Without prejudice to subsection (5), this section shall, so far as it relates to the Restrictive Trade Practices Act 1976, be construed as one with that Act.

Modifications consequent on revision of Code, etc.

12.—(1) Her Majesty may by Order in Council make such provision as she considers appropriate for the purpose of giving effect in the United Kingdom to—

(*a*) any revision of the Code which has been agreed to by Her Majesty's Government in the United Kingdom or is to be treated as agreed to by virtue of Article 51 (amendments circulated without objection);

(*b*) any further international agreement which has been agreed to by Her Majesty's Government in the United Kingdom relating to any of the matters dealt with in the Code;

(*c*) any revision of any such further agreement which has been agreed to by Her Majesty's Government in the United Kingdom or is to be treated as agreed to by virtue of any provision similar in effect to Article 51.

(2) Without prejudice to the generality of subsection (1), an Order under that subsection may in particular include provision—

(*a*) for making such modifications of any provision of this Act or any other statutory provision, whenever passed or made, as appear to Her Majesty to be appropriate;

(*b*) for creating criminal offences punishable on summary conviction with a fine not exceeding £1,000.

(3) In this section " revision ", in relation to the Code or any other international agreement, means an omission from, addition to or alteration of the agreement, and includes the replacement of the agreement to any extent by another agreement.

13.—(1) Where the Secretary of State proposes to make any regulations under section 2(1), he shall consult such persons in the United Kingdom as he considers will be affected by the proposed regulations.

Regulations and orders: consultation and Parliamentary control.

(2) The following shall be subject to affirmative resolution—

(*a*) regulations under section 2(1) made before the expiry of the period of three months beginning with the date on which this Act comes into force ;

(*b*) any Order in Council under section 12.

(3) The following shall be subject to negative resolution—

(*a*) regulations under section 2(1) made after the expiry of the period mentioned in subsection (2)(*a*) ;

(*b*) any regulations under section 4.

(4) In subsection (2) " subject to affirmative resolution " means that the instrument in question shall not be made unless a draft of it has been laid before and approved by a resolution of each House of Parliament ; and in subsection (3) " subject to negative resolution " means that the instrument in question shall be subject to annulment in pursuance of a resolution of either House of Parliament.

General

14.—(1) In this Act—

Interpretation.

" Article " means Article of the Code ;

" the Code " has the meaning given by section 1(1) ;

" conciliation " means international mandatory conciliation under Chapter VI of the Code, and references to the institution or completion of conciliation proceedings shall be construed in accordance with subsection (2) ;

" conference " has the meaning given by Chapter I of the Code ;

" judgment ", in relation to proceedings arising out of the Code, means any judgment, decree, order, award, recommendation or determination of any description given or made in such proceedings, and references to the giving of a judgment shall be construed accordingly ;

" mandatory provision ", in relation to the Code, means a provision identified as such by regulations as mentioned in section 2(2)(*b*) ;

" modifications " includes additions, omissions and alterations ;

" proceedings arising out of the Code " means legal proceedings, conciliation proceedings, arbitration proceed-

ings or any other proceedings for the determination
or resolution of a dispute arising out of the Code ;

1978 c. 30.

" statutory provision " means any provision contained in an
Act, in Northern Ireland legislation, in subordinate
legislation (as defined in section 21(1) of the Interpretation Act 1978) or in any instrument of a legislative
character made under Northern Ireland legislation ;

" trade " has the same meaning as in the Code.

(2) For the purposes of this Act conciliation proceedings relating to a dispute are instituted when a party to the dispute
requests that it be referred to conciliation and are completed
when the conciliators notify the parties of their recommendations.

Short title,
commence-
ment and
extent.

15.—(1) This Act may be cited as the Merchant Shipping
(Liner Conferences) Act 1982.

(2) This Act comes into force on such day as the Secretary
of State may appoint by order made by statutory instrument.

(3) This Act extends to Northern Ireland.

(4) Her Majesty may by Order in Council provide that any
provisions of this Act, or of any instrument made under this
Act, shall extend, with such modifications as are specified in
the Order, to any of the following countries, namely the Isle
of Man, any of the Channel Islands and any colony.

(5) An Order in Council under subsection (4) relating to any
of the countries mentioned in that subsection may direct that
any provision of this Act, or of any instrument made under this
Act, shall have effect, with such modifications as may be specified in the Order, as if references to the United Kingdom included references to that country.

SCHEDULE

THE TEXT OF THE CODE

ARRANGEMENT OF PROVISIONS

CONVENTION ON A CODE OF CONDUCT FOR LINER CONFERENCES

OBJECTIVES AND PRINCIPLES

The Contracting Parties to the present Convention,

Desiring to improve the liner conference system,

Recognising the need for a universally acceptable code of conduct for liner conferences,

Taking into account the special needs and problems of the developing countries with respect to the activities of liner conferences serving their foreign trade,

Agreeing to reflect in the Code the following fundamental objectives and basic principles:

(a) The objective to facilitate the orderly expansion of world sea-borne trade ;

(b) The objective to stimulate the development of regular and efficient liner services adequate to the requirement of the trade concerned ;

(c) The objective to ensure a balance of interests between suppliers and users of liner shipping services ;

(d) The principle that conference practices should not involve any discrimination against the shipowners, shippers or the foreign trade of any country ;

(e) The principle that conferences hold meaningful consultations with shippers' organisations, shippers' representatives and shippers on matters of common interest, with, upon request, the participation of appropriate authorities ;

(f) The principle that conferences should make available to interested parties pertinent information about their activities which are relevant to those parties and should publish meaningful information on their activities,

Have agreed as follows:

PART ONE

CHAPTER I

DEFINITIONS

Liner conference or conference

A group of two or more vessel-operating carriers which provides international liner services for the carriage of cargo on a particular route or routes within specified geographical limits and which has an agreement or arrangement, whatever its nature, within the framework of which they operate under uniform or common freight rates and any other agreed conditions with respect to the provision of liner services.

National shipping line

A national shipping line of any given country is a vessel-operating carrier which has its head office of management and its effective control in that country and is recognized as such by an appropriate authority of that country or under the law of that country.

Lines belonging to and operated by a joint venture involving two or more countries and in whose equity the national interests, public and/or private, of those countries have a substantial share and whose head office of management and whose effective control is in one of those countries can be recognized as a national line by the appropriate authorities of those countries.

Third-country shipping line

A vessel-operating carrier in its operations between two countries of which it is not a national shipping line.

Shipper

A person or entity who has entered into, or who demonstrates an intention to enter into, a contractual or other arrangement with a conference or shipping line for the shipment of goods in which he has a beneficial interest.

Shippers' organization

An association or equivalent body which promotes, represents and protects the interests of shippers and, if those authorities so desire, is recognized in that capacity by the appropriate authority or authorities of the country whose shippers it represents.

Goods carried by the conference

Cargo transported by shipping lines members of a conference in accordance with the conference agreement.

Appropriate authority

Either a government or a body designated by a government or by national legislation to perform any of the functions ascribed to such authority by the provisions of this Code.

Promotional freight rate

A rate instituted for promoting the carriage of non-traditional exports of the country concerned.

Special freight rate

A preferential freight rate, other than a promotional freight rate, which may be negotiated between the parties concerned.

CHAPTER II

RELATIONS AMONG MEMBER LINES

Article 1

MEMBERSHIP

1. Any national shipping line shall have the right to be a full member of a conference which serves the foreign trade of its country, subject to the criteria set out in article 1, paragraph 2. Shipping lines which are not national lines in any trade of a conference shall have the right to become full members of that conference, subject to the criteria set out in article 1, paragraphs 2 and 3, and to the provisions regarding the share of trade as set out in article 2 as regards third-country shipping lines.

2. A shipping line applying for membership of a conference shall furnish evidence of its ability and intention, which may include the use of chartered tonnage, provided the criteria of this paragraph are met, to operate a regular, adequate and efficient service on a long-term basis as defined in the conference agreement within the framework of the conference, shall undertake to abide by all the terms and conditions of the conference agreement, and shall deposit a financial guarantee to cover any outstanding financial obligation in the event of subsequent withdrawal, suspension or expulsion from membership, if so required under the conference agreement.

3. In considering an application for membership by a shipping line which is not a national line in any trade of the conference concerned, in addition to the provisions of article 1, paragraph 2, the following criteria, *inter alia,* should be taken into account:

(a) The existing volume of the trade on the route or routes served by the conference and prospects for its growth ;

(b) The adequacy of shipping space for the existing and prospective volume of trade on the route or routes served by the conference ;

(c) The probable effect of admission of the shipping line to the conference on the efficiency and quality of the conference service ;

(d) The current participation of the shipping line in trade on the same route or routes outside the framework of a conference ; and

(e) The current participation of the shipping line on the same route or routes within the framework of another conference.

The above criteria shall not be applied so as to subvert the implementation of the provisions relating to participation in trade set out in article 2.

4. An application for admission or readmission to membership shall be promptly decided upon and the decision communicated by a conference to an applicant promptly, and in no case later than six months from the date of application. When a shipping line is refused admission or readmission the conference shall, at the same time, give in writing the grounds for such refusal.

5. When considering applications for admission, a conference shall take into account the views put forward by shippers and shippers' organizations of the countries whose trade is carried by the conference, as well as the views of appropriate authorities if they so request.

6. In addition to the criteria for admission set out in article 1, paragraph 2, a shipping line applying for re-admission shall also give evidence of having fulfilled its obligations in accordance with article 4, paragraphs 1 and 4. The conference may give special scrutiny to the circumstances under which the line left the conference.

Article 2

PARTICIPATION IN TRADE

1. Any shipping line admitted to membership of a conference shall have sailing and loading rights in the trades covered by that conference.

2. When a conference operates a pool, all shipping lines members of the conference serving the trade covered by the pool shall have the right to participate in the pool for that trade.

3. For the purpose of determining the share of trade which member lines shall have the right to acquire, the national shipping lines of each country, irrespective of the number of lines, shall be regarded as a single group of shipping lines for that country.

4. When determining a share of trade within a pool of individual member lines and/or groups of national shipping lines in accordance with article 2, paragraph 2, the following principles regarding their right to participation in the trade carried by the conference shall be observed, unless otherwise mutually agreed:

(a) The group of national shipping lines of each of two countries the foreign trade between which is carried by the conference shall have equal rights to participate in the freight and volume of traffic generated by their mutual foreign trade and carried by the conference ;

(b) Third-country shipping lines, if any, shall have the right to acquire a significant part, such as 20 per cent, in the freight and volume of traffic generated by that trade.

5. If, for any one of the countries whose trade is carried by a conference, there are no national shipping lines participating in the carriage of that trade, the share of the trade to which national shipping lines of that country would be entitled under article 2, paragraph 4 shall be distributed among the individual member lines participating in the trade in proportion to their respective share.

6. If the national shipping lines of one country decide not to carry their full share of the trade, that portion of their share of the trade which they do not carry shall be distributed among the

individual member lines participating in the trade in proportion to their respective shares.

7. If the national shipping lines of the countries concerned do not participate in the trade between those countries covered by a conference, the shares of trade carried by the conference between those countries shall be allocated between the participating member lines of third countries by commercial negotiations between those lines.

8. The national shipping lines of a region, members of a conference, at one end of the trade covered by the conference, may redistribute amongst themselves by mutual agreement the shares in trades allocated to them, in accordance with article 2, paragraphs 4 to 7 inclusive.

9. Subject to the provisions of article 2, paragraphs 4 to 8 inclusive regarding shares of trade among individual shipping lines or groups of shipping lines, pooling or trade-sharing agreements shall be reviewed by the conference periodically, at intervals to be stipulated in those agreements and in accordance with criteria to be specified in the conference agreement.

10. The application of the present article shall commence as soon as possible after entry into force of the present Convention and shall be completed within a transition period which in no case shall be longer than two years, taking into account the specific situation in each of the trades concerned.

11. Shipping lines members of a conference shall be entitled to operate chartered ships to fulfil their conference obligations.

12. The criteria for sharing and the revision of shares as set out in article 2, paragraphs 1 to 11 inclusive shall apply when, in the absence of a pool, there exists berthing, sailing and/or any other form of cargo allocation agreement.

13. Where no pooling, berthing, sailing or other trade participation agreements exist in a conference, either group of national shipping lines, members of the conference, may require that pooling arrangements be introduced, in respect of the trade between their countries carried by the conference, in conformity with the provisions of article 2, paragraph 4 ; or alternatively they may require that the sailings be so adjusted as to provide an opportunity to these lines to enjoy substantially the same rights to participate in the trade beween those two countries carried by the conference as they would have enjoyed under the provisions of article 2, paragraph 4. Any such request shall be considered and decided by the conference. If there is no agreement to institute such a pool or adjustment of sailings among the members of the conference, the groups of national shipping lines of the countries at both ends of the trade shall have a majority vote in deciding to establish such a pool or adjustment of sailings. The matter shall be decided upon within a period not exceeding six months from the receipt of the request.

14. In the event of a disagreement between the national shipping lines of the countries at either end whose trade is served by the

conference with regard to whether or not pooling shall be introduced, they may require that within the conference sailings be so
adjusted as to provide an opportunity to these lines to enjoy substantially the same rights to participate in the trade between those
two countries carried by the conference as they would have enjoyed
under the provisions of article 2, paragraph 4. In the event that
there are no national shipping lines in one of the countries whose
trade is served by the conference, the national shipping line or
lines of the other country may make the same request. The conference shall use its best endeavours to meet this request. If, however, this request is not met, the appropriate authorities of the
countries at both ends of the trade may take up the matter if they
so wish and make their views known to the parties concerned for
their consideration. If no agreement is reached, the dispute shall
be dealt with in accordance with the procedures established in this
Code.

15. Other shipping lines, members of a conference, may also
request that pooling or sailing agreements be introduced, and the
request shall be considered by the conference in accordance with
the relevant provisions of this Code.

16. A conference shall provide for appropriate measures in any
conference pooling agreement to cover cases where the cargo has
been shut out by a member line for any reason excepting late
presentation by the shipper. Such agreement shall provide that a
vessel with unbooked space, capable of being used, be allowed to
lift the cargo, even in excess of the pool share of the line in the
trade, if otherwise the cargo would be shut out and delayed beyond
a period set by the conference.

17. The provisions of article 2, paragraphs 1 to 16 inclusive concern all goods regardless of their origin, their destination or the
use for which they are intended, with the exception of military
equipment for national defence purposes.

Article 3

Decision-making Procedures

The decision-making procedures embodied in a conference agreement shall be based on the equality of all the full member lines ;
these procedures shall ensure that the voting rules do not hinder
the proper work of the conference and the service of the trade and
shall define the matters on which decisions will be made by
unanimity. However, a decision cannot be taken in respect of
matters defined in a conference agreement relating to the trade
between two countries without the consent of the national shipping
lines of those two countries.

Article 4

SANCTIONS

1. A shipping line member of a conference shall be entitled, subject to the provisions regarding withdrawal which are embodied in pool schemes and/or cargo-sharing arrangements, to secure its release, without penalty, from the terms of the conference agreement after giving three months' notice, unless the conference agreement provides for a different time period, although it shall be required to fulfil its obligations as a member of the conference up to the date of its release.

2. A conference may, upon notice to be specified in the conference agreement, suspend or expel a member for significant failure to abide by the terms and conditions of the conference agreement.

3. No expulsion or suspension shall become effective until a statement in writing of the reasons therefor has been given and until any dispute has been settled as provided in chapter VI.

4. Upon withdrawal or expulsion, the line concerned shall be required to pay its share of the outstanding financial obligations of the conference, up to the date of its withdrawal or expulsion. In cases of withdrawal, suspension or expulsion, the line shall not be relieved of its own financial obligations under the conference agreement or of any of its obligations towards shippers.

Article 5

SELF-POLICING

1. A conference shall adopt and keep up to date an illustrative list, which shall be as comprehensive as possible, of practices which are regarded as malpractices and/or breaches of the conference agreement and shall provide effective self-policing machinery to deal with them, with specific provisions requiring:

(*a*) The fixing of penalties or a range of penalties for malpractices or breaches, to be commensurate with their seriousness ;

(*b*) The examination and impartial review of an adjudication of complaints, and/or decisions taken on complaints, against malpractices or breaches, by a person or body unconnected with any of the shipping lines members of the conference or their affiliates, on request by the conference or any other party concerned ;

(*c*) The reporting, on request, on the action taken in connection with complaints against malpractices and/or breaches, and on a basis of anonymity for the parties concerned, to the appropriate authorities of the countries whose trade is served by the conference and of the countries whose shipping lines are members of the conference.

2. Shipping lines and conferences are entitled to the full co-operation of shippers and shippers' organizations in the endeavour to
combat malpractices and breaches.

Article 6

CONFERENCE AGREEMENTS

All conference agreements, pooling, berthing and sailing rights
agreements and amendments or other documents directly related to,
and which affect, such agreements shall be made available on request
to the appropriate authorities of the countries whose trade is served
by the conference and of the countries whose shipping lines are
members of the conference.

CHAPTER III
RELATIONS WITH SHIPPERS

Article 7

LOYALTY ARRANGEMENTS

1. The shipping lines members of a conference are entitled to
institute and maintain loyalty arrangements with shippers, the form
and terms of which are matters for consultation between the conference and shippers' organizations or representatives of shippers.
These loyalty arrangements shall provide safeguards making explicit
the rights of shippers and conference members. These arrangements
shall be based on the contract system or any other system which
is also lawful.

2. Whatever loyalty arrangements are made, the freight rate
applicable to loyal shippers shall be determined within a fixed range
of percentages of the freight rate applicable to other shippers. Where
a change in the differential causes an increase in the rates charged
to shippers, the change can be implemented only after 150 days'
notice to those shippers or according to regional practice and/or
agreement. Disputes in connexion with a change of the differential
shall be settled as provided in the loyalty agreement.

3. The terms of loyalty arrangements shall provide safeguards
making explicit the rights and obligations of shippers and of shipping
lines members of the conference in accordance with the following
provisions, *inter alia* :

   (a) The shipper shall be bound in respect of cargo whose
       shipment is controlled by him or his affiliated or subsidiary
       company or his forwarding agent in accordance with the
       contract of sale of the goods concerned, provided that the
       shipper shall not, by evasion, subterfuge, or intermediary,
       attempt to divert cargo in violation of his loyalty commit-
       ment ;

(b) Where there is a loyalty contract, the extent of actual or liquidated damages and/or penalty shall be specified in the contract. The member lines of the conference may, however, decide to assess lower liquidated damages or to waive the claim to liquidated damages. In any event, the liquidated damages under the contract to be paid to the shipper shall not exceed the freight charges on the particular shipment, computed at the rate provided under the contract ;

(c) The shipper shall be entitled to resume full loyalty status, subject to the fulfilment of conditions established by the conference which shall be specified in the loyalty arrangement ;

(d) The loyalty arrangement shall set out:

(i) A list of cargo, which may include bulk cargo shipped without mark or count, which is specifically excluded from the scope of the loyalty arrangement ;

(ii) A definition of the circumstances in which cargo other than cargo covered by (i) above is considered to be excluded from the scope of the loyalty arrangement ;

(iii) The method of settlement of disputes arising under the loyalty arrangement ;

(iv) Provision for termination of the loyalty arrangement on request by either a shipper or a conference without penalty, after expiry of a stipulated period of notice, such notice to be given in writing ; and

(v) The terms for granting dispensation.

4. If there is a dispute between a conference and a shippers' organization, representatives of shippers and/or shippers about the form or terms of a proposed loyalty arrangement, either party may refer the matter for resolution under appropriate procedures as set out in this Code.

Article 8

DISPENSATION

1. Conferences shall provide, within the terms of the loyalty arrangements, that requests by shippers for dispensation shall be examined and a decision given quickly and, if requested, the reasons given in writing where dispensation is withheld. Should a conference fail to confirm, within a period specified in the loyalty arrangement, sufficient space to accommodate a shipper's cargo within a period also specified in the loyalty arrangement, the shipper shall have the right, without being penalized, to utilize any vessel for the cargo in question.

2. In ports where conference services are arranged subject to the availability of a specified minimum of cargo (i.e. on inducement), but either the shipping line does not call, despite due notice by shippers, or the shipping line does not reply within an agreed time

to the notice given by shippers, shippers shall automatically have
the right, without prejudicing their loyalty status, to use any available vessel for the carriage of their cargo.

Article 9

Availability of Tariffs and Related Conditions and/or Regulations

Tariffs, related conditions, regulations, and any amendments thereto shall be made available on request to shippers, shippers' organizations and other parties concerned at reasonable cost, and they shall be available for examination at offices of shipping lines and their agents.   They shall spell out all conditions concerning the application of freight rates and the carriage of any cargo covered by them.

Article 10

Annual Reports

Conferences shall provide annually to shippers' organizations, or to representatives of shippers, reports on their activities designed to provide general information of interest to them, including relevant information about consultations held with shippers and shippers' organizations, action taken regarding complaints, changes in membership, and significant changes in service, tariffs and conditions of carriage.   Such annual reports shall be submitted, on request, to the appropriate authorities of the countries whose trade is served by the conference concerned.

Article 11

Consultation Machinery

1. There shall be consultations on matters of common interest between a conference, shippers' organizations, representatives of shippers and, where practicable, shippers, which may be designated for that purpose by the appropriate authority if it so desires.   These consultations shall take place whenever requested by any of the above-mentioned parties. Appropriate authorities shall have the right, upon request, to participate fully in the consultations, but this does not mean that they play a decision-making role.

2. The following matters, *inter alia*, may be the subject of consultation:

   (*a*) Changes in general tariff conditions and related regulations ;
   (*b*) Changes in the general level of tariff rates and rates for major commodities ;
   (*c*) Promotional and/or special freight rates ;
   (*d*) Imposition of, and related changes in, surcharges ;

(e) Loyalty arrangements, their establishment or changes in their form and general conditions ;

(f) Changes in the tariff classification of ports ;

(g) Procedure for the supply of necessary information by shippers concerning the expected volume and nature of their cargoes ; and

(h) Presentation of cargo for shipment and the requirements regarding notice of cargo availability.

3. To the extent that they fall within the scope of activity of a conference, tthe following matters may also be the subject of consultation :

(a) Operation of cargo inspection services ;

(b) Changes in the pattern of services ;

(c) Effects of the introduction of new technology in the carriage of cargo, in particular unitization, with consequent reduction of conventional service or loss of direct services ; and

(d) Adequacy and quality of shipping services, including the impact of pooling, berthing or sailing arrangements on the availability of shipping services and frieight rates at which shipping services are provided ; changes in the areas served and in the regularity of calls by conference vessels.

4. Consultations shall be held before final decisions are taken, unless otherwise provided in this Code. Advance notice shall be given of the intention to take decisions on matters referred to in article 11, paragraphs 2 and 3. Where this is impossible, urgent decisions may be taken pending the holding of consultations.

5. Consultations shall begin without undue delay and in any event within a maximum period specified in the conference agreement, or in the absence of such a provision in the agreement, not later than 30 days after receipt of the proposal for consultations, unless different periods of time are provided in this Code.

6. When holding consultations, the parties shall use their best efforts to provide relevant information, to hold timely discussions and to clarify matters for the purpose of seeking solutions of the issues concerned. The parties involved shall take account of each other's views and problems and strive to reach agreement consistent with their commercial viability.

CHAPTER IV
FREIGHT RATES

Article 12

CRITERIA FOR FREIGHT-RATE DETERMINATION

In arriving at a decision on questions of tariff policy in all cases mentioned in this Code, the following points shall, unless otherwise provided, be taken into account:

(*a*) Freight rates shall be fixed at as low a level as is feasible from the commercial point of view and shall permit a reasonable profit for shipowners ;

(*b*) The cost of operations of conferences shall, as a rule, be evaluated for the round voyage of ships, with the outward and inward directions considered as a single whole. Where applicable, the outward and inward voyage should be considered separately. The freight rates should take into account among other factors, the nature of cargoes, the interrelation between weight and cargo measurement, as well as the value of cargoes ;

(*c*) In fixing promotional freight rates and/or special freight rates for specific goods, the conditions of trade for these goods of the countries served by the conference particularly of developing and land-locked countries, shall be taken into account.

Article 13

Conference Tariffs and Classification of Tariff Rates

1. Conference tariffs shall not unfairly differentiate between shippers similarly situated. Shipping lines members of a conference shall adhere strictly to the rates, rules and terms shown in the tariffs and other currently valid published documents of the conference and to any special arrangements permitted under this Code.

2. Conference tariffs should be drawn up simply and clearly, containing as few classes/categories as possible, depending on the commodity and, where appropriate, for each class/category ; they should also indicate, wherever practicable, in order to facilitate statistical compilation and analysis, the corresponding appropriate code number of the item in accordance with the Standard International Trade Classification, the Brussels Tariff Nomenclature or any other nomenclature that may be internationally adopted ; the classification of commodities in the tariffs should, as far as practicable, be prepared in co-operation with shippers' organizations and other national and international organizations concerned.

Article 14

General Freight-Rate Increases

1. A conference shall give notice of not less than 150 days, or according to regional practice and/or agreement, to shippers' organizations or representatives of shippers and/or shippers and, where so required, to appropriate authorities of the countries whose trade is served by the conference, of its intention to effect a general increase in freight rates, an indication of its extent, the date of effect and the reasons supporting the proposed increase.

2. At the request of any of the parties prescribed for this purpose in this Code, to be made within an agreed period of time after the

receipt of the notice, consultations shall commence, in accordance with the relevant provisions of this Code, within a stipulated period not exceeding 30 days or as previously agreed between the parties concerned ; the consultations shall be held in respect of the bases and amounts of the proposed increase and the date from which it is to be given effect.

3. A conference, in an effort to expedite consultations, may or upon the request of any of the parties prescribed in this Code as entitled to participate in consultations on general freight-rate increases shall, where practicable, reasonably before the consultations, submit to the participating parties a report from independent accountants of repute, including, where the requesting parties accept it as one of the bases of consultations, an aggregated analysis of data regarding relevant costs and revenues which in the opinion of the conference necessitate an increase in freight rates.

4. If agreement is reached as a result of the consultations, the freight-rate increase shall take effect from the date indicated in the notice served in accordance with article 14, paragraph 1, unless a later date is agreed upon between the parties concerned.

5. If no agreement is reached within 30 days of the giving of notice in accordance with article 14, paragraph 1, and subject to procedures prescribed in this Code, the matter shall be submitted immediately to international mandatory conciliation, in accordance with chapter VI. The recommendation of the conciliators, if accepted by the parties concerned, shall be binding upon them and shall be implemented, subject to the provisions of article 14, paragraph 9, with effect from the date mentioned in the conciliators' recommendation.

6. Subject to the provisions of article 14, paragraph 9, a general freight-rate increase may be implemented by a conference pending the conciliators' recommendation. When making their recommendation, the conciliators should take into account the extent of the above-mentioned increase made by the conference and the period for which it has been in force. In the event that the conference rejects the recommendation of the conciliators, shippers and/or shippers' organizations shall have the right to consider themselves not bound, after appropriate notice, by any arrangement or other contract with that conference which may prevent them from using non-conference shipping lines. Where a loyalty arrangement exists, shippers and/or shippers' organizations shall give notice within a period of 30 days to the effect that they no longer consider themselves bound by that arrangement, which notice shall apply from the date mentioned therein, and a period of not less than 30 days and not more than 90 days shall be provided in the loyalty arrangement for this purpose.

7. A deferred rebate which is due to the shipper and which has already been accumulated by the conference shall not be withheld by, or forfeited to, the conference as a result of action by the shipper under article 14, paragraph 6.

8. If the trade of a country carried by shipping lines members of a conference on a particular route consists largely of one or few basic commodities, any increase in the freight rate on one or more of those commodities shall be treated as a general freight-rate increase, and the appropriate provisions of this Code shall apply.

9. Conferences should institute any general freight-rate increase effective in accordance with this Code for a period of a stated minimum duration, subject always to the rules regarding surcharges and regarding adjustment in freight rates consequent upon fluctuations in foreign exchange rates. The period over which a general freight-rate increase is to apply is an appropriate matter to be considered during consultations conducted in accordance with article 14, paragraph 2, but unless otherwise agreed between the parties concerned during the consultations, the minimum period of time between the date when one general freight-rate increase becomes effective and the date of notice for the next general freight-rate increase given in accordance with article 14, paragraph 1 shall not be less than 10 months.

Article 15

PROMOTIONAL FREIGHT RATES

1. Promotional freight rates for non-traditional exports should be instituted by conferences.

2. All necessary and reasonable information justifying the need for a promotional freight rate shall be submitted to a conference by the shippers, shippers' organizations or representatives of shippers concerned.

3. Special procedures shall be instituted providing for a decision within 30 days from the date of receipt of that information, unless mutually agreed otherwise, on application for promotional freight rates. A clear distinction shall be made between these and general procedures for considering the possibility of reducing freight rates for other commodities or of exempting them from increases.

4. Information regarding the procedures for considering applications for promotional freight rates shall be made available by the conference to shippers and/or shipper's organizations and, on request, to the Governments and/or other appropriate authorities of the countries whose trade is served by the conference.

5. A promotional freight rate shall be established normally for a period of 12 months, unless otherwise mutually agreed between the parties concerned. Prior to the expiry of the period, the promotional freight rate shall be reviewed, on request by the shipper and/or shippers' organization concerned, when it shall be a matter for the shipper and/or shippers' organization, at the request of the conference, to show that the continuation of the rate is justified beyond the initial period.

6. When examining a request for a promotional freight rate, the conference may take into account that, while the rate should promote the export of the non-traditional product for which it is sought, it is not likely to create substantial competitive distortions in the export of a similar product from another country served by the conference.

7. Promotional freight rates are not excluded from the imposition of a surcharge or a currency adjustment factor in accordance with articles 16 and 17.

8. Each shipping line member of a conference serving the relevant ports of a conference trade shall accept, and not unreasonably refuse, a fair share of cargo for which a promotional freight rate has been established by the conference.

Article 16

SURCHARGES

1. Surcharges imposed by a conference to cover sudden or extraordinary increases in costs or losses of revenue shall be regarded as temporary. They shall be reduced in accordance with improvements in the situation or circumstances which they were imposed to meet and shall be cancelled, subject to article 16, paragraph 6, as soon as the situation or circumstances which prompted their imposition cease to prevail. This shall be indicated at the moment of their imposition, together, as far as possible, with a description of the change in the situation or circumstances which will bring about their increase, reduction or cancellation.

2. Surcharges imposed on cargo moving to or from a particular port shall likewise be regarded as temporary and likewise shall be increased, reduced or cancelled, subject to article 16, paragraph 6, when the situation in that port changes.

3. Before any surcharge is imposed, whether general or covering only a specific port, notice should be given and there shall be consultation, upon request, in accordance with the procedures of this Code, between the conference concerned and other parties directly affected by the surcharge and prescribed in this Code as entitled to participate in such consultations, save in those exceptional circumstances which warrant immediate imposition of the surcharge. In cases where a surcharge has been imposed without prior consultation, consultations, upon request, shall be held as soon as possible thereafter. Prior to such consultations, conferences shall furnish data which in their opinion justify the imposition of the surcharge.

4. Unless the parties agree otherwise, within a period of 15 days after the receipt of a notice given in accordance with article 16, paragraph 3, if there is no agreement on the question of the surcharge between the parties concerned referred to in that article, the relevant provisions for settlement of disputes provided in this Code

shall prevail. Unless the parties concerned agree otherwise, the surcharge may, however, be imposed pending resolution of the dispute, if the dispute still remains unresolved at the end of a period of 30 days after the receipt of the above-mentioned notice.

5. In the event of a surcharge being imposed, in exceptional circumstances, without prior consultation as provided in article 16, paragraph 3, if no agreement is reached through subsequent consultations, the relevant provisions for settlement of disputes provided in this Code shall prevail.

6. Financial loss incurred by the shipping lines members of a conference as a result of any delay on account of consultations and/or other proceedings for resolving disputes regarding imposition of surcharges in accordance with the provisions of this Code, as compared to the date from which the surcharge was to be imposed in terms of the notice given in accordance with article 16, paragraph 3, may be compensated by an equivalent prolongation of the surcharge before its removal. Conversely, for any surcharge imposed by the conference and subsequently determined and agreed to be unjustified or excessive as a result of consultations or other procedures prescribed in this Code, the amounts so collected or the excess thereof as determined hereinabove, unless otherwise agreed, shall be refunded to the parties concerned, if claimed by them, within a period of 30 days of such claim.

Article 17

CURRENCY CHANGES

1. Exchange rate changes, including formal devaluation or revaluation, which lead to changes in the aggregate operational costs and/or revenues of the shipping lines members of a conference relating to their operations within the conference provide a valid reason for the introduction of a currency adjustment factor or for a change in the freight rates. The adjustment or change shall be such that in the aggregate the member lines concerned neither gain nor lose, as far as possible, as a result of the adjustment or change. The adjustment or change may take the form of currency surcharges or discounts or of increases or decreases in the freight rates.

2. Such adjustments or changes shall be subject to notice, which should be arranged in accordance with regional practice, where such practice exists, and there shall be consultations in accordance with the provisions of this Code between the conference concerned and the other parties directly affected and prescribed in this Code as entitled to participate in consultations, save in those exceptional circumstances which warrant immediate imposition of the currency adjustment factor or freight-rate change. In the event that this has been done without prior consultations, consultations shall be held as soon as possible thereafter. The consultations should be on the application, size and date of implementation of the currency adjustment factor or freight-rate change, and the same procedures shall

be followed for this purpose as are prescribed in article 16, paragraphs 4 and 5, in respect of surcharges. Such consultations should take place and be completed within a period not exceeding 15 days from the date when the intention to apply a currency surcharge or to effect a freight-rate change is announced.

3. If no agreement is reached within 15 days through consultations, the relevant provisions for settlement of disputes provided in this Code shall prevail.

4. The provisions of article 16, paragraph 6 shall apply, adapted as necessary to currency adjustment factors and freight-rate changes dealt with in the present article.

CHAPTER V
OTHER MATTERS

Article 18
FIGHTING SHIPS

Members of a conference shall not use fighting ships in the conference trade for the purpose of excluding, preventing or reducing competition by driving a shipping line not a member of the conference out of the said trade.

Article 19
ADEQUACY OF SERVICE

1. Conferences should take necessary and appropriate measures to ensure that their member lines provide regular, adequate and efficient service of the required frequency on the routes they serve and shall arrange such services so as to avoid as far as possible bunching and gapping of sailings. Conferences should also take into consideration any special measures necessary in arranging services to handle seasonal variations in cargo volumes.

2. Conferences and other parties prescribed in this Code as entitled to participate in consultations, including appropriate authorities if they so desire, should keep under review, and should maintain close co-operation regarding the demand for shipping space, the adequacy and suitability of service, and in particular the possibilities for rationalization and for increasing the efficiency of services. Benefits identified as accruing from rationalization of services shall be fairly reflected in the level of freight rates.

3. In respect of any port for which conference services are supplied only subject to the availability of a specified minimum of cargo, that minimum shall be specified in the tariff. Shippers should give adequate notice of the availability of such cargo.

Article 20

Head Office of a Conference

A conference shall as a rule establish its head office in a country whose trade is served by that conference, unless agreed otherwise by the shipping lines members of that conference.

Article 21

Representation

Conferences shall establish local representation in all countries served, except that where there are practical reasons to the contrary the representation may be on a regional basis. The names and addresses of representatives shall be readily available, and these representatives shall ensure that the views of shippers and conferences are made rapidly known to each other with a view to expediting prompt decisions. When a conference considers it suitable, it shall provide for adequate delegation of powers of decision to its representatives.

Article 22

Contents of Conference Agreements, Trade Participation Agreements and Loyalty Arrangements

Conference agreements, trade participation agreements and loyalty arrangements shall conform to the applicable requirements of this Code and may include such other provisions as may be agreed which are not inconsistent with this Code.

PART TWO

CHAPTER VI

PROVISIONS AND MACHINERY FOR SETTLEMENT OF DISPUTES

A. GENERAL PROVISIONS

Article 23

1. The provisions of this chapter shall apply whenever there is a dispute relating to the application or operation of the provisions of this Code between the following parties:

(*a*) A conference and a shipping line;

(*b*) The shipping lines members of a conference;

(*c*) A conference or a shipping line member thereof and a shippers' organization or representatives of shippers or shippers ; and

(*d*) Two or more conferences.

For the purposes of this chapter the term " party " means the original parties to the dispute as well as third parties which have joined the proceedings in accordance with (*a*) of article 34.

2. Disputes between shipping lines of the same flag, as well as those between organizations belonging to the same country, shall be settled within the framework of the national jurisdiction of that country, unless this creates serious difficulties in the fulfilment of the provisions of this Code.

3. The parties to a dispute shall first attempt to settle it by an exchange of views or direct negotiations with the intention of finding a mutually satisfactory solution.

4. Disputes between the parties referred to in article 23, paragraph 1 relating to:

(*a*) Refusal of admission of a national shipping line to a conference serving the foreign trade of the country of that shipping line ;

(*b*) Refusal of admission of a third-country shipping line to a conference ;

(*c*) Expulsion from a conference ;

(*d*) Inconsistency of a conference agreement with this Code ;

(*e*) A general freight-rate increase ;

(*f*) Surcharges ;

(*g*) Changes in freight rates or the imposition of a currency adjustment factor due to exchange rate changes ;

(*h*) Participation in trade ; and

(*i*) The form and terms of proposed loyalty arrangements

which have not been resolved through an exchange of views or direct negotiations shall, at the request of any of the parties to the dispute, be referred to international mandatory conciliation in accordance with the provisions of this chapter.

Article 24

1. The conciliation procedure is initiated at the request of one of the parties to the dispute.

2. The request shall be made:

(*a*) In disputes relating to membership of conferences: not later than 60 days from the date of receipt by the applicant of the conference decision, including the reasons therefor, in accordance with article 1, paragraph 4 and article 4, paragraph 3 ;

(*b*) In disputes relating to general freight-rate increases: not later than the date of expiry of the period of notice specified in article 14, paragraph 1 ;

(*c*) In disputes relating to surcharges: not later than the date of expiry of the 30-day period specified in article 16, paragraph 4 or, where no notice has been given, not later than 15 days from the date when the surcharge was put into effect ; and

(*d*) In disputes relating to changes in freight rates or the imposition of a currency adjustment factor due to exchange rate changes: not later than five days after the date of expiry of the period specified in article 17, paragraph 3.

3. The provisions of article 24, paragraph 2 shall not apply to a dispute which is referred to international mandatory conciliation in accordance with article 25, paragraph 3.

4. Requests for conciliation in disputes other than those referred to in article 24, paragraph 2, may be made at any time.

5. The time-limits specified in article 24, paragraph 2 may be extended by agreement between the parties.

6. A request for conciliation shall be considered to have been duly made if it is proved that the request has been sent to the other party by registered letter, telegram or teleprinter or has been served on it within the time-limits specified in article 24, paragraphs 2 or 5.

7. Where no request has been made within the time-limits specified in article 24, paragraphs 2 or 5, the decision of the conference shall be final and no proceedings under this chapter may be brought by any party to the dispute to challenge that decision.

Article 25

1. Where the parties have agreed that disputes referred to in article 23, paragraph 4(*a*), (*b*), (*c*), (*d*), (*h*) and (*i*) shall be resolved through procedures other than those established in that article, or agree on procedures to resolve a particular dispute that has arisen between them, such disputes shall, at the request of any of the parties to the dispute, be resolved as provided for in their agreement.

2. The provisions of article 25, paragraph 1 apply also to the disputes referred to in article 23, paragraph 4(*e*), (*f*) and (*g*), unless national legislation, rules or regulations prevent shippers from having this freedom of choice.

3. Where conciliation proceedings have been initiated, such proceedings shall have precedence over remedies available under national law. If a party seeks remedies under national law in

respect of a dispute to which this chapter applies without invoking the procedures provided for in this chapter, then, upon the request of a respondent to those proceedings, they shall be stayed and the dispute shall be referred to the procedures defined in this chapter by the court or other authority where the national remedies are sought.

Article 26

1. The Contracting Parties shall confer upon conferences and shippers' organizations such capacity as is necessary for the application of the provisions of this chapter. In particular:

(*a*) A conference or a shippers' organization may institute proceedings as a party or be named as a party to proceedings in its collective capacity;

(*b*) Any notification to a conference or shippers' organization in its collective capacity shall also constitute a notification to each member of such conference or shippers' organization;

(*c*) A notification to a conference or shippers' organization shall be transmitted to the address of the head office of the conference or shippers' organization. Each conference or shippers' organization shall register the address of its head office with the Registrar appointed in accordance with article 46, paragraph 1. In the event that a conference or a shippers' organization fails to register or has no head office, a notification to any member in the name of the conference or shippers' organization shall be deemed to be a notification to such conference or organization.

2. Acceptance or rejection by a conference or shippers' organization of a recommendation by conciliators shall be deemed to be acceptance or rejection of such a recommendation by each member thereof.

Article 27

Unless the parties agree otherwise, the conciliators may decide to make a recommendation on the basis of written submissions without oral proceedings.

B. INTERNATIONAL MANDATORY CONCILIATION

Article 28

In international mandatory conciliation the appropriate authorities of a Contracting Party shall, if they so request, participate in the conciliation proceedings in support of a party being a national of that Contracting Party, or in support of a party having a dispute arising in the context of the foreign trade of that Contracting Party. The appropriate authority may alternatively act as an observer in such conciliation proceedings.

Article 29

1. In international mandatory conciliation the proceedings shall be held in the place unanimously agreed to by the parties or, failing such agreement, in the place decided upon by the conciliators.

2. In determining the place of conciliation proceedings the parties and the conciliators shall take into account, *inter alia,* countries which are closely connected with the dispute, bearing in mind the country of the shipping line concerned and, especially when the dispute is related to cargo, the country where the cargo originates.

Article 30

1. For the purposes of this chapter an international panel of conciliators shall be established, consisting of experts of high repute or experience in the fields of law, economics of sea transport, or foreign trade and finance, as determined by the Contracting Parties selecting them, who shall serve in an independent capacity.

2. Each Contracting Party may at any time nominate members of the panel up to a total of 12, and shall communicate their names to the Registrar. The nominations shall be for periods of six years each and may be renewed. In the event of the death, incapacity or resignation of a member of the panel, the Contracting Party which nominated such person shall nominate a replacement for the remainder of his term of office. A nomination takes effect from the date on which the communication of the nomination is received by the Registrar.

3. The Registrar shall maintain the panel list and shall regularly inform the Contracting Parties of the composition of the panel.

Article 31

1. The purpose of conciliation is to reach an amicable settlement of the dispute through recommendations formulated by independent conciliators.

2. The conciliators shall identify and clarify the issues in dispute, seek for this purpose any information from the parties, and on the basis thereof, submit to the parties a recommendation for the settlement of the dispute.

3. The parties shall co-operate in good faith with the conciliators in order to enable them to carry out their functions.

4. Subject to the provisions of article 25, paragraph 2, the parties to the dispute may at any time during the conciliation proceedings decide in agreement to have recourse to a different procedure for the settlement of their dispute. The parties to a dispute which has been made subject to proceedings other than those provided for in this chapter may decide by mutual agreement to have recourse to international mandatory conciliation.

Article 32

1. The conciliation proceedings shall be conducted either by one conciliator or by an uneven number of conciliators agreed upon or designated by the parties.

2. Where the parties cannot agree on the number or the appointment of the conciliators as provided in article 32, paragraph 1, the conciliation proceedings shall be conducted by three conciliators, one appointed by each party in the statement(s) of claim and reply respectively, and the third by the two conciliators thus appointed, who shall act as chairman.

3. If the reply does not name a conciliator to be appointed in cases where article 32, paragraph 2 would apply, the second conciliator shall, within 30 days following the receipt of the statement of claim, be chosen by lot by the conciliator appointed in the statement of claim from among the members of the panel nominated by the Contracting Party or Parties of which the respondent(s) is(are) a national(s).

4. Where the conciliators appointed in accordance with article 32, paragraphs 2 or 3 cannot agree on the appointment of the third conciliator within 15 days following the date of the appointment of the second conciliator, he shall, within the following 5 days, be chosen by lot by the appointed conciliators. Prior to the drawing by lot:

   (a) No member of the panel of conciliators having the same nationality as either of the two appointed conciliators shall be eligible for selection by lot ;

   (b) Each of the two appointed conciliators may exclude from the list of the panel of conciliators an equal number of them subject to the requirement that at least 30 members of the panel shall remain eligible for selection by lot.

Article 33

1. Where several parties request conciliation with the same respondent in respect of the same issue, or of issues which are closely connected, that respondent may request the consolidation of those cases.

2. The request for consolidation shall be considered and decided upon by majority vote by the chairmen of the conciliators so far chosen. If such request is allowed, the chairmen will designate the

conciliators to consider the consolidated cases from among the conciliators so far appointed or chosen, provided that an uneven number
of conciliators is chosen and that the conciliator first appointed by
each party shall be one of the conciliators considering the consolidated case.

Article 34

Any party, other than an appropriate authority referred to in
article 28, if conciliation has been initiated, may join in the proceedings :

either

(*a*) As a party, in case of a direct economic interest ;

or

(*b*) As a supporting party to one of the original parties, in case
   of an indirect economic interest,

unless either of the original parties objects to such joinder.

Article 35

1. The recommendations of the conciliators shall be made in accordance with the provisions of this Code.

2. When the Code is silent upon any point, the conciliators shall
apply the law which the parties agree at the time the conciliation proceedings commence or thereafter, but not later than the time of
submission of evidence to the conciliators. Failing such agreement,
the law which in the opinion of the conciliators is most closely connected with the dispute shall be applicable.

3. The conciliators shall not decide *ex aequo et bono* upon the
dispute unless the parties so agree after the dispute has arisen.

4. The conciliators shall not bring a finding of *non liquet* on the
ground of obscurity of the law.

5. The conciliators may recommend those remedies and reliefs
which are provided in the law applicable to the dispute.

Article 36

The recommendations of the conciliators shall include reasons.

Article 37

1. Unless the parties have agreed before, during or after the
conciliation procedure that the recommendation of the conciliators
shall be binding, the recommendation shall become binding by
acceptance by the parties. A recommendation which has been
accepted by some parties to a dispute shall be binding as between
those parties only.

2. Acceptance of the recommendation must be communicated by the parties to the conciliators, at an address specified by them, not later than 30 days after receipt of the notification of the recommendation ; otherwise, it shall be considered that the recommendation has not been accepted.

3. Any party which does not accept the recommendation shall notify the conciliators and the other parties, within 30 days following the period specified in article 37, paragraph 2 of its grounds for rejection of the recommendation, comprehensively and in writing.

4. When the recommendation has been accepted by the parties, the conciliators shall immediately draw up and sign a record of settlement, at which time the recommendation shall become binding upon those parties. If the recommendation has not been accepted by all parties, the conciliators shall draw up a report with respect to those parties rejecting the recommendation, noting the dispute and the failure of those parties to settle the dispute.

5. A recommendation which has become binding upon the parties shall be implemented by them immediately or at such later time as is specified in the recommendation.

6. Any party may make its acceptance conditional upon acceptance by all or any of the other parties to the dispute.

Article 38

1. A recommendation shall constitute a final determination of a dispute as between the parties which accept it, except to the extent that the recommendation is not recognized and enforced in accordance with the provisions of article 39.

2. " Recommendation " includes an interpretation, clarification or revision of the recommendation made by the conciliators before the recommendation has been accepted.

Article 39

1. Each Contracting Party shall recognize a recommendation as binding between the parties which have accepted it and shall, subject to the provisions of article 39, paragraphs 2 and 3, enforce, at the request of any such party, all obligations imposed by the recommendation as if it were a final judgment of a court of that Contracting Party.

2. A recommendation shall not be recognized and enforced at the request of a party referred to in article 39, paragraph 1 only if the court or other competent authority of the country where recognition and enforcement is sought is satisfied that:

(a) Any party which accepted the recommendation was, under the law applicable to it, under some legal incapacity at the time of acceptance ;

(b) Fraud or coercion has been used in the making of the recommendations ;

(*c*) The recommendation is contrary to public policy (*ordre public*) in the country of enforcement ; or

(*d*) The composition of the conciliators, or the conciliation procedure, was not in accordance with the provisions of this Code.

3. Any part of the recommendation shall not be enforced and recognized if the court or other competent authority is satisfied that such part comes within any of the subparagraphs of article 39, paragraph 2 and can be separated from other parts of the recommendation. If such part cannot be separated, the entire recommendation shall not be enforced and recognized.

Article 40

1. Where the recommendation has been accepted by all the parties, the recommendation and the reasons therefor may be published with the consent of all the parties.

2. Where the recommendation has been rejected by one or more of the parties but has been accepted by one or more of the parties:

(*a*) The party or parties rejecting the recommendation shall publish its or their grounds for rejection, given pursuant to article 37, paragraph 3, and may at the same time publish the recommendation and the reasons therefor ;

(*b*) A party which has accepted the recommendation may publish the recommendation and the reasons therefor ; it may also publish the grounds for rejection given by any other party unless such other party has already published its rejection and the grounds therefor in accordance with article 40, paragraph 2(*a*).

3. Where the recommendation has not been accepted by any of the parties, each party may publish the recommendation and the reasons therefor and also its own rejection and the grounds therefor.

Article 41

1. Documents and statements containing factual information supplied by any party to the conciliators shall be made public unless that party or a majority of the conciliators agrees otherwise.

2. Such documents and statements supplied by a party may be tendered by that party in support of its case in subsequent proceedings arising from the same dispute and between the same parties.

Article 42

Where the recommendation has not become binding upon the parties, no views expressed or reasons given by the conciliators, or concessions or offers made by the parties for the purpose of the conciliation procedure, shall affect the legal rights and obligations of any of the parties.

Article 43

1. (*a*) The costs of the conciliators and all costs of the administration of the conciliation proceedings shall be borne equally by the parties to the proceedings, unless they agree otherwise.

(*b*) When the conciliation proceedings have been initiated, the conciliators shall be entitled to require an advance or security for the costs referred to in article 43, paragraph 1(*a*).

2. Each party shall bear all expenses it incurs in connexion with the proceedings, unless the parties agree otherwise.

3. Notwithstanding the provisions of article 43, paragraphs 1 and 2, the conciliators may, having decided unanimously that a party has brought a claim vexatiously or frivolously, assess against that party any or all of the costs of other parties to the proceedings. Such decision shall be final and binding on all the parties.

Article 44

1. Failure of a party to appear or to present its case at any stage of the proceedings shall not be deemed an admission of the other party's assertions. In that event, the other party may, at its choice, request the conciliators to close the proceedings or to deal with the questions presented to them and submit a recommendation in accordance with the provisions for making recommendations set out in this Code.

2. Before closing the proceedings, the conciliators shall grant the party failing to appear or to present its case a period of grace, not exceeding 10 days, unless they are satisfied that the party does not intend to appear or to present its case.

3. Failure to observe procedural time-limits laid down in this Code or determined by the conciliators, in particular time-limits relating to the submission of statements or information, shall be considered a failure to appear in the proceedings.

4. Where the proceedings have been closed owing to one party's failure to appear or to present its case, the conciliators shall draw up a report noting that party's failure.

Article 45

1. The conciliators shall follow the procedures stipulated in this Code.

2. The rules of procedure annexed to the present Convention shall be considered as model rules for the guidance of conciliators. The conciliators may, by mutual consent, use, supplement or amend the rules contained in the annex or formulate their own rules of procedure to the extent that such supplementary, amended or other rules are not inconsistent with the provisions of this Code.

3. If the parties agree that it may be in the interest of achieving an expeditious and inexpensive solution of the conciliation proceedings, they may mutually agree to rules of procedure which are not inconsistent with the provisions of this Code.

4. The conciliators shall formulate their recommendation by consensus or failing that shall decide by majority vote.

5. The conciliation proceedings shall finish and the recommendation of the conciliators shall be delivered not later than six months from the date on which the conciliators are appointed, except in the cases referred to in article 23, paragraph 4(*e*), (*f*), and (*g*), for which the time limits in article 14, paragraph 1 and article 16, paragraph 4 shall be valid. The period of six months may be extended by agreement of the parties.

C. INSTITUTIONAL MACHINERY

Article 46

1. Six months before the entry into force of the present Convention, the Secretary-General of the United Nations shall, subject to the approval of the General Assembly of the United Nations, and taking into account the views expressed by the Contracting Parties, appoint a Registrar, who may be assisted by such additional staff as may be necessary for the performance of the functions listed in article 46, paragraph 2. Administrative services for the Registrar and his assistants shall be provided by the United Nations Office at Geneva.

2. The Registrar shall perform the following functions in consultation with the Contracting Parties as appropriate:

(*a*) Maintain the list of conciliators of the international panel of conciliators and regularly inform the Contracting Parties of the composition of the panel ;

(*b*) Provide the names and addresses of the conciliators to the parties concerned on request ;

(*c*) Receive and maintain copies of requests for conciliation, replies, recommendation, acceptances, or rejections, including reasons therefor ;

(*d*) Furnish on request, and at their cost, copies of recommendations and reasons for rejection to the shippers' organizations, conferences and Governments, subject to the provisions of article 40 ;

(*e*) Make available information of a non-confidential nature on completed conciliation cases, and without attribution to the parties concerned, for the purposes of preparation of material for the Review Conference referred to in article 52 ; and

(*f*) The other functions prescribed for the Registrar in article 26, paragraph 1(*c*) and article 30, paragraphs 2 and 3.

CHAPTER VII

FINAL CLAUSES

Article 47

IMPLEMENTATION

1. Each Contracting Party shall take such legislative or other measures as may be necessary to implement the present Convention.

2. Each Contracting Party shall communicate to the Secretary-General of the United Nations, who shall be the depositary, the text of the legislative or other measures which it has taken in order to implement the present Convention.

Article 48

SIGNATURE, RATIFICATION, ACCEPTANCE, APPROVAL AND ACCESSION

1. The present Convention shall remain open for signature as from 1 July 1974 until and including 30 June 1975 at United Nations Headquarters and shall thereafter remain open for accession.

2. All States are entitled to become Contracting Parties to the present Convention by:

   (*a*) Signature subject to and followed by ratification, acceptance or approval ; or

   (*b*) Signature without reservation as to ratification, acceptance or approval ; or

   (*c*) Accession.

3. Ratification, acceptance, approval or accession shall be effected by the deposit of an instrument to this effect with the depositary.

Article 49

ENTRY INTO FORCE

1. The present Convention shall enter into force six months after the date on which not less than 24 States, the combined tonnage of which amounts to at least 25 per cent of world tonnage, have become Contracting Parties to it in accordance with article 48. For the purpose of the present article the tonnage shall be deemed to be that contained in *Lloyd's Register of Shipping—Statistical Tables 1973*, table 2 "World Fleets—Analysis by Principal Types", in respect to general cargo (including passenger/cargo) ships and container (fully cellular) ships, exclusive of the United States reserve fleet and the American and Canadian Great Lakes fleets.

2. For each State which thereafter ratifies, accepts, approves or accedes to it, the present Convention shall come into force six months after deposit by such State of the appropriate instrument.

3. Any State which becomes a Contracting Party to the present
Convention after the entry into force of an amendment shall, failing
an expression of a different intention by that State:

> (a) Be considered as a Party to the present Convention **as**
> amended ; and

> (b) Be considered as a Party to the unamended Convention in
> relation to any Party to the present Convention not bound
> by the amendment.

Article 50

DENUNCIATION

1. The present Convention may be denounced by any Contracting
Party at any time after the expiration of a period of two years
from the date on which the Convention has entered into force.

2. Denunciation shall be notified to the depositary in writing, and
shall take effect one year, or such longer period as may be specified
in the instrument of denunciation, after the date of receipt by the
depositary.

Article 51

AMENDMENTS

1. Any Contracting Party may propose one or more amendments
to the present Convention by communicating the amendments to the
depositary.   The depositary shall circulate such amendments among
the Contracting Parties, for their acceptance, and among States
entitled to become Contracting Parties to the present Convention
which are not Contracting Parties, for their information.

2. Each proposed amendment circulated in accordance with
article 51, paragraph 1 shall be deemed to have been accepted if
no Contracting Party communicates an objection thereto to the
depositary within 12 months following the date of its circulation
by the depositary. If a Contracting Party communicates an objection
to the proposed amendment, such amendment shall not be considered as accepted and shall not be put into effect.

3. If no objection has been communicated, the amendment shall
enter into force for all Contracting Parties six months after the
expiry date of the period of 12 months referred to in article 51,
paragraph 2.

Article 52

REVIEW CONFERENCES

1. A Review Conference shall be convened by the depositary
five years from the date on which the present Convention comes

SCH.   into force to review the working of the Convention, with particular
reference to its implementation, and to consider and adopt appropriate amendments.

2. The depositary shall, four years from the date on which the
present Convention comes into force, seek the views of all States
entitled to attend the Review Conference and shall, on the basis
of the views received, prepare and circulate a draft agenda as
well as amendments proposed for consideration by the Conference.

3. Further review conferences shall be similarly convened every
five years, or at any time after the first Review Conference, at the
request of one-third of the Contracting Parties to the present
Convention, unless the first Review Conference decides otherwise.

4. Notwithstanding the provisions of article 52, paragraph 1, if the
present Convention has not entered into force five years from the
date of the adoption of the Final Act of the United Nations Conference of Plenipotentiaries on a Code of Conduct for Liner Conferences, a Review Conference shall, at the request of one-third of
the States entitled to become Contracting Parties to the present Convention, be convened by the Secretary-General of the United Nations,
subject to the approval of the General Assembly, in order to review
the provisions of the Convention and its annex and to consider and
adopt appropriate amendments.

Article 53

FUNCTIONS OF THE DEPOSITARY

1. The depositary shall notify the signatory and acceding States
of:

   (a) Signatures, ratifications, acceptances, approvals and acces-
   sions in accordance with article 48 ;

   (b) The date on which the present Convention enters into force
   in accordance with article 49 ;

   (c) Denunciations of the present Convention in accordance with
   article 50 ;

   (d) Reservations to the present Convention and the withdrawal
   of reservations ;

   (e) The text of the legislative or other measures which each
   Contracting Party has taken in order to implement the present Convention in accordance with article 47 ;

   (f) Proposed amendments and objections to proposed amendments in accordance with article 51 ; and

   (g) Entry into force of amendments in accordance with article
   51, paragraph 3.

2. The depository shall also undertake such actions as are necessary under article 52.

Article 54
AUTHENTIC TEXTS—DEPOSIT

The original of the present Convention, of which the Chinese, English, French, Russian and Spanish texts are equally authentic, will be deposited with the Secretary-General of the United Nations.

IN WITNESS WHEREOF the undersigned, having been duly authorized to this effect by their respective Governments, have signed the present Convention, on the dates appearing opposite their signatures.

....

ANNEX TO THE CONVENTION
MODEL RULES OF PROCEDURE FOR INTERNATIONAL MANDATORY CONCILIATION

Rule 1

1. Any party wishing to institute conciliation proceedings under the Code shall address a request to that effect in writing, accompanied by a statement of claim to the other party, and copied to the Registrar.

2. The statement of claim shall:

    (*a*) Designate precisely each party to the dispute and state the address of each ;

    (*b*) Contain a summary statement of pertinent facts, the issues in dispute and the claimant's proposal for the settlement of the dispute ;

    (*c*) State whether an oral hearing is desired and, if so, and to the extent then known, the names and addresses of persons to give evidence, including experts' evidence, for the claimant ;

    (*d*) Be accompanied by such supporting documentation and relevant agreements and arrangements entered into by the parties as the claimant may consider necessary at the time of making the claim ;

    (*e*) Indicate the number of conciliators required, any proposal concerning the appointment of conciliators, or the name of the conciliator appointed by the claimant in accordance with article 32, paragraph 2 ; and

2 F 2

(*f*) Contain proposals, if any, regarding rules of procedure.

3. The statement of claim shall be dated and shall be signed by the party.

Rule 2

1. If the respondent decides to reply to the claim, he shall, within 30 days following the date of his receipt of the statement of claim, transmit a reply to the other party and copied to the Registrar.

2. The reply shall:
- (*a*) Contain a summary statement of pertinent facts opposed to the contentions in the statement of claim, the respondent's proposal, if any, for the settlement of the dispute and any remedy claimed by him with a view to the settlement of the dispute;
- (*b*) State whether an oral hearing is desired and, if so, and to the extent then known, the names and addresses of persons to give evidence, including experts' evidence, for the respondent;
- (*c*) Be accompanied by such supporting documentation and relevant agreements and arrangements entered into by the parties as the respondent may consider necessary at the time of making the reply;
- (*d*) Indicate the number of conciliators required, any proposal concerning the appointment of conciliators, or the name of the conciliator appointed by the respondent in accordance with article 32, paragraph 2; and
- (*e*) Contain proposals, if any, regarding rules of procedure.

3. The reply shall be dated and shall be signed by the party.

Rule 3

1. Any person or other interest desiring to participate in conciliation proceedings under article 34 shall transmit a written request to the parties to the dispute, with a copy to the Registrar.

2. If participation in accordance with (*a*) of article 34 is desired, the request shall set forth the grounds therefor, including the information required under rule 1, paragraph 2 (*a*), (*b*) and (*d*).

3. If participation in accordance with (*b*) of article 34 is desired, the request shall state the grounds therefor and which of the original parties would be supported.

4. Any objection to a request for joinder by such a party shall be sent by the objecting party, with a copy to the other party, within seven days of receipt of the request.

5. In the event that two or more proceedings are consolidated, subsequent requests for third-party participation shall be transmitted to all parties concerned, each of which may object in accordance with the present rule.

Rule 4

By agreement between the parties to the dispute, on motion by either party, and after affording the parties an opportunity of being heard, the conciliators may order the consolidation or separation of all or any claims then pending between the same parties.

Rule 5

1. Any party may challenge a conciliator where circumstances exist that cause justifiable doubts as to his independence.

2. Notice of challenge, stating reasons therefor, should be made prior to the date of the closing of the proceedings, before the conciliators have rendered their recommendation. Any such challenge shall be heard promptly and shall be determined by majority vote of the conciliators in the first instance, as a preliminary point, in cases where more than one conciliator has been appointed. The decision in such cases shall be final.

3. A conciliator who has died, resigned, become incapacitated or disqualified shall be replaced promptly.

4. Proceedings interrupted in this way shall continue from the point where they were interrupted, unless it is agreed by the parties or ordered by the conciliators that a review or rehearing of any oral testimony take place.

Rule 6

The conciliators shall be judges of their own jurisdiction and/or competence within the provisions of the Code.

Rule 7

1. The conciliators shall receive and consider all written statements, documents, affidavits, publications or any other evidence, including oral evidence, which may be submitted to them by or on behalf of any of the parties, and shall give such weight thereto as in their judgement such evidence merits.

2. (*a*) Each party may submit to the conciliators any material it considers relevant, and at the time of such submission shall deliver certified copies to any other party to the proceedings, which party shall be given a reasonable opportunity to reply thereto ;

(*b*) The conciliators shall be the sole judges of the relevance and materiality of the evidence submitted to them by the parties ;

(*c*) The conciliators may ask the parties to produce such additional evidence as they may deem necessary to an understanding and determination of the dispute, provided that, if such additional evidence is produced, the other parties to the proceeding shall have a reasonable opportunity to comment thereon.

Rule 8

1. Whenever a period of days for the doing of any act is provided for in the Code or in these rules, the day from which the period begins to run shall not be counted, and the last day of the period shall be counted, except where that last day is a Saturday, Sunday or a public holiday at the place of conciliation, in which case the last day shall be the next business day.

2. When the time provided for is less than seven days, intermediate Saturdays, Sundays and public holidays shall be excluded from the computation.

Rule 9

Subject to the provisions relating to procedural time-limits in the Code, the conciliators may, on a motion by one of the parties or pursuant to agreement between them, extend any such time-limit which has been fixed by the conciliators.

Rule 10

1. The conciliators shall fix the order of business and, unless otherwise agreed, the date and hour of each session.

2. Unless the parties otherwise agree, the proceedings shall take place in private.

3. The conciliators shall specifically inquire of all the parties whether they have any further evidence to submit before declaring the proceedings closed, and a noting thereof shall be recorded.

Rule 11

Conciliators' recommendations shall be in writing and shall include:

(*a*) The precise designation and address of each party ;

(*b*) A description of the method of appointing conciliators, including their names ;

(*c*) The dates and place of the conciliation proceedings ;

(*d*) A summary of the conciliation proceedings, as the conciliators deem appropriate ;

(*e*) A summary statement of the facts found by the conciliators ;

(*f*) A summary of the submissions of the parties ;

(*g*) Pronouncements on the issues in dispute, together with the reasons therefor ;

(*h*) The signatures of the conciliators and the date of each signature ; and

(*i*) An address for the communication of the acceptance or rejection of the recommendation.

Rule 12

The recommendation shall, so far as possible, contain a pronouncement on costs in accordance with the provisions of the Code. If the recommendation does not contain a full pronouncement on costs, the conciliators shall, as soon as possible after the recommendation, and in any event not later than 60 days thereafter, make a pronouncement in writing regarding costs as provided in the Code.

Rule 13

Conciliators' recommendations shall also take into account previous and similar cases whenever this would facilitate a more uniform implementation of the Code and observance of conciliators' recommendations.

Northern Ireland Act 1982

1982 CHAPTER 38

An Act to make new provision for the resumption of legislative and executive functions by the Northern Ireland Assembly and by persons responsible to it; to amend the Northern Ireland Constitution Act 1973 and the Northern Ireland Assembly Act 1973; and for connected purposes.   [23rd July 1982]

BE IT ENACTED by the Queen's most Excellent Majesty, by and with the advice and consent of the Lords Spiritual and Temporal, and Commons, in this present Parliament assembled, and by the authority of the same, as follows:—

1.—(1) Subject to the provisions of this section, the Northern Ireland Assembly may, with a view to the making of one or more Orders in Council under section 2 below, submit to the Secretary of State— *Proposals for general or partial suspension of direct rule.*

> (a) proposals for the resumption by the Assembly and by persons responsible to it of all the functions that would be exercisable by them apart from Schedule 1 to the Northern Ireland Act 1974 (direct rule); or *1974 c. 28.*
>
> (b) proposals for the resumption as aforesaid of those functions so far as relating to any transferred matters within the responsibilities of any one or more Northern Ireland departments.

(2) Proposals under paragraph (a) of subsection (1) above shall include proposals as to the composition of a Northern Ireland Executive and as to the other appointments to be made under section 8 of the Constitution Act; and proposals under paragraph (b) of that subsection shall include proposals as to the appointment under that section of a head of the Northern Ireland department or, as the case may be, each Northern

2 F 4

Ireland department to which the proposals relate and may include proposals as to the appointment under that section of a person to assist any person appointed as head of any such department.

(3) Proposals under subsection (1) above may also include proposals for further provisions in the standing orders of the Assembly for the better conduct of any functions that would become exercisable by it in pursuance of those proposals.

(4) The Assembly shall not submit any proposals under this section unless—

(a) the proposals have the support of at least 70 per cent. of the members of the Assembly ; or

(b) the proposals have the support of a majority of those members and the Secretary of State has notified the Assembly that he is satisfied that the substance of the proposals is likely to command widespread acceptance throughout the community.

(5) The Secretary of State shall lay before Parliament any proposals submitted to him under this section.

General or partial suspension of direct rule.

1974 c. 28.

2.—(1) At any time after proposals have been laid before Parliament under section 1 above Her Majesty may by Order in Council—

(a) suspend the operation of the provisions of Schedule 1 to the Northern Ireland Act 1974 ; or

(b) suspend the operation of those provisions so far as relating to the transferred matters within the responsibilities of such Northern Ireland department or departments as are specified in the Order.

(2) No recommendation shall be made to Her Majesty to make an Order under subsection (1) above unless each House of Parliament has passed a resolution approving a draft of the Order and stating that its provisions are, in the opinion of that House, likely to command widespread acceptance throughout the community.

(3) An Order may be made under paragraph (a) of subsection (1) above without any Order having been made under paragraph (b) of that subsection or, if one or more Orders have been made under paragraph (b) of that subsection, so as to supersede that Order or those Orders.

(4) No Order under subsection (1)(b) above shall specify the Department of Finance and Personnel or any matters within its responsibilities.

(5) An Order under paragraph (a) of subsection (1) above shall have effect as provided in Part I of Schedule 1 to this Act ; and an Order under paragraph (b) of that subsection shall have effect as provided in Part II of that Schedule.

(6) An Order under subsection (1) above may contain such transitional provisions as appear to Her Majesty to be required in consequence of the Order.

3.—(1) During any period for which no Order is in force Matters for under paragraph (*a*) of subsection (1) of section 2 above, the consideration Assembly— by Assembly

    (*a*) may, without prejudice to its powers by virtue of any pending general Order under paragraph (*b*) of that subsection, consider suspension of any matter affecting Northern Ireland which is not direct rule. an excepted matter ;

    (*b*) shall consider any matter affecting Northern Ireland (whether or not an excepted matter) which is referred to it by the Secretary of State.

(2) Without prejudice to the generality of subsection (1)(*b*) above, the Secretary of State may refer to the Assembly for its consideration—

    (*a*) any proposal for the making of an Order under paragraph 1(1)(*b*) of Schedule 1 to the Northern 1974 c. 28. Ireland Act 1974 ;

    (*b*) any instrument or draft of an instrument to which paragraph 3 of that Schedule applies ;

but the reference to the Assembly under this section of an instrument or draft shall not be regarded for the purposes of the said paragraph 3 as laying it before the Assembly.

(3) The Assembly may report to the Secretary of State the views expressed in the Assembly on any matter considered by it under this section and shall do so if the Secretary of State so requests ; and any such request may require the report to be made within a specified period.

(4) The Secretary of State shall lay before Parliament any report received by him under this section which relates to a transferred matter considered by the Assembly under subsection (1)(*a*) above or to a matter which has been referred to it under this section by the Secretary of State.

(5) For the purposes of section 26(1) of the Constitution Act (privilege) any report made under this section shall be treated as an official record of the proceedings of the Assembly.

4.—(1) The Assembly shall by its standing orders make Assembly provision— committees in relation to

    (*a*) for the establishment, in relation to each Northern departments Ireland department whose functions are for the time under control being subject to paragraph 2(2) of Schedule 1 to the of Secretary Northern Ireland Act 1974, of a committee of of State.

members of the Assembly for the purpose of considering the exercise of those functions ; and

(*b*) for the appointment by the presiding officer of the Assembly of the members of each such committee and of a chairman and a deputy chairman (or two deputy chairmen) of each such committee from among its members.

(2) The appointments made pursuant to subsection (1)(*b*) above shall be such as to secure, so far as practicable, that the balance of parties in the Assembly is reflected—

(*a*) in the membership of each committee exclusive of the chairman and deputy chairman or chairmen ;

(*b*) in the chairmen taken as a whole ; and

(*c*) in the deputy chairmen taken as a whole.

(3) Special provision may be made by Order in Council under section 26(2) of the Constitution Act (salaries etc. of members of the Assembly) in respect of the members who are appointed as chairmen or deputy chairmen of committees established under this section, and different provision may be made as respects chairmen and deputy chairmen respectively.

(4) The foregoing provisions are without prejudice to the establishment by the Assembly of other committees to assist it in the discharge of its functions.

Dissolution of Assembly and revocation of Orders.

5.—(1) If it appears to Her Majesty after taking into account any relevant proceedings in the Assembly—

(*a*) that no proposals are likely to be submitted under section 1 above that could lead to the making of an Order under section 2 above or, if any such Order is or has been revoked, to the making of a further Order under that section ; and

(*b*) that it is in the public interest that the Assembly should be dissolved,

Her Majesty may by Order in Council direct that the date of dissolution for the Assembly, instead of being determined in accordance with section 27 of the Constitution Act, shall be such earlier date as may be specified in the Order.

(2) Subsections (7), (8) and (9) of the said section 27 (ancillary provisions in case of dissolution) shall have effect in relation to any dissolution and any Order under subsection (1) above as they have effect in relation to any dissolution and any Order under subsection (5) of that section.

(3) If at any time when an Order is in force under section 2 above it appears to Her Majesty, after taking into account any relevant proceedings in the Assembly, that the continued operation of the Order does not command widespread

acceptance throughout the community Her Majesty may by Order in Council revoke that Order or, if it was made under subsection (1)(*b*) of that section and applies to two or more Northern Ireland departments, revoke it so far as it applies to any of them.

(4) No recommendation shall be made to Her Majesty to make an Order under subsection (3) above unless a draft of the Order has been approved by a resolution of each House of Parliament.

(5) An Order under subsection (3) above may contain such transitional provisions as appear to Her Majesty to be required in consequence of the Order.

6. The Constitution Act and the Northern Ireland Assembly Act 1973 shall be amended in accordance with Schedule 2 to this Act.

Amendments of Constitution and Assembly Acts.

1973 c. 17.

7.—(1) This Act may be cited as the Northern Ireland Act 1982.

(2) In this Act " the Constitution Act " means the Northern Ireland Constitution Act 1973 and any expression which is also used in that Act has the same meaning as in that Act.

Short title, interpretation and repeals.

1973 c. 36.

(3) The enactments mentioned in Schedule 3 to this Act (which include spent provisions) are hereby repealed to the extent specified in the third column of that Schedule.

SCHEDULES

SCHEDULE 1

SUSPENSION OF DIRECT RULE

PART I

GENERAL SUSPENSION

1. Where an Order is made under section 2(1)(*a*) of this Act—

    (*a*) the interim period referred to in subsection (3) of section 1 of the Northern Ireland Act 1974 shall expire on the coming into force of the Order ; but

    (*b*) if the Order is revoked that period shall run again for the period of one year beginning with the date of revocation and may be continued thereafter as provided by subsection (4) of that section.

2. Where an Order under paragraph (*a*) of subsection (1) of section 2 of this Act comes into force at a time when one or more Orders are in force under paragraph (*b*) of that subsection the Order or Orders under paragraph (*b*) shall thereupon cease to have effect.

PART II

PARTIAL SUSPENSION

Preliminary

3.—(1) While an Order is in force under section 2(1)(*b*) of this Act the interim period referred to in subsection (3) of section 1 of the Northern Ireland Act 1974 shall continue without the need for any order under subsection (4) of that section ; and if an Order under section 2(1)(*b*) of this Act is revoked (and no other Order under that provision is in force) that period shall further continue as aforesaid for the period of one year beginning with the date of revocation.

(2) In this Part of this Schedule—

    " the relevant order " means the Order under section 2(1)(*b*) of this Act ;

    " the specified matters " and " the specified department " mean the transferred matters and the Northern Ireland department (or each Northern Ireland department) in relation to which the relevant order is in force ;

    " Schedule 1 " means Schedule 1 to the Northern Ireland Act 1974.

Legislative functions

4.—(1) While the relevant order is in force—

    (*a*) paragraph 1(1)(*a*) of Schedule 1 shall not preclude the Assembly from passing Measures ; but (*b*) transferred matters other than the specified matters shall be treated for the purposes of sections 5 and 6 of the Constitution Act as if they were reserved matters.

(2) It is hereby declared for the avoidance of doubt that the Assembly may, as part of its power to legislate for the specified matters, pass Measures appropriating moneys for the services administered by the specified department or charging sums on, or providing for the payment of sums into, the Consolidated Fund of Northern Ireland in respect of the specified matters.

Executive functions

5.—(1) Notwithstanding paragraph 2(1)(*a*) of Schedule 1 the Secretary of State may under section 8(1) of the Constitution Act appoint—

(*a*) a person to be head of the specified department while the relevant order is in force ; and

(*b*) a person to assist the person appointed as mentioned in paragraph (*a*) above.

(2) Subsections (2), (5) and (6) of section 8 of the Constitution Act (appointments to Northern Ireland Executive and appointment of persons who are not members of the Assembly etc.) shall not apply to any appointment made by virtue of sub-paragraph (1) above.

(3) While the relevant order is in force paragraph 2(1)(*b*) and (2) of Schedule 1 shall not apply to the specified department.

Subordinate instruments, etc.

6.—(1) While the relevant order is in force paragraph 3(1) to (6) of Schedule 1 shall not apply in relation to the specified matters.

(2) For the purposes of this paragraph an instrument shall not be treated as not relating to the specified matters by reason only that it requires the consent or concurrence of a Northern Ireland department other than the specified department or that it contains provisions creating offences or imposing penalties.

Parliamentary Commissioner and Commissioner for Complaints

7.—(1) Paragraph 4(1) of Schedule 1 shall not apply to any report which relates only to matters that are the responsibility of the specified department at the time when the report is made.

(2) Where, apart from this sub-paragraph, a report to which the said paragraph 4(1) applies would relate both—

(*a*) to such matters as are mentioned in sub-paragraph (1) above ; and

(*b*) to other matters,

the report shall be made in separate parts relating to those matters respectively and the said paragraph 4(1) shall apply only to the part dealing with the matters referred to in paragraph (*b*) above.

Accounts

8.—(1) Paragraph 5(1) of Schedule 1 shall not apply to any accounts or reports required by any provision of the Exchequer
and Audit Act (Northern Ireland) 1921 (other than section 10) which relate to—

(*a*) the specified department ; and

(*b*) a period for which the relevant order is in force ;

and where any such accounts or reports relate to a financial year of which only part falls within the period mentioned in paragraph (*b*) above the accounts or reports shall be prepared separately for that part and for the remainder of the financial year in question.

(2) Notwithstanding paragraph 5(3) of Schedule 1 the functions of any such committee as is there mentioned shall extend to the application of moneys by the specified department during the period for which the relevant order is in force.

SCHEDULE 2

AMENDMENTS OF CONSTITUTION AND ASSEMBLY ACTS

Appointment of heads of Northern Ireland departments and members of the Northern Ireland Executive

1. In section 8 of the Constitution Act for subsections (1) to (7) there shall be substituted—

" (1) The Secretary of State may on behalf of Her Majesty appoint—

(*a*) persons to be heads of the Northern Ireland departments ; and

(*b*) persons to discharge such other functions as he may determine.

(2) The Secretary of State may likewise appoint all or any of the persons appointed under subsection (1) above to be members of the Northern Ireland Executive and, if he thinks fit, one of those persons to preside over the Executive as chief executive member.

(3) The total number of persons at any time holding appointments under this section shall not exceed thirteen but the Secretary of State may by an order made by statutory instrument increase or further increase that number and any such order shall be subject to annulment in pursuance of a resolution of either House of Parliament.

(4) Subject to subsections (5) and (6) below, appointments under this section—

(*a*) shall be from among persons who are members of the Assembly ; and (*b*) shall be such as will in the opinion of the Secretary of State command widespread acceptance throughout the community.

(5) Without prejudice to subsection (6) below, two of the persons at any time holding appointments under this section may be persons who were not appointed from among members of the Assembly but not more than one of them shall be the head of a Northern Ireland department.

(6) If at any time it appears to the Secretary of State that it is not possible to make an appointment which complies with the requirements of subsection (4) above he may make an appointment which does not comply with those requirements but any person so appointed shall not hold office for more than six months.

(7) Before making any appointment under this section (otherwise than by virtue of subsection (6) above) the Secretary of State shall so far as practicable consult with the parties represented in the Assembly and take into account any proposals submitted to him under section 1 of the Northern Ireland Act 1982."

Abolition of statutory consultative committees

2. In the Constitution Act—

(*a*) section 7(4) (which requires the head of a Northern Ireland department to consult with a consultative committee of the Assembly established in relation to that department); and

(*b*) section 25(4) to (7) (which requires the standing orders of the Assembly to provide for the establishment of such consultative committees),

shall cease to have effect.

Privileges and remuneration of the Assembly

3.—(1) Section 26 of the Constitution Act shall be amended as follows.

(2) For subsection (1) there shall be substituted—

" (1) Subject to subsection (1A) below and to any provision made by Measure, the powers, privileges and immunities of the Assembly and of its members and committees shall be the same as those for the time being held and enjoyed by the House of Commons and its members and committees.

(1A) Neither the Assembly nor its committees shall have power—

(*a*) to require any person to give evidence, or to produce any papers, relating to any matter other than one in respect of which the Assembly has power to pass a Measure not requiring the consent of the Secretary of State ; or

SCH. 2

    (*b*) to require any person to give evidence, or to produce any papers, relating to any matter which is or has been within his responsibility as a Minister of the government of the United Kingdom or as an officer of a department under the control of any such Minister."

(3) After subsection (2) there shall be inserted—

    " (2A) An Order in Council under subsection (2) above increasing the salaries or allowances payable to members of the Assembly may be made with retrospective effect."

    4. The matters referred to in section 26(1A)(*b*) of the Constitution Act include any matter which is or has been within the responsibility of the Secretary of State by virtue of paragraph 2 of Schedule 1 to the Northern Ireland Act 1974 or within the responsibility of an officer of a Northern Ireland department under the control of the Secretary of State by virtue of that paragraph.

1974 c. 28.

Dissolution and prorogation of Assembly

    5.—(1) Section 27 of the Constitution Act shall be amended as follows.

    (2) For subsections (2) to (4) there shall be substituted—

    " (2) Any Assembly elected following the dissolution of its predecessor by Order in Council shall by virtue of this subsection be dissolved on the fourth anniversary of the day appointed for the election of the members of that Assembly ; and any Assembly elected otherwise than as aforesaid shall by virtue of this subsection be dissolved on the fourth anniversary of the dissolution of its predecessor.

    (3) If, apart from this subsection, the date of dissolution under subsection (2) above would fall on a Saturday, Sunday, public holiday or bank holiday it shall fall on the next subsequent day which is not a Saturday, Sunday, public holiday or bank holiday.

1971 c. 80.

    In this subsection " bank holiday " means a day which by virtue of the Banking and Financial Dealings Act 1971 is a bank holiday in Northern Ireland.

    (4) The Secretary of State may by order direct that any date of dissolution under subsection (2) above shall, instead of being determined in accordance with that subsection and subsection (3) above, be a date specified in the order, being a date falling not more than two months before or after the date so determined."

    (3) For subsection (6) there shall be substituted—

    " (6) Her Majesty may by Order in Council prorogue or further prorogue the Assembly."

Power to legislate by Order in Council for reserved and other matters

6.—(1) Section 38 of the Constitution Act shall be amended as follows.

(2) In subsection (1) for paragraph (*b*) there shall be substituted—

" (*b*) any reserved matter."

(3) In subsection (2) the words " passed before this Act " shall be omitted.

(4) For subsection (5) there shall be substituted—

" (5) Subject to subsection (6) below, no recommendation shall be made to Her Majesty to make an Order in Council under this section unless a draft of the Order has been approved by resolution of each House of Parliament.

(6) Subsection (5) above does not apply to an Order in Council which—

(*a*) is made under subsection (1)(*b*) above ; and

(*b*) declares that it has been made to appear to Her Majesty that by reason of urgency the Order requires to be made without a draft having been approved as mentioned in subsection (5) above ;

but any such Order shall be laid before Parliament after being made and, if at the end of the period of forty days after the date on which it is made the Order has not been approved by resolution of each House, shall then cease to have effect (but without prejudice to anything previously done under the Order or to the making of a new Order).

In reckoning the period mentioned in this subsection no account shall be taken of any time during which Parliament is dissolved or prorogued or during which both Houses are adjourned for more than four days.

(7) References to Measures in any enactment or instrument shall, so far as the context permits, be deemed to include references to Orders in Council under paragraph (*b*) of subsection (1) above ; and Orders in Council under that paragraph may be omitted from any annual edition of statutory instruments required to be prepared under regulations made by virtue of section 8 of the Statutory Instruments Act 1946."

1946 c. 36.

7.—(1) No recommendation shall be made to Her Majesty to make an Order in Council under section 38(1)(*b*) of the Constitution Act during the interim period referred to in section 1(3) of the Northern Ireland Act 1974.

1974 c. 28.

(2) Orders in Council under section 38(1)(*b*) of the Constitution Act shall not be regarded as subordinate legislation for the purposes of section 23(1) or (2) of the Interpretation Act 1978 but shall be Northern Ireland legislation for the purposes of section 24 of that Act.

1978 c. 30.

Power to make consequential amendments

8. In section 39(1) of the Constitution Act the reference to that Act and an Order under section 3 of that Act shall include a reference to this Act and any Order under section 2 or 5(3) of this Act.

Excepted matters

9. In paragraph 15 of Schedule 2 to the Constitution Act—

> (*a*) after the words "the Northern Ireland Assembly Act 1973 or this Act" there shall be inserted the words "or by the Northern Ireland Act 1974 or the Northern Ireland Act 1982";

1974 c. 28.

> (*b*) after the words "an Order in Council under section 6(4) or (5), 38 or 39 of this Act" there shall be inserted the words "or under paragraph 1 of Schedule 1 to the said Act of 1974".

Costs of Assembly elections

1973 c. 17.

10. Section 4(2) of the Northern Ireland Assembly Act 1973 shall apply also to any subsequent election of members of the Assembly, including bye-elections.

Alteration of number of members to be returned by constituencies

11. In the Schedule to the Northern Ireland Assembly Act 1973 for the number of members specified in relation to each of the constituencies mentioned in the first column of the following Table there shall be substituted the number of members specified in relation to that constituency in the second column of that Table.

TABLE

Constituency	Substituted number of members to be returned
East Belfast	6
North Belfast	5
South Belfast	5
West Belfast	4
North Antrim	8
South Antrim	10
Armagh	7
North Down	8
South Down	7
Fermanagh and South Tyrone ...	5
Londonderry	7
Mid Ulster	6

SCHEDULE 3

Section 7(3).

REPEALS

Chapter	Short Title	Extent of Repeal
1973 c. 17.	The Northern Ireland Assembly Act 1973.	Section 1(3), (5) and (6). Section 2(1) and (2). Section 4(1).
1973 c. 36.	The Northern Ireland Constitution Act 1973.	Section 7(4). Section 13(4). Section 25(4) to (7). Section 26(8) and (9). In section 27, subsection (1) and in subsection (7) the words " (1)(*b*) or ". In section 38(2) the words " passed before this Act ".
1973 c. 69.	The Northern Ireland Constitution (Amendment) Act 1973.	In section 1, subsection (1) and in subsection (2) the words following the semi-colon.
1974 c. 28.	The Northern Ireland Act 1974.	Section 1(2). Section 2. Schedule 2.
1975 c. 25.	The Northern Ireland Assembly Disqualification Act 1975.	In Schedule 2, paragraph 3.

Finance Act 1982

1982 CHAPTER 39

An Act to grant certain duties, to alter other duties, and to amend the law relating to the National Debt and the Public Revenue, and to make further provision in connection with Finance.   [30th July, 1982]

Most Gracious Sovereign,

WE, Your Majesty's most dutiful and loyal subjects, the Commons of the United Kingdom in Parliament assembled, towards raising the necessary supplies to defray Your Majesty's public expenses, and making an addition to the public revenue, have freely and voluntarily resolved to give and grant unto Your Majesty the several duties hereinafter mentioned; and do therefore most humbly beseech Your Majesty that it may be enacted, and be it enacted by the Queen's most Excellent Majesty, by and with the advice and consent of the Lords Spiritual and Temporal, and Commons, in this present Parliament assembled, and by the authority of the same, as follows:—

PART I

CUSTOMS AND EXCISE

1.—(1) In section 5 of the Alcoholic Liquor Duties Act 1979 (excise duty on spirits) for the words from "at the rates" to the end of the section there shall be substituted the words "at the rate of £14·47 per litre of alcohol in the spirits".

Duties on spirits, beer, wine, made-wine and cider.
1979 c. 4.

(2) In section 36 of that Act (excise duty on beer) for " £18·00 " and " £0·60 " there shall be substituted " £20·40 " and " £0·68 " respectively.

(3) For the provisions of Schedule 1 to that Act (rates of excise duty on wine) there shall be substituted the provisions of Schedule 1 to this Act.

(4) For the provisions of Schedule 2 to that Act (rates of excise duty on made-wine) there shall be substituted the provisions of Schedule 2 to this Act.

(5) In section 62(1) of that Act (excise duty on cider) for " £7·20 " there shall be substituted " £8·16 ".

(6) This section shall be deemed to have come into force on 10th March 1982.

Tobacco products.
1979 c. 7.

2.—(1) For the Table in Schedule 1 to the Tobacco Products Duty Act 1979 there shall be substituted—

" Table

1. Cigarettes	An amount equal to 21 per cent. of the retail price plus £20·68 per thousand cigarettes.
2. Cigars	£39·00 per kilogram.
3. Hand-rolling tobacco ...	£33·65 per kilogram.
4. Other smoking tobacco and chewing tobacco	£24·95 per kilogram ".

(2) This section shall be deemed to have come into force on 12th March 1982.

Hydrocarbon oil, etc.
1979 c. 5.

3.—(1) In subsection (1) of section 6 of the Hydrocarbon Oil Duties Act 1979 (rates of duty on hydrocarbon oil) for the words " £0·1382 a litre " (light oil) there shall be substituted the words " £0·1554 a litre " and for the words " £0·1191 a litre " (heavy oil) there shall be substituted the words " £0·1325 a litre ".

(2) In Schedule 1 to that Act (vehicles which are not road vehicles within the meaning of that Act) in sub-paragraph (*a*) of paragraph 2 (exclusions by reference to exemptions from duty

1971 c. 10.

under the Vehicles (Excise) Act 1971) for the word " or " there shall be substituted the words " section 4(1)(i) of that Act (gritting vehicles) " and at the end of that sub-paragraph there shall be added the words " or section 7(3) of that Act (snow ploughs etc.) ".

(3) Subsection (1) above shall be deemed to have come into force at 6 o'clock in the evening of 9th March 1982.

4.—(1) The Hydrocarbon Oil Duties Act 1979 shall have effect subject to the following modifications.

(2) In section 6 (rates of duty on hydrocarbon oils)—

   (*a*) in subsection (1) for the words " subsection (2) " there shall be substituted the words " subsections (2) and (3) " ; and

   (*b*) at the end of the section there shall be inserted the following subsections—

      " (3) In the case of aviation gasoline, the duty of excise charged under subsection (1) above shall be at one half of the rate specified in that subsection in relation to light oil.

      (4) In this Act " aviation gasoline " means light oil which—

        (*a*) is specially produced as fuel for aircraft ; and

        (*b*) is not normally used in road vehicles ; and

        (*c*) is delivered for use solely as fuel for aircraft."

(3) In section 24 (power to control use of duty-free oil etc.) in subsection (1) after the words " for the purposes of " there shall be inserted the words " section 6(3) ".

(4) In subsection (1) of section 27 (interpretation) after the words " In this Act " there shall be inserted the words—

      " " aviation gasoline " has the meaning given by section 6(4) above".

(5) In Part I of Schedule 3 (regulations under section 21 relating to hydrocarbon oil) after paragraph 10 there shall be inserted the following paragraphs—

      " 10A. Amending the definition of " aviation gasoline " in subsection (4) of section 6 of this Act.

      10B. Conferring power to require information relating to the supply or use of aviation gasoline to be given by producers, dealers and users.

      10C. Requiring producers and users of and dealers in aviation gasoline to keep and produce records relating to aviation gasoline."

(6) In Schedule 4 (regulations under section 24) after paragraph 18 there shall be inserted the following paragraphs—

      " 18A. Prohibiting the use of aviation gasoline otherwise than as a fuel for aircraft.

      18B. Prohibiting the taking of aviation gasoline into fuel tanks for engines other than aircraft engines."

(7) Subsections (1) and (2) above shall be deemed to have come into force at 6 o'clock in the evening of 9th March 1982.

Vehicles
excise duty:
Great Britain.
1971 c. 10.

5.—(1) The Vehicles (Excise) Act 1971 shall be amended as follows.

(2) For the provisions of Part II of Schedules 1 to 5 (annual rates of duty) there shall be substituted the provisions set out in Schedule 3 to this Act.

(3) In subsection (5) of section 16 (rates of duty for trade licences), including that subsection as set out in paragraph 12 of Part I of Schedule 7, for " £35 " and " £7 " there shall be substituted respectively " £40 " and " £8 ".

(4) For Schedule 4 (annual rates of duty on goods vehicles) there shall be substituted the provisions of Part A of Schedule 5 to this Act (which shall, accordingly, have effect as Schedule 4 to the Act of 1971).

(5) In section 2(1) (duration of licences), for paragraph (c) there shall be substituted the following paragraph—

1972 c. 20.

" (c) in the case of any vehicle which is authorised to be used on roads by virtue of an order made under section 42(1) of the Road Traffic Act 1972 and—

(i) in respect of which duty is chargeable by reference to an annual rate applicable in accordance with the provisions of Schedule 3 to this Act ; or

(ii) which is a goods vehicle the unladen weight of which exceeds eleven tons ;

for any period of seven consecutive days (such a licence being referred to in this Act as a ' seven day licence ') ; "

(6) In section 38(4) (meaning of " unladen weight "), after the word " Act " there shall be inserted the words ", except in Schedule 4," ; and in Schedule 6 (provisions as to the computation of unladen weights) paragraphs 3 and 5 shall cease to have effect and in paragraph 4 for the words " Schedules 3 and 4 " there shall be substituted the words " Schedule 3 ".

(7) Subsections (2) and (3) above apply in relation to licences taken out after 9th March 1982 and subsections (4) to (6) above apply in relation to licences first having effect after 30th September 1982.

Vehicles
excise duty:
Northern
Ireland.
1972 c. 10
(N.I.)

6.—(1) The Vehicles (Excise) Act (Northern Ireland) 1972 shall be amended as follows.

(2) For the provisions of Part II of Schedules 1 to 5 (annual rates of duty) there shall be substituted the provisions set out in Schedule 4 to this Act.

(3) In subsection (6) of section 16 (rates of duty for trade
licences), including that subsection as set out in paragraph 12 of
Part I of Schedule 9, for " £35 " and " £7 " there shall be substituted respectively "£40 " and " £8 ".

(4) For Schedule 4 (annual rates of duty on goods vehicles)
there shall be substituted the provisions of Part A of Schedule
5 to this Act, modified in accordance with Part B of that
Schedule ; and Part A, as so modified, shall accordingly have
effect as Schedule 4 to the Act of 1972.

(5) In section 2—

    (*a*) in subsection (1) (duration of licences), for paragraph (*c*)
    there shall be substituted the following paragraphs—

        " (*c*) in the case of a vehicle which is chargeable
        with duty by reference to the annual rate applicable
        in accordance with Schedule 2, being a hackney car
        riage having a seating capacity for more than twenty
        persons and used only during such holiday seasons
        as may be prescribed, for any period of seven con
        secutive days ;

        (*d*) in the case of any vehicle which is authorised
        to be used on roads by virtue of an Order under
        Article 29(3) of the Road Traffic (Northern Ireland) S.I. 1981/154
        Order 1981 and—   (N.I.).

            (i) in respect of which duty is chargeable by
            reference to an annual rate applicable in
            accordance with the provisions of Schedule
            3 to this Act ; or

            (ii) which is a goods vehicle the unladen weight
            of which exceeds eleven tons ;

        for any period of seven consecutive days." ;

    (*b*) after subsection (1) there shall be inserted the following
    subsection—

        " (1A) In this Act a licence taken out under para
        graph (*c*) or (*d*) of subsection (1) is referred to as a
        ' seven day licence '."

(6) In section 35(1) (interpretation), in the definition of
" seven day licence " for the words " section 2(1)(*c*) " there shall
be substituted the words " section 2(1A) ".

(7) In section 35(4) (meaning of " unladen weight "), after the
word " Act " there shall be inserted the words ", except in
Schedule 4," ; and in Schedule 7 (provisions as to the computation of unladen weights) paragraphs 3 and 5 shall cease to have
effect and in paragraph 4 for the words " Schedules 3 and 4 "
there shall be substituted the words " Schedule 3 ".

(8) Subsections (2) and (3) above apply in relation to licences taken out after 9th March 1982 and subsections (4) to (7) above apply in relation to licences first having effect after 30th September 1982.

Additional
liability in
relation to
alteration of
vehicle or
its use.
1971 c. 10.

7.—(1) In the Vehicles (Excise) Act 1971 the following section shall be inserted after section 18—

"Additional
liability in
relation to
alteration of
vehicle or
its use.

18A.—(1) Where a person convicted of an offence under section 18 of this Act is the person by whom the vehicle in respect of which the offence was committed was kept at the time it was committed, the court shall, in addition to any penalty which it may impose under that section, order him to pay an amount (the " additional duty ") calculated in accordance with this section.

(2) The additional duty shall, subject to subsections (7) and (8) below, be an amount equal to one three-hundred-and-sixty-fifth of the appropriate annual rate of duty for each day in the relevant period.

(3) The following Cases are referred to in subsections (5) and (6) below—

CASE A

Where—

(*a*) at the time of the offence the vehicle in question had a plated weight (the " higher plated weight ") which exceeds the plated weight (the " previous plated weight ") which it had when the current licence was taken out ; and

(*b*) the current licence was taken out at the rate of duty applicable to the previous plated weight.

CASE B

Where—

(*a*) the vehicle in question is a tractor unit (within the meaning of paragraph 15 of Schedule 4 to this Act) ;

(*b*) the current licence was taken out at a rate of duty applicable to the use of the vehicle only with semi-trailers having not less than two axles or, as the case may be, only with semi-trailers having not less than three axles ; and

(*c*) the offence consisted in using the vehicle with a semi-trailer with a smaller number of

axles than that mentioned in paragraph (*b*)
above, in circumstances in which it was not
treated by virtue of paragraph 14(2) of
Schedule 4 to this Act as being licensed in
accordance with the requirements of this
Act.

CASE C

Where—

> (*a*) the current licence was taken out at the rate
> of duty applicable, by virtue of paragraph
> 8 of Schedule 4 to this Act, to a weight
> lower than the plated weight of the vehicle
> in question ; and
>
> (*b*) the offence consisted in using the vehicle in
> contravention of a condition imposed by
> virtue of paragraph 8(3) of Schedule 4.

CASE D

Where the current licence was taken out at a rate
of duty lower than that applicable to the vehicle in
question by reference to its plated weight and the
circumstances of the case do not bring it within Case
A, B or C.

CASE E

Where the current licence was taken out at a rate
of duty lower than that at which duty was chargeable
in respect of that condition or manner of use of the
vehicle which constituted the offence and the circumstances of the case do not bring it within Case A,
B, C or D.

(4) In this section "current licence" means the
licence in relation to which the offence was committed.

(5) In this section "appropriate annual rate of
duty" means the difference between the rate of duty
at which the current licence was taken out and—

> (*a*) in Case A, the rate which would have been
> applicable had the current licence been
> taken out by reference to the higher plated
> weight ;
>
> (*b*) in Case B, the rate which would have been
> applicable had the current licence been
> taken out by reference to that use of the
> vehicle which constituted the offence ;

(c) in Case C, the rate which would have been applicable had the current licence been taken out by reference to the plated weight of the vehicle ;

(d) in Case D, the rate which would have been applicable had the current licence been taken out by reference to the plated weight of the vehicle ; and

(e) in Case E, the rate which would have been applicable had the current licence been taken out by reference to that condition or use of the vehicle which constituted the offence.

(6) In this section ' relevant period ' means the period ending with the day on which the offence was committed and beginning—

(a) in relation to Case A, with the day on which the vehicle in question was plated with the higher plated weight ; and

(b) in relation to each of the other Cases, with the day on which the current licence first took effect.

(7) Where the person convicted proves—

(a) that throughout any day comprised in the relevant period he was not the keeper of the vehicle in question ;

(b) that throughout any such day the vehicle in question was neither used nor kept by him on a public road and that he was exempt by virtue of section 10(2)(b) or (c) of this Act from liability under subsection (1) of that section in respect of that day ;

(c) that he had, before his conviction, paid the higher of the two rates of duty referred to in the relevant paragraph of subsection (5) above in respect of the vehicle for any such day, whether or not on a licence ; or

(d) that throughout any such day the vehicle was not chargeable with duty ;

the additional duty shall be calculated as if that day were not comprised in the relevant period.

(8) Where a person is convicted of more than one contravention of section 18 of this Act in respect of

the same vehicle (whether or not in the same proceedings) the court shall, in calculating the additional duty payable in respect of any one of those offences, reduce the amount calculated in accordance with the preceding provisions of this section in relation to a particular period by the amount of the additional duty ordered to be paid under this section in relation to that period in respect of the other offence or, as the case may be, offences.

(9) Except so far as it is proved to have fallen within some other description for the whole of any day comprised in the relevant period, the vehicle in question shall be taken for the purposes of this section to have belonged throughout the relevant period to that description of vehicle to which it belonged for the purposes of duty at the date of the offence.

(10) Where, on a person's conviction of an offence under section 18 of this Act, an order is made under Part I of the Powers of Criminal Courts Act 1973 placing him on probation or discharging him absolutely or conditionally, this section shall apply as if the conviction were deemed to be a conviction for all purposes.

1973 c. 62.

(11) This section shall have effect subject to the provisions (applying with the necessary modifications) of any enactment relating to the imposition of fines by magistrates' courts, other than one conferring a discretion as to their amount; and any sum payable by virtue of an order under this section shall be treated as a fine, and the order as a conviction, for the purposes of Part III of the Magistrates' Courts Act 1980 (including any enactment having effect as if contained in that Part) and of any other enactment relating to the recovery or application of sums ordered to be paid by magistrates' courts.

1980 c. 43.

(12) In its application to Scotland, this section shall have effect as if for subsections (10) and (11) there were substituted the following subsections—

' (10) Where a person is convicted on indictment of, or is charged before a court of summary jurisdiction with, an offence under section 18 of this Act, and an order is made under section 182 or 383 of the Criminal Procedure (Scotland) Act 1975 discharging him absolutely, or under section 183 or 384 of that Act placing him

1975 c. 21.

on probation, this section shall apply as if the making of the order were a conviction for all purposes.

(11) Any sum payable by virtue of an order under this section shall be treated as a fine imposed by a court of summary jurisdiction.'

(13) This section is subject to Schedule 7 to this Act.".

1972 c. 10
(N.I.).
(2) In the Vehicles (Excise) Act (Northern Ireland) 1972, after section 18 there shall be inserted the section set out in subsection (1) above, modified as follows—

(*a*) in subsection (1) for the word ' penalty ' there shall be substituted the word ' fine ' ;

(*b*) for any reference in subsections (3) and (5) to a plated weight there shall be substituted a reference to a relevant maximum weight or, as the case may be, a relevant maximum train weight ;

(*c*) in subsection (6)—

(i) after the words ' ending with ' there shall be inserted the words ' and including ' ;

(ii) in paragraph (*a*) after the word ' with ' (where it first occurs) there shall be inserted the words ' and including ' and for the words ' plated with the higher plated weight ' there shall be substituted the words ' rated at the higher relevant maximum weight or, as the case may be, the higher relevant maximum train weight ' ; and

(iii) in paragraph (*b*) after the word ' with ' there shall be inserted the words ' and including ' ;

1973 c. 62.
1950 c. 7
(N.I.).
(*d*) in subsection (10) for the reference to Part I of the Powers of Criminal Courts Act 1973 there shall be substituted a reference to the Probation Act (Northern Ireland) 1950 ;

(*e*) for subsection (11) there shall be substituted the following subsection—

1954 c. 9
(N.I.).
' (11) A sum payable by virtue of any order made under this section by a court shall be recoverable as a sum adjudged to be paid by a conviction and treated for all purposes as a fine within the meaning of section 20 of the Administration of Justice Act (Northern Ireland) 1954.' ;

(*f*) for subsection (12) there shall be substituted the following subsection—

' (12) In this section " relevant maximum weight " and " relevant maximum train weight " have the same meaning as in Schedule 4.' ; and

(*g*) in subsection (13) for the reference to Schedule 7 there shall be substituted a reference to Schedule 9.

(3) In Schedule 7 to the Act of 1971 (transitional provisions), the following paragraph shall be inserted after paragraph 17—

" 17A. Section 18A shall have effect as if—

(*a*) in subsection (2) for the words " one three-hundred-and-sixty-fifth " there were substituted the words " one twelfth " and for the words " day in the relevant period " there were substituted the words " calendar month or part of a calendar month in the relevant period " ;

(*b*) in subsection (7)—

(i) in paragraph (*a*), for the word " day " there were substituted the words ' month or part of a month ' ;

(ii) in paragraph (*b*), for the word " day " there were substituted the words " month or part " and the words from " and that he was exempt " onwards were omitted ;

(iii) in paragraphs (*c*) and (*d*) and in the words following paragraph (*d*), for the word " day " there were in each case substituted the words " month or part " ;

(*c*) in subsection (9), for the words " any day comprised in the relevant period " there were substituted the words " any month or part of a month comprised in the relevant period.".

(4) In Schedule 9 to the Act of 1972 (transitional provisions in Northern Ireland), the paragraph set out in subsection (3) above shall be inserted after paragraph 17 ".

8.—(1) Schedule 6 to this Act shall have effect for the purposes of—

Betting and gaming duties.

(*a*) increasing pool betting duty, other than in the case of pool competitions bets ;

(*b*) increasing gaming licence duty ;

(c) amending the law relating to bingo duty ; and

(d) increasing, and otherwise amending the law relating to, gaming machine licence duty.

(2) Part II of Schedule 6 shall have effect in relation to bets made at any time by reference to an event taking place after 31st March 1982, Part III of that Schedule shall have effect in relation to gaming licences for any period beginning after 31st March 1982, Part IV of that Schedule shall have effect in relation to bingo played after 26th September 1982 and Part V of that Schedule shall have effect in relation to gaming machine licences for any period beginning after 30th September 1982.

Immature spirits for home use and loss allowance for imported beer.

1979 c. 4.

9.—(1) The Treasury may by order—

(a) substitute for the period of three years or that of two years referred to in subsection (1) of section 31 of the Alcoholic Liquor Duties Act 1979 (restriction on delivery of immature spirits for home use) or for both such periods such shorter period or periods as they think fit ;

(b) amend the said section 31 so as to exempt rum from any restriction imposed by that subsection ; and

(c) repeal the said section 31.

(2) An order under subsection (1) above shall be made by statutory instrument which shall be laid before the Commons House of Parliament and shall cease to have effect at the end of the period of twenty-eight days beginning with the day on which it was made unless it is approved by resolution of the Commons House of Parliament before the end of that period (but without prejudice to anything previously done in pursuance of the order or to the making of a new order).

In reckoning that period no account shall be taken of any time during which Parliament is dissolved or prorogued or during which the Commons House of Parliament is adjourned for more than four days.

(3) At the end of section 40 of the Alcoholic Liquor Duties Act 1979 (charge of duty on imported beer) there shall be added the following subsection:—

" (3) The duty chargeable on beer to which subsection (1) above applies and which is imported or removed into the United Kingdom in containers having a capacity of more than 10 litres shall be charged on a quantity which is 2 per cent. less than the quantity so imported or removed."

(4) Subsection (3) above has effect in relation to beer imported or removed into the United Kingdom on or after 1st October 1982.

10.—(1) In subsection (2) of section 1 of the Excise Duties (Surcharges or Rebates) Act 1979 (regulator powers) for the words from " groups of duties " to " every right " there shall be substituted the words " duties to which this section applies, provide for an adjustment—

PART I
Regulator powers.
1979 c. 8.

(*a*) of any liability to such a duty ; and

(*b*) of any right ".

(2) For subsections (3) and (4) of section 2 of that Act there shall be substituted the following subsection—

" (3) An order—

(*a*) may specify different percentages for different cases ; but

(*b*) may not provide for both an addition to any amount payable and a deduction from any other amount payable.".

(3) In subsection (7) of that section (procedure for certain orders) for the words from " with respect to " to the end of paragraph (*b*) there shall be substituted the words " —

(*a*) specifies a percentage by way of addition to any amount payable or increases a percentage so specified ; or

(*b*) withdraws or reduces a percentage specified by way of deduction from any amount payable,".

11.—(1) Notwithstanding that—

Power of Commissioners with respect to agricultural levies etc.
1972 c. 68.

(*a*) agricultural levies, within the meaning of section 6 of the European Communities Act 1972, which are charged on goods exported from the United Kingdom are, in accordance with subsection (4) of that section, paid to and recoverable by the Intervention Board for Agricultural Produce, and

(*b*) payments made by virtue of Community arrangements to which subsection (3) of that section applies are made by that Board,

proceedings for an offence under the Theft Act 1968, the Theft Act 1978, the Theft Act (Northern Ireland) 1969 or the Theft (Northern Ireland) Order 1978 relating to any such levies or payments may be instituted by the Commissioners.

1968 c. 60.
1978 c. 31.
1969 c. 16 (N.I.).
S.I. 1978/1407 (N.I. 23).
1979 c. 2.

(2) At the end of Part V of the Customs and Excise Management Act 1979 (control of exportation) there shall be added the following section:—

" Offences in relation to agricultural levies.

68A.—(1) Without prejudice to section 11(1) of the Finance Act 1982, if any person is, in relation to any goods, in any way knowingly concerned in any fraudulent evasion or attempt at evasion of any agricultural levy chargeable on the export of the goods, he shall be guilty of an offence and may be detained.

(2) Any person guilty of an offence under this section shall be liable, on summary conviction, to a penalty of three times the value of the goods or £200, whichever is the greater.

(3) Any goods in respect of which an offence under this section is committed shall be liable to forfeiture.

(4) In this section "agricultural levy" has the same meaning as in section 6 of the European Communities Act 1972 and the provisions of this section apply notwithstanding that any such levy may be payable to the Intervention Board for Agricultural Produce."

(3) At the end of section 136 of the Customs and Excise Management Act 1979 (offences in connection with claims for drawback etc.) there shall be inserted the following subsection: —

" (6) Without prejudice to section 6(5) of the European Communities Act 1972 (which provides for the application of certain enactments, including this section, if the Commissioners are charged with the performance on behalf of the Intervention Board for Agricultural Produce, of certain duties in relation to the payment of refunds or allowances on goods exported or to be exported from the United Kingdom)—

(a) references in this section to amounts by way of drawback include amounts payable by the Intervention Board for Agricultural Produce by virtue of Community arrangements to which section 6(3) of that Act applies ; and

(b) in relation to such amounts, subsection (3) above shall have effect with the omission of the words from " but in the case " onwards."

12. In subsection (1) of section 8 of the Customs and Excise Management Act 1979 (functions of Commissioners may be exercised by secretaries, assistant secretaries, etc.) for paragraphs (b) and (c) there shall be substituted the following paragraph: —

" (b) any officer or other person acting under the authority of the Commissioners " ;

and at the end of that subsection there shall be added the words " and any statement signed by one or more of the Commissioners certifying that a person specified in the statement was, at a time

or for a purpose so specified, acting under the authority of the   PART I
Commissioners shall be admissible in evidence, and in Scotland
shall be sufficient evidence, of the fact so certified."

PART II

VALUE ADDED TAX AND CAR TAX

13.—(1) In paragraph 1 of Schedule 1 to the Finance Act   Registration.
1972 (liability to be registered)—   1972 c. 41.

(*a*) for " £5,000 " there shall be substituted " £6,000 ", and

(*b*) for " £15,000 ", in each place, there shall be substituted
" £17,000 " ;

and in section 20(1) of that Act (registration of local authorities)
for the words following " one year " there shall be substituted the
words " does not exceed the sum for the time being specified in
paragraph 1(*a*)(ii) of that Schedule, as if that value exceeded
that sum ".

(2) In paragraph 2 of that Schedule (termination of liability to
be registered)—

(*a*) for " £15,000 ", in both places, there shall be substituted
" £17,000 ", and

(*b*) for " £14,000 " there shall be substituted " £16,000 ".

(3) After paragraph 11 of that Schedule there shall be
inserted—

" 11A. The Treasury may by order substitute for any
of the sums for the time being specified in paragraphs 1
and 2 of this Schedule such greater sums as they think
fit.".

(4) Subsection (1) above shall be deemed to have come into
force on 10th March 1982 and subsection (2) on 1st June 1982.

14.—(1) In subsection (5) of section 3 of the Finance Act   Input tax.
1972 (payment of excess credit for input tax against output tax
by Commissioners) after the words " the amount of the excess
shall " there shall be inserted the words " subject to subsection
(6A) below ", and after subsection (6) of that section there shall
be inserted the following subsection—

" (6A) Where at the end of any period an amount is
due under subsection (5) above to a taxable person who
has failed to submit returns or to pay tax for any earlier
period as required by this Part of this Act, the Commissioners may withhold payment of that amount until he has
complied with that requirement."

2 G 2

(2) In subsection (8)(*b*) of that section (power to enable taxable persons to count tax on the supply or importation of goods as their input tax) for the words " supply to him, or paid by him on the importation, of goods " there shall be substituted the words " supply to him of goods or services or paid by him on the importation of goods ".

Supplies
spanning
change of
rate etc.

1972 c. 41.

15.—(1) This section applies where there is a change in the rate of value added tax in force under section 9 of the Finance Act 1972, or in the descriptions of exempt or zero-rated supplies.

(2) Where—

(*a*) a supply affected by the change would, apart from sub-sections (4) to (6A) of section 7 of that Act (time of supply), be treated under subsection (2) or (3) of that section as made wholly or partly at a time when it would not have been affected by the change, or

(*b*) a supply not so affected would apart from subsections (4) to (6A) be treated under subsection (2) or (3) of that section as made wholly or partly at a time when it would have been so affected,

the rate at which tax is chargeable on the supply, or any question whether it is zero-rated or exempt, shall if the person making it so elects be determined without regard to subsections (4) to (6A).

(3) Any power to make regulations under Part I of the Finance Act 1972 with respect to the time when a supply is to be treated as taking place shall include power to provide for this section to apply as if the references in subsection (2) above to section 7(4) to (6A) included references to specified provisions of the regulations.

(4) Regulations under section 30 of the Finance Act 1972 may make provision for the replacement or correction of any tax invoice which—

(*a*) relates to a supply in respect of which an election is made under this section, but

(*b*) was issued before the election was made.

(5) No election may be made under this section in respect of a supply to which paragraph 6 of Schedule 2 to the Finance Act 1972 (sales in satisfaction of debts) or section 19(4) of the Finance (No. 2) Act 1975 (invoice provided by recipient) applies.

1975 c. 45.

Treatment of
partnerships.

16.—(1) In section 22 of the Finance Act 1972 (partnerships) in subsection (1) (registration of partners in the name of the

firm and provisions as to changes of members of the partnership)—

    (*a*) after the words " in determining " there shall be inserted
        the words " for any purpose of this Part of this Act " ;
        and

    (*b*) the words from " or of a change " onwards shall be
        omitted.

(2) After that subsection there shall be inserted the following
subsections : —

    " (1A) Without prejudice to section 36 of the Partnership 1890 c. 39.
Act 1890 (rights of persons dealing with firm against
apparent members of firm) until the date on which a change
in the partnership is notified to the Commissioners, a person
who has ceased to be a member of a partnership shall be
regarded as continuing to be a partner for the purposes
of this Part of this Act and, in particular, for the purpose
of any liability for tax on the supply of goods or services
by the partnership.

    (1B) Where a person ceases to be a member of a part-
nership during a prescribed accounting period (or is treated
as so doing by virtue of subsection (1A) above) any notice,
whether of assessment or otherwise, which is served on the
partnership and relates to, or to any matter arising in, that
period or any earlier period during the whole or part of
which he was a member of the partnership shall be treated
as served also on him.

    (1C) Without prejudice to section 16 of the Partnership
Act 1890 (notice to acting partner to be notice to the firm)
any notice, whether of assessment or otherwise, which is
addressed to a partnership by the name in which it is
registered by virtue of subsection (1) above and is served in
accordance with this Part of this Act shall be treated for
the purposes of this Part of this Act as served on the partnership and, accordingly, where subsection (1B) above
applies, as served also on the former partner."

(3) In subsection (2) of that section for " Subsection (1) "
there shall be substituted " Subsections (1) and (1B) ".

    17.—(1) In section 31 of the Finance Act 1972 (assessment Recovery of
to tax) after subsection (1) there shall be inserted the following over-payment
subsections : —
        of value
        added tax,
    " (1A) In any case where— etc.

    (*a*) an amount has been repaid to any person as being 1972 c. 41.
        a repayment of tax, which ought not to have been
        repaid, or

(*b*) an amount has been paid to any person as being
due to him in accordance with section 3(5) of this
Act, which ought not to have been paid to him,

the Commissioners may assess that amount as being tax
due from him in the prescribed accounting period in which
the amount was repaid or, as the case may be, paid and
notify it to him accordingly.

(1B) Where a person is assessed under subsections (1)
and (1A) above in respect of the same prescribed accounting period the assessments may be combined and notified
to him as one assessment."

(2) In subsections (2), (4) and (6) of that section after the
words " subsection (1) " there shall be inserted the words " or
subsection (1A) ".

1972 c. 41.   (3) In section 40(1)(*b*)(i) of the Finance Act 1972 (appeals
against assessments) after the words " subsection (1) " there shall
be inserted the words " or (1A) ".

(4) The preceding provisions of this section shall not have
effect in relation to any amounts repaid or paid to any person
before the passing of this Act.

Car tax:
reduction for
motor
caravans.   **18.** In subsection (2) of section 52 of the Finance Act 1972
(car tax) after the words " 10 per cent. of " there shall be inserted the words—

" (*a*) in the case of a caravan, three-fifths of its wholesale
value ; and

(*b*) in any other case ".

Car tax:
transfer of
liability on
transfer of
stocks.   **19.** In paragraph 26 of Schedule 7 to the Finance Act 1972
(regulations relating to car tax) after paragraph (*e*) there shall
be inserted the following paragraph—

" (*ee*) for transferring liability for the tax in respect of any
chargeable vehicles to a person to whom the property
in the vehicles is transferred where the circumstances
of the transfer are of a description specified in the
regulations and are such that tax does not become due
on or before the transfer, and for applying to the
transferee, with or without modifications, provisions of
this Schedule applicable to a person who is liable for
tax as a person registered under this Schedule."

PART III

INCOME TAX, CORPORATION TAX AND CAPITAL GAINS TAX

CHAPTER I

GENERAL

20.—(1) Income tax for the year 1982-83 shall be charged at the basic rate of 30 per cent. ; and—

  (*a*) in respect of so much of an individual's total income as exceeds £12,800 at such higher rates as are specified in the Table below ; and

  (*b*) in respect of so much of the investment income included in an individual's total income as exceeds £6,250 at the additional rate of 15 per cent.

Part of excess over £12,800				*Higher rate*
The first £2,300	...	...	...	40 per cent.
The next £4,000	...	...	...	45 per cent.
The next £6,200	...	...	...	50 per cent.
The next £6,200	...	...	...	55 per cent.
The remainder	...	...	...	60 per cent.

(2) Section 24(4) of the Finance Act 1980 (increase of basic rate limit, higher rate bands and investment income threshold) shall not apply for the year 1982-83.

21. Corporation tax shall be charged for the financial year 1981 at the rate of 52 per cent.

22. The rate of advance corporation tax for the financial year 1982 shall be three-sevenths.

23.—(1) The small companies rate for the financial year 1981 shall be 40 per cent., and for that year the fraction mentioned in subsection (2) of section 95 of the Finance Act 1972 (marginal relief for small companies) shall be two twenty-fifths.

(2) For the financial year 1981 and subsequent financial years subsection (3) of the said section 95 shall have effect with the substitution for any reference to £80,000 of a reference to £90,000 and with the substitution for any reference to £200,000 of a reference to £225,000.

(3) Where by virtue of subsection (2) above the said section

Part III

95 has effect with different relevant amounts in relation to different parts of the same accounting period, those parts shall be treated for the purposes of that section as if they were separate accounting periods and the profits and income of the company for that period (as defined in that section) shall be apportioned between those parts.

Personal
reliefs.
1980 c. 48.

24.—(1) Section 24(5) of the Finance Act 1980 (increase of personal reliefs) shall not apply for the year 1982-83.

(2) In section 8 of the Taxes Act (personal reliefs)—

(a) in subsection (1)(a) (married) for " £2,145 " there shall be substituted " £2,445 " ;

(b) in subsections (1)(b) (single) and (2) (wife's earned income relief) for " £1,375 " there shall be substituted " £1,565 " ;

(c) in subsection (1A) (age allowance) for " £2,895 " and " £1,820 " there shall be substituted " £3,295 " and " £2,070 " respectively ; and

(d) in subsection (1B) (income limit for age allowance) for " £5,900 " there shall be substituted " £6,700 ".

Relief for
interest.
1974 c. 30.

25.—(1) In sub-paragraph (1) of paragraph 5 of Schedule 1 to the Finance Act 1974 (limit on relief for interest on certain loans for the purchase or improvement of land) the references to £25,000 shall have effect for the year 1982-83 as well as for previous years of assessment.

(2) At the end of that paragraph there shall be added the following sub-paragraph—

" (6) In determining whether the amount on which interest is payable under a loan exceeds the limit in sub-paragraph (1) above, no account shall be taken of so much (if any) of that amount as consists of interest which has been added to capital and does not exceed £1,000."

Deduction
of tax from
certain loan
interest.

1972 c. 41.

26.—(1) If a person who is a qualifying borrower makes a payment of relevant loan interest to which this section applies, he shall be entitled, on making the payment, to deduct and retain out of it a sum equal to income tax thereon at the basic rate for the year of assessment in which the payment becomes due ; and, accordingly, section 75 of the Finance Act 1972 (relief for payment of interest), section 54 of the Taxes Act (certain payments of interest to be made under deduction of tax) and section 343(4) of the Taxes Act (no deduction of income tax from payment of interest to building societies) shall not apply to that payment of relevant loan interest.

(2) Where a sum is deducted under subsection (1) above from a payment of relevant loan interest,—

    (*a*) the person to whom the payment is made shall allow the deduction on receipt of the residue ;

    (*b*) the borrower shall be acquitted and discharged of so much money as is represented by the deduction as if the sum had been actually paid ; and

    (*c*) the sum deducted shall be treated as income tax paid by the person to whom the payment is made.

(3) Part I of Schedule 7 to this Act shall have effect to determine what is relevant loan interest, Part II of that Schedule shall have effect with respect to the application of this section to any such interest and Parts III and IV of that Schedule shall have effect with respect to qualifying borrowers and qualifying lenders respectively.

(4) Where payments of relevant loan interest to which this section applies become due in any year, the borrower shall be charged with tax at the basic rate for that year on an amount of income equal, subject to subsection (5) below, to the deduction which, in computing his total income, falls to be made on account of those payments.

(5) In any case where—

    (*a*) payments of relevant loan interest to which this section applies become due in any year ; and

    (*b*) the total income of the borrower for that year is such that he cannot benefit from any or, as the case may be, the full amount of the relevant personal reliefs to which he is entitled,

so much of that full amount as cannot be deducted from his total income shall be deducted from the amount of income on which he is chargeable to tax by virtue of subsection (4) above.

(6) In subsection (5) above " relevant personal relief " means any relief to which the borrower concerned is entitled under Chapter II of Part I of the Taxes Act, other than—

    (*a*) relief under section 19 of that Act (premiums on life insurance policies) which is given either by deduction by virtue of paragraph 5 of Schedule 4 to the Finance Act 1976 or in accordance with paragraph 15 of that Schedule ; and   1976 c. 40.

    (*b*) relief under section 20 of the Taxes Act (deferred annuities) ;

and for the purposes of subsection (5) above the full amount of those reliefs means the amount of them determined without regard to section 25 of the Taxes Act (under which reliefs are limited so as not to exceed total income).

PART III   (7) Sections 240(5) and 246(3) of the Taxes Act (which require income tax deducted from payments received by certain companies to be set off against corporation tax and denies the company the right to repayment of income tax) shall not apply to a payment of relevant loan interest to which this section applies which is received by any company, but, in accordance with regulations under section 29 below, any person by whom such a payment is received shall be entitled to recover from the Board an amount equal to the sum which, by virtue of subsection (2)(*c*) above is treated as income tax paid by him ; and any amount so recovered shall be treated for the purposes of the Tax Acts in like manner as the payment of relevant loan interest to which it relates.

(8) Notwithstanding paragraph (*l*) of section 130 of the Taxes Act (prohibition on deduction of annual payments other than interest in computing profits or gains of a trade etc.) no sum shall be deducted in respect of relevant loan interest in computing the amount of the profits or gains to be charged under Case I or II of Schedule D and, accordingly, no sum shall be so deducted in computing the profits or gains to be charged under Case VI of that Schedule.

1976 c. 40.   (9) In the Finance Act 1976—

    (*a*) in section 66 (taxation of benefit of employment linked loans) at the end of subsection (8) there shall be added the words " or which would be so eligible apart from section 26 of the Finance Act 1982 " ; and

    (*b*) in paragraph 8 of Schedule 8 (provisions supplementary to section 66) the following sub-paragraph shall be substituted for sub-paragraph (1)—

        " (1) Interest is elegible for relief for the purposes of this Part of this Schedule if it is eligible for relief

1972 c. 41.   under section 75 of the Finance Act 1972 or would be eligible for such relief apart from section 26 of the Finance Act 1982."

Termination of the option mortgage schemes.   **27.**—(1) Subject to the provisions of this section, Part II of the 1967 Act (assistance for house purchase and improvement in Great Britain) and Part VIII of the 1981 Order (option mortgages in Northern Ireland) shall cease to have effect on 1st April 1983.

(2) Nothing in this Act affects the continuing operation of—

    (*a*) sections 24(2)(*a*) and 28 of the 1967 Act (entitlement to and calculation of subsidy) with respect to payments falling to be made by the Secretary of State and related to amounts due from the borrower before 1st April 1983 or treated as so due by virtue of section 28(1A) of that Act ; or (*b*) section 28A of the 1967 Act (recovery of subsidy in certain cases) in its application to any such payments ; or

(*c*) Articles 142(2)(*a*) and 149 of the 1981 Order (entitlement to and calculation of subsidy) with respect to payments falling to be made by the Department of the Environment for Northern Ireland and related to amounts due from the borrower before 1st April 1983 or treated as so due by virtue of Article 149(2) of that Order ; or

(*d*) Article 150 of the 1981 Order (recovery of subsidy in certain cases) in its application to any such payments.

(3) Nothing in this Act affects the continuing operation of Part II of the 1967 Act in relation to a loan in respect of which an option notice is in force on 31st March 1983 if—

(*a*) on that date the residence condition in section 24B of that Act is not fulfilled ; and

(*b*) as a result either of the lender having first become aware of the fact on or before that date or of a notification having been given on or before that date, the option notice will (assuming the continuation in force of the said Part II) cease to have effect after that date by virtue of paragraph (ix) or paragraph (x) of subsection (3) of section 24 of that Act.

(4) Nothing in this Act affects the continuing operation of Part VIII of the 1981 Order in relation to a loan in respect of which an option notice is in force on 31st March 1983 if—

(*a*) on that date the residence condition in Article 145 of that Order is not fulfilled ; and

(*b*) as a result either of the lender having first become aware of that fact on or before that date or of a notification having been given on or before that date, the option notice will (assuming the continuation in force of the said Part VIII) cease to have effect after that date by virtue of sub-paragraph (*i*) or sub-paragraph (*j*) of paragraph (4) of Article 142 of that Order.

(5) In this section—

" the 1967 Act " means the Housing Subsidies Act 1967 ; and 1967 c. 29.

" the 1981 Order " means the Housing (Northern Ireland) Order 1981. S.I. 1981/156 (N.I. 3).

28.—(1) If relevant loan interest payable by a qualifying borrower— Variation of terms of repayment of certain loans.

(*a*) is payable under a loan agreement requiring combined payments, and (*b*) is payable to a qualifying lender who, in accordance with subsection (5) below, is specified for the purposes of this section, and

(*c*) is interest on a loan made before 1st April 1983, or if it is interest in respect of which the Board have notified an earlier date to the lender under paragraph 2(5) of Schedule 7 to this Act, before that earlier date,

then, subject to subsection (2) below, the terms of repayment of the loan are by virtue of this section varied in accordance with subsection (3) below.

(2) Subsection (1) above does not apply to any combined payment unless—

(*a*) the qualifying lender concerned has, in accordance with regulations, given notice to the qualifying borrower that this section is to apply to combined payments which the borrower is required to make under the loan agreement ; and

(*b*) the qualifying borrower has not, in accordance with regulations, given notice to the qualifying lender that he wishes to continue with combined payments which, allowing for any sums he is entitled to deduct by virtue of section 26 above, do not exceed the combined payments which he would have been required to make but for the provisions of that section.

(3) Where subsection (1) above applies, the amount of any combined payment payable by the qualifying borrower concerned which includes a payment of relevant loan interest shall be determined by the lender so as to secure, so far as practicable,—

(*a*) that the principal and interest are repaid over the period which is for the time being agreed between the lender and the borrower ; and

(*b*) that, unless there is a change in that period or in the basic rate of income tax or in the rate of interest charged by the lender, the amount of each net payment due from the borrower to the lender will be of the same amount ;

and for the purposes of paragraph (*b*) above a " net payment " means a payment which, so far as it is a payment of interest, consists of interest from which the sum provided for by section 26(1) above has been deducted.

(4) Where the qualifying borrower gives a notice under subsection (2)(*b*) above, the amount of any combined payment payable by him which includes a payment of relevant loan interest and the period over which the principal and interest on the loan are to be repaid shall be determined by the lender so as to

secure, so far as practicable, that, unless there is a change in the basic rate of income tax or in the rate of interest charged by the lender,—

(*a*) the amount of each net payment, as defined in subsection (3) above, which is due from the borrower to the lender will be of the same amount ; and

(*b*) the amount of each such payment does not exceed what, apart from section 26 above, would have been the amount of the first combined payment payable by the borrower after the date referred to in subsection (1)(*c*) above, less tax at the basic rate for the year 1983-84 on so much of that combined payment as would have consisted of interest ;

but nothing in this section or in the loan agreement shall prevent the borrower from making, at such time or times as he chooses, additional repayments of capital of any amount so as to secure that the principal and interest on the loan are repaid within a period which is not shorter than that referred to in subsection (3)(*a*) above.

(5) A building society within the meaning of the Building 1962 c. 37. Societies Act 1962 or the Building Societies Act (Northern Ire- 1967 c. 31 land) 1967 is by virtue of this subsection specified for the pur- (N.I.). poses of this section ; and the Treasury may by order made by statutory instrument specify any other qualifying lender or class of qualifying lender for the purposes of this section.

(6) The giving of a notice under paragraph (*a*) or paragraph (*b*) of subsection (2) above does not affect the right of the qualifying lender and the qualifying borrower to vary, by agreement, the terms on which interest or capital or both is to be repaid.

(7) In this section—

" loan agreement " means an agreement governing the terms of payment of interest and repayment of capital of a loan the interest on which is relevant loan interest ;

" combined payment " means one of a number of regular payments which are attributable in part to repayment of capital and in part to payment of interest ; and

" regulations " means regulations made by the Board under section 29 below ;

and other expressions have the same meaning as in section 26 above.

29.—(1) The Treasury may by regulations made by statutory Supple- instrument make provision for the application of sections 26 and mentary 28 above and Schedule 7 to this Act in relation to— regulations.

(*a*) a housing association which is for the time being approved for the purposes of section 341 of the Taxes

Act and which borrows or has borrowed from a qualifying lender on the security of a freehold or leasehold estate of that association on land in Great Britain or Northern Ireland ; and

1974 c. 44.
(b) a self-build society, within the meaning of Part I of the Housing Act 1974, which is for the time being approved for the purposes of section 341A of the Taxes Act and which borrows or has borrowed from a qualifying lender on the security of a freehold or leasehold estate of that society on land in Great Britain.

(2) Regulations under subsection (1) above—

(a) may contain such modifications of the provisions of sections 26 and 28 above and Schedule 7 to this Act, and

(b) may make the application of any of those provisions subject to such special conditions,

as appear to the Treasury to be appropriate.

(3) The Board may by regulations made by statutory instrument make provision—

(a) for the purposes of any provision of section 26 or section 28 above or Schedule 7 to this Act which relates to any matter or thing to be specified by or done in accordance with regulations ;

(b) for the application of sections 26 and 28 above and Schedule 7 to this Act in relation to loan interest paid by personal representatives and trustees ;

(c) with respect to the furnishing of information by borrowers or lenders, including, in the case of lenders, the inspection of books, documents and other records on behalf of the Board ;

(d) for, and with respect to, appeals to the General Commissioners or the Special Commissioners against the refusal of the Board to issue a notice under paragraph 7(1)(b) of Schedule 7 to this Act or the issue of a notice under paragraph 10 of that Schedule ; and

(e) generally for giving effect to sections 26 and 28 above and Schedule 7 to this Act.

(4) In the application of this section to Scotland—

(a) " a freehold or leasehold estate " means any interest in land ;

1970 c. 35.
(b) any reference to a loan on the security of such an estate is a reference to a loan upon a heritable security within the meaning of section 9(8)(a) of the Conveyancing and Feudal Reform (Scotland) Act 1970.

(5) A statutory instrument by which the power to make regulations conferred by subsection (1) or subsection (3) above is

exercised shall be subject to annulment in pursuance of a reso-
lution of the Commons House of Parliament.

30.—(1) In section 219(1) of the Taxes Act (social security   Exemption
benefits charged to tax unless specifically exempted) after the   from
words " attendance allowance " there shall be inserted the words   income tax:
" mobility allowance ".   mobility
allowance.

(2) Paragraph (*b*)(ii) of subsection (2) of section 8 of the Taxes
Act (mobility allowance of wives to be treated as earned income)
shall cease to have effect.

(3) This section shall have effect in relation to mobility allowance paid in respect of periods beginning on or after 6th April
1982.

31.—(1) The following section shall be inserted in the Taxes   Income
Act after section 219—   taxable under
    Schedule E.

" Other   **219A.**—(1) The following payments shall be
payments   charged to income tax under Schedule E by virtue
charged   of this section if they would not otherwise be, that
under   is to say—
Schedule E.

       (*a*) allowances paid under a scheme of the kind
         described in the Job Release Act 1977,   1977 c. 8.
         being a scheme which provides for the
         payment of allowances for periods begin-
         ning earlier than one year before the date
         on which the recipient attains pensionable
         age, as defined in that Act ;

       (*b*) maternity pay (whether paid during the sub-
         sistence of a contract of employment or
         not) within the meaning of section 33 of
         the Employment Protection (Consolidation)   1978 c. 44.
         Act 1978 or, in Northern Ireland, Article
         15 of the Industrial Relations (No. 2) (Nor-
         thern Ireland) Order 1976 ; and   S.I. 1976/2147
                                                     (N.I. 28).
       (*c*) payments of statutory sick pay within the
         meaning of section 1 of the Social Security
         and Housing Benefits Act 1982 or, in Nor-   1982 c. 24.
         thern Ireland, any corresponding provision
         contained in an Order in Council under
         the Northern Ireland Act 1974.   1974 c. 28.

     (2) This section has effect in relation to payments
     made in respect of periods beginning on or after
     6th April 1982."

(2) In subsection (2)(*c*) of section 530 of the Taxes Act (certain
payments to be " earned income "), after the words " section
219(1) " there shall be inserted the words " or section 219A ".

32.—(1) In section 27 of the Finance Act 1981 (provisions relating to the taxation of social security payments)—

    (*a*) in subsection (3) (taxation of certain supplementary allowances)—

        (i) the words " (except so far as made by virtue of section 4 of that Act) " shall cease to have effect ; and

        (ii) for paragraph (*a*) there shall be substituted the following paragraphs : —

            " (*a*) his right to the allowance is subject to any condition contained in section 5 of that Act (requirements as to registration and availability for employment) ; or

            (*aa*) the allowance is paid to him under Regulation 12, 16 or 19 of the Supplementary Benefit (Urgent Cases) Regulations 1981, and his right to the allowance is not subject to the said section 5 by virtue only of Regulation 3(2) of those Regulations ; or " ;

    (*b*) after subsection (3) there shall be inserted the following subsection—

        " (3A) An allowance shall not be charged to tax under Schedule E by virtue of subsection (3)(*b*) above to the extent that it is made by virtue of section 4 of the said Act of 1976." ;

    (*c*) in subsection (5) (relevant amounts) the following paragraph shall be substituted for paragraph (*a*)—

        " (*a*) in a case where the supplementary allowance is paid to a person—

            (i) to whom subsection (3)(*a*) above applies and he is for the purposes of the said Act of 1976 one of a married or unmarried couple the other one of whom is within section 8 of that Act and the said paragraph 10 applies to him, or

            (ii) to whom subsection (3)(*b*) above applies,

    to the amount specified in the said paragraph 10 ; " ; and at the end of that subsection there shall be inserted the following words—

        " Any reference in this subsection to an amount or rate or increase specified in any provision is a reference to the amount or rate or increase so specified for the week in question." ;

    (*d*) at the end of paragraph (*c*) of subsection (8) (Northern Ireland adaptations) there shall be added the words " and

(*d*) for any reference to the Supplementary Bene-   Part III
fit (Urgent Cases) Regulations 1981 there were sub-   S.I. 1981/1529.
stituted a reference to the Supplementary Benefit   S.R. 1981/372
(Urgent Cases) Regulations (Northern Ireland)   (N.I.).
1981 " ; and

(*e*) in subsection (11) (commencement of section 27) for
the words " 5th April 1982 " there shall be substituted
the words " 4th July 1982 ".

(2) In section 29 of the Finance Act 1981 (pay as you earn
repayments) in paragraph (*b*) for the words from " to the condition " to " or " there shall be substituted the words " to any
condition contained in section 5 of the said Act of 1976 or,
in Northern Ireland, Article 7 of the said Order (requirements
as to registration and availability for employment) ; or ".

(3) Any reference in section 27 or section 29 of the Finance   1981 c. 35.
Act 1981 to section 5 of the Supplementary Benefits Act 1976   1976 c. 71.
or to Article 7 of the Supplementary Benefits (Northern Ireland)   S.I. 1977/2156
Order 1977 includes a reference to that section or Article as   (N.I. 27).
amended by any other enactment including an enactment passed
or made after the passing of this Act.

(4) Paragraph (*e*) of subsection (1) above shall be deemed
to have come into force on 5th April 1982 and the remainder
of this section shall be deemed to have come into force on 5th
July 1982.

33.—(1) Section 65 of the Taxes Act (certain small mainten-   Small
ance payments to be made without deduction of tax) shall be   maintenance
amended as follows.   payments.

(2) For subsection (1) there shall be substituted the following
subsections—

" (1) In this section ' small maintenance payments '
means payments under an order made by a court in the
United Kingdom—

(*a*) by one of the parties to a marriage (including a
marriage which has been dissolved or annulled) to
or for the benefit of the other party to that marriage for that other party's maintenance,

(*b*) to any person under 21 years of age for his own
benefit, maintenance or education, or

(*c*) to any person for the benefit, maintenance or education of a person under 21 years of age,

in respect of which the two conditions mentioned in subsection (1A) below are satisfied ; and ' small maintenance

order' means an order providing for the making of small maintenance payments.

(1A) The first of the conditions referred to in subsection (1) above is—

(*a*) in the case of payments falling within paragraph (*a*) of that subsection, that the order for the time being requires them to be made—

(i) weekly at a rate not exceeding £33 per week, or

(ii) monthly at a rate not exceeding £143 per month,

(*b*) in the case of payments falling within paragraph (*b*) (but not within paragraph (*a*)) of that subsection, that the order for the time being requires them to be made—

(i) weekly at a rate not exceeding £33 per week, or

(ii) monthly at a rate not exceeding £143 per month,

(*c*) in the case of payments falling within paragraph (*c*) (but not within paragraph (*a*) or (*b*)) of that subsection, that the order for the time being requires them to be made—

(i) weekly at a rate not exceeding £18 per week, or

(ii) monthly at a rate not exceeding £78 per month,

and the second of those conditions is that the payments would, apart from this section, fall within section 52 or section 53 above (deduction of income tax from annual payments)."

(3) For subsection (5) there shall be substituted the following subsection—

" (5) The Treasury may from time to time, by order made by statutory instrument subject to annulment in pursuance of a resolution of the Commons House of Parliament, increase any, or all, of the amounts for the time being specified in subsection (1A) above."

(4) In subsection (6) for the words from " or further ", where they first occur, to " weekly amount " there shall be substituted the words " the amount for the time being specified in sub-paragraph (i) of paragraph (*a*), (*b*) or (*c*) of subsection (1A) above shall increase the amount for the time being specified in sub-paragraph (ii) of that paragraph so that it is 52 twelfths of the amount specified in sub-paragraph (i) by virtue of the order ".

(5) This section applies—

    (*a*) in the case of payments under orders made, varied or revived after the passing of this Act, to those falling due after that date, and

    (*b*) in the case of payments under other orders, to those falling due on or after 6th April 1983.

34.—(1) Where, as a result of a variation in the life or lives for the time being assured, a qualifying policy (in this section referred to as " the earlier policy ") is replaced by a new policy (in this section referred to as " the later policy ") which, in accordance with the rules in paragraph 9 of Schedule 1 to the Taxes Act, is also a qualifying policy, then, subject to subsection (3) below, for the purposes of— Life assurance: variation in life or lives assured.

    (*a*) the enactments specified in subsection (2) below, and

    (*b*) any second or subsequent application of this section,

the later policy and the earlier policy shall be treated as a single policy issued in respect of an insurance made at the time of the making of the insurance in respect of which the earlier policy was issued ; and, accordingly, so long as the later policy continues to be a qualifying policy, the single policy shall also be treated as a qualifying policy for those purposes.

(2) The enactments referred to in subsection (1) above are—

    (*a*) sections 394 and 395 of the Taxes Act (life policies: chargeable events and computation of gains) ; and

    (*b*) sections 7 to 9 of the Finance Act 1975 (payments becoming due on certain surrenders etc. of life policies). 1975 c. 7.

(3) Subsection (1) above does not apply unless—

    (*a*) any sum which would otherwise become payable by the insurer on or in connection with the coming to an end of the earlier policy is retained by the insurer and applied in the discharge of some or all of the liability for any premium becoming due under the later policy ; and

    (*b*) no consideration in money or money's worth (other than the benefits for which provision is made by the later policy) is receivable by any person on or in connection with the coming to an end of the earlier policy or the coming into existence of the later policy.

(4) Any sum which is applied as mentioned in subsection (3)(*a*) above,—

    (*a*) shall be left out of account in determining, for the purposes of the enactments specified in subsection (2) above, the total amount which at any time has been

PART III

paid by way of premiums under the single policy referred to in subsection (1) above ; and

(*b*) shall not be regarded, in relation to that single policy, as a relevant capital payment, within the meaning of section 395 of the Taxes Act.

(5) Any reference in this section to a qualifying policy is a reference to a qualifying policy within the meaning of Part I of Schedule 1 to the Taxes Act.

(6) This section applies where the later policy comes into existence on or after 25th March 1982.

Life assurance: qualifying policies and policies on the lives of children.
1976 c. 40.
1974 c. 49.
1981 c. 31.

35.—(1) In paragraph 2A of Schedule 4 to the Finance Act 1976 (qualifying life policies: exclusion of accident policies)—

(*a*) in sub-paragraph (1), for the words " subsection (2)(*a*) of section 83 of the Insurance Companies Act 1974 " there shall be substituted the words " Class I or Class III in Schedule 1 to the Insurance Companies Act 1981 " ; and

(*b*) in sub-paragraph (2), for the words " falling within subsection (2)(*b*) of the said section 83 " there shall be substituted the words " which—

(*a*) are expressed to be in effect for a period of not less than five years or without limit of time ; and

(*b*) either are not expressed to be terminable by the insurer before the expiration of five years from their taking effect or are expressed to be so terminable before the expiration of that period only in special circumstances therein mentioned ".

(2) In paragraph 11(3) of Schedule 4 to the Finance Act 1976 (maximum annual premium for policies on lives of children or grandchildren) for " £52 " there shall be substituted " £64 ".

1980 c. 48.

(3) In section 30 of the Finance Act 1980 (certain policies not to be qualifying policies) in subsection (3) (definition of " policy " by reference to ordinary long-term insurance business) for the words " within the meaning of section 83(2) of the Insurance Companies Act 1974 " there shall be substituted the words " as defined in section 85(1) of the Insurance Companies Act 1974, as amended by Schedule 4 to the Insurance Companies Act 1981 ".

(4) This section applies to policies issued in respect of insurances made on or after 25th March 1982.

36.—(1) In section 338 of the Taxes Act (which, as amended by section 57(3) of the Finance Act 1980, provides for exemption for income and gains of a trade union precluded by Act or rules from assuring to any person a sum exceeding £2,000 by way of a gross sum or £416 a year by way of annuity if the income or gains is or are applied for purpose of provident benefits) for " £2,000 " and " £416 " there shall be substituted respectively " £2,400 " and " £500 ".

(2) Subsection (1) above has effect in relation to income or gains which are applicable and applied as mentioned in the said section 338 on or after 1st June 1982.

37.—(1) Where for any year of assessment an individual—

    (*a*) is chargeable to income tax in respect of relevant earnings derived from Lloyd's underwriting activities ; and

    (*b*) there is an amount of unused relief attributable to those earnings,

the individual may, subject to subsection (2) below, elect that there shall be treated as paid in that year any qualifying premium paid by him in the next year of assessment but two.

(2) An election under this section shall not have effect in relation to so much of any qualifying premium as exceeds the amount of unused relief referred to in subsection (1)(*b*) above.

(3) Any election under this section shall be made before the end of the year of assessment in which the premium is paid.

(4) Where an election is made under this section the provisions of Chapter III of Part IX of the Taxes Act (retirement annuities), other than section 227(1BB), shall have effect as if the premium or, as the case may be, the part of the premium in question had been paid in the year specified in the election and not in the year in which it was actually paid.

(5) In this section " qualifying premium " and " relevant earnings " have the same meaning as in the said Chapter III, " unused relief " has the same meaning as in section 227A of the Taxes Act and " relevant earnings derived from Lloyd's underwriting activities " means relevant earnings as an underwriting member of Lloyd's or by way of commission calculated by reference to the profits of Lloyd's underwriting business.

(6) This section has effect in relation to any premium paid in the year 1982-83 or any subsequent year of assessment.

38.—(1) In subsection (4) of section 228 of the Taxes Act (relief for premiums under retirement annuity contracts limited by reference to percentage of earnings dependent upon age) the words " Subject to subsection (5) below " shall be omitted and for the Table set out in that subsection there shall be substituted the following Table:—

" Table

Year of birth	Percentage
1916 to 1933	20
1914 or 1915	21
1912 or 1913	24
1910 or 1911	$26\frac{1}{2}$
1908 or 1909	$29\frac{1}{2}$
1907	$32\frac{1}{2}$ "

(2) Subsection (5) of the said section 228 (which restricts relief in relation to any year in which the individual concerned benefits from pensionable employment) shall cease to have effect.

(3) This section has effect for the year 1982-83 and subsequent years of assessment.

Partnership retirement annuities.
1974 c. 30.

39.—(1) In section 16 of the Finance Act 1974 (partnership retirement annuities) in paragraph (*a*) of subsection (2) after the word " is " there shall be inserted the words " subject to subsection (2A) below " and at the end of that subsection there shall be inserted—

" (2A) If the retail prices index for the month of December in the last of the seven years referred to in paragraph (*c*) of subsection (2) above is higher than it was for the month of December in any of the other years referred to in that paragraph, the amount which, for that other year, was the former partner's share of the relevant profits or gains shall be treated for the purposes of that subsection as increased by the same percentage as the percentage increase in the retail prices index."

(2) This section has effect in relation to annual payments falling within section 16(1) of the Finance Act 1974 which are income of the year 1982-83 or any subsequent year of assessment.

Share options.

40.—(1) In any case where—

(*a*) for the year 1982-83 or any subsequent year of assessment a person is chargeable to tax under Schedule E, by virtue of section 186 of the Taxes Act (directors and employees of companies granted rights to acquire shares), on an amount equal to a gain realised by the exercise of a right to acquire shares ; and

(*b*) the shares acquired in the exercise of that right were acquired for a consideration which, subject to subsection (2) below, was not less than the market value (determined as for the purposes of the Capital Gains Tax Act 1979) of shares of the same class at the time the right was granted or, if the right was granted before 6th April 1982, 90 per cent. of that market value ; and

1979 c. 14.

(c) following an assessment for the year in which that right
    was exercised (in this section referred to as " the rele-
    vant year ") an amount of tax chargeable by virtue
    of section 186 of the Taxes Act in respect of the
    amount referred to in paragraph (a) above and exceed-
    ing £250 is payable to the collector pursuant to regu-
    lations under section 204 of that Act ; and

(d) the person concerned makes an election in accordance
    with subsection (3) below,

he shall be entitled to pay tax by instalments in accordance
with subsection (4) below.

(2) Shares which are acquired for a consideration less than
that required by paragraph (b) of subsection (1) above by reason
only of a diminution in the market value of shares of that class
(determined as aforesaid) which is attributable solely to the share
capital of the company issuing the shares being varied after the
right to acquire the shares was granted, shall for the purposes of
that paragraph be regarded as having been acquired for a consideration not less than that required by that paragraph.

(3) An election under this section shall be made by notice
in writing to the inspector before the expiry of the period of sixty
days beginning immediately after the end of the relevant year.

(4) Where an election has been made under this section the
tax referred to in subsection (1)(c) above shall, subject to subsections (5) and (6) below, be paid in three equal instalments
as follows—

(a) the first shall be due and payable at the expiry of the
    period of fourteen days beginning on the date on
    which application for the tax is made pursuant to
    regulations under the said section 204 ;

(b) the third shall be due and payable on the last day
    of the third year following the end of the relevant
    year ; and

(c) the second shall be due on such date as falls midway
    between the dates on which the first and third instal-
    ments are due and payable.

(5) In any case where the date which, apart from this subsection, would be the due date for the third instalment of tax
under subsection (4) above is earlier than the due date referred
to in paragraph (a) of that subsection, all three instalments shall
be due on the later date.

(6) Tax which, by virtue of an election under this section, is
not yet due and payable in accordance with subsection (4) above
may nevertheless be paid at any time and shall become due and
payable forthwith if the person who made the election becomes
bankrupt under the law of any part of the United Kingdom.

PART III

(7) Subject to any other provision of the Income Tax Acts requiring income of any description to be treated as the highest part of a person's income, for the purposes of paragraph (c) of subsection (1) above in determining what tax is chargeable on a person by virtue of section 186 of the Taxes Act in respect of the amount referred to in paragraph (a) of that subsection, that amount shall be treated as the highest part of his income for the relevant year.

1980 c. 48.

(8) In Schedule 10 to the Finance Act 1980 (savings-related share option schemes) in paragraph 26 (interpretation) at the end of the definition of " associated company " in sub-paragraph (1) there shall be added the words " except that, for the purposes of paragraph 12 of this Schedule, subsection (1) of that section shall have effect with the omission of the words ' or at any time within one year previously ' ".

Share options etc.: restrictions on insider dealing.
1973 c. 51.

41. Paragraph 5 of Schedule 8 to the Finance Act 1973 and paragraph 18 of Schedule 10 to the Finance Act 1980 (certain matters deemed to be restrictions attaching to shares) shall each have effect and shall be deemed always to have had effect as if the references in those paragraphs to any contract, agreement, arrangement or condition did not include a reference to so much of any contract, agreement, arrangement or condition as contains provisions similar in purpose and effect to any of the provisions of the Model Rules set out in the Model Code for Securities Transactions by Directors of Listed Companies issued by the Stock Exchange in April 1981.

Approved profit sharing schemes.
1978 c. 42.

42.—(1) In section 56 of the Finance Act 1978 (capital receipts in respect of approved profit sharing schemes) in subsection (1)—

(a) after the words " trustees become ", in each place where they occur, there shall be inserted the words " or the participant becomes " ;

(b) before the words " the amount or value " there shall be inserted the words " so much of " ; and

(c) at the end there shall be added the words " as exceeds the appropriate allowance for that year, as determined under subsection (6) below ".

(2) For subsection (6) of that section there shall be substituted the following subsection—

" (6) For the purposes of subsection (1) above, the appropriate allowance for any year of assessment means a sum which, subject to a maximum of £140, is the product of multiplying £20 by 1 plus the number of years which fall within the period of 7 years immediately preceding the year in question and in which shares were appropriated to the participant under the scheme; and if in any year (and before the release date) the trustees become or the participant becomes entitled, in respect of or by reference to any of his shares, to more than one capital receipt, the receipts shall be set against the appropriate allowance for that year in the order in which they are received."

(3) In subsections (1) and (2) of section 58 of the Finance Act 1978 (shares in excess of initial market value of £1,000) for " £1,000 " there shall be substituted " £1,250 ".

(4) In paragraph 1(4) of Schedule 9 to that Act (profit sharing schemes to provide that total initial market values of shares appropriated to one participant yearly must not exceed £1,000) for " £1,000 " there shall be substituted " £1,250 ".

(5) Subsections (1) and (2) above apply to receipts to which the trustees become or the participant becomes entitled on or after the passing of this Act; subsection (3) above applies in relation to shares appropriated on or after 6th April 1982; and subsection (4) above shall be deemed to have come into force on that date.

43.—(1) Schedule 8 to the Taxes Act (tax on payments for loss of employment etc.) shall have effect with the insertion at the beginning of paragraph 7 of the words " Subject to sub-paragraph (2) below " and with the addition, at the end of that paragraph, of the following:—

" (2) In the case of a payment which exceeds £50,000, this paragraph applies as if it were a payment of £50,000 exactly.

7A.—(1) Subject to sub-paragraph (2) below, in the case of a payment which exceeds £50,000 and in respect of which tax is chargeable under section 187 of this Act, the following relief shall be allowed by way of deduction from the tax chargeable by virtue of that section, that is to say, there shall be ascertained—

(a) the amount of tax which would be chargeable apart from this paragraph and paragraph 7 above in respect of the income of the holder or past holder of the office or employment for the chargeable period of which the payment is treated as income, and

(b) the amount of tax which would be so chargeable if the amount of the payment had been £50,000 exactly,

and the amount to be deducted shall be one-quarter of the difference between the amount ascertained at (a) and the amount ascertained at (b).

(2) In the case of a payment which exceeds £75,000, this paragraph applies as if it were a payment of £75,000 exactly.

(3) Any relief allowed by virtue of this paragraph shall be in addition to that allowed by virtue of paragraph 7 above."

(2) This section has effect in relation to any payment which, by virtue of section 187(4) of the Taxes Act, is treated as income received on or after 6th April 1982.

44.—(1) Section 36 of the Finance (No. 2) Act 1975 (taxation of benefits in kind provided by means of vouchers other than cash vouchers) shall be amended as follows.

(2) In subsection (1)—

(*a*) after the words " in relation to a voucher ", in the passage following paragraph (*b*), there shall be inserted the words " (other than a cheque voucher) " ; and

(*b*) at the end there shall be added the words " ; and in relation to a cheque voucher is the one in which the voucher is handed over in exchange for money, goods or services (a voucher which is posted being treated as handed over at the time of posting)."

(3) For subsection (2) there shall be substituted the following subsection—

" (2) There shall be deductible under section 189, 192 or 194(3) of the Taxes Act (necessary expenses etc.) from the amount taxable under subsection (1) above such amounts, if any, as would have been so deductible if the cost of the goods or services in question had been incurred by the employee out of his emoluments."

(4) After subsection (3) there shall be inserted the following subsection—

" (3A) Subsection (1) above shall not apply in relation to a transport voucher provided for an employee of a passenger transport undertaking under arrangements in operation on 25th March 1982 and intended to enable that employee or a relation of his to obtain passenger transport services provided by—

(*a*) his employer ;

(*b*) a subsidiary of his employer ;

(*c*) a body corporate of which his employer is a subsidiary ; or

(*d*) another passenger transport undertaking."

(5) For subsections (4) and (4A) there shall be substituted the following subsection—

" (4) In this section—

'cheque voucher' means a cheque provided for an employee and intended for use by him wholly or mainly for payment for particular goods or services or for goods or services of one or more particular classes; and, in relation to a cheque voucher, references to a voucher being exchanged for goods or services shall be construed accordingly;

'employee' means the holder of any office or employment the emoluments in respect of which fall to be assessed under Schedule E; and related expressions shall be construed accordingly;

'passenger transport undertaking' means an undertaking whose business consists wholly or mainly in the carriage of passengers and includes a subsidiary of such an undertaking;

'relation', with respect to an employee, means his spouse, parent or child, the spouse of his child and any dependant of that employee;

'subsidiary' means a wholly owned subsidiary within the meaning of section 150(4) of the Companies 1948 c. 38. Act 1948;

'transport voucher' means any ticket, pass or other document or token intended to enable a person to obtain passenger transport services (whether or not in exchange for it); and, in relation to a transport voucher, references to a voucher being exchanged for services shall be construed as references to it being exchanged for, or otherwise used to procure, services;

'voucher' does not include a cash voucher within the meaning of section 37 of this Act but, subject to that, means any voucher, stamp or similar document or token capable of being exchanged (whether singly or together with other such vouchers, stamps, documents or tokens and whether immediately or only after a time) for money, goods or services (or for any combination of two or more of those things) and includes a transport voucher and a cheque voucher."

(6) After subsection (5) there shall be inserted the following subsection—

" (5A) Subsections (6) and (7) of section 36A of this Act shall apply for the purposes of this section in relation to vouchers as they apply for the purposes of that section in relation to credit-tokens."

(7) This section has effect for the year 1982-83 and subsequent years of assessment.

Benefits in
kind:
credit-tokens.
1975 c. 45.

45.—(1) Section 36A of the Finance (No. 2) Act 1975 (taxation of benefits in kind provided by means of credit-tokens) shall be amended as follows.

(2) In subsection (1), paragraph (a) and, in paragraph (b), the words " (including any interest paid in connection therewith) " shall cease to have effect ; and accordingly in subsection (3) for the words " paragraphs (a) and " there shall be substituted the word " paragraph ".

(3) For subsection (4) there shall be substituted the following subsections—

" (4) In this section ' credit-token ' means, subject to subsection (4B) below, a card, token, document or other thing given to a person by another person who undertakes—

(a) that on the production of it (whether or not some other action is also required) he will supply money, goods and services (or any of them) on credit ; or

(b) that where, on the production of it to a third party (whether or not some other action is also required), the third party supplies money, goods and services (or any of them), he will pay the third party for them (whether or not taking any discount or commission).

(4A) For the purposes of subsection (4) above, use of an object to operate a machine provided by the person giving the object, or by a third party, shall be treated as production of the object to that person or, as the case may be, third party.

(4B) In this section—

' credit-token ' does not include a voucher within the meaning of section 36, or a cash voucher within the meaning of section 37, of this Act ; and

' employee ' has the same meaning as in section 36(4) of this Act."

(4) This section has effect for the year 1982-83 and subsequent years of assessment.

Benefits in
kind: cars
and car fuel.
1981 c. 35.
1976 c. 40.

46.—(1) In Chapter III of Part IV of the Finance Act 1981 (benefits in kind)—

(a) subsections (2), (4) and (5) of section 68 (which, for the year 1982-83 and subsequent years of assessment, amend section 64 of the Finance Act 1976 with respect to certain benefits relating to cars available for private use) shall be deemed not to have been enacted and, accordingly, the said section 64 shall have effect for the year 1982-83 and subsequent years of assessment without regard to the amendments made by those subsections ; and

(b) section 69 (new provision relating to car fuel) shall not have effect until the year 1983-84 and, accordingly, in subsection (2) of that section for " 1982-83 " there shall be substituted " 1983-84 ".

(2) Subsection (2A) of section 64 of the Finance Act 1976 (removal of double or alternative charges for car and car fuel benefits) shall be amended—

(a) by the substitution, for the words from the beginning to " under this section ", of the words " Subject to subsection (2B) below, where in any year the benefit of a car is chargeable to tax under this section as the employee's income " ; and

(b) by the substitution, in paragraph (c), for the words " made by him " of the words " made to him " ;

and in section 69(2)(a) of that Act (calculation of emoluments in relation to benefits in kind) after the words " amounts as come " there shall be inserted the words " or would but for section 64(2A) of this Act come ".

(3) After the said subsection (2A) there shall be inserted the following subsection :—

" (2B) If, in the year 1982-83, the benefit of a car is chargeable to tax under this section, subsection (2A) above shall have effect for that year as if—

(a) the reference in paragraph (a) to a liability in connection with the car did not include a reference to liability for fuel ;

(b) the references in paragraph (b) to goods or services in connection with the car did not include fuel ; and

(c) the reference in paragraph (c) to expenses incurred in connection with the car did not include expenses incurred in the provision of fuel."

(4) In section 64A of the Finance Act 1976 (taxation of amounts equal to value of car fuel benefits), in subsection (1) for the words from " he shall be treated " to the end of the subsection there shall be substituted the words " an amount equal to whatever is the cash equivalent of that benefit in that year shall be treated as emoluments of the employment and, accordingly, shall be chargeable to income tax under Schedule E." ; and subsections (7) and (8) of that section shall be omitted.

(5) For the Tables in subsection (2) of the said section 64A there shall be substituted the following Tables:—

TABLE A

Cylinder capacity of car in cubic centimetres	Cash equivalent
1300 or less	£325
More than 1300, but not more than 1800	£425
More than 1800	£650

TABLE B

Original market value of car	Cash equivalent
Less than £4,300	£325
£4,300 or more but less than £6,100 ...	£425
£6,100 or more	£650

(6) In subsection (4) of the said section 64A (power for Treasury by order to vary Tables of cash equivalents for the year 1983-84 and subsequent years) for " 1983-84 " there shall be substituted " 1984-85 ".

1970 c. 9.

1981 c. 35.

(7) Section 15 of the Taxes Management Act 1970 (returns of employees' emoluments etc.) shall have effect for the year 1982-83 as if the amendments made by section 69 of the Finance Act 1981 (as amended by this section) had effect for that year.

Sub-contractors in the construction industry.

1975 c. 45.

47. Chapter II of Part III of the Finance (No. 2) Act 1975 shall have effect subject to the provisions of Schedule 8 to this Act (which authorises the issue of certificates under section 70 of that Act to certain individuals who would not otherwise qualify, and makes certain minor amendments).

Contributions to local enterprise agencies.

48.—(1) Notwithstanding anything in section 130 of the Taxes Act (general rules as to deductions not allowable in computing profits or gains) but subject to the provisions of this section, where a person carrying on a trade, profession or vocation makes any contribution (whether in cash or in kind) to an approved local enterprise agency, any expenditure incurred by him in making the contribution which would not otherwise be so deductible may be deducted as an expense in computing the profits or gains of the trade, profession or vocation for the purposes of tax.

(2) Where any such contribution as is referred to in subsection (1) above is made by an investment company, within the meaning of section 304 of the Taxes Act, any expenditure allowable as a deduction under subsection (1) above shall for the purposes of that section be treated as expenses of management.

(3) Subsection (1) above does not apply in relation to a contribution made by any person if either he or any person connected with him receives, or is entitled to receive, a benefit of any kind whatsoever for or in connection with the making of that contribution, whether from the agency concerned or from any other person.

(4) In this section " approved local enterprise agency " means a body approved by the Secretary of State for the purposes of this section; but the Secretary of State shall not so approve a body unless he is satisfied that—

    (*a*) its sole objective is the promotion or encouragement of industrial and commercial activity or enterprise in a particular area in the United Kingdom with particular reference to encouraging the formation and development of small businesses; or

    (*b*) one of its principal objectives is that set out in paragraph (*a*) above and it maintains or is about to maintain a fund separate from its other funds which is or is to be applied solely in pursuance of that objective;

and where the Secretary of State approves a body by virtue of paragraph (*b*) above, the approval shall specify the fund concerned and, in relation to a body so approved, any reference in this section to a contribution is a reference to a contribution which is made wholly to or for the purposes of that fund.

(5) A body may be approved under subsection (4) above whether or not it is a body corporate or a body of trustees or any other association or organisation and whether or not it is described as a local enterprise agency; but no body may be so approved unless it is precluded, by virtue of any enactment, contractual obligation, memorandum or otherwise from making any direct or indirect payment or transfer to any of its members or to any person charged with the control and direction of its affairs of any of its income or profit by way of dividend, gift, division, bonus or otherwise howsoever by way of profit (but for this purpose the payment of reasonable remuneration for goods, labour or power supplied, or for services rendered, of reasonable interest for money lent or of reasonable rent for any premises does not constitute a payment or transfer which is required to be so precluded).

(6) Any approval given by the Secretary of State may be made conditional upon compliance with such requirements as to

PART III   accounts, provision of information and other matters as he considers appropriate ; and if it appears to the Secretary of State—

> (*a*) that an approved local enterprise agency is not complying with any such requirement, or
>
> (*b*) that one or other of the conditions for his approval contained in subsection (4) above or the precondition for his approval in subsection (5) above has ceased to be fulfilled with respect to an approved local enterprise agency,

he shall by notice in writing withdraw his approval from the body concerned with effect from such date as he may specify in the notice (which may be a date earlier than the date on which the notice is given).

(7) In any case where—

> (*a*) a contribution has been made to an approved local enterprise agency in respect of which relief has been given under subsection (1) above, and
>
> (*b*) any benefit received in any chargeable period by the contributor or any person connected with him is in any way attributable to that contribution,

the contributor shall in respect of that chargeable period be charged to tax under Case I or Case II of Schedule D or, if he is not chargeable to tax under either of those cases for that period, under Case VI of Schedule D on an amount equal to the value of that benefit.

(8) Section 533 of the Taxes Act (connected persons) applies for the purposes of subsections (3) and (7) above.

(9) This section applies to contributions made on or after 1st April 1982 and before 1st April 1992.

Relief for interest: loans for investment in close companies.
1974 c. 30.

49.—(1) Paragraphs 9 and 10 of Schedule 1 to the Finance Act 1974 (relief for interest paid on loans for investment in close companies) shall have effect subject to the following provisions of this section.

(2) In paragraph 9(1) for the words following sub-paragraph (*c*) there shall be substituted the words—

> " and either the conditions stated in sub-paragraph (1) of paragraph 10 below or those stated in sub-paragraph (2) of that paragraph are satisfied.".

(3) In paragraph 10 for all the words preceding sub-paragraph (*a*) there shall be substituted the following words—

> " (1) The conditions first referred to in paragraph 9 above are—"

and the following shall be inserted in paragraph 10 as sub-   PART III
paragraph (2)—

"(2) The conditions secondly referred to in paragraph 9
above are—

> (a) that, when the interest is paid, the company con-
> tinues to satisfy any of the conditions of para-
> graph 3A(2) of Schedule 16 to the Finance Act   1972 c. 41.
> 1972 and the individual holds any part of the
> ordinary share capital of the company ; and

> (b) that in the period from the application of the pro-
> ceeds of the loan to the payment of the interest the
> individual has worked for the greater part of his
> time in the actual management or conduct of the
> company or of an associated company of the
> company ; and

> (c) that he shows in the period from the application of
> the proceeds of the loan to the payment of the
> interest he has not recovered any capital from the
> company, apart from any amount taken into
> account under paragraph 13 below."

(4) This section has effect in relation to interest paid on or
after 10th March 1982.

50. In section 39(1) of the Finance Act 1980 (relief for pre- Relief for
trading expenditure incurred within a year of the time the trader   pre-trading
began to carry on the trade) for the words "one year" there   expenditure.
shall be substituted the words "three years".   1980 c. 48.

51.—(1) In section 52 of the Finance Act 1981 (investment   Investment
in new corporate trades)—   in new
    corporate
> (a) in subsection (3)(a) (claim for relief not allowed until   trades.
> company has traded for twelve months) for the words   1981 c. 35.
> "twelve months" there shall be substituted the words
> "four months" ;

> (b) in subsection (6) (effect of subsection (3)(a) where com-
> pany is wound up before expiry of the twelve month
> period) for the words "twelve months" there shall be
> substituted the words "four months" ; and

> (c) after subsection (8) there shall be inserted the follow-
> ing subsection—

>> "(8A) No account shall be taken of the relief,
>> in so far as it is not withdrawn, in determining
>> whether any sums are excluded by virtue of sec-
>> tion 33 of the Capital Gains Tax Act 1979 (ex- 1979 c. 14.
>> clusion of expenditure by reference to tax on in-
>> come) from the sums allowable as a deduction in the

computation of gains and losses for the purposes of that Act."

(2) In section 53 of that Act (limits of the relief) for subsection (2) there shall be substituted the following subsection—

" (2) The relief shall not be given—

    (a) to the extent that the amount or total amount subscribed by an individual for ordinary shares issued to him (whether or not by the same company) in the years 1981-82 and 1982-83 exceeds £30,000 ; and

    (b) to the extent that the amount or total amount subscribed by an individual for ordinary shares issued to him (whether or not by the same company) in the year 1983-84 exceeds £20,000 ;

but paragraph (a) above shall not authorise relief to be given to an individual in respect of so much of the total amount subscribed by him for shares issued to him in the year 1981-82 as exceeds £10,000."

1981 c. 35.
(3) In subsection (7) of section 55 of the Finance Act 1981 (restrictions as to share capital for qualifying company for purposes of section 52 of that Act) for the words " at any time in the relevant period include " there shall be substituted the words " include at any time in the period of three years beginning with the date of issue of the shares in respect of which relief is claimed ".

(4) In subsection (1) of section 64 of that Act (reduction of sums allowable as deductions for capital gains tax) for the words from " reduced " to the end of paragraph (b) there shall be substituted the words " determined without regard to that relief, except that where those sums exceed the consideration they shall be reduced by an amount equal to—

    (a) the amount of that relief, or

    (b) the excess,

whichever is the less ".

Subsidiaries of qualifying companies.
52.—(1) In subsection (1) of section 65 of the Finance Act 1981 (application of sections 52 to 67 of that Act to subsidiaries) for the words from " did not commence business " to the end there shall be substituted the words " and if any subsidiary commenced business before the qualifying company did so, it was incorporated or (if later) commenced business not more than five years before the date of issue of the shares in respect of which relief is claimed ; and

    (c) the subsidiary or each subsidiary complies with the requirements of subsections (2) to (6) of section 55 above ".

(2) In paragraph 2(1) of Schedule 12 to that Act (modification of section 54 of that Act in relation to subsidiaries of qualifying companies) for the words from the beginning to " company if " there shall be substituted the following—

" (1) In subsections (2), (4) and (6) of section 54, references to the company (except, in each subsection, the first such reference) include references to a company which is during the relevant period a subsidiary of that company, whether it becomes a subsidiary before, during or after the year of assessment in respect of which the individual concerned claims relief and whether or not it is such a subsidiary while he is such an employee, partner or director as is mentioned in subsection (2) or while he has or is entitled to acquire such capital or voting power or rights as are mentioned in subsections (4) and (6).

(1B) Without prejudice to the provisions of section 54 (as it has effect in accordance with sub-paragraph (1) above), an individual shall be treated as connected with a company if—

(a) he has at any time in the relevant period had control (within the meaning of section 534 of the Taxes Act) of another company which has since that time and before the end of the relevant period become a subsidiary of the company ; or

(b) ".

(3) In paragraph 4 of that Schedule (modification of sections 58 and 59 in relation to subsidiaries of qualifying companies) for the words " a subsidiary of the company " there shall be substituted the words " any company which during the relevant period is a subsidiary of that company, whether it becomes a subsidiary before or after the individual concerned receives any value from it,".

(4) After that paragraph there shall be inserted the following paragraph—

" 4A. In subsection (2) of section 59 (redemption etc. of shares by company) the references to the company (except the first) shall include references to a company which during the relevant period is a subsidiary of the company whether it becomes a subsidiary before or after the redemption, repayment, repurchase or payment referred to in that subsection."

53.—(1) References in the Corporation Tax Acts to distribu- Purchase of tions of a company shall not include references to a payment own shares by made by a company on the redemption, repayment or purchase unquoted of its own shares if— trading company.

(a) the company is an unquoted company and either a trading company or the holding company of a trading group ; and

2 H 2

    (*b*) the redemption, repayment or purchase is made wholly or mainly for the purpose of benefiting a trade carried on by the company or by any of its 75 per cent. subsidiaries, and does not form part of a scheme or arrangement the main purpose or one of the main purposes of which is—

        (i) to enable the owner of the shares to participate in the profits of the company without receiving a dividend, or

        (ii) the avoidance of tax ; and

    (*c*) the conditions in paragraphs 1 to 9 of Schedule 9 to this Act, so far as applicable, are satisfied in relation to the owner of the shares.

(2) References in the Corporation Tax Acts to distributions of a company shall not include references to a payment made by a company on the redemption, repayment or purchase of its own shares if—

    (*a*) the company is within subsection (1)(*a*) above, and

    (*b*) the whole or substantially the whole of the payment (apart from any sum applied in paying capital gains tax charged on the redemption, repayment or purchase) is applied by the person to whom it is made in discharging a liability of his for capital transfer tax charged on a death, and is so applied within the period of two years after the death ;

but this subsection shall not apply to the extent that the liability could without undue hardship have been discharged otherwise than through the redemption, repayment or purchase of shares in the company or another company within subsection (1)(*a*) above.

(3) Schedule 9 to this Act shall have effect for supplementing this section ; and in that Schedule " the purchase " means the redemption, repayment or purchase referred to in subsection (1) above, and " the vendor " means the owner of the shares at the time it is made.

(4) This section has effect in relation to payments made on or after 6th April 1982.

54.—(1) Where on or after 6th April 1982 a company purchases its own shares from a dealer, the purchase price shall be taken into account in computing the profits of the dealer chargeable to tax under Case I or II of Schedule D ; and accordingly—

    (*a*) tax shall not be chargeable under Schedule F in respect of any distribution represented by any part of the price, and

    (*b*) the dealer shall not be entitled in respect of the distribution to a tax credit under section 86 of the Finance Act 1972, and

(c) sections 232(4) (duty to provide statements) and 239 (distributions not chargeable to corporation tax) of the Taxes Act shall not apply to the distribution.

(2) For the purposes of subsection (1) above a person is a dealer in relation to shares of a company if the price received on their sale by him otherwise than to the company would be taken into account in computing his profits chargeable to tax under Case I or II of Schedule D.

(3) In subsection (1) above,—

(a) the reference to the purchase of shares includes a reference to the redemption or repayment of shares and to the purchase of rights to acquire shares, and

(b) the reference to the purchase price includes a reference to any sum payable on redemption or repayment;

but subject to subsection (4) below.

(4) Subsection (1) above shall not apply in relation to—

(a) the redemption of fixed-rate preference shares, or

(b) the redemption, on terms settled or substantially settled before 6th April 1982, of other preference shares issued before that date,

if (in either case) the shares were issued to and continuously held by the person from whom they are redeemed.

(5) In this section—

" fixed-rate preference shares " means shares which—

(a) were issued wholly for new consideration, and

(b) do not carry any right either to conversion into shares or securities of any other description or to the acquisition of any additional shares or securities, and

(c) do not carry any right to dividends other than dividends which—

(i) are of a fixed amount or at a fixed rate per cent. of the nominal value of the shares, and

(ii) together with any sum paid on redemption, represent no more than a reasonable commercial return on the consideration for which the shares were issued;

" new consideration " has the same meaning as in Part X of the Taxes Act; and

" shares " includes stock.

2 H 3

PART III
Application
of advance
corporation
tax on
purchase of
company's
own shares.
1972 c. 41.

55. In section 92 of the Finance Act 1972 (setting of company's advance corporation tax in respect of dividends against subsidiary's liability) after subsection (7) there shall be inserted—

" (7A) References in this section to dividends shall be construed as including references to distributions made on or after 6th April 1982 on the redemption, repayment or purchase by a company of its own shares, and references to the payment of dividends shall be construed accordingly."

Close
companies:
apportionment
of income.
1980 c. 48.

56.—(1) In Schedule 16 to the Finance Act 1972 references to distributions shall be construed as including references to anything that would be a distribution but for one or both of—

(a) paragraph 1 of Schedule 18 to the Finance Act 1980 (demergers), and

(b) section 53 of this Act.

(2) In paragraph 12 of that Schedule, after sub-paragraph (2A) there shall be inserted—

" (2B) References in sub-paragraphs (1)(a) and (2)(b) above to the redemption or repayment of a company's share capital shall be construed as including references to the purchase by the company of its own shares."

(3) This section has effect in relation to events occurring on or after 6th April 1982.

Eurobond
dealers:
exemption
from
bond-washing
provisions.

57. Section 472 of the Taxes Act (application of bond-washing provisions to dealers in securities) shall have effect, and be deemed always to have had effect, with the addition, at the end of the section, of the following subsection:—

" (5) Subsection (1) of this section shall not apply if the securities are Eurobonds bought by the first buyer in the ordinary course of his trade as a dealer in Eurobonds; and in this subsection " Eurobond " means a security—

(a) which is neither preference stock nor preference share capital ; and

(b) which is issued in bearer form ; and

(c) which carries a right to interest either at a fixed rate or at a rate bearing a fixed relationship to a standard published base rate ; and

(d) which does not carry a right to any other form of benefit, whether in the nature of interest, participation in profits or otherwise ; and

(e) the interest on which is payable without any deduction in respect of income tax or of any tax of a similar character imposed by the laws of a territory outside the United Kingdom ;

but, notwithstanding anything in paragraph (*d*) above, a security is not prevented from being a Eurobond by reason only that it carries a right to convert into a security of another description or to subscribe for further securities (whether of the same description or not)."

58.—(1) This section has effect with respect to the following Treasury Stock, namely— Index-linked Treasury Stock.

(*a*) 2 per cent. Index-linked Treasury Stock 1996 ; and

(*b*) 2 per cent. Index-linked Treasury Stock 2006 ; and

(*c*) 2½ per cent. Index-linked Treasury Stock 2011 ;

and in this section any such stock is referred to as " existing index-linked stock ".

(2) The variation of the prospectuses relating to existing index-linked stock which was effected by a supplement to those prospectuses dated 9th March 1982 shall not be regarded as having affected the status of such stock as restricted government securities for the purposes of section 41 of the Finance Act 1981 1981 c. 35. (treatment of any income, gains or losses of insurance companies relating to such securities).

(3) Subject to subsection (4) below, on or after 27th March 1982 existing index-linked stock shall not be regarded as restricted government securities for the purposes of section 41 of the Finance Act 1981.

(4) If any existing index-linked stock was on 27th March 1982 held by an insurance company against and applied solely towards meeting the liabilities of its pension business, then, if and so long as the stock continues to be so held by that company, it shall continue to be treated as restricted government securities for the purposes of section 41 of the Finance Act 1981.

(5) If, on or after 27th March 1982, any existing index-linked stock which on that date was held by an insurance company ceases to be restricted government securities for the purposes of section 41 of the Finance Act 1981, otherwise than by virtue of being actually disposed of or being redeemed, then, on the day on which it so ceases, the stock shall be deemed for the purposes of corporation tax, including, subject to subsection (6) below, corporation tax on chargeable gains, to have been disposed of and immediately re-acquired at its market value on that date.

(6) For the purposes of sections 67 and 68 of the Capital Gains Tax Act 1979 (gilt-edged securities)— 1979 c. 14.

(*a*) in ascertaining the date on which securities were acquired,

2 H 4

no account shall be taken of any deemed disposal and re-acquisition resulting from subsection (5) above ; and

(b) so long as any existing index-linked stock continues, by virtue of subsection (4) above, to be treated on and after 27th March 1982 as restricted government securities for the purposes of section 41 of the Finance Act 1981, it shall be regarded as being stock of a different kind from existing index-linked stock which is not so treated.

(7) In this section " insurance company " and " pension business " have the same meaning as in section 323 of the Taxes Act.

Manufactured
dividends:
extension to
certain
securities
issued by
building
societies.

59.—(1) In section 477 of the Taxes Act (manufactured dividends: treatment of tax deducted) in subsection (2) (exclusion of cases where interest is payable without deduction of tax) after the word " where ", in the first place where it occurs, there shall be inserted the words " otherwise than by virtue of section 343(3)(a) of this Act ".

(2) This section has effect in relation to contracts for the sale of securities entered into after 9th March 1982.

Limitation on
meaning of
" distri-
bution " for
corporation
tax.

60.—(1) Any interest or other distribution which—

(a) is paid out of the assets of a company (in this section referred to as " the borrower ") on or after the relevant day to another company which is within the charge to corporation tax, and

(b) which is so paid in respect of securities of the borrower which fall within any of sub-paragraphs (i) to (iii) and (v) of paragraph (d) of subsection (2) of section 233 of the Taxes Act (meaning of " distribution "),

shall not be a distribution for the purposes of the Corporation Tax Acts unless the application of this subsection is excluded by subsection (2), subsection (3) or subsection (4) below.

(2) Subsection (1) above does not apply in a case where the consideration given by the borrower for the use of the principal secured represents more than a reasonable commercial return for the use of that principal ; but, where this subsection does apply, nothing in section 233(2)(d) of the Taxes Act shall operate so as to treat as a distribution for the purposes of the Corporation Tax Acts so much of the interest or other distribution as represents a reasonable commercial return for the use of that principal.

(3) Subsection (1) above does not apply in the case of any interest or other distribution which is paid in respect of a sec-

urity of the borrower falling within section 233(2)(*d*)(iii) of the
Taxes Act if—

(*a*) the principal secured does not exceed £100,000 ; and

(*b*) the borrower is under an obligation to repay the principal and interest before the expiry of the period of five
years beginning on the date on which the principal was
paid to the borrower ; and

(*c*) that obligation either was entered into before 9th March
1982 or was entered into before 1st July 1982 pursuant
to negotiations which were in progress on 9th March
1982 ; and

(*d*) where the period for repayment of either principal or
interest is extended on or after 9th March 1982 (but
paragraph (*b*) above still applies), the interest or other
distribution is paid within the period which was applicable immediately before that date ;

and for the purposes of paragraph (*c*) above negotiations shall
not be regarded as having been in progress on 9th March 1982
unless, before that date, the borrower had applied to the lender
for a loan and had supplied the lender with any documents required by him to support the application.

(4) Subsection (1) above does not apply in a case where the
company to which the interest or other distribution is paid is
entitled under any enactment, other than section 239 of the
Taxes Act (U.K. company distributions not chargeable to corporation tax), to an exemption from tax in respect of that
interest or distribution.

(5) In subsection (1)(*a*) above " the relevant day " means—

(*a*) in the case of any interest or other distribution which
is payable before 1st April 1983 pursuant to an
obligation entered into before 9th March 1982, 1st
April 1983 ; and

(*b*) in any other case, 9th March 1982.

(6) This section shall be construed as if it were included in
Part X of the Taxes Act.

61.—(1) This section applies to income arising from settled
property in respect of which a direction under section 93 below
has effect if the income—

Maintenance
funds for
historic
buildings:
reimbursement
of settlor.

(*a*) is treated by virtue of Part XVI of the Taxes Act as
income of the settlor for the year 1982-83 or a subsequent year of assessment, and

(*b*) is applied in reimbursing the settlor for expenditure
incurred by him for a purpose within subsection (3)(*a*)(i)
of section 93,

and if that expenditure is (or would apart from the reimbursement be) deductible in computing the profits of a trade carried on by the settlor.

(2) Income to which this section applies shall not be treated as reducing the expenditure deductible in computing the profits referred to in subsection (1) above, and shall not be regarded as income of the settlor otherwise than by virtue of Part XVI of the Taxes Act.

Maintenance funds: miscellaneous amendments. **62.**—(1) Where settled property in respect of which a direction has effect under section 93 below constitutes part only of the property comprised in a settlement, it and the other property shall be treated as comprised in separate settlements for the purposes of the enactments specified in subsection (2) below.

(2) The enactments referred to in subsection (1) above are—

    (*a*) sections 168 to 173 of the Taxes Act ;

    (*b*) Part XVI of the Taxes Act ;

1973 c. 51.   (*c*) sections 16 and 17 of the Finance Act 1973 ;

1977 c. 36.   (*d*) section 38 of the Finance Act 1977 ;

1980 c. 48.   (*e*) sections 52 and 53 of the Finance Act 1980.

(3) Schedule 10 to this Act (which makes amendments relating to maintenance funds) shall have effect.

Sums paid to settlor otherwise than as income. **63.**—(1) In section 451 of the Taxes Act (sums paid to settlor otherwise than as income) subsection (1) shall have effect in accordance with subsections (2) and (3) below and shall be presumed so to have had effect in relation to any capital sum paid to the settlor on or after 6th April 1981.

1981 c. 35. (2) In paragraph (*b*) the amendment made by section 42(2)(*c*) of the Finance Act 1981 shall be presumed not to have been made and, accordingly, the words following " up to the end of " shall read " the next following year, be treated for the purposes aforesaid as income of the settlor for the next following year ".

(3) In the words following paragraph (*b*) (as amended by section 42(2)(*b*) of the Finance Act 1981) after the words " each subsequent year " there shall be inserted the words " up to a maximum of ten subsequent years ".

(4) Where a capital sum was paid in a relevant year ending before 6th April 1981 (the operative date for sections 42 and 43 of the Finance Act 1981) and the circumstances are such that—

    (*a*) subsection (1) of section 451 of the Taxes Act applies to that sum, but

    (*b*) on that date the whole or some part of that sum (in this subsection referred to as " the balance ") had not been treated, in accordance with that subsection, as the income of the settlor for any relevant year ending before that date,

the balance shall be deemed for the purposes of that section to have been paid not at the time the capital sum was in fact paid but on 6th April 1981.

(5) Expressions used in subsections (1) and (4) above have the same meaning as in section 451(1) of the Taxes Act.

64.—(1) In section 131(2)(*c*)(ii) (deduction of certain interest payments to non-residents in computing profits or gains) and section 249(1)(*c*)(ii) (similar provision in relation to corporation tax) of the Taxes Act, for the words " the currency of a territory outside the scheduled territories " there shall be substituted, in each case, the words " a currency other than sterling ". Payments of interest in currencies other than sterling.

(2) In section 416(1) of the Taxes Act (local authority borrowing in foreign currencies) for the words from " the currency " to " territories " there shall be substituted the words " a currency other than sterling ".

(3) Subsection (1) has effect in relation to payments of interest made, and subsection (2) has effect in relation to securities issued, on or after 6th April 1982.

65.—(1) This section applies in a case where— Double taxation relief:

> (*a*) in any chargeable period the profits of any person (in this section referred to as " the lender ") which are brought into charge to income tax or corporation tax include an amount, computed in accordance with section 503 of the Taxes Act, in respect of interest (in this section referred to as " foreign loan interest ") on a loan made to a person resident in a territory outside the United Kingdom ; and interest on certain overseas loans.

> (*b*) in determining the liability of the lender to income tax or corporation tax, expenditure related to the earning of the foreign loan interest is deductible in computing the profits referred to in paragraph (*a*) above ; and

> (*c*) the lender is entitled in accordance with Chapter II of Part XVIII of the Taxes Act (double taxation relief) to credit for foreign tax chargeable on or by reference to the foreign loan interest.

(2) If, in a case where this section applies, the foreign tax referred to in subsection (1)(*c*) above is or includes an amount of spared tax, then, for the purposes of income tax or corporation tax, the amount which, apart from this subsection, would be the amount of the foreign loan interest shall be treated

as increased by so much of the spared tax as does not exceed the permitted amount, as defined in subsection (3) below ; but nothing in this subsection prejudices the operation of section 503 of the Taxes Act in relation to foreign tax which is not spared tax.

(3) In this section " spared tax " means foreign tax which, although not payable, falls to be taken into account for the purposes of credit by virtue of section 497(3) of the Taxes Act ; and the permitted amount, in relation to spared tax which is referable to the whole or any part of the foreign loan interest, is an amount which does not exceed—

    (*a*) 15 per cent. of the interest to which the spared tax is referable, computed without regard to any increase under subsection (2) above ; or

    (*b*) if it is less, the amount of that spared tax for which, in accordance with any arrangements applicable to the case in question, credit falls to be given as mentioned in subsection (1)(*c*) above.

(4) If, in a case where this section applies,—

    (*a*) the foreign tax referred to in subsection (1)(*c*) above is or includes an amount of tax which is not spared tax, and

    (*b*) that amount of tax exceeds the amount of the credit which, by virtue of Chapter II of Part XVIII of the Taxes Act and subsection (5) below, is allowed for that foreign tax against income tax or corporation tax,

then, for the purposes of income tax or corporation tax, the amount which, apart from this subsection, would be the amount of the foreign loan interest shall be treated as reduced by a sum equal to the excess.

(5) Where this section applies, the amount of the credit for foreign tax referred to in subsection (1)(*c*) above which, in accordance with Chapter II of Part XVIII of the Taxes Act, is to be allowed against income tax or corporation tax shall not exceed 15 per cent. of the foreign loan interest, computed without regard to any increase under subsection (2) or any reduction under subsection (4) above.

(6) This section shall be construed as if it were included in Chapter II of Part XVIII of the Taxes Act.

(7) Where the loan on which the foreign loan interest is payable was made pursuant to an agreement entered into before 1st April 1982, this section does not apply in relation to interest payable before 1st April 1983, but subject thereto, this section applies in relation to interest payable on or after 1st April 1982.

66.—(1) This section applies in a case where—

(a) a bank or a company connected with a bank makes a claim for an allowance by way of credit in accordance with Chapter II of Part XVIII of the Taxes Act ; and

(b) the claim relates to underlying tax on a dividend paid by the overseas company, within the meaning of section 508 of that Act ; and

(c) that underlying tax is or includes tax payable under the law of a territory outside the United Kingdom on or by reference to interest on a loan made in the course of its business by that overseas company or by such a third, fourth or successive company as is referred to in subsection (2) or subsection (3) of that section ; and

(d) if the company which made the loan had been resident in the United Kingdom, then, in determining its liability to corporation tax, expenditure related to the earning of the interest on the loan would be deductible in computing the profits of the company brought into charge to tax.

(2) If, in a case where this section applies, the underlying tax is or includes an amount of spared tax, then, for the purposes of corporation tax, the amount which, apart from this subsection, would be the amount of the dividend shall be treated as increased by an amount equal to so much of that spared tax as does not exceed the permitted amount, as defined in subsection (3) below ; but nothing in this subsection prejudices the operation of section 503 of the Taxes Act in relation to foreign tax which is not spared tax.

(3) In this section " spared tax " has the same meaning as in section 65 above ; and the permitted amount, in relation to spared tax which is referable to the whole or any part of the interest referred to in subsection (1)(c) above, is an amount which does not exceed—

(a) 15 per cent. of the interest to which that spared tax is referable ; or

(b) if it is less, the amount of that spared tax which under any arrangements is to be taken into account for the purpose of allowing credit against corporation tax in respect of the dividend concerned.

(4) If, in a case where this section applies,—

(a) the underlying tax is or includes an amount of tax which is not spared tax, and

(b) that amount of tax exceeds 15 per cent. of the interest to which it is referable,

then, for the purposes of corporation tax, the amount which, apart from this subsection, would be the amount of the dividend shall be treated as reduced by a sum equal to the excess.

(5) Where this section applies, the amount of the credit referred to in paragraph (a) of subsection (1) above which is referable to the underlying tax payable as mentioned in paragraph (c) of that subsection shall not exceed 15 per cent. of so much of the interest referred to in that paragraph as is included in the relevant profits of the company paying the dividend ; and for the purposes of this subsection—

(a) " relevant profits " has the same meaning as, by virtue of section 506 of the Taxes Act, it has for the purposes of the computation of underlying tax ; and

(b) the amount of the interest shall be determined without making any deduction in respect of any foreign tax.

(6) In subsection (1) above " bank " means a company carrying on, in the United Kingdom or elsewhere,—

(a) a banking business ; or

(b) another business which includes the making of loans where the circumstances of the business are such that, in determining the liability of the company to corporation tax, expenditure related to the earning of the interest on those loans is deductible in computing the profits brought into charge to tax ;

and section 533 of the Taxes Act (connected persons) applies for the purposes of subsection (1) above.

(7) This section shall be construed as if it were included in Chapter II of Part XVIII of the Taxes Act.

(8) Where the loan referred to in subsection (1)(c) above was made pursuant to an agreement entered into before 1st April 1982 this section does not apply to any underlying tax which is referable to interest on that loan payable before 1st April 1983 but, subject thereto, this section applies where the underlying tax is referable to interest payable on or after 1st April 1982.

Double taxation relief: branches of non-resident banks.

67. At the end of paragraph (b) of the proviso to section 502 of the Taxes Act (exceptions, in relation to unilateral relief, from the requirement that the person claiming relief must be resident in the United Kingdom) there shall be added " and

(c) for tax paid under the law of any territory in respect of interest on a loan where the following conditions are fulfilled, namely,—

(i) that the person in question is a company which, for the chargeable period in question, carries on a banking business in the United Kingdom through a branch or agency ; and

(ii) that the loan was made by the company through the branch or agency in the United Kingdom ; and

(iii) that the territory under whose law the tax was paid is not one in which the company is liable to tax by reason of domicile, residence or place of management ; and

(iv) that the amount of relief claimed does not exceed (or is by the claim expressly limited to) that which would have been available if the branch or agency had been a company resident in the United Kingdom and the loan had been made by it in the course of its banking business.

68.—(1) In section 55 of the Taxes Management Act 1970 (postponement of recovery of tax) in subsection (2) for the words " If no application is made under subsection (3) below " there shall be substituted the words " Except as otherwise provided by the following provisions of this section ".

Postponement of recovery of tax.
1970 c. 9.

(2) After subsection (3) of that section there shall be inserted the following subsection—

" (3A) An application under subsection (3) above may be made more than thirty days after the date of the issue of the notice of assessment if there is a change in the circumstances of the case as a result of which the appellant has grounds for believing that he is over-charged to tax by the assessment."

(3) In subsection (6) of that section (determination of application) in paragraph (*a*) after the words " subsection (3) above " there shall be inserted the words " other than an application made by virtue of subsection (3A) above ".

(4) This section has effect in relation to notices of assessment to tax issued after the passing of this Act.

69.—(1) In section 86 of the Taxes Management Act 1970 (interest on overdue tax) in subsection (3) (date when interest becomes payable)—

Interest on unpaid tax.

(*a*) the following paragraph shall be inserted after paragraph (*a*)—

" (*aa*) in relation to any tax payable in accordance with the determination of an appeal against an assessment but which had not been charged by the assessment, the date which if it had been charged would by virtue of paragraph (*a*) above have been the reckonable date ; and " ;

PART III   **and**

(b) in paragraph (b) after the words " paragraph (a) " there shall be inserted the words " or paragraph (aa) ".

(2) This section has effect in relation to notices of assessment to tax issued after the passing of this Act.

CHAPTER II
CAPITAL ALLOWANCES

Allowances for assets leased outside the United Kingdom.

70.—(1) The provisions of this section have effect with respect to expenditure on the provision of machinery or plant for leasing where the machinery or plant is at any time in the requisite period used for the purpose of being leased to a person who—

(a) is not resident in the United Kingdom, and

(b) does not use the machinery or plant for the purposes of a trade carried on there or for earning profits or gains chargeable to tax by virtue of section 38(4) of the Finance Act 1973,

1973 c. 51.

and where the leasing is not short-term leasing.

(2) In its application to expenditure falling within subsection (1) above, section 44 of the Finance Act 1971 (writing-down allowances and balancing adjustments) as it has effect—

1971 c. 68.

1980 c. 48.

(a) in accordance with section 65 of the Finance Act 1980 (assets leased in the course of a trade), or

(b) in accordance with paragraph 6 of Schedule 8 to the Finance Act 1971 (effect of subsidies towards wear and tear of assets), or

(c) in accordance with paragraph 10 of that Schedule (cars costing more than £8,000), or

(d) with respect to any motor car to which paragraph 11 of that Schedule applies (contributions towards expenditure on cars costing more than £8,000), or

(e) with respect to machinery or plant to which section 46 of the Finance Act 1971 applies (assets leased otherwise than in the course of a trade),

shall have effect, subject to subsection (4) below, as if the reference in subsection (2) of section 44 to 25 per cent. were a reference to 10 per cent.

(3) In any case where—

(a) machinery or plant is used for the purpose of being leased to such a person as is referred to in paragraphs (a) and (b) of subsection (1) above, and

(b) the circumstances are such that the machinery or plant is used otherwise than for a qualifying purpose, within the meaning of section 64 of the Finance Act 1980 (exclusion of first-year allowances for certain leased assets), any question whether that use falls within the requisite period, as defined in subsection (8) of that section, shall be determined as if, for each reference in that subsection to four years, there were substituted a reference to ten years ; and any reference to the requisite period in sections 66 and 67 of that Act shall be construed accordingly.

(4) No first year allowances, balancing allowances or writing-down allowances shall be available in respect of expenditure falling within subsection (1) above if the circumstances are as mentioned in subsection (3)(*b*) above and—

   (*a*) there is a period of more than one year between the dates on which any two consecutive payments become due under the lease ; or

   (*b*) any payments other than periodical payments are due under the lease or under any agreement which might reasonably be construed as being collateral to the lease ; or

   (*c*) disregarding variations made under the terms of the lease which are attributable to—

      (i) changes in the rate of corporation tax or income tax, or

      (ii) changes in the rate of capital allowances, or

      (iii) changes in any rate of interest where the changes are linked to changes in the rate of interest applicable to inter-bank loans, or

      (iv) changes in the premiums charged for insurance of any description by a person who is not connected with the lessor or the lessee,

    any of the payments due under the lease or under any such agreement as is referred to in sub-paragraph (*b*) above, expressed as monthly amounts over the period for which that payment is due, is not the same as any other such payment expressed in the same way ; or

   (*d*) either the lease is expressed to be for a period which exceeds thirteen years or there is, in the lease or a separate agreement, provision for extending or renewing the lease or for the grant of a new lease so that, by virtue of that provision, the machinery or plant could be leased for a period which exceeds thirteen years ; or

   (*e*) at any time the lessor or a person connected with him will, or may in certain circumstances, become entitled to receive from the lessee or any other person a payment, other than a payment of insurance moneys, which is of an amount determined before the expiry of the lease and which is referable to a value of the machinery or plant at or after that expiry (whether or not the payment relates to a disposal of the machinery or plant).

(5) Where a first year allowance, a balancing allowance or a writing-down allowance has been made in respect of expenditure incurred in providing machinery or plant and, at any time in the requisite period, an event occurs such that, by virtue of subsection (4) above, there is no right to that allowance, an amount equal to any such allowance which has previously been given (less any excess reliefs previously recovered by the operation of

section 66 of the Finance Act 1980) shall, in relation to the person to whom the machinery or plant belongs immediately before the occurrence of that event, be treated as if it were a balancing charge to be made on him for the chargeable period in which, or in the basis period for which, the machinery or plant is used at the time that event occurs.

(6) Subsections (3) and (4) of section 66 of the Finance Act 1980 apply in relation to the allowances mentioned in subsection (5) above as they apply in relation to the allowances mentioned in subsection (2) of that section.

(7) In subsection (1) above " short-term leasing " has the same meaning as in subsection (2)(*b*) of section 64 of the Finance Act 1980, and in subsection (3) of that section (which defines that expression) at the beginning of sub-paragraph (ii) of paragraph (*b*), there shall be inserted the words " subject to subsection (3A) below " and at the end of that subsection there shall be added—

" (3A) In a case where the requisite period exceeds four years the reference in subsection (3)(*b*)(ii) above to that period shall be construed as a reference to any period of four consecutive years which falls within the requisite period."

(8) The provisions of Schedule 11 to this Act shall have effect for supplementing the preceding provisions of this section.

(9) In subsections (1) and (5) above " the requisite period " has the same meaning as, in a case where subsection (3) above applies, it has in sections 64 to 68 of the Finance Act 1980 ; and section 73 of that Act (interpretation), with the exception of subsection (4) thereof, has effect in relation to the preceding provisions of this section and the provisions of Schedule 11 to this Act—

(*a*) as if those provisions were comprised in the foregoing provisions of Chapter II of Part III of that Act ; and

(*b*) as if the reference in subsection (1) of that section to section 72 of that Act included a reference to subsection (10) below.

(10) Subject to subsection (11) below, this section applies to expenditure incurred on or after 10th March 1982 unless—

    (*a*) the expenditure consists of the payment of sums payable under a contract entered into before that date by the person incurring the expenditure ; or

    (*b*) the expenditure consists of the payment of sums payable under a contract entered into not later than 31st March 1984 and the conditions in subsection (12) below are fulfilled ;

and, in either case, the machinery or plant concerned is brought into use not later than 31st March 1985.

(11) In its application to subsections (4) to (6) above, subsection (10) above has effect as if for the references to 10th March 1982 there were substituted references to 23rd June 1982.

(12) The conditions referred to in paragraph (*b*) of subsection (10) above are—

    (*a*) that the expenditure referred to in that paragraph is incurred in fulfilment of arrangements (not necessarily amounting to contractual obligations) under which the person incurring the expenditure (in this subsection referred to as " the lessor ") would lease the machinery or plant in question to another person (in this subsection referred to as " the lessee ") ; and

    (*b*) that those arrangements were in existence on 10th March 1982 and are evidenced by writing dating from a time before that date ; and

    (*c*) that. in reliance upon the arrangements and before 10th March 1982, the lessee had entered into a contract with a third party (in this subsection referred to as " the supplier ") to incur expenditure on the provision of the machinery or plant in question ; and

    (*d*) that, pursuant to the arrangements,—

        (i) the obligations of the lessee under the contract referred to in paragraph (*c*) above are, before 31st March 1984, either taken over by the lessor or discharged on the lessor entering into a new contract with the supplier ; or

        (ii) the lessee purchases the machinery or plant in question and transfers it to the lessor before 8th July 1982 ; and

    (*e*) that, on or before 31st March 1984, the lessor enters into a contract to lease the machinery or plant to the lessee ; and

    (*f*) that, disregarding any use before 8th July 1982, the machinery or plant in question is not brought into use by the lessee before it is leased to him by the lessor ; and

(g) that the lessor and the lessee are not connected persons and neither of them is connected with the supplier ;

and section 533 of the Taxes Act (connected persons) applies for the purposes of this section.

Restriction on first-year allowances in respect of ships and aircraft let on charter.
1980 c. 48.

71.—(1) In subsection (5) of section 64 of the Finance Act 1980 (first-year allowances to be available in respect of ships and aircraft let out on certain charters) after the words " subsection (2) above " there shall be inserted the words " but subject to subsection (6A) below ".

(2) At the end of subsection (6) of that section there shall be inserted the following subsection :—

" (6A) Subsection (5) above does not apply if the main object, or one of the main objects, of the letting of the ship or aircraft on charter, or of a series of transactions of which the letting on charter was one, or of any of the transactions in such a series was to obtain a first-year allowance in respect of expenditure incurred on the provision of the ship or aircraft, whether by the person referred to in subsection (5)(a) above or some other person."

(3) This section applies in relation to expenditure incurred on or after 10th March 1982 unless—

(a) the expenditure consists of the payment of sums payable under a contract entered into before that date by the person incurring the expenditure ; and

(b) the ship or aircraft concerned is brought into use not later than 31st March 1984.

Expenditure on production and acquisition of films etc.

1971 c. 68.

72.—(1) Expenditure which—

(a) is incurred on or after 10th March 1982 on the production or acquisition of a film, tape or disc, and

(b) would, apart from this subsection, constitute capital expenditure on the provision of machinery or plant for the purposes of Chapter I of Part III of the Finance Act 1971 (first-year and other allowances in respect of machinery and plant),

shall be regarded for the purposes of the Tax Acts as expenditure of a revenue nature unless it is expenditure falling within subsection (7) below.

(2) In this section—

(a) any reference to a film is (except where, in subsection (8) below, the context otherwise requires) a reference to an original master negative of the film and its soundtrack (if any) ;

(*b*) any reference to a tape is a reference to an original master film tape or original master audio tape ; and

(*c*) any reference to a disc is a reference to an original master film disc or original master audio disc ;

and any reference to the acquisition of a film, tape or disc includes a reference to the acquisition of any description of rights in a film, tape or disc.

(3) Subject to the following provisions of this section, in computing the profits or gains accruing to any person from a trade or business which consists of or includes the exploitation of a film, tape or disc, expenditure which—

(*a*) is incurred on or after 10th March 1982 on the production or acquisition of a film, tape or disc, and

(*b*) is expenditure of a revenue nature (whether by virtue of subsection (1) above or otherwise),

shall be allocated to relevant periods in accordance with subsection (4) below ; and in this subsection and subsection (4) below " relevant period " means a period for which the accounts of the trade or business concerned are made up or, if those accounts are not made up for any period, a period the profits or gains of which are taken into account in assessing the income of the trade or business for any chargeable period.

(4) The amount of expenditure falling within subsection (3) above which falls to be allocated to any relevant period shall be such as is just and reasonable, having regard to—

(*a*) the amount of that expenditure which remains unallocated at the beginning of that period ;

(*b*) the proportion which the estimated value of the film, tape or disc which is realised in that period (whether by way of income or otherwise) bears to the aggregate of the value so realised and the estimated remaining value of the film, tape or disc at the end of that period ; and

(*c*) the need to bring the whole of the expenditure falling within subsection (3) above into account over the time during which the value of the film, tape or disc is expected to be realised.

(5) Subsections (3) and (4) above do not apply to the profits or gains of a trade in which the film, tape or disc concerned constitutes trading stock, as defined in section 137(4) of the Taxes Act.

(6) In a case where any expenditure on the production or acquisition of a film, tape or disc is expenditure to which subsection (1) above applies, sums received from the disposal of that film, tape of disc shall be regarded for the purposes of the Tax Acts as receipts of a revenue nature (if they would not

be so regarded apart from this subsection); and the reference in this subsection to sums received from the disposal of any film, tape or disc shall be construed as including—

> (a) sums received from the disposal of any interest or right in or over the film, tape or disc, including an interest or right created by the disposal ; and

> (b) insurance or compensation moneys and other moneys of a like nature which are derived from the film, tape or disc.

(7) The preceding provisions of this section do not apply to expenditure which is incurred by any person on or before 31st March 1984 if it consists of the payment of sums payable under a contract entered into by him before 10th March 1982 or it is incurred—

> (a) by a person who carries on a trade or business which consists of or includes the exploitation of films, tapes or discs ; and

> (b) on the production or acquisition of a film, tape or disc which is certified by the Secretary of State for the purposes of this section as a qualifying film, tape or disc and the value of which is expected to be realisable over a period of not less than two years.

(8) The Secretary of State shall not certify a film, tape or disc as a qualifying film, tape or disc for the purposes of this section unless he is satisfied that it is the master negative, master tape or master disc of a film which, in his opinion,—

1981 c. 16.
> (a) is an eligible film for the purposes of regulations made or having effect as if made under section 6 of the Film Levy Finance Act 1981 (payments by the British Film Fund Agency to the makers of British films) and in force immediately before the passing of this Act ; or

> (b) would be such an eligible film if it were not a television film within the meaning of those regulations.

(9) In this section " expenditure of a revenue nature " means expenditure which, if it were incurred in the course of a trade the profits or gains of which are chargeable to tax under Case I of Schedule D, would be taken into account for the purpose of computing the profits, gains or losses of the trade ; and " receipts of a revenue nature " means receipts which, if they were receipts of such a trade, would be taken into account for that purpose.

Industrial buildings allowance: very small workshops.

1968 c. 3.
1980 c. 48.

73.—(1) Chapter I of Part I of the Capital Allowances Act 1968 (industrial buildings allowances) shall apply with the modifications specified in paragraphs 1 to 3 of Schedule 13 to the Finance Act 1980 in relation to capital expenditure on the construction of an industrial building to which this section applies if the expenditure is incurred after 26th March 1983 and before 27th March 1985.

(2) This section applies to an industrial building if the gross internal floor space of the whole building will not exceed 1,250 square feet.

(3) Subsections (3) to (6) of section 75 of the Finance Act 1980 (small workshops allowance) shall apply for the purposes of this section as they apply for the purposes of that section and accordingly—

> (*a*) in subsection (3) the reference to subsection (2) of that section shall be construed as including a reference to subsection (2) of this section ; and
>
> (*b*) in subsections (4) and (5) the references to subsection (1) of that section shall be construed as including a reference to subsection (1) of this section.

(4) The Tax Acts shall have effect as if this section were contained in Chapter I of Part I of the said Act of 1968.

74.—(1) In section 1 of the Capital Allowances Act 1968 (initial allowances) the following subsection shall be inserted after subsection (1)—

> " (1A) The reference in subsection (1) above to the occupation of a building or structure for the purposes of a trade carried on by the person who incurred the capital expenditure on that building or structure shall include a reference to the use of that building or structure for the purposes of a trade carried on by a licensee of that person or of a lessee of that person."

(2) Section 6 of that Act (method of making allowances and charges) shall apply where the building or structure in question is used by a licensee of the person entitled to the relevant interest as if that interest were subject to a lease.

(3) In section 7 of that Act (definition of " industrial building or structure ") the following subsection shall be inserted after subsection (3)—

> " (3A) Where a building or structure is used by more than one licensee of the same person that building or structure shall not be an industrial building or structure unless each of the licensees uses the building or that part of it to which his licence relates for the purposes of a trade which falls within subsection (1) above."

(4) Subsections (1) and (3) above shall apply in relation to licences granted on or after 10th March 1982.

PART III
Industrial
buildings
allowance:
maintenance
of goods etc.
1968 c. 3.

75.—(1) In section 7 of the Capital Allowances Act 1968 (definition of " industrial building or structure ") the following subsection shall be inserted after subsection (2)—

" (2A) The reference in paragraph (e) of subsection (1) above to the subjection of goods or materials to any process shall include a reference to the maintaining or repairing of any goods or materials but, notwithstanding subsection (2) above, paragraph (e) shall not apply to the maintenance or repair by any person of goods or materials employed by that person in any trade or undertaking unless that trade or undertaking itself falls within any of the paragraphs of that subsection (including paragraph (e))."

(2) In subsection (3) of that section (retail shops etc. not to constitute industrial buildings or structures) for the words " subsection (1) or subsection (2) " there shall be substituted the words " the preceding provisions ".

(3) This section shall be deemed to have come into force on 10th March 1982.

Allowances
for dwelling-
houses let on
assured
tenancies.

76.—(1) The provisions of Schedule 12 to this Act shall have effect to provide for reliefs in respect of expenditure incurred on the construction of buildings consisting of or including dwelling-houses let on assured and certain other tenancies.

(2) Schedule 12 to this Act has effect only where the expenditure concerned is incurred on or after 10th March 1982 and before 1st April 1987 or is deemed to have been so incurred by virtue of paragraph 8 of that Schedule.

Teletext
receivers and
teletext and
viewdata
adaptors.
1980 c. 48.

77.—(1) Paragraph 7 of Schedule 12 to the Finance Act 1980 (transitional period for 100 per cent. first year allowances for television sets) shall be amended in accordance with the following provisions of this section.

(2) In sub-paragraph (2) (definition of " the transitional period ") in paragraph (a) after the words " other than " there shall be inserted the words " a teletext receiver or " and at the end of paragraph (a) there shall be inserted : —

" (aa) in relation to expenditure on the provision of a teletext receiver, the period of five years beginning with that date ".

(3) In sub-paragraph (3) (definition of " viewdata receiver ") after the words " television set " in the first place where they occur, there shall be inserted the words " which is not a teletext receiver but which is " and the words from " and a television set " to the end of the sub-paragraph shall be omitted.

(4) After sub-paragraph (3) there shall be inserted the following sub-paragraphs:—

" (4) In this Part of this Schedule " a teletext receiver " means a television set—

    (*a*) which is constructed for receiving teletext transmissions, that is to say, transmissions intended for general reception and consisting of a succession of visual displays (with or without accompanying sound) each capable of being selected and held for separate viewing or other use ; and

    (*b*) which is not also constructed for displaying information received as mentioned in sub-paragraph (3) above.

(5) In relation to expenditure incurred after 9th March 1982—

    (*a*) this Part of this Schedule, other than sub-paragraph (6) below, shall have effect as if any reference to a television set included a reference to a teletext adaptor or a viewdata adaptor ; and

    (*b*) sub-paragraph (2) above shall have effect as if any reference to a teletext receiver included a reference to a teletext adaptor and as if any reference to a viewdata receiver included a reference to a viewdata adaptor.

(6) In this Part of this Schedule—

    (*a*) " teletext adaptor " means a device external to a television set which, after it is connected to that television set, allows the set to display transmissions in the same manner as a teletext receiver ; and

    (*b*) " viewdata adaptor " means a device external to a television set which, after it is connected to that television set, allows the set to display information received in the same manner as a viewdata receiver."

78.—(1) In section 515(1) of the Taxes Act (postponement of capital allowances to secure double taxation relief) for the words " tax in respect of a trade under Case I of Schedule D " there shall be substituted the words " tax under Schedule D in respect of a trade ".

Extension of section 515 relief to Case V of Schedule D.

(2) This section applies in relation to claims made on or after 6th April 1982.

79.—(1) This section applies in any case where a person is entitled to an allowance or relief for a year of assessment and—

(*a*) he and the inspector have come to an agreement, in writing, as to the extent to which the allowance or relief is to be given effect in that year (whether by deduction from profits or gains or by discharge or repayment of tax, or both) ; and

(*b*) no assessment giving effect to the allowance or relief is made for that year.

(2) In a case to which this section applies the allowance or relief shall be taken to have been given effect in the year of assessment in question, as if an assessment had been made, to the extent set out in the agreement mentioned in subsection (1) above.

(3) In this section—

1968 c. 3.

" allowance " means an allowance to which section 70 or 71 of the Capital Allowances Act 1968 applies (income tax allowances in taxing a trade) ; and

1981 c. 35.

" relief " means a relief to which Part II of Schedule 9 to the Finance Act 1981 applies (income tax: stock relief).

(4) This section has effect in relation to agreements made on or after 6th April 1982.

CHAPTER III

CAPITAL GAINS

Increase and
indexation of
annual exempt
amount.
1979 c. 14.

80.—(1) In section 5 of the Capital Gains Tax Act 1979 (exemption for first £3,000 of gains)—

(*a*) for " £3,000 ", in each place where it occurs, there shall be substituted " the exempt amount for the year " ; and

(*b*) for " £5,000 ", where it occurs in subsection (5)(*b*), there shall be substituted " an amount equal to twice the exempt amount for the year."

(2) After subsection (1) of that section there shall be inserted the following subsections—

" (1A) Subject to subsection (1B) below, the exempt amount for any year of assessment shall be £5,000.

(1B) If the retail prices index for the month of December preceding the year 1983-84 or any subsequent year of assessment is higher than it was for the previous December, then, unless Parliament otherwise determines, subsection (1A) above shall have effect for that year as if for the amount specified in that subsection as it applied for the previous year (whether by virtue of this subsection or otherwise) there were substituted an amount arrived at by increasing the amount for the previous year by the same percentage as the percentage increase in the retail prices index and, if the result is not a multiple of £100, rounding it up to the nearest amount which is such a multiple.

(1C) The Treasury shall, before the year 1983-84 and each subsequent year, make an order specifying the amount which by virtue of this section is the exempt amount for that year ; and any such order shall be made by statutory instrument ".

(3) In Schedule 1 to that Act—

(*a*) the heading shall be changed to " APPLICATION OF EXEMPT AMOUNT IN PARTICULAR CASES " ;

(*b*) for the words " the amount of £3,000 ", where they occur in paragraphs 2(1) and 5(1D), and for " £3,000 " in every other place where it occurs, there shall be substituted the words " the exempt amount for the year " ;

(*c*) for " £300 ", where it occurs in paragraphs 5(1B) and 6(4), there shall be substituted the words " one tenth of that exempt amount " ;

(*d*) for " £1,500 ", in each place where it occurs in sub-paragraphs (2) and (4) of paragraph 6, and for " the amount of £1,500 ", where it occurs in sub-paragraph (6) of that paragraph, there shall be substituted the words " one half of the exempt amount for the year " ; and

(*e*) in sub-paragraph (3) of paragraph 6 for the words from " £5,000 " onwards there shall be substituted the words " ' twice the exempt amount for the year ' of ' one half of the exempt amount for the year ' and ' the exempt amount for the year ' respectively ".

(4) In section 24(8) of the Finance Act 1980 (definition of " retail prices index " for the purposes of the Income Tax Acts) after the word " Acts " in each place where it occurs, there shall be inserted the words " or the Capital Gains Tax Act 1979 ". 1980 c. 48.

1979 c. 14.

(5) This section has effect for the year 1982-83 and subsequent years of assessment.

81.—(1) In the following enactments, namely,— Increase of chattel exemption.

(*a*) section 128 of the Capital Gains Tax Act 1979 (chattel exemption by reference to consideration of £2,000),

(*b*) section 12(2)(*b*) of the Taxes Management Act 1970 (information about assets acquired), and 1970 c. 9.

Part III

(c) section 25(7) of that Act (information about assets disposed of),

for " £2,000 ", in each case where it occurs, there shall be substituted " £3,000 ".

(2) This section applies to disposals on or after 6th April 1982 and, accordingly, in relation to subsection (1)(b) above, to assets acquired on or after that date.

Extension of general relief for gifts.
1980 c. 48.
1981 c. 35.

82.—(1) Section 79 of the Finance Act 1980 (which gives relief for disposals between individuals and, by virtue of section 78 of the Finance Act 1981, disposals by individuals to trustees) shall have effect as if references to an individual included references to the trustees of a settlement; but a claim for relief under that section in respect of a disposal to the trustees of a settlement shall be made by the transferor alone (instead of by the transferor and the transferee).

(2) In subsection (4) of that section, the words from " or " onwards shall cease to have effect.

(3) In subsection (5) of that section—

(a) in paragraph (a), for the words from " chargeable " to " purposes " there shall be substituted the words " attributable to the value of the asset " ; and

(b) the words from " and where " onwards shall cease to have effect.

(4) In section 78 of the Finance Act 1981 (subsections (1) and (3) of which are superseded by this section) in subsection (2) for the words " that section " there shall be substituted the words " section 79 of the Finance Act 1980 ".

(5) This section applies to disposals on or after 6th April 1982.

Relief on compulsory purchase.
1979 c. 14.

83. After section 111 of the Capital Gains Tax Act 1979 there shall be inserted the following sections—

" Rollover relief on compulsory acquisition.

111A.—(1) This section applies where—

(a) on or after 6th April 1982 land (in this section referred to as " the old land ") is disposed of by any person (in this section referred to as " the landowner ") to an authority exercising or having compulsory powers ; and

(b) the landowner did not take any steps, by advertising or otherwise, to dispose of the old land or to make his willingness to dispose of it known to the authority or others ; and

(c) the consideration for the disposal is applied by the landowner in acquiring other land (in this section referred to as "the new land ") not being land excluded from this paragraph by section 111B below.

(2) Subject to section 111B below, in a case where the whole of the consideration for the disposal was applied as mentioned in subsection (1)(c) above, the landowner, on making a claim as respects the consideration so applied, shall be treated for the purposes of this Act—

  (a) as if the consideration for the disposal of the old land were (if otherwise of a greater amount or value) of such amount as would secure that on the disposal neither a gain nor a loss accrues to him ; and

  (b) as if the amount or value of the consideration for the acquisition of the new land were reduced by the excess of the amount or value of the actual consideration for the disposal of the old land over the amount of the consideration which he is treated as receiving under paragraph (a) above.

(3) If part only of the consideration for the disposal of the old land was applied as mentioned in subsection (1)(c) above, then, subject to section 111B below, if the part of the consideration which was not so applied (in this subsection referred to as " the unexpended consideration ") is less than the amount of the gain (whether all chargeable gain or not) accruing on the disposal of the old land, the landowner, on making a claim as respects the consideration which was so applied, shall be treated for the purposes of this Act—

  (a) as if the amount of the gain so accruing were reduced to the amount of the unexpended consideration (and, if not all chargeable gain, with a proportionate reduction in the amount of the chargeable gain) ; and

  (b) as if the amount or value of the consideration for the acquisition of the new land were reduced by the amount by which the gain is reduced (or, as the case may be, the amount by which the chargeable gain is proportionately reduced) under paragraph (a) above.

(4) Nothing in subsection (2) or subsection (3) above affects the treatment for the purposes of this

Act of the authority by whom the old land was acquired or of the other party to the transaction involving the acquisition of the new land.

(5) For the purposes of this section—

   (*a*) subsection (2) of section 115 below shall apply in relation to subsection (2)(*a*) and subsection (2)(*b*) above as it applies in relation to subsection (1)(*a*) and subsection (1)(*b*) of that section ; and

   (*b*) subsection (3) of that section shall apply as if any reference to the new assets were a reference to the new land, any reference to the old assets were a reference to the old land and any reference to that section were a reference to this.

(6) Where this section applies, any such amount as is referred to in subsection (2) of section 110 above shall be treated as forming part of the consideration for the disposal of the old land and, accordingly, so much of that subsection as provides for a deemed disposal of other land shall not apply.

(7) The provisions of this Act fixing the amount of the consideration deemed to be given for the acquisition or disposal of assets shall be applied before this section is applied.

(8) In this section—

   " land " includes any interest in or right over land ; and

   " authority exercising or having compulsory powers " shall be construed in accordance with section 108(5) above.

Provisions supplementary to section 111A.

111B.—(1) Land is excluded from paragraph (*c*) of subsection (1) of section 111A above if—

   (*a*) it is a dwelling-house or part of a dwelling-house (or an interest in or right over a dwelling-house), and

   (*b*) by virtue of, or of any claim under, any provision of sections 101 to 105 above (private residences) the whole or any part of a gain accruing on a disposal of it by the landowner at a material time would not be a chargeable gain ;

and for the purposes of this subsection " a material time " means any time during the period of six years

beginning on the date of the acquisition referred to
in the said paragraph (c).

(2) If, at any time during the period of six years
referred to in subsection (1) above, land which at
the beginning of that period was not excluded from
section 111A(1)(c) above by virtue of that subsection becomes so excluded, the amount of any chargeable gain accruing on the disposal of the old land
shall be redetermined without regard to any relief
previously given under section 111A above by reference to the amount or value of the consideration for
the acquisition of that land ; and all such adjustments of capital gains tax, whether by way of
assessment or otherwise, may be made at any time,
notwithstanding anything in section 34 of the Taxes
Management Act 1970 (time limit for assessments). 1970 c. 9.

(3) Where the new land is a depreciating asset,
within the meaning of section 117 below, that section has effect as if—

(a) any reference in subsection (1) or subsection
(3) to section 115 or section 116 were a
reference to subsection (2) or subsection
(3) respectively of section 111A above ; and

(b) paragraph (b) of subsection (2) were omitted ; and

(c) the reference in subsection (4) to section
115(3) were a reference to that provision as
applied by section 111A(5) above.

(4) No claim may be made under section 108 above
in relation to a transfer which constitutes a disposal
in respect of which a claim is made under section
111A above.

(5) Expressions used in this section have the same
meaning as in section 111A above."

84.—(1) In section 55 of the Capital Gains Tax Act 1979, in Termination
subsection (1), for the words from the beginning to " market of life interest
value of the asset " there shall be substituted— etc.

" On the termination, on the death of the person entitled 1979 c. 14.
to it, of a life interest in possession in all or any part of
settled property—

(a) the whole or a corresponding part of each of the
assets forming part of the settled property and not
ceasing at that time to be settled property shall
be deemed for the purposes of this Act at that
time to be disposed of and immediately re-acquired
by the trustee for a consideration equal to the

whole or a corresponding part of the market value of the asset ; but

(b) no chargeable gain shall accrue on that disposal." ;

and subsection (2) of that section shall cease to have effect.

(2) In section 56 of that Act, after subsection (1) there shall be inserted—

" (1A) Where the life interest referred to in subsection (1) above is an interest in part only of the settled property to which section 54 applies, subsection (1)(a) above shall not apply but any chargeable gain accruing on the disposal shall be reduced by a proportion corresponding to that represented by the part.

(1B) The last sentence of subsection (1) of section 55 above, and subsection (6) of that section, shall apply for the purposes of subsection (1A) above as they apply for the purposes of section 55(1)." ;

and subsection (2) of section 56 shall cease to have effect.

(3) After section 56 of that Act there shall be inserted—

" Effect on sections 55 and 56 of relief under Finance Act 1980, section 79.

1980 c. 48.

56A.—(1) This section applies where—

(a) a claim for relief was made under section 79 of the Finance Act 1980 in respect of the disposal of an asset to a trustee, and

(b) the trustee is deemed to have disposed of the asset, or part of it, by virtue of section 54(1) or 55(1)(a) above.

(2) Sections 56(1)(a) and 55(1)(b) shall not apply to the disposal of the asset or part by the trustee, but any chargeable gain accruing to the trustee on the disposal shall be restricted to the amount of the held-over gain (or a corresponding part of it) on the disposal of the asset to him.

(3) Subsection (2) above shall not have effect in a case within section 56(1A) above ; but in such a case the reduction provided for by section 56(1A) above shall be diminished by an amount equal to the proportion there mentioned of the held-over gain.

(4) In this section " held-over gain " has the same meaning as in section 79(1) of the Finance Act 1980."

(4) This section applies in relation to interests terminating on or after 6th April 1982.

85.—(1) Section 148 of the Capital Gains Tax Act 1979 (maintenance funds for historic buildings) shall be amended as follows.

(2) In subsection (1) for the words " section 84 of the Finance Act 1976 " there shall be substituted the words " section 95 of the Finance Act 1982 ".

(3) In subsection (1A) for the words from " section 89(4)(*d*) " to " of that Act " there shall be substituted the words " paragraph 1(1) or (5) or 3(1) of Schedule 16 to the Finance Act 1982 no charge to capital transfer tax in respect of the asset deemed to be disposed of or a reduced charge to that tax by virtue of paragraph 1(2) or (8) or 3(4) of that Schedule."

(4) After subsection (1A) there shall be inserted—

" (1B) This section applies also where a trustee disposes (or is deemed to dispose) of an asset comprised in a settlement if on the disposal the asset becomes settled property in respect of which a direction has effect under section 93 of the Finance Act 1982."

86.—(1) This section applies to any disposal of an asset—

- (*a*) which occurs on or after 6th April 1982, or, if the disposal is by a company, on or after 1st April 1982 ; and
- (*b*) which occurs after the expiry of the period of twelve months beginning on the date on which the asset in question was acquired or provided (which period is in the following provisions of this Chapter referred to, in relation to a disposal, as " the qualifying period ") ; and
- (*c*) on which, disregarding the indexation allowance for which provision is made below, a gain would accrue (whether or not that gain would be wholly a chargeable gain).

(2) In relation to a disposal to which this section applies—

- (*a*) " the gross gain " means the amount of the gain referred to in subsection (1)(*c*) above, computed in accordance with Chapter II of Part II of the Capital Gains Tax Act 1979 ; and
- (*b*) " relevant allowable expenditure " means, subject to subsection (3) below, any sum which, in the computation of the gross gain, was taken into account by virtue of paragraph (*a*) or paragraph (*b*) of subsection (1) of section 32 of that Act.

(3) In determining what sum (if any) was taken into account as mentioned in subsection (2)(*b*) above, account shall be taken of any provision of any enactment which, for the purpose of the

computation under the said Chapter II, increases, excludes or reduces the whole or any part of any item of expenditure falling within the said section 32 or provides for it to be written-down.

(4) The following provisions of this Chapter have effect to provide for an allowance (in those provisions referred to as " the indexation allowance ") which, on a disposal to which this section applies, is to be allowed against the gross gain so as to give the gain for the purposes of the Capital Gains Tax Act 1979 or, if the indexation allowance equals or exceeds the gross gain, so as to extinguish it ; and, accordingly, at the end of subsection (1) of section 28 of that Act (computation of gains accruing on the disposal of assets) there shall be added the words " and sections 86 and 87 of the Finance Act 1982 ".

(5) Notwithstanding anything in section 29 of the Capital Gains Tax Act 1979 (losses to be computed in like manner as gains)—

(*a*) this section does not apply to a disposal on which a loss accrues ; and

(*b*) in any case where, on a disposal to which this section does apply, the indexation allowance exceeds the gross gain, no loss shall result and, accordingly, the disposal shall be one on which, after taking account of the indexation allowance, neither a gain nor a loss accrues.

(6) The provisions of Schedule 13 to this Act have effect for supplementing this section and the following provisions of this Chapter and the preceding provisions of this section have effect subject to the provisions of that Schedule.

Calculation of indexation allowance.   **87.**—(1) The provisions of this section have effect for the purpose of computing the indexation allowance on a disposal to which section 86 above applies.

(2) The indexation allowance is the aggregate of the indexed rise in each item of relevant allowable expenditure ; and, in relation to any such item of expenditure, the indexed rise is a sum produced by multiplying the amount of that item by a figure expressed as a decimal and determined, subject to subsections (3) and (4) below, by the formula $(RD-RI) \div RI$ where—

RD is the retail prices index for the month in which the disposal occurs ; and

RI is the retail prices index for March 1982 or the month which is the twelfth month after that in which the expenditure was incurred, whichever is the later.

(3) If, in relation to any item of expenditure,—

(*a*) the month in which the expenditure was incurred is less than thirteen months before the month in which the disposal occurs. or

    (*b*) RD, as defined in subsection (2) above, is equal to or
      less than RI, as so defined,
the indexed rise in that item is nil.

(4) If, in relation to any item of expenditure, the figure determined in accordance with the formula in subsection (2) above would, apart from this subsection, be a figure having more than three decimal places, it shall be rounded to the nearest third decimal place.

(5) For the purposes of this section—

    (*a*) relevant allowable expenditure falling within paragraph
      (*a*) of subsection (1) of section 32 of the Capital Gains 1979 c. 14.
      Tax Act 1979 shall be assumed to have been incurred
      at the time when the asset in question was acquired or
      provided ; and

    (*b*) relevant allowable expenditure falling within paragraph
      (*b*) of that subsection shall be assumed to have been
      incurred at the time when that expenditure became due
      and payable.

88.—(1) With respect to securities held on, or acquired on Identification or after, 6th April 1982 or, in the case of a company, 1st April of securities 1982 the provisions of this section (other than subsection (8)) etc. disposed and section 89 below have effect in place of sections 65 and 66 of: general of the Capital Gains Tax Act 1979 (pooling and other rules for rules. identification of securities) ; and, in taking account of those provisions,—

    (*a*) this section, section 89 below and Part II of Schedule
      13 shall have effect subject to section 58 of the Finance 1975 c. 45.
      (No. 2) Act 1975 (disposal of shares and securities
      within prescribed period of acquisition) ; and

    (*b*) the reference in section 68(4) of the Capital Gains Tax
      Act 1979 (general identification rules for gilt-edged
      securities) to section 66(1) of that Act shall be con-
      strued as including a reference to subsection (4) below.

(2) Where a person disposes of securities, the securities disposed of shall be identified in accordance with the rules contained in this section with the securities of the same class acquired by him which could be comprised in that disposal, and shall be so identified notwithstanding that they are otherwise identified by the disposal or by a transfer or delivery giving effect to it (but so that where a person disposes of securities in one capacity, they shall not be identified with securities which he holds or can dispose of only in some other capacity).

(3) Securities disposed of on an earlier date shall be identified before securities disposed of on a later date, and the identification of the securities first disposed of shall accordingly determine the securities which could be comprised in the later disposal.

(4) Securities disposed of for transfer or delivery on a particular date or in a particular period—

(*a*) shall not be identified with securities acquired for transfer or delivery on a later date or in a later period; and

(*b*) shall be identified with securities acquired for transfer or delivery on or before that date or in or before that period, but on or after the date of the disposal, rather than with securities not so acquired.

(5) The securities disposed of shall be identified—

(*a*) with securities acquired within the twelve months preceding the disposal rather than with securities not so acquired, and with securities so acquired on an earlier date rather than with securities so acquired on a later date, and

(*b*) subject to paragraph (*a*) above, with securities acquired on a later date rather than with securities acquired on an earlier date; and

(*c*) with securities acquired at different times on any one day in as nearly as may be equal proportions.

(6) The rules contained in the preceding subsections shall have priority according to the order in which they are so contained.

(7) Notwithstanding anything in subsections (3) to (5) above, where, under arrangements designed to postpone the transfer or delivery of securities disposed of, a person by a single bargain acquires securities for transfer or delivery on a particular date or in a particular period and disposes of them for transfer or delivery on a later date or in a later period, then—

(*a*) the securities disposed of by that bargain shall be identified with the securities thereby acquired; and

(*b*) securities previously disposed of which, but for the operation of paragraph (*a*) above in relation to acquisitions for transfer or delivery on the earlier date or in the earlier period, would have been identified with the securities acquired by that bargain—

(i) shall, subject to subsection (3) above, be identified with any available securities acquired for such transfer or delivery (that is to say, any securities so acquired other than securities to which paragraph (*a*) above applies and other than securities with which securities disposed of for such transfer or delivery would be identified apart from this subsection); and

(ii) in so far as they cannot be so identified shall be treated as disposed of for transfer or delivery on the later date, or in the later period, mentioned above.

(8) The provisions of Part II of Schedule 13 to this Act have effect with respect to securities acquired before 6th April 1982 or, in the case of a company, before 1st April 1982.

(9) In this section and Schedule 13 to this Act " securities " means—

(a) shares or securities of a company ; and

(b) any other assets where they are of a nature to be dealt in without identifying the particular assets disposed of or acquired ;

and shares or securities of a company shall not be treated for the purposes of this section and that Schedule as being of the same class unless they are so treated by the practice of The Stock Exchange or would be so treated if dealt with on The Stock Exchange.

89.—(1) Where, in a case of a man and his wife living with him, one of them—

Identification of securities: special rules.

(a) disposes of securities to his wife or her husband on or after 6th April 1982, and

(b) disposes of other securities, which are of the same kind as those disposed of to the wife or husband, to another person (in this section referred to as "a third party "), the provisions of subsections (3) and (4) below have effect with respect to any securities acquired by the person making those disposals which, but for the provisions of section 88 above, could have been comprised in either of those disposals.

(2) Where a company which is a member of a group of companies—

(a) disposes of securities to another member of the group on or after 1st April 1982, and

(b) disposes of other securities, which are of the same kind as those disposed of to that other company, to another person (in this section referred to as a "third party ") not being another member of the same group, the provisions of subsections (3) and (4) below have effect with respect to any securities acquired by the company making those disposals which, but for the provisions of section 88 above, could have been comprised in either of those disposals.

(3) If, apart from the provisions of this subsection, securities disposed of to a third party—

(a) would be indexed securities, and

(b) but for the disposal referred to in subsection (1)(a) or, as the case may be, subsection (2)(a) above would be unindexed securities,

213

PART III   the identification shall be reversed so that the securities disposed
of to the third party (or, if the quantity disposed of to the third
party was greater than the quantity disposed of to the wife or
husband or, as the case may be, to the other company, a part
of them equal to the quantity so disposed of) shall be unindexed
securities.

(4) If there is more than one disposal falling within subsection
(1)(*a*) or, as the case may be, subsection (2)(*a*) above, or more
than one disposal to a third party, the provisions of subsection
(3) above shall be applied to securities disposed of on an earlier
date before being applied to securities disposed of on a later date,
and the re-identification of the securities first disposed of shall
accordingly determine the way in which this section applies to
the securities comprised in the later disposal.

(5) In this section " indexed securities " means securities which
were acquired or provided more than twelve months before the
date of the disposal concerned and " unindexed securities " shall
be construed accordingly.

(6) Section 272 of the Taxes Act (groups of companies) shall
apply for the purpose of this section as it applies for the purposes
of sections 273 to 281 of that Act.

(7) Subsection (9) of section 88 above applies for the purposes
of this section as it applies for the purposes of that.

PART IV

CAPITAL TRANSFER TAX

CHAPTER 1

GENERAL

Reduction of   **90.**—(1) For the Tables in section 37(3) of the Finance Act
tax.   1975 there shall be substituted the Tables in Schedule 14 to this
1975 c. 7.   Act.

(2) This section applies to any chargeable transfer made on
or after 9th March 1982.

Indexation of   **91.**—(1) If the retail prices index for the month of December
rate bands.   in 1982 or any later year is higher than it was for the previous
December, then, unless Parliament otherwise determines, section
37 of the Finance Act 1975 shall apply to chargeable transfers
made on or after 6th April in the following year with the substitution in subsection (3) of new Tables for the Tables applying
(whether by virtue of this section or otherwise) to earlier chargeable transfers.

(2) The new Tables shall differ from the Tables they replace in that for each of the amounts specified in the first and second columns there shall be substituted amounts arrived at by increasing the previous amounts by the same percentage as the percentage increase in the retail prices index and, if the result is not a multiple of £1,000, rounding it up to the nearest amount which is such a multiple.

(3) The references in this section to the retail prices index are references to the general index of retail prices (for all items) published by the Department of Employment ; and if that index is not published for a month of December those references shall be construed as references to any substituted index or index figures published by that Department.

(4) The Treasury shall before 6th April 1983 and each subsequent 6th April make an order specifying the amounts which by virtue of this section will be treated, in relation to chargeable transfers on or after that date, as specified in the Tables in section 37(3) of the Finance Act 1975 ; and any such order 1975 c. 7. shall be made by statutory instrument.

(5) In section 85(3) of the Finance Act 1980 (transitional 1980 c. 48. provisions on reduction of tax by that section or subsequent enactments) for the words " which reduces tax by substituting " there shall be substituted the words " by virtue of which tax is reduced by the substitution of ".

92.—(1) In paragraph 1(2) of Schedule 6 to the Finance Act Exemptions. 1975 (exemption limit for transfers to non-domiciled spouses) for " £50,000 " there shall be substituted " £55,000 ".

(2) In paragraph 10(1)(*b*) of that Schedule (limit on exempt gifts made to charities on or within one year of death) for " £200,000 " there shall be substituted " £250,000 ".

(3) This section applies to any transfer of value made on or after 9th March 1982.

93.—(1) On a claim made for the purpose, the Treasury shall Maintenance give a direction under this section in respect of property com- funds: prised in a settlement if the conditions mentioned in subsection Treasury (2) below are fulfilled. directions.

(2) The conditions are—

    (*a*) that the Treasury are satisfied—

        (i) that the trusts on which the property is held comply with the requirements mentioned in subsection (3) below, and

        (ii) that the property is of a character and amount appropriate for the purposes of those trusts ; and

    (*b*) that the trustees—

        (i) are approved by the Treasury,

(ii) include a trust corporation (as defined in section 94(1) below) or a solicitor or an accountant (as so defined) or a member of such other professional body as the Treasury may allow in the case of the property concerned, and

(iii) are, at the time the direction is given, resident in the United Kingdom (as specified in section 94(1) below).

(3) The requirements are—

(a) that none of the property held on the trusts can at any time in the period of six years beginning with the date on which it became so held be applied otherwise than—

(i) for the maintenance, repair or preservation of, or making provision for public access to, property which is for the time being qualifying property (as defined in section 94(2) below), for the maintenance, repair or preservation of property held on the trusts or for such improvement of property so held as is reasonable having regard to the purposes of the trusts, or for defraying the expenses of the trustees in relation to the property so held ;

(ii) as respects income not so applied and not accumulated, for the benefit of a body mentioned in paragraph 12 of Schedule 6 to the Finance Act 1975 (museums etc.) or of a qualifying charity (as defined in section 94(4) below) ; and

(b) that none of the property can, on ceasing to be held on the trusts at any time in that period or, if the settlor dies in that period, at any time before his death, devolve otherwise than on any such body or charity ; and

(c) that income arising from property held on the trusts cannot at any time after the end of that period be applied except as mentioned in paragraph (a)(i) or (ii) above.

(4) Subject to subsection (5) below, paragraphs (a) and (b) of subsection (3) above do not apply to property which—

(a) was previously comprised in another settlement ; and

(b) ceased to be comprised in that settlement and became comprised in the current settlement in circumstances such that by virtue of paragraph 3(1) of Schedule 16 to this Act there was no charge (or, but for paragraph 3(4) of that Schedule, there would have been no charge) to tax in respect of it ;

and in relation to any such property paragraph (c) of that subsection shall apply with the omission of the words " at any time after the end of that period ".

(5) Subsection (4) above shall not have effect if the time when the property comprised in the previous settlement devolved otherwise than on any such body or charity as is mentioned in paragraph (*a*) of subsection (3) above fell before the expiration of the period of six years mentioned in that paragraph ; but in such a case subsection (3) above shall apply to the current settlement as if for the references to the period of six years there mentioned there were substituted references to the period beginning with the date on which the property became comprised in the current settlement and ending six years after the date on which it became held on the relevant trusts of the previous settlement (or, where this subsection has already had effect in relation to the property, the date on which it became held on the relevant trusts of the first settlement in the series).

(6) If in the Treasury's opinion the facts concerning any property or its administration cease to warrant the continuance of the effect of a direction given under this section in respect of the property, they may at any time by notice in writing to the trustees withdraw the direction on such grounds, and from such date, as may be specified in the notice ; and the direction shall cease to have effect accordingly.

(7) Where a direction under this section has effect in respect of property, the trustees shall from time to time furnish the Treasury with such accounts and other information relating to the property as the Treasury may reasonably require.

(8) Where a direction under this section has effect in respect of property, the trusts on which the property is held shall be enforceable at the suit of the Treasury and the Treasury shall, as respects the appointment, removal and retirement of trustees, have the rights and powers of a beneficiary.

(9) The Treasury may give a direction under this section in respect of property proposed to be comprised in a settlement or to be held on particular trusts, and the preceding provisions of this section shall be read accordingly.

(10) This section shall have effect in relation to events after 8th March 1982.

94.—(1) For the purposes of section 93(2) above—

Provisions supplementary to section 93.

    (*a*) " accountant " means a member of an incorporated society of accountants ;

    (*b*) " trust corporation " means a person that is a trust corporation for the purposes of the Law of Property Act 1925 or for the purposes of Article 9 of the Administration of Estates (Northern Ireland) Order 1979 ;

1925 c. 20.

S.I. 1979/1575 (N.I. 14).

(c) trustees shall be regarded as resident in the United Kingdom at any particular time if the general administration
of the trusts is ordinarily carried on in the United Kingdom and the trustees or a majority of them (and, where
there is more than one class of trustees, a majority of
each class) are resident in the United Kingdom ;

and, where a trustee is a trust corporation, the question whether
the trustee is resident in the United Kingdom shall, for the purposes of paragraph (c) above, be determined as for the purposes
of corporation tax.

(2) Property is qualifying property for the purposes of section
93(3) above if—

(a) it has been designated under section 34(1) of the Finance
Act 1975 or section 77(1)(b), (c), (d) or (e) of the Finance Act 1976 ; and

(b) the requisite undertaking has been given with respect to
it under the said section 34 or under section 76, 78(5)
(b) or 82(3) of the Finance Act 1976 ; and

(c) tax has not (since the last occasion on which such an
undertaking was given) become chargeable with respect to it under the said section 34 or under section
78 or 82(3) of the Finance Act 1976.

(3) If it appears to the Treasury that provision is, or is to
be, made by a settlement for the maintenance, repair or preservation of any such property as is mentioned in subsection (1)
(b), (c), (d) or (e) of section 77 of the Finance Act 1976, they
may, on a claim made for the purpose—

(a) designate that property under this subsection ; and

(b) accept with respect to it an undertaking such as is
described in subsection (4) of that section ;

and, if they do so, subsection (2) above shall have effect as if
the designation were under that section and the undertaking
under section 76 of the Finance Act 1976 and as if the reference
to tax becoming chargeable were a reference to the occurrence
of an event on which tax would become chargeable under section 78 of that Act if there had been a conditionally exempt
transfer of the property when the claim was made and the
undertaking had been given under the said section 76.

(4) A charity is a qualifying charity for the purposes of
section 93(3) above if it exists wholly or mainly for maintaining,
repairing or preserving for the public benefit buildings of historic
or architectural interest, land of scenic, historic or scientific
interest or objects of national, scientific, historic or artistic
interest ; and in this subsection " national interest " includes
interest within any part of the United Kingdom.

(5) Property comprised in a settlement by virtue of a transfer of value made before the coming into force of this section and exempt under section 84 of the Finance Act 1976 shall be treated as property in respect of which a direction has been given under section 93 above.

(6) Designations, undertakings and acceptances made under section 84(6) of the Finance Act 1976 shall be treated as made under subsection (3) above and, in relation to them, subsections (2) and (3) above shall be treated as having been in force when they were made.

95.—(1) Subject to the provisions of Part II of Schedule 6 to the Finance Act 1975 as applied by this section, a transfer of value is an exempt transfer to the extent that the value transferred by it is attributable to property which by virtue of the trans- fer becomes, or immediately after the transfer remains, comprised in a settlement and in respect of which—

(a) a direction under section 93 above has effect at the time of the transfer, or

(b) such a direction is given after the time of the transfer.

(2) Sub-paragraphs (1), (2), (2A), (3)(a), (b) and (ba) and (4B) of paragraph 15 of Schedule 6 to the Finance Act 1975 shall apply to this section as they apply to paragraphs 10 to 13 of that Schedule, and for the purposes of the said sub-paragraph (4B) the trustees of a settlement in relation to which a direction under section 93 above has effect shall be treated as a body within paragraph 13 of that Schedule.

(3) In paragraph 16 of Schedule 6 to the Finance Act 1975 for the words " sections 76 and 84 of the Finance Act 1976 " there shall be substituted the words " section 76 of the Finance Act 1976 and section 95 of the Finance Act 1982 ".

(4) This section shall have effect in relation to events after 8th March 1982.

96.—(1) In determining for the purposes of capital transfer tax the value of the estate immediately before his death of a person to whom this section applies there shall be left out of account the balance on—

(a) any qualifying foreign currency account of his, and

(b) subject to subsection (3) below, any qualifying foreign currency account of the trustees of settled property in which he is beneficially entitled to an interest in possession.

(2) This section applies to a person who is not domiciled in the United Kingdom immediately before his death, and is neither resident nor ordinarily resident there at that time.

(3) Subsection (1)(*b*) above does not apply in relation to settled property if the settlor was domiciled in the United Kingdom when he made the settlement, or if the trustees are domiciled, resident or ordinarily resident in the United Kingdom immediately before the beneficiary's death.

(4) For the purposes of this section—

    (*a*) the question whether a person is resident or ordinarily resident in the United Kingdom shall, subject to paragraph (*b*) below, be determined as for the purposes of income tax ; but

    (*b*) the trustees of a settlement shall be regarded as not resident or ordinarily resident in the United Kingdom unless the general administration of the settlement is ordinarily carried on in the United Kingdom and the trustees or a majority of them (and, where there is more than one class of trustees, a majority of each class) are resident and ordinarily resident there.

(5) In this section " qualifying foreign currency account " means a foreign currency account with the Bank of England, the Post Office, a recognised bank or licensed institution ; and for this purpose—

    (*a*) " foreign currency account " means any account other than one denominated in sterling, and

    (*b*) " recognised bank " and " licensed institution " have the same meanings as in the Banking Act 1979.

1979 c. 37.

(6) This section has effect in relation to deaths occurring after 8th March 1982.

Scottish
agricultural
leases.

97.—(1) Subject to subsections (2) and (3) below, where any part of the value of a person's estate immediately before his death is attributable to the value of the interest of a tenant of agricultural property in Scotland, being an interest held by virtue of tacit relocation ; and

    (*a*) either he had been tenant of the said property continuously for a period of at least two years immediately preceding his death or he had become tenant of the said property by succession ; and

    (*b*) the said interest is acquired on his death by a new tenant, the value of the said interest shall be left out of account in determining the value transferred on the death.

(2) The value to be left out of account under subsection (1) above shall not include the value of any rights to compensation in respect of tenant's improvements.

(3) Subsections (1) and (2) above apply to deaths on or after 15th November 1976.

(4) The Finance Act 1981 shall be amended as follows—

    (*a*) in section 98 at the beginning there shall be inserted " (1) ", and at the end there shall be inserted the following new subsection—

        " (2) This section applies to deaths on or after 15th November 1976." ;

    (*b*) section 99 and Schedule 15 shall cease to have effect.

98.—(1) Paragraph 17 of Schedule 5 to the Finance Act 1975 shall be amended in accordance with subsections (2) to (5) below.

(2) In sub-paragraph (1)(*a*) for the words " profession or undertaking " (where they first occur) there shall be substituted the words " or profession ".

(3) In sub-paragraph (1) the words " or (*c*) charities " shall be omitted.

(4) After sub-paragraph (1) there shall be inserted—

    " (1A) Where settled property is held on trusts permitting the property to be applied for the benefit of persons within paragraph (*a*) or (*b*) of sub-paragraph (1) above, those trusts shall not be regarded as outside the description specified in that sub-paragraph by reason only that they also permit the settled property to be applied for charitable purposes."

(5) For sub-paragraph (2) there shall be substituted—

    " (2) Where any class mentioned in sub-paragraph (1) above is defined by reference to employment by or office with a particular body, this paragraph applies to the settled property only if—

        (*a*) the class comprises all or most of the persons employed by or holding office with the body concerned ; or

        (*b*) the trusts on which the settled property is held are those of a profit sharing scheme approved in accordance with Schedule 9 to the Finance Act 1978."

(6) In paragraph 17A(1) of that Schedule for the words " to (*c*) " there shall be substituted the words " and (*b*) ".

(7) This section shall have effect in relation to events after 8th March 1982.

PART IV
Close
companies.
1975 c. 7.

99.—(1) Paragraph 24 of Schedule 5 to the Finance Act 1975 shall have effect with the following amendments in relation to events after 8th March 1982.

(2) In sub-paragraph (2), for paragraph (*b*) there shall be substituted—

" (*b*) if no qualifying interest in possession subsists in the settled property, Chapter II of Part IV of the Finance Act 1982 shall have effect as if on the making of the transfer the trustee had made a disposition as a result of which the value of the settled property had been reduced by an amount equal to the part so apportioned less the amount specified in sub-paragraph (3) below ";

and for the words " an interest in possession " in each place where they occur there shall be substituted the words " a qualifying interest in possession ".

(3) In sub-paragraph (5) for the words from " as " to " beneficially " there shall be substituted the words " and of Chapter II of Part IV of the Finance Act 1982 as being the persons ".

(4) After sub-paragraph (5) there shall be inserted—

" (5A) Where—

(*a*) the participators mentioned in sub-paragraph (5) above include the trustees of a settlement, and

(*b*) a person is beneficially entitled to an interest in possession in the whole or part of the settled property by virtue of which the trustees are participators,

that person shall be treated for the said purposes as beneficially entitled to the whole or a corresponding part of the interest to which the trustees would otherwise be treated as entitled under that sub-paragraph."

(5) In sub-paragraph (6), at the end, there shall be added the words " and " qualifying interest in possession " has the meaning given by section 103 of the Finance Act 1982."

Apsley House.
1947 c. 46.

100. The enactments relating to capital transfer tax shall not apply in respect of the rights conferred by section 3 of the Wellington Museum Act 1947.

CHAPTER II

SETTLEMENTS WITHOUT INTERESTS IN POSSESSION

Preliminary

Preliminary.
1975 c. 7.

101. This Chapter, which supersedes paragraphs 6 to 14 of Schedule 5 to the Finance Act 1975, shall have effect in relation to events after 8th March 1982, but subject, in the case of any

settlement which commenced before 27th March 1974, to the   PART IV
provisions of Schedule 15 to this Act.

Principal definitions

102.—(1) In this Chapter " relevant property " means settled Relevant
property in which no qualifying interest in possession subsists, property.
other than—

  (a) property held for charitable purposes only, whether for
    a limited time or otherwise ;

  (b) property to which section 114 below applies ;

  (c) property to which paragraph 2 of Schedule 16 to this
    Act applies ;

  (d) property which is part of or held for the purposes of a
    fund or scheme to which paragraph 16 of Schedule 5
    to the Finance Act 1975 applies (superannuation 1975 c. 7.
    schemes) ;

  (e) property to which paragraph 17 of that Schedule applies
    (trusts for employees etc. and newspaper trusts) ;

  (f) property which is held on trusts to the like effect as those
    specified in section 33(1)(ii) of the Trustee Act 1925 1925 c. 19.
    (protective trusts) and which became held on those
    trusts on the failure or determination before 12th April
    1978 of trusts to the like effect as those specified in
    section 33(1)(i) ;

  (g) property within paragraph 19 of Schedule 5 to the
    Finance Act 1975 (trusts for disabled persons), as it
    applies to property which was transferred into settle-
    ment before 10th March 1981 ;

  (h) property comprised in a trade or professional compensa-
    tion fund ; and

  (i) excluded property.

(2) The reference in subsection (1)(d) above to property which
is part of or held for the purposes of a fund or scheme does
not include a reference to a benefit which, having become payable under the fund or scheme, becomes comprised in a
settlement.

103.—(1) In this Chapter " qualifying interest in possession " Qualifying
means an interest in possession to which an individual, or where interest in
subsection (2) below applies a company, is beneficially entitled. possession.

(2) This subsection applies where—

  (a) the business of the company consists wholly or mainly
    in the acquisition of interests in settled property, and

  (b) the company has acquired the interest for full considera-
    tion in money or money's worth from an individual
    who was beneficially entitled to it.

(3) Where the acquisition mentioned in paragraph (*b*) of subsection (2) above was before 14th March 1975—

(*a*) the condition set out in paragraph (*a*) of that subsection shall be treated as satisfied if the business of the company was at the time of the acquisition such as is described in that paragraph, and

(*b*) that condition need not be satisfied if the company is authorised to carry on long-term business under section 3 or 4 of the Insurance Companies Act 1981.

1981 c. 31.

Commencement of settlement.

104. In this Chapter references to the commencement of a settlement are references to the time when property first becomes comprised in it.

Ten-year anniversary.

105.—(1) In this Chapter " ten-year anniversary " in relation to a settlement means the tenth anniversary of the date on which the settlement commenced and subsequent anniversaries at ten-yearly intervals, but subject to subsections (2) to (4) below.

(2) The ten-year anniversaries of a settlement treated as made under section 120 below shall be the dates that are (or would but for that section be) the ten-year anniversaries of the settlement first mentioned in that section.

(3) No date falling before 1st April 1983 shall be a ten-year anniversary.

(4) Where—

(*a*) the first ten-year anniversary of a settlement would apart from this subsection fall during the year ending with 31st March 1984, and

(*b*) during that year an event occurs in respect of the settlement which could not have occurred except as the result of some proceedings before a court, and

(*c*) the event is one on which tax is (or, apart from Part II of Schedule 15 to this Act, would be) chargeable under this Chapter,

the first ten-year anniversary shall be taken to be 1st April 1984 (but without affecting the dates of later anniversaries).

Related settlements.

106.—(1) For the purposes of this Chapter two settlements are related if and only if—

(*a*) the settlor is the same in each case, and

(*b*) they commenced on the same day,

but subject to subsection (2) below.

(2) Two settlements are not related for the purposes of this Chapter if all the property comprised in one or both of them was immediately after the settlement commenced held for charitable purposes only without limit of time (defined by a date or otherwise)

Principal charge to tax

107. Where immediately before a ten-year anniversary all or any part of the property comprised in a settlement is relevant property, tax shall be charged at the rate applicable under sections 109 and 110 below on the value of the property or part at that time.

108.—(1) Subject to the following provisions of this section, there shall be a charge to tax under this section—

    (*a*) where the property comprised in a settlement or any part of that property ceases to be relevant property (whether because it ceases to be comprised in the settlement or otherwise) ; and

    (*b*) in a case in which paragraph (*a*) above does not apply, where the trustees of the settlement make a disposition as a result of which the value of relevant property comprised in the settlement is less than it would be but for the disposition.

(2) The amount on which tax is charged under this section shall be—

    (*a*) the amount by which the value of relevant property comprised in the settlement is less immediately after the event in question than it would be but for the event, or

    (*b*) where the tax payable is paid out of relevant property comprised in the settlement immediately after the event, the amount which, after deducting the tax, is equal to the amount on which tax would be charged by virtue of paragraph (*a*) above.

(3) The rate at which tax is charged under this section shall be the rate applicable under section 111 or 112 below.

(4) Subsection (1) above does not apply if the event in question occurs in a quarter beginning with the day on which the settlement commenced or with a ten-year anniversary.

(5) Tax shall not be charged under this section in respect of—

    (*a*) a payment of costs or expenses (so far as they are fairly attributable to relevant property), or

    (*b*) a payment which is (or will be) income of any person for any of the purposes of income tax or would for any of those purposes be income of a person not resident in the United Kingdom if he were so resident,

or in respect of a liability to make such a payment.

(6) Tax shall not be charged under this section by virtue of subsection (1)(*b*) above if the disposition is such that, were the

trustees beneficially entitled to the settled property, section 20(4) of the Finance Act 1975 (disposition not intended to confer gratuitous benefit) or section 97 of the Finance Act 1981 (grant of tenancies of agricultural property) would prevent the disposition from being a transfer of value.

(7) Tax shall not be charged under this section by reason only that property comprised in a settlement ceases to be situated in the United Kingdom and thereby becomes excluded property by virtue of paragraph 2(1)(*a*) of Schedule 5 to the Finance Act 1975.

(8) If the settlor of a settlement was not domiciled in the United Kingdom when the settlement was made, tax shall not be charged under this section by reason only that property comprised in the settlement is invested in securities issued as mentioned in paragraph 3 of Schedule 7 to the Finance Act 1975 and thereby becomes excluded property by virtue of sub-paragraph (2) of that paragraph; and section 45 of that Act (domicile) shall not apply to determine the settlor's domicile for the purposes of this subsection in relation to property which became comprised in a settlement before 10th December 1974.

(9) For the purposes of this section trustees shall be treated as making a disposition if they omit to exercise a right (unless it is shown that the omission was not deliberate) and the disposition shall be treated as made at the time or latest time when they could have exercised the right.

Rates of principal charge

Rate of
ten-yearly
charge.
109.—(1) Subject to subsection (2) below, the rate at which tax is charged under section 107 above at any time shall be three tenths of the effective rate (that is to say the rate found by expressing the tax chargeable as a percentage of the amount on which it is charged) at which tax would be charged on the value transferred by a chargeable transfer of the description specified in subsection (3) below.

(2) Where the whole or part of the value mentioned in section 107 above is attributable to property which was not relevant property, or was not comprised in the settlement, throughout the period of ten years ending immediately before the ten-year anniversary concerned, the rate at which tax is charged on that value or part shall be reduced by one-fortieth for each of the successive quarters in that period which expired before the property became, or last became, relevant property comprised in the settlement.

(3) The chargeable transfer postulated in subsection (1) above is one—

    (*a*) the value transferred by which is equal to an amount determined in accordance with subsection (4) below;

(*b*) which is made immediately before the ten-year anniversary concerned by a transferor who has in the preceding ten years made chargeable transfers having an aggregate value determined in accordance with subsection (5) below ; and

(*c*) for which the appropriate Table of rates is the second Table set out in section 37(3) of the Finance Act 1975. 1975 c. 7.

(4) The amount referred to in subsection (3)(*a*) above is equal to the aggregate of—

(*a*) the value on which tax is charged under section 107 above ;

(*b*) the value immediately after it became comprised in the settlement of any property which was not then relevant property and has not subsequently become relevant property while remaining comprised in the settlement ; and

(*c*) the value, immediately after a related settlement commenced, of the property then comprised in it.

(5) The aggregate value referred to in subsection (3)(*b*) above is equal to the aggregate of—

(*a*) the values transferred by any chargeable transfers made by the settlor in the period of ten years ending with the day on which the settlement commenced, disregarding transfers made on that day, and

(*b*) the amounts on which any charges to tax were imposed under section 108 above in respect of the settlement in the ten years before the anniversary concerned ;

but subject to section 110 below.

110.—(1) This subsection applies where, after the settlement Added commenced and after 8th March 1982, but before the anniversary property etc. concerned, the settlor made a chargeable transfer as a result of which the value of the property comprised in the settlement was increased.

(2) For the purposes of subsection (1) above, it is immaterial whether the amount of the property so comprised was increased as a result of the transfer, but a transfer as a result of which the value increased but the amount did not shall be disregarded if it is shown that the transfer—

(*a*) was not primarily intended to increase the value, and

(*b*) did not result in the value being greater immediately after the transfer by an amount exceeding five per cent. of the value immediately before the transfer.

(3) Where subsection (1) above applies, section 109(5)(*a*) above shall have effect as if it referred to the greater of—

(*a*) the aggregate of the values there specified, and

(b) the aggregate of the values transferred by any chargeable transfers made by the settlor in the period of ten years ending with the day on which the chargeable transfer falling within subsection (1) above was made, disregarding transfers made on that day and excluding the values mentioned in subsection (4) below ;

and where the settlor made two or more chargeable transfers falling within subsection (1) above, paragraph (b) above shall be taken to refer to the transfer in relation to which the aggregate there mentioned is the greatest.

(4) The values are—

(a) any value attributable to property whose value is taken into account in determining the amount mentioned in section 109(4) above ; and

(b) any value attributable to property in respect of which a charge to tax has been made under section 108 above and by reference to which an amount mentioned in section 109(5)(b) above is determined.

(5) Where the property comprised in a settlement immediately before the ten-year anniversary concerned, or any part of that property, had on any occasion within the preceding ten years ceased to be relevant property then, if on that occasion tax was charged in respect of the settlement under section 108 above, the aggregate calculated under section 109(5) above shall be reduced by an amount equal to the lesser of—

(a) the amount on which tax was charged under section 108 (or so much of that amount as is attributable to the part in question), and

(b) the value on which tax is charged under section 107 above (or so much of that value as is attributable to the part in question) ;

and if there were two or more such occasions relating to the property or the same part of it, this subsection shall have effect in relation to each of them.

(6) References in subsection (5) above to the property comprised in a settlement immediately before an anniversary shall, if part only of the settled property was then relevant property, be construed as references to that part.

(7) In relation to the first ten-year anniversary of a settlement which commenced after 26th March 1974 and before 9th March 1982, section 109(5) above shall have effect with the addition after paragraph (b) of the words " and

(c) the amounts of any distribution payments (determined in accordance with the rules applicable before 9th March 1982 under paragraph 11 of Schedule 5 to the

Finance Act 1975) made out of the settled property after 26th March 1974 but before 9th March 1982 and within the period of ten years before the anniversary concerned ".

111.—(1) The rate at which tax is charged under section 108 above on an occasion preceding the first ten-year anniversary after the settlement's commencement shall be the appropriate fraction of the effective rate at which tax would be charged on the value transferred by a chargeable transfer of the description specified in subsection (4) below.

(2) For the purposes of this section the appropriate fraction is three tenths multiplied by so many fortieths as there are complete successive quarters in the period beginning with the day on which the settlement commenced and ending with the day before the occasion of the charge, but subject to subsection (3) below.

(3) Where the whole or part of the amount on which tax is charged is attributable to property which was not relevant property, or was not comprised in the settlement, throughout the period referred to in subsection (2) above, then in determining the appropriate fraction in relation to that amount or part—

(a) no quarter which expired before the day on which the property became, or last became, relevant property comprised in the settlement shall be counted, but

(b) if that day fell in the same quarter as that in which the period ends, that quarter shall be counted whether complete or not.

(4) The chargeable transfer postulated in subsection (1) above is one—

(a) the value transferred by which is equal to an amount determined in accordance with subsection (5) below ;

(b) which is made at the time of the charge to tax under section 108 by a transferor who has in the period of ten years ending with the day of the occasion of the charge made chargeable transfers having an aggregate value equal to that of any chargeable transfers made by the settlor in the period of ten years ending with the day on which the settlement commenced, disregarding transfers made on that day ; and

(c) for which the appropriate Table of rates is the second Table set out in section 37(3) of the Finance Act 1975.

(5) The amount referred to in subsection (4)(a) above is equal to the aggregate of—

(a) the value, immediately after the settlement commenced, of the property then comprised in it ;

(b) the value, immediately after a related settlement commenced, of the property then comprised in it ; and

(c) the value, immediately after it became comprised in the settlement, of any property which became so comprised after the settlement commenced and before the occasion of the charge under section 108 (whether or not it has remained so comprised).

Rate between ten-year anniversaries.

112.—(1) Subject to subsection (2) below, the rate at which tax is charged under section 108 above on an occasion following one or more ten-year anniversaries after the settlement's commencement shall be the appropriate fraction of the rate at which it was last charged under section 107 (or would have been charged apart from section 109(2)).

(2) If at any time before the occasion of the charge under section 108 and on or after the most recent ten-year anniversary—

(a) property has become comprised in the settlement ; or

(b) property which was comprised in the settlement immediately before the anniversary, but was not then relevant property, has become relevant property,

then, whether or not the property has remained comprised in the settlement or has remained relevant property, the rate at which tax is charged under section 108 shall be the appropriate fraction of the rate at which it would last have been charged under section 107 (apart from section 109(2)) if immediately before that anniversary the property had been relevant property comprised in the settlement with a value determined in accordance with subsection (3) below.

(3) In the case of property within subsection (2) (a) above which either—

(a) was relevant property immediately after it became comprised in the settlement ; or

(b) was not then relevant property and has not subsequently become relevant property while remaining comprised in the settlement,

the value to be attributed to it for the purposes of subsection (2) above is its value immediately after it became comprised in the settlement ; and in any other case the value to be so attributed is the value of the property when it became (or last became) relevant property.

(4) For the purposes of this section the appropriate fraction is so many fortieths as there are complete successive quarters in the period beginning with the most recent ten-year anniversary and ending with the day before the occasion of the charge ; but

subsection (3) of section 111 above shall have effect for the PART IV
purposes of this subsection as it has effect for the purposes of
subsection (2) of that section.

Special cases

113.—(1) This section applies to settled property held for Property
charitable purposes only until the end of a period (whether leaving
defined by a date or in some other way). temporary
charitable

(2) Subject to subsections (3) and (4) below, there shall be a trusts.
charge to tax under this section—

> (*a*) where settled property ceases to be property to which
> this section applies, otherwise than by virtue of an
> application for charitable purposes, and

> (*b*) in a case in which paragraph (*a*) above does not apply,
> where the trustees make a disposition (otherwise than
> by an application of property for charitable purposes)
> as a result of which the value of settled property to
> which this section applies is less than it would be but
> for the disposition.

(3) Tax shall not be charged under this section in respect of—

> (*a*) a payment of costs or expenses (so far as they are
> fairly attributable to property to which this section
> applies), or

> (*b*) a payment which is (or will be) income of any person
> for any of the purposes of income tax or would for
> any of those purposes be income of a person not resi-
> dent in the United Kingdom if he were so resident,

or in respect of a liability to make such a payment.

(4) Tax shall not be charged under this section by virtue of
subsection (2)(*b*) above if the disposition is such that, were the
trustees beneficially entitled to the settled property, section 20(4)
of the Finance Act 1975 (disposition not intended to confer 1975 c. 7.
gratuitous benefit) or section 97 of the Finance Act 1981 (grant 1981 c. 35.
of tenancies of agricultural property) would prevent the disposition from being a transfer of value.

(5) The amount on which tax is charged under this section
shall be—

> (*a*) the amount by which the value of property which is
> comprised in the settlement and to which this section
> applies is less immediately after the event giving rise
> to the charge than it would be but for the event, or

> (*b*) where the tax payable is paid out of settled property
> to which this section applies immediately after the
> event, the amount which, after deducting the tax, is

equal to the amount on which tax would be charged by virtue of paragraph (a) above.

(6) The rate at which tax is charged under this section shall be the aggregate of the following percentages—

(a) 0·25 per cent. for each of the first forty complete successive quarters in the relevant period,

(b) 0·20 per cent. for each of the next forty,

(c) 0·15 per cent. for each of the next forty,

(d) 0·10 per cent. for each of the next forty, and

(e) 0·05 per cent. for each of the next forty.

(7) In subsection (6) above " the relevant period " means the period beginning with the later of—

(a) the day on which the property in respect of which tax is chargeable became (or last became) property to which this section applies, and

(b) 13th March 1975,

and ending with the day before the event giving rise to the charge.

(8) Where the property in respect of which tax is chargeable—

(a) was relevant property immediately before 10th December 1981, and

(b) became (or last became) property to which this section applies on or after that day and before 9th March 1982,

subsection (7) above shall have effect as if the day referred to in paragraph (a) of that subsection were the day on which the property became (or last became) relevant property before 10th December 1981.

(9) For the purposes of this section trustees shall be treated as making a disposition if they omit to exercise a right (unless it is shown that the omission was not deliberate) and the disposition shall be treated as made at the time or latest time when they could have exercised the right.

114.—(1) Subject to subsection (2) below, this section applies to settled property if—

(a) one or more persons (in this section referred to as beneficiaries) will, on or before attaining a specified age not exceeding twenty-five, become beneficially entitled to it or to an interest in possession in it, and

(b) no interest in possession subsists in it and the income from it is to be accumulated so far as not applied for the maintenance, education or benefit of a beneficiary.

(2) This section does not apply to settled property unless either—

    (*a*) not more than twenty-five years have elapsed since the commencement of the settlement or, if it was later, since the time (or latest time) when the conditions stated in paragraphs (*a*) and (*b*) of subsection (1) above became satisfied with respect to the property, or

    (*b*) all the persons who are or have been beneficiaries are or were either—

        (i) grandchildren of a common grandparent, or

        (ii) children, widows or widowers of such grandchildren who were themselves beneficiaries but died before the time when, had they survived, they would have become entitled as mentioned in subsection (1)(*a*) above.

(3) Subject to subsections (4) and (5) below, there shall be a charge to tax under this section—

    (*a*) where settled property ceases to be property to which this section applies, and

    (*b*) in a case in which paragraph (*a*) above does not apply, where the trustees make a disposition as a result of which the value of settled property to which this section applies is less than it would be but for the disposition.

(4) Tax shall not be charged under this section—

    (*a*) on a beneficiary's becoming beneficially entitled to, or to an interest in possession in, settled property on or before attaining the specified age, or

    (*b*) on the death of a beneficiary before attaining the specified age.

(5) Subsections (3) to (7) and (9) of section 113 above shall apply for the purposes of this section as they apply for the purposes of that section (with the substitution of a reference to subsection (3)(*b*) above for the reference in section 113(4) to section 113(2)(*b*)).

(6) Where the conditions stated in paragraphs (*a*) and (*b*) of subsection (1) above were satisfied on 15th April 1976 with respect to property comprised in a settlement which commenced before that day, subsection (2)(*a*) above shall have effect with the substitution of a reference to that day for the reference to the commencement of the settlement, and the condition stated in subsection (2)(*b*) above shall be treated as satisfied if—

    (*a*) it is satisfied in respect of the period beginning with 15th April 1976, or

(b) it is satisfied in respect of the period beginning with 1st April 1977 and either there was no beneficiary living on 15th April 1976 or the beneficiaries on 1st April 1977 included a living beneficiary, or

(c) there is no power under the terms of the settlement whereby it could have become satisfied in respect of the period beginning with 1st April 1977, and the trusts of the settlement have not been varied at any time after 15th April 1976.

(7) In subsection (1) above " persons " includes unborn persons ; but the conditions stated in that subsection shall be treated as not satisfied unless there is or has been a living beneficiary.

(8) For the purposes of this section a person's children shall be taken to include his illegitimate children, his adopted children and his stepchildren.

Property becoming subject to employee trusts.

1975 c. 7.

115.—(1) Tax shall not be charged under section 108 above in respect of shares in or securities of a company which cease to be relevant property on becoming held on trusts of the description specified in paragraph 17(1) of Schedule 5 to the Finance Act 1975 if the conditions in subsection (2) below are satisfied.

(2) The conditions referred to in subsection (1) above are—

(a) that the persons for whose benefit the trusts permit the settled property to be applied include all or most of the persons employed by or holding office with the company ;

(b) that, at the date when the shares or securities cease to be relevant property or at a subsequent date not more than one year thereafter, both the conditions mentioned in subsection (2) of section 67 of the Finance Act 1978 (read with subsections (3) and (6)) are satisfied, without taking account of shares or securities held on other trusts ; and

1978 c. 42.

(c) that the trusts do not permit any of the settled property to be applied at any time (whether during any such period as is referred to in the said paragraph 17(1) or later) for the benefit of any of the persons mentioned in subsection (4) of the said section 67 (read with subsections (5) and (6)) or for the benefit of the settlor or of any person connected with him.

(3) In its application for the purposes of subsection (2)(c) above, section 67(4) of the Finance Act 1978 shall be construed as if—

(a) references to section 67(1) were references to subsection (2) above ; and

(b) references to the time of the transfer of value were references to the time when the property ceases to be relevant property.

116.—(1) This section applies to settled property to which paragraph 17 of Schedule 5 to the Finance Act 1975 applies if no qualifying interest in possession subsists in it.

(2) Subject to subsections (4) and (5) below, there shall be a charge to tax under this section—

  (a) where settled property ceases to be property to which this section applies, otherwise than by virtue of a payment out of the settled property, and

  (b) where a payment is made out of settled property to which this section applies for the benefit of a person within subsection (3) below, or a person connected with such a person, and

  (c) in a case in which paragraphs (a) and (b) above do not apply, where the trustees make a disposition (otherwise than by way of a payment out of the settled property) as a result of which the value of settled property to which this section applies is less than it would be but for the disposition.

(3) A person is within this subsection if—

  (a) he has directly or indirectly provided any of the settled property otherwise than by additions not exceeding in value £1,000 in any one year ; or

  (b) in a case where the employment in question is employment by a close company, he is a participator in relation to that company and either—

      (i) is beneficially entitled to, or to rights entitling him to acquire, not less than 5 per cent. of, or of any class of the shares comprised in, its issued share capital, or

      (ii) would, on a winding-up of the company, be entitled to not less than 5 per cent. of its assets ; or

  (c) he has acquired an interest in the settled property for a consideration in money or money's worth.

(4) If the trusts are those of a profit sharing scheme approved in accordance with Schedule 9 to the Finance Act 1978, tax shall not be chargeable under this section by virtue of subsection (3)(b) above on an appropriation of shares in pursuance of the scheme.

(5) Subsections (3) to (9) of section 113 above shall apply for the purposes of this section as they apply for the purposes of that section (with the substitution of a reference to subsection (2)(c) above for the reference in section 113(4) to section 113(2)(b)).

(6) In this section—

   (a) " close company " and " participator " have the same meanings as in section 39 of the Finance Act 1975 ; and

   (b) "year " means the period beginning with 26th March 1974 and ending with 5th April 1974, and any subsequent period of twelve months ending with 5th April ;

and a person shall be treated for the purposes of this section as acquiring an interest for a consideration in money or money's worth if he becomes entitled to it as a result of transactions which include a disposition for such consideration (whether to him or another) of that interest or of other property.

117. Schedule 16 to this Act shall have effect.

118.—(1) This section applies to—

   (a) settled property which is held on trusts to the like effect as those specified in section 33(1)(ii) of the Trustee Act 1925 and which became held on those trusts on the failure or determination before 12th April 1978 of trusts to the like effect as those specified in section 33(1)(i), and

   (b) settled property within paragraph 19 of Schedule 5 to the Finance Act 1975, as it applies to property which was transferred into settlement before 10th March 1981.

(2) Subject to subsection (3) below, there shall be a charge to tax under this section—

   (a) where settled property ceases to be property to which this section applies, otherwise than by virtue of a payment out of the settled property for the benefit of the relevant beneficiary, and

   (b) in a case in which paragraph (a) above does not apply, where the trustees make a disposition (otherwise than by way of such a payment) as a result of which the value of settled property to which this section applies is less than it would be but for the disposition.

(3) Subsections (3) to (9) of section 113 above shall apply for the purposes of this section as they apply for the purposes of that section.

(4) In this section " the relevant beneficiary " means—

   (a) where this section applies by virtue of subsection (1)(a) above, the principal beneficiary within the meaning of section 33 of the Trustee Act 1925 :

(*b*) where this section applies by virtue of subsection (1)(*b*) above, the person mentioned in paragraph 19(1) of Schedule 5 to the Finance Act 1975.

119.—(1) Subject to the following provisions of this section, tax shall not be charged under this Chapter in respect of property which ceases to be relevant property, or ceases to be property to which section 113, 114, 116 or 118 above or paragraph 2 of Schedule 16 to this Act applies, on becoming—

(*a*) property held for charitable purposes only without limit of time (defined by a date or otherwise) ;

(*b*) the property of a political party qualifying for exemption under paragraph 11 of Schedule 6 to the Finance Act 1975 ;

(*c*) the property of a body mentioned in paragraph 12 of that Schedule (national purposes etc.) ; or

(*d*) the property of a body not established or conducted for profit.

(2) Subsection (1)(*d*) above shall not apply unless the Treasury so direct, whether before or after the time when the property becomes the property of the body in question, and the property is within sub-paragraph (2) of paragraph 13 of Schedule 6 to the Finance Act 1975 ; and sub-paragraphs (3) to (8) of that paragraph shall apply for the purposes of this subsection as they apply for the purposes of that paragraph.

(3) If the amount on which tax would be charged apart from this section in respect of any property exceeds the value of the property immediately after it becomes property of a description specified in paragraphs (*a*) to (*d*) of subsection (1) above (less the amount of any consideration for its transfer received by the trustees), that subsection shall not apply but the amount on which tax is charged shall be equal to the excess.

(4) The reference in subsection (3) above to the amount on which tax would be charged is a reference to the amount on which it would be charged—

(*a*) assuming (if it is not in fact so) that the tax is not paid out of settled property, and

(*b*) apart from Schedule 10 to the Finance Act 1976 (business property) and Schedule 14 to the Finance Act 1981 (agricultural property) ;

and the reference in that subsection to the amount on which tax is charged is a reference to the amount on which it would be charged on that assumption and apart from those Schedules.

(5) Subsection (1) above shall not apply in relation to any property if the disposition by which it becomes property of the relevant description is defeasible; but for this purpose a disposition which has not been defeated at a time twelve months after the property concerned becomes property of the relevant description and is not defeasible after that time shall be treated as not being defeasible, whether or not it was capable of being defeated before that time.

(6) Subsection (1) above shall not apply in relation to any property if it or any part of it may become applicable for purposes other than charitable purposes or purposes of a body mentioned in subsection (1)(*b*), (*c*) or (*d*) above.

(7) Subsection (1) above shall not apply in relation to any property if, at or before the time when it becomes property of the relevant description, an interest under the settlement is or has been acquired for a consideration in money or money's worth by an exempt body otherwise than from a charity or a body mentioned in subsection (1)(*b*) or (*c*) above.

(8) In subsection (7) above " exempt body " means a charity or a body mentioned in subsection (1)(*b*), (*c*) or (*d*) above; and for the purposes of subsection (7) above a body shall be treated as acquiring an interest for a consideration in money or money's worth if it becomes entitled to the interest as a result of transactions which include a disposition for such consideration (whether to that body or to another person) of that interest or of other property.

Miscellaneous

Initial Interest of settlor or spouse.

120.—(1) Where a settlor or his spouse is beneficially entitled to an interest in possession in property immediately after it becomes comprised in the settlement, the property shall for the purposes of this Chapter be treated as not having become comprised in the settlement on that occasion; but when the property or any part of it becomes held on trusts under which neither of those persons is beneficially entitled to an interest in possession, the property or part shall for those purposes be treated as becoming comprised in a separate settlement made by that one of them who ceased (or last ceased) to be beneficially entitled to an interest in possession in it.

(2) References in subsection (1) above to the spouse of a settlor include references to the widow or widower of a settlor.

(3) This section applies whether the occasion first referred to in subsection (1) above occurred before or after the passing of this Act, but not if it occurred before 27th March 1974.

121.—(1) Where property which ceases to be comprised in one settlement becomes comprised in another then, unless in the meantime any person becomes beneficially entitled to the prop- erty (and not merely to an interest in possession in the property), it shall for the purposes of this Chapter be treated as remaining comprised in the first settlement.

(2) Subsection (1) above applies only if the date on which property ceases to be comprised in a settlement falls after 9th December 1981 ; but where property ceased to be comprised in one settlement before 10th December 1981 and after 26th March 1974 and, by the same disposition, became comprised in another settlement, it shall for the purposes of this Chapter be treated as remaining comprised in the first settlement.

122.—(1) For the purposes of this Chapter property to which section 120 or 121 above applies shall not be taken to be exclu- ded property by virtue of paragraph 2(1)(*a*) of Schedule 5 to the Finance Act 1975 unless the condition in subsection (3) below is satisfied (in addition to the conditions in that paragraph that the property is situated outside the United Kingdom and that the settlor was not domiciled there when the settlement was made).

(2) Section 108(8) above shall not have effect in relation to property to which section 120 or 121 above applies unless the condition in subsection (3) below is satisfied (in addition to the condition in section 108(8) that the settlor was not domiciled in the United Kingdom when the settlement was made).

(3) The condition referred to in subsections (1) and (2) above is—

    (*a*) in the case of property to which section 120 above applies, that the person who is the settlor in relation to the settlement first mentioned in that section, and

    (*b*) in the case of property to which subsection (1) or (2) of section 121 above applies, that the person who is the settlor in relation to the second of the settlements mentioned in the subsection concerned,

was not domiciled in the United Kingdom when that settlement was made.

(4) In determining for the purposes of section 108(8) whether the condition in subsection (3) above is satisfied in relation to property which became comprised in the settlement before 10th December 1974, section 45 of the Finance Act 1975 shall be disregarded.

PART IV
Property
becoming
settled on a
death.

123. Property which becomes comprised in a settlement in pursuance of a will or intestacy shall for the purposes of this Chapter be taken to have become comprised in it on the death of the testator or intestate (whether it occurred before or after the passing of this Act).

Income
applied for
charitable
purposes.

124. For the purposes of this Chapter, where the trusts on which settled property is held require part of the income of the property to be applied for charitable purposes, a corresponding part of the settled property shall be regarded as held for charitable purposes.

Annual
charges under
Finance Act
1975.
1975 c. 7.

125. No charge to tax shall be imposed under paragraph 12(2) of Schedule 5 to the Finance Act 1975 by reference to any year ending after 31st December 1981 ; and any tax charged under that provision and not already allowed as a credit under paragraph 12(3) of that Schedule or under this section shall be allowed as a credit against tax chargeable under this Chapter in respect of the settled property or part concerned.

Minor
interpretative
provisions.

126.—(1) In this Chapter, unless the context otherwise requires—

" payment " includes a transfer of assets other than money ; and

" quarter " means a period of three months.

(2) In this Chapter " trade or professional compensation fund " means a fund which is maintained or administered by a representative association of persons carrying on a trade or profession and the only or main objects of which are compensation for or relief of losses or hardship that, through the default or alleged default of persons carrying on the trade or profession or of their agents or servants, are incurred or likely to be incurred by others.

Amendments.

127. Schedule 17 to this Act (which makes amendments relating to the preceding provisions of this Chapter) shall have effect.

PART V

STAMP DUTY

Reduction of
duty on
conveyances
and leases.
1963 c. 25.

128.—(1) In subsection (1) of section 55 of the Finance Act 1963 and in the Table in Part I of Schedule 11 to that Act (under which stamp duty is not chargeable on conveyances and transfers certified at £20,000 and is chargeable at reduced rates on those certified at £25,000, £30,000 and £35,000) and in sub-

section (1) of section 4 of the Finance Act (Northern Ireland)
1963 and in the Table in Part I of Schedule 1 to that Act (which
make similar provision for Northern Ireland) for " £20,000 ",
" £25,000 ", " £30,000 " and " £35,000 ", wherever occurring,
there shall be substituted respectively " £25,000 ", " £30,000 ",
" £35,000 " and " £40,000 ".

(2) In subsection (2) of the said section 55 and of the said
section 4 (under which the relief afforded by subsection (1) of
those sections is not available as respects the duty chargeable
in respect of the premium for a lease if the consideration includes rent exceeding £250 a year) for " £250 " there shall be
substituted " £300 ".

(3) In the heading " Lease or Tack " in Schedule 1 to the
Stamp Act 1891 as it applies throughout the United Kingdom—

(a) in paragraph (2)(a) (duty where definite term less than a
year of furnished dwelling-house and rent exceeds
£400) for " £400 " there shall be substituted " £500 ",
and

(b) in the Table in paragraph (3) (which provides for duty
on rent in the case of any other term and the first
column of which indicates the rent, the second column
the duty where the term does not exceed 7 years or is
indefinite, the third column the duty where the term
exceeds 7 years but not 35 years, the fourth column the
duty where the term exceeds 35 years but not 100 years
and the fifth column the duty where the term exceeds
100 years) for the last entry there shall be substituted—

" Exceeding £400 and not exceeding £450.	Nil	9·00	54·00	108·00
Exceeding £450 and not exceeding £500.	Nil	10·00	60·00	120·00
Exceeding £500: for any full sum of £50 and also for any fractional part thereof.	0·50	1·00	6·00	12·00 "

(4) This section applies to instruments executed on or after
22nd March 1982 and shall be deemed to have come into force
on that date.

129.—(1) Where any conveyance, transfer or lease is made or
agreed to be made to a body of persons established for charitable
purposes only or to the trustees of a trust so established or to
the Trustees of the National Heritage Memorial Fund, no stamp
duty shall be chargeable by virtue of—

(a) any of the following headings in Schedule 1 to the Stamp
Act 1891, namely, " Conveyance or Transfer on Sale ",

PART V

1910 c. 8.

" Conveyance or Transfer of any kind not hereinbefore described " and " Lease or Tack ", or

(b) section 74 of the Finance (1909-10) Act 1910 (gifts inter vivos),

on the instrument by which the conveyance, transfer or lease, or the agreement for it, is effected.

(2) An instrument in respect of which stamp duty is not chargeable by virtue only of subsection (1) above shall not be treated as duly stamped unless it is stamped in accordance with 1891 c. 39. section 12 of the Stamp Act 1891 with a stamp denoting that it is not chargeable with any duty.

(3) This section applies to instruments executed on or after 22nd March 1982 and shall be deemed to have come into force on that date.

Exemption from duty for substituted life policies.

130.—(1) In any case where, for the purposes of the enactments specified in subsection (2) of section 34 of this Act, policies which are the earlier policy and the later policy, within the meaning of that section, are treated as a single policy, stamp duty shall not be chargeable on the policy of life insurance which is the later policy if it comes into existence on or after 25th March 1982.

(2) This section shall be deemed to have come into force on 25th March 1982.

Maintenance funds for historic buildings.

1980 c. 48.

131. In section 98(1) of the Finance Act 1980 (maintenance funds for historic buildings) for the words from " section 89(4)(d) " to " section 90(3) above " there shall be substituted the words " paragraph 1(5) or 3(1) of Schedule 16 to the Finance Act 1982 no charge to capital transfer tax in respect of the property ceasing to be comprised in the settlement or a reduced charge to that tax by virtue of paragraph 1(8) or 3(4) of that Schedule ".

PART VI

OIL TAXATION

CHAPTER I

GENERAL

Increase of petroleum revenue tax and ending of supplementary petroleum duty.

1981 c. 35.

132.—(1) With respect to chargeable periods ending after 31st December 1982, section 1(2) of the principal Act (rate of petroleum revenue tax) shall be amended by substituting for the words " 70 per cent." the words " 75 per cent.".

(2) At the end of subsection (5) of section 122 of the Finance Act 1981 (the chargeable periods for which supplementary

petroleum duty is chargeable) for the words " and 30th June 1982 " there shall be substituted the words " 30th June 1982 and 31st December 1982 and to no other periods ".

133.—(1) In section 2 of the principal Act (assessable profits Export sales and allowable losses) at the beginning of subsection (5) there of gas. shall be inserted the words " Subject to subsection (5A) below " and at the end of that subsection there shall be inserted the following subsection—

" (5A) In any case where oil consisting of gas is disposed of in a sale at arm's length and the terms of the contract are such that the seller is required to transport the gas from a place on land in the United Kingdom for delivery at a place outside the United Kingdom or to meet some or all of the costs of or incidental to its transportation from and to such places then, for the purposes of this Part of this Act—

   (*a*) the price received or receivable for the gas shall be deemed to be that for which it would have been sold, and

   (*b*) the gas shall be deemed to be delivered at the time it would have been delivered,

if the terms of the contract required the gas to be delivered as mentioned in paragraph 2(2)(*b*) of Schedule 3 to this Act and did not require the seller to meet any such costs as are mentioned above."

(2) In section 122(3) of the Finance Act 1981 (gross profit 1981 c. 35. for purposes of supplementary petroleum duty) for " 2(4) and (5) " there shall be substituted " 2(4) to (5A) ".

(3) This section has effect with respect to chargeable periods ending after 31st December 1981.

134.—(1) Where an election is made under this section and Alternative accepted by the Board, the market value for taxation purposes valuation of of any ethane to which the election applies shall be determined, ethane used for not in accordance with paragraphs 2, 2A and 3 of Schedule 3 purposes. to the principal Act (value under a notional contract), but in accordance with a price formula specified in the election ; and, in relation to any such ethane, any reference to market value in any other provision of the principal Act shall be construed accordingly.

(2) Subject to subsection (3) below, an election under this section applies only to ethane—

   (*a*) which, during the period covered by the election, is either disposed of otherwise than in sales at arm's length or relevantly appropriated ; and

2 K 2

(b) which is used or to be used for petrochemical purposes by or on behalf of the person to whom it is so disposed of or, as the case may be, by or on behalf of the participator by whom it is appropriated ; and

(c) which is not subjected to fractionation between the time at which it is disposed of or appropriated as mentioned in paragraph (a) above and the time at which it is used as mentioned in paragraph (b) above.

(3) In any case where—

(a) at a time during the period covered by an election, a market value falls to be determined for ethane to which subsection (4)(b) or subsection (5)(d) of section 2 of the principal Act applies (oil stocks at the end of chargeable periods), and

(b) after the expiry of the chargeable period in question, the ethane is disposed of or appropriated and used as mentioned in subsection (2) above,

the market value of that ethane at the time referred to in paragraph (a) above shall be determined as if it were then ethane to which the election applies.

(4) Where any ethane is used principally for the petrochemical purposes specified in the election but some of it is used for fuel, as an incident of the principal use, the whole of it shall be regarded as ethane to which the election applies ; but, subject thereto, the market value of ethane used otherwise than for those purposes shall be determined as if no election had been made.

(5) The provisions of Schedule 18 to this Act shall have effect for supplementing this section.

(6) In the preceding provisions of this section—

(a) " ethane " means oil consisting of gas of which the largest component by volume over any chargeable period is ethane and which—

(i) before being disposed of or appropriated as mentioned in subsection (2)(a) above either is not subjected to initial treatment or is subjected to initial treatment which does not include fractionation, or

(ii) results from the fractionation of gas before it is disposed of or relevantly appropriated ;

(b) " taxation purposes " means the purposes of Part I of the principal Act and of Part VIII of the Finance Act 1981 (supplementary petroleum duty).

1981 c. 35.

(7) In this section " fractionation " means the treatment of gas in order to separate gas of one or more kinds as mentioned

in paragraph 2A(3) of Schedule 3 to the principal Act; and for
the purposes of subsection (6)(*a*) above,—

    (*a*) the proportion of ethane in any gas shall be determined
at a temperature of 15 degrees centigrade and at a
pressure of one atmosphere; and

    (*b*) " component " means ethane, methane or liquefied
petroleum gas.

135.—(1) In any case where a determination of an oil field Determination
is made under Schedule 1 to the principal Act and before the of oil fields.
date of the determination oil has been won from the oil field
so determined,—

    (*a*) Part I of the principal Act, except Schedule 7, and Part
VIII of the Finance Act 1981 (supplementary petro- 1981 c. 35.
leum duty) shall apply as if the determination had been
made immediately before oil was first won from the
field;

    (*b*) where the actual date of the determination is later than
the date which by virtue of paragraph (*a*) above is the
end of a chargeable period for the oil field, then as
respects that chargeable period sections 33(1) and 34
of the Taxes Management Act 1970 (in their applica- 1970 c. 9.
tion by virtue of paragraph 1 of Schedule 2 to the
principal Act), paragraphs 2(1), 5(1) and 13 of
Schedule 2 to the principal Act and paragraph 9 of
Schedule 16 to the Finance Act 1981 shall have effect
as if any reference to the end of a chargeable period
were a reference to the actual date of the determination;

    (*c*) where the actual date of the determination is later than
the date which by virtue of paragraph (*a*) above is the
end of a claim period in relation to the oil field, then
as respects that claim period paragraph 2(1) of Schedule
5 to the principal Act and paragraph 1(2) of Schedule
6 to that Act shall have effect as if any reference to the
end of the claim period in which the expenditure is
incurred were a reference to that actual date; and

    (*d*) where the actual date of the determination is later than
the date which by virtue of paragraph (*a*) above is the
end of the transfer period, within the meaning of
Schedule 17 to the Finance Act 1980, in relation to the 1980 c. 48.
oil field, then as respects that transfer period paragraph
3(1) of that Schedule shall have effect as if the reference
to the end of the transfer period were a reference to
that actual date.

(2) In any case where—

    (*a*) a determination is made under paragraph 5 of Schedule

PART VI   1 to the principal Act (variation of fields) varying an
                       earlier determination ; and

                    (b) in consequence of that variation an existing oil field
                       is altered to any extent ;

1981 c. 35.   then Part I of the principal Act and Part VIII of the Finance Act
               1981 shall apply in relation to the oil field subject only to the
               modifications provided by subsection (3) below.

               (3) Where subsection (2) above applies—

                    (a) the time allowed—

                          (i) by paragraph 2 or paragraph 5 of Schedule 2
                          to the principal Act for making returns, or

1980 c. 48.   (ii) by paragraph 3 of Schedule 17 to the Finance
                          Act 1980 for delivering notices,

                       shall as respects returns or notices containing such
                       particulars as may be required in consequence of the
                       later determination be extended to a period ending, in
                       the case of a return under paragraph 2 or a notice
                       under paragraph 3, two months and, in the case of a
                       return under paragraph 5, one month after the actual
                       date of that determination ;

                    (b) any claim falling to be made in accordance with Schedule
                       5 or 6 to the principal Act in respect of any expendi-
                       ture incurred before the actual date of the later deter-
                       mination which could not have been made before that
                       determination may be made at any time before the
                       expiry of the period of six years beginning with that
                       date ;

1980 c. 1.   (c) section 1 of the Petroleum Revenue Tax Act 1980 (pay-
                       ments of tax on account), section 105 of the Finance
                       Act 1980 (advance payments of tax) and paragraph
                       10 of Schedule 16 to the Finance Act 1981 (payments
                       on account of supplementary petroleum duty) shall
                       not apply in relation to any return made under para-
                       graph 2 of Schedule 2 to the principal Act in so far
                       as it is made by virtue of paragraph (a) above ; and

                    (d) section 139 below (advance petroleum revenue tax)
                       shall not apply in relation to so much of the gross
                       profit as accrues to any person in a chargeable period
                       ending before the actual date of the later determina-
                       tion by virtue only of that later determination.

               (4) In subsection (3) of section 12 of the principal Act (re-
               ferences to things done etc. before determination of field) the
               words from " as regards " to " any oil field " shall cease to have
               effect.

               (5) This section has effect in relation to determinations made
               after 31st December 1981.

136.—(1) In section 13 of the principal Act (treatment of oil extraction activities etc. for purposes of income tax and corporation tax) after subsection (2) there shall be inserted the following subsection—

" (2A) In any case where—

(*a*) in any chargeable period a person incurs a loss in activities (in this subsection referred to as " separate activities ") which, for that or any subsequent chargeable period, are treated by virtue of subsection (1) above as a separate trade for the purposes specified in that subsection, and

(*b*) in any subsequent chargeable period any of his trading income is derived from activities (in this subsection referred to as " related activities ") which are not part of the separate activities but which, apart from subsection (1) above, would together with those activities constitute a single trade,

then, nothwithstanding anything in that subsection, the amount of the loss may be set off, in accordance with section 171 or section 177(1) of the Taxes Act, against so much of his trading income in any subsequent chargeable period as is derived from the related activities."

(2) At the end of section 15 of the principal Act (oil extraction activities: charges on income) there shall be added the following subsection—

" (5) In any case where—

(*a*) such of the charges on income which are paid by a company and allowable under section 248 of the Taxes Act as, by virtue of the preceding provisions of this section, are not allowable against that part of the company's profits referred to in subsection (2) above exceed the remaining part of its profits (in this subsection referred to as the company's " non-oil profits "), and

(*b*) the amount of that excess is greater than the amount (if any) by which the total of the charges on income which are allowable to the company under that section exceeds the total of the company's profits,

then, for the purpose of enabling the company to surrender the excess referred to in paragraph (*a*) above by way of group relief, subsection (6) of section 259 of the Taxes Act shall have effect as if—

(i) the reference therein to the amount paid by the surrendering company by way of charges on income were a reference to so much of that amount as is allowable only against the company's non-oil profits ; and

(ii) the reference therein to the surrendering company's profits were a reference to its non-oil profits alone."

(3) The amendments made by subsections (1) and (2) above,—

(a) so far as they relate to corporation tax, shall be deemed to have had effect for accounting periods beginning before the passing of this Act and on or after 1st January 1980 and shall have effect for subsequent accounting periods ; and

(b) so far as they relate to income tax, shall be deemed to have had effect for the years 1980-81 and 1981-82 and shall have effect for subsequent years of assessment ;

and accordingly subsection (1) above applies to losses incurred in any such accounting period or year of assessment and subsection (2) above applies to charges on income paid in any such accounting period.

Expenditure met by regional development grants to be disregarded for certain purposes.

137.—(1) In paragraph 8 of Schedule 3 to the principal Act (certain subsidised expenditure to be disregarded) in sub-paragraph (1) the words from " unless it is so met by a grant " onwards shall be omitted.

(2) Subject to subsection (3) below, in any case where, by virtue of the said paragraph 8 as amended by subsection (1) above, expenditure which has been or is to be met by a regional development grant is not to be regarded for any of the purposes of Part I of the principal Act as having been incurred by any person, that particular grant shall be regarded as not falling within the reference to a regional development grant in—

1968 c. 3.

(a) section 84(1) of the Capital Allowances Act 1968 (treatment of subsidised expenditure for the purposes of the main reliefs for capital expenditure) ; or

(b) section 95(6) of that Act (treatment of subsidised expenditure for the purposes of allowances relevant to scientific research).

(3) If, in a case falling within subsection (2) above, only a proportion of the expenditure which has been or is to be met by a regional development grant is expenditure which, if it were not so met, would be allowable under section 3 or section 4 of the principal Act, only a corresponding proportion of the grant shall be regarded as not falling within the reference to regional development grant in the provisions referred to in subsection (2) above.

(4) Subsection (5) below applies in any case where—

    (*a*) a person has incurred expenditure (by way of purchase, rent or otherwise) on the acquisition of an asset in a transaction to which paragraph 2 of Schedule 4 to the principal Act applies (transactions between connected persons and otherwise than at arm's length), and

    (*b*) the expenditure incurred by the other person referred to in that paragraph in acquiring, bringing into existence or enhancing the value of the asset as mentioned in that paragraph has been or is to be met by a regional development grant and, in whole or in part, falls to be taken into account under Chapter I of Part I, or under Part II, of the Capital Allowances Act 1968 (industrial 1968 c. 3. buildings and structures and scientific research) or Chapter I of Part III of the Finance Act 1971 (machin- 1971 c. 68. ery and plant).

(5) Where this subsection applies, for the purposes of the charge of income tax or corporation tax on the income arising from those activities of the person referred to in subsection (4)(*a*) above which are treated by virtue of subsection (1) of section 13 of the principal Act as a separate trade for those purposes, the expenditure referred to in subsection (4)(*a*) above shall be treated as reduced by the amount of the regional development grant referred to in subsection (4)(*b*) above.

(6) In this section " regional development grant " means a grant made under Part I of the Industry Act 1972 or such grant 1972 c. 63. made under an enactment of the Parliament of Northern Ireland or Measure of the Northern Ireland Assembly as has been or may be declared by the Treasury under section 84 or section 95 of the Capital Allowances Act 1968 to correspond to a grant made under the said Part I.

(7) This section applies in any case where—

    (*a*) the expenditure to which the regional development grant relates is incurred after 9th March 1982 ; and

    (*b*) the regional development grant concerned is paid after that date.

138.—(1) The provisions of this section apply where— Provisions

    (*a*) expenditure incurred by any person in relation to an supplementary asset in any relevant period (in this section referred to to section 137. as " the initial period ") has been or is to be met by a regional development grant ; and

    (*b*) notwithstanding the provisions of section 137 above, in determining that person's liability to income tax or corporation tax for the initial period the whole or some part of that expenditure falls to be taken into account under Chapter I of Part I, or under Part II, of the Capital Allowances Act 1968 (allowances in respect of industrial buildings and structures and scientific research) or Chapter I of Part III of the Finance Act 1971 (allowances in respect of machinery and plant) ; and

(c) in a relevant period subsequent to the initial period, either expenditure on the asset becomes allowable under section 3 or section 4 of the principal Act or the proportion of any such expenditure which is so allowable is different as compared with the initial period ;

and in the following provisions of this section, the subsequent relevant period referred to in paragraph (c) above is referred to as " the adjustment period ".

(2) Where this section applies, there shall be redetermined for the purposes of this section the amount of the expenditure referred to in paragraph (a) of subsection (1) above which would have been taken into account as mentioned in paragraph (b) of that subsection if the circumstances referred to in paragraph (c) of that subsection had existed in the initial period ; and according to whether the amount as so redetermined is greater or less than the amount actually taken into account as mentioned in subsection (1)(b) above, the difference is in the following provisions of this section referred to as the increase or the reduction in the allowance.

(3) If there is an increase in the allowance, then, for the purposes of the provisions referred to in subsection (1)(b) above, an amount of capital expenditure equal to the increase shall be deemed to have been incurred by the person concerned in the adjustment period on an extension of or addition to the asset referred to in subsection (1)(a) above.

(4) If there is a reduction in the allowance, then, for the purpose of determining the liability to income tax or corporation tax of the person concerned, he shall be treated as having received in the adjustment period, as income of the trade in connection with which the expenditure referred to in subsection (1)(a) above was incurred, a sum equal to the amount of the reduction in the allowance.

(5) In this section " relevant period " means an accounting period of a company or a year of assessment.

ADVANCE PETROLEUM REVENUE TAX

139.—(1) For each of the following chargeable periods, namely— Liability for APRT and credit against liability for petroleum revenue tax.

(*a*) the first chargeable period ending after 31st December 1982 in which, subject to sections 140 and 141 below, a gross profit accrues to a participator from an oil field, and

(*b*) every one out of the nine immediately succeeding chargeable periods in which, subject to those sections, a gross profit accrues to him from that field,

the participator shall be liable to pay an amount of petroleum revenue tax (to be known as " advance petroleum revenue tax " and in this Chapter referred to as " APRT ") in accordance with this section.

(2) Subject to sections 140 and 141 below, APRT shall be payable on the gross profit accruing to the participator in the chargeable period in question and shall be payable at the rate of 20 per cent.

(3) The aggregate of—

(*a*) the APRT which is paid by a participator in respect of any chargeable period and not repaid, and

(*b*) any APRT which is carried forward from the previous chargeable period by virtue of subsection (4) below,

shall be set against the participator's liability for petroleum revenue tax charged in any assessment made on him in respect of the assessable profit accruing to him in the period referred to in paragraph (*a*) above from the oil field in question (which liability is in this Chapter referred to as his liability for petroleum revenue tax for a chargeable period) and shall, accordingly, discharge a corresponding amount of that liability.

(4) If, for any chargeable period, the aggregate of—

(*a*) the APRT which is paid by a participator for that period and not repaid, and

(*b*) any APRT carried forward from the previous chargeable period by virtue of this subsection,

exceeds the participator's liability for petroleum revenue tax for that period, the excess shall be carried forward as an accretion to the APRT paid (and not repaid) for the next chargeable period ; and any reference in this Chapter to a participator's APRT credit for a chargeable period is a reference to the aggregate of the APRT paid for that period and not repaid and any APRT carried forward from the previous chargeable period by virtue of this subsection.

(5) The references in section 1 of the Provisional Collection of Taxes Act 1968 to petroleum revenue tax include a reference to APRT.

(6) The provisions of Schedule 19 to this Act shall have effect for supplementing this section and, accordingly, section 105 of the Finance Act 1980 (advance payments of petroleum revenue tax) shall cease to have effect with respect to chargeable periods ending after 30th June 1983.

(7) This Chapter shall be included in the Oil Taxation Acts for the purposes of sections 107 and 108 of the Finance Act 1980 (transmedian fields and gas banking schemes).

Increase of
gross profit
by reference
to royalties in
kind.
1934 c. 36.

140.—(1) This section applies where part of a participator's share of the oil won and saved from an oil field is delivered by him in a chargeable period to the Secretary of State pursuant to a requirement imposed under the terms of a licence granted under the Petroleum (Production) Act 1934.

(2) In determining for the purposes of APRT the gross profit accruing to the participator from the field in the chargeable period the aggregate of the amounts mentioned in paragraphs (*a*), (*b*) and (*c*) of subsection (5) of section 2 of the principal Act shall be increased by multiplying it by a fraction of which—

(*a*) the numerator is the total of the quantity of oil won from the field which is delivered or relevantly appropriated by him in the period including the oil delivered to the Secretary of State ; and

(*b*) the denominator is that total excluding the oil delivered to the Secretary of State.

(3) Where oil is delivered pursuant to a requirement which relates to oil of one or more kinds but not to others, subsection (2) above shall apply only in relation to oil of the kind or kinds to which the requirement relates ; and where oil is delivered pursuant to a requirement which specifies different proportions in relation to different kinds of oil, that subsection shall apply separately in relation to each of those kinds.

(4) For the purposes of subsection (5) of section 2 of the principal Act as it applies in determining for the purposes of APRT the gross profit accruing to a participator, the exclusion by paragraph 4 of Schedule 3 to that Act of oil delivered to the Secretary of State under the terms of a licence granted under the said Act of 1934 shall be deemed to extend to oil which is inadvertently delivered to him in excess of the amount required ; and oil so delivered shall be treated for the purposes of this section as delivered pursuant to a requirement imposed under the terms of such a licence.

(5) Any reference in this section or in section 141 below to the purposes of APRT includes a reference to the purpose of determining whether APRT is payable for a chargeable period by virtue of section 139(1) above.

PART VI

141.—(1) For the purposes of APRT there shall be for each oil field in each chargeable period an exempt allowance of 500,000 metric tonnes of oil divided between the participators in shares proportionate to their shares of the oil won and saved from the field during the period.

Reduction of gross profit by reference to exempt. allowance.

(2) If the gross profit accruing to a participator in a chargeable period from a field exceeds the cash equivalent of his share of the exempt allowance, the gross profit shall be reduced to an amount equal to the excess.

(3) If the gross profit accruing to a participator in a chargeable period from a field does not exceed the cash equivalent of his share of the exempt allowance, the gross profit shall be reduced to nil.

(4) Subject to subsection (5) below, the cash equivalent of a participator's share of the exempt allowance for an oil field for a chargeable period shall be equal to such proportion of the gross profit accruing to him from the field in that period (before any reduction under this section) as his share of the exempt allowance bears to his share, exclusive of excluded oil within the meaning of section 10 of the principal Act, of the oil won and saved from the field during the period.

(5) If a participator in an oil field so elects by notice in writing given to the Board at the time when he makes his return under paragraph 2 of Schedule 2 to the principal Act for a chargeable period, the cash equivalent of his share of the exempt allowance for the field for that period shall be determined under subsection (4) above—

  (*a*) to the extent that his share of that exempt allowance does not exceed his share of the oil (other than gas) won and saved from the field in the period, as if in computing the gross profit accruing to him in the period all amounts relating to gas fell to be disregarded ; and

  (*b*) to the extent, if any, that his share of that allowance exceeds his share of the oil (other than gas) so won and saved, as if in computing the gross profit so accruing all amounts relating to oil other than gas fell to be disregarded.

(6) In this section references to a participator's share of the oil won and saved from a field are to his share as expressed in metric tonnes and for that purpose 1,100 cubic metres of oil

consisting of gas at a temperature of 15 degrees centigrade and pressure of one atmosphere shall be counted as equivalent to one metric tonne of oil other than gas.

Consequences
of crediting
APRT
against
liability for
petroleum
revenue tax.

142.—(1) If it appears to the Board—

    (*a*) that any amount of APRT credit which has been set off against a participator's assessed liability to petroleum revenue tax for any chargeable period ought not to have been so set off, or that the amount so set off has become excessive, or

    (*b*) that, disregarding any liability to or credit for APRT, a participator is entitled to a repayment of petroleum revenue tax for any chargeable period,

then, for the purpose of securing that the liabilities of the participator to petroleum revenue tax and APRT (including interest on unpaid tax) for the chargeable period in question are what they ought to have been, the Board may make such assessments to, and shall make such repayments of, petroleum revenue tax and APRT as in their judgment are necessry in the circumstances.

(2) In a case falling within paragraph (*a*) of subsection (1) above, any necessary assessment to petroleum revenue tax may, where the revised amount of set off is ascertained as a result of an appeal, be made at any time before the expiry of the period of six years beginning at the end of the chargeable period in which the appeal is finally determined ; and in a case falling within paragraph (*b*) of that subsection any necessary assessment to APRT may be made at any time before the expiry of the period of six years beginning at the end of the chargeable period in which the participator became entitled as mentioned in that paragraph.

(3) In subsection (1) of section 17 of the principal Act (corporation tax: deduction of petroleum revenue tax in computing income)—

    (*a*) after the words " has paid " there shall be inserted the words " or is treated by virtue of subsection (1A) below as having paid " ;

    (*b*) after the words " chargeable period ", in the first place where they occur, there shall be inserted the words " not being advance petroleum revenue tax " ; and

    (*c*) after the words " petroleum revenue tax paid " there shall be inserted the words " or treated as having been paid ".

(4) After that subsection there shall be inserted the following subsection:—

" (1A) If and so far as any liability to an amount of petroleum revenue tax for any chargeable period is satisfied by an amount of advance petroleum revenue tax paid for that or any earlier chargeable period, that amount of petroleum revenue tax shall be treated for the purposes of this section as having been paid on the date on which it became due."

(5) Paragraphs 13, 14 and 15 of Schedule 2 to the principal Act (payment of tax, appeals and interest on tax) apply in relation to an assessment to petroleum revenue tax under subsection (1) above as they apply to an assessment under that Schedule.

Part VII

Miscellaneous and Supplementary

143.—(1) Subject to subsection (2) below, in section 1(1) of the National Insurance Surcharge Act 1976 (surcharge of $3\frac{1}{2}$ per cent. on secondary Class 1 contributions) for the words " $3\frac{1}{2}$ per cent." there shall be substituted the words " $2\frac{1}{2}$ per cent.". Reduction of national insurance surcharge. 1976 c. 85.

(2) Subject to subsections (3) and (4) below, this section has effect in relation to any contribution in respect of earnings which are paid on or after 2nd August 1982 ; but with respect to earnings paid in a tax week beginning before 6th April 1983, subsection (1) above shall have effect as if the words substituted for " $3\frac{1}{2}$ per cent." were " 2 per cent.", not " $2\frac{1}{2}$ per cent.".

(3) The amendments made by subsections (1) and (2) above do not apply to any secondary Class I contribution which any of the bodies specified in subsection (4) below is liable to pay in respect of earnings paid in a tax week beginning before 6th April 1983 ; and accordingly in the case of any such contributions, the rate of surcharge shall continue to be $3\frac{1}{2}$ per cent.

(4) The bodies referred to in subsection (3) above are—

(a) in England and Wales, those which, by virtue of section 53(5) of the Local Government, Planning and Land Act 1980, are local authorities for the purposes of Part VI of that Act ; 1980 c. 65.

(b) in Scotland, regional, islands and district councils ;

(c) the Receiver for the Metropolitan Police District and the police authority for every police area other than that District ;

(d) in Scotland, the fire authority for every area falling within a combined area ;

(e) the committees established under paragraph 2 of Schedule 3 to the Powers of Criminal Courts Act 1973 (probation and after-care committees) ; and

(f) magistrates' courts committees, within the meaning of section 19 of the Justices of the Peace Act 1979, and the committee of magistrates referred to in section 35(1) of that Act (the committee for the inner London area).

(5) In this section " tax week " has the same meaning as in the Social Security Act 1975.

144.—(1) In paragraph 5 of Schedule 4 to the Broadcasting Act 1981 (accounting periods of programme contractors which are bodies corporate)—

(a) after sub-paragraph (2) there shall be inserted the following sub-paragraph—

" (2A) Where two parts of such a period as is mentioned in sub-paragraph (1) fall to be divided from each other under sub-paragraph (2)(a), section 32(4) shall have effect as if the profits and advertising receipts for each part were the profits and advertising receipts for the whole multiplied by $\dfrac{X}{X+Y}$ where X and Y are respectively the number of weeks in that part and the number of weeks in the other part, counting (in each case) an odd 4 days or more as a week." ; and

(b) in sub-paragraph (3) for the words " sub-paragraph (2) ", in both places where they occur, there shall be substituted the words " sub-paragraph (2)(b) ".

(2) Subsection (1) above applies where the relevant order under section 32 of that Act (payments by programme contractors) is made after the passing of this Act.

(3) Any contract between the Independent Broadcasting Authority and a programme contractor under which television programmes or local sound broadcasts are to be provided by the contractor, being a contract which is in force immediately before the passing of this Act, shall, until it is varied or superseded by a further contract or expires or is otherwise terminated, whichever first occurs, be deemed to be modified by virtue of this subsection so as—

(a) to substitute provisions in conformity with subsection (1) above for so much (if any) of the contract as is not in conformity with that subsection ; and (*b*) to incorporate in the contract such additional provisions as the contract is required to include in accordance with that subsection.

(4) If it appears to the Independent Broadcasting Authority that subsection (1) above calls for the inclusion of additional provisions in any such contract as is mentioned in subsection (3) above, but does not afford sufficient particulars of what those provisions ought to be, the Authority may, after consulting the programme contractor, decide what those provisions are to be.

(5) The first order made under section 32 of the Broadcasting Act 1981 after the passing of this Act may make, so as to take effect from 1st April 1982, provision which reduces the amount of any payments payable by virtue of subsection (1)(*b*) of that section ; and if that order makes any such provision so as to take effect from that date, that section and paragraph 5 of Schedule 4 to that Act shall have effect in relation to the order as if any reference (however worded) to its commencement were a reference to that date.

145. For the purposes of certificates of tax deposit issued by the Treasury under section 12 of the National Loans Act 1968 on terms published before 31st July 1980, the date which is the due date in relation to—

(*a*) income tax charged at a rate other than the basic rate, and

(*b*) capital gains tax,

is by virtue of this section postponed, with respect to the year 1980-81 and any subsequent year of assessment, from the date specified in the prospectuses concerned to 1st December following the end of the year of assessment for which the tax is payable.

146.—(1) In this section—

" the Corporation " means the British National Oil Corporation ;

" 75 per cent. subsidiary " has the meaning given by section 532(1)(*b*) of the Taxes Act ;

" the subsidiary " means a 75 per cent. subsidiary of the Corporation to which any of the Corporation's assets or any of the assets of any other 75 per cent. subsidiary of the Corporation are transferred in pursuance of a scheme made under section 2(2) of the Oil and Gas (Enterprise) Act 1982 ; and

" transferred assets " means any of the assets so transferred

(2) Section 278 of the Taxes Act (deemed disposals of assets for capital gains tax where member leaves group) and section 21 of the Development Land Tax Act 1976 (deemed disposals of assets for development land tax where member leaves group) shall not have effect as respects any of the transferred assets on the subsidiary's ceasing on or after 6th April 1982 to be a 75 per cent. subsidiary of the Corporation.

147.—(1) In this section—

" the Corporation " means the British Gas Corporation ; and

" 75 per cent. subsidiary " has the meaning given by section 532(1)(*b*) of the Taxes Act.

(2) If, in pursuance of a scheme made under section 10(2) of the Oil and Gas (Enterprise) Act 1982, any of the assets of the Corporation or of a 75 per cent. subsidiary of the Corporation are transferred to another 75 per cent. subsidiary of the Corporation, neither—

(*a*) section 278 of the Taxes Act (deemed disposals of assets for capital gains tax where member leaves group), nor

(*b*) section 21 of the Development Land Tax Act 1976 (deemed disposals of assets for development land tax where member leaves group),

shall have effect as respects any of the assets so transferred on that other subsidiary's ceasing to be a 75 per cent. subsidiary of the Corporation.

(3) If, for the purpose of enabling the Corporation to comply with a direction given under section 7(2) of the Gas Act 1972 requiring any asset to be disposed of, the asset to which the direction relates is transferred to a 75 per cent. subsidiary of the Corporation, neither section 278 of the Taxes Act nor section 21 of the Development Land Tax Act 1976 shall have effect as respects any of the assets of that subsidiary on the subsidiary's ceasing to be a 75 per cent. subsidiary of the Corporation.

148.—(1) For the purposes of the Capital Gains Tax Act 1979, the transfer by virtue of the Hops Marketing Act 1982 of any asset from the Hops Marketing Board to any person or persons specified as mentioned in section 2(1) of that Act (in this section referred to as " the transferee ") shall be deemed to be for a consideration such that no gain or loss accrues to the Board ; and Schedule 5 to the Capital Gains Tax Act 1979 shall have effect in relation to any asset so transferred as if the acquisition or provision of it by the Board had been the acquisition or provision of it by the transferee.

(2) Any transfer by virtue of the Hops Marketing Act 1982 of any interest in land from the Hops Marketing Board to the transferee shall be deemed to be a disposal to which subsection (1) of section 20 of the Development Land Tax Act 1976 (groups of companies) applies.

149.—(1) The following section shall be substituted for section 30 of the Taxes Management Act 1970—

30.—(1) Where an amount of tax has been repaid to any person which ought not to have been repaid to him, that amount of tax may be assessed and re-covered as if it were unpaid tax.

(2) In any case where—

    (*a*) a repayment of tax has been increased in accordance with section 47 or 48 of the Finance (No. 2) Act 1975 (supplements added to repayments of tax, etc.) ; and

    (*b*) the whole or any part of that repayment has been paid to any person but ought not to have been paid to him ; and

    (*c*) that repayment ought not to have been in-creased either at all or to any extent ;

then the amount of the repayment assessed under subsection (1) above may include an amount equal to the amount by which the repayment ought not to have been increased.

(3) In any case where—

    (*a*) a payment, other than a repayment of tax to which subsection (2) above applies, is in-creased in accordance with section 47 or 48 of the Finance (No. 2) Act 1975 ; and

    (*b*) that payment ought not to have been in-creased either at all or to any extent ;

then an amount equal to the amount by which the payment ought not to have been increased may be assessed and recovered as if it were unpaid income tax or corporation tax.

(4) An assessment to income tax or corporation tax under this section shall be made under Case VI of Schedule D.

(5) An assessment under this section shall not be out of time under section 34 of this Act if it is made before the end of the chargeable period following that in which the amount so assessed was repaid or paid as the case may be.

(6) Subsection (5) above is without prejudice to sections 36, 37 and 39 of this Act.

(7) In this section any reference to an amount repaid or paid includes a reference to an amount allowed by way of set-off."

1978 c. 42.

(2) Subsection (5) of section 22 of the Finance Act 1978 (recovery of repayments of tax to spouses) shall not apply in relation to any amount repaid on or after 6th April 1982.

(3) Subsection (1) above has effect in relation to any amount repaid or paid on or after 6th April 1982.

Investment in gilt-edged unit trusts.
1961 c. 62.

150. In Part II of Schedule 1 to the Trustee Investments Act 1961 (" narrower-range investments " in which trust property may be invested) the following paragraph shall be inserted after paragraph 10—

1970 c. 10.

1980 c. 48.

" 10A. In any units, or other shares of the investments subject to the trusts, of a unit trust scheme which, at the time of investment, is an authorised unit trust, within the the meaning of section 358 of the Income and Corporation Taxes Act 1970, in relation to which, by virtue of section 60 of the Finance Act 1980, section 354 of the said Act of 1970 does not apply."

National savings accounts.
1971 c. 29.

151.—(1) The National Savings Bank Act 1971 shall have effect subject to the amendments specified in Schedule 20 to this Act.

(2) This section and Schedule 20 to this Act shall come into force on the expiry of the period of three months beginning with the day on which this Act is passed.

Additional power of Treasury to borrow.
1968 c. 13.

152.—(1) At the beginning of subsection (1) of section 12 of the National Loans Act 1968 (power of Treasury to borrow) there shall be inserted the words " Any money which the Treasury consider it expedient to raise for the purpose of promoting sound monetary conditions in the United Kingdom and ".

(2) After the said subsection (1) there shall be inserted the following subsection:

" (1A) The terms (as to interest or otherwise) on which any balance for the time being in the National Loans Fund is to be held shall be such as may be agreed between the Treasury and the Bank of England."

(3) In section 19(4) of the National Loans Act 1968 (meaning of liabilities and assets of the Fund) after the words " the assets of that Fund shall be " there shall be inserted the words " the aggregate of any balance in that Fund and ".

153.—(1) For section 5 of the National Loans Act 1968 (rates of interest) there shall be substituted the following section—

PART VII
Variable rates
of interest for
government
lending.
1968 c. 13.

" Rates of
interest.

     5.—(1) This section has effect as respects any rate of interest—

> (a) which under any provision in Schedule 1 to this Act is to be determined in accordance with this Act, or
>
> (b) which is to be determined by the Treasury under section 3 of this Act,

and, where any enactment passed after this Act provides for the payment of interest on advances or loans made out of the National Loans Fund, and for the rate at which that interest is to be payable to be determined or approved by the Treasury, then, except as otherwise expressly provided, this section has effect as respects that rate of interest.

    (2) For any loan or class of loans the Treasury may determine or approve either—

> (a) a fixed rate of interest, that is to say a specified rate or a formula rate which is to be applied, throughout the period of the loan or any loan of that class, with the value which it has when the loan is made, or
>
> (b) a variable rate of interest, that is to say a formula rate which is to be applied, for each of the successive periods of the loan or any loan of that class which are of a length specified in the determination or approval (in this section referred to as interest periods), with the value which it has at the beginning of that period ;

and in this subsection " formula rate " means a rate which is so expressed (whether by means of a formula or otherwise) that it will or may have different values at different times.

    (3) The Treasury shall, on each occasion when they determine or approve a fixed rate of interest for a loan or class of loans, satisfy themselves that the rate would be at least sufficient to prevent a loss if—

> (a) the loan, or any loan of that class—
>> (i) were made forthwith, and
>> (ii) were met out of money borrowed by the Treasury at the lowest rate at which the Treasury are for the time being

able to borrow money (of whatever amount) for a comparable period, and on other comparable terms, and

(*b*) the interest on the money so borrowed, together with the Treasury's expenses of borrowing, were set off against the interest received on the loan.

(4) The Treasury shall, on each occasion when they determine or approve a variable rate of interest for a loan or class of loans, satisfy themselves that the rate would be at least sufficient to prevent a loss if—

(*a*) the loan, or any loan of that class,—

(i) were made forthwith,

(ii) were to be repaid at the end of its first interest period, and

(iii) were met out of money borrowed by the Treasury at the lowest rate at which the Treasury are for the time being able to borrow money (of whatever amount) for a comparable period, and

(*b*) the interest on the money so borrowed were set off against the interest received on the loan.

(5) If at any time the Treasury are satisfied that a rate of interest determined or approved for a class of loans, of for a loan not yet made, would not meet the requirements of subsection (3) or, as the case may be, subsection (4) above if it were determined or approved at that time, that determination or approval shall be withdrawn ; and another rate shall be determined or approved in accordance with that subsection for further loans of that class or, as the case may be, for that loan.

(6) The Treasury may in determining or approving a rate of interest take into account any consideration justifying a rate higher than that required by subsection (3) or (4) above.

(7) Different fixed rates of interest may be determined or approved in respect of loans which are to be made for the same length of time ; and different variable rates of interest may be determined or approved for loans which are to have interest periods of the same length.

(8) The Treasury shall cause—

(*a*) all rates of interest determined from time to time by them in respect of local loans, and

(*b*) all other rates of interest determined from PART VII
time to time by them otherwise than by
virtue of subsection (6) above,

to be published in the London and Edinburgh Gazettes as soon as may be after the determination of
those rates."

(2) The enactments amended by Schedule 1 to that Act (government lending and advances) shall have effect as if in the third
column of that Schedule for the word " fixed ", wherever it
occurs, there were substituted the word " determined ".

(3) In subsection (9) of section 47 of the Housing (Financial 1958 c. 42.
Provisions) Act 1958 (loans for certain housing purposes) for the
word " prescribed " there shall be substituted the word " determined ".

(4) In subsection (5) of section 20 of the Crown Agents Act 1979 c. 43.
1979 (grants and loans by Minister) for the words " section 5(2)
of the National Loans Act 1968 (criteria for fixing " there shall 1968 c. 13.
be substituted the words " section 5(3) and (4) of the National
Loans Act 1968 (criteria for determining ".

154.—(1) Loans in pursuance of section 3 of the National Local loans.
Loans Act 1968 may be made by the Public Works Loan Commissioners, in addition to any loans made by them under section 78 of the Finance Act 1978, but the aggregate of— 1978 c. 42.

(*a*) the commitments of the Commissioners outstanding at
any time in respect of undertakings entered into by
them to grant such loans ; and

(*b*) the advances in respect of such loans made by them
under this section up to that time,

shall not exceed £4,000 million or such greater amount as may
be specified in an order under subsection (2) below.

(2) The Treasury may, on not more than three occasions, by
order made by statutory instrument increase or further increase
the limit imposed by subsection (1) above by such sum not exceeding £4,000 million as may be specified in the order.

(3) No order shall be made under this section unless a draft
of it has been laid before and approved by a resolution of the
Commons House of Parliament.

155.—(1) In so far as any charity continues, on 9th March Extinguish-
1982, to have a liability for development land tax which is defer- ment of
red by virtue of section 25 of the Development Land Tax Act deferred
1976 (development by charities on land acquired after 12th liability of
September 1974) that liability is hereby extinguished with effect development
from that date. land tax.

1976 c 24.

PART VII
1976 c. 24.

1980 c. 48.

(2) Subsection (1) above shall be construed as one with the Development Land Tax Act 1976 and the reference in that sub-section to section 25 of that Act is a reference to that section as it had effect before it was replaced by section 111 of the Finance Act 1980.

Dissolution of
Board of
Referees.
1968 c. 3.

156.—(1) The Board of Referees mentioned in section 26 of the Capital Allowances Act 1968 is hereby dissolved and the functions of the Board transferred to the tribunal established under section 463 of the Taxes Act.

(2) Schedule 21 to this Act shall have effect for the purpose of making provision consequential on this section.

Short title,
interpretation,
construction
and repeals.
1970 c. 10.

157.—(1) This Act may be cited as the Finance Act 1982.

(2) In this Act " the Taxes Act " means the Income and Corporation Taxes Act 1970.

(3) Part III of this Act, so far as it relates to income tax, shall be construed as one with the Income Tax Acts, so far as it relates to corporation tax, shall be construed as one with the Corporation Tax Acts and, so far as it relates to capital gains tax, shall be construed as one with the Capital Gains Tax Act 1979.

1979 c. 14.

(4) Part IV of this Act shall be construed as one with Part III of the Finance Act 1975.

1975 c. 7.

(5) Part VI of this Act shall be construed as one with Part I of the Oil Taxation Act 1975 or, in the case of section 136, with Part II of that Act and references in Part VI to the principal Act are references to that Act.

1975 c. 22.

(6) The enactments and Orders mentioned in Schedule 22 to this Act (which include spent enactments) are hereby repealed to the extent specified in the third column of that Schedule, but subject to any provision at the end of any Part of that Schedule.

1947 c. 46.
1975 c. 45.

(7) The provisions of Part XI of Schedule 22 to this Act, except in so far as they relate to the Wellington Museum Act 1947 and the Finance (No. 2) Act 1975, shall have effect in substitution for the provisions of Section B of Part VI of Schedule 20 to the Finance Act 1980 and, accordingly, that Section shall be deemed not to have taken effect at the beginning of the year 1982-83.

SCHEDULES

SCHEDULE 1

Section 1(3).

WINE: RATES OF DUTY

Description of wine	Rates of duty per hectolitre
	£
Wine of a strength—	
not exceeding 15 per cent. ...	106·80
exceeding 15 but not exceeding 18 per cent.	137·90
exceeding 18 but not exceeding 22 per cent.	162·30
exceeding 22 per cent. ...	162·30 plus £14·47 for every 1 per cent. or part of 1 per cent. in excess of 22 per cent.; each of the above rates of duty being, in the case of sparkling wine, increased by £23·45 per hectolitre.

SCHEDULE 2

Section 1(4).

MADE-WINE: RATES OF DUTY

Description of made-wine	Rates of duty per hectolitre
	£
Made-wine of a strength—	
not exceeding 10 per cent. ...	73·10
exceeding 10 but not exceeding 15 per cent.	103·80
exceeding 15 but not exceeding 18 per cent.	127·80
exceeding 18 per cent. ...	127·80 plus £14·47 for every 1 per cent. or part of 1 per cent. in excess of 18 per cent.; each of the above rates of duty being, in the case of sparkling made-wine, increased by £10·75 per hectolitre.

SCHEDULE 3

PROVISIONS SUBSTITUTED IN VEHICLES (EXCISE) ACT 1971 (c. 10)

I

PROVISIONS SUBSTITUTED FOR PART II OF SCHEDULE 1

Description of vehicle	Rate of duty
	£
1. Bicycles and tricycles of which the cylinder capacity of the engine does not exceed 150 cubic centimetres	8·00
2. Bicycles of which the cylinder capacity of the engine exceeds 150 cubic centimetres but does not exceed 250 cubic centimetres; tricycles (other than those in the foregoing paragraph) and vehicles (other than mowing machines) with more than three wheels, being tricycles and vehicles neither constructed nor adapted for use nor used for the carriage of a driver or passenger	16·00
3. Bicycles and tricycles not in the foregoing paragraphs ...	32·00

II

PROVISIONS SUBSTITUTED FOR PART II OF SCHEDULE 2

Description of vehicle	Rate of duty
Hackney carriages	£ 40·00 with an additional 80p for each person above 20 (excluding the driver) for which the vehicle has seating capacity.

III

PROVISIONS SUBSTITUTED FOR PART II OF SCHEDULE 3

	Weight unladen of vehicle		Rate of duty	
1.	**2.**	**3.**	**4.**	**5.** Additional for each ton or part of a ton in excess of the weight in column 2
Description of vehicle	Exceeding	Not exceeding	Initial	
			£	£
1. Agricultural machines; digging machines; mobile cranes; works trucks; mowing machines; fishermen's tractors.	—	—	13·50	—
2. Haulage vehicles, being showmen's vehicles.	—	7¼ tons	130·00	—
	7¼ tons	8 tons	156·00	—
	8 tons	10 tons	183·00	—
	10 tons	—	183·00	28·00
3. Haulage vehicles, not being showmen's vehicles.	—	2 tons	155·00	—
	2 tons	4 tons	278·00	—
	4 tons	6 tons	402·00	—
	6 tons	7¼ tons	525·00	—
	7¼ tons	8 tons	642·00	—
	8 tons	10 tons	642·00	109·00
	10 tons	—	860·00	123·00

IV
PROVISIONS SUBSTITUTED FOR PART II OF SCHEDULE 4
TABLES SHOWING ANNUAL RATES OF DUTY ON GOODS VEHICLES

TABLE A
GENERAL RATES OF DUTY

1. Description of vehicle	Weight unladen of vehicle		Rate of duty	
	2. Exceeding	3. Not exceeding	4. Initial	5. Additional for each $\frac{1}{4}$ ton or part of a $\frac{1}{4}$ ton in excess of the weight in column 2
			£	£
1. Farmers' goods vehicles ...	—	12 cwt.	46	—
	12 cwt.	16 cwt.	50	—
	16 cwt.	1 ton	54	—
	1 ton	3 tons	53	7
	3 tons	4 tons	106	5
	4 tons	7 tons	126	4
	7 tons	9 tons	176	2
	9 tons	—	233	6
2. Showmen's goods vehicles ...	—	12 cwt.	46	—
	12 cwt.	16 cwt.	50	—
	16 cwt.	1 ton	54	—
	1 ton	3 tons	53	7
	3 tons	4 tons	106	5
	4 tons	6 tons	126	4
	6 tons	9 tons	156	7
	9 tons	—	278	10
3. Tower wagons	—	12 cwt.	62	—
	12 cwt.	16 cwt.	69	—
	16 cwt.	1 ton	78	—
	1 ton	4 tons	77	8
	4 tons	6 tons	171	9
	6 tons	9 tons	242	8
	9 tons	—	394	15
4. Goods vehicles not included in any of the foregoing provisions of this Part of this Schedule.	—	1 ton	80	—
	1 ton	1¼ tons	90	—
	1¼ tons	1½ tons	100	—
	1½ tons	3 tons	130	22
	3 tons	4 tons	264	23
	4 tons	9 tons	340	40
	9 tons	10 tons	1,351	48
	10 tons	—	1,537	57

TABLE B
RATES OF DUTY ON GOODS VEHICLES USED FOR DRAWING TRAILERS

1. Description of vehicle	Weight unladen of vehicle		4. Rate of duty
	2. Exceeding	3. Not exceeding	
			£
1. Showmen's goods vehicles	—	—	41
2. Other goods vehicles	—	1½ tons	41
	1½ tons	3 tons	55
	3 tons	4 tons	92
	4 tons	6 tons	139
	6 tons	9 tons	173
	9 tons	—	210

V
PROVISIONS SUBSTITUTED FOR PART II OF SCHEDULE 5

Description of vehicle	Rate of duty
	£
1. Vehicles not exceeding seven horse-power, if registered under the Roads Act 1920 for the first time before 1st January 1947	57·00
2. Vehicles not included above	80·00

SCHEDULE 4
PROVISIONS SUBSTITUTED IN VEHICLES (EXCISE) ACT (NORTHERN IRELAND) 1972 (N.I. c. 10)

Section 6(2).
1972 c. 10.
(N.I.).

I
PROVISIONS SUBSTITUTED FOR PART II OF SCHEDULE 1

Description of vehicle	Rate of duty
	£
1. Bicycles and tricycles of which the cylinder capacity of the engine does not exceed 150 cubic centimetres	8·00
2. Bicycles of which the cylinder capacity of the engine exceeds 150 cubic centimetres but does not exceed 250 cubic centimetres; tricycles (other than those in the foregoing paragraph) and vehicles (other than mowing machines) with more than three wheels, being tricycles and vehicles neither constructed nor adapted for use nor used for the carriage of a driver or passenger	16·00
3. Bicycles and tricycles not in the foregoing paragraphs ...	32·00

II

Provisions Substituted for Part II of Schedule 2

Description of vehicle	Rate of duty
Hackney carriages	£ 40·00 with an additional 80p for each person above 20 (excluding the driver) for which the vehicle has seating capacity.

III

Provisions Substituted for Part II of Schedule 3

1. Description of vehicle	Weight unladen of vehicle		Rate of duty	
	2. Exceeding	3. Not exceeding	4. Initial	5. Additional for each ton or part of a ton in excess of the weight in column 2
1. Agricultural machines; digging machines; mobile cranes; works trucks; mowing machines; fishermen's tractors.	—	—	£ 13·50	£ —
2. Haulage vehicles, being showmen's vehicles.	— 7¼ tons 8 tons 10 tons	7¼ tons 8 tons 10 tons —	130·00 156·00 183·00 183·00	— — — 28·00
3. Haulage vehicles, not being showmen's vehicles.	— 2 tons 4 tons 6 tons 7¼ tons 8 tons	2 tons 4 tons 6 tons 7¼ tons 8 tons —	139·00 248·00 355·00 464·00 572·00 572·00	— — — — — 123·00

IV

PROVISIONS SUBSTITUTED FOR PART II OF SCHEDULE 4
TABLES SHOWING ANNUAL RATES OF DUTY ON GOODS VEHICLES

TABLE A

GENERAL RATES OF DUTY

1. Description of vehicle	Weight unladen of vehicle		Rate of duty	
	2. Exceeding	3. Not exceeding	4. Initial	5. Additional for each $\frac{1}{4}$ ton or part of a $\frac{1}{4}$ ton in excess of the weight in column 2
			£	£
1. Farmers' goods vehicles ...	—	12 cwt.	46	—
	12 cwt.	16 cwt.	50	—
	16 cwt.	1 ton	54	—
	1 ton	3 tons	53	7
	3 tons	6 tons	111	2
	6 tons	8 tons	143	1
	8 tons	9 tons	157	2
	9 tons	—	201	4
2. Showmen's goods vehicles; tower wagons.	—	12 cwt.	60	—
	12 cwt.	16 cwt.	62	—
	16 cwt.	1 ton	70	—
	1 ton	2 tons	73	3
	2 tons	3 tons	84	4
	3 tons	5 tons	97	6
	5 tons	6 tons	144	5
	6 tons	9 tons	158	7
	9 tons	—	278	10
3. Goods vehicles not included in any of the foregoing provisions of this Part.	—	1 ton	80	—
	1 ton	1$\frac{1}{4}$ tons	90	—
	1$\frac{1}{4}$ tons	1$\frac{1}{2}$ tons	100	—
	1$\frac{1}{2}$ tons	3 tons	116	16
	3 tons	4 tons	209	25
	4 tons	6 tons	310	32
	6 tons	9 tons	569	37
	9 tons	—	1,218	50

TABLE B

RATES OF DUTY ON GOODS VEHICLES USED FOR DRAWING TRAILERS

1. Description of vehicle	Weight unladen of vehicle		4. Rate of duty
	2. Exceeding	3. Not exceeding	
			£
1. Showmen's goods vehicles	—	—	41
2. Other goods vehicles	— 1½ tons 3 tons 4 tons 6 tons 9 tons	1½ tons 3 tons 4 tons 6 tons 9 tons —	41 55 92 139 173 210

V

PROVISIONS SUBSTITUTED FOR PART II OF SCHEDULE 5

Description of vehicle	Rate of duty
	£
1. Vehicles first registered under the Roads Act 1920 before 1st January 1947, or which, if its first registration for taxation purposes had been effected in Northern Ireland would have been so first registered as aforesaid under the Act as in force in Northern Ireland:	
(i) not exceeding 6 horse-power	48·00
(ii) exceeding 6 horse-power but not exceeding 9 horse-power—for each unit or part of a unit of horse-power	8·00
2. Other vehicles	80·00

SCHEDULE 5

Sections 5(4) and 6(4).

ANNUAL RATES OF DUTY ON GOODS VEHICLES

PART A

PROVISIONS HAVING EFFECT AS SCHEDULE 4 TO THE VEHICLES (EXCISE) ACT 1971 AND (AS MODIFIED BY PART B OF THIS SCHEDULE) AS SCHEDULE 4 TO THE VEHICLES (EXCISE) ACT (NORTHERN IRELAND) 1972

1971 c. 10.

1972 c. 10 (N.I.).

PART I

GENERAL PROVISIONS

Vehicles chargeable at the basic rate of duty

1.—(1) Subject to paragraphs 5 and 6 below, the annual rate of duty applicable to a goods vehicle—

(*a*) which has a plated gross weight or a plated train weight which does not exceed 7·5 tonnes ; or

(*b*) which has neither a plated gross weight nor a plated train weight but which has an unladen weight which exceeds 1,525 kilograms ; or

(*c*) which is a tower wagon, having an unladen weight which exceeds 1,525 kilograms ;

shall be £170.

(2) Any reference in the following provisions of this Schedule to the basic rate of duty is a reference to the annual rate of duty for the time being applicable to vehicles falling within sub-paragraph (1) above.

Vehicles exceeding 7·5 but not exceeding 12 tonnes plated weight

2. Subject to paragraphs 1(1)(*c*) above and 6 below, the annual rate of duty applicable to a goods vehicle which has a plated gross weight or a plated train weight which exceeds 7·5 tonnes but does not exceed 12 tonnes shall be £360.

Rigid goods vehicles exceeding 12 tonnes plated gross weight

3.—(1) Subject to the provisions of this Schedule, the annual rate of duty applicable to a goods vehicle which is a rigid goods vehicle and has a plated gross weight which exceeds 12 tonnes shall be determined in accordance with Table A in Part II of this Schedule by reference to—

(*a*) the plated gross weight of the vehicle ; and

(*b*) the number of axles on the vehicle.

(2) If a rigid goods vehicle to which sub-paragraph (1) above applies is used for drawing a trailer which—

(*a*) has a plated gross weight exceeding 4 tonnes ; and

(*b*) when so drawn, is used for the conveyance of goods or burden ;

Part I

2 L

SCH. 5   the annual rate of duty applicable to it in accordance with that sub-paragraph shall be increased by the amount of the supplement which, in accordance with Table B in Part II of this Schedule, is appropriate to the gross plated weight of the trailer being drawn.

Tractor units exceeding 12 tonnes plated train weight

4.—(1) This paragraph applies to a tractor unit which has a plated train weight exceeding 12 tonnes.

(2) The annual rate of duty applicable to a tractor unit to which this paragraph applies and which has not more than two axles shall be determined, subject to the following provisions of this Schedule, in accordance with Table C in Part II of this Schedule by reference to—

> (*a*) the plated train weight of the tractor unit ; and

> (*b*) the types of semi-trailers, distinguished according to the number of their axles, which are to be drawn by it.

(3) The annual rate of duty applicable to a tractor unit to which this paragraph applies and which has three or more axles shall be determined subject to the following provisions of this Schedule in accordance with Table D in Part II of this Schedule by reference to—

> (*a*) the plated train weight of the tractor unit ; and

> (*b*) the types of semi-trailers, distinguished according to the number of their axles, which are to be drawn by it.

Special types of vehicles

5.—(1) This paragraph applies to a goods vehicle—

> (*a*) which has an unladen weight exceeding 1,525 kilograms ; and

> (*b*) which does not comply with regulations under section 40 of the Road Traffic Act 1972 (construction and use regulations) ; and

> (*c*) which is for the time being authorised for use on roads by virtue of an order under section 42 of that Act (authorisation of special vehicles).

1972 c. 20.

(2) The annual rate of duty applicable to a goods vehicle to which this paragraph applies and which falls within a class specified by an order of the Secretary of State made for the purposes of this paragraph shall be determined, on the basis of the assumptions in sub-paragraph (3) below, by the application of Table A, Table C or Table D in Part II of this Schedule, according to whether the vehicle is a rigid goods vehicle or a tractor unit and, in the latter case, according to the number of its axles.

(3) The assumptions referred to in sub-paragraph (2) above are—

> (*a*) where Table A applies, that the vehicle has a plated gross weight which exceeds 30 tonnes but does not exceed 30.49 tonnes ; and

(*b*) where Table C or Table D applies, that the vehicle has a plated train weight which exceeds 32 tonnes but does not exceed 32·52 tonnes.

(4) In the case of a goods vehicle to which this paragraph applies and which does not fall within such a class as is referred to in sub-paragraph (2) above, the annual rate of duty shall be the basic rate of duty.

(5) The power to make an order under sub-paragraph (2) above shall be exercisable by statutory instrument; but no such order shall be made unless a draft of it has been laid before Parliament and approved by a resolution of each House of Parliament.

Farmer's goods vehicles and showmen's goods vehicles

6.—(1) If the unladen weight of—

(*a*) a farmer's goods vehicle; or

(*b*) a showman's goods vehicle;

does not exceed 1,525 kilograms, the annual rate of duty applicable to it shall be £60.

(2) If a farmer's goods vehicle or a showman's goods vehicle has a plated gross weight or a plated train weight, the annual rate of duty applicable to it shall be—

(*a*) £100, if that weight does not exceed 7·5 tonnes;

(*b*) £130, if that weight exceeds 7·5 tonnes but does not exceed 12 tonnes; and

(*c*) the appropriate Part II rate, if that weight exceeds 12 tonnes.

(3) In sub-paragraph (2) above the " appropriate Part II rate " means the rate determined in accordance with paragraph 3 or, as the case may be, 4 above but by reference—

(*a*) in the case of a farmer's goods vehicle, to Table A(1), Table B(1), Table C(1) or, as the case may be, Table D(1) in Part II of this Schedule, in place of the corresponding Table referred to in that paragraph; and

(*b*) in the case of a showman's goods vehicle, to Table A(2), Table B(2), Table C(2) or, as the case may be, Table D(2) in Part II of this Schedule, in place of the corresponding Table referred to in that paragraph.

(4) In the case of any other farmer's goods vehicle or showman's goods vehicle, the annual rate of duty applicable to it shall be £100.

Smaller goods vehicles

7. If a goods vehicle—

(*a*) has an unladen weight which does not exceed 1,525 kilograms; and

(*b*) does not fall within paragraph 6 above;

the annual rate of duty applicable to it shall be £80.

Vehicles treated as having reduced plated weights

8.—(1) The Secretary of State may by regulations provide that, on an application made in accordance with the regulations, the goods vehicle to which the application relates shall be treated for the purposes of this Schedule as if its plated gross weight or plated train weight were the lower gross weight or train weight (the " operating weight ") specified in the application.

(2) Where, following an application duly made in accordance with the regulations, a licence is issued for the vehicle concerned at the rate of duty applicable to the operating weight, that weight shall be shown on the licence.

(3) The regulations may provide that the use of any vehicle in respect of which a lower rate of duty is chargeable by virtue of this paragraph shall be subject to prescribed conditions and to such further conditions as the Secretary of State may think fit to impose in any particular case.

(4) In any case where a vehicle in respect of which a lower rate of duty has been charged by virtue of this paragraph is used in contravention of a condition imposed by virtue of sub-paragraph (3) above, then—

    (*a*) the higher rate of duty applicable to its plated gross weight or plated train weight shall become chargeable as from the date of the contravention ; and

    (*b*) section 19 of this Act shall apply as if—

        (i) that higher rate had become chargeable under subsection (1) of that section by reason of the vehicle being used as mentioned in that subsection ; and

        (ii) subsections (5) to (9) were omitted.

Plated and unladen weights

9.—(1) Any reference in this Schedule to the plated gross weight of a goods vehicle or trailer is a reference—

1972 c. 20.
    (*a*) to that plated weight, within the meaning of Part II of the Road Traffic Act 1972, which is the maximum gross weight which may not be exceeded in Great Britain for the vehicle or trailer in question ; or

    (*b*) in the case of any trailer which may lawfully be used in Great Britain without a plated gross weight, to the maximum laden weight at which the trailer may lawfully be used in Great Britain.

(2) Any reference in this Schedule to the plated train weight of a vehicle is a reference to that plated weight, within the meaning of the said Part II, which is the maximum gross weight which may not be exceeded in Great Britain for an articulated vehicle consisting of the vehicle in question and any semi-trailer which may be drawn by it.

(3) A mechanically propelled vehicle which—

    (*a*) is constructed or adapted for use and used for the conveyance of a machine or contrivance and no other load except articles used in connection with the machine or contrivance ; and

(b) is not a vehicle for which an annual rate of duty is specified in Schedule 3 to this Act ; and

(c) has neither a plated gross weight nor a plated train weight,

shall, notwithstanding that the machine or contrivance is built in as part of the vehicle, be chargeable with duty at the rate which would be applicable if the machine or contrivance were burden.

Goods vehicles used partly for private purposes

10.—(1) Where a goods vehicle is partly used for private purposes, the annual rate of duty applicable to it shall, if apart from this paragraph it would be less, be the rate determined in accordance with Schedule 5 to this Act.

(2) A vehicle shall not be prevented from being a farmer's goods vehicle for the purposes of this Schedule solely by reason of its being used partly for private purposes.

(3) In this paragraph " partly used for private purposes " means used partly otherwise than for the conveyance of goods or burden for hire or reward or for or in connection with a trade or business.

Exempted vehicles

11. Duty shall not be chargeable by virtue of this Schedule in respect of—

(a) a vehicle chargeable with duty by virtue of Schedule 1 to this Act ;

(b) an agricultural machine which is a goods vehicle by reason of the fact that it is constructed or adapted for use, and used, for the conveyance of farming or forestry implements fitted to it for operation while so fitted ;

(c) a mobile crane, works truck or fisherman's tractor ; or

(d) a vehicle which, though constructed or adapted for use for the conveyance of goods or burden, is not so used for hire or reward or for or in connection with a trade or business.

12.—(1) This paragraph and paragraph 13 below apply to agricultural machines which do not draw trailers.

(2) Subject to paragraph 13 below, a vehicle to which this paragraph applies shall not be chargeable with duty by virtue of this Schedule by reason of the fact that it is constructed or adapted for use and used for the conveyance of permitted goods or burden if they are carried in or on not more than one appliance and the conditions mentioned in sub-paragraph (3) below are satisfied.

(3) The conditions are that—

(a) the appliance is fitted either to the front or to the back of the vehicle ;

(b) the appliance is removable ;

(c) the area of the horizontal plane enclosed by vertical lines passing through the outside edges of the appliance is not, when the appliance is in the position in which it is carried when the vehicle is travelling and the appliance is loaded, greater than—

(i) 0·65 of a square metre, if the appliance is carried at the front ; or

(ii) 1·394 square metres, if it is carried at the back.

(4) In sub-paragraph (2) above " permitted goods or burden " means goods or burden the haulage of which is permissible under paragraph 2(1) of Schedule 3 to this Act.

(5) Sub-paragraph (2) above does not apply—

(a) to the use of a vehicle on a public road more than 15 miles from a farm occupied by the person in whose name the vehicle is registered under this Act ;

(b) to three-wheeled vehicles ; or

(c) to any vehicle in respect of which the distance between the centre of the area of contact with the road surface of the relevant wheel and that of the nearest wheel on the other side of the vehicle is less than 1·22 metres.

(6) In sub-paragraph (5)(c) above " relevant wheel " means—

(a) in a case where only one appliance is being used for the carriage of goods or burden and that appliance is fitted to the back of the vehicle, a back wheel ; and

(b) in any other case, any wheel on a side of the vehicle.

(7) For the purposes of this paragraph a vehicle which has two wheels at the front shall, if the distance between them (measured between the centres of their respective areas of contact with the road) is less than 46 centimetres, be treated as a three-wheeled vehicle.

13.—(1) This paragraph shall have effect in relation to any vehicle fitted with an appliance of any description prescribed for the purposes of all or any of the provisions of this paragraph by regulations under this paragraph.

(2) The limitation in paragraph 12(2) above to one appliance shall have effect as a limitation to two appliances of which at least one must be an appliance prescribed for the purposes of this sub-paragraph ; but if two appliances are used they must be fitted at opposite ends of the vehicle.

(3) Regulations under this paragraph may provide for all or any of the following matters where an appliance prescribed for the purposes of this paragraph is being used, that is to say, that paragraph 12(2) above shall not apply unless the prescribed appliance is fitted to the prescribed end of the vehicle, or unless the use of the prescribed or any appliance is limited to prescribed goods or burden or to use in prescribed circumstances.

(4) Regulations under this paragraph may provide that paragraph 12(3)(*c*) above shall not have effect in relation to appliances prescribed for the purposes of this sub-paragraph, but that in relation to those appliances paragraph 12(5)(*a*) above shall have effect with the substitution of such shorter distance as may be prescribed.

(5) In sub-paragraphs (2) to (4) above references to use are references to use for the carriage of goods or burden ; and regulations under this paragraph may make different provision in relation to different descriptions of prescribed appliances.

Tractor units used with semi-trailers having only one axle when duty paid by reference to use with semi-trailers having more than one axle

14.—(1) This paragraph applies in any case where—

(*a*) a vehicle licence has been taken out for a tractor unit having two axles which is to be used only with semi-trailers with not less than two axles or for a tractor unit having two axles which is to be used only with semi-trailers with not less than three axles ; and

(*b*) the rate of duty paid on taking out the licence is equal to or exceeds the rate of duty applicable to a tractor unit having two axles—

(i) which has a plated train weight equal to the maximum laden weight at which a tractor unit having two axles may lawfully be used in Great Britain with a semi-trailer with a single axle ; and

(ii) which is to be used with semi-trailers with any number of axles.

(2) If, in a case to which this paragraph applies, the tractor unit is used with a semi-trailer with a single axle and, when so used, the laden weight of the tractor unit and semi-trailer taken together does not exceed the maximum laden weight mentioned in sub-paragraph (1)(*b*)(i) above, the tractor unit shall, when so used, be taken to be licensed in accordance with the requirements of this Act.

Interpretation

15.—(1) In this Schedule, unless the context otherwise requires—

" agricultural machine " has the same meaning as in Schedule 3 to this Act ;

" axle " includes—

(i) two or more stub axles which are fitted on opposite sides of the longitudinal axis of the vehicle so as to form—

(*a*) a pair in the case of two stub axles, and

(*b*) pairs in the case of more than two stub axles,

(ii) a single stub axle which is not one of a pair ; and

(iii) a retractable axle ;

" basic rate of duty " has the meaning given by paragraph 1(2) ;

" business " includes the performance by a local or public authority of its functions ;

2 L 4

" farmer's goods vehicle " means, subject to paragraph 10(2) above, a goods vehicle registered under this Act in the name of a person engaged in agriculture and used on public roads solely by him for the purpose of the conveyance of the produce of, or of articles required for the purposes of, the agricultural land which he occupies, and for no other purposes ;

" fisherman's tractor " has the same meaning as in Schedule 3 to this Act ;

" goods vehicle " means a mechanically propelled vehicle (including a tricycle as defined in Schedule 1 to this Act and weighing more than 425 kilograms unladen) constructed or adapted for use and used for the conveyance of goods or burden of any description, whether in the course of trade or otherwise ;

" mobile crane " has the same meaning as in Schedule 3 to this Act ;

" rigid goods vehicle " means a goods vehicle which is not a tractor unit ;

" showman's goods vehicle " means a showman's vehicle which is a goods vehicle and is permanently fitted with a living van or some other special type of body or superstructure, forming part of the equipment of the show of the person in whose name the vehicle is registered under this Act ;

" showman's vehicle " has the same meaning as in Schedule 3 to this Act ;

" stub axle " means an axle on which only one wheel is mounted ;

" tower wagon " means a goods vehicle—

(*a*) into which there is built, as part of the vehicle, any expanding or extensible contrivance designed for facilitating the erection, inspection, repair or maintenance of overhead structures or equipment ; and

(*b*) which is neither constructed nor adapted for use nor used for the conveyance of any load, except such a contrivance and articles used in connection therewith ;

" tractor unit " means a goods vehicle to which a semi-trailer may be so attached that part of the semi-trailer is superimposed on part of the goods vehicle and that when the semi-trailer is uniformly loaded not less than 20 per cent. of the weight of its load is borne by the goods vehicle ;

" trailer " shall be construed in accordance with sub-paragraph (2) below ;

" unladen weight " has the same meaning as it has for the purposes of the Road Traffic Act 1972 by virtue of section 194 of that Act ; and

" works truck " has the same meaning as in Schedule 3 to this Act.

(2) In this Schedule " trailer " does not include—

(*a*) an appliance constructed and used solely for the purpose of distributing on the road loose gritting material ;

(*b*) a snow plough ;

(*c*) a road construction vehicle as defined in section 4(2) of this Act ;

(*d*) a farming implement not constructed or adapted for the conveyance of goods or burden of any description, when drawn by a farmer's goods vehicle ;

(*e*) a trailer used solely for the carriage of a container for holding gas for the propulsion of the vehicle by which it is drawn, or plant and materials for producing such gas.

PART II

TABLE A

RATES OF DUTY ON RIGID GOODS VEHICLES EXCEEDING 12 TONNES PLATED GROSS WEIGHT

GENERAL RATES

Plated gross weight of vehicle		Rate of duty		
1	2	3	4	5
Exceeding	Not exceeding	Two axle vehicle	Three axle vehicle	Four or more axle vehicle
tonnes	tonnes	£	£	£
12	13	450	360	360
13	14	550	360	360
14	15	610	360	360
15	16	670	360	360
16	17	730	360	360
17	18	—	420	360
18	19	—	490	360
19	20	—	560	360
20	21	—	640	360
21	22	—	730	430
22	23	—	820	520
23	24	—	920	620
24	25	—	1,030	730
25	26	—	—	850
26	27	—	—	980
27	28	—	—	1,120
28	29	—	—	1,270
29	30	—	—	1,430
30	30·49	—	—	1,620

TABLE A(1)

RATES OF DUTY ON RIGID GOODS VEHICLES EXCEEDING
12 TONNES PLATED GROSS WEIGHT

RATES FOR FARMERS' GOODS VEHICLES

Plated gross weight of vehicle		Rate of duty		
1 Exceeding	2 Not exceeding	3 Two axle vehicle	4 Three axle vehicle	5 Four or more axle vehicle
tonnes	tonnes	£	£	£
12	13	150	130	130
13	14	155	130	130
14	15	160	135	130
15	16	165	140	130
16	17	170	145	130
17	18	—	150	130
18	19	—	155	135
19	20	—	160	140
20	21	—	165	145
21	22	—	170	150
22	23	—	175	155
23	24	—	180	160
24	25	—	190	165
25	26	—	—	180
26	27	—	—	200
27	28	—	—	220
28	29	—	—	240
29	30	—	—	260
30	30·49	—	—	280

TABLE A(2)

Rates of Duty on Rigid Goods Vehicles Exceeding 12 Tonnes Plated Gross Weight

Rates for Showmen's Goods Vehicles

Plated gross weight of vehicle		Rate of duty		
1 Exceeding	2 Not exceeding	3 Two axle vehicle	4 Three axle vehicle	5 Four or more axle vehicle
tonnes	tonnes	£	£	£
12	13	150	130	130
13	14	155	130	130
14	15	160	135	130
15	16	165	140	130
16	17	170	145	130
17	18	—	150	135
18	19	—	155	140
19	20	—	165	145
20	21	—	175	155
21	22	—	185	165
22	23	—	195	175
23	24	—	210	185
24	25	—	225	200
25	26	—	—	220
26	27	—	—	245
27	28	—	—	270
28	29	—	—	295
29	30	—	—	320
30	30·49	—	—	350

TABLE B

Supplementary Rates of Duty on Rigid Goods Vehicles Over 12 Tonnes Used for Drawing Trailers Exceeding 4 Tonnes Plated Gross Weight

General Rates

Gross weight of trailer		Duty supplement
Exceeding	Not exceeding	
tonnes	tonnes	£
4	8	75
8	10	100
10	12	125
12	14	175
14	—	250

TABLE B(1)

SUPPLEMENTARY RATES OF DUTY ON RIGID GOODS VEHICLES OVER 12 TONNES USED FOR DRAWING TRAILERS EXCEEDING 4 TONNES PLATED GROSS WEIGHT

RATES FOR FARMERS' GOODS VEHICLES

Gross weight of trailer		Duty supplement
Exceeding	Not exceeding	
tonnes	tonnes	£
4	8	75
8	10	100
10	12	125
12	14	175
14	—	250

TABLE B(2)

SUPPLEMENTARY RATES OF DUTY ON RIGID GOODS VEHICLES OVER 12 TONNES USED FOR DRAWING TRAILERS EXCEEDING 4 TONNES PLATED GROSS WEIGHT

RATES FOR SHOWMEN'S GOODS VEHICLES

Gross weight of trailer		Duty supplement
Exceeding	Not exceeding	
—	—	£ 75

TABLE C

RATES OF DUTY ON TRACTOR UNITS EXCEEDING 12 TONNES
PLATED TRAIN WEIGHT AND HAVING ONLY 2 AXLES

GENERAL RATES

Plated train weight of tractor unit		Rate of duty		
1. Exceeding	2. Not exceeding	3. For a tractor unit to be used with semi-trailers with any number of axles	4. For a tractor unit to be used only with semi-trailers with not less than two axles	5. For a tractor unit to be used only with semi-trailers with not less than three axles
tonnes	tonnes	£	£	£
12	13	470	470	470
13	14	520	470	470
14	15	570	470	470
15	16	620	470	470
16	17	680	470	470
17	18	730	470	470
18	19	790	470	470
19	20	850	470	470
20	21	920	520	470
21	22	990	580	470
22	23	1,060	650	470
23	24	1,130	730	470
24	25	1,210	820	470
25	26	1,210	920	550
26	27	1,210	1,040	650
27	28	1,210	1,160	750
28	29	1,280	1,280	870
29	30	1,400	1,400	990
30	31	1,530	1,530	1,110
31	32	1,670	1,670	1,230
32	32·52	1,820	1,820	1,350

TABLE C(1)

RATES OF DUTY ON TRACTOR UNITS EXCEEDING 12 TONNES PLATED TRAIN WEIGHT AND HAVING ONLY 2 AXLES

RATES FOR FARMERS' GOODS VEHICLES

Plated train weight of tractor unit		Rate of duty		
1. Exceeding	2. Not exceeding	3. For a tractor unit to be used with semi-trailers with any number of axles	4. For a tractor unit to be used only with semi-trailers with not less than two axles	5. For a tractor unit to be used only with semi-trailers with not less than three axles
tonnes	tonnes	£	£	£
12	13	150	150	150
13	14	155	150	150
14	15	160	150	150
15	16	165	150	150
16	17	170	150	150
17	18	175	150	150
18	19	180	150	150
19	20	185	150	150
20	21	190	150	150
21	22	195	155	150
22	23	200	160	150
23	24	210	165	150
24	25	220	170	150
25	26	220	180	150
26	27	220	190	160
27	28	220	200	170
28	29	220	215	180
29	30	235	235	190
30	31	255	255	210
31	32	275	275	230
32	32·52	295	295	250

TABLE C(2)

RATES OF DUTY ON TRACTOR UNITS EXCEEDING 12 TONNES
PLATED TRAIN WEIGHT AND HAVING ONLY 2 AXLES

RATES FOR SHOWMEN'S GOODS VEHICLES

Plated train weight of tractor unit		Rate of duty		
1. Exceeding	2. Not exceeding	3. For a tractor unit to be used with semi-trailers with any number of axles	4. For a tractor unit to be used only with semi-trailers with not less than two axles	5. For a tractor unit to be used only with semi-trailers with not less than three axles
tonnes	tonnes	£	£	£
12	13	150	150	150
13	14	155	150	150
14	15	160	150	150
15	16	165	150	150
16	17	170	150	150
17	18	175	150	150
18	19	180	150	150
19	20	190	155	150
20	21	200	160	150
21	22	215	170	150
22	23	230	180	160
23	24	245	190	170
24	25	260	200	180
25	26	260	215	190
26	27	260	235	200
27	28	260	255	210
28	29	275	275	225
29	30	295	295	240
30	31	320	320	260
31	32	345	345	285
32	32·52	370	370	310

Table D

Rates of Duty on Tractor Units Exceeding 12 Tonnes Plated Train Weight and having 3 or more Axles

General Rates

Plated train weight of tractor unit		Rate of duty		
1.	2.	3.	4.	5.
Exceeding	Not exceeding	For a tractor unit to be used with semi-trailers with any number of axles	For a tractor unit to be used only with semi-trailers with not less than two axles	For a tractor unit to be used only with semi-trailers with not less than three axles
tonnes	tonnes	£	£	£
12	20	470	470	470
20	21	520	470	470
21	22	580	470	470
22	23	650	470	470
23	24	730	470	470
24	25	820	470	470
25	26	920	470	470
26	27	1,040	470	470
27	28	1,160	470	470
28	29	1,280	540	470
29	30	1,400	610	470
30	31	1,530	680	470
31	32	1,670	750	470
32	32·52	1,820	820	470

TABLE D(1)

RATES OF DUTY ON TRACTOR UNITS EXCEEDING 12 TONNES
PLATED TRAIN WEIGHT AND HAVING 3 OR MORE AXLES

RATES FOR FARMERS' GOODS VEHICLES

Plated train weight of tractor unit		Rate of duty		
1. Exceeding	2. Not exceeding	3. For a tractor unit to be used with semi-trailers with any number of axles	4. For a tractor unit to be used only with semi-trailers with not less than two axles	5. For a tractor unit to be used only with semi-trailers with not less than three axles
tonnes	tonnes	£	£	£
12	20	150	150	150
20	21	150	150	150
21	22	155	150	150
22	23	160	150	150
23	24	165	150	150
24	25	170	150	150
25	26	180	155	150
26	27	190	165	150
27	28	200	175	160
28	29	215	190	170
29	30	235	210	185
30	31	255	230	205
31	32	275	250	225
32	32·52	295	270	245

Sch. 5

Table D(2)

Rates of Duty on Tractor Units Exceeding 12 Tonnes Plated Train Weight and having 3 or more Axles

Rates for Showmen's Goods Vehicles

Plated train weight of tractor unit		Rate of duty		
1. Exceeding	2. Not exceeding	3. For a tractor unit to be used with semi-trailers with any number of axles	4. For a tractor unit to be used only with semi-trailers with not less than two axles	5. For a tractor unit to be used only with semi-trailers with not less than three axles
tonnes	tonnes	£	£	£
12	18	150	150	150
18	19	150	150	150
19	20	155	155	150
20	21	160	160	150
21	22	170	165	150
22	23	180	170	150
23	24	190	175	150
24	25	200	180	160
25	26	215	190	170
26	27	235	200	180
27	28	255	220	190
28	29	275	240	210
29	30	295	260	230
30	31	320	285	255
31	32	345	310	280
32	32·52	370	335	305

Part B

Modifications for Northern Ireland

16.—(1) The following are the modifications subject to which, by virtue of section 6(4) of this Act, the preceding provisions of this Schedule have effect as Schedule 4 to the Vehicles (Excise) Act (Northern Ireland) 1972.

1972 c. 10 (N.I.).

(2) For any reference to a plated gross weight or a plated train weight there shall be substituted a reference to a relevant maximum weight or a relevant maximum train weight.

(3) For any reference in paragraph 5(1) to section 40 or 42 of the Road Traffic Act 1972 there shall be substituted a reference to Article 28 or 29(3) of the Road Traffic (Northern Ireland) Order 1981.

1972 c. 20.
S.I. 1981/154 (N.I. 1).

(4) In paragraph 8(4)(*b*)(ii) for the words " subsections (5) to (9) " there shall be substituted the words " subsections (5) to (8) ".

(5) For paragraph 9(1) and (2) there shall be substituted—

" (1) Any reference in this Schedule to the relevant maximum weight of a goods vehicle or trailer is a reference—

> (*a*) where the vehicle or trailer is required by regulations under Article 28 of the Road Traffic (Northern Ireland) S.I. 1981/154 Order 1981 to have a maximum gross weight in Great (N.I. 1). Britain for the vehicle or trailer marked on a plate attached to the vehicle or trailer, to the maximum gross weight in Great Britain marked on such a plate ;
>
> (*b*) where a vehicle or trailer on which the maximum gross weight in Great Britain is marked by the same means as would be required by regulations under the said Article 28 if those regulations applied to the vehicle or trailer, to the maximum gross weight in Great Britain so marked on the vehicle or trailer ;
>
> (*c*) where a maximum gross weight is not marked on a vehicle or trailer as mentioned in sub-paragraph (*a*), to the notional maximum gross weight of the vehicle or trailer ascertained in accordance with the Goods S.R. 1976/241 Vehicles (Ascertainment of Maximum Gross Weights) (N.I.). Regulations (Northern Ireland) 1976 (or any regulations replacing those regulations, whether with or without amendments).

(2) Any reference in this Schedule to the relevant maximum train weight of a vehicle is a reference to the maximum gross weight which may not be exceeded in Great Britain for an articulated vehicle consisting of the vehicle in question and any semi-trailer which may be drawn by it."

(6) In paragraph 12(5)(*a*) for the words " a farm " there shall be substituted the words " agricultural land ".

(7) In paragraph 15(1), in the definition of " unladen weight ", for the references to the Road Traffic Act 1972 and section 194 of 1972 c. 20. that Act there shall be substituted, respectively, references to the Road Traffic (Northern Ireland) Order 1981 and Article 2(3) of that Order.

SCHEDULE 6

Section 8.

BETTING AND GAMING DUTIES

PART I

GENERAL

1. In this Schedule—

> the " 1981 Act " means the Betting and Gaming Duties Act 1981 c. 63. 1981 ; and
>
> the " 1972 Act " means the Miscellaneous Transferred Excise 1972 c. 11 Duties Act (Northern Ireland) 1972. (N.I.).

PART II

POOL BETTING DUTIES

2. In section 7 of the 1981 Act and section 18(1) of the 1972 Act (rates of duty), as modified by section 2(2) of the Finance Act 1974, for the words " 40 per cent. " there shall be substituted the words " 42½ per cent.".

PART III

GAMING LICENCE DUTY

3. In section 14 of the 1981 Act (rate of duty) for the Table set out in subsection (1) there shall be substituted the following Table—

" TABLE

Part of gross gaming yield	Rate
The first £500,000	5 per cent.
The next £1,750,000	12½ per cent.
The remainder	25 per cent.".

PART IV

BINGO DUTY

4. In section 17 of the 1981 Act (bingo duty) in subsection (2)(*a*) (duty by reference to amount paid for bingo cards) after the words " the money taken " there shall be inserted the words " (if any) ".

5.—(1) Schedule 3 to the 1981 Act (exemptions from bingo duty) shall have effect subject to the following provisions of this paragraph.

(2) For paragraphs 2, 3 and 4 there shall be substituted the following paragraph—

" *Small-scale bingo*

2.—(1) Bingo duty shall not be charged in respect of bingo promoted by any person and played on any day in a week (the " chargeable week ") at any premises, other than premises which are licensed under the Gaming Act 1968, if—

(*a*) where a person's eligibility to participate in that bingo depends upon his being a member of a particular society or his being a guest of such a member or of the society—

(i) the total value of the prizes won on any day in a relevant week at those premises in bingo played by members of that society or by guests of such members or of the society does not exceed £300 ; and

(ii) the total value of prizes won during any relevant week at those premises in bingo played by any such persons does not exceed £1,000 ; and

(*b*) in any other case—

(i) the total value of the prizes won on any day in a relevant week at those premises in bingo promoted by that person does not exceed £300 ; and

(ii) the total value of the prizes won during any relevant week at those premises in bingo promoted by that person does not exceed £1,000.

(2) In sub-paragraph (1) above—

" relevant week ", in relation to any chargeable week, means (subject to sub-paragraph (3) below that week or any of the preceding twelve weeks ; and

" society " includes any club, institution, organisation or association of persons, by whatever name called, and any separate branch or section of such club, institution, organisation or association but a branch or section shall not be treated as a separate branch or section unless it occupies separate premises.

(3) For the purposes of this paragraph there shall be disregarded any bingo which—

(a) is played in any week beginning before 27th September 1982 ; or

(b) is exempt from duty by virtue of paragraph 5 or 6 below."

(3) In paragraph 10 (registration of bingo promoters)—

(a) the following sub-paragraph shall be inserted after sub-paragraph (1)—

" (1A) Any person who is a bingo-promoter but is not registered as such and is not a person to whom sub-paragraph (1) above applies shall within five days of the date on which he became a bingo-promoter (disregarding any day which is a Saturday or a Sunday or a Bank Holiday) notify the Commissioners of that fact and of the place where the bingo was and (if he intends to continue to promote the playing of bingo which will or may be chargeable with duty) is to be played and apply to be registered as a bingo-promoter." ; and

(b) in sub-paragraph (2) of that paragraph for the words " notifies his intention as aforesaid " there shall be substituted the words " gives notice to the Commissioners under sub-paragraph (1) or (1A) above " and at the end of that sub-paragraph there shall be inserted the words—

" Conditions shall not be imposed under this sub-paragraph if the premises at which the bingo in question is or is to be played are not licensed under the Gaming Act 1968." 1968 c. 65.

(4) In paragraph 12 (preservation of records by bingo-promoters)—

(a) in sub-paragraph (1) for the word " bingo-promoter " there shall be substituted the words " promoter of bingo other than bingo which is exempt from duty by virtue of paragraph 1, 5 or 6 above " :

(b) in sub-paragraph (3) for the words " A bingo-promoter " there shall be substituted the words " Any such promoter of bingo " ; and

SCH. 6

(c) in sub-paragraph (4) for the word " bingo-promoters " there
shall be substituted the words " such promoters of bingo
as aforesaid ".

(5) In paragraph 15 (computation of amount of payments for cards
and of the value of prizes) in sub-paragraph (1)—

(a) for the words from " a bingo-promoter " to " any prize "
there shall be substituted the words " a promoter of bingo
as to the amount taken by him or on his behalf on a particular occasion as payment by players for cards or as to the
value of the prizes won in bingo promoted by him or by any
other promoter on one or more occasions," ;

(b) in sub-paragraph (a) for the words " the bingo-promoter "
there shall be substituted the words " the promoter " ; and

(c) in sub-paragraph (b) after the words " amount of duty " there
shall be inserted the words " (if any) ".

(6) The following sub-paragraph shall be inserted in paragraph 15
after sub-paragraph (3)—

" (4) In any case where a promoter of bingo disputes the
amount of duty chargeable to and recoverable from him by reference to bingo which is chargeable to duty by reason only that
one or other (or both) of the conditions specified in sub-paragraph
(1)(a) of paragraph 2 above is not satisfied with respect to that
bingo, any information obtained in pursuance of this Schedule
relating to bingo promoted by any other person may be disclosed
to him and shall be admissible in evidence in any proceedings
against him."

PART V
GAMING MACHINE LICENCE DUTY
Great Britain

6. In sections 21(1) and 24(1) of the 1981 Act (gaming machines
which require licences) for the words " a penny machine " there shall
be substituted the words " a two-penny machine ".

7. In subsection (2) of section 21 of the 1981 Act (duration of
licences) at the end of paragraph (b) there shall be added the words
" or

(c) a quarter-year licence for any period of three months beginning on 1st January, 1st April, 1st July or 1st October."

8. In subsection (1) of section 22 of the 1981 Act (charge to
duty) in paragraph (b) for the words " the higher or the peak rate "
there shall be substituted the words " or the higher rate ".

9. In subsection (5) of section 22 of the 1981 Act (lower rate,
higher rate and peak rate machines)—

(a) in paragraph (a) for " 2p " there shall be substituted the
words " 5p ; and " ; and

(b) in paragraph (b) for sub-paragraphs (i) and (ii) there shall
be substituted the words " in any other case " ; and

(c) paragraph (c) shall be omitted.

10. In section 23 of the 1981 Act (amount of duty) the following
Tables shall be substituted for the Tables set out in subsection (1)—

TABLE A
Premises with local authority approval

Description of machines authorised by the licence	Duty on whole-year licence
Chargeable at the lower rate	£120 per machine
Chargeable at the higher rate	£300 per machine

TABLE B
Premises without local authority approval

Description of machines authorised by the licence	Duty on whole-year licence
Chargeable at the lower rate	£300 per machine
Chargeable at the higher rate	£750 per machine

11. In subsection (2) of section 23 (rate of duty for half-year licence) after the word " eleven-twentieths " there shall be inserted the words ", and on a quarter-year licence six-twentieths,".

12. In subsection (6) of section 24 of the 1981 Act (penalty for knowingly or recklessly contravening section 24) for sub-paragraph (*a*) there shall be substituted the following sub-paragraph—

" (*a*) on summary conviction to a penalty—

(i) of the prescribed sum, or

(ii) of an amount equal to three times the amount of duty payable on a whole-year gaming machine licence for those premises and that machine or, where more than one machine has been provided on those premises in contravention of this section, those machines (whether or not the duty has been paid),

whichever is the greater, or to imprisonment for a term not exceeding six months or to both such penalty and imprisonment ; ".

13. In subsection (4) of section 25 of the 1981 Act (gaming machines playable by more than one person)—

(*a*) after the words " a machine " in the second place where they occur, there shall be inserted the words " other than a two-penny machine " ;

(*b*) in paragraph (*a*) for " 2p " there shall be substituted " 5p " ;

(*c*) in paragraph (*b*) for the words from the beginning to " 5p " there shall be substituted the words " in a case not falling within paragraph (*a*) above ; " and

(*d*) paragraph (*c*) shall be omitted.

14.—(1) In section 26 of the 1981 Act, in subsection (2) (interpretation) for the definition of " penny machine " there shall be substituted the following definition :—

" " two-penny machine " means a gaming machine which can only be played by the insertion into the machine of a coin or coins of a denomination, or aggregate denomination, not exceeding 2p ".

(2) At the end of that section there shall be inserted the following subsection :—

" (4) Where the game playable by means of a gaming machine can be played more than once for the insertion of a coin or coins of a denomination, or aggregate denomination, exceeding any sum in pence mentioned in section 22(5) or subsection (2) above, the machine is to be treated for the purposes of those provisions as if it can only be played by the insertion into it of a coin of a denomination not exceeding that sum if, in effect, the amount payable to play the game once does not exceed that sum or, where the machine provides differing numbers of games in differing circumstances, cannot exceed that sum."

15. In paragraph 4 of Schedule 4 to 1981 Act (licences not required for March or October in certain cases) for the words from " during March or October " to the end there shall be substituted the words " which have local authority approval under the Gaming Acts—

    (*a*) during March of any year if the provision of the machine on the premises during April of that year has been authorised by a half-year licence or a quarter-year licence ;

    (*b*) during October of any year if the provision of the machine on the premises during September of that year has been authorised by a half-year licence or a quarter-year licence.".

16. At the end of sub-paragraph (3) of paragraph 7 of Schedule 4 to the 1981 Act (expiry of licences) there shall be added the words " and a quarter-year licence shall expire at the end of 31st March, 30th June, 30th September or 31st December, as the case may be, after the date on which it is expressed to take effect.".

17. In paragraph 13 of Schedule 4 to the 1981 Act (regulations as to the marking of gaming machines) for the words from " the higher rate " to " penny machines " there shall be substituted the words " or the higher rate or, as the case may be, as being two-penny machines ".

Northern Ireland

18. At the end of subsection (3) of section 43 of the 1972 Act (duration of licences) there shall be added the words " or a quarter-year licence for any period of three months beginning on 1st January, 1st April, 1st July or 1st October ".

19.—(1) In subsection (2) of section 44 of the 1972 Act (charge to duty) for the words " the higher or the peak rate " there shall be substituted the words " or the higher rate ".

(2) In subsection (3) of that section (lower rate, higher rate and peak rate machines)—

SCH. 6

> (*a*) in paragraph (*a*) for " £0·02 " there shall be substituted " £0·05 " ;
>
> (*b*) in paragraph (*b*) for the words from " if it can " to the end of the paragraph there shall be substituted the words " in any other case " ; and
>
> (*c*) paragraph (*c*) shall be omitted.

(3) In subsection (4) of that section (rate of duty) for the Table there set out there shall be substituted the following Table—

TABLE

Description of machines authorised by the licence	Duty on whole-year licence
Chargeable at the lower rate	£300 per machine
Chargeable at the higher rate	£750 per machine

(4) In subsection (5) of that section (rate of duty for half-year licences) after the word " eleven-twentieths " there shall be inserted the words " , and on a quarter-year licence six-twentieths,".

(5) In subsection (6) of that section—

> (*a*) after the words " a machine ", in the first place where they occur, there shall be inserted the words " other than a two-penny machine " ;
>
> (*b*) in paragraph (*a*) for " £0·02 " there shall be substituted " £0·05 " ;
>
> (*c*) paragraph (*aa*) shall be omitted ; and
>
> (*d*) in paragraph (*b*) for the word " peak " there shall be substituted the word " higher ".

20. In section 46 of the 1972 Act (gaming machine licences) at the end of subsection (1) there shall be inserted the words " or the machine is a two-penny machine ".

21. In subsection (4) of section 48 of the 1972 Act (interpretation) after the definition of " coin " there shall be inserted the following definition—

> " " two-penny machine " means a gaming machine which can only be played by the insertion into the machine of a coin or coins of a denomination, or aggregate denomination, not exceeeding 2p ".

22. At the end of sub-paragraph (2) of paragraph 9 of Schedule 3 to the 1972 Act (expiry of licences) there shall be added the words " and a quarter-year licence shall expire at the end of 31st March 30th June, 30th September or 31st December, as the case may be, after the date on which it is expressed to take effect ".

23. In paragraph 13 of Schedule 3 to the 1972 Act (regulations as to marking of gaming machines) the words "the peak rate" shall cease to have effect.

24. In paragraph 14(1) of Schedule 3 to the 1972 Act (penalties for knowingly or recklessly contravening section 46) the following sub-paragraphs shall be substituted for sub-paragraphs (i) and (ii)—

"(i) on summary conviction to a penalty not exceeding £1,000 or, if greater, of an amount equal to three times the amount of duty payable on a whole-year gaming machine licence for those premises and that machine or, where more than one machine has been provided on those premises in contravention of this section, those machines (whether or not the duty has been paid), or to imprisonment for a term not exceeding 6 months or to both such penalty and imprisonment ;

(ii) on conviction on indictment to a penalty of any amount or to imprisonment for a term not exceeding 2 years or to both such penalty and imprisonment."

Section 26.

SCHEDULE 7

Deduction of Tax from Certain Loan Interest

Part I

Relevant Loan Interest

Interpretation

1. In this Schedule—

1967 c. 29.　"the 1967 Act" means the Housing Subsidies Act 1967 ;

1972 c. 41.　"the 1972 Schedule" means Schedule 9 to the Finance Act 1972 (relief for interest on loans for purchase or improvement of land etc.) ;

1974 c. 30.　"the 1974 Schedule" means Schedule 1 to the Finance Act 1974 (modification of rules for relief for interest) ;

S.I. 1981/156 (N.I. 3).　"the 1981 Order" means the Housing (Northern Ireland) Order 1981 ;

"notice" means notice in writing ;

"prescribed", except in Part IV, means prescribed by the Board ;

"the principal section" means section 26 of this Act ; and

"regulations" means regulations made by the Board under section 29 of this Act.

Qualifying conditions

2.—(1) Subject to the following provisions of this Schedule, interest which is paid and payable in the United Kingdom to a qualifying lender and to which sub-paragraph (2) or sub-paragraph (3) below applies is "relevant loan interest".

(2) This sub-paragraph applies to interest if—

  (*a*) it is interest falling within paragraph 1 of the 1972 Schedule (interest on loans for purchase or improvement of land) or paragraph 24 of the 1974 Schedule (interest on loans to purchase life annuities) ; and

  (*b*) apart from subsection (1) or subsection (8) of the principal section and, where applicable, paragraph 5 or paragraph 24(3) of the 1974 Schedule (the tax relief limit) the whole of the interest either would be eligible for relief under section 75 of the Finance Act 1972 or would be taken into account in a computation of profits or gains or losses for the purposes of Case I, Case II or Case VI of Schedule D for any year of assessment ; and

  1972 c. 41.

  (*c*) except in the case of interest falling within paragraph 24 of the 1974 Schedule, at the time the interest is paid, the condition in either paragraph 4 or paragraph 4A of the 1974 Schedule is fulfilled with respect to the land, caravan or houseboat to which the loan concerned relates ;

but, unless sub-paragraph (4) or sub-paragraph (5) below applies, this sub-paragraph does not apply to interest which becomes due before 6th April 1983.

(3) This sub-paragraph applies to interest which becomes due on or after 1st April 1983 and is payable on a loan—

  (*a*) in respect of which there is in force on 31st March 1983—

    (i) an option notice given under section 24(2) of the 1967 Act (option mortgages), other than one falling within section 27(3)(*b*) of this Act ; or
    (ii) an option notice given under Article 142(2) of the 1981 Order (option mortgages in Northern Ireland), other than one falling within section 27(4)(*b*) of this Act ; and

  (*b*) which relates to a dwelling in respect of which, at the time the interest is paid, the condition in paragraph 4 of the 1974 Schedule is fulfilled.

(4) Sub-paragraph (2) above applies to interest which becomes due on or after 1st April 1983 (instead of 6th April 1983) if the qualifying lender to whom it is payable is either a building society, within the meaning of the Building Societies Act 1962 or the Building Societies Act (Northern Ireland) 1967, or a local authority.

1962 c. 37.
1967 c. 31.
(N.I.).

(5) If an application in that behalf is made to the Board by a qualifying lender, sub-paragraph (2) above applies to interest which becomes due on or after such date as may be specified by the Board for the purposes of that sub-paragraph (instead of 6th April 1983).

(6) The Board shall not under sub-paragraph (5) above specify a date earlier than 1st March 1983 or later than 5th April 1983 and the Board shall notify the qualifying lender concerned of the date specified under that sub-paragraph.

(7) Sub-paragraph (2) above does not apply to interest payable on a loan the only security for which is a contract of insurance on human life or a contract to pay an annuity on human life.

3.—(1) In determining whether sub-paragraph (2) of paragraph 2 above applies to any interest, paragraph 1 of the 1972 Schedule and paragraph 24 of the 1974 Schedule shall each have effect as if the words " or the Republic of Ireland " were omitted.

(2) In determining whether sub-paragraph (2)(*c*) of paragraph 2 above applies to any interest, sub-paragraph (1) of paragraph 4 of the 1974 Schedule (restrictions on reliefs under the 1972 Schedule) shall have effect as if—

(*a*) in paragraph (*a*) after the word " used ", where it first occurs, there were inserted the words " wholly or to a substantial extent " ; and

(*b*) paragraph (*b*) (commercial lettings) and the word " or " immediately preceding it were omitted.

(3) In determining for the purposes of paragraph 2(3)(*b*) above whether the condition in paragraph 4 of the 1974 Schedule is for the time being fulfilled with respect to any dwelling,—

(*a*) sub-paragraph (1) of that paragraph shall have effect as if for the words from " Part I of Schedule 9 " to " used " (where it first occurs) there were substituted the words " interest shall not be relevant loan interest for the purposes of section 26 of the Finance Act 1982 unless the dwelling to which the loan relates is at the time the interest is paid used wholly or partly " and paragraph (*b*) and the word " or " immediately preceding it were omitted ; and

(*b*) sub-paragraph (3) of that paragraph shall have effect as if for the words " land, caravan or house-boat " there were substituted the word " dwelling ".

(4) Where at a time when interest on a loan (in this sub-paragraph referred to as " the first loan ") is relevant loan interest, the borrower raises another loan to defray money to be applied as mentioned in paragraph 1 of the 1972 Schedule with a view—

(*a*) to the use of other land or another caravan or house-boat wholly or partly as that person's only or main residence, and

(*b*) to the disposal of the land, caravan, house-boat or dwelling to which the first loan relates,

then, in relation to interest payable within twelve months from the making of the other loan, the condition in paragraph 4 of the 1974 Schedule shall be treated as continuing to be fulfilled.

(5) If in a case falling within sub-paragraph (4) above, the interest on the first loan referred to in that sub-paragraph is interest to which paragraph 2(2) above applies and a direction is given under paragraph 6 of the 1974 Schedule extending the period within which Part I of the 1972 Schedule applies to that first loan, sub-paragraph (4) above shall have effect in relation to that case as if for the

reference to twelve months there were substituted a reference to such longer period as is specified in the direction.

(6) If, in a case falling within sub-paragraph (4) above, the interest on the first loan is interest to which paragraph 2(3) above applies and, having regard to the circumstances of that case, it appears to the Board reasonable to do so, they may direct that, in relation to that case, that sub-paragraph shall have effect as if for the reference to twelve months there were substituted a reference to such longer period as meets the circumstances of that case.

4.—(1) Notwithstanding anything in paragraph 2 above, interest on a home improvement loan is not relevant loan interest unless—

> (a) the qualifying lender to whom the interest is payable is a building society, within the meaning of the Building Socie- 1962 c. 37. ties Act 1962 or the Building Societies Act (Northern 1967 c. 31 (N.I.). Ireland) 1967, or a local authority or the Northern Ireland Housing Executive ; or

> (b) the qualifying lender to whom the interest is payable has given notice to the Board in accordance with regulations that he is prepared to have those home improvement loans in respect of which he is the lender and which were made after such date as he may specify in the notice brought within the tax deduction scheme.

(2) A qualifying lender may not specify a date in a notice under sub-paragraph (1) above which is earlier than the earliest date on which paragraph 2 above applies to interest on any loan (whether or not a home improvement loan) made by him.

(3) In this paragraph " home improvement loan " means a loan made to defray money applied wholly in improving or developing land or buildings on land or in paying off another loan which was itself to defray money so applied.

(4) Paragraphs 3 and 4 of the 1972 Schedule (construction of references to money applied in improving or developing land or buildings) shall apply for the purposes of this paragraph as they apply for the purposes of Part I of that Schedule.

Loans over the tax relief limit

5.—(1) The provisions of this paragraph have effect in relation to a loan where, by virtue of sub-paragraphs (1) and (2) of paragraph 5 or paragraph 24(3) of the 1974 Schedule (the limit on eligibility for tax relief), only part of the interest on the loan would (apart from the principal section) be eligible for relief under section 75 of the Finance Act 1972 ; and in this paragraph any such loan is referred 1972 c. 41. to as a " limited loan ".

(2) None of the interest on a limited loan is relevant loan interest unless the qualifying lender to whom the interest is payable has given notice to the Board in accordance with regulations that he is prepared to have limited loans of a description which includes that limited loan brought within the tax deduction scheme.

SCH. 7

(3) If, in a case where sub-paragraph (2) above applies, paragraph 5(2) of the 1974 Schedule requires another loan to be taken into account for the purpose of determining that part of the limited loan interest on which would (apart from the principal section) be eligible for relief as mentioned in sub-paragraph (1) above, none of the interest on the limited loan is relevant loan interest unless that other loan was made by the same qualifying lender as the limited loan.

1972 c. 41.

(4) Where notice has been given as mentioned in sub-paragraph (2) above and, if sub-paragraph (3) above also applies, the condition in that sub-paragraph is fulfilled only so much of the interest as (apart from the principal section) would be eligible for relief under section 75 of the Finance Act 1972 is relevant loan interest.

Joint borrowers

6.—(1) Where a loan on which interest is payable by the borrower was made jointly to the borrower and another person who is not the borrower's husband or wife, the interest on the loan is not relevant loan interest unless—

    (a) each of the persons to whom the loan was made is a qualifying borrower ; and

    (b) in relation to each of them considered separately, the whole of that interest is relevant loan interest, in accordance with the preceding provisions of this Part of this Schedule.

(2) References in this paragraph to the borrower's husband or wife do not include references to a separated husband or wife, and for this purpose " separated " has the same meaning as in Part II of the 1974 Schedule.

PART II

APPLICATION OF THE PRINCIPAL SECTION

7.—(1) The principal section does not apply to any relevant loan interest unless either—

    (a) in the case of a loan of a description specified by regulations for the purposes of this sub-paragraph, the borrower or, in the case of joint borrowers, each of them has given notice to the lender in the prescribed form certifying—

        (i) that he is a qualifying borrower ; and

        (ii) that the interest is relevant loan interest ; and

        (iii) such other matters as may be prescribed ; or

    (b) the Board have given notice to the lender and the borrower that the interest may be paid under deduction of tax ; or

    (c) it is interest to which paragraph 2(3) above applies ; or

    (d) the loan to which the interest relates was made, subject to sub-paragraph (4) below, before 1st April 1983 and is of a description specified by regulations for the purposes of this sub-paragraph.

(2) Where notice has been given as mentioned in paragraph (a) or paragraph (b) of sub-paragraph (1) above, the principal section applies to any relevant loan interest to which the notice relates and

which becomes due on or after the relevant date, as defined in sub-paragraph (3) below ; and in a case falling within paragraph (*c*) or paragraph (*d*) of sub-paragraph (1) above, the principal section applies to the relevant loan interest referred to in that paragraph.

(3) In the case of a notice under paragraph (*a*) of sub-paragraph (1) above, the relevant date is the date the notice is given and, in the case of a notice under paragraph (*b*) of that paragraph, the relevant date is a date specified in the notice as being the relevant date (which may be earlier than the date so specified as the date from which the interest may be paid under deduction of tax).

(4) In the case of relevant loan interest—

    (*a*) which falls within sub-paragraph (2) of paragraph 2 above, and

    (*b*) to which sub-paragraph (4) or sub-paragraph (5) of that paragraph does not apply, for the reference in sub-paragraph (1)(*d*) above to 1st April 1983 there shall be substituted a reference to 6th April 1983.

(5) In the case of relevant loan interest—

    (*a*) which falls within sub-paragraph (2) of paragraph 2 above, and

    (*b*) to which sub-paragraph (5) of that paragraph applies,

for the reference in sub-paragraph (1)(*d*) above to 1st April 1983 there shall be substituted a reference to the date specified by the Board and notified under sub-paragraph (6) of paragraph 2 to the qualifying lender to whom the interest is payable.

8.—(1) If at any time—

    (*a*) the interest on a loan ceases to be relevant loan interest, or

    (*b*) a person making payments of relevant loan interest ceases to be a qualifying borrower,

the borrower shall give notice of that fact to the lender.

(2) Without prejudice to sub-paragraph (3) below, in relation to a payment of interest—

    (*a*) which is due after the time referred to in sub-paragraph (1) above and before the date on which notice is given under that sub-paragraph, and

    (*b*) from which a deduction was made as mentioned in sub-section (1) of the principal section,

the principal section, except subsection (8), shall have effect as if the payment were a payment of relevant loan interest made by a qualifying borrower.

(3) Nothing in sub-paragraph (2) above entitles the borrower to any relief from tax or other benefit and, accordingly, where the amount of any such relief or other benefit which is allowed by virtue of that sub-paragraph exceeds that which ought to have been allowed, he shall be liable to make good the excess and an inspector may make such assessments as may in his judgment be required for recovering the excess.

(4) The Taxes Management Act 1970 shall apply to an assessment under this paragraph as if it were an assessment to tax for the year of assessment in which the relief was given and as if—

    (a) the assessment were among those specified in sections 55(1) (recovery of tax not postponed) and 86(2) (interest on overdue tax) of that Act ; and

    (b) the sum charged by the assessment were tax specified in paragraph 3 of the Table in section 86(4) of that Act (reckonable date).

9.—(1) If, as a result of receiving a notice under paragraph 8 above or otherwise, a qualifying lender has reason to believe that any interest is no longer relevant loan interest or that a borrower is no longer a qualifying borrower, the lender shall furnish the Board with such information as is in his possession with respect to those matters.

(2) At the end of the second column of the Table in section 98 of the Taxes Management Act 1970 (penalty for failure to furnish information etc.) there shall be inserted—

    " Paragraph 9(1) of Schedule 7 to the Finance Act 1982 ".

10.—(1) Where it appears to the Board that any of the provisions of Part I of this Schedule is not or may not be fulfilled with respect to any interest, or that a qualifying borrower has or may have ceased to be a qualifying borrower, they shall give notice of that fact to the lender and the borrower specifying the description of relevant loan interest concerned or, as the case may be, that the borrower has or may have ceased to be a qualifying borrower.

(2) The principal section shall not apply to any payment of relevant loan interest of a description to which a notice under sub-paragraph (1) above relates and which becomes due or is made after such date as may be specified in the notice and before such date as may be specified in a further notice given by the Board to the lender and the borrower.

11. In any case where—

    (a) the principal section applies to any relevant loan interest by virtue of a notice under paragraph 7(1)(b) above, and

    (b) the relevant date specified in the notice is earlier than the date from which the interest begins to be paid under deduction of tax, and

    (c) a payment of that interest was made on or after the relevant date but not under deduction of tax,

regulations may provide for a sum to be paid by the Board of an amount equal to that which the borrower would have been able to deduct from that payment by virtue of the principal section if it had been made after the relevant date.

12.—(1) No obligation as to secrecy imposed by statute or otherwise on persons employed in relation to Inland Revenue shall prevent information relating to any loan in respect of which an option notice has been given as mentioned in paragraph 2(3)(a) above from

being disclosed to the Secretary of State or the Department of the   Sch. 7
Environment for Northern Ireland, or to an officer of either of
them authorised to receive such information, in connection with the
exercise by the Secretary of State or that Department of any of his
or their functions in relation to any such loan.

(2) Sub-paragraph (1) above extends only to disclosure by or under
the authority of the Inland Revenue ; and information which is disclosed to any person by virtue of sub-paragraph (1) above shall not
be further disclosed to any other person unless—

    (*a*) it could have been disclosed to that other person in accord-
        ance with sub-paragraph (1) above ; or

    (*b*) the disclosure is made for the purposes of any civil or
        criminal proceedings concerned with the loan to which the
        disclosure relates.

PART III

QUALIFYING BORROWERS

13.—(1) Subject to the provisions of this paragraph, an individual
is for the purposes of the principal section and this Schedule a
qualifying borrower with respect to the interest on any loan.

(2) In relation to interest paid at a time when the borrower or the
borrower's husband or wife holds an office or employment in respect
of the emoluments of which he or she would but for some special
exemption or immunity from tax be chargeable to tax under Case I,
Case II or Case III of Schedule E, the borrower is not a qualifying
borrower.

(3) In sub-paragraph (2) above references to the borrower's husband
or wife do not include references to a separated husband or wife,
and for this purpose " separated " has the same meaning as in Part
II of the 1974 Schedule.

PART IV

QUALIFYING LENDERS

14.—(1) The following bodies are qualifying lenders for the purposes of the principal section and Parts I to III of this Schedule : —

    (*a*) a building society within the meaning of the Building Societies   1962 c. 37.
        Act 1962 or the Building Societies Act (Northern Ireland)   1967 c. 31
        1967 ;   (N.I.).

    (*b*) a local authority ;

    (*c*) the Bank of England ;

    (*d*) the Post Office ;

    (*e*) a company which is authorised under section 3 or section 4
        of the Insurance Companies Act 1981 to carry on in the   1981 c. 31.
        United Kingdom any of the classes of business specified in
        Schedule 1 to that Act ;

SCH. 7
1981 c. 65.

1974 c. 56.
1970 c. 31
(N.I.).
1981 c. 64.
1968 c. 16.

(f) a trustee savings bank within the meaning of the Trustee Savings Bank Act 1981 ;

(g) a registered friendly society or branch, within the meaning of the Friendly Societies Act 1974 or the Friendly Societies Act (Northern Ireland) 1970 ;

(h) a development corporation within the meaning of the New Towns Act 1981 or the New Towns (Scotland) Act 1968 ;

(j) the Commission for the New Towns ;

(k) the Housing Corporation ;

(l) the Northern Ireland Housing Executive ;

(m) the Scottish Special Housing Association ;

(n) the Development Board for Rural Wales ;

(o) any of the following which is prescribed under sub-paragraph (2) below, namely, a recognised bank or licensed institution, within the meaning of the Banking Act 1979, a company which is authorised as mentioned in paragraph (e) above to carry on in the United Kingdom any of the classes of business specified in Schedule 2 to the Insurance Companies Act 1981, and a 90 per cent. subsidiary of any such bank, institution or company or of a company within paragraph (e) above.

(2) The Treasury may by order prescribe for the purposes of this Part of this Schedule generally or in relation to any specified description of loan any of the bodies referred to in paragraph (o) of sub-paragraph (1) above ; and a body which is prescribed by such an order shall become a qualifying lender for the purposes referred to in that sub-paragraph generally or, as the case may be, in relation to such description of loan as is specified in the order with effect from the beginning of the first year of assessment which begins after the date on which the order is made.

15. Without prejudice to paragraph 14 above, in relation to interest to which sub-paragraph (3) of paragraph 2 above applies, the person who, as a qualifying lender for the purposes of Part II of the 1967 Act or Part VIII of the 1981 Order, was the lender in relation to the loan referred to in that sub-paragraph shall also be a qualifying lender for the purposes of the principal section and Parts I to III of this Schedule.

SCHEDULE 8

SUB-CONTRACTORS IN THE CONSTRUCTION INDUSTRY

1. In section 70 of the Finance (No. 2) Act 1975, at the beginning of subsection (1) there shall be inserted the words " Subject to the provisions of regulations under this section or section 70A of this Act ".

2. In subsection (2)(c) of that section, for the words " by virtue of " there shall be substituted the words " in accordance with ".

3. In subsection (4) of that section, at the end there shall be added the words " (not being a certificate to the holder of which section 70A below would apply) ".

4. In subsection (7) of that section, after paragraph (*g*) there shall be inserted the words " and

(*h*) excluding payments from the operation of this section where, in such circumstances as may be specified in the regulations, the requirements of regulations relating to the production of certificates or the obtaining, production or surrender of vouchers have not been complied with ; ".

5. After that section there shall be inserted—

" Provision for limited exception from section 69.

70A.—(1) This section applies to the holder of a certificate in force under section 70 of this Act if it was issued to him on the basis—

    (*a*) that the condition in paragraph 2 of Part I of Schedule 12 to this Act was inapplicable to him by reason of sub-paragraph (1)(*b*) of that paragraph, or

    (*b*) that he satisfied that condition by virtue of sub-paragraph (5) of that paragraph.

(2) The Board may make regulations securing that a person to whom this section applies shall not be excepted from section 69 of this Act in relation to a payment to the extent that the amount of the payment, or the aggregate amount of the payment and such other payments as may be prescribed by the regulations, exceeds a limit so prescribed.

(3) Regulations under this section shall be made by statutory instrument which shall be subject to annulment in pursuance of a resolution of the House of Commons."

6. In section 71 of that Act, for subsection (5) there shall be substituted—

" (5) A payment (including a payment by way of loan) that has the effect of discharging an obligation under a contract relating to construction operations shall be taken to be made under the contract ; and if—

    (*a*) the obligation is to make a payment to a person within paragraphs (i) to (iii) of section 69(1) of this Act, but

    (*b*) the payment discharging that obligation is made to a person not within those paragraphs,

the payment shall be taken to be made to the first-mentioned person."

7. In paragraph 2 of Part I of Schedule 12 to that Act, in sub-paragraph (1) for the words from the beginning to " must " there shall be substituted the words " Unless the applicant—

    (*a*) is the holder of a certificate in force under section 70 of this Act (other than a holder to whom section 70A applies), or

SCH. 8

(*b*) supplies the Board with a guarantee by such person, for such amount and in such form as may be prescribed in regulations made by the Board,

he must ".

8. In sub-paragraph (2) of that paragraph for the words from " who " to " this condition " there shall be substituted the words " shall be treated as satisfying the condition in sub-paragraph (1) above ".

9.—(1) At the end of that paragraph there shall be added—

" (5) If the applicant satisfies the Board that he has during any period within six years before the date of his application attended a school or other establishment for the purpose of receiving full-time education or full-time training, this paragraph shall have effect as if that period were one during which he was employed as mentioned in sub-paragraph (1) above."

(2) This paragraph shall not have effect in relation to applications made before the coming into operation of regulations under section 70A of the Finance (No. 2) Act 1975.

1975 c. 45.

10. After paragraph 2 of Part I of Schedule 12 to that Act there shall be inserted—

" 2A. The applicant must not be receiving full-time education or full-time training ".

11. In paragraph 3 of Part I of that Schedule, in sub-paragraph (1) for the words " the Income Tax Acts " there shall be substituted the words " the Tax Acts ".

12. After sub-paragraph (1) of that paragraph there shall be inserted—

" (1A) An applicant who at any time in the qualifying period had control of a company shall be taken not to satisfy the condition in sub-paragraph (1) above unless the company has satisfied that condition in relation to periods ending at a time within that period when he had control of it ; and for this purpose " control " has the meaning assigned to it by section 534 of the Taxes Act.".

13. In sub-paragraph (2) of that paragraph for the word " who " there shall be substituted the words " or company that ".

14. In paragraph 1 of Part II of that Schedule, in sub-paragraph (1) after the words " this Act " where they first appear there shall be inserted the words " (other than a holder to whom section 70A applies) ".

15. In paragraph 2 of Part IV of that Schedule, in sub-paragraph (1) for the words " the Income Tax Acts, the Corporation Tax Acts " there shall be substituted the words " the Tax Acts ".

SCHEDULE 9

PURCHASE OF OWN SHARES BY UNQUOTED TRADING COMPANY

Conditions for application of section 53(1)

1.—(1) The vendor must be resident and ordinarily resident in the United Kingdom in the year of assessment in which the purchase is made and if the shares are held through a nominee the nominee must also be so resident and ordinarily resident.

(2) The residence and ordinary residence of trustees shall be determined for the purposes of this paragraph as they are determined under section 52 of the Capital Gains Tax Act 1979 for the purposes 1979 c. 14. of that Act.

(3) The residence and ordinary residence of personal representatives shall be taken for the purposes of this paragraph to be the same as the residence and ordinary residence of the deceased immediately before his death.

(4) The references in this paragraph to a person's ordinary residence shall be disregarded in the case of a company.

2.—(1) The shares must have been owned by the vendor throughout the period of five years ending with the date of the purchase.

(2) If at any time during that period the shares were transferred to the vendor by a person who was then his spouse living with him then, unless that person is alive at the date of the purchase but is no longer the vendor's spouse living with him, any period during which the shares were owned by that person shall be treated for the purposes of sub-paragraph (1) above as a period of ownership by the vendor.

(3) Where the vendor became entitled to the shares under the will or on the intestacy of a previous owner—

(a) any period during which the shares were owned by the previous owner or his personal representatives shall be treated for the purposes of sub-paragraph (1) above as a period of ownership by the vendor, and

(b) that sub-paragraph shall have effect as if it referred to three years instead of five.

(4) Where the vendor is a personal representative of a deceased owner—

(a) any period during which the shares were owned by the deceased shall be treated for the purposes of sub-paragraph (1) above as a period of ownership by the vendor, and

(b) that sub-paragraph shall have effect as if it referred to three years instead of five.

(5) In determining whether the condition in this paragraph is satisfied in a case where the vendor acquired shares of the same class at different times—

(a) shares acquired earlier shall be taken into account before shares acquired later, and

2 M 3

(b) any previous disposal by him of shares of that class shall be assumed to be a disposal of shares acquired later rather than of shares acquired earlier.

(6) If for the purposes of capital gains tax the time when shares were acquired would be determined under any provision of Chapter

II of Part IV of the Capital Gains Tax Act 1979 (reorganisation of share capital, conversion of securities, etc.) then, subject to sub-paragraph (7) below, it shall be determined in the same way for the purposes of this paragraph.

(7) Sub-paragraph (6) above shall not apply to shares allotted for payment or comprised in share capital to which section 34 of the

Finance (No. 2) Act 1975 (stock dividends) applies.

3.—(1) If immediately after the purchase the vendor owns shares of the company, then, subject to paragraph 9 below, his interest as a shareholder must be substantially reduced.

(2) Subject to sub-paragraph (3) below the vendor's interest as a shareholder shall be taken to be substantially reduced if and only if the total nominal value of the shares owned by him immediately after the purchase, expressed as a fraction of the issued share capital of the company at that time, does not exceed 75 per cent. of the corresponding fraction immediately before the purchase.

(3) The vendor's interest as a shareholder shall not be taken to be substantially reduced where—

(a) he would, if the company distributed all its profits available for distribution immediately after the purchase, be entitled to a share of those profits, and

(b) that share, expressed as a fraction of the total of those profits, exceeds 75 per cent. of the corresponding fraction immediately before the purchase.

(4) In determining for the purposes of sub-paragraph (3) above the division of profits among the persons entitled to them, a person entitled to periodic distributions calculated by reference to fixed rates or amounts shall be regarded as entitled to a distribution of the amount or maximum amount to which he would be entitled for a year.

(5) In sub-paragraph (3) above " profits available for distribution " has the same meaning as it has for the purposes of Part III of the

Companies Act 1980, but subject to sub-paragraph (6) below.

(6) For the purposes of sub-paragraph (3) above the amount of the profits available for distribution (whether immediately before or immediately after the purchase) shall be treated as increased—

(a) in the case of every company, by £100, and

(b) in the case of a company from which any person is entitled to periodic distributions of the kind mentioned in sub-paragraph (4) above, by a further amount equal to that required to make the distribution to which he is entitled in accordance with that sub-paragraph :

and where the aggregate of the sums payable by the company on the purchase and on any contemporaneous redemption, repayment or purchase of other shares of the company exceeds the amount of the profits available for distribution immediately before the purchase, that amount shall be treated as further increased by an amount equal to the excess.

(7) References in this paragraph to entitlement are, except in the case of trustees and personal representatives, references to beneficial entitlement.

4.—(1) If immediately after the purchase any associate of the vendor owns shares of the company then, subject to paragraph 9 below, the combined interests as shareholders of the vendor and his associates must be substantially reduced.

(2) The question whether the combined interests as shareholders of the vendor and his associates are substantially reduced shall be determined in the same way as is (under paragraph 3 above) the question whether a vendor's interest as a shareholder is substantially reduced, except that the vendor shall be assumed to have the interests of his associates as well as his own.

5.—(1) This paragraph applies where the company making the purchase is immediately before the purchase a member of a group and either—

    (*a*) immediately after the purchase the vendor owns shares of one or more other members of the group (whether or not he then owns shares of the company making the purchase), or

    (*b*) immediately after the purchase the vendor owns shares of the company making the purchase and immediately before the purchase he owned shares of one or more other members of the group ;

and in the following provisions of this paragraph "relevant company" means the company making the purchase and any other member of the group in which the vendor owns shares immediately before or immediately after the purchase.

(2) Where this paragraph applies then, subject to paragraph 9 below, the vendor's interest as a shareholder in the group must be substantially reduced.

(3) The vendor's interest as a shareholder in the group shall be ascertained by—

    (*a*) expressing the total nominal value of the shares owned by him in each relevant company as a fraction of the issued share capital of the company,

    (*b*) adding together the fractions so obtained, and

    (*c*) dividing the result by the number of relevant companies (including any in which he owns no shares).

(4) Subject to sub-paragraph (5) below, the vendor's interest as a shareholder in the group shall be taken to be substantially reduced if and only if it does not exceed 75 per cent. of the corresponding interest immediately before the purchase.

(5) The vendor's interest as a shareholder in the group shall not be taken to be substantially reduced if—

(a) he would, if every member of the group distributed all its profits available for distribution immediately after the purchase (including any profits received by it on a distribution by another member), be entitled to a share of the profits of one or more of them, and

(b) that share, or the aggregate of those shares, expressed as a fraction of the aggregate of the profits available for distribution of every member of the group which is—

(i) a relevant company, or

(ii) a 51 per cent. subsidiary of a relevant company,

exceeds 75 per cent. of the corresponding fraction immediately before the purchase.

(6) Sub-paragraphs (4) to (6) of paragraph 3 above shall apply for the purposes of sub-paragraph (5) above as they apply for the purposes of paragraph 3(3).

(7) Subject to the following sub-paragraphs, in this paragraph " group " means a company which has one or more 51 per cent. subsidiaries, but is not itself a 51 per cent. subsidiary of any other company, together with those subsidiaries.

(8) Where the whole or a significant part of the business carried on by an unquoted company (" the successor company ") was previously carried on by—

(a) the company making the purchase, or

(b) a company which is (apart from this sub-paragraph) a member of a group to which the company making the purchase belongs,

the successor company and any company of which it is a 51 per cent. subsidiary shall be treated as being a member of the same group as the company making the purchase (whether or not, apart from this sub-paragraph, the company making the purchase is a member of a group).

(9) Sub-paragraph (8) above shall not apply if the successor company first carried on the business there referred to more than three years before the time of the purchase.

(10) For the purposes of this paragraph a company which has ceased to be a 51 per cent. subsidiary of another company before the time of the purchase shall be treated as continuing to be such a subsidiary if at that time there exist arrangements under which it could again become such a subsidiary.

6.—(1) This paragraph applies where the company making the purchase is immediately before the purchase a member of a group and at that time an associate of the vendor owns shares of any member of the group.

(2) Where this paragraph applies then, subject to paragraph 9 below, the combined interests as shareholders in the group of the vendor and his associates must be substantially reduced.

(3) The question whether the combined interests as shareholders in the group of the vendor and his associates are substantially reduced shall be determined in the same way as is (under paragraph 5 above) the question whether a vendor's interest as a shareholder in a group is substantially reduced, except that the vendor shall be assumed to have the interests of his associates as well as his own (and references in paragraph 5(3) to (5) to a relevant company shall be construed accordingly).

(4) For the purposes of this paragraph " group " has the same meaning as it has for the purposes of paragraph 5 above.

7.—(1) The vendor must not immediately after the purchase be connected with the company making the purchase or with any company which is a member of the same group as that company.

(2) For the purposes of this paragraph " group " has the same meaning as it has for the purposes of paragraph 5 above.

(3) This paragraph has effect subject to paragraph 9 below.

8.—(1) The purchase must not be part of a scheme or arrangement which is designed or likely to result in the vendor or any associate of his having interests in any company such that, if he had those interests immediately after the purchase, any of the conditions in paragraphs 3 to 7 above could not be satisfied.

(2) A transaction occurring within one year after the purchase shall be deemed for the purposes of sub-paragraph (1) above to be part of a scheme or arrangement of which the purchase is also part.

(3) This paragraph has effect subject to paragraph 9 below.

9.—(1) Where—

(a) any of the conditions in paragraphs 3 to 8 above which are applicable are not satisfied in relation to the vendor, but

(b) he proposed or agreed to the purchase in order that the condition in paragraph 4(1) or 6(2) could be satisfied in respect of the redemption, repayment or purchase of shares owned by a person of whom he is an associate,

this paragraph applies to the purchase to the extent that that result is produced by virtue of the purchase.

(2) Where this paragraph applies, section 53(1) of this Act shall have effect as if the conditions in paragraphs 3 to 8 above were satisfied in relation to the vendor.

Administration

10.—(1) A payment made by a company on the redemption, repayment or purchase of its own shares shall be deemed to be one to which section 53 of this Act applies if, before it is made, the Board have on the application of the company notified the company that they are satisfied that the section will apply.

(2) A payment made by a company on the redemption, repayment or purchase of its own shares shall be deemed to be one to which

section 53 of this Act does not apply if, before it is made, the Board have on the application of the company notified the company that they are satisfied that the section will not apply.

(3) An application under this paragraph shall be in writing and shall contain particulars of the relevant transactions ; and the Board may, within thirty days of the receipt of the application or of any further particulars previously required under this sub-paragraph, by notice require the applicant to furnish further particulars for the purpose of enabling the Board to make their decision.

(4) If a notice under sub-paragraph (3) above is not complied with within thirty days or such longer period as the Board may allow, the Board need not proceed further on the application.

(5) The Board shall notify their decision to the applicant within thirty days of receiving the application or, if they give a notice under sub-paragraph (3) above, within thirty days of the notice being complied with.

(6) If particulars furnished under this paragraph do not fully and accurately disclose all facts and circumstances material for the decision of the Board, any resulting notification by the Board shall be void.

11.—(1) A company which treats a payment made by it as one to which section 53 of this Act applies shall within sixty days after making the payment make a return to the inspector giving particulars of the payment and of the circumstances by reason of which section 53 is regarded as applying to it.

(2) Where a company treats a payment made by it as one to which section 53(1) of this Act applies, any person connected with the company who knows of any such scheme or arrangement affecting the payment as is mentioned in paragraph 8 above shall, within sixty days after he first knows of both the payment and the scheme or arrangement, give a notice in writing to the inspector containing particulars of the scheme or arrangement.

12.—(1) Where the inspector has reason to believe that a payment treated by the company making it as one to which section 53(1) of this Act applies may form part of a scheme or arrangement of the kind referred to in subsection (1)(b) of that section or in paragraph 8 above, he may by notice in writing require the company or any person who is connected with the company to furnish him within such time, not being less than sixty days, as may be specified in the notice with—

(a) a declaration in writing stating whether or not, according to information which the company or that person has or can reasonably obtain, any such scheme or arrangement exists or has existed, and

(b) such other information as the inspector may reasonably require for the purposes of the provision in question and the company or that person has or can reasonably obtain.

(2) The recipient of a payment treated by the company making it as one to which section 53 of this Act applies, and any person on whose behalf such a payment is received, shall if so required by the inspector state whether the payment received by him or on his behalf is received on behalf of any person other than himself and, if so, the name and address of that person.

13.—(1) The Table in section 98 of the Taxes Management Act 1970 shall be amended as follows.

(2) At the end of the first column there shall be added—
" Paragraph 12 of Schedule 9 to the Finance Act 1982."

(3) At the end of the second column there shall be added—
" Paragraph 11 of Schedule 9 to the Finance Act 1982."

Interpretation

14.—(1) Any question whether a person is an associate of another in relation to a company shall be determined for the purposes of this Schedule in accordance with the following provisions of this paragraph.

(2) A husband and wife living together are associates of one another.

(3) A person under the age of eighteen is an associate of his parents, and his parents are his associates.

(4) A person connected with a company is an associate of the company and of any company controlled by it, and the company and any company controlled by it are his associates.

(5) Where a person connected with one company has control of another company, the second company is an associate of the first.

(6) Where shares of a company are held by trustees (other than bare trustees) then in relation to that company, but subject to sub-paragraph (9) below, the trustees are associates of—

   (a) any person who directly or indirectly provided property to the trustees or has made a reciprocal arrangement for another to do so, and

   (b) any person who is, by virtue of sub-paragraph (2) or (3) above, an associate of a person within paragraph (a) above, and

   (c) any person who is or may become beneficially entitled to a significant interest in the shares ;

and any such person is an associate of the trustees.

(7) Where shares of a company are comprised in the estate of a deceased person, then in relation to that company the deceased's personal representatives are associates of any person who is or may become beneficially entitled to a significant interest in the shares, and any such person is an associate of the personal representatives.

(8) Where one person is accustomed to act on the directions of another in relation to the affairs of a company, then in relation to that company the two persons are associates of one another.

(9) Sub-paragraph (6) above shall not apply to shares held on trusts which—

(a) relate exclusively to an exempt approved scheme as defined in Chapter II of Part II of the Finance Act 1970, or

(b) are exclusively for the benefit of the employees, or the employees and directors, of the company referred to in that sub-paragraph or of companies in a group to which that company belongs, or their dependants (and are not wholly or mainly for the benefit of directors or their relatives);

and for the purposes of this sub-paragraph " group " means a company which has one or more 51 per cent. subsidiaries, together with those subsidiaries.

(10) For the purposes of sub-paragraphs (6) and (7) above a person's interest is significant if its value exceeds 5 per cent. of the value of all the property held on the trusts or, as the case may be, comprised in the estate concerned, excluding any property in which he is not and cannot become beneficially entitled to an interest.

15.—(1) Any question whether a person is connected with a company shall be determined for the purposes of this Schedule in accordance with the following provisions of this paragraph.

(2) A person is connected with a company if he directly or indirectly possesses or is entitled to acquire more than 30 per cent. of—

(a) the issued ordinary share capital of the company, or

(b) the loan capital and issued share capital of the company, or

(c) the voting power in the company.

(3) Where a person—

(a) acquired or became entitled to acquire loan capital of a company in the ordinary course of a business carried on by him, being a business which includes the lending of money, and

(b) takes no part in the management or conduct of the company,

his interest in that loan capital shall be disregarded for the purposes of sub-paragraph (2) above.

(4) A person is connected with a company if he directly or indirectly possesses or is entitled to acquire such rights as would, in the event of the winding up of the company or in any other circumstances, entitle him to receive more than 30 per cent. of the assets of the company which would then be available for distribution to equity holders of the company; and for the purposes of this sub-paragraph—

(a) the persons who are equity holders of the company, and

(b) the percentage of the assets of the company to which a person would be entitled,

shall be determined in accordance with paragraphs 1 and 3 of
Schedule 12 to the Finance Act 1973, taking references in paragraph
3 to the first company as references to an equity holder and references
to a winding up as including references to any other circumstances
in which assets of the company are available for distribution to its
equity holders.

(5) A person is connected with a company if he has control of it.

(6) References in this paragraph to the loan capital of a company
are references to any debt incurred by the company—

    (*a*) for any money borrowed or capital assets acquired by the
        company, or

    (*b*) for any right to receive income created in favour of the com-
        pany, or

    (*c*) for consideration the value of which to the company was (at
        the time when the debt was incurred) substantially less than
        the amount of the debt (including any premium thereon).

(7) For the purposes of this paragraph a person shall be treated
as entitled to acquire anything which he is entitled to acquire at
a future date or will at a future date be entitled to acquire.

(8) For the purposes of this paragraph a person shall be assumed
to have the rights or powers of his associates as well as his own.

16.—(1) In section 53 of this Act and in this Schedule—

    " control " has the meaning assigned to it by section 534 of the
        Taxes Act ;

    " holding company " means a company whose business (disre-
        garding any trade carried on by it) consists wholly or
        mainly of the holding of shares or securities of one or more
        companies which are its 75 per cent. subsidiaries ;

    " personal representatives " means persons responsible for ad-
        ministering the estate of a deceased person ;

    " quoted company " means a company whose shares (or any
        class of whose shares) are listed in the official list of a
        stock exchange ;

    " shares " includes stock ;

    " trade " does not include dealing in shares, securities, land or
        futures and " trading activities " shall be construed accord-
        ingly ;

    " trading company " means a company whose business consists
        wholly or mainly of the carrying on of a trade or trades ;

    " trading group " means a group the business of whose members,
        taken together, consists wholly or mainly of the carrying
        on of a trade or trades, and for this purpose " group "
        means a company which has one or more 75 per cent.
        subsidiaries together with those subsidiaries ;

    " unquoted company " means a company which is neither a
        quoted company nor a 51 per cent. subsidiary of a quoted
        company.

(2) References in section 53 of this Act and in this Schedule to the owner of shares are references to the beneficial owner except where the shares are held on trusts (other than bare trusts) or are comprised in the estate of a deceased person, and in such a case are references to the trustees or, as the case may be, to the deceased's personal representatives.

(3) References in section 53 of this Act and in this Schedule to a payment made by a company include references to anything else that is, or would but for section 53 be, a distribution.

SCHEDULE 10

INCOME TAX: MAINTENANCE FUNDS FOR HISTORIC BUILDINGS

Finance Act 1977

1.—(1) Section 38 of the Finance Act 1977 shall be amended as follows.

(2) In subsection (1) for the words from "the Treasury" to "1976" there shall be substituted the words "a direction has effect under section 93 of the Finance Act 1982".

(3) For subsection (5) there shall be substituted—
" (5) Where—
(*a*) for part of a year of assessment a direction under the said section 93 has effect and circumstances obtain by virtue of which income arising from property comprised in the settlement is treated as income of a settlor under the said Part XVI ; and
(*b*) for the remainder of that year either no such direction has effect, or no such circumstances obtain, or both,
the foregoing provisions of this section shall apply as if each of those parts were a separate year of assessment and separate elections may be made accordingly."

Finance Act 1980

2.—(1) Section 52 of the Finance Act 1980 shall be amended as follows.

(2) In subsection (1)—
(*a*) for the words from "the Treasury" to "1976" there shall be substituted the words "a direction has effect under section 93 of the Finance Act 1982" ;
(*b*) after paragraph (*b*) there shall be inserted the words "or (*c*) the direction ceases to have effect".

(3) In subsections (2) and (3) for the words "subsection (3)(*a*)(i) or (ii) of the said section 84" there shall be substituted the words "subsection (3)(*a*)(i) or (ii) of the said section 93".

(4) In subsection (7) for the words from "if" to the end there shall be substituted the words "if either—
(*a*) it ceases to be comprised in the first-mentioned settlement and becomes comprised in the other settlement in circum-

stances such that by virtue of paragraph 3(1) of Schedule
16 to the Finance Act 1982 there is (or, but for paragraph
3(4), there would be) no charge to capital transfer tax in
respect of the property, or

(*b*) both immediately before and immediately after the transfer
it is property in respect of which a direction has effect
under section 93 of that Act.".

3.—(1) Section 53 of the Finance Act 1980 shall be amended as
follows.

(2) In subsection (1)—

(*a*) for the words " subsection (3) of section 84 of the Finance
Act 1976 " there shall be substituted the words " subsection (3) of section 93 of the Finance Act 1982 " ;

(*b*) in paragraph (*a*) for the words " section 84 " there shall be
substituted the words " section 93 " ; and

(*c*) at the beginning of paragraph (*b*) there shall be inserted the
words " while such a direction has effect ".

(3) In subsection (2) after the word "shall " there shall be inserted
the words " (while such a direction has effect) ".

(4) In subsection (4) for the words from " if " to the end there shall
be substituted the words " if either—

(*a*) it becomes comprised in another settlement in circumstances
such that by virtue of paragraph 3(1) of Schedule 16 to the
Finance Act 1982 there is (or, but for paragraph 3(4), there
would be) no charge to capital transfer tax in respect of
the property so ceasing, or

(*b*) both immediately before and immediately after its so ceasing
it is property in respect of which a direction has effect under
section 93 of that Act."

SCHEDULE 11

Capital Allowances for Assets Leased Outside the United Kingdom

Interpretation

1. In this Schedule " the principal section " means section 70 of
this Act.

Separate pooling of writing-down allowances

2. In any case where section 44 of the Finance Act 1971 has
effect as mentioned in paragraphs (*a*) to (*e*) of subsection (2) of the
principal section, section 44 shall apply separately with respect to
expenditure falling within subsection (1) of the principal section and
with respect to other expenditure.

Recovery of excess relief

3.—(1) In relation to expenditure falling within subsection (1) of
the principal section, section 66 of the Finance Act 1980 shall apply
subject to the following modifications :—

(*a*) any reference in that section to machinery or plant (or a
new ship) being used otherwise than for a qualifying pur-

2

pose shall be construed as a reference to its being used as mentioned in paragraphs (*a*) and (*b*) of subsection (3) of the principal section ; and

(*b*) any reference in section 66 to a first-year allowance shall be construed as including a reference to a writing-down allowance of an amount determined without regard to subsection (2) of the principal section ; and

(*c*) the reference in subsection (1)(*b*) of section 66 to section 44 of the Finance Act 1971, as it has effect in accordance with section 65 of the Finance Act 1980, shall be construed as including a reference to section 44 as it has effect as mentioned in paragraphs (*b*) to (*e*) of subsection (2) of the principal section ; and

(*d*) in determining the amount of any excess relief under section 66 in a case where that section had previously applied, account shall be taken of the relief already recovered.

(2) If subsection (7) of section 66 of the Finance Act 1980 has already applied in relation to expenditure on a new ship before subsection (1) of the principal section applied to that expenditure, then, on the subsequent application of the said subsection (7) by virtue of sub-paragraph (1)(*a*) above, paragraph (*b*) of that subsection shall not again apply.

4.—(1) Subject to sub-paragraph (3) below, the provisions of sub-paragraph (2) below apply where—

(*a*) by virtue of subsection (5) of the principal section any amount falls to be treated as if it were a balancing charge, and

(*b*) the person on whom the balancing charge is, by virtue of that subsection, to be made acquired the machinery or plant in question as a result of a transaction which was, or a series of transactions each of which was, between connected persons, and

(*c*) a first-year allowance, a balancing allowance, or a writing-down allowance in respect of expenditure on the provision of that machinery or plant has been made to any of those persons.

(2) Where this sub-paragraph applies—

(*a*) subsection (5) of the principal section shall have effect as if it referred to the allowances specified in sub-paragraph (1)(*c*) above ; and

(*b*) for the purposes of that subsection any consideration paid or received on a disposal of the machinery or plant between connected persons shall be disregarded ; and

(*c*) if a balancing allowance or balancing charge is made in respect of the machinery or plant, there shall be made such adjustments of the relief falling to be taken into account by virtue of paragraph (*a*) above as are just and reasonable in the circumstances.

(3) Sub-paragraph (2) above does not apply where section 154(2), SCH. 11
section 155(1), or section 255(2) of the Taxes Act or sub-paragraph
(*a*) or sub-paragraph (*b*) of paragraph 13 of Schedule 8 to the Fin- 1971 c. 68.
ance Act 1971 (succession to trades) applied on the occasion of the
transaction or transactions referred to in sub-paragraph (1)(*b*).

(4) Section 533 of the Taxes Act (connected persons) applies for the
purposes of this paragraph.

Information

5.—(1) The obligation to give notice by virtue of subsection (2)
or subsection (3) of section 67 of the Finance Act 1980 where 1980 c. 48.
machinery or plant becomes used otherwise than for a qualifying
purpose shall arise a second time where machinery or plant which
has been used otherwise than for a qualifying purpose but not as
mentioned in paragraphs (*a*) and (*b*) of subsection (3) of the principal section subsequently becomes used as mentioned in those
paragraphs.

(2) In the case of any expenditure in respect of which a first-
year allowance has not been made but a writing-down allowance
of an amount determined without regard to subsection (2) of the
principal section has been or may be made, then—

(*a*) any reference in subsections (2), (3) and (4) of section 67 of
the Finance Act 1980 to a first-year allowance shall be construed as a reference to a writing-down allowance of an
amount so determined ; and

(*b*) any reference in those subsections to the use of machinery
or plant otherwise than for a qualifying purpose shall be
construed as a reference to the use of machinery or plant
as mentioned in paragraphs (*a*) and (*b*) of subsection (3)
of the principal section.

Joint lessees

6.—(1) The provisions of this paragraph have effect where machinery or plant is leased to two or more persons jointly and at least
one of the joint lessees is a person falling within paragraphs (*a*) and
(*b*) of subsection (1) of the principal section (in this paragraph referred to as a " non-resident lessee ").

(2) Where this paragraph applies, any reference in section 68 of
the Finance Act 1980 to the requisite period shall be construed in
accordance with subsection (3) of the principal section, whether or
not there is also a joint lessee who is not a non-resident lessee.

(3) If the circumstances are such that no first-year allowance has
been or may be made in respect of any part of the expenditure on
the provision of the machinery or plant in question, the principal
section shall apply in relation to that expenditure as if all the joint
lessees were non-resident lessees.

(4) Where, by virtue of subsection (3), subsection (4) or subsection
(5) of section 68 of the Finance Act 1980 (cases of joint lessees
where first-year allowances may be or have been made) section 44 of

the Finance Act 1971 has effect (directly or through the operation
of section 66 of the Finance Act 1980) in relation to the whole or any
part of the expenditure on the machinery or plant in question, it
shall have effect, in accordance with subsection (2) of the principal
section, as if that expenditure were expenditure falling within subsection (1) of that section.

Section 76.

SCHEDULE 12

Capital Allowances for Dwelling-Houses Let on Assured Tenancies

Initial allowances

1.—(1) Subject to the provisions of this Schedule, where an approved body incurs capital expenditure on the construction of a
building which is to be or to include a qualifying dwelling-house,
then, for the chargeable period related to the incurring of that expenditure an allowance (in this Schedule referred to as an " initial
allowance ") shall be made to that body in respect of each qualifying
dwelling-house to be comprised in the building.

(2) An initial allowance in respect of a qualifying dwelling-house
shall be of an amount equal to three-quarters of the capital expenditure appropriate to that dwelling-house.

(3) No initial allowance shall be made in respect of any expenditure
if, when the dwelling-house to which it relates comes to be used, it is
not a qualifying dwelling-house ; and where an initial allowance has
been granted in respect of any expenditure otherwise than in accordance with the provisions of this paragraph, all such assessments shall
be made as are necessary to secure that effect is given to those provisions.

(4) For the purposes of this Schedule, the capital expenditure
appropriate to a dwelling-house shall be determined as follows : —

  (*a*) if the building concerned consists of a single qualifying dwel-
      ling-house, then, subject to the relevant limit, the whole
      of the capital expenditure referred to in sub-paragraph (1)
      above is appropriate to that dwelling-house ; and

  (*b*) in the case of a dwelling-house which forms part of a build-
      ing, the capital expenditure appropriate to it is, subject to
      the relevant limit, the aggregate of—

      (i) that proportion of the capital expenditure referred
      to in sub-paragraph (1) above which is properly attribu-
      table to the construction of that dwelling-house ; and

      (ii) where there are common parts of the building, such
      proportion of the capital expenditure on those common
      parts as it is just and reasonable to attribute to the dwel-
      ling-house and as does not exceed one-tenth of that pro-
      portion of the capital expenditure referred to in paragraph
      (i) above ;

and in this Schedule " the relevant limit " means £60,000, if the
dwelling-house is in Greater London, and £40,000 if it is elsewhere

(5) In sub-paragraph (4) above " common parts ", in relation to a SCH. 12 building, means common parts of the building which—

(*a*) are not intended to be in separate occupation (whether for domestic, commercial or other purposes) ; and

(*b*) are intended to be of benefit to some or all of the qualifying dwelling-houses included in the building ;

and the capital expenditure on any such parts of the building is so much of the expenditure referred to in sub-paragraph (1) above as it is just and reasonable to attribute to those parts.

Writing-down allowances

2.—(1) Subject to the provisions of this Schedule, where—

(*a*) an approved body or a body which has been an approved body is, at the end of a chargeable period or its basis period, entitled to an interest in a building, and

(*b*) at the end of that chargeable period or its basis period, the building is or includes a qualifying dwelling-house or two or more qualifying dwelling-houses, and

(*c*) that interest is the relevant interest in relation to the capital expenditure incurred on the construction on that building,

an allowance (in this Schedule referred to as " a writing-down allowance ") shall be made to that body for that chargeable period in respect of the dwelling-house or, as the case may be, each dwelling-house falling within paragraph (*b*) above.

(2) The writing-down allowance in respect of a dwelling-house shall be equal to one twenty-fifth of the capital expenditure which is appropriate to that dwelling-house, except that for a chargeable period of less than a year that fraction shall be proportionately reduced.

(3) If, in the case of a building which is or includes a qualifying dwelling-house,—

(*a*) the interest which is the relevant interest in relation to any expenditure is sold, and

(*b*) the sale is an event to which paragraph 4(1) below applies,

then (subject to any further adjustment under this sub-paragraph on a later sale) the writing-down allowance in respect of that dwelling-house for any chargeable period, if that chargeable period or its basis period ends after the time of the sale, shall be the residue, as defined in paragraph 7(1) below, of that expenditure immediately after the sale, reduced in the proportion (if it is less than one) which the length of the chargeable period bears to the part unexpired at the date of the sale of the period of 25 years beginning with the time when the building was first used.

(4) Notwithstanding anything in the preceeding provisions of this paragraph, in no case shall the amount of a writing-down allowance made to a body for any chargeable period in respect of any expenditure exceed what, apart from the writing-off falling to be made

by reason of the making of that allowance, would be the residue of that expenditure at the end of that chargeable period of its basis period.

Qualifying dwelling-house

3.—(1) In this Schedule " qualifying dwelling-house " means, subject to the following provisions of this paragraph, a dwelling-house let on a tenancy which is for the time being an assured tenancy, 1980 c. 51. within the meaning of section 56 of the Housing Act 1980.

(2) Without prejudice to section 57 of the Housing Act 1980 (by virtue of which certain tenancies continue to be treated as assured tenancies notwithstanding that the landlord has ceased to be an approved body by reason of a variation in the description of bodies for the time being approved) a dwelling-house which has been a qualifying dwelling-house by virtue of sub-paragraph (1) above shall be regarded as a qualifying dwelling-house at any time when—

(*a*) it is for the time being subject to regulated tenancy or a housing association tenancy ; and

(*b*) the landlord under that tenancy either is an approved body or was an approved body but has ceased to be such for any reason.

(3) Notwithstanding that a dwelling-house is let as mentioned in sub-paragraph (1) or sub-paragraph (2) above, it is not a qualifying dwelling-house for the purposes of this Schedule—

(*a*) unless the landlord is for the time being entitled to the relevant interest in the dwelling-house or is the person who incurred the capital expenditure on the construction of the building in which the dwelling-house is comprised ; or

(*b*) if the landlord is a housing association which is approved for the purposes of section 341 of the Taxes Act (co-operative housing associations) or is a self-build society, 1974 c. 44. within the meaning of Part I of the Housing Act 1974 ; or

(*c*) if the landlord and the tenant are connected persons ; or

(*d*) if the tenant is a director of a company which is or is connected with the landlord ; or

(*e*) if the landlord is a close company and the tenant is, for the purposes of Chapter III of Part XI of the Taxes Act, a participator in that company or an associate of such a participator ; or

(*f*) if the tenancy is entered into as part of an arrangement between the landlords (or owners) of different dwelling houses under which one landlord takes a person as a tenant in circumstances where, if that person was the tenant of a dwelling-house let by the other landlord, that dwelling-house would not be a qualifying dwelling-house by virtue of any of paragraphs (*c*) to (*e*) above ;

and section 533 of the Taxes Act (connected persons) applies for the purposes of this sub-paragraph.

(4) In this paragraph "regulated tenancy" and "housing associa- Sᴄʜ. 12
tion tenancy" have the same meaning as in the Rent Act 1977.   1977 c. 42.

Balancing allowances and balancing charges

4.—(1) Where any capital expenditure has been incurred on the
construction of such a building as is referred to in paragraph 1(1)
above and any of the following events occur while a dwelling-house
comprised in that building is a qualifying dwelling-house, that is to
say—

    (*a*) the relevant interest in the dwelling-house is sold, or

    (*b*) that interest, being a leasehold interest, comes to an end
        otherwise than on the person entitled to it aquiring the
        interest which is reversionary on it, or

    (*c*) the dwelling-house is demolished or destroyed or, without
        being demolished or destroyed, ceases altogether to be
        used,

then, subject to sub-paragraph (2) below, for the chargeable period
related to that event an allowance or charge (in this Schedule referred to as a "balancing allowance" or a "balancing charge") shall,
in the circumstances mentioned below, be made to or, as the case
may be, on the person entitled to the relevant interest immediately
before that event occurs.

(2) No balancing allowance or balancing charge shall be made
by reason of any event occurring more than twenty-five years after
the dwelling-house was first used.

(3) Subject to paragraph 5 below, where there are no sale, insurance, salvage or compensation moneys, or where the residue
of the expenditure immediately before the event exceeds those moneys,
a balancing allowance shall be made and the amount of it shall
be the amount of that residue or, as the case may be, of the excess
of that residue over those moneys.

(4) Subject to paragraph 5 below, if the sale, insurance, salvage
or compensation moneys exceed the residue, if any, of the expenditure immediately before the event, a balancing charge shall be
made, and the amount on which it is made shall be an equal amount
to the excess or, where the residue is nil, to those moneys.

(5) The provisions of section 78 of and Schedule 7 to the Capital 1968 c. 3.
Allowances Act 1968 (special provisions as to certain sales) apply for
the purposes of this Schedule as they apply in relation to the sale of
an industrial building and as if—

    (*a*) any reference in those provisions to Part I of that Act
        included a reference to this Schedule ; and

    (*b*) for the words in sub-paragraph (2)(*a*) of paragraph 4 of that
        Schedule following "the case of" there were substituted
        the words "a qualifying dwelling-house, the residue of the
        expenditure immediately before the sale, computed in accord-
        ance with paragraph 7 of Schedule 12 to the Finance Act
        1982" ; and

(*c*) for paragraphs (*a*) and (*b*) of sub-paragraph (3) of paragraph 4 of that Schedule there were substituted the words " both the seller and the buyer are at the time of the sale approved bodies, as defined in section 56(4) of the Housing Act 1980 ".

(6) For the purposes of this Schedule, any transfer of the relevant interest in a dwelling-house, otherwise than by way of sale, shall be treated as a sale of that interest for a price other than that which it would have fetched if sold on the open market ; and if Schedule 7 to the Capital Allowances Act 1968 would not, apart from this sub-paragraph have effect in relation to a transfer treated as a sale by virtue of this sub-paragraph, that Schedule shall have effect in relation to it as if it were a sale falling within paragraph 1(1)(*a*) of that Schedule.

(7) Notwithstanding anything in the preceding provisions of this paragraph (or in paragraph 5 below), in no case shall the amount on which a balancing charge is made on any person in respect of any expenditure on the construction of a dwelling-house comprised in a building exceed the amount of the initial allowance, if any, made to him in respect of the expenditure appropriate to that dwelling-house together with the amount of any writing-down allowances made to him in respect of that expenditure for chargeable periods which end on or before the date of the event giving rise to the charge or of which the basis periods ends on or before that date.

5.—(1) If, in a case where paragraph 4(1) above applies, a dwelling-house which had been a qualifying dwelling-house was not, for any part of the relevant period, such a dwelling-house, the provisions of this paragraph shall have effect instead of sub-paragraphs (3) and (4) of paragraph 4 above.

(2) Subject to sub-paragraph (4) below, where the sale, insurance, salvage or compensation moneys are not less than the capital expenditure appropriate to the dwelling-house, a balancing charge shall be made and the amount on which it is made shall be an amount equal to the allowances given.

(3) Subject to sub-paragraph (4) below, where there are no sale, insurance, salvage or compensation moneys or where those moneys are less than the capital expenditure appropriate to the dwelling-house, then—

(*a*) if the adjusted net cost of the dwelling-house exceeds the allowances given, a balancing allowance shall be made and the amount thereof shall be an amount equal to the excess ;

(*b*) if the adjusted net cost of the dwelling-house is less than the allowances given, a balancing charge shall be made and the amount on which it is made shall be an amount equal to the shortfall.

(4) No balancing charge or allowance shall be made under this paragraph on the occasion of a sale if, by virtue of paragraph 4 of Schedule 7 to the Capital Allowances Act 1968, as applied by para-

graph 4(5) above, the dwelling-house is treated as having been sold   SCH. 12
for a sum equal to the residue of the expenditure before sale.

(5) In this paragraph—

" the relevant period " means the period beginning at the time
when the dwelling-house was first used for any purpose and
ending with the event giving rise to the balancing allowance or balancing charge, except that where there has been
a sale of the dwelling-house after that time and before
that event the relevant period shall begin on the day
following that sale or, if there has been more than one
such sale, the last such sale ;

" the capital expenditure " means—

(a) where paragraph (b) of this definition does not
apply, the capital expenditure incurred (or by virtue of
paragraph 8 below deemed to have been incurred) on the
construction of the dwelling-house ;

(b) where the person to or on whom the balancing
allowance or balancing charge falls to be made is not
the person who incurred (or is deemed to have incurred)
that expenditure the residue of that expenditure at the
beginning of the relevant period,

together (in either case) with any amount to be added to
the residue of that expenditure by virtue of paragraph 7(9)
below ;

" the allowances given " means the allowance referred to in
paragraph 4(7) above ;

" the adjusted net cost " means—

(a) where there are no sale, insurance, salvage or compensation moneys, the capital expenditure appropriate
to the dwelling-house ; and

(b) where those moneys are less than that expenditure,
the amount by which they are less,

reduced (in either case) in the proportion that the part or the
aggregate of the parts, of the relevant period for which the
building is a qualifying dwelling-house bears to the whole
of that period.

6.—(1) If a dwelling-houses ceases to be a qualifying dwelling-
house otherwise than by reason of a sale or transfer of the relevant
interest in it, that relevant interest shall be treated for the purposes
of this Schedule as having been sold, at the time the dwelling-house
ceases to be a qualifying dwelling-house, for the price which it would
have fetched if sold in the open market.

(2) For the purposes of this Schedule, a dwelling-house shall not
be regarded as ceasing altogether to be used by reason that it falls
temporarily out of use, and where, immediately before any period
of temporary disuse, it is a qualifying dwelling-house, it shall be
regarded as continuing to be a qualifying dwelling-house during the
period of temporary disuse.

Writing off of expenditure and meaning of " residue of expenditure "

7.—(1) Any expenditure appropriate to a qualifying dwelling-house shall be treated for the purposes of this Schedule as written off to the extent and as at the times specified below, and the references in this Schedule to the residue of any such expenditure shall be construed accordingly.

(2) Where an initial allowance is made in respect of a qualifying dwelling-house, the amount of that allowance shall be treated as written off as at the time when the qualifying dwelling-house is first used.

(3) Where, by reason of the whole or part of a building being at any time a qualifying dwelling-house, a writing-down allowance is made for any chargeable period in respect of the expenditure, the amount of that allowance shall, subject to sub-paragraph (4) below, be treated as written off as at that time.

(4) Where, at a time which is material for the purposes of sub-paragraph (3) above, an event occurs which gives rise or may give rise to a balancing allowance or balancing charge, the amount directed to be treated as written off by that sub-paragraph as at that time shall be taken into account in computing the residue of that expenditure immediately before that event for the purpose of determining whether any and if so what balancing allowance or balancing charge is to be made.

(5) If, for any period or periods between the time when the whole or part of a building was first used for any purpose and the time at which the residue of the expenditure falls to be ascertained, the building or part, as the case may be, has not been a qualifying dwelling-house, there shall in ascertaining that residue be treated as having been previously written off in respect of the said period or periods amounts equal to writing-down allowances made for chargeable periods of a total length equal thereto at such rate or rates as would have been appropriate having regard to any sale on which paragraph 2(3) above operated.

(6) Where, on the occasion of a sale, a balancing allowance is made in respect of the expenditure, there shall be treated as written off as at the time of the sale the amount by which the residue of the expenditure before the sale exceeds the net proceeds of the sale.

(7) Where, on the occasion of a sale, a balancing charge is made in respect of the expenditure, the residue of the expenditure shall be deemed for the purposes of this Schedule to be increased as at the time of the sale by the amount on which the charge is made.

(8) Where, on the occasion of a sale, a balancing charge is made under paragraph 5(3)(*b*) above in respect of the expenditure and, apart from this sub-paragraph, the residue of the expenditure immediately after the sale would by virtue of sub-paragraph (7) above be deemed to be greater than the net proceeds of the sale, the residue immediately after the sale shall be deemed for the purposes of this Schedule to be equal to the net proceeds.

(9) Where a dwelling-house is demolished, and the demolition gives rise, or might give rise, to a balancing allowance or charge under this Schedule to or on the person incurring the cost of demolition, the net cost to him of the demolition (that is to say the excess, if any, of the cost of the demolition over any moneys received for the remains of the property) shall be added for the purposes of this Schedule to the residue, immediately before the demolition, of the expenditure appropriate to the dwelling-house; and if this sub-paragraph applies to the net cost to a person of the demolition of any property, the cost or net cost shall not be treated, for the purpose of this Schedule, as expenditure incurred in respect of any other property by which that property is replaced.

Buildings bought unused

8.—(1) Subject to sub-paragraph (2) below, where expenditure is incurred on the construction of such a building as is referred to in paragraph 1(1) above and the relevant interest in that building is sold before any of the dwelling-houses comprised in it are used,—

(*a*) the expenditure actually incurred on the construction of the building shall be left out of account for the purposes of the preceding provisions of this Schedule; but

(*b*) the person who buys that interest shall be deemed for those purposes to have incurred, on the date when the purchase price becomes payable, expenditure on the construction of the building equal to the expenditure actually incurred or to the net price paid by him for that interest, whichever is the less.

(2) Where the relevant interest in such a building as is referred to in paragraph 1(1) above is sold more than once before any of the dwelling-houses comprised in it is used, the provisions of sub-paragraph (1)(*b*) above shall have effect only in relation to the last of those sales.

(3) Where the expenditure incurred on the construction of such a building as is referred to in paragraph 1(1) above was incurred by a person carrying on a trade which consists, as to the whole or any part thereof, in the construction of buildings with a view to their sale, and, before any of the dwelling-houses comprised in it is used, he sells the relevant interest in the building in the course of that trade, or, as the case may be, of that part of that trade, paragraph (*b*) of sub-paragraph (1) above shall have effect subject to the following modifications—

(*a*) if that sale is the only sale of the relevant interest before any of the dwelling-houses comprised in the building is used that paragraph shall have effect as if the words "the expenditure actually incurred or to" and the words "whichever is the less" were omitted, and

(*b*) in any other case, that paragraph shall have effect as if the reference to the expenditure actually incurred on the construction of the building were a reference to the price paid on that sale.

Manner of making allowances and charges

9.—(1) Any allowance under this Schedule shall be made to a person by way of discharge or repayment of tax and shall be available primarily against the following income, that is to say—

    (*a*) income taxed under Schedule A in respect of any premises which at any time in the chargeable period consist of a qualifying dwelling-house ; or

    (*b*) income which is subject of a balancing charge under this Schedule.

(2) Effect shall be given to a balancing charge to be made on a person—

    (*a*) if it is a charge to income tax, by making the charge under Case VI of Schedule D,

    (*b*) if it is a charge to corporation tax, by treating the amount on which the charge is to be made as income of the description in sub-paragraph (1)(*a*) above.

Expenditure on repair of buildings

10. This Schedule shall have effect in relation to capital expenditure incurred by a person on repairs to any part of a building as if it were capital expenditure incurred by him in the construction for the first time of that part of the building.

Exclusion of double allowances

11. No allowance shall be made under this Schedule in respect of any expenditure on a building or in respect of a dwelling-house if for the same or any other chargeable period an allowance is or can be made under any provisions of Chapter V of Part I of the Capital Allowances Act 1968 (agricultural land or buildings) in respect of that expenditure or that dwelling-house.

1968 c. 3.

Holding over by lessee etc.

12.—(1) Where the relevant interest in relation to the capital expenditure incurred on the construction of a building is an interest under a lease, this Schedule shall have effect subject to the following provisions of this paragraph, and in those provisions—

    (*a*) except in sub-paragraph (5), any reference to a lessor or lessee is a reference to the lessor or lessee under that lease ; and

    (*b*) in sub-paragraph (5) the reference to the first lease is a reference to that lease.

(2) Where, with the consent of the lessor, a lessee of any building remains in possession thereof after the termination of the lease without a new lease being granted to him, that lease shall be deemed for the purposes of this Schedule to continue so long as he remains in possession as aforesaid.

(3) Where, on the termination of a lease, a new lease is granted to the lessee in pursuance of an option available to him under the terms of the first lease, the provisions of this Schedule shall have effect as if the second lease were a continuation of the first lease.

(4) Where, on the termination of a lease, the lessor pays any sum
to the lessee in respect of a building comprised in the lease, the
provisions of this Schedule shall have effect as if the lease had come
to an end by reason of the surrender thereof in consideration of the
payment.

(5) Where, on the termination of a lease, another lease in granted
to a different lessee and, in connection with the transaction, that
lessee pays a sum to the person who was the lessee under the first
lease, the provisions of this Schedule shall have effect as if both
leases were the same lease and there had been an assignment thereof
by the lessee under the first lease to the lessee under the second lease
in consideration of the payment.

Meaning of " the relevant interest "

13.—(1) Subject to the provisions of this paragraph, in this Schedule " the relevant interest " means,—

(*a*) in relation to any expenditure incurred on the construction
of a building, the interest in that building to which the
person who incurred the expenditure was entitled when he
incurred it ; and

(*b*) in relation to a dwelling-house comprised in such a building as is referred to in paragraph 1(1) above, that interest,
to the extent that it subsists in the dwelling-house, which is
the relevant interest in relation to the capital expenditure
incurred on the construction of that building.

(2) Where, when it incurs expenditure on the construction of a building, a body is entitled to two or more interests in the building and
one of those interests is an interest which is reversionary on all the
others, that interest shall be the relevant interest for the purposes of
this Schedule.

(3) An interest shall not cease to be the relevant interest for the
purposes of this Schedule by reason of the creation of any lease or
other interest to which that interest is subject, and where the relevant interest is a leasehold interest and is extinguished by reason
of the surrender thereof or on the body entitled thereto acquiring
the interest which is reversionary on it, the interest into which that
leasehold interest merges shall thereupon become the relevant interest.

Application of provisions of Capital Allowances Act 1968

14. The following provisions of the Capital Allowances Act 1968, 1968 c. 3.
namely—

section 71 to 74 (income tax and corporation tax allowances and
charges),

section 76 (companies not resident in the United Kingdom),

subsections (1) to (3) of section 77 (apportionment of consideration etc.),

section 81 (procedure on apportionments),

subsections (1) and (3) of section 82 (interpretation of certain
references to expenditure etc.),

section 84 (subsidies),

section 86 (meaning of "sale, insurance, salvage or compensation moneys"), and

subsections (1), (3) and (6) of section 87 (interpretation of Part I),

shall apply for the purposes of this Schedule as they apply for the purposes of Part I of that Act and, accordingly, any reference in those provisions to Part I of that Act shall include a reference to this Schedule.

Interpretation

15.—(1) In this Schedule—

"approved body" has the meaning given by section 56(4) of the Housing Act 1980;

"building", except where the context otherwise requires, includes part of a building;

"dwelling-house" except where the context otherwise requires, has the same meaning as in the Rent Act 1977;

"expenditure appropriate to a dwelling-house" has the meaning given by paragraph 1(4) above; and

"qualifying dwelling-house" has the meaning given by paragraph 3 above.

(2) References in this Schedule to expenditure incurred on the construction of a building do not include any expenditure incurred on the acquisition of, or of rights in or over any land.

(3) A person who has incurred expenditure on the construction of a building shall be deemed, for the purposes of any provision of this Schedule referring to his interest therein at the time when the expenditure was incurred, to have had the same interest therein as if the construction thereof had been completed at that time.

(4) Without prejudice to any of the other provisions of this Schedule relating to the apportionment of sale, insurance, salvage or compensation moneys, the sum paid on the sale of the relevant interest in a building or structure, or any other sale, insurance, salvage or compensation moneys payable in respect of any building or structure, shall, for the purposes of this Schedule, be deemed to be reduced by an amount equal to so much thereof, as, on a just apportionment, is attributable to assets representing expenditure other than expenditure in respect of which an allowance can be made under this Schedule.

SCHEDULE 13

THE INDEXATION ALLOWANCE

PART I

GENERAL

Part disposals

1. For the purpose of determining the indexation allowance (if any) on the occasion of a part disposal of an asset, the apportionment under section 35 of the Capital Gains Tax Act 1979 of the sums

which make up the relevant allowable expenditure shall be effected before the application of section 87 of this Act and, accordingly, in relation to a part disposal—

(a) references in section 87 to an item of expenditure shall be construed as references to that part of that item which is so apportioned for the purposes of the computation under Chapter II of Part II of that Act of the gross gain on the part disposal ; and

(b) no indexation allowance shall be determined by reference to the part of each item of relevant allowable expenditure which is apportioned to the property which remains undisposed of.

Disposals on a no-gain/no-loss basis

2.—(1) This paragraph applies to a disposal of an asset which falls within subsection (1)(a) of section 86 of this Act if, by virtue of any enactment other than subsection (5)(b) of that section or any provision of this Schedule, the disposal is treated as one on which neither a gain nor a loss accrues to the person making the disposal.

(2) In relation to a disposal to which this paragraph applies—

" the transferor " means the person making the disposal of the asset concerned ; and

" the transferee " means the person acquiring the asset on the disposal.

(3) On a disposal to which this paragraph applies and which falls within subsection (1)(b) of section 86 of this Act, the amount of the consideration shall be calculated for the purposes of the Capital Gains Tax Act 1979 on the assumptions that—

(a) the disposal is one to which that section applies ; and

(b) on the disposal a gross gain accrues to the transferor which is equal to the indexation allowance on the disposal ;

and, accordingly, the disposal shall be one on which, after taking account of the indexation allowance, neither a gain nor a loss accrues.

(4) Except as provided by paragraph 3 below, for the purposes of the application of sections 86 and 87 of this Act there shall be disregarded so much of any enactment as provides that, on the subsequent disposal by the transferee of the asset acquired by him on a disposal to which this paragraph applies, the transferor's acquisition of the asset is to be treated as the transferee's acquisition of it.

Subsequent disposals following no-gain/no-loss disposals

3.—(1) The provisions of this paragraph apply in relation to a disposal by the transferee of the asset acquired by him on a disposal to which paragraph 2 above applies ; and in this paragraph—

(a) " the initial disposal " means the disposal to which paragraph 2 above applies ;

(*b*) " the subsequent disposal " means the disposal to which this paragraph applies ; and

(*c*) " the transferor " and " the transferee " have the same meaning as in paragraph 2 above.

(2) If the subsequent disposal is one on which a loss accrues (and, accordingly, is one to which section 86 of this Act does not apply) then, for the purposes of the Capital Gains Tax Act 1979, the amount of that loss shall be taken to be reduced by—

(*a*) an amount equal to the indexation allowance (if any) on the initial disposal ; or

(*b*) such an amount as will secure that, on the subsequent disposal, neither a gain nor a loss accrues,

whichever is the less.

(3) The following provisions of this paragraph apply where the initial disposal is one to which paragraph 2 above applies by reason only of any of the following enactments applying to the initial disposal, namely—

(*a*) section 267 or section 273 of the Taxes Act ; or

(*b*) section 44 of the Capital Gains Tax Act 1979 ; or

(*c*) section 148 of this Act.

(4) For the purpose of calculating the indexation allowance (if any) to which the transferee is entitled on the subsequent disposal in a case where the initial disposal falls within sub-paragraph (3) above and the transferor made that disposal outside the qualifying period,—

(*a*) subsection (1) of section 86 of this Act shall have effect with the omission of paragraph (*b*) ; and

(*b*) the indexed rise in any item of relevant allowable expenditure falling within section 32(1)(*a*) of the Capital Gains Tax Act 1979 shall be calculated as if, in the definition of RI in the formula in section 87(2) of this Act, the words " which is the twelfth month after that " were omitted, and as if section 87(3)(*a*) of this Act were also omitted.

(5) For the purpose of calculating the indexation allowance (if any) to which the transferee is entitled on the subsequent disposal in a case where the initial disposal falls within sub-paragraph (3) above and the transferor made that disposal within the qualifying period (so that he was not entitled to any indexation allowance) the transferor's acquisition of the asset shall be treated as being the transferee's acquisition of it.

(6) If, in a case where sub-paragraph (5) above applies, the subsequent disposal is itself a disposal to which paragraph 2 above applies, that sub-paragraph shall again apply so that the original transferor's acquisition of the asset shall be treated as being the acquisition of it by the transferee under the subsequent disposal ; and so on if there is a series of disposals to which paragraph 2 above applies, all occurring within twelve months of the first such disposal.

Receipts etc. which are not treated as disposals but affect relevant allowable expenditure

4.—(1) This paragraph applies where, in determining the relevant allowable expenditure in relation to a disposal to which section 86 of this Act applies, account is required to be taken, as mentioned in subsection (3) of that section, of any provision of any enactment which, by reference to a relevant event occurring after the beginning of the qualifying period, reduces the whole or any part of an item of expenditure as mentioned in that subsection.

(2) For the purpose of determining, in a case where this paragraph applies, the indexation allowance (if any) to which the person making the disposal is entitled, no account shall in the first instance be taken of the provision referred to in sub-paragraph (1) above in calculating the indexed rise in the item of expenditure to which that provision applies but, from that indexed rise as so calculated, there shall be deducted a sum equal to the indexed rise (determined as for the purposes of the actual disposal) in a notional item of expenditure which—

(*a*) is equal to the amount of the reduction effected by the provision concerned ; and

(*b*) was incurred on the date of the relevant event referred to in sub-paragraph (1) above.

(3) In this paragraph "relevant event" means any event which does does not fall to be treated as a disposal for the purposes of the Capital Gains Tax Act 1979.

1979 c. 14.

Reorganisations, reconstructions etc.

5.—(1) This paragraph applies where,—

(*a*) by virtue of section 78 of the Capital Gains Tax Act 1979, on a reorganisation the original shares (taken as a single asset) and the new holding (taken as a single asset) fall to be treated as the same asset acquired as the original shares were acquired ; and

(*b*) on the reorganisation, a person gives or becomes liable to give any consideration for his new holding or any part of it.

(2) Where this paragraph applies, so much of the consideration referred to in sub-paragraph (1)(*b*) above as, on a disposal to which section 86 of this Act applies of the new holding, will, by virtue of section 79(1) of the Capital Gains Tax Act 1979, be treated as having been given for the original shares, shall be treated for the purposes of section 87 of this Act as an item of relevant allowable expenditure incurred not at the time the original shares were acquired but at the time the person concerned gave or became liable to give the consideration (and, accordingly, subsection (5) of section 87 of this Act shall not apply in relation to that item of expenditure).

(3) In the preceding provisions of this paragraph the expressions "reorganisation", "the original shares" and "the new holding" have the meanings assigned by section 77 of the Capital Gains Tax Act 1979 except that in a case where, by virtue of any other provision

SCH. 13   of Chapter II of Part IV of that Act (which extends to conversion of securities, company reconstructions and amalgamations etc.) sections 78 and 79 of that Act apply in circumstances other than a reorganisation (within the meaning of section 77 of that Act), those expressions shall be construed in like manner as they fall to be construed in sections 78 and 79 as so applied.

Calls on shares etc.

6.—(1) Sub-paragraph (2) below applies where,—

(*a*) on a disposal to which section 86 of this Act applies, the relevant allowable expenditure is or includes the amount or value of the consideration given for the issue of shares or securities in, or debentures of, a company ; and

(*b*) the whole or some part of that consideration was given after the expiry of the qualifying period.

(2) For the purpose of computing the indexation allowance (if any) on the disposal referred to in sub-paragraph (1)(*a*) above,—

(*a*) so much of the consideration as was given after the expiry of the qualifying period shall be regarded as an item of expenditure separate from any consideration given during that period ; and

(*b*) subsection (5) of section 87 of this Act shall not apply to that separate item of expenditure which, accordingly, shall be regarded as incurred at the time the consideration in question was actually given.

Options

7.—(1) This paragraph applies where, on a disposal to which section 86 of this Act applies, the relevant allowable expenditure includes both—

(*a*) the cost of acquiring an option binding the grantor to sell (in this paragraph referred to as " the option consideration ") ; and

(*b*) the cost of acquiring what was sold as a result of the exercise of the option (in this paragraph referred to as " the sale consideration ").

(2) Where this paragraph applies, the qualifying period in relation to the disposal referred to in sub-paragraph (1) above shall not begin until the date of the sale resulting from the exercise of the option.

(3) For the purpose of computing the indexation allowance (if any) on the disposal referred to in sub-paragraph (1) above,—

(*a*) the option consideration and the sale consideration shall be regarded as separate items of expenditure ; and

(*b*) subsection (5) of section 87 of this Act shall apply to neither of those items and, accordingly, they shall be regarded as incurred when the option was acquired and when the sale took place, respectively.

1979 c. 14.   (4) The preceding provisions of this paragraph have effect notwithstanding section 137 of the Capital Gains Tax Act 1979 (under which the grant of an option and the transaction entered into by the

grantor in fulfilment of his obligations under the option are to be
treated as a single transaction) ; but expressions used in this paragraph have the same meaning as in that section and subsection (6)
of that section (division of consideration for option both to sell and
to buy) applies for the purpose of determining the cost of acquiring
an option binding the grantor to sell.

PART II

EXISTING SHARE POOLS

8.—(1) The provisions of this Part of this Schedule have effect in
relation to a number of securities of the same class which, immediately before the operative date, are held by one person in one
capacity and, by virtue of section 65 of the Capital Gains Tax Act 1979 c. 14.
1979 are to be regarded for the purposes of that Act as indistin-
guishable parts of a single asset (in that section and in this Part of
this Schedule referred to as a holding).

(2) Subject to paragraph 9 below, on and after the operative
date,—

(a) the holding shall continue to be regarded as a single asset
for the purposes of the Capital Gains Tax Act 1979 (but one
which cannot grow by the acquisition of additional securities
of the same class) ; and

(b) the holding shall be treated for the purposes of section 86 of
this Act as having been acquired twelve months before
the operative date ; and

(c) every sum which, on a disposal of the holding occurring
after the operative date, would be an item of relevant
allowable expenditure shall be regarded for the purposes of
section 87 of this Act as having been incurred at such a
time that the month which determines RI, in the formula
in subsection (2) of that section, is March 1982.

(3) Nothing in sub-paragraph (2) above affects the operation of
section 78 of the Capital Gains Tax Act 1979 (equation of original
shares and new holding on a reorganisation etc.) in relation to the
holding, but without prejudice to paragraph 5 above.

(4) In this Part of this Schedule " the operative date " means—

(a) where the holding is held by a company, 1st April 1982 ;
and

(b) in any other case, 6th April 1982.

9.—(1) For the purposes of this paragraph there shall be ascertained—

(a) the amount which would be the relevant allowable expenditure on a disposal of the whole of the holding on the day
in 1982 which immediately precedes the operative date ; and

(b) the amount which would have been the relevant allowable
expenditure on a disposal of the whole of the holding (as
then constituted) on the same day in 1981 ;

and in this paragraph these amounts are referred to as the 1982 amount and the 1981 amount respectively.

(2) If the 1982 amount exceeds the 1981 amount, paragraph 8(2) above shall not apply to the holding and the following provisions of this paragraph shall have effect in relation to it.

(3) Where sub-paragraph (2) above applies, the identification rules set out in sub-paragraph (4) below shall be assumed to have applied in relation to every acquisition or disposal of securities which occurred after the day referred to in sub-paragraph (1)(b) above and before the operative date and which, apart from this paragraph, would have increased or reduced the size of the holding; and accordingly—

(a) only such of the securities (if any) which constituted the holding on that day as are not identified, by virtue of those rules, with securities disposed of before the operative date shall be regarded as constituting the holding on the operative date; and

(b) all securities acquired after that day and before the operative date, so far as they are not so identified with securities disposed of before the operative date, shall be regarded as separate assets.

(4) The identification rules referred to in sub-paragraph (3) above are—

(a) that securities disposed of on an earlier date shall be identified before securities disposed of on a later date, and the identification of the securities first disposed of shall accordingly determine the securities which could be comprised in the later disposal; and

(b) that securities disposed of shall be identified with securities acquired on a later date rather than with securities acquired on an earlier date; and

(c) that securities disposed of shall be identified with securities acquired at different times on any one day in as nearly as may be equal proportions;

and these rules shall have priority according to the order in which they are set out above.

(5) In this paragraph and paragraph 10 below—

(a) " the reduced holding " means the securities referred to in sub-paragraph (3)(a) above; and

(b) " relevant allowable expenditure " has, in relation to a disposal taking place at any time, the meaning assigned to it by subsection (2)(b) of section 86 of this Act in relation to a disposal to which that section applies.

(6) Sub-paragraph (2) of paragraph 8 above shall apply in relation to the reduced holding but, so far as paragraph (c) of that sub-paragraph is concerned, subject to paragraph 10(1) below.

10.—(1) For the purpose of computing the indexation allowance (if any) on a disposal of—

(a) the reduced holding, or

(*b*) any other securities which, by virtue of sub-paragraph (3)(*b*)
of paragraph 9 above, constitute one or more separate
assets,

the 1982 amount, as defined in that paragraph, shall be apportioned
between the reduced holding and that asset or those assets in proportion to the number of securities comprised in each of them on the
operative date.

(2) In relation to a disposal on or after the operative date, the
amount apportioned to the reduced holding or to any asset by virtue
of sub-paragraph (1) above shall be regarded for all purposes of
capital gains tax as the relevant allowable expenditure attributable
to the securities comprised in the reduced holding or, as the case may
be, in the asset in question.

(3) For the purposes of section 87(5) of this Act any relevant allowable expenditure which is attributable to any securities by virtue of
sub-paragraph (2) above shall be deemed to be expenditure falling
within paragraph (*a*) of subsection (1) of section 32 of the Capital 1979 c. 14.
Gains Tax Act 1979.

11. In paragraph 2(2) of Schedule 5 to the Capital Gains Tax
Act 1979 (identification of quoted securities held on 6th April 1965
with—among other cases—shares or securities subsequently disposed
of) and in paragraph 13(3) of that Schedule (corresponding provisions for unquoted securities etc.) for the words "earlier time"
there shall be substituted the words "later time" and for the words
"later time" there shall be substituted the words "earlier time".

SCHEDULE 14

RATES OF CAPITAL TRANSFER TAX

FIRST TABLE

Portion of value		Rate of tax
Lower limit £	Upper limit £	Per cent.
0	55,000	Nil
55,000	75,000	30
75,000	100,000	35
100,000	130,000	40
130,000	165,000	45
165,000	200,000	50
200,000	250,000	55
250,000	650,000	60
650,000	1,250,000	65
1,250,000	2,500,000	70
2,500,000	—	75

SECOND TABLE

Portion of value		Rate of tax
Lower limit £	Upper limit £	Per cent.
0	55,000	Nil
55,000	75,000	15
75,000	100,000	17½
100,000	130,000	20
130,000	165,000	22½
165,000	200,000	25
200,000	250,000	30
250,000	650,000	35
650,000	1,250,000	40
1,250,000	2,500,000	45
2,500,000	—	50

Section 101.

SCHEDULE 15

CAPITAL TRANSFER TAX

SETTLEMENTS COMMENCING BEFORE 27TH MARCH 1974

PART I

PERMANENT PROVISIONS

Introductory

1. In relation to settlements which commenced before 27th March 1974, sections 109 to 111 of this Act shall have effect subject to the following provisions of this Part of this Schedule.

Rate of ten-yearly charge

2.—(1) Section 109(4) shall have effect with the omission of paragraphs (*b*) and (*c*).

(2) Where tax is chargeable under section 107 by reference to a settlement's first ten-year anniversary, section 109(5) shall have effect with the substitution of the following paragraph for paragraph (*a*)—

" (*a*) the amounts of any distribution payments (determined in accordance with the rules applicable before 9th March 1982 under paragraph 11 of Schedule 5 to the Finance Act 1975) made out of the settled property after 26th March 1974 but before 9th March 1982 and within the period of ten years before the anniversary concerned ".

(3) Where tax is chargeable under section 107 by reference to the second or a subsequent ten-year anniversary of a settlement, section 109(5) shall have effect with the omission of paragraph (*a*).

3. Section 110 shall have effect with the substitution of the following for subsection (3)—

" (3) Where subsection (1) above applies section 109(5) above shall have effect as if there were added to the aggregate value there mentioned the aggregate of the values transferred by any chargeable transfers made by the settlor in the period of ten years ending with the day on which the chargeable transfer falling within subsection (1) above was made, disregarding transfers made on that day and excluding the values mentioned in subsection (4) below ; and where the settlor made two or more chargeable transfers falling within subsection (1) above, this subsection shall be taken to refer to the transfer in relation to which the aggregate to be added is the greatest."

Rate before first ten-year anniversary

4.—(1) For the reference in section 111(1) to the appropriate fraction there shall be substituted a reference to three tenths or, in the case of a charge to which sub-paragraph (2) below applies, one fifth.

(2) This sub-paragraph applies to a charge imposed under section 108 on an occasion before 1st April 1983 or, where the event occasioning the charge could not have occurred except as the result of some proceedings before a court, before 1st April 1984, if the occasion is one on which settled property ceases to be relevant property either—

    (*a*) on becoming property to which, or to an interest in possession in which, a qualifying person becomes beneficially entitled, or

    (*b*) on becoming property to which section 114 applies in circumstances where each of the beneficiaries mentioned in section 114(1)(*a*) and living when the charge is imposed is a qualifying person.

(3) A person is a qualifying person for the purposes of sub-paragraph (2) above if he is an individual who is domiciled in the United Kingdom when the charge is imposed and has not at or before that time acquired an interest under the settlement for a consideration in money or money's worth directly or indirectly from a person not so domiciled.

(4) For the purposes of this paragraph a person shall be treated as acquiring an interest for a consideration in money or money's worth from a person not domiciled in the United Kingdom if he becomes entitled to it as a result of transactions which include a disposition of that interest or of other property made for such consideration (whether to him or another) by a person not so domiciled.

5. Section 111(4) shall have effect with the substitution of the following paragraphs for paragraphs (*a*) and (*b*)—

    " (*a*) the value transferred by which is equal to the amount on which tax is charged under section 108 above ;

    (*b*) which is made at the time of that charge to tax by a transferor who has in the period of ten years ending with the day of the occasion of the charge made chargeable transfers having an aggregate value equal to the aggregate of—

        (i) any amounts on which any charges to tax have been

imposed under section 108 above in respect of the settlement in that period of ten years ; and

(ii) the amounts of any distribution payments (determined in accordance with the rules applicable before
9th March 1982 under paragraph 11 of Schedule 5 to
the Finance Act 1975) made out of the settled property
after 26th March 1974 but before 9th March 1982 and
within the said period of ten years ".

PART II

ELECTION DURING TRANSITIONAL PERIOD

6.—(1) This paragraph shall apply to a settlement which commenced before 27th March 1974 if—

(a) an event occurs before 1st April 1983 on which tax would
(apart from this paragraph) be chargeable under this Chapter
in respect of the settlement, and

(b) a person who would be liable for the tax gives to the Board,
not later than the permitted time, written notice that this
paragraph is to apply.

(2) Where this paragraph applies this Chapter shall have effect in
relation to events after 31st March 1983 (and not 8th March 1982) ;
and accordingly—

(a) for the references to 8th March 1982 in sections 93(10), 95(4),
98(7) and 99(1) of this Act there shall be substituted
references to 31st March 1983,

(b) for the references to 9th March 1982 in sections 109(5)(a),
111(4)(b)(ii) and 113(8)(b) of this Act there shall be substituted references to 1st April 1983, and

(c) sections 62(3), 85 and 131 of this Act and Schedule 10 shall
have effect in relation to events after 31st March 1983.

7.—(1) This paragraph shall apply to a settlement in respect of
which a notice is duly given under paragraph 6 above if—

(a) after 31st March 1983 and before 1st April 1984 an event
occurs in respect of the settlement which could not have
occurred except as the result of some proceedings before a
court,

(b) the event is one on which tax would (apart from this
paragraph) be chargeable under this Chapter, and

(c) the Board have not, before the event occurs, accepted a payment in full satisfaction of tax charged under this Chapter
in respect of the settlement on another event.

(2) Where this paragraph applies, paragraph 6(2) above shall have
effect with the substitution of " 1984 " for " 1983 ".

8.—(1) This paragraph shall apply to a settlement which commenced before 27th March 1974 if—

(a) no event occurs before 1st April 1983 on which tax would (apart from paragraph 6 above) be chargeable under this Chapter in respect of the settlement,

(b) after 31st March 1983 and before 1st April 1984 an event occurs in respect of the settlement which could not have occurred except as the result of some proceedings before a court,

(c) the event is one on which tax would (apart from this paragraph) be chargeable under this Chapter, and

(d) a person who would be liable for the tax gives to the Board, not later than the permitted time, written notice that this paragraph is to apply.

(2) Where this paragraph applies, this Chapter shall have effect in relation to events after 31st March 1984 (and not 8th March 1982) ; and accordingly—

(a) for the references to 8th March 1982 in sections 93(10), 95(4), 98(7) and 99(1) of this Act there shall be substituted references to 31st March 1984,

(b) for the references to 9th March 1982 in sections 109(5)(a), 111(4)(b)(ii) and 113(8)(b) of this Act there shall be substituted references to 1st April 1984, and

(c) sections 62(3), 85 and 131 of this Act and Schedule 10 shall have effect in relation to events after 31st March 1984.

9. In paragraphs 6 and 8 above " the permitted time ", in relation to an event, means the latest time at which an account could be delivered in respect of the event in accordance with paragraph 2 of Schedule 4 to the Finance Act 1975 or, if earlier, the time when the 1975 c. 7. Board first accept a payment in full satisfaction of tax charged under this Chapter in respect of the settlement on that or another event.

SCHEDULE 16

Section 117.

CAPITAL TRANSFER TAX: MAINTENANCE FUNDS
FOR HISTORIC BUILDINGS

Property becoming comprised in maintenance funds

1.—(1) Subject to sub-paragraphs (2) and (3) below, tax shall not be charged under section 108 of this Act in respect of property which ceases to be relevant property on becoming property in respect of which a direction under section 93 of this Act then has effect.

(2) If the amount on which tax would be charged apart from sub-paragraph (1) above in respect of any property exceeds the value of the property immediately after it becomes property in respect of which the direction has effect (less the amount of any consideration for its transfer received by the trustees of the settlement in which it was comprised immediately before it ceased to be relevant property), that sub-paragraph shall not apply but the amount on which tax is charged shall be equal to the excess.

(3) Sub-paragraph (1) above shall not apply in relation to any property if, at or before the time when it becomes property in respect of which the direction has effect, an interest under the settlement

in which it was comprised immediately before it ceased to be relevant property is or has been acquired for a consideration in money or money's worth by the trustees of the settlement in which it becomes comprised on ceasing to be relevant property.

(4) For the purposes of sub-paragraph (3) above trustees shall be treated as acquiring an interest for a consideration in money or money's worth if they become entitled to the interest as a result of transactions which include a disposition for such consideration (whether to them or to another person) of that interest or of other property.

(5) Subject to sub-paragraphs (7) and (8) below, tax shall not be charged under section 108 of this Act in respect of property which ceases to be relevant property if within the permitted period an individual makes a transfer of value—

>   (a) which is exempt under section 95 of this Act, and

>   (b) the value transferred by which is attributable to that property.

(6) In sub-paragraph (5) above " the permitted period " means the period of thirty days beginning with the day on which the property ceases to be relevant property except in a case where it does so on the death of any person, and in such a case means the period of two years beginning with that day.

(7) Sub-paragraph (5) above shall not apply if the individual has acquired the property concerned for a consideration in money or money's worth ; and for the purposes of this sub-paragraph an individual shall be treated as acquiring any property for such consideration if he becomes entitled to it as a result of transactions which include a disposition for such consideration (whether to him or another) of that or other property.

(8) If the amount on which tax would be charged apart from sub-paragraph (5) above in respect of any property exceeds the value of the property immediately after the transfer there referred to (less the amount of any consideration for its transfer received by the individual), that sub-paragraph shall not apply but the amount on which tax is charged shall be equal to the excess.

(9) The references in sub-paragraphs (2) and (8) above to the amount on which tax would be charged are references to the amount on which it would be charged apart from—

>   (a) paragraph (b) of section 108(2) of this Act, and

>   (b) Schedule 10 to the Finance Act 1976 (business property) and Schedule 14 to the Finance Act 1981 (agricultural property) ;

and the references in those sub-paragraphs to the amount on which tax is charged are references to the amount on which it would be charged apart from that paragraph and those Schedules.

Property leaving maintenance funds : charge to tax

2.—(1) This paragraph applies to settled property which is held on trusts which comply with the requirements mentioned in sub-section (3) of section 93 of this Act, and in respect of which a direction given under that section has effect.

(2) Subject to paragraphs 3 and 4 below, there shall be a charge to tax under this paragraph—

> (*a*) where settled property ceases to be property to which this paragraph applies, otherwise than by virtue of an application mentioned in paragraph (*a*)(i) or (ii) of subsection (3) of section 93 of this Act or by devolving on any such body or charity as is mentioned in paragraph (*a*)(ii) of that sub-section ;

> (*b*) in a case in which paragraph (*a*) above does not apply, where the trustees make a disposition (otherwise than by such an application) as a result of which the value of settled property to which this paragraph applies is less than it would be but for the disposition.

(3) Subsections (4), (5) and (9) of section 113 of this Act shall apply for the purposes of this paragraph as they apply for the purposes of that section (with the substitution of a reference to sub-paragraph (2)(*b*) above for the reference in section 113(4) to section 113(2)(*b*)).

(4) The rate at which tax is charged under this paragraph shall be determined in accordance with paragraphs 5 to 9 below.

(5) The devolution of property on a body or charity shall not be free from charge by virtue of sub-paragraph (2)(*a*) above if, at or before the time of devolution, an interest under the settlement in which the property was comprised immediately before the devolution is or has been acquired for a consideration in money or money's worth by that or another such body or charity ; but for the purposes of this sub-paragraph any acquisition from another such body or charity shall be disregarded.

(6) For the purposes of sub-paragraph (5) above a body or charity shall be treated as acquiring an interest for a consideration in money or money's worth if it becomes entitled to the interest as a result of transactions which include a disposition for such consideration (whether to that body or charity or to another person) of that interest or of other property.

Property leaving maintenance funds : exceptions from charge

3.—(1) Subject to sub-paragraphs (3) and (4) below, tax shall not be charged under paragraph 2 above in respect of property which, within the permitted period after the occasion on which tax would be chargeable under that paragraph, becomes comprised in another settlement as a result of a transfer of value which is exempt under section 95 of this Act.

(2) In sub-paragraph (1) above " the permitted period " means the period of thirty days except in a case where the occasion referred to is the death of the settlor, and in such a case means the period of two years.

(3) Sub-paragraph (1) above shall not apply to any property if the person who makes the transfer of value has acquired it for a consideration in money or money's worth; and for the purposes of this sub-paragraph a person shall be treated as acquiring any property for such consideration if he becomes entitled to it as a result of transactions which include a disposition for such consideration (whether to him or another) of that or other property.

(4) If the amount on which tax would be charged apart from sub-paragraph (1) above in respect of any property exceeds the value of the property immediately after it becomes comprised in the other settlement (less the amount of any consideration for its transfer received by the person who makes the transfer of value), that sub-paragraph shall not apply but the amount on which tax is charged shall be equal to the excess.

(5) The reference in sub-paragraph (4) above to the amount on which tax would be charged is a reference to the amount on which it would be charged apart from—

  (a) section 113(5)(b) of this Act (as applied by paragraph 2(3) above), and

1976 c. 40.
1981 c. 35.

  (b) Schedule 10 to the Finance Act 1976 (business property) and Schedule 14 to the Finance Act 1981 (agricultural property);

and the reference in that sub-paragraph to the amount on which tax is charged is a reference to the amount on which it would be charged apart from section 113(5)(b) and those Schedules.

4.—(1) Subject to the following provisions of this paragraph, tax shall not be charged under paragraph 2 above in respect of property which ceases to be property to which that paragraph applies on becoming—

  (a) property to which the settlor or his spouse is beneficially entitled, or

  (b) property to which the settlor's widow or widower is beneficially entitled if the settlor has died in the two years preceding the time when it becomes such property.

(2) If the amount on which tax would be charged apart from sub-paragraph (1) above in respect of any property exceeds the value of the property immediately after it becomes property of a description specified in paragraph (a) or (b) of that sub-paragraph (less the amount of any consideration for its transfer received by the trustees), that sub-paragraph shall not apply but the amount on which tax is charged shall be equal to the excess.

(3) The reference in sub-paragraph (2) above to the amount on which tax would be charged is a reference to the amount on which it would be charged apart from—

  (a) section 113(5)(b) of this Act (as applied by paragraph 2(3) above), and

  (b) Schedule 10 to the Finance Act 1976 (business property) and Schedule 14 to the Finance Act 1981 (agricultural property);

and the reference in sub-paragraph (2) above to the amount on which tax is charged is a reference to the amount on which it would be charged apart from section 113(5)(*b*) and those Schedules.

(4) Sub-paragraph (1) above shall not apply in relation to any property if, at or before the time when it becomes property of a description specified in paragraph (*a*) or (*b*) of that sub-paragraph, an interest under the settlement in which the property was comprised immediately before it ceased to be property to which paragraph 2 above applies is or has been acquired for a consideration in money or money's worth by the person who becomes beneficially entitled.

(5) For the purposes of sub-paragraph (4) above a person shall be treated as acquiring an interest for a consideration in money or money's worth if he becomes entitled to the interest as a result of transactions which include a disposition for such consideration (whether to him or to another person) of that interest or of other property.

(6) Sub-paragraph (1) above shall not apply in respect of property if it was relevant property before it became (or last became) property to which paragraph 2 above applies and, by virtue of paragraph 1(1) or (5) above, tax was not chargeable (or, but for paragraph 1(2) or (8), would not have been chargeable) under section 108 of this Act in respect of it ceasing to be relevant property before becoming (or last becoming) property to which paragraph 2 above applies.

(7) Sub-paragraph (1) above shall not apply in respect of property if—

(*a*) before it last became property to which paragraph 2 above applies it was comprised in another settlement in which it was property to which that paragraph applies, and

(*b*) it ceased to be comprised in the other settlement and last became property to which that paragraph applies in circumstances such that by virtue of paragraph 3(1) above there was no charge (or, but for paragraph 3(4), there would have been no charge) to tax in respect of it.

(8) Sub-paragraph (1) above shall not apply unless the person who becomes beneficially entitled to the property is domiciled in the United Kingdom at the time when he becomes so entitled.

Property leaving maintenance funds : rates of charge

5.—(1) This paragraph applies where tax is chargeable under paragraph 2 above and—

(*a*) the property in respect of which the tax is chargeable was relevant property before it became (or last became) property to which that paragraph applies, and

(*b*) by virtue of paragraph 1(1) or (5) above tax was not chargeable (or, but for paragraph 1(2) or (8), would not have been chargeable) under section 108 of this Act in respect of it ceasing to be relevant property on or before becoming (or last becoming) property to which paragraph 2 above applies.

(2) Where this paragraph applies, the rate at which the tax is charged shall be the aggregate of the following percentages—

(*a*) 0·25 per cent. for each of the first forty complete successive quarters in the relevant period,

(*b*) 0·20 per cent. for each of the next forty,

(*c*) 0·15 per cent. for each of the next forty,

(*d*) 0·10 per cent. for each of the next forty, and

(*e*) 0·05 per cent. for each of the next forty.

(3) In sub-paragraph (2) above " the relevant period " means the period beginning with the latest of—

(*a*) the date of the last ten-year anniversary of the settlement in which the property was comprised before it ceased (or last ceased) to be relevant property,

(*b*) the day on which the property became (or last became) relevant property before it ceased (or last ceased) to be such property, and

(*c*) 13th March 1975,

and ending with the day before the event giving rise to the charge.

(4) Where the property in respect of which the tax is chargeable has at any time ceased to be and again become property to which paragraph 2 above applies in circumstances such that by virtue of paragraph 3(1) above there was no charge to tax in respect of it (or, but for paragraph 3(4), there would have been no charge), it shall for the purposes of this paragraph be treated as having been property to which paragraph 2 above applies throughout the period mentioned in paragraph 3(1).

6.—(1) This paragraph applies where tax is chargeable under paragraph 2 above and paragraph 5 above does not apply.

(2) Where this paragraph applies, the rate at which the tax is charged shall be the higher of—

(*a*) the first rate (as determined in accordance with paragraph 7 below), and

(*b*) the second rate (as determined in accordance with paragraph 8 below).

7.—(1) The first rate is the aggregate of the following percentages—

(*a*) 0·25 per cent. for each of the first forty complete successive quarters in the relevant period,

(*b*) 0·20 per cent. for each of the next forty,

(*c*) 0·15 per cent. for each of the next forty,

(*d*) 0·10 per cent. for each of the next forty, and

(*e*) 0·05 per cent. for each of the next forty.

(2) In sub-paragraph (1) above " the relevant period " means the period beginning with the day on which the property in respect of which the tax is chargeable became (or first became) property to which paragraph 2 above applies, and ending with the day before the event giving rise to the charge.

(3) For the purposes of sub-paragraph (2) above, any occasion on which property became property to which paragraph 2 above applies, and which occurred before an occasion of charge to tax under that paragraph in respect of the property, shall be disregarded.

(4) The reference in sub-paragraph (3) above to an occasion of charge to tax under paragraph 2 does not include a reference to—

(*a*) the occasion by reference to which the rate is being determined in accordance with this Schedule, or

(*b*) an occasion which would not be an occasion of charge but for paragraph 3(4) above.

8.—(1) If the settlor is alive, the second rate is the effective rate at which tax would be charged, on the amount on which it is chargeable, under the appropriate Table if the amount were the value transferred by a chargeable transfer made by him on the occasion on which the tax becomes chargeable.

(2) If the settlor is dead, the second rate is (subject to sub-paragraph (3) below) the effective rate at which tax would have been charged, on the amount on which it is chargeable, under the appropriate Table if the amount had been added to the value transferred on his death and had formed the highest part of it.

(3) If the settlor died before 13th March 1975, the second rate is the effective rate at which tax would have been charged, on the amount on which it is chargeable ("the chargeable amount"), under the appropriate Table if the settlor had died when the event occasioning the charge under paragraph 2 above occurred, the value transferred on his death had been equal to the amount on which estate duty was chargeable when he in fact died, and the chargeable amount had been added to that value and had formed the highest part of it.

(4) Where, in the case of a settlement ("the current settlement"), tax is chargeable under paragraph 2 above in respect of property which—

(*a*) was previously comprised in another settlement, and

(*b*) ceased to be comprised in that settlement and became comprised in the current settlement in circumstances such that by virtue of paragraph 3(1) above there was no charge (or, but for paragraph 3(4), there would have been no charge) to tax in respect of it,

then, subject to sub-paragraph (5) below, references in sub-paragraphs (1) to (3) above to the settlor shall be construed as references to the person who was the settlor in relation to the settlement mentioned in paragraph (*a*) above (or, if the Board so determine, the person who was the settlor in relation to the current settlement).

(5) Where, in the case of a settlement ("the current settlement"), tax is chargeable under paragraph 2 above in respect of property which—

(*a*) was previously comprised at different times in other settlements ("the previous settlements"), and (*b*) ceased to be comprised in each of them, and became comprised in another of them or in the current settlement, in circumstances such that by virtue of paragraph 3(1) above there was no charge (or, but for paragraph 3(4), there would have been no charge) to tax in respect of it,

references in sub-paragraphs (1) to (3) above to the settlor shall be construed as references to the person who was the settlor in relation to the previous settlement in which the property was first comprised (or, if the Board so determine, any person selected by them who was the settlor in relation to any of the other previous settlements or the current settlement).

    (6) Sub-paragraph (7) below shall apply if—

      (*a*) in the period of ten years preceding a charge under paragraph 2 above (the " current charge "), there has been another charge under that paragraph where tax was charged at the second rate, and

      (*b*) the person who is the settlor for the purposes of the current charge is the settlor for the purposes of the other charge (whether or not the settlements are the same and, if the settlor is dead, whether or not he has died since the other charge) ;

and in sub-paragraph (7) below the other charge is referred to as the " previous charge ".

    (7) Where this sub-paragraph applies, the amount on which tax was charged on the previous charge (or, if there have been more than one, the aggregate of the amounts on which tax was charged on each)—

      (*a*) shall, for the purposes of calculating the rate of the current charge under sub-paragraph (1) above, be taken to be the value transferred by a chargeable transfer made by the settlor immediately before the occasion of the current charge, and

      (*b*) shall, for the purposes of calculating the rate of the current charge under sub-paragraph (2) or (3) above, be taken to increase the value there mentioned by an amount equal to that amount (or aggregate).

    (8) References in sub-paragraphs (1) to (3) above to the effective rate are to the rate found by expressing the tax chargeable as a percentage of the amount on which it is charged.

    (9) For the purposes of sub-paragraph (1) above the appropriate Table is the second Table in section 37 of the Finance Act 1975, and for the purposes of sub-paragraphs (2) and (3) above it is (if the settlement was made on death) the first Table in that section and (if not) the second.

    9. Where property is, by virtue of section 94(5) of this Act, treated as property in respect of which a direction has been given under section 93 of this Act, it shall for the purposes of paragraphs 5 to 8 above be treated as having become property to which paragraph 2 above applies when the transfer of value mentioned in section 94(5) was made.

SCHEDULE 17

Capital Transfer Tax

Settlements Without Interests in Possession

Finance Act 1975

1. In section 25(3) of the Finance Act 1975 after the words " under 1975 c. 7. Schedule 5 to this Act " there shall be inserted the words " or under Chapter II of Part IV of the Finance Act 1982."

2. In section 25(9) of that Act for the words from " any question " to the end there shall be substituted the words " trustees of a settlement shall be regarded as not resident in the United Kingdom unless the general administration of the settlement is ordinarily carried on in the United Kingdom and the trustees or a majority of them (and, where there is more than one class of trustees, a majority of each class) are for the time being resident in the United Kingdom.".

3. For section 43(5) of that Act there shall be substituted—

" (5) Chargeable transfers under Chapter II of Part IV of the Finance Act 1982 shall if they relate to the same settlement be treated for the purposes of subsections (2) and (3) above as made by the same person."

4. For subsection (1A) of section 47 of that Act there shall be substituted—

" (1A) Where property comprised in a person's estate immediately before his death is settled by his will and, within the period of two years after his death and before any interest in possession has subsisted in the property, an event occurs on which tax would (apart from this subsection) be chargeable under any provision, other than section 107, of Chapter II of Part IV of the Finance Act 1982, then—

(a) tax shall not be charged under that Chapter on that event, and

(b) this Part of this Act shall apply as if the will had provided that on the testator's death the property should be held as it is held after the event."

5. For subsection (2A) of section 51 of that Act there shall be substituted—

" (2A) Except where the context otherwise requires, references in this Part of this Act to chargeable transfers, to their making or to the values transferred by them shall be construed as including references to occasions on which tax is chargeable under Chapter II of Part IV of the Finance Act 1982, to their occurrence or to the amounts on which tax is then chargeable."

6. In section 51(5) of that Act, the words " (except paragraph 11(10) of Schedule 5) " shall be omitted and at the end there shall be added the words " ; but the preceding provisions of this subsection do not apply for the purposes of section 103 of the Finance Act 1982 ".

7. In paragraph 2 of Schedule 4 to that Act—

(a) in sub-paragraph (1)(c) for the words from " a capital distribution " to the end there shall be substituted the words " an occasion on which tax is chargeable under Chapter II of Part IV of the Finance Act 1982, or would be so liable if tax were chargeable on the occasion ; " ;

(b) in sub-paragraphs (1), (2) and (3) for the words "relevant property " there shall be substituted the words " appropriate property " ;

(c) in sub-paragraph (7) after the words " section 78 " there shall be inserted the words " or 82(3) ".

8. For paragraph 4(3) of that Schedule there shall be substituted—

" (3) For the purposes of this paragraph trustees of a settlement shall be regarded as not resident in the United Kingdom unless the general administration of the settlement is ordinarily carried on in the United Kingdom and the trustees or a majority of them (and, where there is more than one class of trustees, a majority of each class) are for the time being resident in the United Kingdom."

9. In paragraph 6(6) of that Schedule for the words from " capital distributions " to the end there shall be substituted the words " occasions on which tax is chargeable under Chapter II of Part IV of the Finance Act 1982 or to the amounts on which tax is then chargeable.".

10. In paragraph 12(4) of that Schedule after the words " section 78 " there shall be inserted the words " or 82(3) ".

11. In paragraph 13 of that Schedule—

(a) in sub-paragraph (5)(b) for the words " paragraph 4, 6(2), 12 or 15 of Schedule 5 to this Act " there shall be substituted the words " paragraph 4 of Schedule 5 to this Act, or is an occasion on which tax is chargeable under Chapter II of Part IV of the Finance Act 1982," ;

(b) in sub-paragraph (6)(c) for the words " made under paragraph 6, 12 or 15 of Schedule 5 to this Act " there shall be substituted the words " an occasion on which tax is chargeable under Chapter II of Part IV of the Finance Act 1982 ".

12. In paragraph 14(4)(b) of that Schedule for the words " paragraph 4, 6(2), 12 or 15 of Schedule 5 to this Act " there shall be substituted the words " paragraph 4 of Schedule 5 to this Act, or is an occasion on which tax is chargeable under Chapter II of Part IV of the Finance Act 1982, ".

13. In paragraph 19(1)(c) of that Schedule after the words " section 78 " there shall be inserted the words " or 82(3) ".

14. In paragraph 20(1)(b) of that Schedule after the words " under Schedule 5 to this Act " there shall be inserted the words " or under Chapter II of Part IV of the Finance Act 1982 ".

15. In paragraph 25(5) of that Schedule for the words from " to a capital distribution " to the end there shall be substituted the words " to an occasion on which tax is chargeable under Chapter II of Part IV of the Finance Act 1982 or to the amount on which tax is then chargeable.".

16. In paragraph 1(8) of Schedule 5 to that Act, after the word " Act " there shall be inserted the words " and Chapter II of Part IV of the Finance Act 1982 ".

17. In paragraph 16(6) of that Schedule, for the words from the beginning to " settlement is " there shall be substituted the words " Where a benefit has become payable under a fund or scheme to which this paragraph applies, and the benefit becomes comprised in a settlement ".

18. In paragraph 17(3)(*b*) of that Schedule, after the word " Schedule " there shall be inserted the words " and of Chapter II of Part IV of the Finance Act 1982 ".

19.—(1) Paragraph 3 of Schedule 7 to that Act shall be amended as follows.

(2) In sub-paragraph (1)(*b*), for the words " beneficially entitled to an " there shall be substituted the words " entitled to a qualifying ".

(3) In sub-paragraph (2)—

  (*a*) for the words " no interest " there shall be substituted the words " no qualifying interest " ; and

  (*b*) after the word " who " there shall be inserted the words " are or ".

(4) In sub-paragraph (2A) for the words from " by " to " another " there shall be substituted the words—

  " (*a*) property ceased to be comprised in one settlement before 10th December 1981 and after 19th April 1978 and, by the same disposition, became comprised in another settlement, or

  (*b*) property ceased to be comprised in one settlement after 9th December 1981 and became comprised in another without any person having in the meantime become beneficially entitled to the property (and not merely to an interest in possession in the property) ".

(5) After sub-paragraph (3) there shall be added—

  " (4) In this paragraph ' qualifying interest in possession ' has the meaning given by section 103 of the Finance Act 1982."

20. In paragraph 4 of Schedule 10 to that Act, for sub-paragraph (2) there shall be substituted—

  " (2) Sub-paragraph (1) above shall not apply where the chargeable transfer is made under Schedule 5 to this Act or under Chapter II of Part IV of the Finance Act 1982 and the gain accrues to the trustees of the settlement ; but if in such a case any capital gains tax chargeable on the gain is borne by a person who becomes absolutely entitled to the settled property concerned, the amount of the tax so borne shall be treated as reducing the value transferred by the chargeable transfer ".

21. In paragraph 9A of that Schedule for the words " relevant property " (wherever they occur) there shall be substituted the words " property concerned ".

22. In paragraph 11 of that Schedule, for sub-paragraph (5) there shall be substituted—

" (5) References in sub-paragraphs (1) and (4) above to a transfer of value shall be construed as including references to an event on which there is a charge to tax under Chapter II of Part IV of the Finance Act 1982, other than an event on which tax is chargeable in respect of the policy or contract by reason only that its value (apart from this paragraph) is reduced."

Finance Act 1976

23. In section 73 of the Finance Act 1976, for paragraph (*b*) there shall be substituted—

" (*b*) the amount on which tax is chargeable under Chapter II of Part IV of the Finance Act 1982 ".

24.—(1) Section 79 of that Act shall be amended as follows.

(2) In subsection (1)(*b*) for the words " relevant transferor " (in each place) there shall be substituted the words " relevant person ".

(3) Subsections (2), (5) and (6) shall be omitted.

(4) After subsection (7) there shall be inserted—

" (8) In this section " relevant person " and " appropriate Table " have the meanings given by section 82A below.

(9) Subsection (1)(*b*) above shall have effect subject to section 82A(6) and (7) below."

25.—(1) Section 80 of that Act shall be amended as follows.

(2) In subsections (2) and (3) for the words " relevant transferor " there shall be substituted the words " relevant person ".

(3) At the end of the section there shall be inserted—

" (5) In this section " relevant person " has the meaning given by section 82A below."

26. For sections 81 and 82 of that Act there shall be substituted—

" Con-
ditionally
exempt
occasions.
    81.—(1) A transfer of property or other event shall not constitute an occasion on which tax is chargeable under any provision of Chapter II of Part IV of the Finance Act 1982 other than section 107 if the property in respect of which the charge would have been made has been comprised in the settlement throughout the six years ending with the transfer or event, and—

(*a*) the property is, on a claim made for the purpose, designated by the Treasury under section 77 above ; and (*b*) the requisite undertaking described in that section is given with respect to the property by such person as the Treasury think appropriate in the circumstances of the case.

(2) References in subsections (3) and (4) below and in sections 82, 82A and 83 below to a conditionally exempt occasion are to—

(*a*) a transfer or event which by virtue of subsection (1) above does not constitute an occasion on which tax is chargeable under the Chapter there mentioned ;

(*b*) a conditionally exempt distribution (within the meaning given by this subsection as it had effect in relation to events before 9th March 1982).

(3) Sections 78 and 79 above shall have effect as if—

(*a*) references to a conditionally exempt transfer and to such a transfer of property included references respectively to a conditionally exempt occasion and to such an occasion in respect of property ;

(*b*) references to a disposal otherwise than by sale included references to any occasion on which tax is chargeable under any provision of that Chapter other than section 107 ; and

(*c*) references to an undertaking given under section 76 above included references to an undertaking given under this section.

(4) Section 80 above shall not apply where—

(*a*) tax has become chargeable under section 78 above by reference to a chargeable event in respect of any property, and

(*b*) the last conditionally exempt transaction regarding the property before the event was a conditionally exempt occasion ;

and for the purposes of this subsection conditionally exempt transactions regarding property are conditionally exempt transfers of it and conditionally exempt occasions in respect of it.

82.—(1) Where property is comprised in a settlement Exemption and there has been a conditionally exempt transfer of the from property on or before the occasion on which it became ten-yearly comprised in the settlement, section 107 of the Finance charge. Act 1982 (charge at ten-year anniversary) shall not have effect in relation to the property on any ten-year anniversary falling before the first occurrence after the transfer of a chargeable event with respect to the property.

(2) Where property is comprised in a settlement and there has been, on or before the occasion on which it became comprised in the settlement, a disposal of the property in relation to which subsection (4) of section

147 of the Capital Gains Tax Act 1979 (capital gains tax relief for works of art etc.) had effect, the said section 107 shall not have effect in relation to the property on any ten-year anniversary falling before the first occurrence after the disposal of an event on the happening of which the property is treated as sold under subsection (5) of the said section 147.

(3) Where property is comprised in a settlement and there has been no such transfer or disposal of the property as is mentioned in subsection (1) or (2) above on or before the occasion on which it became comprised in the settlement, then, if—

> (*a*) the property has, on a claim made for the purpose, been designated by the Treasury under section 77 above ; and
>
> (*b*) the requisite undertaking described in that section has been given by such person as the Treasury think appropriate in the circumstances of the case ; and
>
> (*c*) the property is relevant property for the purposes of Chapter II of Part IV of the Finance Act 1982,

the said section 107 shall not have effect in relation to the property ; but there shall be a charge to tax under this subsection on the first occurrence of an event which, if there had been a conditionally exempt transfer of the property when the claim was made and the undertaking had been given under section 76 above, would be a chargeable event with respect to the property.

(4) Tax shall not be charged under subsection (3) above in respect of property if, after the occasion and before the occurrence there mentioned, there has been a conditionally exempt occasion in respect of the property.

(5) The amount on which tax is charged under subsection (3) above shall be an amount equal to the value of the property at the time of the event.

(6) The rate at which tax is charged under subsection (3) above shall be the aggregate of the following percentages—

> (*a*) 0.25 per cent. for each of the first forty complete successive quarters (that is, periods of three months) in the relevant period,
>
> (*b*) 0.20 per cent. for each of the next forty,
>
> (*c*) 0.15 per cent. for each of the next forty,
>
> (*d*) 0.10 per cent. for each of the next forty, and
>
> (*e*) 0.05 per cent. for each of the next forty.

(7) In subsection (6) above " the relevant period " means the period beginning with the latest of—

> (*a*) the day on which the settlement commenced,

(*b*) the date of the last ten-year anniversary of   Sch. 17
the settlement to fall before the day on which
the property became comprised in the settlement,
and

(*c*) 13th March 1975,

and ending with the day before the event giving rise to
the charge.

(8) The persons liable for tax in respect of a charge
under subsection (3) above are—

(*a*) the trustees of the settlement ; and

(*b*) any person for whose benefit any of the property
or income from it is applied at or after the time
of the event occasioning the charge.

(9) Subsection (10) below shall have effect where—

(*a*) by virtue of subsection (3) above, section 107 of
the Finance Act 1982 does not have effect in
relation to property on the first ten-year anniversary of the settlement to fall after the making
of the claim and the giving of the undertaking,

(*b*) on that anniversary a charge to tax falls to be
made in respect of the settlement under the
said section 107, and

(*c*) the property became comprised in the settlement,
and the claim was made and the undertaking
was given, within the period of ten years ending
with that anniversary.

(10) In calculating the rate at which tax is charged
under the said section 107, the value of the consideration
given for the property on it becoming comprised in the
settlement shall be treated for the purposes of section
109(5)(*b*) of the Finance Act 1982 as if it were an amount
on which a charge to tax was imposed in respect of the
settlement under section 108 of that Act at the time of
the property becoming so comprised.

(11) In this section " ten-year anniversary " in relation
to a settlement has the same meaning as in Chapter II of
Part IV of the Finance Act 1982.

Relevant   82A.—(1) Subsections (2) to (4) below have effect to
person; and   determine, for the purposes of sections 79 and 80 above,
appropriate   the relevant person in relation to a chargeable event in
Table.   respect of any property.

(2) In this section references to transactions regarding
the property are to conditionally exempt transfers of the
property and conditionally exempt occasions in respect
of the property ; and " the last transaction " means—

(*a*) if there has been only one transaction regarding
the property before the event, that transaction ;

   (*b*) if there have been two or more such transactions and the last was before, or only one of them was within, the period of thirty years ending with the event, the last of those transactions ;

   (*c*) if there have been two or more such transactions within that period, whichever transaction the Board may select.

(3) If the last transaction was a conditionally exempt transfer the relevant person is the person who made the transfer ; and if the last transaction was a conditionally exempt occasion the relevant person is the person who is the settlor in relation to the settlement in respect of which the occasion occurred (or, if there is more than one such person, whichever of them the Board may select).

(4) The conditionally exempt transfers and occasions to be taken into account for the purpose of subsection (2) above in relation to a chargeable event do not include those made or occurring before any previous chargeable event in respect of the same property or before any event which apart from section 78(4) above would have been such a chargeable event.

(5) For the purposes of section 79(1)(*b*)(ii) above—

   (*a*) if the relevant person is the person who made a transfer, the appropriate Table is, if the transfer was made on death, the first Table and, if not, the second ;

   (*b*) if the relevant person is the person who is the settlor in relation to a settlement, the appropriate Table is, if the settlement was created on his death, the first Table and, if not, the second.

(6) If the last transaction regarding property before a chargeable event was a conditionally exempt occasion, and the relevant person died before 13th March 1975, section 79(1)(*b*)(ii) above shall (subject to subsection (7) below) be taken to read as follows : —

   " (ii) the rate or rates that would have applied to that amount (" the chargeable amount ") under the appropriate Table in that section if the relevant person had died when the chargeable event occurred, the value transferred on his death had been equal to the amount on which estate duty was chargeable when he in fact died, and the chargeable amount had been added to that value and had formed the highest part of it."

(7) If the last transaction regarding property before a chargeable event was a conditionally exempt occasion, the rate (or each of the rates) mentioned in section 79(1)(*b*)(i) or (ii) above—

   (*a*) shall, if the occasion occurred before the first ten-year anniversary to fall after the property became comprised in the settlement concerned, be 30 per cent. of what it would be apart from this subsection ; and

(*b*) shall, if the occasion occurred after the first and before the second ten-year anniversary to fall after the property became so comprised, be 60 per cent. of what it would be apart from this subsection,

and in this subsection " ten-year anniversary " in relation to a settlement has the same meaning as in Chapter II of Part IV of the Finance Act 1982.".

27. In section 83 of that Act, after subsection (3) there shall be inserted—

" (3A) References in subsection (3) above to a conditionally exempt transfer of property include references to a conditionally exempt occasion in respect of property.".

28. For subsection (8) of section 114 of that Act there shall be substituted—

" (8) This section shall apply to occasions on which tax is chargeable under section 108 of the Finance Act 1982 in cases within paragraph 5 of Schedule 15 to that Act in the same way as it applies to transfers of value ; and for this purpose references in this section to transfers made by the same person shall be construed as references to occasions relating to, or distribution payments made out of property comprised in, the same settlement.".

29. For subsection (6) of section 122 of that Act there shall be substituted—

" (6) Anything which is done in compliance with an order under the said Act of 1975 or occurs on the coming into force of such an order, and which would (apart from this subsection) constitute an occasion on which tax is chargeable under Chapter II of Part IV of the Finance Act 1982, shall not constitute such an occasion ; and where an order under the said Act of 1975 provides for property to be settled or for the variation of a settlement, and (apart from this subsection) tax would be charged under paragraph 4(2) of Schedule 5 to the Finance Act 1975 on the coming into force of the 1975 c. 7. order, the said paragraph 4(2) shall not apply.".

30. For paragraph 1 of Schedule 10 to that Act there shall be substituted—

" 1. In this Schedule references to a transfer of value include references to an occasion on which tax is chargeable under Chapter II of Part IV of the Finance Act 1982, and

(*a*) references to the value transferred by a transfer of value include references to the amount on which tax is then chargeable, and

(*b*) references to the transferor include references to the trustees of the settlement concerned."

Finance Act 1980

31. In Schedule 15 to the Finance Act 1980, after paragraph 2 there shall be inserted—

" 2A. Where tax is chargeable under section 108 of the Finance Act 1982 on any occasion after a reduction and the rate at which it is charged is determined under section 112 of that Act by reference to the rate that was (or would have been) charged under section 107 of that Act on an occasion before the reduction (or before that and one or more previous reductions), the rate charged on the later occasion shall be determined as if the second of the Tables in section 37(3) as substituted by the reduction (or by the most recent of those reductions) had been in force on the earlier occasion.".

32. For paragraph 6 of that Schedule there shall be substituted—

" 6. Where tax is chargeable under paragraph 2 of Schedule 16 to the Finance Act 1982 on any occasion after a reduction and the rate at which it is charged falls to be determined under paragraph 8 of that Schedule by reference to a death which occurred before that reduction (or before that and one or more previous reductions) that paragraph shall apply as if the Tables in section 37(3) as substituted by that reduction had been in force at the time of the death.".

Finance Act 1981

33. In section 96(1) of the Finance Act 1981, for paragraph (*b*) there shall be substituted—

" (*b*) the amount on which tax is chargeable under **Chapter II** of Part IV of the Finance Act 1982 ".

34. In Schedule 14 to that Act, for sub-paragraph (1) of paragraph 1 there shall be substituted—

" (1) In this Schedule references to a transfer of value include references to an occasion on which tax is chargeable **under** Chapter II of Part IV of the Finance Act 1982, and—

(*a*) references to the value transferred by a transfer of **value** include references to the amount on which **tax is then** chargeable, and

(*b*) references to the transferor include references to **the** trustees of the settlement concerned ".

Section 134.

SCHEDULE 18

ALTERNATIVE VALUATION OF ETHANE USED FOR PETROCHEMICAL PURPOSES

The election

1.—(1) An election shall be made—

(*a*) in so far as it is to apply to ethane which is relevantly appropriated, by the participator alone ; and

(*b*) in so far as it is to apply to ethane which is disposed of, by the participator and the person to whom it is disposed of.

(2) An election shall be made in such form as may be prescribed by the Board and shall—

(a) identify, by reference to volume, chemical composition and initial treatment, the ethane to which the election is to apply ;

(b) specify the period, beginning on or after the date of the election and not exceeding fifteen years, which is covered by the election ;

(c) specify the price formula which is to apply for determining the market values of ethane during that period ;

(d) specify the petrochemical purposes for which ethane to which the election applies will be used ; and

(e) specify the place to or at which any such ethane is to be delivered or appropriated.

(3) The reference in sub-paragraph (2)(a) above to initial treatment is a reference to such initial treatment (if any) as the ethane will have been subjected to before it is disposed of or relevantly appropriated.

Conditions for acceptance of an election

2.—(1) Subject to sub-paragraphs (2) and (3) below, the Board shall accept an election if they are satisfied that, under a relevant contract (as defined in paragraph 3 below) for the sale at arm's length of the ethane to which the election applies, the contract prices would not differ materially from the market values determined in accordance with the price formula specified in the election ; and if the Board are not so satisfied they shall reject the election.

(2) The Board shall reject an election if they are not satisfied that the price formula specified in the election is such that the market value of ethane disposed of or relevantly appropriated at any time during the period covered by the election will be readily ascertainable either by reference to the price formula alone or by reference to that formula and to information—

(a) which is, or is expected to be at that time, publicly available ; and

(b) which is not related or dependent, in whole or to any substantial degree, to or on the activities of the person or persons making the election or any person connected or associated with him or them.

(3) The Board shall reject an election if, after receiving notice in writing from the Board, the person or, as the case may be, either of the persons by whom the election was made—

(a) fails to furnish to the Board, before the appropriate date, any information which the Board may reasonably require for the purpose of determining whether the election should be accepted ; or

(b) fails to make available for inspection, before the appropriate date, by an officer authorised by the Board any books, accounts or documents in his possession or power which contain any information relevant for that purpose.

(4) In sub-paragraph (3) above " the appropriate date " means such date as may be specified in the notice concerned, being a date not earlier than one month after the date on which the notice was given.

(5) Any notice under sub-paragraph (3) above shall be given within the period of three months beginning on the date of the election in question.

3.—(1) In paragraph 2 above " relevant contract " means a contract which is entered into,—

> (a) if the price formula specified in the election is derived from an actual contract which is identified in the election and was entered into not more than two years before the date of the election, at the time at which that contract was entered into, and
>
> (b) in any other case, at the time of the election in question,

and which incorporates the terms specified in sub-paragraph (2) below, but is not necessarily a contract for the sale of ethane for petrochemical purposes.

(2) The terms referred to in sub-paragraph (1) above are—

> (a) that the ethane is required to be delivered at the place in the United Kingdom at which the seller could reasonably be expected to deliver it or, if there is more than one such place, the one nearest to the place of extraction ; and
>
> (b) that the price formula may be varied only in the event of a substantial and lasting change in the economic circumstances surrounding or underlying the contract and that any such variation may not take place before the expiry of the period of five years beginning on the date of the first delivery of ethane during the period covered by the election.

Notice of acceptance or rejection

4.—(1) Notice of the acceptance or rejection of an election shall be given to the party or, as the case may be, each of the parties to the election before the expiry of the period of three months beginning on—

> (a) the date of the election, or
>
> (b) if a notice has been given under paragraph 2(3) above relating to the election, the date or, as the case may be, the last date which is the appropriate date, as defined in paragraph 2(4) above, in relation to such a notice.

(2) If no such notice of acceptance or rejection is so given, the Board shall be deemed to have accepted the election and to have given notice of their acceptance on the last day of the period referred to in sub-paragraph (1) above.

(3) After notice of the acceptance of an election has been given under this paragraph, a change in the identity of the participator or, where appropriate, of the person to whom the ethane in question is disposed of shall not, of itself, affect the continuing operation of the election.

Market value ceasing to be readily ascertainable

5.—(1) In any case where—

(a) it appears to the Board that, at some time during the period covered by an election, the market value of ethane to which the election applies has ceased or is ceasing to be readily ascertainable as mentioned in paragraph 2(2) above, and

(b) the Board give notice of that fact to the party or, as the case may be, each of the parties to the election and in that notice specify a date for the purposes of this paragraph (which may be a date earlier than that on which the notice is given),

then, subject to sub-paragraph (2) below, on the date so specified the election shall cease to have effect.

(2) If—

(a) within the period of three months beginning on the date of a notice under sub-paragraph (1)(b) above, the party or parties to the election by notice in writing given to the Board specify a new price formula, and

(b) the new price formula is accepted by the Board in accordance with paragraph 7 below,

the election shall continue to have effect and, subject to paragraph 9 below, for the purpose of determining the market value, on and after the date specified in the notice under sub-paragraph (1)(b) above, of ethane to which the election applies, section 134 of this Act shall have effect as if the new price formula were the formula specified in the election.

Price formula ceasing to give realistic market values

6.—(1) If, at any time after the expiry of the period of five years beginning on the date of the first delivery or relevant appropriation of ethane during the period covered by an election,—

(a) it appears to the party or parties to the election or, as the case may be, to the Board that, by reason of any substantial and lasting change in any economic circumstances which were relevant at the time referred to in paragraph 3(1) above, the market values determined in accordance with the price formula specified in the election are no longer realistic ; and

(b) the party or parties to the election give notice of that fact to the Board, or the Board give notice of that fact to the party or, as the case may be, each of the parties to the election,

then, subject to the following provisions of this paragraph, sub-paragraph (2) below shall apply.

(2) Where this sub-paragraph applies, the election shall not have effect with respect to any chargeable period beginning after the date of the notice under sub-paragraph (1)(b) above.

(3) Before the expiry of the period of three months beginning on the date on which a notice under sub-paragraph (1)(b) above given

Sch. 18

by the party or parties to the election is received by the Board, the Board shall give notice of acceptance or rejection of that notice to the party or parties concerned ; and

(a) if the Board give notice of rejection, sub-paragraph (2) above shall not apply ; and

(b) if no notice of acceptance or rejection is in fact given as required by this sub-paragraph, the Board shall be deemed to have given notice of acceptance on the last day of the period of three months referred to above.

(4) If a notice under sub-paragraph (1)(b) above which has been given by the party or parties to the election contains a new price formula, the Board shall first consider the notice without regard to that formula and if, following upon that consideration, the Board give a notice of acceptance under sub-paragraph (3) above, they shall then proceed to consider the new price formula.

(5) In any case where—

(a) sub-paragraph (4) above applies and the new price formula contained in the notice under sub-paragraph (1)(b) above is accepted by the Board in accordance with paragraph 7 below, or

(b) within the period of three months beginning on the date of a notice given by the Board under sub-paragraph (1)(b) above, the party or parties to the election by notice in writing given to the Board specify a new price formula which is accepted by the Board in accordance with paragraph 7 below,

sub-paragraph (2) above shall not apply and for the purpose of determining, for any chargeable period beginning after the date of the notice under sub-paragraph (1)(b) above, the market value of ethane to which the election applies, section 134 of this Act shall have effect as if the new price formula were the formula specified in the election.

(6) If, by virtue of sub-paragraph (5) above or an appeal under paragraph 8 below, a new price formula has effect for determining the market value of ethane to which an election applies, sub-paragraph (1) above shall thereafter have effect in relation to the market value of any such ethane as if—

(a) the reference therein to the date of the first delivery or relevant appropriation of ethane during the period covered by the election, and

(b) the reference therein to the time referred to in paragraph 3(1) above,

were each a reference to the beginning of the first chargeable period for which the new price formula has effect.

Acceptance or rejection of new price formula

7.—(1) Subject to sub-paragraph (3) below, the Board shall accept a new price formula specified in a notice under paragraph 5(2) above if they are satisfied that the new formula provides for readily ascertainable market values which correspond, so far as practicable, with those which were intended to be provided for under the original price formula ; and if the Board are not so satisfied they shall reject such a new price formula.

(2) Subject to sub-paragraph (3) below, sub-paragraphs (1) and (2) of paragraph 2 above and paragraph 3 above shall apply to determine whether the Board shall accept—

   (*a*) a new price formula contained in a notice under paragraph 6(1)(*b*) above which has been accepted by the Board under paragraph 6(3) above, or

   (*b*) if the Board have given notice under paragraph 6(1)(*b*) above, a new price formula specified in a notice under paragraph 6(5)(*b*) above,

as if the new price formula were specified in an election made at the time the notice under paragraph 6(1)(*b*) above was given.

(3) The Board shall reject such a new price formula as is referred to in sub-paragraph (1) or sub-paragraph (2) above if, after receiving notice in writing from the Board, the party or, as the case may be, either of the parties to the election—

   (*a*) fails to furnish to the Board, before the appropriate date, any information which the Board may reasonably require for the purpose of determining whether the new formula should be accepted in accordance with sub-paragraph (1) or, as the case may be, sub-paragraph (2) above, or

   (*b*) fails to make available for inspection, before the appropriate date, by an officer authorised by the Board any books, accounts or documents in his possession or power which contain information relevant for that purpose.

(4) Sub-paragraph (4) of paragraph 2 above applies in relation to sub-paragraph (3) above as it applies in relation to sub-paragraph (3) of that paragraph.

(5) Notice of the acceptance or rejection of a new price formula—

   (*a*) specified in a notice under paragraph 5(2) or paragraph 6(5)(*b*) above, or

   (*b*) contained in a notice under paragraph 6(1)(*b*) above which has been accepted by the Board by a notice under paragraph 6(3) above,

shall be given to the party or, as the case may be, each of the parties to the election concerned before the expiry of the period of three months beginning on the relevant date (as defined in sub-paragraph (6) below), and if no notice of acceptance or rejection is in fact given as required by this sub-paragraph, the Board shall be deemed to have accepted the formula and to have given notice of their acceptance on the last day of that period.

(6) In sub-paragraph (5) above " the relevant date " means—

   (*a*) if a notice has been given under sub-paragraph (3) above relating to the price formula in question, the date or, as the case may be, the last date which is the appropriate date, within the meaning of that sub-paragraph, in relation to such a notice ; and

     (b) if no such notice has been given, then—

         (i) in relation to a new price formula falling within paragraph (a) of sub-paragraph (5) above, the date on which the notice referred to in that paragraph was received by the Board ; and

         (ii) in relation to a new price formula falling within paragraph (b) of that sub-paragraph, the date of the notice from the Board under paragraph 6(3) above.

8.—(1) Where the Board give notice to any person or persons—

     (a) under paragraph 4 above, rejecting an election ; or

     (b) under paragraph 5 above, that the value of any ethane has ceased or is ceasing to be readily ascertainable ; or

     (c) under paragraph 6(1)(b) above, that a price formula is no longer realistic ; or

     (d) under paragraph 6(3) above, rejecting a notice given under paragraph 6(1)(b) above ; or

     (e) under paragraph 7(5) above, rejecting a new price formula ;

that person or, as the case may be, those persons acting jointly may appeal to the Special Commissioners against the notice.

(2) An appeal under sub-paragraph (1) above shall be made by notice in writing given to the Board within thirty days after the date of the notice in respect of which the appeal is brought.

(3) Where at any time after the giving of notice of appeal under this paragraph and before the determination of the appeal by the Commissioners, the Board and the appellant agree that the notice in respect of which the appeal is brought should be accepted or withdrawn or varied, the same consequences shall ensue as if the Commissioners had determined the appeal to that effect.

(4) If, on the hearing of an appeal under this paragraph it appears to the majority of the Commissioners present at the hearing that the appeal should be allowed they shall allow the appeal and—

     (a) where the appeal is against a notice of rejection of an election or proposed new price formula, they shall substitute a notice of acceptance of the election or price formula without modification or with such modifications as they think fit ;

     (b) where the appeal is against a notice under paragraph 5 or paragraph 6(1)(b) above, they may direct that the price formula in question shall continue to have effect as if the notice had not been given ; and

     (c) where the appeal is against a notice under paragraph 6(3) above rejecting a notice under paragraph 6(1)(b) above, the Commissioners shall substitute a notice of acceptance.

(5) Sub-paragraphs (2), (8) and (11) of paragraph 14 of Schedule 2 to the principal Act shall apply in relation to an appeal against any such notice as is referred to in sub-paragraph (1) above as they apply in relation to an appeal against an assessment or determina-

tion made under the principal Act, but with the substitution, for any reference to the participator, of a reference to the person or persons who gave notice of appeal under sub-paragraph (2) above.

(6) Where notice of appeal is duly given against a notice given by the Board under paragraph 5 or paragraph 6(1)(*b*) above, the period of three months referred to in paragraph 5(2)(*a*) or, as the case may be, paragraph 6(5)(*b*) above shall not begin to run until the appeal is withdrawn or finally determined.

(7) Any reference in section 134 of this Act or the preceding provisions of this Schedule to an election accepted by the Board shall be construed as including a reference to an election accepted in pursuance of an appeal under this paragraph.

Returns

9. In any case where a notice under paragraph 5(1)(*b*) above or paragraph 6(1)(*b*) above relating to an election has been given to a party to the election or to the Board then, unless the notice has been withdrawn (whether in pursuance of an appeal or otherwise) or a price formula different from that to which the notice referred has effect as if specified in the election, any party to the election, in making a return under paragraph 2 of Schedule 2 to the principal Act with respect to ethane to which that election applies or which by virtue of that election falls within section 134(3) of this Act—

(*a*) where the notice was given under paragraph 5 above, may include the market value on and after the date specified in the notice of any such ethane determined on such basis as appears to him to be the best practical alternative to that provided by the price formula to which the notice referred ; and

(*b*) where the notice was given under paragraph 6 above, shall include the market value of any such ethane determined in accordance with the price formula to which the notice referred.

Penalties for incorrect information etc.

10.—(1) Paragraphs 8 and 9 of Schedule 2 to the principal Act (which penalise inaccurate returns etc. and are in this paragraph referred to as " the penalty provisions ") shall apply, in accordance with sub-paragraph (2) or sub-paragraph (3) below, in relation to inaccurate information—

(*a*) contained in an election ; or

(*b*) furnished pursuant to a notice under paragraph 2(3) or paragraph 7(3) above ; or

(*c*) contained in any books, accounts or documents made available as mentioned in paragraph 2(3)(*b*) or paragraph 7(3)(*b*) above.

(2) Where the inaccurate information is provided by a participator, the penalty provisions shall apply—

(*a*) as they apply in relation to an incorrect return under paragraph 2 of Schedule 2 to the principal Act ; and

Sᴄʜ. 18   (*b*) as if the reference in paragraph 8(2)(*a*)(i) of that Schedule to the chargeable period to which the return relates were a reference to each chargeable period which falls within the period covered by the election and which is affected by any decision of the Board in connection with which the provision of the information was material.

(3) Where the incorrect information is provided by a person other than a participator, the penalty provisions shall apply—

(*a*) as they apply to an incorrect return under paragraph 5 of Schedule 2 to the principal Act ; and

(*b*) as if that person were the responsible person for an oil field.

Interpretation

11.—(1) Subsection (6) of section 134 of this Act has effect in relation to this Schedule as it has effect in relation to the preceding provisions of that section.

(2) In this Schedule, any reference to an election is a reference to an election under section 134 of this Act ; and any reference to the date of an election is a reference to the date on which the election (made as mentioned in paragraph 1 above) is received by the Board.

(3) Any reference in the preceding provisions of this Schedule to the party to an election is relevant only to an election applying to ethane which is relevantly appropriated and is a reference to the participator by whom the ethane is for the time being so appropriated.

(4) Any reference in the preceding provisions of this Schedule to the parties to an election is relevant only to an election applying to ethane which is disposed of as mentioned in section 134(2)(*a*) of this Act and is a reference to the participator by whom and the person to whom the ethane is for the time being so disposed of.

Section 139(6).

SCHEDULE 19

Sᴜᴘᴘʟᴇᴍᴇɴᴛᴀʀʏ Pʀᴏᴠɪsɪᴏɴs Rᴇʟᴀᴛɪɴɢ ᴛᴏ APRT

Pᴀʀᴛ I

Cᴏʟʟᴇᴄᴛɪᴏɴ ᴏꜰ Tᴀx

Payment of tax

1.—(1) APRT which a participator is liable to pay in respect of any chargeable period for an oil field shall be due on the date on which the return for that period and that field is made by the participator in accordance with paragraph 2 of Schedule 2 to the principal Act or, if a return is not so made, on the last day of the second month following that period ; and APRT which is due shall be payable without the making of an assessment.

(2) Subject to sub-paragraph (3) below, every participator in an oil field shall, at the time when he delivers to the Board the return for a chargeable period required by paragraph 2 of Schedule 2 to the principal Act,—

(*a*) deliver to the Board a statement showing whether any, and if so what, amount of APRT is payable by him for that chargeable period in respect of the field ; and (*b*) subject to the following provisions of this Schedule, pay to the Board the amount of APRT, if any, shown in the statement.

(3) In relation to any oil field, sub-paragraph (2) above does not apply with respect to any chargeable period after the last of the nine chargeable periods referred to in section 139(1(*b*) of this Act.

(4) The statement under sub-paragraph (2)(*a*) above shall be in such form as the Board may prescribe.

(5) Paragraphs 3, 8 and 9 of Schedule 2 to the principal Act shall apply in relation to statements required to be made under this paragraph as they apply in relation to returns required to be made under paragraph 2 of that Schedule.

2.—(1) Subject to sub-paragraph (2) below, if for any chargeable period for an oil field ending on or after 30th June 1983—

(*a*) an amount of APRT is shown to be payable by the participator in the statement delivered by him in accordance with paragraph 1 above in respect of that period and that field ; or

(*b*) an amount is payable by the participator on account of petroleum revenue tax in accordance with section 1 of the Petroleum Revenue Tax Act 1980 in respect of that period and that field ; or 1980 c. 1.

(*c*) both such amounts are so payable by the participator,

then the participator shall pay to the Board six monthly instalments commencing in the second month of the next chargeable period each equal to one-eighth of the amount referred to in paragraph (*a*) or paragraph (*b*) above or, where paragraph (*c*) applies, of the aggregate of those amounts.

(2) With respect to the chargeable period which, for an oil field, is the last of the nine chargeable periods referred to in section 139(1)(*b*) of this Act and with respect to any subsequent chargeable period for that field, sub-paragraph (1) above shall have effect as if—

(*a*) for paragraphs (*a*) to (*c*) there were substituted the words " an amount of tax is shown to be payable in the statement delivered in respect of that period in accordance with section 1(1)(*a*) of the Petroleum Revenue Tax Act 1980 " ; and

(*b*) for the words from " the amount referred to in paragraph (*a*) " onwards there shall be substituted the words " that amount ".

(3) Instalments paid in accordance with sub-paragraph (1) above shall be regarded as being paid in respect of the next chargeable period referred to in that sub-paragraph.

(4) The aggregate amount paid by a participator in accordance with sub-paragraph (1) above in respect of a chargeable period for an oil field—

(*a*) to the extent that it is equal to or less than his liability, if any, to pay an amount of APRT under paragraph 1 above in

respect of that oil field for that chargeable period shall be
deemed to be an amount of APRT paid by him in respect
of that field for that period ; and

(*b*) to the extent that it exceeds any such liability of his to pay
an amount of APRT and is equal to or less than his liability,
if any, to pay an amount in respect of that field for that
period in accordance with paragraph (*b*) of subsection (1)
of section 1 of the Petroleum Revenue Tax Act 1980 (payments on account of petroleum revenue tax), shall be
deemed to be an amount paid by him under that paragraph.

3.—(1) If in any month a participator in an oil field—

(*a*) has not delivered (otherwise than to the Secretary of State)
any of the oil which has been won from the field and disposed of by him at any time in or before that month ; and

(*b*) has not relevantly appropriated any of the oil which has
been so won by him at any such time,

he shall be entitled to withhold the instalment due, under paragraph 2 above, for that field in the following month.

(2) An instalment shall not be withheld by virtue of the conditions
in sub-paragraph (1) above being fulfilled in any month unless a
notice to that effect, in such form as the Board may prescribe, is
given to the Board before the end of the following month and—

(*a*) where the Board are not satisfied with any such notice,
the powers conferred by paragraph 7 of Schedule 2 to the
principal Act (production of accounts etc.) shall be exercisable as if the notice were a return under paragraph 2 of
that Schedule ; and

(*b*) paragraph 8 of that Schedule (penalties) shall apply to an
incorrect notice as it applies to an incorrect return under
paragraph 2.

4. Certificates of tax deposit issued by the Treasury under section
12 of the National Loans Act 1968 on terms published on or before
14th May 1979 may be used for making payments of APRT and
of instalments under paragraph 2 above ; and for that purpose those
terms shall have effect with the necessary modifications and as if
the tax in or towards the payment of which a certificate is used
were due—

(*a*) in the case of APRT payable under paragraph 1 above, two
months after the end of the chargeable period to which it
relates ;

(*b*) in the case of an instalment payable under paragraph 2
above, at the end of the month in which the instalment is
required to be paid.

Assessments and appeals

5.—(1) Where it appears to the Board that any APRT payable
in accordance with paragraph 1 above has not been paid on the
due date they may make an assessment to tax on the participator
and shall give him notice of any such assessment.

(2) APRT due under an assessment under this paragraph shall be due within thirty days of the issue of the notice of assessment.

(3) A notice of assessment shall state that the participator may appeal against the assessment in accordance with paragraph 7 below.

(4) After the service of a notice of assessment the assessment shall not be altered except in accordance with the express provisions of this Part of this Schedule or any of the provisions of the Taxes Management Act 1970 which apply by virtue of paragraph 1 of 1970 c. 9. Schedule 2 to the principal Act in relation to the assessment.

6.—(1) Where it appears to the Board that any gross profit charged to tax on a participator for any chargeable period in respect of an oil field by an assessment under paragraph 5 above ought to have been larger or smaller or that no gross profit accrued to the participator from that oil field during that chargeable period, they may make such amendments to the assessment or withdraw the assessment, as the case may require.

(2) Where the Board amend an assessment under sub-paragraph (1) above they shall give notice to the participator of the amendment ; and sub-paragraphs (2) to (4) of paragraph 5 above shall apply in relation to any such notice as they apply in relation to a notice of assessment under paragraph 5.

7.—(1) A participator may appeal to the Special Commissioners against an assessment or amendment of an assessment under paragraph 5 or paragraph 6 above by notice of appeal in writing to the Board given within thirty days of the date of issue of the notice of the assessment or amendment of assessment.

(2) Sub-paragraphs (2) to (11) of paragraph 14 of Schedule 2 to the principal Act shall apply in relation to an appeal under this paragraph as they apply in relation to an appeal under sub-paragraph (1) of that paragraph except that—

(a) for each reference in sub-paragraph (3) to tax there shall be substituted a reference to APRT ;

(b) where in determining the gross profit accruing to a participator from a field in a chargeable period the aggregate of the amounts mentioned in paragraphs (a) to (c) of subsection (5) of section 2 of the principal Act falls to be increased under section 140 of this Act (whether as respects all oil or as respects a particular kind or kinds of oil), the difference mentioned in sub-paragraph (3)(b) (or as the case may be, the difference so far as relating to oil of the particular kind or kinds in question) shall be increased by multiplying it by the fraction mentioned in subsection (2) of section 140 ;

(c) for each reference in sub-paragraph (10) to an assessable profit there shall be substituted a reference to a gross profit ; and

(d) any reference in sub-paragraph (10) to an allowable loss shall be omitted.

8. Paragraphs 5(2) to (4) and 7 above shall apply in relation to an assessment to APRT under section 142(1) of this Act as if it were an assessment under paragraph 5.

Overpayment of tax

9.—(1) Where in respect of any oil field a participator has paid an amount of APRT for a chargeable period which exceeds the amount of APRT payable therefor the amount of that excess shall be repaid to him.

(2) Where in respect of any oil field the amount paid for any chargeable period by a participator by way of instalments under paragraph 2 above exceeds the aggregate of his liabilities mentioned in sub-paragraph (4) of that paragraph, the amount of that excess shall be repaid to him.

Interest

10.—(1) APRT payable for a chargeable period but not paid before the end of the second month after the end of that period shall carry interest from the end of that month until payment.

(2) Any amount payable by a participator as an instalment in respect of a chargeable period for a field and not paid by him in the month in which it ought to be paid shall carry interest from the end of that month until—

    (*a*) payment of the amount, or

    (*b*) two months after the end of that period,

whichever is the earlier.

(3) Where, in accordance with paragraph 14 of Schedule 2 to the principal Act as applied by paragraph 7 above, APRT may be withheld until the determination or abandonment of an appeal, the interest on that APRT may also be withheld until the determination or abandonment of that appeal.

(4) Where an amount of APRT or an amount paid by way of instalment becomes repayable, that amount shall carry interest from—

    (*a*) two months after the end of the chargeable period in respect of which the APRT or the instalment was paid, or

    (*b*) the date on which the amount was paid,

whichever is the later, until repayment.

(5) For the purposes of sub-paragraph (2) above a payment on account of an overdue instalment shall, so far as possible, be attributed to the earliest month for which an instalment is overdue ; and for the purposes of sub-paragraph (4) above any instalment or part of an instalment that becomes repayable shall, so far as possible, be regarded as consisting of the instalment most recently paid.

(6) In its application (by virtue of paragraph 1 of Schedule 2 to the principal Act) to interest payable under sub-paragraph (1) or sub-paragraph (2) above, section 69 of the Taxes Management Act 1970 shall have effect with the omission of the words " charged and due and payable under the assessment to which it relates ".

(7) Interest paid to a participator under sub-paragraph (4) above shall be disregarded in computing his income for the purposes of income tax and corporation tax.

(8) Any reference in this paragraph to interest is a reference to interest at the rate applying under paragraph 15 of Schedule 2 to the principal Act.

Transitional provisions

11.—(1) In any case where, by virtue of section 105 of the Finance 1980 c. 48. Act 1980, a sum is paid by a participator as an advance payment of tax in respect of an oil field for the chargeable period ending on 30th June 1983 then,—

    (*a*) to the extent that the sum so paid does not exceed his liability to APRT for that period, it shall be deemed to be a payment of APRT for that period ; and

    (*b*) subsection (5) of that section (treatment of advance payments) shall apply to any such sum only to the extent that it exceeds that liability to APRT.

(2) In subsection (7) of that section the reference to tax assessed on a participator in respect of a field for a chargeable period shall include, for the chargeable period ending on 30th June 1983, a reference to the amount (if any) of APRT payable by him in respect of that field for that period.

12.—(1) Every participator in an oil field shall in March 1983 and in each of the four succeeding months pay to the Board an amount equal to one-fifth of the amount, if any, shown in the statement delivered by the participator under paragraph 10(1)(*a*) of Schedule 16 to the Finance Act 1981 as supplementary petroleum duty payable 1981 c. 35. by him in respect of the field for the chargeable period ending on 31st December 1982.

(2) Paragraphs 2(4) and 9 above shall apply in relation to any payment made by the participator under sub-paragraph (1) above as if it were an instalment under paragraph 2 above paid in respect of the chargeable period ending on 30th June 1983 ; but for the purposes of this sub-paragraph the amount of the participator's liability to pay any APRT as mentioned in paragraph 2(4) above shall be reduced by the amount of any APRT deemed to have been paid by him in accordance with paragraph 11 above.

(3) Paragraphs 3, 4 and 10 above shall apply in relation to a payment under sub-paragraph (1) above as if it were an instalment under paragraph 2 above.

13.—(1) If, in respect of the chargeable period ending on 30th June 1983, any sum is payable by a participator in accordance with section 1 of the Petroleum Revenue Tax Act 1980, then, so far 1980 c. 1. as the net amount of that sum is concerned, only one-fifth shall become payable at the time specified in that section and the remaining four-fifths shall be paid in four equal monthly instalments in the months of September to December 1983, inclusive.

(2) The reference in sub-paragraph (1) above to the net amount of any sum payable in accordance with section 1 of the Petroleum Revenue Tax Act 1980 is a reference to the sum specified in paragraph (*b*) of subsection (1) of that section less any amount which is treated as (or deemed to be) paid as part of that sum—

    (*a*) by virtue of section 105(5) of the Finance Act 1980, as applied by paragraph 11(1)(*b*) above ; or

    (*b*) by virtue of paragraph 2(4)(*b*) above, as applied by paragraph 12(2) above.

(3) Any amount payable by a participator as an instalment by virtue of sub-paragraph (1) above and not paid by him in the month in which it ought to be paid shall carry interest from the end of that month until payment.

(4) Paragraph 15 of Schedule 2 to the principal Act (interest on assessed tax) shall not apply in relation to so much of the tax charged in an assessment on the participator for the chargeable period referred to in sub-paragraph (1) above (excluding any APRT so charged) as is equal to or less than the net amount referred to in that sub-paragraph and payable by him, and in relation to so much if any of that tax as exceeds that net amount paragraph 15 shall apply with the substitution for the words " two months after the end of the period " of the words " the end of October 1983 ".

(5) If, in respect of the chargeable period referred to in sub-paragraph (1) above, any amount of tax charged by an assessment to tax or paid on account of tax so charged becomes repayable under any provision of Part I of the principal Act, paragraph 16 of Schedule 2 to the principal Act (interest on such repayments) shall have effect in relation to that amount with the substitution for the words following " per annum " of the words " from the end of October 1983 until repayment ".

(6) Sub-paragraphs (5) to (8) of paragraph 10 above shall apply for the purposes of sub-paragraphs (3) and (5) above as they apply for the purposes of sub-paragraphs (2) and (4) of paragraph 10.

PART II

MISCELLANEOUS

Repayment of APRT

14.—(1) If a participator in an oil field has an excess of APRT credit for the last of the chargeable periods referred to in section 139 (1)(*b*) of this Act, then, on the making of a claim the amount of that excess shall be repaid to him.

(2) For the purposes of this paragraph there is an excess of APRT credit for the last of the chargeable periods referred to in subsection (1)(*b*) of section 139 of this Act if any of that credit would, apart from this paragraph, fall to be carried forward to the next chargeable period in accordance with subsection (4) of that section ; and the amount of the excess is the amount of the credit which would fall to be so carried forward.

(3) A claim under sub-paragraph (1) above shall be made not earlier than two months after the expiry of the last chargeable period referred to in that sub-paragraph.

(4) In any case where—

    (*a*) a claim is made under sub-paragraph (1) above before an assessment is made for the chargeable period referred to in that sub-paragraph, and

    (*b*) the APRT credit for that period exceeds the amount of tax which, in the statement delivered under section 1(1)(*a*) of the Petroleum Revenue Tax Act 1980, is shown to be 1980 c. 1 payable by the participator concerned in accordance with the Schedule to that Act for that period in respect of the oilfield in question,

the amount of the excess shall be repaid to the participator and that repayment shall be regarded as a payment on account of any amount which may fall to be repaid to him by virtue of sub-paragraph (1) above.

(5) Paragraph 10(4) above shall not apply to any amount of APRT which is repayable only on the making of a claim under sub-paragraph (1) above.

(6) Amounts repaid to a participator by virtue of this paragraph shall be disregarded in computing his income for the purposes of income tax or corporation tax.

Transfer of interest in fields

15.—(1) This paragraph has effect in a case where Part I of Schedule 17 to the Finance Act 1980 applies (transfer of interests 1980 c. 48. in oil fields) and expressions used in the following provisions in this paragraph have the same meaning as in that Schedule.

(2) For the purpose of determining whether the new participator is liable to pay an amount of APRT, but for no other purpose, subsection (1) of section 139 of this Act shall apply as if any gross profit which at any time before the transfer had accrued to the old participator from the field had accrued at that time to the new participator or, if the transfer is of part of the old participator's interest in the field, as if a corresponding part of that gross profit had at that time accrued to the new participator.

(3) There shall be treated as the APRT credit of the new participator the whole or, if the transfer is of part of the old participator's interest in the field, a corresponding part of so much, if any, of the old participator's APRT credit in respect of that field for the transfer period as exceeds his liability for petroleum revenue tax for that period.

(4) For the purposes of computing whether any, and if so what, amount of APRT is payable by the old participator and the new participator for the transfer period or any later chargeable period, it shall be assumed that any application or proposal made in relation to the transfer under paragraph 4 or paragraph 5(1) of

Schedule 17 to the Finance Act 1980 and in respect of which the
Board have not notified their decision will be accepted by the Board.

Net profit periods

16.—(1) For the purposes of sections 111, 112 and 113 of the
Finance Act 1981 (determination of net profit periods etc.) the
total assessable profits which have accrued to a participator from an
oil field at the end of a chargeable period may in addition to being
set against allowable losses be set against the APRT paid by the
participator in respect of that oil field for chargeable periods up
to and including that period and accordingly those sections shall
have effect subject to the following modifications.

(2) In subsection (2) of section 111 (calculation of net profit) for
the words from "exceed the total" to the end there shall be
substituted the words "exceed the aggregate of the total allowable
losses that have so accrued to him and the total amount of advance
petroleum revenue tax paid by him in respect of that field for chargeable periods up to and including that period." and at the end of
that subsection there shall be inserted the following subsection—

"(2A) For the purposes of subsection (2) above the total
amount of advance petroleum revenue tax paid by the participator does not include any amount of that tax repaid to him
before the end of the chargeable period first referred to in that
subsection or any amount of that tax subsequently repaid to
him under section 142(1) of the Finance Act 1982 or under
paragraph 9 of Schedule 19 to that Act.".

(3) In section 112 (application of section 111 where an interest in
an oil field is transferred) the following subsection shall be inserted
after subsection (4)—

"(4A) Subsections (2) and (2A) of section 111 shall have
effect as if references to the amount of advance petroleum
revenue tax paid by the new participator or repaid to him
included references to the amount of that tax paid by or repaid
to the old participator or, where the old participator has transferred part of his interest, such part of that amount as is just
and reasonable.".

(4) In section 113 (relief where total allowable losses exceed total
allowable profits after the net profit period) the following subsection
shall be substituted for subsection (1)—

"(1) This section has effect where the aggregate of—

(a) the total allowable losses that have accrued to a
participator from an oil field in chargeable periods up
to and including a chargeable period ending not more
than three years after his net profit period, and

(b) the amount of advance petroleum revenue tax paid by
him in respect of that field for those periods less any
such tax repaid to him before the end of those periods
or repaid subsequently under section 142(1) of the
Finance Act 1982 or paragraph 9 of Schedule 19 to
that Act,

exceeds the total assessable profits (without any reduction under section 7 or 8 of the principal Act) that have so accrued to him."

Abandoned fields

17.—(1) The provisions of this paragraph apply where—

(a) the responsible person for an oil field has given notice under paragraph 1 of Schedule 8 to the principal Act that the winning of oil from the field has permanently ceased ; and

(b) he has been notified of a decision (whether of the Board or on appeal from the Board) that the winning of oil has so ceased ; and

(c) the date stated in that decision as the date on which the winning of oil from the field ceased is earlier than the expiry of the last of the chargeable periods specified in section 139(1)(b) of this Act.

(2) Where a participator in the field in question has an amount of APRT credit—

(a) which cannot be set against a liability for petroleum revenue tax under section 139(3) of this Act, and

(b) which is not repayable by virtue of any other provision of this Schedule,

then, on the making of a claim, that amount shall be repaid to him.

(3) Paragraph 10(4) above shall not apply to any amount of APRT which is repayable only on the making of a claim under sub-paragraph (2) above.

(4) Any claim under sub-paragraph (2) above shall be made before any claim for any unrelievable field loss allowance under section 6 of the principal Act ; and any amount of APRT which is repayable by virtue of such a claim shall be left out of account in determining the amount of any such loss.

(5) Amounts repaid to a participator under this paragraph shall be disregarded in computing his income for the purposes of income tax and corporation tax.

PART III

AMENDMENTS

18. In section 2 of the principal Act, at the beginning of subsection (4), there shall be inserted the words " For the purposes of the tax (including advance petroleum revenue tax) ".

19.—(1) In paragraph 13 of Schedule 2 to the principal Act for the words from " so far as " to " four months " there shall be substituted the words " and payable shall be due within six months ".

(2) This paragraph has effect with respect to chargeable periods ending on or after 30th June 1983.

20. In sub-paragraph (2) and (4) of paragraph 5 of Schedule 3 to the principal Act (liability for petroleum revenue tax and interest in

Sch. 19 the case of transfers to associated companies) the references to tax and to interest payable under Part I of that Act shall include references to APRT and to interest payable under paragraph 10 or paragraph 13 above.

1980 c. 1. 21. In section 1 of the Petroleum Revenue Tax Act 1980 (payments on account of petroleum revenue tax)—

(*a*) at the end of paragraph (*b*) of subsection (1) (computation of payments) there shall be added the words " less an amount equal to his APRT credit for that chargeable period in respect of that oil field." ; and

(*b*) in subsection (3) (repayment of excess) after the words " tax so charged " there shall be inserted the words " less the amount of the APRT credit deducted in accordance with subsection (1)(*b*) above from the tax shown in the statement " ; and

(*c*) the following subsections shall be inserted after subsection (3)—

" (3A) In subsections (1) and (3) above " APRT credit " has the meaning given by section 139(4) of the Finance Act 1982.

(3B) Paragraphs 3, 8 and 9 of Schedule 2 to the principal Act (penalties for failure to make returns under paragraph 2 of that Schedule) shall apply in relation to statements required to be made under subsection (1)(*a*) above as they apply in relation to returns required to be made under paragraph 2 of that Schedule."

Section 151.

SCHEDULE 20

NATIONAL SAVINGS ACCOUNTS

1971 c. 29. 1. The National Savings Bank Act 1971 shall have effect subject to the following amendments.

2. In subsection (2) of section 3 (provisions as to investment and ordinary deposits)—

(*a*) after the words " investment deposits " there shall be inserted the words " and with respect to investment deposits of different descriptions " ; and

(*b*) after the words " investment deposit " there shall be inserted the words " or an investment deposit of a particular description ".

3.—(1) In section 4 (power by order to limit amount of deposits) the following subsection shall be inserted after subsection (1)—

" (1A) The Treasury may by order prescribe an amount as the minimum balance for investment accounts and may provide for converting into a different description of investment account any account into which investment deposits of any description are made if the balance of that account falls below the minimum balance so prescribed for an account of that description."

(2) At the end of paragraph (*a*) of subsection (2) of section 4 there shall be inserted the words " and with respect to investment deposits of different descriptions ".

4.—(1) In subsection (1) of section 5 (interest on ordinary deposits) after the words " other rate " there shall be inserted the words " or rates " and at the end of the subsection there shall be added the words " and the Treasury may determine different rates of interest in relation to amounts deposited in any ordinary deposit account by reference to any one or more of the following factors, namely—

(*a*) the balance of the account at any time or over any period or the aggregate balance of that account and the depositor's other ordinary deposit accounts at any time or over any period ; and

(*b*) the number of withdrawals from that account over any period or the number of withdrawals from that account and the depositor's other ordinary deposit accounts."

(2) In subsection (5) of that section, for the words " the rate " there shall be substituted the words " any of the rates ".

5.—(1) In section 6 (interest on investment deposits) at the end of subsection (1) there shall be added the words " and different terms may be prescribed in relation to different descriptions of investment deposits ".

(2) In subsection (2) of section 6, after the words " in relation to " there shall be inserted the words " different descriptions of investment deposits and ".

(3) After subsection (2) of section 6 there shall be inserted the following subsection : —

" (2A) Without prejudice to the generality of subsection (2) above, the Treasury may determine, in relation to an account into which investment deposits of any description are made, different rates of interest by reference to any one or more of the following factors, namely,—

(*a*) the balance of that account at any time or over any period or the aggregate balance of the account and the depositor's other accounts of the same description, or the depositor's other investment accounts of any description, at any time or over any period ; and

(*b*) the number of withdrawals from that account over any period or the number of withdrawals from that account and the depositor's other accounts of the same description, or the depositor's other investment accounts of any description, over any period."

(4) In subsection (3) of section 6 for the words following " investment deposits " there shall be substituted the words " or investment deposits of a particular description ; and any such alteration may affect deposits received at or before, as well as after the time the alteration is made ".

6. In section 7 (withdrawal of deposits)—

(*a*) in subsection (1) for the words " deposit, or part of a deposit," there shall be substituted the words " ordinary deposit, or part of an ordinary deposit," ; and

(*b*) the following subsection shall be substituted for subsection (2)—

" (2) The terms as to withdrawal of investment deposits shall be such as may from time to time be prescribed.".

7. In subsection (1) of section 8 (matters which may be included in regulations under section 2 of the Act)—

(*a*) the following paragraph shall be substituted for paragraph (*b*)—

" (*b*) for the giving of statements of accounts or the issuing of depositors' books and for prescribing the entries to be made in such books ; " ; and

(*b*) in paragraph (*d*) of that subsection (entries, etc. to be proof of certain matters) for the words " or acknowledgements made " there shall be substituted the words " , acknowledgements or statements of accounts made or given ".

8. In section 27 (interpretation) after the definition of " the Commissioners " there shall be inserted the following definition—

" ' interest ', in relation to investment deposits, includes any bonus or other payment, whether payable annually or otherwise, which constitutes income derived from the whole or any part of the deposits."

Section 156.

SCHEDULE 21

Dissolution of Board of Referees : Consequential Provision

Capital Allowances

1968 c. 3.   1.—(1) Section 26 of the Capital Allowances Act 1968 (determination and review of percentage rates, for tax purposes, on wear and tear allowances for plant and machinery) shall be amended as follows.

(2) In subsection (2) for the words from " a Board of Referees " to " and the Referees " there shall be substituted the words " the tribunal, who ".

(3) In the proviso to subsection (2), and in subsection (3), for the word " Referees " in each place where it occurs there shall be substituted the word " tribunal ".

(4) For subsection (7) there shall be substituted the following subsection—

" (7) In this section ' tribunal ' means the tribunal established under section 463 of the principal Act."

S.I. 1950/3.   2. The Income Tax (Applications for Increase of Wear and Tear Percentages) Regulations 1950 shall have effect as if for references to the Board of Referees there were substituted references to the tribunal.

The tribunal

3.—(1) For paragraph (*a*) of section 463 of the Taxes Act (constitution of tribunal) there shall be substituted the following paragraph—

" (*a*) a chairman, appointed by the Lord Chancellor, and ".

(2) In this Schedule "tribunal" means the tribunal established under section 463 of the Taxes Act.

Savings and transitionals

4.—(1) Section 54 of the Taxes Management Act 1970 (settling of appeals by agreement) shall apply to the tribunal in relation to the exercise of functions transferred by section 156 of this Act as it applied, by virtue of paragraph 8 of Schedule 4 to that Act, to the Board of Referees. 1970 c. 9.

(2) Section 156 of this Act shall not affect the validity of anything done by or in relation to the Board of Referees before the commencement of that section ; and anything which at that date is in process of being done by or in relation to the Board may be continued by or in relation to the tribunal.

SCHEDULE 22
REPEALS
PART I
MISCELLANEOUS CUSTOMS AND EXCISE AND VALUE ADDED TAX

Section 157.

Chapter	Short title	Extent of repeal
1981 c. 35.	The Finance Act 1981.	In section 1, subsections (1), (3) and (4). Section 2. In section 12, subsections (1) and (2). Schedules 1 and 2.

PART II
VEHICLES EXCISE DUTY

Chapter	Short title	Extent of repeal
1971 c. 10.	The Vehicles (Excise) Act 1971.	In Schedule 6, paragraphs 3 and 5.
1972 c. 10 (N.I.).	The Vehicles (Excise) Act (Northern Ireland) 1972.	In Schedule 7, paragraphs 3 and 5.
1981 c. 56.	The Transport Act 1981.	Section 33. Section 34. Schedule 11.
1981 c. 35.	The Finance Act 1981.	In section 7, subsections (2) and (3). In section 8, subsections (2) and (3). Schedule 3. Schedule 4.

The repeals in the Finance Act 1981 do not affect licences **taken** out before 10th March 1982.

PART III
GAMING MACHINE LICENCE DUTY

Chapter	Short title	Extent of repeal
1972 c. 11 (N.I.).	The Miscellaneous Transferred Excise Duties Act (Northern Ireland) 1972.	In section 44, subsections (3)(*c*) and (6)(*aa*). In paragraph 13 of Schedule 3 the words " the peak rate ".
1980 c. 48.	The Finance Act 1980.	In Schedule 6, paragraph 15(2) and (4).
1981 c. 35.	The Finance Act 1981.	Section 9(6).
1981 c. 63.	The Betting and Gaming Duties Act 1981.	In section 22, subsections (5)(*c*) and (6). In section 25(4), the word " and ", at the end of paragraph (*b*), and paragraph (*c*).

These repeals do not affect licences for periods beginning before
1st October 1982.

PART IV
INCOME AND CORPORATION TAX: GENERAL

Chapter	Short title	Extent of repeal
1970 c. 10.	The Income and Corporation Taxes Act 1970.	Section 8(2)(*b*)(ii). Section 131(6). Section 228(5). Section 249(5). Section 416(4).
1975 c. 45.	The Finance (No. 2) Act 1975.	Section 36(5)(*a*). In section 36A(1), paragraph (*a*) and, in paragraph (*b*), the words " (including any interest paid in connection therewith) ".
1976 c. 40.	The Finance Act 1976.	Section 64A(7) and (8).
1980 c. 48.	The Finance Act 1980.	In Schedule 12, in paragraph 7(3) the words from " and a television set " onwards.
1981 c. 35.	The Finance Act 1981.	Section 24. In section 27(3), the words " (except so far as made by virtue of section 4 of that Act) ". In section 27(8) the word " and " where it appears at the end of paragraph (*b*). Section 42(2)(*c*). In section 68, subsections (2), (4) and (5).

1. The repeals of sections 131(6) and 249(5) of the Income and
Corporation Taxes Act 1970 have effect in relation to payments of
interest made, and the repeal of section 416(4) has effect in relation to
securities issued, after 5th April 1982.

2. The repeals in section 36 and 36A of the Finance (No. 2) Act 1975 have effect for the year 1982–83 and subsequent years of assessment.

PART V
OPTION MORTGAGE SCHEMES

Chapter or Number	Short title	Extent of repeal
1967 c. 29.	The Housing Subsidies Act 1967.	Sections 24 to 32.
1969 c. 33.	The Housing Act 1969.	Sections 78 and 79.
1970 c. 10.	The Income and Corporation Taxes Act 1970.	In Schedule 15, the entry in Part II relating to the Housing Subsidies Act 1967.
1971 c. 68.	The Finance Act 1971.	Section 66.
1974 c. 44.	The Housing Act 1974.	Section 119. Schedule 11.
1980 c. 51.	The Housing Act 1980.	Sections 114 to 116. Schedule 14.
S.I. 1981/156 (N.I. 3).	The Housing (Northern Ireland) Order 1981.	Articles 141 to 152.

These repeals have effect on 1st April 1983, but subject to subsections (2) to (4) of section 27 of this Act.

PART VI
CAPITAL GAINS

Chapter	Short title	Extent of repeal
1979 c. 14.	The Capital Gains Tax Act 1979.	Section 55(2). Section 56(2). In section 146(3)— the words " or 55 "; the words from " or (*b*) " to " paragraph 12 "; the words " or the assets are so held "; the words from " or of the assets " to " (*b*) above "; the words " and 55 ". In section 147(3), the words " or 55(1) ". In Schedule 4— in paragraph 2(1) the words " or 55(1) "; paragraph 2(3)(*b*); in paragraph 3(1)(*a*), the words " or 55(1) ".
1980 c. 48.	The Finance Act 1980.	In section 79(4), the words from " or " onwards. In section 79(5), the words from " and where " onwards.
1981 c. 35.	The Finance Act 1981.	Section 78(1) and (3).

SCH. 22   The repeals of section 55(2) and 56(2) of the Capital Gains Tax Act 1979 have effect in relation to interests terminating after 5th April 1982 and the remaining repeals have effect in relation to disposals after that date.

PART VII
CAPITAL TRANSFER TAX

Chapter	Short title	Extent of repeal
1975 c. 7.	The Finance Act 1975.	In section 20(7) the words "(within the meaning of Schedule 5 to this Act)". Section 26(2A). In section 51, in subsection (1) the definition of "capital distribution", and in subsection (5) the words "(except paragraph 11(10) of Schedule 5)". In Schedule 4, in paragraphs 2(7), 12(4) and 19(1)(c) the words "or section 89 of the Finance Act 1980" and the words "or paragraph 3 of Schedule 15 to the Finance Act 1981". In Schedule 5— paragraphs 6 to 15; paragraph 16(5); in paragraph 17, in subparagraph (1) the words "or (c) charities", subparagraph (3)(c) to (e) and the word "and" immediately preceding paragraph (c), and sub-paragraphs (4) and (5) to (9); in paragraph 18 (as it applies where the failure or determination of the trusts concerned was before 12th April 1978), sub-paragraphs (2) and (3); in paragraph 19 (as it applies to property transferred into settlement before 10th March 1981), sub-paragraphs (2) and (3); paragraphs 20 and 21; in paragraph 24, sub-paragraph (4). In Schedule 6, paragraphs 10(2), 11(1A), 12(2), 13(1A) and 15(6).
1976 c. 40.	The Finance Act 1976.	Section 79(2), (5) and (6). Section 84. In section 105, in subsection (1) the words "(2) and" and "paragraph 6(7) were omitted and", and subsection (2).

Chapter	Short title	Extent of repeal
1976 c. 40. *cont.*	The Finance Act 1976. *cont.*	Section 106. Section 107(3) and (4). Section 110(3). In section 111, subsections (1) to (3), in subsection (4) the words from " after sub-paragraph (1) " to " Schedule 5 to this Act ", and subsection (5). In section 118(2) the words from " and subsection (4) " onwards. Section 118(4). In Schedule 11, paragraph 4. In Schedule 14, paragraphs 2, 3, 8, 11, 12, 13(*c*) and (*d*), 14, 15, 16 and 17.
1977 c. 36.	The Finance Act 1977.	Section 50. In section 51, subsections (3) and (4).
1978 c. 42.	The Finance Act 1978.	In section 64, subsection (6), and in subsection (7) the words from the beginning to " and " and the word " other ". In section 69, subsections (2) and (3), and in subsection (6) the words " 6(6B) and 14(5) ". Section 70. In section 71(2) the words from " but " to the end. In section 72(2) the words from " and " onwards. In Schedule 11, paragraph 1.
1979 c. 47.	The Finance (No. 2) Act 1979.	Section 23.
1980 c. 48.	The Finance Act 1980.	In section 86, subsection (4), and in subsection (5) the words " and (4) ". Section 88(1) to (6). Sections 89 to 91. In Schedule 15, paragraphs 3 and 4A, and in paragraph 5 the words " or 81(4)(*b*) ", " or a settlement which ceased to exist " and " or when the settlement ceased to exist ". Schedule 16.
1981 c. 35.	The Finance Act 1981.	In section 92, subsection (3), in subsection (4) the words " or 81(4)(*b*), ", " or a settlement which ceased to exist " and " or when the settlement ceased to exist ", and subsection (5).

Chapter	Short title	Extent of repeal
1981 c. 35. *cont.*	The Finance Act 1981. *cont.*	Section 99. Section 102. Schedule 15.

1. The repeals of—

    (*a*) section 26(2A) of the Finance Act 1975,

    (*b*) paragraph 4A of Schedule 15 to the Finance Act 1980, and

    (*c*) section 99 of and Schedule 15 to the Finance Act 1981,

together with the repeals in Schedule 4 to the Finance Act 1975 relating to Schedule 15 to the Finance Act 1981, have effect in relation to deaths on or after 15th November 1976.

2. The repeal of paragraph 12(1) and (2) of Schedule 5 to the Finance Act 1975 has effect as from 1st January 1982.

3. The remaining repeals, except those in section 86 of the Finance Act 1980, have effect in relation to events after 8th March 1982 (or, in a case within Part II of Schedule 15 to this Act, 31st March 1983 or, as the case may be, 31st March 1984).

PART VIII

STAMP DUTY

Chapter	Short title	Extent of repeal
1974 c. 30.	The Finance Act 1974.	In section 49, subsections (2) and (3).
1980 c. 48.	The Finance Act 1980.	In section 118(3) the words " section 49(2) of the Finance Act 1974 (relief from stamp duty) ".

PART IX

OIL TAXATION

Chapter	Short title	Extent of repeal
1975 c. 22.	The Oil Taxation Act 1975.	In section 12(3) the words from "as regards" to "any oil field ". In Schedule 3, in paragraph 8(1) the words from "unless it is so met by a grant" onwards.
1980 c. 48.	The Finance Act 1980.	Section 105.
1981 c. 35.	The Finance Act 1981.	Sections 122 to 128. Schedule 16.

1. The repeal in section 12(3) of the Oil Taxation Act 1975 has effect in relation to determinations made after 31st December 1981.

2. The repeal of section 105 of the Finance Act 1980 does not have effect in relation to chargeable periods ending on or before 30th June 1983.

3. The repeal of sections 122 to 128 of and Schedule 16 to the Finance Act 1981 does not have effect in relation to chargeable periods ending on or before 31st December 1982.

PART X

BOARD OF REFEREES

Chapter	Short title	Extent of repeal
1970 c. 9.	The Taxes Management Act 1970.	Section 6(1)(*b*). In Schedule 4, paragraph 8.
1971 c. 62.	The Tribunals and Inquiries Act 1971.	In Schedule 1, paragraph 29(*c*).
1975 c. 24.	The House of Commons Disqualification Act 1975.	In Schedule 1, in Part III, the entry relating to the Board of Referees appointed for the purposes of section 26 of the Capital Allowances Act 1968.
1975 c. 25.	The Northern Ireland Assembly Disqualification Act 1975.	In Schedule 1, in Part III, the entry relating to the Board of Referees appointed for the purposes of section 26 of the Capital Allowances Act 1968.

Part XI

Spent Enactments

Chapter	Short title	Extent of repeal
1947 c. 46.	The Wellington Museum Act 1947.	Section 4(3).
1970 c. 10.	The Income and Corporation Taxes Act 1970.	Section 10. Section 11(1), (2), (3) and (6), In section 39(1)(*d*) the words " relief in respect of a child under section 10(1)(*b*) or " and the word " child " in the second place where it occurs.
1971 c. 68.	The Finance Act 1971.	In Schedule 4, paragraph 3(1)(*a*). In Schedule 6, paragraph 6.
1975 c. 7.	The Finance Act 1975.	In Schedule 6, paragraphs 1(3) and (4) and 10(4) and (5).
1975 c. 45.	The Finance (No. 2) Act 1975.	In Schedule 12— paragraph 5 of Part I; paragraph 3 of Part III; paragraph 4 of Part IV.
1976 c. 40.	The Finance Act 1976.	Section 29(3).
1977 c. 36.	The Finance Act 1977.	Section 25.
1978 c. 42.	The Finance Act 1978.	Section 20(3) and (5).
1979 c. 25.	The Finance Act 1979.	Section 1(4).
1980 c. 48.	The Finance Act 1980.	Section 25.

PRINTED IN ENGLAND BY W. J. SHARP
 Controller and Chief Executive of Her Majesty's Stationery Office and Queen's Printer of Acts of Parliament

INDEX

TO THE

PUBLIC GENERAL ACTS

AND

GENERAL SYNOD MEASURE 1982

A

ACQUISITION OF LAND. *See* LAND.

ADMINISTRATION OF JUSTICE ACT: 1982 c. 53   ...   .   II, p. 1993

PART I
DAMAGES FOR PERSONAL INJURIES ETC.
Abolition of certain claims for damages etc.

§1. Abolition of right to damages for loss of expectation of life, II, p. 1994.
 2. Abolition of actions for loss of services etc, II, p. 1994.

Fatal Accidents Act 1976

 3. Amendments of Fatal Accidents Act 1976, II, p. 1994.

Claims not surviving death

 4. Exclusion of Law Reform (Miscellaneous Provisions) Act 1934, II, p. 1997.

Maintenance at public expense

 5. Maintenance at public expense to be taken into account in assessment of damages, II, p. 1998.

Provisional damages for personal injuries

 6. Award of provisional damages for personal injuries, II, p. 1999.

PART II
DAMAGES FOR PERSONAL INJURIES ETC.—SCOTLAND

 7. Damages in respect of services, II, p. 2000.
 8. Services rendered to injured person, II, p. 2000.
 9. Services to injured person's relative, II, p. 2000.
 10. Assessment of damages for personal injuries, II, 2001.
 11. Maintenance at public expense to be taken into account in assessment of damages: Scotland, II, p. 2002.
 12. Award of provisional damages for personal injuries: Scotland, II, p. 2002.
 13. Supplementary, II, p. 2003.
 14. Amendment and repeal of enactments, II, p. 2004.

PART III
POWERS OF COURTS TO AWARD INTEREST

 15, and schedule 1. Interest on debts and damages, II, p. 2005.
 16. Interest on lump sums in matrimonial proceedings, II, p. 2005.

AGRICULTURAL TRAINING BOARD ACT: 1982 c. 9   ...   ...   I, p. 41

THE AGRICULTURAL TRAINING BOARD

§ 1, and schedule 1.   The Agricultural Training Board, I, p. 41.
  2.   Establishment of committees, I, p. 42.
  3.   Amendment or revocation of order establishing the Board, I, p. 43.

Functions of the Board

  4.   Functions of the Board, I, p. 44.
  5.   Training for employment overseas, I, p. 45.
  6.   Directions by the Ministers, I, p. 45.
  7.   Disclosure of information to the Board, I, p. 45.
  8.   Reports and accounts, I, p. 46.

General

  9.   Financial assistance and investment, I, p. 46.
 10.   Industrial injuries benefit for accidents in training, I, p. 47.

Supplemental

 11, and schedule 2.   Consequential provisions, repeals and savings, I, p. 47.
 12.   Short title, extent and commencement, I, p. 48.
Schedule 1   The Agricultural Training Board, I, p. 49.
Schedule 2   Repeals, I, p. 50.

APPEALS.   Under—

PART I

OFFENCES AGAINST THE SAFETY OF AIRCRAFT ETC.

PART II

PROTECTION OF AIRCRAFT, AERODROMES AND AIR
NAVIGATION INSTALLATIONS AGAINST ACTS OF VIOLENCE

General purposes

Powers of Secretary of State

Supplemental provisions with respect to directions

Air navigation installations

Miscellaneous supplemental provisions

C

PART III

CONTROL OF SEX SHOPS

PART IV

OFFENCES, POWERS OF CONSTABLES ETC.

The Secretary of State

CIVIL AVIATION (AMENDMENT) ACT: 1982 c. 1   ...   .   I, p. 1

CIVIL JURISDICTION AND JUDGMENTS ACT: 1982 c. 27   ...   ...   I, p. 509

PART I

IMPLEMENTATION OF THE CONVENTIONS

Main implementing provisions

Supplementary provisions as to recognition and enforcement of judgments

Other supplementary provisions

D

Trade disputes

15. Actions in tort against trade unions and employers' associations, II, p. 1493.
16. Limit on damages awarded against trade unions in actions in tort, II, p. 1495.
17. Recovery of sums awarded in proceedings involving trade unions and employers' associations, II, p. 1495.
18. Meaning of " trade dispute ", II, p. 1496.
19. Amendment of sections 13 and 30 of the 1974 Act, II, p. 1498.

Periods of continuous employment

20, and schedule 2. Change of basis of computation of period of continuous employment, II, p. 1498.

Supplemental

21, and schedules 3 and 4. Interpretation, minor and consequential amendments and repeals, II, p. 1499.
22. Short title, commencement and extent, II, p. 1499.

Schedule 1. Compensation for certain dismissals, II, p. 1500.
Schedule 2. Change of basis of computation of period of continuous employment II, p. 1503.
Schedule 3. Minor and consequential amendments.
Part I. Minor amendments, II, p. 1509.
Part II. Consequential amendments, II, p. 1512.
Schedule 4. Repeals, II, p. 1517.

ENTRY. Powers of, under—

EVIDENCE. Provisions under—

F

PART I

CUSTOMS AND EXCISE

§ 1, and schedules 1 and 2. Duties on spirits, beer, wine, made-wine and cider, I, p. 917.
2. Tobacco products, I, p. 918.
3. Hydrocarbon oil, etc., I, p. 918.
4. Aviation gasoline, I, p. 919.
5, and schedules 3 and 5. Vehicles excise duty: Great Britain, I, p. 920.
6, and schedules 4 and 5. Vehicles excise duty: Northern Ireland, I, p. 920.
7. Additional liability in relation to alteration of vehicle or its use, I, p. 922.
8, and schedule 6. Betting and gaming duties, I, p. 927.
9. Immature spirits for home use and loss allowance for imported beer, I, p. 928.
10. Regulator powers, I, p. 929.
11. Powers of Commissioners with respect to agricultural levies etc., I, p. 929.
12. Delegation of Commissioners' functions, I, p. 930.

PART II

VALUE ADDED TAX AND CAR TAX

PART III

INCOME TAX, CORPORATION TAX AND CAPITAL GAINS TAX

CHAPTER I

GENERAL

PART VII

MISCELLANEOUS AND SUPPLEMENTARY

FIREARMS ACT: 1982 c. 31　...　　...　　...　　...　　...　　...　　I, p. 739

FIRE SERVICE COLLEGE BOARD (ABOLITION) ACT: 1982 c. 13　...　I, p. 117

I

L

Part III

Planning

LOCAL GOVERNMENT (MISCELLANEOUS PROVISIONS) ACT: 1982 c. 30   I, p. 631

PART I

LICENSING OF PUBLIC ENTERTAINMENTS

§ 1. and schedules 1 and 2. Licensing of public entertainments, I, p. 632.

PART II

CONTROL OF SEX ESTABLISHMENTS

2. and schedule 3. Control of sex establishments, I, p. 633.

PART III

STREET TRADING

3. and schedule 4. Power of district council to adopt Schedule 4, I, p. 634.

M

MAGISTRATES' COURTS.   Jurisdiction, powers, under—

PART I

DEFINITION OF MENTAL DISORDER

PART II

COMPULSORY ADMISSION TO HOSPITAL AND GUARDIANSHIP

Admission to hospital

Reception into guardianship

Care and treatment of detained patients

Duration of detention or guardianship and discharge of patients

Functions of relatives of patients

Applications and references

PART III

PATIENTS CONCERNED IN CRIMINAL PROCEEDINGS ETC.

Hospital orders

Transfer directions

O

PART I

OIL

P

PASTORAL (AMENDMENT) MEASURE: 1982 No. 1 ... ... II, p. 2073

PART I

AMENDMENTS OF THE PASTORAL MEASURE 1968

Procedure for making pastoral schemes and orders

PLANNING INQUIRIES (ATTENDANCE OF PUBLIC) ACT: 1982 c. 21   [I, p. 317

PUBLIC PROSECUTOR.

RESERVE FORCES ACT: 1982 c. 14 ...   .   I, p. 118

S

SEARCH.   Powers of, under—

c

THIS PUBLICATION
relates to
the Public General Acts
and General Synod Measures
which received the Royal Assent in 1982
in which year ended the THIRTIETH
and began the THIRTY-FIRST YEAR
of the Reign of HER MAJESTY
QUEEN ELIZABETH THE SECOND
and
ended the Third Session
and began the Fourth Session
of the Forty-Eighth Parliament of the
United Kingdom of Great Britain
and Northern Ireland.

d

Produced in England by W. J. SHARP
Controller and Chief Executive of Her Majesty's Stationery Office
and Queen's Printer of Acts of Parliament